Landscapes in History

Landscapes
in History

DESIGN AND PLANNING IN
THE WESTERN TRADITION

Philip Pregill
Nancy Volkman

VAN NOSTRAND REINHOLD
New York

Copyright © 1993 by Van Nostrand Reinhold

Library of Congress Catalog Card Number 91-48094
ISBN 0-442-31804-9

I(T)P   Van Nostrand Reinhold is an International Thomson Publishing company.
         ITP logo is a trademark under license.

Printed in the United States of America

Van Nostrand Reinhold   International Thomson Publishing GmbH
115 Fifth Avenue   Königswinterer Str. 418
New York, NY 10003   53227 Bonn
                                         Germany

International Thomson Publishing   International Thomson Publishing Asia
Berkshire House,168-173   221 Henderson Bldg. #05-1
High Holborn, London WC1V 7AA   Singapore 0315
England

Thomas Nelson Australia   International Thomson Publishing Japan
102 Dodds Street   Kyowa Building, 3F
South Melbourne 3205   2-2-1 Hirakawacho
Victoria, Australia   Chiyoda-Ku, Tokyo 102
                                         Japan

Nelson Canada
1120 Birchmount Road
Scarborough, Ontario
M1K 5G4, Canada

16 15 14 13 12 11 10 9 8 7 6 5 4 3 2

Library of Congress Cataloging-in-Publication Data

Pregill, Philip, 1944-
    History of landscape architecture / Philip Pregill, Nancy Volkman.
    p.   cm.
    Includes bibliographical references.
    ISBN 0-442-31804-9
    1. Landscape architecture—History. I. Volkman, Nancy, 1949-
II. Title.
SB470.5.P74   1992
    304.2'3—dc20   91-48094

Contents

Preface

The history of human interaction with the landscape spans the scope of cultural achievement. During the past ten millennia—the period of human evolution defined by settlement and technological advancement—religion, philosophy, economics, politics, and aesthetics have directed the course of human activity in the landscape. While landscape does not determine human endeavors, it has set limits to human activity and has directed subsequent human strategies. In the large scale these strategies include broad land use patterns, often leading to metaphysical interpretations of physical reality. In the small scale, landscape often functioned like an environmental toy, molded to express human abstractions of natural landscapes. Sometimes these particular schema have led to artificial fantasy environments with little relationship to the natural landscape, save for the need to feed some real or perceived human need. This book explores these patterns of human utilization of the landscape from prehistory to the present, illuminated by pertinent physical and cultural circumstances.

As much as we are tied to modern perceptions of the landscape, earlier periods reaching back to early human hunting and gathering also influence our values and understanding of the environment. Migration, early sedentarism, agriculture, and preindustrialization all contribute to the layers of human predilection regarding the land, especially in forming our perennial fascination with the pastoral and the idealized landscape.

Our modern concern with planned and designed landscapes is a relatively new concern, stemming from Renaissance interest in great architectural and landscape architectural works from antiquity. The classical revival of the Renaissance established the study of past architectural works, an important cultural activity that fostered broader design vocabularies beyond traditional, vernacular themes. Then, in the eighteenth and nineteenth centuries, the expanding field of archeology exposed deeper layers of past environmental works. These revelations expanded the scope of earlier design concepts and made designers more aware of the range of design solutions—including some that were ill fitted to their own era. The nineteenth century was an especially important period in this incipient study of past designs, fueled by European and American nationalism and romanticism, which encouraged serious organized study of historic built environments. In addition, improvements in printing and publication and the growth of literacy allowed greater dissemination of historical information. These factors led to a florescence of serious study of landscape architectural history in the early twentieth century, when the Beaux Arts revival focused on history and precedents. The outcome was a series of garden design histories, with an attenuated regard for the history of large-scale land use and land planning, except among those pursuing the emerging geographical disciplines.

Among the first works to address comprehensively the subject of landscape architectural history was Newton's *Design on the Land,* first published in 1971. This book and three other standard references—G.B. Tobey's *A History of Landscape Architecture: The Relationship of People to the Environment,* Susan and Geoffrey Jellicoe's *The Landscape of Man,* and W. Mann's *Space and Time in Landscape: Architectural History,* are major syntheses of landscape architectural history. In addition, since its inception in 1910, the periodical *Landscape Architecture* had included articles dealing with the history of the profession, most of which focused on Renaissance design or American design since the colonial period. However, in the past twenty-five years a more academic strategy has imbued landscape architectural history with a greater sense of scholarship. Much of this effort has combined traditional art and architectural methodologies with new investigative methods suitable to the scale and transigence of landscapes. Lately, research in design, geography, and landscape ideology had added to our comprehension of the environment. It is the purpose of this book to combine the substance of earlier summary histories with the new research and interpretations into a overview of the human landscape as it is now understood.

Certainly it is necessary to synthesize traditional and contemporary information about land planning and design; however a mere update of landscape architectural history would overlook the larger implications of the subject, especially the need to place it within a broader social and environmental setting. Therefore, this book examines the role of six issues in human interaction with the environment: the relationship of people to the natural environment; the effect of technology; human values concerning urban, rural, and natural landscapes; symbolism of the landscape; the social role of design; and the role of aesthetics in land planning and design.

Discussion of the first issue, the relationship of humans to the natural environment must reach back to humankind's early migrations in the landscape, and concludes with a summary of contemporary environmental issues. In between, the discussion engages physical and psychic dimensions, both of which are relevant to attitudes and values about the landscape. Throughout, humans have established a relative relationship to the landscape as master, servant, steward, or interpreter of the natural world. These roles rest in large part on the level of technology possessed by a particular society at a given time. For example, mastery of a region could not have occurred without the development of agriculture and reclamation techniques in the earliest cultures, nor would a sense of stewardship have emerged without the effects of eighteenth- and nineteenth-century industrialization, including the introduction of new forms of transportation after the eighteenth century, which altered the use and appearance of the landscape.

Thus for some time people have viewed the environment as either natural—unaltered by human activity—or urban and rural. These categories stem from prevailing attitudes and values about the landscape. For example, prehistoric cultures, in the early stages of forming urban patterns, were likely to be more influenced by the natural environment, while within a few thousand years, agricultural societies had clearly distinguished urban and rural environments. Within the recent past, as humans commodified the landscape, the urban, rural, and natural distinction became more pertinent. During each phase, humans have evidenced a preference for one or more of these landscapes over the others; recently, contradictory preferences for either urban or rural living have emerged as people idealize one and malign the other. These preferences indicate a deeper consciousness regarding the landscape, beyond a desire that it merely satisfy functional needs. Every culture has had some symbolic attachment to the landscape, including the earliest prehistoric settlements, whose inhabitants maintained vigorous animistic religions. Much later, certain environments—for example, Walden Pond—symbolized human spiritual freedom, while others—the Dutch polders, for example—symbolized human ingenuity and persistence. Modern cultures maintain a symbolic vocabulary as well, apparent in designed landscapes including cemeteries, monuments, and, lately, avant-garde works in urban settings. Regionally, landscapes such as the Black Forest in southwestern Germany and the Hudson River valley in North America reign as symbols for natural beauty.

At the personal level, landscapes have also been a vehicle for social expression, a way of indicating status. Design in the hands of individuals and powerful groups has left an indelible mark on the landscape, notably in the building of sumptuous pleasure landscapes. Early on, the possession of lands allowed certain individuals to establish a superior position in society. Soon after, planning and design of private landscapes increased one's social status, and later, less fortunate individuals began to create their own distinctive landscapes within the urban realm. The possession of some part of the landscape is still regarded as a measure of social worth, especially as democratic capitalism spreads throughout the globe. Implied in the issue of social status is the concept of aesthetics, the presentation of some sense of order in the design and planning of the landscape. Each major phase of human activity carries an aesthetic label, certain cultures bearing a more graceful tag than others. Regardless, this last issue sums up the previous five by expressing a particular culture's sense of order within the perceived randomness of the natural world.

This text's exploration of these six issues within the context of landscape architectural history relies on two sources of information: existing literature and documentation in design, archaeology, geography, and aesthetics, and field observation and analysis. By using documentary sources, including unpublished material, it is possible to form a better impression of the recent past within the backdrop of earlier history. However, field study is also essential to confirm with the eye the impressions gathered from the literature. The material presented by the authors includes the results of years of travel and field observation and analysis. However, as with any summary work only a selection of relevant issues and material could be addressed in this book.

The book consists of two sections. Part One examines the European region, including adjacent Near Eastern and North African lands, and traces the development of human activity in the landscape through early settlement, agricultural societies, industrialization, and the modern period. Much of the material deals with landscape design and planning before the inception of formal landscape architectural practice. This section emphasizes the development of techniques and values that are antecedent of the North American experience, though it does not exclude events that have occurred in the recent past within or near the European region. Part Two reviews landscape precedence in North America from prehistoric to contemporary times, with particular emphasis on the emergence and the philosophical development of the profession of landscape architecture.

PART ONE

THE EUROPEAN LANDSCAPE

Introduction to Part One
The European Landscape

Only ten thousand years have passed since the first settlements appeared in the Near Eastern foothills, a short duration in human evolution. In those ten millennia, human culture has evolved from occupying a tentative place in the landscape to near control over many of its environmental elements. In the process there has been a perceptible cycle in which cultural efflorescence preceded social stagnation and decline, often the result of economic expansion reaching the limits of landscape sustainability. All of these achievements and failures—the agriculture, industrial, and early modern phases of landscape utilization—have an influence on how we, as contemporary individuals, perceive and utilize the landscape.

Within this broad framework of events, we will examine two aspects of human utilization of the environment in the Near East and Europe that cause us to form conclusions about landscape history. The first has to do with how and why humans have shaped the landscape over the millennia, and how certain values influenced the use of particular technical strategies over others. The second aspect has to do with perception—or idealization—of the landscape, itself a function of human values relative to time and place. Together these aspects stimulated societies to create patterns in the landscape, public and personal, that over time have created a rich layering of form and meaning in the old world and European region. Each of these layers is stamped with exemplary evidence of human endeavor, as well as a sense of how far a culture could expand before the environment limited human advancement.

In the European Region—by which we mean here the lands surrounding the Mediterranean basin, including the Near East and continental Europe—time and human activity define several broad periods of landscape development. The first phase, prehistory, is the period of human activity through the end of the most recent Ice Age, 9200 B.C., during which humans had a minimal impact on the structure and function of the landscape. The second phase is the period of agricultural civilizations, beginning with the small communities in the uplands of southwestern Asia and concluding with the beginning of industrialization in Western Europe in 1400 A.D. The third phase includes the period of industrialization and rapid urbanization in the West; the emergence of national political regions and the influence of the Renaissance, Baroque, and Romantic aesthetics. This phase corresponds to a period when the "idea" of landscape—landscape as an economic and aesthetic entity—prevailed in Western Europe. The fourth and last phase includes the period from the middle of the nineteenth century to the present, when changes in science, politics, and art altered the way we currently view and affect the landscape.

MIGRATION AND ADAPTATION

Before settlements began to appear in the foothills of the Near East, humans went through a period of slow adaptation to the landscape. The process accompanied a rapid evolution in the human species, culminating in modern individuals. Part of these evolutionary advances stemmed from environmental changes, many of which induced humans to migrate from the African continent into regions of Asia and Europe. By 500,000 B.P. humans existed in most of the landscapes in these regions, mostly in favorable habitats south of the large mountain ranges.

Technologically, early humans were limited in their range of achievement, and concentrated their industry on manufacturing rudimentary tools that were suitable for hunting, gathering, and primitive camp building. Even with these devices, humans assured themselves of a reasonable supply of protein, mostly derived from the herds of migrating animals that foraged on the continents. To a great degree, it was the habit and availability of these great herds that kept humans from establishing permanent settlements: an accessible source of protein, albeit on the move, selected against a sedentary existence. Not until these sources became scarce did the need to form subsistence communities develop. Permanent settlements, based on agricultural economics, became the vehicle for human advancement.

AGRICULTURAL CIVILIZATIONS

The earliest planned landscapes, including gardens, town spaces, and parks, occurred in Mesopotamia during the Sumerian, Assyrian, and neo-Babylonian periods. The Sumerians maintained small gardens as a complement to their larger agricultural holdings. They utilized irrigation and drainage techniques to assure adequate food production in the lower Tigris-Euphrates region. The Assyrians, who ruled Mesopotamia from 1250 to 612 B.C., introduced the concept of private parks into the Middle East, notably the hunting parks of the various kings. These gardens contained ornamental plants brought into the region during Assyrian expeditions to foreign lands and were watered by elaborate irrigation systems. The neo-Babylonians (612–539 B.C.) reinstituted the Babylonian culture in southern Mesopotamia and during the reigns of Nebuchadnessar I and II, built elaborate settlements, including Babylon, noted for its broad avenues and the fabled hanging gardens. Recent scholarship indicates that these gardens were elaborate terraced spaces, enclosed by a high wall, which created the appearance of plants hovering above the ground. When the Persians invaded the region in 539 B.C., they borrowed many of the Mesopotamian horticultural techniques, preserving many technologies for posterity. Throughout the Mesopotamian era, the landscape was constantly depleted by excessive irrigation, which caused salinity of the soil and a drop in agricultural productivity.

In the Nile Valley, small agricultural settlements gradually coalesced into a kingdom under Menes (c. 3200 B.C.), who unified Upper and Lower Egypt into one society. For three thousand years agriculture was the primary activity of the Egyptian society. Because the Nile deposited precious silts along its banks each year, thereby assuring a decent agricultural yield, the Egyptians were able to maintain a stable, monolithic society, with few cultural changes over time. The Egyptians also utilized irrigation techniques to convey water to their fields located on levees above the river, though their particular strategy, basin irrigation, was less extensive than the Mesopotamian version. However the Egyptian approach was sufficient to allow the state to maintain large temple estates; the various pharaohs maintained their own elaborate landholdings, where farms and gardens added to the wealth of their dynasties. Less influential individuals, namely merchants and bureaucrats, also owned elegant homes. Many of these smaller estates included enclosed gardens, symmetrically arranged, and detailed with formal pools and groves of figs and palm trees. During the New Kingdom (1567–1085 B.C.) Egyptian rulers including Rameses III ordered the urban improvement of Thebes, including the planting of papyrus and trees; in the Nile delta similar improvements occurred with the planting of vineyards, lotus, and papyrus, and the construction of shaded walks, lined with exotic plants imported from foreign lands.

As the Egyptian culture began to wane by the fourth century B.C., Greek and Roman societies controlled the quality of landscape utilization in the Mediterranean region. The Greeks were less expansive, agriculturally, than their Near Eastern and Egyptian predecessors; the geography of the Greek mainland, which consisted of innumerable mountains, hills, and valleys, intersected by small drainage channels and arable plains, simply favored small-scale agricultural activity. Nevertheless, by carefully farming the small plains that surrounded their isolated communities, the Greeks produced sufficient agricultural produce to maintain their society. They borrowed irrigation technology from their predecessors: rudimentary dams and irrigation elements were part of the Greek agricultural strategy. The Greeks also improved their urban areas with groves and orchards, especially at Athens and at sacred sites. They were able to site structures, including temples, theaters, and stadiums, in precipitous locations by working with the prevailing contours of the land. Outstanding examples of Greek land-planning sensitivity exist at Delphi, Corinth, Athens, and Syracuse.

The Romans, noted for their ambitious political expansion, commanded the entire Mediterranean region by the first century A.D. Their strategy included the conquest of lands suitable for sufficient agricultural production to feed Rome and the other major Roman cities. The Nile, North Africa, Asia Minor, southern France, and Spain all yielded vast agricultural outputs, leading to rapid deterioration of arable landscapes. Mostly, this was a result of intensive agricultural practices, and the clearing of forests for new agricultural lands. Leptus Magnus and Ephesus are prime examples of poor land management.

In contrast, the Romans produced elegant gardens in association with their villas and towns. Pompeii, buried in 79 A.D. by the eruption of Mt. Vesuvius, contained sumptuous town houses, built around interior spaces, which included an atrium, tablinium, and peristyle garden. Many of these gardens contained ornamental plants and carefully clipped topiary (geometrically formed evergreen material). Walls, painted in scenes of vistas and rural landscapes, surrounded the gardens, helping to ameliorate the enclosed feeling of the houses. The public areas, or *fora,* at Pompeii contained extensive groves, often planted in olive and fig trees. Larger estates or villas, including Horace's Sabine villa, Pliny's Laurentine villa, and Hadrian's expansive villa-city near Tivoli, exhibited extensive formal gardens, which contained pools, flower beds, topiary, statuary, and garden structures. All were fed by irrigation systems that conveyed water from streams and reservoirs by gravity flow.

The post-Roman medieval period was a time of political instability throughout the Mediterranean and northwestern Europe. Ambitious princes, commanding small kingdoms, ruled the land, until Charles the Great reunified Western Europe into the Holy Roman Empire in 800 A.D. His empire was short-lived due to family treachery and the resurgence of invasions by migrating groups, particularly the Lombards, Normans, and Mohammedans. Each group brought new design ideas into Europe, especially the Islamic groups who occupied North Africa and southern Spain (711–1492). They were especially successful in transferring agricultural techniques into Western Europe, notably irrigation technology, which the Romans had only slightly developed in Spain and the Western Mediterranean. The Arabs also introduced new plant material into the region, especially citrus, and successfully planned, constructed, and outfitted sumptuous gardens for local rulers. The gardens at the Court of the Oranges at Cordoba, the Alcazar Gardens at Seville, and the superb gardens at the Alhambra at Granada are testaments to Islamic expertise. Unlike their Greek and Roman predecessors, the Moors tended to plan their landscapes as a series of self-contained spaces, without an all-encompassing symmetry. Their inspiration was the garden of paradise described in the Koran, an intellectual ideal inspired by generations of societies inhabiting arid lands. Thus gardens contained water channels, flower beds, shade, and music. The gardens of the Alhambra are the best example of this sensibility, with each space—the Court of the Myrtles, the Court of the Lions—devoted to a particular function within the regimen of the palace.

Outside Islamic-influenced Spain, the quality of landscape articulation in medieval Europe depended on the resources, needs, and ingenuity of the local culture. Perhaps the most successful planned landscapes were those associated with the monasteries in Italy, Switzerland, and France. Essentially these establishments were self-sufficient enclaves, modeled after earlier Roman patterns and influenced by Islamic treatment, especially in the inclusion of irrigation, plant material, architectural elements, and cloister gardens. A notable example was the monastery at St. Gall in Switzerland, one of the most successful religious enterprises after the ninth and tenth centuries. The plan of the establishment illustrates an efficiently organized entity, containing shops, hospital, gardens, living quarters, and dining halls.

Only the estates of the secular princes rivaled the monasteries. The village of Carcassonne in southern France, dominated by an eleventh-century fortress, is one of the few medieval castles to survive relatively intact. Most of these establishments depended on the labor of individuals living around the fortress to produce sufficient agricultural produce for the community. For several centuries the feudal relationship between landowner and peasant held firm; its decline began in the thirteenth century, when in Italy, small settlements began to attract individuals from the countryside who were seeking a better life and relief from the feudal system.

Private gardens in the Middle Ages were not as elaborate as those of former periods, owing to the constricted nature of the societies and their estates. Generally gardens were small-scale affairs, organized in a quasi-formal manner, and containing ornamental plants, and in some instances, a pool for bathing.

INDUSTRIAL SOCIETIES: LANDSCAPE IDEAL

The appearance of politically independent cities, first in Italy, then later in France and England, began the third phase of human impact on the European landscape. Individuals living in these settlements, prosperous from their mercantile and industrial activity, reinvested in the surrounding landscapes, and began an era when the landscape acquired the status of a commodity, valued for its economic potential and leisure qualities. The concept of landscape as an idealized environment stimulated wealthy individuals to establish elaborate estates, which contained elegant, repetitive classical gardens. At first these estates were modest, including the Medici villas at Caffagiola and Fiesole near Florence. At Fiesole, Giuliano Medici constructed an estate that was carefully sited into a hillside overlooking Florence. Each of the villa gardens was a self-contained entity, formally arranged, and featuring small pools, *boschi*, paved terraces, and ornamental plant material. On innumerable occasions the gifted and wealthy of Tuscany met in the *giardino segreto* to exchange ideas, to gossip, and to plot strategies. Later estates, including the Villa d'Este at Tivoli, the Villa Lante at Bagnaia, the Villa Aldobrandini at Frascati, the Villa Isola Bella at Lago Maggiore, and Palladio's villas in the Veneto illustrate the progressive evolution of the Italian garden from pure Renaissance idealism to Baroque exuberance. The distinctive qualities of these establishments are the formal arrangement of space, the profusion of plant material, and the ingenious use of water.

The Italian Renaissance spread to northern Europe through French political involvement in Italy. Charles VIII transferred the Italian sensibility to French culture, succeeded in this effort by Henry II, III, and IV, and Francis I. Francis I attempted to affect the Italian style at chateaux Blois, Amboise, and Chambord in the Loire Valley, but the terrain and the siting of these establishments did not allow for the implementation of traditional Italian gardens. At Blois the Italian garden was an awkward attempt at Italian design, sited across a ravine from the chateau structure. At Chambord the level terrain was not ideal for exuberant water features. Instead the chateau features expansive allées and ronds, for the benefit of guests who wished to observe hunting parties moving through the surrounding forest. These features appeared in seventeenth-century chateaux at Vaux-le-Vicomte and Versailles. The Vaux, built by the hapless Nicolas Fouquet, was the supreme achievement of garden art at the time. The chateau consists of an elegant structure facing an elaborate symmetrical garden, crisply outlined in paths, topiary, parterre, large geometric pools, and baroque fountains. At this estate André Le Notre realized the potential of the Baroque sensibility with a grand sight line that moved the eye to infinity. Only Versailles, Le Notre's grand achievement, outshines the Vaux, if not in proportion and restraint, in sheer scale and excessiveness. Versailles was the most grandiose estate of the seventeenth century, and remains the most expansive garden in Europe. Enormous pools, parterres, bosques, and terraces surrounded the western end of the site. Architectural elements, including the Grand and Petite Trianon, punctuate the vast gardens. At its completion in 1685, Versailles became the model for subsequent urban design in Europe, and later, the United States.

During the sixteenth and seventeenth centuries, Italian and French styles affected landscape design in Britain in a limited way. Mostly, continental influence was evident in manor houses constructed in the English countryside. Hatfield House, St. Catherine's Court, and Hampton Court sustained Italian, French, and, at Hampton Court, Dutch influences. However most of these works lacked the spatial integrity of Italian examples and the quality of detail found in French works. Hatfield House, for example, was conceived as a collection of formal spaces, lacking vertical definition. Hampton Court is also a collection of parts: a Dutch flower garden, an English park-preserve, and a French *patte d'oie*. By the eighteenth century, the British began to question the validity of pure classicism as a landscape rationale, as influential essayists and designers, including Pope, Addison, and Steele, promoted a naturalistic landscape style based on a romantic idealization of nature. Wealthy landowners sought designers who could implement the new style, which counterposed classical architecture and informal landscape planning. Henry Hoare's estate at Stourhead attempted to link classical literature to the landscape allegorically. Architecturally, Stourhead and other examples owe their inspiration to Andrea Palladio and his villas in the Veneto. At Stowe House, three designers, Bridgeman, Kent, and Capability Brown successively altered the gardens; their redesigns reflect the development of Romantic concepts during the eighteenth century. Brown's approach was the most severe: house and grounds were juxtaposed with scant connection between interior and exterior spaces. At Blenheim Palace, Brown's work—the lake and outlying landscape—stands in contrast to the formal gardens near the manor house. Brown's lack of sensitivity resulted in a reevaluation of landscape design approaches, headed by Humphrey Repton and J. C. Loudon. Repton advocated a greater attention to interior and exterior spatial relationships. His Red Books are a compelling record of landscape design theory and execution. Loudon, an advocate of the picturesque sensibility, championed the use of horticultural elements to solve landscape design problems. His ideas were favorably received by the general public, which was increasingly exposed to exotic plant materials in public aboretums and parks. Loudon's ideas were a subsquent influence on American practitioners during the early nineteenth century.

OBJECTIVITY AND MODERNISM

The middle of the nineteenth century saw a shift in science, politics, and art from allegorical reasoning to objective judgment. This was the beginning of a fourth phase in human utilization of the landscape, with the "idea" of landscape fading in favor of an objective analysis and use of landscape phenomena. This change in attitude took visual form in the work of early twentieth-century artists, including Georges Braque and Pablo Picasso. In land planning the British produced revolutionary community design schemes, led by Ebenezer Howard's pioneering Garden City concepts. On the continent similar attempts at suburban planning appeared with early modernism and the influence of Gropius and Le Corbusier. Theirs was a landscape environment somewhat detached from individuals, who were envisioned as living in multistoried residential units floating above the ground plane. Some relief from these utlitarian environments appeared in the Scandinavian countries, including Finland, where new towns like Tapiola promised environments that combined landscape ideal with utility.

In rural landscapes, planning has produced a succession of parks and preserves throughout Europe, and in recent years the formation of national parks in many European states. The purpose, in many cases, has been to protect scenic and scientific environments from excessive human intrusion, but also to provide the public with reasonable access to selected lands. Nearer to urban areas, once strictly agricultural lands have sustained urbanization, fueled by a rising standard of living and the desire of urban dwellers to relocate to rural residential enclaves. To prevent wholesale conversion of prime agricultural lands to urbanization, European states have attempted to regulate agriculture; regulatory attempts include the drafting of a Common Agricultural Plan for the Mediterranean lands.

Contemporary urban landscapes that are planned for public benefit fall into two categories, those that attempt to reinforce the identity of a historic district, and those that seek an identity through the imposition of contemporary forms and materials. The distinction between the two is clearly visible in the differences between a Mariensplatz in Munich and a Parc La Villette on the outskirts of Paris. These disparate examples demonstrate the range of expression persistent in European urban landscapes. And, in concert, they are consistent with the era: the presence of urban spaces equally successful at evoking the senses and logic.

In sum, each phase has sustained unique examples of human adaptation and utilization of the landscape, marked by utility and ideals. Presently, the European landscape bears the compounded effects of prolonged agricultural, industrial, and modernist activity. It is useful to note these effects, first for their relationship to human achievement, and second, for their reappearance in successive cultures, as societies continue to push the limits of landscape sustainability. The response of contemporary Europe—with its traditional systems in decline, and on the threshold of economic unity and political realignment—to current environmental conditions will signal the advent of another phase of human design in the landscape. Very likely this phase will be as dynamic as the ones that have preceded it.

1

Prehistory: Migration and Adaptation

The imprint of human culture on the landscape is a recent phenomenon, of short duration within the time frame of earth history. The first postglacial settlements appeared roughly ten thousand years ago in the uplands of the Near East, and it was another five thousand years before the first civilizations began to flourish in the alluvial plains of Mesopotamia, the Indus Valley, and Egypt. But before they began to form temporary, and then permanent, settlements, humans passed through a slow period of adaptation to the environment, first in Africa, then in Asia and Europe.

In the process of environmental adaptation, early humans came in contact with a range of geographical regions that had resulted from dynamic global processes: continental drift, vulcanism, uplift, erosion, alluvial formation, and glaciation. They encountered lands built over four billion years of earth history, a period when the earth's surface evolved from a single land mass to a collection of continents, all adrift on techtonic plates that eventually produced terrestrial folding and uplifting. The great mountain ranges of Europe and Asia, the eroded valleys in East Africa, and the calcareous outcroppings in the Mediterranean are a few examples of these protracted geological processes.

By about five hundred thousand years ago ancestral humans had begun their intercontinental migrations. Africa had long since separated from South America and had drifted northward to help form the Mediterranean ocean and the European Alps. Subsequently, the Mediterranean region underwent a period of prolonged drought, resulting in the disappearance and reappearance of the Mediterranean Sea. Later, massive glaciation scoured the northern latitudes, the only major geographical event to occur within the span of late human evolution. The regions of Africa, Asia, and Europe where early humans wandered had landscapes that were extremely diverse, and often very different from the landscapes of the present day. For example, as late as twelve thousand years ago, the mountainous regions of North Africa possessed thick cedar forests, as did the mountains of the Near East. The Northern Mediterranean rim was a blanket of mixed fir and hardwoods, a continuous forest stretching to the sea.

PREHISTORIC HUMAN ADAPTATION

Due to limited technology, initial human adaptation to the landscape was extremely modest by modern standards. Only within the past half million years has technology accompanied human activity, often revolving around the use of fire and primitive stone tools. During the Pleistocene, advances in tool and weapon technology accompanied a slow cycle of glacial activity. The first of four successive glacial periods began about three million years ago and the last ceased at about twelve thousand years before the present. Each glacial period terminated with an interglacial warming condition; animal, plant, and landscape associations changed with the cooling and warming cycles. By the end of the Pleistocene, the radical changes in the environment helped to eliminate several members of the human evolutionary family, with the surviving *Homo sapiens* line apparently being the one best able to adapt to a range of environmental stresses.

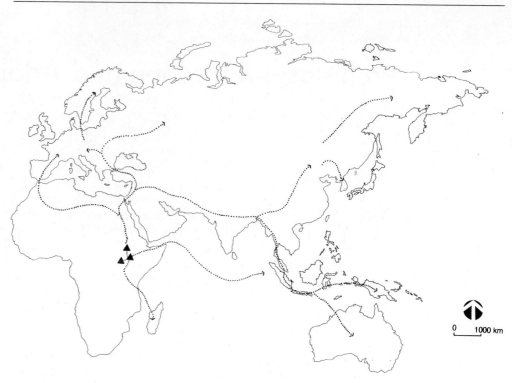

Human migration from Africa into Europe and Asia began over 500,000 years ago. Early migrations were confined to lands south of the major mountain ranges in Asia.

Pleistocene glaciation extended into the middle European latitudes and in alpine regions. Seasonal camps normally occurred south of the ice flows.

An important point in this process occurred midway through the second Pleistocene Ice Age, at about 800,000 B.P., when humans began to show signs of rudimentary cultural formation. This occurred as advances in tool and weapon technology took place, stemming from mid-Pleistocene hominids' use of temporary camps for tool manufacturing and food preparation. *Homo erectus,* the dominant hominid line at this time, established temporary camps for tool manufacturing in a range of habitats in East Africa. Also, *erectus* may also have acquired the ability to control fire and cook food by the Late Middle Paleolithic period.

The use of fire, along with improved tool technology, coincided with the movement of humans into less hospitable habitats, specifically northern Africa, Europe, and Asia. Concomitantly intercontinental migration at about 800,000 B.P. signaled a change in the relationship of humans to the landscape: anthropological finds in Africa and Asia indicate greater human control over the environment by the Middle Paleolithic period. Again the index for gauging hominid impact on the environment is the quality of tool and weapon industry. Middle Paleolithic hunter-gatherers possessed the dexterity to manufacture an array of stone implements for specific hunting or food preparation purposes. Tool makers constructed hand axes, scrapers, cleavers, notched blades, and smaller stone chips to mash, pound, cut, and parcel pieces of flesh and hide from large animals. Bone and wood combined with stone were the materials used to make the array of tools and weapons.

Despite these gains in technology toolmaking and food preparation did not appreciably alter the configuration of the mid-Pleistocene landscape. Even though the hunter-gatherers paused for a day or two to produce the implements required for the next round of hunting and gathering, the modest encampments did not include permanent shelters requiring conscious shaping of the land.

However, armed with these tools hunting groups successfully captured a range of animals for food. Horses, pigs, elephants, birds, and fish were among the broad variety of game killed by the hunter-gatherers. These hunters cleverly used available resources and even the landscape in their pursuit of game. For example, they often drove larger animals into swamps and bogs; leather thongs tied around stones brought down swifter animals; the hunting parties possibly conducted evening ambushes using sticks, clubs, and spears.

Though the hunter-gatherers of the mid-Pleistocene remained unspecialized in their efforts to maintain a satisfactory level of subsistence, their consumption of animal protein had increased significantly. Higher protein intake stimulated population growth, resulting in a need for more temporary encampments. By the mid-Pleistocene, four to thirty individuals made up these typical camps; some were no more than stopping places for the consumption of a single animal. Longer occupation of sites occurred when tool manufacture or butchering of large animals was necessary. As a result, effective hunting-gathering put pressure on the carrying capacities of the mid-Pleistocene, East African landscapes. But unlike other animals of the grassland savannahs and thickets, the hunter-gatherers were not relegated to competing for finite resources in specific habitats. Intelligence, adaptability, and technological skills, along with the rudimentary use of fire, permitted groups to disperse into formerly less hospitable environments in North Africa, Asia, and Europe.

In response to these pressures, five hundred thousand years ago, the initial migration of hunter-gatherers into new regions was ongoing; migration into more arid areas of western and southern Africa occurred later in the Middle Pleistocene. The archaeological remains of hunter-gatherer sites in Africa, Asia, and Europe reveal discrete responses to environmental conditions during this period of adaptation. Generally, settlement sites in the African savannah had been near sources of water, and lake shores, springs, streams, and rivers continued to attract migrating groups of humans. Early human migration in Asia centered in areas south of the major mountain ranges; hunter-gatherers established few sites in the cold steppes or plains of Central Asia. Further east, hunting groups founded temporary camps in the Indian subcontinent, particularly near the river valleys of the Himalayan foothills and in the open plains of the Deccan region. In both Asia and India, hunter-gatherers preferred sites similar to the landscapes of East Africa, specifically well-water locations near food sources.

In contrast, the middle European latitudes sustained a slightly different response from migrating humans as initial movement into the colder latitudes of Europe occurred during the warmer interglacial period. Also, hunter-gatherers preferred the open landscapes for campsites—a majority of French, English, German, and Italian archaeological sites exist in grass and steppe landscapes, and few sites were in dense, wooded environments. Presumably, hunter-gatherer groups selected landscapes consisting of open rather than closed vegetation patterns for economic reasons: larger game, a major source of protein, inhabited the open landscape. Similarly, the food resources of the lake shores, streams, and riverine habitats of Central Europe also attracted the hunter-gatherers. In summary, Late Paleolithic hunter-gatherers were able to exist in a range of habitats in Africa, Asia, and Europe. Improved technology, the rudimentary use of fire, and a functional social structure produced a greater ease of movement in the landscape and a general ability to adapt to formerly inhospitable environments. Thus, human impact on the environment at this time reflected the prevailing low level of technology. Archaeological data point to a generally unspecialized hunting and

Fragments of postglacial landscapes remain in isolated pockets in the interior of contemporary, eastern Mediterranean lands.

Nomadism persists in areas of Anatolia, the Near East, and Asia most often in conjunction with pastoralism.

gathering mode, with the tools and weapons of the period being effective in capturing a range of game, large and small. However, the human population during this period was not great enough to adversely affect the existence of any particular animal species. Of all technological advances the use of fire probably contributed more to human alteration of later Pleistocene landscapes in Europe, especially as fire became a technique for clearing wooded sites for use as hunting grounds.[1]

LATE PLEISTOCENE ADAPTATION

The first archaic forms of *Homo sapiens* appeared about three hundred thousand years ago, and they proceeded to occupy the habitats of the earlier *Homo erectus* group. The emergence of more evolved forms of *Homo sapiens,* including the Neanderthals later in the Pleistocene, signaled an acceleration of human cultural evolution and an expanded impact on the land, coinciding with a gradual shift in the locus of technological advancement from Africa to Asia and Europe. By 175,000 years ago, during the third interglacial period, tool and weapon technology in Europe and Asia surpassed the level of the earlier hunter-gatherer toolmaking of the Middle Pleistocene. The shift in technological development away from Africa stimulated increased human expansion into Europe and Asia.

As noted, this change in cultural focus from the African tropics to Asia and the middle European latitudes accompanied the decline of the earlier *Homo erectus* line in Africa, Asia, and Europe. In their stead, the Neanderthals appeared about 175,000 years ago during the late third interglacial. By the beginning of the fourth glacial period the Neanderthal species possessed a sophisticated tool and weapon technology, knowledge about the use of fire, and the ability to produce adequate clothing and shelter to survive the colder climates of the European and Asian subarctic regions. Often we use the term ''Neanderthal'' derisively, to describe primitive appearance and behavior, but in fact the species was an adaptable and industrious contributor to the human evolutionary record. The Neanderthals possessed a large cranial capacity, about 1450 millimeters, and had the intelligence and dexterity to produce refined tools and weapons. Most Neanderthal achievements, technically and socially, occurred in the forest, tundra, and cold steppes of Europe and Asia, rather than the warm, mixed woods and grasslands of the Mediterranean rim.

The Neanderthals' ability to survive in the glacial European and Asian landscapes was a major step in human cultural and technological advancement. Their key to success was an ability to utilize the resources of the tundra-like lands of middle latitude Europe and Asia. During the fourth glacial period, the open lands of these regions were prime habitats for large herbivores, including horses and woolly mammoths. Neanderthals tapped these rich food sources, combining tool and weapon technology and efficient socialization into a viable economic strategy. The result was a diet better than that of earlier human groups, and the food resources of the fourth glacial landscape of Europe and Asia inevitably stimulated human population expansion. Consequently, primary hunting-gathering groups soon reached the limits of manageable size, forcing groups to abandon the larger tribes. The result was a proliferation of hunting-gathering clans and the movement of humans into specialized environments. For the first time in human evolution, individuals began to occupy the more severe environments in Africa, Europe, and Asia: the sub-Arctic tundra of the Late Pleistocene, the African rain forests, and the cave environments of Central and southern Europe.

Human migration into a wider range of environments was a response to the demands of an expanding population and a major event in human evolution during the fourth glacial period. But human culture continued to be based on a migratory or, at best, semimigratory pattern. Neanderthal hunting parties habitually followed the herds of reindeer, mammoth, and bison into semiwooded environments during the winter and returned with the herds to the open, her-

Semipermanent settlement during the glacial epoch often occurred in the south-facing limestone caves in southern France and northern Spain.

Distribution of major cave sites in southwestern Europe during the glacial epochs.

baceous landscapes in the summer. The procedure can be seen as involving a quid pro quo: following the large herds over areas of Africa, Asia, and Europe helped to assure a constant food supply, but at the expense of producing the cultural achievements we associate with a less nomadic way of life. A few groups possibly managed to develop a semipermanent existence in the caves and natural shelters of Central and southern Europe; animal remains indicate at least a seasonal occupation of natural enclosures. In all likelihood, groups of Neanderthals traded use of the shelters from one period of the year to another. In addition to these natural shelters, primitive tents or windbreaks were a common form of enclosure in open lands of Europe and Asia. Often, bones, animal skins, and stones made up the material of the tents and windbreaks. In less open terrain and especially cave environments, windbreaks and campfires placed at the opening of natural enclosures helped to improve the quality of the shelters.

EARLY POSTGLACIAL ADAPTATION

For nearly one hundred thousand years, the Neanderthals managed to sustain a viable culture in the landscapes of Central and southern Europe. Their demise was due to increased environmental stresses, notably the appearance of modern *Homo sapiens sapiens*. Most likely, competition between the two groups for preferred environments forced the less resourceful Neanderthals out to the fringes of the best environments and into marginal landscapes at a time when the effects of the fourth glacial period made such landscapes uninhabitable. By then competition with modern *Homo sapiens* for preferred habitats and resources resulted in the gradual elimination of the Neanderthal line.

The decline of the Neanderthal hunter-gatherer and the emergence of *Homo sapiens sapiens* in Western Europe was another major stage of human adaptation and technical achievement. Modern *Homo sapiens* hunter-gatherers of the fourth glacial maintained a sophisticated blade tool technology, possibly originating in the Middle East and spreading to the middle latitudes of Europe and Asia. Their long, parallel-sided blade tools helped turn wood and bone into an array of implements, including handles, shafts, awls, hooks, harpoons, needles, and pins. These implements made possible a new level of achievement in hunting, food preparation, clothing, and shelter manufacture—and these tools appeared in new locales when migrating groups of humans spread the technology into Australia and the Americas for the first time in human history. Use of these artifacts was accompanied by the construction of clever hunting devices such as snares, pitfalls, traps, and enclosures to capture large and small varieties of game. Landscape features including cliffs and ravines rounded out the hunting strategy of Upper Paleolithic humans. For example, hunting parties stampeded large herds of grazing animals over precipices, while the open grasslands were ideal for using arrows and spears to pursue and kill the large grazing animals.

Despite improvements in technology and expansion into newer habitats, Upper Paleolithic humans did not produce any appreciable advances in settlement quality over earlier human forms. The hunter-gatherers continued to occupy open landscapes and cave environments as long as food resources permitted. Caves were probably still used as seasonal or semipermanent shelter, although with improved techniques for constructing tents and windbreaks, hunting groups may have occupied the open landscapes for longer periods of time. Modern humans continued the tendency towards specialized food acquisition and the adaptation to specific habitats in the Late Pleistocene. Reindeer were the favored food resource in Western Europe, mammoth in east central Europe, reindeer and horses in Central Asia, and bison in southern Asia. Though these animals were the preferred protein resource of each region, smaller animals contributed as well. Thus, the respective hunting-gathering groups adapted to the landscape on the basis of the quality and quantity of the resources, including the supply of animals, and whether or not they were migratory.

In a protein-rich environment, economic specialization was not a priority as long as available resources remained high. However, with the population of the species expanding, the quest for newer habitats led some groups to develop a dependency on the resources of particular habitats. This shift to specialization had immediate and long-range effects on human occupation of the landscape. In the short term, hunting and gathering groups slowly refined the techniques for occupying a landscape, and raised the quality of food acquisition and shelter construction. Continuous involvement with one habitat resulted in environmental specialization, essential for human adoption of a sedentary mode of life at the end of the Pleistocene.

Some of the most revealing data about the quality of landscape occupation during the Upper Paleolithic is the graphic information in the natural shelters used by modern *Homo sapiens* during the period. Cro-Magnon cave drawings and paintings in southwestern France, for example, depict groups of humans organizing a camp in the open landscape. Bronowski sees in these paintings an indication of the human imagination, the capacity to function within a time frame

Drawings from the interior of a cave illustrates hunting activities during the Pleistocene in Europe.

and the ability to influence the future—in these instances, the outcome of the hunt.[2] If Bronowski is correct, the cave paintings are the earliest graphic indications in Europe of human consciousness about the landscape, and about the ability of humans to control aspects of the environment through collective effort.

Archaeological data, combined with the cave drawings and paintings, indicate that the hunting-gathering groups used elaborate tents and huts as shelter in the open landscapes. The huts were perhaps as large as 30 by 45 feet and open to the sky during the warmer summer months. Hearths placed in regular distribution in the huts helped to keep the shelters warm throughout the year. An example of a winter habitation is provided by a Late Pleistocene camp in Germany, consisting of a large circular dwelling measuring 18 feet in diameter. The builders of the shelter employed sophisticated construction techniques, including the use of a partial retaining wall. Poles covered with animal hides and branches enclosed the remainder of the walls and ceiling of the structure. Open areas adjacent to the huts included fire pits and tool-manufacturing spots. Up to 25 people occupied the shelter; since the camp consisted of at least five dwellings, population of the camp numbered from 100 to 125 individuals.

From these and other archaeological data about Upper Paleolithic technology, it appears that humans had learned to successfully occupy all environments except extreme Arctic regions and deserts. Hunting and gathering remained the economic base for the late Pleistocene inhabitants of Europe and Asia. Their advanced level of tool industry and landscape adaptation produced the highest standard of living of the Paleolithic, and an established economic base allowed some individuals within each group to spend time on activities other than the acquisition of food. The result was the beginning of cultural specialization leading to numerous creative expressions, including the imaginative cave paintings in France and Spain.

A Paleolithic camp site in northern Germany where small groups manufactured hunting and gathering tools.
(Benevolo, Leonardo. *The History of the City.* Copyright © 1980 MIT Press.)

MESOLITHIC ADAPTATION AND EARLY SEDENTARISM

The Late Pleistocene marked the end of the latest major glacial event and the beginning of a period of rapid expansion of human cultural activity. Most important for humans was the change from a glacial to a postglacial climate at the end of the Pleistocene, marked by the shift from cold to warm climate conditions. The result was series of shorter warmer and colder shifts in weather accompanying an overall warming trend ending about 10,300 years ago. The climate change reduced the Arctic tundra association and stimulated the growth of a birch-pine associations through the final phases of Late Pleistocene glaciation in Europe. In addition, the reduction of the European tundra accompanied the gradual extinction of faunal species, including the mammoth, woolly rhinoceros, giant elk, and musk ox. The reindeer, a major food source for humans in the Late Pleistocene, ceased to inhabit Central Europe by 9500 B.P. At that point, new animal species began to adapt to the woodlands of the European postglacial landscape, while foxes, squirrels, hares, and horses continued to populate the woods and prairies of the region.

The effect these changes had on humans was evident in the quality of day to day economic activity. In many instances, subsistence on the great herds of the Pleistocene shifted to a reliance on less migratory animal food sources such as deer, wild cattle, and boar. Hunter-gatherers deemphasized the large-scale, organized hunting activities in favor of subsistence on localized resources. In addition, hunting-gathering at the end of the Pleistocene and beginning of the Holocene tended to focus on middle latitude Europe. Near Eastern hunter-gatherers did not develop specialized hunting-gathering in the tradition of their European counterparts. Rather, by 10,000 years ago, small subsistence farming settlements began to emerge in parts of the Middle Eastern landscape. Significantly, humans had crossed the threshold to agriculture and urbanization.

ENVIRONMENTAL ISSUES

The emergence of agricultural economies in the late Pleistocene–early Holocene period signaled a change in the quality of impact humans had on the landscape. During the earlier Pleistocene their effect was negligible, due to a limited technology and an economy based on continual migration. But by the Upper Paleolithic, early humans were producing a perceptible effect on the environment. For example, Upper Paleolithic sites in Belgium, The Netherlands, and Germany have a high charcoal content, perhaps resulting from the use of fire as a hunting and plant control mechanism, since the technique of clearing by fire was a simple way of creating pastures for large game animals. Also plant regeneration in cleared areas attracted grazing animals, which in turn provided hunter-gatherers with a convenient food supply.

Whether persistent hunting resulted in wholesale overkill or extinction of certain animal species is difficult to ascertain. No doubt the elimination of some habitats by fire and the intense selection of specific game species by humans coincided with the general extinction of a number of animals including woolly mammoth, woolly rhinoceros, steppe bison, giant elk, and the cave bear. A scientific debate continues as to whether the extinctions were caused by changes in climate and habitats or by the intense hunting practices of Upper Paleolithic humans. Since some species managed to survive human activities during the Pleistocene, it is likely that human presence was not the sole factor in extinction. But, with more control than ever over the landscape, Paleolithic hunter-gatherers had some effect on the environment, contributing to the demise of certain plants and animals. In sum, early in the human evolutionary record individuals depended on prevailing environmental conditions for survival. Humans could not wander far from water, food, or relative warm climate; hunting and gathering was the economic mechanism used to sustain primitive, nomadic groups. Beyond localized alteration of the environment, the impact humans had on the landscape through most of the Pleistocene appears negligible.

NOTES

1. Karl W. Butzer, 1982. Archeology as Human Ecology. *Chicago University. See pp. 123–156 for a discussion concerning the impact of fundamental human activity on landscape quality. See also Butzer,* Environment and Archaeology: An Introduction to Pleistone Geography. *Chicago: Adline, pp. 136–148 regarding Pleistocene floral and faunal categories as well as human distributions.*

2. Jacob Bronowski. 1973. The Ascent of Man. *Boston: Little, Brown.*

2

The Near Eastern Landscape: Neolithic Settlements

For more than half a million years early humans migrated over the African, Asian, and European continents, dependent on prevailing environmental conditions and available resources. Gradually, this long-standing dependency began to fade when, at the end of the Pleistocene, their interminable migrations slowly gave way to settled existence. At first this change in lifestyle began in the uplands of western Asia, between lowland and alpine environments, where humans settled into lands that offered them the chance to exert more control over their surroundings. Then, between 8000 B.C. and 5000 B.C., humans began to abandon traditional hunting and gathering activities and to develop new economic systems based on agriculture and animal husbandry. As this new economic strategy emerged, small permanent settlements began to appear in regions that contained favorable natural resources—water, soils, plant material, game—and to lay the foundation of the Neolithic revolution. Jacob Bronowski eloquently expresses the significance of these events in *The Ascent of Man,*[1] when he observes that this agricultural and urban revolution transformed humans from mere *figures* in the landscape to *shapers* of the landscape. In the process, humans acquired the ability to create habitable environments throughout the middle latitudes, setting into motion the spread of urbanization east and west. Further, the demands and opportunities of settled existence reversed a long-standing relationship between humans and the environment: for better or worse, people were acquiring the power to control nature, a control that was rather tenuous at first, but that gradually, with time and technological advancement, shifted from being secondary to human existence to an absolute requirement for the survival of the species. Subsequent human adaptation to the landscape is essentially a chronicle of this process, beginning inauspiciously in the foothills of the Near East.

ENVIRONMENTAL CONTEXT; SETTLEMENTS AND AGRICULTURE

Nearly all of the early formation of settlements occurred along an arc described by a series of mountain ranges facing the northern and eastern Mediterranean Sea. This geographical area, where the Neolithic revolution began between 9000 and 8000 B.C., includes the Syro-Palestinian Levant, the hilly flanks of the Zagros Mountains in Iraq and Iran, and the Anatolian plateau south of the Taurus Mountains in Turkey. In general the landscapes of these regions were similar, consisting of hilly, forested uplands.

Geologically the region lies within several lands that constitute the greater eastern Mediterranean region. The area that contains the so-called fertile crescent, an arc of territory from Turkey to the Persian Gulf, includes two major structural zones. The northwestern portion consists of a complex geological zone that has

The location of principal Neolithic settlements in the Near East. Many of these communities occupied upland sites to take advantage of game, forage, water, and favorable climate.

sustained significant folding, fracturing, and vulcanism, and remains seismically unstable to this day. The southerly portion includes an intermediary zone of sedimentary rocks, overlying earlier layers of folded and faulted material. Subsequent erosion and sedimentation here produced soils that spawned forests, marshes, and meadows.

At the time of the Neolithic occupation of the region and the emergence of the first settlements, three distinctive ecological zones constituted the environment of the Near East. The first was the coastal region along the edge of the eastern Mediterranean near the shores of southeastern Turkey and below the Taurus Mountains, including a strip of land along the eastern Mediterranean running through the western edges of Syria, Lebanon, and Israel. The predominant plant forms here were varieties not suitable to colder inland climates, notably cedars and temperate grasses. The second zone included the deserts of Syria, Jordan, and Iraq, and adjacent steppes, including Mesopotamia, the land between the Tigris and Euphrates Rivers. This region is one of scant rainfall, between 5 and 10 inches annually, producing sparse ground cover. Lastly, between and partly surrounding these two zones, lies the highland zone, including the Lebanon Mountains of the Levant, the Taurus Mountains of eastern Turkey, and the Zagros Mountains, which extend into the western border of Iran and into the northern portion of Iraq. The elevation of the region often exceeds 8,000 feet, with peaks averaging 10,000 feet in height.

Due to local rainfall patterns and vertical elevation variation, major plant associations varied within these three broad zones. Rainfall was not sufficient to support large perennials, and much of the plant cover consisted of quick-growing

The terrain of present-day Turkey south of the Taurus mountains, a region favored by Neolithic settlers. Catal Hüyük is located about sixty miles north of this site in upland terrain.

perennials. Here the harvest period is short, but early collectors could have extended the season by migrating to higher elevations, moving from lowland to upland in the spring and reversing the process in the fall. While in the highlands, humans encountered vegetation associations found in temperate forests, including oak, fir, pistachio, and juniper. In addition to these species, many edible fruits, nuts, and wild cereals existed in the region, along with native sheep, goats, cattle, and pigs. Such plant and animal diversity allowed initial settlers to pursue a mixed economic strategy, consisting of local hunting and gathering that augmented rudimentary agricultural production.

TRANSITION TO PERMANENT SETTLEMENT

The abandonment of a hunting and gathering tradition after nearly 500,000 years of activity is hard to reconcile with the fact that hunter-gatherer groups maintain a sufficient level of nourishment, and have more leisure time than agriculturalists. Flannery[2] believes the transition from hunting and gathering to sedentarism and agriculture most likely occurred as a result of a change in economic strategies. According to this reasoning, by the late Mesolithic (40,000–10,000 B.C.) and the early Neolithic, humans had begun to deplete the supply of available wild game. To augment the food supply, hunters and gatherers learned to move into more varied ecological niches and to depend more on grains and seeds as a food supply; however, expanding economic possibilities—a more eclectic strategy in a wider range of environments—inevitably led to greater population increases. Larger populations selected for the development of a stable and permanent economic system, which would consistently assure an adequate food supply.

For some time specialists believed that sedentarism and the development of agriculture coincided with sudden changes in climate that forced humans to concentrate near sources of water. Part of the reasoning behind this theory had to do with certain ecological changes that occurred at the end of the last major Ice

Age about 12,000 years ago. Briefly, the retreat of the glaciers affected the pattern of the rainbelts, causing a drying of the Near Eastern landscape and the concentration of humans, animals, and plants into oases, where it was asserted that proximity of resources led to domestication and sedentarism. For other theorists, the "oasis" hypothesis fails since it does not explain why sedentarism did not begin during one of the earlier interglacial periods. Also there is little evidence to support the notion that plants and animals of an upland environment would easily adapt to lowland oasis conditions.

Paleoclimatic data support this contention since they do not indicate a change in the climate of the Middle East and eastern Africa comparable to the change in Europe. The climate of the hilly regions of western Asia in the Late Pleistocene produced a fairly stable and well-watered environment at the end of the fourth glacial period. River and stream drainage from upper elevations of the hill country provided reliable sources of water. The native vegetation of the region included temperate woodland associations containing a range of plant species suitable for domestication. Updated archaeological theories, then, tend to place emphasis on the development of early agriculture in areas of the landscape that contained localized, reliable sources of food supply, rather than in the Near Eastern floodplains.

Another important factor that influenced the development of permanent settlements in the Near East is related to the presence of semipermanent camps in prime foraging areas in the Near Eastern uplands. As in other areas of Africa, Asia, and Europe, semipermanent camps near areas of prime food resources were a common feature by the end of the last Ice Age. As the available natural resources near these camps declined, humans gradually came to rely on a mixed economic strategy for existence, including the domestication of plants and animals.

By 8000 B.C. the typical pattern of human existence in the upland slopes of the Near East had begun to develop towards increased sedentarism and greater economic diversity. The archaeological record of human activity in the region for this period indicates a lifestyle based on hunting and gathering and rudimentary plant and animal domestication. But as available natural food sources declined, humans became increasingly dependent on animal husbandry and plant cultivation to augment the food supply. Two-row barley *(Hordeum vulgare)*, einkorn wheat *(Triticum monococcum)*, and emmer wheat grew naturally in the region and were actively collected by inhabitants as a protein source. At about the same time, wild emmer underwent a series of biological mutations that produced a strain of wheat suitable for cultivation. The new strain had a sturdier spike and the individual kernels held fast to the ear, enhancing net yields. At first this new strain of wheat had a negligible effect on the economies of the region, since livestock husbandry and hunting-gathering still yielded sufficient quantities of food. But as livestock began to deplete the supply of natural plant resources, humans began to emphasize plant cultivation.

The consequence of this gradual shift away from the gathering of naturally existing plant sources to cultivation in the Near East tended to lessen the dependency of humans on the immediate natural resources of the landscape. With the new strain of wheat and sufficient water, groups of individuals began to locate settlements in areas of the Near Eastern foothills less blessed with natural reserves of food. In these communities humans began to pay more attention to the development of a new economic system based on agriculture, thereby quickening the onset of sedentarism.

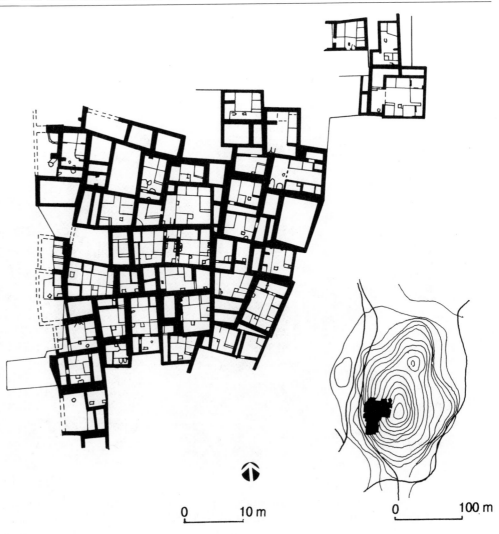

Site plan and detail of Catal Hüyük, a principal Anatolian Neolithic settlement. By this time communities had adopted a functional, rectilinear arrangement to their organization.

0   10 m

0   100 m

NEOLITHIC COMMUNITIES IN THE NEAR EASTERN FOOTHILLS

The effect of this new economic strategy on the quality of the Near Eastern landscape around 6500 B.C. was evident in the proliferation of small settlements in the region. Most of these communities did not appear particularly advanced by modern standards; the basic amenities of the settlements included food and shelter without the level of embellishment preferred by us today. One way of understanding the quality of settlement in the Near East during the Neolithic is to examine several communities in chronological order, with an eye to the effect such development had on the subsequent quality of the landscape of the Near East. Four communities, Zawi Chemi Shanidar in the foothills of the northern Zagros, Jarmo in the southern Zagros, Jericho in the Syria–Palestine region, and Catal Hüyük in Anatolia, are worthy examples of settlement quality and human landscape adaptation of the period.

Zawi Chemi Shanidar

Zawi Chemi Shanidar, located in the foothills of northern Iraq, provides an example of an early Neolithic community beginning to shift from a pure hunting and gathering mode of existence to a sedentary lifestyle. The overall form of the community resembled a compound of circular structures arranged around shared

Contemporary site and structure in central Turkey. The forms and materials are similar to constructions from the period of earliest settlement in the region.

storage and open spaces. Excavation of the site has shown the presence of a continuous stone tool industry and building foundations that qualify Zawi Chemi as a year-round site. Lower levels of the site show a preponderance of wild goat and red deer bones, while upper levels reveal the presence of domesticated sheep remains. Evidence of cultivated plants is conspicuously absent from all levels of the site. The likely explanation for these findings is that the community was located in a region of initially sufficient plant and animals resources; as the game supply became depleted through overhunting, the occupants of the settlement gradually adopted a more sedentary mode of existence based on gathering of available plant resources and the domestication of sheep. The effect of Zawi Chemi and other communities of the period on the region's landscape was probably localized and confined to the alteration of habitat through the husbanding of livestock. The impact was greater than that of humans during the Late Mesolithic, but was still negligible by contemporary standards.

Zawi Chemi is an example of an early Neolithic settlement that was a transition from hunting and gathering to the development of agriculture as a significant increase in human control over the environment. Braidwood[3] described these sites as "nuclear areas" where wild plants and animals suitable for domestication existed at the crucial moment in human development of agriculture. Normally the nuclear areas in the Near East generally possessed common qualities including (1) locations in the intermediate upland region between 1,000 and 5,000 feet elevation adjacent to the fertile crescent, (2) presence of several members of the animal-plant complex which was eventually domesticated, and (3) annual rainfall levels that were low, but sufficient for dry farming.

**Jarmo, Jericho, and
Catal Hüyük**

Jarmo, Jericho, and Catal Hüyük all flourished by the eighth or seventh century B.C., shortly after the first steps towards food production had occurred in the Near East. In the broadest sense the sites lie within the nuclear area along the fertile crescent, but the specific environmental setting of each is strikingly different; as a group, the sites represent the beginning of the early diffusion of animal domestication and plant cultivation from the uplands to lower elevations.

Jarmo Lying in the western foothills of the Zagros Mountains in Iraq in the same general region as Zawi Chemi and other preagricultural settlements, the prehistoric agricultural settlement of Jarmo serves as a good example of an agriculturally based economy at about 9000 years ago. From the archaeological data, the general character of the landscape near the site was one of alternately open and wooded plains and hillsides combined with freshwater streams and ponds. The site of Jarmo itself is about 2,000 feet above sea level; the settlement existed on a bluff about 80 feet above a stream, which served as the major source of water for the community. A pollen study of the community has confirmed the existence of wild einkorn wheat, barley, acorns, pistachio nuts, lentils, field peas, and blue vetchling. Animal remains on the site consist of goats and pigs plus an array of locally hunted animals such as fox, wolf, and wild cattle. Even the remains of a large number of terrestrial snails, along with freshwater crabs and fish, are part of the animal remains of the site.

By 6750–6500 B.C. the settlement consisted of about twenty houses situated on 4 acres atop the bluff. The boundaries of Jarmo included a land area of about 2.6 acres. There was no formal plan to the village; Jarmo was a loosely organized grouping of houses, storage structures, and animal shelters. At its peak, the community contained about twenty-five houses with five to seven people living in each. The inhabitants fashioned the rectangular village structures from sun-dried mud, of which they built walls laid on rough stone foundations. The interior of the dwellings included spaces for cooking, sleeping, and storage; an interior courtyard used for the grinding of grains adjoined the day rooms.

The change from the circular floor plans of the earlier Neolithic settlements to a rectilinear arrangement probably reflects a change in social organization, as the nuclear family gradually replaced the hunting and gathering group as the unit of economic production. Unlike the circular arrangement of preagricultural compounds, in which the storage facilities are shared and the economic unit is the group, in communities like Jarmo the basic unit is the family, which maintains its own storage of supplies and has a greater incentive for intensification of production. The rectilinear arrangement allowed for the easy expansion of the dwelling as the family grew, without causing the overall size of the community to become unwieldy.

Jericho The environment at the site of ancient Jericho differs sharply from those of earlier preagricultural communities in the Near East. The site is located about 700 feet below sea level in the deepest part of the Jordan River valley, near a large natural spring. Because the community sat in a small valley surrounded by dry uplands in which some wild cereals were present, it is considered a part of the Near Eastern nuclear area.

From Mesolithic times, hunting and gathering groups used this site as a toolmaking camp, and several layers of occupation lead some authorities to conclude that Jericho may be the oldest community in the Near East. A preagricultural group known as the Natufians occupied the site about 8000 B.C.; by 7000 B.C. the settlement covered about 10 acres and had nearly 3,000 inhabitants. Excavation of earlier levels reveals a settlement pattern consisting of small mud structures with curved walls. Subsequent occupants constructed rectilinear dwellings with wide doorways and rooms grouped around courtyards. Well before 6000 B.C. Jericho had the appearance of an established community complete with a massive surrounding town wall.

The community had the advantage of being situated near a spring and stream, rendering agricultural production a natural alternative, and by the seventh millennium B.C. the center of economic activity at Jericho was plant cultivation. Neither wild wheat nor barley is native to the dry hills surrounding the site, indicating that these grains were introduced to the area from the uplands of the Jordan Valley.

Catal Hüyük   Catal Hüyük in Anatolia is the third Neolithic community considered here as an example of the gradual development of settlements away from the Near Eastern uplands. Like Jericho and Jarmo, Catal Hüyük was an established agricultural community by the seventh century B.C. The unique aspect of the settlement is the location of the site about 3,000 feet above sea level in the Konya plain of the south central region of the Anatolian plateau in Turkey. Part of the attraction of the area was the richness of the soil and the presence of numerous species of wild game and cereal grasses. A small river in the vicinity of the site provided sufficient moisture for plant cultivation in an arid area receiving no more than 16 inches of rainfall a year. In addition, abundant quantities of obsidian were present in the region.

Catal Hüyük covers 32 acres, about three times the area of Jericho. From a distance, the community appeared fortresslike, with solid, blank walls facing the periphery. In its earlier stages, the settlement was sited near the river, with subsequent development occurring beyond the river bank. Catal Hüyük contained a mass of structures constructed of mud brick. Entrance to dwellings was through an opening in the roof; communication between dwellings occurred via rooftops. The interior organization of these residences was fairly uniform and included rooms for cooking, sleeping, and production. Courtyards between structures were dumping spaces for refuse. The landscape immediately adjacent to the structures included spaces for animal husbandry and plant propagation. Corrals on the edge of the settlement contained a variety of livestock, including cattle, sheep, goats, and pigs. Inhabitants cultivated at least fourteen species of plant foods, including einkorn, emmer wheat, peas, and lentils. Hunting and gathering continued to add to the diet.

By the seventh century B.C., Catal Hüyük was a dominant site in the area, figuring in the trading activities of the region; like so many other communities, it specialized in a particular commodity in the local trading economy, in this instance obsidian, which the community actively traded for timber and other materials. Eventually the economic superiority enjoyed by the community imbued the settlement with religious and political authority. For example, modest shrines housed wall paintings and stylized sculptural representations of animals and human female forms. The depiction of human and animal forms focused on the concept of fertility, the basis of the local religion. Through the symbolic powers of art, religious activity focused on aspects of the environment that appeared to affect community livelihood.

AGRICULTURAL DISPERSAL

Despite success in maintaining viable economies, the Near Eastern settlements did not maintain a monopoly on agricultural development. Eventually major civilizations emerged along the floodplains that eclipsed the foothill communities. This process began when dispersal of agricultural technology east and west of the region spawned settlement and plant propagation. Quite likely, early intensive farming in the woodlands depleted the arable soils near the early settlements,

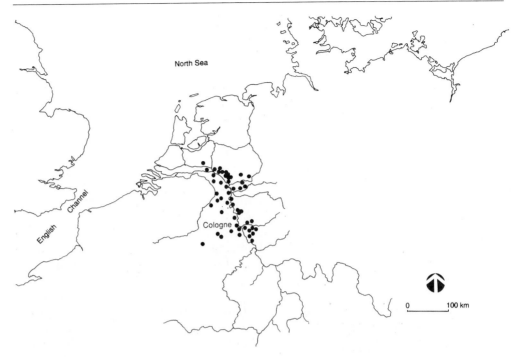

Distribution of Neolithic Rhineland settlements. Most of these settlements were associated with subsistence farming.

prompting villagers to abandon their settlements and relocate in areas of arable land. Dispersal may also have been caused by rapid population growth within the agricultural settlements, which outstripped the agricultural resources of a community. With few alternatives but to trim populations, individuals may have elected to break away from the parent community and resettle in an uninhabited, arable locality.

It is also interesting to consider the adaptations necessary for the introduction of agricultural practices into disparate regions of Africa, Europe, and Asia. For example, the Central European landscape was generally unsuitable for many of the Mediterranean techniques of agricultural production, since other plant materials were required to fit the climate, soils, and parasitic conditions of Central Europe. Cereal farming was not suited to the semi-arid regions of the Sahara; instead, gathering and herding augmented plant cultivation along desert edges. Finally, transfer of agricultural procedures from the wooded slopes of the Near East into the river floodplains required early gatherer-farmers to adapt to spring flooding and a summer growing season, and to solve the problems of farming in heavy, saline, alluvial soils.

The transfer of agricultural techniques into southern Europe coincided with a warming trend in the region and the transition of pine-hazel woodlands to oak and elm plant associations in the western part of the continent. As in earlier periods, the change in plant association reduced the biomass resources of larger animals such as wild cattle and red deer; the formation of bogs in preexisting lakes also reduced the fish and waterfowl populations. These ecological changes stimulated a relocation of settlement to major river and coastal environments. The plentiful waterfowl, fish, and mammals in these environments were an incentive for a more sedentary lifestyle and encouraged the development of an agricultural component. As a result, settlements gradually appeared that were similar to communities in southeastern Europe in pattern and agricultural practice. The architecture of these villages consisted of one-room structures built from baked mud; their agricultural activities included the propagation of wheat, barley, peas, and lentils and the husbanding of cattle, goats, pigs, and sheep.

Further north, groups of individuals founded agricultural settlements along the tributaries and floodplains of the Danube and Rhine rivers. Agriculture began with the clearing of the thick oak woodlands and the subsequent propagation of barley, einkorn, and emmer wheat. Villages consisted of structures built of wood and wickerware measuring 20 to 60 feet in size; storage buildings, pits, fences, animal and plant spaces helped give the settlements the sense of an organized community. As many as 400 individuals occupied the villages; after about ten years the inhabitants abandoned many of the settlements for more fertile regions. Subsequent groups of gatherer-farmers reinhabited the villages after allowing the soils near the settlements to lie fallow for about fifty years. Butzer[4] summarizes human landscape adaptation during this period as a three-part cycle: forest clearance and the conscious elimination of native plant material through slash and burn and grazing; introduction of domesticated plant species; and the subsequent degradation of soil by overuse and erosion.

REGIONAL SETTLEMENT PATTERNS; ENVIRONMENTAL ISSUES

The transition from hunting and gathering to cultures based on an agricultural economic system occurred in towns like Jarmo, Jericho, and Catal Hüyük. As early as 6000 B.C. a number of such communities participated in regional trading activities, bartering obsidian, timber, and building stone along footpaths or waterways such as the Tigris River. Thus, by that date, the pattern of settlement in the Near East consisted of emerging agricultural communities loosely connected by modest trading routes.

The effect of this pattern of settlement was to escalate gradually the transformation of the environment by humans. Until this time, such alteration con-

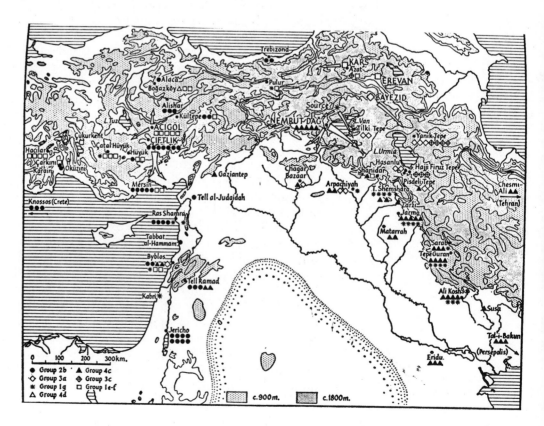

Principal obsidian production and trading centers in the Near East during the Neolithic. Source locations are in capital letters. Groupings pertain to archaeological designations.

sisted of activities related to the hunting and gathering mode of existence: the building of small, seasonal camps and the clearing of small areas of forest to enhance hunting prospects; but sedentarism encouraged higher settlement densities and intensive agricultural activities. Jarmo, for example, contained about 150 to 200 people, roughly 27 people per square mile. Economically, the area of landscape required to support such a community depended on the particular agricultural specialty of the settlement and the amount of space needed to accommodate a combination of animal husbandry and plant cultivation. As more communities emerged in areas of the Near Eastern landscape away from the resource-rich nuclear zones, areas which were often naturally suitable for small-scale cultivation, migrants had to create suitable conditions by clearing woodlands. In sum, Neolithic settlements were a critical link between the earlier migratory bands and later agricultural societies; they retained some of the habits of earlier human activity, including localized clearing for hunting. Equally important, the Neolithic settlements presaged the subsequent process of landscape alteration that was to occur on a far greater scale in the floodplains of the Near East.

NOTES

1. *Jacob Bronowski. 1973.* The Ascent of Man. *Boston: Little, Brown, p. 19.*

2. *Kent V. Flannery. 1972.* The Origins of Villages as a Settlement Type in Mesoamerica and the Near East: A Comparative Study. *Man, Settlement and Urbanism. (P.J. Ucko and G.W. Dimbleby, eds.). London: Duckworth, pp. 337–45.*

3. *Robert J. Braidwood. 1960. "The Agricultural Revolution."* Scientific American, *203 (3), 130–48. See also R. J. Braidwood. "Near Eastern Prehistory,"* Science 77, *pp. 1428–29.*

4. *Karl W. Butzer. 1982.* Archaeology as Human Ecology. *Cambridge: Cambridge University Press. pp. 38–42; 123–156.*

3

Mesopotamia and the Indus Valley

At the end of the late Neolithic, about 6000 B.C., human settlement and subsistence in the landscapes of the Near East began to shift from the lands adjacent to upland regions to the alluvial plains of the Tigris and Euphrates rivers and their tributaries. Elsewhere in the region similar migrations were occurring in Anatolia, the Levant, Iran and the Indus Valley. However, the settlements that appeared in Mesopotamia, the "land between the rivers," were unique in their eventual impact on the region. From these early migrations, the settlements in the Tigris and Euphrates landscape evolved into the first major floodplain cultures.

Human settlement in Mesopotamia began in the northern Tigris and Euphrates region and proceeded southward into the delta formed by the two rivers. The initial communities in the northern Mesopotamian region resembled the earlier settlements of the uplands in social organization, economic quality, and environmental impact, but subsequent communities in the delta were considerably more sophisticated in organization and economies. Their economic strategy depended on intensive agriculture and artificial irrigation, and as each settlement prospered, the surrounding lands sustained agricultural expansion and rural development. Eventually, these settlements evolved into urban centers with all the advantages and disadvantages associated with cities. Only persistent over-utilization of the landscape, due mostly to intensive agriculture and artificial irrigation, kept many of these communities from surviving in the long term.

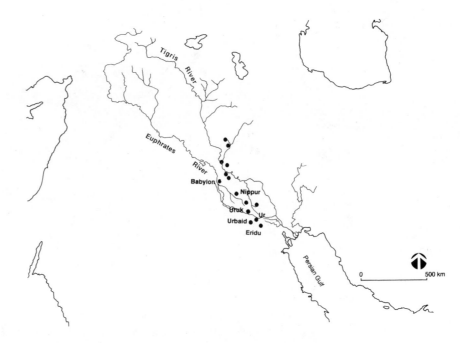

Distribution of important settlements and urban centers within the Mesopotamian region. Most of these communities were important centers during the city-state phase in Mesopotamia, between 2600 and 1800 B.C.

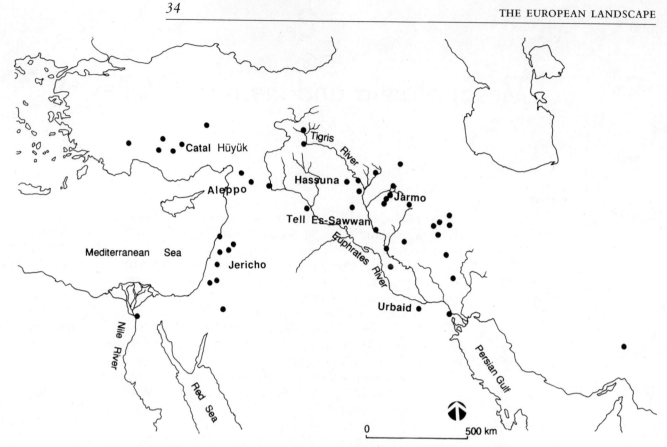

Near-eastern agricultural centers within the larger "fertile crescent" region.

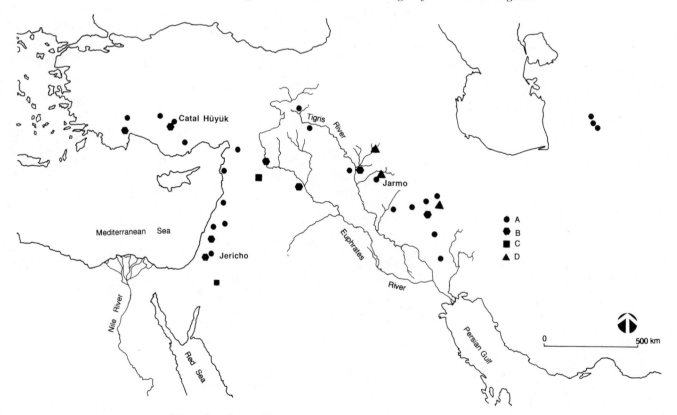

Hierarchy of agricultural settlements in the Near East. (A) sites with established food production (B) successive occupation, some with food production (C) no food production (D) incipient food production.

LANDSCAPE CONTEXT

In present-day northern Iraq, where the first communities flourished below the surrounding uplands, the landscape consists of rolling plains intersected by the Tigris and Euphrates rivers. From late prehistoric times, this undulating landscape supported a thick grassland suitable for grazing. However, unlike the foothills and rolling plains adjacent to the Taurus and Zagros Mountains, the lower-lying territory is generally arid, with an annual rainfall insufficient for unirrigated agriculture. Closer to the tributaries, where migrants settled on the alluvium, the rivers were depositing most of their silt and clay on their own beds. Occasional flooding occurred beyond the rivers, resulting in the deposit of a thick blanket of fertile soil adjacent to the river margins. But at about 2000 B.C., when the river had aggraded above the floodplains, movement in the earth's crust caused the rivers to cut down through the alluvium to many meters below the plains, creating natural levees along the watercourses.

Similarly, the southern delta formed by the two rivers is an arid land, geographically unprotected, an open region with insufficient rainfall for year-round dry farming. Further, the land lacks usable building stone, timber, or metals. Since the region lies at the terminus of two great rivers, alluvium created by the annual buildup of silt and clay from the Tigris and Euphrates formed the region into meandering drainageways and lowlands that support usable wild plants, including flax and rushes, and a variety of fish, which early on supplied adequate protein to early human inhabitants. Despite the heat and intense sunlight of the summer months, the lands in the delta—with adequate irrigation—were ideal for the cultivation of wheat, barley, olive trees, citrus, onions, garlic, and many other crops.

NORTHERN MESOPOTAMIAN SETTLEMENTS

The first Neolithic society to flourish in the Mesopotamian region was the culture associated with Tell Hassuna, which grew up on the west side of the middle Tigris in northern Iraq. Early Hassunan culture resembled that of upland settlements such as Jarmo, with the exception of improvements in residential construction. The Hassunan inhabitants pursued rudimentary farming, augmented by local hunting and gathering.

To the south of Tell Hassuna, at the juncture of the arid northern plains and the northern alluvium, another settlement flourished called Tell as-Sawwan, dating from between 5000 and 6000 B.C. A simple farming community of several hundred people, Tell as-Sawwan subsisted on a mixture of plant cultivation, animal husbandry, and hunting; plants and animals domesticated included wheat and barley, and goats, sheep, and cattle. Architecturally, Tell as-Sawwan resembled other communities of the region: small, rectangular, mud brick structures served as residences and storage spaces, while open courtyards provided space for animal pens and refuse. A narrow ditch buttressed by a thick clay wall that surrounded the site was probably a defensive element.

The economic focus of the community was on plant propagation, and various rudimentary artificial irrigation strategies were employed. The most successful techniques relied on working with the river and levees. By breaching the river banks that were above the flood plain, and diverting the water along rudimentary canals, the early farmers of northern Mesopotamia successfully cultivated their small fields and achieved sufficient agricultural production for their settlements.

Eventually the communities of Northern Mesopotamia formed a pattern of settlement that was closely tuned to the resources of the region's environment. Most were located in close proximity to natural resources, including tributaries and arable land. But as the movement of people and goods between settlements became more important within the unrestricted, open agricultural landscape, the pattern of subsequent settlement eventually evolved into a series of regularly spaced villages and towns.

PREDYNASTIC AND EARLY SETTLEMENT IN SOUTHERN MESOPOTAMIA

Around 4300 B.C. the tempo of settlement in southern Mesopotamia increased, shifting the focus of community formation to areas closer to the southern Mesopotamian delta. The proliferation of communities into the northern delta was part of a larger expansion of new communities instigated by competition for arable land, a phenomenon that continued in the region until about 4000 B.C. South of present-day Baghdad the landscape changes into a broad, flat, desertlike series of alluvial valleys and marshlands. Rainfall is rare, and, with periodic flooding, renders the region a combination of desert and swamp. Early communities in the region occupied the lands along natural watercourses, domesticated animals foraged in the area, and plant cultivation occurred along swamp edges and stream banks. After this period, population increases often transformed small towns into urban centers. Communities became more stratified socially and began to display a rudimentary political and religious hierarchy; economies based on subsistence agriculture quickly evolved into stratified entities, with a complex division of labor and substantial technological advancement. By the third millennium B.C., Bronze Age settlements flourished in Mesopotamia, leaving behind the Neolithic stage of cultural achievement. The earliest cultures in the area were the Urbaid, Warka, protoliterate, and early dynastic societies. Supported by a viable agricultural economic base, the group produced a series of cultural advances beginning around 4000 B.C. and lasting until 3000 B.C. The quality and diversity of production included the use of sophisticated techniques of fabrication and metallurgy, supervised by a class of secular and religious administrators.

The cultures of southern Mesopotamia sought ways to expand their economic base by exploiting landscape resources to increase plant cultivation and animal husbandry. However, there were obstacles to such a strategy stemming from environmental conditions. The hot summer months constricted the amount of natural pasture available for animal forage. In addition, during droughts, the

Aerial view of contemporary irrigation channels in Iraq.

best natural vegetation occurred along the edges of watercourses, in areas used for agriculture. Not wanting to infringe on naturally arable land, inhabitants were obliged to expand arable lands to produce adequate forage.

Accelerated competition for arable land soon made the old technique of simple irrigation by breaching stream banks obsolete, and improvements in irrigation technology became a priority to assure adequate agricultural production in the face of expanding populations. Consequently, small-scale irrigation methods evolved into increasingly sophisticated techniques, including the building of irrigation canals, and later the construction, maintenance, and administration of canal network systems.

Expansion of arable land and improvements in irrigation technology spawned changes in urban patterns during the Urbaid period, and by 4000 B.C. the regional settlement pattern had evolved into a mix of towns and villages, with larger settlements surrounded by satellite communities. Urbaid towns and villages occupied sites adjacent to the various smaller tributaries and channels of the major rivers. Mostly they depended on short channels running from the rivers as sources for their irrigation needs. In a number of instances, towns developed a linear configuration to reflect their relationship to channels. Larger towns functioned as markets and religious centers; smaller communities provided a focus for outlying agricultural establishments. Because the area lacked major natural resources, the towns also functioned as trading centers: agricultural goods were exchanged for imported timber, stone, and metals. Revenues derived from

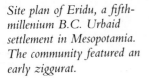

Site plan of Eridu, a fifth-millenium B.C. Urbaid settlement in Mesopotamia. The community featured an early ziggurat.

0   50 m

the trading of imported goods for local produce probably remained in the hands of administrators in the form of tributes and taxes paid to the religious authority, which progressively strengthened the position of the priest class in the culture.

By 4350 B.C. the Urbaid culture existed over most of the alluvial plain. All settlements occupied sites that were near waterways; few settlements exceeded 20 acres in size. The precise form of these communities remains a matter of speculation, due to the insubstantial quality of the mud brick material used to construct settlements. From what evidence exists, there is some reason to believe that these early towns may have been built up and organized in a regular grid of streets and lanes. We know that virtually all Urbaid settlements contained a large public building, usually a temple, fashioned from mud brick and some imported stone. These temples began as small elevated structures, which were to evolve into the larger multilevel ziggurats of later Mesopotamian cultures. Eridu, founded as an Urbaid settlement, typified community arrangement during the period.

CITY-STATES

In the succeeding millennium, the pace of urbanization quickened, and communities in southern Mesopotamia began to acquire the characteristics of sophisticated cities, including increased population densities, a complex economy with a division of labor, and a management class. By 3500 B.C. most of the larger settlements were politically autonomous and functioned as independent city-states. The trend to urbanization and the formation of city-states stemmed from a migration of individuals to fortified centers, leading to a reduction in the rural population. Agriculture remained the economic base for these early cities, with land nearest the urban centers being the most intensely exploited for agricultural purposes.

The precise social structure of villages and cities of the later predynastic period remains obscure, due to the lack of written materials from the era. Mostly, villages remained relatively unchanged from earlier times, consisting of a few acres near streams or marshes. The layout of larger cities was rarely formal. Most important urban centers had a fortified ring wall giving them an overall circular form; beyond the wall, farmers worked irrigated tracts of land. Unpaved and dusty streets radiated from large public buildings, large and sufficiently straight for the movement of carts and chariots. Residences belonging to the affluent lined the streets; most of these were multiroomed with spacious courtyards. Meanwhile, the less well-to-do occupied smaller structures along alleyways between larger structures. There was usually no marketplace for private commerce in these early cities, since most commercial activity was conducted by the religious elite; public, open space amenity was usually absent.

Toward the end of the predynastic period in southern Mesopotamia major urban centers often covered 250 acres or more and had populations numbering in the thousands. The city of Uruk, for example, occupied over 1,100 acres and had a population of 50,000 people. As these centers acquired more wealth through production and trade, their religious edifices became more monumental, making the cities dominant visual elements in the landscape. Also, the emergence of religious structures coincided with the appearance of a specialized priest class, subsidized by tribute derived from agricultural production and trade. The White Temple of Uruk, built at about 3500 B.C. during the Warka period, is one of the few extant examples of temple architecture of the predynastic era. The complex consisted of a one-level ziggurat, or "holy mountain," supporting a flat-roofed temple. The ziggurat and temple measured over 200 feet by 200 feet at the base and over 42 feet to the temple roof. As a visual element the White Temple functioned as a counterpoint to the maze of winding streets and one- and two-storied mud brick structures.

Erbil. The settlement retains the look of early communities with its circular wall enclosing a tightly knit urban structure.

Several other cities in the region attained city-state status during the Urbaid period, including the settlements of Ur and Umma, the former important for its relatively good state of preservation and its monumental temple, the ziggurat of Ur. Through time the city of Ur evolved to include three parts: an older walled city, a religious district, and a surrounding town. The old city resembled other settlements of its genre; its layout was irregular, abutting two small ports on the Euphrates. What open spaces there were ran through the religious district, an area near the northwest quarter of the city, consigned to priests and royalty. The remainder of the city within the old walls was a compact and densely occupied area, reserved for residential housing. Most residences were of mud brick construction, though they were less constricted spatially than homes in earlier communities. One notable aspect of the housing at Ur was the use of interior courtyards as open space, a feature highly prized in an environment devoid of public open space.[1]

URBANIZATION IN SOUTHERN MESOPOTAMIA: SUMERIA

Population growth in the communities of southern Mesopotamia signaled the beginning of a new era of landscape occupation in the region. A once fertile plain with isolated pockets of permanent settlement changed to a landscape of densely occupied urban centers.[2] We have seen that in the alluvial plans adjacent to the riverways south of Baghdad, cities were no longer simply agricultural centers, but had acquired the status of city-states with authority over adjacent landscapes. In the interest of trade these cities began to function as a unified society, with a common language and social system. By 3000 B.C. the cities, towns, and villages of southern Mesopotamia had been organized into the Sumerian culture, the first major civilization in the region. City-states evolved in the region, with Babylon becoming the capital of a single empire in 2250 B.C.

The foundation of the Sumerian civilization was an intensive agricultural system based on effective artificial irrigation and production management. At its

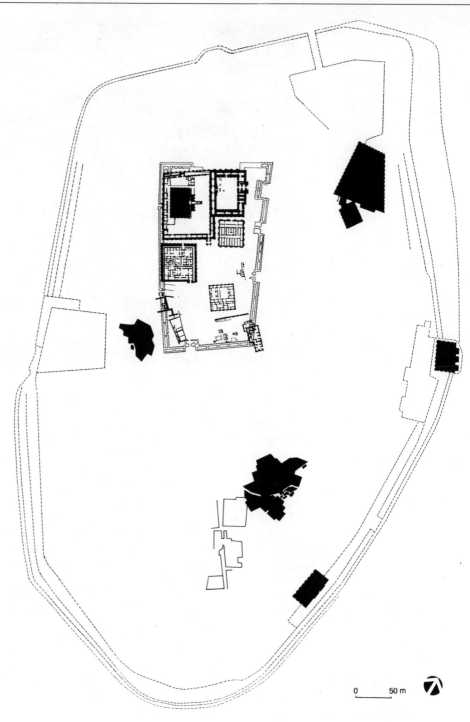

Ur with its protective walls and religious district, upper center; solid lines and dark areas indicate excavated portions. (Morris, A.E.J. History of Urban Form. John Wiley and Sons, 1979.)

0   50 m

most powerful in the early second millennium, the society had produced a language based on cuneiform, and invented the plough, wagon wheel, and sailboat. A mathematical system based on the number 60 and the invention of measuring and surveying instruments provided the society with the means to measure land, record agricultural production, and tax production. Farming had evolved into a sophisticated endeavor, featuring a farmers' almanac, which gave precise advice on plant husbandry, irrigation technique, and farm management.

Most agricultural strategies, especially irrigation techniques, stemmed from the methods employed by earlier communities in the southern alluvium, to which the Sumerians made relatively modest improvements. Earthen dams retained small streams and tributaries and formed reservoirs from which water flowed through short canals to fields. Though rudimentary, the technique allowed the Sumerians to expand the amount of arable land around the major cities, with fields often extending 9 miles from the center of the settlement. As a result, watercourses near the main urban centers acquired a canal-like form, as the inhabitants worked to straighten and deepen their channels for boat traffic. Written evidence for the construction of larger structures and reservoirs is rare; references in Sumerian writings to dams, weirs, and dykes does not occur before the middle of the third millennium B.C.

Despite the emphasis on agricultural production in Sumeria, an important portion of everyday life focused on activities within the urban centers. In fact, it was improved agricultural production resulting from the Sumerians' effective irrigation techniques which freed a portion of the population from direct involvement in cultivation, allowing them to engage in trade, craft, and administration. Merchants, craftsmen, administrators, farmers, herdsmen, and fishermen all occupied dwellings within the cities; artisans and itinerant craftsmen exchanged their goods for money in the central markets. As the cities and towns grew into economic centers, more people migrated from rural areas to urban centers. Rapid urbanization took place throughout the third millennium, increasing the number of urban sites occupying large areas of landscape; by this time up to 78 percent of the urban sites in southern Mesopotamia occupied sites larger than 100 acres or more.[3] Visually, the landscape was a composite of town and pasture, the latter existing as the part of the environment, "fructified with water, the moistened ground."[4] Irrigated lands surrounding population centers produced substantial yields of agricultural produce, including cereals, dates, and gar-

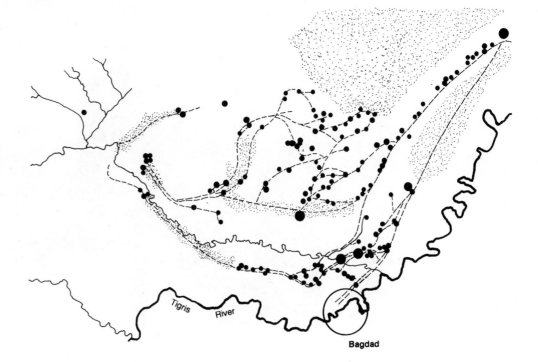

Settlements and irrigation system in the Diayan Plain during the second millenium B.C.

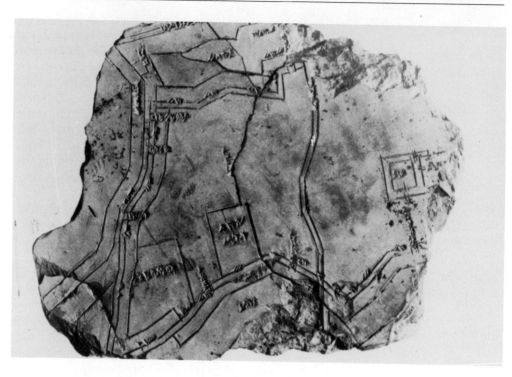

Fragment of a clay tablet depicting an urban district within Nippur. Structures, walls, and the river appear in the artifact.

Model of a Sumerian Urban neighborhood with a ziggurat in the distance. Communities were tightly arranged environments with little public open space.

A clay tablet illustrating a part of an Assyrian hunting park. Such spaces contained exotic plant material and a requisite irrigation network.

den crops. Intensely cultivated and highly irrigated lands, including gardens and orchards, occupied areas close to the cities and towns; large-scale cultivation areas lay on the periphery of the higher-yield lands.[5]

Sustained by the yields from the agricultural lands, the major urban settlements functioned as economic, social, and religious centers in the southern alluvium. Within these roughly circular, walled enclaves, citizens went about their business in relative freedom. Even the poorest inhabitants managed to own a house and garden or a farm and cattle. Homes of the less affluent tended to be one-story mud brick structures, containing several rooms organized around a central courtyard. More affluent individuals possessed two-story dwellings of a dozen rooms or more with space for servants and room for a private chapel and, in some instances, a mausoleum in the basement. Often the residences and accompanying workspaces encircled the major public and religious structures. In Nippur, a principal Sumerian religious and cultural center, and in ancient Khafje, the major public and private structures had a south-southwest orientation to take advantage of the *shamal,* the prevailing summer breezes. Residential and commercial districts surrounded the structures, forming a concentric urban pattern. Consistent with Nippur's function as the religious heart of the larger settlements, a multileveled ziggurat, sited on an elevated terrace, loomed above the smaller community structures.

THE NORTHERN ALLUVIUM: ASSYRIAN URBANIZATION

Eventually, constant strife between competing factions in southern Mesopotamia, and the general enervation that eventually affects any civilization, shifted the cultural focus in Mesopotamia from the southern alluvium to the region of the northern plains nearer the Zagros Mountains. The Assyrians, a Semitic group from western Asia, assumed control of the northern Mesopotamian region in 1250 B.C., supplanting the indigenous Babylonians. The Assyrians tended to be more militaristic than their predecessors and produced a society based on strong central authority. Assyrian cities contained palaces, temples, and residential and commercial districts; towns and villages dotted the countryside, providing the labor to maintain the artificially irrigated agricultural lands. Assyrian royalty maintained botanical gardens and hunting preserves, the latter evolving over time from places of ritual to recreational sites for royalty.

At the time of Assyrian ascendency in the northern plains, many of the agricultural techniques used by the Sumerians were common practice in the northern alluvium. Therefore, all the constraints related to the maintenance of a viable irrigation system fell to the Assyrians, who quickly adopted the technologies of the earlier societies. Irrigation canals and channels fed water to outlying agricultural zones. Agricultural production supported commerce within the larger urban centers. The care taken by the Assyrians to maintain a healthy agricultural base is apparent from the written record on clay tablets, with illustrations delineating the various methods used to assure maximum benefits from intensified agricultural practices. From small plots to medium-sized farms to large-scale agricultural estates, the Assyrians successfully produced a range of agricultural products, including barley—a prime staple—onions, garlic, lettuce, endive, carrots, melons, pomegranates, apricots, plums, peaches, figs, dates, grapes, and olives. To maintain this output, all the agricultural lands, large and small, received water through an irrigation system that ranged from simple channels cut from local tributaries to larger, more ambitious canals and channels that conducted large volumes of water to outlying lands. *Qanats,* or horizontal wells, conveyed water some distances from the foot of mountains to arable lands. Qualitatively, the systems, large and small, were similar to those of the southern alluvium: natural channels were dredged into a more linear configuration, thereby improving the flow of water and facilitating the conveyance of boats from one urban area to another along the channels. In the agricultural lands adjacent to the Assyrian city of Nineveh, for example, records indicate that, during the reign of Sennacherib, specific projects increased the size of the irrigation system. These included the canalization of the Khosr River to irrigate the orchards and royal park, which contained rare flora collected by the king during his foreign campaigns. A second, more ambitious project included the diversion of the Gomel River into the Khosr River by the construction of a diversion canal from the mountains, at a distance of 30 miles northeast of Nineveh. Both projects fed water to all the orchards in the hot summer months, and to the extensive alluvial agricultural sites to the south of the city. A royal park, with its exotic plants, produced reeds from swamp plants, while wood from the cypress and mulberry trees furnished material for the construction of the royal palaces.

Efficient irrigation techniques and plentiful agricultural yields helped to stimulate a general trend toward urbanization in the Assyrian cities of northern Mesopotamia. Whether for cultural or economic reasons, increasing numbers of individuals migrated into the larger cities in search of the rewards available in a socially stratified milieu. In these centers, people lived and worked in the residential and commercial districts surrounding the important royal and religious structures. In form, the cities resembled the urban areas of the southern alluvium: residential and commercial areas emanating from the center to the city wall in a roughly circular configuration. The size of one's residence indicated social rank, with the less affluent occupying modest dwellings while the wealthier occupied sumptuous structures. However, urban amenities, including parks and open spaces, were not normally a feature of the Assyrian urban environments.

Despite the dearth of urban open space, life for the ruling and managerial classes was probably quite comfortable, judging from the large palaces found within the urban centers. At Khorsbad, home of several important Assyrian rulers, the extensive palace of Sargon II clearly illustrates the level of urban

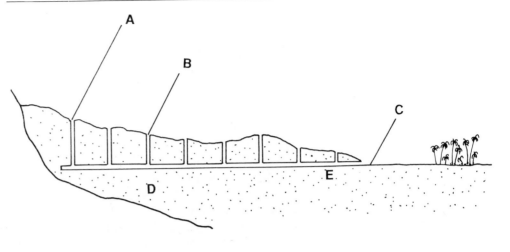

Section showing a qanat water system. The technique permitted communities to draw water from subterranean streams. (A) primary well (B) qanat shaft (C) surface stream (D) water table (E) channel.

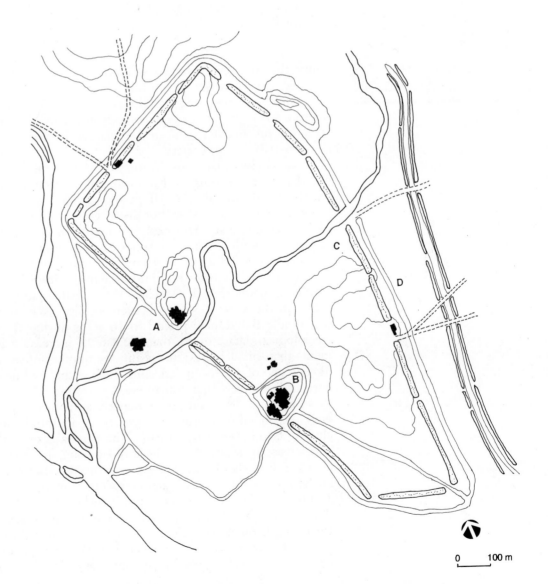

Nineveh with (A) citadel (B) arsenal (C) city walls (D) city moat. The Khosr River cuts across the site.

0   100 m

planning and design attained in the large Assyrian cities in the early first millennium B.C. The site of the palace and town is a short distance from Nineveh, away from the Mosul River and the stifling summer heat. Sargon ordered that the palace be located on an artificial terrace to protect the structure from inundation during peak flood periods. Half of the palace complex lay inside the town walls, while the remainder jutted beyond the enclosure to form a projection into the landscape. Early excavations led researchers to conclude that the plan of the complex was symmetrical, consistent with nineteenth-century European ideals concerning urban form, but subsequent interpretations showed the plan to be slightly trapezoidal in shape.

The main terrace, constructed of unbaked brick and supporting the palace complex, contained an advanced internal drainage system that conveyed all run-off into large, vaulted sewers. Ramps led up along the sides of the terrace to convey draft animals and chariots. The various structures situated on the main terrace formed a complex of interior spaces and exterior courtyards. Courtyard surfaces were made of flat bricks or a layer of bitumen and rammed earth; each sloped slightly toward the center so that water could be easily drained into the underground sewer system. A few courtyards had richly embellished surfaces of yellow, blue, or green enamelled brick, sometimes depicting the image of plants or animals.

NEO-BABYLONIAN URBANIZATION

While the Assyrians worked assiduously to maintain control of the Mesopotamian region, elements within the society, most notably some of the progeny of the earlier Sumerians and Babylonians, were slowly undermining Assyrian domination. Invasion by the Medes, a group from the eastern Zagros, and the destruction of Nineveh reduced Assyrian authority and hastened the formation of the neo-Babylonian society.

Neo-Babylonian consolidation of Mesopotamia accompanied a rapid growth of urban areas in southern Mesopotamia, reversing a trend of urban decline that had begun during the Ur III period (2113–2006 B.C.). Growth of the urban areas accompanied a "slow but distinct expansion of population and resettlement of long abandoned territories."[6] Some of the growth accrued from population expansion, while a portion resulted from the return to the region of people who had been exiled during Assyrian rule. Also large numbers of individuals may have been forcibly transferred into the mid-Mesopotamian region during the rule of Nebucchadnezzar II (604–562 B.C.). All these factors contributed to an increase in the average size of settlement sites, which rose from 11 acres during the middle Babylonian period to 16 acres during the neo-Babylonian era.[7] Archaeological data indicate that the rate of increase was greater for larger settlements than smaller sites, increasing the number of sites of 24 acres or more from 36 percent of the occupied sites during the middle Babylonian period to 51 percent in the neo-Babylonian era.

Intensive urbanization influenced agricultural practices: irrigation systems were expanded and improved yearly agricultural yields were emphasized, including two harvests per season. The emphasis on maximizing yields stimulated an increase in seed use per hectare—during the earlier Ur III period requiring about .5 bushels of seed per acre; in the neo-Babylonian period, the figure increased to over 1.5 bushels per acre. Yields increased proportionally, from about 14 bushels of barley per acre during the Ur III period to 625 to 830 bushels. If these figures are accurate, the neo-Babylonians must have maintained strict irrigation schedules to avoid excessive irrigation and salination.

Increased yields were also tied to the use of more sophisticated irrigation strategies and techniques. In contemporary records the use of new technical terms that referred to sluice gates may have indicated development of new techniques that made better use of available water. Also, the old Babylonian strategy, employing linear irrigation channels branching from parallel and widely spaced canals or river branches was changed in neo-Babylonian times, giving form to an interlocking grid of channels that broke large areas of landscape into uniform units of cultivable land. The change was significant, for in the older scheme large areas between irrigation channels remained uncultivated, while with the neo-Babylonian approach large, continuous cultivated areas became common.

Life in the neo-Babylonian cities, supported by these intensive agricultural practices, was similar in many ways to that in earlier Mesopotamian urban centers. People lived and worked in the commercial and residential districts, while the important administrative functions occurred in the palaces, temples, and public edifices. Babylon, the most important of these centers, epitomized urban life. Straddling the Euphrates River, the 355-acre city had a roughly rectangular configuration within its perimeter moat and wall. Wide thoroughfares divided districts into rectilinear areas that contained houses and workspaces for laborer and merchant classes. The wealthy lived in larger structures featuring interior spaces opening to courtyards. Between the river and the Processional Way leading from the Ishtar Gate, several important structures loomed above the residential and commercial districts. These included the Marduk temple, the imposing ziggurat (Tower of Babel), and the royal palace. The palace complex, including the king's abode and neighboring royal residences, lay protected within a boundary wall. On a terraced hill adjacent to the palace were planted numerous horticultural specimens, including rare plants, as in the garden of Sennacherib near

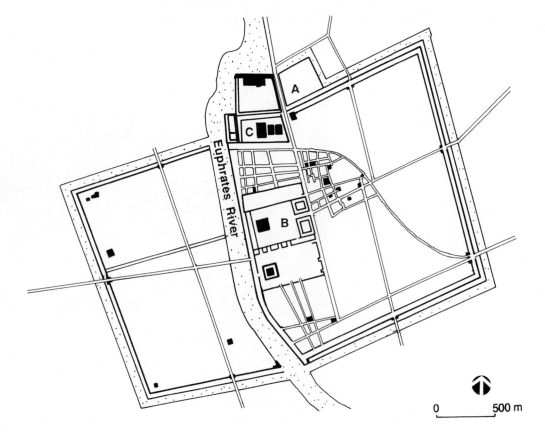

Babylon and the Palace of Marduk including (A) the Ishtar Gate (B) temple (C) Hanging Gardens.

Nineveh. Seen from a distance beyond the wall, the larger plant specimens appeared to float in the air, helping to perpetuate the tradition of the "hanging gardens of Babylon."

Urbanization and neo-Babylonian supremacy halted abruptly in the fourth century B.C. with the invasion of the Persians from the lands northeast of the Zagros Mountains. From the middle of the third century B.C. to well into the sixth century A.D., Mesopotamia became part of the Persian civilization, ruled by outsiders. Unlike earlier invasions and political changes, the demise of the neo-Babylonians meant the end of control of the Mesopotamian landscape by indigenous factions. Despite this political disruption, not all that had been accomplished by the previous dynasties in Mesopotamia fell into neglect. The Per-

Recent drawing of a proposed restoration of the Palace of Marduk and its gardens.

Aerial photo of the ruins of Persepolis with the line of qanats to the right of the palace.

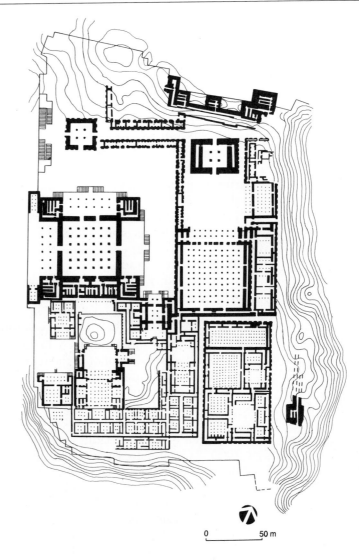

Plan of palace at Persepolis. Showing rectilinear organization to the site.

0   50 m

sians, like the earlier Sumerians and Assyrians, adopted many of the agricultural practices and irrigation techniques used by the indigenous Mesopotamians. At Persepolis, the Persian capitol, Darius I and Xerxes oversaw the construction of a sumptuous palace covering 33 acres, which included gardens with an ornamental lake, embellished with plant material.

Both the Sassanian and later Islamic societies relied on the neo-Babylonian strategies and technologies of irrigation and cultivation. Later, as the great empires in the Mediterranean flourished, some of these techniques would accrue to the western cultures, especially in Spain during Moorish occupation.

THE INDUS VALLEY

The Indus Valley culture was another prominent ancient society to flourish in an alluvial environment. Formerly it appeared to be less spectacular, culturally, than either the Mesopotamian or Egyptian civilization; perhaps the fact that the Indus Valley, or Harappan, culture evolved later than that of Egypt or Mesopotamia made the society seem less significant. However, recent archaeological information has helped to place the Indus culture in proper perspective, as a major ancient society occupying a distinct region, producing a written language, constructing large, well-planned cities with sophisticated drainage and water systems, and eventually, controlling more territory—over 494,000 square miles—than any other ancient Near Eastern culture.

The physical essence of the Indus culture was the Indus River valley landscape, its tributaries, and adjacent environments. East of Mesopotamia along the Arabian Sea, the Indian subcontinent, responding to movements in the earth's crust 50 million years ago, had collided with the Eurasian land mass and forced the intervening land mass upward, forming the Himalayan Mountains. Spring snow melt from these mountains generated billions of cubic feet of water that rushed into the Indus Valley and carried large amounts of silt and clay to form the Indus River plain. Eventually, two major rivers, the Indus and the Ghaggar-Haskra, and their tributaries formed the drainage system along the length of the valley. The Indus is an *aggrading* river, depositing alluvium along its course, while in portions of the Ghaggar–Hakra system, the river flow is *degrading*, continuing to cut into the land.

The Indus Valley has two principal ecological zones, the Baluchistan Plateau with the western highlands, and the lower Indus Valley including the western and eastern valley areas and the delta. The Thar Desert on the eastern edge of the valley isolates the Indus environment from the rest of India. The regional climate is hot and arid, even in the western uplands and Baluchistan Plateau, though the sparse rainfall in the region is sufficient to support an adequate amount of vegetation suitable for grazing. In arable regions, the lands yielded several crops a year, especially with artificial irrigation on the rich alluvial soils of the valley.

Most of the permanent settlement in the Indus Valley occurred after several millennia of seminomadic occupation in the western uplands and plateaus. By 7000 B.C. humans were cultivating wheat and tending sheep in Afghanistan and Baluchistan. Agriculture and pastoralism slowly spread throughout the uplands, where dry farming was made possible by sufficient rainfall and irrigation from local streams. In the highlands west of the valley, small settlements subsisted on farming, pastoralism, and occasional hunting and gathering. Between 3500 B.C. and 2500 B.C. permanent villages existed in the foothills, and individuals were beginning to migrate into the Indus Valley. Initial settlement occurred along the margins between the foothills and the floodplains and spread eastward into the valley. Several factors influenced the growth of settlements within the valley, including general behavior of the major rivers, their navigability, the climate, the availability of natural resources, and, finally, the location of east-west trade routes. Ideal sites were those along the rivers and tributaries that linked settlements to the sea. Along these locations, the Indus alluvial environment favored cultivation of many plants, with wheat and barley being the most important economically. Evidence of the plough appears near a few communities, but usually the natural fertility of the alluvium allowed for plant growth without ploughing or fertilizing: fields near natural flood channels protected by earth embankments were ideal for plant cultivation.

At the height of the Harappan culture the pattern of settlement in the valley featured large agricultural and trading centers surrounded by smaller, local settlements. Some authorities contend that the location of the major cities represents a "central place" settlement configuration, while others argue for a "gateway" rationale for the location of large settlements, particularly those located along the frontiers near major trading routes. The settlement pattern is perhaps best described as a mixture of communities including major cities, medium-sized centers, and small villages.

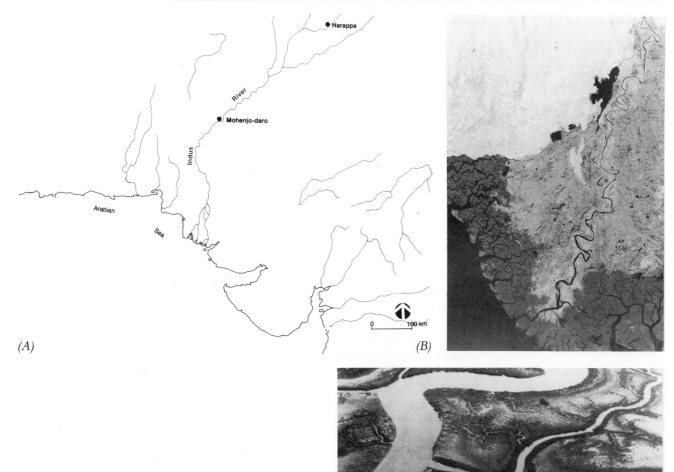

(A) Alluvial landscape in the Indus region. The smaller channels were ideally suited for settlement and small-scale agriculture. (B)Aerial view of Indus Valley. (C) Location of Mohenjo-Daro and Haraffa.

MOHENJO-DARO, HARAPPA, AND ALLAHDINO

Large, planned cities and smaller settlements were a familiar feature in the Indus Valley region by 2200 B.C. Most of the human activity within the settlements depended on agriculture, with some individuals participating in trade, crafts, and administration. The major settlements show a surprising degree of conformity in town planning, including regular thoroughfares, evenly spaced cross streets, and rectilinear alignment of structures. Residences often sat on raised platforms as a safeguard against flooding.

Mohenjo–daro was one of several large settlements in the Indus Valley to exhibit the Harappan sense of town planning and site detailing. The community evolved from a small settlement dating from the early third millennium B.C., occupying a site midway along the Indus River in the central valley. At its zenith the town covered an area of nearly 2 square miles. The layout of the settlement formed a large grid, with thoroughfares and cross streets aligned with the city's main street, a road nearly 30 feet wide and drained by adjacent, wide drainage ditches. Businesses, residences, and public buildings made up the various districts; public toilets and an underground sewage system conveyed effluence from the community. Most residential structures were of fired-brick construction, and included major interior spaces surrounding an open courtyard. Houses contained a number of amenities, including showers and toilets that drained into the municipal sewage system.

The most striking structure at Mohenjo-daro was the great 3-acre fortified citadel, located about 400 feet to the northwest of the main settlement. For some reason, the land between the citadel and the community remained unoccupied, though inhabitants may have flooded the space periodically to produce a pond for fishing or bathing. Spatially, the largest element of the citadel was a 36-foot brick platform, perhaps used as a refuge during flood periods. A large bath facility, halls, garrisons, and granaries completed the complex. Religious structures, such as the Mesopotamian ziggurat were not a part of the citadel since apparently no monumental public structures existed in the Indus communities.

At its zenith, Mohenjo-daro was a prosperous community of nearly 40,000 individuals, who labored as farmers, craftspeople, herders, brick masons, and builders. They cultivated wheat and barley and augmented their diet with dates, melons, legumes, and various other crops, while husbanding animals, including cattle, goats, sheep, pigs, and fowl.

To the north of Mohenjo-daro, situated in a zone of high agricultural productivity and south of present day Lahore on the Ravi River, rested the town of Harappa, the most prominent of the northern Indus Valley settlements. The community occupied a sliver of high ground that protruded into the valley near the alluvium. The site, with its high ground for protection and alluvium for cultivation, was ideal for occupation. The size of the settlement, roughly 65 hectares, placed Harappa in the category of contemporary major cities. Due to its location on the Indus frontier, it may have experienced much commercial activity as a gateway city to the Hindu Kush, Baluchistan, and Afghanistan: several important trade routes converged on the town, and the Indus River drainage afforded communication with the plains.

Unfortunately, intrusion by railway builders in the nineteenth century obscured the original organization of Harappa. However, we do know that the town had a gridiron configuration and included residential and public structures similar to those of Mohenjo-daro.

Smaller settlements in the Indus Valley do not reveal themselves as readily as the larger communities. Generally the smaller towns patterned their way of life after that of the larger ones; agriculture, basic crafts, and arts occupied the time of inhabitants of cities, large and small. One smaller community that has been extensively studied is the settlement of Allahdino near the delta region in the southwestern Indus alluvium. The first occupants of the site were pastoralists, and were succeeded by individuals who settled the site and built permanent structures, a period of occupation that lasted no more than one hundred years. Wheat and barley were the agricultural mainstay; cattle, sheep, goats, and water buffalo, fish and fowl augmented the diet. Eventually, the town occupied a site on a low hill at the confluence of two small tributaries, the Malir and Basaar Nadi Rivers. In its day it was a modest-sized community, extending no more than 75 yards in any direction and home to fewer than 80 individuals. Yet within the site a number of human-built features exist to provide a record of human occupation of a small village during the Harappan period.

One important urban element was an open, paved court measuring 20 yards by 8 yards, surrounded by several mud brick one-story structures. The court is

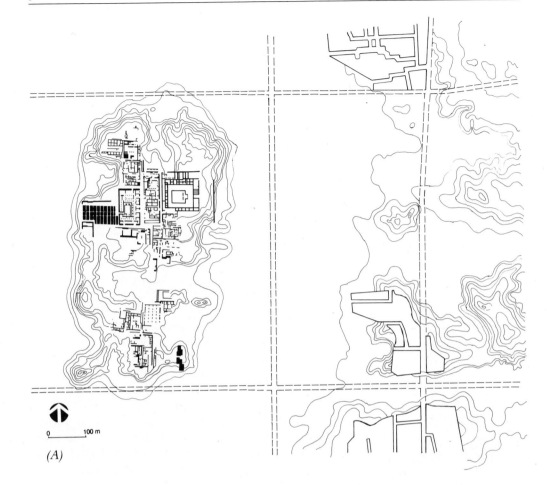

(A)

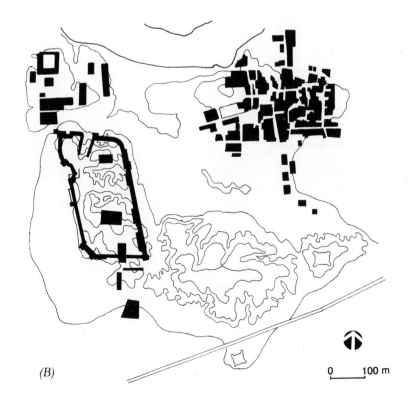

(B)

Plan of the excavations of
(A) Mohenjo-daro (B) Harappa.

at the highest point on the site, and at the southern edge of the space, two water wells spill out into stone basins. Access to the central court is from between the buildings. In addition to the large court, several architectural elements exhibit evidence that reasonably commodious structures existed on the site. For example, the largest structure contains an interior courtyard; other structures contain interior baths that drain by way of stone-lined channels. Allahdino lacks the formal site organization common in larger settlements of the time, and there was no enclosing wall around the site, a usual feature at smaller settlements.

The most intriguing feature of Allahdino is the two water wells. The small opening of the wells, and the possible artesian effect from rising water in a shallow natural underground reservoir, have led a few investigators to conclude that the inhabitants of Allahdino used gravity flow to convey water from the elevated, open courtyard along stone channels to open fields below the settlement. If so, they avoided having to convey water from the rivers through open canals to the fields, a procedure which would have required an extensive canal system.

As successful as the Harappans were in their occupation of the Indus River valley, theirs was a relatively short-lived experience, lasting about 500 years. By 1800 B.C. evidence of cultural decline began to appear; the Harappans' ability to design artifacts of high quality, particularly in pottery, began to wane, and a general deterioration in quality in art and architecture signaled a loss of cultural direction. Theories concerning the cause of the decline range from possible invasion to a large-scale geological cataclysm. Hydrologists speculate that a tectonic disturbance altered the flow of the Lower Indus River, creating a large lake at the mouth of the Indus River. Wenke[8] ties the demise of the civilization to a combination of factors, including natural and social events, both of which precipitated wholesale abandonment of major Harappan centers. As the Harappan society gradually lost control of the Indus Valley, cultural power began to shift to adjacent regions. After 1100 B.C. large cities developed in the Ganges River valley, where expertise in metallurgy, agriculture, and construction helped to propel the Ganges cultures to prominence.

ENVIRONMENTAL ISSUES: AGRICULTURE AND URBAN DECLINE

At the end of the predynastic period in southern Mesopotamia, villages, towns, and cities formed the pattern of settlement in the region. Economic complexity and social stratification mirrored the rapid increase in settlement expansion. By the late fourth century B.C., people were no longer living solely in small towns and villages, but on adjacent lands possessing agricultural potential. At this point the settlement pattern had become more differentiated: major cities dominated the alluvium, surrounded by dependent villages and towns. These autonomous city-states functioned as production and exchange nodes for the inhabitants of the agricultural areas.

As populations increased in urban areas of the southern delta, competition between farmers and shepherds for use of the desirable lands near waterways stimulated the development of more effective techniques for supplying water to potentially arable lands. The simple technique of breaching a stream bank was enough to supply irrigation to a small village, but was generally insufficient to supply the needs of larger settlements. The technological advance that solved this problem was the refinement of artificial irrigation. The result was the development of complex systems of small ditches and canals to convey water to fields near urban areas. In the process farmers converted greater areas of natural lands to agricultural use. Eventually, flooding and overirrigation exposed arable lands to the recurring problem of salinity. Finally, as alluviation extended the delta

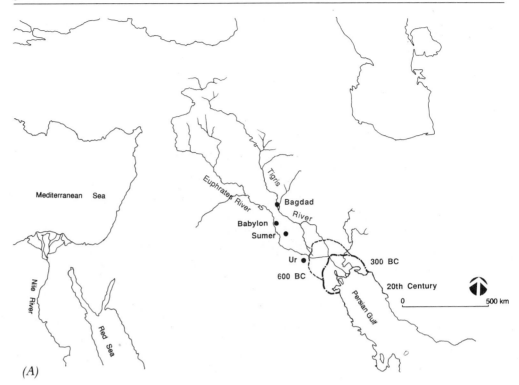

(A) *Stages of alluviation from the seventh century B.C. to the present. (B) A present-day example of salination in the alluvial soils in the Indus region of southern Pakistan. (C) Timber was a precious commodity in the ancient Near East. Due to protracted urbanization and pastoralism, only small patches of cedar forests now remain along the uplands surrounding the ancient alluvial landscapes.*

(A)

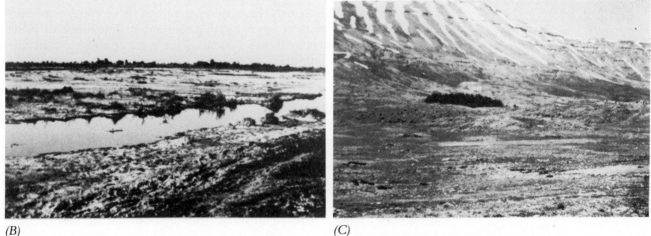

(B)   (C)

into the Persian Gulf, farmers used their knowledge of canal building to drain low-lying land.

The conversion of natural landscape to agricultural use was only a part of the change in the quality of human adaptation to the landscape. With less contact with rural existence and more dependence on urban life, humans were relatively free for the first time from immediate dependence on the environment and more dependent on the interplay of a complex social structure and division of labor. Physically and socially, the very shape of cities like Uruk, with its fortified and ziggurat-dominated organization, epitomized a new relationship between humans and the landscape.

Eventually, the Sumerian economic and social system could not withstand the constant internecine strife between competing cities. By 2300 B.C. the society was weakened to the point that the cultural focus began to shift northward to the area south of Baghdad, home of the Akkadians, a Semitic group from west Asia. The Akkadians destroyed Nippur, the Sumerian holy city, and for about two hundred years dominated the region, until the Sumerians regained control of the territory in the name of the Third Dynasty of Ur. The effect of this cultural exchange was to create a climate of cultural ebb and flow in Mesopotamia that would continue into successive millennia.

The effect of the shift in power from Sumeria to Akkadia and back to the Third Dynasty of Ur, on the pattern of landscape occupation in southern Mesopotamia, is an issue that tends to be submerged by consideration of the cultural achievements of the time. The intense urbanization, which had proceeded at a rapid pace from the time of Uruk through the Sumerian period, began to wane, with fewer individuals migrating into the urban centers and more electing to remain in rural settlements. As a result, the percentage of urban centers occupying 100 acres or more dropped from the high 78 percent in the Sumerian period to 55 percent in the Ur III period.

Despite the shift in population from urban centers to rural areas, large-scale canal systems appeared during the Third Dynasty of Ur. By the second millennium B.C. newer channels crossed the plain from the west-northwest. These artificial canals, some more than 60 miles in length and large in carrying capacity, helped to solve the problem of maintaining a continuous water supply from the Euphrates as the river continued to shift westerly away from the center of the alluvium.[9] In addition, zonal irrigation, in contrast to the restricted irrigation system stemming from the back slopes of main levees of earlier times, became a common feature during the Ur III period. Networks of irrigation channels, often forming lattice or dendritic configurations, reached beyond the main tributaries to irrigate orchards and fields. The main channels of these systems became more linear, with intensive human labor applied to their maintenance to prevent recurrent meanders. The system was beneficial for river commerce and for irrigation agriculture, with minimal loss of fields and gardens to uncontrolled erosion caused by meandering.[10]

These remarkable changes in irrigation practices, fully replacing one system with another, affected not only the quality of irrigation in the region but the lands the new systems watered. For example, in terms of the labor required to keep each system functioning, the new channels, with less gradient than earlier systems, had a tendency to accumulate silt, making the older levees more advantageous for irrigation. More significantly, the increased volume of water possible in the newer systems tended to favor overirrigation of arable lands. On land near major population centers, farmers placed greater emphasis on very high yields. Plentiful water supply assured greater yields and several harvests on the same land each year. However, multiple yields violated the principle of fallow; lands in Mesopotamia had formerly been allowed to lie uncultivated during alternate years. Intensification and overirrigation hastened the rise in saline groundwater into plant root zones. Within a few seasons, oversalinized lands fell out of production, and replacement of these lands was slow. The progressive loss of cultivatable lands merely put more pressure on available lands, compounding the problem of maintaining yields. For example, an annual agricultural yield of 23 bushels per acre during the Sumerian period declined to 13 bushels during the Ur III era. Agriculture output continued to decline substantially throughout the Ur III period, and by 1700 B.C. the problem had become acute.

Agricultural deterioration, political instability, and a general social decline spelled the end of the Ur III period and the beginning of the Old Babylonian period at the beginning of the second millennium B.C. Beyond the achievements of Hammurabi, which included an articulated legal code, the Old Babylonian period was a time of economic and demographic retrenchment.[11] Few new settlements or irrigation projects appear in the archaeological record. The percentage of urban areas occupying sites larger than 100 acres continued to decline, reaching a low of 16 percent. Smaller, dispersed settlements became the rule. By the middle Babylonian period, the typical settlement pattern consisted of a string of small settlements around irrigation canals, separated by some distance from other concentrations of settlements.[12] One or two larger settlements along this line dominated the region, though most of the population lived in the smaller settlements. Gradually the settlement pattern became more decentralized, with the smaller villages held together by a landed patriarchal authority. In all the pattern had changed dramatically since the Ur III period. The number of occupied sites dropped by 40 percent, reducing the area of occupied land by 77 percent. Many large urban centers had disappeared, though Babylon, the capital, continued to flourish as a city of considerable size.

NOTES

1. A.E.J. Morris. 1979. History of Urban Forms. *New York: Wiley, p. 8.*

2. Robert McC. Adams. 1978. Heartland of Cities. *Chicago and London: University of Chicago Press, p. 130.*

3. Ibid., p. 137.

4. Ibid., p. 138.

5. Hans Nissen and Robert Adams. 1972. The Uru Countryside. *Chicago: University of Chicago Press, p. 23.*

6. Stolper. 1974. p. 199.

7. Adams. 1978, op. cit., p. 178.

8. Robert J. Wenke. 1980. Patterns in Prehistory: Mankind's First Three Million Years. *New York: Oxford University Press, 1980.*

9. Adams. 1978, op. cit, p. 158.

10. Ibid., p. 164. See also T. Jacobsen and R.M. Adams, 1958, "Salt and Silt in Ancient Mesopotamian Agriculture," Science, 120, p. 1251; and R.M. Adams, "Agriculture and Urban Life in South-Western Iran," Science, 136, pp. 109–22 (1962).

11. Adams, 1978, op. cit, p. 165.

12. Ibid., p. 168.

4

Egypt and the Nile Valley

The Nile River Valley landscape is a dramatic element in an otherwise stark environment. Searing reddish deserts bound the dark, rich soils of the Nile channel, providing a narrow linear matrix suitable for human occupation. Historically, inhabitants of the Nile region have been acutely aware of this particular landscape duality, and have linked most aspects of their culture to the river. Agricultural systems, settlement patterns, administrative bodies, and architectural monuments all have antecedents in the river valley and its constituent elements. Physically, the clear distinction between desert and river valley has imbued the Nile cultures with a consistent identity, only occasionally affected by predilections of rulers during more than three thousand years of Egyptian history.

At the heart of this duality is the river, a composite of two major drainage systems, the silt-laden Blue Nile and the clearer White Nile. From prehistoric times to the present, this system has supplied the biological essentials to the inhabitants of the region, producing one of the most enduring examples of human interaction with the landscape. As the Nile Valley became the site for villages, towns, and cities, clever inhabitants tapped into the river to supply moisture, thereby assuring economic survival. The testament to their perseverance and to their close ties to the environment is visible at ancient sites where the Egyptians eventually built impressive monuments that have survived to act as a reminder of their skill in organizing the land.

Satellite photograph of the Nile region.

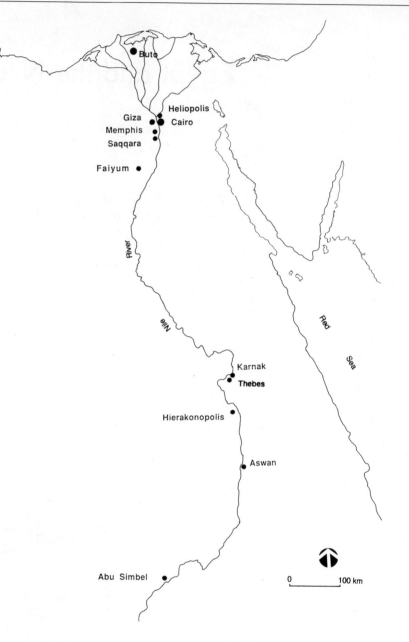

The Nile region with the location of important settlements during the ancient Egyptian kingdoms.

PHYSICAL CONTEXT

Long before the first humans set foot in the Nile Valley, the region had undergone a series of geological events that formed the structure and shape of Egypt. Fifty million years ago, the region was part of the floor of an ancient sea covering much of North Africa to the twenty-third parallel. The ancient seabed contained a mixture of metamorphic and igneous material, now visible at the Second Cataract of the Nile. Sedimentary material appears in southern Egypt and Nubia as limestone, shales, and sand clays in the oases of the western deserts and the northern Nile Valley. Between forty and fifty million years ago, during the Eocene Period, a tilting of the land northward conveyed the waters covering most of Egypt into the Mediterranean Sea. Portions of the northernmost part of Egypt remained submerged for a short period, allowing for deposition of limestone material. Subsequent drainage of water from the African highlands flowed into the Nile valley on the way to the Mediterranean, creating channels, or *wadis*. A second uplift occurred as late as eight million years ago, initiating vertical cutting into the land by the water rushing to the Mediterranean sea. The result was a deep gorge nearly 9 miles wide, which confined the Nile river to its present course. The new channel continued to erode into the old seabed and to expose geological strata that, today, give identity to the Egyptian landscape. Some of the most visible elements from this process are limestone outcrops, which intermittently line the Nile from Cairo to Aswan.

The most recent geological events occurred between 2.5 million and sixteen thousand years ago, when sedimentation carried by the river came to rest near the middle Nile. These deposits created a series of terraces that completed the Nile Valley profile, a topographic succession from arable lowlands to high deserts. By this time the Nile River was a composite of two major sources, the White Nile originating at Lake Victoria and providing a consistent water source to the Valley and the Blue Nile, carrying runoff and silt from the Ethiopian plateaus. The full impact of these two tributaries occurred at the peak flood stage in September when, until recently, 350,000 cubic feet of water and tons of nitrogen-rich silt pushed past the First and Second Cataracts. These processes formed the arable land along the river bank, along with the levees and basins that would be the basis of Egyptian agriculture. A few miles north of Cairo, the Nile breaks into two branches, the Rosetta and the Damietta, to form the Nile Delta. The area of the Delta evolved from protracted sedimentation to encompass nearly 10,000 square miles of alluvium to a depth of 30 to 120 feet. As a result of these events, the Nile became a geographically symmetrical element along its length, with only one interruption, occurring south of Cairo, and due to an ancient depression and lake. The depression, called the Faiyum, and the ancient Lake Moeris extend west of the river for an area of 3,000 square miles; in prehistoric times, the lake received waters from the Nile River.

Human adaptation in the region began with local occupation. Lower Egypt, including the sediment-rich Delta, was ideal for subsistence agriculture. Further

The Nile with adjacent alluvium providing the matrix for agricultural activity.

south along the Nile into Upper Egypt, the rich alluvium along the river margins was also suitable for cultivation and settlement, aided by the limestone outcrops and adjacent deserts that were natural barriers to invasion. Past Aswan and into the Nubian region, a series of cataracts impeded movement on the river: below this point boats can navigate the river northward to the Delta. Throughout the valley, the climate has remained fairly consistent, apart from occasional periods of drought and flooding. Temperatures routinely approach 100 degrees Fahrenheit during the summer and rainfall is infrequent. In late summer and early fall, during the flood period, the heat creates a humid condition ideal for plant cultivation. In its natural state the Nile floods northward, filling the basins and flooding the land to a depth of 3 to 5 feet; after the drenching of the soil, the flood waters remain about forty days. As the flood waters recede, the basins remain filled, sufficient to irrigate surrounding levees, which are suitable for cultivation by October or November. In this context, modest labor will produce a range of edible plants, including wheat, barley, legumes, onions, radishes, cucumbers, melons, and figs and dates.[1] Additionally, pastures along the alluvium support sheep, goats, cattle, and fowl; the Nile River teems with fish and crustaceans; stands of reeds, flax, and papyrus are suitable for basketry, linen, and paper.

PREDYNASTIC SETTLEMENT

Human settlements appeared in the wadis and along the Nile alluvium as early as ten to fifteen thousand years ago. The economic strategy depended on available resources: hunting, fishing, and gathering. By the middle of the ninth millennium B.C. the Nile region became more arid, causing desiccation of Saharan pasturage and rendering the interior wadis less desirable for human occupation. Human response was predictable; people moved into more favorable regions along the Nile, increasing the size of the local population. At this time settlements occurred in areas of alluvium with high percentages of river frontage and natural basins. The landscape around Hierakonopolis in lower Egypt was a prime site during this period.

The quality of life at this point still revolved around modest economic strategies. Butzer[2] supports the hypothesis that the Nile Valley supported hunting and gathering as early as 12,000 B.C. By 5000 B.C. the alluvium was home to a predynastic culture, which relied primarily on cattle and goat pastoralism, in addition to hunting and gathering. Settlements in Upper Egypt retained a hunting and gathering lifestyle until 4000 B.C., when the Badarian culture began to produce fine pottery and the first metal implements in Egypt. Successive predynastic cultures advanced the art of stoneworking and various crafts, but the economic base was still principally hunting and gathering, with pastoralism and plant cultivation retaining a secondary role. Many settlements in upper Egypt favored the desert alluvium margin to take advantage of the seasonal pasturage in the deserts.

Then in the late predynastic period larger settlements, such as the Gerzan town near Hierakonopolis, expanded to contain public buildings, cemeteries, and tombs. Also at this time, Egypt began to coalesce into two "kingdoms," a northern kingdom with Buto as its capital, and a southern kingdom with Heirakonopolis as its center. These two lands in historic times were called To-Mehu and Shemau, Lower and Upper Egypt, and abutted in the vicinity of ancient Memphis. Historically, the two lands consisted of subdivision, or *nomes,* a Greek term for many small settlements clustered around a larger town; in early Egypt sixteen of these existed in Upper Egypt and ten in the Lower Egyptian Delta. Nomes formed in the vicinity of natural basins; during the Old Kingdom most of these

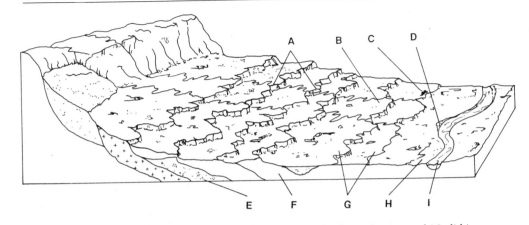

Section of the Nile River Valley showing the location of major landscape features and Neolithic settlement. (A) upper terraces (B) desert spurs (C) prehistoric settlement (D) levee (E) early Nile deposits (F) older Nile and wadi sediments (G) flood plain (H) sandbar (I) Nile River.

divisions had attained their geographical limits. For some time the nomes retained some autonomy, particularly at moments of regional disturbances. For nearly 3,000 years, Egypt and the nome provinces remained aloof from the outside world, sustaining contact with communities in Western Asia. In turn, ships from the Near East plied the Egyptian ports in the Delta.

EARLY DYNASTIES AND AGRICULTURE

Until the close of the forth millennium B.C. environmental conditions remained ideal in the Nile River valley for hunting and gathering, pastoralism, and minor plant cultivation. However, a general climactic drying began at this time that eliminated vegetation and game from the great wadis. Pressure for control of the most productive lands in the Nile Valley resulted in the first unification of Upper and Lower Egypt by one or more rulers from Upper Egypt. According to legend, Menes (c. 4000 B.C.) was responsible for the political unification of the two lands; during his reign Memphis became the capital of the Nile region. From 3100 B.C. to 2700 B.C. craftsmen acquired the ability to work skillfully in stone, metal, and papyrus; by the end of the Second Dynasty, knowledge of astronomy, geometry, medicine, and other arts gradually became part of the culture.[3]

At this point during the Second Dynasty, a shift began from pastoralism and small-scale agriculture to more concentrated agricultural activity. Trade with Near Eastern societies was now common, but most individuals continued to live in unsophisticated small villages. Few large centers existed apart from Memphis, and long stretches of the middle Nile Valley remained sparsely populated. Gradually, increases in population within the settlements along the Nile began to exert pressure on available resources, with increased agricultural output seen as an effective way to provide sufficient food for the expanded population. Thus, in areas where rudimentary agriculture occurred, basin irrigation helped to supply water to the fields during the warmer months preceding the floods. Just when this method came into common use is hard to determine from the few records extant from the period; however, artificial techniques, including flood irrigation, the control of water by sluice gates, and the containment of water by dykes, began by the First Dynasty. Traditionally, local rulers dignified a new irrigation system by ceremonially opening the channels.

Drawing from the Scorpion Macehead depicting the ceremonial opening of an irrigation basin. Rulers often initiated an irrigation system by breaking a small dam.

COSMOLOGY, SETTLEMENT, AGRICULTURE, AND IRRIGATION

At the middle of the third millennium B.C., the climate of the Nile region reached its present quality, and the Nile floods became more of an environmental issue, flood levels being lower between the Old Kingdom (2686–2181 B.C.) and the First Intermediate period (2181–1900 B.C.). The change in the character of the Nile floods made it possible for Dzozer, the second king of the Old Kingdom, to organize Egypt into a productive agricultural society. Along with his chief vizier, Imhotep, he instituted the creation of monumental architecture and an equally monumental royal bureaucracy.

When societies shift from dispersed settlements to centralized systems, perceptions of a common philosophy begins to form, aided by intellectuals and priests. Often this process spawns a formal religion, through which individuals contemplate life and death. From the records, we have some knowledge about this process in Egypt; a sense of how the Egyptians viewed the world at this juncture, and how their perceptions influenced their relationship to the landscape. According to ancient Egyptian tradition each individual life was a miniature representation of a larger cosmic process. The cycle of birth, maturity, and death reiterated the natural processes that occurred everywhere in the environment: the rising and setting of the sun and moon, the rise and fall of the Nile floods, the seasons of the year. The physical world, the world of the senses, was essentially a replica of a preordained pattern; while the physiography of Egypt represented the organization of eternal realms. Before the existence of the physical world, Nun, the waters of Chaos, described a limitless void, until the waters began to recede to reveal an island, the place of creation. The sanctuary of each major Egyptian temple is considered, symbolically, to have been on the island of creation. Throughout Egyptian history the temple has stood as the abode of the creator and various gods; the king, or Pharaoh, was the temporal link to the occupants of the temples, and it was his responsibility to oversee all of Egypt—as a surrogate to the gods.

Since all the land of Egypt belonged to the Pharaoh as heir to the gods, private ownership of land was rare. If lesser individuals owned land, built up estates, and obtained wealth, power, and some economic independence, they normally did so after receiving a grant from the Pharaoh as recognition for service to the state or its gods. Under this system, the produce of all the land, including temple lands, was subject to state taxation. The larger centers and nome capitals served as centers for administration and taxation purposes; cult centers of the gods and Pyramid towns built by the pharaohs became the nuclei of cities. During the Old Kingdom, areas were opened up for cultivation by creating new villages. At this time, the close tie that each Egyptian had to the landscape, supported by a common cosmology and encouraged by a rural lifestyle, stimulated the development of numerous small villages rather than a few large centers, making it easier to utilize the river to farm the alluvium and to produce products for local and regional distribution. Generally most settlements developed in the northern or southern extremities of the Nile, with areas in between sustaining sparse human occupation, possibly due to the difficulty of managing the large flood basins in these areas. In addition, colonization in the middle Nile may have been restricted by the politics of the nome provinces, which were based on earlier tribal subdivisions of the Nile flood basins.

At the local level, each village had to maintain enough land for both plant cultivation and adequate pasturage. Often the two overlapped, so that additional land was converted to agricultural purposes. The techniques for irrigation followed the methods used by earlier groups, including the manipulation of natural flood basins, containment of water by dykes, and distribution of irrigation water by sluice gates. Generally, the lands associated with the small villages of the Old Kingdom and First Intermediate period could rely on tapping the natural basins for irrigation purposes during the drier part of the year. In the smaller agricultural settlements, minor adjustments to the natural basins were sufficient for small-scale irrigation. More ambitious tinkering with the natural configuration of the Nile alluvium produced larger basins and in turn, increased arable land by providing irrigation to the periphery of the floodplains. Farmers formed these artificial basins by trapping floodwaters between the higher terraces and parallel dykes near the Nile, with cross-banks or *salibas,* which enclosed the basin to the north and south. More ambitious villagers sometimes created artificial terraces with basins that could be drained toward lower elevations in the spring and summer. Generally, the basins averaged a few acres in size, though later efforts produced basins as large as 60,000 acres. In some instances these adjustments permitted second or third yields in smaller gardens.

In the dry season, farmers labored to keep the basins clear until the flood was high enough to fill them through holes in the dyke nearest the Nile. Once the basin was filled, laborers closed the holes, and after about forty days, when the flood waters had receded, opened the holes by lifting sluice gates, letting the water flow over the fields. After about a week, farmers cast seed on the fields, and waited for the sun and soil to mature the crop.

Further refinement of the irrigation process ensued with the development of more sophisticated construction technology. For example, feeder canals brought water from higher up the river so that elevated lands could receive nitrogen-rich flood waters. Also, short canals called "red water feeders" lay below the main feeder canals and connected the river directly to the basins. Water moved through the various channels and past brick sluices; during periods of artificial irrigation, the sluices regulated water volume from higher to lower basins. In the hot season, when the Nile was low and little water remained in the basins, water had to be drawn from the river by lift devices, the most common of which was the *shaduf*. This mechanism—invented during the Late Kingdom— was a simple tool made of a long pole balanced on a beam that was supported by two columns of dried mud, wood, or stone. One end of the pole supported a counterweight, the other end a leather bucket. The shaduf was better suited for irrigating small fields than large tracts.

Artificial irrigation, including basins and sluice gates, functioned best in the small flood basins of southern Upper Egypt and further north on the east bank of the Nile. In these areas, plant cultivation progressively eliminated pastoral activities and natural pasturage. Yet irrigation technology of the Old Kingdom often suffered from the lack of efficient lifting devices that could bring water directly from the Nile to the fields in times of low flooding or during periods of insufficient water containment in the basins. Thus, irrigation techniques relied on the regulation of water during and after high floods. For example, during good flood periods the population labored to increase the vertical and horizontal extent of the natural levees, enlarge and dredge natural diverging overflow channels, and block natural basins by cross-dikes and dams. Workers subdivided the large natural flood basins into manageable subunits and controlled water flow with temporary cuts in the dykes or levees, or by short canals and masonry sluice gates. Also, management of the artificial irrigation system, dependent on the vagaries of the river, relied on the systematic control of the opening and closing of the sluice gates during periods of high floods. Despite the Egyptians' sophisticated use of artificial irrigation, cultivation of plants on the higher levees was impossible due to the lack of suitable lifting devices until the Eighteenth Dynasty. Finally, the irrigation systems were generally a local phenomenon and were not adequate for major flooding or protection of settlements from catastrophic inundation.

Agricultural production involved most of the citizenry, particularly during the planting and harvesting seasons. Farming activities are part of the hieroglyphic images in Old Kingdom tombs in Giza. One scene depicts the distribution of seeds, another illustrates the breaking of the soil with mallets in preparation for ploughing, and a third image shows people cutting down trees and clearing land. Ploughing, hoeing, and seeding follow in subsequent hieroglyphics. The illustrations conclude with scenes of harvesting and the inevitable taxation of the yield by the Pharaoh's representative, who could efficiently judge the amount of tax to be paid by a farmer by measuring the field with a knotted cord.

The harvest was the most important and festive occasion in ancient Egypt; harvest scenes even appear frequently in the illustrations in the tombs. Reaping, threshing, separating, and storing were the activities of the harvest, and all members of the farm or village participated in the process. The major crops were grain, wheat or barley, but many other plants contributed to the cultivation output—including flax, onions, lettuce, beans, melons, dates and figs, and pomegranates—and even flowers were harvested and grown in garden plots. The Egyptians, though heavy consumers of beer, also propagated grapes for wine, and processed them using the traditional grape trough and foot-mashing technique.[4]

Farm scene illustrating agricultural activity and an accounting by the tax assessor who is measuring a field for its output.

EARLY CEREMONIAL SITES

The Pharaoh's power during the Old Kingdom was absolute, and permitted him to share in the agricultural output. Often he or his representatives visited the monarchial estates along the Nile to collect tribute from the various semiautonomous nome districts. Part of this income financed major construction projects, especially tombs at the Old Kingdom sites in Lower Egypt. For the pharaohs, these cemeteries were the point of departure to the hereafter; to students of Egyptian site planning, the burial grounds provide important information concerning land planning and design during the Old Kingdom. Preeminent are the cemeteries at Saqqara on the west bank of the Nile near Cairo, where royal burials occurred from the First Dynasty onward. At this site, *mastabas,* elevated platform structures, housed the remains of the early pharaohs and nobility. From the Third Dynasty onward, the tombs gradually evolved from "step" pyramids to the imposing structures of the Fourth and Fifth Dynasties. One of the most ambitious burial complexes of the Old Kingdom was the tomb complex of King Dzozer, built by Imhotep at the beginning of the Third Dynasty (2778 B.C.).

Dzozer's burial complex has given us much information about site planning in a land where much ancient building lies buried under alluvium deposited by Nile flooding. The reason for its survival is its siting on a terrace overlooking the countryside, protected from Nile floods. On this natural platform, builders constructed a limestone rampart 10 feet high, 1790 feet long, and 912 feet wide that enclosed the site within a rectangular space whose long axis points northward. Viewing the complex from outside the wall, the most prominent feature is the massive stone step pyramid that looms over adjacent chambers, colonnaded courts, temples, and sanctuaries. At its completion, the extensive necropolis covered nearly 16 million square feet, and contained the extensive burial complexes of three pharaohs, including tombs of various queens and burial structures of the nobility. The queens' pyramids and the mastaba tombs of the royal princes surround the kings' pyramid, while, on their periphery, a grid of parallel streets

View of Dzoser's burial complex including the step pyramid.

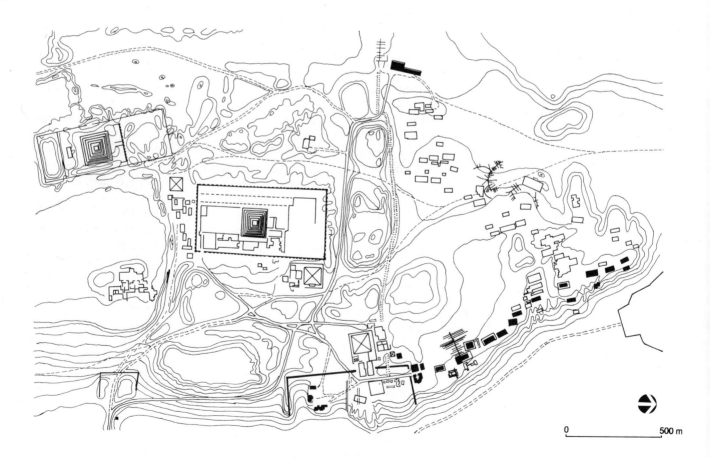

Dzoser's burial complex at Saqqara. The siting of Old Kingdom tombs reflected an orthogonal arrangement in the placement of structures.

contain the mastabas of officials in descending order of rank. Spatially the complex exhibits a clear interplay of architectural mass and void, balanced by open courtyards, smaller structures, and colonnades.

The same concept of rectilinear planning, with lesser volumes clustering around major architectural forms, exists at the archaic necropolis of Giza north of Saqqara. Situated on a terrace overlooking Cairo on the east bank, above the flood level of the Nile, the various tombs, temples, and cemeteries combine with the pyramids to give the complex a sense of overwhelming scale uncommon at this point in Egyptian history. Part of the spatial drama derives from the formal order of the site. Most architectural elements sit at right angles to one another, with the notable exception of the slightly oblique processional connection between the pyramid of Chefren and the Sphinx and Valley Temple complex on the eastern edge of the site. Filling out the complex are secondary structures aligned with the three massive pyramids, whose corners are precisely oriented to the four cardinal points.

0   100 m

Plan of the burial complex at Giza. The pyramids are aligned to the cardinal points. This arrangement is reinforced by the north-south orientation of the Nile River Valley.

The Pyramids of Giza site on a terrace above the Nile River to the east. Most tombs occupied sites on the west bank of the Nile above the flood plain.

The accessible location of the Giza necropolis, and its vulnerability to theft, compelled the kings of the Fifth Dynasty to abandon the necropolis and site their burial complexes at Abusirm, between Saqqara and Giza, where they built burial monuments of more modest scale. Coincidentally, the decline in the scale of burial sites accompanied a gradual weakening of the pharaonic central authority. Most likely the cause was a cessation of wet climate conditions and lower Nile floods that interrupted the system of basin irrigation and the fruitful harvests. As conditions worsened, the power of state rulers weakened, causing the splintering of Egypt into feudal states, each controlled by a local ruler. Faced with agricultural problems, provincial governors instituted plans to conserve water and to improve food resources by driving out nonnative individuals from their localities. But consistent low floods fueled internecine strife, further constricting areas of cultivation. For the remainder of Egyptian history, this decline at the end of a period of spectacular cultural achievements forced the Egyptians to confront the boundaries of human ambition in the face of environmental limits.

POLITICAL REUNIFICATION AND TEMPLE LANDS

At the beginning of the Middle Kingdom (2133–1782 B.C.), central control of the landscape returned with the ascendency of Menuhotep as Pharaoh, under whose leadership Upper and Lower Egypt once again functioned as a unified entity. This change was not entirely the result of adroit political management, since flood levels rose during the Middle Kingdom, sometimes exceptionally high. Despite the improved conditions, the pharaohs of the Middle Kingdom maintained only an uneasy alliance with the nomes and had to devote time to trying to placate powerful regional authorities. However, in 1999 B.C. Amenemhet assumed power, and the capital of Egypt once again rested at Memphis. The Pharaoh streamlined the state administration, surveyed the country, improved the irrigation system, restored the temples, and established the great temple at Karnac. In addition, he and subsequent rulers exerted sufficient central authority to reestablish control over Nubia and to undertake large-scale land reclamation projects in the Faiyum. The only unattainable objective at this point was colonization of lands along the central Nile, an objective that failed due to continued political solidarity of the regional nomes.

Two events occurred in the landscape during the Middle Kingdom that indicate the degree to which the kings of the period were able to affect the built environment. These were the organization and management of temples and the construction of funerary complexes. Due partly to a shift in burial practices during the Middle Kingdom, when the royal tombs began to be located in secret chambers in the surrounding foothills, tombs became less important architecturally than the burial temple. At this point, there was less interest in older burial practices, and a higher priority for the maintenance of temples as houses for specific gods, or their temporal surrogates, the pharaohs. Consequently, two categories of temple evolved: those dedicated to specific gods and those built as royal burial temples. Both mortuary and cult temples had similar spatial ingredients: a main axis that linked an open walled court, the hypostyle hall, and a private sanctuary. The hypostyle hall, with its rows of papyrus- or lotus-shaped columns, invoked the primal swamp that emerged as the waters began to recede at the time of creation.

Concentration on the architectural arrangement of the cult temples, however, obscures the larger impact such structures had on the landscape. For example, the cult temples, whose sole owner was the Pharaoh, included landholdings, sometimes bequeathed to the temple by a subsequent ruler. In practical terms the temples operated like any other large household and landholding, and the respective temple god retained the status of any landed nobility. Therefore, temples had their own laborers to maintain the landholding and to conduct the cultivation and harvest of agricultural products. A sharecropper system was not uncommon, with the temple dividing its agricultural output with the tenant laborers. Workers were also needed to tend the various bequests to the temple, including animal herds, fishing and fowling rights, flax fields, vegetable beds, vineyards, and beehives. In sum, the temples were a part of the diverse economy, employing individuals who worked for a profit and incurred tax liabilities like any other agricultural enterprise.

Workers harvesting grain on an estate farm. A portion of the production went to the state as a source of revenue.

Funerary temple of Mentuhotep, left, adjacent to the later temple of Queen Hatshepsut. Both structures complemented the color and form of the surrounding terrain.

Mortuary temples, the other major temple category to appear during the Middle Kingdom, became common as rulers began to prefer burial in secret rock-cut chambers in the hills west of Thebes. These temples were important in assuring the divine status of the deceased ruler. Ceremonially, they were important in the funeral processional rite; the temple signified both terminus and departure for the deceased kings and queens—the point at which the deceased ruler began the journey from the temporal world to the afterlife.

One of the best-preserved mortuary temples from the Middle Kingdom belonged to Mentuhutep of the Eleventh Dynasty (c. 1950 B.C.). The structure shares a site with a later New Kingdom temple on the western edge of a preexisting Nile River "bay" across the river from Thebes. Conceived as a series of architectural levels, the temple gracefully moves from one elevation to another, aligned on a central axis that links a series of interior and colonnaded spaces. A walled causeway tied the temple to a valley building, three-quarters of a mile to the east. From the causeway, a path moved through a grove of tamarisk and sycamore figs, and continued along an inclined ramp through two colonnaded chambers, culminating in the uppermost hypostyle hall. At its completion, the complex exhibited a bilateral arrangement, with the shaded forecourt gracefully linked to the hillside and tomb beyond.

The significance of the temple is its compatibility to the surrounding landscape. Its scale, repetition of vertical form, color of material, all visually complement the massive cliffs west of the complex. The placement of spatial elements bilaterally along a central axis is a direct response to the processional ceremony and the larger, symmetrical Nile context of which the temple and its site are a part.

THE NEW KINGDOM: TOWNS, TEMPLES, AND ESTATES; SETTLEMENT PATTERNS

The cultural gains made by the Egyptians during the Middle Kingdom lasted until 1782 B.C., after which date a series of ineffectual rulers and an invasion of Asian Hyksos in 1663 B.C. weakened the authority of indigenous Egyptians. However, with the expulsion of the Hyksos by Ammose I in 1570 B.C., the Egyptian society once again began to function as a state poised on the brink of empire. With control of states in west Asia and Nubia as far south as the Fifth Cataract, Thebes once again emerged as the political center.

Scholars have been able to form a more complete picture of the quality of life in towns and estates during this phase of Egyptian life than they have of earlier ones. Temples, both cult and funerary, continued to be an important element in the landscape. New Kingdom (1567–1085 B.C.) governments undertook resettlement of populations, including military veterans and mercenaries, and began to colonize the broad floodplains north of Abydos. Documents from the period attest to a highly complex pattern of landholding, where a farm was not necessarily a contiguous area of agricultural land, but a series of scattered plots either held in private ownership or rented on a sharecropper basis from a temple or some other landowner. These, in turn, received political and administrative directions from a nearby town. A property such as this, if privately owned, would operate on an economic cycle identical with that of a temple. Part of the production would go to royalties and taxes, part to payments to the owner's servants and managers, and part to feeding and maintaining his family.

Beyond the agricultural holdings, capitals of nomes, ports, and frontier towns all had official quarters of some size, generally situated on the Nile or a main canal, providing a focus for residential quarters. Numerous new towns also emerged in these times of prosperity, since it was constantly necessary for the state to support and reward civil and military officials with grants of land, to feed an increasing population, and to bring productive land under cultivation by marsh clearance and canal building. New settlements on marginal lands were the means of achieving this objective. The various settlements along the Nile continued to function as centers for the control of the river and the cultivation of surrounding land. In the New Kingdom the king always had major residences at Memphis and Thebes. There were also small palaces attached to major temples in the provinces, where the king and his retinue could live during festivals. In Thebes, one of the few major urban centers during the New Kingdom, most inhabitants lived in simple, dusty, whitewashed houses, with few amenities.

For a few lucky individuals who possessed a particular skill, such as stone-cutting or painting, there was the opportunity to occupy one of the worker communities founded by the state to house craftsmen. An example is Deir el-Medina, one of the best preserved of these worker villages; here craftsmen and their families could live in a well-organized community, situated on the west bank of the Nile in a small valley depression formed by hills across the river from Thebes. Most of the occupants labored in the royal tombs as artisans, and handed down their privileged status from one generation to another.

First established during the Old Kingdom by Amenhotep I, Deir el-Medina functioned as state-maintained enclave, with the workers' needs—shelter, food, water, clothing—supplied by the state. Presumably Egyptian rulers wanted to maintain the community as an isolated entity, at some distance from the royal tombs and protected from intrusion by inhabitants along the Nile. By the time of the New Kingdom, the village consisted of about seventy structures surrounded by long rectangular walls and accessible at the northern end through a small doorway. The doorway opened onto a main street, which ran the length of the village—140 yards—and was sometimes only 10 feet wide. Between the main street and the perimeter wall, residential and small commercial structures sharing common walls abutted one another. Overhead, a roof covered the main street, giving the settlement the appearance of being a single, low, dusty brown monolith, filling the bottom of the small valley. The residential structures were small by modern standards, and they were more regular and compact than the dwellings in Thebes. The interiors were lighted by small slits in the roofs that cast light on the whitewashed interior walls. The largest room in the house was reserved for gatherings of friends, a necessary amenity since the community lacked an open meeting place where people could congregate in the evenings.

Deir-al-Medina, the tomb workers village near the Valley of the Kings. Life in the village was a privilege handed down from one generation to another.

Beyond the large room lay a kitchen with ovens and a stairway to the roof. Outside the north wall of the town, on high ground, was a group of temples, dedicated to various state gods; the land beyond the south wall was used as a rubbish dump.

Few town sites give so complete a picture of village life during the New Kingdom as Deir el-Medina. But El Amarna, built during the reign of Akenahten (1350–1334 B.C.), and occupied for less than a generation, provides an additional picture of contemporary life, undisturbed by subsequent settlements. The town was sited on the east bank of the Nile, midway between Upper and Lower Egypt, where Akenahten was able to build free from the constraints of a pre-existing town plan.

The result was a city consisting of two parts, a north suburb and a main city, which served as the king's residence and official headquarters, respectively. The city extends for about 5 miles along the edge of the Nile, and the only fortifications were those which surrounded a small temple in the main city, and the palace in the north suburb; the rest of the community remained unfortified. The overall configuration of both the main city and the north suburb stemmed from the location and orientation of the main palaces and temples, which faced a common street frontage. The main city contained the administrative structures of the community and was planned in a strict rectilinear mode. A main thoroughfare linked this district with the north suburb and residences beyond. To the east lay a necropolis workmen's village; to the south, additional suburbs. Back from the primary structures, building alignment appears to have been determined by the location of the incoming streets from the south suburbs, arriving at an angle. Additional palaces, temples, and estates lay beyond the city and suburbs.

The El Amarna suburbs were a series of self-contained and economically self-sustaining neighborhoods. Most of the owners of the smaller residences were

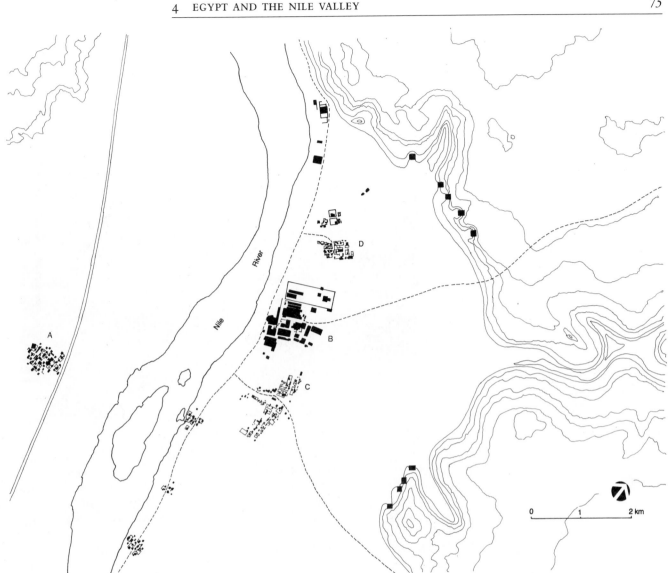

Plan of El Amarna.
(A) worker's village (B) main
city (C)south suburb
(D) north suburb.

living adjacent to or fairly near their source of employment. The neighborhood units were divided on a north-south axis by a continuous 75- to 90-feet-wide space that functioned as a thoroughfare to the main city. Narrow cross streets linked parts of the neighborhoods to the main street. Within the general road layout, the neighborhoods followed their own plans; as a result, roughly rectangular compounds formed the larger residences, while the smaller houses filled in the intervening spaces between larger structures in an irregular manner. In the central portion of the north suburb, the community plan resembled the layout of medieval European and North African towns, with its network of narrow twisting streets and juxtaposed of houses that belonged to individuals from all economic levels. Formal open space for gathering was limited to areas around wells, which often functioned as small market centers. Within this maze of residential living, one would occasionally encounter the residence of a fairly important official or noble.

Drawing showing the organization of a New Kingdom estate.

At El Amarna and other communities along the Nile, larger private residences had a fair number of amenities even by modern standards. A plan of these residences, as revealed by paintings on the walls of tombs near Thebes, gives a clear indication of the level of lifestyle enjoyed by the well-to-do during this period. A typical mansion at El Amarna and other locations was an enclosed affair, sometimes as large as three-quarters of an acre, with a main entrance, living quarters, kitchens, craft and storage facilities, and extensive gardens with pools. The general feeling of the complex was one of containment and self-sufficiency, cushioned by the presence of open space, plant material, and water. Plants not only provided shade but furnished the household with additional food: grapes, pomegranates, almonds, and apples; pools, if large enough, were ideal for fish cultivation, another food source. The individual apartments and ancillary structures were small and airy to allow for ventilation during the hot summer months. In addition, the residence often had a porch or some other elevated terrace from which its occupants could enjoy the north breezes and breathe in the fragrances from the trees and flowers in the garden.

The sort of amenity found in these residences—shade, water, and relative calm—was not a feature common in the villages or cities in ancient Egypt. The open fields and dry, dusty village streets scarcely provided the shade and scenery so prized by the most humble Egyptian. However, certain rulers attempted to humanize the condition of a few of the more important centers, especially Ramses III, during his reign between 1182 and 1151 B.C. With an eye on civic improvement, the king ordered the planting of trees and papyrus in Thebes, and at a new town in the Delta, he financed the construction of vineyards, walks shaded by a variety of sweet fruit trees, and a sacred way resplendent with flowers from foreign lands; Ramses assigned foreign slaves to tend the gardens and to dig water tanks in which to grow lotus plants.

NEW KINGDOM TEMPLES: PLANNING AND SITING

The principal achievement in site design during the New Kingdom occurred in the planning of the extensive temples, both funerary and cult. Some were extensions and reworkings of older complexes, other were newly built—often as funerary temples for an important king or queen. Two temples near Thebes remain well enough preserved for us to understand the values and consciousness behind their construction. The first is Queen Hatshepsut's (1503–1488 B.C.) funerary complex at Deir el-Bahari, adjacent to the funeral temple of the Pharaoh Ahmenhotep I. Though the complex is similar to its predecessor in basic conception, it nonetheless surpassed the earlier example in its gracefulness and the fine bas-relief carvings on its walls. Similar to older work, Queen Hatshepsut's temple is a trilevel complex with colonnades flanking the central inclined ramps, echoing the configuration of limestone cliffs immediately to the west. Symmetrically arranged, the strict spatial formality of the temple complements the dynamic sense conveyed by its spaciousness and the movement from the two lowest levels, with their large, open forecourt, to the upper level that terminates with its sanctuary carved out of the hillside. Along the walls under the second-level colonnade, carvings depict Queen Hatshepsut's expedition to Punt. One shows a ship laden with flora and fauna, including myrrh trees, setting sail for Egypt.

The other outstanding temple from the New Kingdom is the cult Temple of Ammon at Karnac, adjacent to Thebes. As in earlier periods, cult temples flourished during the New Kingdom, due to the general prosperity of the state. At its height, the temple at Karnac was the center of a vast corporation that owned land throughout Egypt. The temple was, officially, the home—the household—of a god and was managed like any large estate household, private or royal. The vast complex consists of a central core, dating from the Twelfth Dynasty (c. 2153 B.C.), from which the remainder of the temple expands outward. The entire site covers an area of nearly a square mile, enclosed by a 20- to 30-inch-thick wall and linked to a companion temple at Luxor by an avenue of sphinxes. The heart of the temple lies along a central axis which bilaterally disposes the various chambers along its length. A huge hypostyle hall containing 134 columns capped with papyrus flower capitals recreates the papyrus thicket in the Delta, where, in Egyptian mythology, Isis protected the child Horus from Set. From the hypostyle hall the complex gently rises by a series of ramps and stairways to a columned vestibule containing wall reliefs depicting flora and fauna to the sanctuary of Ammon.

While these temples flourished, gradual colonization of the Nile alluvium and state investment in large-scale monument construction continued throughout the second millennium B.C. However, a breakup of the Asiatic empire and the loss of control over Nubia in 1000 B.C. placed Egypt in direct confrontation with west Asian states. During the first millennium B.C., colonization resumed in the Delta, and the demographic center of the country shifted from the Nile Valley to the Delta. During the rule of the Ptolemies, land reclamation projects ensued in the Faiyum, reducing the size of Lake Moeris. A system of radial irrigation appeared in the region, increasing the amount of arable land nearly threefold. However, the new irrigation system required artificial regulation systems at each distributional node, a technique never before used with basin irrigation. The new system marked a radical change in irrigation strategy along the length of the Nile. It also marked the decline of the ancient Egyptian approach to agriculture, irrigation, and settlement in the Nile Valley.

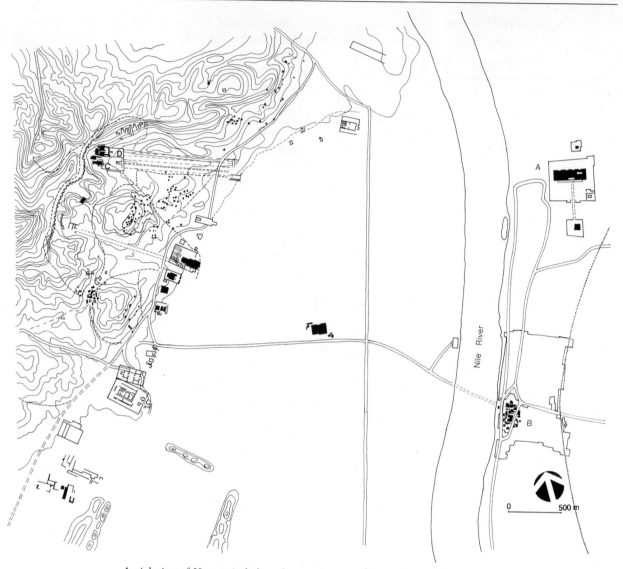

Aerial view of Karnac including the temples and avenues. Plan of Thebes and Karnac. (A) Karnac with temple (B) Luxor (C) tomb of Mentuhotep (D) tomb of Queen Hatshepsut.

ENVIRONMENTAL ISSUES

The decline of the traditional Egyptian culture, and the successive dominance of Greek and Roman authority in the Nile Valley, brought to a conclusion the longest sustained society in the region. The Nile-oriented Egyptian culture had successfully wrested arable land from the banks of the river, and produced a viable agricultural economy through the application of irrigation technology. Success lay with adapting to the presence of the Nile River, which, unlike the Tigris and Euphrates, was distinctive in its yearly regenerative habit, namely the deposition of silt and nutrients necessary for agricultural activity. The yearly floods also cleansed agricultural lands by leaching salt from the soils, a benefit which the inhabitants of Mesopotamia did not enjoy. However, the Nile did present certain problems, mostly associated with the effects of seasonal flooding, which could occur in greater or lesser quantities depending on the amount of rainfall in the hinterlands. Too little rain constricted agricultural production, too much caused severe flooding of towns and villages near the Nile. At times the

The temple at Karnac with its central axis leading to the interior chamber.

flooding was catastrophic, and it continued to be a threat until a few decades ago, when the Aswan High Dam controlled flood waters and provided hydro-electric power to modern Egypt.

In general the extent of early environmental alteration within the region may be gauged by the quality of agriculture and urbanization along the Nile. In both instances urban and rural activity proceeded at a pace less dramatic than that in Mesopotamia. For example, extensive canals were not required for basin irrigation; the scale of urban centers in Egypt rarely approached that of Meso-potamian counterparts. Later, during the New Kingdom and subsequent periods, rulers attempted to alter the landscape for specific purposes, most notably through reclamation projects in the Delta and at Lake Moeris. One ambitious Pharaoh, Necho II, decided to link the Mediterranean and the Red Sea, but abandoned the project after, as Herodotus noted, more than 100,000 workers died in the course of construction. In 520 B.C. King Darius of Persia successfully commanded the building of a link between the lower Nile and the Red Sea, wide enough to accommodate war galleys. Maintenance of the channel plagued successive rulers, including the Romans and the Arabs, the latter of which filled in the channel out of frustration.[5]

In sum, human activity along the Nile was spectacular for its successive levels of cultural achievements in planning, architecture, and fine arts. Environ-mental alteration occurred locally, associated with small-scale adjustments to landscape form and function, mostly to assure adequate water at peak agricultural periods. By observing the habit of the Nile River, the Egyptians were able to produce a level of agricultural output that enabled them to evolve from a local-ized society to rule, for a time, parts of the Near East and northeast Africa.

NOTES

1. *Williams, Martin A. J. and Hughes Faure. 1980.* The Sahara and the Nile. *Rotterdam: Balkema. See discussion of the origin of the Nile Basin, pp. 204–224; Pleistocene history of lower Nile Valley, pp. 253–280; prehistoric settlements, pp. 421–450; plant domestication, pp. 503–526.*

2. *Karl Butzer. 1976.* Early Hydraulic Civilization in Egypt. *Chicago: University of Chicago Press.*

3. *Agricultural production in Egypt followed a prescribed regimen from soil preparation to harvest and storage. See Erhman, pp. 424–445.*

4. *Kemp, Barry J. 1989.* Ancient Egypt: Anatomy of a Civilization. *London: Routledge. See chapters on culture, model communities, and the city of Amarna.*

5. *David Attenborough. 1987.* The First Eden: The Mediterranean World and Man. *Boston: Little, Brown.*

5

The Mediterranean Landscape:
The Aegean and Greece

Human settlement in the Mediterranean region produced vigorous cultures notable for their distinctive adaptations to a range of landscape zones. At first, human occupation of the Mediterranean landscape was negligible; small groups of people occupied advantageous niches along the coasts or inland from the sea. Eventually, a series of societies dominated the region, beginning with the Aegeans and the Phoenicians, followed by the Greeks, Cathaginians, Romans, and later, medieval feudal societies. A period of agricultural development ensued, lasting several millennia, from about 6000 B.C. to 1400 A.D. In the process, humans converted a veritable Eden, endowed with a wide range of flora and fauna, into a pattern of villages, towns, and urban centers which were supported by extensive agricultural and pastoral lands. The impact that this had on the region is undeniable: from Spain to the levant, urban and rural landscapes still retain traces of their classical and feudal heritage.

PHYSICAL CONTEXT

The plains, mountains, peninsulas, and islands that give the Mediterranean region its identity evolved as the result of a complex series of geological events beginning nearly sixty million years ago during the Cretaceous, when Africa and Arabia were islands separated from Europe by a wide oceanic gap. Slowly, the African continent drifted northward on a tectonic plate, gradually closing the gap between Africa and the European continent. At about forty million years ago, tectonic movement thrust up the sediments that had accumulated on the ocean floor, forming the Alps. At this time, the gap between Africa and Europe had narrowed sufficiently that the basic conformation of the contemporary Mediterranean Sea was established—except that the sea was open at its eastern and western ends. Subsequent tectonic movement at the eastern end of the sea resulted in the closing of the straits, halting the migration of marine life between the Indian Ocean and the Mediterranean Sea. However, the plants and animals on the African and European continents began to mingle for the first time, due in part to the continued movement of the two land masses, which closed the Mediterranean sea at the western end, forming the Straits of Gibraltar.

As important as this conjunction of the two land masses was for the evolution of plant and animal species in Europe and North Africa, the constricting of the Mediterranean also initiated a period of rapid desiccation of the enclosed sea and the creation of an inhospitable, arid basin. Thus, by six million years ago, when the climate was somewhat hotter than it is today, the waters of the Mediterranean completely evaporated. The floor of the basin became an arid, stifling environment, occasionally punctuated by volcanic mountains, which form modern Corsica, Sardinia, and a number of the central Aegean islands.

Occasionally, water from the Atlantic Ocean spilled over into the arid basin. Finally, about five and a half million years ago the Mediterranean filled with water, due to the breaking of the land connection between Gibraltar and North Africa. A spectacular cascade, nearly 10,000 feet high, poured 40 cubic miles per day of water from the Atlantic into the basin. In little more than a year, the entire Mediterranean basin was once again full. Today, the Atlantic continues to feed the Mediterranean through a narrow channel, only 9 miles wide, and less than 1,000 feet deep. As the Mediterranean refilled, small rivers and streams continued to cut into the lands surrounding the sea, creating a varied topography that complemented the existing mountain ranges that had evolved through uplift and vulcanism. Due to these processes, there are few extensive plains in the eastern Mediterranean landscape. Rather hills, ravines, small alluvial valleys, and modest drainage ways characterize much of the land.

About five hundred thousand years ago, at the time of human entry into the Mediterranean region, the land and sea had evolved into its present-day topography, accompanied by an equally varied flora and fauna. Since the conclusion of the most recent Ice Age, the coastal lands adjacent to the Mediterranean shores have included an array of semideciduous and evergreen species. Many are drought-resistant plants, including heat- and fungus-resistant flowering annuals, such as vetch, toadflax, lupin, and pimpernel. Many shrubs are evergreens, ideally suited for the summer droughts: their thick, leathery, silver and gray leaves helped plants retain moisture during the summer months. Thyme, sage, and rosemary, among others, served as the shrub layer of plant cover along the dry shores of the Mediterranean lands. In the shallow soils, low-level shrubs sprout from

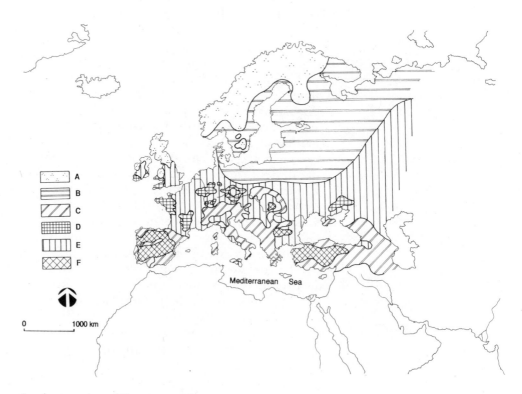

Landscape regions of Europe (A) pre-cambrian and paleozoic mountains (B) glaciated plains (C) alpine mountains (D) Hercynian mountain system (E) plains and low plateaux (F) plateaux with alpine system.

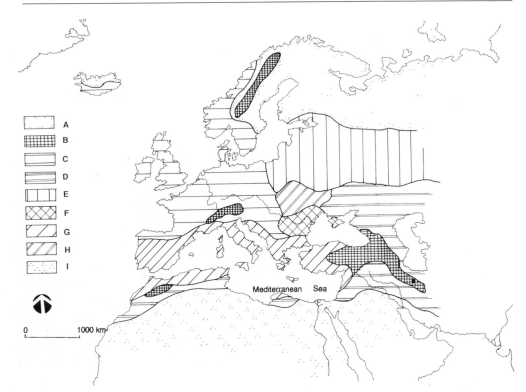

Climate zones of the Mediterranean and European regions. (A) cold winter (B) highland and alpine (C) north-west coast marine (D) Africa: hot steppe; Asia: cold winter steppe (E) humid with cool summer (F) humid subtropical with warm summer (G) warm Mediterranean (H) humid with warm summer (I) hot desert.

(A)

(B)

(A) Aerial view from a weather satellite of the eastern Mediterranean region. (B) The physiography of the Greek landscape, with its small valleys enclosed by hills and mountains, favored the formation of independent, self-sustaining communities.

Native eastern Mediterranean plant community. Such sites were home to important species including the olive and oak.

between the rocky cover to form the *garrigue* along the French coast, and in slightly deeper soils the *maquis,* denser and taller plants including oleander, broom, gorse, myrtle, rockrose, and arbutus, cover the land. In addition to the maquis, myrtle, laurel, arbutus, cistus, juniper, evergreen oak, wild olive, and various herbs and grasses persist and flourish after the winter rains, with some species dying back during the protracted summer heat.

From north to south the plant associations of the Mediterranean basin form a rich gradation of plant material. In the north the forms merge with the dense forests, mostly deciduous trees and herbaceous plants of continental Europe. Forests of pine, holm oak, cork oak, juniper, cypress, and wild olives were common forms in existence as early as the first human occupation of the region. Fir, hardwoods, and cedar forests shade higher elevations along the uplands and mountainous slopes, including the Atlas Mountain region in North Africa. Along the southern rim in North Africa, the Mediterranean plant associations gradually fade into desert and steppe associations. In these regions, the plants are thick-leaved, thorny shrubs that can resist the prolonged drought of the south. Standing above the typical lower-slope Mediterranean vegetation pattern—at 2,000 to 5,000 feet above sea level—are the forests, ranging from maritime pines and evergreen oaks on the lower slopes to deciduous oak, elm, chestnut, and beech at higher elevations. The vegetation pattern followed the typical association noted by Pliny (200 B.C.), with deciduous trees appearing in greater numbers from lower to higher altitudes and from south to north.

Such a rich floral composition constituted an ideal habitat for a number of animal species, including amphibians, reptiles, birds, dwarf antelopes, deer, pigmy hippos, and elephants, some of which survived to as late as ten thousand years ago. Of the important species to survive into the Holocene, the wild bull was arguably the most formidable creature along the Mediterranean shores, the source of myth, and the basis for numerous early religions.

PREHISTORIC
ACTIVITY

As early as 400,000 B.P. humans regularly built rudimentary camps along the Mediterranean. Near Nice, France, bands of humans camped in the pine and oak forest shores and built leaf-covered branch huts, some as long as 45 feet. Other groups chose to occupy the innumerable caves in the limestone extrusions in Spain and France. All these settlements were temporary, due to the need to follow herds of game for food.

By 100,000 B.P. *Homo sapiens* had evolved physiologically to the level of modern humans, and had succeeded in eliminating competing subspecies, notably the Neanderthal line, by either absorption or competition. Through the third interglacial and forth glacial phases, and into the period of presettlement, humans roamed the shores and forests of the Mediterranean lands, following the great migrating herds and foraging for edible plant life. Semipermanent encampments fashioned from animal skins or plant material were the predominant forms of shelter, though hunters and gatherers also spent time occupying caves, particularly those within close proximity to a reliable animal food source.

As noted above, one of the best records of this phase of human occupation of the Mediterranean region exists in a number of the caves in the limestone formations of central and western lands. Along the walls of these labyrinthine caverns colorful paintings document the hunting process, illustrating the strategy of the hunt in vivid imagery. The interior of the caves with their bold representations of the hunt were ritual places for a successful expedition. With a creative spontaneity remarkable in the history of artistic expression, the cave painters brought to life the vicissitudes of hunting: deer, horses, and the ferocious wild bull dominate the interior of the caves, sometimes as solitary forms, at other times being pursued by bands of humans intent on bringing down their prey by spear and arrow. Most important, the paintings reveal aspects of human control of the Mediterranean landscape at 30,000 B.P. From these scenes we can see that, though humans were far from totally dominating the land, they had begun to manipulate animal life, one of the major elements in the landscape, and a source of sustenance. Additional anthropological data indicate that humans cleared land for pasturage and hunting grounds, thereby taking another major step toward control of the environment.

HUMAN ADAPTATION TO THE EASTERN MEDITERRANEAN LANDSCAPE

The eastern half of the Mediterranean landscape, including the lands along the coasts and uplands of Asia Minor, and modern Syria, Lebanon, and Israel, nurtured the seeds of subsequent human occupation and settlement of the central and western Mediterranean region. As early as 10,000 B.P., prefarming settlements existed in the uplands, in areas similar to the lands above the riverine civilizations of the Indus Valley, the Tigris and Euphrates rivers. With abundant wild grain and game, the eastern Mediterranean uplands supported these first communities, which by 8000 B.P. had evolved into full-fledged agricultural settlements. In the interior regions of Asia Minor successful agricultural communities such as Catal Hüyük flourished, with mud brick dwellings, animal pens, and subsistence gardens. Nearer the east end of the Mediterranean, ancient communities such as Jericho, with its hillside site and year-round spring, supported nearly eight thousand years of human occupation; and along the eastern Mediterranean coast, near modern Lebanon, additional Neolithic camps evolved into agricultural settlements. The Phoenicians, for example, a tenacious seafaring society, evolved from these early coastal settlements to control a good part of the Mediterranean Sea.

Adaptation to the region required time and persistence, but, gradually, migrants from early Eastern settlements moved westward over the seas to settle in the central and western Mediterranean, in Greece, Sicily, and perhaps even

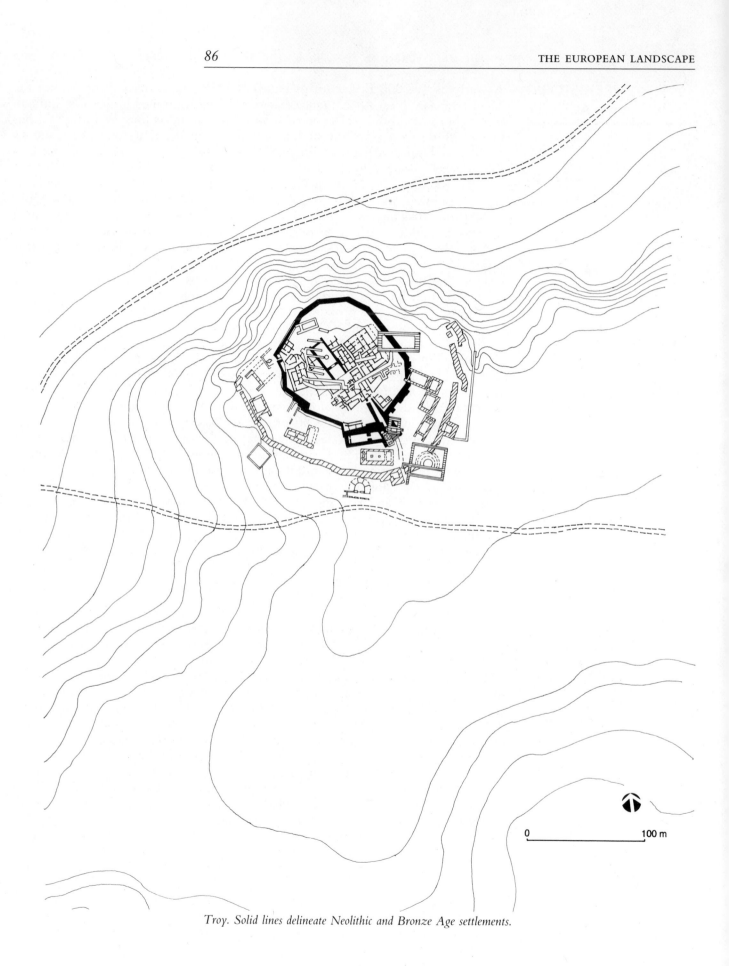

Troy. Solid lines delineate Neolithic and Bronze Age settlements.

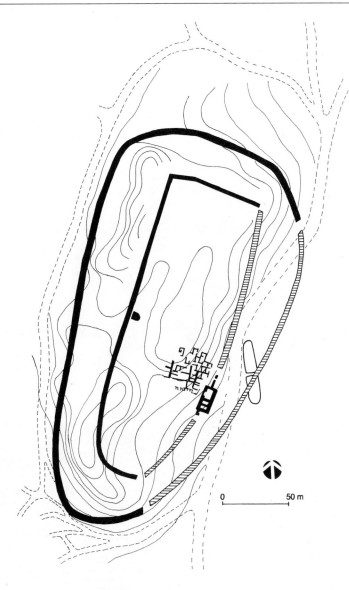

*Jericho. Solid lines indicate
excavated elements.*

Spain, bringing with them technical knowledge about agriculture and community formation. By 5000 B.P. these and other immigrants from central Europe had mixed with the various indigenous groups to form viable agricultural communities.

Other migrating groups who chose to form settlements in the eastern Mediterranean produced some of the most vigorous societies by developing permanent settlements in isolated locations, especially on the islands in the eastern Mediterranean region. Though previous occupation of island locations had tended to work against the growth of a community by isolating it from essential mating pools, the general spread of human occupation throughout the Mediterranean by the third and fourth centuries B.C. included the occupation of islands. By this time competition for arable land had accelerated, rendering these locations, which were naturally defensible, ideal for settlements. In the southern Aegean, for example, individuals from the Mediterranean mainland colonized Crete and formed a brilliant culture, one that endured until around 1600 B.C.[1]

Neolithic settlement on Crete began at least as early as the seventh millennium with the occupation of early sites along the north and south coasts. Around

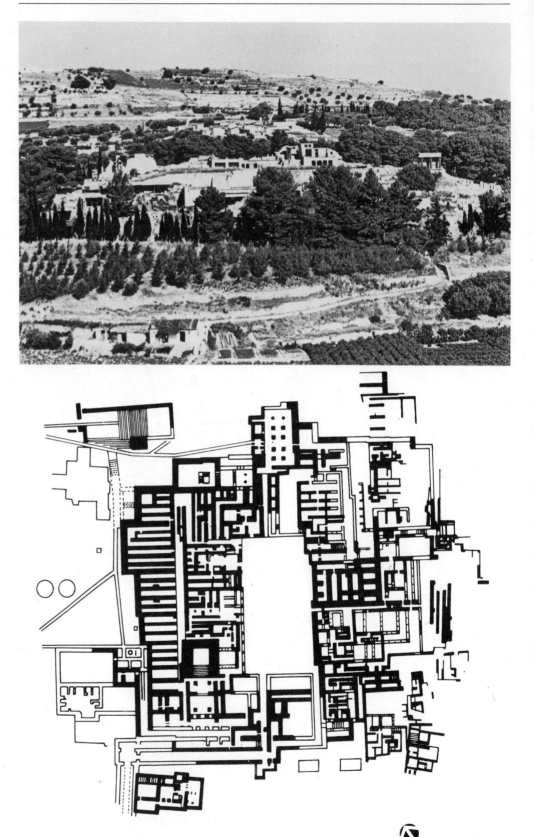

Ancient Knossos, sited on a
hill overlooking a steam and
surrounding agricultural lands
and protected from intermittent
flooding.

Plan of Knossos during the
Minoan period, c. 1600 B.C.,
depicting rectilinear arrangement
of architectural components
adjacent to exterior spaces.

0   25 m

6000 B.C., the earliest settlers established a community on a hill overlooking a small river and modest alluvial plain. Below the hill, the villagers cultivated wheat and six-row barley and tended sheep, goats, and pigs. The community that was to become the city of Knossos began as a modest, prepottery camp of less than an acre, consisting of no more than a dozen families. By the middle and late Neolithic the island contained a number of sites, and at about 5000 B.P. Knossos had evolved into a full-fledged agricultural community. Small, rectangular mud brick structures housed the occupants, who numbered roughly 100, in an area no larger than 50,000 square feet. The settlement grew and flourished through the fourth and third millennia B.C., and maintained a high level of social and cultural achievement.

SETTLEMENT CRITERIA

Throughout the Mediterranean, as additional communities began to form in advantageous locations, settlers tended to employ similar criteria in selecting a site. For example, they normally favored sites possessing ample arable land, a year-round source of water, and protection from flood and invasion. Consequently, promontories, hilltops, and slopes were favored locations for settlements throughout the region. For example, Dimini, located on the eastern shore of Greece on a site that fulfilled all the settlement criteria. It evolved over several centuries into an important, fortified community, commanding the natural resources of the immediate territory.

The question of water supply was at the forefront of Mediterranean consciousness from the time of the very earliest settlements since insufficient water supply during the summer drought spelled disaster for a community. Therefore, early settlements tended to appear either as small clusters around sparse springs or as a group of smaller settlements strung out along the landscape in line with existing springs. Despite these locations, intensive droughts caused devastating famines in the plain of Boetia, and later in Athens—and, in 490 B.C., in the less arid Italian Peninsula. Much later, Greek and Roman authorities, including Themistocles, Cato the Censorer, and Frontinus, promoted the need to understand the importance of an adequate water supply for the viability of a settlement.

URBAN AND RURAL PATTERNS

The beginning of a larger-scale urban and rural landscape development appeared after the decline of the Cretan society, around 1600 B.C., accompanying the development of larger and more politically ambitious settlements in the Peloponessus and the Greek mainland. The shift in cultural focus from the southern Aegean and Crete to the Greek mainland in the sixteenth century B.C. coincided with the development of numerous independent settlements on hilly sites overlooking the small, fertile plains of southern Greece. This pattern of early settlement was the backbone of subsequent urbanization and agricultural development of the rural landscape in the region.

Greek contribution to landscape development occurred in two stages. First were the events that occurred in the Greek homeland in concert with the activities of the various city-states; the second, and perhaps more dynamic, stage was associated with the period of Greek colonization beginning in the sixth century B.C.

During the first stage, many of the city-states were prosperous communities dominated by one or several powerful individuals. Eventually the tight social order that resulted from the political systems of the cities and from diminishing natural resources fostered the disenfranchisement of groups on the lower rungs of the economic ladder. Lack of opportunity led to migration from Greece, motivated by the emigrants' desire to improve their economic and social position.

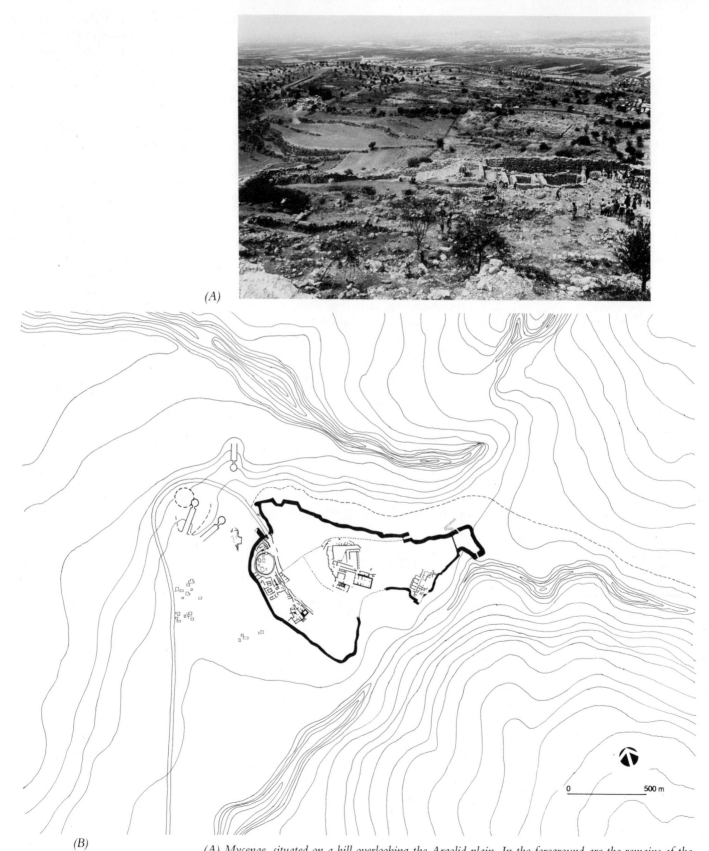

(A)

(B)

(A) Mycenae, situated on a hill overlooking the Argolid plain. In the foreground are the remains of the Bronze Age settlement. (B) Plan of Mycenae; solid lines indicate excavated elements.

Asia Minor, the coast of North Africa, and lands in the central and western Mediterranean became home to successive waves of colonists.

Before the colonization period, Greek society had undergone several phases of invasion and assimilation, a process that added to the sophistication of the society. Beginning at the late period of Aegean influence on the southern islands, the major settlement activity in the region occurred in conjunction with the activities of fledgling city-states, and including a period of Greek revival in the twelfth century B.C. From Asia Minor waves of Dorian settlers brought a fresh perspective to a land that had been dominated by the Mycenaeans. Attica, the region around Athens, became the location for the largest population in Greece. By the tenth century B.C. Athens, already an established sea power from Mycenaean times, had become the strongest community in the region.[2] Sparta, Athens' chief competitor, located inland about 20 miles from the coast on the Eurotus River, occupied an elevated site in the upper basin of the river, secure from periodic flooding. Less notable communities formed from the remnants of earlier native communities, often banding together to form larger settlements as the waves of Dorian immigrants swept over Greece. Most of the important city-states by this time centered around a citadel, or *acropolis,* and were often located some distance from the coasts as a protection from invading seafarers. A few communities ended up on elevated spurs that jutted seaward. All had need for a measure of arable land to help sustain their communities, but ordinarily the amount of territory commanded by the city-states was modest, averaging 70 square miles for the Boetian states. Only three city-states had populations of more than 20,000.[3]

AGRICULTURE, IRRIGATION, AND RECLAMATION

Economically, the lands within the territories of the city-states offered less opportunity for agricultural exploitation than the alluvial plains of the Near East or the Nile River. Scant rainfall during the hot summer months and few year-round rivers rendered the landscape of the Greek mainland a difficult environment for agriculture. Farmers used the least useful irrigated lands as pastures for goats, cows, horses, and oxen, while prime agricultural lands supported the propagation of wheat, barley, beans, figs, and peas. In the period of domination of the city-states, the traditional Mediterranean agricultural triad of cereals, wine, and oil became the focus of agricultural activity. Several regions produced fine crops of wheat, especially in Boeotia and Thessaly, though a number of other city-states perennially worried about sufficient produce.

Part of the success of the Greeks in producing grain and other produce rested on a concerted effort to maintain the best agricultural soils. In the Attican plain near Athens, farmers kept the soils loose and workable by ploughing farmlands three times a year. After breaking up of the soil in the spring, subsequent cross-ploughings occurred in the summer and fall, the last of which was in preparation for sowing. October was a time of rejoicing for the Greeks, for the process of sowing wheat symbolized the reuniting of life with the mother earth, a preparation for the rebirth of life in the spring. Mild winters had little effect on the seeds, so that in February or March, light hoeing removed unwanted weeds and prepared the soil for spring rains and subsequent growth and harvesting of the wheat.[4] The process also included leaving half the land unplanted as fallow. The fallow land was used as pasture, and with sufficient manure and ploughing, again became ready for cultivation.

A problem with the fallow technique was the diminution of yields due to withholding a portion of the land from cultivation. The Greeks responded to this problem by cultivating wheat between olive trees and vines, a technique transferred to the western Mediterranean during the Roman era. This method was particularly suited to the local conditions: the shallow wheat roots did not interfere with the moisture requirements of the trees and vines, while the wheat functioned as a cover crop, helping to prevent unnecessary erosion of the orchard terraces. Traditionally both crops—olives and grapes—were important to the Greek culture. According to Greek folklore, Athena won the right to command Athens by offering the olive tree as a gift to the citizens of the city. The vine was also an important element of Greek culture, both physically and intellectually; Homer refers to viticulture in the Odyssey, and legend held that wine was the divine mechanism for communication with Dionysus.

It is believed that the olive tree, native to the eastern Mediterranean, appeared as an important species as early as 2000 B.C., based on the remains of olive presses found associated with ancient Thera. And it is known that the Mycenaeans maintained groves to produce the fruit for food and household uses. The olive, more than any other natural element, reflects the condition of the landscape and climate of Greece, and in some ways mirrors the tenacious, sturdy quality of its people as well. Few plants are as well suited to the calcareous soils and long summer droughts as this specimen. The plant is hardy, able to survive in many soil types as long as drainage is good; it can withstand the parching summers because its root system not only penetrates down to the moist layers of soil but also spreads outward, allowing it to accumulate moisture during the rainy season.

In ancient Attica, where the olive had been revered from time immemorial, farmers were mindful of its invasive root system. Laws forbade the planting of the tree closer than 9 feet to a neighbor's land. Near Athens, the olive groves received an extra supply of nutrients from the sewage system that carried material from the city to a reservoir and then out along a canal to the orchards and farms on the small plains nestled in the nearby valleys.[5] Ample watering helped to produce bigger fruit, though the best oil resulted from dry-farming methods. With sufficient irrigation, the plant produces more foliage; the olive trees in the sacred grove of Pallas Athena in the Academy, which received moisture from streams from the Cephisios River, produced the "deep impenetrable shade" noted by Sophocles.[6]

As we have noted, Mediterranean landscapes, composed of hills, mountains, and small, intermittent alluvial valleys are problematic for agriculture, due to scant arable land and an arid climate. Generally nonalluvial lands are difficult to cultivate in the summer and the alluvial valleys are prone to inundation during spring floods. In order to survive in such landscapes, farmers have had to devise forms of artificial irrigation, as well as methods for rendering lowlands free from severe flooding. The Greeks were not exempt from this requirement and, along with their counterparts throughout the Mediterranean, they devised irrigation and reclamation techniques to create sufficient arable lands. With few major rivers to draw from and scant moisture during the summer drought, the Greeks practiced irrigation with a cautious eye to economy of water use. Since the dry summers alternated with torrential precipitation during the rainy seasons, they relied on combined irrigation and drainage strategies to both water and preserve important agricultural lands. Dykes and drainage ditches functioned as irrigation channels; small dams created reservoirs for storing runoff from mountain torrents. Plants accustomed to growing in dry soils received a small amount of irrigation during the summer. Young trees growing in nurseries received regular watering, but mature trees in orchards received water only during the driest months, July and August. Also, a proportion of the irrigation supply flowed from the underground streams contained in the limestone substrata that underlay a good portion of the Greek landscape. Surface vents from these underground streams and rivers formed fountainheads, or *kephalari,* that furnished water to the fields on the small plains. Ironically, in areas where these sources occurred in some abundance, the Greeks actually had to undertake reclamation projects to free the lands near the springs from overinundation during peak flow periods. Unlike the Mesopotamians, who had to contend with an accumulation of salts and alkalies in their soils, the Greeks were able to avoid this problem with sufficient drainage and restricted irrigation.[7]

Boeotia, underlain by the karst limestone that contained underground streams, was an area that underwent constant reclamation efforts. The excellent soils in the district needed constant attention to avoid unwanted inundation, particularly during the rainy season, when the underground streams could not carry off the excess precipitation. About every nine years, Lake Copais sustained a period of flooding, which inundated 90 square miles of land. Very early, inhabitants of the area attempted to counteract the effect of the floods by constructing canals and attempting to enlarge the openings to the underground channels, wherein excess water ran along ancient tunnels, under the surrounding hills, and drained as large springs. By maintaining this drainage system, the Greeks were able to render large tracts of land usable for agriculture. Numerous villages, tucked along the hillsides surrounding the lake, fed off these lands, though from time to time extreme flooding isolated the settlements from each other. Another clever approach to utilizing the arable land on Boeotia was employed in the western portion of the district at ancient Thisbe. There the inhabitants built a longitudinal dike along the gradient of a small lake. Biannually they diverted water to one side of the dike, and farmed the land on the other side, thereby assuring themselves arable land that contained moisture and nutrients from decaying plants.[8]

Reclamation projects were not restricted to Boeotia. The highlands of Arcadia, underlain by limestone deposits, contained some of the best arable land in the region. In ancient times Lake Pheneos was a fertile plain, sustaining periodic inundation from the backing up of underground streams. The inhabitants of the area created an embanked channel along the length of the stream, 1,100 feet long and 30 feet deep. In the best of times, the system helped to reclaim 9 square miles of arable land, but it did not make the areas immune to floods during severe storm periods. Consequently the largest city occupied a relatively safe site about 6 miles from the channel on the rim of the lake basin.

As the rural areas of Greece rapidly converted to agriculture and pasturage, urban areas, particularly the larger city-states, grew in size and cultural influence. By the fifth century B.C. Athens had a population of nearly 150,000 and commanded an area 50 by 30 miles in extent.

Attica, the area ruled by Athens, consisted of hills and mountains that divided the land into smaller units. Its coastline, indented with small coves and bays, was ideal for small ports and maritime activity. Between the uplands and coast were the numerous small plains, covered with woods and scrub land, a land suitable for marginal, small-scale farming and pastures. The greater portion of the plains region belonged to the lands adjacent to the Cephisus River, the narrow plain of Eleusis, northwest of the city; and the plain between Mts. Pentelicon and Hymettus, the largest at slightly less than 8 miles in width.

Both agriculture and pastoralism occurred marginally in the plains of Attica. Few of the plains named above contained moist valleys suitable for stock breeding, and due to the marginal quality of their soils most of the grain produced was barley rather than wheat. Even the fig-bearing orchards and the vineyards were of less than premium quality due to insufficient rainfall and frequent drought—for, in addition to their other drawbacks, the plains were in a rain shadow created by adjacent mountains.

Not surprisingly, the landscape placed severe constraints on the amount of food produced in the region. Only those who were quick-witted enough to adapt to the landscape were able to prosper, and food shortages were common, though actual famine was uncommon except in times of siege.[9] Typically food shortages would occur as a result of protracted low harvests rather than a single crop failure, exacerbated by populations attempting to feed their ever increasing numbers off a landscape with a mediocre agricultural capacity.

AGORA, THEATERS, GROVES, TEMPLE SITES

Hard and often unyielding agriculturally, the Greek land nevertheless was wonderfully suited for outdoor activity. From January to March assemblies, councils, law courts, and spirited arguments by philosophers often took place outdoors during the winter months, between sowing and the harvest. The larger urban areas, including Athens, reflected the Greek predilection for life outdoors, where the prolonged sunshine fostered a quick intelligence and clarity of mind.[10] Life outdoors also stimulated social exchange and fostered the attitude of inquiry that was an important component of the Greek sensibility. Exposure to nature made the Greeks acutely aware of their physical surroundings, fostering a sensitivity to the spirit of site, or *genius loci*.[11] The earliest Greek philosophers, including Thales of Miletus, Anaxemeter, and Anaximenes, sought to explain natural phenomena through observation and inquiry. Subsequent Greek philosophers, including Pythagorus, endeavored to expand upon the rational approach by delving into mathematics. At the height of Athenian supremacy shortly after her defeat of the Persians in 480 B.C., philosophical activity acquired an elevated social status, first through the works of Anaxagoras, and later, those of Socrates, Plato, and Aristotle. Athenians complemented their love of philosophical inquiry with the theater. Both Greek comedy and tragedy, epitomized by Aeschylus, Sophocles, Euripides, and Aristophanes, plumbed the range of the human condition.

Greek urban centers existed to facilitate commerce, small industry, and political activity. But urban structure and form also evolved to accommodate the practice of the philosophical and theatrical arts. Every major urban center, and many smaller settlements as well, contained theaters, groves, schools, and public open spaces—places devoted to intellectual and artistic expression. Athens, like all the principal classical Greek cities, had its share of open spaces for public activity, these elements having accrued to the city over time, beginning with its founding as a small settlement adjacent to an impregnable citadel.

By the sixth century B.C. Athens had evolved from a small community surrounding a hilltop fortress to one of over 150,000 individuals. Physically, the town conformed to the style of architectural organization common to the eastern Mediterranean: domestic structures were built of sun-dried brick on stone or rubble foundations. Well-to-do families occupied commodious residences built around an open courtyard, bounded by living and working quarters. Often these residences were organized to allow their occupants to shift living quarters to the north and south ends of the dwelling, depending on the time of year and prevailing climatic conditions. Streets and ways connecting neighborhoods to commercial districts loosely followed the existing topography and the alignment established by ancient inhabitants of the city.

Life in Athens typified the response many communities made to the opportunities for activities outdoors, which was to fuse the various forms of Greek expression—philosophical, commercial, and political—into the physical structure of the community. Of the several important spaces within the communities for public activity, the *agora* was preeminent. Day to day commercial and political activities centered on this space, which in Athens commanded an important location in the community at the foot of the Acropolis, or upper city, and at the terminus of the Panathenaic Way, the ancient road from the seaport of Piraeus to Athens. The agora was approximately 10 acres in area, and lacked the sense of formal arrangement so common in later Mediterranean town spaces; instead, the space took its shape from the location of important commercial and political buildings sited along its periphery. The *stoa* of Attalus II, a long colonnaded structure, bounded the north edge of the space, while additional stoa and commercial structures enclosed the space from the other sides.

The Theater of Dionysius, directly opposite the agora on the south slope of the Acropolis, was another important exterior public space. As with all theaters in Greece, the roots of the architectural and siting choices made by its builders can be traced to the Greek habit of performing theater in the open. From earliest times, inhabitants gathered on open hillsides to participate in the production of important ancient plays. Often actors and participants were one, all reciting important lines in the production. Eventually, theaters acquired a more formal arrangement, with the audience separated from the actors. As early as the sixth century B.C. important writers presented plays to the Athenians, who reciprocated by bestowing poetry prizes on the authors of the most stimulating plays.

The Greek theater, whether at Athens, Delphi, or Epidauros, epitomized the Hellenic sensitivity to building in the landscape. Rather than attempting to site theaters on terrain that was topographically inappropriate, especially on land that was susceptible to flooding, the Greeks selected sites along hillsides, taking advantage of prevailing slope and the elevation above seasonal flooding. Hillside siting also allowed the Greeks to sculpt the structure out of the land and to form acoustically functional space. For example Epidauros, sited on the eastern edge of the Argolid region, flourished as an important hilltop settlement from the first millennium. In its prime, the city boasted a *hieron,* or sacred enclosure, consisting of a circular *tholos,* stoa, temples, and stadium. But the most enduring element of the community to survive from antiquity is its theater. Constructed in 350 B.C.,

The Acroplis of Athens.

The agora of Athens seen from the Acropolis. Beyond the city lies the port of Piraeus.

The agora, Stoa of Attalus, and the Acropolis.

the well-preserved, semicircular volume measuring 387 feet across occupies a north-facing hillside providing a spectacular view to the landscape beyond.

Not all important exterior sites relied on formal architecture for definition. Following a tradition that predates classical temples, specific landscape units acquired special status as places for contemplation and recreation. Preeminent were the sacred groves, derived from stands of forest trees. Later, these sites, embel-

The Theater of Epidauros sited into a hillside with spectacular views to the surrounding landscape.

lished with ornamental trees, shrubs, and flowers, were dedicated to an important deity. An example of such a grove was the Garden of Daphne, dedicated to Apollo, near the city of Antioch.[12] At Athens one of the most important sacred groves was a stand of olive trees in the Cephisus Valley, a small, narrow plain near Eleusis, the eventual site of the Academy of Athens. In the late sixth century B.C., Hipparchus surrounded the site with walls, and subsequent important Athenians embellished the site with walks, trees, and fountains. As a place of ritual where the ancient Mysteries were performed, Eleusis linked human and natural cycles; and here Greeks conducted pagan rituals to initiate individuals into the realm of extrasensory experience.

At Athens, above the theaters, agora, and groves, loomed the striking composition of temples and structures on the Acropolis. Once the site of a fortified "upper city," the site, measuring 1,000 by 445 feet, became the location of outstanding architectural elements, including the Dorian temples constructed during the sixth century B.C., and the Parthenon, Propylaea, and Erectheum constructed during and after the leadership of Pericles in the late fifth century B.C. Most of the fine marble used to construct the various structures originated from Mt. Pentelicon, 12 miles distant, or from nearby Mt. Hymettus. The fine-grained, glossy marble was the material favored by the builders and sculptors; the bluish-white marble from Hymettus and the dark-gray limestone from Eleusis functioned beautifully for embellishments and contrasting effects.[13] As a complement to the materials, the various architects of the Acropolis took care to place their structures in an arrangement that formed a spatial composition visible from a prime station point at the Propylaea. Scholars have argued about the rationale for this and other urban arrangements, with some attributing the decision to mathematical standards,[14] and others inferring a more intuitive approach.[15]

Athens was far from being the only urban area in Greece to display sophisticated settlement patterns. Another striking example of sensitive response to

Delphi, situated on a south-facing hillside; structures at Delphi include temples, theater, and stadium.

landscape qualities was Delphi, resting on a hillside in the shadow of Mt. Parnassus. A site dedicated to the god Apollo, Delphi contained domestic and commercial structures and spaces, but its most important feature was a fine arrangement of architectural elements. Initially, local inhabitants constructed a Doric temple about midway along the slope facing the Gulf of Corinth some 15 miles to the south. Subsequent structures followed the siting of the temple, including additional temples, a theater, and a stadium. The temple to Apollo, the most dominant of the structures in this sequence, rested midway on the slope above the treasuries and below the theater. A path leading from the bottom of the slope to the stadium near the top of the site linked various architectural elements in a sequence, allowing viewers to perceive each element successively.

COLONIZATION; PRIENE AND MILETUS

While urbanization and agricultural production proceeded apace in Greece, small settlements of Greek origin were forming along the shores of the eastern and western Mediterranean. Marseilles, Paestum, Pompeii, Syracuse, Miletus, and Priene all trace their origins to this period of colonization. Mainly these communities evolved from an out-migration from Greece of people seeking relief from political oppression and scarcity of resources. Beginning around 750 B.C. cities in Greece solved their population problems by establishing colonies, a policy that also helped to broaden trade for the parent cities. Originally the colonial settlements conformed to the social and economic arrangements of their respective parent cities, but physically they were quite different. Part of the credit for the more rigorous organization of these colonial cities belongs to planners, who imparted a sense of order unfamiliar to most parent cities in Greece.

Priene and Miletus, colonies near the coast of Asia Minor, epitomized Greek colonial urban planning. Both were the work of Hippodamus of Miletus, a fifth-century planner who is traditionally credited with leading the movement to formal order in urban organization. His approach reflects a reliance on geometry, especially the gridiron and right angles, though such urban arrangement had occasionally occurred in earlier societies, especially the Indus valley. From a view of the remains of both Priene and Miletus, the effect of the Hippodamian approach is clear. Priene, perched on a precipice above the Meander Valley, dispenses with the sequential placement of architectural elements, a technique favored in Greece. Rather, temples, theaters, shops, streets, and ways conform to a predetermined grid arrangement. East-west streets run parallel to contours, and the agora, also with its longer dimension aligned along contours, seems suited to the steep site; north-south streets, however, incline steeply across the contours, underscoring the prime drawback of the grid-iron approach: though efficient as a spatial concept, it is awkward on hilly terrain. On level topography, the grid configuration permits an orderly urban arrangement.

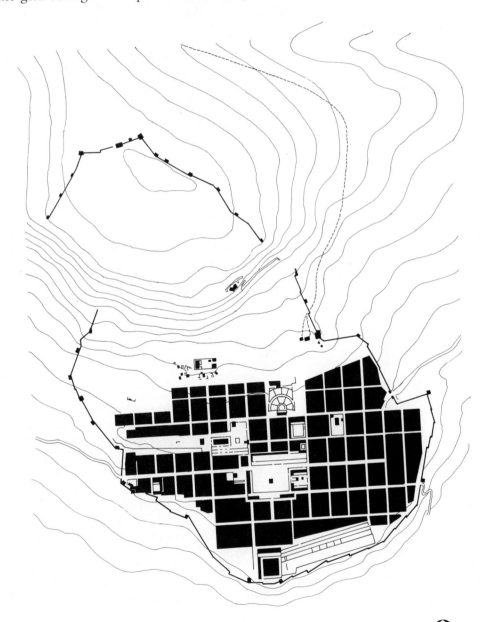

Plan of Priene, a sixth-century B.C. Greek colonial site organized in the Hippodamian mode.

0   100 m

(A) Priene near the agora looking upslope to the Acropolis. (B) Reconstruction of the city.

Miletus, older than Priene, sits on an elevated site on the Meander Plain, inland from the sea about 4 miles. In antiquity, the city was an important seaport, but intensive agricultural activity in the region generated excessive siltation, which eventually isolated the town from the coast. In 494 B.C., a destructive invasion by the Persians left the community in need of serious restoration. Hippodamus won a commission to plan the city, and in 479 B.C. began to fashion a new community based on his spatial theories. Its distinction lay in the planner's application of the gridiron which in this instance was suited to the relative level topography of the site. Within its 220 acres, the new town encompassed three residential districts, a rectangular forum and theater, gymnasium, and stadium.

ENVIRONMENTAL ISSUES

Before the development of sophisticated settlements with their public spaces, temples, and theaters, large stands of native vegetation covered areas of the eastern Mediterranean region. Among these were oak, fir, cedar, and cypress, which flourished along mountain slopes and in many of the plains. For example, Cape Sunion, on the south coast of Attica, was a forested promontory overlooking the sea.[16] However, intensive agriculture in the small arable plains and valleys, goat herding along the hillsides and mountain slopes, and the removal of forests for the production of charcoal for use in shipbuilding and as firewood, progressively eliminated many of the natural stands of timber. Especially the hills and mountains, which in ancient times had imparted to the landscape a sense of scale and enclosure, bore the consequences of agriculture and deforestation. Further, stripped of the plants that held the soil, the steep slopes could not endure the long droughts and the intermittent powerful winter rains without extensive soil erosion. In response to these conditions Plato observed that the land "seemed a mere decayed carcass with the bare bones sticking through the soil."[17]

These insidious changes to the landscape appear to contradict the brilliant achievements attributed to Greek culture. But rather than being an indictment

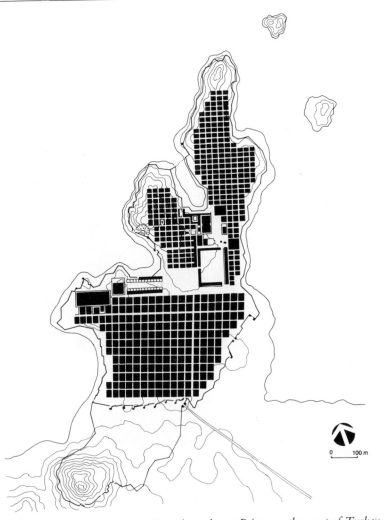

Plan of Miletus and important Greek colonial site located near Priene on the coast of Turkey.

View of Miletus and the coast from the theater. Siltation from the Meander River has long since isolated the settlement from the sea.

Extensive grazing in many areas of the eastern Mediterranean landscape has deforested hillsides.

An example of forest land in Greece protected from overgrazing.

of the society, landscape alteration can be seen as the inevitable product of population growth and stiff competition for natural resources. Also with colonialism offering the opportunity to expand into undeveloped lands, the effects of urban and rural expansion probably did not appear dire in a region with sufficient resources. In fact, rather than appearing on the brink of cataclismal decline, the environment was a source of continuous inspiration. The Greeks enjoyed nature, and were inclined to express their interpretations of natural phenomena in their art and architecture. In literature, themes often revolved around aspects of the land and its denizens. Philosophers asked questions about ecological issues. Sacred rites, including Eleusis, conferred upon individuals an everlasting link between human birth, mortality, and rebirth, and the cyclic seasons in nature. Aristotle promoted the observation and classification of biological phenomena. Except for occasional storms and floods, the Greeks maintained a sanguine attitude about nature, tempered by reverence for the deities that ruled the cosmos.[18]

Yet despite these influences, extensive removal of forests occurred between 600 and 200 B.C. Nearly every industry relied on wood, whether for carpentry, pottery, adhesives for binding and waterproofing, or for winemaking. Hughes estimates that half the land originally had forest cover, reduced to one-tenth by modern times. Certain rulers attempted to stem deforestation, including the Cypriot kings in the fourth century B.C., only to be reversed by subsequent rulers who encouraged rural settlement. In each instance, deforestation lessened soil quality and erosion quickly became a problem. Added to this was the Greek predilection for pastoralism—four-fifths of the usable land supported grazing—and the rapid elimination of soil cover by voracious sheep and goats. One solution was to encourage terracing, which was intended to mitigate the effects of grazing and the need to extend arable land. Finally, agriculture and deforestation eliminated habitats, reducing the faunal population along the entire food chain. Significantly, all of these effects on the environment occurred in a society associated with the modest gains in agricultural production, far less than the large-scale industry associated with later cultures, especially the Romans.

NOTES

1. *A. B. Knapp. 1985.* Prehistoric Production and Exchange: The Aegean and the Eastern Mediterranean. *Los Angeles: University of California Press.*

2. *Michael Grant. 1969.* The Ancient Mediterranean. *New York: Scribners, p. 134. The author discusses settlement activities throughout the successive stages of Greek activity in the Mediterranean.*

3. *Ibid., p. 136.*

4. *Ibid., p. 186.*

5. *E. C. Semple. 1971.* The Geography of the Mediterranean Region. *New York: AMS Press, p. 414. See Semple for a thorough discussion of Mediterranean geography and land use.*

6. *Ibid., p. 435.*

7. *Ibid., p. 446.*

8. *Ibid., p. 448.*

9. *Peter Garnsey. 1988.* Famine and Food Supply in the Greco-Roman World. *Cambridge: Cambridge University Press, p. 37.*

10. *Grant, op. cit., p. 202.*

11. *Christian Norberg-Schulz. 1970.* Genius Loci: Towards a Phenomenology of Architecture. *New York: Rizzoli.*

12. *Semple, op. cit., p. 489.*

13. *William Fleming. 1980.* Arts and Ideas. *New York: Holt, Rinehart and Winston, p. 24.*

14. *Konstaninos Doxiades. 1972.* Architectural Space in Ancient Greece. *Cambridge, Mass.: MIT Press.*

15. *Norberg-Schulz, op. cit.*

16. *Grant, op. cit., p. 98.*

17. *Ibid., p. 98. Also see Semple, 1971, p. 289 for comments regarding deforestation.*

18. *Donald J. Hughes. 1975.* Ecology in Ancient Civilizations. *Albuquerque: University of New Mexico Press. See Semple, 1971, for a discussion of the Mediterranean timber industry.*

6

The Mediterranean Landscape: Roman Hegemony

During the first millenium B.C., as agriculture, pastoralism, and urbanization spread throughout the Mediterranean, competition for territory and natural resources stimulated Roman ascendancy in the region. Through military prowess, economic ability, and legal acumen, the Romans were by far the most successful culture in the Mediterranean by the first century B.C. As demand for agricultural production and raw materials compelled Rome to expand its boundaries, the region soon became the storehouse for Roman appetites. By the first century A.D., the Roman Empire had replaced its efficient small farms with a system of large-scale agricultural industries, urban centers, and rural reclamation projects. After several centuries of expansion Rome gradually declined, handing over authority to groups who had migrated into the realm to staff the military and the government. By the fifth century A.D., the Roman Mediterranean landscape began to fracture into disparate regional political units, with northern cultures slowly imposing new patterns on the region.

CULTURAL AND PHYSICAL CONTEXT

The Romanization of the Mediterranean landscape began around the eighth century B.C., when Rome emerged as a settlement on the banks of the Tiber River. The small community was one of several settlements in Latium, which included the area around modern Rome, and was also one of several communities com-

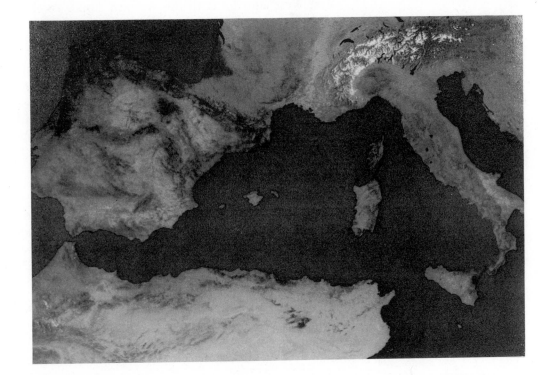

Satellite view of the western Mediterranean.

Physiography of the landscape of Etruria, a region dissected by streams and ravines.

peting with the Etruscans to the north for regional supremacy. Geographically, the portion of Italy where these settlements appeared includes uplands and small river valleys, one of four alluvial areas on the peninsula suitable for agriculture. The other alluvial areas lay in the Po Valley; in Latium and the lowlands of Etruria and the Campagna near Naples; and further south, in the broad, warm lands, which sustained Greek colonization between the sixth and fourth centuries B.C. The north-south Appenine mountain range, rising nearly 9,600 feet in the central peninsula, bisects the peninsula and also contributes to the distinctive, east-west climate, with the western slopes receiving more annual rainfall than the eastern.

Even before the Latin tribes occupied central Italy, small communities had existed on the peninsula, pursuing a mixture of hunting-gathering and, later, rudimentary agriculture. Based on archaeological evidence from Neolithic hunting-gathering sites near estuaries and shorelines, the earliest sites display rudimentary farming, as early as 6000 B.C. along the Italian peninsula at Rendina, on Sardinia, and possibly on Corsica.[1] In addition to farming, perennial hunting, gathering, and stock breeding supplemented the economic base of these early Neolithic settlements. By 4500 B.C., in the Apulia region of the southern Italian peninsula, small farming communities dotted the region; in the fifth and fourth millennia B.C. settlement activity appeared further south near Terranto. Even the islands surrounding the peninsula supported prehistoric settlement: in the fourth and third millennia, aboveground "aviolian" tombs dotted the island of Malta; on other remote islands, small farming communities pooled their labor and resources to build temples as monuments to local deities.

The first Italic farmers and pastoralists migrated across the Adriatic from beyond the Balkan peninsula prior to the third millennium B.C. Later immigrants from beyond the Alps crossed the Brenner Pass; these settlers introduced metallurgy to the region and built timbered, moated structures. In the late second millennium B.C. subsequent groups occupied the same region, building settlements around the Po Valley and as far south as the Campagna. Grant[2] speculates that these various groups eventually combined to form the later Etruscan culture.

The Etruscans, whose territory spanned what is now northern Tuscany and northern Lazio, produced an outstanding culture, especially in the arts and in the management of their communities. The Etruscans occupied one of the most varied landscapes in Italy, characterized by coasts, headlands, sandy bars, plains, hills, uplands, and mountains. At the time of early Etruscan activity, dense stands of evergreen oaks and beech forests covered the land. In addition, there were numerous pockets of fertile land, protected by the Appenines to the east and warmed by the Tyrrhenian Sea to the west, a sea that is warmer than the Adriatic, helping to produce a winter temperature about five degrees higher than that in the eastern half of the peninsula.

ETRUSCAN AND ROMAN DEVELOPMENT

Despite the availability of water and rich soil in the alluvial plains, the Etruscans, like other early societies in the Mediterranean, tended to avoid settling directly in low-lying areas, preferring to build their communities along the slopes of hills and mountains. These elevated sites escaped the winter flooding of the local drainage channels, and to some degree protected inhabitants from malaria in the summer, a phenomenon the Etruscans attributed to marsh mist.

Tuned to the resources and limitations of the surrounding landscape, the Etruscans responded to specific site conditions in the formation of their communities. As noted, Etruscan towns occupied higher elevations, lying above arable lands. Traditionally, these city-states were twelve in number, but aerial photography shows that many hills that had natural defenses on three sides supported an Etruscan town.[3] To facilitate communication between towns, they built good roads to link one city-state to another.

By the seventh century B.C., settlements in the southern alluvial portion of Etruria began to assume political command of the region. Tarquinia, perhaps the richest of the Etruscan city-states, along with other communities in southern Etruria, frequently traded with the Greeks, exchanging their elegant bronze artifacts for Greek products. At both Tarquinia and Caere, the Etruscans built elaborate tombs to house the remains of well-to-do inhabitants. The necropolis at Ceverteria, near Tarquinia, contains a number of tombs fashioned out of native rock, and elaborately carved to resemble the interior of houses owned by the deceased.

In the sixth century B.C., as the Etruscans expanded their authority into the northern section of the Italian peninsula, adjacent tribes were extending their influence in the southern peninsula. Latium, the Samnite lands, the islands of Sicily, Sardinia, and Corsica all supported settlements, and were not unknown to the Etruscans, who actively traded with these groups. At the southern edge of the territory, a few miles south of Veii, indigenous tribes, possibly descended from Indo-Europeans, began to compete for the lands around the Tiber River. Two of these tribes, the Latins and the Sabines, settled on the the north bank of the river on the surrounding seven hills around 800 B.C., about half a century before the traditional founding of Rome.

The site selected by the two tribes was perhaps the most advantageous of any along the Italian peninsula. Lying midway between the Italian Alps and the tip of the Italian peninsula, it occupied a position near the last ford and ferry point along the course of the Tiber River on its flow to the sea. The crossing spanned the only firm ground where the river turns westward and falls through the low mountain range to meet the coastal plain. It was well-watered, defensible, adjacent to rich, fertile lands, and accessible to ample winter pasturage. Within a short time the local inhabitants had extended their settlements to near the coast and to 17 miles upstream.

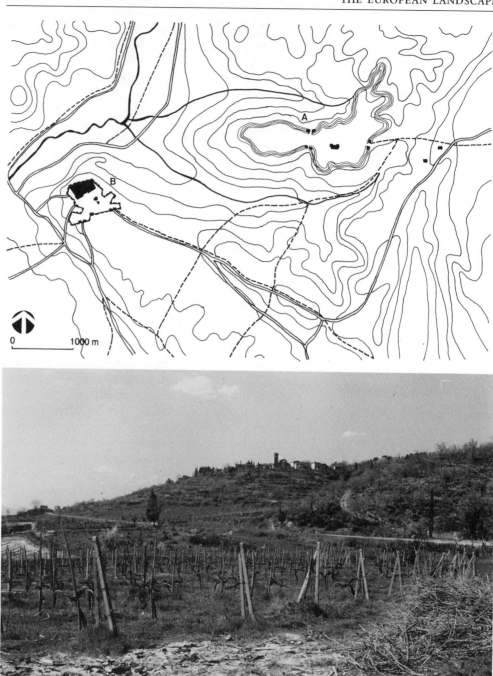

Etruscan settlements such as Tarquinia took advantage of elevated sites above narrow floodplains and prime agricultural land. Top: (A) ancient site (B) medieval and modern towns. Below: contemporary Tuscan community founded during Etruscan-Roman times showing the siting of the settlement above the flood plain and prime agricultural land.

By the sixth century B.C. the Etruscans had expanded their domain to include the two villages along the Tiber. They encouraged the inhabitants to pursue agricultural activity, prompting farmers to cultivate the heavy soil to produce a variety of coarse emmer wheat. In addition pasture land near the river supported livestock; the area was also the town center in the earliest days of the settlement. A sixth century B.C. wooden bridge linked the community to an Etruscan fortress on the north side of the river.

Etruscan tombs at Tarquinia carved from native tufa. Interior of the tombs replicated the organization of the deceased's residence.

Advantageous siting is evident in this Tuscan settlement surrounded by agricultural lands.

Throughout Etruria, from the Po Valley to the southern lands, each community cultivated arable lands near its settlement—mostly as a complement to pastoralism, primarily the tending of sheep and goats. Much of their success stemmed from intelligent agricultural practices, due in part to the comprehension of agriculture and irrigation borrowed from the Greeks and other Mediterranean societies. This included knowledge of irrigation techniques; soil management, including the use of fallow; and an understanding of the habit of important agricultural specimens, such as the olive and vine that were introduced into the peninsula by the Greeks.

Armed with technical knowledge about irrigation and agricultural practice, the various cities evolved patterns to suit the local conditions. For example, at towns like Veii near Rome, the inhabitants stored water in cisterns fed by rock-cut channels, connected to rivers and streams. In addition, in lands that had been too marshy for cultivation, the inhabitants of Veii dug elaborate drainage channels, thereby significantly increasing the amount of arable land.

Etruscan domination of central Italy, the Po Valley, and the Campagna began to wane in the sixth century B.C., as Greek and other non-Latin inhabitants of the region began to compete for territory. Eventually, competing forces defeated the Etruscans in a series of land and sea battles, which eventually resulted in the expulsion of Etruscan settlers from Sicily and Corsica. Around 400 B.C., the Etruscan settlements in the Po Valley fell to Gallic invaders, effectively shrinking Etruscan peninsular authority to its original homeland in central Italy. Soon after, Veii capitulated to its rival, Rome, which had established itself as a viable city in 753 B.C., and a republic in 509 B.C. What had been a domain stretching from the Italian Alps to the Straits of Messina disintegrated, leaving the Romans to continue the process of cultural expansion in the central Mediterranean.

Like the Greeks in their own homeland, the Etruscans never achieved true unity of the Italian landscape. The Romans, however, applied their intelligence and energy to unifying the Italian peninsula and subjugating the Mediterranean region. Roman rule in the region left an indelible mark; what was a relatively pristine natural setting was changed to one which reflected the voracious Roman appetite for land and natural resources. At the heart of this consumption of the natural environment was an economic system that depended on a constant inflow of resources to support the expanding Roman population. Most important, all economic activities, commercial and industrial, were subordinate to the needs of agriculture, which was Rome's prime industry and the greatest source of its wealth.[4] As a result, Rome sought to solidify its economic base by constantly expanding its agricultural lands, a process that spawned new settlements in undeveloped regions.

SETTLEMENT INFLUENCES

Despite what appeared to be a greater percentage of arable land in the Italian peninsula than in Greece, Italy possessed a limited amount of land suitable for cultivation, mostly occurring between drainage ways and along low-lying formations at the outfall of rivers and streams. As in other Mediterranean regions, the limited amount of fertile land compelled early inhabitants to carefully focus their agricultural activities on small alluvial plains.[5] Good land was often diminished by an inadequate water supply: year-round streams were a rarity, particularly in the southern peninsula. Therefore, in areas underlain by dry, porous limestone, where springs and wells are sparsely scattered in the landscape, people tended to form large settlements near these water sources. On volcanic soils, with numerous springs, the settlement pattern was more dispersed, consisting of smaller communities. Finally, on the alluvial plains, with plenty of groundwater, or in piedmont areas possessing perennial springs, the good soils and sufficient water were favorable for the maintenance of numerous small villages.

Thus, from earliest times, the combination of geological, geographical, and climatic conditions in the Italian peninsula favored a broad distribution of agricultural towns and villages, from the extensive deposits of tufa and volcanic ash in Etruria, Latium, and the Campagna to the medium-sized alluvial plains in the Po Valley. Adequate rainfall, which fed smaller steams and springs, combined to support small agricultural communities and farms; the Po Valley, the region around Etruria, and the Campagna were especially suited for the formation of numerous small settlements. In these areas, tribes, formed by the association of

Landscape in the Campagna. The region was a favorite locale during ancient times due to its fine soil and climate.

clan villages, united to form a coherent settlement, with a nearby hill, or *capitolium,* used as a meeting ground and as a refuge in times of war. Gradually, the elevated part of the settlement evolved into the nucleus of a town and developed into a small city, surrounded by farms, which used the town as a market center and political focal point. Ancient Tivoli (Tibur) and Veii evolved in this manner, as did numerous other settlements founded on rocky hilltops flanked by deep gullies cut into the soft volcanic material.[6]

This settlement process, reminiscent of the founding of Rome, itself a community that evolved from several villages near the Tiber, occurred from region to region, where the local inhabitants owned and cultivated their own lands, eventually uniting and forming tribes. The nearest hill, the capitolium, became a refuge from invasion—the *arx,* or stronghold—and later the center of the town. Early on, local inhabitants preferred to live in surrounding hamlets, using towns for market and meeting purposes; thus, through the peninsula, during Etruscan and Roman times, the settlement pattern was often similar: towns surrounded by outlying villages. The only limiting factor was the availability of water, which, as we have seen, prevented an even distribution of settlements.[7] Therefore, whether in the rocky uplands of the Alps or Appenines, on isolated volcanic extrusions such as the Alban Mountains southeast of Rome, or along the the river peninsulas adjacent to deep gullies, the effect was the same: Citadels and hamlets, perched on rocky protrusions for defensive purposes and the avoidance of flood-prone ravines and lowlands, loomed over surrounding agricultural lands. Occasionally, an overriding need for security compelled people to settle in the mountains; if they settled in the fertile plains, they tended to locate on the best defensible site above the plain, often at the foot of mountains where ridges butted into the alluvium. Many of these fertile plains constricted upland to form valleys that connected various regions within the peninsula, thereby affording invading armies access to the territory. Consequently, towns located near these valleys occupied sites as far from these routes as possible. An example of this strategy was ancient Iguvium (Gubbio), located high in the uplands near the foot of Mt. Calvo, with its arable land at the lower wedge of the site.

Despite favorable siting, inundation from floods during the winter months was always a problem for rural settlements, especially as farmers cleared more land for agriculture, accelerating the denuding of the forests. In addition clearing increased the volume of debris at the mouths of valleys, expanding the potential for widespread flooding during the rainy season. The reverse prevailed during the summer in low-lying areas where undrained lands existed; during warmer months these areas sustained malaria, thereby motivating the population to select elevated sites along slopes above the marshy lowlands. Today, the results of these concerns are evident in the valleys in central Italy—in Valdarno, for example, where many towns along the slopes occupy sites of ancient settlements dating from the Etruscan period. The Romans followed these customs, since settlements founded during the early Roman period occupied sites at elevations from 500 to 1,300 feet.[8] In neighboring Latium, the settlement pattern resembled that throughout the alluvial areas of the peninsula: individuals grouped in small towns and villages along the line formed by the connection between plain and slope. Half a dozen agricultural communities hugged the slopes of the Alban hills east of Rome.[9] In the plain of Latium few settlements occurred between the uplands and the coast; only a few lonely coastal towns such as Ostia and Laurentium punctuated the 10-mile stretch between the sea and hills.

Further north, in Tuscany, the settlement pattern often resembled the configuration seen around Rome. The Arno River, with its succession of ancient lake basins strung along its length, flooded during the spring from runoff from the springs and streams emanating from the Appenine Mountains, and ancient towns clung to the hillsides along the Arno from Arezzo to Lucca. South of the Italian Alps in the Po Valley, towns occupied defensible sites along the lower edges of the hillsides that protruded from the Alps and Appenines, protecting inhabitants from floods and marauders. Rome was the lone settlement directly on the Tiber, and the hilly aspect of that locale afforded the city an elevated prospect above the floodplain. Only the low-lying site of the Circus Maximus and adjacent areas were prone to inundation, which occurred with some devastation to fields and houses during the third and fourth centuries B.C. Despite recurrent flooding, the rich alluvium of the Tiber floodplain continued to attract settlers, who sought to exploit the soils for agriculture; more astute inhabitants generally located their dwellings near their fields, but above the floodplain.

SETTLEMENT PATTERNS IN SOUTHERN FRANCE AND SPAIN

Despite Neolithic, Greek, Phoenician, and Roman colonization in Spain and southern France, early development of an extensive settlement pattern along the western edge of the Mediterranean was impeded by a variety of factors. The mountainous quality of the region and the lack of sufficient rainfall for dry farming obliged the inhabitants to locate small settlements near watercourses or on pockets of alluvial deposits near the outfalls of drainage ways. As in Italy, waterways always threatened flooding; therefore, most settlements ended up on hills or spurs next to the arable lands. Few settlements occurred along the floodplains of tributaries, although numerous small seaport towns dotted the coastline. At the Rhone Delta, Massila (Marseilles) and Narbo clung to elevated land above the floodplain; Arles, situated at the head of the delta on a hill, developed into a sizable commercial town, probably as an exchange point for ships coming up the delta and indigenous southward commercial traffic. A later Roman road connected Italy with Spain, crossing the Rhone about 10 miles to the north of Arles. Further west and above the potentially devastating floodplain, Narbo developed into the busiest Roman seaport in the locality. Further westward, the Roman road continued along the edge of the coast and then proceeded over a gap in the Pyrenees to Gerona, Spain.[10]

Settlements along the Spanish coast of Phoenician, Carthaginian, or Greek origin were essentially fortresses, containing an acropolis (Malaga), or were located within a defensible inlet (Rhoda), or occupied a defensible islet or peninsula (Cadiz and Gibraltar). The Phoenicians chose to locate their settlements on the spurs of the Sierra Nevada and other coastal ranges. During the Roman era, both the agricultural potential and defensive qualities of a site influenced settlement. Consequently, many Roman communities in Iberia ended up on the piedmont at the juncture of coastal and continental landforms. Further inland, where annual precipitation amounted to 8 to 20 inches, indigenous inhabitants chose sites that were defensible and near reliable springs. Subsequent Roman settlement tended to follow the ancient traditions, with communities located along slopes within reach of natural springs. These arable slopes supported a range of agricultural endeavors, while the drier plains sufficed for olive orchards and pasture. The Guadalquivir River, fed by numerous large tributaries from the southern highlands, was an attraction for ancient and Roman settlers, who sought out its springs; closer to the the boundary with Gaul, communities occupied elevated sites several hundred yards from the shore.[11]

Across the Straits of Gibraltar and along the western coast of North Africa, early Phoenician settlements had dotted the coastline, marking an attempt to establish trading centers along the coast. Later Cathaginian cities, including Utica and Carthage, straddled the mouths of the major rivers flowing from the North African hinterland. Carthage, located on a promontory overlooking the east-west Sicilian Straits and amply supplied by water via a 38-mile aqueduct from the Zaghouan Mountains, was perhaps the most ideally sited for protection and commerce.[12]

URBAN AND RURAL LANDSCAPE DEVELOPMENT

By the time the Roman Senate had conferred imperial status on Augustus in the first century B.C., the Roman society was well on the way to dominating the entire Mediterranean. Early in this process, Rome had pinned its expansionist strategy to the subjugation of the ancient communities tucked into the hillsides and hilltops in Latium, Etruria, and elsewhere. Veii, the nearest Etruscan community to Rome, fell under her rule in 396 B.C., making Rome the most powerful and largest state in the region. Further expansion in the following century doubled Rome's territory to include the Latin League, and later the entire territory once dominated by the Etruscans.

Rome's success at expanding its territory, the *Ager Romanus,* depended on a sophisticated policy of internal, and later external, colonization. Unlike those of other societies, the Roman colonization effort was not left to entrepreneurs in search of fresh enterprise on new lands, but, rather to the state, which annexed territories to the Roman sphere as public lands. After annexation, lands not leased as farmsteads by wealthy Romans became the private property of agrarian settlers, called *coloni,* or cultivators. The earliest colonies were formed primarily to protect Roman boundaries, and it was not until the middle of the second century B.C. that Rome began to recognize the economic potential of these colonies.[13] From this point on, two distinct colonial designations existed: the Latin colonies, whose settlers were not Roman citizens; and the citizen colonies, mostly coastal settlements, whose inhabitants were Roman citizens. The Latin colonies were distinct from other colonies in their origins, and included early settlements founded in the lands southeast of Rome, lands belonging to the Latin League, and the lands annexed from the Sabines. Together, the colonies extended Roman authority across the Italian peninsula to the Adriatic Sea.

By the third century B.C., Rome had instituted an active policy of colonization along the frontiers of its expanding domain. Part of the plan was to form a protective shield from invasion, especially from the sea. To this end, Rome established maritime settlements, the *Coloniae Maritimea,* along the western coast. Ostia, the chief Roman port on the western peninsula, was part of the maritime colony scheme, and functioned early as a defender against marauding seafarers. In 272 B.C., at the end of the Pyrrhic wars, Rome extended its influence southward, establishing a maritime colony at Paestum, principally as a safeguard from attacks by Carthaginians. By 260 B.C., at least eight colonies existed along the coast to protect inland communities from invasion; often these were modest in size, with as few as 330 inhabitants. Livy (59 B.C.–17 A.D.) noted ten maritime colonies, all of which were similar in organization. Most were modest holdings, generally occupied by around 300 families. After the Second Punic War, Rome founded eight more maritime colonies, and added more colonies to the Latium and citizen category to bring the total number near fifty. Not surprisingly, Rome had a difficult time attracting inhabitants to the settlements, due to the threat of attack and uncomfortable living conditions. Regardless, the Roman government successfully founded eight new citizen colonies in 194 B.C., populated by many ex-soldiers. Colonies founded between 100 and 30 B.C., *colonia civica,* were intended for nonmilitary settlers.

Ideally, the colonies were to have the appearance of Rome itself. However, though the colonies attempted to imitate Rome, they differed in population size, area of urban centers, size of land allotments, and physical appearance. Seaside Ostia was about 5 acres in area, while Nemausus was nearly 800. Some settlers received small holdings, about 1.25 acres; larger private holdings sometimes reached 60 or more acres. The lands surrounding smaller colonies, the dependent *territoria,* were modest in scope, 50 square miles or less, while the larger *colonia* might cover hundreds of square miles.[14] Since the settlements needed to "function as organized, self-governing units with a well-defined urban center and

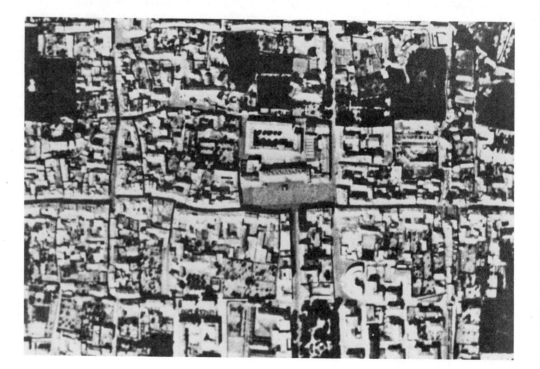

Aerial of the citizen colony, Nepet. Axial arrangement dates from the Roman period.

Aerial view of the Maritime colony, Pyrgi, seen in the bottom center of the photograph.

Ostia, an important maritime colony surrounded by a modern settlement.

administrative locus," the Roman Senate required that a newly formed colony be carefully planned and supervised.[15] After the Senate had given permission for the founding of the colony, a three-man commission assigned land to prospective settlers. The exact planning of the settlement followed a procedure dating back to the early Republic; it stipulated that before settlers could begin breaking soil and constructing structures, surveyors had to subdivide the *territorium* into parcels for individual occupation. With the aid of a *groma*, the standard Roman surveying instrument, engineers subdivided the colony lands by *centuriation*.

A hereditary land plot of two *iugera,* or 1.25 acres, constituted the basic unit of the centuriation square, which in its entirety included 200 *iugera.* Right-angle field boundaries separated the *centuriae.* Often the boundaries formed roads called *decumani* and *cardi,* running east-west and north-south, respectively. At the intersection of the boundaries, the *decumanus* and *cardo* formed a *maximus,* the prime reference point from which the boundaries were numbered serially. An inscribed boundary stone marked the corner of each *centuria.* Centuriation applied to citizen colonies, while the Latin colonies rarely conformed to the system: their lands consisted of strips and rectangles unrelated to an overall grid.[16] After 200 B.C. most new colonies were of the citizen form and featured centuriated lands. Once surveyed, rural lands acquired the appearance of a large grid, a checkerboard of centuriated holdings.

Territorial lands were not the only element to display the effects of grid surveying and subdivision. Many colonial towns conformed to a grid pattern when the town's boundaries circumscribed the centuriation *cardo, maximus,* and *decumanus.* But other towns did not exactly conform to centuriation, particularly those located on hilly terrain or on nonarable land. Also, town formation was not always a mechanical process of conducting an engineering survey. Ritual accompanied the founding of many settlements—for example, individuals who had volunteered for a new colony marched to the site, where priests performed auspices and sacrifices to ensure the blessing of the gods. Chief commissioners, resplendent in ceremonial robes, marked the limits of the town wall by inscribing a line in the earth with a bronze plow drawn by a white steer and heifer. At the location of each of the town's three gates, the commissioner designated the spot by lifting the plow from the earth. At the conclusion of the ritual, the *coloni* received their plots, or *sortes,* by lot. By the end of the third century, after the Second Punic War, land grant allotments tended to be based on rank, especially in Imperial times when retired soldiers received lands based on their military rank and record.[17]

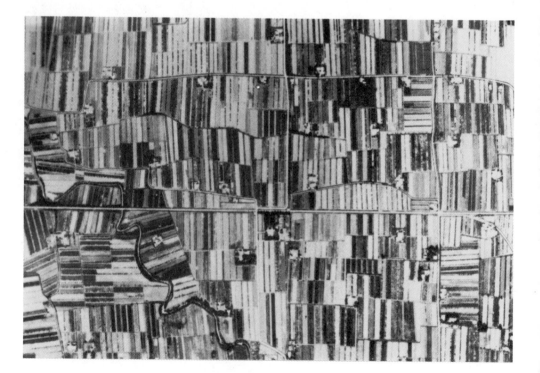

Centuriation in the region of the Po Valley.

Despite a gradual increase in sophistication of town planning over time, the basic organization remained remarkably similar to the earliest antecedents. Even in settlements where topographic conditions did not allow for an ideal grid layout and town walls followed site contours, some semblance of symmetry was always apparent. Generally the urban centers had a protective ring wall, just inside of which was a narrow road. A town square, or *forum,* lay in the center of the community, usually irregular in form during early Republican times and more geometric by the third century B.C. Important public buildings adjoined the forum, including temples, *curia, basilica,* and, in some instances, triumphal arches, baths, and theaters. Toward the end of the Republican period, some fora contained porticoes, which partially or fully enclosed the space. However, space was so limited within the town walls that only citizens with lands close to the settlement lived within the walls, while others lived in small hamlets beyond the towns to be nearer their landholdings.

MILITARY COLONIES: REGIONAL SETTLEMENT

Roman colonization did not end with the founding of the colonies along the Italian peninsula. By the first century B.C. Rome had a population of nearly 1 million; to feed this enormous population it had to import grain from beyond the Italian peninsula. Sicily, Sardinia, North Africa, and Egypt eventually became major contributors to Roman stores. To ensure that these regions maintained a consistent agricultural production schedule, Rome established a policy of forming colonies to protect and govern these regions. North of the Mediterranean, beyond the Alps and westward along the coast into Spain, they established colonies to hold the frontiers, and sometimes to form the nucleus of agricultural communities.

The most visible colonial settlements were the *coloniea militares.* As early as 194 B.C., a few of these communities existed along the edges of the Roman frontier, especially in regions where the threat of local uprisings made the presence of seasoned soldiers necessary to protect the Roman boundaries. After 100 B.C. veteran colonies became a principal form of Roman colonization, due in part to increased Roman expansion beyond Italy.[18] The military colonies were a convenient way of satisfying the property needs of military retirees, many of whom had been indigent conscripts serving an established period of service. Sulla (138–78 B.C.), during his tenure as general, established military colonies in the southern peninsula, including a military camp at the old Greek colonial site at Pompeii. Julius Caesar preferred to found colonies beyond Italy, including new settlements, which were accessible by roads and by sea. He also seized the opportunity to revitalize once flourishing communities beyond Italy, including settlements at Corinth and Carthage on the North African coast. During his rule, nearly 80,000 *coloni* settled in the provinces. Augustus, after the battle of Actium, demobilized nearly 120,000 soldiers and settled them in Italian colonies. The foundations of these colonies still appear in communities such as Florence, Turin, and Verona.

Augustan colonies followed the pattern established during earlier days. Many colonies were considered self-sufficient, and little attention was paid to their economic well-being.[19] Thus, as protectors of the frontier, towns such as Ostia and Turin contained stout walls on protected sites, linked by the well-maintained roads. Further from Italy—in Britain, France, Spain, and North Africa—the organization and construction of the colony was the same: well-fortified, defensible, populated by military veterans, fit to preserve the *Pax Romana.*

Timgad, site of a North African colony established by the emperor Trajan in A.D. 100.

ROMAN ROADS

The earliest Roman roads appeared during the period of expansion, when the Republic was founding colonies. These roads functioned as an all-weather link from Rome to the colonies and provinces. The empire relied on the road system to bring food and supplies to the capital, and Roman engineers carefully followed construction methods that assured longevity. Construction techniques evolved from those used by the engineers of the Near Eastern and Mediterranean cultures and adopted by the Etruscans. But most of these roads, though they linked the regions of Italy, were not fully engineered until after the Punic Wars.[20] Often road building followed the construction of a colony, rather than the reverse.

The via Latina, constructed in 370 B.C. was the earliest of the ancient roads, fashioned from native lava rock overlying an ancient path. The via Appia, begun in 312 B.C., traversed the foothills south of Rome and eventually connected the city with Brindisi on the Adriatic coast. The earliest roads hugged the base of hills and mountains, maintaining an alignment above the valleys and drainage ways. The via Aemilia, constructed in 187 B.C., followed the northern edge of the Appenines, connecting colonial towns along its course. At Vicencia the road turned south, wound through the Venetian plain and skirted the drainage ways, and ran "by the roots of the Alps and encircling the marshes."[21] Between Rome and Florence the road alignment strategy was the same as for the principal highways that linked the various colonial towns above the floodplains. Conversely, the via Aemelia, had to be engineered to withstand the muddy landscape of the Venetian plain. By the beginning of the first century B.C., there were eighteen principal roads on the Italian peninsula, used mainly as military connectors to the numerous colonies. Eventually, the roads formed a network throughout Italy and the provinces. A fine road connected Italy with the lands along the western Mediterranean. Nime, Marseilles, and Nice lay along this coastal highway.

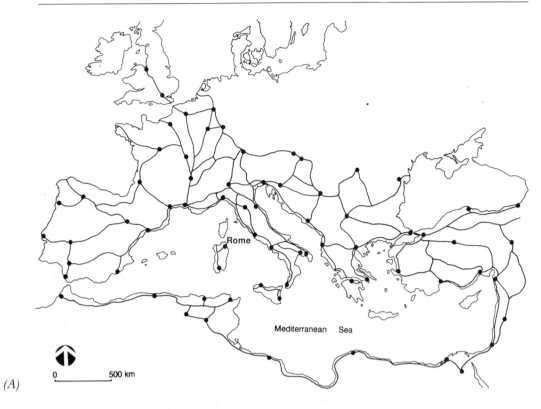

(A)

(A) Map of Roman road
network in the European
region. (B) Example of a
Roman road at Paestum.

(B)

AGRICULTURE, FARMS, AND VILLAS

Farming was the principal occupation throughout the Roman Mediterranean, including along the coast of North Africa and Asia Minor, reflecting the constant need to feed the rapidly expanding urban centers, especially Rome. This need was not always met: food shortages were common throughout the Republican and Imperial eras, even with substantial production in the colonies. Thus, along with those in peninsular Italy, some of the primary agricultural centers included the lands dominated by Syracuse on Sicily, the inland plains in Spain, and the area near Leptus Magnus, a seacoast town in North Africa, all of which helped to feed Rome.

Agricultural practices in the Mediterranean followed methods originally perfected in the Near East and later transferred to Rome through the Phoenicians and Greeks. The Mediterranean triad, olives, vines, and grain, continued to be the most prized agricultural commodities. Wheat was the preferred grain, although barley was often a dietary staple in areas where wheat did not flourish. The farmstead was the productive unit throughout the realm, and, initially, it was a modest enterprise, originally belonging to a single extended family. As the society continued to expand, the plots owned by individual farmers gradually fell into the hands of wealthier individuals through purchase or confiscation.

Much of what we know about Roman agriculture we have learned from the chronicles of agricultural authorities, many of whom owned their own extensive farms. One such authority was Cato the Elder (234–149 B.C.), whose book *On Agriculture* details the procedures and materials needed for a successful agricultural operation. He praised the concept of a small farm managed by the owner and his family and worked by farmhands. In many parts of Italy the system worked well; however, in areas where warfare had caused the displacement of farm owners, the smaller allotments of 5 to 30 acres gave way to combined lands of more than 300 acres.

The agricultural strategy employed by the Romans to assure sufficient farm production was similar from locale to locale. Both stock raising and plant propagation occupied the Roman farmer. Generally, large-scale stock raising included the husbanding of sheep and goats, an activity that required sufficient pasturage. To assure the minimum of interference with plant growing, the large flocks tended to remain in the upland pastures during the prime plant-growing season, returning to the lowlands after the harvest to graze on field stubble. During the later Republican period, an extensive large mountain estate, or *saltus,* functioned as a center for large-scale stock grazing. Separation of the flocks from the home fields meant less fertilizer for the plots, a situation farmers attempted to solve by using supplemental fertilizers, including the ploughing in of green plants, a technique that never fully compensated for the qualities of animal fertilizers.[22] In addition, farms had to be carefully organized to function productively, since arable lands were scarce in a predominantly mountainous landscape. Farms included areas for field crops, orchards, vineyards, olive groves, and gardens. Due to the need for irrigation during the summer months, hay and forage production was expensive. Consequently farmers often relied on natural meadows near wetlands for pasturage for milk cattle and horses.

The initial smaller farms, generally 1.25 to 2.5 acres in extent, were self-sufficient and tuned to the vagaries of local conditions, and were normally established in areas near sufficient water and soil for plant propagation. From earliest times farmers preferred to locate their farms at the base of the mountain ranges, where runoff from the highlands deposited good agricultural soils, and where the elevated location of the site protected the farmstead from flooding. A south-facing aspect was the best for solar advantage; mountain ranges protected farms from excessively cold winds, while elevated locations afforded air drainage and protected orchards from frosts. From ancient times farmers attempted to respond to these influences as they selected a site, though local conditions always influenced the selection process.

As natural sites became more scarce, the early Romans, like their counterparts in other Mediterranean regions, turned to techniques to increase the amount of arable land. Terracing of mountain slopes by elaborate retaining walls in upland areas and manuring of shallow soils helped to increase the agricultural output in less than favorable areas. Even on better lands—on the prized valley fields—repeated fertilization of the soil increased agricultural yields, as did proper tillage, the use of the best crops for the region, and even the introduction of foreign seeds. Winter rains were the primary source of moisture for the farms. The summer drought, which affected lands in the southeast, required supplemental techniques to provide adequate moisture to plants, including legumes, vegetables, and fruit trees. Other strategies used to promote soil moisture included specific field rotation methods. The rule in Italy, as well as most Mediterranean locations, was the two-field rotation system: alternate fields sat unused from year to year to build up soil nutrients and fertilizers. The technique not only gave the land a period of rest, but it allowed for the accumulation of moisture in the soil for the subsequent year's crop. In addition, farmers often subjected fallow lands to three or more ploughings annually to build up vegetable matter and to increase soil moisture. The first ploughing was done in September to catch the autumn showers, the second in midwinter in anticipation of winter frost and rain, the third in the late spring, and finally, a fourth in midsummer to break up the surface sufficiently to prevent loss of moisture from soil capillary attraction. Crop rotation was another way of sustaining productivity. Roman farmers often rejuvenated a plot by rotating beans, wheat, and clover over a three-year period. Generally, though, farmers tended to refrain from crop rotation and to concentrate on the planting of a specific crop, primarily due to the limited cropland, a factor that selected against crop rotation and fallow and favored overcropping and the intense use of manures.

In addition to tending annual crops, farmers had to care for their orchards. The olive was the most widely propagated orchard specimen, due to its acclimation to the Mediterranean environment. Pliny identified fifteen varieties, claiming that the best fruit grew in Italy. Part of the success of the plant was due to its suitability to calcareous, clayey, or sandy soils, wherever drainage was adequate. However, solar exposure was an important factor in the location of an orchard, with west-facing slopes, or any aspect that reduced frost hazard, being the best.

Viticulture required the same attention to environmental conditions as orchards. In Roman Italy, farmers preferred southerly aspects for their vines. Virgil did not recommend a westerly exposure, and an easterly aspect was often avoided altogether. Specific localities often required adjustments to these rules, including the Po Valley, where the vineyards faced the north or northeast, or in humid areas where the vines flourished along drier south slopes. Thus all manner of vineyard siting occurred in Italy, based on the needs of the plant variety and the peculiarities of local conditions. The soils surrounding olive orchards supported wheat propagation, but, in contrast, farmers were careful to keep the soil between vines free of any other plant material, in order to facilitate cultivation and to afford the vines access to moisture and soil nutrients.

The painstaking work of the individual farmer helped sustain the Roman society through the second century B.C., but, soon after, wealthy individuals began to form large farms, or *latifundia*. The dislocation of farmers during the Second Punic War, together with subsequent Roman law, made it easier for wealthy individuals to accumulate lands through the purchase of public lands, a procedure that helped to reduce state debt. Also, admission to the Roman Senate,

Present-day Italian landscape with olive trees sharing space with cover crops.

a prized political appointment, required the possession of large landholdings, a qualification that further stimulated the evolution of large farms. As a result the formation of the large farming estates, from 60 to 150 acres or more, marked the end of the old agricultural structure, and eventually led to the demise of the small, independent farmer. Instead, these large farms, or villas, relied mostly on slave labor, and functioned as agricultural factories, producing large quantities of important staples.

Cato's opinion regarding the management of a villa sheds some light on late Republican agricultural practices. These included the presence of a suitable dwelling in proportion to the size of the landholding, large enough to be comfortable to the owner, but not so grand as to require undue expense for its upkeep. The work of the estate was to be overseen by a trusted steward, capable of managing the slaves who were responsible for the orchards, vineyards, and agricultural plots, the size of which might be 350 iugera or larger.

Of all the changes in landscape activity between the Republican and Imperial periods, the shift from the small agricultural landholding to the large latifundia was perhaps the most significant. The years from 241 to 31 B.C. saw a progessive shift of the Italian landscape into wealthy hands. Wealthy individuals with economic interests in the provinces accelerated the process, fostering greed and bribery, which inevitably subverted any movement to reform the agricultural system. Due to these events, the concept of a free-farming peasantry died out. Worse, the prime goal of the small farmer, agricultural production, gradually gave way to the use of agricultural lands as pasturage on the large estates, preferred by landowners for its better return on their investment.[23]

Another attraction of estate ownership was the potential for creating specialized gardens for recreation and propagation of selected horticultural varieties. For the once practical Romans, interest in ornamental materials signaled a shift from utilitarian horticulture to gardening practiced as an aesthetic exercise. Part of this shift stemmed from a time-honored tradition in the Mediterranean, which emphasized the presence of gardens that were both economically productive and aesthetically pleasing. Cato stated that all farm gardens should include ceremonial plants, including laurel and myrtle, in areas near the farmhouse. Columella, in his second-century A.D. treatise, *Carmen Hortorum,* describes the garden of a typical large estate, which featured roses, daffodils, pomegranate flowers, marigolds, poppies, and fragrant flowers from foreign lands. The gardens he described contained irrigation channels, sunken paths, raised flower beds, all laid out in a formal pattern and enclosed by a wall or hedge to keep out intruders. So popular were these gardens that Horace noted that flower gardens had become the great national pastime, replacing interest in field crops. This shift was partly due to the increased reliance on imported grain from the provinces, which freed grain lands for propagation of specialized fruits and vegetables, and the development of horticultural refinement.

All the above events coincided with an interest among wealthy urban dwellers in acquiring rural retreats in which they could escape the political and economic activity of major urban centers and the unhealthful conditions of such areas during the hot summer months. The wealthy began to convert older farms into such retreats, and the *villa rustica,* complete with pavilions, shaded groves, and formal gardens, became fashionable. The wealthy also built smaller *suburbana,* villas nearer the main cities, to use as convenient daily retreats. These villas had the amenities associated with the larger *villa rustica,* including formal gardens. Pliny the Younger's *suburbano* near Laurentum and Diomedes' villa near Pompeii were fine examples of the style of estates fashioned by the wealthy as a way of escaping urban stress.

ROMAN IRRIGATION PRACTICES

Properly irrigated lands were a source of pride to the Roman landholder. Horace praised the "orchards watered by the flowing rills," but was quick to admonish the farmer who produced insipid vegetables by overirrigating his fields.[24]

Roman irrigation practice derived from ancient regulations that controlled the distribution of water between adjacent landowners. The earliest laws prohibited the construction of devices that illegally altered the normal flow of a public or perennial river, or that caused the diversion of a river or stream into a channel, which would alter the riparian rights of a landholder. Also, the quantity of water drawn from a stream depended on the size of the landholding. Individuals sharing the same water channel, or *rivus,* were competitors for the use of the water, and if an individual was prevented by a "rival" from getting his share of the water, any damage to the crops of the offended party was grounds for a lawsuit.[25]

During both the Republican and Imperial periods, water rights controlled Roman irrigation strategies. Water usage by the individual farmer was a function of the supply of water, the size of the estate, season, and even the landowner's purchasing power.[26] There was a distinction between daily water rights and summer water rights, a distinction based on use but also determined by the actual supply of water during the summer months. The summer water rights permitted the use of water for farming, but varied from district to district depending on the climatic conditions of the locale. Some farmers were allowed to draw water only during the day, others only at night or every other day or during designated hours or months. In addition, farmers could only draw water from specific sources; failure to observe this condition could result in the forfeiture of the right. Domestic water was available throughout the year, while summer water, drawn from perennial sources, was used mainly for irrigation. All citizens contributed to the building and maintenance of the irrigation system by paying taxes or contributing labor, and all were entitled to the use of the system. The overall aim of the laws was to assure an equitable supply of water to all citizens throughout the day, by assuring a steady flow without sudden shortages resulting from unscheduled heavy overdraft.

LAND RECLAMATION

As the Roman population continued to expand in the Italian peninsula, the quantity of arable lands was insufficient to produce necessary foodstuffs for urban areas. From the Republican period onward, the solution to the problem lay with the reclamation of forests and lowlands. For example, by the first century B.C., the lands along the via Aemelia exhibited a pattern of centuriation, revealing the results of active land reclamation. In this region, more than 40,000 plots, between 5 and 30 acres in size, gave testimony to the effort expended by the Romans to keep the rich sedimentary land of the Po Valley accessible to colonists.

Land reclamation had been an issue prior to Roman occupation of the Italian peninsula. The Etruscans had undertaken reclamation projects, and the ancient site of Rome itself had been reclaimed from the marshy land between the Palatine and Capitoline Hills. Towns beyond Rome, including Clusium adjacent to the Clanis River, maintained extensive underground passages to conduct water away from elevated sites. The early Romans based part of their reclamation strategy on the construction of brick-lined dams used to check runoff and to preserve spring waters for irrigation. Many of the Alban lakes southeast of Rome had been tapped as sources of irrigation water by cutting holes through the crater walls holding the water, including a 1,300-yard channel that drained Lake Albanus.

A major reclamation project in the third century B.C. focused on drainage problems east of Rome. Specifically, the drainage basin described by the Velinus River in the Sabine territory contained meadows and pastures, though the lands were subject to inundation at peak flood periods. Beginning in 271 B.C. the Romans built a series of drainage channels and continued to maintain the system by clearing old channels and building new ones.[27] Later, the variable water level of the lakes of the Appenines invited drainage schemes to free the rich soils around their shores from excessive inundation. This was one of the largest projects during the period and was attempted by several emperors and finally accomplished in 1875 A.D. To the north, in the Po Valley, the Etruscans had initiated reclamation projects by diverting the Po River into the coastal swamps. Initially, these projects were undertaken as a means of improving communications between communities. The Romans followed this objective in the first century B.C., building navigable canals, thereby draining the land south of the Po Valley in the effort to construct the via Aemelia. During centuriation, reclaimed land became sites for homesteads, which helped to solidify Roman power in the region.

Despite the size of the projects, the land reclamation techniques of the Romans were similar to the smaller-scale techniques used by Etruscan and Roman peasants. In his writings, Cato directed the individual farmer to begin clearing drainage ditches with pick and shovel to drain excess waters brought by the autumn rains. Virgil recalls life as a youth on his father's farm in the Po region, and refers to the countryside as "afloat with brimming ditches during the winter rains."[28] Often the layout of these canals conformed to the prevailing gridiron configuration, picking up the water running from the furrows, and conveying the runoff to open ditches. To prevent complaints from adjacent landowners, the Romans enforced laws that governed drainage. For example, the law required neighbors to keep trenches and dikes free of debris. Low-lying estates, generally having better soils, were responsible for the drainage quality of higher lands.

Roman-era reclamation and farming activities.

Landholders had the right to impound water for irrigation, but could not create a drainage situation that could endanger a neighbor. By law a landholder also had the right to construct dikes or ditches on a neighbor's land if necessary for flood control.

SUBURBAN AND RURAL ESTATES

For the wealthy, private estates, prized for their sumptuous gardens, were an integral part of life in suburban and rural areas. On both sides of the Tiber, stretching over the hills for at least 2 miles, wealthy Romans maintained elegant estates, many of which lay beyond the city's Servian walls,[29] transforming the landscape around Rome into a swath of verdure. In the ancient *collis hortorum* along the Pincian Hill, prosperous Romans, including Pompey, Lucullus, and the historian Sallust, built estates, some of which were to become the sites for late-Renaissance villas. East and south of the city, Augustus' prime minister converted an old potter's field on the Esquiline Hill into an expansive garden, the *Horti Maecenatis*. On level terrain and the slopes of the Janiculum and Vatican Hills west of the city, other important estates flourished.

Many estates in this vicinity were large, some at least 7 or 8 acres in size, and the techniques used to embellish their grounds reveal the Romans' horticultural expertise. Their planning derived from established siting and garden organizational procedures, drawn from centuries of landscape utilization on small and large farms in rural areas. Some of this knowledge appeared in formal writing, including Vitruvius's *Ten Books of Architecture*, a first-century A.D. account of planning and design featuring concepts about site planning and the use of geometry in design. To the modern observer, Vitruvius's ideas seem common sensical: select an elevated, well-drained site; respond to solar orientation and favorable air movement when siting structures; possess a reliable water supply; and use indigenous materials in the construction of the estate.

Not all the land connected to the estates functioned as garden space; structures, including palaces, offices, and pavilions, occupied a good proportion of the site. In many cases the size of planted areas was modest, though the ruins of the Imperial palace on the Palatine Hill include a garden with water covering nearly 2 acres. The gardens of the Campus Martius consisted of 3 miles of covered walkway, a 6-acre sheltered area, and 16 acres of enclosed garden spaces. Augustus' public garden on the Esquiline Hill, the *Porticul Liviae,* included a sunken garden about 2 acres in extent. The site included a pool, trees, flower beds, and a marble arcade.

Further from Rome, near the main highways, the size and design of estates varied, limited only by the financial resources of the owner. A favorite location was the region around the Alban Mountains 15 miles southeast of Rome. The area was renowned for its rich volcanic soils, copious springs, and verdant woods. A few miles northwest, Cicero sited his Tusculum villa near Frascati; the grounds included gardens, terraces, and groves. Further inland, on the western slopes of the Appenines in the area of the Sabine Mountains, near modern Tivoli, Augustus, Hadrian, and others built extensive villas. Hadrian's villa was an immense property—nearly the size of a small town—and included large gardens, water features, and finely detailed living and working quarters. To the west along the coast near Ostia and Laurentum and south near Naples, villas dotted the landscape. During the Imperial period, Pliny the Younger's suburban villa near Laurentum typified the art of villa planning, with its formal, geometrical gardens facing the villa structure. The details found at many villas included a portico, which opened onto a garden terrace, or *zystus,* featuring turf, violets, lilies, or crocuses, each surrounded by box hedges or other suitable shrubs. The *zystus* often overlooked a lower garden, or *ambulatio.* Ramps and steps connected garden and terrace levels; designers were careful to use a combination of plant material stimulating to the senses. After meals the owner of the villa walked and conversed with his guests along the shaded portions of the lower terrace. From the lower terrace the owner could view the *gestatio,* an area of the garden designed for horse riding or as a place in which to be carried along on a litter by slaves. The *gestatio* often included examples of the Syrian art of topiary, featuring the pruning and shaping of box hedges and dwarf plane trees.

The Nilus at Hadrian's Villa, one of several major site elements that comprise the extensive villa.

Aerial view of Hadrian's villa.
(Benevolo, Leonardo.
The History of the City.
Copyright © 1980 MIT
Press.)

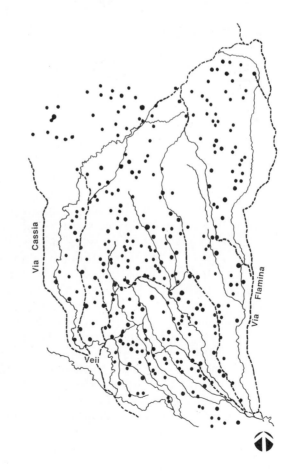

*Distribution of villas and farms
north of Rome during the first
century A.D.*

Mosaic of a rural villa illustrating the various agricultural activities common to a North African estate.

URBAN LANDSCAPES

Life in Roman urban centers was an amalgam of trade, politics, social intrigue, and survival. Urban expansion, especially in Rome, accompanied the shift from small, single-family farms—the traditional foundation of the Roman agricultural system—to large agricultural estates. At the end of the Second Punic War in 201 B.C., many farmers were dispossessed, and chose to migrate from rural areas to urban centers. Also, colonization of Italian lands began to decline during the Second Punic War, further complicating the distribution of the population throughout Italy. After the wars, individuals were disinclined to pursue the life of the farmer-soldier, principally due to the rigors of agricultural life and the risks involved in supporting a colony. As commoners migrated to urban areas, wealthy landowners also chose to live in the urban centers for the convenience of being close to public affairs. Despite these dislocations and adjustments, the pattern of urbanization continued to resemble earlier regional patterns. The central peninsula, including Umbria and Latium, contained urban centers founded on ancient settlements, surrounded by smaller urban nodes and farmsteads. The remainder of the peninsula remained a loose aggregation of isolated, small farms and modest-sized urban nodes.

Life in the center of the cities focused on commercial and residential activities. Apartment buildings often housed the urban masses, while wealthier individuals retreated to their urban estates. The wealthy also had the advantage of being able to leave the cities during the hot summer months, when malaria was most prevalent. But gradually crowding prompted urban renewal, often to the detriment of existing amenities. As noted earlier, by the first century A.D. the population of Rome approached 1 million, necessitating the elimination of many private homes to provide space for the construction of multistory apartment complexes. The result was loss of small gardens, though the ingenious Romans attempted to rectify this situation by constructing roof gardens; many of these gardens included grape arbors, fruit and shade trees planted in containers, and, for the wealthier, marble-rimmed fish pools.[30]

By the third century A.D., Rome had evolved from a collection of small settlements on the hills and plains surrounding the Tiber to a crowded and often inhospitable community, particularly in the summer months, when the low-lying areas of the city were susceptible to oppressive heat and malaria. Despite these conditions, the city remained the nerve center of the Roman Empire, the locus of important political and economic activity. Owing to the physiography of the site, with its hills and depression, and the age of the settlement, nearly six hundred years old by the time Augustus assumed power, the city did not exhibit the typical arrangement found at many colonial towns, which traced their form to the *cardo-decamanus* organization. As the capital of the Empire, though, the city had acquired an urban form befitting its position. Important government and commercial buildings, formally detailed in the classical style of architecture, lent it a grandiose scale. Its principal public meeting spaces included the Forum Romanum, the Fora of the Emperors, the Circus Maximus, and the Coliseum, all of which complemented the city's major architectural elements and contributed to its imperial appearance.

Roman urban planning differed from the Hellenic in the way it conceived spatial arrangement of architectural elements. Unlike Hellenic cities, where the siting of structures reinforced the perception of architectural elements as spatial objects, Roman planning used structures to form exterior space. The result in Rome and other major cities was a sense of spatial sequence in important urban spaces. The Roman Forum and the Fora of the Emperors exemplified this quality. For instance, the Roman Forum, lying within the depression formed by the Palatine and Capitoline Hills, began as a pasture and drainage way, and later, the *cloaca maxima,* the major sewer for the community. As a public meeting place, the Forum owes its existence to a series of improvements, which gradually gave spatial articulation to the site.[31] A few of the more notable architectural additions included temples, basilica, and ceremonial arches. In combination with the site, the structures gave the Forum a trapezoidal shape, bisected by the sight line that terminates at the Temple of the Divine Julius. Nearby, the Fora of the Emperors, built through the first and second centuries A.D., exhibited a strong sense of geometric arrangement and spatial sequence. By using sight lines to link spaces, Roman planners created a majestic series of public spaces, including Trajan's Forum, Vespasian's Forum of Peace, and the Forum of Nervae. The result was a sequence of open and enclosed, large and small spatial elements befitting the capital city.

South of Rome in the Campagnia, towns flourished in less grandiose settings, especially communities populated by well-off merchants. One of the best examples of a well-planned and commodious urban landscape was Pompeii, a Greco-Roman community located on the Bay of Naples. Throughout its long history, Pompeii was a prosperous settlement, mainly due to its location near the sea on a bed of rich volcanic soil, which, with adequate irrigation, often produced three crops a year. Remains of Greek activity from the sixth century B.C. appear on the site, though the Samnites, a local tribe, conquered the Campagnia and transformed the community into a Samnite settlement. In 89 B.C., the community became an official Roman settlement and *colonia,* the result of Sulla's conquests in the area.

Pompeii's siting fit the opportunities and constraints of its context. Its slightly elevated position prevented the community from being blanketed in the fog that covered most of the plain during the rainy season, and its southeast

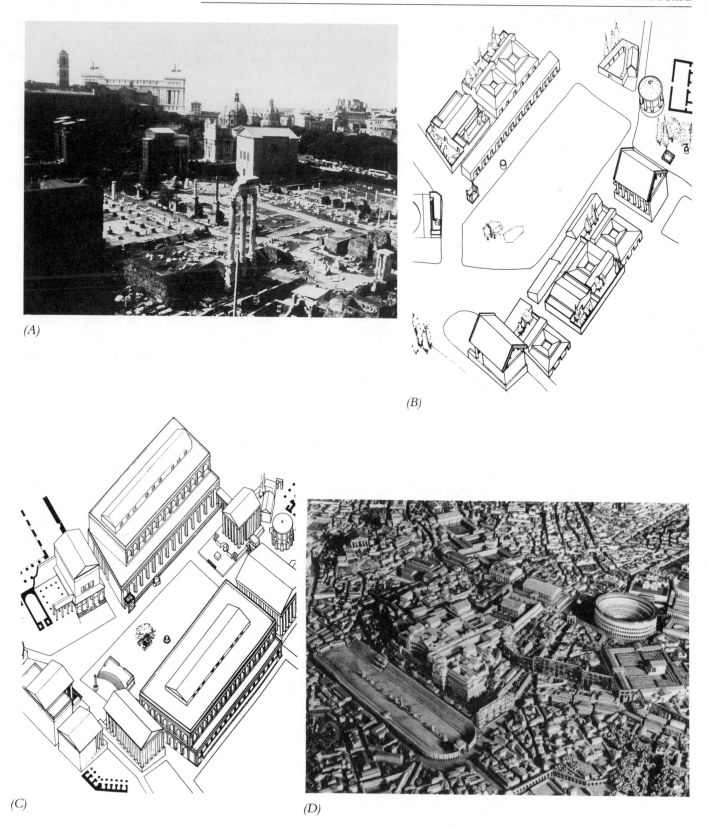

(A) *The Roman forum from the Palatine hill.* (B) *The forum in the first century B.C. and* (C) *the third century A.D.* (D) *Model of Imperial Rome.* (Benevolo, Leonardo. *The History of the City.* Copyright © 1980 MIT Press.)

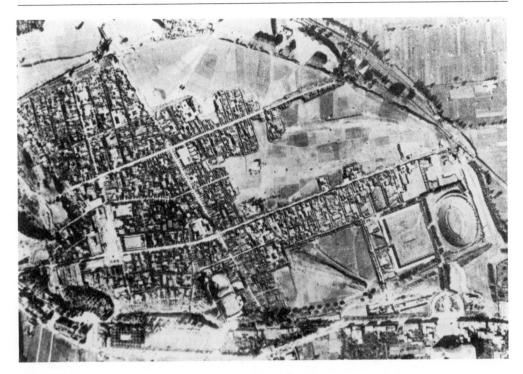

Aerial view of Pompeii showing the Greek colonial influence of town organization.

aspect and east-west axis along the slope of Mt. San Angelo assured the inhabitants of ample solar exposure during most days. A major constraint was the lack of water, owing to the difficulty of digging wells through the volcanic stratum, a problem the inhabitants overcame through the use of cisterns, subterranean chambers that were filled by collecting runoff from the roofs of town structures; despite these measures, the water problem was not resolved until the Augustan period, when the government constructed an aqueduct to supply additional water to the community.

The eruption of Mt. Vesuvius in 79 A.D. destroyed Pompeii, leaving the community buried under a deep layer of volcanic material. However, extensive archaeological research at the site has revealed much about the organization of the town and the quality of its urban landscape. Prior to the eruption, the town covered an area of 155 acres (63 hectares), enclosed by a perimeter wall that followed the contours of an old lava bed. The oldest portion of the community, an area to the southwest around the forum, consisted of irregularly shaped blocks of dwellings and commercial establishments, a contrast to the orderly grid of *insulae* at the northeastern, newer end of the town. The via Stabiana, running along a southeast-northwest depression on the site, connected the highest and lowest portions of the community. Two major streets crossed the via Stabiana. One of these, the via dell'Abbondanza, connected to the forum, which was the site of an earlier market square and the principal public space in the community. Adjacent to the forum were temples, basilica, library, public buildings, and the city treasury. In addition to the main forum, other important public spaces in Pompeii include the triangular forum, theaters, *palaestrae,* and baths. In addition to these public areas were the food-producing gardens, vineyards, orchards, and vegetable plots, which took up about 10 percent of the space in the community.

Pompeii was renowned for its success as a commercial center. Its streets were lined with shops and commercial establishments: bakeries, butchers, fish shops, cloth manufacturers and cleaners, inns, hotels, and wine shops. Many of the inns and restaurants had a small garden at the rear of the establishment where patrons would dine in the evening in the cool air. In all, the public space, including streets and public squares, amounts to nearly 18 percent of the excavated area, while recreational space, including theaters and exercise areas, accounts for roughly 11 percent—thus, the total area of open space is nearly 30 percent of the excavated area of Pompeii, showing the city to have been a spacious habitat, rather than a crowded, congested environment.

Part of Pompeii's reputation stemmed from the quality of its residential structures, common wall buildings that lined the town's streets and housed the population in commodious surroundings. The most notable structures were the *atrium* houses, so named for the roofless space at the entry to the structure. Many atrium houses also had a peristyle garden at the rear, surrounded by walls that extended from the side of the structure and terminated by a cross-wall at the back of the garden.

Upon entering the structure, one moved from the entry space, or *fauces,* past the atrium with the *impluvium,* or pool, used to catch and convey rainwater that fell through a roof opening, or *compluvium,* into the house cistern, then through the *tablinium,* or summer dining room, and into the peristyle garden, surrounded by a portico and terminating with an *exedra* at the rear. From archaeological evidence, the peristyle garden contained both ornamental and food-producing plants, including olive trees, nut and fruit trees, ivy, box hedges, laurel, myrtle, acanthus, and rosemary. It was not unusual to find informal plantings interspersed with formal evergreen plant varieties, though by the Augustan era, many homes, such as the House of the Vettii, had formal gardens with clipped hedges, pools, statuary, and topiary work. Some of the most sumptuous of the Pompeiian residences featured two peristyle gardens—for example, the House of the Faun. Additional elements of many peristyle gardens were paintings on the side or rear walls, which, from the vantage of one entering the structure and viewing the garden through the atrium and *tablinium,* gave the illusion that the house and garden were larger than they actually were.[32]

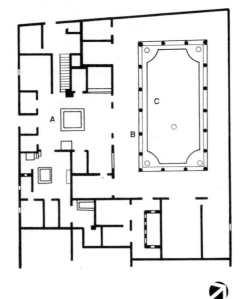

Plan for the House of the Vettii including (A) atrium (B) tablinium (C) perisyle court.

0   10 m

The peristyle court within the house of the Vettii.

ENVIRONMENTAL ISSUES

With over a million people inhabiting Rome by the first century A.D. and the rapid expansion of the Empire beyond the Mediterranean into central Europe, North Africa, and the Near East to Mesopotamia, environmental change due to organized human activity occurred in the region at a scale unknown in earlier times. Behind this expansion was an attitude that had begun in the east and had spread westward: the idea that people must and should acquire or convert land for agriculture and settlement. Intensive use of natural resources—minerals, plants, animals—was necessary to sustain the growth of Rome, as it had been to sustain the growth of earlier societies. But because the Romans mastered the management of a large empire, the scale of landscape alteration and resource depletion surpassed that of earlier cultures.

The process began in the Italian peninsula, where large tracts of arable land were created by reclamation of marshes and low-lying lands, especially around the Po Valley.[33] Further south, the large estates shifted from agricultural production to the raising of livestock, an activity that tended to render the landscape less useful for smaller farms and for small-scale agricultural activity. By the conclusion of the Second Punic War, a large, and increasing, proportion of the agricultural production required to maintain the urban centers came from external sources, especially from North Africa, Spain, and, later, Egypt. For the next five centuries, Rome's insatiable demand for agricultural products and raw materials accelerated urbanization and reclamation along the Mediterranean rim.

The rich lands along the North African shore were particularly suited to fill Rome's needs. The city of Leptis Magna, located on the North African coast, was one of six hundred cities that flourished in the region that helped to supply the Empire. The city, which boasted a population of 100,000 by the first century A.D., was an important wheat-exporting center. The land around Leptis Magna was sufficiently fertile to produce very rich harvests, and helped to contribute to the half million tons of wheat shipped yearly from North Africa to supply Rome

View to the old port of Ephesus that once existed beyond the grove in the middle ground. Siltation eventually rendered the port inaccessible and isolated the community from the coast that now exists beyond the far hill.

with nearly two-thirds of its grain requirement. Pliny claimed that the soil was so fertile that 1 grain of wheat could produce an ear with 150 grains.[34] In the process, the dense forests near the North African shores quickly evolved into open land for agriculture, supplying the wood needed to heat homes, build ships, and fuel industries. The soil no longer benefited from the moisture-holding cover provided by the forests; instead the land lay exposed to the sun and wind.

Large-scale agriculture in these regions began at a time when the region was experiencing diminished rainfall. Combined with the interminable ploughing to increase yields, the increasingly arid conditions caused the parched land to erode during the windy summer months and add to the erosion that occurred during the rainy season, as runoff carried topsoil to the coast, forming ever enlarging deltas. For example, Ephesus, once a bustling port on the coast of Asia Minor, lost its harbor, being clogged with silt from the runoff from agricultural lands inland. Within a few decades a settlement that was one of the most important in the Roman Empire ceased to function as a vital city. It now lies in ruins in marshy terrain 3 miles from the coast.

In some areas, the Romans attempted to rectify the situation by restoring lands with plant material that would help prevent erosion. Along the North African coast, the once rich farmlands became too dry to produce sufficient yields of wheat, thus obliging the farmers to plant olives, a plant that normally does well in arid conditions. But the parched soil along the coast was now unsuitable even for the hardy olive, and as a result the population of the region began to decline. Leptis Magna could not keep up with the effects of erosion and soil depletion. It too fell into ruin, choked by the soil which for a few years gave it its wealth.[35]

NOTES

1. D. H. Trump. 1980. Prehistory of the Mediterranean. *New Haven and London: Yale University Press.*

2. Michael Grant. 1980. The Ancient Mediterranean. *New York: Scribners.*

3. *Grant, op. cit.*

4. Ellen C. Semple. 1971. The Geography of the Ancient Mediterranean. *New York: AMS Press.*

5. *Ibid., p. 540.*

6. *Ibid., p. 542. Cato and Vittuvius also recommended elevated sites for health reasons.*

7. Civy. 1982. Rome and Italy. *Translated by Betty Radile. New York: Penguin.*

8. *Ibid., p. 545. Roman siting is apparant in Valdarno at Ponti Agli Stoli and Incisa.*

9. Strabo, 1967. V, Chapt. III. Geography of Strabo. *Cambridge, MA: Harvard University Press.*

10. Polybius. 1962. Histories. *Bloomington: Indiana University Press.*

11. *Semple, op. cit., p. 559.*

12. *Ibid., p. 560.*

13. Edward T. Salmon. 1970. Roman Colonization under the Republic. *Ithaca, N.Y.: Cornell University Press, p. 14.*

14. *Ibid., p. 18. Salmon maintains that a territory of 500 square miles may have been smaller than normal during the Empire.*

15. *Ibid., p. 10. After 200 B.C. the decision to found colonies lay with the military dictators and later with the emperors.*

16. *Ibid., p. 22.*

17. *Ibid., p. 25.*

18. *See Barbara P. Levick. 1967. Roman Colonies in Southern Asia Minor. Oxford: Clarendon Press.*

19. Tactus, Ann. I. M. Annales. *Harmondsworth, Middlesex: Penguin Books.*

20. Nigel H. Sitwell. 1981. Roman Roads in Europe. *London: Cassell.*

21. *Strabo, op. cit., V. Chapt. I, II.*

22. W. F. Brooks. 1905. Agriculture. *Vol. II. Springfield: Home Course School, p. 65.*

23. W. E. Heitland. 1970. Agricola. *Westport, CT: Greenwood, p. 203.*

24. Horace. 1977. Satires, II. *Translated by Jacob Fuchs. New York: Norton, pp. 4, 16.*

25. *Semple, op. cit., p. 467.*

26. *Ibid., p. 370.*

27. W. Deecke. 1904. Italy. *London: S. Sonnenschein and Co., p. 102.*

28. Virgil. 1871. Georgic I. *pp. 214–216.*

29. *Semple, op. cit., p. 494.*

30. Pliny, 1938. Natural History. *Cambridge, MA: Harvard University Press.*

31. Norman T. Newton. 1971. Design on the Land: The Development of Landscape Architecture. *Cambridge, MA: Harvard University Press, p. 15.*

32. W. F. Jashemski. 1979. The Gardens of Pompeii. *New Rochelle: N.Y., Caratzas, p. 56.*

33. Donald J. Hughes. 1975. Ecology in Ancient Civilizations. *Albuquerque: University of New Mexico Press.*

34. David Attenborough. 1987. The First Eden: The Mediterranean World and Man. *Boston: Little, Brown, p. 112.*

35. *Ibid., p. 118.*

7

Continental Europe: Agriculture, Feudalism, and Community

With Roman decline ensuing by the third century A.D., religion, art, and law, the foundations of Mediterranean society, sustained profound changes. The landscape, which the Romans had exploited to supply their cities with food and raw materials, also altered, as Latin authority gradually capitulated to subregional and local control. The most visible signs of this transformation appeared in the formation of new settlements north of Italy. Continental Europe—lands north and west of the Alps that experience Atlantic climatic influences—began to sustain waves of immigrant incursions into the south and west in search of lands for settlements and farming. By most accounts, the scale and duration of these migrations were large and persistent; a number of continental European settlements owe their founding to this period.

The decline of Roman influence in continental Europe instituted a slow reestablishment of regional power centers, eventually forming the various independent states of modern Europe. Roman decline also precipitated an enduring oscillation of power between western and eastern European political centers, including territorial conflicts between Rome and Byzantium. Amid the wrenching dislocation of classical culture and the effects of the gradual formation of new political strongholds, the 700 years from about A.D. 472 to A.D. 1200 saw the formation of the values and habits of modern Europe.

Agriculture, which had been the prime economic activity of Roman society, continued to be the basis of economies throughout Europe during this period. Medieval societies had to solve problems of drainage, soil management, crop rotation, and animal husbandry to maintain viable settlements. Their ability to form these settlements and to produce sufficient agricultural output for subsistence partly resulted from the lessons they took from the Roman world. Despite the rigors of the era—plagues, warfare, political reorganization—people laboring in the agricultural landscapes of continental Europe forged a link between the classical and modern worlds. By the thirteenth century, when urbanization began to challenge agrarian economies, the European landscape bore the mark of these centuries of accomplishment in the form of permanent urban and rural systems.

PHYSICAL CONTEXT

The landscape of continental Europe forms a distinct physiographic unit. Along the south, the Alps and the Pyrennees separate Italy and Spain from the north; the Mediterranean Sea forms an edge along the French coast, as does the Atlantic Ocean along the west. To the east the physiographic limits of Europe fall along the Ural Mountains and the Ural River, which empties into the Caspian Sea. To the southeast the line forms along the Caucasus range and the Black Sea.

137

Diverse landforms exist within this landmass of nearly 4 million square miles, a result of particular geological and atmospheric forces. Geologically the region began to form with the appearance of the Atlantic ranges, derived from the folding and uplifting of the Hercynian folds, which covered most of Western and Central Europe. Subsequent terrestrial leveling and marine inundation formed a sedimentary layer over the Hercynian strata, whereupon the Hercynian layer underwent dramatic recombination during the late tertiary formation of the southern Alpine system. The land fractured into blocks, forming a patchwork of uplifted, submerged, fractured, and faulted elements. As a result, Central Europe contains uplifted material that forms uplands and massifs, including the central plateau of France, the massifs of western Germany, and the mountain ranges of Czechoslovakia.

Pleistocene glaciation was the other major geological event to modify the form of the Central European landscape during prehistory. Ice sheets, often 10,000 feet thick, eroded the landscape, reducing the height of the Alps by almost one-half. The material from this scouring moved with the ice, creating landforms, including hills and depressions. Crisp V-shaped valleys, earlier formed by stream erosion, quickly changed into U-shaped valleys due to the force of the ice flows. After the ice sheets receded, subsequent erosion by surface runoff created scattered lakes connected by drainage channels.

The soil structure that resulted from glaciation consists of either damp clay soils frequently found in Northwestern Europe or the thick layers of loess formed south of the glacial region, possibly carried along by strong winds during the interglacial periods. Also, in the north, older preglacial podsols are common, while further south, the results of glacial forces contribute to soil structure. For example, in glaciated areas on the Hercynian massifs, sections of loess alternate with rich loams. In Central Europe, loams cover limestone plateaus, while fertile alluvial deposits occur in river valleys. Newer soils, especially alluvial deposits, tend to be more fertile than older soils of the same kind. Older soils often develop a solid crust from periods of leaching, due to the action of climate on the older granitic soils, which produce a heavy, clayey, nonpermeable matrix. As a result of all these geological and climatic factors, the interior of the Central and Northern European landmass consists of disparate physiographic regions, forming what Gottmann[1] calls an irregular checkerboard. Within this composite, three distinct landscape regions exist, including older, worn mountains, which now form uplands and plateaus; younger mountain ranges including the Alpine system; and lowlands and interior planes.

Since the last Ice Age, climate and the action of surface erosion have continued to affect the Central European landscape. Generally, marine air from the Atlantic is the prime influence on the soils of continental Europe, and continues to affect the growth of forests and grasslands, though the specific climate varies from region to region. Northwest and Central Europe have climates derived from Atlantic influences, while further east the climate is more susceptible to continental air masses originating deep within the eastern areas of Europe and Asia. Also, since continental Europe lies between Arctic and subtropical belts, the region is affected by unstable air currents, which convey centers of low pressure from west to east. Therefore, the interior polar air masses in the winter and low-pressure air masses in the summer make the region more susceptible to extremes of temperature and climatic conditions, while coastal areas tend to experience less extreme climates. Except for the far north, the climate is moderate, with an average rainfall of between 20 to 40 inches per year.

The action of climate on the continental European landscape formed much of the drainage pattern in the region. Many rivers developed partially after the retreat of the Pleistocene glaciers, though some were formed prior to that time,

Primal forest in southeastern Europe. Many of these regions are protected as national forests.

particularly in Norway, Scotland, and the Alps. Others were unable to occupy their old courses, and, diverted by glacial debris, created new courses across old valleys, forming numerous waterfalls and lakes. Both old and newer courses still depend on precipitation for flow, including the Danube, which relies on the winter runoff from the Black Forest and the melting snows of the Alps, while the Seine and Loire rivers derive their flow from the marine climate.

With rich soils and sufficient rainfall, the region has evolved a complex vegetation pattern, distinct from that of the Mediterranean. From pollen analysis, it is possible to trace the evolution of plant communities in the region and to learn much about prehistoric habitats. Since the retreat of the last ice sheets, four plant associations have appeared: boreal, Atlantic, subboreal, and sub-Atlantic. Starting with the proliferation of spruce, fir, and pine during the warmer boreal stage in Scandinavia, stands of oak, elm, and linden appeared during the Atlantic phase in central Europe. Beech forests began to appear in Western and Central Europe, mostly in river valleys during the subboreal and sub-Atlantic phases. This period corresponds to the Neolithic in Europe, a time when the landscape consisted of dense stands of trees and undergrowth.[2] Most of these major native plant associations have ceased to exist due to pressures from agricultural and industrial activities since the Neolithic.

Presently, in the northern latitudes near Scandinavia, tundra is the major plant association, while south of the tundra, coniferous forests, including firs, pines, and spruces, mixed with birch trees, occur in dense stands. Further south, in the warmer latitudes of central and western Europe, broad-leafed stands of oak, beech, and firs formed dense forests prior to extensive agricultural activity. Today a few stands of the original associations still exist, especially along the primary mountain ranges, in the northern areas of Europe, and in the marshes of Eastern Europe. At the moment, most contemporary forests contain a mixture of introduced species, imported from foreign lands for either agricultural or ornamental purposes.

PREHISTORIC SETTLEMENT

Humans first entered Western Europe during the Paleolithic and Mesolithic periods; human culture began to flourish at least by 3000 B.C. in central, western, and northern Europe. The development of Neolithic cultures in these regions resembled the general trend of human settlement that first occurred in the Near East and gradually spread from the eastern Mediterranean to western Europe. The attraction for humans of central Europe was the opportunity to settle near the edges of forests or on the margins of the steppes and to gradually convert these regions to agricultural lands. Successive generations labored to keep these lands cleared and free from the reemergence of the forests. The large stands of heath in northwestern Germany stem from the efforts of Neolithic groups to keep the lands clear through agriculture and grazing.[3]

Two other landscape environments became the focus of Neolithic development in continental Europe. The first was land adjacent to lakes in Switzerland, Germany, Austria, Hungary, the Balkans, and northern Italy. Lake Neuchatal in Switzerland had at least fifty small villages along its shore, Lake Geneva had forty, and Lake Constance nearly the same number. The villages consisted of structures made of logs and brush, situated on platforms supported by pilings. The village dwellers relied on the natural resources of the locale for sustenance. Refuse found near the sites includes the remains of 170 different species of plants, including fruits, vegetables, nuts; animal skins supplied the dwellers with the material to fashion clothing and textiles.[4]

The second major location for Neolithic settlement was along the coasts from the Baltic to the Bay of Biscay. These settlements consisted of undistinguished structures located near coastal waters, where groups searched for shellfish and fished for herring and cod; these modest communities represented the successful transition from hunting and gathering to the development of economies based on the resources of a specific location. Over time, camp refuse sites or kitchen middens formed large mounds; inhabitants relocated their camps when these refuse mounds began to crowd out the village. Remains from the middens include shellfish and waterfowl, along with the tools used to capture and clean the marine life.

Apart from the location and function of early Neolithic settlements, another aspect of human ordering of the landscape during the period of late prehistory is the remains of impressive megalithic structures in western Europe and Britain. Megaliths date from the Neolithic and from the Bronze Age, which began about 1800 B.C., and attest to the high level of logistical skill and craft possessed by

Neolithic lake shore village.

early Europeans. *Megaliths* (large stones), *dolmens* (stone chambers), *tumuli* (earth-covered dolmens), *cromlechs* (stone circles), and *menhirs* (upright stones placed in ovals and rows), appeared in one form or another throughout Western Europe, with some of the best preserved located in France and Great Britain. For example, in France, over 4,500 megalith sites exist, many functioning later as stone quarries.[5] At Carnac in Brittany, Stonehenge at Wiltshire, and Avebury in Devonshire, rows and circles of stones still punctuate the landscape, monuments to Neolithic activity in these regions. The physical origin of these monuments remains obscure; many of the massive stones had to be transported miles from distant quarries. Though the scale and arrangement of the stone elements point to ritual functions, the exact nature of their use remains conjectural.

Neolithic farmstead in Sussex, England.

Megaliths near Avebury, Devonshire, England.

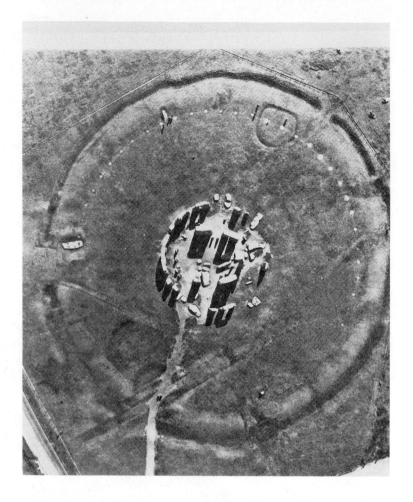

Aerial view of Stonehenge revealing the successive stages of annular development.

EARLY HISTORIC SETTLEMENT

Archaeological evidence indicates that plains, plateaus, river valleys, and terraces overlain by light soils were preferred sites for agricultural development in western continental Europe during late prehistory. During the Bronze Age, agriculture was the focus of economic activity in such places as the Rhine plains, portions of which the inhabitants converted from marshlands to agricultural zones. In central Europe, especially in southwest Germany, and as far north as the North Sea plains, these settlements appeared in zones of loess soils.

These lands include, in part, areas occupied by early Germanic groups in search of agricultural land. As early as the second millennium B.C. German settlements appeared in the lands along the lower Rhine and the Oder and in southern Sweden. In 200 B.C. German migrants moved south into lands occupied by Celts, perhaps as a consequence of periods of wetter weather. Where open, arable lands permitted, agriculturalists formed permanent settlements or established scattered homesteads; social rank determined the amount of land an individual could claim. Physically the settlements, which included structures and arable lands, complemented the *mark,* or fringe of unsettled area around a village. The mark provided pasture and timber, as well as forming a natural protection for the settled lands.[6] Traditionally the mark consisted of woodland, and villagers had the right of common use of its resources.

The forces that compelled Eastern Europeans to migrate westward and move through the Roman frontiers were the same forces that had induced migrations in early societies in the Near East. Settlements in eastern Europe were founded on a combination of extensive agricultural activity and stock raising, utilizing large areas of open land. Open land was a prime commodity in relation to forest, marshes, and moors. As population growth increased the competition for arable land, the eastern tribes either had to reclaim adjacent land, an undertaking requiring considerable labor, or migrate into lands that were already usable; therefore groups began to migrate from eastern and central Europe south and west toward the Mediterranean and the Atlantic coasts. By 166 A.D. the Romans could no longer restrain migration into western Europe, and the first major Germanic migrations ensued.

ROMAN INFLUENCE, DECLINE, AND LEGACY

Through the Republic and Empire, Roman authority in Europe depended on maintaining local control by central administration. North of the Alps, military outposts formed the nucleus of agricultural settlement. Along the Mediterranean in Gaul, the Romans maintained cities and villas, connected by roadways and watered by aqueducts. As Roman authority began to fade, so too did the appearance of the Romanized European landscape begin to change.

The causes for the decline of the Roman Empire were many, including the lack of political will, the failure of the economic system, and the dissolution of moral standards. Factors affecting the quality of Roman landscape use and management may also have had an influence.

The first indication that the Roman system was in decline was the failure of the ruling authority to maintain an effective line of succession. Roman dominance, the cultural anchor in the region, reached its zenith in the third century A.D., but Rome's political structure did not assure peaceful succession to the throne. Thus ensued an unending struggle for the Imperial crown, which, by 472 A.D., had resulted in the accession of the last emperor in the West. Roman economic structure had also become ineffectual by the third century, due mainly to the reliance on slave labor to produce goods and services in the Italian peninsula. With much slave labor on hand, there was little incentive to develop labor-saving devices and methods. The quality of invention at the mercantile level remained low, freezing the society in an endless cycle of basic agricultural production and political expansion. Romans also invested heavily in imported goods from the eastern Mediterranean, inevitably weakening their balance of payments. Rome eventually felt the economic strain, for though it was the political center of the Empire, its inhabitants had grown into an unruly mob that either was treated cruelly by the reigning emperor or placated by a "bread and circuses" strategy.

In addition to these problems in commerce and politics, changes in Roman agricultural practices, particularly the shift from small-scale independent farming to large estates during the Republic, deprived the Empire of its mainstay: the independent farmer, long the cornerstone of the economic and military system. By the second century A.D., and to the long-standing consternation of Roman writers such as Virgil and Pliny, the local farmer had become a rare commodity, further compounding the problem of maintaining an army of adequate size. Thus the old farmer-soldier system began to fade from the society, and with it the concept of a ready militia. Increasingly the Empire relied on the use of foreigners to fill the army's ranks, mostly conscripts from the northern provinces. By the late second century the Germans had become particularly eager to join the Mediterranean world and were allowed to join and in some instances command Roman legions. Eventually, foreigners began to move up the ranks of the military hierarchy to a point where they occupied many positions of authority.

For a time during the reign of Diocletian (284–304) some of the troubles plaguing the Empire seemed to abate, due to a new economic strategy based on increased taxation and the bonding of individuals to the trades of their forebears. But the burden of taxation on the middle class helped to destroy the remaining viable economic element in the realm. From Diocletian through the reign of Constantine I, Rome maintained its presence, though it was little more than a stopgap until the church was able to take over the administration of the society in the fifth century. A millenium of Roman rule in the Mediterranean basin had strained the natural and human resources of the region to the point where a single, unified empire was no longer feasible.

The legacy left by Roman activity in the Mediterranean and continental Europe was greater than that of any society that had preceded it. At its height during the third century A.D., Roman dominions stretched from the Mediterranean eastward to the Black Sea and north to the North Sea, and east across the Danube River. Roman expansion, though, was mostly a function of local colonization rather than the founding of Latin settlements, since few individuals from the Italian peninsula actually settled in Central and Western Europe. Most of the population increase came from the migration of peoples from the northeast toward the Atlantic and the Mediterranean. However, Roman activity in these landscapes helped to establish a model for subsequent landscape occupation through the Middle Ages. Though later landscape practices had other antecedents as well—for the western Germans had developed techniques of settlement and agricultural practice—Roman efficiency and technology left an indelible mark on the landscape, especially in matters related to the production and conveyance of resources for use within the heart of the old Empire.

The most visible of these was the existing engineered road system, which exerted an influence on the routes of in-migration of peoples from the northeast.[7] Another visible contribution was the extensive aqueduct systems built by Roman engineers and laborers to convey water from upland regions to large inhabited areas along the Mediterranean rim in Gaul. Fragments of this system remain near Nimes, where the Pont du Gard, part of a Roman aqueduct, spans the Rhone River. Finally, the Roman settlements themselves, whether urban centers or rural estates, provided newcomers with a measure of structure to pattern urban and rural activities. Mostly these were founded as Roman military camps, *castrum,* though usually occupied and managed by local inhabitants. With few exceptions Roman towns founded on military camps adhered to the *cardo* and *decumanus* plan, though towns differed in shape due to the constraints of local topography. London, founded as a bridgehead on the Thames, was quite small, covering only half a square mile; Lyons, the capital of Gaul, was larger. Many contemporary communities, including Milan, Bordeaux, Vienna, and Strasbourg occupy sites near or on Roman foundations. Not all Roman towns experienced continuous occupation after the decline of the Empire, though many in Italy and Gaul managed to weather the vicissitudes of medieval impact and alteration. In London the Roman street pattern did not survive; remains of the Roman community lie several feet below the present city. Farther from major Roman centers, numerous present day communities in continental Europe with names ending in "ingen" trace their origin to Roman settlement and agricultural activity either as small nucleated villages or scattered settlements.

Perhaps the most important legacy left by the Romans was their agricultural system, which was founded on Mediterranean concepts of landscape management and production. Northern Europeans, like their Mediterranean counterparts, were attuned to the rigors of rural life, and considered that their purpose in the world was to devise ways to survive in a hostile environment, primarily through the activity of agriculture. Some individuals were fortunate enough to assume the position of landlords of the large Roman estates. Many others were

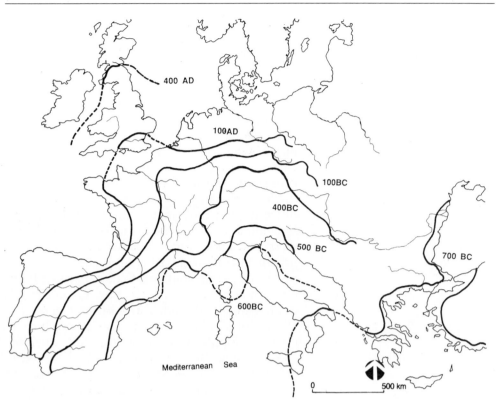

Progression of urbanization in the European region during Greek and Roman domination preceding the Middle Ages.

consigned to individual labor on communal agricultural land, or as feudal serfs tied to an estate.

For most of the northern Roman Empire, agricultural techniques stemmed from ancient methods used in the Mediterranean basin, some of which were not suitable for the wet climate of northern Europe, including dry farming and the propagation of figs and olives. This system was carried to the northern Empire by Roman soldiers who were compelled to farm to produce à portion of their food. Soldiers and civilians received land to farm, which they owned, and normally laid out and farmed according to the standards of the Mediterranean.

Mediterranean farming depended on a crop and fallow system, with the major crops being the vine, olive, and cereals. A light plough, or *ard,* could break through the friable Mediterranean soil and prepare a seedbed in the shallow rut in the ground. The Romans carefully maintained a fertilization schedule through the use of manures or the plowing in of legumes. Cereals, vegetables, and fruit trees, including the olive and citrus, formed the list of cultivable plants. Livestock rounded out the agricultural activity in the Mediterranean. Horses, sheep, goats, pigs, and cattle supplied food and energy to the Roman farms, while transhumance occurred in mountainous areas.

In the northern provinces, the Romans utilized the two-field rotation system, introduced the vine, promoted the use of manures, and forced the wheelless *ard* into the deep, wet soils of Central Europe. But the Romans had little experience with spring-sown crops that could be propagated in the northern region. Agriculture was essentially an individual endeavor performed near villages and hamlets on small rectangular plots, yielding peas, lentils, oats, barley, wheat, rye, and spelt. In Gaul and Britain the Romans built villas, and used servile labor to produce goods for profit. Members of the Roman senatorial class, the individuals who profited most from the imperial system, maintained large *latifundia,* which a few foreign individuals managed to acquire during the period of Roman decline in continental Europe.[8]

Late Roman occupation of continental Europe bequeathed other elements to the region, principally the practice of agricultural slaveholding. The system of tying people to the land as slaves or indentured *coloni* was an acceptable part of maintaining a farm in Gaul, as it was in Italy. The practice stemmed from social change during the late Empire, when individuals placed themselves under the protection of a local leader. Also, in the third century A.D., under Diocletian, the authorities instituted laws to help reduce inflation, including the reduction of freedom of movement from one occupation to another. Peasants and military individuals collectively formed the *clientela rusticorum,* and put themselves and their land under the protection of a local lord. In the northwestern lands, feudalism first flourished between the Loire and the Rhine, and spread to other places, including southern France, parts of Italy, Spain, and Britain, but had little effect in Scandinavia and the Low Countries.[9] The practice contained the nucleus of later medieval feudalism with its manorial system. Unlike slavery, feudalism allowed individuals the freedom to produce a modicum of goods for personal consumption. Service to the local lord in either labor or tribute, along with the lack of ownership of land, provided the wealthy in Central Europe with the means to establish a feudal system, an arrangement that endured in some areas of Europe until the nineteenth century.

GERMANIC MIGRATIONS

Diocletian, Constantine I, and subsequent emperors made attempts to revive the Roman Empire by resisting migrations, but Germanic incursion into the Empire resumed in 376. The migrations originated from three areas in Eastern Europe, including northern Europe between the Rhine and Vistula, Galicia in east-central Europe, and the steppe margins of southeastern Europe.[10] The first occurred when pressures for arable land drove the Germanic people into the Empire, in retreat from waves of eastern nomadic groups who were forcing their way westward, putting pressure on the Romanized societies in Gaul and western Germany. For centuries groups had migrated westward through the Mediterranean and eastward to the Black Sea as a function of either Greek or Roman colonization. The movement of people into continental Europe and the Mediterranean during the third and fourth centuries A.D. was tied to a different phenomenon, namely the desire of peoples to establish settlements in the more desirable landscapes in Western Europe, preferably in areas of security and relative stability. The Roman realm, with its apparent umbrella of prosperity and security, functioned as a vacuum for the intruding groups that swept across the European continent from the third to the tenth centuries.

The first of these groups to migrate into continental Europe and the Mediterranean region were from lands that were beginning to feel the pinch of limited resources. This western branch spawned the Angles, Saxons, and Jutes who settled Germany and Britain and the Franks who under Charles the Great helped to establish the Holy Roman Empire in 800. The eastern groups, who had established settlements in the steppe area north of the Black Sea, and eventually migrated westward to southern Gaul, Italy, and the Iberian peninsula, included, in succession, the Ostrogoths, Visigoths, Vandals, Burgundians, and Lombards. To some extent the configuration of the European continent helped to encourage the migration. Physiographically, central Europe has an east-west alignment, making movement and communication possible along this axis. For example,

Alaric, the Visigoth chief, led his invaders from the region around the Black Sea into Italy, and pillaged the land for eleven years. Thereafter the Visigoths established a kingdom in the Iberian peninsula that lasted until the eighth century. The Vandals and the Burgundians were successful in establishing settlements in North Africa, and the latter in Gaul near the Rhine. The Huns, originating from southern Russia, attempted to claim Italy in 452 under the leadership of Attila. Their ambitions were thwarted: Attila lost his army to illness in northern Italy, an event that presaged his own death the following year and the dissolution of his holdings. Some semblance of stability was restored in the old Empire in 534 when Justinian established the western Byzantine kingdom in Ravenna, reclaimed Africa, and ended the Vandal occupation of the region. Two distinct disruptions to the central and southern European landscape occurred after the founding of the Byzantine Empire: these were, first, the incursions of the Norse from Scandinavia in the ninth century, and second, the rapid expansion of Islam from the Middle East that spread the teachings of Mohamet along the north coast of Africa, and into Spain and portions of France and Italy during the seventh and eighth centuries.

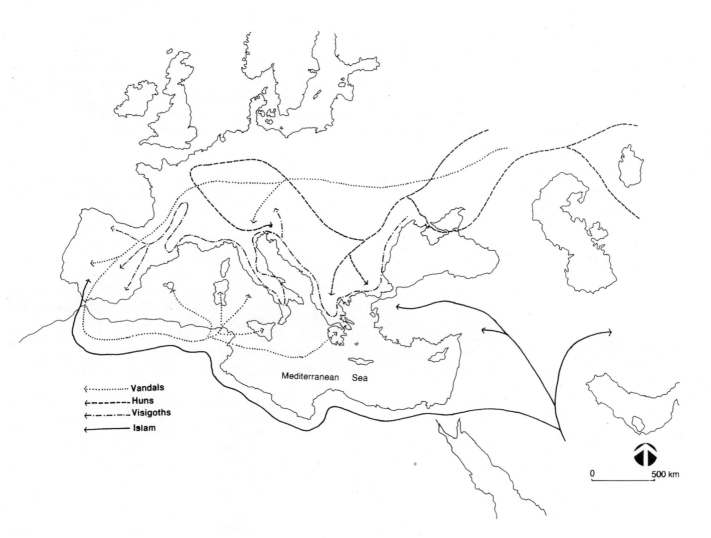

Migration routes into post Roman Europe used by groups originating in Eastern Europe and Asia.

The result of these continuing migrations into the western European landscape by groups living on its periphery was to lessen the Roman influence in the region and imbue the continental European landscape with a distinctive identity. Politically, great shifts in power ensued up to the fourteenth century, giving rise to the eventual formation of the individual European states. The key to this transformation was the displacement of Rome in northern Europe by the migrating groups and the development of settlements independent of Roman authority. As a landscape phenomenon, it was a time when the region came into its own.[11] The more ambitious migrants acquired and assumed the management of the great estates, though the Roman system of cultivation soon faded, replaced by a new system based on the collective use of arable lands surrounding small settlements. During the early medieval period, few individuals left this system for careers in the towns or with the church. Most of the population devoted its energy to the maintenance of an agricultural system, which consigned each person to the expansion of agricultural territory through forest clearing and the reclamation of less arable lands. However, converting the denser, moister soils in northern Europe required more effort and commitment to labor than had been needed in the Mediterranean. Often farmers opted for marginal soils rather than attempting to convert heavy forest lands into arable landscapes.

Eventually some resistance developed to the westward migrations, and stimulated the development of boundaries that cut across topographic and climatic zones from north to south. Within these regions settlements gradually rose to prominence as the nuclei of provinces. Often these settlements occurred in proximity to an important trade route, whether near an important mountain pass, navigable river, or natural marine port. Even the lofty Alps yielded to migration through the deep passes cut by glacial activity. Only the Mediterranean peninsulas, with their mountainous interiors that define these landscapes as a series of ranges, basins, and valleys, opposed easy movement of migrants.

EARLY MEDIEVAL SETTLEMENT

The pattern of landscape use in the Middle Ages began with migration and settlement and evolved into a complex interplay between lay, ecclesiastical, and monastic settlements. As the population began to expand in continental Europe, the aristocracy and the church encouraged the expansion of human activity into areas of the continental European landscape where, before, few people had wanted to live. At the secular level, the strategy used by settlers often differed from Roman antecedents in both the organization of agricultural space and the methods and techniques used for farming. Regardless of strategy, medieval settlements formed the nuclei for agricultural activity, and the pattern of landscape activity in continental Europe, for a millennium. Several influences determined the location and quality of settlement in these lands, including the incidence of existing Roman-Gallo settlements, the location of roads and waterways, the occurrence of Roman-style *latifundia,* the establishment of fortified domains, and the location of ecclesiastical centers.

Urban formation, which during the early Middle Ages amounted to the establishment of small settlements and individual rural establishments, first occurred in or near preexisting settlements and arable lands. Soil, vegetation pattern, topographic relief, and the existing cultural features, including farmsteads, roads, cities, and plantations, all played a role in determining settlement location and quality. For example, early place names in Belgium suggest that migrants tended to avoid forests, marshes, and heath for established lands in plains and valleys.

By the late fifth century villages and farms existed west of the Rhine, along the line of westward advancement. The processes of colonization into Western

Europe proceeded with the cutting and firing of woodlands and the draining of marshes. Within these newly established lands, settlers formed villages as agricultural outposts. Further west in Roman Gaul, where the landscape had consisted of farms and villages during the Roman occupation, villas dotted the landscape, mostly in natural clearings or areas where individuals had cleared patches of land for agriculture and livestock raising. Though some farmsteads in northern Gaul failed to survive Roman decline, other villas in southern Gaul persisted, eventually falling into the hands of northeastern inheritors.

AGRICULTURAL STRATEGY

Throughout continental Europe, remnants of the medieval agricultural order persist. Evidence of these early activities in the landscape exists in northern France, the Low Countries, and western Germany, where agricultural fields fan out from villages and form long, unfenced strips. In southern France, parts of western Britain, and northern Scandinavia, the farmlands surround hamlets in rectangular plots. For some of these locations the difference in field form stems from the kind of plough used to prepare the soil. The Mediterranean *ard,* used for cross-ploughing, produced the rectangular form, while the heavier wheeled plough, with coulter and moldboard, performed more effectively in elongated strips.[12] The precise date for the introduction of the wheeled plough is uncertain, probably evolving from central Europe sometime after the sixth century.

Another significant modification of earlier Roman agricultural technique was the adoption of the three-field rotation system. Use of the Mediterranean two-field system continued in continental Europe during the fifth and sixth centuries: one field was sown in winter or spring corn, while the adjacent field was left fallow; land surrounding the arable fields was held in common with few individual restrictions concerning use. But by the eighth century farmers had adopted the three-field system, whereby two crops and a fallow were rotated annually, thereby enhancing the agricultural output of the region. This system, most likely

Aerial view of contemporary middle European farming village with surrounding agricultural lands.

invented in western France, spread from north of the Loire into the Low Countries, Germany, Denmark, and England. The two-field system remained in those regions where soil quality was poor and in remote areas—for example, western Britain, northern Scandinavia, and southern France. The two systems appear to have existed, if not contiguously, then at the same time in northern Europe and parts of Britain.[13] The three-field system increased the yield a farmer could anticipate, although estimates as to the magnitude of the increase vary. Theoretical increases of 3:1 for barley could be expected in good years, perhaps even as high as 6:1 in the best of times, though less was more likely. The use of the three-field system could increase the number of harvests on a field from three harvests every six years to four.

Typically a village consisted of common arable land that was divided into three large fields. Each of these formed elongated strips separated by narrow paths; the size of a strip was an acre; each farmer in the village managed several strips in various fields. Some individuals held many strips, while others farmed only a few. After the harvest all the fields became common pasture, usually forage for the village livestock. Meadows were also common property, often consigned by lot to individuals who wanted to produce hay; woodlands were considered common property, used for grazing and apportioned based on the size of each farmer's arable holdings.

The technical aspects of medieval farming varied from region to region, depending on landscape qualities and local customs. Fussel[14] notes the practice of "wild field grass husbandry," a method persisting in regions with exposed, hilly areas with less than fertile soils. Farmers plowed up natural grassland and grew crops for a few years until the soil was exhausted. The land was then abandoned and permitted to return to natural cover. Another adaptation was the infield-outfield system, used in hills and moorlands: here lower-elevation, "infield" farmland functioned as annual cropland, often receiving most of the pre-

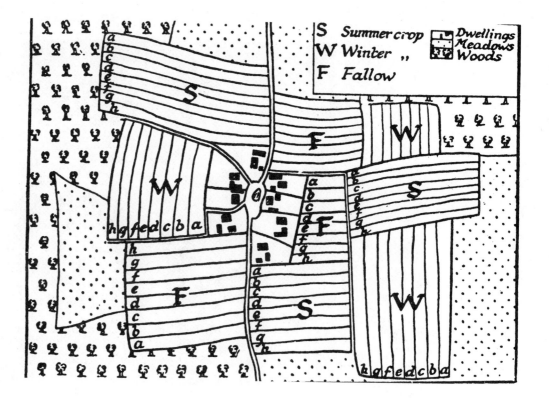

Organization of medieval farming village in England. Field designations reflect the three-field system.

Aerial view of preexisting medieval village revealing Anglo-Saxon ridge and furrow pattern.

cious fertilizers; the "outfield" consisted of rough pasture, with some parts used for cultivation.

Classical literature appears to have had little effect on agricultural technique during the early medieval period. But by the ninth century, during the Carolingian period, classical and contemporary writings, including the *Geoponika,* began to influence the agricultural strategy of the region. The author of the *Geoponika* relied on Varro and other classical sources for guidance, along with additional contemporary sources. As meager as the available literature was, farmers now had a few references to agricultural procedures from earlier periods. For example, there was information in these references about Roman techniques for selecting a site. The texts encouraged the farmer to examine the soil for sight, smell, and taste. By digging a hole and refilling it, the prospective landowner could determine soil structure: that which overflowed when refilled was apt to be heavy after ploughing; if it refilled evenly, the soil was friable and expected to yield good crops. Also the texts advised farmers to qualify land according to slope and aspect, with south and west slopes preferred for their orientation to the sun. Finally, medieval writers continued the Latin tradition of classifying land into three categories—plain, hill, and mountain—carrying on a tradition that lasted until the seventeenth century.[15]

Regarding soil preparation and maintenance, farmers usually adhered to the Roman habit of three ploughings; one each during the spring, summer, and fall was common, with manure added during the second ploughing to assure proper fertility. The third often was merely a light mixing of the soil surface. Manures included animal wastes, vegetable matter, or marl. On the prepared soils, farmers broadcast seed that was likely to give the highest yield, favoring wheat and barley seed that appeared full, firm, smooth, and golden in color. Certain farmers used seed from the largest ears of wheat or barley, others tested the seed on small manured plots, while others relied on seed from plants grown on different soils.

Also, from the literature, they knew that Latin writers prescribed certain lands for particular crops: wheat should be cultivated in soils that were clayey and moist; barley was suitable for dry soils, as were peas, beans, and lentils. Agriculturalists propagated lucern for forage; with proper care one seeding could produce plant material for twenty years. Agricultural yields were unpredictable; rye, wheat, and millet were popular cereals; also common were peas, beans, barley, oats, flax, hemp, and various fruit trees, including apple, cherry, plum, and pear. The olive continued to be important in southern continental lands, and the vine eventually flourished in many parts of France and Germany.

Plant propagation was only half the agricultural equation during the Middle Ages. Animal husbandry formed part of farmstead activity, and most farm animals familiar to us today were equally familiar to medieval agriculturalists. They included horses, oxen, donkeys, cattle, sheep, and goats; most survived on local fodder, acorns, chestnuts, and barley. Horses were less useful as draft animals, but were prized for transportation and warfare. More often oxen, donkeys, and mules furnished the energy to pull ploughs; advice on the the care of draft and farm animals appeared in some references, along with a list of the duties for the shepherd and animal tender.

MANORIAL LANDS

Large landholdings had existed in continental Europe before Germanic settlement, often as Roman *latifundia.* These estates persisted in some areas of continental Europe, especially in Britain and southern France. The estates that survived the migrations often fell into the hands of resourceful immigrants from the Germanic lands and were managed on the classical villa model. These lands and newer holdings constituted the manorial system, whose origins lie north of Paris and whose influence spread throughout France, Britain, the Low Countries, and Germany.

Thus, small villages and individual farms formed only part of the landscape pattern of the early Middle Ages. Large landholdings, both lay and ecclesiastical, rounded out the settlement pattern in Western Europe and made a significant mark on the continental landscape. Just as farmlands sustained small villages and individual holdings, the agricultural portions of the manorial lands bore the economic load, and determined the form and viability of the estate. Larger landholdings would often include a mixture of small settlements, housing individual laborers. In southern France the *mas,* or *massio,* signified a large holding, whereas in Britain the term *manor* was used. These large holdings appeared and disappeared as the fortunes of powerful families waxed and waned; ecclesiastical holdings often expanded during the Middle Ages, as important families gradually bequeathed lands to the church. At times, a manorial land might also form part of a royal holding, belonging to a local or regional lord, and enlarged over time as individuals relinquished their lives and property to a lord in exchange for protection.

All manorial holdings, from Britain to east-central Europe, shared certain characteristics, including some form of the feudal social system and the use of common or open fields. A lord, or *seigneur,* perhaps a baron, local ruler, or an administrator of an ecclessiastical holding, was the nominal possessor of the manorial land. Within his realm the seigneur had total legal authority. Manorial lands consisted of two parts, the *demesne,* the land held and worked directly for the lord, and the tenancies, the small landholdings farmed by the peasants. By the ninth century the demesne was the greater part of the manor, and was worked by slaves or hired laborers. Later in the Middle Ages and with the decline of the feudal system, villeins worked the land in exchange for a plot of land for their families.[16] In the hierarchy of the feudal system, the work on the estate was performed by peasants, both free and unfree, as payment for their use of a part of the land for their own subsistence. The amount of land farmed by a peasant varied, but from 35 to 40 acres was common.

One of the most prominent landholdings during the Middle Ages in France was the extensive estate belonging to the Abbey of St. Germain-des-Pres; at its peak the abbey controlled nearly 80,000 acres. Another important manor of the period appeared on the list of ecclesiastical holdings of the Abbey of Westminster. The landholding originated as a Saxon settlement, first as a cluster of farmsteads and then as an agricultural village. The lands evolved into a prosperous classical holding, ruled by an abbot and administered by his monks. Fifteen tenant farmers worked lands ranging in size from 20 to 30 acres; each was responsible for ploughing and maintaining 12 acres of the abbot's demesne land. In addition, sixteen minor tenants farmed a few acres each, and were required to pay rent in labor or produce to the abbot.[17]

MONASTERIES AND FORTIFIED SETTLEMENTS

Though manorial lands and independent villages, with their open field arrangement, were instrumental in helping to form a pattern of settlement in continental Europe, two additional settlement elements helped to shape the continental landscape during the Middle Ages: monasteries and fortified settlements. These settlements were more than just agricultural centers: they provided additional security or stability to regions accustomed to internecine strife.

Monasticism first appeared in Western Europe in Italy during the sixth century, with the founding of the Monastery at Monte Cassino by St. Benedict. This and other early monasteries along the edge of the old Roman Empire—for example, in Ireland and Greece—were depositories for classical literature and culture, locations where individuals labored to conserve and produce manuscripts that documented earlier classical sources. Conceived as communal enterprises dedicated to work and piety, monasteries relied on the application of traditional agricultural practices and landscape use to sustain their lands. Some of the most prosperous functioned by emulating secular manorial establishments, with abbots and monks functioning as overseers of all economic activity. Agricultural space and technique conformed to the habits of the day: open field, two- and three-field systems, and feudal social arrangement. Monte Cassino and other monasteries gradually evolved into extensive holdings through donations of lands from wealthy individuals who sought asylum within the church.

A prime example of the organization of a highly successful monastic settlement was the Benedictine monastery of St. Gall in Switzerland. The plan for the site, with its various structures, first appeared in 816 as a model for the ideal layout of a monastery. Many of the elements in the plan attest to classical influences, including the garden, reminiscent of a Roman *villa rusticus,* and planned to include fruit trees, vegetable gardens, flowers, and medicinal herbs.[18] The south end of the site included pens, barns, and workers' quarters, while at the north end were the abbot's residence, guest facilities, and a school. For those in need of a place for meditation, an arcaded cloister garden lay on the south side of the church. The self-contained and self-sufficient organization of St. Gall and many other monasteries added to their sense of insularity, perhaps intended to assure a separation from the influences of the secular world. The plan left little opportunity for distraction from chores and prayer; it encouraged a separation of the brothers from other laborers, who were responsible for the field work, including serfs who tilled the fields and tended to the livestock.[19]

The Cistercian order strove to shed the relative sumptuosness of monasteries such as St. Gall, and dedicated their efforts to forming agricultural establishments on the fringes of medieval settlement. High in the uplands of the Ardennes and

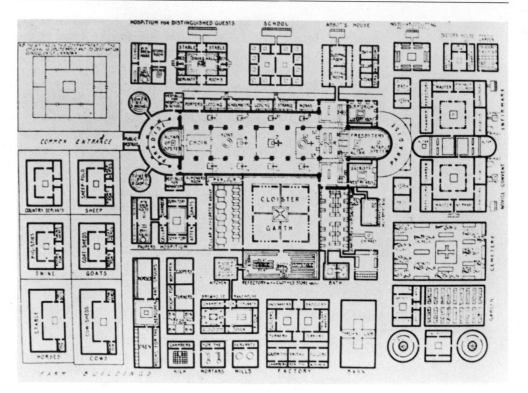

The plan for the Monastery of St. Gall, Switzerland, founded in the ninth century during a period of monastic development in continental Europe.

Cloister garden of late medieval monastery in Orange, France.

Remains of the Cistercian Abby of St. Antimo. The Abby was founded in the ninth century and controlled a large agricultural landholding.

the Vosges, and in the western Alps, the Cistercians labored in the elevated, wet forest lands to carve out agricultural lands. Typically, they farmed blocks of land, the outlying portions of which were farmed by brothers inhabiting granges, or small farmsteads. They were determined to live by their own resources and they became outstanding agriculturalists. Many of their farms and granges became the nuclei of villages.[20]

While monasteries provided one form of shelter from the harsher aspects of medieval life, fortified settlements provided the inhabitants with protection in areas prone to strife. Fortifications dotted the French Midi. They also appeared in southwestern France, due to hostilities between the British and French in the later Middle Ages, and in Provence, which was prone to attack in the western Alps from Saracen invaders or seaward from pirates. These new villages, or *Bastides,* appeared on elevated sites when the threat of attack seemed endemic to the locality. In southern France over a thousand Bastide towns evolved during the later Middle Ages, becoming small economic centers. We will discuss the organization of Bastides later, but it is important to note that the location for these communities evolved from older fortifications, such as the walled town of Carcassonne in southwestern France. Carcassonne traces its origins to the Roman period and later to its use as a Visigoth site during the fifth century. Eleventh-century walls complete the form of the community, which today still dominates the surrounding landscape. Carcassonne was a compact community, with its inner and outer walls separated by an earthen barrier. The interior of the town lacked any formal open space; its arrangement and function were utilitarian. What planned outdoor spaces there were at fortified sites generally were on a small scale, and had an inward-oriented appearance. Berrall[21] cites painting from the late Middle Ages for examples of castle garden arrangement, particularly images in *The Book of Hours.* In these paintings, the gardens inside the walls of fortified sites appear loosely formal with fruit trees, small water features, medicinal plants, and flowering specimens embellishing the walled garden. From

Carcassone.

Petrus Crecentius's thirteenth-century comments regarding garden arrangement, there were at least three possible styles, one each for the common individual, the middle class, and the nobility.

RURAL SETTLEMENTS, TOWNS, AND TRADE ROUTES

During the early Middle Ages, ecclesiastical, noble, and lay settlements formed a cultural structure in the western European landscape that was prone to change whenever local conditions shifted resources or security away from the locality. From the ninth to the thirteenth century, a more permanent structure began to form. Charles the Great, crowned Holy Roman Emperor in Rome on Christmas Day 800, instituted policies during his brief reign that had some effect on the direction of landscape use within his domains. His efforts were principally aimed at securing his frontiers by establishing military districts as buffers between the eastern cultures, the Slavs and Avars. Upon his death and in accordance with the Treaty of Verdun, his grandsons inherited the Empire, albeit as a tripartite entity. The treaty made France, Thuringia, and the Germanic lands the three major political regions of continental Europe, and the boundaries of subsequent national states are roughly indicated in its provisions.

Between 900 and 1300 permanent Germanic settlement finally appeared in the eastern lands near the Baltic. Existing Slavic settlements were typically rudimentary, consisting of a circle of dwellings enclosing a pasture. Acquisition of land proceeded in response to the rise in the value of property in established regions of continental Europe, following a rise in the population in the later Middle Ages. With the Germanic advance came the church, which, with the various kings, strove to acquire and exploit inexpensive land. By the end of the tenth century new settlements had formed along the Germanic frontiers. Many of these were founded around fortified *burgs*, settlements functioning as military and ecclesiastical centers. A number of village place names reflect this period of colonization. Present-day towns bearing names containing "roth," "metz," "au," and "brand" trace their origins to this era.[22]

From 1100 to 1400, rural settlement in continental Europe was a complex process that defies easy categorization. Some authorities explain the phenomenon by describing three forms of rural settlement during this period: nucleated, diffuse, and an intermediate pattern between the two. The first existed as a tightly arranged collection of farmsteads, the second as scattered farmsteads, and the third a collection of scattered homesteads around a nucleated site. Demangeon[23] presented a model for nucleated village settlement pattern that included three forms. The first was the communal open-field village surrounded by arable strips, meadow, and woodland. The second was the village with contiguous fields, including the linear villages founded in forest clearings and drained marshes. Arable lands adjacent to the settlement were individually owned. This configuration was common in the Low Countries, northwest Germany, and the Hercynian Highlands. The third form occurred whenever topography and the need for defense dictated the siting of the village on an elevation, a form common to Mediterranean lands. It should be noted that few accurate maps exist from the later Middle Ages that show the exact distribution and size of settlements. Mainly this is the result of permanent settlements occurring in uninhabited areas and the slow conversion of native landscape to urban and agricultural lands, neither of which favors documentation.

Despite the dearth of graphic data, we do have some information about medieval community organization. Typically, site location and the organization of nucleated villages differed from earlier Mediterranean examples in several aspects. First, the climate and landforms of the Mediterranean produced fluctuations between dry and torrential stream and river conditions that made rivers difficult to use as transportation routes and that produced malarial conditions. Settlements often occurred on elevated sites with agricultural zones occurring on slopes or in lowlands, areas reclaimed for agricultural use. In continental Europe the opposite siting tending to occur. Oceanic and continental weather patterns and the prevailing topography afforded settlers the opportunity to site settlements near rivers on well-drained terraces above floodplains. Some settlements occurred on elevated sites, particularly when adjacent lands were ill drained. Good sites also existed in upland areas in the rims of sheltered basins and on the edges of lakes, marshes, lagoons, and springs.[24]

The form of rural settlements in continental Europe depended on local factors, although from region to region there is evidence of some organizational similarities. Topography, soils, and other physical conditions normally determined settlement form, as much as local customs. For example Slavic villages took one of several forms; circular, elongated, oval, and gridiron configurations were common. The elongated village often reflected community siting along a road, while an oblong, roughly circular form might be the result of hilltop topography. And as in Mediterranean locales different lands near settlements functioned for specific uses. The prime arable land, which was used to grow cereals, needed to be well drained and cleared of all native vegetation cover. Natural meadowland, necessary for the pasturing of stock and the growing of fodder, was the second most important landscape resource. Finally, settlements needed to maintain lands consisting of woodlands, marshes, and heath for rough pasture, and as the source of fowl and fish, wood and peat.

Even if a village possessed ample landscape resources, inhabitants, ever aware of their precarious economic status, normally elected to function collectively. Often, neither annoying political systems nor burdensome taxation prevailed in these communities, and subsistence through self-sufficient effort was the rule. Thus anyone traveling through continental Europe during this time would be

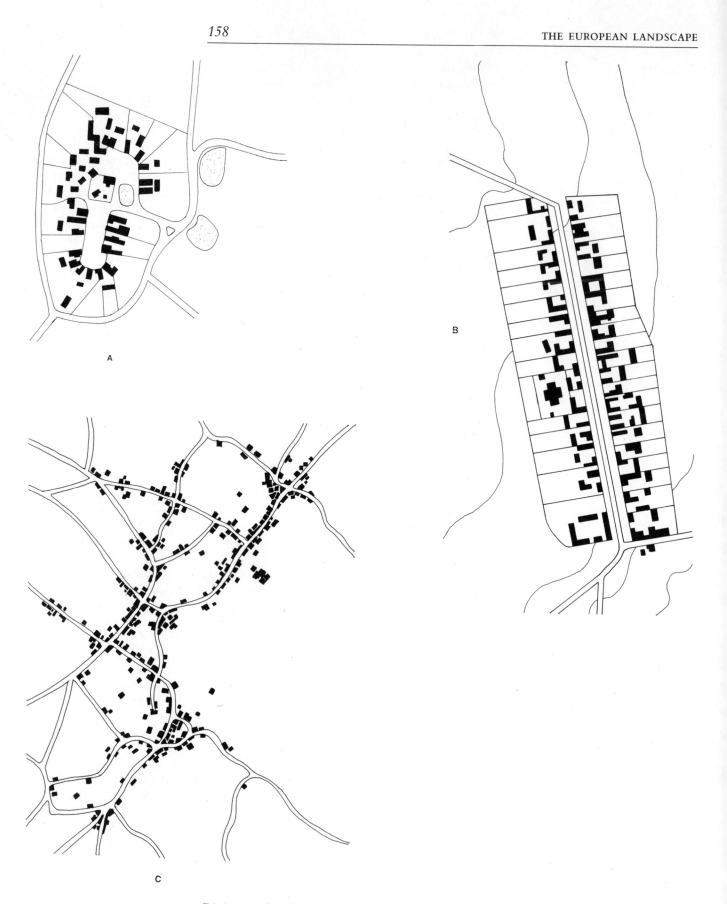

Distinctive village forms in continental Europe. (A) round (B) roadside linear (C) nebular

struck by the relative uniformity of agricultural strategy from region to region. The open field, three-field rotation strategy prevailed in the low plains from Britain to Germany. In upland areas with marginal soils, the run-rig system was common, identified by its enclosed, arable infield, surrounded by temporary enclosures for cultivation in woodlands. Further south the open field concept prevailed, accompanied by the two-field rotation system. In form, northern fields were elongated, reflecting the use of the wheeled plough; in the south, the fields were squarer. Also, terraces supporting vines, olives, oranges, and figs were a common feature of southern continental landscapes.

No doubt, some exceptions existed where local conditions required a modification of the customary standard. But throughout the continental European landscape, the nucleated village and the open field agricultural strategy prevailed. Villages consisted of timber and thatched-roof structures, a manor house and small church, enclosed demesne land, gardens surrounded by fields, meadows, and woodlands, heath or bog. The fields featured elongated tracts, formed by the wheeled furrow plough, which, in turn, consisted of smaller plots for the individual farmer.[25]

Rural settlement was, then, an unspecialized endeavor, fusing traditional practices with the demands of the particular locality. Soil, climate, aspect, and relief dictated the particularities. Everything required by the village for its sustenance came from the fields, meadows, and woodlands. Few specializations were prevalent, except for the olive and vine, the latter of which had been introduced into central and northern Gaul by the Romans.

Medieval village life followed an established seasonal routine as illustrated in this depiction of spring farming activities from "la vie and miracles de Notre Dame" by Jean de Nielot.

Towns and Cities   Urban communities, as distinct from rural settlements, existed in continental Europe through the early and later Middle Ages, though urban centers began to be a more prominent element in the landscape at the close of the age. The origins of these towns cannot always be determined with certainty but there is little argument against the notion that some evolved as early as the Neolithic period while others emerged during the classical period or during the formation of settlements during the Middle Ages. Also the idea that towns were the direct outgrowth of a particular settlement phenomenon, monastic or seignorial, assumes that economic activities during the Middle Ages were solely agricultural, without taking into account other industrial or mercantile functions at particular locations.

What is important is the recognition of certain elements, including landscape phenomena, that tend to give a certain settlement the prominence to evolve into a complex town. These include a favorable, elevated site, protected from natural or human disturbance. This might be a position along a waterway, trade route, or as some have postulated, the proximity to an important ecclesiastical center, fortified complex, or manor, each of which relied on a reasonably efficient agricultural base for existence. Towns in Belgium, for example, tend not to occur on Roman foundations but in the proximity of an important stronghold or monastery. However, many urban sites in former Roman lands trace part of their origin to Roman influence, including cities in Gaul and the Rhine-Danubian borderlands. Regardless of their origins, towns served multiple functions: social, economic, ecclesiastic, and even military.

Roman Gaul is the most prominent region to examine when considering the evolution of towns founded on classical activities. The Romans did not avoid founding towns on existing Gallic sites, since many of these were established regional centers and were part of a preexisting route system. In some cases, as at Autun, new towns sprang up below the old defensive site when the need for military advantage no longer existed. Other communities evolved directly from Romanized settlements to become regional centers. Many Roman towns have subsequent settlements occupying the original site and were continuous settlements from the Roman period. Some dropped their Romanized names and took up the name of the indigenous people as the name of the community—for example, Lutetia, which became Paris, for the native Parisii. The tendency for people to continuously occupy Roman sites is attributable to Gallic site selection skill as well as Roman engineering ability in the construction of improvements, roads, bridges, aqueducts, and foundations.

In France, Christianity helped to preserve many of these communities. As the religion spread northward from Provence to the Rhone and Soane valleys, certain towns became important religious centers, including Lyons, the first bishop's see in the region. The conversion of the population in towns like Arles, Narbonne, Toulouse, and Tours followed. During and after the Carolingian period, the migrations from the east enabled additional towns to be added to the ecclesiastical roster, so that, by the tenth century, there were seventeen archbishopric centers. Though these centers formed the nuclei of ecclesiastical divisions in France, it was not until 1000 A.D. that ecclesiastical communities were able to shed their fortified purpose and become flourishing centers of trade and industrialization.[26]

In the later Middle Ages, towns also evolved around castles, monasteries, bishops' landholdings, manors, and kings' residences, since artisans, tradespeople, and agriculturalists could expect some economic benefit from living in proximity to these settlements. Tenth- and eleventh-century strongholds spawned towns at Chateauroux, Nort, Alençon, Mirepoix, Cluny, Sens, and Narbonne. Some royal estates, including Charles the Great's residence at Aachen, eventually

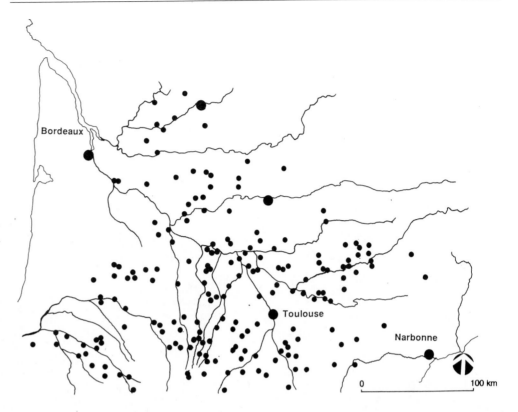

General distribution of French Bastides in southwestern France after 1240.

developed into towns. Bastides, though a slightly later phenomenon in places like the Garonne region, were newly created settlements, and were organized in a geometric form, usually rectangular. At times, a particular landform might dictate another settlement form, circular in the case of a hillside, elongated for a valley. Regardless, the Bastides were often the limits of the agricultural frontier, perched on the edge of a forest. Their economic base was agricultural, but their fortified quality and free population—a result of being founded by either a noble or royal individual—helped to imbue these communities with an independent spirit.

Roads and Trade Routes

Villages, towns, manors, and monasteries formed centers of economic and cultural activity in the continental landscape, but equally significant were the routes that linked these centers to one another, and at times, helped to stimulate village formation. For some, including individuals from Italy or Spain, roads afforded the opportunity to bring finished goods to northern markets. For others, the roads were important as pilgrimage routes to important ecclesiastical sites, the roads to Santiago and Rome being major examples. From London, then by ship across the channel, one could travel along an established route that crossed France, passed Lyons, snaked through the Alps via the Mt. Cenis pass, linked with Turin, and terminated at Rome. Similarly the roads from west-central European towns, including Paris, Bourges, and Arles, conveyed pilgrims through the town of Ostabat to Santiago.

Roman roads, constructed by military personnel, formed the basis of the engineered road system south of the Danube and west of the Rhine. Roman engineers had carefully constructed the road to conform to existing physical conditions, but, though the system remained useful for merchants, soldiers, and others, the roads suffered from lack of maintenance after the decline of centralized government. Yet many of the Roman roads survived to convey individuals to

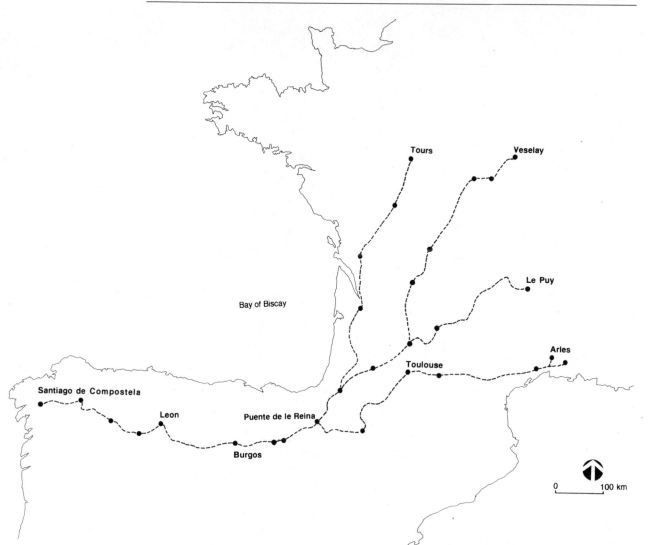

Pilgrimage routes within southwestern Europe during the eleventh century.

various points, and there is evidence that many were improved during the Middle Ages. By the later Middle Ages the road system in continental Europe formed a pattern of north-south, east-west routes. During the Middle Ages, routes into Italy brought visitors to Rome along circuitous roads through the Alps. Not until the thirteenth century was direct north-south access achieved. The St. Bernard, Mt. Cenis, St. Gotthard, and Brenner Passes connected French and German lands with Rome and important trading centers in Italy. The Gotthard Pass, opened in the early thirteenth century, formed a direct link between Basle and Milan. Further east, the Brenner Pass played an important role in the extension of Venetian commerce into south Germany. The Crusades, begun in the eleventh century and enduring for a hundred years, added to the traffic along these routes, and others that were established to convey the nobility and their armies to the Levant.

FEUDAL DECLINE

While rural communities, monasteries, manors, and fortified settlements together gave form to the continental European landscape throughout the Middle Ages, feudalism, the economic mechanism that linked these elements, began to decline by the thirteenth century. The demesne, for example, was at its height in the ninth and tenth centuries, primarily directed to the production of cereal crops.

By the eleventh century the demesne concept also had declined, due to changes in the manorial system. Specifically, tenants, rather than serfs, were farming more and more demesne land.

After 1200 the system weakened further when landowners began to demand cash instead of labor from their tenants. Also, from about 950 to 1300 economic objectives began slowly to shift from low-yield agricultural production, enough to sustain the individual settlement, to more intense production stimulated by a population increase, the upsurge in urban centers, industialization, and the spread of the monetary economy. Then followed the Black Death in the fourteenth century, which caused a dramatic decline in the population and a shortage of labor. A smaller labor force left major landholders with fewer workers, affecting agricultural production and reclamation. As a result, successive centuries witnessed the upsurge in peasant holdings, consisting of leased but inheritable allotments. At this point European culture had crossed the threshold from the older agricultural order to the new urban system.

ENVIRONMENTAL ISSUES

Between the fourth and twelfth centuries continental Europe acquired the foundation of much of its urban and rural pattern. Not surprisingly, these changes in the landscape accompanied alterations in terrestrial and aquatic environments. Mostly these changes were the consequences of a gradual expansion of human activity into uninhabited regions. Smith identified agricultural practices, pastoralism, and urbanization as significant changes to the environment.[27] The occurrence of these events during the early Middle Ages in continental Europe combined with long-term activity in the Mediterranean to confirm essential human habits that would affect the quality of the entire European landscape throughout the succeeding millennium.

Before humans began to significantly alter the quality of the European landscape, nearly 80 percent of the land was covered in forests. About two-thirds of this cover has disappeared during the last thirty-five hundred years. Deforestation during the early Middle Ages occurred on the local level, interrupting the essential functions of the woodland ecosystem by breaking down the exchange of water and energy between the soil and atmosphere. Clearing wooded lands for agriculture also eliminates habitats. The creation of arable land from preexisting forest lands removes the forest debris and exposes the soil, especially during fallow or before the crop has matured. Even with a crop at a mature stage, a portion of the land is exposed to the elements, thereby hastening the effects of rain and wind.

During the early Middle Ages, population growth necessitated an expansion of cultivation. The manorial system and the spread of settlement stimulated agricultural production until the later Middle Ages, when plague reduced the population and the labor force. Prior to the plague severe erosion due to agricultural practices may have been the exception rather than the norm. Bayless-Smith's[28] data indicate that only two out of fifteen cases of alluvial aggradation in medieval Britain were related to agriculture.[29] Though the effects of agricultural expansion up to the thirteenth century did not include massive erosion, the Black Death altered this balance, by reducing the peasant population to levels insufficient to maintain feudal landscapes. The rate of erosion appears to accelerate in the fourteenth century, coinciding with population and economic decline.

Blaikie and Brookfield clarify Bayless-Smith's findings by identifying three issues affecting the relationship of humans to the landscape during this period. The first pertains to local social customs and the effect certain habits have on landscape quality. Land allocation, ploughing techniques, and land maintenance are primary concerns. The second involves particular demographic conditions, population counts for example, and the extent such numbers effect the agricultural system and the landscape, possibly rendering one or both susceptible to physical extremes, including flood and drought. The third concerns the health of the social system and its ability to care for the landscape, including stress and exploitation of the labor pool and their effect on management of the landscape.[30] Inevitably, each is tied to the amount of energy a society has to put into the task of preventing landscape degradation.

Since the principal economic strategy of the early Middle Ages was agriculture, most human energy was devoted to developing, maintaining, and protecting the components of the agricultural system. Whether the activity was practiced in manorial, monastic, or independent settlements, the demands on the landscape resources were the same. Sufficient land had to be available for the benefit of a community. Medieval agricultural settlements faced the same dilemma as communities of earlier civilizations, as they grew and natural arable land became scarce. The open field system anticipated the need to expand arable land by designating forest and moor as common property to be used as auxiliary agricultural space when required.

Draining of marshes and low-lying areas was another method of assuring sufficient arable land. During the phase of early German settlement in Gaul, most draining of low-lying areas had only a local effect, usually to extend the arable landscape enough to provide for the needs of the community. Colonization stimulated the cutting and burning of forests and the creation of dikes and embankments in poorly drained areas along the Rhine and beyond into Western Europe. Marshy lands in the plains of France were not appreciably affected by Roman activities, but were slowly reclaimed during the eleventh, twelfth, and thirteenth centuries through engineering efforts associated with the abbeys. In the region around Flanders, small hamlets appeared along the dikes within the drained lands. Settlers performed rudimentary drainage tasks between the Elbe and Gascony, thereby establishing free colonies. Larger-scale draining began in the northern areas of continental Europe in The Netherlands, Britain, and northern Germany. In The Netherlands, land reclamation began by the year 1000 and reclaimed lands from rivers and the sea. Reclamation in these areas has been conducted on a grand scale during the twentieth century, but the concepts stem from local practices during the Middle Ages.

The exact degree of impact these reclamation activities had on the landscape during this period is difficult to assess without precise data, but we suspect that it was noticeable. Tribal groups migrating into alpine regions cleared beech forests to make loess lands available for cultivation. After the decline of Roman authority in the region and the increase in population, there was extensive clearing of forest lands on older soils and glacial moraines. However, severe erosion was not as prevalent in continental Europe as it was in the Mediterranean, due to landform, vegetation pattern and quality, and agricultural practices. Also, a forest area could be expected to regenerate within a short span of time. Only when extensive grazing continually occurred in an area would the land not revert to timberland. In Britain, which was extensively forested, livestock raising resulted in the development of moorland vegetation associations on preexisting forest lands. Roughly one-twentieth of the early forests of Britain survive the extensive clearing of lands for cropland and pasture.[31]

The link between urban activity and landscape degradation is more difficult to substantiate, but Blaikie and Brookfield[32] contend that the period between the eleventh and thirteenth centuries stands as an indicator of urban impact on landscape quality. As we shall see, continental Europe was overpopulated in relation to the technical means of assuring adequate agricultural production. As a result, the rapid extension of settlement into lands previously unused for agricultural purposes occurred at this time. Further, most of the effects associated with modern urbanization, including air pollution, temperature alteration, landform reconfiguration, increased storm runoff, and urban encroachment on arable lands were features of settlements during this period, though on a smaller scale than at present. As such, the significance of these activities is the adoption of environmentally deleterious habits that humans have carried into modern times.

In sum, it appears that urbanization, agriculture, and reclamation in continental Europe during the early Middle Ages established a pattern of urban and rural development for subsequent centuries. Settlement occurred either in areas established by previous Roman activity or in lands that were suited to the formation of communities and the establishment of agriculture. Larger landholdings eventually accrued to the nobility, clergy, and ambitious lay individuals. By the thirteenth century, when the feudal system waned and settlements flourished, urbanization began to accelerate qualitative changes in the landscape.

NOTES

1. Jean Gottman. 1969. A Geography of Europe. *New York: Holt, Rinehart and Winston.*

2. George Hoffman. 1977. A Geography of Europe: Problems and Prospects. *New York: Wiley, p. 5.*

3. Ibid., p. 9.

4. George Hubbard. 1937. The Geography of Europe. *New York: Appleton-Crofts, p. 54.*

5. Ibid., p. 59.

6. Ibid., p. 58.

7. Gordon East. 1966. An Historical Geography of Europe. *New York: E. P. Dutton, p. 57.*

8. D. B. Grigg. 1975. The Agricultural Systems of the World. *London: Cambridge University Press, p. 136.*

9. Robert Trow-Smith. 1967. Life from the Land. *London: Longmans, p. 56.*

10. Hoffman, op. cit., p. 48.

11. Donald Matthew. 1983. Atlas of Medieval Europe. *New York: Facts on File, pp. 10–11.*

12. Grigg, op. cit., p. 140.

13. G. E. Fussell. 1972. The Classical Tradition in West European Farming. *Rutherford, N.J.: Farleigh Dickinson University Press, p. 65.*

14. G. E. Fussell. 1968. Farming Technique from Prehistoric to Modern Times. *Oxford: Pergamon Press, p. 36.*

15. Fussell, 1972, op. cit., p. 66.

16. Grigg, op. cit., p. 160.

17. Trow-Smith, op. cit., p. 52.

18. Fussell, 1972, op. cit., p. 51.

19. Spiro Kostof. 1985. A History of Architecture. *New York: Oxford University Press, pp. 283–84.*

20. East, op. cit., p. 76.

21. Julia S. Berrall. 1966. The Garden. *New York: Viking.*

22. East, op. cit., p. 86.

23. Albert Demangeon. 1947. Problems of Human Geography. *Paris: Armand Colin.*

24. East, op cit., p. 96.

25. Ibid., p. 100.

26. Ibid., p. 115.

27. *Catherine Delano Smith. 1979.* Western Mediterranean Europe. *London and New York: Academic Press.*

28. *T. P. Bayless-Smith. 1979. "Prehistoric Soil Erosion in Britain: Evidence from Fenibog and Mire Deposits," unpublished paper. Detail cited in Piers Blaikie 1987.*

29. *Piers Blaikie and Harold Brookfield. 1987.* Land Degradation and Society. *London and New York: Methuen, p. 139.*

30. *Ibid., pp. 139–40.*

31. *Ibid., pp. 78–79. See also Hoffman, 1977, pp. 1125–27.*

32. *Piers Blaikie and Harold Brookfield, op. cit., p. 140.*

8

The Late Middle Ages: Urban and Rural Landscape Development

For the seven centuries after Roman decline, European landscape development centered on agricultural and settlement expansion within regional and local political centers, much of it occurring in the lands north of the Alps, where migrants labored to convert the land to agrarian settlements. Despite constant instability instigated by the internecine warfare and the economic inequities of the feudal system, agriculturalists slowly expanded their activities into unsettled lands in western Europe as agricultural production attempted to keep pace with the demands of an expanding population. Gradually, European lands were domesticated, as settlements—some linked to a feudal arrangement, others evolving from the efforts of independent agriculturalists—were established.

Between 1200 and 1400, agrarianism gradually shifted to urbanization. The year 1200 marked the beginning of a perceptible decline in the feudal system, which could no longer serve the best interests of common individuals. First in northern Italy, and later throughout Europe, urban centers began to compete with the rural feudal system by offering individuals the opportunity to pursue a livelihood free from the constraints of the landowner and peasant arrangement. During this period, Europe sustained the rise of the Lombard cities, the Crusades, strife between empire and papacy, and the rise of scholasticism. The fourteenth and fifteenth centuries witnessed a decline in institutions and the formation of modern counterparts. Many of these events grew out of gradual political transformations, beginning with Charles the Great and concluding with Frederick II's inevitable failure to preserve the Holy Roman Empire. The loss of empire on the death of Frederick in 1250 shifted authority away from the aristocracy and onto the urban centers, especially the communities that comprised the Lombard League in northern Italy.

POLITICAL AND SOCIAL CONTEXT

By 1200 European cultural geography had acquired a structure that roughly defined the boundaries of subsequent European states. The process began in 843 with the Treaty of Verdun and divided Western Europe into three compartments, spanning the landscape from north to south, creating three political regions: to the west, the French lands; to the east, Germanic areas; and in between, Thuringia, running from the Baltic through Italy. The reason the division crossed physiographic boundaries was to assure an equitable share of natural resources to each of the three regions. The boundaries established by the treaty remained in contention through subsequent centuries, with Thuringia forming the bulk of the disputed area. Meanwhile, Moorish kingdoms continued to exist on the Spanish peninsula. Isabella and Ferdinand expelled the last Islamic rulers from Granada in 1492, a milestone in the gradual development of Christian kingdoms and accompanying reconquest.

Throughout the period there was a progressive shift from the small, autonomous feudal domains to the formation of larger states. Islamic influence in Spain had existed for some time, and the Ottoman Empire solidified into the dominant political force in the eastern Mediterranean by the thirteenth century. Eastern Europe witnessed the emergence of Poland, Russia, and Hungary. Western Europe was slowly taking shape politically despite the internecine fighting between competing kingdoms in France and England. Only Italy, the heart of the old Roman Empire, failed to attain political unity until later in European history.

At the beginning of this period, numerous smaller units—duchies, ecclesiastical lands, church properties, and small urban settlements—formed a mosaic of landscape ownership. Some would remain intact in subsequent centuries, namely the urban lands; others would gradually disappear with the development of larger political states in Western Europe in the sixteenth and seventeenth centuries. But as long as feudalism prevailed in various regions, so too would competing forms of agrarian activity. Thus, physical alteration of the landscape remained a function of local activity around farms and villages throughout Europe.

Unlike the period of Germanic migrations into western Europe, the late Middle Ages were initially calm and prosperous, allowing a population explosion to take place through the early fourteenth century. However, the aristocracy continued to focus its attention on fighting over local disputes. The appalling losses by the French at Agincourt and the interminable strife of the Hundred Years War in the fourteenth century cast a pall over the continent, and with the Black Death of 1347–49, depleted the populations of all the social classes. The fifteenth century was a period of slow recovery. Thus, the years between the twelfth and fifteenth centuries fall into two phases: an earlier period of rapid population growth and land reclamation, and the later, after plague and wars in the thirteenth and fourteenth centuries, a slow recovery phase.

The formation of settlements and the conversion of the landscape into agricultural lands brought western Europe to a point where the business of agricultural economies, fostered by the feudal system, spawned the development of urbanization in the region, first in Italy, then in surrounding countries. Settlements had always relied on their surrounding landscapes for sustenance; this dependency on the resources of the land continued to be a primary economic consideration for communities in Europe. Nowhere was this more apparent than in the Italian peninsula, where in classical times, cities had been the predominant cultural and economic centers; after centuries of decline in these areas, the cities in Italy once again were the major element of the cultural fabric. For Western Europe, the decline of feudalism and the rise of commercial centers throughout the landscape constituted an urban revolution, the precursor to the Industrial Revolution of the eighteenth century. Technological innovation, economic diversity, and entrepreneurship flourished in these centers, thereby lessening the dependency on agriculture as an economic base.

The expansion of population and the development of urban centers altered the social and economic system of Western Europe and fostered a shift from a feudal to a monetary economy, notably the payment for services in cash. Due partly to population declines in the fourteenth century and the rise in the influence of the Church, which endeavored to discredit the aristocracy as a useless anachronism, the feudal aristocracy found it increasingly difficult to maintain a labor force on the large estates. As the cities began to prosper, individuals accumulated extra cash and bought goods and services with the local currency, the Florentine florin being the first minted by a medieval city, in the early thirteenth century. With cash on hand, and an expanding population, wealthy urban dwellers began to invest in agricultural lands, further subverting the old feudal order.

By the end of the thirteenth century a settlement pattern had formed in Western Europe, consisting of farms, small villages, and larger communities. Outward from these settlements individuals attempted to extend arable lands by reclaiming forests and lowlands. Depending on the particular region in Western Europe and certain agricultural practices inherited from antiquity, agriculturalists worked according to the needs of the local inhabitants and available resources. By the fourteenth century, rural life began to wane due to effects of plague and warfare, stimulating the decline in feudalism and the rise of urban centers and urban industry. Towards the end of the 1300s the age of agriculture began to decline as cities offered individuals the opportunity to develop alternative livelihoods. By 1400 the European landscape reflected this shift in economic strategies, as urban and rural landscapes acquired distinctive identities.

AGRICULTURAL SETTLEMENT SYSTEMS: NUCLEATED AND DISPERSED COMMUNITIES

Agricultural communities were the focus of rural landscape identity during the late Middle Ages, as the population continued to expand. The previous millennium had been a period of human adaptation to a range of environments, along with a gradual increase in the population. For example, by 1300 the population in the western Mediterranean was roughly the same it had been in the first century A.D.; between the tenth and fourteenth centuries the population in Italy, Britain, and the Rhineland doubled, necessitating an expansion of arable lands beyond established communities. As we have noted, Demangeon identified general categories of settlement at this time in Europe:[1] one resulted from nucleated villages, settlements formed around a prominent physical or cultural feature; the other featured dispersed settlements, individual occupied holdings spread throughout a region and not forming concentrated settlement patterns.

The oldest nucleated settlement pattern was the open field village, consisting of scattered landholdings surrounding the community. As noted, the landholdings were an agglomeration of arable strips, and also included meadows and communal pasture. The second form of nucleated settlement was the linear village, appearing in cleared forest margins and drained marshes, whose adjacent agricultural lands were divided into individually owned parcels. Many of these occurred in the Low Countries and northwestern Europe, and on the Hercynian lands of the Black and Bohemian Forests. The latter included landscapes containing villages with dissociated fields, a configuration particular to Mediterranean Europe. Topography influenced the evolution of this pattern: from the earliest times settlers founded communities on elevated sites, some quite precipitous, to afford protection from invasion and natural disaster.

According to Demangeon, there were three major categories of dispersed agricultural settlement. The first resulted from primary dispersion, and appeared early in the landscape, generally in the Masssif Central, Cornwall, Wales, and Norway. The second was a secondary phenomenon when peasants moved from villages to the surrounding landscape to form individual farmsteads. These included the Bastides of Provence and many villages in Britain that formed due to the enclosure of common lands from the fifteenth to nineteenth centuries.[2] The third category was dispersed settlement that evolved into nucleated villages due the clearing of land around a landholding and the subsequent establishment of a community by individuals migrating from established villages. Many feudal and monastic landholdings acquired this pattern when peasants were allowed to form settlements on the demesne. Individuals received land from the overlords, but were required to cultivate the remaining demesne, a practice lasting until 1200 when the growth of a monetary exchange system caused the landowners to

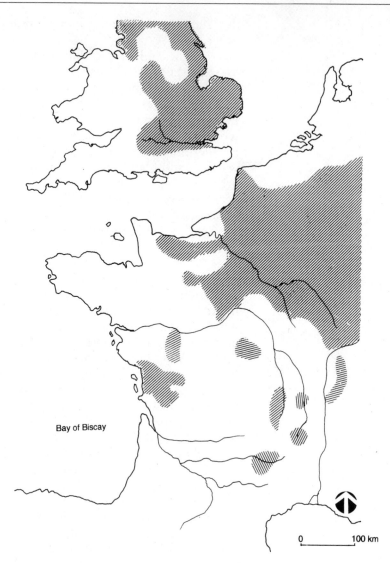

Conjectural distribution of nucleated settlements during the Middle Ages in western France and southern England.

Bay of Biscay

0   100 km

demand cash for rent. This pattern of rural settlement was not an absolute standard, but the general composition in the late Middle Ages. Death and warfare depleted the overall population of Europe in the fourteenth and fifteenth centuries. France, for example, had a population of about 19 million, which by the end of the Hundred Years War had declined by one-third. The demise of the demesne quickened with the population decline due to the Black Death in the fourteenth century; not until the fifteenth and sixteenth centuries was there a reversal in the decline of rural activity.

LANDSCAPE RECLAMATION

Near the end of the first century A.D., Tacitus remarked that the lands of Central Europe were "either bristling with woods or festering with swamps." We have seen how conditions prior to the eleventh century necessitated local reclamation measures if a community outgrew its arable lands. During the early Middle Ages, when the population increase was negligible, the forests functioned as an important local resource. Forest lands provided pasture for cattle, horses, and pigs, and were especially valued for the amount of food they could produce for swine. Some attempts at land reclamation occurred during the early period of settlement after the decline of Roman influence. In the sixth century individuals established farms, planted vines, and cleared lands, and during the rule of Charles the Great, officials were ordered to clear lands and to prevent the return of the forests. In general, though, the instability wrought by the Norse in the north and the Moors in the south prevented the spread of arable lands and settlements until the eleventh century. Most areas of Europe were still blanketed by native cover consisting of woodlands, gorse, heath in the north, and in the south, garrigue and maquis scrub.[3]

By the eleventh century political stability had begun to return to western Europe. The fierce invaders from the north and south had gradually been absorbed into the social fabric, and the decline of feudalism and the beginnings of the formation of monarchial states laid the foundation for peaceful settlement and land reclamation. Settlers successfully reclaimed extensive areas of marsh and forest lands for agricultural use, instituting the great age of land clearance. France, for example, sustained major land reclamation in forest and marsh areas. Forest clearing changed continuous stretches of woodland into fragmented segments.

In coastal zones, marshes, and forests, farmers transformed poorly drained and overgrown regions into lands suitable for settlements and farming activity.[4] In the northwest corner of the Continent, inhabitants of Flanders and Holland instigated the first attempts to wrest from the sea lands that had been inundated by it centuries before. During Roman times, the sea had invaded coastal Flanders and covered an area occupied by Roman colonists. Inhabitants along the Flemish coast constructed artificial mounds for settlements, and then in the eleventh century began the long process of reclaiming the submerged lands. The struggle to reclaim the land included accompanying marine inundations, but by the late Middle Ages the inhabitants of the region had established *polders,* areas of drained and diked lowlands, putting into effect a reclamation strategy that persists into the present. So skilled were the inhabitants of the lowlands at reclaiming lands, that their methods were applied to the fens and marshlands of Britain and to the marshlands of Germany. The Italians followed the lead of their neighbors to the north by reclaiming lands in the Po Valley that had been lost due to the neglect of Roman land reclamation efforts. Major gains in land reclamation occurred there between the eleventh and thirteenth centuries. The effort yielded large areas of land for cultivation and pasture. Near Mantua citizens were responsible for embanking and maintaining the river thereby preserving holdings in the region, which were generally small and shared on a leased basis. In the heart of the French landscape, around Rochefort and La Rochelle and north of the Loire Valley, agricultural areas grew with successive reclamation efforts. These marshy lands, unaffected by Roman settlement activities, progressively became the sites for settlement and agriculture between the eleventh and thirteenth centuries.

Land reclamation during this period included aggressive removal of forests to make way for settlements. It was not until after the primary stages of settlement that forest clearance occurred on a large scale, excluding the stretches of forests removed along the Rhine during Charles the Great's reign. Earlier, during the time of the Caesars, the Germans viewed the forests as the home of their divinities and as protection for their small villages, an attitude echoed by the Slavic and Scandinavian peoples, who saw the great stretches of woodlands as the repository of important resources, including fuel, timber, game, honey, and rough grazing land. When the German settlers, in particular, settled in former Roman lands, they applied their energies first to the reestablishment of arable areas, then to forest clearance, as their settlements required more agricultural land. In Britain, forest removal began after the incursion of Anglo-Saxons and Danes. Germans and Flemings worked to clear forest lands in Transylvania.

Aerial view of Dutch polders.

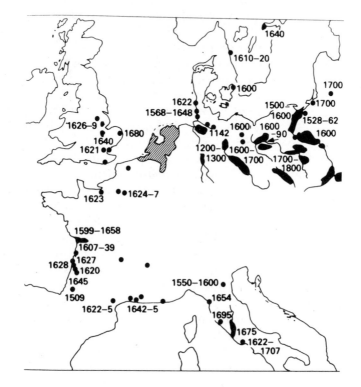

Incidence of land reclamation activities from the sixteenth to nineteenth centuries in Western Europe.

Around established communities, *assarting,* or the clearance of forests around a settlement, extended arable lands. The exception to the clearing activity was the large stretches of forests protected by royal authority for hunting purposes.

Nor was all forest clearance a result of agricultural expansion. Shipbuilding in the Mediterranean helped to deplete forests in southern Europe. In England, Germany, and Russia the demand for charcoal by local iron smelters also hastened forest clearance. By the end of the Middle Ages, the landscape had begun to alter appreciably from the combined forces of reclamation.

AGRICULTURAL STRATEGIES; COMMON LAND AND TRANSHUMANCE

During the late Middle Ages, urban areas demanded constant supplies of agricultural produce; most of this was grown within a relatively short distance of the settlement. In rural areas large and small land holdings continued to support a range of agricultural activity. In northern Italy and in Central Europe agriculture and animal husbandry helped shape the landscape; southern Italy and substantial areas of Spain supported large-scale pastoralism.

Despite such diverse land uses, agriculturalists relied on one of two traditional approaches to farming. The first stemmed from classical practices, mostly applicable to the thinner, drier soils of the Mediterranean. These persisted in the south and consisted of a two-field rotation system and reliance on the Mediterranean triad: wheat, vines, and olives. The growth of cities in the north stimulated investment in agriculture and the expansion of arable lands. Population growth and the expansion of agricultural land spurred the revival of irrigation in the Po Valley. Though this region, with its ample areas of arable lowlands, boasted one of the most advanced agricultural systems in Europe, a majority of the agricultural progress in Italy by the fourteenth century was the result of the

Aerial view revealing cleared and forested lands within an English agricultural zone.

production of small farms. Some of the agricultural activity produced goods for the textile industries, including mulberry trees and woad, the source of a yellow dye. Other farms directed their energies to food production for the cities and towns, dispensing with the traditional fallow system. By the fourteenth century new crops were appearing in the region, particularly in Lombardy, where mulberry flourished in the uplands and rice, flax, and fodder at lower elevations.

The second approach can be traced to the response by the Germanic settlers in the lands north of the Alps to the climate and soil conditions of the region and consists of the advances in agricultural procedure effected by these groups. Vigorous land reclamation activities in western France opened up lands to tenancy, and stimulated the building of small farmsteads protected by a ditch, hedge, and embankment. Farms included a dwelling and garden plot for the propagation of peas, beans, flax, and hemp. Outlying plots were for growing wheat, the surrounding forest provided pannage for livestock and timber for farmstead construction. In the east settlers cut into the forests, and with the aid of Dutch and Flemish workers, contained streams and drained marshes, including the bogs between the Elbe and Oder Rivers. Some technical advances in agriculture, namely a new harness, the stirrup, refinement of the iron horseshoe, improvements in the plough, and the use of the three-field rotation system, allowed the settlers in the landscape north of the Alps to produce crops in the soils of the region. Aided by the horse and larger draft teams, farmers adopted an intensive approach to cultivation, including more use of existing lands as the supply of new land began to decline after 1250.

In addition to these strategies, certain regions adopted measures to secure lands for priviledged factions. For example, as a response to the need for greater agricultural output on manorial lands, individual feudal lords in England began to enforce the enclosure of lands which had traditionally been consigned to the peasants as common landscape. The old system of shared land, in which the holdings of one worker were scattered through the manorial lands, had become inefficient, and a hindrance to individual initiative. By consolidating the scattered parcels, the farmworker obtained 20 or 30 acres in large enclosed fields. Around 1236 the Statute of Mertain became law in England, giving landlords the authority to enclose part of the common waste, woods, and pasture. But few of these early enclosure attempts were successfully enforced, since peasants uprooted hedges and filled in ditches at night. Only later, during the reign of the Tudor kings, did the enclosure acts begin to have an impact on the organization and form of the landscape in England.

In the Mediterranean region, Spain and southern Italy both sustained an increase in pastoralism by the thirteenth century, stimulated by the development of the commercial potential of wool in northern Italy, Flanders, and England. Transhumance had been a feature of the Italian peninsula during the early Middle Ages, but by the middle of the fourteenth century, after the Black Death, the practice spread in the south, especially when the Dogana acquired royal support for its sheep-raising and herding activities. The *latifundia* in southern Italy, for example, were ideally suited for large-scale pastoralism. As in Spain, where sheep raising had expanded with Moorish occupation, the size of the flocks in Italy rapidly increased. In both Spain and Italy the pastoralists were able to generate support from the government due to the sizable taxes the states realized from the exportation of wool. Governments enacted legislation to support the woolen trade, which favored the pastoralist over the farmer.[5]

URBANIZATION

Urban centers, as opposed to rural agricultural settlements, existed in Western Europe from the decline of Roman authority to the formation of monarchical states in the late Middle Ages. Some communities persisted on the sites of former Roman centers; others evolved from agricultural, commercial, monastic, or other ecclesiastical activities. "Copenhagen" means "the merchants' harbor," and Paris was the geographical center for several rivers and important land routes. Trade and merchandizing gave life to Venice, Florence, Ghent, and Bruges. Regional fairs spawned cities in the Middle Ages, including Milan, Lyons, and Frankfurt. As these communities began to mature, Europe began to display a dichotomy of urban and rural landscape patterns.

Several factors helped to stimulate urban growth by the thirteenth century, principally the decline of feudalism and population expansion. Competition between the aristocracy and the church stimulated the formation of states, whose rulers formed free cities. Also the introduction of a monetary exchange system, a result of the weakening of the feudal system, whetted people's appetite for monetary gain through investment and made the opportunities in the independent cities appealing to ambitious individuals. Specialization of labor and production, which in turn produced goods and services that were not within the purview of the agriculturist, further strengthened the position of the towns in Europe.

Though in the thirteenth century the bulk of economic activity still centered around agriculture and rural life, cities such as Florence, Venice, Paris, and London were quickly gaining in population and in importance as economic centers. Textile centers in northern Italy, Flanders, and England, prosperous cities of the Hanseatic League along the Baltic coast, ecclesiastical centers, and coastal ports all sought to maintain and improve their position in the trading economy of Europe. Some of the most dynamic communities first appeared in central and northern Italy, due to the region's location along east-west trade routes and a

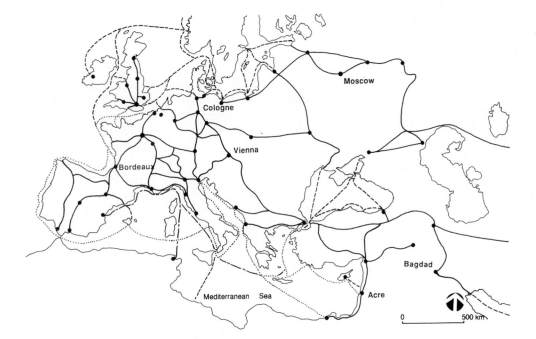

Principal trade routes and merchant centers.

less effective feudal system. By the thirteenth century lively trading centers dominated the northern Italian landscape, each claiming economic authority over its respective region and each contributing to the emergence of powerful city-states. Not until the Black Death decimated their populations was the growth of these centers halted, and in many instances temporarily, since many of these communities have survived into contemporary times.

By the fifteenth century, it is possible to distinguish diverse categories of urban patterns in the Mediterranean and Western Europe. Morris groups towns into five categories: towns of Roman origin, fortified military bases or burgs, towns founded as village settlements, Bastide towns, and planned towns or towns established during the Middle Ages for commercial purposes.[6] Some of these tended to predominate in specific regions. Bastides, for example, appeared in France, England, and Wales; burgs tended to exist north of the Mediterranean in Western Europe. Each of these centers manifested political and social processes that encouraged the founding and development of the urban landscape during the late Middle Ages.

URBAN AND RURAL DICHOTOMY

With the ascendancy of urban centers, Europe began to regain a system that reestablished a clear distinction between urban and rural existence, a custom traceable to earlier societies. During the Roman Imperial era, the wealthy expended energy and money to create residences in the countryside in order to escape the congestion and unhealthy quality of the urban areas. Cities primarily functioned as commercial centers where the masses jostled for survival, an environment that the wealthy avoided during unhealthful summer months. The Roman cities that survived Imperial decline hung on as administrative centers for the Church. During the Middle Ages, the development of cities happened slowly, picking up momentum only as population growth and economic output increased after the eleventh century.

Medieval urban centers grew out of the local economies, mostly as nodes of agricultural exchange. Excluding settlements of Roman origin that functioned as church administrative centers, cities of the late Middle Ages evolved over centuries, acting as centers for the production and exchange of goods that were outside the purview of traditional agricultural activity. The wealthy of the late Middle Ages rarely viewed urban centers as cultural hubs, as did some Romans who were privileged to live in the better merchant centers—Pompeii, for instance. Twelfth-century communities represented the culmination of rural effort; they were the coalescence of agricultural societies: settlements that produced enough surplus to support the urban dwellers who had the responsibility to produce specialized nonagricultural goods for trade.

The formation of urban centers and the increase in urban populations created a new locus for many individuals. The structure and function of urban landscapes reemerged in the consciousness of the later Middle Ages, albeit in a somewhat altered form. Despite the presence of Roman patterns in some of the centers, few evolved in the Middle Ages as clones of the classical city. The European attempt to reconcile apparent dualities—church and landlord, Latin Christianity and Germanic Aryanism, reason and superstition—removed from the classical precepts of form, imbued these early centers with a distinctive morphology. Not until the fifteenth century, when the Renaissance produced individuals with the confidence to challenge medieval precepts, would the urban centers of Europe begin to reacquire the formality of the classical past.

In the northern half of Italy, the death of Frederick II in 1250 opened the way for cities to function as independent and autonomous communities. The opportunity for economic gain attracted individuals from the countryside, who were encouraged to adopt a trade and become citizens. Guilds maintained standards of production and conduct; citizens were eligible to participate in the community government. By the fifteenth century powerful ruling families controlled many Italian cities and successfully extended their authority into the surrounding countryside. The result was a landscape in northern Italy consisting of discrete political entities ruled for generations by powerful families, including the Sforzas of the Duchy of Milan, the Medici of the Republic of Florence, and the Orsini families in Rome.

As the fortunes of the ruling elite increased, the towns also acquired greater physical complexity. All space within towns had a relative value, depending on proximity to the market square. Intensive use of every square foot was preferable to the expensive undertaking of tearing down the town walls and adding more space. When pressure from the surrounding suburbs made the prospect of town expansion a certainty, community leaders would initiate the construction of new walls. Often the land acquired by this expansion was carefully apportioned to guarantee sufficient open space, including provisions for new market spaces, market gardens, and groves. Florence initiated the construction of new walls in 1172, and again in the sixteenth century, primarily to fill the need for adequate town space. A decline in the population during the fourteenth century left Florence with more space than it needed, which made the city appear more spacious during the Renaissance. Not until the nineteenth century, during a phase of rapid urban growth, did the city acquire the structure that it has today.

A graphic summary of the relationship of these towns to the landscape appears in the work of Italian painters during the thirteenth and fourteenth centuries, including the Sienese painter Ambrosio Lorenzetti. Lorenzetti's frescoes in the public palace in Siena are often cited for their quality of pictorial technique, but the subject of the works, models for good and bad government, also communicates contemporary notions about the relationship of urban elements and surrounding landscapes. In his painting of good government the city is the focus

Medieval Florence circumscribed by sixteenth-century walls. (Benevolo, Leonardo. *The History of the City.* Copyright © 1980 MIT Press.)

Ambrosio Lorenzetti's Good Government *wherein town and surrounding landscape from a cohesive unit.*

San Gimignano occupies ridge lines, a traditional pattern that left hillsides open for agricultural activity.

of the composition, with the landscape, a secondary focus, providing the natural context to the scene.[7] The civic core appears to support prosperity and liveliness; the surrounding landscape contains evidence of rural industry and stability. Similarly, Sereni's[8] twentieth-century impression of the landscape as viewed by fifteenth-century travelers to the region includes a sense of order to the cultivation of trees and shrubs along the slopes of northern and central Italy.

Lorenzetti's paintings illustrate the theoretical level of urban and rural accomplishment of the period. How accurate his images were for all cities remains conjectural. Each prosperous city in the northern Italian region had its own history of formation and growth. Despite some commonalty of terrain or material, communities evolved in distinct patterns, mostly in response to the configuration of the immediate landscape and the aspirations of the citizens. Hill towns spread out along ridge lines, low-lying communities formed around important natural or human-made elements, coastal communities clung to elevated terrain. The forms of these towns embody complex physical and social issues, many of which belong in other discussions. But the result was the eventual formation of communities that, despite their sophistication, owed their identity to the qualities of the site and to the spatial sensitivity of their inhabitants. The growth of towns initiated the formation of urban landscapes in concert with existing rural landscape use, forming a dichotomy of urban and rural landscape quality for the succeeding centuries.

ITALIAN URBAN LANDSCAPES: SITING AND SPATIAL ORGANIZATION

No one factor determined the location of cities and towns in the northern half of Italy in the thirteenth century. Some flourished along major trade routes; some evolved around ecclesiastical centers; others sprang up on preexisting Etruscan or Roman foundations. Florence, which was by the late Middle Ages a major center, was a holdover from prior Roman and Lombard settlements, occupying the floodplain along the Arno River. Venice, no more than a small coastal village on mudflats in the ninth century, grew into the most powerful community on the Adriatic. Only the possibility of severe flooding discouraged the formation of towns in unsuitable locations, at least until the fourteenth century when technology allowed for the drainage of lowands.

In central Italy many prominent communities evolved elevated sites, in response to prevailing natural conditions. Often these sites had accommodated previous human occupation, especially during the Etruscan and Roman periods. A millennium separated classical Rome from the thirteenth and fourteenth centuries, but latter-day inhabitants of these sites placed as much value on the intrinsic qualities of elevated lands as had their predecessors. Hilltops and ridges were above the floodplains, and were blessed with natural light, ventilation, views, and drainage.

Thirteenth-century towns in central Italy had a spatial order determined by functional necessity. Unlike the Romans, with their predilection for geometrical ordering of civic spaces, builders of thirteenth- and fourteenth-century cities tied civic form to prevailing physical conditions. Also, people living in the towns and countryside of late medieval Italy were the inheritors of both Latin and Teutonic traditions; both formed the sensibility of the society, one that combined the experiences of cultures from north and south of the Alps. The Romanesque architectural elements that appear in artists' frescoes attest to Mediterranean and northern European sensibilities that inspired Italian urban form of the period. Classical order, especially in the structuring of a form, stems from Roman logic; the articulation of architectural detail, including the expression of organic forms, contains shapes and patterns that attest to pagan northern European influences. Consequently, late medieval towns in Italy had a dual quality in their arrangements, both intuitive and logical. Building masses appear to grow out of specific utility, from the need to enlarge a structure to accommodate an addition to the family. Urban space has a similar utilitarian appearance, stemming from the need to function as an outdoor commercial space, as a place for gathering in front of an important civic or religious structure, or, on occasion, as a stage for important civic festivals.

What distinguished one community from another was its landscape context, specifically the nuance of existing topographic form and elements; these determined the pattern of urban space and the form of each community. Since many of these communities occupied elevated sites, especially in Tuscany and Umbria, there was a similarity of form between one town and another when viewed from a distance. But each hilltop or slope had topographic features that could not be erased in the process of urban articulation. Instead these features were the armature around which the towns took shape, and, on close inspection, imbued each town with a distinct morphology.

Two hilltop cities in central Italy, Siena and San Gimignano, typify urban landscape development between the thirteenth and fifteenth centuries. Siena, tracing its origin to Etruscan and Roman occupation and during the early Middle Ages the site of an influential monastery, remains as one of the important examples of urban form dating from the late Middle Ages. The community was the focus of commercial activity stemming from grape and olive production and animal husbandry in the region. Siena, like the model in Lorenzetti's frescoes, dominates its hillside location and commands the surrounding landscape.

Viewed from an aerial perspective the modern town and surrounding landscape interpose, amoebalike, reflecting the ridge line and valley configuration of the site. Major streets align with the contours along the hillside; some connecting streets run steeply across the slope; building heights, materials, and detailing still conform to city codes enacted in 1242. The principal public urban space, the Piazza del Campo, rests in a small, natural cleft in the hillside, and functions as the forecourt to the public palace and as the site of the twice-yearly *palio*. Since

Aerial view of Siena and the Piazza del Campo and Palazzo Pubblico.

the thirteenth century this spirited horse race between competing city quarters has turned the space into the site of one of the principal social events in central Italy.

As the most dramatic response to the original site configuration and the principal urban landscape feature, the Piazza del Campo is neither classically formal nor entirely intuitive in its shape and structure. The fan-shaped space derives its form from a depression in the hillside, and, faithful to the natural site, is contoured to convey drainage to its lowest point. Only a fifteenth-century fountain, situated at the upper elevation of the space, interrupts its simple, organic configuration. Narrow streets, enclosed by three- and four-story structures, link the various city quarters to the piazza.

Not all communities in north central Italy acquired the cultural significance that Siena enjoyed. But many were quite prosperous and, with sufficient capital and public spirit, evolved remarkable urban landscapes. San Gimignano, about 20 miles north of Siena, occupies several ridges above the Val di Chianti. The economic foundation for the town was the local production of saffron, used in the manufacture of drugs and dyes, and the annual yield of fine grains and wines. The present-day community remains well preserved, though only fifteen of its seventy-two original towers remain standing. In its prime the town bristled with towers, projecting an imposing image on the surrounding landscape. The hillsides surrounding the community enveloped it in a swath of agriculture and open space. The town's interior was a compact assembly of residences, shops, and *palazzi*. Its chief magisterial building, the Palazzo Popolo, dominated the town center, bounded by a college and important private palaces.

Unlike Siena, with streets and small piazzas issuing from the grand Piazza del Campo, San Gimignano had an urban landscape more typical of the smaller communities in the region. The principal town space, the Piazza della Cisterna, roughly triangular in shape and less than 150 feet long at its greatest extent, is only slightly larger than an adjoining space, the Piazza del Duomo. The two, linked by a narrow street and arcade, form the principal public spaces and the

The Piazza della Cisterna, San Gimignano.

meeting point for the main streets of the community. Smaller streets and ways wind through the community, occasionally punctuated by small neighborhood squares. Within these smaller streets and spaces, form and material express a conscious unity: window and doorway details, reminiscent of those specified by Siena's building codes, lend visual stability to the spaces.

RIVER AND COASTAL SITES: FLORENCE AND VENICE

While the hill sites in north central Italy were ideal for the development of independent communities in the thirteenth and fourteenth centuries, some of the most important economic centers in Italy evolved in low-lying landscapes. River margins and coastal edges at both the east and west coasts of the Italian peninsula were the sites of these cities. Genoa, Pisa, Amalfi, and Venice were viable commercial centers, due to their proximity to established trade routes. Each was a fledgling maritime republic by the tenth century and enjoyed the fruits of commerce generated during the Crusades.

Florence: Cultural Developments and Urban Form

Florence, sited on the banks of the Arno River, evolved into a major Italian commercial center during the Middle Ages. Bolstered by its dye industry and successful banking activities, the city remained one of the most independent communes in the region, dominated by wealthy families, especially the Medici.

Though each of the towns named above figured prominently in the economic growth of northern Italy during the thirteenth century, each began life prior to the late Middle Ages, often inauspiciously. Florence first appeared along the banks of the Arno at about 200 B.C., founded by individuals from the nearby Etruscan hill town, Fiesole. The site of the original village lay east of the later historic city until Sulla's army destroyed the community in 82 B.C. Under Julius Caesar, the Romans established a new community along the Arno, west of the original Etruscan settlement. Founded as a military camp, the settlement featured a rectilinear layout. The camp was no larger than 500 meters on each side, enclosed by a wall with gates through which ran the north-south and east-west main roads. At the intersection of these roads lay the forum—in medieval times the Mercato Vecchio, or Old Market—and now the site of the Piazza Vittorio Emmanuele. The Romans built a bridge across the Arno River, the venerable Ponte Vecchio, to facilitate north-south movement along the via Cassia. Though at this time the community did not rate above the rank of a provincial town, it boasted baths, temples, aqueducts, and an amphitheater.

With the decline of Roman dominance, Florence and its neighbors sustained invasions from Germanic tribes, beginning in 405 and lasting through the period of the Holy Roman Empire. Florence was home to successive German groups, including the Lombards, who maintained authority in the region from 568 to 774, and later the Franks and Hohenstaufens. The legacy from this period included the division of Tuscany into counties, or *comitati*, jurisdictions administered by the major cities in the region. Also during this long period of foreign domination, the cities slowly evolved their own local authority, at first consisting of small assistance groups, and by the thirteenth century a unified civic authority, or *commune*. With the death of Frederick II many of the Italian communes assumed an independent position in the political fabric of Italy. A few, including Florence, while attempting to steer a course between the church's ambitions and invading armies, capitalized on their independent status to create a cultural florescence in the fine arts, architecture, and literature. Dante, Petrarch, and Machiavelli were all products of Florentine culture.

By the middle of the thirteenth century, Florence had evolved into a major production center, with a range of artisans and merchants concentrated in the

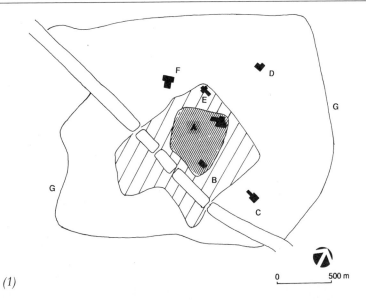

(1)

(2)

(1) Organization of Florence during the Roman era (A) Roman quarter (B) medieval quarter straddling the Arno River and enclosed by twelfth-century walls (C) Santa Croce (D) San Marco (E) San Lorenzo (F) Santa Maria Novella (G) 16th century wall. (2) Present-day site of Roman settlement.

historic town center, still defined by the original Roman walls. Bolstered by its own silver and gold coinage, the city maintained vital links with France, where Florentine products sold briskly.

Part of the wealth generated by this activity was applied to improvements to the city. During the earlier Middle Ages most of the Roman urban elements had been buried under refuse; subsequent accumulation raised the level of the city 6 to 10 feet by the thirteenth century. Upon this material rose the late Middle

Ages settlement; it still exists within the heart of modern Florence. At this time, one important improvement was the construction of new walls, the first in a succession of structures to enclose the suburbs that had grown beyond the old Roman walls. The project, begun in 1172 and completed four years later, expanded the city's area threefold, and for the first time enclosed a part of the town on the left bank of the arno. Another project instituted by the community was the paving of the city streets, begun in 1235, and completed in 1339. Between 1320 and 1380, the city established a new residential area north of San Lorenzo. Unlike the compact neighborhoods of the old quarter that opened onto small squares, dwellings within this district were built on elongated lots to face the street and a rear garden. Since most of these dwellings did not contain an interior courtyard, the exterior gardens were the principal spaces where a family could spend time tending to plants in the fresh air.

Urban space in Florence also began to show signs of change in form as the city changed from a medieval town to a prominent commercial center. For six hundred years the Piazza della Signoria, adjacent to the Palazzo Vecchio, had been the center of Florentine civic activity. By the fifteenth century the space had begun to shed its purely medieval appearance, mostly by physical additions that lent a modicum of Renaissance structure to the space. These included the line of sculpture that projected beyond the palazzo and joined the two volumes of the piazza. In addition the Loggia dei Lanzi, a fourteenth-century addition, forms a spatial link between the Uffizi and the piazza.

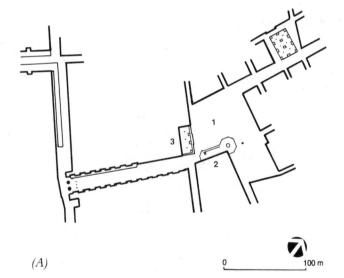

(A)

0   100 m

(B)

(A) Piazza della Signoria, a late medieval urban space. (1) piazza (2) Palazzo Vecchio (3) Loggia dei Lanzi. (B) View into the piazza with the fountain of Neptune and a bronze statue of Cosimo the Elder projecting from the facade of the Palazzo Vecchio.

Venice: Site Evolution and Organization

When northern invaders began to attack Mediterranean lands in the fifth century, inhabitants along the northeast coast of Italy sought refuge on the small islands in the brackish lagoon formed by the Brenta, Sile, and Piave Rivers. The 500-square-mile lagoon, most of it a few feet deep, studded with shoals and occasionally cut by river channels, was an ideal site for small villages during periods of invasion. Protecting the lagoon from the open Adriatic were the *Lidi,* a line of outlying sandbanks.

During the Roman period the lagoon supplied salt and fish to the prosperous cities along the northern Adriatic coast. But northern invaders, beginning with Alaric's Goth army in 402, spilled into the peninsula, forcing coastal inhabitants to gradually expand their occupation of the small islands in the lagoon. At first coastal inhabitants occupied the islands only during times of invasion. However, by 466 there were enough permanent settlers to form a tribunal government. During the Lombard invasions in 568, permanent settlements appeared on the islands of the Rialto, forming the heart of contemporary Venice. Around 726 the Venetians banded together to elect their first administrative leader, bestowing the title of Doge.

In 811 a peace treaty between Charles the Great and his Byzantine adversaries brought stability to the region and stimulated an increase in building activity on the Venetian islands. However, the poorly drained islands could not at this time sustain an increase in population, since the Lidi appeared insufficient to protect the expanding community from the Adriatic Sea. The inhabitants responded to these conditions by instituting land reclamation projects, including the construction of canals to drain the islands and the buttressing of the Lidi. As the islands were drained, new one- and two-story buildings appeared, built from lightweight materials to prevent subsidence. A few of the more important structures required stone facades, especially the firm, white variety from Istria, across the Adriatic. To compensate for the subsidence, builders drove pilings into the ooze to form a platform foundation for the stone structures. Many of these pilings remain today, almost a thousand years after they were driven into the soil.

These reclamation and construction projects eventually defined the configuration of Venice and established the morphology of the city. For the next several centuries, the populace continued to add to the initial pattern by constructing important ecclesiastical and administrative structures, including the church of St. Mark, begun in 832 and rebuilt after the fire of 976 that destroyed more than 300 buildings. Gradually, residences appeared along the canals and formed neighborhoods, each with a small piazza. Eventually the city became a honeycomb of small squares surrounding the dominant Piazza San Marco. Adjacent to the entry to the basilica, the piazza first appeared in 1177, as part of urban improvements undertaken to upgrade the appearance of the town. Previously the space had been the site of the old church of San Geminiano and an orchard. The Doge purchased the orchard and removed the church; the space was then paved in brick in a herringbone pattern. He also required the owners of the structures surrounding the space to link their buildings with arcades and arches. The present trapezoidal shape of the piazza was the result of these improvements, including the two long north and south facades of the Procuratie, built between 1480 and 1640.

A smaller piazzetta also took form at this time, mostly resulting from the removal of a wall that blocked access from the piazza to the water and by the placement of two columns brought back from the Middle East by a Venetian adventurer. In 1264 workers paved the space; between 1329 and 1415, builders replaced the wooden bell tower built in 888 with a brick structure that stood until its collapse in 1901. The newest additions include three flagpoles erected in

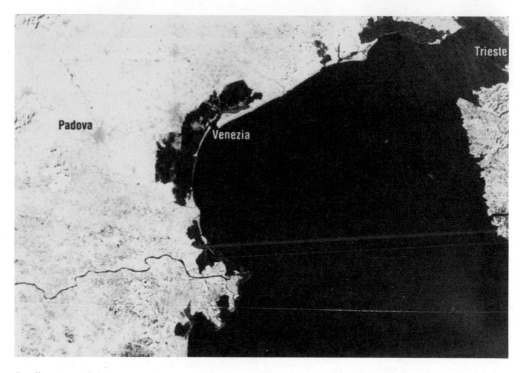

Satellite view of the Venetian region. The lagoon and Lido are in the upper center of the photograph.

Aerial oblique view of Venice, the lagoon, and the modern causeway.

(A)

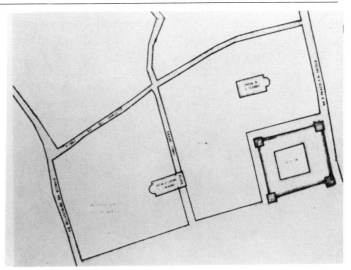

(B)

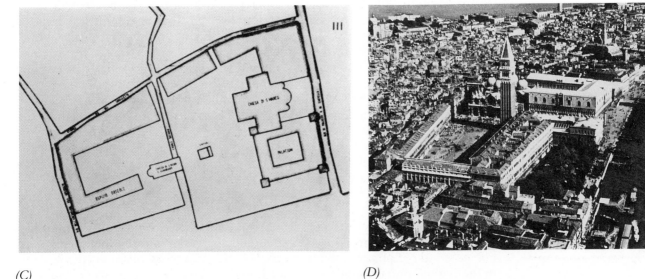

(C)

(D)

Piazza San Marco, Venice, during early stages of its development. (A) A.D. 700 (B) A.D. 900 (C) A.D. 1100 (D) the piazza today.

1505 and a new paving pattern installed between 1722 and 1735. After nearly a thousand years of development, the result is one of the most dramatic public spaces in Italy. Unlike the staid Piazza della Signoria or the bold Piazza del Campo, the Piazza San Marco is a medieval form dressed in Renaissance attire. Surrounded by neighborhoods and small squares, the piazza is the spatial heart of the city, itself dominated by its imposing campanile. The arrangement of piazza and piazzetta, and the secondary presence of implied spaces, including the area between the flagpoles and the small space off the north facade of the basilica, imbue the site with a dynamic spatial hierarchy.

SATELLITE COMMUNITIES AND RURAL ESTATES

Part of the economic and political strategy of the important northern Italian cities was the formation of satellite communities: towns that established territorial control for the main cities. For example, between 1280 and 1320 Florence undertook steps to establish control in the region by establishing *terra murata,* or walled new towns, to protect its interests in the surrounding countryside. Terranuova, one of twelve new towns, guarded the southern end of Valdarno. The town and its companion communities were roughly rectilinear in form, and featured a perimeter wall and two principal streets, with a town square at their intersection.

Through the fifteenth century farmers and pastoralists continued to derive a livelihood from the landscape by producing agricultural commodities for the bustling markets of the expanding cities and towns in the northern half of Italy. Wealthy merchants added to this agricultural activity by investing in farmsteads for their capital potential. And many of these merchants eventually established villas on these farms to provide a respite from the stress of urban life. Gradually these villas lost much of their agricultural function, as they became extensive gardens for contemplation and pleasure, as well as very visible proof of the wealth of the powerful merchant families.

By the early fifteenth century, villas, many of which retained a fortified appearance, were a feature of the landscape surrounding prosperous towns. The Villa Medici at Cafaggiola, in the valley of the Mugello on the road to Pistoia, was one of these early country retreats. It was built by Cosimo the Elder as a family refuge in times of trouble or plague; its high towers, battlement arches, and moat gave the villa a fortified appearance. Cosimo also built less imposing estates, such as the Medici villa at Careggi, where he could occasionally work in the orchards and talk with the local inhabitants.

It was inevitable that wealthy individuals would build villas that were designed for social functions rather than agricultural activity, and the next generation of Medicis did that. At Fiesole, on the hill overlooking Florence, Cosimo's son, Giovanni, commissioned the design of a villa that could be used as a site for entertaining the gifted and wealthy of Florence. As we shall discuss later, the result was a rural establishment that linked the agrarian past of important Florentine families with the urban life of the fifteenth century and the revival of classical idealism in Italy.

URBAN AND RURAL LANDSCAPES: SPAIN

Beginning in the early fifth century, Spain experienced waves of northern invasions, notably the migration of Vandals and Visigoths into the Iberian peninsula. For nearly three hundred years, until 711, the Visigoths maintained a kingdom in the region, outlasting all other northern invaders. In 629, however, followers of the prophet Mohamet began their conquests of the Middle East, beginning with the conquest of Syria, then swiftly moving eastward through Persia, and, in 643, to the Indian frontier. Turning westward, the Moslem conquerors extended their conquests across North Africa. In 711 they invaded Spain and pressed northward until they were repelled by Charles Martel in 732 at Poitiers. During the Islamic conquest of Spain, 20,000 Arabs and Berbers settled the Iberian peninsula. By the middle of the eighth century Islamic leadership in the Near East had passed from the Umayyads to the Abbasids, prompting Islamic Spain to establish an independent Western Caliphate under the leadership of Abd-al-Raqhman. In 929 Abd al-Raqhman III established a caliphate in Spain, designating Cordoba as his capital. Christian kings gradually countered Muslim efforts to rule the entire Spanish peninsula. In 1034, Sancho the Great extended the Christian lands to include Castile, Aragon, and Navarre. By the middle of the thirteenth century, Islamic activity was limited to the kingdom of Granada.

From 1100 to 1500, the landscapes and urban centers of Spain gradually shifted from Moorish control to Christian dominance. By 1300, Christian forces had retaken Toledo, Cordoba, and Seville. Only the kingdom of Granada, hugging the southern tip of the peninsula, remained in Muslim hands until 1492. Muslim influence in Spain left an indelible mark on the landscape, and during their rule, Muslim cities were renowned as cultural centers: Cordoba became one of the most cultured cities in the world, rivaled by few other European cities.

In Spain, as in other regions of the Mediterranean, settlements varied in size from large cities to small villages. A Spanish *pueblo* was any settlement, large or small, devoted to agricultural activity. Often, very small settlements were called *castillas* or *villas*. In southern Spain, villages were similar to their counterparts in France or Italy: structures grouped on a hill, ridge line, or mountain flank, most of which were walled by the later Middle Ages. A *cortijos* was an estate farm, where as many as a hundred people might live. Usually the primary estate structures faced gardens and orchards, and were surrounded by agricultural lands devoted to cereal farming. The Moors extended irrigation into dry-farming lands, forming *huertas* in otherwise inhospitable regions. A typical *huerta* near Valencia in the nineteenth century had 283 persons per square kilometer, many of whom occupied isolated farmsteads. During the thirteenth century, small irrigated plots (*rahals*) developed near villages. Later these plots evolved into sites for estates, planted with vines and fruit trees, including apples, oranges, figs, and date palms.[9] Other plots were eventually occupied as farmstead sites by colonists who banded together to form new villages.

Throughout the Spanish Reconquest, rulers attempted to reestablish settlements in reclaimed lands. In Castile and Valencia all social levels received land allotments from the crown as a way of holding new territories. Many larger cities governed smaller, peripheral villages, thereby extending urban authority into the landscape beyond the city. At the end of the 1300s, wealthy urban dwellers began to invest in rural property, beginning with the building of rural retreats near cities, followed by the purchase of land as a hedge against business problems, and concluding with the development of rural property for its agricultural potential. All of these measures tended to blur the distinction between urban and rural landscapes. Many cities in Spain, as well as in the rest of the Mediterranean, had a countrified appearance, while the countryside sustained urbanization, including the founding of villages and private agricultural centers. Some cities had large agricultural areas and much open space. Within the fifteenth-century walls enclosing Valencia, for example, were open lands used for intensive agricultural purposes; these lands remained unbuilt for at least two centuries following the building of the walls.

In the kingdom of Granada, where important Islamic cities steadfastly held out against the Spanish reconquest, town organization reflected that of medieval Islamic cities. The market was the heart of the city, consisting of narrow ways lined with shops; normally the market area lay close to the mosque. Wider streets, sufficient to allow pack animals to pass one another, connected the city gates with the marketplace. Outward from the market, residences spread to the city walls. Very little formal planning was evident in the arrangement of the residential quarter; housing units grew together as families increased in size. Within these housing districts, narrow, winding roads connected residential entrances. Houses were traditionally Mediterranean in their organization: the interior of the structures opened to courtyards, some of which contained gardens. Few cities featured the spatial sense of organization found in Roman cities or their progeny in the Middle Ages. The traditional cross-axis, four-part town division of Roman towns was generally absent in Spanish Islamic cities. So was the open square in the middle of the town, which initially functioned as both market and public meeting space. Islamic cities echoed the Arab arrangement, which was that of a temporary camp: houses clustered around the market and the sanctuary. In reality, the apparently haphazard organization of these cities conformed to a social logic, controlled by the mosques, fed by the marketplace, and rejuvenated by the airy residential interiors. For the average inhabitant, returning from the market or a shop to the residential quarter meant coursing along narrow streets past small squares containing fountains and arbors. Smaller mosques, providing peaceful sanctuary to the tired worker, opened to these intimate squares. In Cordoba many smaller mosques also served as schools, often directly supported by the Caliph.[10]

AGRICULTURE AND IRRIGATION PRACTICES IN SPAIN

Near Eastern agricultural practices, including irrigation techniques and the introduction of Middle Eastern plant materials, formed part of the Moorish legacy in Spain. A major influence were Islamic practices, established by the thirteenth century in southern Spain. The Islamic rulers of the Iberian peninsula included the Umayyad faction from the Middle East and Berbers from North Africa. The former transferred Middle Eastern agricultural technology and materials to the western Mediterranean, while the latter established pastoralism on a grand scale. North Africa, Italy, Sicily, and southern France were the most affected by Islamic agricultural techniques, helping to improve the quantity and quality of output.

Muslim success with agriculture stemmed from techniques practiced in the Middle East, including Syria, Iraq, and Persia. Since antiquity the foundation for agriculture in these regions was irrigation. When the Persians acquired Mesopotamia in the second century B.C., they inherited irrigation technology from the local inhabitants. By the second century A.D. the Sassanids had successfully instituted new irrigation techniques in lands above the floodplains by using *qanats,* or inclined tunnels that conveyed water from an aquifer to an agricultural area. They also constructed shallow terraces to impound runoff. Check dams across intermittent drainage ways also helped to retain soil and water carried from unterraced areas. The soils behind the check dams were ideal for cultivation, provided farmers maintained runoff during severe thunderstorms. In addition to these irrigation techniques, the Persians and their Islamic usurpers also constructed irrigation channels and drop towers to convey water from springs to farms. The result of these strategies was the proliferation of farmsteads in the piedmont region east of the Mesopotamian floodplains.[11]

Upon conquering Spain, the Moors transferred these techniques to the region, many of which were similar to Roman practices. The Romans, however, had not developed extensive irrigation systems in Spain, relying instead on dry farming to produce grain, olives, and wine for Rome. It was the Moors who introduced hydrologic techniques that enabled inhabitants to pursue intensive farming. Much of their knowledge concerning irrigation had been gleaned from Mesopotamia and Egypt at the time of Arab ascendency in those regions, thence transferred to the western Mediterranean. They were the first to irrigate riparian fields and gardens, and to construct canals, and to lift water with waterwheels.[12] They established the *huertas* in Valencia, constructed sophisticated canal systems, and encouraged the use of the *noria,* the large, scoop waterwheel.

By the late Middle Ages many Spanish huertas included sizable landholdings. The huerta of Valencia was 50 square kilometers in area, composed of numerous irrigated units acquired over the centuries. Irrigated land on these huertas fell into two categories. The first was the *rahals,* where irrigation was in constant supply. Outlying, extensive landscapes, or *regadio alfayt,* received irrigation only during times of ample water resources, including flood periods. After the reconquest, Moorish irrigation efforts continued to benefit the development of the huertas, since Moorish engineers had constructed extensive irrigation systems that included dams; minor canals; and main canals, or *acequias,* to convey water to a wide area. Moslem water rights laws helped to extend irrigation into the landscape, since water was considered common property.[13] The Moors also took care to limit the amount of runoff in hilly areas during stormy periods by constructing elaborate terraces. In addition, their engineers gave specific details for surveying and constructing retaining walls to form terraces.

Irrigation allowed Moslem farmers to successfully cultivate a range of fruits and vegetables; they were renowned for their encouragement of horticulture, and it may have helped to give the Mediterranean cultures their only technological lead over northern Europe. They introduced alfalfa, carob, rice, lemons, melons, apricots, oranges, sugar cane, cotton, and saffron. The two agricultural commodities that were not actively propagated were wine and pigs, though Islamic settlers encouraged the propagation of vines to produce currants and sultanas.[14]

Many of the Moslems' agricultural practices influenced agricultural procedure in other parts of Western Europe, a measure of their success. Contemporary scholars attempted to document whatever information, past and present, was available on the subject. Ibn al-Awam, a twelfth-century Arabic writer, compiled a work from a number of sources, that, with the *Geoponika* documented earlier Mediterranean thinking on the subject. In the following century Petrus Crescentius compiled a work that attempted to take the concepts from earlier works and apply them to the conditions of northern Italy, and Albertus Magnus also wrote extensively on agriculture.

PASTORALISM IN SPAIN

From Visigothic times through the later Middle Ages, part of the agricultural strategy in Spain was stock raising, especially sheep herding. Visigoth rulers instituted laws to allow livestock access to open lands. The Moors, with varying success, attempted to raise livestock, including cattle, sheep, horses, and goats. The horse was especially prized by the Spanish Moors, who cherished the animal for its speed and beauty, but it was sheep raising that proved to be most valuable to them. One contributing factor was the development of pastoralism in North Africa due to the incursion of Bedouins during the seventh and eleventh centuries and the transfer of transhumance to Spain. Pastoralism expanded in the Spanish lands after the Arab conquest with the migration of Berbers into the region and the introduction of merino sheep in the 1300s. By then the south to north migration of large flocks was common in Spain; the Mesta, a powerful sheepherders guild, had been formed by 1273, and by the mid-fifteenth century more than 250,000 sheep took part in the migrations. Large areas of landscape, the *mesata,* remained open to the Spanish herders, a factor that prevented the enclosure of lands in Spain.

PALACES AND GARDENS IN SPAIN

Often the ruler of a Moorish community lived outside the city in a sumptuous residence, though many cities contained a royal residence, or *alcazar.* Cordoba possessed an elaborate alcazar, although between 987 and 990, Al-Mansur built an additional administrative center outside the city walls. In 1002 civil war broke out in the region, leading to the destruction of the administrative center and an accompanying royal palace. Despite the loss of these two centers, enough remains of the Alcazar of Cordoba to provide some knowledge of Islamic garden design. Its garden, like those of other similar establishments in Spain, gives evidence of the attention paid to garden design by the ruling elite.

In both form and material, the Islamic garden owes much to Middle Eastern attitudes and techniques dating back as far as the neo-Babylonian period in Mesopotamia. As we have seen, societies in the Tigris-Eurphrates region had been sensitive to the vagaries of plant cultivation and irrigation strategy. Eventually, societies occupying the plateaus beyond Mesopotamia also became adept at producing irrigated gardens, by drawing water from below the surface through qanats.

When the Persians, under Abbasid rule, conquered Mesopotamia, a natural conjunction of technology and garden theory ensued. The Persians interpreted the Koran strictly, applying their own concepts of "paradise"—the Persian word for "garden"—to the planning of private open spaces. The emphasis on private urban open space stems from Near Eastern traditions going back as far as the neo-Babylonian period in Mesopotamia. The epitome of the Islamic garden occurred in Persia, where the Muslim concept of the "paradise garden" found acceptance and was nourished by both Persian intellectual rigor and Persia's traditional respect for irrigation and horticultural practice. The blueprint for the Islamic garden in Persia came from the Koran, which describes paradise as a lush garden, resplendent with water, vegetation, color, and pleasing sounds.[15] Islamic attention to private gardens in Persia, for example, carried this tradition into the Middle Ages, spurred on by Near Eastern concepts of paradise gardens.[16] When the Western Caliphate established its presence in Spain, many Middle Eastern design and construction techniques flowed into the society, including Persian concepts of garden design and construction.

An important example of the organization and detail of exterior spaces during Moorish rule is the courtyard of the Great Mosque of Cordoba, known as the Court of the Oranges. Construction of the Mosque begun near the end of the eighth century, after Abd ar-Rahman I purchased the Christian church that existed on the site in 785. By 796 the mosque stood on the site, supported by its horseshoe-shaped arches and elegant *mihrab,* or prayer wall. A courtyard is one of three elements included in the organization of any mosque: these elements, derived from the organization of Mohamet's house in Medina, are the *minaret,* or prayer tower; an enclosed courtyard, often containing a pool for cleansing prior to entering the sanctuary; and an interior sanctuary. What distinguishes the Court of the Oranges is the grove of orange trees that extend the line of interior columns into the courtyard.

The Great Mosque and the Court of the Oranges represent the epitome of Islamic religious design in Spain. But some of the most elegant Moorish landscapes in the region were the property of Islamic princes and wealthy individuals. One of the most outstanding is the Alcazar gardens in Seville. This lush enclave is a composite of elements produced over time by successive owners of the property. The earliest site treatment occurred during the construction of a Moorish palace on Roman foundations in the twelfth century. The palace was so large at this point that the site extended to the edge of the Guadalquivir River. A siege in 1248 completely destroyed the structure, and Peter the Cruel replaced it with a smaller palace in the fourteenth century. Because many of the builders of this new palace were Moorish craftsmen, much of the spirit of Islamic garden planning pervades the site. Seville experiences hot, dry weather during the summer, and designers of the garden took care to provide ample opportunity for individuals to spend time on the site in relative comfort. Small, compartmentalized patios, shaded by evergreen trees, instill a sense of intimacy. Water moves from a reservoir adjacent to the palace through pipes to small fountains at the centers

Court of the Oranges at the Great Mosque at Cordoba.

of the various gardens, each modestly spouting a small jet of water. The shade and sound of water are a backdrop to specific visual details, particularly the *azulejo,* glistening polychrome tiles. Later additions to the garden, especially the Pavilion of Charles V, compound the Islamic tradition, notably in the use of scale and materials. Only the later, English-style garden on the edge of the site contradicts the original Moorish design concepts.

After 1248 and the decline of Seville as one of the last strongholds of Moorish resistance in Andalusia, Ibn Ahmar turned his attention to enriching the city of Granada with public works. His attention to the well-being of the community established a base for Moorish activity—the last in Spain—to endure until 1492. For more than two centuries Granada retained Moorish traditions, often appearing more aligned to North Africa than Iberia. Part of the success of the community stemmed from its physiographic context, particularly the natural fortification afforded by the Sierra Nevada, which loom over the defensible plateau site of the city.

The Alhambra, the spectacular fortress of Ibn Ahmar, rests above the city on a spur projecting from the the foothills of the Sierra Nevada. As the last outpost of the Moorish empire the reddish citadel (it derives its Arabic name from its color) has inspired poets and designers down to the present day. When Ibn Ahmar began construction of the complex, only the scant remains of a Ziridian fortress, the *alcazaba,* remained on the site. It was he who saw the need to provide water to the palace, and did so by diverting the waters of the Darro River to the structure. To strengthen the fortified appearance of the site, he ordered the construction of walls and towers to enclose the palace. The result was an imposing fortress from whose internal chambers it is possible to view the city below. Organizationally, the citadel consisted of three parts: the older *alcazaba;* the palace, or *alcazar;* and a small village, or *medina.* The heart of the complex was the palace, consisting of interior and exterior spaces connected by passageways. Overall, the complex is an asymmetrical grouping of spaces,

The Alcazar gardens of Seville.

The Alhambra overlooking Grenada. Various rulers inhabited the site since before Roman times. The Alcazaba is on the far right; the Alcazar and Medina are in the center.

The Court of Myrtles.

The Court of the Lions. The use of animal forms was unusual for an Islamic palace.

The Canal Garden of the Generalife.

devoid of a central axis. Two important spaces—the Court of the Myrtles and the Court of the Lions—lie at its heart. The Court of the Myrtles, named for the myrtle hedges bordering the long reflecting pool, is a testament to Moorish taste and design expertise. The Court of the Lions, less restrained ornamentally, contains intersecting water channels that divide the space into quadrants. At the intersection of the channels is an elegant fountain defined by twelve lions. The two spaces create an interesting contrapuntal mood, with the lavish use of water in one space balanced by restrained use of water in the other. Before the Moors relinquished control of the Alhambra, they built a summer retreat on a hill across the ravine from the palace. This addition, the Palace of the Garden of the Generalife, fits comfortably into the hillside as a series of garden terraces crowned by an elongated courtyard with its Canal Garden. Combined with the other chambers within the palace, these spaces epitomize the Koran's image of paradise: a shaded retreat cooled by streams.

URBAN AND RURAL LANDSCAPES: NORTHWESTERN EUROPE

While the landscapes along the Mediterranean rim south of the Alps and Pyrenees evolved into distinct urban and rural patterns, the lands north of the Alps in Western Europe were undergoing similar transformations. From Germany to the British Isles, urban and rural landscapes were slowly evolving from their medieval origins, dominated by a feudal system, toward modern environments. The process of change in these lands was similar to the events in southern Europe, though the feudal ideal managed to endure longer in the north. Until the fifteenth century, the feudal aristocracy north of the Alps held out against central governments. Mainly it was the power of the nobility in the north that restrained the shift toward the style of landscape use that appeared in Italy. Eventually, feudalism lost its political and economic authority to an alliance of kings and merchants.

The transformation of urban and rural landscapes between 1200 and 1400 in the lands north of the Alps stemmed from the influence of feudalism and the slow demise of the aristocracy and the rise of monarchies in France, Germany, and England. Agricultural practices tended to be fixed by tradition: nearly all the basic agricultural techniques used by the settlers of northern Europe in the 1300s were still in use until the nineteenth century. Farmers had but one major objective: the production of wheat and rye for flour, and in the spring, the planting of oats and barley, fodder for horses. Dairying and stock breeding were secondary to the care of draft animals.

During the late Middle Ages, France, Germany, and Britain were not subject to the political or cultural forces that affected northern Italy or southern Spain, though Islamic culture had an effect on southern France along its Mediterranean coast, including influence on agricultural technique. The Lombard cities in northern Italy influenced Western Europe through their trading activities and their dedication to playing the pope against the emperor. North of the Alps the political structure reflected a gradual movement toward centralized government, stemming from tripartite division of Europe established by the Treaty of Verdun. Though this partition did not last even a generation, it set the stage for a succession of monarchial claims. Along with the move to central authority, an urban and rural landscape structure gradually appeared, distinct from the relatively insignificant urban cultures of the ninth century. Generally, the siting of settlements during the later Middle Ages, if not already determined by earlier occupation, depended on traditional criteria: the availability of water, natural resources, and security. By the twelfth century the urban pattern in Western Europe included towns of Roman origin, burgs, towns expanded from village settlements, and Bastides.

FRENCH BASTIDES

From the early Middle Ages in France, both nucleated and dispersed settlements formed communities that would evolve into urban centers. Nucleated settlements formed around prominent physical or cultural features: old Roman settlements or a strategic topographic location, for example. Dispersed settlements formed as offshoots from established settlements. Many Bastide towns and *faubourgs* (towns that sprang up beyond original burgs) fit into this latter category. The Bastide town was an important settlement strategy during the thirteenth century in southwestern France. Since these communities were dedicated to agricultural activity, inhabitants were granted agricultural land outside the community. Many of these towns exhibited common site design principles: their builders normally attempted to lay them out in a rectangular form, subdividing the interior into residential lots of equal size. Often, though, town form conformed to local topographic conditions, and the gridiron applied only to part of the community. Most were fortified, with a ditch and a perimeter wall, the latter strong enough to afford protection from small-scale attack. Inhabitants built their residences along the street frontage on their assigned plots. There was a main square, located at the crossing of the two main streets of the town; a town hall, the focus of commercial activity, normally stood in the main square.[17]

Carcassonne, originally a Roman settlement and then a Visigoth community located on a hilltop adjacent to the river Aude in Languedoc, expanded beyond its walls and formed a Bastide settlement in 1240. From then on the *cité,* the older fortification, functioned as a military fortress, while the Bastide, or *ville-basse,* grew into an agricultural and merchant center. The *cité* included two rows of walls, spiked with fifty-three towers. Its interior included a church and a castle, but does not appear to have contained a large public open space. The *ville-basse,* across the river from the fortified town, conformed to the planning ideals associated with Bastides. The town consisted of a gridiron of housing plots arranged along the two principal streets. The town square was in the center of the community off the principal north-south street.

Another important Bastide town was Aigues-Mortes, built by Louis IX in 1240 as a port for his ships bound for the Levant during the Crusades. By 1272

Aigues-Mortes, an important French coastal city dating from 1240. (Morris, A.E.J. History of Urban Form. John Wiley and Sons, 1979.)

the town was surrounded by a defensive wall with fifteen towers. Within the walls were streets laid out in a gridiron, a town square, and public buildings. Effective as a staging point during the Crusades, the community lost its port by the end of the fourteenth century due to rapid siltation of its harbor. Today the town is separated from the Mediterranean by salt marshes, and linked to the coast by a canal.

GERMAN RHINE TOWNS; HANSEATIC CITIES

The Rhine region has supported settlement from the Neolithic period and was a center of Roman activity until the dissolution of the Empire. Cologne, Coblenz, Strasbourg, Colmar, Frankfurt, Worms, and other communities accommodated pre-Roman settlers, and continued to thrive past the Roman era into the present. Cologne, named for its Roman title of Colonia Agrippina, was one of the most populated and vital cities in Europe during the Middle Ages. The town evolved from a legionary fortress on the left bank of the Rhine, and Roman streets and walls still survive. Despite a siege with the Alamanns in 355, recapture by the Romans in 356, and subsequent domination by the Franks, the town survived to be a principal Hanseatic center.

In the twelfth century local rulers added to this settlement pattern by constructing towns along the Rhine in southern Germany and Switzerland. These *zahringer*, named for their founders, the Dukes of Zahringer, were new towns built to secure the region. Those that survived, including Freiburg, Villingen, and Rottweil, formed a collection of twelve successful communities. Morris[18] cites several planning principles common to these communities: a market thoroughfare, the absence of interior spaces, a gridiron arrangement of streets, the separation of public buildings from the market street, a fortress, and a sewage system. Few towns had stone perimeter walls; instead they protected themselves with a wooden palisade and moat.

Distribution of Hanseatic communities.

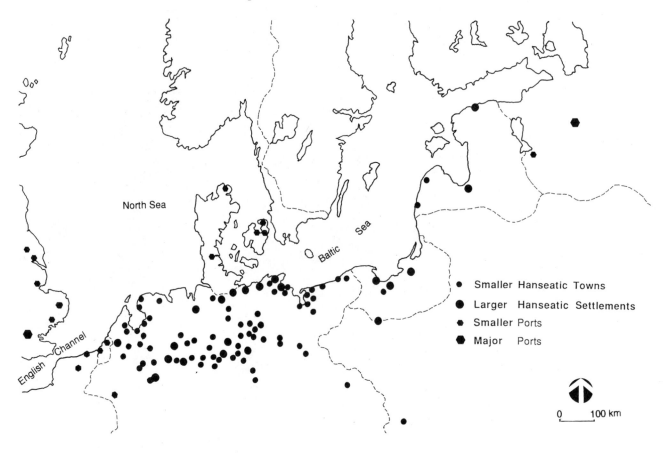

North Sea

Baltic Sea

English Channel

• Smaller Hanseatic Towns
● Larger Hanseatic Settlements
• Smaller Ports
⬢ Major Ports

0   100 km

Economically, the northern Rhine region supported numerous settlements that fed off the trading opportunities associated with the river and the Baltic coast. By the twelfth century the Rhine delta began to develop trading centers that included Bruges, Ghent, and Ypres. Flanders and Holland gradually added settlements to the region. From these lands settlements extended along the North Sea to the Baltic. Italian traders shipped goods through Gibraltar to Flanders. In the thirteenth century the Hanse league formed with Lubeck as its center. The word *hanse,* German for "fellowship," referred to the northern guilds; the league's code ordered the activities of member communities, which numbered about nineteen in the 1300s.

Trade and commerce flourished for the Hanseatic cities. They policed the waters of the Baltic coast, allowing goods from the east to reach the Baltic ports. By 1418 the league had nearly 100 members, and met in Lubeck whenever necessary. Soon after, pressure from the King of Poland and the rise of trading centers in the Low Countries ended the league's supremacy.

Part of the economic strategy of the German lands in the Middle Ages also depended on sustaining a flourishing trading activity along the Baltic. The Rhine cities were important in facilitating trade from the south to the north. The town of Cologne, for example, took the role of the principal regulator of trade on the Rhine. It controlled traffic on the river, and prospered by imposing taxes on goods delivered and sold within the city as well as goods bound for other destinations on its own vessels.

BRITISH LANDS: ENCLOSURES AND FORESTS

The quality of the British landscape in the late Middle Ages was the product of sustained human occupation dating from the Neolithic period. From as early as 7000 B.P. inhabitants of the British Isles have actively utilized their natural resources to sustain settlements. By 1500 B.C. Neolithic inhabitants had placed parts of Britain under cultivation; the Romans remarked that the population of Kent was large and the landscape was "studded with homesteads."[19] Before the Romans abandoned Britain around 410 A.D. most of the main towns and principal roads existed, the primary ports were in full operation, and London was a renowned trading center.

Human adaptation to the British landscape by the eleventh century resembled the patterns produced by the economic and settlement strategies of western continental Europe. Agriculture was the overwhelming economic force in the landscape. After the invasion of the Normans and the development of the manorial system, feudalism reigned on the Islands as it did in France and Germany.

After 1066, the Normans quickly divided the country into two parts: one was the settled portions governed by ordinary laws; the other was large areas designated by the kings as Crown lands and governed by strict forest laws. The term "forest lands" can be misleading in this instance, because many of these lands were not heavily covered with trees; many included settlements. The kings were interested in sites that could support game, and, therefore selected both open and covered landscapes. Proximity was also an issue; thus forest lands occurred mainly in lowland Britain, within reasonable reach by the king.[20]

Often the forest lands lay on poorer soil, the Normans being aware of the need to leave the best soils for agriculture. The kings avoided creating forests on cleared land. Forests at Sherwood and Exmore lie on marginal lands; others that occurred on better soil eventually gave way to agriculture. Forest laws protected game from heavy encroachment, and red deer, fallow deer, roe deer, and wild boar lived in these environments. Predators such as wolves, foxes, and cats were unwelcome; kings encouraged the hunting of such predators. Occasionally, a wealthy individual had permission to establish a private forest, though the practice was rare.

Eventually, portions of forests or lands adjacent to them became parks, mainly conceived as enclosures from which deer could not stray; Windsor Park, for example, evolved as an enclosure inside the larger Windsor Forest. Eventually, the laws protecting the forests eventually became less stringent. Two years after the Magna Charta, the Forest Charter abolished penalties, including death or dismemberment, for people hunting in forest lands. Many of the public forests in Britain today owe their existence to the laws of the Norman kings.

Enclosure did not occur only on forest lands. A distinctive feature of the British landscape by the thirteenth century was the introduction of enclosure laws to reduce the labor needed to cultivate fields at some distance from each other. Through the Anglo-Saxon period, agricultural practice depended on open field cultivation, wherever the best soils occurred in a region. The strategy fit the individualism of Anglo-Saxon life. With the introduction of the manorial system and the need to devise a communal economic strategy, the scattered landholdings gradually became consolidated into large landholdings enclosed by a hedge, or, in some instances, a stone wall.

Late medieval enclosures first appeared around 1236, legalized by the Statute of Merton, granting manor owners the right to enclose portions of woodlands and pasture. From then on, the lands functioned in various ways: some produced crops, others were suited for pasture or meadow. In some instances the lands helped to foster the rotation of crops, and, eventually, the pasturing of sheep. After the Statute of Merton, tenants also moved to enclose lands, mostly as a result of local reallotment, particularly in the coastal counties of Essex, Kent, and Devonshire. Subsequent enclosure activity occurred during the Tudor and later periods. The legacy of the enclosures for contemporary Britain is the miles of hedgerows in the countryside, imbuing the land with an important animal habitat.

BRITISH SETTLEMENTS AND NEW TOWNS

Both nucleated and dispersed settlements existed in Britain from the earliest periods through the Middle Ages. During Anglo-Saxon times, villages formed the nucleus of parishes, areas of land surrounding the villages needed to sustain the settlement. Rich landscapes yielded smaller parishes, while poorer lands meant a larger area was needed to support the village. In the Midlands the average size of a parish was roughly 4 square miles. During the manorial era, the parish included a manor house and an inn, and later a residence for the parish priest. Individuals inhabited small settlements or independent farmsteads. Most of the 13,000 villages in existence today were functioning by the time of the Domesday survey in 1086. These formed the basis for subsequent stages of landscape change in Britain, including initial settlement and clearing, enclosures, and recent reorganization of small holdings into large agricultural tracts. Formally, villages fell into one of three categories: enclosed or nucleated villages; linear, roadside villages; and dispersed villages,[21] although most often settlements did not fit neatly into one category.

Towns arose in Britain during the Middle Ages when a village grew into a trading center and small-scale industrial node. As these settlements prospered, their agricultural function tended to diminish in favor of trade and industry. Some of these commercial centers, including London, continued to flourish during the later Middle Ages. Other towns, such as Oxford, Cambridge, York, and Chester, grew in size as the economy of Britain quickened in the fourteenth and fifteenth centuries. Cambridge, a pre-Roman settlement, and Oxford, founded during Anglo-Saxon times, grew into prominence then. These and other historic towns had the advantage of affecting trade by their location on waterways, and all derived a part of their urban form from Roman or Anglo-Saxon organization.[22]

Only two Bastides appeared in England during the late Middle Ages, Winchelsea and Kingston-upon-Hull; ten appeared in Wales, built by Edward I. The English Bastides were built near preexisting harbors and were lightly fortified. Welsh Bastides appeared as fortifications during Edward's campaign to eliminate the Welsh from the region. Eight occupied sites along the coastline, and guarded important river crossings and harbors.

In addition to the Bastides, new towns were formed during the trading activity of the later Middle Ages. Most of these benefited from nearby trading roads, rivers, or ports; in fact the key to success for these settlements was the proximity of either a road or river. Some evolved along older Roman roads, often dividing parishes; others sprang up at the intersection of major routes or crossing a river. Morris[23] cites Salisbury as an example of a new town that evolved from an earlier hill town. Like Carcassonne, the old fortified part of Salisbury gave way to a new town nearer a river, the Avon.[24] The town plan was roughly gridiron in form, without any attempt to provide fortifications. In addition there was a market square and a parish church. By 1220 construction of Salisbury's Gothic cathedral had begun, which, with the Bishop's palace, occupied a prime site near the river.

ENVIRONMENTAL ISSUES

The period between 1200 and 1400 was crucial for the formation of European landscapes, a watershed for urban and rural development. Political forces north and south of the Alps drove disparate cultures to consolidate their holdings, regionally and locally, into the most coherent units since the end of the Roman period. Germanic and Moslem rulers carved out dominions in the lands west of the Elbe River, forming landscape patterns that would influence development for several centuries. Most visible were the urban centers, functioning as nodes for trade, and inspiring their wealthy inhabitants to build sumptuous country estates, so beginning the transformation of rural lands into places for leisure.

By the end of the Middle Ages, Western Europe was gradually entering the modern era. In northern Italy the old medieval system and values had begun to fade by the fourteenth century, and by the fifteenth, a new economic and social conception was in place. The process of moving from a closed agricultural society to a culture based on urbanization and industrial activity had clear effects on the quality of the European landscape, effects caused by agriculture, pastoralism, reclamation, urban expansion, and industrialization.

Agriculture in the Middle Ages followed the general practices that had been in place since the Neolithic period. Since technology had remained stable, except for the introduction of the heavy plough head and of field systems, there is little evidence of radical change in the landscape resulting from agricultural practices. The significant factor was population: as populations rose and declined during the period, demand for agricultural production expanded and contracted concomitantly. In general the population in Europe increased substantially from about the middle of the eleventh century to the Black Death in 1347–49, doubling in some areas, including England and the Rhineland. Along with this population growth, agricultural activity continued to increase until the middle of the fourteenth century.

Though not extreme, agricultural practices had two direct effects on the landscape. The first was a reduction in the extent of covered land—dense forest and mixed woodlands—that stood in the way of cultivation. The second was alteration of soil quality. Early on, inhabitants recognized distinct agricultural divisions within Europe. One, along the Mediterranean, allowed for biennial rotation (one year crops, the other fallow); the other, in the lands north of the Alps, depended on triennial rotation (grains, roots, and fallow in sequence). During this period woodlands succumbed to the axe; in other instances soils became depleted by insufficient fallow, especially in areas where intensive farming was the aim. Clearing accelerated runoff, thus removing valuable soils from a site.

In Spain and other regions where Arab irrigation technology affected agricultural practices, the use of artificial irrigation expanded intensive farming. Especially in regions where such crops as oranges, sugar cane, cotton, and rice were grown, artificial environments for agricultural production became more sophisticated.

Land reclamation often accompanied agricultural expansion and followed the rise and decline of the population during the later Middle Ages. Prior to the Black Death the agricultural economies were in a period of growth, giving impetus to a great period of land reclamation. Between 1050 and 1300, forests and marsh areas fell victim to aggressive reclamation activities. The process produced considerable arable land, but continuous forests became fragmented, resulting in a substantial reduction in the total amount of forest lands. Forest soils were often thin and subject to erosion without their usual cover. Areas not actively cleared remained forage lands. But domesticated animals feeding in these areas hastened retardation of plant associations by consuming young shoots.

One of the prime reclamation sites was the Po Valley, where clearing and drainage accelerated the rate of erosion, helping to form deltaic plains in the Po region and off the Ebro in Spain. Today we view this activity as not solely the elimination of trees and shrubs but the reduction of habitat as well. Landscape reclamation in the Middle Ages affected habitats, particularly in wetland areas which are home to indigenous flora and fauna, including fish and bird species.

Following the Hundred Years War and the Black Death, diminished populations instigated techniques to improve agricultural output. In the French

Picturesque lake that originated from medieval excavations in Britain.

Dombes region between the Soane and Upper Rhone, villagers formed artificial lakes to create fisheries. Other farmers periodically drained the lakes for use as agricultural land. But the extended area of water produced fevers, further weakening the human population.[25] Finally, reclamation was not only a matter of draining and clearing lands for agricultural production: coastal areas experienced intense reclamation efforts, especially in Flanders.

Transhumance was another human activity that affected the European landscape during the late Middle Ages. A surge in pastoralism occurred in the Mediterranean region, especially in Spain, with the introduction of merino sheep. In Britain, due to a labor shortage after the Black Death and less labor required for animal raising, there was also more interest in sheep raising than farming. By 1447 transhumance accounted for 2,500,000 sheep in Spain. In Italy by 1400 there were approximately 5,600,000 sheep in the Appenine-Apulia region, and Britain claimed nearly 12,000,000 sheep by 1340. Land for sheep raising was at a premium in all of these regions. As a result, sheep enclosures were forbidden in England during the fourteenth century, despite an increase in enclosed grazing land and the fall in the production of corn. To make room for the sheep, entire villages fell in the path of the sheep herders. In Spain, where the King controlled pastoralism, wide swaths were cut through the landscape from the south to north to permit the movement of large flocks; farmers were not allowed to block pastoralists. What once were areas of diverse vegetation associations quickly became grasslands, eliminating natural habitats.

Extractive and manufacturing activities also had an effect on the Western European landscape during the later Middle Ages. Both produced effects on local and regional environments by fostering the construction of roads and canals to bring raw resources to manufacturing centers. For example, extractive industries changed the appearance of the landscape: in Norfolk, England, where woodland

Central Spanish landscape rendered treeless by centuries of transhumance.

was scarce, industrialists used peat for fuel in the salt-making process; nearly 2,600 acres of peat were used in the process, leaving a 900-million-cubic-foot cut in the landscape. Also, farmers excavated chalk for use in agriculture, leaving pits in the landscape at sites in England and Wales.

Finally, urbanization during the late Middle Ages produced cities in which the population had risen significantly, though accurate surveys were few. London numbered 34,971 individuals by 1377. Russell[26] estimated the total urban population of England at this time to be roughly 15 percent of the total population. Life in the cities varied with the location and resources of the settlement. Mumford[27] contends that life in urban areas was not as uncomfortable as it might seen. Many of the communities had a few thousand inhabitants at most, and afforded their residents an improved standard of living compared with the vicissitudes of rural life.

Of the salient effects of urbanization, pollution stands out as a primary issue at this juncture. Most of the wastes produced during the Middle Ages were degradable materials, some used as soil fertilizers. Air quality was a problem for communities that produced goods from coal firing. Ore smelting and glass and clay manufacturing added to the pollution produced by cooking stoves and heaters. In 1273 officials in London took steps to limit coal burning. Despite these measures pollution from this source had local effects on human health as well as on the quality of vegetation in the area.

Urbanization also affected rural areas, especially as the level of affluence in cities generated a new social class intent on reinvesting its profits in the resources of rural landscapes. By the early fifteenth century, this attitude spawned new perceptions and issues related to the landscape, spawning new forms and patterns in the European region.

NOTES

1. Albert Demangeon. 1947. Problems of Human Geography. *Paris: Armand Colin.*

2. Ibid.

3. George Hoffman. 1977. A Geography of Europe. *New York: Wiley, p. 51.*

4. Gordon East. 1966. An Historical Geography of Europe. *New York: E. P. Dutton, p. 74.*

5. G. E. Fussell. 1972. The Classical Tradition in Western European Farming. *Rutherford, N.J.: Farleigh Dickinson University Press, p. 175.*

6. A. E. J. Morris. 1979. History of Urban Form. *New York: Wiley.*

7. D. B. Grigg. 1975. The Agricultural Systems of the World. *London: Cambridge University Press, pp. 137–38.*

8. E. Sereni. 1974. Storia del paessagio agrario Italiano. *Bari, Italy: Lateza.*

9. Grigg, op. cit., p. 136.

10. John White. 1987. The Birth and Rebirth of Pictorial Space. *Cambridge, Mass.: Harvard University Press, p. 97.*

11. T. Downing and M. Gibson, eds. 1974. Irrigation's Impact on Society. *Tucson: University of Arizona Press, pp. 27–34.*

12. Catherine D. Smith. 1979. Western Mediterranean Europe. *London: Academic, p. 62.*

13. Ibid., p. 180.

14. Titus Burkhardt. 1980. Moorish Culture in Spain. *London: Allen and Unwin, pp. 49–52.*

15. Julia S. Berrall. 1966. The Garden. *New York: Viking, pp. 55–56.*

16. G. B. Tobey. 1973. A History of Landscape Architecture. *New York: American Elsevier; Newton, 1971.*

17. Morris, op. cit., p. 96.

18. *Morris, op. cit, p. 109.*

19. *Clive H. Knowles. 1973.* Landscape History. *London: The Historical Association.*

20. *L. D. Stamp. 1955.* Man and the Land. *London: Collins.*

21. *Morris, op. cit., p. 82. See Hoskins, W. G. The Making of the English Landscape.*

22. *Ibid., p. 91.*

23. *Ibid., p. 108.*

24. *Ibid.*

25. *East, op. cit., p. 79.*

26. *Bertrand Russell. 1945.* A History of Western Philosophy. *New York: Simon and Schuster.*

27. *Lewis Mumford. 1970.* The Culture of Cities. *New York: Harcourt Brace Jovanovich, pp. 13–51.*

9

Humanism and Ideal Landscapes

The early 1400s were a critical transition from feudal to modern worlds, and a significant turning point in the evolution of the European landscape. Despite the persistence of feudalism and petty warfare throughout Western Europe, certain regions evolved a new landscape order based on urbanization and free market economies. Notably in northern Italy, where feudal forces had been less pervasive than in other parts of Western Europe, the landscape gradually evolved into a multifunctional entity, engendering both agricultural and leisure activity. In Italy both of these functions accrued from the rapid development of market systems, enabling resourceful and successful individuals to invest in land for monetary gain and sensual pleasure. The force behind this shift in landscape use stemmed from a fascination with classical theory, which stimulated wealthy communities in Italy to become the locus of free-spirited expression in painting, sculpture, city planning, and garden design. After centuries of religious fatalism, learned individuals in Italy proclaimed the supremacy of the human intellect in temporal matters, echoing Leon Battista Alberti's proclamation of human superiority of mental and sensory faculties.[1] Soon entire regions bore the mark of Renaissance humanism, fueled by market capitalism and the habit of prosperous individuals of viewing land as a commodity in the market system.

Free from medieval notions about land and agricultural production, merchants developed a new conception of urban and rural landscapes, based on classical formalism and linear perspective. Their legacy was a new spirit, laying the foundation for modern science and technology but producing an environmental ethic based on industrial growth and accelerated natural resource consumption. During the sixteenth and seventeenth centuries, similar and even more grandiose expressions of wealth began to appear in the land north of the Alps, especially in France, where wealthy and powerful individuals designed landscapes on a grand scale.

The catalyst for the change from medieval agrarianism to Renaissance mercantilism was a shift from feudalism to capitalism in the Mediterranean and northern Europe. By 1400 local and regional economies began to change to meet the demands of an emerging monetarism. As noted, agricultural production, for centuries dominated by the aristocracy, had maintained the feudal order and the configuration of regional landscapes. Throughout this period, cities and adjoining rural communities continued to depend on agricultural production for sustenance. Certain individuals and families continued to labor on farms as they had during earlier feudal periods, though now they traded cash rent payments for the old, feudal work-as-payment system. But as war and plague depleted the labor force many individuals could either work in the fields in exchange for cash payment or, as many chose to do, migrate to urban areas where merchants paid well for semiskilled labor. Thus, by the fifteenth century the structure of urban and rural lands began to change, resulting in the gradual demise of feudalism and the rise of wealthy individuals who imposed humanist concepts on their land-holdings. Older, feudal relationships evolved into formal landlord-tenant arrangements; sumptuous estates began to replace simple, utilitarian farmsteads.

As the landscape became a commodity in a monetary system, and as humanist attitudes began to alter the management and structure of occupied land, individuals rapidly evolved an attitude toward the landscape based on rationalism and the formal concepts of antiquity. From the beginning of the fifteenth century to the middle of the seventeenth, the approach to organizing urban and rural landscapes stemmed from a faith in experience, classical form, and linear perspective. Armed with this attitude, and bolstered by the emergence of science in the seventeenth century, Europeans delighted in creating idealized landscapes. Their fascination with the landscape as an abstract ideal prevailed, until the economic and social priorities associated with nineteenth-century industrialization and urbanization made such intellectual play irrelevant. Along the way, market economies and Renaissance humanism prepared Europe for the eventual birth of Modernism, distinguishable by its consumption of natural resources for commercial purposes and its accelerated rate of environmental exploitation.

GEOGRAPHICAL AND POLITICAL CONTEXT

The radical changes in economic conditions and philosophical attitudes described above were accompanied by equally momentous changes in the geopolitics of Western Europe. Before the fifteenth century, the political geography of the rural lands of Western Europe was related to the strength of the feudal system and the extent of decentralized authority in various regions. From 1250, when Frederick II relinquished control of the important lands he held within the Holy Roman Empire, Europe north and south of the Alps began to evolve along divergent paths. The Italians, who had managed to avoid feudalism in its extreme form, relished the opportunity to play wealthy landowners and the church against one another, which they did throughout an interminable period of regional feuding. From locality to locality, their objective was to establish local and regional autonomy, dominated early on by an important trading center such as Florence, Siena, or Venice—or later, by their fortunes of a particular ruling family, the Medici in Florence or the Visconti near Milan. Consequently, Italy evolved into a group of autonomous but interrelated regional districts, and retained this geopolitical pattern in one form or another until the middle of the nineteenth century.

North of the Alps, where feudalism had been a major economic strategy throughout the medieval period, the political structure of the landscape was beginning to evolve along national lines. Though far from consolidated, France, the Low Countries, Germany, Switzerland, Spain, and England all showed signs of falling under centralized, absolute rule. From 834, when northern European rulers had divided the land into three regions, the north moved to the unification of these regions into the modern states of France, the Low Countries, Switzerland, and Germany. By the sixteenth century these states showed greater signs of consolidation, with France emerging as a major power.

MARKET ECONOMIES AND THE ROLE OF ART AND SCIENCE

As we have noted, Europe after the first part of the fourteenth century experienced a gradual shift from feudalism to market economies. This shift had antecedents in the devastating plague during 1347–49 and the equally disastrous Hundred Years War from 1294 to 1400. The two events left Europe short of agricultural labor, thereby weakening the centuries old dynamics between serf and landowner. Yet to lay the shift from feudalism to capitalism on a declining population would be to overlook other factors that may also have weakened the feudal bond. These include the influence of long-distance trade,[2] which, until the rise of the cities of Italy and Provence, was external to the feudal network, and the possibility that tension between serf and landowner for the control of agricultural surpluses stimulated revolts. Such factors led to monetization of rents and greater peasant control over mobility, and the development of specialized skills.[3] Each of these events occurred in various regions as social context permitted.

As individuals fought to establish the terms of land ownership and use during the transition from feudalism to capitalism, they also developed a new vision of themselves in relation to the land. Far from the feudal concepts of common ownership and the cycle of labor and subsequent extraction of a part of the agricultural surplus for payment, a condition that imbued the peasant with the sense of being an inextricable element of production, the transition from feudalism established in the minds of fifteenth-century individuals the notion that land had value as a commodity in a system of private ownership and production. A pronounced objectivity accompanied the transition to capitalism, one that removed the individual from the structure of interminable production to the status of owner of land, by contract, for profit. The clear distinction at this juncture is the perceived locus of humans; the individual has shifted from the internal in the feudal system to a position of external observer and owner of land. Nowhere was this posture more distinctly illustrated than in the arts—painting, sculpture, and design—which in the fifteenth century led the way to the conception of the landscape as an objective ideal.

The arts, however, entail qualitative judgments that are not solely attributable to shifts in economic circumstances. More likely such judgments evolve in tandem with socioeconomic shifts, as new places and circumstance compel people to reevaluate values and standards. At the middle of the thirteenth century, for example, Catholic scholasticism directed intellectual life; by the middle of the fourteenth century, the Church was racked with dissent and schism, and the populace began to take the opportunity to ignore church authority and to form independent models for intellectual judgment. Wealthy Italians in the fifteenth century cast their lot with antiquity, finding inspiration in the classical worlds of Greece and Rome. New knowledge (that is, information based on scientific data) did not affect the Europeans of the early Renaissance, since individuals put more stock in classical concepts than scientific experimentation. But, in succession, Leonardo, Copernicus, and finally Kepler and Galileo, eventually established the authority of science over dogma, paving the way for modern philosophy.

Perception and Landscape Ideal

Philosophically, the principal achievement of the early Renaissance was the replacement of church authority by the intellectual order of the ancient world. Greek scholars fleeing Constantinople after the invasion of the Turks in 1453 contributed eastern philosophy to the Renaissance. The effect this had on the perception and organization of the landscape during the 1400s resulted in a substitution of Platonic idealism for Aristotelian logic. Medieval scholars tended to apply empirical deduction to their analysis of the world, while early Renaissance thinkers, though respectful of the intellectual rigor of the Scholastics, believed, according to Russell,[4] in a "reminiscent vision." At first this intellectual direction appealed to a narrow spectrum of society, which encouraged social interaction based on intellectual activity, free from the constraints of church orthodoxy. Among the adherents of Plato were Cosimo and Lorenzo de' Medici, who both supported the Florentine Academy. From Plato, learned Renaissance designers and planners established a formal system based on simple geometric figures—the circle and square—that they were convinced expressed perfection. They also had a passion for mathematics—but unlike medieval mathematical applications, which produced complex systems, Renaissance mathematics produced a formal language of simplicity and elegance. The circle, for example, symbolized the cosmos, ruled by God, and relating all subordinate parts to a whole. The geometry of the circle determined the proportions and relationship of all elements perceived by the senses. This belief in the inherent perfection of simple geometric forms was the model to which artists and planners tied their reason and emotions as they undertook creative activity.

These ideals about the landscape, which stemmed from fifteenth-century humanism, fit the communities in Europe where the shift from feudalism to capitalism removed many individuals from the agricultural production cycle of the medieval landscape. Not all individuals, certainly, but those who by birth or fortune established themselves within the new social convention of urban commercialism. Individuals who remained to toil in rural areas did so under an order bent on establishing class power. Meanwhile the urban rich applied routine mathematical concepts to maintain accurate estimates of the fruits of their holdings: the relative yield of a landholding for an upcoming year or the risk of venturing into a new agricultural enterprise. Land became a prime commercial commodity to be utilized and traded as a part of a monetary economy. If anyone dedicated to these principles could not follow this logic, they only had to view any number of the paintings produced during the period, which depicted the landscape as a place of rural production. During the fifteenth century, rural images in painting often appeared as backgrounds, filling the middle and far space in a painting. Usually these backgrounds contained the idealized elements of rural life including structures, figures, landforms, plants, and animals. Initially the paintings all had religious themes, but increased demand for the skill with which artists rendered nature eventually lessened the sacred content of paintings and heightened the temporal.

This shift in pictorial emphasis was an important step in establishing landscape painting as a genre. Realism in painting had been an element of image making as early as the fourteenth century. Fifteenth-century realism, *il vero,* played to the distinction between classes, the distinction between urban and rural, and the relationship of community to countryside. Realism reinforced the fifteenth-

(Bottom left) Idealized landscape from the fifteenth-century painting, Allegory.

(Bottom right) A Renaissance structure with an idealized landscape in the background in this fifteenth-century painting, Christ Delivering the Keys to St. Peter, *by Perugino.*

century perception of the individual as an observer of the natural order, removed from the medieval concepts of the individual as an internal element in the rural economy. It is perception, mediated by an ideal formal language and ordered pictorially by linear perspective, that controls human perception of the landscape during the 1500s. In Cosgrove's[5] estimation the "idea of landscape" at this moment reinforces the dichotomy of land as commodity and land as a subjective phenomenon communicable through art.

The effect of Renaissance thought on the perception of rural lands first appeared in northern Italy, where a modern rather than medieval outlook first prevailed in the minds of wealthy individuals. Prior to the fifteenth century lands beyond the walls of hill towns were thought to be places of agricultural hardship. Urban dwellers considered travel unsafe through wilderness areas, which everyone believed harbored beasts and marauders. The literature of the late medieval period often contained foreboding images of nature, including Dante's opening lines in his *Divine Comedy,* in which a "dark wood" alludes to error, a darker side of human nature. In fact, it wasn't until the latter half of the fourteenth century that individuals began to consider wilderness areas more favorably. In 1340 Petrach, for example, climbed a mountain simply to enjoy the view. Leonardo spent time trekking through the Alps to study flora and geology, and subsequently filled his paintings with impressions of the land. From these and other instances it is clear that a new vision of the meaning of individual presence and the way it determined environmental order had come into being.

Rural Order in Renaissance Italy

The allusory images produced by Renaissance artists, with their precisely ordered rural landscapes, did not tell the whole truth about rural life: many facets of rural existence remained unaltered by the shift from feudalism to market economies. Rural lands were still primarily devoted to agricultural production. Certain individuals owned land, others spent their days producing agricultural goods. In many regions descendents of the old aristocracy continued to own the best agricultural lands, even if the bulk of their time was spent living and trading in towns. In Italy the rural pattern evolved into a city-state model, with powerful communes controlling sizable lands. In northern Europe, community autonomy was less common, as the various regions shifted toward central government. Regardless, there was a need to sustain agricultural production, and in areas where sufficient labor was lacking, including Britain, landowners encouraged alternative agricultural activities—the raising of livestock—to assure productivity.

Northern and central Italy were the first regions to sustain changes in the landscape stemming from the new Renaissance ideal. The reason these areas experienced a burst of commercial activity was partly due to the decline in feudalism, although the secession of northern invasions, weakening Islamic influence in the region, Italy's central location along Mediterranean trade routes, and its long-standing urban tradition undoubtedly contributed to the rise of capitalist economies and Renaissance culture.[6] As numerous cities and towns gained prominence through the mercantile activity of the fourteenth century, the lands surrounding urban areas furnished the raw material required for urban survival. Migration to urban centers increased as individuals sought to improve their standard of living. Northern Italy, which had maintained a weak feudal system during the Lombard and Carolingian periods, formed independent communities, which pursued their own commercial and agricultural interests. Before the fifteenth century, the communes had aligned themselves with landowners, who had acquired outright ownership of land in 1037. Merchant and landowner factions had the means to control rural lands, and through the fourteenth century had the power to compete with established aristocratic landholders. The tension between rival factions stimulated rural investment, as the results of bourgeois material success became evident in the countryside where, as we have seen, rich merchants invested in land for capital gain and leisure.

The locus of rural authority during the fifteenth century in Italy was the city-states and their lesser town and village subordinates. Martines lists several urban and rural qualities common to many cities during this period: economic prosperity; property ownership and social contact in rural areas; control over tolls and customs incomes; and alliances with important urban families.[7] Florence, for example, controlled the landscape beyond the city as far south as present day Cortona and Castiglion Fiorentino.[8] Thus, the northern Italian landscape was characterized by a network of larger urban centers, often exceeding 20,000 residents, surrounded by smaller trading centers, which maintained regular markets and controlled the economic and political quality of the surrounding countryside.

With bustling commercial centers acting as population nodes in the northern Italian countryside, urban and rural agricultural patterns tended to respond to urban autonomy. Cities were the exchange points for land and landscape commodities. Agricultural activity generally decreased in intensity as distance from a city increased. Often some of the most productive agricultural lands lay within city walls or on lands attached to dwellings in suburban districts. Town gardens consistently produced good vines and fruit. For several miles beyond city walls and between suburban structures, farmers intensively cultivated wheat and and fruit trees on small parcels. Certain trees, including elms, supported vines and supplied wood fuel to the population during colder months. In sum, rural lands in northern Italy formed a picture of order and productivity. Foreign visitors often favorably commented on the pattern of tree and shrub cultivation, which gave the countryside the appearance of a "delicate embroidery."[9] Though the pattern appeared to stem from conscious planning, in reality it resulted from innumerable agreements between landowners and resident farmers.

The landscape near Castiglion Fiorentino.

In addition to the intensive agricultural activity near towns, traditional feudal life also persisted on large ecclesiastical or aristocratic landholdings. Open fields used for growing grains, and later in the year for pasture, remained a feature in the uplands beyond the close-in city holdings. Certain lands reverted to a natural condition during the agricultural decline of the fourteenth century; however, by the early fifteenth century land prices in Italy had risen sufficiently for authorities to reinstate woodland clearance restrictions.

AGRICULTURE AND LANDSCAPE RECLAMATION

A major problem faced by late medieval landowners was maintaining adequate production in the face of demographic changes. In France one of the most urgent problems was the need to reclaim lands lost during periods of population decline. When plague and warfare decimated the rural work force, landowners were forced to abandon marginal lands and to concentrate agricultural production on the best sites. England and Germany sustained losses similar to those of France, though Italy, especially in the north, did not experience a severe decline in production. Along the central coast in Tuscany, in the Roman Campagna, and in the south, conditions were most severe, as lands reverted to natural conditions and smaller settlements ceased to exist.

In northern Italy, land reclamation and agricultural activity proceeded with the growth of market activity in the cities. Italy's varied terrain of mountains, hills, and valleys made reclamation a necessity. In the Veneto, where lands often sustained flooding from the regional drainage pattern, the state oversaw reclamation efforts, which, between 1550 and 1650, significantly increased the available agricultural holdings. In hilly regions deforestation and soil erosion necessitated the construction of terraces retained by stone walls, though many rectangular fields lay across contours, thereby increasing runoff and the loss of valuable agricultural soils. Though writers advised farmers to adhere to ancient practices of contour farming, these practices did not appeal to farmers, due to the risk of creating standing water around vines. Also, to avoid malarial low-

Rural Tuscany still evokes the landscape order that inspired fifteenth-century sensibility.

lands, farmers in central Italy chose hillsides for agricultural production. In Lombardy, the most advanced agricultural region during the fourteenth and fifteenth centuries, drainage and irrigation systems opened lands for the planting of trees and fodder and fostered regular crop rotation and manure application.

Farmers continued to rely on agricultural techniques that had been employed since classical times. Fussell[10] summarized the general agricultural strategy through the fifteenth century, and noted a dearth of new literature on the subject of farming in Western Europe. Instead, landowners and laborers referred to the *scriptores rei rusticae,* if available, or to the works of Crescentius and other thirteenth-century writers. Few ancient texts were available in the vernacular; when printing became common in the fifteenth century, few books appeared on the new technology. Consequently, Roman authorities continued to be popular, notably Varro and Cato. In the sixteenth and seventeenth centuries the number of agricultural texts increased, including important works by Fitzherbert (1523) in England and Gallo (1556) in Italy.

The major distinction between northern and southern Europe continued to be the field systems utilized in each region. Along the Mediterranean, two-field systems, adaptable to smaller, arid lands, predominated, while three-field systems prevailed in northern regions. In Italy, where the rule was intensive farming near towns, newer crops appeared, including citrus, rice, and mulberry. Advances in technical procedures were not overwhelming, though there was some progress: for example, the use of animals for traction accompanied the introduction of the horse collar. The principal effort was an intensification of production and a habit of overusing land. In northern Italy farmers attempted to maintain the fertility of land by planting catch crops, a practice derived from Roman procedure. Also dating from classical times was the practice of growing two crops on the same land: vines grew on trees or posts; lower to the earth, farmers planted and harvested grains, which thrived in the shade during severe hot spells. Further south crops grew separately, with vines, olives, and fruit on individual plots; wheat grew on large acreages, and open lands provided pasture for sheep, cattle, and horses.

To understand what landowners and farmers north of the Alps had to confront during the second half of the fourteenth century, one must again recall the effect plague and war had had on their lands. The climate had also been a problem between the thirteenth and fifteenth century, with the occurrence of a "little Ice Age" that produced lower summer temperatures and heavy rains. By 1360 cultivation had nearly disappeared in some regions, leaving the landscape open to the regrowth of native plant material. Deserted villages dotted the land; farms stood empty where in the thirteenth century successful farmsteads had produced foodstuffs for the manor. With a population decline of 50 percent in some areas, labor was scarce, spurring a shift to sheep raising and other intensive land uses. As the feudal system continued to wane, people abandoned their traditional ways of rural survival. The most resourceful adopted commercial strategies, concentrating on producing forage crops for sale at market.

In the north European region farmers adhered to a specific routine based on three-field rotation. Only on the best lands of the southern region, such as those in Lombardy, in the areas maintained by the Moors in southern Spain, and in Flanders on land reclaimed from the sea, was there notable progress in the production of specialized agricultural products. Several countries embarked on reclamation projects, often with the assistance of Flemish technicians who had worked to expand arable lands seaward in the Low Countries. In England reclamation projects drained fens and made solid land out of marshes.

By the end of the fifteenth century, agricultural activity in regions north of the Alps was showing recovery from the rigors of the previous two centuries.

In England, where cooler weather and plague had ended population expansion into marginal agricultural areas, numerous small villages were abandoned, especially in the Midlands. Dwindling populations were insufficient for the demands of large landholdings, private and monastic. Wherever legally possible, landlords evicted remaining villagers to free open fields for use as large enclosures for cattle and sheep. Freeman or yeoman farmers also began to emerge as a potent force in the agricultural structure of England, and eventually many of these independent farmers were able to expand their holdings into sizable properties. The forces that propelled the yeoman farmer to the forefront were the same that had been important a century earlier in Italy. These included a declining population and a shift to a monetary economy, along with institution of long-term leases, insulating the leaseholder from inflation. Many yeoman farmers also embarked on livestock raising, an enterprise that required less effort than plant production and gave a greater monetary return.

RURAL INDUSTRY

By the beginning of the fifteenth century agriculture was only one of several industries to occupy a place in the rural environments of Western Europe. Depending on the resources and economic strategy of a region, industrial activity became common throughout Europe from the 1400s onward. The earliest and most successful industrial activities in Europe centered on the manufacture of woolen goods. The Flemish and the Italians both developed cloth-manufacturing centers, with the Italians gaining a virtual monopoly by controlling the dye trade. As purchasers of raw wool, the Italians stimulated sheep raising in less developed areas of Europe with ample land for animal husbandry.

By the fifteenth century the demand for wool was having a measurable effect on English agriculture. Hoskins[11] remarks that by 1500 the distinguishing feature of English lands was the preponderance of sheep, nearly three for every human. As we have seen, the shortage of labor and the net return from sheep raising favored a shift from traditional agricultural production. Livestock raising required little labor, at least compared to the effort required for traditional farming, yet it produced a high value for weight: a pound of wool, butter, or meat brought a larger monetary return than an equivalent weight of wheat. And sheep raising was feasible on land unsuitable for other agricultural activities. Because of these advantages, livestock farming became a major land use in Britain by the sixteenth century.

Wherever sheep raising occurred, there were changes in the landscape. The stretches of pasture that ran from south to north in Spain have been noted, as have the large estates in southern Italy that catered to sheep raising. In Britain the most notable change was the elimination of common fields, and their conversion to enclosed pastures. Enclosures were not new to the English landscape in the fifteenth century; portions of England had sustained enclosure activities as early as the Celtic period. These more recent enclosures stemmed from an interest in wool production and benefited the farmer by allowing him to regulate his stock and protect the flock from diseases borne by a neighbor's stock. So pervasive was the practice of enclosure that by the 1500s very little open field remained in Devon, for example.[12] In the Midlands, where some of the largest open fields persisted, landowners successfully removed tenants and enclosed the fields by planting hawthorn hedgerows. The government generally frowned on private enclosures, though it was ineffective in halting the practice. After 1640 the government ceased to discourage the practice, thereby hastening enclosure of open lands and facilitating the transformation of the English rural landscape to its modern form.[13] In contrast, the arrangement of fields in continental Western Europe continued to evidence a communal pattern due to the ability of free

Rural enclosure began in the thirteenth century in Britain and remains an important landscape element.

farmers to maintain common pastures, a practice guaranteed in writing from the late medieval period. In Germany, Switzerland, Austria, France, and The Netherlands communal law controlled village life and land use. Mostly due to these early arrangements, a great portion of Western Europe remained hedgeless and open to communal plant and stock raising. Trow-Smith[14] contends that the emphasis on enclosures and the presence of enterprising yeomen gave England an eventual technical edge in agricultural activity and hastened the "Great rebuilding" of rural England and Wales.

Another significant industrial activity that began to appear in England was stimulated by an increasing demand for cloth in Europe. The Flemish and Italian woolen industries were in decline by the end of the fifteenth century due to labor disputes, taxes, and the scarcity of wool. As England began to intensify its woolen industry, the English began to construct fulling mills that utilized water-powered mechanical beaters rather than human trampling. These mills had to be located near water, away from the large towns that had previously supplied mill labor; the result was a new rural industry that formed the nuclei of small towns in the Welsh border hills, the Cotswolds, and the Devon valleys.

URBAN DESIGN AND IDEAL CITIES

Urban centers persisted in Western Europe despite the population decline of the fourteenth century, although few new cities appeared. Northern Italy showed resilience by maintaining many of its urban centers. Of the twenty or more late medieval cities in the region, many survived into the Renaissance, though more than a few showed a decline in population by 1400. Prato had 10,600 inhabitants in 1339, but by 1357 the population had dropped to 6,000. Florence began to show some gains in population by 1460 with about 40,000 inhabitants. By 1552 the number had increased to 59,000, though the count was half of what it was in the mid-fourteenth century. These figures fit the general decline in population experienced after the plague of 1348: during the 1300s Europe had about 75 million people; by 1450 the population had decreased to 50 million. Figures similar to those quoted for Florence held for urban populations in most other parts of Western Europe, with some urban areas losing 50 percent of their population to plague alone.[15]

Population decline, though it at first severely reduced the number of people living, in the cities, was one of the chief factors in the growth of market economies and the move to urbanization and eventual industrialization. Individuals were attracted to the cities for disparate reasons: employment, a better standard of living, and security. All these factors, with the infusion of capital, stimulated creativity in commerce and the arts. Intellectually, city dwellers, especially those who managed to amass sizable fortunes, adopted a humanistic attitude toward life and the world around them. They spent time and money learning about earlier cultures, especially those that appeared to express the philosophical ideals of the fifteenth century. Though this process began in northern Italy, it spread northward into Flanders, France, and England. Between 1350 and 1500, new villages and structures gradually appeared in Britain, as new fields were being added to farmsteads. Some individuals also financed the construction of small harbors and piers, while others paid to have potentially valuable lands reclaimed from marsh and lowlands.

Each region made strides toward expanding urban environments. Yet the focus of urban evolution as a spatial event unrelated to medieval sensibilities was in the northern Italian communities, which had begun to internalize the effects of material gain at an earlier time. We have already noted the general pattern or urban and suburban order associated with these cities through the middle of the seventeenth century; urban centers tended to dominate the surrounding countryside in a paternalistic manner, with cities functioning as centers of market activity. Florence, Siena, Milan, and Venice all had a role to play in maintaining urban and rural order, often clouded by internecine strife.

City life and humanism spawned a new way for individuals to see and express the physical structure of a community and the relationship of a city to its surroundings. Technically, linear perspective and the application of classical form permitted artists and designers to visualize urban environments unrestrained by medieval concepts. A dramatic graphic expression of the medieval conception of the city is Ambrogio Lorenzetti's "Good Government in Town and Country," executed on the walls of the Palazzo Pubblico in Siena. This fourteenth-century work shows the organic arrangement of the community, with its inhabitants going about their routine. Architecture and human form appear visually unified, without the visual hierarchy associated with Renaissance spatial organization.[16] However, the relationship of the town to the countryside is distinct; the city dominates the surrounding landscape, agricultural patterns decrease outwardly from the city. Another Renaissance work, Piero della Francesco's painting "Ideal Town," shows the city as a Renaissance individual thought it to be: ordered, arranged in space by linear perspective, defined from the human point of view. The surrounding landscape is absent, implying that it is unnecessary to the comprehension of urban order. As Cosgrove states, the city *is* landscape. Yet it is a landscape without the integration of architectural and human form that appears in earlier medieval work. Reduced to geometrical abstractions, all forms assume an idealized shape or poise, while the linear perspective dictates urban order within a rational context.[17]

Florence, the birthplace of this new visual order, was a highly civilized city and the principal source of Renaissance ideas. Very early in the fifteenth century, Florentine artists and architects evolved an intellectual strategy to order pictorial space, and quickly expanded their ideas to the realm of urban order. As we have

(A)

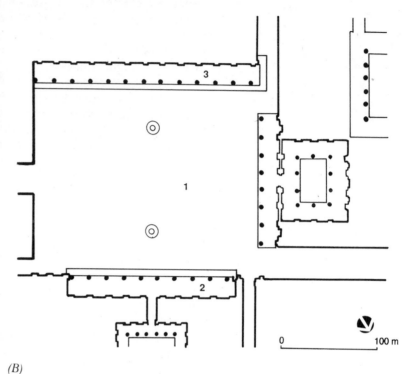

(B)

(A) Piazza Pio II in the
fifteenth-century planned
community of Pienza.
(B) Piazza Annunciata, an
example of fifteenth-century
Renaissance planning.
(1) piazza (2) foundling
hospital (3) Sangallo addition.

seen, fifteenth-century humanists eschewed the Aristotelian world of the Scholastics and adopted a new sensibility based on Platonic concepts. Their study of the ancient past engendered precise aesthetic rules, though these standards lacked the natural flexibility inherent in antique sensibilities. The circle and square, because of their geometrical purity, were thought to apply to the human form and architectural design. The Roman architectural theorist Vitruvius had had similar ideas, and judging from the presence of his manuscript at Cluny, medieval designers were also aware of these concepts.[18]

Linear perspective was the other major visual device adopted by Renaissance designers to order two- and three-dimensional space. From the scientific work of Alhazen, an Arabic mathematician, knowledge of this technique spread to Italy. Alhazen had correctly observed that the eye sees light rays reflected from an object, and that these rays form a cone from the object to the observer. Renaissance artists, including Brunelleschi and Ghiberti, formed the school of the *perspectivi* and applied the results of their optical investigations as they worked to create the illusion of lifelike form and movement in space. The full significance of perspective appeared in the theoretical writings of Leon Battista Alberti, who is credited with laying the foundation for Renaissance spatial theory. Armed with these visual techniques, Renaissance designers and artists were equipped to translate humanist ideals into space and form. In the process they rejected medieval informality for symmetry and balance; they sought to articulate the horizontal rather than the vertical; and they imbued space with visual stability and order.

Across northern Italy the effect of Renaissance spatial theory appeared in many urban centers. Generally, Renaissance urban designers relied on certain components to give form to city interiors: primary straight streets, enclosed spaces, and gridiron districts.[19] In Florence, for example, the Piazza Annunciata, designed by Brunelleschi, terminated a sight line from the Duomo at a rectilinear volume bounded by the Foundling hospital. Unlike earlier medieval spaces, which do not appear to conform to a classical ideal, the Piazza Annunciata appeared as a conscious, unified volume, contained and formal. Fully articulated by 1516, it can be considered a standard of Renaissance urban landscape. Its originality stems from a spatial symmetry imposed by complementary architectural elements, notably Brunelleschi's arcade to the Foundling Hospital; Michelozzo's porch to the Church of Santissima Annunciata, constructed in 1454; and Sangallo's 1516 sensitive refrain, the arcade facing the hospital. Added to these were two fountains and an equestrian statue. Each reinforced the symmetrical arrangement of the space, and in the case of the statue, terminated the sight line along the via Servi. South of Florence, at the elegant hilltop community of Pienza, Pope Pius II commissioned a redesign of the town's civic core to conform to Renaissance design principles. The result is a beautifully proportioned piazza surrounded by an arcade, church, and palace. Eastward on the Adriatic coast, Venice bore marks of Renaissance idealism in the articulation of the Piazza San Marco, primarily in the architectural refinement of the structures surrounding the space. In 1483 and after a fire in 1577, the government added a classical wing to the main structure; in 1513 and 1590, designers supervised construction of continuous loggias surrounding the main Piazza.

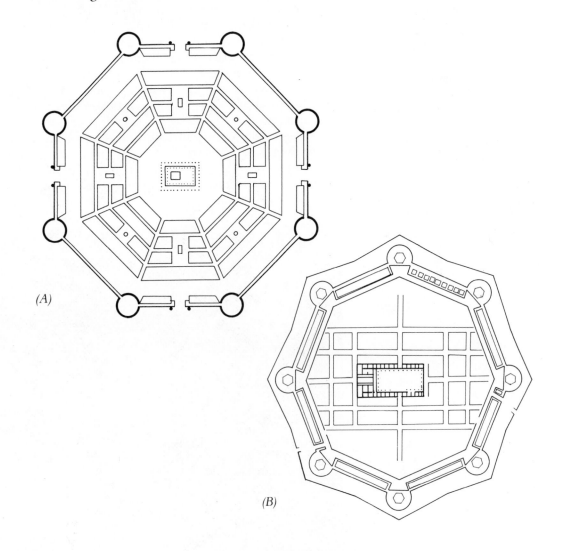

(A) Vitruvius' first-century A.D. ideal town (B) Filarete's fifteenth-century version.

In addition to the redesign of urban elements, Morris[20] identified four other planning elements related to Renaissance design: fortification systems, urban growth along extended streets, new districts, and new towns. Of these, new towns offered an opportunity for designers to test their theories of urban spatial organization. Fortification systems had an important influence on cities throughout Western Europe, including Vienna and Paris. British towns often had walls, but often these were used as commercial barriers. At continental cities successive perimeter walls forced cities to grow vertically; when the walls were no longer useful, the abandoned spaces became ring boulevards. Structurally, the walls changed when heavy cannon became common in the fifteenth century, and thicker walls were needed to withstand the heavier shot.

The need to fortify towns stimulated an interest in military engineering, and more important, in the elaboration of ideal city proposals by Renaissance urban designers. However, the idea of the ideal city rests with Alberti, Antonio Filarette, and Francesco Martini, drawing from the earlier work of Vitruvius. They envisioned the ideal city as a unified space, protected by a circular or polygonal wall, with a central open space surrounded by civic and military structures. Road patterns within the city were to function as visual links to important buildings or monuments. In typical humanist fashion, the city is considered a visual phenomenon, with each mass and space within the community contributing to the sense of formal perfection. Nor was the city intended to be entirely democratic: designers and theorists recommended design elements—specific districts for the wealthy and the poorer—for the health and safety of the ruling elite. Apart from leisurely activities at a comfortable villa, urban theorists had few recommendations for rural life, since the city was conceived as the home of upstanding individuals.

Alberti focused his attention on design and planning theory and produced few drawings or plans of ideal cities, but Filarette, Martini, Pietro Cataneo, and Buonaiuto Lorini all contributed to the planning of ideal cities. Most of their schemes followed the circular or polygonal form prescribed by Alberti, but, as

Aerial view of Palma Nova, a sixteenth-century planned community near Venice.

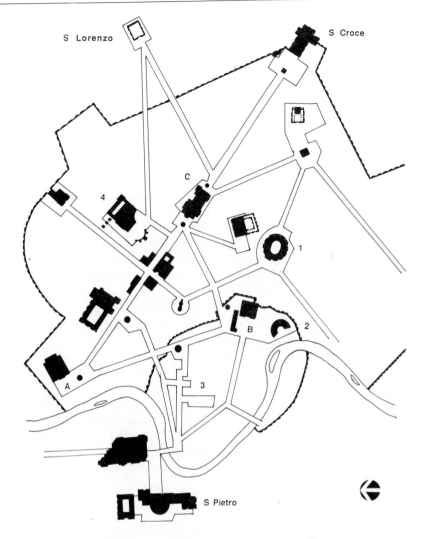

Renaissance Rome with the major avenues and obelisks. (A) Piazza del Popolo (B) Capitolium (C) Santa Maria Maggiore (1) Coliseum (2) Theatre of Marcellus (3) Piazza Navona (4) Baths of Diocletian.

Morris notes, none of the plans contained proposals for the siting of houses, though they clearly illustrated the layout of streets, squares, and walls. Perhaps for these reasons the plans had little effect on urban form in the early Renaissance except in the area of fortification design.

The first urban theorist to have his plans implemented was Vincenzo Scamozzi, whose work appeared during the latter half of the sixteenth century. His most notable achievement was the planning of Palma Nova, begun in 1593 as a defensive outpost for Venice. A modern aerial view of Palma Nova reveals the strict geometry envisioned for the town by Scamozzi. The town's outer contour is polygonal, a nine-sided star configuration; its center is a regular hexagon. Public buildings face the main square; major streets radiate from the center; three concentric streets echo the perimeter wall. Unlike many urban works from the period, Palma Nova retains much of its original form and detail.

URBAN DESIGN: ROME

While the wealthy citizens of northern Italian communities were investing in the talent of Renaissance designers and planners, the Church was spending time and resources to improve the physical quality of its temporal home, Rome. The city that Augustus had found in brick and left in marble had deteriorated over the centuries to a point where, when Gregory XI returned the papacy to the community in 1377, Rome was an insignificant town of about 17,000 inhabitants. Not until Nicholas V assumed the papacy and applied his influence to establishing the Renaissance in Rome did the city begin to shed its medieval form. Most of his effort went into rectifying basic ills: establishing an urban focal point at the bridge crossing near the Castel Sant'Angelo, encouraging residential development in deserted areas of the city, reconstructing of the Aqua Virgine to furnish the city with additional fresh water.[21] Subsequent Popes, including Sixtus IV and Alexander VI, made contributions to the revitalization of the city, including Alexander VI's bold move to rebuild St. Peter's basilica.

The most ingenious planning initiatives, however, were undertaken when Sixtus V implemented his comprehensive urban program in 1585. As Morris[22] points out, Sixtus V inherited two projects instigated by his predecessors, which gave impetus to his own ideas: the design of the Compigdolio and reorganization of the Piazza del Popolo. But Sixtus V's vision went beyond individual works to reworking major systems in Rome. One of his primary concerns was the general environmental quality of Rome, physically and visually. He recognized the need for an improved water supply system, refuse collection, better drainage systems, and solutions for chronic unemployment within the city. With Domenico Fontana as his chief architect and planner, he attempted to remedy these problems. His major successes included an increased water supply to higher elevations in the city, improved spatial quality of streets and squares, and the creation of a unified street system out of the existing road pattern.

The goal of Sixtus V's street plan was to link the seven pilgrimage churches in Rome. The principal element in his scheme was to align a new road, the Strada

View from St. Peters through the Piazza San Pietro and Via della Consolazione.

Caffagiola, formerly a medieval farmstead, converted to a villa by Cosimo Medici.

Felice, between the future Piazza del Popolo and Santa Croce in Gerusalemme at the southeast end of the city. The chief difficulty in completing this task was the terrain between the piazza and the church: 2.5 miles of hills and valleys that required substantial cutting and filling of landform. Because of these obstacles, the street terminated at Santa Trinita dei Monte; the impressive Scale di Spagna, constructed in 1721–25, subsequently connected the Strada Felice and the lower-level Strada del Babuino at the Piazza di Spagna.

To assure that other parts of his plan would be carried out, Sixtus V had four obelisks placed at locations in the city that he believed would evolve into important spaces. He located one at the intersection of three streets in the Piazza del Popolo, one on the Strada Felice near Santa Maria Maggiore, another facing San Giovanni in Laterano, and one in front of St. Peter's. Sixtus V's death in 1590 prevented him from seeing all of his ideas implemented, but the spirit of his vision encouraged subsequent planning and improvements. Many of these later projects, such as Compigdolio and the Piazza del Popolo, were completed between the seventeenth and nineteenth centuries.

ITALY: VILLAS AND ESTATES

By no means were all resources during the Renaissance applied to urban environments. As we have seen, wealthy individuals, seizing on the opportunity to extend capitalization to the countryside, continued during this period to purchase agricultural lands. Initially, these lands functioned as *fattoria,* productive farms, similar to the early Medici farmstead at Caffagiola, north of Florence. According to Cosgrove,[23] ownership of rural lands by urban merchants in the fourteenth century was an important aspect of rural landscape control for a city, a way of exploiting the resources of an area in a semifeudal manner. By the 1400s, however, Renaissance humanism extended far beyond city walls to the farmsteads, transforming strictly agricultural lands into *villas,* elegant country sites built by the rich for pleasure and show. For the wealthy, villas were an important link between urban commercial dynamism and rural agricultural existence, without the arduous aspects of production associated with city and farm.

The theoretical foundation for the design of fifteenth-century estates in Italy was laid by Alberti and others who applied the spatial principles they had developed for urban design to the countryside to create an extension of urban order. Alberti considered the spatial aspects of the townhouse to be appropriate for villas, and he stressed the need for comfort and luxury in the country villa, a pleasure house that should be less formal than an urban residence. With these amenities, the affluent city dweller could eschew business and politics for contemplation in a setting free from urban and rural production. This goal required special environments that would support solitary reflection, or, on occasion, conversation with artists and intellectuals. For these purposes the private garden was as Petrarch emphasized, the ideal location—a physical link between urban geometry and organic nature—and much time and energy went into making villa gardens the epitome of humanist reason and order.

Not all the credit for the design of villas belongs to fifteenth-century theorists. Renaissance humanists were keenly aware of ancient precedents, including the country homes of Pliny, Horace, and the Roman aristocracy. Vitruvius, a first-century A.D. engineer and architect, had outlined site-planning criteria in his *De Architectura.* His recommendations are deceptively straightforward; they included good drainage, favorable natural ventilation and sun angles, sufficient water supply, and the use of local building materials.

An early example of an estate constructed for leisure and contemplation is the Villa Medici at Fiesole, overlooking Florence and the Arno floodplain. The property was one of several villas built for the Medici clan, whose founder, Cosimo the Elder, had built country estates at Cafaggiola in the valley of the Mugello and at Careggi. According to Vasari, Cafaggiola was a distinguished country house with a pleasant garden, groves, and fountains, though the villa's high towers, battlement arches, and moat also gave it a fortresslike appearance. These villas were favorites with Cosimo, and he enjoyed working in their groves, planting and pruning trees, or exchanging stories with the local inhabitants. Occasionally he would invite a friend to a villa to play chess, to discuss Plato, or to "discover the true road to happiness."[24]

The true road to happiness for Cosimo's son, Giovanni, did not include rustic sites where one could spend time working in gardens or conversing with peasants. Rather, he planned his Villa Medici at Fiesole to be a place where leisure activities could occur in shaded, private gardens in the company of artists and intellectuals. If Giovanni intended to avoid agricultural activity, he could not have selected a better site than Fiesole—interestingly, Cosimo considered the surrounding lands excessively steep and stoney, requiring expensive site alterations simply for the purpose of having a good view of Florence. Nevertheless, in 1458, Giovanni de' Medici commissioned Michelozzo to design the villa, which the architect completed in 1458. The result was an elegant testimony to humanist order in design, and the fulfillment of the Renaissance ideal of the villa as a perfect intermediate landscape between urban and rural environments. Michelozzo carefully positioned structures and terraces into the hillside to create a balance between vertical and horizontal planes. Connection between one level and another was by modest ramps and stairs near the ends of the terraces or by small staircases midway along terrace retaining walls. The high retaining walls gave each level a sense of enclosure, and each terrace had a simple, geometrical arrangement, delineated by plant material and an occasional small fountain.

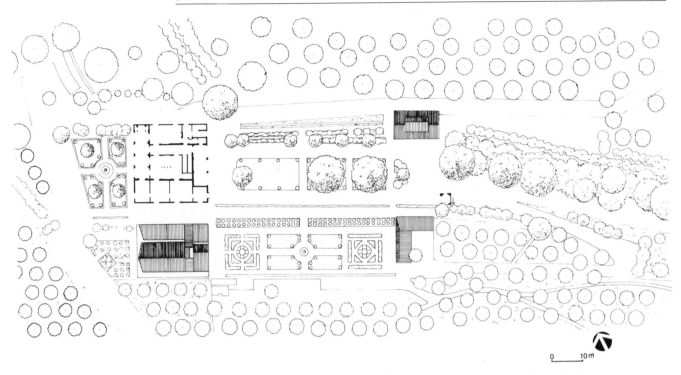

Plan of Villa Medici at Fiesole. The villa epitomized early Italian Renaissance site planning.

(A)   *(B)*

(A) View of Villa Medici at Fiesole showing the relationship of site to structures and garden terraces.
(B) View from the upper terrace of the villa to the lower garden.

Soon after Giovanni's death in 1463 the villa at Fiesole passed into the hands of Lorenzo de' Medici, who turned it into an important literary center, where the most gifted artists and writers of the region gathered for contemplation and conversation. Since many members of important families, including the Medici, eventually held important positions in the church hierarchy, the concept of the villa flourished on the hillsides outside Rome during the sixteenth and seventeenth centuries. The chief distinction between fifteenth-century Florentine estates and the later Roman villas was the sheer grandeur and opulence of the latter.

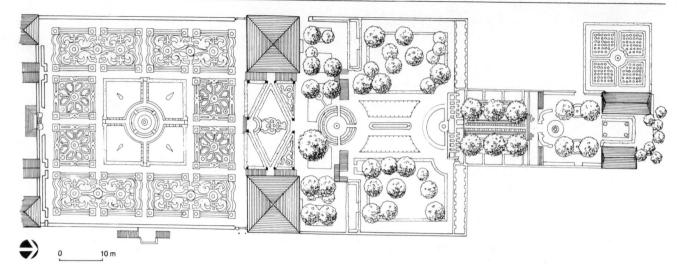

0   10 m

Plan of Villa Lante at Bagnaia. Spatial balance and the restrained use of materials make this villa one of the finest Renaissance examples.

At Tivoli and the Villa d'Este (1549), at Frascati and the Villas Aldobrandini (1518), Torlonia (1621), and Mondragone (1567), at Bagnaia and the elegant Villa Lante (1566), wealthy popes and cardinals imbued these sites with a spatial and material splendor unequalled in Europe. Newton[25] provides a description of the entire villa phenomenon near Florence and Rome between 1400 and 1750. His descriptions identify a distinguishing feature of many of the villas in those regions: the ingenious and often effusive use of water in fountains, water chains, pools, and garden details. The Villa Lante, built for Cardinal Gianfrancesco Gambara, is the epitome of the Renaissance sensibility applied to the landscape. The spatial order of the site aligns along a central axis that links various garden levels and features. Hard and soft material complement an ever present and ingenious use of water: fountains, water chains, pools, and fanciful water table. Twin *casini* provide shelter from the elements; in scale and detail, rather than dominating the site, these two architectural components function as integral elements within the overall organization of the garden. The spatial and material precision of the Villa Lanta is a contrast to seventeenth-century villas in the region, notably the baroque Villa Garzoni at Collodi.

The influence of Italian villas on subsequent northern European estate development and the evolution of a postmedieval landscape ideal did not come only from Florence and Rome; other regions were important, particularly the Veneto surrounding Venice. In the early 1400s certain wealthy families in Venice, the Cornari and Barbari, for example, had broken with Venetian tradition and extended their property holdings into the *terraferma* through drainage and reclamation of low-lying lands. Cosgrove notes a link between property, politics, and humanism at this time. Part of the phenomenon was a gradual shift from strictly maritime activity to investments and revenues from estates in the Veneto. Eventually attitudes concerning work began to move away from active participation in agricultural production to the exploitation of lessees, who provided increased revenues through more stringent rental agreements. As these investments continued to enrich the landowners, some of their wealth was invested in pleasure villas. On the Guidecca and the *terraferma,* villas appeared in greater numbers, as landowners and merchants began to invest their time in

Lower garden at Villa Lante. The fountain sculpture commemorates the original owners of the villa.

Fountain of the Giants, Villa Lante. Sufficient water pressure at many villa sites made fanciful water features a common element in the gardens.

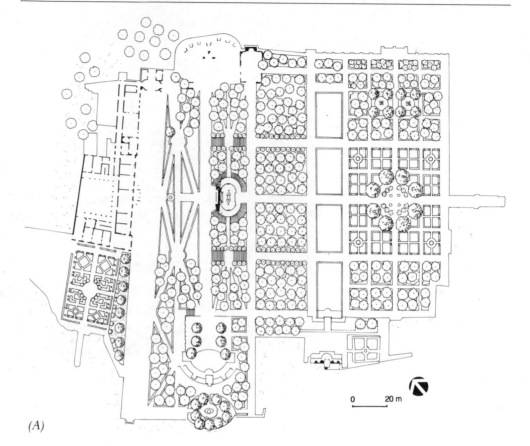

(A)

(B)

Villa d'Este, (A) plan and (B) Water Organ. The villa is a composite of water features fed by a diverted stream above the site.

Palladio's Villa Capra, Vicenza. This villa was the inspiration for a series of architectural works in subsequent centuries.

Villa Garzoni, Collodi. Baroque manipulation of materials are evident in the fanciful staircase.

humanist activities within the confines of villa gardens. The Venetians strove to create environments where city problems disappeared, replaced by meditation and discussion. But though their intentions were similar to those of the Florentines, the Venetians tended to arrange their estates to allow boundaries to fade into one another. Unlike Florentine villas, where space was strictly controlled by geometric form, Venetian estates "emphasized informal transition," to "allow the passage from culture into nature."[26]

The Venetians also combined urban spatial theory and perspectival space in the organization of their villas. These concepts were especially evident in the villa designs of Andrea Palladio during the sixteenth century. Palladio came from the ranks of Vicenza's schooled elite and rose to prominence as an architect when he received a commission to rebuild the loggias of the council building in Vicenza. Vincentine nobility subsequently commissioned Palladio to design rural villas, many of which captured the sense of Venetian landscape ideology. Pevsner[27] sums up Palladio's achievements with his observation that these villas were the first to connect architecture and landscape into a unified conception. According to Puppi, the villa designs were planned to control estate production while visually separating social classes.[28] At the Villa Capra near Vicenza, Palladio combined circular and cubic forms to produce the most quoted of his works, though the villa is considered by some critics to be the least functional of his efforts. But at the Villa Emo near Fanzola, Palladio brought his genius to bear in a brilliant organization of the site and structure. Surrounded by an 80-acre garden, the central residence, flanked by arched arcades, provides views into the countryside, undisturbed by workers' residences obscured by masses of plant material.

FRANCE AND ENGLAND: CHATEAUX, ESTATES, AND PARKS

As the Renaissance humanist tradition in Italy moved into a Baroque phase, epitomized by the infusion of spatial dynamics into urban design and villa organization, similar transformations were occurring in the countries north of the Alps. Generally, the stimulus for change in these regions stemmed either from the accumulation of wealth by landowners or from the political consolidation of a region under an absolute monarchy. In both France and Spain absolute monarchies were in place by the middle of the sixteenth century. The Italians had negotiated property rights in the eleventh century, and the English had secured land rights through the Magna Charta, but the French and Spanish had acquired no such rights due to the strength of the feudal system in France and Moorish dominance in Spain. While Italy was evolving into powerful duchies or ecclesiastical provinces, Charles V of Spain acquired The Netherlands in 1506 and the German Holy Roman Empire in 1520. Gradually, the Spanish monarchy lost control of its holdings, allowing France to solidify its position of absolute authority in continental Europe by the seventeenth century.

The first region of the French landscape to manifest the gradual shift to absolutism was the Loire Valley, especially the lands around Tours. At the conclusion of the Hundred Years War in 1453, many of the structures and lands in the region became sites for *chateaux,* French estates for leisure activity. Unlike Italian villas, which were the property of individuals connected with the church, many of these estates belonged to members the French monarchy, beginning with Charles VIII at Loches, Louis XII and Francis I at Amboise (1490), and Francis I at Bois (1515). Francis I brought important Italian Renaissance figures into his court at Amboise, including Vignola, the architect at the Villa Lante, and Leonardo da Vinci, who died at Amboise in 1519. But despite the presence of competent designers, the grounds of early chateaux were mostly restricted by site limitations to modest garden spaces. Many of the early chateaux occupied

Chateau Amboise. Most of the early chateaux retained their earlier fortified character.

medieval defensible sites—promontories overlooking towns and plains—which limited the extent of site development.

As newer chateaux appeared on less constricted sites, designers placed greater emphasis on expansive gardens, including those at the elegant chateau at Villandry (1530) built by Jean le Breton, minister to Francis I. Here the site and structure affect the spatial and material balance seen at Italian villas. At Chambord (1519) Francis I planned an expansive hunting lodge that tied the chateau to the outlying landscape with *allées* and *ronds,* thereby permitting viewers to enjoy the progress of hunting parties in the surrounding preserve. Two other chateaux built for Francis I, Chenonceaux (1519) and Fountainbleau (1528–40), incorporated water into the site, notably a 1200-meter-long grand canal at Fountainbleau and the siting of the chateau structure over the river Cher at Chenonceaux. All of these chateaux contributed to the tradition of estate design in France and helped to lay the foundation for the creation of even greater private estates in the mid-seventeenth century.

Absolute monarchy in England was relatively short-lived, lasting from the end of Tudor rule to the Civil War in 1640. We have noted the enclosure phenomenon during this period and the general development of the English countryside, with significant building and reconstruction by all classes, except the very poor, in the cities and in rural areas.

Behind the English interest in acquiring estates lay social motives imbedded in the ability of industrious, nonaristocratic individuals to own land and to order their environment, not unlike the attitudes that shaped the landscape in Renaissance Italy. Thus estates occurred on sites owned by long-term landowners or by yeomen who had risen up the social scale by accumulating property through their own enterprise. The country house, constructed for leisure, became a common element in the English landscape during Henry VIII's reign, a phenomenon aided by Henry's confiscation and redistribution of monastic lands. Some of the

Chateau Villandry. Italian influences are evident in the gardens and the sight line that cuts through the bosque.

Chateau Chenonceaux on the River Cher.

earliest country houses occupied former village sites; many utilized building materials from confiscated or abandoned structures.

Spatially, many of the earlier estates conformed to medieval planning conventions, with an emphasis on a large hall and haphazard arrangement of ancillary spaces. Longleate (1550), Montecute (1580), Hatfield House (1611), and Hampton Court (1550–1689) illustrate applications of Renaissance concepts to estates of different sizes and locations. In general few of these estates exhibit the clear geometrical order of their Italian counterparts.

Often the spatial articulation of the grounds immediately surrounding the manor house shows an eclectic assembly of French and Italian influences—a good

Aerial oblique of Hatfield House. Site spaces lack sufficient vertical definition for a clear sense of spatial volume.

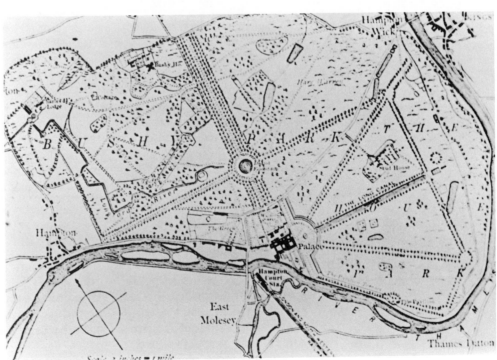

Hampton Court. The site is a composite of English and continental influences, including Dutch and French.

example being the grounds of Hampton Court, with their medieval, French, and Dutch elements.

Further from the manor, the outlying landscape often served as a private park, originally an enclosed area, preferably a woodland, for the protection of game for hunting. The practice of setting aside private holdings as game preserves was an ancient one, as we have seen: some of the earliest parks were

*Compton Wynyates,
Warwickshire, and surrounding
park.*

established before the eleventh century, others a little later in the eleventh and twelfth centuries. Hatfield House, Woodstock Park at Blenheim, and Bushy Park at Hampton Court originated as private game preserves before the sixteenth century. Parks were also a convenient way for the wealthy, new and old, to isolate themselves from the daily routine of agricultural life and labor. Out of this isolation grew an aesthetic which conspired to limit the lower classes' rights to the land. Eventually, parks began to acquire a naturalistic visual quality, which further separated the landowner from the outlying rural countryside.[29] Eventually, as landowners solidified their holdings and increased their wealth from emerging trade and mercantilism in seventeenth- and eighteenth-century Britain, an idea of landscape appeared that was a logical outgrowth of the upper classes' leisure.

ENVIRONMENTAL ISSUES

The introduction of market economies in the fourteenth and fifteenth centuries added another element to the list of human activities that affected environmental quality in Western Europe. In Northern Italy humanist attitudes concerning land gradually transformed medieval agricultural properties into a component of the market system. Land was now viewed as a commodity, another means of increasing an individual's financial status by providing revenues from rents and the sale of agricultural products.

Few of the wealthy urban inhabitants who invested in agricultural land sought to improve agricultural techniques. Landowners preferred *villagiatura,* the pursuit of leisure activity within quiet villa gardens, to spending time managing their farms. As a result, few improvements occurred in crop rotation, seed quality, or stock breeding during the fifteenth and sixteenth centuries in northern Italy. Ancient techniques accompanied ancient problems: excessive soil erosion; siltation of streams, lakes, and lagoons; and accelerated soil depletion due to intensive farming. As a remedy for excessive soil loss landowners used retaining walls and terraces to hold back soil, and they utilized the olive tree as a source of agricultural revenue, and secondarily, a method of holding the soil in place.

As we have noted, the woolen trade was also having an effect on land quality in Spain, Italy, and England. We have seen how a diminished labor force after 1349 and the rise in the value of woolen products drove many landowners in Britain to convert common agricultural land to enclosed pastures. Forests had continued to disappear since the Roman occupation of Britain, and enclosures created habitats for small animals, who preferred the shelter of hawthorn, maple, oak, dogwood, and elm that flourished along property boundaries.

In Spain and southern Italy sheep raising required extensive open lands, and custom and the influence of the Mesta kept lands open for the passage of sheep to market. When the Spanish monarchy drove the last of the Moors from Spain in 1492, additional lands in Andalusia and Estramadura became available for sheep raising. By the middle of the sixteenth century the number of merino sheep in Spain had increased to three and a half million, and constituted a major part of the Spanish economy. The earlier, wide *canadas,* which provided pasture for the flocks, had to be enlarged to accommodate the larger numbers of sheep. The result was further cutting of forests to widen the pathways that ran from the south to north. Eventually the paths grew to 250 feet in width; any farmer refusing to allow sheep to pass over his land was subject to the death penalty. At higher elevations, herders felled forests to connect higher- and lower-elevation pastures. By the middle of the sixteenth century, the forests that had covered Spain were nearly gone. With the forests went precious topsoil, whose absence robbed the country of its agricultural potential. The effect of sheep raising on forests in Italy was similar.

Attenborough[30] notes another influence on Italian forests during the fifteenth and sixteenth century: shipbuilding. Major cities along the coasts of Italy, including Pisa, Genoa, and Venice, needed wood to maintain their trading fleets. Venice, the most powerful maritime city during this period, built large merchant ships and low-slung galleys for its burgeoning sea trade. Both types of ship required a range of forest materials for construction: beech, oak, pine, and firs. And when the Venetian fleets had to battle their way along the trade routes, the loss of material was staggering. At the battle of Leptano in 1571, for example, the Venetians and the Turks lost the equivalent of 250,000 mature trees—not to mention the loss of 28,000 lives. Landward the cost was also apparent. In the early 1400s, forests stretched from the edge of the Venice lagoon to the Alps. By the end of the sixteenth century, reclamation and forest clearing had pushed the forest line to the Alps and the Appenines.

Once the forest lands had disappeared to the shipbuilding industry, maquis and garrique spread from marginal soils into former forest lands, aided by voracious goats, who retard forest regrowth by eating tender shoots and leaves as soon as they appear. By the seventeenth century the southern Mediterranean lands faced a future of agricultural hardship, magnified by the loss of the forests and the topsoil needed for long-term agricultural activity. With these changes Europeans had imposed a new order in the landscape, which superseded nearly a thousand years of feudal activity. Trade accelerated the advent of the capitalist market system and scientific inquiry, both of which helped form new landscapes dominated by industrialization, urbanization, and political absolutism.

NOTES

1. *Kenneth Clark. 1969.* Civilization. *New York: Harper & Row, p. 91.*

2. *Ferdinand Braudel. 1972.* Civilization and Capitalism, 15th–18th Centuries. *Vol. II:* The Wheels of Commerce. *London: Collins.*

3. *Denis E. Cosgrove. 1984.* Social Formation and Symbolic Landscape. *Totowa, N.J.: Barnes and Noble, p. 51.*

4. *Bertrand Russell. 1945.* A History of Western Philosophy. *New York: Simon and Schuster.*

5. *Cosgrove, op. cit, p.26.*

6. *Clark, op. cit., p. 72.*

7. *L. Martines. 1980.* Power and Imagination: City States in Renaissance Italy. *New York: Vintage.*

8. *The Medici insignia still appears on the walls of many of these communities.*

9. *E. Sereni. 1974.* Storia del paessagio agrario Italiano. *Bari, Italy: Luteza, p. 223.*

10. *G. E. Fussell. 1972.* The Classical Tradition in Western European Farming. *Rutherford, N.J.: Farleigh Dickinson University Press.*

11. *W. G. Hoskins. 1969.* The Making of the English Landscape. *London: Hodder and Stoughton.*

12. *Ibid., p. 113.*

13. *Ibid., p. 119.*

14. *Robert Trow-Smith. 1967.* Life From the Land. *London: Longmans.*

15. *Paul M. Hobenberg and L. H. Lees. 1984.* The Making of Urban Europe, 1000–1950. *Cambridge, Mass.: Harvard University Press, p. 74.*

16. *Cosgrove, op. cit, p. 91.*

17. *Ibid., p. 92.*

18. *Clark, op. cit., p. 97.*

19. *A. E. J. Morris. 1979.* History of Urban Form. *New York: Wiley, p. 123.*

20. *Ibid, p. 123.*

21. *Ibid., p. 142.*

22. *Ibid, p. 143.*

23. *Cosgrove, op. cit, p. 71.*

24. *Christopher Hibbert. 1975.* The House of the Medici. *New York: Morrow, p. 77.*

25. *Norman T. Newton. 1971.* Design on the Land: The Development of Landscape Architecture. *Cambridge, Mass.: Harvard University Press, pp. 55–131.*

26. *Cosgrove, op. cit., p. 120.*

27. *N. Pevsner. 1975.* An Outline of European Architecture. *Harmonsworth: U.K., Penguin.*

28. *L. Puppi. 1972. "The Villa Garden in the Veneto," in David R. Coffin, ed.,* The Italian Garden. *Washington, D.C.: Dumbarton Oaks.*

29. *Tom Williamson and Liz Bellamy. 1987.* Property and Landscape. *London: Philip, p. 116.*

30. *David Attenborough. 1987.* The First Eden: The Mediterranean World and Man. *Boston: Little, Brown, p. 166.*

10

Enlightenment and Romanticism

By 1650 Europeans again significantly changed their perception of the landscape. Two factors played an important role in this change: the Reformation and advances in science. The Reformation pitted less sophisticated states against the intellectual dominance of the church in Italy. After the Thirty Years War, the uselessness of Catholic or Protestant dominance was apparent to civilized individuals, who now had the opportunity to think openly about fundamental issues. Science, which had slowly overcome church authority through the efforts of Leonardo, Copernicus, Kepler, and Galileo, became preeminent with Newton, and with the production of scientific instruments to observe and measure natural phenomena. By the end of the seventeenth century, scientific law captured the imagination, eliminating mysticism and transforming medieval attitudes into a modern outlook. Russell[1] eloquently describes this transformation by stating that the medieval world had been preoccupied with the implication of sin, held in place by the prospect of retribution from God for prideful conduct. Previously natural calamities and political upheavals both seemed to validate this conception, until science illuminated nature and nature's laws.

Intellectually, northern Europe played a critical role in the appearance of ecclestiastical reform and scientific development. Italy, which had dominated the artistic world in the fifteenth century, fell victim to the Counterreformation and the Inquisition in the 1600s, shutting out scientific development for several centuries. In Protestant countries, the clergy were eager to contain scientific development, but their inability to control those countries' governments allowed scientists to adopt the heliocentric theory of Copernicus. A shift in trading activity from the Mediterranean to the Atlantic coast also helped to put the northern European countries in a position to foster new intellectual inquiry. Ironically, the advances in seafaring and trade along the northern Atlantic coast echoed the several millennia of Mediterranean supremacy in trade, begun by the Phoenicians and the Greeks. Early trade across the Mediterranean Sea created a mentality based on innate inquisitiveness that combined adventure with logic into a mode of original thought. But the power of the church in the seventeenth century effectively eliminated this tradition in Mediterranean countries, handing free inquiry to the northern European states.

Intellectual inquisitiveness in the north slowly transformed people's conception of the landscape, from the purely logical approach of the Italian Renaissance to the highly literary romantic idealism of the eighteenth and nineteenth centuries. As we have seen, the earlier Italian Renaissance was rife with ostentatious display of learning and material gain. Land acquired the status of a cash commodity, and wealthy Italian merchants and princes spent money on the design and construction of urban and rural landscape elements, while they relied on Greek and Roman ideals as standards for the organization of public and private environments. Yet as bold as these works were, the roots of their conception lay in the past—especially in Italy, where artists and intellectuals eschewed scholasticism but maintained a reverence for authority, substituting the classical order of the ancients for the power of the church. As Russell[2] noted, few fifteenth-century Italians would have maintained an opinion for which there was no basis in ancient authority. Only individuals such as Leonardo da Vinci attempted to look to the future by proposing that there was some value in scientific procedure.

Though these ideas filtered into northern Europe, primarily in the planning and design of elaborate estates in France and Britain, freer inquiry there stimulated technical advances, which revolutionized agriculture and the shape of rural landscapes. With the power of the absolute monarchies in France and Germany bolstered by the application of practical science to industry, trade, and warfare, urban landscapes began to acquire the scale and grandiosity befitting the increasing wealth and power in the northern European states. At the beginning of the 1600s, there was little in the way people shaped the land that differed from earlier pre-Renaissance methods. But slowly the intention and scale of landscape works shifted with the growth of the middle class in northern Europe, and with advances in agricultural practices and scientific technique, investment in urban industrial enterprises, and the revolution of land transportation. Then in the eighteenth century the process took another direction, this time resulting in a romantic treatment of the land founded on contemporary art and literature. Finally by the mid-nineteenth century European culture began to dispense with classical and romantic ideas in favor of objective perceptions of the world, supported by scientific and social revolutions.

SCIENCE AND ENLIGHTENMENT

The idea of science prevalent during the seventeenth century had little in common with the conception prevalent during the nineteenth and twentieth centuries. During the 1600s, science was the purview of the informed amateur, an uneven activity practiced by dedicated individuals with little formal training. Yet from the moment Newton set forth his concepts in the *Principia* in 1687, English researchers proposed ever more insightful theories on the laws of nature: by the eighteenth century, patient scientific observers were on the way to proposing theories on light, navigation, celestial phenomena, electricity, and gases. All the attention given to the power of observation and experimentation helped to instill an interest in nature.

Two aspects of scientific activity directly influenced landscape order in northern Europe from 1650 to 1850. The first was observation, the desire to examine the structure of natural phenomena. Precedents for scientific inquiry were established by, among others, artistic practitioners in Renaissance Italy: Leonardo and Michelangelo, for example, were patient observers of nature who dissected organisms to get a clearer understanding of their morphology. Such empirical activity helped lay the foundation for considering the idea of order in nature. The second scientific aspect was theory, the exposition of concepts that could explain natural phenomena: light; the motion of the stars and planets; and as proposed by Newton, an explanation for universal gravitation and motion. Combined into an intellectual strategy, observation and theory led seventeenth- and eighteenth-century aestheticians to evolve concepts about the geometrical potential of landscape space. One form this kind of thinking took was the application of mathematical concepts to landscape order—for example, Pascal's notions of geometry and space, which may have influenced Le Notre's work at Vaux-le-Vicomte and Versailles. As scientific activity expanded to include the investigation of life processes epitomized by Gregor Mendel's genetic theories and Wallace and Darwin's model for biological evolution, conceptions about landscape order concomitantly shifted from seventeenth-century geometrical solutions to landscape order based on nineteenth-century naturalistic conventions.

Enlightenment, distinct from strict objectivity, led to a conception of the landscape rooted in reason. The philosophers of the Enlightenment were responsible for maintaining belief in justice, tolerance, and natural law. And as Clark[3] observes, it was in England that the French commitment to reason and tolerance flourished: the 1700s in Britain were a time when thinkers could avoid the persecutions common on the Continent. People with convictions about political, social, or aesthetic issues vented their thoughts in print, and some of them, including Alexander Pope and the essayists Addison and Steele, significantly influenced ideas about the landscape in England. Pope was the first of these to apply aesthetic concepts to landscape design, and his writings about nature reflect the appreciation for observation and natural phenomena prevalent in the eighteenth century; his descriptions of natural scenes contain numerous references to color and light in the landscape:

> The bright-ey'd Perch with Fins of Tyrian Dye
> The Silver Eel, in shining Volumes roll'd,
> The yellow Carp, in Scales bedrop't with Gold
> Swift Trout, diversify'd with Crimson Stains.

But unlike fifteenth- and sixteenth-century practitioners, who operated within the structure of church doctrine, these inheritors of Renaissance humanism eschewed the religious conviction common to their predecessors. They sought to establish a new morality based on natural law and the ethic of Republican Rome. Embedded in this philosophy is the belief in the goodness of "natural man" over sophisticated individuals. As a political matter, thinkers of the Enlightenment concluded that the selfless attitudes embodied in the actions of early Roman leaders fit the new order of eighteenth-century Europe.

POLITICAL ABSOLUTISM

While the driving forces behind the changes in intellectual and aesthetic attitudes toward the landscape were scientific inquiry and an enlightened philosophy, we cannot overlook the influence of the political structure in northern Europe, in which these ideas evolved, and the consequences these had for the landscape during the seventeenth and eighteenth centuries. Notably, the appearance of absolute monarchies, briefly in England, fully in France, established social orders that influenced the development of ideas, especially by providing patronage to thinkers, artists, and designers.

The French succeeded in solidifying their political structure at the conclusion of the Hundred Years War with England, Charles VIII and Francis I both reaped the benefits of regaining lands along the Atlantic coast. As we discussed earlier, within the region, including the Loire Valley, there were many fine chateaux, which the monarchy converted into country estates. By 1500 Francis I had refurbished or built chateaux in the region around Tours, including Amboise, Blois, Chenonceaux, Villandry, and Chambord. Then, political solidarity received a boost from Louis XIII, who, with Cardinal Richelieu, strengthened monarchial authority by calming internal strife stemming from the Reformation. And France held to its medieval social structure, with the landowning aristocracy ruling the countryside. As a result, the relationship between merchant class and landscape ownership, common in northern Italy, had little currency in France at this time. The aristocracy maintained its position, bolstering the monarchy; when Louis XIV assumed the throne in 1661, his power was absolute.

The power of the king was most conspicuously displayed in the building of the grand chateaux constructed for the monarchy, notably the town and estate at Versailles. Why Louis XIV chose to build Versailles is part of the lore surrounding the largest garden in Europe. Apparently, when Nicholas Fouquet, finance minister to the crown, completed the construction of his sumptuous chateau Vaux-le-Vicomte southwest of Paris in 1661, he unwittingly stirred the envy of Louis XIV. No doubt the king was impressed by both the scale and detail of the estate. Conceiving his chateau as a grand stage upon which the French elite could act out their social fantasies, Fouquet commissioned the architect Le Vau, the painter Le Brun, and the site designer André Le Notre to evolve a scheme that would match his ambitions. Evidently, Le Notre's schooling in the fine arts and his training as a designer at the Tuilleries gardens in Paris under Claude Mollet gave him the skill and confidence needed to articulate the site design of the chateau.

Le Notre's concept was to organize Vaux-le-Vicomte as a rational, symmetrical environment, ordered by a central sight line. A forecourt, with carriage houses and quarters for attendants, lay adjacent to the chateau structure, effectively separating carriage traffic from the gardens. The central axis tied garden spaces, cross-axis, and water elements along a gently undulating site to a turf allée. Seventeenth-century theoretical science, including mathematics and optics, account for the geometry of the garden spaces and elements and the visual autonomy of the central axes. What Le Notre achieved was a unified, ordered arrangement of site and structure, with an emphasis on geometry in the disparate garden spaces and elements. But unlike earlier chateaux, Vaux-le-Vicomte was a Baroque conception throughout, as is especially visible in the sense of infinity conveyed by the reflection of the sky on large, flat water elements and the forceful movement of the eye along the central axis. Cross-axes tie the edge of the site to the primary sight line.

By all measures Le Notre's design for Vaux-le-Vicomte outmatched previous chateau planning in scale, proportion, unity, and material. But Louis XIV, after arresting Fouquet and confiscating Vaux-le-Vicomte, was determined to construct a chateau which would outshine all competitors. For this task he commissioned Le Vau, Le Brun, and Le Notre to propose and execute a plan for a

The Tuilleries garden, a major influence on Le Notre's design strategy.

(A)

(B)

(A) Vaux-le-Vicomte, Foquet's impressive chateau and one of Le Notre's finest gardens.
(B) Plan of the Vaux-le-Vicomte. A dominant central axis ties the various garden spaces into a unified composition.

new palace and grounds. What emerged was Versailles, the most grandiose of all projects implemented during the age of absolutism.

By the time the project was begun in 1661, Louis XIV had decided to begin moving his court from the Louvre Palace in Paris to a location that could accommodate his large retinue and provide some insulation from the annoyances of urban existence. The king chose an old stone hunting lodge, built by Louis XIII and located on a swampy site west of Paris. To make the site fit for a grand palace, Louis enlisted an army to plant trees and construct a lake. By 1668, Le Vau had begun to add structures onto the original lodge; he was followed in 1678 by Hardoin-Mansart, who added the enormous north-south wings. However it was the garden that gave Versailles its grandeur.

Within the approximately 5 square miles of the site, Le Notre transformed the sleepy little village of Versailles into the political and social hub of the French state. Le Notre's plan rested on a grand east-west axis, linking the king's bedroom with the west horizon. A large cross-axis cuts along the west face of the palace, extending north and south to the north parterre and the Swiss lake, respectively. Along the central axis, Le Notre positioned a water parterre, fountains, a turf allée, and a "grand canal" that extended to the horizon. Because of the surrounding terrain and the scale of the plan, many of the fountains had to be activated by mechanical pumps, in succession, as the king moved through the gardens. Sebastien Vauban (1633–1707) proposed an ambitious scheme to divert the River Eure 50 miles to provide an adequate water supply for the gardens,

Plan of Versailles.

Versailles: View from the palace looking westward to the grand canal.

but the plan failed due to the unhealthy conditions in the intervening marshlands. Despite hydraulic problems, more than ninety sculptors produced statues to line the allées and decorate the various fountains, reinforcing the Baroque sense of motion and infinity conveyed by Le Notre's scheme. Twenty-five years after the project was begun, Louis XIV's chateau was complete, a model for subsequent estate and town planning, especially in urban areas where broad, paved boulevards fanning out from "ronds" permitted military forces to maintain order in times of urban upheaval. But until Louis XIV's death in 1715, Versailles was principally a monument to absolutism, a counterpoint to the equally ambitious urban designs in papal Italy.

EIGHTEENTH-CENTURY URBAN CLASSICISM

French and Italian Baroque ideals inspired the redesign of existing urban sites and the design of new urban areas, and sustained a phase of planning in the tradition of Bernini, Borromini, and Le Notre. Versailles, the Piazza del Popolo, and the Piazza San Pietro loomed over Europe as principal urban design models for monarchies that could absorb the cost of planning on an extravagant scale. Paris acquired most of its Renaissance structures between the reigns of Francis I and Louis XV, principally in the construction of small squares, the Champs Elysées, and the Grandes Boulevards. The Place Vosges (1612) and the Place Vendome (1702) began as real estate ventures and as sites for important statues of royalty. Formally they are contained spaces, modest in scale, with strong focal points. The Champs Elysées, however, falls in with Baroque concepts of urban form. It was conceived to link the Tuileries gardens and the Bois de Boulogne along an east-west spine. Le Notre's plan (1667) for the axis was to add a dynamic element to the Tuileries gardens by projecting the Champs Elysées westward. In addition to this major axis extending from the gardens, several of the old fortifications surrounding Paris evolved into Grandes Boulevards, consisting of a central vehicular space enclosed by tree-lined pedestrian allées.

The idea of converting city fortifications into boulevards took hold in other European cities, and spread the classical sensibility beyond Rome and Paris. During the eighteenth century, Vienna acquired the feel of French and Italian classicism in the design of the Belvedere Palace (1723) and the Schönbrunn summer palace (1740). In the eighteenth century, the construction of boulevards along

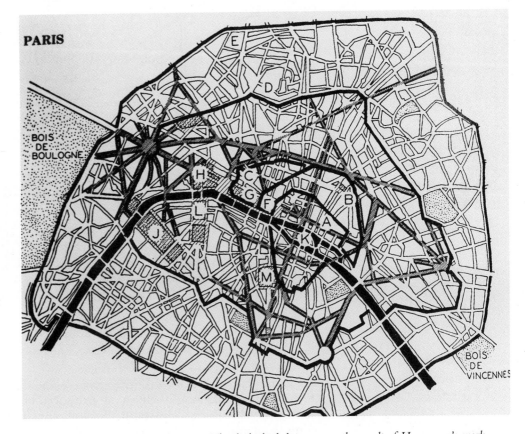

Paris: Successive stages of development. The dark shaded streets are the result of Haussman's work. A series of walls include (A) twelfth century (B) fourteenth century (C) seventeenth century (D) eighteenth century (E) nineteenth century. Urban features include (F) the Louvre (G) the Tuilleries (H) the Champs Elysees (J) the Champs de Mars (K) the Ile de la Cité (L) the Invalides (M) the Luxemborg.

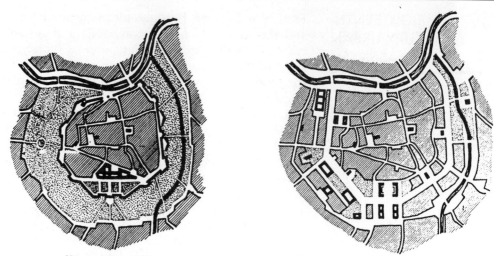

Urban alteration of Vienna after 1857.

Vienna before 1857

Vienna after 1857

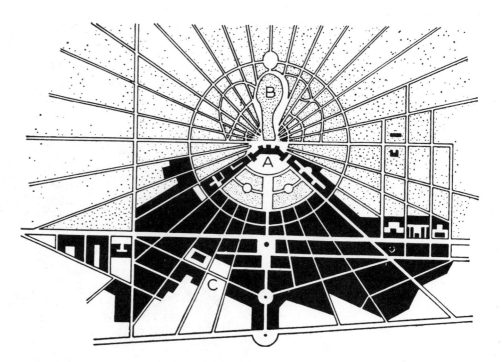

Diagram of Karlsruhe in the early eighteenth century. (A) palace (B) park (C) town

the alignment of older fortifications gave the city its radial-concentric appearance. Rational planning in Germany produced classical designs for Karlsruhe and Wilhelmshohe. Karlesruhe, built in 1709, consisted of thirty-two avenues radiating from an octagonal center. An even more grandiose scheme was devised for Wilhelmshohe, which included a 4-mile-long road leading from Kassel to a Baroque cascade.

The full potential of classicism as an ordering theory for urban design was fulfilled in the plan for St. Petersburg, on the Neva River on the Gulf of Finland.

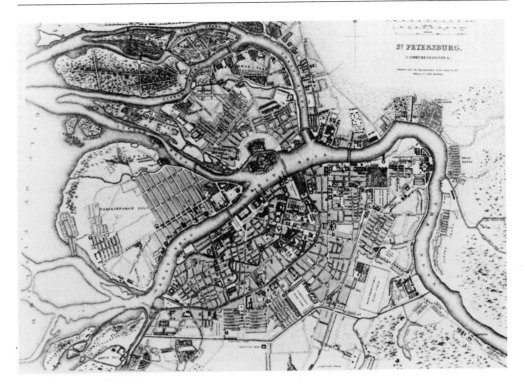

Plan of St. Petersburg as it appeared in 1837. South of the Neva River, three main avenues converge on the Admiralty. (Morris, A.E.J. History of Urban Form. John Wiley and Sons, 1979.)

The site chosen for this city lacked many advantages usually associated with new settlements, principally a stable substratum. The site was poorly drained; solid building material, including stone, had to be imported. Despite these drawbacks, the Russian government proceeded to found a major city there. Beginning with the construction of a military outpost in 1703, the city expanded to include a cathedral (1712), the Summer Palace (1710), and later the Winter Palace (1754). Originally, Le Blonde, a student of Le Notre, received a commission to organize Vasileski Island as a focus for development on the two adjacent banks of the river. His scheme was not approved, and a subsequent plan was made (1846) for the modern city. The heart of the plan was the three avenues radiating from the Admiralty, crossing a gridiron street layout to the east. Morris[4] sees similarities in the radiating street and gridiron combination at the town of Versailles, and later at Washington, D.C.

LANDSCAPE CONCEPTION IN BRITAIN

Political absolutism in England developed along lines different from European continental states. Though Henry VIII (1491–1547) built the authority of the crown by confiscating ecclesiastical lands, many of these properties eventually accrued to individuals not directly tied to the aristocracy. Some lands went to individuals who had emerged from the commercial sector, unaligned with the aristocracy. Two groups eventually appeared as a result of this process. One traced their origins to the old, feudal ruling class, the other came from the ranks of the commercial entrepreneurs. As Anderson[5] observes, English landowners possessed common roots from the sixteenth and seventeenth centuries, they were "unusually civilian in background, commercial in occupation, and commoner in rank." Mercantilism drove a wedge into the old aristocracy with its reliance on land warfare to hold its authority. Landholdings in Britain complemented the industrial centers, supplying the raw materials, especially wool, for manufacture. London, for example, became the prime market for agricultural goods, influencing the agricultural pattern over the southern and Midland regions of England. An urban and rural model evolved from this association, a miniature of later colonial enterprise and empire.

Societal and mercantile accomplishments in the eighteenth century tend to overshadow events in Britain during the seventeenth century that led to the formation of a landscape conception. We have noted an increase in centralized authority and a change in the nature of the landowning class, the sort of social change that helped to stimulate the Italian Renaissance. One of the first descriptions of a landscape conception appeared in 1590 in Philip Sidney's *New Arcadia,* at about the same time the term "landscip" first occurred in English.[6] During Stuart rule, Baroque spatial concepts and Italian urban theories permeated British design consciousness. As an interest in rural landscape order grew, important artists, including Peter Paul Rubens, popularized a landscape genre. The pictorial investigation of landscape preoccupied other continental artists, including Jacob van Ruisdael, Claude Lorrain, and Salvatore Rosa, who helped to conceive the visual imagery that would help found the Romantic tradition in Britain. Rubens, according to Cosgrove,[7] was especially adept at portraying the country house in an ideal setting. His pictures illustrated rural life at its genteel best, fit for the landowning class of the 1600s.

Artistic expression in painting and poetry gradually formed an ideal of nature from the point of view of the landed observer. Paintings of rural scenes tended to emphasize landscape elements—hills, valleys, forests—by arranging these components to fit the demands of perspective. Perspective was, as it had been in Italy, a convenient method of imposing order on nature. In England, the use of perspective in painting and the organization of country estates fit the intimations of absolutism bound to Stuart rule.[8] Socially and politically, the rural estate epitomized prevailing landscape theory, which was tied to absolutism. The country

Drawing by Lorrain illustrating a pastoral scene. Such images had an influence on the development of the Romantic sensibility.

house, a self-contained agricultural factory, was a miniature example of the mercantile state, self-sufficient and productive.

The efforts of architects to respond to seventeenth-century aesthetic ideology are best exemplified by Inigo Jones, a careful student of Vitruvian and Palladian antecedents. Jones's journey to the Veneto in 1613–14 ended in a commitment to instill into British architecture a Renaissance sensibility, and both James I and Charles I made use of his expertise in the remodeling of London. Jones's proposals called for a Palladian classicism for the Palace of Westminster, and a grand plan for Covent Garden. Only the reluctance of Parliament and the inability of the crown to furnish funding prevented these schemes from becoming reality. The same fate befell later architects, including Nicholas Hawksmoor, John Vanbrugh, and Christopher Wren, with the latter achieving some success at realizing his schemes during the rebuilding of London after the fire of 1666. But the downfall of the Stuarts and the institution of parliamentary authority over the monarchy bolstered the ambitions of the landowning classes, who proceeded headlong into capitalistic production. By the eighteenth century the country estate had become the locus of rural production and the source of wealth for the aristocracy and the ingenious. The country estate was also becoming the focus of cultural expression, exemplified by a formal transition in landscape planning from perspective-driven symmetry to free-flowing naturalism. The sources of this transition attest to the complexity of the change: included were aesthetic theory, literature, and seventeenth-century painting. The very best landscapes to emerge from the Romantic ideal—Stourhead, Stowe, Blenheim—established a model for landscape organization which would influence design on the European continent and in the Americas.

ROMANTICISM AND RURAL ORDER

The great leap in the eighteenth-century British imagination was the emergence of the Romantic tradition. However, the sources of romanticism lay on the European continent, in Germany, Holland, and Italy. Russell[9] points to late eighteenth-century German influences on British literary figures, including Coleridge and Shelley. Cosgrove refers to a succession of pictorial images produced in Holland, which promoted a realistic perception of nature, wrapped in an ordered materialism.[10] From Italy the great Baroque forms represent a rapidly decaying urban culture. French painters, seeking to establish fresh pictorial sources, developed methods of observation that revealed a formal order in nature and an original comprehension of urban structure. While visiting Rome, Claude Lorrain sketched the action of natural phenomena on urban forms, including light and shapes that were to inspire his major paintings. In combination, these European resources visually anticipated a shift in the relationship of humans to political and economic systems by substituting absolutism for the possibility of a new social order founded on natural harmony and sensual appeal.

Two events fueled the development of the Romantic tradition in England: the worship of nature and the ownership of property. At a time when scientific inquiry was beginning to produce theories about primary physical phenomena, aesthetics bore the mark of being derived from the senses rather than reason. Perhaps, as Clark[11] states, the lack of formal religion in England by the eighteenth century created a vacuum into which flowed a faith in the divinity of nature. We might also note the effect scientific activity was probably having on traditional faith. Regardless, the interest in nature blossomed in England, by the 1700s, into a full-fledged sensibility, visually reminiscent of the landscape paintings of Lorrain, Rosa, and van Ruisdael. In addition the Romantic attitude attracted various proponents, especially literary figures who extolled the virtues of untamed nature. The most prominent were essayists, including Alexander Pope, Richard Steele, and Joseph Addison. Pope wrote of Newton's theories,

> Nature and Nature's Laws lay hid in Night
> God said, Let Newton be! and all was Light.

However, Pope carefully distinguished between Renaissance perception of natural phenomena, which rested on objective rules, and the subjective apprehension of nature posited by eighteenth-century theorists:

> Those rules of old discover'd, not divis'd,
> Are Nature still but Nature methodis'd
> Nature, like Liberty, is but restrain'd
> By the same rules which first herself ordain'd.[12]

Nature remains part of the divine order, but the perception of this order now depends on intuition, rather than classical logic, or as David Hume (1711–1776) maintained, "All reason is nothing but a species of sensation." Rousseau, safely ensconced in his cottage at Lake Bienne, Switzerland, proclaimed that "existence was a succession of moments perceived through the senses." The extension of this belief led theorists to propose a mental state which transcended sensation and produced, in the mind of genius, the sublime. Early eighteenth-century writers associated the sublime with the greatest literature of the past, which touched upon the insignificance of human order in the face of divine authority.

Initially, the landscape in its natural state was thought to have little affinity with the sublime; beauty could occur in nature, and the most astute artists, including Lorrain, might capture it in a painting. Gradually eighteenth-century aestheticians refined their theories to include the possibility that landscape also had the potential to elicit the sense of the sublime, if it contained sufficient historical references to elevate a scene beyond mere natural effect. Cosgrove[13] singles out Rosa as a painter who often captured the sublime in his painting. Rosa's images usually balanced the awesome potential latent in nature with a human event, often one drawn from a classical epic. Though none of these images became the precise model for organizing landscapes, the attitude individuals, particularly landowners, had concerning the structure of the landscape derived from contemporary literature, which attempted to delineate the boundaries of the Romantic in the landscape.

Little of the Romantic ideal might have appeared in the landscape had theorists not taken the opportunity to extol the virtues of the new sensibility. As we have seen, the shift from Stuart rule to a balance between Crown and Parliament furnished a political model where liberty prevailed over the monarchy and property replaced the medieval landholding system. Pope advocated a balance between nature and its allusion to liberty and the monarchy and its claim to order. Of course the concept of liberty applied to landowners and successful merchants, both of whom had access to property. But Pope was careful to point out the value of landscape and the people who were responsible for producing goods from it. Where landowners such as Walpole and Cadogan freely removed tenants from their estates to provide room for lawns and trees, Pope advocated social accommodation in the production and management of the estates. His is a paternalistic view, where the landowner is responsible for the care of all elements of the landholding, tenants and livestock included.

Formally, the Baroque absolutism of France was unsuited to this new political and aesthetic conception. Essayists explored the relationship between naturalistic form and the country estate and proposed design concepts consistent with the new order. Joseph Addison in *The Spectator* railed against the lack of sensitivity within the formal gardens in England, with their carefully clipped hedges trimmed to form "cones, globes, and pyramids." Without a doubt, these formal gardens, which traced their existence to French and Dutch antecedents, seemed out of step with the new naturalism. Ironically, however, it was through Palladianism that neoclassicism and naturalism joined to form a recognizable image. Regardless, Pope characteristically criticized Lord Burlington and other Palladians for their lack of sensitivity to the landscape as a traditional source of economic well-being and formal integrity.

How all these disparate points of view eventually converged is evident in the design and construction of large estates between 1700 and 1800. Not only is it important to understand the qualitative aspects of these landholdings, but it is important to recognize the personalities involved. We might begin with Charles Bridgeman (d. 1730), who, in 1715, teamed up with Vanbrugh to produce the palace and grounds at Stowe in Buckinghamshire. Bridgeman is best known for developing the *ha-ha,* a retaining-wall technique that eliminated traditional fences. Formally, however, Bridgeman's contribution to the planning of Stowe House was a tenuous scheme, marked by a combination of straight sight lines and ambiguous curves. When William Kent (1685–1784) agreed to improve the gardens at Stowe in 1769, he concentrated on eliminating the stiff geometry of Bridgeman's earlier plan. Kent was well prepared to deal with the formal qualities of the garden. In 1727 he had collaborated with Lord Burlington on Chiswick House in Middlesex and around 1737 had planned the gardens at Rousham, Oxfordshire, after Bridgeman's initial work. Horace Walpole praised the garden at Rousham as a "characteristic and charming" example of Kent's work. In fact the spatial organization of the garden most closely approximated Claude Lorrain's ideal image of the landscape. At Stowe, however, Kent was less successful, concentrating on adjustments to Bridgeman's scheme.

In the midst of the planning and replanning of large gardens, there appeared an enduring, sensitive estate plan, Stourhead, designed by Henry Hoare in 1740.

Successive stages of landscape development at Stowe (A) 1739, Bridgeman and Wise (B) 1769, Kent (C) 1780, Brown

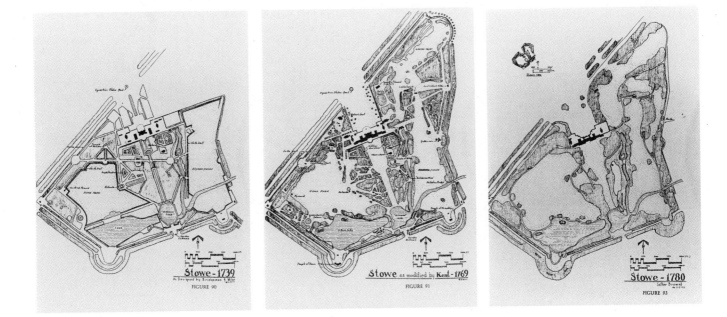

Hoare, a banker and the owner of the Wiltshire property, organized the site as a classical allegory of humankind's travels through the world, perhaps drawn from Virgil's *Aeneid*. Similar to other gardens of the period, Stourhead appears to be influenced by the naturalism of the French painters. Also, Hoare probably owed a debt to Kent, especially in the way water was used on the site. Kent had effectively removed formal water features from consideration in his proposals, preferring "the gentle stream to serpentize seemingly at its pleasure." Hoare, in turn, arranged his scheme around an artificial lake, where, along a path, an observer moves sequentially from one classical feature to another. Beyond the water's edge, Hoare planted trees and shrubs to heighten the sense of seclusion.

Toward the end of the eighteenth century, various approaches to estate planning began to coalesce around major practitioners. Bridgeman had earlier established a *picturesque* approach to design, based on naturalistic images in painting and literature. Richard Payne Knight advocated the picturesque in his commentaries, which appeared in the *The Landscape*. Essentially this school was preoccupied with perceiving the landscape as as personal, elemental phenomenon. Often, gardens designed by followers of the picturesque, including Kent, appeared fragmented, delineated by random clumps of plant material. Lancelot (Capability) Brown (1716–1783) espoused a different line of reasoning, based on a reductive view of the landscape. His concern was for the formal aspects of landscape arrangement. Most of his designs attempted to produce the sublime in the landscape. Thus his schemes were usually large, heroic conceptions defined by rolling hills; large, naturalistic water features; and masses of trees. Often the relationship between the interior of a structure and its exterior surroundings

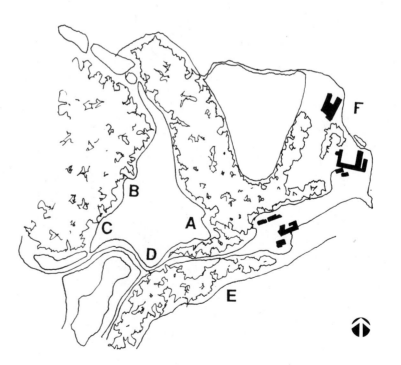

Plan of Stourhead showing the location of (A) Temple of Flora (B) grotto (C) Pantheon (D) arch (E) Temple of Apollo (F) manorhouse

0   100 m

View to the Pantheon at Stourhead. The structure was inspired by Palladio's earlier work near Vicenza.

appeared unarticulated, lacking formal interconnection. Even more problematic was Brown's habit of remaking a preexisting design by eliminating existing, valuable architectural and organic detail.

The forcefulness of Brown's work is evident at both Stowe and Blenheim Palace. At Stowe, Brown reworked Kent's scheme by eliminating any semblance of geometry proposed in the Bridgeman scheme. A plan of Stowe in 1780 clearly illustrates Brown's intentions. Gone are the rigid sight lines and formal spatial elements. Removed also is any hint of a spatial connection between interior and exterior spaces. Blenheim Palace, originally designed by Vanbrugh and the garden designer Henry Wise, was equally formal in its original state. Brown, in 1764, retained some of the original formality of the landscape plan, though he subtly altered the outlying portions of the site to fit his sensibility. He joined the various water features to form a continuous lake, and defined the boundaries of the site with groves, skillfully unifying the 2,500-acre site.

As popular as Brown's work was, it was not until the end of the eighteenth-century that the various design theories began to dovetail into a single, distinguishable aesthetic. The individual most responsible for synthesizing the various landscape theories was Humphrey Repton (1752–1818). Repton adhered to his predecessors' general concepts, but proposed to solve certain spatial problems by greater attention to interior and exterior connections. In *Sketches and Hints on Landscape Gardening* (1795) Repton defended Brown; in his Red Books he delved into the optical and psychological implications of design. Each Red Book was an account of a specific project, with before and after drawings included to help the client understand his proposals. By the end of the eighteenth century Repton had created a theoretical position which attracted other practitioners, including the urban designer M. A. Laugier. In 1840 J. C. Loudon published Repton's writings in conjunction with the emergence of the "Gardenesque" school of landscape design. As Newton[14] points out, the Gardenesque school tended to emphasize a botanical approach to design, resulting in formlessness and inarticulation of space.

Aerial view of Blenheim with Brown's lake beyond the palace.

Sketch by Repton of a landscape plan.

By the early 1800s the argument concerning form and content had come full circle. As Brown had criticized Knight for his picturesque sensibility, Loudon, with his Gardenesque theories, repudiated Repton, who had endeavored to instill into landscape design a greater spatial consciousness.

RURAL INDUSTRY

The great landholdings in England during the eighteenth and nineteenth centuries accounted for a significant amount of England's economic activity. In 1760, agriculture accounted for almost three-fourths of the country's wealth, and manufacturing, which was beginning to expand, for only 7 percent. But a century later manufacturing industry had increased to 24 percent and agriculture had declined to 36 percent.[15] By 1850 the rural landscape had evolved into a composite of farms, small manufacturing centers, and transportation networks.

Rural industry in England and on the European continent grew out of a general revolution in agriculture and manufacturing, facilitated by advances in practical science, beginning in the later seventeenth century. At the same time, the middle class in Britain—small landowners and urban merchants—acquired rural property for agricultural purposes—unlike their continental counterparts, who had less access to property ownership. Property and commercial enterprise were part of the general movement toward market capitalism in England during the eighteenth century, and developed in tandem in rural areas. Largely this occurred because of the resources available in outlying areas: land for raising sheep, and water for powering early woolen mills. Therefore both the agricultural revolution and the Industrial Revolution were initially rural phenomena and English. Bronowski[16] cites statistics which illustrate the point: England was an early, albeit small-scale, manufacturing society, a nation of cottage industries, of watchmakers, blacksmiths, and millwrights living and working in villages. Before 1760 merchants brought piecework to villager's homes. By 1820 workers customarily produced goods in factories, under the watchful eye of the shop foreman.[17] The independent factory appeared only when resources and the market could justify the investment required. The earliest, such as Abraham Darby's ironworks at Coalbrookedale (1707), appeared on sites with water, wood, or coal. Visually, these early factories appealed to the sensibilities of Romantic painters, who, like Joseph Wright of Derby, produced luminous scenes of industrial activity in the rural landscape. In fact these factories imposed a new scale on the landscape, especially at night when structures glowed from within, spilling light into the surrounding countryside.

By midcentury, successful industrial villages were beginning to enlarge. Communities tended to specialize in particular goods, and it wasn't long before

Nineteenth-century rural industrial landscape.

the need to improve the movement of these goods inspired the development of transportation alternatives. England had innumerable roads and paths, some dating to the Neolithic,[18] but most of them were unsuitable for moving industrial goods. James Brindley, a sharp-minded millwright, expanded his engineering expertise to canal building, and by the end of his career had laid out nearly 400 miles of canals, including a connection between Manchester and Liverpool. Brindley's concept was to keep the water in the canals as level as possible. To achieve this goal, he constructed aqueducts to span streams and ravines, traversed valleys by embankments, and when necessary, cut through hillsides.

At the beginning of the nineteenth century nearly 3,000 miles of canals stretched across the British landscape. Many were concentrated in the industrial regions, especially in the Midlands and the south. Snaking across the landscape, the canals introduced a new element into the settlement pattern of rural areas. Towpaths, canal inns, lockkeepers' dwellings, and horse stables came into existence along the canals. New materials brought from distant factories permitted homeowners to upgrade their structures. Formerly inundated lands were drained, and fertilizers, shipped toll-free along the canals, enriched the reclaimed fields.

Road and canal networks played an equally important role in the development of commerce on the Continent. Though Britain maintained an economic edge during the Industrial Revolution, by the nineteenth century the rise of major industrial and trade centers in Holland, France, and Germany stimulated the development of transportation networks. By 1850, The Netherlands and Germany possessed an extensive canal system; by that date also the road systems on the Continent had evolved from localized elements to a regional network, with London and Paris functioning as the hubs of national systems.[19]

Improved roads and extensive canal systems changed the appearance of the British and continental landscape, though, as Hoskins points out, these changes were mostly localized. The appearance of the railroad, however, brought larger changes in landscape quality. With their extensive bridges and tunnels, railroads surpassed the canal systems in both scale and complexity of accomplishment.[20] Naturally, contemporary pundits expressed their opinion in print regarding the effect canal and railroad construction had on country life, especially the genteel solitude of the landed class. But even less privileged individuals objected to the potential despoliation of "beloved solitudes," echoed in Wordsworth's lines,

> Is there no nook of English ground secure
> From rash assault?

Gradually conservatives, as Hoskins notes, lost the battle, as the railroads "slashed like a knife through the delicate tissue of a settled rural civilization, leaving their scars on park and copse and raising high walls of earth across the meadows." Part of the alteration caused by the railways was due to limitations on gradients that necessitated severe cutting and filling. The London to Southampton route, for example, required 16 million cubic feet of earthwork to complete the line. Near settlements, inhabitants accustomed to the quiet rhythm of country life found their solitude rudely disturbed by the change in the local social composition wrought by the influx of construction crews. Visually, the outlying communities gradually changed in appearance as building materials from distant sources began to supplant local materials. By 1850 many ancient sources of local building materials—slate pits and mines—were ceasing production as industrial materials, including asbestos and corrugated iron, became common throughout the land. Eventually only wealthy individuals could afford to build in the "old manner," while less affluent individuals had to live in structures built of industrially produced materials.[21]

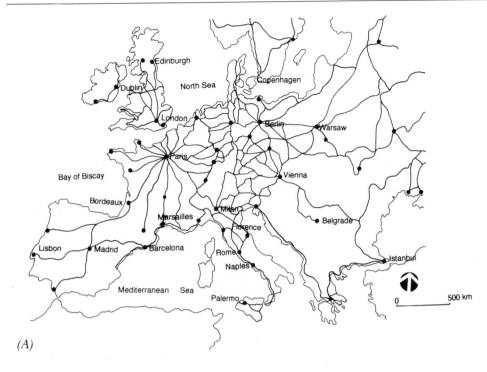

(A)

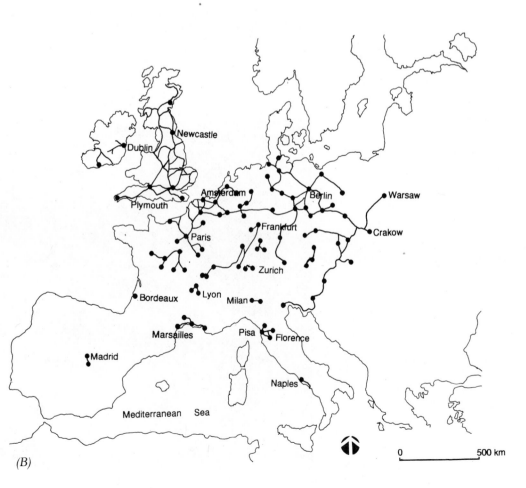

Distribution of nineteenth-century (A) railroads (B) highways.

(B)

Meanwhile, agriculture continued to make a significant mark on the land. Part of the "agricultural revolution" was due to advances in scientific method, which put animal and plant production on a more objective basis. Machinery and breeding techniques improved plant and stock quality and yields. Also, agricultural journalism expanded the general awareness of technique and technology. During the later 1700s, William Marshall and Arthur Young collectively produced fifty-eight volumes on agricultural history and methodology, and established the intellectual basis for agricultural activity in the nineteenth century.

The catalyst for agricultural improvements in Europe during the nineteenth century included refinements in the enclosure movement in Britain, and to a lesser extent, continental Europe. Between 1750 and 1850, the parliamentary enclosure movement in Britain produced 6.75 million acres of enclosed land, far exceeding the 400,000 enclosed acres in 1750. By the mid-nineteenth century, enclosure acts had converted an additional 2 million acres of less arable "waste" and into usable farm land. Mostly the parliamentary enclosure acts affected the Midlands and eastern England. Many of the enclosures in this region were small holdings, roughly 5 to 10 acres in size; larger farms were 50 to 60 acres. The law required the landholding to be fenced within one year of occupancy, and in areas of scant tree cover, this resulted in loss to the small forests. Sheep and cattle breeders subdivided their larger holdings to increase stock production by rotating fields to assure fresh grass for grazing. Plant production also improved with the enclosures. In the heath and moorland districts, former "wastes" became productive lands. In East Norfolk, for example, much traditional sheep-grazing land eventually produced barley, wheat, and rye. Enclosure also provided habitat for small game in the hedgerows that lined the property boundaries of enclosed lands. Often a shallow ditch and a line of hawthorn, sometimes ash or elm, formed the new hedgerow, with other plant species appearing over time.[22]

Contemporary enclosure in Britain.

OBJECTIVITY AND LANDSCAPE ORDER

By the early nineteenth century the structure of market capitalism and the focus of material production began to shift from the countryside to towns and cities. More manufacturing plants were appearing near urban areas, where displaced rural inhabitants, seeking a better life in the cities, furnished the labor to produce finished goods. As European economies became more diversified, slowly shedding their predominantly agricultural emphasis, property became less valuable as a center for production and cultural status; large landholdings gradually became anachronisms, retained to satisfy the nostalgia of long-term landowners. Between the wealthy landowners and the displaced rural laborer, an expanding middle class emerged with hope, energy, but, as Clark notes, without a "scale of values."[23]

Unfortunately artists and theorists were of little help to the prosperous middle class. As science rapidly assumed an uppermost position in the way individuals understood the environment, capped by Wallace and Darwin's theories, the Romantic sensibility, founded on a religious belief in nature, began to lose its grip on the creative imagination. Science had the power to confirm or deny phenomena by objective analysis of causal relationships. Art could no longer claim, as Ruskin believed, to fuse object and subject into a unified response. Though the paintings of J. M. W. Turner, for example, attempted to bring experience and emotion into coherent imagery, resulting in numerous sublime images, the fusion of subject and object in his work fell outside the requirements of positive science with its demand for strict objectivity. Moreover, the ability to experience the essence of landscape, as Ruskin knew it, was the chief means of comprehending moral truths embedded in the structure and function of nature. Ruskin extended his reasoning to argue for an architectural style derived from the forms of the natural landscape, rather than geometry, which was the underpinning of classicism. Inevitably, science prevailed, and began to influence political and social theory in Britain. And as scientists succeeded in separating subject and object in nature, practitioners began to apply objectivity to the ordering of landscapes.

The idea of objective treatment of landscape emerged with the rise of the middle class in Britain and its desire to acquire Romantic tastes. As middle-class suburbs began to appear, a market evolved for landscape treatment around suburban dwellings. Repton championed a synthesis of pictorial composition with horticultural knowledge. Loudon, on the other hand, viewed Repton's aesthetic with disdain, calling it lacking in scientific and agricultural credibility.[24] By the mid-nineteenth century, there was a general interest in horticulture and botany throughout British society. Botanical gardens, full of exotic species, were popular with the middle class, and helped to form a horticultural aesthetic for prosperous suburbanites. Loudon's Gardenesque landscape treatment founded on botanical principles, mirrored the sensibility of the bourgeoisie and spawned a suburban landscape dominated by disparate plant species, crowded into confined gardens. Eventually, as urban areas began to receive more attention from planners and designers, the Gardenesque approach influenced the design of public spaces.

URBAN LANDSCAPES

The Romantic legacy, with its Gardenesque overtones, first appeared as a major influence on serious urban design strategy in 1754, when John Wood II (1728–1781) proposed an addition to the northwest section of Bath, in Somerset. Wood's plan for the Royal Crescent, an architectural arc of thirty fashionable residential structures, combined classicism with English romanticism. Beyond the half-ellipse of residential frontages, the landscape moves outward, allowing a beautiful view of the countryside to the south.

Beech plantations dating from the early nineteenth century in southern England, a holdover from picturesque influence of the Romantic tradition.

In 1811, John Nash (1752–1835) in his plan for Regent's Park, London, worked to create an illusion of the countryside in the city. Nash was an acquaintance of the Prince of Wales and an associate of Repton, a fortunate combination of financial backing and aesthetic collaboration. Regent's Park, sited on part of Marylebone hunting park, was a real estate venture aimed at wealthy urbanites. The plan featured terraced houses sited to afford their owners the "sense of living in a vast mansion in its own grounds." Repton's influence appears in the illusion of vistas and the "detailed use of trees and waters."[25] Even though the final scheme for the site was less ambitious than the original plan, Regent's Park received praise from contemporary critics for its positive influence on surrounding neighborhoods, providing "breathing space between town and country," and for mitigating the unending construction of brick buildings in the district[26].

By the mid-nineteenth century politicians and planners had proposed park schemes for other regions of Britain's major cities. Victoria Park, located in London's East End, combined residential housing with Gardenesque site planning. Birkenhead Park, across the Mercy River from Liverpool, offered housing and open space for working families. Through several improvement Acts, Liverpool authorities purchased 225 acres, and in 1843 commissioned Joseph Paxton (1803–1865) to evolve a plan for a "country park." His proposal avoided the Gardenesque approach to site arrangement. Housing was placed on the periphery; carriage roads loop through the site, compartmentalizing the land to some degree. Despite the eclectic quality of the structures built around the site and the imposing nature of the road system, the park was a major influence on urban open space theory. Frederick Law Olmstead, who visited the site in 1850, was impressed with the public park, a concept yet undeveloped in America.

Olmstead was not the only one to sense the potential of British park theories. Two designers, Prince von Puckler-Muskau (1785–1873) and Baron Georges Haussman, succeeded in establishing a direction to park planning in Prussia and France, respectively. Puckler, who had visited Britain and formed opinions on

Royal Crescent at Bath.
Neoclassical structures embrace
a naturalistic landscape.

Regents Park, London.

the relative merits of the proponents of the English landscape school—notably Brown, Repton, and Loudon—criticized the German interpretation of the English style, which often resulted in stiff imitations of the original. In his plan for Muskau Park, built on a portion of his own large estate, Puckler aimed at producing an environment tuned to country life, by weaving natural and human-

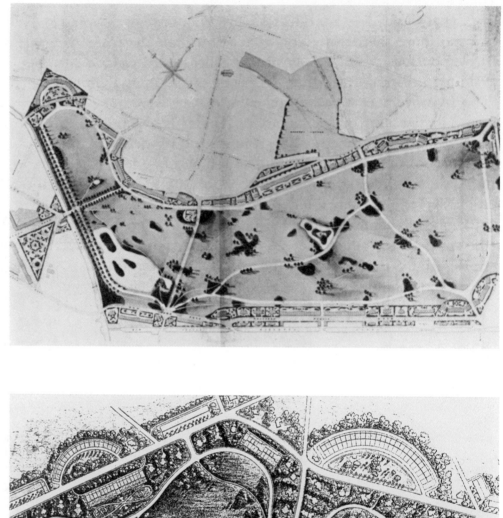

Victoria Park, London. Despite its design flaws, the project was one of the first attempts in England to provide commodius urban housing.

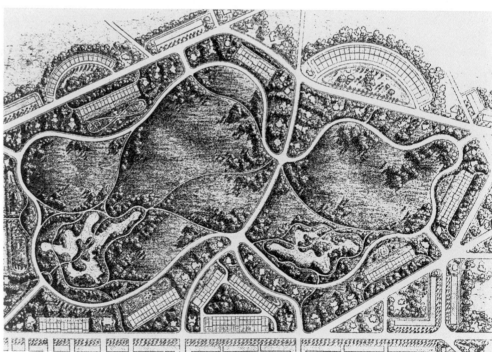

Birkenhead Park, Liverpool.

made elements into a coherent unit. His guide was a set of self-evolved "hints" on site design, which included standards for the spatial and ecological planning of a site.[27] Most prescient was Puckler's eye for site dynamics and ecology, concepts that are timely in the late twentieth century.[28]

Baron Haussman stands out for his ambitious reorganization of important parks in Paris during the reign of Napoleon III. Part of the credit for the redesign

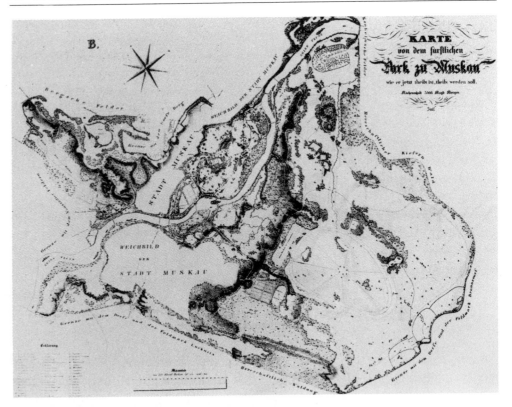

Estate of Prince Puckler-Muskau.

of the Bois de Boulogne, a 110-acre site with allées and ronds, rests with Louis Napoleon, who was interested in the English landscape style and wished to model Parisian parks after the English style. Though Puckler consulted with the Emperor concerning the design of the Bois, the plan for the park originally fell to Vare, who succeeded in creating major engineering problems. In 1853 the Emperor appointed Baron Haussman to administer planning activities for Paris. Haussmann identified three planning objectives: clearing the city; linking urban center, railway terminals, and boulevards; and creating main roads and intersections in outer districts.[29] Many of the major streets and parks of modern Paris stemmed from Haussman's influence. For the Bois de Boulogne, however, Haussman enlisted Jean Alphand, a civil engineer, to assist in the redesign of the park. Alphand rectified Vare's scheme by dividing the lake and by transforming long allées into winding roads. The result was an urban space modified to fit the naturalistic sensibility occuring in Britain, western Europe, and, eventually, under Olmstead's influence, America.

INDUSTRIAL LANDSCAPES

Nineteenth-century industrial workers, many of whom were emigrants from rural areas, toiled in oppressive factory environments with no prospect of substantial economic advancement. Early in the 1800s social reformers became interested in improving the living standards of industrial laborers. Ruskin characterized the plight of the laborer as a testament to the separation of human experience from nature, instigated by industrial capitalism. But Ruskin's attempt to link social progress with art was conservative in comparison to the concepts of social theorists, including Engels and Marx, who sought to expose the structure and operation of capitalism by objective analysis. Public consciousness spawned reform legislation in Britain, including the Factory Act in 1819 and the Reform Bill in 1832, both in reaction to the conditions of industrial workers. A few industrialists sought to improve the living conditions of their workers, prominently Robert Owen, a Manchester textile manufacturer. Owen envisioned planned communities for workers, with a maximum population and land area, and ample open space and gardens. Owen was ahead of his time; few of his contemporaries appreciated his vision. Frustrated by his attempts to form a community in Britain, Owen transplanted his ideas to America, and in 1825 founded New Harmony, Indiana.

By the mid-nineteenth century, however, the squalid conditions of industrial towns in Britain prompted industrialists to propose solutions to the situation. In 1853 Sir Titus Salt founded Saltaire on the edge of the river Aire in Yorkshire. Around 1880, the Cadbury Brothers founded Bournville near Birmingham, as a housing and open space plan independent of the Cadbury industry. Recreational facilities were included, and the residences, each of which had a garden, were grouped around a central open space. By 1900 the 330-acre site had 313 residences, administered by the Bournville Village Trust. In 1887 Lever Brothers, the soap-manufacturing firm, established Port Sunlight a few miles outside Liverpool. Port Sunlight, unlike Bournville, was intended to house employees of the firm. The village had a "superblock" arrangement, with open space for gardens and active and passive recreation; by the early 1900s the community consisted of 230 acres. The village plan did not possess a distinctive visual quality, nor was it revolutionary socially. Its chief distinction lies in the effort made by an industry to improve the quality of life of its workers.[30]

Theoretical advancement in housing at the end of the Victorian age appeared with the work of Ebenezer Howard, who originated the "Garden City" concept. Howard was more a social planner than a designer, and his concepts had a mix of classical and Romantic flavor. His diagram (1898) for an ideal Garden City has the appearance of a sixteenth-century Italian plan, with its formal geometry

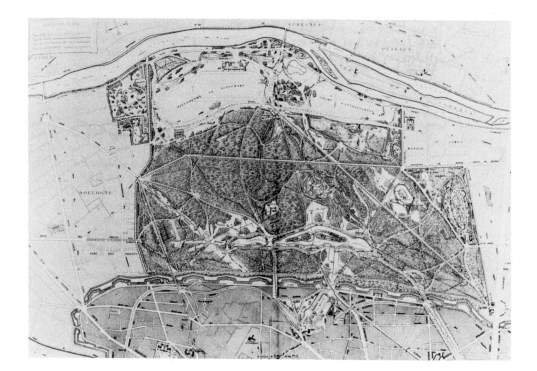

Bois de Boulogne, Haussmann and Alphand's 1853 plan.

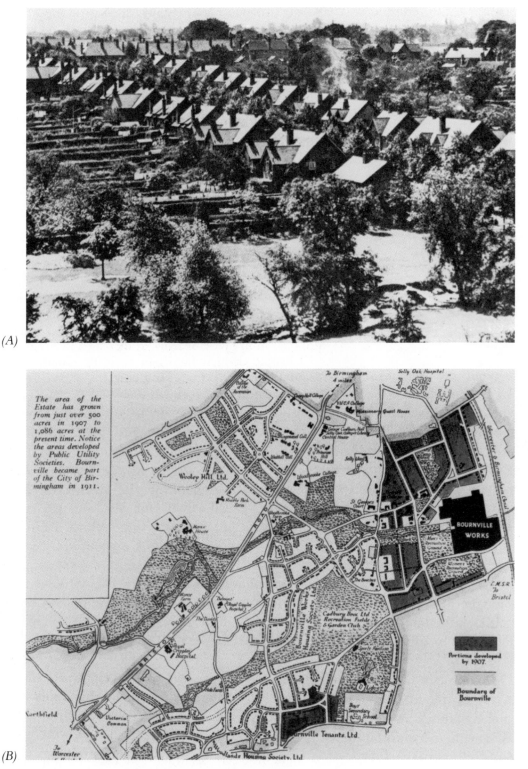

Bournville with (A) workers' homes (B) the town plan.

(A)

(B)

linking various site functions into a unified whole. Morris points to antecedents in Greek colonialism and Renaissance urban planning, especially Leonardo, for Howard's work. For example, similar to Leonardo's schemes his Garden City concept embodied specific planning standards based on a "town and country magnet." Howard believed that a successful community must combine the advantages of town and country life—economics and recreation—for vitality. He advocated restrictions on community size, and called for the inclusion of a transportation link, an industrial component, and a community planning authority. Missing from Howard's proposal is an emphasis on the pictorial, or the link between landscape and sensibility that motivated Ruskin in the earlier part of the nineteenth century. Human association with the landscape in Britain and Europe was quickly evolving into an urban phenomenon, which could not rely on rural standards. Regardless, Letchworth (1903) and Welwyn (1920) were successful as model Garden Cities and examples of Howard's genius; perhaps more important they were clearly conceived to address the most pressing issues concerning the landscape, which, by the beginning of the twentieth century, were becoming social and ecological issues.

ENVIRONMENTAL ISSUES

In Western Europe, the two and a half centuries between 1650 and 1900 witnessed radical changes in intellectual activity, political structure, and economic process. Science seriously challenged religion for intellectual superiority, romanticism absorbed classical theory, and the medieval landlord and tenant relationship, still lingering in parts of the region, succumbed to capitalism. Each of these events contributed to extreme social changes, including a rapid decline in rural population in favor of marked increases in urban growth.

People flocked to urban areas to obtain employment and attain a better standard of living. In 1701, Berlin had a population of 30,000 people; by 1800, its population had increased to 170,000.[31] As populations concentrated in urban areas, the natural resources of the countryside supplied the power and raw materials for industrial production. Initially, factories appeared near natural resources, especially water power, but, with the invention of steam power and the locomotive, industrialization tended to center near urban areas. In Prussia, public funding encouraged new industries, which necessitated changes in urban form, including the addition of suburbs to house the emerging middle class.[32] By 1900, slightly more than 293 million people lived in Europe, with urban centers, many of them industrial satellites of older urban areas, having sustained a nearly sixfold increase in population since 1700. In the capitalistic market system, rife with abuses socially and ecologically, land itself acquired the status of a commodity, first as a mark of distinction for the wealthy landowner, then as an investment for the new urban rich.

By the nineteenth century, urban environmental quality was class-specific, with wealthier individuals likely to enjoy the best housing and access to open space. Certain areas in large cities, the East End of London, for example, saw the implementation of housing and open space plans for industrial workers, but these schemes were the exception, rather than the rule. Generally, living conditions in urban areas may be summed up in the words of Ruskin, who railed against the "loathsome mass of sultry and foul fog, like smoke" that cast a pall over urban areas.[33] Other social observers, such as Louis Waurin, counseled against the headlong migration to cities by rural workers, warning of crime, psychological stress, and moral decay. Hohenberg and Lees[34] point to subtler changes in society resulting from urbanization, mostly changes in social structure and values. Life in the cities meant an opportunity to raise one's standard of living, and higher standards of living created increasing demands on natural resources—coal, metals, water, timber—and accelerated the rate of effluence from urban industry and housing. By 1900 the rate of urban growth appeared to be greater than any conceivable planning strategy could control. Slowly, cities crept outward, insidiously nibbling away at rural lands.

The regional effect of urbanization and intensive agricultural practices on the Western European landscape from 1650 to 1900 varied with the degree of industrialization in the region. Britain, Holland, and parts of France and Germany sustained higher rates of industrialization and agricultural improvement than other areas. The Dutch, in need of additional agricultural lands to support a high population density, continued to retrieve lands from the sea, constructing massive polders along the North Sea. Britain, the industrial leader through the nineteenth century, relied on Dutch engineers to transform fens into agricultural areas. These activities, added to pre-seventeenth century deforestation and large-scale transhumanance, produced a indelible pattern of regional transformation in Europe and the Mediterranean. In the Middle Ages, disease and war had periodically reduced the population and allowed parts of the landscape to revert to natural conditions, but industrialization and capitalization, combined with population growth, transformed the European region into a permanently altered urban and regional system.

By the end of the nineteenth century the layers of human impact on the European, Mediterranean, and Near Eastern landscape produced a complex settlement pattern. Though the essential constituents of the landscape were present over the 250 years of industrial and urban activity in these regions, including soils and geomorphology, surface and subsurface waters, vegetation, and animal habitat, the relative quality of these components through the Industrial Revolution sustained major changes, sometimes with surprising results.[35] For example, as Britain instituted its enclosure acts, landowners, by law, delineated their holdings by erecting fences. In thinly wooded regions, fence building further reduced woodlands. Many other landowners enclosed their lands by planting boundary hedgerows. These linear thickets quickly gave the landscape in south and central Britain a compartmentalized appearance. Moreover, the hedgerows became habitats for small and medium-sized animals. As Hoskins[36] notes, the hedgerows added greatly to the bird population, while limiting some populations, including heathland species.

At the beginning of the nineteenth century popular interest in plant material, fostered by the Gardenesque treatment of landscapes, encouraged the introduction of exotic species into the European landscape. The planting of exotics dates back to early European and Mediterranean history. The Greeks and Romans promoted olive culture—the plant was an eastern Mediterranean native—and later the Arabs introduced sugar cane and citrus to Spain. Nineteenth-century Europeans added to this plant list numerous species from abroad. Attenborough refers to these new species as "terrestrial invaders from the west,"[37] some nutritional, such as potatoes, tomatoes, and sunflowers, others decorative, including cacti and agave; still others restorative like the eucalyptus, which appeared in Europe around 1804 and was used to reforest lands around the Mediterranean. Occasionally, the importation of plant material resulted in the introduction of unwanted parasitic organisms, such as phylloxera, a variety of aphid native to eastern America, which by 1863 had begun to devastate French vineyards, threatening to eliminate a major European agricultural commodity. At first the magnitude of the problem prompted vintners to apply toxins, deadly to the insect and to humans, with little positive results. Only by replacing established vines with imported rootstock were the Europeans able to preserve the wine industry.

The phylloxera debacle is an illustration of how complex the European landscape had become in the 250 years between 1650 and 1900. Much of the complexity was due to human alteration, a process that had a protracted history. Political, social, economic, technical, and aesthetic factors dovetailed during this period to produce compelling personal and public landscapes, many unattainable today, due to financial and material considerations, and the legacy of this period clearly remains within the regional European fabric. Part of this legacy is a Romantic attitude about the landscape, which helps us to retain an ideal about the landscape, but which obscures ecological issues behind a naturalistic mask. The other, equally onerous, part is the need to maintain a range of landscapes, from urban spaces to rural lands, as European society evolves to greater complexity in the twentieth century. Finally, the period brought Europeans face to face with the issue of the landscape as an element of the environment, which, with finite resources available to an expanding population, eventually required collaboration in its planning and management.

NOTES

1. *Bertrand Russell. 1945.* A History of Western Philosophy. *New York: Simon & Schuster, p. 495.*

2. *Ibid.*

3. *Kenneth Clark. 1969.* Civilization. *New York: Harper & Row, p. 246.*

4. *A. E. J. Morris. 1979.* History of Urban Form. *New York: Wiley.*

5. *Perry Anderson. 1975.* Lineages of the Absolutist State. *London: New Left Books, p. 127.*

6. *Denis E. Cosgrove. 1984.* Social Formation and Symbolic Landscape. *Totowa, N.J.: Barnes and Noble, p. 192.*

7. *Ibid, p. 193.*

8. *Ibid., p. 194.*

9. *Russell, op. cit., p. 724.*

10. *Cosgrove, op. cit., p. 160.*

11. *Clark, op. cit., p. 269.*

12. *Alexander Pope. 1711.* An Essay on Criticism. *lines 88–91.*

13. *Cosgrove, op. cit., p. 228.*

14. *Norman T. Newton. 1971.* Design on the Land: The Development of Landscape Architecture. *Cambridge, Mass.: Harvard University Press, p. 228.*

15. *Cosgrove, op. cit., p. 223.*

16. *J. Bronowski. 1973.* The Ascent of Man. *Boston: Little, Brown, p. 259.*

17. *Ibid., p. 260.*

18. *W. G. Hoskins. 1955.* The Making of the English Landscape. *London: Hodder and Stoughton, p. 30.*

19. *Hoffman, 1977, op. cit., p. 45.*

20. *Hoskins, op. cit., p. 199.*

21. *Hoffman, 1977, op. cit., p. 47.*

22. *Hoskins, 1977, op. cit., p. 152.*

23. *Clark, op. cit., p. 327.*

24. *Cosgrove, op. cit., p. 240.*

25. *A. E. J. Morris. 1979.* History of Urban Form. *New York: Wiley, p. 231.*

26. *Ibid., p. 231.*

27. *Newton, op. cit., p. 239.*

28. *Geoffrey and Susan Jellicoe. 1975.* The Landscape of Man. *New York: Viking, p. 253.*

29. *Newton, op. cit., p. 451.*

30. *Paul M. Hohenberg and L. H. Lees. 1985.* The Making of Urban Europe, 1000–1950. *Cambridge, Mass.: Harvard University Press, p. 324.*

31. *Ibid., p. 215.*

32. Ibid., p. 215.

33. John Ruskin. 1886. The Stormcloud of the Nineteenth Century. *New York: Wiley. Cosgrove, op. cit.,*
p. 251.

34. Hobenberg and Lees, op. cit., p. 264.

35. Charles F. Bennett, Jr. 1975. Man and Earth's Ecosystems. *New York: Wiley.*

36. Hoskins, op. cit., p. 153.

37. David Attenborough. 1987. The First Eden: The Mediterranean World and Man. *Boston: Little, Brown,*
p. 182.

11

The Twentieth Century: Modernism and Planning

At the beginning of the twentieth century, science, art, and planning inspired the formation of another conception of the European landscape. Along with this conception appeared a new logic, partly formed by reason and partly shaped by objectivity. The two united to produce a distinctive style in Europe called Modernism, whose influence is only now beginning to fade. However, its legacy remains clearly imbedded in the European landscape, from efficient concrete and glass urban centers to planned suburbs to rural lands.

Though the modernist vision stems from radical changes in science, art, and planning, these were foreshadowed by conditions within urban and industrial landscapes during the nineteenth century that compelled farsighted individuals to propose plans for improved environmental quality. These proposals attempted to respond to cultural and economic changes in urban areas—and especially to living conditions in industrial neighborhoods, viewed by many as inimical to social justice. For instance, we noted earlier that socially inspired planning appeared in Great Britain with Robert Owen, followed by the largesse of conscientious industrialists, and culminating in Ebenezer Howard's Garden City schemes in the early twentieth century. Concern for social and environmental improvement increased as revolutionary fervor rose in Russia and parts of Europe, and a series of events began that for many European states involved the assimilation of socialist concepts into established political theories. In most instances, these concepts evolved from the thoughts of nineteenth-century radical socialists, including Karl Marx and Friedrich Engels, who sought to challange capitalist authority over social policy. For example, Engels, in his *The Condition of the Working Class in England in 1844,* focused on the neglect of the working poor in industrial centers. Marx strove to give socialism a scientific basis, and to shift the fruits of production from the industrialist to the wage-earner. Marx and Engels' publication, the *Communist Manifesto* (1848), fueled a drive to dismantle the prevailing social order, which has had far-reaching, and sometimes cataclysmic, consequences in Europe throughout the twentieth century. In the most extreme case, the Russian Revolution completely overthrew the old aristocratic order, instigating authoritarian state control of social, economic, and physical planning. In less extreme cases—for example, Great Britain, France, Germany, and Italy—political change produced a synthesis of democratic and socialist ideals.

In every instance, these attempts to alter social policy contributed to the demise of the nineteenth-century landscape, and set the stage for a new vision. For example, Ruskin's romantic ideal could no longer accommodate the moral and social burden associated with late nineteenth- and early twentieth-century theoretical changes.[1] Rather, twentieth-century concepts depended on a realistic appraisal of social and environmental conditions, leading to a new vision of the landscape. If there was a loss in the process, it accrued to the side that viewed the landscape as a mechanism for resolving moral issues, an idea that lost its currency as objective efficiency became the byword of the twentieth century.

Arguably, certain patterns remained, mostly holdovers linked to rural life and agricultural practices. However, migration to urban centers, instigated by eighteenth- and nineteenth-century industrialization, inexorably shifted the focus of landscape activity from the countryside to the cities. The burgeoning of European urban centers intensified the need to solve landscape problems endemic to the new, urban social structure. The seedbed was ready for the changes to be wrought by new concepts in science, art, and planning. The result was the development of a new landscape sensibility, suitable for maintaining a balance between urban and rural landscape development.

OBJECTIVITY IN SCIENCE, ART, AND PLANNING

The distinctive feature of twentieth-century landscape perception and planning is objectivity. Radical advances in science, art, and planning stemmed from objective analysis, which produced from a shift away from analogically derived assumptions about nature to reliance on quantitative methods for acquiring scientific information about natural phenomena. The processes began in the first half of the nineteenth century, as scientists rapidly developed quantitative methods for proposing theories in biology and physics. Gregor Mendel invested his adult life in research on genetics, and—although with little immediate attention from the scientific community—established a mathematical model for biological inheritance. By 1858, Darwin and Wallace, after extensive research in South America, independently produced the theory of natural selection, and further helped to establish an objective basis for comprehending the biological world. In chemistry and physics, researchers produced increasingly complex models for the structure and function of nature, culminating in Einstein's theories about space, time, and matter. By the early twentieth century science had swept away romantic notions about the physical world and had replaced them with objective, verifiable models.

Few graphic images better describe the shift in the mode of comprehending the landscape that took place at the beginning of the twentieth century than Georges Braque's cubist depictions of rural Mediterranean settlements. In these images we see landscapes derived from a new logic, unencumbered by traditional perspective and romantic ideals. Absent is the vocabulary, inspired by history and literature, which was standard in much nineteenth-century art. Instead Braque's paintings record the act of observing the landscape, free of traditional pictorial devices. Just as scientific theory was peeling back the layers of the visible world to reveal the physical structure of nature, so too was cubist painting revealing nature's interior.

Most likely the habit of closely observing nature evolved late in the nineteenth century from the Postimpressionist aesthetic. In theory, the Postimpressionists were in step with the general shift to objectivity in science and aesthetics. For example, Paul Cézanne probed the visual world for deeper meaning and produced solid images of the Provençal landscape, portraying nature in constant transition, with organic forms appearing to shift and realign on his canvasses. By the beginning of the twentieth century younger artists, influenced by Cézanne and other progressive artists, abandoned traditional spatial techniques, including formal perspective, and launched on a course of presenting the world in nonrepresentational methods. The result was a plethora of artistic styles during the first half of the twentieth century—Cubism, Surrealism, Dada, Constuctivism, Abstract Expressionism—each attempting to examine the world in a nontraditional manner. Braque and Picasso, who were early exponents of this new system, and whose cubist landscapes epitomize the era, succeeded in portraying a new view of the world, unfettered by classicism and representation. From their efforts, two worlds emerged: one empirical, guided by the experience of forms,

Houses at L'Estaque,
1908, by Georges Braque.

the other, positivist, concerned with formal relationships. Throughout most of the twentieth century, the tension produced by these two positions has driven aesthetic theory, with Modernism dominating European aesthetics until late in the century.

In the field of landscape planning, science and art created adherents to powerful and opposing design versions. Jellicoe[2] singles out Antonio Gaudi and Le Corbusier as examples of the two extremes. Gaudi, a modernist master at improvising form intuitively, contrived environments inspired by the logic of nature and materials, while Le Corbusier produced environments based on the logic of form and function. Applied to early twentieth-century design and planning, which evolved from social concerns, the dual forces of intuition and logic gave rise to numerous aesthetic directions, some of which continue to shape planning and design in the late twentieth century. On balance, the objective side of the equation, in the name of Modernism, has had the greater impact during this century. For example, Modernism's effect on environmentalism during the nineteenth century operated from a romantic locus, linking environmental analysis with an objective, geographical methodology. Consequently, environmentalism has been bolstered by a new, more scientifically rigorous, geography.[3] In the second half of the twentieth century, environmentalism in Europe has slowly regained its authority to direct physical planning.

URBAN LANDSCAPE PLANNING

In the midst of Barcelona's visually stimulating urban fabric is one of the most lyrical urban landscape components to grace a twentieth-century European city. Parc Guell, designed by Antonio Gaudi in 1900, swirls along a hillside, an imag-

Parc Guell, Barcelona.

inative combination of form and material. Gaudi, a keen observer of the structure of nature, achieved a synthesis of logical and intuitive form in the terraces and columns of the park structures. At first his solution for the park appears driven by purely romantic ideals, an impression of nature. But behind the free-form assemblage lies a study of the structure and forces of nature, a prescient view of twentieth-century planning and design, which underscores the value of utilizing organic models in design.

In contrast to Gaudi's bold concepts, the preponderance of twentieth-century urban landscape design evolved from concepts of objectivity and analysis rooted in the modernist sensibility. Leaders on the Continent were Adolph Loos, Le Corbusier, Walter Gropius, and Mies van der Rohe, all of whom were instrumental in developing Modernism in architecture and planning. Their concepts fostered a change in the perception of landscape, from the value-laden nineteenth-century view to one embracing a strictly utilitarian application of function in design.

In many ways, modernist ideas fit the rapidly changing lifestyles evolving within the urban centers in Western Europe. As migration to industrial centers continued, people's relationship to the landscape shifted—the landscape becoming less a place of work and psychological reference than a place of retreat from the rigors of urban existence. In Britain, especially in the housing projects planned for the middle and upper classes, community open space embodied intimations of romantic landscapes, in what were essentially utilitarian environments. On the Continent, Le Corbusier repudiated Beaux Arts classicism with his revolutionary modernist planning schemes, notably in his design for La Ville Radieuse (1935). Here were architecture and landscape conceived as disparate components, ostensibly to free the land for pedestrian and vehicular uses. Yet Bacon[4] argues that Le Corbusier's goals led to the separation of landscape and architecture, which, in the hands of an inspired master, had the potential to produce dynamic planning proposals. However, many adherents to Le Corbusier's concepts interpreted his vision as an opportunity to develop architecture at the expense of landscape, depriving the urban dweller of the opportunity to maintain sufficient physical contact with the land. Hughes contends that Le Corbusier's plan for the Ville Radieuse stretches the limit of human involvement with landscape by proposing broad, efficient open space components as a foil for imposing and impersonal architectural elements. However, Hughes qualifies his assessment by noting that Le Corbusier also envisioned a new class of urbanite in his proposals, one who possessed the "right state of mind for living in mass-produced houses."[5] Hughes acknowledges the need for solutions to living conditions of the urban dweller at the turn of the century, but like Bacon's opinion his observations about the application of Modernism to social problems have a familiar ring: the founders of Modernism sought solutions to social ills by relying on objectivity and mass production, but, as noble as these pioneers were in their goals, they were off the mark in supposing that a new category of individual would evolve within their utopia, an individual able to adapt to the efficient steel and glass environments of modernity.[6]

Not all cities in Europe embraced modernist theories in the organization of their urban landscapes. For example, Denmark's Aarhaus University, designed by C. Th. Sorenson in 1932, evinces a rural mood, with its buildings and open spaces sited around a glacial ravine. Jellicoe[7] contends that Stockholm, Sweden, was one of the first urban areas to plan the growth of the city with attention to prevailing natural features. Because Stockholm did not sustain industrial blight during the nineteenth century, planners were free to concentrate on preserving the existing natural amenities of the city, which evolved into verdant corridors within the urban core. In Amsterdam, Bos Park, designed by a collaboration of academics, scientists, designers, and planners, furnishes the city with a naturalistic setting for active and passive recreation activities.

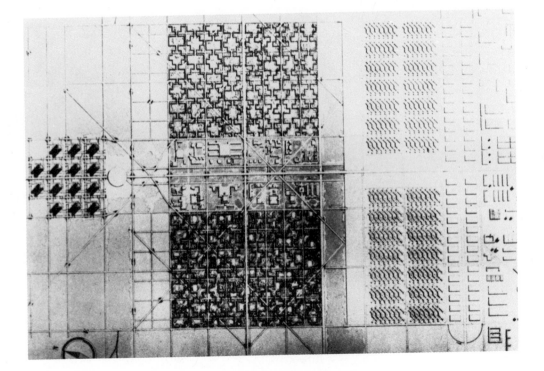

Le Corbusier's utopian scheme for La Ville Radieuse.

Aarhaus University, Denmark.

Stockholm.

Bos Park, Amsterdam.

In Central and southern Europe, post-World War II landscape planners devised imaginative solutions in or near urban centers. One of the most ambitious examples is the 1972 Olympic site, 1.5 miles from the center of Munich. The center of the project, a one-time airstrip, exhibition ground, and dump site for subway excavations, roughly 1 square mile in area, metamorphosed into a dynamic combination of landscape and architecture under the guidance of Gunter Behnisch, who envisioned an "Olympic in Green" where buildings, landform, and flora fuse to produce an environment which would inspire a festival attitude.[8] Behnisch's concept was to use landscape as the prime spatial element. He achieved this objective by interweaving all architectural elements with the landscape, and by avoiding spatial disconnections: the stadium appears to emanate from landform; the natatorium glistens in natural light; water, hills, and paths allow visitors to see and feel naturalistic forms and materials. Tension structures, inspired by Ewald Bubner, carry the lines of the landforms into the architectural elements, further enhancing spatial unity.

Another bold project near the periphery of an urban center is Parc La Villette, on a 125-acre site once occupied by the slaughterhouses of Paris. This park was designed by Bernard Tschumi, who explicitly attempted to apply late twentieth-century deconstructionist theory to the planning of an urban landscape. Because the old industrial site contained few elements suitable for a new park, Tschumi was free to rebuild the landscape in the spirit of a twenty-first-century park.[9] Despite the site's location on the urban fringe, the designer conceived of the park as a part of the city. Therefore Tschumi elected to save important structures, including the Museum of Science and Industry and the nineteenth-century Grand Halle, and combine these with new structures, which do not have the historical associations of the older buildings, but which project late twentieth-century cultural disjunction. Paths, sunken gardens, water features, and broad lawns are the only features that allude to traditional parks;

1972 Munich Olympic park. Landforms and architecture combine to form a coherent scheme.

Tschumi sees these elements fitting into European modernist concepts of urban space, rather than as concessions to naturalistic urban landscapes. Because of its deconstructionist arrangement, La Villette does not have the landscape and architectural cohesion of traditional parks, or even modernist parks, including the Munich Olympic site, which successfully combine architectonic and landscape form. Its strength lies in the questions it asks about the future of architecture in recreational settings.

In its attempt to impose a late modern pattern on an urban park, La Villette is the exception to most urban landscape planning. Most urban centers in the large European cites are variants of the pedestrian-oriented urban space. In some instances these districts evolved from the need to impede the automobile from coming into close contact with historical features—architecture, sculpture, painting—and in other situations the need to clear urban centers of vehicular traffic to improve commercial and social prospects. Cologne, Stockholm, Paris, Munich, Rome, and Barcelona, among others, each feature a district devoted to pedestrian activity. Less populated centers, including relatively small cities, usually possess equally pleasant pedestrian districts including Perugia, Strasbourg, Seville, Cortona, Bologna, and a long list of other communities.[10]

Except in cities that sustained heavy damage during World War II, most of these pedestrian districts rely on their historic contexts to give them identity. Less frequently—examples are the Ramblas in Barcelona and Les Halles in Paris—they feature nearly contemporary planning solutions. The Ramblas is a linear urban landscape element defined by trees and elegant paving; Les Halles plays to late nineteenth-century detailing within a modern spatial organization. West of Paris, La Defense is a late modernist collection of imposing urban forms and spaces. Recently certain cities have initiated ambitious urban art projects as part of their overall urban renewal plans.[11] Barcelona, host to the Summer Olympics in 1992, continues to expand its urban landscape program of art and parks *(Espais Urbans)*, and now has 50 sculptures and 200 parks and plazas. Most of the works

Aerial photograph of Parc La Villette, Paris.

Parc La Villette. Contemporary spaces and forms complement a naturalistic landscape treatment.

have a contemporary quality to their form and material, notably Richard Serra's installation at the Plaza de la Palmera and Andres Nagel's sculpture and water feature at the Parc de l'Espanya Industrial. Many of the works occupy sites in working-class and middle-class neighborhoods, rather than in locations that adorn civic sites. Late twentieth-century urban planning, with an eye for spreading amenities throughout cities, fits the socialist context of Barcelona and its problem of imbuing disparate neighborhoods with a sense of place, by employing contemporary art as a mechanism for imparting visual energy to the "otherwise lackluster neighborhoods."[12] Many of the projects succeed in accomplishing this task, mostly by upholding the basic tenets of twentieth-century art and design in urban landscapes by juxtaposing intuition with objectivity.

The Ramblas, Barcelona.

Pedestrian spaces at La Defense, west of Paris.

SUBURBAN PLANNING

At the beginning of the twentieth century the weight of industrial activity in Europe pressed on urban areas and stimulated advance in land planning and design. In Britain, where the pace of industrial activity stimulated early attempts to plan habitable landscapes for factory personnel, planners continued to propose increasingly sophisticated schemes for social benefit. We have noted Ebenezer Howard's pioneering theories, embodied in his Garden City plans. The legacy of his work appeared in early twentieth-century planned communities, notably at Letchworth and Welwyn.

Letchworth, located in Hertfordshire about 35 miles north of London, began to take shape in 1902. Within a year surveyors had completed their work on the site, completing requisite engineering for water supply and drainage. Letchworth was not a perfect model of Howard's Garden City concept: the site was 4,000 acres, 2,000 less than his model; the existing railway, rather than encircling the interior of the community, bisects the site. Working within these limitations, the principal site planners, Barry Parker and Raymond Unwin, designed a community center with a town square, main street, and residential and industrial districts. Early difficulty in obtaining sufficient financing, coupled with competition from other housing schemes, retarded the development of the community. But by 1919, the town boasted a population of about 10,000, sufficient for Howard to propose a second Garden City, Welwyn, 12 miles away.

At 3,000 acres, Welwyn was even smaller than its predecessor, half the size originally recommended by Howard. Despite this limitation, Welwyn fulfilled Howard's essential recommendations: a rail link, town square, and parkway formed the central core of the plan, flanked by industrial and residential components, surrounded by an agricultural belt. Newton[13] praises the Welwyn plan for its sensitivity—especially in the design of the residential component, which responded to existing topography, in the use of existing lanes to "soften" the plan, and in the preservation of existing landscape features. The population of the community numbered about 8,000 ten years after construction had commenced.

Substantial population increases at each project finally occurred during World War II, as workers migrated from the threatened industrial centers. At the conclusion of the war, Britain came to grips with urban growth and the specter of uncontrolled development during reconstruction of the country, by instituting planning measures to assure orderly growth. To guide urban growth, the British government instituted the New Towns Act in 1946, aimed at regulating the

Letchworth (A) aerial view of surrounding countryside (B) residential area. (Benevolo, Leonardo, The History of the City. Copyright © 1980 MIT Press.)

(A)

(B)

planning and construction of new communities. The Act cleared up ownership questions at Letchworth and Welwyn, and led to the development of new towns at Harlow, Stevenage, and Hemel Hempstead.

Britain was by no means the only country in the nineteenth century to pursue improved living conditions for urban dwellers. France, Holland, and Germany also proposed plans for urban growth. In France, Jean Baptiste Godin began building a worker's community at his foundry at Guise in 1860. His plan included apartments, day-care centers, educational and recreational facilities. Within twenty years, the workers were managing the community, tapping factory profits to finance community projects.[14] In Germany, conscientious factory owners also proposed housing schemes for their workers. The Krupp industry backed the planning of several worker communities near Essen, including one at Friedrichshof, begun in 1860, which had community facilities, recreational spaces, and a lower than normal density apartment house component. Subsequent planning efforts in Germany tended to focus on preserving city centers by encouraging and managing urban expansion into the surrounding countryside. As in Britain, much of the effort in urban design and improvement of existing urban settings in the later part of the nineteenth century centered on amenities for the middle and upper classes. Planning for factory workers in the spirit of Howard's concepts was not synonymous with German planning. Instead, worker housing was part of the overall strategy to direct growth into districts that were expanding outward from the urban core. Regardless of specifics, planning both in Britain and on the Continent signified a change in human occupation of the landscape through rational planning.

After World War II a less utilitarian approach to suburban landscape design began to emerge in the Scandinavian countries, where Hohenberg and Lees see Howard's Garden City concepts forming the basis for new settlements, fusing community with the natural environment.[15] Olwig contends that Scandinavian lands, including the heath lands of Denmark, are the locus of an age-old con-

Nineteenth-century planned workers neighborhood.

junction of nature and human activity, stemming from an Anglo-Saxon pastoral conception of the landscape. Moreover this conception fostered the appearance of a gothic sensibility in Denmark during the seventeenth century, opposed to the neo-classical conception of the landscape, that Olwig contends was a result of political absolutism during the eighteenth and nineteenth centuries.[16]

Modern suburban landscapes in Scandinavia often evince a belief in nature as a source of regeneration, inspiring the arrangement of landscape forms in an approximation of naturalness. Even such an ambitious landscape project as Tapiola, Finland (1972), with its various housing densities and commercial elements, contains elements of the gothic pastoral in the open spaces wending through its residential and commercial districts. Conceived as a Finnish rendition of Howard's Garden City model, Tapiola occupies a site on the Gulf of Finland, 10 miles west of Helsinki. The community is part of a Seven Cities regional plan, with each city housing 50,000 to 200,000 persons. Tapiola epitomizes planning theory applied to new towns in Scandinavia, with its hierarchy of residential units dominated by a town center. Separate pedestrian and vehicular systems link the various parts of the site, with the pedestrian system fanning from the town center to the residential districts.[17] Part of the early success of Tapiola was due to its low density, about 57 persons per acre compared to Stockholm's 200 to 300 persons per acre, and its social diversity (the population is a mix of professional and industrial workers). Physically the community projects a "naturescape" rather than a "cityscape," including the use of water for recreational use and spatial interest; the inclusion of fields, forests, and gardens within the community; and a mix of high- and low-cost dwellings in the same housing cluster. The Seven Cities project was scheduled to accommodate nearly 1.5 million people by 1990.

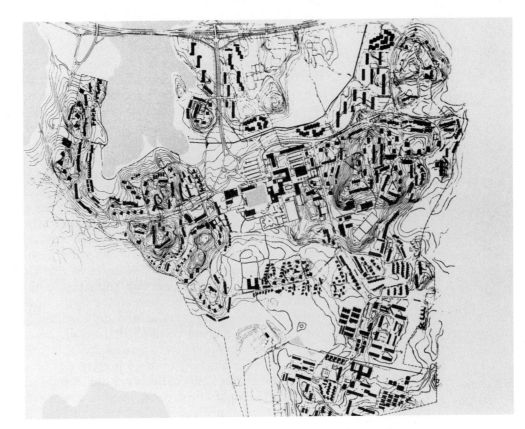

Plan for Tapiola, Finland.

Tapiola, Finland.

RURAL LANDSCAPES

Though urban and suburban centers continue to attract people who seek to improve their standard of living by participating in the diverse economic and cultural activities they offer, rural landscapes have also become the focus of interest for many who have the inclination and resources to live beyond cities. Since World War II and the diversification of the European economies, many rural areas have sustained a gradual qualitative change in their appearance. Within the last forty years, rural landscape planning has taken on great urgency, as agricultural and open space areas succumb to residential uses. Partly this is due to a persistent decline in the number of agriculturalists in rural areas, many of whom are now middle-aged or elderly and without offspring interested in pursuing an agricultural lifestyle. For example, between 1960 and 1980, the agricultural population in Britain declined 1.6 percent. In Italy the decline was 20 percent over the same period; West Germany posted an 8.3 percent decline.[18]

For some countries, notably Italy, the decline began to ease in the 1960s with the out-migration of individuals from historic centers to rural areas. Added to these were individuals interested in acquiring second homes in rural areas. Berry,[19] Fielding,[20] and Dematteis[21] all characterize this reinvestment in rural lands by city dwellers as *counterurbanization,* a phenomenon roughly analogous to American suburbanization. The effect of this trend in such countries as Italy is visible in the landscapes surrounding cities, which are slowly losing their wholly agricultural image. In the process, the visual integrity of historic centers is weakening as contemporary residential and institutional structures occupy agricultural lands, thereby helping to obscure the traditional edges of the centers.[22]

Despite these changes in rural areas, farming is still the predominant land use in Western Europe, with 44 percent of the landscape devoted to agricultural activity in the late 1970s; however, many individuals participating in farming are doing so on a part-time basis. Various European initiatives, including the Common Agricultural Plan and the Mansholt Plan, have helped to foster an enlightened approach to rural land management. Included in these plans are measures for insuring technical, marketing, and small farming strategies. In 1978 the Common Agricultural Plan focused on the Mediterranean region, including improved irrigation techniques in the Italian Mezzogiorno. According to Clout et al.,[23] the prospect for rural lands is cloudy and depends on the formulation of a land policy which will allow the continuation of agricultural activity while accommodating competing interests.

PUBLIC LANDS: PARKS AND RESERVES

Since some of the pressure on rural landscapes has occurred in areas of scientific and scenic value, the various European states have pursued measures to set aside these lands as reserves and parks. Historically, public park planning in Europe is a recent phenomenon, dating from the middle of the nineteenth century. The application of scientific rigor to geographical disciplines helped set the course of environmentalism in Europe and shifted the concept of landscape from an intuitive to an objective phenomenon. By viewing the landscape in a scientific manner, planners were better equipped to distinguish salient qualities of disparate landscapes. The ability to make such distinctions created a new sensibility about the European landscape and lent credence to those advocating the preservation of land for scientific, scenic, and recreational purposes.

The idea of selecting lands for use as reserves was current early in European history, notably during the medieval era when the aristocracy created hunting preserves for their personal use. But not until the nineteenth century were lands beyond urban areas identified for public use. The French forest at Fountainbleu, cherished for its scenic quality by artists, became a reserve in 1858, a landmark event in the history of public lands in Europe. In 1895 the British National Trust began acquiring lands for use as private reserves; by 1905 similar measures were in effect in The Netherlands. By 1909 France and Germany saw the creation of reserves at Sept Iles and Luneburger Heide, the latter designated a "nature protection park." By the beginning of the twentieth century reserves had acquired a value beyond the scenic. Planners recognized the need to set aside lands that contributed to important ecological functions, including physical processes and maintenance of habitat.

As important as these events were, true national parks did not begin to appear in Europe until 1909, when Sweden established parks at Sarek, Stora, Sjofallet, and Abisko, followed by a similar proclamation by the Swiss, who established the Engadine national park. For the first time in Europe, governments identified criteria for park lands, including recreation, ecosystem, and scientific significance. Both Sweden and Switzerland dedicated their park systems to scientific activity, due to the efforts of the scientific communities in each country. The Swiss park immediately became an alpine field laboratory for the study of flora and fauna. Geographically the park, 39,520 acres in extent and surrounded by mountain ranges, consists of fifteen valleys in the lower Engadine. Throughout the twentieth century, the Swiss Academy of Sciences has sponsored research at the site, enabling scientists to publish significant environmental data.[24]

The second phase of park development began immediately following World War I in 1919, concluding with the outbreak World War II in 1939. Initially, recreational need was the motive for the creation of parks, especially in Italy, where park development began with the conversion of the Grand Paradiso reserve into a national park, followed by the Abruzzi (1923), the Stelvio (1935), and soon after the Circero. In 1918 Spain logged in with national parks at Ordesa and Cavadonga; Sweden added to its national park lands at Vadvetjjakko (1920) and Tofsingdalen (1930); Holland established the "Hogte Veluwe" national park in 1935; and, three years later, Finland founded national parks at Pallus-Ounas and Pyhatunturi—the same year Greece established parks at Parnassus and Olympus.

The years after World War II constituted the third phase of park development, noted for the establishment of the majority of Western Europe's parks and reserves. Most of the European states expanded their park lands during this period, resulting in a total by 1970 of 269 nature reserves and national parks with an aggregate area of 30,007,783 acres, or about 2.1 percent of the area of Western and Eastern Europe.[25] However, several Western European countries exceed the percentage, including the Federal Republic of Germany (West Germany) (11.5%), France (10%), Great Britain (9.7%), and Norway (4.4%). These percentages are more significant when compared with the amount of land area in the United States devoted to public parks, which amounted to 29,515,265 acres in 1972.

In addition, the Western European countries have endeavored to form intereuropean parks, beginning with a German-Luxembourg reserve (1965), followed by a German-Belgian reserve (1971). By 1970 the concept of transfrontier parks and preserves was a top priority and stimulated proposals for a German-Dutch park, along with discussions between Germany, France, Switzerland, and Austria about similar parks. The French and Italians contemplated a link between the Vanoise and Grand Paradiso parks, and proposed a similar connection between Finland's Lemmenjoki park and adjacent Swedish lands.

With Europeans enjoying a high standard of living, including one in three persons owning an automobile in 1980, demand for recreational space continues to put pressure on landscape that had traditionally functioned as agricultural lands and open space.[26] Urbanites now have the opportunity to travel into the countryside and as a result have had a major impact on rural areas.[27] For instance, Britain emphasizes public access to rural landscapes, where sightseers may view pastoral and agricultural lands. In West Germany, the approach is somewhat the reverse: more than 1,100 nature reserves attest to the government's emphasis on nature conservation. Added to these divergent approaches to rural recreation is the now ambiguous term *national park,* which in contemporary Europe is a loose designation for lands ranging from public wilderness, often closed to intensive, public use, to private farmland, which is actively promoted for rural recreation uses.

The International Union for Conservation of Nature and Natural Resources (IUCN) has attempted to establish a rational basis for designating lands as national parks. By 1974 IUCN standards, a landscape must have specific qualities to qualify as a national park. These include a large area consisting of one or more ecosystems relatively unaffected by human activity; scientific, educational, or visual interest; and the commitment of respective national governments to protect the resources of the national park and to restrict public use of the land to recreational, educational, cultural, or spiritual purposes. To avoid confusing national park land with other parks, the IUCN has removed from consideration any land that is a restricted scientific reserve; a private or local public natural reserve; a plant or animal game reserve; or a recreational landscape devoted to tourism that favors recreation over the protection of ecosystems. Based on these standards, the number of national parks varies from country to country, with Sweden having the highest percentage of land area devoted to national parks, and Denmark the smallest.

In addition to national parks, the IUCN has promoted the identification and protection of wetlands and other significant habitats. Beginning in 1965, IUCN has maintained a list of sites that require special protection as wetlands, marshes, or bogs—the so-called MAR list, which by 1975 had named over 163 locations in eighteen countries. A boost to the program occurred in 1971 with the Ramsar, Iran, convention, which sought to draw attention to the fragility of these sites in the face of worldwide rapid urbanization and increased rural recreational activity.

The result of all these national and international measures to form reserves, parks, and recreational areas has been a complex arrangement of specially designated lands set aside for conservation and recreation. In West Germany, armed with its 1976 Federal Nature Conservation Law, the government continues to favor the preservation of natural habitats, and seeks to protect rare plants and animals, rather than picturesque landscapes. Many of the sites are 125 acres or less in size, compounding the difficulty of protecting sensitive landscapes from pollution and urbanization. In France, rural landscape conservation received a boost from the 1967 proclamation, which created the *parcs naturels regionaux.* The purpose of these parks is to furnish the nation with lands that enhance and preserve the natural, cultural, and rural aspect of the countryside. There are now twenty regional parks ranging in size from 508,820 acres in southwest France to a small 25,441-acre site near the Belgian border.[28] Of all the Western European countries, Britain appears to have created the most elaborate system of reserves and parklands. Beginning with the National Nature Reserves initiative in the

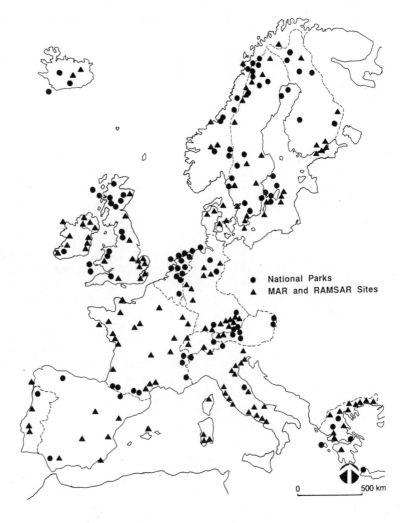

● National Parks
▲ MAR and RAMSAR Sites

0   500 km

Distribution of European parks and reserves.

European Reserve in Denmark.

1940s, the British government, by 1982, had created 219 reserves in England, Northern Ireland, Scotland, and Wales. Many of these lands are owned or leased by the Nature Conservancy, thereby providing some safeguards against indiscriminate land use.

ENVIRONMENTAL ISSUES: PROSPECTS AND PLANNING

In 1990 the population of Western Europe was projected to reach 358 million people, with a majority of the population concentrated in urban areas. In the industrial sectors of Great Britain, The Netherlands, Germany, and Belgium, the population density per square mile exceeds 650, much higher than Sweden, for example, with a density of 55 persons per square mile. These numbers tell only part of the story, since for the past several thousand years Western Europe has been part of a larger arena of human activity centering on the Mediterranean. Thus we must include all the nations of the region, including the North African and eastern Mediterranean states, in any discussion of environmental issues affecting landscape quality. For example, Egypt presently has a population of 49 million, mostly concentrated along the Nile River channel. The population density along most of the river exceeds 1,100 persons per square mile, with areas around Cairo and Aswan exceeding 2,800 persons per square mile. These figures, added to the European estimate, raise the total population of the region to roughly 420 million, many of whom are involved in modern industrial and agricultural activities.

However, population projections are only a part of the picture. Of equal significance is the change in lifestyles, fueled by economic prosperity throughout most of the region. The average European today has attained a standard of living such that his or her material and leisure demands are exacting an increased toll on the landscape. Even in areas, such as Egypt, where a good portion of the population remains involved in agricultural activities, changes in agricultural techniques have stimulated a gradual rise in standard of living, creating increased demands for energy, natural resources, housing, and recreation space.

The Egyptian example is pertinent at this point. For nearly seven thousand years the Egyptians have relied on the Nile River to provide moisture and nutrients for their agricultural activities. Until recently, water from the White and Blue Niles has conveyed nutrients and silt into the lower Nile River valley during the autumn flood season. At times these floods were disastrous, overfilling agricultural lands and inundating settlements; in other instances insufficient rainfall in the Ethiopian highlands produced scant runoff. To overcome these problems, the Egyptian government embarked on a plan to control the flooding by constructing the Aswan High Dam.[29] The project, begun in 1971 with Soviet assistance, produced a high dam and large reservoir, Lake Nassar. The projected benefits of the project seemed to support the building of the dam: the builders promised it would increase arable land in Egypt from 7 million to 9 million acres and enable the country to maintain high yields of rice and wheat. In addition, the project produced an annual hydroelectric output of 10,000 million kilowatts.

Though the Aswan High Dam project has helped to control flooding and to produce needed electrical energy, the project, like so many efforts undertaken in the region to tap the resources of the landscape, has also produced several negative environmental consequences. The most significant is the loss of sediments that now accrue behind the dam, rapidly building up due to the high evaporation rate at Lake Nasser. Farmers now must rely on artificially produced fertilizers for their fields. Ironically, a portion of the electrical output at the High Dam must be used to produce these fertilizers. Even with these substitutes, farmers now contend with increased rates of salination and the spread of schistosomiasis. In addition the projected increase in arable land was not realized; building of the dam has actually resulted in a net *loss* of 106 million square yards of land below the dam. Further north along the Nile Delta, there is a problem with shoreline erosion resulting from the lack of sediment reaching the sea. Finally, the once fecund sardine fishing industry has declined due to insufficient nutrients reaching the Mediterranean.

Along the northern rim of the Mediterranean, pressures to utilize undeveloped landscapes for new industrial, residential, and recreational sites have produced similar alterations in the environment. Attenborough[30] paints a vivid picture of the conditions along the Mediterranean rim during the summer vacation months when more than 60 million people invade the region in search of sun and relaxation. Visitors from northern European companies along with tourists from America, Australia, and Asia cram the resort communities from the Spanish to the Turkish coasts. Between seasons developers hustle to keep up with the demand for resort facilities, appropriating sensitive landscapes like the the coastal stretch of the Carmarque near Cannes, which lacked a natural beach but, with the application of modern engineering techniques, now accommodates numerous boats and sunbathers. Along other stretches of the coast, developers plant high-rise hotels on sites once distinguished by dunes and esturarian lands. To reach these sites, highways and local roads link one development with another, crossing sensitive lands. Once these developments fill to capacity, tourists add to the intrusion by wearing footpaths into the landscape in their wanderings into the hinterlands in search of nature.

By 1972 sufficient data on the consequences of human activity had appeared to alert the European community to the need to institute measures to help protect the environmental health of the region. Part of the reaction stemmed from a United Nations conference in Stockholm that focused on worldwide environmental issues. Following this conference, the United Nations established an en-

Erosion of Nile River Delta occurs as less silts are conveyed along the Nile River.

Mediterranean beach exhibiting one of the most pressing environmental problems: tourism.

vironmental program, a part of which centered on the problems of continental and Mediterranean Europe. A major objective of the program was to establish accurate environmental monitoring methods and to report on the extent of human influence on environmental quality. Various scientific groups have now produced revealing data on the status of human-environmental relations in the Mediterranean region. Since 1973, at least 90 tons of pesticides have entered the coast from landward agricultural operations. Spillage and tanker cleaning had dumped 800 tons of oil into the sea; 430 billion tons of household waste and sewage entered the Mediterranean, most of it untreated. And coastal industries have managed to flush high levels of zinc, lead, and mercury into the waters.

All nations surrounding the Mediterranean had to assume some blame for the problem, and accordingly strict regulations have been put in place to reduce the level of degradation. How well these initiatives will succeed in ameliorating the problems remains to be seen. However, as recently as the summer and fall of 1990, thirty-five nations from the region met at Palma de Majorca, Spain, under the auspices of the Conference on Security and Cooperation in Europe to push for better management of the situation. According to Meisler,[31] the situation was less than sanguine. To give one example, striped dolphin were washing up on the Spanish beaches, due to an immune system deterioration instigated by industrial contamination. Despite this and other revelations, the conference could do little to cope with the problematic politics of international environmental regulation—resulting in acrimonious charges being leveled against European and United States interests by Mediterranean countries for subverting tough environmental legislation. Not an auspicious outcome at a time when the environmental quality of the Mediterranean, and, by extension, the well-being of the nations within the region is at a crossroads.

In Britain, efforts to rectify environmental problems occurred as early as 1821 with legislation aimed at curbing problems associated with air pollution. By 1861 Parliament had enacted the Alkali Act, instituted to reverse the pervasive emission of hydrochloric acid into the atmosphere. After World War II, Britain gradually expanded its regulations regarding air and water pollution, coupled with the founding of the Nature Conservancy to oversee reserves. Following devastating fogs in London, which killed 4,000 people in 1952, the British government tightened air pollution laws and eventually reduced air pollution in major cities by 80 percent.[32] Public regard for environmental quality in Britain helped sustain membership in various conservation organizations, and by the mid-1970s, terrestrial and aquatic waste acts were in place to help stem pollution.

Similar efforts have occurred in continental Europe, especially in West Germany, Sweden, Austria, and France, where the Green Party made political inroads during the 1970s and 1980s.[33] Responding to this and other influences, public opinion in West Germany now places environmental quality at the top of the list of national concerns. Degradation of the Black Forest from acid rain and pollution of the Rhine River has helped to stir public interest in the environment and subsequent regulation requiring emission controls at coal-fired plants and regulating the disposal of phosphates into rivers.

Each of these national efforts has helped to ameliorate the degradation of land, water, and atmospheric environments. However, the European Community has recognized the need for a comprehensive strategy, which will assess environmental problems and implement responses across the various national boundaries. Officials have identified critical issues common to all the nations which must be dealt with if a comprehensive plan is to work. The first is the need for regulatory parity across the Continent to assure strict conformity to environmental regulations. For instance, it does Norway little good to impose strict regulations when nations to the west, who contribute to eastward-moving pollution, fail to uphold similar standards. Second, the European Community recognizes that environmental legislation has a critical effect on productivity in many industries. With economic union looming in 1992, all industries need to function on the same standards. Therefore as the European Community looks to the next century, it appears that it will gradually adopt an environmental policy similar to the American approach, placing the responsibility for regulation with its governmental bureaucracy, chiefly the Environmental Protection Agency, and backing it up with constitutional authority—as distinct from the European approach, which traditionally has allowed governmental officials to bargain directly with industry without the intervention of the courts. The result will be more confrontation, but greater control of environmental problems throughout Europe.

At the end of the twentieth century the Near Eastern, Mediterranean, and Western European cultures appear to be approaching another critical juncture regarding the quality of their landscapes, a juncture often repeated throughout the history of the region. However, unlike earlier periods, when individuals could migrate to an uninhabited locale and establish a new community, or later, when individuals had the option to migrate from farmsteads to the cities for an improved standard of living, the contemporary inhabitants of the region no longer have the luxury of mobility. Even for those who move from one place to another, the resources and problems appear similar: coastal lands in Spain are as populated with tourists as the beaches in Turkey; farmland and forests in Western Europe sustain effects of urbanization similar to lands in Yugoslavia and Greece. But with intelligent planning and the resolve to make critical decisions regarding the stewardship of urban and rural lands, future generations could have the opportunity to live in healthy and inspiring landscapes.

NOTES

1. *Denis Cosgrove. 1985.* Social Formation and Symbolic Landscape. *Totowa, N.J.: Barnes and Noble, p. 254.*

2. *Geoffrey and Susan Jellicoe. 1975.* The Landscape of Man. *New York: Viking, p. 285.*

3. *Cosgrove, op. cit., p. 260*

4. *Edmond Bacon. 1978.* Design of Cities. *New York: Penguin, p. 231.*

5. *Robert Hughes. 1980.* The Shock of the New. *New York: Knopf. Hughes contends that Le Corbusier's architectural concepts mirrored his image of the modern human: the modular figure, bred to be suited for a high-speed life based on socialism and aesthetic order.*

6. *Ibid., pp. 167–68.*

7. *Jellicoe, op. cit., p. 299.*

8. *Faber Birren. 1972. "The Olympics Landscape."* AIA Journal, *58(2):20–21.*

9. *Ginger Danto. 1989. "Parc de la Villette. Rough and Reddish."* Art News, *vol. 88, no. 5:103. Also see Artforum International Magazine, vol. 26, no. 6:82.*

10. *Roberto Brambillo and Gianni Longo. 1977.* For Pedestrians Only. *New York: Watson-Guptill. The authors present an overview of pedestrian districts in several European cities and discuss planning and design strategies for creating viable pedestrian areas.*

11. *Garry Apgar. 1991. "Public Art and the Remaking of Barcelona."* Art in America, *1985 (2):108–17.*

12. *Ibid., p. 108. Apgar notes the difficulty the city has had in maintaining the works, many of which are abstract—a style unfamiliar to local residents.*

13. *Norman T. Newton. 1971.* Design on the Land. *Cambridge, Mass.: Harvard University Press.*

14. *Paul M. Hobenberg and L. H. Lees. 1985.* The Making of Urban Europe, 1000–1950. *Cambridge, Mass.: Harvard University Press, p. 322.*

15. *Ibid., p. 330.*

16. *Kenneth Olwig. 1984.* Nature's Ideological Landscape. *London: Allen & Unwin. Olwig distinguishes between the conception of nature as a source of change and regeneration, and the modern perception of nature as a thing or place.*

17. *Morris Ketchum. "From Three Emerged One."* AIA Journal, *48(1):36–58, July 1967. This article discusses the issue of community architecture and planning and profiles Stockholm, Sweden; Tapiola, Finland; and Cumbernauld, Scotland.*

18. *B. J. L. Berry, 1978. "The Counterurbanization Process: How General?" in N. M. Hansen, ed.,* Human Settlement Systems. *Cambridge, U.K.: Ballinger, pp. 25–49.*

19. *Ibid., p. 123.*

20. *A. J. Fielding. 1982. "Counterurbanization in Western Europe."* Progress in Planning, *17:1–52.*

21. *Giuseppe Dematteis. 1986. "Urbanization and Counterurbanization in Italy."* Ekistics *316, 317:22.*

22. *Giancarlo De Carlo. 1966.* Urbini, *Padova, Marsilio Editoro. Dimatteis, op. cit. Alberto Gasparini. 1982.* "The Historical Center as an Integrative Value for Outlying Areas: Italy," *Ekistics, 295, 1982. See these sources for discussions of the implications of counterurbanization near Italian hill towns.*

23. *Hugh Clout et al. 1985.* Western Europe, Geographical Perspectives. *London: Longmans.*

24. *Richard Van Osten. 1972.* World National Parks: Progress and Opportunity. *Brussels: Hayez, p. 32.*

25. *Ibid., p. 123.*

26. *Clout et al., op. cit., p. 137.*

27. *I. G. Simmons. 1975.* Rural Recreation in the Industrial World. *London: Arnold.*

28. *Clout et al., op. cit. The authors point to the advantages and disadvantages of the plan, including the need to maintain cooperation between the various authorities, as well as the positive aspect of local input into the planning of the park.*

29. *Gupta Avijit. 1988.* Ecology and Development in the Third World. *London: Rutledge.*

30. *David Attenborough. 1988.* The First Eden: The Mediterranean World and Man. *Boston: Little, Brown, p. 194.*

31. *Stanley Meisler. "Pollution and Deep Blue Sea."* Los Angeles Times, *October 20, 1990, p. A3.*

32. *Norman J. Vig and Michael E. Craft. 1990.* Environmental Policy in the 1990s: Toward a New Agenda. *Washington, D.C.: C. Q. Press, p. 258–64.*

33. *J. F. Pilat. 1980.* Ecological Politics: The Rise of the Green Movement. *Beverly Hills: Sage.*

PART TWO

THE NORTH AMERICAN LANDSCAPE

Introduction to Part Two
The North American Landscape

In Part Two we will change both the geographical location and scale of our discussion. North America is significant as a distinctive human-made landscape because of its distinctive natural landscapes, its unusual settlement pattern—especially that it was not widely inhabited until a fairly modern period—and as the location where landscape architecture as a distinctive profession involving land planning, design, and management was established. In addition, the period covered by this part is limited, with the exception of Chapter 1, to the past five hundred years. This allows for the discussion of more site-specific details, as well as in-depth discussion of specific issues, especially the relationship of the natural environment to the designed landscape.

The six themes introduced in the preface to this book will continue to be the basis for discussion, but in the specific cultural and natural context of North America. The natural landscape of North America was particularly important in determining the pattern of land use that evolved following human settlement—Native American, African-American, and European—because of the dramatically different characteristics of each region. In particular, the presence of two major mountain groups tended to slow settlement and intergroup contacts until the nineteenth century. This segmentation led to regionally variable cultural development that continues to impact the built landscape today.

Nowhere else has the paradoxical attitude of Europeans and their descendants toward natural, rural, and urban landscapes been as obvious as in North America. Arriving in the first large "wilderness" to be settled by Europeans, immigrants encountered situations in the undeveloped landscape that both challenged and terrified them. The drive to "pastorialize" the landscape became a key theme of most political decisions of the eighteenth and nineteenth centuries. This idealization of the rural tended to lead to an undervaluation of the natural, which was viewed as completely hostile to human life and in need of modification. Similarly, the rural landscapes that were so valued in the nineteenth century were often considered detrimental to human cultural development in the twentieth century. Rural living for all but the wealthy was viewed as substandard—a kind of agrarian slum life, in which few services were available. At the same time, cities were maligned as places that bred evil human traits, which the country could purify. These ambiguous attitudes led to mid-twentieth-century programs to upgrade rural life to urban standards of comfort, through rural road improvement and electrification, and to late twentieth-century efforts at urban renewal.

Many symbols were embodied in the North American landscapes as a whole and in specific landscapes. At the broadest level, to early Euroamerican immigrants the continent represented freedom from the oppressive and constrained physical environments of Europe, as well as from suffocating cultural traditions that limited individual freedom and initiative. Of course, to another group, the African and Caribbean slaves forced to emigrate from their homelands, North America symbolized just the opposite. Individual landscapes have also been imbued with specific meanings. For Native Americans, distinctive places such as

Devil's Rock in Wyoming have a spiritual meaning. For Euroamericans, few landscapes have such a metaphysical connotation, but symbolize ideals of beauty, power, and history. Plymouth Rock is a landscape of miniscule proportions that symbolizes the entire spirit of American settlement by Europeans. Regions like the Hudson River valley, the Yosemite area, and the Grand Canyon are both impressive natural landscapes and symbols both of the dynamic character of presettlement America and of Euroamerican ideals of natural beauty.

The designed environment has always had an important social role. At times this was asserted by methods as simplistic as the setting of important buildings on high ground, either natural or artificial, a technique used to impress the populace in urban plans from the Aztec capital at Tenochtitlan to the U.S. capital at Washington, D.C. In other more subtle ways the landscape influenced human behavior, either adding to what we would today call "stress," or ameliorating it. One interesting aspect of the development of the profession of landscape architecture in the nineteenth century is that this social role was explicitly recognized, and designed landscapes organized in attempts to alleviate negative conditions of human life and promote desired values.

The influence of technology on the development of the North American landscape is particularly apparent, because so much of it was occupied during and after the Industrial Revolution, when the rate of technological change was increasing with great speed. Among the most important technologies to influence North America have been those associated with agriculture, such as the self-scouring steel plough, and transportation, such as the long-distance railroad line. At the broadest scale, each of these allowed new areas of the continent to be settled, while at the local level they led to particular patterns of land use and occupation.

Finally, Americans in all periods have viewed the designed landscape as a place to express aesthetic principles, sometimes in conjunction with symbolic land uses. The most exceptional example of this was the effigy mounds of pre-Columbian peoples, particularly the beautiful undulating Serpent Mound in Ohio, which continues to influence modern artists. Elsewhere different aesthetic principles were expressed at all scales, from the gardens of individual homeowners to the designed cityscapes of the early twentieth-century City Beautiful Movement.

While many North American land use practices derive from European precedents, the ways in which they were assembled proved to be distinctive to the continent. It is the distinctive set of relationships to both the natural and cultural landscapes which resulted from this process that had a direct impact on the formation of the new profession of landscape architecture, whose adherents differed markedly from older landscape design practitioners in the depth of their theoretical justification for alterations of the landscape.

12

The Pre-Columbian Landscape

Many moons ago, there was a vast expanse of water, seemingly boundless in extent. Above it was the great blue arch of air, but no signs of anything solid or tangible. High above the lofty blue expanse of the clear sky was an unseen floating island, sufficiently firm to allow trees to grow upon it, and there men-beings were. There was one great Chief who gave the law to all the Ongweh or beings on the Island. In the center of the Island there grew a tree so tall that no one of the beings who lived there could see its top. On its branches, flowers and fruit hung all the year around, for there was no summer or winter there, or day or night.

Seneca myth of the origin of the world[1]

SHAPING THE NORTH AMERICAN LANDSCAPE

Glaciers of the Pleistocene period were important shapers of the landscape that we see today, both physical and cultural. In North America, one of the most important cultural impacts of the geoclimatic events of the Pleistocene has to do with the role that the Wisconsin glaciation played in immigration of the first known humans to this continent. The Wisconsin glaciation, which took place from approximately 100,000 to 15,000 B.P. (before the present), had many important landscape effects such as the scouring of the Great Lakes and creation of much of the northern Mississippi River drainage basin; no effect was as important from the standpoint of human activity, however, as the impact it had on the elevation of the oceans. At about 35,000 B.P., when huge quantities of atmospheric moisture were trapped in glaciers, sea level was about 400 feet below present levels. This lowering exposed many areas of the continental shelf, creating new dry land. In the area now called the Bering Strait a sea level drop of as little as 150 feet exposed a continuous ice-free isthmus from northeastern Russia to Alaska. It has long been hypothesized that it was this link that provided the path of entry for successive waves of Mongoloid peoples from Asia into North America. If this theory of migration is accurate, then human occupation of the Americas can be conservatively dated to 30,000 B.P.[2]

The landscape which these early settlers encountered was conspicuously different from the landscape today. The climate is believed to have been generally wetter and cooler, but with less seasonal variation than at present. This, coupled with differences in soils and landforms, produced a flora and fauna no longer present either in type or in extent. Among the animals known to have existed in parts of the Americas were the small, native horse, which may have looked somewhat like a mule; the American camel; and the saber-toothed cat. Vegetation distribution also differed markedly from present patterns, with cold and mountain zone materials extending much further south. These landscape characteristics surely affected early Native Americans, just as the landscape influences us today. The climatic consistency and greater moisture levels over much of North America may help explain, in part, why the vast length of the Americas was so quickly occupied. Areas of the two continents that are today semi-arid were then far more fertile and would not have presented the barrier to movement and settlement which they have in historic times.

NORTH AMERICAN LANDSCAPE ZONES

Climate changes led to a generally warmer, but drier, landscape by about 12,000 B.P. These changes seem to have produced a climate and landscape much like the one we see today at the macro scale. The following general discussion of the climate and vegetation at the time of European discovery will provide a basis for later discussions of particular physical features of the landscape and their relationship to human landscape use. The scheme we will present is obviously a simplification of the true complexity of North American ecozones. However, the continent can be categorized as having nine distinctive types of regions, some with subzones, as defined by vegetation and climate. These nine regions are: Eastern Woodlands, Plains/Prairies, High Mountains, Great Basin, Arid Regions, High Plateaus, Semitropics, Coastal Areas, and Arctic Region.

The Eastern Woodlands cover most of the continent from the Atlantic to the Mississippi, with a mixture of hardwoods and softwoods within that zone. The region is generally rolling or hilly, with many well-defined drainage systems. A major watershed break occurs along the ridge of the Appalachians, where rivers which flow directly to the Atlantic are separated by now highly eroded mountains from those that flow to the Gulf of Mexico, most via the Mississippi River. This zone has been an important landscape for human development since prehistoric times when, first the Hopewellian, and later the Mississippian, Native American cultures dominated extensive areas. It was this woodland zone which also became a cultural hearth for northern European settlement in North America.

Although the Great Plains or Prairie Zone is most often identified by its flat topography, this feature alone is not determinative. A distinctive vegetation complex, consisting almost entirely of forbs and deeply rooted tall grasses dominated the landscape, producing a fertile soil. In pre-Columbian times this land supported a large, diverse fauna, and then, following European encroachment, a highly productive agriculture. Two natural forces controlled this landscape: water and fire. Water influenced species distribution as well as plant size. A distinction between short-grass and tall-grass prairie is largely based on differences in overall annual rainfall, with taller grasses appearing in wetter, usually eastern portions of the region. Water was also a factor in distribution of woody plant material, especially trees, as large stands appeared only along streams, where annual water availability met their needs. Fire was also a factor in tree distribution. It was the major agent in controlling the spread of trees and their intrusion into grasslands, since only trees near water or wet ground were likely to survive a prairie fire. Savannahs were subzones where grasslands and woods intermixed, with neither truly dominant.

The term "High Mountain Zone" refers to the western portion of the continent where mountains and ranges over 4,000 feet in elevation predominate. The Rocky Mountains are the principal mountain group, but other ranges such as the Sierra Nevada in the United States and the Mackenzie Mountains in Canada also form this zone. Rapid elevation changes in this mountain region have created a variety of climatic, microclimatic, and vegetative zones, but most of the region is semi-arid, with much moisture received in the form of snow. The most obvious vegetative differences occur above and below the tree line, which marks the limits of woody plant viability. Other, more subtle, changes occur depending on orientation to the sun, amount and direction of wind, and position in the watershed. The High Mountain Zone offers the greatest ecosystem variability within a short distance. From the standpoint of human landscape activity, the High Mountains have had two major impacts. The first was as a barrier to movement between east and west. The second was their impact on inland climate, particularly by limiting the amount of moisture delivered to inland basins and plains.

One inland area which receives limited rainfall due to its leeward location is the Great Basin. This is an unusual zone in that its identifying characteristic is an inward drainage pattern. The zone has a variety of landforms, including mountainous areas and arid plains, as well as fertile valleys. All drain inland toward the former Lake Bonneville, of which the Great Salt Lake in Utah is a remnant.

The Arid Regions are not one distinctive zone, but rather a series of dispersed deserts or dry areas which occur west of the 100 degree longitude mark and south of the 40th parallel. Although there are important and famous arid areas in the United States, such as the Mojave Desert, it is in Mexico that the largest contiguous dry stretch exists. This is the Chihuahuan Desert. The Arid Regions are characterized by limited biomass production and a distinctive flora of shrubs, short grasses, succulents, and seasonal wildflowers. Although the soils of this region may be fertile, low levels and inconsistency of rainfall limited their exploitation until irrigation technology was introduced.

High Plateaus are flat lands found in areas with poorly developed drainage systems. They are usually in semi-arid regions that have a natural vegetative cover of short grass mixed with some arid zone plants. In the eastern portion of the High Plateau Zone (northwest Texas), the plateaus are very large and relatively moist, with a fertile soil developed under prairie grasses. Proceeding westward, the plateaus are increasingly dissected by the deep draws of intermittent streams, have shallow soils, and receive less than 10 inches of rain annually. In Central Mexico another plateau zone exists which supported scrub pine vegetation in the pre-Columbian period.

Semitropical and Tropical Zones are found primarily in the Caribbean Islands and Central America. They are moist areas frequently associated with lowlands, and have a dense, diverse vegetative cover. Their climates range from very hot and humid in the lowlands, to moist and temperate in the uplands. Their soils, although initially fertile, are quickly depleted once the native forests have been removed. Prior to modern medical advances the tropics were very unhealthful environments for humans, although several very successful pre-Columbian civilizations did develop in these areas.

The Coastal Areas of North America can be separated into two general types: the coastal plains, such as those along the Atlantic Ocean; and the rocky coast, such as is found along the Pacific Ocean in much of California. Coastal plains are lowlands extended from eroding interior land as material carried by streams is deposited. These areas are generally quite flat. Plant types differ regionally due to soil and climate variations and can range from marsh flora to grasses. The rocky coasts meet the water's edge with a sheer embankment that generally has hilly or mountainous lands behind it. In the north, coniferous woodlands cover these coastal areas. From central California to central Mexico coastal vegetation is Mediterranean or semi-arid in type, while in Central America tropical hardwood forests have developed. Plate tectonics theory has identified these rocky coastal areas of the Pacific as among the most geologically active areas in the world. Coastal areas of each type do occur on both the Atlantic and Pacific sides of the continent.

The Arctic Region has two general subregions: tundra and taiga. Tundras have the coldest average temperatures of any areas of the continent, with very severe winters. Precipitation is also generally low, and the ratio of sunlight to darkness changes completely from almost sunless winters to nearly 24 hours of sunlight in midsummer. No trees grow in the tundra, and grasses, shrubs, lichens, and sedges are the region's major vegetation types. The taiga is also a very cold zone, but one with warmer temperatures in which trees do grow. Human settlement in the Arctic has been generally limited to cultural groups such as Eskimo and Aleut, who have developed special survival techniques.

NATIVE AMERICAN SETTLEMENT OF NORTH AMERICA

These nine landscape zones have had very important effects on human settlement in North America from its beginnings. One of the most important of these effects was the role of the landscape in fostering diversity among Native Americans. Habitation in new ecological zones required new subsistence strategies, and these in turn led to variations in ways of life, even among population groups with the same ancestors. An interesting example of this can be found among the Athabascan-speaking peoples of North America, the Athabascans of Canada, and the Navajo and Apache of the United States. Linguistic similarities indicate that all three groups are descended from a parent stock, yet important cultural differences in economy, settlement pattern, and religious practices exist. Both the Athabascans and Apache remained nomadic hunters and gatherers, while the Navajo eventually became pastoralists with semi-permanent settlements.

Such differences between related peoples are indicative of the variety found in Native American cultures at the time of European discovery. Over twenty major language groups and uncountable local dialects existed. Economic activities ranged from hunting and gathering to agriculture or trade. Hunting and gathering was the dominant form of livelihood practiced by groups in all ecological zones. Agriculture was far more limited, being practiced by some Eastern Woodland peoples, such as the Iroquois and Creek; a few plains tribes, such as the Hidatsa of Missouri; the pueblo peoples of the southwest; and some communities on the Pacific coast. Trade was to an extent practiced by all, with some groups making it a specialty.

The impact which Native Americans had on both the American landscape and the European immigrants to North America is often considered to have been minimal, but despite their small number (estimated to have been between 200,000 and 4 million in 1492[3]), their activities created distinctive pre-Columbian landscape elements—many of which remain, in disguised form, today. While the effects of their environmental activities may seem fleeting compared to the drastic changes wrought by Euroamerican cultures, it is important to have some understanding of the environmental alterations that occurred in the pre-Columbian period. There are several reasons why. First, Euroamericans ethnocentrically attribute any landscape alteration of permanence to their own cultural group. This is not the case, and in studying the landscape, whether designed or vernacular, one should be aware that all peoples alter their physical environments to suit their various needs. Second, native landscape alterations had an effect on later European settlement. Finally, there are instances in which Native American landscape decisions continue to influence the modern landscape. How many modern roads follow the routes of ancient trails? Which cities occupy sites initially settled by a Native American band? To what extent have prehistoric earthworks inspired a new genre of art which uses the land itself as a material? The landscape alterations of all Native American peoples would be a subject of great interest, but any full discussion of it is a book in itself.[4] For purposes of this text, three cultures that have left dramatic evidence of human interaction with the landscape have been selected as representatives of the variety and magnitude of pre-Columbian landscape activities. The three regional groups we will look at are the cultures of the Valley of Mexico, the Mound Builders of the Midwest, and the Anasazi people of the pueblo Southwest.

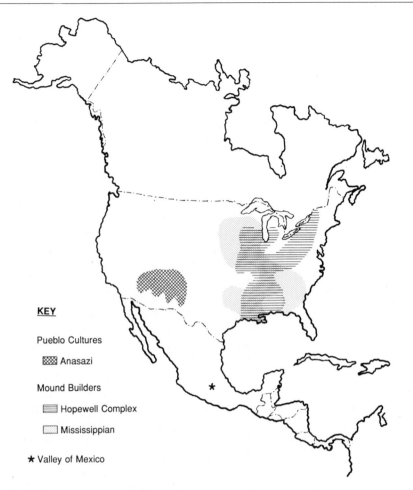

Map of North America showing principal territories of Native American cultures discussed in text. (Drawing by Rita Hodge).

KEY

Pueblo Cultures

▨ Anasazi

Mound Builders

▤ Hopewell Complex

▢ Mississippian

★ Valley of Mexico

The Valley of Mexico

Cultural ascendency in the Valley of Mexico, the site of modern Mexico City, had its origins nearby in the Tehuacan Valley southwest of Mexico City and in the Olmec cultural region along the Gulf of Mexico coast. The Tehuacan Valley was one, if not the sole, origin site for the domestication of corn. Around 5000 B.C. the species *Zea mays* developed as a mutation of wild grass. The first maize or corn was very small, with hard kernels, and calorically unproductive. It provided the stock plant, though, that succeeding generations and cultures hybridized to larger, more nutritious forms. By the year 2000 B.C., in what is known as the Meso-American Formative period, domestication of corn led to a series of cultural advances, particularly sedentarism. This set the stage for the emergence of the advanced civilizations of central Mexico. The Olmec culture was the first of these, arising around 1500 B.C. in the humid coastal region southeast of modern Veracruz. The Olmecs are known today primarily for their sculpture, particularly the giant basalt heads discovered at San Lorenzo. We know little of their architecture or site planning because they built of impermanent materials, but fieldwork has shown that they did make use of artificial moundlike landforms, this being the first evidence of a site feature typical of many later Native American civilizations. Around 400 B.C. Olmec culture declined. In Central Mexico this created a cultural vacuum, which continued until the first century A.D. when the urban area of Teotihuacan emerged. Teotihuacan was the center of the first great indigenous culture of the Valley of Mexico, but its direct origins are unclear. Its impact on Central Mexico, though, is vivid: it generated a vital culture that dominated the region, persisting in various forms until conquest of the Aztecs by Spaniards.

The culture of Teotihuacan is associated with one central place—the city of Teotihuacan. This great urban center required a highly developed agriculture, which in turn relied upon two innovations in farming: (1) hybridization of increasingly larger, more nutritious types of corn, which along with amaranth, was the major food source, and (2) creation of cropping systems that improved plant viability in the unpredictable climate of the Valley. One technique, which the Teotihuacans were among the first to develop and which they devised prior to 1000 A.D., is now called the *chinampa* system. *Chinampas* are long, linear earthen mounds surrounded by water, which utilize swampy land as both a moisture and nutrient source. In later times the Aztecs utilized this same system to support their own agriculture. Chinampas will be discussed in more detail when we look at the later Aztec city of Tenochtitlan.

The developed agriculture of Teotihuacan provided food to support a large population, many of whom were engaged in service activities. Estimates of the ultimate population of Teotihuacan vary widely, but a population figure for the city of 125,000 people by 500 A.D. would certainly not be excessive. To accommodate such a large population, a complex urban infrastructure based on careful planning was created. The developed area of Teotihuacan was about 7½ square miles, with most of this laid out in a grid of modules, each module being a square with a side of 57 meters (or about 187 feet). This grid had as its lines of origination two major perpendicular street systems. The "main" street of the city is today called the Street of the Dead, after an early and erroneous European belief that the structures which lined it were tombs. The Street of the Dead is an impressive space about 300 feet across at its widest point, with the width gradually being reduced toward its northern terminus. The "cross" streets, which do not actually physically cross it, are know as East Avenue and West Avenue. These three streets served both as urban axes and as sight lines linking the most important structures of the city.

Four critical structures are related to these central streets: the Pyramid of the Moon, the Pyramid of the Sun, the Great Compound, and the Citadel, which contained the temple of Quetzalcoatl.[5] The Pyramid of the Moon and Pyramid of the Sun are stone-faced earthen mounds similar in profile to the ziggurats of Mesopotamia. The Pyramid of the Moon, although the smaller of the two, is the more critical in terms of urban form because it provides a visual and physical terminus to the Street of the Dead. The Pyramid of the Sun, though, is believed to be the most important ceremonial structure in Teotihuacan. It is the largest in the city, in fact the largest prehistoric structure in the Americas, the earliest built (c. 100 A.D.), and was located to cover and enclose a natural cave. Visually, it dominated the horizon and would have been a beacon for those approaching the city. Both pyramids were approached through plazas containing structures which might be called "pulpits"—flat, raised platforms. These squares may have been sites of activities related to ceremonies that occurred at the pyramids or places from which an audience viewed those ceremonies. It must be noted that, unlike Egyptian pyramids, which were important for their interior spaces, those in the New World were utilized primarily for their exterior surfaces. At both the Pyramid of the Moon and Pyramid of the Sun, the uppermost level was once topped by small buildings, believed to have been associated with religious activities. The pyramid's key function was probably to elevate these structures. Some pyramids do have interior rooms, but these are generally small and probably were not used on a regular basis. Today these structures look very barren and solemn, but when in use they would have been brightly painted nodes of great activity.

The Great Compound, an open space of about 14 acres surrounded by terraced walls, and the Citadel, another large enclosed open space, sat directly across from each other along the Street of the Dead. The Great Compound was spatially

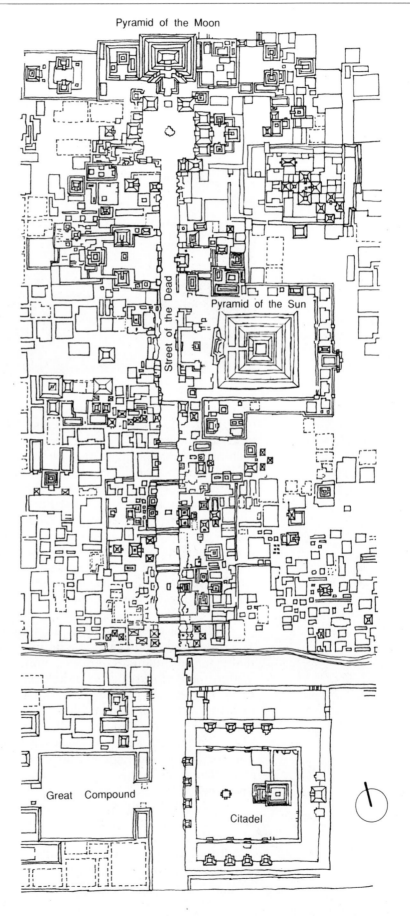

Pyramid of the Moon

Street of the Dead

Pyramid of the Sun

Great Compound

Citadel

Plan of Teotihuacan as excavated up to 1970. (Data from Millon, 1973; drawn by Garret Rossi.)

View in Teotihuacan looking down Street of the Dead from atop the Pyramid of the Moon. The Pyramid of the Sun is to the left, with the Citadel and Great Compound in the distance.

an extension of West Avenue, while the Citadel is almost symmetrical to an imaginary extension of East Avenue. These two enclosures mark the southern limit of "downtown" Teotihuacan and are believed to have served civic functions such as a marketplace, a military command post, or residence of a prominent official. Analysis of the site plan gives some credence to interpretations that say this southern area of the Street of the Dead served a different function than the more ceremonially oriented northern end. First, the street itself is significantly wider near the Compound and Citadel. This suggests that it was designed to hold a greater volume of pedestrians or vehicles, such as might be required at a public market. Second, the purposefully diverted San Juan River created a boundary between the two zones about 150 feet north of the Citadel. This alteration suggests that the river separated the town into two distinctive use areas; the north, the religious/ceremonial center, and the south, the civil/commercial center.

Teotihuacan was not solely a ceremonial or administrative city. It also served as a residential center. Those who lived near the city center occupied one-story, multiroomed building complexes which were arranged in neighborhood blocks. Within these blocks, both residential and ceremonial structures have been identified. In addition, there appears to have been a hierarchy of open spaces within each block. One excavated block, known as Yayahuala, may illustrate a typical pattern. Here three buildings called temples were located on three sides of a large plaza. The fourth side was enclosed by a long, narrow structure of unknown purpose. These nonresidential structures occupied roughly one third of the block. Its remainder was covered with apartment-like structures and their associated open spaces, these all being smaller than the temple plaza. The block as a whole was enclosed and elevated from the street by a retaining wall, with access via several entry stairways. Thus, each block appears to have been a self-contained, physically distinct social or political unit.

Teotihuacan, as an urban center, declined in the seventh century A.D.[6] This decline may have merely been a population shift or economic downturn, rather

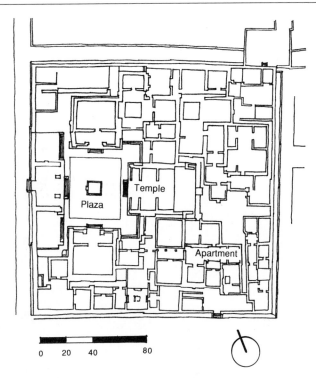

Plan of Teotihuacan apartment block known as Yayahuala. Other residential blocks that have been excavated are similar in arrangement but not exact duplicates. (Data from Millon, 1980; drawn by Rossi.)

than complete annihilation. In any event, for the next two to three hundred years, no dominant cultural group controlled the Valley of Mexico. Around 900 A.D. the Toltecs emerged as a political and cultural force in the Valley. Material evidence suggests, though, that Toltec culture was influenced by the Maya rather than by their regional predecessors at Teotihuacan. In turn, Toltec kingdoms were replaced in Central Mexico by the Aztecs in the fourteenth century. The Aztecs were not native to the Valley and according to their legends came from the north, a land termed the *Chichimeca,* or "home of barbarians." The Aztecs have been called the Romans of the New World, because they were so successful in making the traits of another civilization their own. This is precisely what they did by borrowing from the Toltecs, the Mayans, and in particular from the culture of Teotihuacan. Aztecs so revered Teotihuacan that their rulers made an annual pilgrimage to that city's ruins.

From the ancient culture of Teotihuacan the Aztecs acquired skill in two areas of planning—city form and agricultural systems. The Aztec capital city of Tenochtitlan was founded on an island at the southwest corner of Lake Texcoco, where Mexico City today stands. The city plan itself was organized on a north-south and east-west grid, very similar to that of Teotihuacan in orientation. Although Tenochtitlan apparently lacked the overall design strength of Teotihuacan, particularly in not having as imposing a ceremonial core area, several other planning characteristics were adopted by the Aztecs. Tenochtitlan was divided into four quarters by major streets. Running east to west was a major roadway that passed through the ceremonial district and continued westward as a causeway to the mainland. There were also three major north-south routes. Two of these roads led to the great market and the third formed a causeway to the north. In addition to the roads, a series of canals crossed the city following the same grid as the roads. Tenochtitlan, like Teotihuacan, had distinctive use zones. The mercantile district was located to the north in the Tlatelolco area, while the ceremonial district with palaces and temples was central to the island, located where roads leading to causeways crossed. The remainder of the city was devoted to residential areas and farmland.

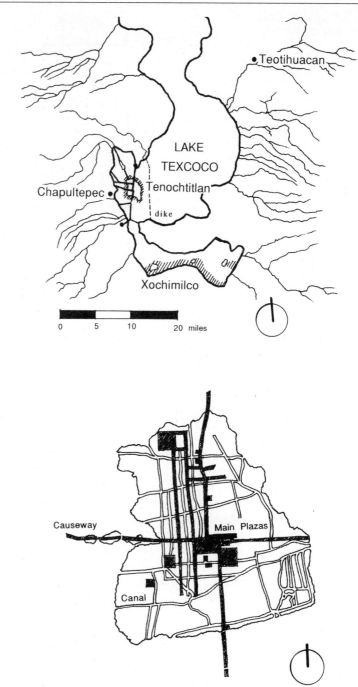

Map of the Valley of Mexico as it appeared at the end of the fifteenth century, showing causeways from Tenochtitlan to the mainland and the position of the dike across the western end of Lake Texcoco. (Data from Coe, 1986; drawn by Rossi.)

Plan of Tenochtitlan in the early sixteenth century. (Data from Hardoy, 1968; drawn by Rossi.)

The Aztecs also borrowed agricultural technology from Teotihuacan, using three systems initially developed there: terracing, irrigation, and chinampas. These systems were utilized at both cities to ameliorate environmental problems of unpredictable spring and fall frosts; unpredictable rainfall, especially in the spring; erosion of thin soils; and reduction in soil fertility from annual cropping. Terraces were constructed on steep slopes where erosion and moisture runoff reduced production. Both stone and earthen retaining walls terraced down the hillsides. Irrigation utilized both permanent water flow from numerous hillside springs in the Valley and storm runoff. The system for utilizing spring flow consisted of diversion structures, reservoirs, and canals, while the system for handling runoff consisted largely of check dams in swales. These small dams stored small volumes of water for a brief period after rainfall, but enough to allow additional water to be transferred to fields or to soak into the soil.

As discussed earlier, chinampas were long, narrow, mounded peninsulas of earth constructed by excavating lake sediments and piling up soil within retaining structures. The typical chinampas of the Valley of Mexico were from 15 to 30 feet wide and up to 300 feet long. Canals created by excavations were generally about 15 feet wide, but some larger "highways" were much wider. In Aztec times chinampas surrounded Tenochtitlan itself, and were also located on the southern shores of Lakes Xochimilco and Chalco. Today only nine chinampa villages remain, the most famous of these being Xochimilco, where visitors or Mexico City residents can go for a boat ride through the misnamed "Floating Gardens."

If the past can be judged by present production, the chinampas were incredibly fertile fields. Today seven crops a year can be harvested and fish caught in the canals. Chinampas may have supplied about 50 percent of the food needs of the estimated half million pre-Columbian inhabitants of the city and suburbs of Tenochtitlan. This high productivity was a result of the complete recycling that was part of the chinampa system. Canal bottoms were continuously built up by nutrient-laden organic matter from decaying plants and animals. Before each new planting, a layer of mud was excavated from the canal and placed on top of the mound. Since the lakes of the Valley had no outlet, nothing was ever permanently lost to erosion.

While the nutrient-recycling benefits of the chinampa system were quite important, there were other advantages as well. The most obvious was the constant presence of moisture near plant roots. Another was that fields could be easily worked and crops harvested using water transport. Perhaps the greatest benefit, and one that would have been difficult to replicate through other means, was that the standing water ameliorated climatic extremes. Field research has shown that on cold nights heat absorbed by canal water is reradiated, warming the surrounding fields by several degrees Fahrenheit. In marginal seasons, when frost may be imminent, these few warming degrees would be enough to protect the crops and extend the growing season. At Lake Titicaca on the Peru-Bolivia border, where a similar system was in use by the Tiwanaku culture, chinampas allowed crop growth to continue even when night temperatures fell to 20 degrees.[7] Chinampas, then, provided a viable agricultural system for farmers who occupied unpredictable climatic zones and relied on organic fertilizers. This legacy from Teotihuacan allowed the Aztecs to prosper in the Valley of Mexico,

Cross-section diagram of a typical chinampa showing tree roots used to retain the artificial islands. (Data from Coe, 1986, and Nuttall, 1919; drawn by Rossi.)

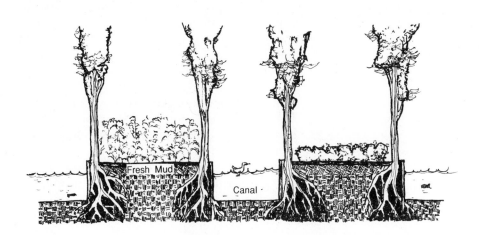

View of the Xochimilco chinampas—or, as they are called today, the Floating Gardens. The canal on which these colorful modern recreational barges takes visitors is one of the larger "highways" in the system.

and, had the Spanish not arrived, would likely have helped them to spread their culture over much more of Mexico.

The lack of a drainage outlet for Lake Texcoco did create one critical problem for the chinampa system—salinization of lake waters that could kill plants or retard growth. Water flowing into the lake came from two sources, runoff from rain and hillside springs. Both sources picked up salts as they flowed to the lake, and, with no outlet, salt concentrations constantly increased. High evaporation rates in the dry climate hastened this process. To correct the problem, and to keep water levels high near chinampas, the Aztecs constructed a dike about 9 miles long to enclose and elevate the western inlet of Lake Texcoco. (The dike is shown on the map in Figure 1-5.) This created a freshwater zone around Tenochtitlan and in Lakes Xochimilco and Chalco. Since most of the springs were on the west and south, spring water continued to feed the agricultural zones, sometimes via aqueducts, while brackish water was allowed to run into the rest of Lake Texcoco, which remained at a lower elevation.

The Mound Builders

The Mound Builders have been so named due to the dramatic landforms that they built and that have survived them. The people grouped under this title had highly varied cultures, and the mounds that each group built differ in both function and form. All, though, are believed to represent the cultural climax of eastward movement of Amerindians that had begun in the Archaic Period around 8000 B.C. This movement resulted in settlement of the Eastern Woodlands, with population concentrations on uplands along rivers. Three major mound-building peoples were the Adena culture, the Hopewell culture, and the Mississippian culture.

The Adena were an early cultural group centered in the Ohio River valley, active from about 700 B.C. to 400 A.D. Like the Hopewell, who would succeed them in that region, they used large mounds that covered a collection of graves. The huge conical mound at Miamisburg, Ohio, has been attributed to this group. Even more dramatic than these artificial burial landforms were the animal effigy mounds that dotted the Adena region. The most famous effigy mound is Serpent Mound near Locust Grove, Ohio. Located on a narrow finger of land above bluffs cut by two small creeks, this sinuous landform winds its way between the bluffs for a distance of more than 1200 feet. The snake's head points toward the juncture of the streams, while its body curves in a broad arch to conform to the topography. Excavations here and at other effigy mound sites have demonstrated that mounds were carefully constructed for durability, with stone cores overlaid with compacted clay layers under the earthen surface. Although interpreted as religious/ceremonial monuments, the true meaning and use of Adena effigy mounds including Serpent Mound can only be guessed.

Following the Adena People, or perhaps overlapping them temporally, was the cultural tradition that has been termed "Hopewell." Named for the Euroamerican owner of the site where their artifacts were first discovered, this tradition dominated the Ohio River valley from 200 B.C. to about 900 A.D. The Hopewell tradition is not necessarily tied to one ethnic group, but is now considered to represent a loose trade and ceremonial confederation with shared physical and behavioral traits, much as diverse ethnic groups today may share similar physical artifacts and popular behaviors.[8] Among these shared traits were use of mounds for burial, development of burial/ceremonial complexes separated by some distance from villages, presence of burial offerings at grave sites, and development of silhouette art using mica as the material. All these characteristics are known from excavations at mound ceremonial centers, where most archaeological work has been done. Far less is known about the daily life of these people, because few village sites have been excavated. For purposes of this discussion it is the Hopewell use of landscape as a ceremonial setting that is of interest: in particular, their construction of the mounds themselves—artifacts that permanently altered the landscape—and their purposeful creation of defined outdoor spaces in which to set these mounds.

Each burial mound was actually a small cemetery containing from a few to more than fifty burials. Each mound site began as a single grave enclosed by a charnel house, in which the burial process occurred. The body, along with an impressive collection of grave goods, was placed on a low clay platform. The deceased was then either cremated or buried under earth. Layers of sand, clay, loam, or stones then covered the grave to make a small mound. Succeeding burials took place in the same charnel house until the floor area was filled. The house was then either moved or burned, and a larger mound built to cover all

Plan of Serpent Mound, an Adena site in Ohio. (Squier and Davis, 1848.)

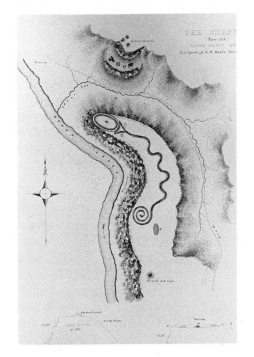

View of Serpent Mound as it appears today, seen from an observation platform. Serpent Mound has often been cited by twentieth-century environmental artists as an important influence on their work.

the burials. It is these terminal mounds enclosing a collection of graves that remain today as prominent landscape features.

Hopewell burial mounds took several forms. Many were cone-shaped with a slightly rounded tip. Other mounds had sloping sides, but a level top surface. A final mound style was the elongated ridge. No clear explanation for these distinctive mound types has been developed, but two theories being tested are that their form related to social status of the deceased and that different forms had different secondary functions, beyond burial. Mound sizes, both in terms of surface area covered and of height, also differ noticeably. There is some relationship of size to number of burials contained, but size may also relate to social status, with influential groups receiving more prominent mounds.

Hundreds of Hopewell mound groups are known to exist, but only a portion of those have been scientifically studied. The Mound City group in Ohio is a significant site that has been partially excavated. As its name suggests, Mound City is an assembly of twenty-two individual mounds, but mounds are not the only prominent landforms present. Other features were two linear berms that surrounded the mounds and eight nonnatural depressions, borrow pits, just beyond the berms.

The two perimeter earthen berms, now about 2½ feet high but 3 to 4 feet in 1846, were separated by openings, each about 5 feet wide.[9] The position of these breaks, which were likely entrances to the mound zone, does not appear to have any cosmological importance, although the reason for their location is unknown. It also seems unlikely that they had a defensive purpose. Although today the two berm openings do not align, according to nineteenth-century investigators each did create a sight line to a mound within the enclosure. It is most likely that the berms established a sacred zone within which burials and perhaps other ceremonies occurred. Thus, they indicate purposeful creation of outdoor spaces and clearly indicate the Hopewellians understood the power of psychosymbolic space.

The 13-acre area of Mound City was roughly square and oriented about 3 degrees off square to the cardinal points, with the east side being the most distorted. This adjustment may have been an accommodation to the location and angle of the Scioto River, above which the site sits. Within this enclosed precinct the mounds themselves were arranged with little perceptible order. Several appear to have been paired, since the interval separating them is smaller than that between other mounds. The one mound group which seems most purposefully arranged is that of five mounds evenly spaced in a line across the northern portion of the site. Several lines of berms running north to south also appear in the

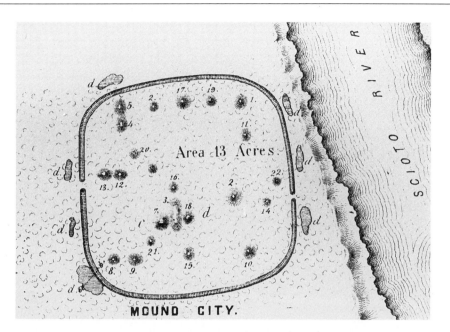

Plan of Mound City, a Hopewell site in Ohio. (Squier and Davis, 1848.)

View of Mound City as it appears today, following reconstruction in the mid-twentieth century according to Squier and Davis's plan. View was taken from a modern interpretive path looking north. Modern enclosure to the left covers an excavated burial.

western half of the site. The sole ridge mound was oriented north-south and may have served as a direction marker from which other mound positions were surveyed. Unfortunately, the purpose of any of these spatial relationships, if in fact planned, is unknown. There were several open areas inside the enclosure, the most notable being a roughly rectilinear area about 2 acres in size in the northern part of the site. This area was bounded by eight mounds and adjoined the largest mound on the site. Configuration of the open space suggests that it may have served as a plaza for ceremonies. On the other hand it may merely have been an open area awaiting future burials.

Burial mounds are not the only type of earthworks associated with Hopewellian people. There are a number of earthwork systems without a significant number of burials, suggesting that these sites had another primary purpose such as defense or nonmortuary ceremonies. One such site is the Newark complex, covering around 2 square miles. There, geometric earthen enclosures ranging in size from 20 to 50 acres were connected by berm-lined causeways 150 feet in width. Configuration of the earthworks indicates that this site most likely served a ceremonial function. For example, a 30-acre "circle" at the southeast portion of the complex has an interior moat rather than an exterior one, thus hindering defense. Berms were generally low, with gently sloping sides. Enclosing walls were built to greater heights at entries, but the height change seemed to signal spatial change rather than fortification. Types of ceremonies held at Newark are open to speculation, with suggestions ranging from large-scale political meetings to community fairs.

Hopewell culture ceased to dominate eastern North America around 900 A.D. Typical speculative causes of this cultural decline have included overpopulation, disease, warfare, and environmental catastrophe. None of these causes, though, has yet been supported by archaeological evidence. At the same time as Hopewell culture declined, a new cultural group arose in the valley of the Mississippi River, the river after which this people was named. Although this culture shares some characteristics with Hopewell, it also has an array of traits which linked it to other, more distant, peoples.

Mississippian culture, dating from about A.D. 900 to A.D. 1400 or 1500, centered on the valleys of the Mississippi River and its tributaries, including the Ohio, but extended over much of the present eastern United States. Mississippians were primarily agriculturalists, who supplemented their farming with hunting and gathering. They were also active traders, interacting with other peoples in a large exchange network throughout the Great Plains, eastern United States, and perhaps into Central America.

From the standpoint of site planning, the Mississippians are of particular interest because they developed a hierarchy of strategically placed urban centers. Those thus far identified range in size from small hamlets that were home to a few families to large, multipurpose cities that functioned as administrative and ceremonial centers. Two technological advances are believed to have allowed such population concentrations to develop. The first was the replacement of the spear, as a hunting tool, with the bow and arrow. While the bow may have been less accurate than the spear, it had the advantage of faster repetition of action,

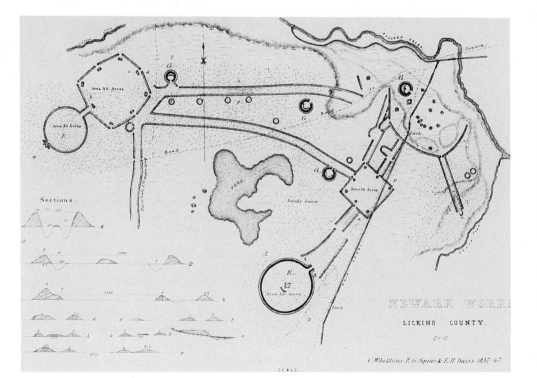

Plan of the Hopewell complex known as Newark. (Squier and Davis, 1848.)

since arrows need not be retrieved. The second advance was the introduction of domesticated corn, either from the southwestern United States or from Central America. Both of these changes created a more plentiful and dependable food supply, which could support a large, diversified culture. Also, as traditional theories of early settlement postulate, the needs of intensive agriculture both required and allowed an extensive settled population.

Studies of Mississippian settlements from various regions indicate that there were six different types of community, defined largely in terms of size and function: city, town, village, hamlet, homestead, and camp. Most Mississippian habitation sites seem to share several characteristics. First, regardless of whether the site served as a farmstead or a town, it was located near a permanent body of water, usually a river, although settlements are also common on the oxbow lakes of the Mississippi River floodplain. Second, all communities were organized around a series of open spaces, commonly called "plazas." Third, larger towns included not only habitation sites, but mounds of three types: platform mounds, frequently topped with permanent structures; conical mounds often containing burials; and ridge mounds, which may have been boundary markers. Of the three characteristics named above, location near a body of water was most critical to the Mississippian settlement system. Two benefits of water-related locations are obvious: first, there was a constant water and nutrient source that aided agriculture, and second, there was a ready means of transportation for trade, but more importantly for the redistribution of food in times of local need. Recent analysis of the regional cultural groups with complex intragroup linkages, such as the Mississippians and Anasazi, have demonstrated the benefits of networks for food redistribution in unpredictable environments where agriculture supported large populations.

River valley locations had other advantages. Mississippian agriculture, generally dependent on corn, beans, and squash as primary crops, would have required a constant renourishing of the soil, so that nutrient depletion of intensively farmed land would not lead to reduced yields. Seasonal natural replenishment through flooding had the advantage of requiring no additional labor; in addition, floodplain and terrace soils are easily worked. Further, waterside locations extended the growing season just as the chinampas did in Mexico. The disadvantage of farming in floodplains is, of course, the potential for flooding at planting and harvesting times. Waterways were also important to a secondary economic activity, hunting and gathering; migratory wildfowl, fish, and game mammals such as deer, all prime protein sources, require water habitats to varying degrees.

Trade within the Mississippian system was very important, although perhaps not as important as to the Hopewell. The location of Cahokia, the largest known Mississippian settlement, suggests that trade with peoples of the Great Lakes and Upper Mississippi regions may have been vital to Mississippians. Evidence suggests that much of the extra-Mississippian trade was in luxury, rather than subsistence, goods while intra-Mississippian trade was for both luxuries and staples critical to life maintenance.

Of the six typical Mississippian settlement types, the city was the largest and most complex. Cities covered an extensive area, influenced an entire region, served diverse functions, had large and numerous mounds, and had a variety of open spaces, including a large central plaza. Only one Mississippian settlement fulfills all these qualifications: Cahokia. Cahokia, located in present day Illinois just east of St. Louis, Missouri, is believed to have been occupied by Mississippian peoples from A.D. 800 to 1400, with a cultural and population peak occurring between 1100 and 1200. During that period it had an estimated population of about 30,000 to 40,000, while the entire population of the present territory of the United States is estimated to have been no more than 3 million. Thus, Cahokia had a surprisingly high percentage of total population for an agrarian community. Cahokia, though, was more than simply a larger version of other Mississippian towns: It was a major political and economic center serving both its immediate 125 square mile market zone and the entire Mississippian culture region.

Aside from sheer size, the site plan and features at Cahokia attest to its importance. The most obviously impressive feature was the platform mound known as Monks Mound.[10] Monks Mound was the largest solely earthen structure in North America, covering a base area of about 15 acres and rising to over 100 feet in height. This massive size was acquired over many building stages spanning at least two hundred years, in which smaller mounds and the small buildings they supported were buried under a mantle of new material. Today Monks Mound looks like a huge grassed berm ideal for children's play or, in winter, for sledding, but its current appearance is deceptive. During the Mississippian Period it, like most other platform mounds, had an architectonic appearance, with steeply angled sides meeting platform edges at pronounced angles. In addition, it was not covered by any vegetation, at least at upper levels, but by compacted clay.

Unfortunately, due to its impressiveness, Monks Mound has dominated popular literature about Cahokia to the exclusion of discussion of the city's other features and its purposefully organized plan. Cahokia was planned like the best of modern cities, with a hierarchy of spaces and use areas. The most important spaces were the open areas, or plazas, around which buildings and mounds were placed. The largest of these plazas, Grand Plaza, covered about 40 acres directly south of Monks Mound. At a smaller scale, clusters of houses, much like neighborhoods, each centered on a plaza or plaza/mound complex. Still smaller open spaces were located between individual houses, providing courtyards for outdoor

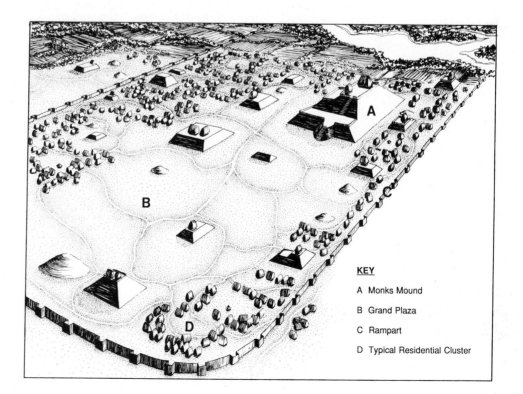

Cahokia from the southeast, as it may have looked at the height of its power. (Data from Fowler, 1977; Fowler, 1989. Drawn by Hodge.)

KEY

A Monks Mound

B Grand Plaza

C Rampart

D Typical Residential Cluster

work and family activities. The distribution of all of these open spaces appears to have been random, but this appearance may simply be due to insufficient information.

It is quite clear that the *overall* organization of the city was not random, but based on careful geometric arrangements and consistent spacing of elements. The point of origination for this plan is unclear, but it may have been at the central plaza adjoining Monks Mound. Support for this theory can be drawn from the fact that this plaza is the most regular, clearly defined space in the city and its integrity was respected by other built elements. From this central space the arrangement of mounds and neighborhoods followed a grid oriented approximately north to south and east to west, rather than to any natural site feature. The grid was in units of 57 meters, a particularly intriguing figure since the same basic planning unit was used at the city of Teotihuacan. A direct link between the Mississippian culture and those of the Valley of Mexico has been postulated from evidence such as this, but has not been conclusively proven.

Toward the end of its occupation period, about 200 acres in the heart of Cahokia were enclosed within a U-shaped wooden rampart. Although the full extent of this wall has not been excavated, a combination of posthole remnants and surficial evidence supports the conclusion that it went around the whole of "downtown" Cahokia with the exception of the north side, where a small stream provided a natural defensive barrier. The purpose of the wall is usually assumed to have been an increased need, or perception of a need, for protection.

A second noteworthy built feature at Cahokia was a series of circles composed of evenly spaced wooden posts, dubbed "Woodhenge." At least three such circles are known to have existed east of Monks Mound, just outside the rampart. Although complete evidence for all of these wooden rings has not been exposed or was destroyed by modern road excavations, archaeologists feel that enough data exist to speculate as to their purpose. Field observation confirmed early hypothesizes that the circles were astronomical observatories for sun and moon movement, much like Stonehenge in England, hence their name. Trial observations at a reconstructed circle demonstrated that alignments between outer posts and a central observer post did occur on equinoxes and solstices. In addition, Warren Witty, the principal Woodhenge archaeologist, believes that sight lines also marked movement of the star Capella. This dual notation system may help explain the unusual Woodhenge arrangement, with a central post surrounded by four markers set 5 feet out from it. Others have speculated that Woodhenge may, in fact, have been used to locate or at least record some of the major survey lines on which the layout of Cahokia was based.

Typical Mississippian towns were much smaller than Cahokia, but still had ceremonial structures, especially platform mounds, and large open spaces. Villages ranged from 12 to 25 acres in size, and had mounds, but usually only one. Caddo Mounds in Texas is an example of a medium-sized village that served as a local trading center. Excavations at Caddo have revealed an inner village area where most buildings and mounds were located and an outer village that defined the limits of habitation. The inner village was a dense zone dominated by conical "beehive" houses reaching to 45 feet. Nearby were two "temple" mounds—that is, artificial landforms on which buildings were placed—and a large, conical mound that was used for burial purposes.

At the level of the village, a major functional break appeared: smaller settlements usually had no mounds or other ceremonial structures; they served chiefly as centers of agriculture. Of this type of settlement the largest was the hamlet, about 2½ acres in size, which contained several family groups. Its only open spaces were small courtyards between structures. Below the hamlet in scale were farmsteads, very small in area and serving only one family group. Finally, there

Artist's view of a Caddo Mississippian village in Texas based upon archaeological evidence from Caddo Mounds State Park. Caddoan beehive-style houses were much taller than those used in more northern Mississippian towns. (Original painting by Nola Montgomery, Texas Department of Parks and Wildlife.)

were camps, which ranged from a few square yards to half an acre in size, that served seasonal or specialized craft functions. Typically, a camp might have been used in a particular hunting season or as a workshop for an intensive craft such as pottery or tanning.

What is particularly important about this hierarchy of settlement types is that it demonstrates the sophistication of Mississippian adaptations to exploit different environmental and economic needs. They were able to adapt the size and scope of a settlement to best exploit resources with minimal input of energy, while still ensuring the maintenance of communal social life.

Siting of settlements of each type loosely followed the principles of central place theory. Settlements were distributed so that larger centers were farther apart. For example, Cahokia was the only Mississippian settlement classed as a city. To find another place of equal size one would have had to travel to Mexico. Thus, highest-level centers were thousands of miles apart. Distances between towns were also considerable. Among the Caddoan Mississippians along the Arkansas River, Spiro and Norman were two sites at the town level, and they are about 175 miles apart. Environmental conditions, of course, influenced town spacing. In more productive areas such as American Bottom,[11] around Cahokia, town-sized settlements were within 10 miles of each other.

The human-altered landscape inhabited by Mississippian peoples was complex. Extensive environmental changes occurred as the Mississippians pursued their highly developed agriculture. At the least, this meant clearing large tracts of native plant species and some animal habitat destruction. In flood-prone areas it also led to artificial drainage or field elevating. To support large populations concentrated in some regions, resources may have been locally exhausted. It has been suggested that in the area around Cahokia no tree larger than a sapling grew within a mile of the central city—all having been cut for fuel and construction. These environmental changes differed from those caused by modern development only in scale.

Decline of Mississippian culture, around A.D. 1400, has been attributed to the effects of such environmental degradation. While it may be appealing to believe that prehistoric peoples were as guilty of pollution as modern cultures, there is no clear evidence that this was the sole cause of decline. In fact rather than "dying," Mississippian culture may have simply been transformed. Ethnographic information from early European explorers suggests that many southern tribes, such as Caddoans and Creeks, had Mississippian physical culture traits, including house type and burial practices, and may have been their direct descendants.

Pueblo Cultures

The decades around the end of the first millennium A.D. were important ones for the development of indigenous cultures in North America. Not only were the Mississippians creating an extensive cultural network in the east, but in the southwestern portion of the United States and northern Mexico native peoples developed another cultural network that, like the Mississippian system, was based on agriculture and permanent settlements. These were the peoples who today are grouped together under the term "Pueblo cultures." The key factor linking these diverse groups was the introduction of corn and the associated agricultural techniques allowing its cultivation in semi-arid areas. In the Pueblo region corn was not cultivated until around 2800 B.C.,[12] probably following introduction from central Mexico. It must be noted that even at this relatively late date, the corn being grown had small cobs (less than 3 inches long) with blue kernels, rather than the large ears which have been developed by modern hybridization. Even with this limitation, the species cultivated represented a significant horticultural advance over the nutrient and calorie levels that could have been provided by wild corn with ears no larger than wheatsheaves.

Four southwestern cultural groups, Mogollon, Hohokam, Patayan, and Anasazi, eventually developed settled lifestyles based on corn agriculture. In addition, except for the Patayan, all developed pit-style houses, which, like contemporary earth-sheltered dwellings, helped mitigate climatic extremes. The Hohokam and Anasazi are also known for their sophisticated irrigation systems. The physical cultures of these groups demonstrated knowledgeable use, but sometimes also abuse, of the environment, and the ability to use that knowledge to dominate large geographical zones. The Anasazi,[13] in particular, are of interest to this discussion, because their adaptation to the environment included purposeful site planning, urban development, planned agriculture utilizing irrigation, and development of an extensive road system.

The Anasazi lived in what is termed the "four corners" region of the United States—the area where the states of Colorado, New Mexico, Arizona, and Utah meet. Typical Anasazi site locations were in the valleys at the upper reaches of intermittent streams. These streams cut deep ravines through the rock plateaus of the region and deposited the outwash in valley floors. Thus, this landscape was dominated by the visual and physiographic extremes of flat valleys, plains, and plateaus and the sheer, vertical planes of mesa walls.

The Anasazi, one of the older groups in the region, are believed to have been the first corn agriculturalists in the Southwest. Like other groups, they used new agricultural food sources to supplement an existing hunting and gathering economy. Before A.D. 700 they lived in small villages of pit-style houses, which were sometimes located in open plains or at others set within the protecting confines of shallow caves. Around 700 a significant housing innovation—the multifamily pueblos—occurred. Establishment of pueblos has been linked to other changes in material culture, such as development of irrigation. This suggests that some decisive environmental or cultural alteration, such as an increase in the annual average rainfall or a change in the seasonal rainfall pattern, may have occurred then. While data on past climatic conditions is not always precise, evidence does suggest that the period from 700 to about 1130 may have had higher rainfall levels than at present.

A second change postulated to have influenced Anasazi cultural development around 700 was increased contact with peoples from the Valley of Mexico. The evidence to support this is the quantity of trade goods, such as copper bells and conch shells, excavated in pueblos. An often cited example indicating trade contact is the discovery of the skeletons of parrots, obviously not a bird indigenous to the southwestern United States. While it is certain that interchange did occur, questions remain as to whether it was direct or indirect. Direct trade would have required long-distance travel of Mexicans or Anasazi, which many researchers feel was out of the question. Another more easily accepted point of view is that the Anasazi were at the northern end of a trade network through which they acquired goods and ideas from Mexico, but without direct contact with the region. Unfortunately, neither type of contact seems adequate to explain that most obvious Anasazi artifact, the pueblo, since housing in prehistoric Valley of Mexico, while multifamily, was not multistoried.

The pueblos, as the Spanish termed Anasazi settlements, were the most obvious vestige of their culture and have always inspired great respect from European explorers. Pueblos have been called the first American apartment buildings because they were multiroomed and usually had at least two levels. The term "apartment house," though, does not adequately describe the pueblos, which were actually self-contained, multiuse villages. The four primary functions that they served were habitation, food and resource storage, religious ceremonies, and work space.

Although Anasazi pueblos differed in size and form, they were all organized around a central open space, much like later plazas in Spanish colonial towns. Typical pueblos had a broad, U-shaped, multiroomed structure, which encircled the plaza on three sides. The fourth side was either open or enclosed by a thin, slightly curvilinear wall which generally faced south. Rooms in the U-shaped structure could be either round or rectangular in form. The round rooms were termed *kivas*,[14] but their function has been interpreted as storage of grain. Some rectangular rooms may also have served as warehouses, but most were used for housing.

A significant number of pueblos lacked the enclosing walls on the south side of the plaza. An archaeologist (Lekson, 1984) has concluded that the wall, when built, came at a later stage of a pueblo's development. Lekson's evidence supports the idea that pueblos were purposefully planned and constructed according to that plan, over periods as much as a hundred years long. It has also been suggested that the walls were an afterthought, a response to real or perceived security threats that emerged later. The consistency of building stages of pueblos, coupled with the fact that many pueblos never did have such a wall, suggests that security was not the chief rationale for enclosure of the plaza.

The plaza itself was a soil or stone-surfaced open space. Open areas of plazas were used as outdoor workrooms for crafts, such as leatherwork, and communal cooking. Larger pueblos also had kivas serving religious functions sited in the plaza. The most famous pueblo exemplifying these planning and design characteristics was Pueblo Bonito, located in Chaco Canyon, New Mexico, at the heart of Anasazi territory.[15]

Pueblo Bonito was constructed in at least seven stages beginning about A.D. 900. In overall form Pueblo Bonito transposes the typical arrangement of rectangular living quarters and curved plaza wall. Instead, its multiroomed apartment area was roughly semicircular, with the enclosing south wall a straight line. Another significant deviation from the norm was placement of a line of rooms that separated the plaza into two distinct parts. In distribution of rooms and use areas Pueblo Bonito appears to have been similar to other pueblos, having both square and circular rooms as well as one large kiva. The name of this unusual structure, Pueblo Bonito, is of course, not an Anasazi term, but the name which early Mexican guides used to indicate the European impression of the structure.

The "beautiful town" has always intrigued visitors with its unique form, impressive scale, and picturesque location, near Chaco Wash at the base of buff-colored mesas.

Pueblo Bonito was but one of the communities that made up the important Anasazi cultural center in Chaco Canyon. Chaco was in fact the *very* center of Anasazi culture, variously interpreted as its principal trade city or a place of religious pilgrimage. For whatever purpose the community was developed, Chaco Canyon as a whole, as well as the individual pueblos within the valley, demonstrated the Anasazi's careful application of environmental knowledge to site planning and design.

Sites for pueblos were consciously selected with regard to three factors:

View of the ruins of Pueblo Bonito, with Chaco Wash in the background. (State of New Mexico, Economic Development and Tourism Department.)

Casa Rinconada was the largest kiva in Chaco Canyon and detached from any pueblo. It has been interpreted as the central religious building—much like a cathedral—for special ceremonies or large communal services.

climatic amelioration through orientation, orientation for specific settlement functions, and location for efficient collection of water. Southern orientation for pueblos was remarkably consistent regardless of whether the pueblo was located in a valley or on a mesa top. This orientation served two purposes. First, the buildings created a solar heat trap which would aid in heat absorption by masonry during cold periods. This heat could then be radiated into the plaza area, warming it by several degrees on cool days or at sunset. In addition, some pueblos were located directly below south-facing mesas to also use these massive rock walls as solar traps. Second, the same structures that trapped solar energy when oriented southward served as windbreaks screening cool north winds from the plaza.

Anasazi pueblos were also planned to accommodate specific functions. Two distinct types of pueblos, each serving a different community need, have been identified. Pueblos located in valleys were agricultural villages, where farmers lived and crops were stored, while mesa top communities functioned as control centers for security or communication. These guard pueblos did not differ remarkably from others in form, only in placement.

Pueblos in the Chaco Wash were located specifically to serve their agricultural functions. First, they were set above flood level, both to protect stored grain and to preserve naturally fertilized land for crops. Second, they were built in areas with the rockiest soils, which would have been least usable for agriculture. Third, they were built on steeper areas of the valley floor, where rapid water runoff and limited moisture infiltration would have been an obstacle to high rates of crop production. The land on which these pueblos were built was the least suitable for farming, and removing it permanently from production would have been no great economic loss.

Other site constraints related to efficient water collection were also considered by the Anasazi. Evidence strongly suggests that the most important source of water for crops was not Chaco Creek, as might be expected, but the ephemeral gully streams created by runoff from mesas. The key element in Chacoan gravity-flow irrigation systems was diversion of water from these small gullies to more viable cultivation land at the base of the mesas between washes. This necessitated a system of channels and flow regulators to control runoff direction and rate. A typical field irrigation system began with a diversion dam located at the bottom of an arroyo where water began to slow down naturally. This dam directed the runoff laterally to a canal. The canal then carried water to a stone headgate directly above fields. This gate regulated water flow through use of movable partitions in the channel course. From this headgate, water flowed through secondary canals to secondary control gates that in turn controlled water flow into the fields. The fields themselves were divided into a series of small, earth-bordered plots, probably much like Navajo "waffle" gardens, with the borders serving as miniature dams to hold moisture inside individual plots.

Construction of these systems required careful manipulation of grades, keen observation of storm patterns and hydraulic behavior, and careful channel and gate construction. Channels and gates were excavated and then lined with stone slabs, probably to prevent erosion where they cut through soil and also for ease in clearing them of sediment. At the headgate in particular, use of stone for walls and channel entrances assured that water flow could be carefully controlled. Capstones over canals were used to protect standing water from evaporation.

A recent study of the efficiency of Anasazi irrigation used contemporary hydraulic and watershed models to compare the runoff volumes and patterns found in Chaco Canyon today to the storm retention design of a particular irrigation system. This study found that flow from a high-intensity, short-duration storm typical of the region exceeded the design volume of the headgate by only 12 percent. Given the variables involved in any runoff calculation, increased by climatic and landscape changes during the ensuing gap of nine hundred years, the correlation is quite remarkable. Researchers conclude that Chacoans designed their system to maximize use of rain from typical summer storms. When storms of greater volume occurred, the system was either flooded or, perhaps, excess waters were diverted. In either case, it is likely that these irrigation systems required extensive, although routine, upkeep.

Other systems of moisture management found in the Southwest, but not always at Anasazi sites, deserve mention because they demonstrate the variety of adaptations developed by pre-Euroamerican peoples to life in agriculturally marginal zones. These "appropriate technologies" may prove useful once again as high-technology irrigation approaches become too costly or environmentally destructive. Five additional irrigation and conservation techniques used in the southwest were terracing of hillsides; check dams in gullies; mesa top reservoirs; akchim farming; and gravel mulching.

Terracing involved regrading hillsides to construct a series of small barrier dams in front of narrow, level bands of land. Terracing had three key advantages: it allowed farming on fairly steep land, it reduced erosion, and it retarded runoff of water and sediment. Check dams were small obstructions, often of stone, placed in swales or stream beds perpendicular to the line of water flow. They slowed runoff, spread it laterally across slopes, and created miniature detention areas. At sites in the Southwest, the principal purpose of check dams was probably to reduce gully erosion, thereby preventing the grades of gully-facing slopes from being steepened.

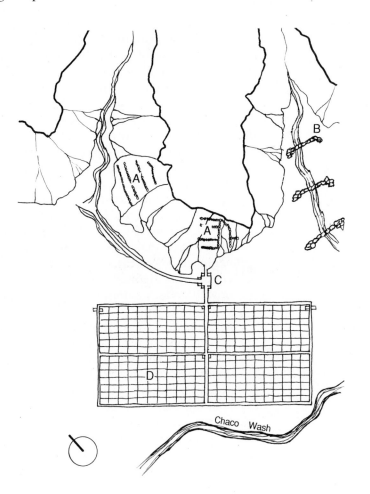

Diagram of some typical irrigation and water conservation systems used by Pueblo peoples, including the Anasazi and Hohokam: A = terracing; B = check dams; C = headgate; D = "waffle fields." (Date from Cordell, 1984; drawn by Rossi.)

Most reservoirs in Anasazi regions and throughout the pre-Columbian Southwest were located on flat mesa tops, for domestic rather than agricultural use. Smaller reservoirs for agriculture were created by canals. Canals had one obvious advantage as retention areas over pool reservoirs—they would be easier to clean of sediment—in fact, storm water would have cleaned them without additional human labor. Two factors mitigated against the efficiency of reservoirs in the Southwest. First, their useful life was limited due to filling from water-borne and aeolian sediments. Second, high evaporation rates made standing shallow pools inefficient, while the presence of rock near the surface made it impossible to dig more usable deep tanks. In the end, Southwestern peoples may have concluded that their best strategy was to maximize water use when rain fell through conservation within the soil, rather than surface storage.

Akchim farming was a technique that made use of natural erosion patterns as a method of water conservation. Farmers located fields on the moisture- and nutrient-rich soils that were deposited in alluvial fans or outwashes. This technique merely required appropriate site selection rather than construction of any water-retaining structures. Its key disadvantage in areas with unpredictable storms was that one unusually intense storm could wash out an entire crop. Another important water conservation technique used by Pueblo peoples was the application of gravel to fields as mulch. This reduced evaporation of soil moisture and had the additional advantage of moderating soil temperature fluctuations, especially by radiating heat from the rocks to the soil after sundown.

The Anasazi relied upon highly developed agriculture to feed their people and upon sophisticated urban planning to house and protect them. To keep their extensive territory unified, as well as supplied with resources, they developed two impressive communication systems: roads and signal stations. Indian trails were very common in the Americas, but the Anasazi system was much more than a series of paths. It was a well-integrated pedestrian system, planned and designed to allow rapid long-distance travel. The most surprising characteristic of these roads was that they were straight, even though they were often more than 50 miles long.[16] No change in direction was made to accommodate landforms along the route. Thus, a traveler literally went up and down mesas, using ladderlike stairways to move from valley to plateau. To contemporary designers, this approach seems at odds with an assumed Native American emphasis on symbiosis with natural systems, but it has been demonstrated that straight roads are more efficient in human calorie expenditure than would be a more modern circuitous route fitted to the topography.[17] To date, seven major routes leading directly to Chaco Canyon, but few lateral linkages, have been identified. Chaco was definitely the hub of the entire system. Recent aerial and field analysis has determined that, in addition to having precise routes, Anasazi roads were also engineered. Widths, usually 30 feet, were uniform across long distances, and road edges were defined with low rock berms. In some heavily traveled or easily eroded areas, paving, of adobe or wood, was added.

The second communication system developed by the Anasazi relied on visual transfer of verbal information. This was a system of signal stations. Evidence for this system is based primarily on the location of a series of masonry structures known as "shrines." A nighttime field experiment in which flares were lighted at shrines demonstrated that they, along with some of the major pueblos, provided a continuous sight line system. While the type of light used by the Anasazi is unknown, as is their cipher system, consensus is emerging that these stations functioned as part of a Chacoan "telegraph."

Anasazi culture is, at least in terms of material culture, one of the most sophisticated ways of life found among Native American peoples. They had a wide geographical influence, which may have been political as well as cultural.

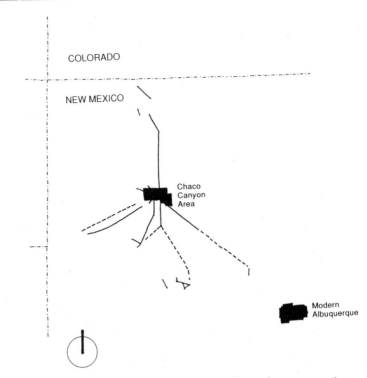

COLORADO

NEW MEXICO

Chaco
Canyon
Area

Modern
Albuquerque

Diagram showing locations and alignments of principal Anasazi roads. (Data from Cordell, 1984; drawn by Rossi.)

They developed technological systems that allowed construction of large masonry buildings, irrigation systems adapted to local rainfall patterns, and an extensive road network. The Anasazi were not immune to cultural disruption, however. Shortly after the beginning of the twelfth century signs of change appear. These include new, more primitive styles of building construction, population decline in Chaco Canyon, and the enlargement of smaller satellite communities such as Mesa Verde and Canyon de Chelley. Reasons suggested for these changes are typical of those proposed for any cultural decline, ranging from warfare to environmental degradation. One of the most reasonable theories is that the Anasazi were forced from upper watershed sites by an extended period of drought.[18] It is believed that the population adapted to these conditions by moving lower in the watershed and living in smaller communities. Contemporary Pueblo peoples such as those of Taos and Acoma are often considered the descendants of the Anasazi.

NATIVE AMERICAN INFLUENCES ON THE NORTH AMERICAN LANDSCAPE

While the land design and planning practices of prehistoric Native Americans, such as the chinampas of the Aztecs or the urban place hierarchy of the Mississippians, are graphic proof of the high levels of culture of pre-Columbian peoples, the reader might rightly ask if they had any lasting impact on patterns of land use in the New World; that is, is the study of Amerindian design merely of esoteric interest, or of importance to our understanding of the present physical arrangement of the North American landscape. Many authors have struggled with this issue in attempting to build a case for Native American influences. Three problems immediately emerge when this is attempted. First, dramatic cultural differences may make it difficult for modern, usually Euroamerican, observers to see and appreciate those influences that do persist. Second, much indigenous planning and design was not documented at the time of Euroamerican contact, so we may simply be unaware of it. Third, antipathy toward Native Americans by early settlers may have, in some cases, led to disguising of their influences, lest the European be seen as having "gone native" for utilizing existing landscape alterations or adaptive techniques. In spite of these limitations, Native American influences on Euroamerican land use can be documented in five important areas: in location of overland transportation routes, in settlement locations, in agricultural site choices and agricultural techniques, in the spread of plant communities, and in site planning.

Many early trails used by European settlers were of Native American origin. Some of these routes persist in use today, although for very different types of transport. The best evidence for Indian trails existed in the wooded lands of the eastern United States. There, cuts through dense forests were necessary if travel was to occur at any reasonable rate. These trails, unlike those of the Anasazi, were narrow, usually only wide enough for single-file passage, and conformed to natural features, such as landform and stream crossings, to make travel easier. Some of the better known Euroamerican routes which followed, at least in part, Native American trails were the Natchez Trace, the Occaneechi Path, and the Camino Real. The Natchez Trace, which was authorized as a federal road from Nashville, Tennessee, to Natchez, Mississippi, in 1806, was originally the Middle Tennessee Chickasaw Trace. It had served both as a route for European settlement and as a Native American warpath. The Occaneechi Path running from Virginia to Georgia was an example of a relatively unimportant trail that, with the advent of European trade, became a critical turnpike. Later, it became the route for parts of U.S. Highway 40. The Camino Real, the longest road network in colonial times, ran from San Antonio, Texas, to St. Augustine, Florida, utilizing sections of former Indian trails over its 1100-mile length.[19] While Europeans would surely have developed comparable routes had Native American trails not existed, the presence of these trails provided quicker access and they were probably more efficient, having been based on the greater environmental knowledge of the original inhabitants.

Just as Euroamericans utilized indiginous trails, so too did they usurp village and farmland locations. Many early colonial towns were built on or adjacent to existing villages, thus utilizing the advanced site selection skills of Native American peoples. Tenochtitlan, as has been mentioned, became the site of Spanish Mexico City, with many Spanish urban elements, such as the *zocalo* and Cathedral, occupying Aztec sites of similar function. Unfortunately for present inhabitants of that city, the site was far better adapted to the needs of a pedestrian, agricultural people than to those of a motorized, industrialized culture, which now suffers from serious environmental problems due to the city's basin location.[20] Other important North American cities grew on Native American sites: the city of Savannah, Georgia, was located on the same bluff above the Savannah River as a Yamacraw Indian village. New York and Chicago both occupy prominent navigational crossroads that were formerly utilized by Native Americans. In the Southwest some of the more picturesque urban settings, such as Santa Fe, were probably originally pueblos. Elsewhere, as at Taos, dual cities—one Native American, one Euroamerican—shared an area.

In addition to utilizing Native American sites for towns, Europeans also farmed on fields that, in many instances, had been previously cleared by Native Americans. This practice was well documented in New England, where use of Native American farmland meant a great saving of labor, since land clearing was a slow activity in the dense forests of the northeast. In addition, either knowingly or unknowingly, the Europeans were utilizing the environmental knowledge of their predecessors to select lands with better soils, more readily available moisture, or more favorable microclimatic factors. This knowledge must have been invaluable to early European settlers, for whom the soil and climate of North America frequently caused unanticipated problems. The Indian Old Fields, as they became known, allowed early agricultural success and probably influenced some New England village locations, as residents took advantage of existing cleared lands.

Native peoples were also of help to Europeans in crop selection and growing techniques. Many crops—including corn, potatoes, certain beans, squash, and tobacco—are unique to the Americas and were developed to be well adapted to local conditions. The indigenous peoples gave settlers initial lots of seeds for these crops and introduced them to cultivation methods. Among the methods widely adopted were that of using raised mounds of earth for crop rows and the addition of organic matter at the time of planting. In addition, cultivation, harvesting, and storage methods were acquired from the Native Americans. This influence was, of the five discussed, that of least continuing importance. Euroamericans quickly altered their agricultural methods as they gained more firsthand environmental knowledge, and, later, as new technologies were developed.

There is evidence to suggest that Native Americans were a force in creating or maintaining some of the ecological zones that Europeans generally considered to be completely natural North American landscapes. In the Eastern Woodlands, the Native Americans cleared meadowlike openings in the forest for wildlife management. This practice allowed invading species to gain a foothold in what was otherwise climax growth. Elsewhere, in prairie regions, the effects of Amerindian activities are more widespread. The spread of grasslands into areas between the Appalachians and the Mississippi River has been credited to fires set to maintain animal habitats or clear land for agriculture. The Black Belt of Alabama and other extensions of prairie vegetation as far east as Indiana may have been the result of these activities. A very different ecozone, the grass balds of the Southern Appalachians, has been interpreted as former Native American campsites, at which soil compaction restricted reforestation by woody species. Thus, views of the indigenous inhabitants as passive preservers of natural systems fail to recognize their role in purposeful alterations of environments that differ primarily in scale from later Euroamerican impacts.

A final area of lasting Native American influence on the landscape can be found at the site-planning scale. A geographer, Daniel Arreola, has concluded that the spatial organization and detailing of Spanish mission church sites were directly related to indigenous designs—specifically, that "the true parent of the atrio [large enclosed courtyard in front of a church] was very likely the *teocalli* court, a distinctive open space in the ceremonial centers of pre-conquest Indian cultures in Mexico" (1986, p. 3). Missionaries may have purposely utilized native site-planning principles to create a link in the minds of the local peoples between their own religion and Catholicism. Other design features of mission churches and sites also appear to have been derived from native prototypes. Atrios, for example, were frequently slightly elevated and churches were brightly painted as had been the Native American temples. Arreola further hypothesizes a direct link between the mission church atrio and the design of modern Mexican-American single-family residences, in which he believes the fence and gateway recreate atrio enclosures and the yard shrine represents the churchyard cross. If these interpretations are accurate, then a direct link with pre-Columbian site designs can be seen today in cities of the Southwest.

CONCLUSION AND SUMMARY

The North America that Europeans "discovered" in 1492 and conquered during the next four centuries was not a blank natural canvas. Rather, it had already been transformed from a natural landscape into a complex cultural landscape, reflecting overlays from thousands of years of occupation by Native Americans. In many instances native landscape modifications were relatively simple and non-intrusive—for example, those caused by buffalo-hunting practices in which kills were often large, but occurred rarely. The cultures that we have examined in this chapter had more significant impacts on their local environment, perhaps to the extent that the very viability of their large populations was threatened.

All Native American lifeways demonstrated a thorough and intimate understanding of environmental process learned over many generations. Such knowledge then became the basis for experimentation to manipulate aspects of the natural environment for human advantage. We will never know how many Anasazi canals were washed away in floods before they identified an appropriate size to accommodate storms. As impressive as their end results were, the long-term learning process through which they were achieved is even more impressive.

It is ironic that so much of this sound, environmentally based knowledge was not only put aside by Euramericans, but actually disparaged as "superstitious" or "nonscientific." In our now more environmentally sensitive era the positive benefits of simple practices are again being recognized, and some of the practices revived. Gravel mulches of the Pueblo peoples of the Southwest have resurfaced in modern "xeriscape" gardens. Chinampa-style agricultural lands are being reconstructed where the economy and environment do not favor agri-business techniques. We can only regret how much landscape knowledge and practice of great value was lost in the rush to transform the Amerindian subsistence landscape into the Euroamerican pastoral paradise.

NOTES

1. In Parker, 1989, p. 411.

2. The land bridge was broken by 13,000 B.P. as glacial meltwater caused sea level to rise. No archaeological evidence exists to prove human settlement in North American prior to 15,000 B.P. Dating of prehistoric events is of course difficult and is always temporary, awaiting new research. Dates used in this section are based on currently accepted chronologies, generally as cited in Fagan, 1987. They will certainly be altered in the future and, if past chronological changes are an indicator, will surely be pushed back even further.

3. Determination of prehistoric population levels is even more speculative than dating of prehistoric events, and very wide ranges frequently exist. Proposed levels have both risen and fallen in recent years, depending on location. Thus all numbers cited in this section should be considered educated "guesstimates" which are constantly under revision.

4. Among those who do treat this subject in greater detail see Morgan, 1980.

5. All of these place names postdate Teotihuacan and do not necessarily indicate the true functions of the structure.

6. To quote Millon:

"One of the most arresting problems surrounding the fall of Teotihuacan is that the city appears to have been flourishing and, with the important exception of a drop in population, was not in an obvious state of decline when it fell, apparently suddenly. There is considerable evidence that many buildings in the city's center burned and collapsed, probably during the eighth century A.D., and never thereafter were rebuilt. The city, therefore, may have met a violent end.

Was it sacked and burned by invaders? Was its center destroyed in a great fire of accidental origin? If so, why was it not rebuilt—or at least reoccupied with some intensity? What happened to the city's population after the catastrophe? Some of its cultivators could have moved out to their fields. But what happened to its craft specialists? Did some of them disperse to other centers where their skills could have been used? Is this part of the explanation for the presence of Teotihuacanoid art in other parts of Middle America during the latter part of the Late Classic Period?

If Teotihuacan fell to invaders, why were the Teotihuacanos unable to successfully resist them? Does this not imply that Teotihuacan society must have faced many problems toward the end of its existence? . . . At the same time, we have found considerable evidence, both from our surface survey and our excavations, of building activity in all parts of the city." (1973, pp. 59–60)

7. The chinampa-style fields at Tiwanaku differ in some construction features from those on Lake Texcoco, probably as an adaptation to local conditions. Their base is a series of coursed stone and gravel layers. Between the bottom stone layer and those above, a sheet of clay was placed, most likely to prevent salty water from being absorbed by roots. Above the finest layer of gravel, topsoil raised the entire mound to about 5 feet. Tiwanakuan raised fields were also larger than those of Mexico, sometimes being almost three-quarters of an acre in size. Reuse of this ancient field system is being encouraged today in the Lake Titicaca area as a way to increase food production for the impoverished and undernourished population of the highlands.

8. In this text, this group will be termed the Hopewell culture. It is sometimes, and probably more accurately, called the Hopewell Interaction Sphere.

9. Where available, nineteenth-century data are used because so much has since occurred to alter Hopewellian mounds. Natural erosion, alteration of profiles by tree roots, and agricultural use of sites are among the more minor alterations which have occurred. On a more drastic scale, mounds have frequently been mined for fill. Mound City was the site of a World War II military base, which destroyed much of the prehistoric fabric. The site which can be visited today is largely reconstructed based on the nineteenth-century survey by Squier and Davis (1848).

10. The mound was named for the Trappist monastery that occupied its summit in the early nineteenth century. As at Teotihuacan, Euroamerican names likely have nothing to do with original functions.

11. This is the name given to the broad floodplain of the Mississippi River located just below its juncture with the Missouri River in Illinois.

12. This dating is reported by several sources, but Berry (and others) contend that "there is no longer any reason to believe that maize made its initial appearance in the Southwest by 2000 B.C., much less 3500 B.C." (1982, p. 31). He would date maize introduction into the Southwest after 1000 B.C.

13. The name Anasazi is a historic term used by the Navajo to identify these prehistoric peoples. It simply means "ancient ones."

14. The term kiva is correctly associated with religious ceremonies. Early explorers erroneously called all round rooms by this term even though most were strictly utilitarian in function. At Chaco Canyon small religious kivas are found within some pueblos, and one large, detached kiva, called Casa Rinconada, also existed.

15. Chaco Canyon will be the focus of this discussion because of the extensive and well-reported investigations that have been conducted there. In addition, Chaco Canyon is now considered to have been the cultural center for the entire Anasazi region.

16. On regional maps they look very straight indeed, but aerial photographs of route traces clearly show that the roads were not ruler-straight. Roads were actually constructed of long tangents which met at angles or were joined by curves of very small radius.

17. These straight road alignments are not unique to Anasazi areas. Similar roads were used in prehistoric California, in northern Mexico, and by the Incas in Peru. Anasazi roads have been most often compared to those in Peru, because they share characteristics other than straightness, such as parallel road segments and the use of rock-cut stairs.

18. Climate history is highly speculative, but various databases recognize the first half of the twelfth century as one of change, and in the Southwest that change was back to a drier pattern. The period of Anasazi expansion in the eleventh century is now believed to have been one of abnormally high rainfall.

19. The Camino Real actually extended all the way to Mexico City, but at San Antonio changed from a path to a highway. Today it is usual to call only the portion east of San Antonio by this name. (See Chapter 4 for further discussion of this important road.)

20. Among the more serious problems which Mexico City is experiencing due to location is the very visible settling of buildings, because their foundations rest on poorly consolidated lake sediments or fill. The rate of destruction from the 1985 earthquake was attributed in part to this problem. There is also very serious air pollution in Mexico City due to its huge population (over 16 million) and the continued use of leaded fuel. The pollution is exacerbated by restricted wind flow, with pollutants frequently trapped and held in the Valley.

13

European Colonial Traditions in the New World

European explorers arriving in the New World found what they considered to be an underpopulated, underexploited, resource-rich, and vegetatively lush landscape. It was also a landscape of incredible challenge. Each cultural group exploring and settling North America met these challenges in a different way, based on national experience and traditions, expectations of gain, attitude toward the native population, and geographical area over which they sought to extend control.[1]

Many nations attempted to establish permanent settlements: the Swedes, the Portuguese, the Germans, the English, the French, the Dutch, and the Spanish. Of these, the last four groups effected the most monumental and lasting impacts on land use and design in North America. The English settled a vast area along the Atlantic seaboard, and, over time, engulfed other groups that had established themselves along the coast. During the eighteenth and nineteenth centuries, their descendants established the modern nations of the United States and Canada, and through them extended English land use practice across much of the continent. The French initially controlled a large, crescent-shaped territory along the principal inland waterways: the Mississippi River, the Great Lakes, and the St. Lawrence River. These lands were eventually lost either directly or indirectly to the English, but French influence persists to this day in language, culture, and land use patterns in isolated regions throughout the continent. The Dutch controlled a relatively small territory, but one central to the development of the new nation of the United States. Their pattern of land development and design along the Hudson River instituted a pastoral landscape which served as an ideal into the nineteenth century. The Spanish occupied vast areas of the New World from Tierra del Fuego to San Francisco Bay. Their consistency of approach to planning and political organization produced a readily identifiable land pattern still viable today. These four cultural groups created a second layer of landscape change, often drawing upon either indigenous precedents or their own practices in Europe. Inevitably the natural environment of North America led to modifications in these practices and a distinctive American approach to use of the land. Three areas, land subdivision and agriculture, city planning, and site and garden design, will be reviewed for each of the four dominant culture groups so that we may begin to understand the origins of Euroamerican land practices on the continent.

LAND SUBDIVISION AND AGRICULTURE

Spanish North America

In the Spanish realm the monarch, through civil administrators, exercised strict control over land ownership. Initially, large land grants were made directly to Spanish subjects in gratitude for their services in conquering land for the crown. Later, developers, known as *empresarios,* became land agents in less fertile regions of northern Mexico and the southwestern United States. These businessmen were responsible for subdividing their grant, selling smaller tracts within it, and assuring that these were settled. Land grants varied in size depending on location and reputation of the *empresario,* but many in arid regions were over a million acres. In Mexico, *conquistadores* were granted not merely land but the native populations on it. This feudal practice, known as the *encomiendas* system, was justified as a way to christianize native people.[2]

The king also set standards for land subdivision since he owned all that had been usurped from the Indians. Size of small grants was based on carrying capacity of the land and the social class of the grantee. Thus, in general, subdivisions in the northern Mexican lands of the *chichimeca* and the Southwest were larger than those in central Mexico or Guatemala. The Spanish carefully assured that allocations were based on the reality of needs in the new colony. Each holding was apportioned to provide areas suitable in both size and natural capacity for a variety of activities. In small grants known as *peonias,* for example, there were individual areas allowed for a farmstead, fields, pastures, orchards, and woodlots.

Individual rural land holdings, known as *haciendas,* were like the plantations of the southeastern United States in many ways. Each was a self-sufficient farm and residential community with work hierarchically organized by class. *Haciendas* were located at a distance from urban areas, and landowners were often absentee managers who preferred to live in the city. *Haciendas* could be as large as 200,000 acres, but often were only several thousand; larger ones were usually subdivided into smaller working units called *ranchos.* In the Southwest the term *rancho* usually referred to a land unit on the scale of a *hacienda* but having stock grazing as its sole or principal activity. Spatial organization of the *hacienda* centered on the main house, which was in reality as much a farm administration and defense structure as it was a home. The main buildings were usually centrally located near the cultivated fields, and designed as a series of interconnected courtyard enclosures. The land around them was often devoid of any ornamental treatment other than an allée of trees lining the main drive. Any garden areas were in the courtyards, with their designs being similar to the town gardens which will be discussed later.

English North America

In English North America land subdivision was less rigid, but all initial control remained in the hands of entrepreneurial organizations such as the Virginia Company, a royally chartered New World development consortium. Company stockholders were often the initial immigrants and grantees, but in some instances, such as at Plymouth Colony, an independent group received a charter.[3] Later a system of distribution to individual immigrants, known as the headright, developed.[4] The type of settler, their reasons for emigration, and the character of the land which they were granted determined the land use pattern which eventually emerged in a region.

Two regionally variant land use and agricultural patterns eventually evolved among English communities. In New England, distribution of property depended on membership in a theocratically governed community, in which the village served as both economic and social focal point. Beginning with Plymouth in 1620, a consistent pattern of centralized residential village with adjoining farmland and dispersed pastures and woodlots developed. The village and the agricultural land assigned to its members became a unit of government and development called a "town" or "township." Each of these had limits of population because the land area was relatively fixed at about 5 or 6 square miles. When no new land remained for newcomers or descendants, an entirely new town was claimed from land belonging to the native population.[5] Thus, the Puritans extended their control over New England in village increments.

Village members were entitled to four types of owned parcels and a share in communal lands. Land allocated to individual families included a town lot for a house and kitchen garden, fields for row crops, a meadow for stock, and a woodlot of fuel and building material. Fields were located as close to the village as practical, with those coming first getting the nearest sites. Often a farmer got several smaller plots rather than one large one to assure some equivalence of land quality between the assigned parcels. Pastures and woodland at a distance from the village were held in common. All the different use parcels were strung out along the primitive roads that connected villages. Individual parcels, whether town lots or farms, had minimal road frontage but were usually quite deep. This configuration assured that a larger number of lots had direct access to circulation links, while reducing the number of roads required in a village.

In the Middle Atlantic and southern areas large farms known as plantations were the major unit of subdivision. Plantations played multiple roles, being both agricultural producers and processors, both farms and hamlets, and both work-places and residences. The first plantation in the region was that of the London Company at Jamestown, Virginia. There, planters were under contract to the company and both lived and worked communally. Later, as an incentive to pro-duction, each planter was granted 100 acres for each share owned in the com-pany. Those emigrants who were not stockholders were awarded a headright land grant of 50 acres provided the settler remained for three years.

Southern plantations remained self-contained villages for more than two centuries following initial settlement due to the labor system, based on Afro-American enslavement, that came to be used there. Since slaves and indentured servants were not free to travel to cities as their masters did, and since masters grouped them for control, their collections of houses functioned socially like a hamlet or small neighborhood. On most plantations slave cabins sat in rows, either facing directly on a road or aligned along it. This clustering, which of course was intended for ease of supervision, had the advantage for residents of creating a strong community with constant social interaction and mutual sup-port.[6] Slave cabins were usually located in rows near the main houses, which sat at the "head" of the row. Singleton believes that this arrangement inadvertently followed an African site-planning tradition in which the chief's residence had a similar dominant position. In America, then, the use of this pattern ". . . would have served to help subjugate an already captive population," but at the same time unknowing Europeans were "caught up in and affected by the creolization process" as European and African traditions merged into new American practices (Singleton, 1985, p. 197).

The small landscapes around their housing that slaves were sometimes per-mitted to control became multifunctional areas for work, recreation, and outdoor living. Since quarters were usually quite small—a family of five or more usually lived in a space not much larger than a modern living room—outdoor rooms between houses were important space extenders during clement seasons. Food preparation, crafts, and child care all took place in these "patios" of bare earth. On many plantations slaves were allowed or even expected to supplement their furnished food supply with leisure time gardening and animal husbandry. Thus areas near, but not directly adjacent to, cabins were often planted with crops or enclosed for poultry or pig pens. This small tradition of independent farming would later in the nineteenth century serve some former slaves well, when they became quasi-independent sharecroppers.

The plantation system of land distribution produced a settlement pattern which contrasted strongly with that of New England. In New England, popu-lation concentrated at small urban units from which farmers went out to work their land. Towns were settled as complete communities to which newcomers

Slave quarters along the main entry drive at Mulberry Plantation near Charleston, South Carolina, illustrating the typical "villagescape" of slave housing.

were assigned. This produced a gradation of settlement density, with the most populated areas being those on the coast, but without voids between areas of development. In the South, each farm family lived on their own plantation or headright, often far from neighbors. In addition each farmer chose their own land from among all the land yet unclaimed, thus leaving large unsettled zones between individual farms. This population dispersal made it difficult for villages to emerge. Southern plantations also differed from New England farms because of their emphasis on production of a single crop for commercial sale. This produced large farming areas dominated by one field type, each of which had very specific parameters for management. Among the plantation crops of importance at various times in the English colonies were indigo, tobacco, and cotton.

Dutch and French North America

The Dutch system was much like that of the Spanish, with huge tracts of land being given to promoters known as *patroons* were who responsible for its subdivision and settlement. Those *patroons* who brought at least fifty adults to New Netherlands for four years were granted a total of 16 linear miles along the spectacular Hudson River running as far back as was "reasonable." Although the length of river frontage and minimum number of settlers was later reduced, a similar land use and ownership pattern persisted throughout the Dutch period: lots were long and narrow, often several miles deep. Since the amount of land allotted for each fifty settlers was excessive, *patroons* had little incentive to bring over more than fifty people, limiting settlement and dispersing populations. As in the Middle Atlantic and the South, large *patroonships* limited the need for towns, and the Hudson Valley remained exclusively rural, with the only large Dutch city being the port of New Amsterdam on Manhattan Island, where roughly half of all Dutch settlers resided.[7]

French settled areas utilized a land subdivision system known as the "long lot" almost exclusively.[8] In this arrangement, each lot had a very narrow frontage—sometimes only 100 feet—on a river, but would extend back from the river a mile or more. This distinctive pattern of lotting persists in areas originally settled by the French, such as Louisiana and the St. Lawrence Valley, but in others such as the Mississippi Valley of Illinois and Missouri, was replaced during subsequent settlement. Long lots offered several advantages. They gave direct river access to large numbers of sites. Settlement was compact, creating strip villages called *côtes.* An otherwise rural population could thus have the advantages of community camaraderie. Long lots also allowed farmers to take advantage of various ecozones, from wetlands to hilltops, each of them suitable for different uses, all within one parcel of land.

The Company of New France, a private corporation like the Virginia Company, initially managed settlement, but was later replaced by direct government control. Both authorities used the seigneurial system, a variant of the *empresario* or *patroonship* systems, but one in which the settlers were legally as well as practically serfs. This feudalistic approach created some social distinctions between landowners and vassals but had little day to day impact. This practice dominated in Canada but by the time the French occupation in the United States had died out. Again, as with the pattern of land subdivision, the seigneurial system fostered a strong sense of local identity and community, in this case due to sense of fealty to the seigneur, or landowner.

The different approaches to land subdivision and agriculture of the Spanish, English, Dutch, and French had a potent influence in the colonial period that often persists today in vestigial form or as a regional variant to national patterns. In New England the pattern of pastoral countryside centered on the small village remains a testament to colonial influences, while in the lower Mississippi contemporary maps show the endurance of the long lot tradition in modern farm boundaries and urban streets.

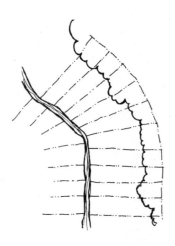

Diagrammatic plan of typical long lot pattern along a river.

CITY PLANNING AND DESIGN
Spanish Settlements

Land subdivision systems not only influenced modern land patterns, but in their own day engendered regionally variant urban paradigms and designs. Of all European powers operating in North America, the Spanish perfected the most progressive and uniform system for settling the continent. They created both a hierarchy of institutions around which specific settlement types were organized, and distinct guidelines for each type of settlement. Through three types of settlement—the *presidio,* the mission, and the *pueblo*—the Spanish furthered their triple aim of conquest, conversion, and occupation. *Presidios* are often identified as forts, because they were stations for military garrisons, but their broader role was as seat of regional government. They usually served as residence of the governor or governor's representative. Missions were the province of religious orders, usually Jesuits or Franciscans, sent to convert and civilize the indigenous people.[9] Missions combined boarding schools, worker's commune, and agricultural estate. *Pueblos,* or *villas* as they were also called, were settlements for Europeans; they combined many functions, but were intended to be commercial and civil centers for the agriculturally based population.

As centers of governmental and military power, *presidios* were sited to take advantage of naturally strategic locations, such as bluffs. They often dominated crucial river locations and sat next to major highways so that internal communications and transportation could be controlled. The *presidio* at Goliad, Texas, located on a hilltop overlooking La Bahia Road, an important east-to-west link, illustrated these principles of siting. Many *presidios* were built as fortifications with high walls and bastions, often in star-shaped Renaissance style; an example is Los Adaes on the frontier with French Louisiana. Others, generally nearer populated areas, were unenclosed collections of buildings around a plaza which

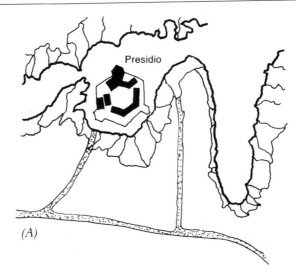

(A)

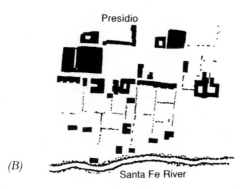

(B)

Diagrammatic plans of two presidios: (A) Los Adaes in Louisiana, an example of a fortified presidio; (B) Santa Fe in New Mexico, an example of an open presidio centered on a military plaza. (Data from Moorhead, 1975; drawn by Rossi.)

served as parade ground; San Fernando de Bexar (at San Antonio) in Texas and Santa Fe in New Mexico were in this style.

Both plans of the period and recent reconstructions show *presidios* as solid, well-built structures capable of withstanding attacks from rain as well as from Comanches and other aggressors. This was not the case. *Presidios* were often erected by the garrisons sent to man them—soldiers with no training in construction—and were built hurriedly of substandard materials, such as unseasoned logs. In many cases, though, this was not of serious consequence since occupation was very short-lived. Los Adaes, for instance, was in active service only about a year. Although usually built as independent institutions, *presidios* served the security needs of nearby missions and *pueblos,* often less than a mile away. In most locations infill construction eventually merged all three, so that *presidios* appeared to have been built in the middle of villages.

Missions were located near native populations deemed suitable for conversion. Of secondary philosophical importance but vital for self-sufficiency was access to fresh water. Since agriculture provided the principal support for missions, location near a reliable water source was essential in the generally arid Spanish-held areas. In California and earlier east coast mission areas such as Florida and Georgia, location was also a function of access to the ocean for transportation.

Post-1760 mission compounds were really small villages with a church, schools for religious instruction and crafts, residences for priests, housing for native families, and indoor and outdoor work areas. Nearby agricultural lands fed the population. To ensure production, most permanent missions in the Southwest had an extensive irrigation system—the first Euroamerican use of this technology in the New World. Water was controlled and managed over a wide area, sometimes an entire watershed. Canals, known as *acequias,* and aqueducts diverted water from streams or reservoirs, carried it to the most fertile fields. In addition to the farmland near the mission complex itself, each mission was assigned more distant ranch lands, for production of livestock both for mission needs and occasionally for sale to the *presidio* or *pueblo.*

The developed grounds of the missions varied based upon particular regional characteristics. Two major mission design concepts can be seen by comparing the missions of California with those of Texas.[10] California missions were shaped by a hospitable and fertile environment where sea access provided relatively regular contact with other missions and with Mexico. There, the native population was peaceful, made up of small tribal bands who in some instances had a history of small-scale agriculture. In Texas, missions were quite isolated—connected only by trails through unpopulated areas. The Native Americans of the area were also more aggressive in protecting their land from Spanish occupation. The Comanche, Kiowa, and Apache in particular habitually raided both Spanish sites and other native settlements. The christianized Native Americans of Texas generally had little prior experience with agriculture or the settled way of life it necessitated. These factors account for important differences in the design of California and Texas missions.

California missions were generally located within view of the coast, but on high ground above it to protect from sea invasion or flooding. The mission at Santa Barbara was one of the most dramatic examples of this siting principle in practice. Mission compounds were made up of a series of small, interconnected patios enclosed by an arcaded walkway fronting small buildings one room deep. These open spaces were designed much like medieval cloisters, with the covered walks offering a shaded area for meditation and the area in the middle divided into four quadrants by paths which met at a central focal point such as a fountain or well. While these courtyards did serve as places for study and reflection, they were also outdoor workrooms for crafts and food preparation. As reconstructed today, most mission courtyards have the appearance of gardens, but this was probably not the case in the eighteenth century. Although there may have been trees for shade, other vegetation would have been for food and medicine production, with most of the ground plain primarily covered in dusty soil.

In California the cloistered areas were primarily the realm of priests and trusted Native American workers. Most of those Native Americans being converted lived and worked in open fields which surrounded the mission buildings. Their small huts were similar in style and arrangement to traditional villages, and many simply carried on usual agricultural practices in a new setting. The mission church, although connected to other buildings, usually fronted on this undefined space allocated to the Native Americans; it was intended to be openly inviting and suggest the way in which native people could gain access to Spanish civilization.

In Texas, the mission had the appearance of a fortified plaza. A single large open space of several acres was separated from the larger landscape by a low, solid wall, which also created the outer wall of native dwellings within the mission. The mission church could be completely within these walls, as at Mission Concepcion near San Antonio, or front on the space with one or more of its walls forming part of the exterior fortification, as at Mission San Antonio de Valero, better known in the United States as the Alamo. The intramural space enclosed by buildings had undifferentiated use areas that could be allocated as

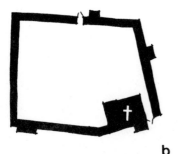

a

b

Diagrammatic plans of two mission types: (A) the open California mission; (B) the enclosed Texas mission.

Mission San Juan Capistrano sans swallows, an example of the open, unfortified plans of California missions. Here one of the open-cornered courtyards is seen through an arcade.

need arose for outdoor work space, stock pens, living and cooking spaces for the native residents, church anteroom, or school. For example, in times of danger this space became the temporary sanctuary of livestock and the native people living outside the mission. Uses changed on a regular basis, as the mission's inhabitants progressed through their daily and seasonal chores. Due to the heavy and diverse usage of these spaces, their appearance was probably quite bleak, with little vegetation other than a few trees for shade and some plots of vegetables.

Missions housed Native Americans welcomed into Christianity, but Spanish or Mexican residents did not want to live side by side with their new coreligionists. They and their government preferred that mission and settler villages be separate entities. The colonist settlement was the *pueblo,* which, as the center of civilian life and commerce, was vital to long-term regional control. For this reason, great care was taken that *pueblos* be well sited and organized. To achieve this, the most comprehensive planning document of its day, the Laws of the Indies, was issued by King Philip II in 1573. The actual authors of the Laws and its myriad provisions are unknown, but the principles upon which it was based date to the writings of Vitruvius. The Laws of the Indies was important not for its innovations, but because it codified and amplified existing rules, making them easily applicable on the frontiers of an expanding empire.

The Laws dealt with two broad areas of colonial administration: just treatment of indigenous peoples and proper planning of towns. Many of the standards relating to the native peoples remained merely statements of good intentions, unimplemented by colonial administrators. In regard to urban planning, the Laws proved more acceptable and had a lasting impact. Planning standards related to two aspects of urbanization: selection of the townsite and internal arrangement of urban elements. Individual ordinances under the Laws dealt with various aspects of each of these much the way modern planning criteria set standards for development today.

In identifying viable townsites the Laws specified that they should be in healthful locations, "that is be of good climate, the sky clear and benign, the air pure and soft, without impediment or alterations and of good temperature, without excessive heat or cold, and having to decide, it is better that it be cold" (Ordinance 34).[11] With an eye to the productivity of the colonies, *pueblos* "should be in fertile areas with an abundance of fruits and fields, of good land to plant and harvest, of grasslands to grow livestock, of mountains and forests for wood and building material for homes and edifices, and of good and plentiful water supply for drinking and irrigation" (Ordinance 35).

Having outlined the general criteria to be considered when exploring for new town locations, the Laws then articulated a series of more specific standards for development of the town center, precepts which today we would call design criteria:

> The main plaza is to be the starting point for the town; if the town is situated on the sea coast, it should be placed at the landing place of the port, but inland it should be at the center of the town. The plaza should be square or rectangular, in which case it should have at least one and a half its width for length in as much as this shape is best for fiestas in which horses are used and for any other fiestas that should be held. (Ordinance 112) The size . . . shall be not less than two hundred feet wide and three hundred feet long, nor larger than eight hundred feet long and five hundred and thirty-two feet wide. A good proportion is six hundred feet long and four hundred wide. (Ordinance 113) From the plaza shall begin four principal streets: One (shall be) from the middle of each side, and two streets from each corner of the plaza; the four corners of the plaza shall face the four principal winds, because in this manner, the streets running from the plaza will not be exposed to the four principal winds . . . (Ordinance 114) Around the plaza as well as along the four principal streets which begin there, there shall be portals [covered walks], for these are of considerable convenience to the merchants who generally gather there . . . (Ordinance 115).

Clearly the plaza was to be the symbolic and physical heart of the pueblo, so great care was to be taken in its arrangement.

The Laws did not neglect other fundamental urban issues, though, and dealt with considerations such as street design, nuisances, and visual unity.

Plaza of Socorro, New Mexico, in 1883, showing the original, prepark appearance of plazas in Spanish colonial towns. (Courtesy Museum of New Mexico.)

In cold places the streets shall be wide and in hot places narrow; but for purposes of defense in areas where there are horses, it would be better if they are wide. . . . (Ordinance 116) Here and there in the town, smaller plazas of good proportion shall be laid out . . . (Ordinance 118) The site and building lots for slaughter houses, fisheries, tanneries, and other business which produce filth shall be so placed the filth can easily be disposed of. . . . (Ordinance 122) Within the town, a commons shall be delimited, large enough that although the population may experience a rapid expansion, there will always be sufficient space where the people may go to for recreation and take their cattle to pasture. . . . (Ordinance 12) They shall try as far as possible to have the buildings all of one type for the sake of the beauty of the town. (Ordinance 134)

The consistency of form found in so many Spanish colonial towns was due to the influence of the Laws. Monclova, the trade center of northern Mexico, and St. Augustine, Florida, are just two examples of the application of the Law to actual towns. The Laws of the Indies should not be viewed as an unyielding edict because, as these two examples show, it was always tempered by local conditions; the standards of the Laws were often disregarded, usually for economic and local environmental reasons. Monterey, California, for example, had little apparent structure and was located almost solely on the basis of access to its excellent harbor. In San Antonio, Texas, the custom of reserving lots around the main plaza for commercial uses was disregarded and land given for homesteads instead.

The physical character of towns created under the Laws emphasized the contrast between public and private spaces, the importance of certain cultural institutions, and the significance of circulation routes both within the town and to the hinterland. Public spaces and structures had a completely open appearance, with ease of access for everyone. Plazas were large, unobstructed areas, with little or no vegetation, with no paving other than soil, and having undifferentiated use areas. There a fiesta could be held, a rancher temporarily store cattle, a farmer sell his produce, or young people promenade. (The contemporary park-like character of most plazas resulted from nineteenth-century alterations, which in the United States usually occurred with Anglo settlement.) Public buildings opened directly onto the main plaza, as at the Palace of the Governors in Santa Fe, while the principal church either faced the plaza or was on an adjoining street. The remainder of the structures facing the plaza were occupied by town offices,

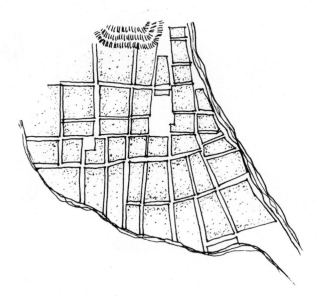

Diagrammatic plan of Monclova, Coahuila, Mexico, founded in the seventeenth century and an example of a city plan that followed in many details the Laws of the Indies. (Data from Moorhead, 1975.)

such as those of the *alcade* (mayor), or by the showrooms of merchants. The plaza was thus surrounded by the essential civic, religious, and commercial institutions of the community.

Residential neighborhoods, on the other hand, turned away from the streets, which often seemed like lifeless alleys. Homes had few openings to the street—usually only a heavy timber door and small windows covered by grilles. The visual and functional focuses of residences were courtyards surrounded by house or perimeter walls.

The grid block and street pattern encouraged by the Laws of the Indies placed great emphasis on circulation systems. They became major lines of sight within the town, as well as important internal and external links. To the non-Spanish eye, this pattern created a rather bleak streetscape, but a visually clean and clear one, with emphasis placed on street activities rather than on street amenities.

English Settlements

English towns were quite different in purpose and appearance from the Spanish *pueblos*. They were also far less consistent in pattern, having no guiding set of regulations. English towns were both seats of commerce and villages for farmers. Their location, planning, and development depended primarily on the religious and educational background of founders, the intended purpose of the community, and local environmental factors affecting the economy. Under the influence of these factors, two broad patterns emerged in two different geographical areas: (1) the pattern of compact village with farm hinterland in New England and English Canada; (2) a pattern of scattered village or crossroads hamlets in an otherwise rural countryside of the Middle Atlantic and South.

The earliest English settlements of any permanence, Plymouth and Jamestown, illustrate the effect of regional factors on land use and design. Plymouth was founded by a group of coreligionists searching for a permanent new home to be established on their distinctive principles. Most did not expect or desire to return to England, so they were equally interested in the social and economic opportunities that the new land afforded. Plymouth was located on the northern Atlantic coast, an area of rugged topography, dense forests, and some danger of access, where the practical functions of a centralized community were quite important. At Plymouth the settlement served as a place of residence for farmers,

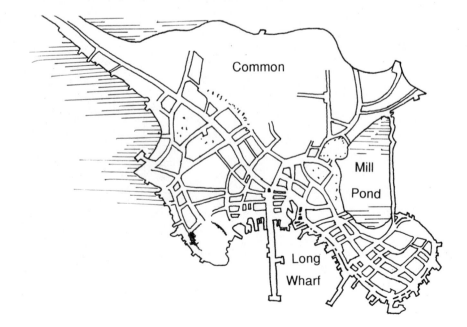

Boston, founded in 1630, was typical of New England towns organized haphazardly around through and local streets. (Data from Powell, 1963; drawn by Rossi.)

Plymouth, Massachusetts, founded 1620, as reconstructed on a site south of the original village.

an exchange point for goods, a religious seat, and the center for participatory government. The village prototype established there set the pattern for almost two centuries of urban development in New England.

Jamestown on the other hand was home base for planters sent to Virginia beginning in 1607 by the Virginia Company. Planters came as individuals, usually with little intention of staying beyond the length of time it took to acquire sufficient wealth for future investments. While they were interested in land acquisition as well, it was for land as an asset rather than as a home. Their interests thus focused on economic rather than community activities.

Founders of many cities established in English North America in the late seventeenth and eighteenth century looked to progressive Renaissance concepts of urban design—concepts which consciously broke from medieval European prototypes that were considered socially repressive and physically unsanitary. The town developers who built these cities, surprisingly to the modern mind, selected grid plans as the most effective way to promote health, equality of opportunity, and community identity.[12] The first developer to use a purposely organized grid pattern in this way was William Penn, in his plan for Philadelphia dating to the 1680s.

Within his 45,000-square-mile land grant, Penn selected almost 1500 acres strategically sited between the Delaware and Schuylkill Rivers for his "garden city" of brotherly love. Penn and his surveyor developed a site plan with an almost unbroken grid of rectangular blocks arranged in four quadrants separated by two broad, perpendicular thoroughfares. At the intersection of these streets, a 10-acre lot was retained for public buildings. Within each quadrangle an offset square—ironically, the only elements which violated an otherwise absolute checkerboard regularity—preserved 8 acres of open space. Original plans were unrelenting in their regularity, making no adjustments for irregular river banks or topography. This lack of adaptation to the landscape naturally caused problems later. One of Penn's purposes in laying out such a large urban plot was to allocate large tracts, usually 1 acre, for house lots. This, he felt, would avoid future congestion and give the city a beautiful country village appearance in which plants rather than buildings dominated the streetscape.[13]

That Penn's scheme was the outgrowth of a European movement toward rational, Cartesian planning which would dominate urban design in the eighteenth century can be seen from other equally geometric schemes for city and country planning. In 1717, Robert Mountgomery proposed one such scheme for the unbuilt South Carolina colony of Azilia. Planned on a massive scale, the farm lot and city zone was to be 14 miles square, with pastures and woodlots beyond that. Mountgomery subdivided this square settlement area into estates of 640 acres—that is, 1 square mile. These surrounded a central city and four "great Parks" to be used for common grazing. Later, Granville Sharp also used the magical square mile as the modular unit for his prototypical town plan. It too had a central urban area with surrounding farmland, but the commons was to be in an encircling band that separated inner from outer town lots.

In the Middle Atlantic and Southern colonies urban development was extremely limited for several reasons. The environment and culture of residents lent themselves well to highly profitable large-acreage agricultural endeavors— the plantations. Each of these was really a rural region which, using forced labor, could both produce products for export and fill its own needs for everyday products and services. Thus, some of the functions of the town were absorbed by the plantation because of its economy of scale. In addition, the wide-mouthed rivers, which were navigable for long distances, became the principal routes of transport; each farm or plantation had immediate frontage on a water route and a dock at which its products could be exchanged for imports. Towns were thus not important as trade centers, usually their most critical function. Finally the fact that a large percentage of the South's residents were kept in bondage either through slavery or indentured servitude, and thus not given full access to the cultural life of the colony, meant that the usual educational and social activities that towns served were underpopulated. Once again, the plantation assumed these roles through tutors and seasonal social gatherings. Of course these factors did not preclude the development of all cities, but it both limited their number and made those which *did* develop even more significant. Charleston, South Carolina, for example was a regional center of plantation culture, and planters from the Indies even came there annually for the social "season."

Towns and cities that were developed in the South often originated for a special purpose or were planned based on the particular philosophy of the colony's founder. Williamsburg and Alexandria in Virginia are examples of towns established for special purposes, while Savannah, Georgia, was a city whose planning very much reflects the philosophy of one person. In 1680 the Virginia House of Burgesses passed an "Act for Cohabitation and Encouragement of Trade and Manufacture," one of a long line of laws intended to create cities. This one stipulated that twenty towns be built in the colony, principally to serve as centers of government-controllable trade. Although the Act itself was revoked the following year, its provisions resurfaced in various forms and a number of towns including Fredericksburg, Tappahannock, Alexandria, and Williamsburg are considered to have resulted from it. All four towns were laid out on grid plans, both for expedience and as a response to contemporary planning theory, which rejected the irregular in favor of the grid. As the capital, Williamsburg was expected to have a more stately plan, as well as more amenities.

The plan of Williamsburg was begun in 1699 by the colonial governor Francis Nicholson, already known for the radial plan of Annapolis, Maryland. For the Virginia capital, which was to be as much a cultural center as one of government and commerce, Nicholson utilized a grid plan, but one in which straight streets served as sight lines as well as routes of passage. Beginning at the existing campus of the College of William and Mary, Duke of Gloucester Street extended as the central business street. At its other end the sight line terminated at the new Capitol. This spine thus linked two major colonial institutions. A cross sight line, Palace Street, led to the residence of the royal governor. This street eventually became a parkway with a green swath dividing the roadways. The principal market was located at the focal intersection of Palace and Duke of Gloucester Streets. This crossed axial plan created a strong central urban core bounded by the major institutions of state, school, and commerce, which were emphasized through their prominent placement. An interesting although short-lived aspect of Nicholson's plan, reported in Reps (1972), was the addition of diagonal streets at the market and Capitol which created the initials of the ruling monarchs, William and Mary.

Elsewhere in the South, other motives prompted the establishment and design of towns. James Oglethorpe's plan for Savannah represented application of progressive planning concepts on the clean slate that was the Georgia frontier. As in Virginia, a grid layout was used, but for reasons other than ease of surveying. To Oglethorpe, as to William Penn in Philadelphia, the grid represented rational thought, order, and a reaction against the unhealthy and cramped medieval urban environments of Europe. In Savannah the grid was also used as a means to preplan future urban expansion.

Peter Gordon's well-known and often cited aerial view illustrated the scheme which Oglethorpe established in Savannah. The town was composed of modular units known as "wards." Each ward had forty house sites of 5500 square feet laid out in four rows with two five-house groupings in each row. Between pairs of rows, in the center of the ward, an area of almost 3 acres was given over to public land uses, including space reserved for a public square and four large lots for public buildings. Circulation was equally well organized. Main arterial streets were those that ran through the squares. These were to be lined with trees and wider than local streets. Of these, Bull Street, which began at the Savannah River next to the wharves became the "main" street. Parallel to these major streets were smaller routes which separated wards. This system of streets provided multiple route choices, while the variety of street treatments allowed drivers or riders to select scenic or speedy alternatives.

View of Nicholson's first effort at colonial town planning, Annapolis, Maryland, which was laid out with streets radiating from two circles reserved for public buildings. Here the Capitol, which occupies one of those circles, provides a visual terminus to the street.

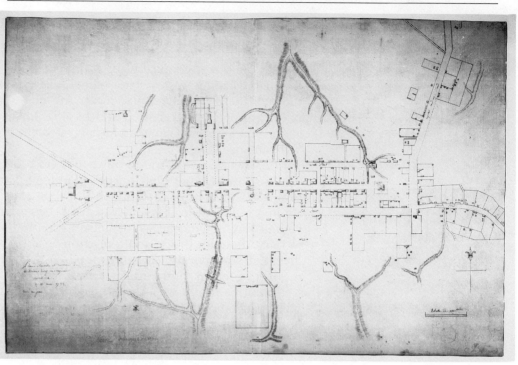

Plan of Williamsburg, Virginia,
designed in 1699 by Francis
Nicholson, as it appeared in
1782 according to "Plan de la
ville et environs de
Williamsburg en Virginie,
America, 11 Mai 1782."
(Swem Library, College of
William and Mary,
Williamsburg, Virginia.)

View from the Governor's
Palace, Williamsburg, to the
Palace Green, the boulevard
that linked the Palace to
Duke of Gloucester Street.
(Department of Landscape
Architecture Collection,
Texas A&M University)

*View of Telfair Square,
Savannah, one of the original
ward squares, in the 1980s.
House lots were originally less
built up, with some space
reserved for productive activities.
The squares were intended as
sites for military drills and did
not become parks until the
nineteenth century.*

*Township Plan, 1798, by John
McKinnon shows land
allotments for colonists in
Savannah, Georgia. In addition
to a town lot of about an eighth
of an acre, each received a 5-
acre garden plot immediately
outside the city and a farm of
almost 45 acres located on the
larger lots at the perimeter, so
that total land holdings equaled
50 acres. Each settler also had
the right of access to the
Common, now Forsyth Park.
(Georgia Historical Society,
Savannah, Georgia.)*

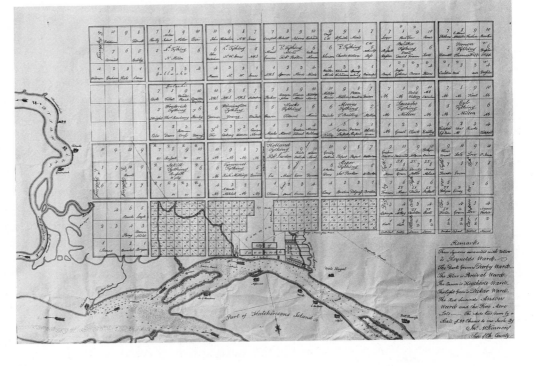

The plan of Savannah included rural as well as urban tracts, making it a comprehensive settlement scheme. The initial subdivision unit was a square mile area subdivided into 45-acre farm sites and 5-acre garden sites. The hierarchy of lands given to each settler made for efficient land use and concentration of population, while maintaining the agricultural base.

French and Dutch Settlements

In French and Dutch America, town patterns were closely related to defense. The town was either itself designed as a fortification or was built around a fort. Thus city plans often resembled those of medieval towns, with densely packed dwellings and alleylike streets. Although many French communities, including Quebec, followed this earlier prototype, other French North American cities developed more regular plans with generous streets, even when built within walls. Montreal, with an irregular but gridlike plan, St. Louis, whose checkerboard street plan adjusted only slightly to topographical conditions, were two examples of the integration of medieval and Renaissance planning concepts in North America.

The Dutch developed cities that were more consistently medieval in character. Initial plans of both new Amsterdam and Albany show similar arrangements, with one or two main thoroughfares, such as Broadway in Manhattan, while the remaining streets were narrow passageways. Streets were totally enclosed by buildings set at the edge of the right-of-way. In New Amsterdam—New York City—a public park was provided at the Battery, and there was additional open space at the rear of buildings in the center of each block. This space was expected to be developed though, and city officials complained about the lack of lots for newcomers because landowners kept back lots for farming, rather than developing them.

GARDEN DESIGN

Although major concerns of both colonial governments and settlers focused on economic and military issues, the amenities of life were not neglected. In the landscape, these amenities took the form of ornamental grounds, particularly gardens. As in political matters, colonial North America depended on European concepts for inspiration in this realm: garden and estate design followed earlier Renaissance prototypes adapted in simple ways to the demands of American landscapes and to the landowner's means.

Spanish Gardens

In Spanish territories garden design had the same consistency of pattern that we have seen in urban design. The design of the inward-looking courtyard-style house, so similar to those from Rome and the Middle East, was based on equally ancient precedents. The tranquil and secluded interior patios were the stage for domestic social and work activities. Most homes, or *adobes* as they were called, had just one patio that served many functions. Homes of the well-to-do often had two patios—one a formal garden, the other a work space or informal garden. The Avila Adobe in Los Angeles, California, and the Casa de Estudillo, in San Diego, California, both restored eighteenth-century *adobes* with gardens, are examples of such upper-class residences, with U-shaped buildings enclosing a formal patio courtyard. A covered walkway surrounded the court and provided a transition from the interior to outdoor spaces. The courts themselves were divided into four quadrants by walks in a cross pattern. At the center of the walks was a fountain, used as much for household water needs as for ornamental purposes. Irregular plantings of shrubs, annuals, perennials, and grasses occupied unpaved ground surfaces and potted plants were set along the walks. As in Islamic gardens, sensual plants with fragrance, bright color, and producing sound were favored. Unplanted ground was often left as swept earth. The overall visual

The restored patio garden at Casa Avila in Los Angeles, California.

effect was much like that of a cloister garden, albeit on a smaller scale. Beyond the enclosing wings of the house was a second courtyard given over to utilitarian functions such as vegetable garden, clothes drying, poultry raising, and storage. These back courts were less regular in plan although some vestigial four-part subdivision may have occurred. At Casa de Estudillo, the back court has been restored as a curvilinear informal garden.

English Gardens

English settlers on the Atlantic coast, like their Spanish cohorts, were interested in recreating the comforting gardens of their homeland in North America. Many early communications among family members on both sides of the ocean dealt with the sending of seeds and plants, and plant exchanges remained one of the more continuous and friendly links between colonists and mother country for several hundred years. Initial serious plant exploration was undertaken by Europeans sent to the New World explicitly to collection unknown materials. Among the earliest of these was John Tradescant, who explored parts of Virginia in the seventeenth century. In the eighteenth century botanists such as Mark Catesby, Peter Collinson, and Peter Kalm extended our knowledge of native materials, and exported species such as tupelo and honey locust to Europe. But the most successful colonial plant explorer and botanist was the self-trained John Bartram. During years of exploration, he traveled and collected materials in much of the original thirteen colonies, with treks to Lake Ontario and Florida. Bartram not only collected material, but he organized it into what was probably the first scientific botanical collection in North America, his garden at Philadelphia. From such collecting, as well as trade with Europe, Americans acquired the plant materials for their gardens.

Early colonial gardens served mixed functions. There was always the need to grow plants useful in household activities—as food, flavorings, medicine, dyes, or materials for tools, but at the same time ornamental beauty could be a psychological boost in a sometimes hostile environment. It is fortunate that many useful plants are also very attractive. Among the oldest North American gardens excavated to date is that at Bacon's Castle in the Tidewater region of Virginia. Dating to the late seventeenth or early eighteenth century, this garden was laid out next to the residence in large, rectangular beds separated from each other by a grid of paths. Although quite simple in plan, it was similar in concept and in details, such as walls and garden structures, to more elaborate later gardens. Researchers have concluded that this garden likely served as both a kitchen and ornamental garden, but how these areas were allotted remains uncertain.

In New England, tight settlement patterns allowed only limited space for gardens not given over to growing major crops. This necessitated intensive use of small areas. The dooryard garden was one response to this need. As their name suggests, these gardens were laid out in the space adjacent to the front door of the house, in a tiny area which separated the residence from the street. "There seemed to be a law which shaped and bounded the front yard; the side fences extended from the corners of the house to the front fence on the edge of the road, and thus formed naturally the guarded parallelogram" (Earle, 1901, pp. 38–39). This precious zone was then intensively planted with carefully tended annuals, perennials, and a few shrubs, such as boxwood. The dooryard garden was the pride of the household and contained all those rare and prized plants which the family struggled to grow. Although useful plants might be grown there, the dooryard garden was, like the modern front yard, a formal space intended to impress the neighbors and create an inviting setting for the home.

Organization of these dooryard gardens relied on a bilaterally symmetrical plan centered on the walkway to the front door. In a small dooryard this would be the only path, but larger gardens had side paths which allowed access to all the planting areas. These could be rectangular or circular in form and paved in brick, gravel, or sand. Unfortunately the dooryard garden was a victim of changing fashions in design, so that no preserved examples survived intact to modern times. But the restoration of gardens at the Mission House in Stockbridge, Massachusetts, suggests the eclectic mixture of annuals and perennials within bordered beds that was probably typical of many dooryard gardens.[14]

Smaller residences often had only these front spaces to use as gardens. Larger establishments with areas not needed for agriculture often devoted more space to formal gardens. These larger rear gardens shared three characteristics with dooryard gardens—bilateral symmetry, use of low hedges to edge walks, and irregular planting schemes for most of the garden, in arrangements inspired by small English gardens such as knot gardens. The Nichols garden in Salem, Massachusetts, illustrated these principles at the prosperous home of a former colonial governor. The design, attributed to architect and builder Samuel McIntire, had four major parts: a dooryard garden, a rear service terrace, an upper ornamental garden, and a lower productive or ornamental garden. These elements were uni-

Reconstructed dooryard garden of the Mission House, Stockbridge, Massachusetts.

fied by a sight line that ran through the house to a rear central path. This path was at an acute angle to the house and not absolutely centered in the rear yard, yet through screening of property lines an illusion of symmetry was created. The rear garden stepped down the hillside, with a view to a nearby river framed by a wooden arch which separated upper and lower gardens. Remnants of the upper garden suggest that it was a tree and shrub garden, possibly with a large turf area, while the lower garden was divided into structured beds for flowers or vegetables. Other, similar colonial gardens were the Derby Garden and Osgood Garden, both in Salem.

In the Middle Atlantic and southern states, town gardens were quite similar to those of New England in following English Renaissance prototypes, with their emphasis on patterning of the ground plane and use of sight lines to connect spaces and views. A typical arrangement for a small garden would have two major perpendicular paths that met at a central circular bed, and an outer rectangular walkway. This simple arrangement was repeated in gardens of every size from Newfoundland to Georgia. Our current image of these gardens comes primarily from restorations such as those at Colonial Williamsburg, but it should be kept in mind that the eighteenth-century gardens which they represent were probably far less regular and less precisely maintained. Thus the axial plans of the restorations are far more authentic than their stiff, clipped appearance.

The greatest differences in garden design between North and South appeared in the arrangement of grounds at large estates. The plantations of the South derived their inspiration primarily from the monarchical French Grand Style. Middleton Plantation in South Carolina was the most complete and sophisticated example of such a formal garden. Begun in 1741, this garden was organized around sight lines that formed a triangle with one side running through the entry drive, across the main house (since destroyed), to the edge of a series of terraces, then to the side forming the hypoteneuse which connected principal features of the formal garden, finally ending in the triangle's base which ran through the center of a long, rectangular reflecting pool. This unusual pattern—which had some crudely sited elements such as the reflecting pool, which reflected little and likely was developed primarily to solve a drainage or other functional problem— was most successful in its sophisticated adaptation to the Ashley River site. Spe-

Nichols Garden, Salem, Massachusetts, looking down the principal sight line path. (Original photo by Mary H. Northend, *Landscape Architecture,* Vol. 2, No. 1.)

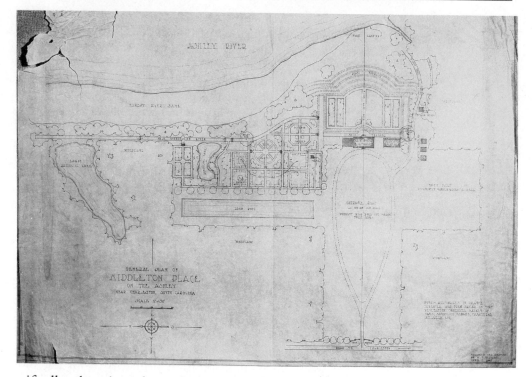

"General Plan of Middleton Place on the Ashley [River] near Charleston, South Carolina, measured and sketched by W. B. Gebhart, April 3, 1925." (Department of Manuscripts and University Archives, Cornell University Libraries, Cornell University, Ithaca, New York.)

cifically, the triangular sight line plan allowed house and garden to be fitted to the angle of the river, while permitting these formal areas to be positioned well above the floodplain. Middleton Place also brilliantly integrated the working landscape of a rice plantation with the formal grounds by using ponds required for cropping and processing as ornamental features.

Other Southern estates also followed French-inspired plans, but with less unity and refinement than did Middleton Place. Such estates, many restored since the 1930s, abound in Virginia; they include Kenmore Plantation and Gunston Hall, which both date to the mid-eighteenth century. Kenmore was built on a site some distance from a river, not a common choice in colonial times, but typically for this period the estate had a large front lawn with circular drive. The sight line up the driveway was extended to the door by a line of trees. Formal gardens appear to have been limited to one side of the house located beyond an outbuilding, but later research may uncover that it had a mirror-image garden on the opposite side. This formal garden was likely laid out with box-edged beds in a geometric pattern. The grounds of Gunston Hall overlooking the Potomac River were more extensive and more clearly unified. As restored, the inland side of the house fronted a grassed lawn set with rows of trees that framed the building. Beyond the house, an expansive formal garden of hedges and beds provided a foreground for a river view that was framed by two garden gazebos. Other impressive colonial estates based on Renaissance French prototypes included Russellborough near Brunswick, North Carolina, perhaps designated by Claude J. Sauthier, Westover near Charles City, Virginia, and Wye near Easton, Maryland.

French and Dutch Gardens

French and Dutch colonial gardens differed little from those built by English colonists, although the choice of plants would have differed somewhat: more clipped plants may have been used. A plan of the residence of a Mr. Veaudreuil in Montreal in the 1720s showed a quite typical geometric arrangement of planting beds separated by generous walkways. Although each of the three major garden areas was internally unified by sight lines, these were not continued from

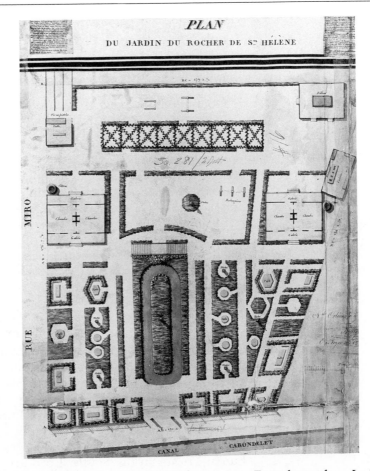

French gardens in Louisiana during the late eighteenth and early nineteenth centuries typically had parterre patterns intended to be viewed from the raised gallery of the house. Here the Garden Du Rocher de St. Helene in New Orleans. (New Orleans Notarial Archives, Plan Drawing Number 35.16.0.2.281.)

one garden to another, as one would expect in a French garden. In less urbane settlements than Montreal, French gardens were far simpler, as recent archaeological excavations at Cahokia, Illinois, have shown. In this frontier community, small fenced yards served as work and food production areas, with what significant vegetation existed being fruit trees or vegetables.

Dutch gardens were perhaps more plentiful than those of French communities. Eighteenth-century plans of both New Amsterdam and Albany show enclosed yards behind buildings to have been carefully structured into geometric beds or orchards. Whether the gardens were ornamental or productive is unknown, but at New Amsterdam the colonial governor did maintain an ornamental garden and esplanade near his palace at the Battery. This had a geometric, symmetrical arrangement similar to many others of the period. It is likely that Dutch colonists followed the contemporaneous design and maintenance practices of their homeland, planting many bulb plants and clipping shrubs and small trees as topiary.

CONCLUSION AND SUMMARY

Euroamerican exploitation of North America, which began in the fifteenth century but became intensive after 1600, varied in its impact depending on geographical location and the European cultural group involved. The landscape patterns that emerged, though, exemplified five processes that the geographer Wilbur Zelinsky (1973) has identified as important in creating American culture. The five processes are:

1. The importation of selected individuals, not necessarily representative of an entire European culture, and thus of selected cultural traits

2. The impact of long-distance transfer of people and their culture in a process called "sea change"

3. Cultural borrowings from native peoples

4. Local evolution of culture in the New World

5. Continuing interchange with other countries

Each of these processes influenced landscape development in different ways. As we have seen, European nations were not uniformly represented in the New World. Some countries such as Spain and England controlled far more extensive geographical areas and had a more lasting influence than others such as the Swedes. From each country certain classes of individuals tended to become colonists. Among the English, younger sons who would not inherit land under the primogeniture inheritance system, landless laborers or peasants, and members of oppressed religious groups were the most likely to emigrate. This produced a distinct class system based on education, social standing, and social alliances.

Long-distance transfer of people and customs produced two different results, depending on the motives of the settlers. Some sought to re-create European prototypes in North America without regard to local environment or economic conditions. Others saw their removal from Europe as a chance to start anew and avoid the problems of the Old World. The New England village system exemplifies the conservative approach, while in Virginia settlers quickly saw the advantages of dispersed settlement given the size of holdings that could be acquired, and they abandoned villages. Of course, regardless of the colonists' intentions, the reality of distance from the home country quickly caused American culture to diverge from that of Europe.

Many colonists downplayed any borrowing from the indigenous peoples, but both outright and subtle influences can be seen, as reviewed in Chapter 1. Euroamericans in the South also borrowed, with acknowledgment, from Africans and Black Caribbean Islanders imported as slaves.

From the integration of diverse cultures in the "melting pot," or as some now call it the "tossed salad," of North America, a new hybrid tradition of land use emerged. Unique settlement and environmental experiences fostered this change. Thus European immigrants were gradually transformed into "Euroamericans" and finally into Americans.

Interchange with other parts of the world did continue during the colonial period, although they were slow and often limited by European powers. This allowed for the continuing transfer of some elements of culture, including the scientific knowledge which would prove so helpful in the process of utilizing American resources. These contacts produced a two-way exchange of goods and ideas, with North America the primary recipient of European exports in the colonial period.

The individual influences of the five processes were less important than the interplay between them, and the way they were shaped by the distinctive qualities of the North American landscape. While landscape does not determine human action, it can be as important a factor in influencing decisions as is culture. European emigrants to the New World were confronted with a radically different physical environment than anything previously experienced or even anticipated, as will be discussed in Chapter 4. At the least this unexpected landscape forced successful settlers to rethink old habits of land use and creatively solve problems of housing, farming, and transportation. The ways in which colonial Europeans solved these problems created patterns of land use and organization that have constrained landscape development ever since.

NOTES

1. In speaking of European discovery and settlement, only those activities which postdate 1490 will be discussed. The very early explorations of the Irish and Norse, among others, while increasingly supported by archaeology and documentary research, did not lead to an intensive or continuous period of European contact. Likewise, the presence of English fishermen in coastal waters did not directly lead to continental settlement, but did contribute to advancing navigational knowledge paving the way for later voyages of discovery.

2. Encomiendas were officially abolished beginning in 1720. In spite of gradual legal changes, the Indians effectively remained feudal tenants into the twentieth century in many places, when land reform made them communal owners rather than serfs.

3. Those stockholders who put up funds but did not travel to the colony were usually termed "adventurers," while those who became settlers were called "planters." The terms "planter" and "plantation" were first used in Ulster, Northern Ireland, to describe the establishment of Protestant communities in the sixteenth century. What was planted was people, not any crop. Thus the word plantation originally referred to a massive resettlement system, not to an agriculture system as it did later in the United States.

4. Headrights simply granted an immigrant, either a free person or a freed former indentured servant, a certain number of unclaimed acres for just coming to North America. Headrights were typically 45 or 50 acres in size, to be claimed on uncleared frontier land.

5. This describes the typical system; the situation, of course, was quite different for dissenters such as Roger Williams and William Coddington, who chose to remove to remote locations for reasons of conscience.

6. It should be noted that only an estimated 50 percent of colonial slaves lived on large plantations. The remainder lived in individual urban households or on small, isolated farms with only a few slaves.

7. Inland Albany was a village of some size, but it could not really be called a city.

8. Long lots are common throughout North America in those riverine situations where transportation was water-dependent. Non-French examples include Spanish long lots along the Rio Grande River.

9. To the Spanish, "conversion" and "civilizing" were really the same activity since Catholicism was so central to Spanish culture. These efforts were not directed toward turning the Indians into Spaniards, since this was considered racially impossible, but simply to making them more acceptable as subjects.

10. Not all missions in the New World follow the patterns of these two areas. In Georgia and Florida, where missions were established in the seventeenth century, they were little more than rustic stockades enclosing a few post and wattle buildings. If the mission was eventually successful, a log church might be built. These were primitive frontier outposts which often were in existence less than a year. In New Mexico, missions were often churches built within or at the edge of an existing Indian pueblo.

11. All quotations from the Laws of the Indies are from Spanish City Planning in North America, *by Dora P. Crouch, Daniel J. Garr, and Axel I. Mundigo, Cambridge, Massachusetts, MIT Press, 1982. This translation preserves the somewhat officious flavor of the Laws while making the Ordinances readable.*

12. The changing meaning of the grid will be a subtheme which will be examined throughout this book. In Chapter 1 possible explanations for the use of this form in pre-Columbian American were considered, but during the historic period there were sufficient writings on the merits or demerits of the grid to allow us to understand its intended meaning. In the colonial period the Laws of the Indies presents one practical rationale, while the plans of Philadelphia and Savannah were based on philosophical principles as well.

13. This scheme was not followed for long, because the plat was too large (at 1 mile by 2 miles) to be effectively traveled in a premotorized age. People preferred to settle compactly in the eastern quarter of the city near the Delaware River. By 1776 the developed "city" consisted of only the six or seven tiers of rows nearest the river.

14. Dooryard gardens had a later descendant, the cottage garden, which is currently enjoying a popular revival.

14

The Early National Period

We hold these truths to be self-evident, that all men are created equal, that they are endowed by their Creator with certain unalienable Rights, that among these are Life, Liberty and the pursuit of Happiness.

Declaration of Independence of the United States, 1776

It was a fine sight . . . a meandering river gliding through, saluting in its various turnings the swelling, green, turfy knolls, embellished with parterres of flowers and fruitful strawberry beds; flocks of turkeys strolling about them; herds of deer prancing in the meads or bounding over the hills; companies of young, innocent Cherokee virgins . . . lay reclined under the shade of floriferous and fragrant native bowers of Magnolia, Azalea, Philadelphus, perfumed Calycanthus, sweet Yellow Jessamine and cerulian Glycine frutescens, disclosing their beauties to the fluttering breeze, and bathing their limbs in the cool fleeting streams; whilst other parties, more gay and libertine, were yet collecting strawberries or wantonly chasing their companions, tantalising them, staining their lips and cheeks with the rich fruit. This sylvan scene of primitive innocence was enchanting. . . .

William Bartram, Travels, *1791.*

Political revolutions are often as much the manifestation of changes that a society has already undergone as they are the producers of change, and this was true of the American Revolution in the eighteenth century. Circumstances leading to it had been evolving over several decades until an inevitable confrontation was finally precipitated by the proverbial "last straw." Just as the transition from colony to republic and the attendant cultural changes actually began well before the first shots were fired at Lexington, the transition from colonial design and planning traditions also began prior to the Revolution. Thus, much design which has been traditionally labeled "colonial" presages the decades of artistic freedom, intellectual stimulation, and experimentation which followed the Revolution in the Early National Period.

INFLUENCES OF PHILOSOPHICAL MOVEMENTS

Before discussing design and planning during this transition period, it is important to understand two philosophical movements that influenced thought in the eighteenth and nineteenth centuries: the Enlightenment and Romanticism. The Enlightenment was an international philosophical movement which began in England at the end of the seventeenth century and by the mid-eighteenth had become centered in France. The Enlightenment can be considered an intellectual offshoot of the Renaissance, although several more immediate events are usually credited with inspiring its philosophers. The penal and intellectual excesses of the Inquisition, as well as renewed attention to the writings of Thomas Aquinas, which elevated faith over reason, stimulated reaction to these conservative tendencies. Intellectual growth brought about by the period of exploration in the fifteenth and sixteenth centuries, and the rise of nationalism, also motivated Enlightenment thought.

Philosophers of the Enlightenment, such as John Locke, Immanuel Kant, and Voltaire, stressed that people can autonomously acquire knowledge directly from experience. The knowledge of which they spoke was empirical and rational. They believed that critical thinking was a moral obligation that followed directly from natural law and that each individual was entitled to freedom of thought. It followed from freedom of thought that there must also be freedom to express that thought. Although the Enlightenment focused on the individual, it did not neglect the importance of human societies. Moral principles of society were derived from interactions of individuals, each of whom acted correctly from knowledge of natural law. Collective decency then followed from individual goodness and could not be imposed by a dogmatic, hierarchical system.

The Enlightenment produced a number of worldwide effects:

- It encouraged the development of science as the method for acquiring empirical knowledge.
- It fostered curiosity about the natural world.
- It led to democratic political movements, especially those in North America and France.
- It produced a pan-European intellectual culture which stimulated the political, scientific, and social reforms that have continued into the twentieth century.

The Enlightenment had a special impact on the Americas, particularly the United States. This was most clearly seen in the Revolution and the process of government formation which followed, but the Enlightenment also influenced policies of land exploitation. Science and adventure came together to promote exploration of the continent, its plants, and its native peoples. The early horticulturists and plant explorers already discussed were participants in this effort. Later the empiricism of the Enlightenment produced a land survey system and a scientifically based agriculture. Both the organized explorations and the formation of a national land allocation policy in the United States can be interpreted as the first application of Enlightenment concepts on a national scale.

A second philosophical movement of the period that affected Europe, North America, and much of the rest of the world was Romanticism. Romanticism dates from the mid-eighteenth century and extends beyond the period of the Enlightenment into the mid-nineteenth century. It was in some ways a reaction to the perceived failures of the Enlightenment, but also shared some of that movement's attitudes, particularly the view that the natural world holds all truths and that individuals can experience these truths directly. Romanticism, though, emphasized that the natural world should be perceived subjectively, rather than rationally. It held that sensuality, spontaneity, emotion, and imagination are more valuable human traits than reason, intelligence, and deductive ability. The Romantics saw the individual as a spirit rather than an intellect, to be the sole source of order, meaning, and value. These attitudes led them to value that which was uncontrolled by external forces, in particular the undeveloped natural world and those exotic, preindustrial peoples who lived most closely with it. William Bartram's travel recollections offer an example of this world view.

While the Enlightenment relied on and promoted scientific query, Romanticism was inspired by and found its clearest expression in the arts, particularity literature and painting. The poems of Lord Byron and novels of James Fenimore Cooper reflect Romantic philosophy. Much nineteenth-century painting was dominated by romantic concepts. In America, the Hudson River School of painting further idealized landscapes already considered sublime[1] by European thinkers.

These artistic efforts were stimulated by events of the eighteenth century which highlighted the contrasts between the Old World and the New. The Industrial Revolution, then centered in Europe, was seen as a dehumanizing economic and social transformation which separated people completely from the natural environment and natural routines of life. Urbanization, usually a result of industrialization, was also seen as a debilitating trend which produced social and physical ill health. Romantics also strongly reacted to the failure of European revolutions, particularly the French, to mitigate excesses of the old political and economic elite. In contrast to all of this, the landscape and peoples of newly discovered lands were envisioned as interacting symbiotically in ideal ways to create a paradise on earth. Jean Jacques Rousseau's "noble savage" was ennobled by a pristine environment which he tended as a steward, while the "ignoble literati" inhabited a moral and physical cesspool of their own making.

The effects of the Romantic movement on the world as a whole were not as far-reaching as those of the Enlightenment, but it had an equal impact on landscape use and design. It encouraged travel and exploration to experience the variety of natural phenomena and human exotica, it fostered an acceptance of non-European cultures, and finally, it produced an artistic perspective which transcended mode of expression and dominated Western art and design through the nineteenth century. In English-speaking North America the influence of Romanticism was particularly strong. It generated expeditions, such as those of the Bartrams, which forged the strongest bond between the Enlightened and the Romantic.[2] It encouraged Europeans to settle in the unsullied lands beyond the limits of civilization. Utopian planners were particularly drawn by this opportunity.[3] It spurred interest in nonclassical design forms, and thus influenced the architectural eclecticism of the nineteenth century. Finally, but of great importance for this study, Romanticism, in both its literary and visual components, was the underlying stimulus for the earliest landscape gardeners, from whose work the profession and discipline of landscape architecture emerged.

The combined influences of the Enlightenment and the Romantic movement most clearly influenced American design in the period which we will call Early National. Although not a design term, this name does properly convey the concept that as a new nation emerged in North America so too did a changed attitude toward the landscape. In political terms this period began in 1775, but to understand the design spirit which is related to political change we will date it to roughly 1760.[4] It continued until the 1830s, when its successor, the Romantic design period, began. Several important trends can be noted during the Early National Period:

• Retention of formal, Renaissance-inspired design motifs
• Interest in naturalistic styles of design which had originated in England
• Increasing integration of formal and naturalistic elements in one design
• Interest in expressing democratic ideals through the landscape
• Implementation of a uniform system of Euroamerican land occupation
• Interest in agriculture and horticulture as scientific endeavors

We will explore how these trends were manifested on the land as we examine the design and planning innovations of this transition period.

GARDEN AND SMALL-SITE DESIGN

Garden design in the Early National Period is best characterized as a hybrid of older fashions based on Renaissance traditions, combined with newer naturalistic styles—the Landscape Gardening School and the Picturesque. In the best work, imaginative transitions effectively blended the old with the new, the formal with the informal, and the rectilinear with the curved. This integration of forms and spaces into unified wholes was clearly seen in a distinctive type of garden known as the Wilderness Garden.

The best documented garden of this sort was the Paca Garden in Annapolis, Maryland, which has been reconstructed after two decades of research, including archaeology. Wilderness Gardens consisted of two thematically different portions. The area nearest the house was divided into formal terraces (all known examples have the house on a high point and the terraces stepping down a hill) which number at least two, as at Paca Garden.[5] These upper, formal terraces had decorative, patterned plantings much like those of parterres or knot gardens, and boxwood was often used as an edging material. Terraces were linked by a sight-line path that terminated in an asymmetrical, naturalistic wooded area called the Wilderness. This lowest terrace—the Wilderness—was planted with irregularly arranged native species, mainly trees, and had a meadow-like lawn. It often contained a focal element such as a mount, a rustic gazebo, or at Paca, an observatory. The Wilderness was used to create a visual transition between the designed garden and the natural landscape beyond the garden. This was usually a woodland, but at Paca the natural landscape was actually a waterscape—Chesapeake Bay, now blocked by buildings of the Naval Academy.

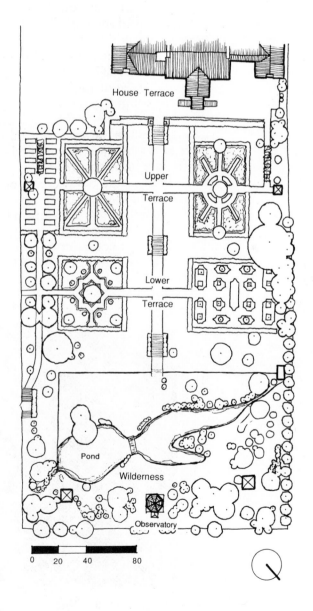

Plan of the Paca Garden as restored. (Data from site brochure; drawn by Rossi.)

The Paca Garden, although having many features typical of other Wilderness Gardens, also had some unusual ones. The most obvious of these was that the sight line linking garden terraces did not align with the rear doorway of the house. This was likely an accommodation necessary because of the small size of the in-town site. Paca-Steele (1986) has recently related the house location and garden spatial arrangement to a geometric pattern based on rectangles made up of two right triangles. Another unusual feature was that the formal terraces were each divided into two outdoor rooms, one to each side of the central path, by tall hedges of clipped Eastern red cedar. This arrangement concealed much of the formal garden and emphasized the Wilderness, while at the same time creating private zones within the small space available.[6] As interpreted at other restorations, the formal gardens were more typically open to view as at Hampton in Ridgely, Maryland.

The Wilderness Garden was the first designed "type" garden to explicitly deal with the integration of old and new styles. Whether this integration of design styles originated in North America is debated, but its practitioners clearly were attempting to resolve an issue that Brown, Repton (at least in his earlier work), Price, and Chambers in England found difficult to tackle. Not all transition gardens of the Early National Period incorporate naturalistic elements in the particular way that the Wilderness Garden does. Some gardens are idiosyncratic and reflect the interests and ideas of their owners rather than following the two-part Wilderness Garden pattern. From the myriad examples that fall into this category, three of the most noted and best documented have been selected for this discussion: Mount Vernon, Monticello, and the Woodlands.

Appropriately, the residence of the first president of the United States can be included among the best transitional gardens of the Early National Period. George Washington acquired Mount Vernon in 1752, but did not take up residence until his marriage in 1759. Although he altered the estate in the 1760s and early 1770s, little is known about its appearance at that time. The best documentation of the house grounds design comes from the 1780s and later, particularly from the 1787 sketch plan by Samuel Vaughan, and the journal of engineer and architect Benjamin H. Latrobe.

These sources describe a composition which integrated a regular plan, geometric in its outline, but with views that were experienced as naturalistic. This

Paca Garden looking from the Wilderness toward the upper terraces and house.

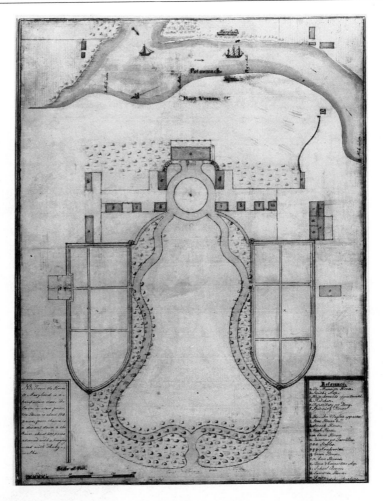

Samuel Vaughan's plan of the house grounds at Mount Vernon as they appeared in 1787. (Mount Vernon Ladies Association of the Union.)

distinction is an important one, since Mount Vernon has often been identified as being a formal-style garden. Such an identification is simplistic and could come from a study of plans only, because the site itself conveys a very different impression. In the Vaughan plan, for example, the symmetrical forms and geometric subdivisions of the kitchen and flower gardens do stand out, as do the equally symmetrical, although curving, serpentine roads lining the Bowling Green. Plan appearances can be deceptive, though, because planting can completely alter the perceived character of a space. This is precisely what occurred at the Bowling Green. Here the roadway trees were not a uniform line of a single species, clipped architectonically into a French-style allée, but were varied to illustrate the horticultural diversity of North America. At the same time species were paired across the green, creating a unique symmetry within an asymmetrical view. Outside the serpentine road trees were denser and more irregularly arranged, to create the illusion that one was passing through a woodland. This area surrounding the Bowling Green was certainly the visual focal point of the landscape design, just as the main house was the focal point of the architectural design. The formal gardens, both originally kitchen gardens,[7] were service landscapes, just as the outbuildings were work areas.

Another significant naturalistic area was to the east of the house on sloping land between it and the Potomac River. Here, according to Latrobe's description, a lawn framed by massed plantings of locust trees on both sides of the house created a foreground to the distant view of the river. Sheer banks right along the river had been carefully planted with trees and shrubs, maintained so that

Aerial view of Mount Vernon. (American Landscape Architect, Vol. 6, No. 5, 1932.)

View from the second story of the main house at Mount Vernon looking down the Bowling Green toward the sight line cut through the woods. (Department of Landscape Architecture Slide Collection, Texas A&M University.)

they never achieved a height sufficient to block the view. This "hanging wood," as it was called, provided seasonal color as it framed the Potomac. On an estate conceived in the formal manner, this dramatic slope would certainly have been terraced into the parterred "falls" then in vogue. Mount Vernon's landscape design represented a sophisticated integration of naturalism into a formal structure. It was truly a transition landscape, one which did not merely copy or crudely link two styles, but rather, skillfully blended the central visual concepts of each to create a coherent whole.

This brings us to the question of the responsibility for this exceptional design. Washington himself is often given credit. We can be certain from diaries that he was actively involved in many details of its organization. He was keenly interested in horticulture as a practical science, and exchanged plants and seeds with both American and European sources. His diaries, particularly for the years 1784 and 1785, record constant construction of landscape features and planting, which he supervised. Whether he can be given equal credit for the site plan remains open to question, however, since his records constantly mention construction, but not design.[8] It may be that Washington served as a kind of "general contractor" for the design as well as for its implementation by integrating planning and design ideas gleaned from books on landscape gardening and from friends, including skilled amateurs such as Jefferson and professionals such as Pierre L'Enfant, the planner of Washington, D.C.

There are no such problems of design attribution at Monticello, where Thomas Jefferson served as landscape architect, architect, horticulturist, and scientific farmer. Jefferson inherited this estate in 1767 and shortly afterwards began the work that became his lifelong preoccupation—development of the property as a *ferme ornée,* or ornamental farm. The agricultural portions of the estate will be discussed a bit later. What is of concern here is the design of the house grounds. From the beginning, Jefferson controlled the entire experience of the environment through placement of the house itself on a small hill from which an overview of the surrounding landscape, particularly the Blue Ridge Mountains in the west, was possible. He further used this location to integrate the house and the hillside by placing "dependencies"—that is, independent building wings—on a downhill slope where they were partially earth-sheltered. From the West Lawn, which became the formal lawn and flower garden, the dependencies appeared to be balustraded walkways which terminated in small pavilions, rather than buildings.

Because Jefferson perceived Monticello to be a working farm as well as a residential estate, ornamental and functional elements often adjoined one another. The best example of this proximity was the vegetable garden location, just to the south of the main house, downhill from the famous entry drive, Mulberry Row.[9] As visitors approached the house, the lawn and flower gardens were vis-

View of West Lawn at Monticello. (Department of Landscape Architecture Slide Collection, Texas A&M University.)

ible slightly uphill to the left, while to the right and below were the vegetable plots and orchards. To link these two areas physically, Jefferson planned to construct a pavilion at the terminus of a sight line which began in the passageway of the south dependencies. A structure of this type was built, but due to poor construction did not long survive.

We know a great deal about the spatial organization and plantings at Monticello from several sources. Jefferson himself was a prolific detailer of everyday life. He kept a Garden Book which recorded plantings, an Account Book which listed purchases, and a Farm Book which recorded both agricultural and horticultural activities. He also wrote extensively to various correspondents. Much of this correspondence touches on land design issues, particularly those related to plant materials and planting techniques. Both the Books and the letters were often illustrated, supplying schematic drawings to supplement verbal descriptions. The final source of quite specific design information is the estate itself. Since 1979, archaeological excavation and related analysis have been used to establish the sequence of construction activities and verify documentary evidence.

These sources of information provide very detailed data on what was intended and on what actually happened, but they leave unanswered the question of the reasons behind the design: that is, what were Jefferson's inspirations and to what degree was the final form of the estate to be the reflection of a larger design concept? To access these issues, researchers have been left to infer from the supporting data. This has, as it naturally would, led to diverse conclusions.

The issue most often discussed is the degree to which Jefferson mimicked existing Landscape Gardening School designs. Those who hold that he was, make much of the tour which he and John Adams made in 1786 of noted English gardens, such as Twickenham and Stowe. However, two factors would mitigate against this being the critical event in Jefferson's design education. First, he had already been at work at Monticello for almost twenty years. The outline and many details of the estate were established. If he had not been called to governmental service, many more of the details executed after 1810 would likely have already been achieved by 1786. Second, Jefferson's recorded European travel observations do not read like those of an awed colonial uncritically impressed by all he saw; rather, they present the critique of an educated and sophisticated design connoisseur. Much of his commentary was of a factual nature, such as locations and costs of garden features, while a good deal of it faulted some illustrious landscapes. For example he concludes that, "in the approach to Stowe, you are brought a mile through a straight avenue, pointing to the Corinthian arch and to the house, till you get to the arch, then you turn short to the right. The straight approach is very ill. The Corinthian arch has a very useless appearance, inasmuch as it has no pretension to any destination. *Instead of being an object from the house, it is an obstacle to a very pleasing distant prospect*" (Betts, 1944, p. 113, emphasis added). This passage not only shows Jefferson's confidence in his understanding of design, but also, as the section in italics indicates, his approach to design, which involved integration of the given site with the distant landscape. This was a theme obviously central to the plan of Monticello.

If Jefferson's design ideas were not formed by these travel experiences, then how did he learn about design? For architecture, Beiswanger (1984) has demonstrated that he learned from books. Every structure built or planned for Monticello has a concept based directly on a design from a book known to be available to Jefferson. From this evidence we can infer that he was also influenced by those books on landscape design known to him.[10] This is not to minimize Jefferson's own inventiveness, which was exceptional. He rarely used an idea in toto, but rather combined patterns and adapted them to the situation at Monticello. The earth-integrated dependencies are the best example of such creative site planning—in this case, adapting the prevailing concept of a main house flanked by outbuildings.

What can be said about the success of this largely self-taught designer with his design for the house grounds at Monticello? The most outstanding feature was, of course, the site plan, which uses the topography so well. Far less successful was the detailed design of the garden areas, particularly the West Lawn. Plans by Jefferson prior to 1800 show only rectilinear forms in this area. Around 1806, a series of drawings begin to explore the use of an ellipse-like walkway; these schemes also play with the arrangements of planting beds within the lawn surrounded by the walk. The oval beds near the house were decided upon within a year, while the form of the beds lining the walk was not finalized until five years later. Beyond the walk Jefferson had always envisioned groves of trees intermixed with shrubs to create a shaded area, yet allow distant views. The fact that the lawn area took so long to work out, while the wooded areas were part of his concept from the start, may give some idea as to why the lawn—probably the most photographed portion of Monticello—is in fact its weakest feature.

Jefferson seems not to have had a feel for design at garden scale. There he was reduced to using motifs from other sources, possibly details which he had seen in Europe. One result was that the West Lawn looked crude in comparison to the rest of the estate. Its curving walk related to very little on the site, and its oval planting beds appeared to float senselessly, more a precursor of the Gardenesque than part of the Virginia landscape which he so loved. As an Early National Period transition landscape, Monticello was less of a success in terms of its detailed design than Mount Vernon, but this was more than compensated for in the overall site plan. Jefferson's was the first American design to rely on the natural landscape as its major source of inspiration, and as such is a precursor to the Romantic design movement of the 1840s.

The final transition garden we will review here is the Woodlands, the Philadelphia estate of William Hamilton.[11] Unfortunately, far less is known or is likely to be known of it than of the sites so far discussed, since much has been covered over by the expanding city, while the rest was converted in 1839 to the Rural Cemetery. Little is known of the details of its design. Thomas Jefferson referred to it as a botanical garden, which could rival in beauty sites in England. Andrew Jackson Downing described it as having "elegance of arrangement" in parklike tree plantations, which made it "the most tasteful and beautiful residence in America" (1875, pp. 25–26). From these two statements alone we can conclude that the Woodlands was at least partially in a naturalistic style (or Downing would not have rated it so highly) and that it was planted with a great variety of plant materials (or it would not have been termed a botanical garden). Terracing has been mentioned in connection with the Woodlands, so the site may also have had more structured garden areas, perhaps near the greenhouses and orangeries. While any arrangement of plant material would be speculative, we can be certain that the planting design relied on diversity. Hamilton's principal activity was the collection and exchange of plants and seeds. While all well-to-do families in his age engaged in this activity, Hamilton was obsessive. His greatest coup was to be one of only two nurseries to receive seeds collected by the Lewis and Clark expedition. Among the then unusual species which Hamilton grew at the Woodlands were gingko, Lombardy poplar, mimosa, purple beech, and zelkova.

No discussion of the Woodlands could really be complete without an update on horticultural exploration in the Early National Period. In sum, the exploration and exchange which had begun in the Colonial Period continued over a wider geographical range as the plains and mountains of the continental interior were explored. The Lewis and Clark expedition of 1804–6 was the seminal event: The expedition collected hundreds of species previously uncultivated in the East and discovered countless others, such as Osage orange and Indian currant. Distribution of the seeds was tightly controlled, with only Hamilton and Philadelphia nurseryman Bernard M'Mahon receiving seed for scientific cultivation. M'Mahon was also responsible for the primary horticultural innovation of the period—publication of the first practical guide to gardening, *The American Gardener's Calendar,* in 1806. The *Calendar* continued to be *the* authority on gardening in the distinctive American environment through eleven editions. M'Mahon may be considered the originator of the early nineteenth-century industry of horticultural and agricultural publication which later resulted in journals such as *American Farmer* and *The Horticulturist and Journal of Rural Arts and Rural Tastes* (referred to as *The Horticulturist*).

The early nineteenth century was also a period of increase in the number of commercial nurseries. When British control of trade was broken after the Revolution, profitability of both inter- and intracontinental plant sales increased, allowing many more to enter what had previously been the domain of a few families such as the Bartrams and the Princes. M'Mahon, André and François Michaux, William Landreth, David Hosack, and Andrée Parmentier were among those to enter this profession. In so doing, they promoted both horticultural materials and design, through the naturalistic displays at nurseries such as Hosack's Elgin Gardens and Parmentier's Botanical Garden.

Many other sites, particularly large estates, combined Renaissance formalism with English naturalism during the period from the 1760s to the 1830s. Drayton Hall in South Carolina, Solitude near Philadelphia, and Clermont on the Hudson River in New York were examples of sites which exhibited eclectic transition designs. Only a few estates, such as The Vale or Gore Place—both in Waltham, Massachusetts, and designed by professional landscape gardeners—had consistently naturalistic plans composed primarily of lawn, massed vegetation, and water. In many cases the naturalistic elements were quickly lost when new designs were implemented. Many may have been so successful that their remnants appear to us today as part of the natural landscape. For these reasons the distinctive transition designs of the Early National Period have been often overlooked and the impression given that American landscape design vaulted almost overnight from the geometry of the colonial garden to the picturesqueness of the Romantic landscape. As we have seen here, the change in style took place gradually over a period of sixty years, through a process of adaptation of European concepts, both old and new, to the unique and diverse landscape of North America.

SITE PLANNING FOR AGRICULTURE

As new ideas about estates were being given physical form at the residences of well-to-do Americans, equally new approaches to the design of agricultural landscapes evolved. Most of these will be discussed in Chapter 4, but one was closely tied to the design transitions of the Early National Period. This was the concept of the farm as an estate, in the sense of the Roman and Renaissance villa. The eighteenth-century term which came to describe this relationship was *ferme ornée. Ferme ornée* literally meant "ornamental farm," and, as we have seen, the term described an estate which was at once planned as a working agricultural manor and an embellished landscape in the landscape gardening fashion. In the Early National Period this type of estate was the prerogative of the well-to-do, but the concept eventually filtered down to the middle class.

As noted above, Mount Vernon and Monticello are both examples of the *ferme ornée* in North America. Both were residences as well as working farms, each had a strong siting concept which exploited natural features as visual amenities, and each had grounds holistically designed so that working and ornamental portions were integrated. Of the two, Mount Vernon was the weaker in overall arrangement because little of the ornamental landscape, besides the sight line from the doorway across the Bowling Green and into the woods, was consciously extended into the almost 1000-acre farm landscape. Rather, Washington exploited existing natural vistas with little elaboration beyond enframement. The principal linking feature was the use of sight lines cut through the woodlands. Latrobe, for example, spoke of seeing the house while about a mile away on the approach drive.

Monticello was a far more convincing example of the *ferme ornée*. From Jefferson's writing, we know that he planned many ornamental features which would unify the entire estate. Just as the functional land uses of vegetable garden and orchard were located near the house, so ornamental areas would extend into the working landscape. Jefferson's basic concept, as shown in a plan of 1809, was for a roughly concentric arrangement of drives—which he called "roundabouts"—and fields centered about the house and lawn. These zones of agricultural use stepped down and encircled the mountaintop, so that the utilitarian land uses would not visually intrude on the panoramic vistas. The first zone, within the first, or uppermost, roundabout, was the house and garden. The second zone included the vegetable garden and orchard to the south and a dense woodland to the north and east. The third zone had plots of about an acre for various fodder plants and livestock display areas. The fourth zone was less precisely planned, but was probably to be meadow. Beyond the roundabouts, cropland, woods, and meadow were mixed.

A number of ornamental features were planned for the farm. The spring north of the house was transformed to a shell- and pebble-lined grotto. An

Sketch plan of Monticello's "roundabouts"—roads—that separated the site into different use areas. (Data from Maccubbin and Martin, 1984; drawn by Rossi.)

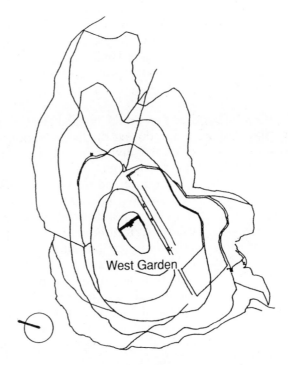

West Garden

"A View of Colonel Lincoln's Seat," circa 1821, by Caroline Betts. The artist was looking across Lake Cazenovia at the main house and surrounding landscape features of Lorenzo, the Linklaen-Ledyard estate. (New York State, Office of Parks, Recreation and Historic Preservation.)

observation tower was to be erected on the hill which Jefferson called Montalto, southwest of the house. Plantings continued this merger of ornamental and functional landscapes. In the grove extending from the West Lawn into the woodland, for example, Jefferson used native trees such as locusts, but planted them in irregular concentric bands rather than with natural randomness.

The *ferme ornée* was not confined to the South. There were many northern examples, although none was as well documented as Monticello. Lorenzo, the Cazenovia, New York, estate of the Lincklaen-Leydard family was one. Founded in 1807, Lorenzo was a simple yet effective ornamental farm that focused on the impressive view from the front of the house up the length of glacially carved Lake Cazenovia. In a primitive 1821 view by Betts, rows of Lombardy poplars extended from the side of the house down the slope toward the lake, creating a broad sight line. To the east and west, orchards occupied the working land nearest the house. Beyond these were outbuildings and meadows. An enclosed garden of formal beds, but surrounded by irregular tree masses, was sited behind the house. The effect was unpretentious, but clearly the entire estate was conceived as a landscape of visual integrity which unified house, formal gardens, agricultural plots, and the surrounding landscape.

CITY PLANNING AND URBAN SITE DESIGN

It is easy to understand American interest in agriculture, horticulture, and garden design during the Early National Period. The country was rural, with 95 percent of citizens living outside population centers. There was space to experiment on, and a corresponding psychological need to fill that space with "civilized" uses. The capture and management of plants and space was one way to assert control over an environment which was, at once, seen as both fruitful and hostile. Americans were less attuned to and adept at urban planning and urban design. European design strictures continued to rule (as in the Spanish towns), or social models of community building, such as the New England town, were followed. The independence of a small part of the continent did not change these attitudes, but did create a demand for urban design which would make manifest the ideals of the new democratic republic. By this demand the first planned city of the "enlightened" age in North America was inspired.

Pierre L'Enfant's plan for Washington, D.C., was the first for a planned national capital. It was significant in two other regards; first, that site selection was based on preestablished criteria, and second, that the design of the entire city was completed before land development began.[12] After the Revolution the national capital had shifted from city to city, and in 1789 Congress finally determined to execute a constitutional provision allowing a federal district. Several regions were considered, but in an early compromise between North and South a Potomac River site was agreed upon. Selection of the exact location along the river anywhere from Williamsport, Maryland, to Georgetown, then also in Maryland, was left to the judgment of President Washington. He chose a site with which he had been long familiar, at the headwaters of the Potomac, near the existing towns of Georgetown, Hamburg, and Carrolsburg, all in Maryland, and Alexandria, Virginia. In 1790 a 10-square-mile district was established and topographic surveys begun.

The selection of L'Enfant, a French citizen, as the designer of the capital may at first thought be surprising. There certainly were Americans who were interested in the commission. Thomas Jefferson, for example, drew two sketch plans for the city, inspired by the rectangular geometry of Philadelphia. But L'Enfant, like many other Frenchmen, had a right to claim identity with the new nation because he had fought for its independence. L'Enfant arrived in America in 1777 as part of a French volunteer brigade; he saw active service in several battles and was an English prisoner of war following the siege of Savannah. During the war L'Enfant became personally acquainted with Washington, and the two continued to work with each other in various ways afterward. L'Enfant also had personal skills which made him well suited to the monumental task of creating a capital city from scratch. He had been trained as painter and sculptor, had learned something of engineering, and was also likely to have been self-trained in architecture, the profession which he followed immediately after the war. L'Enfant asked

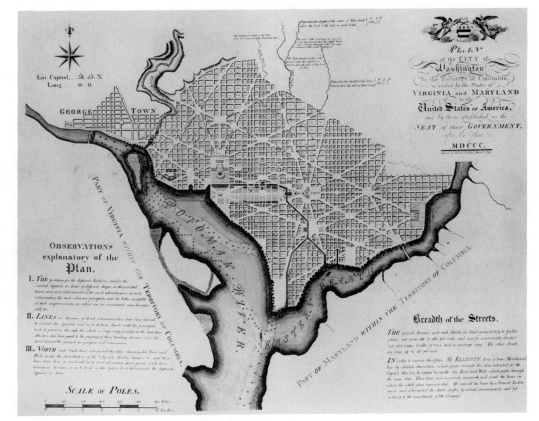

Plan of Washington, D.C., 1792, by Andrew Ellicott after Pierre L'Enfant (Library of Congress, Geography and Map Division.)

Washington directly for the commission in a letter which demonstrated his comprehension of the grand scale required for the projected city.

Through Washington's influence, L'Enfant was appointed as designer in March 1791. He went to work immediately, thoroughly familiarizing himself with the terrain in the selected district. In June, after only three months of work, he presented Washington with the first official report and plan. In it, he established the principal concepts on which his design was to be based. To quote L'Enfant's unpolished English prose:

> I could discover no one [situation] so advantageously to greet the congressional building as is that on the west of Jenkins height which stands as a pedestal waiting for a monument . . . [while] that were I determine the seat of the presidial [presidential] palace, in its difference of nature may be view of advantageous to the object of ading to the sumptuousness of a palace the convenience of a house and the agreeableness of country seat . . . [which from] the west side of the tiber [creek] entrance it will see 10 or 12 miles down the Potowmack . . . having first determined some principal points to which I wished making the rest subordinate I next made the distribution regular with streets at right angle north-south and east west but afterwards I opened others on various directions as avenues to and from every principal places. . . . (Caemmerer, 1950, pp. 151–52)

Two decisions—the strategic siting of the Capitol and White House and the use of a combination grid/diagonal street pattern—established the basic structure within which L'Enfant set other planned features. These included a channelized Tiber Creek that was to emerge from under the Capitol through a 40-foot-high waterfall, the public promenade of the Mall, and the special sites for sculpture, especially the equestrian monument to Washington which was planned to link sight lines from the Capitol and the White House. We can see from L'Enfant's description that his plan was no mere exercise in patterning, but rather an ordered scheme which continued to use natural features, especially topography, as its source of inspiration.

"View of Washington," circa 1851. Edward Sachse, artist, lithographer, and lithographic printer. (I. N. Phelps Stokes Collection, Miriam and Ira D. Wallach Division of Art, Prints and Photographs, The New York Public Library, Astor, Lenox and Tilden Foundations.)

VIEW OF WASHINGTON.

There has been much discussion of the prototypes for L'Enfant's plan. It was known that both Jefferson and Washington made available to him their personal copies of European city plans, which included those for Karlsruhe, Paris, and Milan. L'Enfant was certainly familiar with the major cities of North America. Annapolis and Williamsburg, both planned by Nicholson, may have been evocative. Peets (1928) concluded that the two schemes most related to L'Enfant's were John Evelyn's 1666 reconstruction plan for burned portions of London and André Le Notre's plan for Versailles, since both make use of serial focal points linked by radial and grid sight lines.[13]

Of the two, we can be most certain of the influence of Versailles, since L'Enfant spent several years there as a child while his father was a court painter. It was also likely that he saw the grounds and their plans while a student. In adapting this grand royal park to the more picturesque landscape of the new capital, L'Enfant unintentionally demonstrated in physical form what would become the political reality of the nineteenth and twentieth centuries: the supplanting of the monarchy by the republic.

The stateliness of the plan for Washington was lost, though, from the moment it was presented, in the financial concerns of land development. Landowners in the district wanted prime development on their property, while the federal government wanted quick lot sales to generate needed revenue. Unfortunately, L'Enfant proved far less skillful at public relations than he had at planning. A series of conflicts with landowners escalated into a major confrontation when he refused to display his copy of the plan (the only in existence since none had been printed) at the first lot auction. He felt that the plan still required some revision, as he had worked on it for only six months at that time, and that blind bidding would actually increase government profit. His views were not shared in the government, with the end result that he was dismissed several months later. Andrew Ellicott, the surveyor for the district, completed plan revisions. These events demonstrated an attitude toward the design of the capital which was to persist until 1900. Little attention was paid to anything more than the gross form of L'Enfant's plan. Its corresponding visual character was not achieved, and several significant deviations from the plan threatened its coherence.[14] It is a testament to the strength and appropriateness of the original concept that most of the plan survived these intrusions so that the whole could be restored in this century.

The success of L'Enfant's plan may also be measured by the frequency with which it was copied in emerging cities throughout the country. Among the imitators were Buffalo, New York, laid out by Joseph Ellicott (Andrew's brother);[15] Indianapolis, Indiana, laid out by Alexander Ralston, one of L'Enfant's assistants; and Syracuse, New York. None of these city plans had the unity of L'Enfant's original—because, as so often happens, the form was followed without an understanding of the spirit behind it. The only early nineteenth-century plan to show any of the skill of L'Enfant's was that by Augustus Woodward for Detroit. Woodward, a territorial judge appointed by Jefferson, succeeded in designing a scheme which completely integrated rectangular and radial streets with circular plazas. Unfortunately, this plan did not appeal to the development interests in the city, and it was abandoned after being applied only to the city center. Vestiges of the L'Enfant influence can be seen throughout the United States in the odd diagonal street of small towns.

An equally significant plan, but one for a much, much smaller urban area, was Thomas Jefferson's concept for an "academical village"—the University of Virginia at Charlottesville. Jefferson wrote to a friend that he was "convinced that the people are the only safe depositories of the our liberty, & that they are not safe unless enlightened to a certain degree" (Woods, 1985, p. 282). Thus, the university was essential to liberty, and its founding was one of the three deeds for which Jefferson wished to be remembered.[16] The site plan for the university was Jefferson's most original plan, based weakly if at all on any European prototype.[17] It appears to have issued from Jefferson's lifelong reflections on the relationship of structures to the land and the social role of design.

Jefferson's plan centered on a terraced open space, called the Lawn, about 600 feet long by 200 feet wide, enclosed on three sides by university buildings. On each of the two long sides were five double-story pavilions to be used as lecture rooms below and faculty quarters above. These connected with one-story dormitories whose flat roofs could be used as upper-level walkways between faculty apartments. A colonnade unified facades of the dormitories and physically linked all the buildings on the Lawn. At the north end of the Lawn stood the Rotunda, a Palladian-style interpretation of the Pantheon, which housed the library and science classrooms.[18] Behind the dormitories and pavilions of the Lawn were a second row of single-story dormitories known as the Ranges. At the center and ends of the Ranges were the Hotels, which provided housing for servants and dining halls. Between the Ranges and the Lawn a spacious corridor was reserved for access, outdoor service areas, and gardens. These sundry uses were screened from each other by a system of serpentine walls. In Jefferson's plan the south end of the Lawn was kept open to allow a view to the mountains and to provide for a continuation of the building concept when the need for more space arose.

Jefferson pursued two interesting themes in the design of structures facing the Lawn. First, the facade of each of the ten pavilions was to be in a different architectural style, so that they could be used as a design education tool. Second, Jefferson adroitly manipulated distances between pavilions to distort the viewer's perception of scale. Moving away from the Rotunda, pavilions were progressively farther apart, so that when viewed from either end perspective was distorted; from the south it was foreshortened so that the Rotunda would appear larger and more imposing, while from the Rotunda the view would appear elongated and distant.

The entirety of Jefferson's plan was constructed in about one year, and thus construction was in place when the university enrolled its first class in 1826.

View of the University of Virginia from the South. J. Serz, delineator; H. Weber, printer; C. Bohn, publisher. 1856. (Edwin M. Betts Collection, Special Collections Department, Manuscripts Division, University of Virginia Library.)

Views of the campus show little landscape development until the 1850s. Written evidence suggests, though, that there was planting at the time of the university's opening.[19] Jefferson himself had suggested that the Lawn have grass and trees. One hundred honey locust trees were ordered during 1823, and a report several years later indicated that these had been planted in double, probably offset, rows. Given this number and arrangement, the trees must have been on 24-foot centers to completely line the east and west sides of the Lawn. A single row of trees was also set across the south end of the Lawn. The 1850s view also show planting in the rear gardens, but only of trees. Correspondence indicated that Jefferson did intend these spaces to be ornamental, but there is no evidence that either the university or any faculty member developed them in this way until the early twentieth century.

The suitability of Jefferson's design to its intended purpose has been demonstrated over one hundred and fifty years of use. The Lawn and Ranges still serve as dormitories, today for honor students, while the Rotunda remains a campus, as well as Lawn, focal point. Much of the space has been restored. In the 1950s and 1960s, the Garden Club of Virginia supported research and an interpretive reconstruction of gardens. Original serpentine wall locations were established archaeologically, and the spaces between them were designed by Alden Hopkins, landscape architect of Colonial Williamsburg, to represent typical gardens of the early nineteenth century. Each is unique in its arrangement, to repeat the architectural individuality of the pavilions, but most rely on some combination of the geometric and naturalistic. Only the garden of Pavilion VI is completely naturalistic in style—an arrangement of lawn, path, and woodland reminiscent of Monticello.

The most significant change to the entire Lawn is, of course, that it has been subsumed in the ever expanding twentieth-century campus. The Jeffersonian idea that the buildings of the Lawn and Ranges could be extended indefinitely was never followed through. In the 1850s the first new buildings were added to the campus, but in an irregular pattern on curvilinear walkways. A number of buildings were at the south—especially a circular gymnasium, which interrupted the view to the mountains. Later a power plant was built nearby, creating a very unsightly focal point for the Lawn. In 1899, the visual problems created by these intrusive structures were solved when three new halls were added at the south end of the Lawn. Cabell Hall was placed directly opposite the Rotunda and due to the downward slope effectively screened the power plant while allowing some distant views. Continued development has effectively enclosed the Lawn, so that today it has more the appearance of a courtyard than a space focused on the distant landscape.

Jefferson's concept of the university has inspired designers into this century. As we shall see, Frederick Law Olmsted shared the notion of a college as a community of scholars. The concept of the college as an independent—some might say isolated—community affected the siting of land grant colleges in the late nineteenth century. Unfortunately, few of these adopted plans were as comprehensive and integrated as that of the University of Virginia.

Almost ten years before Jefferson's plan for the University of Virginia campus was implemented, a campus plan equally novel, but less well known in its day, was begun at Union College in Schnectady, New York. Designed by the French architect Joseph Jacques Ramée, the plan called for a formal grouping of college buildings within a naturalistic park. Buildings were grouped in the shapes of a winged U. At the curved end a central building modeled after the Pantheon provided a focal point set on a long terrace. As at the University of Virginia an arcaded walkway connected buildings. Behind the classroom and living buildings were formal gardens and promenades, with a large agricultural garden to one

Plan of Union College, Schenectady, New York, by Joseph Jacques Ramée. 1813. (Schaffer Library, Union College.)

side. This central campus area was surrounded by a sinuous loop drive bordered with irregular masses of trees, organized to screen certain views and open up others. Ramée's plan was the first documented use of a Landscape Gardening-inspired site plan at a public site in North America.

CONCLUSION AND SUMMARY

The Early National Period in the United States has usually been overlooked as a distinctive phase in landscape design and planning. Such an approach minimizes the effect which political and social changes were having on concepts related to the landscape. While many in the United States, Canada, and Mexico continued to utilize concepts from the Renaissance and before, a few individuals were breaking away from these hackneyed traditions. Some naively explored the then popular English naturalistic approaches, often producing less than effective designs. The best work came from the adaptation of European themes to the American landscape, and those who did this work inaugurated an approach to land design which would continue to develop throughout the nineteenth century. But far more important than these small-scale alterations of the landscape were the philosophical ideas that American independence allowed to unfold on the continent. Concepts such as equality of opportunity and government by the people, as well as the perceived need to dominate the continent, would have significant consequences for the landscape as settlement progressed into the wilderness.

NOTES

1. The aesthetic definition of "sublime" is a matter of constant academic controversy. For our purpose here it will refer to that with a beauty so exalted that it produces a strong emotion.

2. William Bartram is often cited as the embodiment of the logical unification of these two philosophies. He was both a natural scientist, who furthered the work begun by his father, and an artist. In painting and words, he presented and interpreted his discoveries for an audience that would never experience them as he had in their natural state.

3. See Chapter 6 for a discussion of utopian planning and design.

4. No "big event" occurred at this date to make it an absolute cutoff point, but it was the year which inaugurated a decade of accelerating change in design as influenced by direct colonial contacts with Europe.

5. Authors tend to disagree on the number of terraces at Paca Garden. For purposes of this discussion, the house terrace is not considered part of the garden.

6. *Mark Leone et al. interpreted the design of Paca Garden and other townhouse gardens as a vehicle "to express their [wealthy merchants and landowners] desire for political power . . . which constituted a web of complex ideological claims. . . . Implicit in such claims was the right to rule" (1989b, pp. 35–36). Such an interpretation, which links specific garden designs to political action, is highly speculative and implies a much more direct link than would ever be possible to establish.*

7. *Sometime in the 1790s the Upper Garden was converted, at least in part, to a flower garden. Latrobe cynically described it as "a neat flower garden laid out in squares, and boxed with great precision. . . . For the first time since I left Germany, I saw a parterre, chipped and trimmed with infinite care into the form of a richly flourished Fleur de Lis: The expiring groans I hope of our Grandfather's pedantry" (Carter, 1977, p. 165). De Forest (1983) concluded that much of the current restoration was inspired by the design of the garden in the first two decades of the nineteenth century. The current restoration thus remains hypothetical but is of the period.*

8. *One exception is a reference to designing a deer paddock on the Potomac River side of the house, on the lawn area discussed earlier.*

9. *Until approximately 1810, Mulberry Row was also the plantation "main street," on which many utilitarian buildings were placed. We know that many of the slave cabins, a blacksmith shop, and smokehouses stood on a ledge between the Row and the garden terraces below. After returning from his service as president, Jefferson began to relocate most of these uses, but this had not been completed at the time of his death in 1826. Jefferson's motives for the moves are unclear, but visitors had commented negatively on the contrast between these rough structures and the temple-like residence.*

10. *A complete list of books owned by Jefferson can be found in* Catalogue of the Library of Thomas Jefferson, *a five-volume set by Millicent Sowerby, published in 1952 by the U.S. Library of Congress. Betts includes, as an appendix, a list of Jefferson's books on agriculture, botany, and gardening. Some of the better known books on landscape design which Jefferson owned were* New Principles of Gardening *by Batty Langley,* The Gardener's Calendar *by Philip Miller, and* Observations on Modern Gardening *by Thomas Whately. The works of George Isham Parkyns were also widely read during this period.*

11. *Woodlands was designed in two major phases. The first was from 1745, when Hamilton inherited it, until 1784, when he left for a European trip. By that time the estate's naturalistic character had already been established. The second design phase began in 1786 when Hamilton returned from Europe and began "remodeling" the garden based on new ideas acquired through travel. This phase ended in 1827 when the land was sold out of the family.*

12. *This is overstating the point a bit, since one of L'Enfant's later difficulties with the Commissioners of the District of Columbia was that he believed they rushed into land clearing and sales before the plan was refined. The fact remains, though, that the essential features of the scheme were established for an area of almost 4 square miles before substantial development began.*

13. *Ironically, the contemporary plan of Washington as established in the McMillan Commission report of 1901 actually bears a greater resemblance to the Evelyn plan, which also has a "kite" pattern of diagonal streets.*

14. *The most significant nineteenth-century changes were:*

- *Disruption of the Pennsylvania Avenue sight line between Capitol and White House when the Treasury building was constructed next to the White House*
- *Construction of the first Smithsonian building on a portion of the Mall*
- *Development of a Romantic landscape park, which blocked views to the Potomac, on the Mall*
- *Construction of a railroad line and station on the Mall near the Capitol*
- *Reduction of the flow in Tiber Creek so that it became a sloughlike dumping ground.*

See Chapters 5 and 11 for further discussion of the Washington, D.C., plan.

15. *There were three Ellicott brothers who were instrumental in various land-planning projects: Andrew, Joseph, and Benjamin.*

16. *In his famous auto-epitaph Jefferson wrote that he wished to be remembered as the author of the Declaration of Independence, as the drafter of the Statute of Virginia for Religious Freedom, and as the father of the University of Virginia.*

17. *See the Woods article for a discussion of possible influences on this plan. (Oddly, Woods does not consider the relationship of the plan to the prevalent Virginia manor house design, with a large central structure and dependencies forming a U.)*

18. *Jefferson's first known sketch plan for a university, dated to about 1815, shows the essential concept of a U-shaped arrangement with two sizes of buildings surrounded by gardens, but it lacks a structural focal point. Benjamin Latrobe has been credited with suggesting the need for a larger focal building at the center of the enclosed end.*

19. *Two factors may explain the confusing discrepancy between descriptions and views. First, the vegetation would have been quite small and unimpressive when first installed and could have been omitted simply for the composition's sake. Second, design interest in the early nineteenth century focused on architecture. Trees would have obscured details of the buildings and may thus have been eliminated. It was not until the 1840s that landscape design began to compete with architecture in public interest and therefore would have been more accurately portrayed.*

15

A New Land to Possess:
Development of Transportation and
Land Tenure Systems

Ambivalence toward landscape is common throughout history. The Babylonians appreciated the valley of the Tigris and Euphrates for its productive abilities, but could not resist erecting a distinctly different symbolic landscape in their ziggurat gardens. In North America such inherently contradictory human thought was magnified by the scope of the uncharted landscape encountered by Euroamericans. Thus, the continent that some termed the "Garden of the World" was to others a malevolent wilderness to be conquered through the surveyor's chain, the axe, and the plough.

A good deal of recent scholarship has focused on limitations of the concepts "wilderness" and "frontier" in explaining the historical development of North America.[1] Although these arguments are persuasive, in that social and physical reality do not necessarily coincide, these terms continue to have valid uses in the study of landscape history. First, as Nash and others have pointed out, they are the terms used by emigrants to describe American landscapes. Second, each term refers to a slightly different level of human interaction with that landscape. "Wilderness," as it will be used here, refers to those areas in which Euroamericans had virtually no control over land use and which were not subject to European systems of land tenure and subdivision. Although these areas may have had points of European contact such as forts, land use was limited quantitatively, geographically, and temporally. Wilderness was a place of confrontation between inexperienced settlers and an unfamiliar, pristine landscape. The "frontier," on the other hand, can be viewed as that zone in which Euroamericans and Native Americans were contending for land control and to which European or American tenure and subdivision systems were in the process of being applied. Frontiers were areas of expanding, but incomplete, Euroamerican control. They were regions of great conflict between native peoples and newcomers because control was often achieved through a process of destruction—of flora, fauna, and existing cultures. The end of the frontier can be dated to the time when all alternative land use patterns, such as those of the Native Americans, had been suppressed. "Civilization" is the term commonly applied to land controlled in this way, but here the term "settled" will be used because it suggests a high level of occupation and control, without proposing that the previous periods were barbaric or lacking a cultural component.

To further clarify the two concepts wilderness and frontier, contrast French settlement of the upper Mississippi in the eighteenth century with that of mid-nineteenth century Americans. The French towns and forts were confined to scattered points along rivers. Excursions inland were for temporary uses such as exploration or hunting. Land grants to settlers were relatively small, in bands along waterways, and did not threaten coexisting Native American uses. In this instance, although there was a European presence, its moderate impact preserved the primeval character of the landscape. Such areas would be considered wilderness. Americans coming into Illinois in the next century brought with them different attitudes toward occupation of the land. Their numbers were large, and it was presumed that they would supplant the Native Americans rather than coexist with them. Although the earliest arrivals settled only on riverine land, the government surveyors who soon followed completely subdivided the land for eventual American ownership. This area, then, was a frontier going progressively through stages of greater European control until earlier systems were eradicated.[2]

"Wilderness" was an evocative term in the seventeenth, eighteenth, and nineteenth centuries. The images that it conjured up could at once be fear-provoking and elevating. Many European settlers found the North American landscape a terrifying enigma devoid of familiar features. Their fear grew out of very real differences—in scale, plants, animals, climate, and indigenous cultures—between the New World and what they had known in Europe. It was psychologically, as well as geographically, a New World. Biblical and Christian religious allusions also fostered this fear: Adam and Eve were punished by being cast out from a paradise into a wilderness, and Christ encountered the devil in the wilderness. Wilderness thus represented both a punishment, a fall from grace, and a place of unspeakable temptations that would alienate one from both God and civilization.

At the same time, wilderness had undeniable attractions. It offered economic benefits of land and other resources to those who were bold enough to claim them. It was a place of social and religious freedom, away from the constraints of organized institutions. While wilderness could corrupt because of its unrestrained freedoms, it was also a refuge from the corrupting materialism of the settled world. The wilderness was also considered a social safety valve—a place to channel the discontent or the undesirable. Thus, it is not surprising that Roger Williams went off into the wilderness when his beliefs threatened established Puritan order. In the nineteenth century, as the wilderness retreated further west, and much of America became urbanized, "wilderness" became a utopian archetype favorably contrasted to the effects of spreading industrialization and mass culture. It also came to symbolize ideal American values of independence, self-reliance, and forthrightness.

When attractive aspects of the wilderness overcame those which were feared, settlement began through formation of a frontier. Of course "the frontier" was never a single place or a line that could be delineated, but rather zones with constantly shifting, usually advancing, but occasionally retreating, edges. In Frederick Jackson Turner's well-known hypothesis, the frontier actually became the stimulus to cultural and economic development of settled areas. A more contemporary view would acknowledge that the presence of the wilderness and the processes of the frontier transformation influenced continental culture, particularly in the English-speaking countries, but that the wilderness and frontier were in reality extensions of the economic, political, and social objectives of the dominant culture of the settled areas.

ROLE OF TRANSPORTATION IN THE SETTLEMENT PROCESS

A process central to the transition from wilderness through frontier to settlement was transportation innovation. Transportation systems were second only to agriculture in their lasting impact on the land, and, prior to this century, were the major engineered alteration of the landscape. Transportation was also central to achieving the expansionist objectives of both colonial powers and native-born North American governments. Edward Everett, in speaking of the situation in the United States, identified what was really a continental perspective: "The destinies of our country run east and west. Intercourse between the mighty interior west and the [eastern] sea coast is the great principle of our commercial prosperity" (quoted in Hulbert, 1920, p. 13). Thus regions of the continent were tied together in symbiotic roles, and none could prosper on its own. Relationships of importance were both commercial and political. Manufacturing and trading areas needed raw materials, of which there were vast supplies, first organic and later inorganic, from the West. And if the interior prospered, this would assure that manufactured goods made from its raw materials could be sold to a national market rather than relying on easily interrupted international trade. Another dimension of commercial need was competition between the major ports on the continent. Boston, New York, Philadelphia, Baltimore, and New Orleans vied for trade to and from the northern United States and the Ohio River valley; Charleston[3] and Savannah the southern trade; and Quebec and Montreal the St. Lawrence and fur country trade.[4] In many ways, the history of nineteenth-century transportation development in North America is the history of competition among these centers to retain their primacy by enlarging their commercial hinterlands.

Politics also played an important role in fostering transportation, as nations sought to acquire and retain new territory. In this age of instantaneous "faxing" and four-hour cross-continental flights it is difficult to imagine the difficulty of keeping nations united when news and products took months to transport. Those at a distance from centers of power often felt overlooked and in some instances sought to establish new political alliances, as in western Pennsylvania's Whiskey Rebellion. In the United States, the Appalachian Mountains created an obstacle that was political, as well as physical and psychological. Breaking this barrier to provide the link between the developed coastal-Piedmont area and the wilderness beyond was a central theme of most of the eighteenth and early nineteenth centuries. In Canada, with a more penetrating water system, serious transportation restraints were not encountered until the railroad era.

The earliest inland transportation routes on the continent were roads and rivers. Roads usually followed routes of Native American or animal trails. In fact, to call them roads suggests an image incompatible with their actual appearance. Most were themselves trails, or what were called "traces," paths gradually worn into the ground through constant use and often only inches wide. Few were fit for wagon transport, except near towns. Not only were they small, but most travelers described them as being in terrible condition—what one called a "veratible [sic] slough of despond." Road "construction" was an unknown or at least unpracticed art. Rights-of-way may have been superficially cleared, but stumps and rocks rarely were. Being ungraded and unpaved, the condition of the roads depended almost solely on the weather. If it was wet, as in the spring, they became impassible quagmires. In summer the road base was stable, but travelers suffered from dust and insects. Winter was often considered a good time to travel because soil was frozen. Of course, ruts could also freeze in place and snowdrifts could trap vehicles or animals.[5] But no matter how hard to travel, roads were essential, especially in parts of the continent with nonnavigable rivers, such as New England. Among the important roads of the seventeenth and early eighteenth centuries were the Great Trail (parts were also known as the Connecticut Path or Bay Path), which connected Boston with towns in Connecticut and, using adjunct paths, Providence, Rhode Island;[6] El Camino Real, a system that connected Veracruz, Mexico City, and the trade centers of northern Mexico via three branches to California, the upper Rio Grande valley, and Spain's southeastern possessions from Texas to St. Augustine, Florida;[7] and the Coastal Post Road from Portsmouth, New Hampshire, to Savannah, Georgia.[8]

In the late eighteenth century demand for land grew so great that neither the old barrier of the Appalachians, nor innumerable treaties with the Native Americans restricting settlement, could deter European movement westward. In 1774–75 Daniel Boone hastened this process by cutting a route known as the Wilderness Road from Virginia across the Cumberland Gap into Kentucky.[9] This route remained nothing but a trace through the woods until it was upgraded to a wagon road in 1795, but by then it had accomplished its mission of routing several hundred thousand newcomers into Kentucky. Similar primitive roads in other areas were Zane's Trace into Ohio and the Natchez Trace between Tennessee and Mississippi.

At the same time that these trails were being pioneered into the West, new road technology improved existing links. The chief development was addition of paved, pay-as-you-go turnpikes. The first one of any scale was the Lancaster Turnpike between Philadelphia and Lancaster, Pennsylvania, begun in 1792, and eventually extended to the Ohio River valley via Pittsburgh. This turnpike differed from earlier roads in alignment, which was straight rather than twisted to fit every vagary of the topography; in construction, which was of compacted gravel in the Telford manner; and in maintenance, which was regular and carried out by experienced workers. Lancaster Turnpike is credited with beginning a new period in road building which emphasized quality of travel rather than mere access. In the three decades following the pike's inception a wave of improved pay roads spread throughout the northeastern United States and part of Canada. Unfortunately for many investors, the distances between toll stations, usually 10 miles or more, allowed a great deal of free usage, and most financially unsuccessful turnpikes deteriorated physically.

In 1835 an engineering variant of these early toll roads—the plank or "cor-

" 'Dark Ages' of the Road," a painting by Carl Rakeman depicting the terrible condition of some American roads in the early nineteenth century. Rakeman prepared this painting and others used in this chapter as part of a series to illustrate articles by Albert Rose published in American Highways in the 1950s. (Courtesy George A. Hay, U.S. Department of Transportation, Federal Highway Administration.)

duroy" road, named for its manner of construction using milled lumber or halved wlogs—was introduced in North America. Plank roads were designed and sited principally to be farm-to-market wagon roads. They lowered transportation cost by reducing wheel friction, so that a greater load per wagon could be carried. The first known plank road in North America was one built to Toronto in 1835. The United States followed with a road to Syracuse in 1837. It was in the agriculturally rich, but poorly drained, Midwest that plank roads became most popular, with three major roads built to Chicago in the 1840s. The plank road era lasted only about twenty years. Plank roads proved expensive to maintain because, of course, untreated lumber in contact with the ground has a very short useful life. Most pavements had to be replaced in five to eight years, more often across the marshy soil they were often used to improve. Competition from railroads and improved stone pavement methods also offered more cost effective and stable alternatives.

There was probably no road technology development that was more important to settlement of the continent than the political decision in the United States to make road infrastructure a federal prerogative. Learning rather belatedly an idea which the Spanish had implemented in the sixteenth century, English-speaking North America finally recognized that transportation was too vital a national cement to be left to uncoordinated efforts of private financiers. The first road in the United States to be constructed with government assistance was the Cumberland or National Road, which began at Cumberland, Maryland.[10] This project was inaugurated by route surveying in 1806, but construction did not begin until the inauspicious year of 1812. Of course the War of 1812, which made the need for the road obvious, also delayed its construction, so that the first major segment—to Wheeling, West Virginia, on the Ohio River—was not completed until 1818. The eventual terminus of the road was to have been St. Louis, so that the entire Northwest Territory would have had an east coast alternative to transport down the Mississippi. This was never achieved, and the road stopped at Vandalia, Illinois, then the state capital. The Cumberland Road lives on as part of U.S. 40 and Interstate 70.[11]

Cumberland Road served many immediate needs. It gave Ohio River valley

Plank Road to Syracuse, New York. As typically constructed, the right-of-way was crudely graded so that a crown and swales were formed. Parallel beams, or "stringers," of rot-resistant wood, such as hemlock or cypress, were laid on the ground, or on a gravel sub-base. Planks or log halves 8 feet in length were then laid perpendicular to the beams and nailed in place. Sets of planks were often staggered so that the total paved width was greater than 8 feet and a vehicle on the shoulder could keep at least one set of wheels on pavement. One plank road was still in use in the Mojave Desert in the 1930s. (From a painting by Rakeman. Courtesy of George A. Hay, U.S. Department of Transportation, Federal Highway Administration.)

Most improved stone roads built in North America were based upon the Telford or Macadam systems of road engineering in which a smooth, crowned subbase was covered with one or more layers of graded, compacted stones. (Painting by Rakeman. Courtesy of George A. Hay, U.S. Department of Transportation, Federal Highway Administration.)

Map showing some of the principal land and water routes discussed in text. (Drawn by Rossi.)

farmers a link to eastern markets, so that they could farm on a commercial scale. It was a mail route to the West and became the principal travel route by which many easterners and Europeans first visited the Northwest Territory. James Silk Buckingham, of "Victoria" fame, commended the road as being "admirable all the way, as good indeed as the road from London to Bath. . . . To us, indeed, who had been jolted and shaken, plunged and precipitated, over the rough roads and . . . corduroy causeways, of various other States . . . it was no ordinary luxury to travel on this smooth and equitable National Road. . . ." (Buckingham, 1842, pp. 268–69).

An account of travel to the wilderness and frontier could never be complete without mention of legendary trails to the Far West. The first great western route was the Santa Fe Trail,[12] running from first Independence, Missouri, and later Westport, Kansas (Kansas City), to New Mexico, a route which was officially surveyed for trade following Mexican independence in 1821, but had been in use far longer. The seventy-five day trip between Santa Fe and Westport was deemed worth the hardship of dust, drought, and Comanche assault because of the value of products from Mexico. An underlying purpose of the road for the United States was to gain knowledge of and a solid foothold in the Louisiana Territory, which was purchased from France two decades earlier. Other western routes served settlers, but also had underlying territorial acquisition motivations. The Oregon Trail, established in the 1830s, allowed Americans to colonize and claim much of the Pacific Northwest, which had been claimed by England since Mackenzie's transcontinental trek of 1789.

Roads served well for local transportation needs, but for long-distance or heavy freight travel they could not compare with waterborne travel. Water travel developed contemporaneously with roads, but expanded more rapidly through infrastructure improvement and vehicular technology innovation, particularly introduction of the steam engine in the early 1800s. Our concern with the landscape, though, relates to development of water routes, both natural and artificial.

Regionally different patterns of river-based intracontinental travel emerged during colonial times. In New England and most of the Middle Atlantic, rivers were short and shallow, limiting their use. In Canada, the St. Lawrence River created a water-paved highway of over a thousand navigable miles. Likewise in the South, there were deep tidal rivers that gave access up to the fall-line of the Appalachians. In Mexico and Central America, inland waterways were of only local importance. Everywhere that water routes existed they were quickly exploited. The James and Rappahannock Rivers in Virginia linked plantations directly with Europe or later New York and Baltimore. The Hudson was a Dutch version of the Virginia rivers, its patroonships having access to both the fur trade of the north and the commercial center of New York City. But the most crucial water route was the great linked system of the Ohio, the Mississippi, and the Great Lakes. Control and exploitation of this route was rightly seen by all colonial powers as critical to dominance of the continent. For almost two centuries, the joining of the two rivers with the Great Lakes became the goal of numerous channelization and canal schemes. As early as 1674 Louis Joliet, the great French explorer, had proposed connecting the Mississippi to the Great Lakes via a channel across northern Illinois, while in 1724 Cadwaller Colden, surveyor general of New York, suggested a Hudson-Mohawk River canal, the precursor of the Erie Canal.

Canals were intended to rectify problems that made river systems imperfect. Most obviously, in the days before engine-driven boats, rivers were essentially unidirectional systems. Travel downstream was relatively rapid and easy, but to get back upstream often took four times as long and required ten times as much muscle power. More often than not, return trips were faster by road. Rivers also had navigational problems due to shifting sandbars, extreme fluctuations in water level, and ice in the water.

Canals are closed water systems into which water flow is controlled by gates at natural water sources. Canals were straight, narrow (30 to 40 feet wide), shallow (about 4 feet deep), and stone-lined. Barges were pulled through the water by mules that walked along towpaths on each side of the water. Travel was slow, roughly 5 miles per hour, but consistent, smooth, and in either direction. It was essential that the grade of the canal be kept nearly level, and this led to construction of structures to deal with natural grade changes. Elevated channels or aqueducts carried canals over natural water features at lower elevations. Hills were crossed by tunnels occasionally, but more common was the use of locks. All canals collected tolls, with the fee based on cargo weight or number of passengers. Special weight locks, one of which is preserved at Syracuse, were used to access fees. Since most canals were built in the North, they could only be used by boats for the warmer eight or nine months of the year. In winter, the thin frozen sheet of residual water at the bottom of a drained canal served many communities as an icy highway, with skates and sleds substituting for barges.

In the eighteenth and early nineteenth centuries, canals were small in scale and were used to improve river travel by circumventing rapids and other impediments, as did the Potomac River Canal. Until 1815, there were only eighteen canals in the United States, with the most lengthy, the Middlesex in Massachusetts, just 27 miles long. Then began what has been called the Canal Era, a period of extensive canal development and use. Building of the Erie Canal across northern New York from the Hudson River to Lake Erie both marked the start of this boom and was the first large-scale, public, civil engineering work in North America.[13]

The Erie Canal was begun in 1817 to serve several purposes. On the national level, it provided the first direct water route from the Midwest to eastern ports, thus reducing farmers' shipping costs. On the state level, it opened for extensive settlement fertile northwest New York, an area attractive to immigrants except for its poor access to commercial markets. On the city level, it created a vast rural hinterland for New York City which assured its financial primacy among American cities for several decades.[14] When its 363 miles[15] were completed in 1825, the route was ceremonially inaugurated by mingling a cask of Atlantic water with Erie water, thereby symbolizing the economic, cultural, and environmental bonds created. The canal demonstrated to Americans that geography, or more precisely physiography, need not be destiny. Those who were ambitious and technologically inventive could remake the continent to suit their needs and desires.

Not everyone was enthusiastic about the canal's opening. Some pointed out

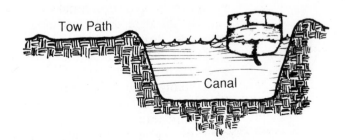

Diagram of typical canal and lock. (Drawn by Rossi.)

A romanticized view of canals entitled "On the Canal" by Edward Lamson Henry. The relationship of towpaths, waterway, and adjacent businesses was typical for the 1830s. (New York State Historical Association, Cooperstown, New York.)

that the canal would exacerbate interstate competition for the western trade, potentially damaging the still shaky federal union. Others, early environmentalists, were concerned that the canal would destroy visual quality in upstate New York. Still others argued that seawater might enter Lake Erie, thereby harming its marine life. Although these concerns were reasonable, they represented a minority view that favored ecological stability over economic advantages that the canal seemed to guarantee.

Following the success of the Erie Canal came a host of projects to connect waterways in other parts of the country. Baltimore countered New York's threat to its commercial role by financing the Chesapeake and Ohio Canal, but this was superseded by a railroad scheme. Pennsylvania, Ohio, and Indiana all developed extensive systems. Only two canals, the Carondelet in Louisiana and the Santee-Cooper in South Carolina, were developed in the South, because density of the river network made canals less profitable there. In Canada, the Rideau Canal, begun in 1826, was the most significant. It provided a short-cut, primarily for the military, from the Ottawa River to Lake Ontario via the site of Ottawa, then little more than a worker's camp.

The Illinois and Michigan Canal (I&M), incorporated in 1825, but delayed in completion for over twenty years, was the last major canal constructed. This canal fulfilled Joliet's vision and completed the Great Lakes-Mississippi-East Coast trade triangle that had long been an American goal, making Chicago the major inland port in the process. The I&M was less than 100 miles long, but those miles were the important ones which separated Lake Michigan from commercially navigable portions of the Illinois River and the Mississippi beyond. Its value to the national economy was indicated by it being the only canal of the period to receive substantial federal assistance through land grants.

By the date of the opening of the Erie, the canals' successor was already emerging. Primitive horse-drawn wagons running on tracks were in use for short-haul transportation in Massachusetts. By the early 1830s several small rail lines were in place, and ambitious plans for the Baltimore and Ohio Railroad were being formed. The advance of transportation technology thus continued as it reshaped the landscape of a continent to suit its new occupants.

While transportation advances are in themselves quite interesting, what concerns us here is their implications for land use, planning, and design. The linear nature of early circulation systems established a regionally diffuse pattern of occupation, but one which could be quite dense along the routes, since everyone wanted direct access to them. Neither roads, rivers, nor canals are essentially nodal in organization—that is, you can disembark at any point although certain points are more favored than others. For roads and rivers, these preferred points are at the junction of two lines of travel, the crossroads or the forks. Major river junctions were crucial locations, with those such as St. Louis or Montreal developed very early. The juncture of any combination of route types became, at least while that form of transport prospered, a center of trade. Canals favored townsites at locks or other breaks in flow: "lockports" across the northeastern part of the United States attest to this.

Although all three types of transportation tended to produce linear land use patterns, urban plans associated with each differed somewhat. Towns along roads, like those in New England, usually had a rambling pattern with density radiating outward from a crossroads or the meeting house. Smaller towns often had no secondary streets; rather, people simply built farther from the center, until distance became prohibitive. In Spanish-influenced areas, application of the Laws of the Indies produced less linear patterns, with towns often off through roads. In the nineteenth century, linear plans for towns generally disappeared, at least on paper, in favor of the isonomic grid. In reality though, most actual development lined the main street while the others remained vacant. River towns of the early 1800s, like Madison, Indiana, had distinctive plans which reflected their economic base in trade. The towns were linear, but densely so, near a wharf area along the river. The wharf served as the loading dock for main street stores which fronted away from it. The shopping district was a double row of stores lining the street, which often meandered with the river. Better residential areas were above the commercial center, out of the floodplain, while poorer housing would be strung out along the river beyond the town center.

Madison, Indiana, on the Ohio River. Main Street, in the center, paralleled the river, while warehouses and docks lined the riverfront.
(Madison Area Chamber of Commerce.)

Canal towns were among the first to have sites purposefully selected in an organized way. Canal companies often developed towns as service centers, selecting prime sites after route surveying was complete. Urban development in northern Illinois was deliberately delayed several years, until the I&M corridor was finalized. Canal towns like Metamora, Indiana, on the Whitewater Canal and Lockport, New York, on the Erie Canal generally occupied both sides of the canal since it was so narrow that bridging was not a problem. Main streets ran with the canal but might face toward or away from it depending on the size of the town. Smaller towns often incorporated the canal into main street, making it the focus of downtown. Canal towns often became industrial, as well as trade, centers since impoundment of water generated power for factories and the canals provided inexpensive transport for the goods produced.

While the impact of transportation improvements was most relevant at the macro-scale of regional and urban planning, the transportation revolution of the early 1800s had impacts on landscape design as well. An intracontinental circulation infrastructure created communication links through which a uniform national and international middle-class culture could be rapidly spread. One of the early manifestations of this culture was the landscape fashion usually termed the Romantic style.[16] That this became a nineteenth-century standard for designed landscapes can, at least in part, be attributed to the ease with which design information could be spread through books, periodicals, and lectures. All of these were made widely accessible through improved road and water, and later railroad, systems.

LAND TENURE SYSTEMS AND THE BEGINNING OF THE AMERICAN LAND PATTERN

Few decisions have the lasting impact on the land that comes from implementation of a land survey system. The persistence of boundaries established in antiquity is well established. Structures may come and go, but property lines, roads, easements, and other basic landholding tracts often become immutable. In North America, land pattern transformations wrought by Euroamericans contrasted strikingly with existing Native American land tenure systems. European tenure was based on absolute, restrictive, and permanent ownership and use, derived initially from imperial claims but eventually dispersed to companies and individuals. While Native Americans occupied land for an indefinite period, it was usually not owned by individuals. Thus, as Indian leaders from Red Jacket of the Seneca to Black Hawk of the Sac and Fox lamented, their treaty signatures were intended to allow whites access, not to alienate their own people from the land. Native American tenure tended to keep natural landscapes entire, while Europeans compartmentalized them into packaged commodities.

Several motivations were at work as first European powers, then American governments, implemented a legal and physical framework of land tenure. First, the opportunity for land ownership motivated many poor or unlanded Europeans to risk the hazardous journey and uncertain New World situation. It was essential that the promise of land could be backed up with assurance of recognized titles. Second, ownership of land tied individuals to places and assured a degree of loyalty not forthcoming from those who were more mobile. The help of landowners in suppressing the Native Americans or protecting colonies from foreign invasion was assured because of their vested interest in the protection of their assets. Third, landowners are more easily controlled than are the nomadic. Their land and possessions can be taxed to support the government or confiscated if they break the law or are treasonous. Thus, in the European approach to land tenure, allotting of certain fixed parcels to individuals was seen as benefiting everyone and fostering development of permanent communities with stable political systems.

In the period since the first European occupation of North America, two major systems of *cadastral* (that is, officially registered) survey, each with distinctive characteristics, advantages, and problems, have been used to apportion land.[17] The oldest is known as the "metes and bounds system," while the more recently implemented is called the Public Land Survey.[18] The metes and bounds system of survey originated in Europe and was used by all the colonial powers in various specific forms. It continued in use as the principal survey system in the United States for a short time after the Revolution, in Canada into the mid-nineteenth century, and in Mexico up to the present day.[19] In metes and bounds surveys, land boundaries were designated through a site-specific combination of natural or human-made landmarks, distances, angles, bearings, and preceding land ownership. Location was recorded only as it was relative to other land parcels or features.

Two examples may make this approach clear. The first description below is from the deed to a tract in Parker County, Texas, originally part of a Spanish land grant; the second is from the deed to a tract in that part of central Ohio once the Virginia Military District:[20]

> Tract or parcel of land . . . beginning at the S.E. corner of the James Veasey 101 acre survey, Abstract No. 1585, and the N. E. corner of the said Hiram E. Swain 24–7/10 acre survey, Abstract No. 1793. Thence West 121.7 vrs [varas—a Spanish and Portuguese measurement which varies locally, but in Texas was equal to 32.9 or 33.3 inches] with fence to corner in the bed of a deep ravine, from which a [round pole] 0.2 ft in dia. standing on the east bank of said ravine brs [bears] East 23 feet. Thence South at 198 vrs to iron stake, located 8 feet N. of the N. W. corner of the . . . red barn. . . . (Parker County, Texas, Deed Records, Vol. 163, p. 48)

> Beginning at a Red Oak and Bur Oak running N 6 E 260 poles [rods; a rod equals 16.5 feet], crossing the Creek at 80 poles passing the Southeast corner of William Heth's Survey No. 4946 at 20 poles with his line passing his Northeast corner at 180 poles to a Stake. Thence S 84 E 250 poles to three Ashes, two from one root; thence S 6 W 345 poles crossing the Creek at 325 poles, to two Hickories and a Bur Oak: Thence N 67 W 260 poles, crossing a branch at 20 poles to the beginning. (Thrower, 1966, p. 31)

From these deeds it is not difficult to imagine some of the problems that metes and bounds surveys created. The imprecision of landmarks made fraud profitable, and even between honest neighbors disputes based on interpretation of landmarks arose. Trees died, iron posts could be moved or rusted out, and streams changed course. When land was first allocated in large tracts to land companies, these problems were relatively minor. As smaller parcels—particularly the 50-acre headrights which made up many of the early individual holdings in the United States—were carved out, differences of several feet could considerably reduce farm size. Beyond the descriptive limitations of metes and bounds was the fact that land was not surveyed prior to occupation in much of the region where it was applied. In most instances a claimant was given a land warrant for a certain acreage, traveled to areas with unclaimed land, established property markers on the preferred site, and then described the area so marked. In principle the claimant was then to return to a recorder's office and have their claim location documented. As settlement proceeded farther from established cities, the period between claiming and recording was often several years. This lapse led to overlapping claims, particularly on uncleared land. In New England, though, the metes and bounds system was used to survey prior to settlement, demonstrating that some of the problems associated with metes and bounds could have been avoided by better planning.

Metamora, Indiana, with its small central business district along one side of the canal.

In spite of problems, metes and bounds surveyed land did have some advantages. Tract size could be easily adjusted to compensate for poor local conditions. The shape of the parcel could also be varied to incorporate a variety of natural capacity zones. The system also allowed natural divides such as streams or ridges to become property limits, generally creating a land use pattern which was visually and ecologically more sensitive to the landscape.[21] Since most settlers selected their land in the field, they had the security of knowing the viability of their claim.

Two factors eventually led to replacement of metes and bounds surveys with the more regular Public Land Survey system.[22] First was the desire to settle the North American continent as rapidly as possible. A cumbersome, imprecise, and uncontrollable system such as metes and bounds would have caused great delay and cost in record keeping. The second factor was the philosophical influence of the Enlightenment, which emphasized both a rational approach to organization of the natural world and the political equality of all citizens.

The Public Land Survey was an absolute land location system in which each parcel could be given a unique and mathematically precise location based on Cartesian geometry. Origins of this approach in American thought are unclear, but in 1781 Pelatiah Webster made the first concrete proposal in a brief essay touching on future use of the public lands.[23] During that decade the system became established in the United States through a series of laws beginning with the Land Ordinance of 1785.[24] This statute, developed under Thomas Jefferson's guidance, had as its major purpose an equitable division of vast areas between the Mississippi and the Appalachians that the federal government had recently been ceded by some of the original thirteen states.[25] Public policy advocated that this area be quickly opened for settlement, because it was generally agreed that settlement would assure U.S. claims threatened by the British, French, and Spanish, as well as create a buffer area to protect developed areas from Native American attack. Federalists, whose views were articulated by Treasury Secretary Alexander Hamilton, also saw public land as a financial asset which could be sold off to pay national debts. The Republicans under Jefferson believed that the resource value of land lay in its potential to ensure a republic of citizens with rights vested in the land. Thus, what was a commodity to Federalists was a moral endowment to Republicans.

Although the Public Land Survey system was put in place in 1785, it was not completely implemented until two years later with passage of the Northwest Ordinance. While the thrust of that law was to establish mechanics under which new states would be admitted to the Union, it also articulated much of the land allocation process that, with minor modifications, is followed today in most of the United States and much of Canada.

There were two essential maxims that established the rectilinear pattern characteristic of the public lands. First, all survey lines were to have uniform orientations, either north-south or east-west. Second, the tracts of land referenced by these lines were to be fixed-size subdivisions. Starting points of the survey were reference lines, known as *principal meridians* if they ran north and south, and *base lines* if they ran east and west. The locations of each of these (in the United States at least) were somewhat arbitrary in that they were placed as need arose rather than having a fixed pattern. For example, in Illinois there were two meridians less than 100 miles apart, while no meridian is located in the larger state of Wyoming. Many meridians do have a locational logic and are, in fact, the only Public Land Survey features tied to the landscape. They often have their point of origin at the junction of large rivers, an example being the third principal meridian, which originated at the fork of the Ohio and Mississippi Rivers.[26]

Once established, the principal meridians became fixed lines of reference which were then used to establish the more visible components of the system—the hierarchy of property-defining lines that began with quadrangle limits. A *quadrangle* was a square area 24 miles on a side, used as the basic mapping subdivision, but which rarely had any land use implications. Quadrangles were subdivided into the more commonly known unit of the *township,* a square that measured 6 miles on a side and is thus 36 square miles in size. In many states townships became important political entities, just as they were in the colonial New England system, but this was not mandatory under the Public Land Survey. Each township was partitioned into thirty-six units of 640 acres each, known as *sections.* Sections were basic units under which land grants to states and businesses were made. Initially sections were considered to be too large for individual farm ownership and were further divided into four parts of 160 acres each—the *quarter section,* which became the land ownership standard in much of the continent. Each quarter section could be still further subdivided using directional designations and fractions of earlier tracts.[27] Thus, the northeastern 40 acres of a township would be described in deeds as the northeast ¼ of the northeast ¼ of section 1 in Township XY.[28] Such precision meant that a tract of any size could be given a unique designation. Coupled with the intention that all land in the public domain was to be surveyed before settlement, this system was intended to assure clarity and validity of title.[29]

In the minds of those who inaugurated this system, it provided only advantages to everyone involved from the government to the farmer. It permitted fast measurement and recording, both because of the ease with which a large number of surveyors could be trained and the rate of completion of field surveys. All tracts had only one legal description, so errors could be quickly noted and overlapping claims prevented.[30] Uniform acreage was assured for all settlers since the "prepackaged" farm units were of equal size. Prior survey meant that distribution could be more easily regulated. Some authors have cited the "psychological comfort" that the regularity gave to those who settled on the topographically uniform prairies of the Midwest, but this concept is questionable since the precision of the system is much more visible today than when first applied and the "disquieting" effect of uniformity to the horizon has not been proven.[31]

Some of the problems inherent in the Public Land Survey system either did not occur to its founders or were overshadowed by the immediacy of its advan-

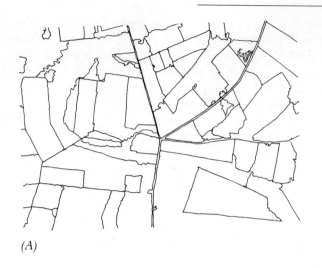

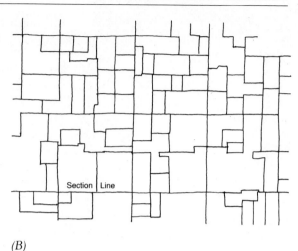

(A)   (B)

Diagrammatic plan comparison of typical land ownership, land use, and road patterns produced under (A) metes and bounds surveys and (B) the U.S. Public Land Survey. (Data from Thrower, 1966; drawn by Rossi.)

tages. Five conditions of so me consequence emerged from the rectangular survey. First, the system would work perfectly on a flat world, but does not on a spherical one. Principal meridians and other north-south lines intended to create square townships actually converge as they move toward the poles. Over long distances these discrepancies become visible. In practice, adjustments were made at section lines to keep them more nearly parallel. Abrupt offsets are often seen at roads that follow section lines and jag 90 degrees at correction points. Next, the importance of naturally occurring land boundaries was ignored. Features such as large streams may divide a quarter section into two or more parts, with access between them difficult. This often produced situations which were uneconomic for owners or aggravated environmental problems. Third, the arbitrary fixed size of quarter-section parcels ignored carrying capacity of different classes of land. This caused serious problems in the 1860s, when drier portions of the central plains and Southwest began to be settled. Eventually a series of laws broke the sovereignty of the quarter section as prototypical parcel so that allocations could be tied to land capacity. Fourth, the grid cannot be easily adjusted to accommodate later systems appended to it. The earliest example of this was the railroad, which followed certain topographical constraints and in most cases disregarded the patterns of the survey, often cutting parcels in two. More recently, the Interstate Highway System has slashed through the public land grid in somewhat the same way.[32] Finally and most significantly, the survey structured most of the human-made world from road pattern to urban design to ploughing pattern into a monotonous grid. What had been developed to make possible immediate land transfer became the key physical formgiver in the landscape. While this need not have been the case, the oppressive regularity of the system overwhelmed other human impulses. The implications of this are diverse. Thrower (1966) demonstrated that roads following survey lines actually increase travel distances by not following the shortest distance between two points. Johnson (1947) found that rectangular tracts increased erosion and gullying along rivers as farmers cultivated upland terraces to the very edge of ravines. Urban minifications of the grid often fostered outright landform removal as topography was altered to facilitate transportation. Ironically, regional uniformity of the midwestern landscape may have been an unanticipated result of the Public Land Survey, but not an undesired one. This pattern would have been seen as the embodiment of both mastery of the wilderness and achievement of agrarian democracy.

The history of the Public Land Survey was both the story of passive land

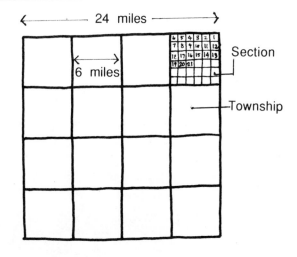

Diagram showing a typical quadrant of the U.S. Public Land Survey and its principal subdivisions. (Drawn by Rossi.)

design through engineering and the history of how that land was transferred from its original Native American owners to new American occupants. The public lands themselves, a resource of over a billion and a half acres, constituted the most significant land development scheme in world history. Through a series of nineteenth-century laws new areas and types of land, along with new rules for acquisition, made it possible for larger numbers of people to take up and maintain claims. Land was both given away and sold. Some have argued that it was actually those lands given away that brought the greatest benefits to the United States and Canada. Officially, public lands were given to two types of organization—to the states for public purposes (much of this was sold or granted to companies), and to corporations as incentives for infrastructure improvements. Grants to states were generally for education and to reward individual service. One or two sections per township were reserved for state or province use as school sites or to support schools. In 1862, assistance for education in the United States was extended to specifically support state technical colleges through provisions of what is commonly called the Morrill Act. States and provinces also redistributed land to individuals who provided special services. Most of these grants were related to military service, but there were some surprising ones such as those to the survivors of the New Madrid, Missouri, earthquake of 1826.

Grants to corporations were extensive and often became the economic rationale for otherwise unworkable public works projects. Although grants were made from every conceivable purpose most extensive grants were for transportation development, such as for canals and railroads. These grants of land have always been controversial, both philosophically and for the amounts of land awarded. Simplistically, nineteenth-century governments used public lands to finance quasi-public projects just as bonds are used today, but in the process distinctions between public and private often became blurred. What is certain is that the use of land grants encouraged development of certain infrastructure elements often before they were needed or could be self-sustaining. In this sense they were an aspect of government expansion policies as much as of public service.

Until 1862, the only way for individuals to acquire land was through a state grant or through purchase. The Jeffersonian notion of free land for all who could make use of it was a noble ideal but one out of step with the practical needs of an undercapitalized continent. Finally, a combination of political and social pressure led to passage of the first true yeomanry act in the United States—the

The U.S. Public Land Survey helped to produce the typical scattered farmsteads of much of North America, in which farm families lived dispersed on their land rather than congregated in villages. (Barker Texas History Center, University of Texas, Austin, Texas.)

A Western Nebraska Soddy.

On the plains, where timber was very limited, nineteenth-century homesteaders often constructed their first buildings of sod, as shown here, or dug into the ground to make a type of earth-sheltered building referred to as a "dugout."

Homestead Act. Provisions of this important law are often misunderstood, but the 1868 Agriculture Report makes the requirements quite clear:

> There are two classes of public lands; the one class at $1.25 per acre, which is designated as minimum, and the other at $2.50 per acre, or double minimum. . . . [The Act] gives to every citizen, and to those who have declared their intentions to become such, the right to a homestead on surveyed lands. This is conceded to the extent of one quarter section, or 160 acres, held at $1.25 per acre, or eighty acres at $2.50 per acre, in any organized district embracing surveyed public lands. (Anonymous, 1869, pp. 466–68)

After a five- to seven-year "proving up" or occupancy period and payment of a small filing fee, the homesteader could acquire legal title. On its surface the Homestead Act was a very good deal for those with little money, but problems existed. Much of the land administered under the Act was not productive, either because of natural limitations or lack of access.[33] The best lands had already been preempted by earlier settlers or acquired as part of railroad grants. Eventually, much of the land claimed under the Homestead Act was abandoned and returned to the public domain until reclaimed in the present century.

CONCLUSION AND SUMMARY

The North American continent is exceptional in that it (along with Australia) was not extensively populated at the time of the Industrial Revolution. The vast areas of land available to arriving Europeans engendered ambivalent feelings of attraction and fear, but the wilderness was eventually explored and became frontier. Once Euroamerican land tenure systems had completely suppressed Native American tenancy, the economic attractions of undeveloped land proved hard to resist. Improved methods and routes of transportation facilitated access to the wilderness, leading to a reshaping of the landscape first for pastoral and later for industrial purposes. The Public Land Survey fostered the greatest "rural renewal" project in history and created the framework for much of the contemporary North American landscape.

There are three concepts of importance to be drawn from the experience of exploration and settlement of the continent. First, Europeans erroneously believed that North American land and resources could be inexhaustibly exploited with little thought as to their management. Time has shown both the error and consequences of this thinking. Second, geographical distance was of less importance than psychological distance, a wilderness several hundred miles from settled areas was farther away to many Americans than a city a thousand miles away. Similarly, political boundaries affected our perception of landscape relationships: Houston is physically closer to Mexico City than to Chicago, but is tied economically directly to the later. Finally, in matters of landscape development, whether one is thinking at the scale of regional planning or at the small scale of specific designs, political decisions are critical. The Erie Canal might never have been built had the United States not feared hostile British attacks on St. Lawrence River and Lake Ontario commerce. Likewise the imposition of a geometric landscape on much of the continent was inspired by a political philosophy of egalitarianism.

NOTES

1. *For a general review of these concepts, in the context of Frederick Jackson Turner's frontier thesis, see* The Turner Thesis Concerning the Role of the Frontier in American History, *George Rogers Taylor, ed., Boston: D. C. Heath, 1956. Patricia N. Limerick suggests that we should "close the frontier and open western history" in* The Legacy of Conquest: The Unbroken Past of the American West, *New York: W. W. Norton, 1987. For discussion of the mythic uses of the concepts see* The Fatal Environment: The Myth of the Frontier in the Age of Industrialization, 1800–1890, *by Richard Slotkin, Middletown, Conn.: Wesleyan University Press, 1985; and by the same author,* Regeneration through Violence: The Mythology of the American Frontier, 1600–1860, *Middletown, Conn.: Wesleyan University Press, 1973.*

2. *Subsequent settlement by other European powers usually recognized initial European land subdivision systems. For example, French settlers in the Mississippi Valley were assured title to their land through the treaty in which Virginia ceded its western claims to the federal government. Although some claims were never recognized due to lack of acceptable evidence, Europeans always fared better than the original occupants of the land in the matter of land rights.*

3. *Even Charleston at one time attempted to capture the Ohio River trade by promoting a road from Columbia, South Carolina, to Cincinnati, Ohio, but distance and rough terrain guaranteed failure.*

4. *In Mexico, Veracruz and Acapulco were the unchallenged Atlantic and Pacific ports, respectively.*

5. *It should be pointed out that at least two twentieth-century authors, Adam Seybert and Alice Morse Earle, are of the opinion that poor road conditions in North America were overemphasized. They believed that conditions, at least in the East, were no worse than those in England. The fact remains that European travelers of the eighteenth and most of the nineteenth century, up to and including Charles Dickens, vigorously complained about deplorable travel conditions in North America.*

6. *Unlike most old trails, which became alignments for later roads or railroads, the Great Trail, as a whole, had been lost by the time of the American Revolution, although portions of it are believed to be followed by contemporary roads.*

7. *Most of "The King's Highway"—as El Camino Real translates into English—is followed by modern highways in both Mexico and the United States. In Texas, the OSR (Old San Antonio Road) is clearly marked to commemorate this important link, although recent evidence suggests that the actual "road" was little more than a constantly changing set of preferred paths.*

8. *U.S. 1 today follows part of this road.*

9. *As with most roads, this alignment was not completely new but was made up of newly blazed links between older trails. Cumberland Gap had for centuries been the Appalachian crossing for the Cherokee trail known as the Warrior's Path.*

10. *Hence its name from the town, not from the gap, through which it did not pass. The road connected at Cumberland to a privately built tollway which terminated at Baltimore, completing an inland to sea link favoring that port. The road was financed with 2 percent of the sale price of public lands in Ohio.*

11. *In the early 1950s George R. Stewart traveled the Route of U.S. 40 and published a photographic essay on the typical landscapes that he found along the route (U.S. 40; Cross Section of the United States, Boston: Houghton Mifflin, 1953). In the early 1980s Thomas and Geraldine Vale retraced Stewart's travels and photographed the same views to record landscape changes over the intervening years (U.S. 40 Today: Thirty Years of Landscape Change in America, Madison: University of Wisconsin Press, 1983). Among the more interesting views related to the original Cumberland Road were those of the 1830s tollhouse, now restored, near Uniontown, Pennsylvania. For comparative pre-1950 views of the road see The National Road, Robert Bruce, Washington, D.C.: National Highways Association, 1916.*

12. *The Atchison, Topeka, and Santa Fe Railroad now follows much of the trail's right-of-way.*

13. *A question often asked is "Why didn't they just use Lake Ontario and save a lot of work?" The author has never encountered a complete scholarly explanation for this, although one surely exists. Among the reasons for preferring an inland route even at greater cost would include that:*

> *Lake Ontario traffic would be exposed to British naval forces, which in the decade after the War of 1812 remained a concern.*
> *Traffic via the Great Lakes and St. Lawrence could bypass New York City.*
> *Need in northwest New York was for better transportation through the fertile Finger Lakes region, not along the lake shore.*
> *The Niagara escarpment was a major grade change between Lake Erie and Lake Ontario, which was not circumvented until the Welland Canal was begun in 1824, but that was in Canada.*
> *Travel on the lakes was more hazardous than on a canal because of winds and ice. Even modern ships have been lost to these threats, as Gordon Lightfoot commemorated in "The Wreck of the Edmund Fitzgerald."*

Of these five reasons, the best guess is that the desire to direct produce to New York City was the deciding factor in construction of the canal.

14. *Ironically, many politicians did not foresee this result, and all New York City representatives voted against the canal in the legislature. It passed due to upstate support and the wisdom of Governor DeWitt Clinton.*

15. *This figure is for the Erie itself, which in 1825 was the longest canal in the world. There are innumerable feeder canals (e.g., the Champlain and Genessee Valley) which branch from it, doubling the navigable distance.*

16. *See Chapter 5.*

17. *There is a third system, known as "block and lot," which applies to urban subdivision of land already recorded in a cadastral system of larger scale.*

18. *The Public Land Survey is variously named by different sources. It is often called the National Survey, the "symmetrical system," the "rectangular" or "grid" system, the "township and section system," or the "geometric system." Each of these appellations indicates some quality of the system.*

19. *Of course once the initial survey, recording, and occupation of land had been completed, the system used was virtually unchangeable. Thus in those areas first laid out by metes and bounds, that system continues in use today. In the United States, the original thirteen colonies, West Virginia, Vermont, Kentucky, Tennessee, eastern Georgia, eastern Texas, certain Spanish-settled areas along the Rio Grande in Texas and New Mexico, Spanish-settled California, the nonprairie provinces of Canada, and all of Mexico are recorded by this method.*

20. *The Virginia Military District or Reserve was the area of land which the state retained in 1784 when it ceded all of its western land claims to the U.S. federal government. The land was kept to be given in payment to Virginians for their military service during the Revolution.*

21. *Exceptions to the generally irregular parcel pattern created under metes and bounds surveys were long lots and several regular lot systems used in Ontario, such as the "single-front system."*

22. *In Canada known as the Dominion Land Survey, which was first established in 1869.*

23. *Such geometric systems were not invented in the New World. They are known to have been used in both ancient Rome and India. With renewed emphasis on regularity of planning in the Renaissance, forms of the system were revised. The first "modern" use of such a survey is considered to be Petts' mapping of Ireland in the seventeenth century.*

   Webster's essay was most concerned with the financial value of the lands. For example, he suggested that mineral rights be retained by the federal government. Among his suggestions later incorporated into law were survey prior to settlement, square townships arranged into tiers, and sale, rather than free grant, of land.

24. *In the at times confusing and always tedious chronology of laws dealing with the public lands and their recording, this statute is sometimes referred to as the Ordinance of 1784. This is due to the fact that requirements of the law were actually outlined in a committee report of that, earlier, year and the content of the statue passed in 1785 was largely a reaction to the report. No attempt will be made in this discussion of the Public Land Survey to deal with the complexity of issues and actions involved in establishing the system, as there is an extensive, if unexciting, literature which already does so. Among the classic works are Hibbard, 1924; Gates, 1968; Carstensen, 1963; and Treat, 1910. For detailed discussion of colonial traditions of tenure see Harris, 1953.*

25. *At the time of independence from Britain, seven of the thirteen colonies had claims to lands west of the Appalachians, many conflicting. In addition, all new states held land confiscated from Loyalists. After several years of debate leading to the Articles of Confederation, states ceded their western territory (with certain reservations such as the Western Reserve of Connecticut) and this territory became the first federal public lands. Later acquisitions came through purchase, such as the Louisiana Territory, or treaty, as did most of the southwestern United States ceded by Mexico in the Treaty of Guadalupe Hidalgo.*

26. *In western Canada, the principal meridians are located at regular intervals of 4 degrees.*

27. *The dimensions and sizes of townships and sections were not arbitrary, but based on surveying units of the day. A rod or pole was equal to 16½ feet. Four rods equaled a chain of 66 feet. Eighty chains (5280 feet) is 1 mile. This length of a mile had been established by decree by Queen Elizabeth in the sixteenth century to make the mile, originally a Roman unit of 5200 feet, compatible with the English distance unit the furlong (220 yards). The nesting of numbers is quite intriguing and could be carried further; 220 yards is 660 feet, which is 10 chains and so on. Of course, this would eventually bring us to human anatomy, from which the "foot" is derived.*

28. *Townships were designated by coordinates called "ranges," which are numbered east and west from the principal meridian, and "tiers," numbered north and south of base lines.*

29. *The reality of the public lands was that many sites, sometimes up to 25 percent of a given area, were occupied by squatters, i.e., preempted, before surveying had ever begun. The problems associated with disregarding these prior claims were more severe in terms of violence and lost time than was the process of recognizing the claims, but restructuring them within the geometry of the survey. Faragher's* Sugar Creek: Life on the Illinois Prairie *(1986) is an excellent discussion of this process at work. Squatters often formed claim clubs to give themselves the force of numbers when they opposed interloping, but legal, claimants who might seek to take the land they had preempted. See Blanchard (1882) for reminiscences about these clubs in Illinois.*

30. *Again this was the theory rather than actual practice since surveying errors could and did result in overlapping claims. A further complication arose when the survey was integrated with less precise mapping of natural features. The so-called Toledo War of 1835 was one large-scale example of this problem. See Saxbe, 1987.*

31. *Original perception of the prairies (used here to mean those landscapes having a plant association in which grasses and forbs are predominant and occurring most often on plains) is the topic of ongoing but as yet inconclusive research. To the authors' knowledge, there has been no complete comparative study of eighteenth- and nineteenth-century impressions, but* The Great Prairie Fact and Literary Imagination, *by Robert Thacker, (Albuquerque, NM: University of New Mexico Press, 1989) comes closest. Regional prairie studies do exist. (See Douglas R. McManis,* The Initial Evaluation and Utilization of the Illinois Prairie, 1815–1840, *Chicago: Department of Geography, University of Chicago, 1964, and David M. Emmons,* Garden in the Grasslands: Boomer Literature of the Central Great Plains, *Lincoln: University of Nebraska Press, 1971, as examples.) Although travel reports communicate both negative and positive opinions, from the readings of the author (possibly biased as a prairie lover) the positive outweighs the negative. (See Buckingham, 1842; Flint, 1826; and Birkbeck, 1818.)*

32. *Although strongly criticized in the 1960s and 1970s for lack of sensitivity to existing features whether natural or human-made, a flight over central Illinois reveals that interstate highways do in fact respond to some established patterns. What appear on the ground to be long straight lines connecting two points are in fact a series of tangents, many along section and township lines, connected by broad S curves.*

33. *In 1871 Henry George estimated that only about one-third of the remaining unclaimed public lands were in fact usable. His estimate, of course, failed to recognize the technological innovations, such as in irrigation and inorganic fertilization, that would allow some additional land to be productive.*

16

The Romantic Period

Deerslayer had not named the borders of the lake amiss. Along their whole length, the smaller trees overhung the water, with their branches often dipping in the transparent element. The banks were steep even from the narrow strand; and, as vegetation invariably struggles toward the light, the effect was precisely that at which the lover of the picturesque would have aimed, had the ordering of this glorious setting of the forest been submitted to his control.

James Fenimore Cooper, The Deerslayer

The impulse toward naturalistic design, which was tentatively expressed in the site plans of some of the great estates of the Early National Period, came to fruition in the 1830s and 1840s when the style of design known as Romantic swept across English-speaking North America. Several forces were at work to encourage the development of what became, within two decades, the accepted standard for designed landscapes. The influence of Romanticism as a philosophical system was, of course, one of the most critical factors, particularly as its ideals were expressed in the arts. Romantic literary works like the Hudson River tales of Washington Irving or the frontier adventures of Cooper's famous Leatherstocking character gave the public written images of idealized natural landscapes—natural compositions so splendid that, as Cooper said, "Salvator Rosa would have delighted to draw" them. At the same time, the Hudson River School of painting was emerging as the quintessential form of American art. Through the work of painters such as Thomas Cole, Asher B. Durand, Washington Allston, and later Frederick Church, the benevolent but awe-inspiring landscapes of North America became icons of natural beauty. As in Europe a century earlier, though, art did more to alter how people viewed the landscape than it did to display the realities of the environment.

Related to Romantic philosophy was the intellectual system and movement known as Transcendentalism. The Transcendentalists, who included Ralph Waldo Emerson and Henry David Thoreau, went beyond Romantic belief in the value of direct sensual experience to advocate the importance of supernaturally inspired human instincts. Although not a religion, Transcendentalism posited the inalienable value of both people and the natural world based on divine creation. Practically, Transcendentalists stressed immediate experience, simple living, social reform for greater egalitarianism, and, most significantly for this discussion, stewardship of the land and animal life.

Of course, the very appearance of the North American landscape, so broad in scale and often with few human intrusions, also inspired Americans to develop a naturalistic design approach. This was especially true since the natural landscape could itself be viewed as the ultimate form of "landscape gardening"—that is, the entire landscape could be treated as the entity to be designed, even if "design" was limited to enframing views of scenic natural features. At this point, at least in the eastern portions of the continent, landscape was no longer feared as it had

The North American landscape as idealized by Hudson River School painters; here, "Scene from 'The Last of the Mohicans,' Cora Kneeling at the Feet of Tamenund," by Thomas Cole, 1827. (Bequest of Alfred Smith, Wadsworth Atheneum, Hartford, Connecticut.)

been in colonial times. Allegorical associations became more positive, with beautiful natural scenery representing the idealism and promise of a new continent, and in the United States a new egalitarian, democratic government.

The final significant influence toward Romantic design was inspiration from England. The works of Repton, Price, and Chambers were required reading for all cultured New World residents, who although they may not always have been able to implement them, were conversant with the general principles of the Landscape Gardening and picturesque theories of design. In the 1830s John C. Loudon's works, advocating a seminaturalistic style which came to be known as the Gardenesque, also began to be widely read. Exposure to illustrated books and artistic prints, and travel to Europe, further helped popularize naturalism as the most appropriate form of expression in the designed landscape.

As these four influences, Romanticism in art, Transcendentalist philosophy, appreciation of native landscapes, and English design, were linked in the late 1820s and 1830s, Romantic-style designs began to influence many public, rather than merely a few private, properties. Of particular importance in the rapid popularization of this style was the spread of an improbable planned and designed landscape type—the Rural Romantic Cemetery.

RURAL ROMANTIC CEMETERIES

Rural Romantic Cemeteries were nineteenth-century innovation in city planning and in design. They were burial places that, unlike the typical churchyard of earlier times, were located outside developed urban areas, usually at a site with some distinguishing natural feature such as dramatic landform, existing woods or water features, or impressive distant views. In addition to this distinctive siting, most cemeteries were designed in naturalistic styles derived from the English Landscape Gardening precedent. Although most mid- to late nineteenth-century cemeteries combined the planning concept of extramural burial with the design concept of naturalistic arrangement, each of these concepts developed from different sources and did at times operate independently.

The notion of burial outside city limits, in what were then rural areas, was advanced primarily as a result of health concerns associated with the typical early American practice of interment in cramped in-town graveyards, usually associated with churches. Since space was limited, burials were often very close together, several deep in each grave, and shallow. One graphic description of a churchyard will serve to illustrate the conditions that drove those concerned with public health to develop an alternative to urban burial: ". . . the graveyard of Trinity Church [was], saturated with dissolved semi-liquid human flesh, oozing from every pore, and the incumbent atmosphere filled with noxious effluvia, concurring with the air of the city . . ." (Coffin, pp. 20–21). Physicians believed that such conditions contaminated the air, causing illness and death. It was not until later in the century that the more critical problems of water contamination and contagion through animal contact were understood. The first urban cemetery in North America to utilize the city planning concept of extramural burial was New Haven, Connecticut. In 1797 that city developed what was called the New Burying Ground north of the city. Although the plan was in a grid form, just as older burial plans had been, it differed from those in having lanes wide enough to accommodate vehicles and in having some ornamental plantings. In addition to these design features, it presaged nineteenth-century practices in being private, nonsectarian, and with plots large enough for extended families. Why no other city adopted the New Haven model in the early nineteenth century is unclear, but the fact that none did certainly suggests just how revolutionary these changes really were.

It was not until the 1830s that the planning idea of rural locations for cemeteries came together with the design idea of naturalistic landscapes to create the pastoral image most often associated with "Rural Cemeteries." In 1831 Mount Auburn Cemetery in Cambridge, Massachusetts, the first Rural Cemetery in Romantic style, was consecrated. Mount Auburn's design became both the prototype for and the instigator of a boom in cemetery development that continued into the 1880s.

As early as 1825, physician Jacob Bigelow had attempted to interest Bostonians in a new, rural cemetery for the city, but the project did not get beyond the discussion stage until his efforts were joined with those of the newly formed Massachusetts Horticultural Society, which hoped to establish an arboretum. Although their joint effort was short-lived, it provided promoters of the cemetery resources to secure a picturesque, hilly, wooded site overlooking the Charles River and to design for this ideal location an equally appealing site plan.

Although Dr. Bigelow was the driving force behind development of Mount Auburn, its design was left to others: War of 1812 general and Massachusetts Horticultural Society president Henry A. S. Dearborn and local civil engineer Alexander Wadsworth.[1] Their plan for Mount Auburn was composed of sinuous roads fitted to the landform, plantings to increase its beauty, small ponds, pavilions, and sites for ornamental tombs. Distinctive natural areas were given descriptive names such as Laurel Hill and The Dell, while paths and roads were named after plants.

Design features such as plantings were believed to have some role in creating a healthful burial place, but their principal function was as a cultural expression of changing social and psychological values. The cemetery functioned as a social statement of family status, the value of the individual, and greater national and individual wealth. Its symbolic connotations were even more significant, expressing in physical form what Linden (1981) has termed "the cult of the melancholy"—that is, a pensive, reflective attitude both toward death and those who have died, commemorated through a sentimental attachment to the outward manifestations of death and its symbols. Among the expressions of this attitude

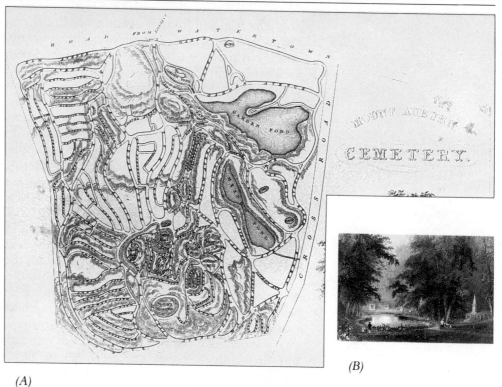

Plan of Mount Auburn Cemetery (A) Cambridge, Massachusetts, 1836, designed by H. A. S. Dearborn and Alexander Wadsworth. Inset (B) shows Forest Pond constructed in a natural site depression. (Engraving by James Smillie, in Walter, 1847.)

(A)

(B)

were the use of weeping trees, particularly the willow, in the cemetery and on gravemarkers; the addition of "ruins" to cemeteries as sites for reflection; and elaborate customs of mourning dress.[2]

So immediate was the popularity of Mount Auburn that within seven years each of the other major cities in the United States—New York, Philadelphia, and Baltimore—had established a similar cemetery, and even Rochester, New York, then still a relatively small city, had established Mt. Hope Cemetery. Mount Auburn's first successor, in 1836, was Laurel Hill Cemetery in Philadelphia, located on a high bank above the Schuylkill River.[3] The Philadelphia cemetery's site plan, by local architect John Notman, differed from that of Mount Auburn in being generally more patterned and having smaller sections. Its composition also relied more on a series of sculptural focal points rather than solely on a naturalistic planting design. Upon entering the classical gateway, there was a sculpted, Gothic grotto enclosing the allegorical figures of "Old Mortality" discoursing with Sir Walter Scott.[4] Above this, at the center of a series of concentric circular paths, a small open area was preserved for a monument. Still farther up the hill and overlooking the river, an oval area in front of the preexisting house provided a site for another commemorative sculpture. The most beautiful area of the cemetery, though, was the bank sloping toward the Schuylkill. There, at the western edge of the plateau, Notman laid out a gently crescent-shaped road below, with parallel crescent tiers for graves. The terracing of these graves allowed each plot to have an unimpeded view of the river valley.

Two years after Laurel Hill was established, the New York City area acquired what would become the first of its many Rural Cemeteries when Greenwood Cemetery was established in the then independent city of Brooklyn. Many considered Greenwood's site to be the most impressive of any early Rural Cemetery. At almost 180 acres it was certainly the largest. That area was comprised of varied landforms, but most of the site was quite hilly and it included the highest point in Brooklyn, from which there were impressive views of the ocean.

View of Mount Auburn in the 1980s looking across Garden Pond.

Greenwood's picturesque, rambling plan was designed by cemetery association president and civil engineer David Bates Douglass. Also in 1838, Baltimore established Green Mount Cemetery, designed by a local architect.[5] Green Mount, although quite hilly, is much more rolling in character than its three contemporaneous cemeteries, a natural characteristic that is reflected in the broad, sweeping curves of its roads. Its most impressive feature was the siting of the Gothic-style chapel, whose spire rose to over 100 feet above the ground, on the highest point of the site.

From this discussion of some of the more famous early Rural Cemeteries it is obvious that, although similar in being naturalistic, their designs do differ in character. In general, nineteenth-century Rural Cemeteries in the Romantic style had four different design characters. Some had a rugged, rustic character which might be described as "picturesque"; Mount Auburn and Greenwood, principally because of their topography, were of this type. Others, such as Green Mount, were much more regular and graceful, following what was termed the "beautiful" aesthetic. A third group, less naturalistic than either the picturesque or beautiful cemeteries, were those like Laurel Hill that introduced regular geometric forms such as ovals and circles into the plan, creating areas of some formality. In the better of these designs, the geometric forms related to landform and thus did not detract from the naturalism. Others, probably not the work of professional designers, used geometric forms as arbitrarily as frontier town planners used the grid, creating designs which mimic Romantic design rather than following its spirit. The final variety of Rural Cemetery was termed the "lawn cemetery" for its emphasis on sweeping, manicured ground planes unbroken by the numerous individual monuments and plot enclosures that were common in the nineteenth century.

The lawn cemetery was a design variation first introduced by Adolph Strauch in his plan for Spring Grove Cemetery in Cincinnati, Ohio. The story of Spring Grove is itself interesting because of the number of prominent designers who worked there, the changes that the design underwent as tastes changed, and because its design was the most highly regarded cemetery design west of the

Appalachians. The original design was prepared in 1845 by John Notman. At least part of this plan—which, based on later criticism, must have had many roads and very small sections for plots—was laid out, but proved unsuited to the topography and too costly. Howard Daniels, trained as an architect but whose largest body of known works is in landscape architecture, was then hired to redo much of the plan and prepare drawings for additional areas. Daniels's plan, located in what is now the center of the cemetery, was distinguished by irregularly curving, almost jagged roads that formed a dense network dividing the grounds into small sections. The roads and smaller paths were generally well adapted to the landform. Naturalistic plantings in areas not assigned to graves completed the design. Although cemetery visitors found the site quite beautiful, perhaps because there was little to compare it with in that area, the proprietors readily accepted the changes proposed by the third designer of Spring Grove, Adolph Strauch.

Strauch, newly arrived from Europe, was a landscape gardener in the European tradition, having worked under Prince Pückler-Muskau at his famous estate in Silesia, Germany. Strauch was obviously skilled in design, horticulture, and technical aspects of site development. His personal view of cemetery design was that "good taste would seem to suggest that a rural Cemetery should partake more of the character of a cheerful park or garden . . ." (Strauch, 1857, p. 31). Although he saw some merits in the design of older portions of Spring Grove, he encouraged the directors to do away with the fencing of graves and plots and to allow only one above-grade grave marker per plot.[6] His purpose in these suggestions was to open up views through the cemetery and emphasize landscape rather than sculpted beauty. Strauch's site plan also differed from the earlier one by Daniels in having fewer roads, with the ones there were laid out on broad, graceful curves, and in being graded to a more gently rolling character. He also created more scenic areas by transforming small wetlands into ornamental ponds.

View of Spring Grove Cemetery in the 1980s.

Although the contrast between the older, Daniels-designed sections and those by Strauch are apparent, there is no glaring dissimilarity, since design differences appear to have been based on some natural differences in landform.

Strauch's concept of open, rolling cemetery grounds—called the "landscape lawn plan"—became the stylish approach to cemetery design after 1855. Strauch himself became the most sought after designer of cemeteries, producing plans for, among others, Forest Lawn Cemetery in Buffalo, New York; Highland Park Cemetery in Fort Mitchell, Kentucky; and Oak Woods Cemetery in Chicago, Illinois. His specialization in cemetery design did not keep him from developing a complete landscape architectural practice, with most of his projects being in the Cincinnati area. He completed site designs for many large estates including Mount Storm and the A. D. Bullock Estate, site plans for subdivisions including Blachly Farm, and the original design of Eden Park on the bluffs above the Ohio River.

Although the earliest Rural Romantic Cemeteries, such as Père Lachaise outside Paris and Kensel Green in London, were established in Europe, they were relatively few in total number and were rarely popular outside urban areas. In North America, on the other hand, Rural Cemeteries became a ubiquitous site type, required of every city or town which sought to be urbane. Writing in 1846, John Jay Smith commented that, "as so often happens, the Americans have decidedly improved on European plans for rural cemeteries; better sites have been usually selected on this side of the water than abroad; more attention to planting and to detail will be observed among us . . ." (p. 5). Rural Cemetery design became a mainstay for landscape architects into the 1880s, when a decline in Rural Cemetery development occurred.[7]

THE ROLE OF ROMANTIC PERIOD HORTICULTURISTS

It was not accidental that Mount Auburn started out as a joint effort of urban reformers and horticulturists, for the early decades of the nineteenth century were a period of great interest and activity in horticulture. Prior to the 1820s, most nurseries had focused on the scientific aspects of horticulture, with little emphasis on design uses of plants. John Bartram's tree rows or André Michaux's rectangular garden in New Jersey were good examples of this approach. As the century progressed, more European horticulturists arrived in North America armed with knowledge of the Landscape Gardening and picturesque styles, having seem them applied to designs for estates and arboretums. From that point on, these progressive horticulturists and nursery professionals advanced naturalistic approaches to design.

One of the first horticulturists of this type was André Parmentier, a Belgian who opened a nursery in Brooklyn, New York, not far from the present location of Prospect Park, in 1828. Although the plan of his property does not appear remarkable to the modern eye, it was one of the first, if not the first, establishments in America to combine a functional, commercial nursery with ornamental areas intended to illustrate how plants might be used in design. To the south and west were geometrically arranged sections with stock, primarily fruit trees, growing in rows. The northern, residential part of the site was more scenic, with meandering paths and focal structures such as the rustic arbor, "in a grotesque style, constructed of crooked limbs of trees in their rough state, covered with bark and moss" (J. W. S., 1832, p. 72).[8] Parmentier's design skills were well regarded by his contemporaries, and he was commissioned to develop plans for a number of estates from Canada to the southern United States, most of which are no longer known by name. Dr. David Hosack, founder of the Elgin Botanical Garden, who had sought Parmentier as the Garden's superintendent, engaged him instead to complete a design for his Hudson River estate, Hyde Park.

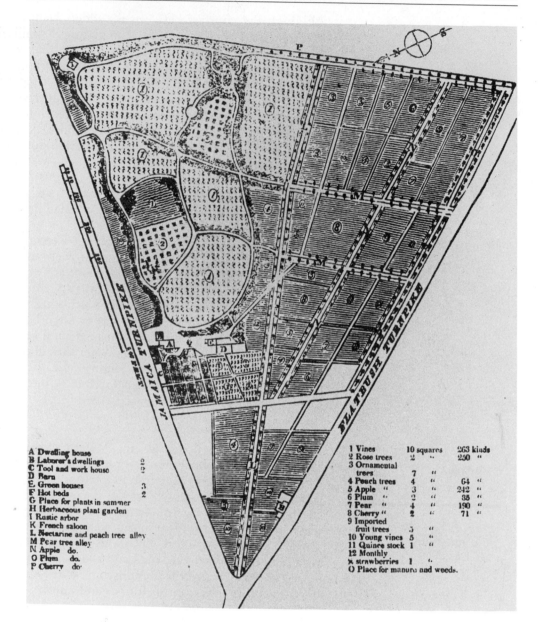

Plan of André Parmentier's Horticultural Garden showing curvilinear Romantic-style paths in the northeastern section. The Romantic theme was carried out further through siting of special features such as the "rustic arbor" at the northeast-most corner (letter I in plan) and the "French saloon" slightly south of that (letter K). (Landscape Architecture, Vol. 39, No. 4.)

A Dwelling house
B Laborer's dwellings
C Tool and work house
D Barn
E Green houses
F Hot beds
G Place for plants in summer
H Herbaceous plant garden
I Rustic arbor
K French saloon
L Nectarine and peach tree alley
M Pear tree alley
N Apple   do.
O Plum   do.
P Cherry   do.

1 Vines	10 squares	263 kinds
2 Rose trees	2 "	250 "
3 Ornamental trees	7 "	
4 Peach trees	4 "	64 "
5 Apple "	3 "	242 "
6 Plum "	2 "	35 "
7 Pear "	4 "	190 "
8 Cherry "	2 "	71 "
9 Imported fruit trees	5 "	
10 Young vines	5 "	
11 Quince stock	1 "	
12 Monthly strawberries	1 "	
O Place for manure and weeds.		

Andrew Jackson Downing called this "one of the finest specimens of the modern style of Landscape Gardening in America," and several authors commented on the way its composition emphasized distant views (1875, p. 29).

Later, even more comprehensive and design-oriented nurseries were developed. Among these was the Mount Hope Gardens and Nursery of Rochester, New York, a precursor of the modern full-service professional horticultural establishment. Founded in 1840 by George Ellwanger and Patrick Barry, the nursery grew over the next three decades from a mere 7 acres to 650 acres, with branches in Canada and Ohio. During this period of growth, the firm provided important services to the western states, supplying newly established farms and towns with a variety of useful and ornamental plants. In addition, the nursery and its owners were active in promoting both quality design and urban improvement. When their grounds were enlarged, they developed a Romantic-style entry garden of diverse tree species set out in a lawn with Gardensque-style flower beds. It was their intention to both illustrate what mature plants looked like and how their customers might design their own grounds. In addition to this display, they advertised that they would design grounds and supply gardeners to care for them.

Ellwanger and Barry were very active in larger-scale projects to improve the quality of life in Rochester. In 1856 they began development of several suburban subdivisions near the nursery, most now in the Mt. Hope–Highland Park Historical District of Rochester. Although these subdivisions did not have the curvilinear street pattern associated with suburbs designed in the Romantic style, they did have large lots, often planted by the nursery in naturalistic designs. Two other important civic projects with which Ellwanger and Barry became involved were Mt. Hope Cemetery, which adjoined their nursery, and Highland Park. Mt. Hope, the first Rural Cemetery established by a municipality rather than by a private association, was improved in the 1840s and 1850s by Ellwanger and Barry through donations of rare plants, which today give the cemetery an arboretum-like character. Later, in the 1880s, the partners donated the 20 acres which became the nucleus of Highland Park, designed by Frederick Law Olmsted.

Although many eastern nurseries became promoters of naturalistic design in the early and mid-nineteenth century, most North American horticulturists remained concerned with plant introductions into new areas rather than their visual use. In the West (at that time, the West meant everything west of the Appalachians), the critical problem was merely to determine what would grow in newly settled soil and climate areas. Pioneer western horticulturists such as John Kennicott of Illinois, Jacob Smith of Arkansas, and Thomas Affleck of Mississippi and Texas, focused on propagation of useful plants such as grapes and fruits. What ornamentals they cultivated were hardy plants, proven under harsh conditions, such as old roses and native trees. Their services did affect design, though, simply by making available a wide selection of plants and encouraging the public to experiment with new introductions.

In these frontier areas, what ornamental planting areas did exist were usually confined to areas adjacent to houses. Following the colonial New England model, dooryard gardens became a practical way to introduce flowers and other tender plants into landscapes largely given over to food production. Unlike the colonial examples though, these yards often were quite large, approximating the modern quarter-acre lot in size. The additional space allowed these yards to be planted with trees and shrubs, as well as annuals, perennials, and food plants. In many cases these nineteenth-century dooryard gardens, which were especially popular in the midwestern part of the continent, differed from modern front yards only in having denser plantings of more species and in being enclosed by fences.

In the South, a distinctive treatment of grounds around houses, the sweep yard, was common. Here the fenced yard around the house was kept devoid of any vegetation by annual hoeing and weekly sweeping with a stiff broom. With herbaceous plants excluded, the main visual features of the yard became large trees that shaded the house. The popularity of sweep yards in the South was usually attributed to practical concerns, such as removal of habitat for snakes and rodents or the fact that grasses in work areas became trampled.

Exceptions to these rather stark sweep gardens did of course exist, and Romantic designs were created in the South, as well as elsewhere. One of the most famous gardens, noted for its great horticultural variety, was the estate known as Magnolia Gardens, near Charleston, South Carolina. Begun as a plantation in the seventeenth century, extensive naturalistic gardens were developed there in the 1840s. These combined existing wetlands and vegetation, such as palmetto and bald cypress, with ornamental features, like bridges and pavilions, and introduced species, most obviously azaleas and nonnative rhododendrons, to create a colorful woodland garden for strolling.

Of all nineteenth-century horticulturists, one proved to have the most pivotal impact on the development of landscape architecture—Andrew Jackson Downing. Downing was born to a family in the nursery business in Newburgh, New York, on the Hudson River. When his father died, Andrew and his brother George inherited this business, although they did not truly become partners until later when Andrew turned sixteen. Their nursery became nationally known for production of fruit and ornamental trees. Like Ellwanger and Barry, the Downings developed the grounds of their home and nursery as a display garden and arboretum. A description from 1836 suggests the design of the grounds: "In the lower parts of the grounds we observed an extensive walk just formed, exhibiting a complete botanical circuit of plants, arranged in a scientific manner [that is, by Linnean classification]—a rockwork for alpine plants, and a pond for aquarian, in which the water-lilies and a number of other aquatic plants were thriving admirably (quoted in Tatum, 1949, p. 41). Perhaps it was from this experience, or from visits to the homes of his wealthy and design-sophisticated clients, that Downing acquired an interest and skill in landscape design. Through whatever combination of circumstances, by the early 1840s he was considered the premier authority on what was termed "tasteful" design in both architecture and landscape architecture.

ANDREW JACKSON DOWNING AND THE DEVELOPMENT OF LANDSCAPE GARDENING IN NORTH AMERICA

Although Andrew Jackson Downing is best known today for his role in the development of landscape architecture in North America, his life's work actually focused on three related areas: horticulture, architectural design, and landscape architecture. Beyond the nursery business, his reputation in horticulture rested on two technical publications, *Fruit and Fruit Trees of America,*[9] which he authored, and *Theory of Horticulture,* which he edited with Asa Gray. He was also founding editor of the very influential periodical *The Horticulturist, and Journal of Rural Art and Rural Taste,* first published in 1846.[10] In addition, Downing wrote extensively on architectural design, particularly that of residences. He helped to popularize revival of historical styles other than the Classical, which he felt was inappropriate for American homes. His two books on architecture, *Cottage Residences* and *The Architecture of Country Houses,* were pattern books much like others of the period.[11] Downing likely designed some of the structures which he illustrated, but he relied primarily on the work of professional architects, notably Alexander J. Davis, John Notman, and after 1850 when Downing employed him, English architect Calvert Vaux, as examples for readers. Although many buildings in the eastern United States are conjectured to have been designed by Downing, only a few have actually been documented. Far more buildings were inspired by those which were illustrated in his books than he actually designed.

His works in horticulture and architecture alone would have assured Downing some recognition in the history of American design, but his real contribution, beyond that which any other individual of the period made, was toward establishing landscape gardening, as this rudimentary practice of landscape architecture was then called, as an acknowledged and respected discipline built on a body of theoretical and practical knowledge. Although Downing only wrote one book on this subject, it proved through its ten nineteenth-century editions and numerous reprints to be one of the most influential written works of the century. He entitled this book *A Treatise on the Theory and Practice of Landscape Gardening,* with the subtitle "Adapted to North America; with a View to the Improvement of Country Residences."

A Treatise on the Theory and Practice of Landscape Gardening precisely fulfilled what the title identified as its mission. It was an explanation of the naturalistic Landscape Gardening style as combined with the picturesque, revised and explained for American environments and residents, particularly those of the middle class with rural homes. In his own time and since, Downing has been disparaged because the book reiterated so much from English sources. This criticism is unfair since only a few eighteenth-century writers such as Pope, Repton, and Price really said anything original about the style, and all later writers built on their publications. In addition, Downing clearly acknowledged both in the title and in the text that his work was not novel except in that it addressed American concerns directly. He freely admitted his reliance on the publications of his English contemporary J. C. Loudon, by referring to them and quoting often from them. Such negative views cover up the significant contributions that Downing did make. Perhaps most important was the very lucid way he explained the somewhat convoluted theoretical premises of landscape gardening, and put principles into understandable, practical form. While his work is not easy for the modern reader, it was a model of clarity compared to earlier or contemporaneous works. Second, just as he promised, Downing interpreted landscape gardening for New World audiences. This was most obvious in his discussion of plants, but also affected the discussion of design issues, where he made two contributions. First, he concluded that the two types of naturalistic design over which Repton and Price had exchanged such acrimonious correspondence were really not opposites which could not occur at the same site, but were points along a visual continuum from the simplified naturalism of "beautiful" landscapes to the more realistic naturalism of the "picturesque." Second, he emphasized the importance of the purposeful design of sites to enframe distant views of majestic American landscapes and thus made them a part of the designed composition. These two design ideas, the relatedness of the beautiful and picturesque and the desirability of capturing distant views, were linked when Downing inferred that the beautiful was more appropriate to the developed part of the grounds near the main building, while the picturesque could provide a transition to the natural landscape.

A Treatise on the Theory and Practice of Landscape Gardening became a text which influenced at least four decades of landscape architects, as well as defined the basic principles of the Romantic style of design. The book had three major parts, each related to one of Downing's areas of interest, and beginning with a general history of garden design. His objective in this first part was to differentiate modern naturalistic styles from the ancient or geometric styles. The section on landscape design then continued with a detailed exposition of the beautiful[12] and picturesque aesthetics in landscape architecture. An extensive descriptive catalogue of trees suitable for American, or at least eastern, conditions rounded out the horticultural discussion. The last portion of the book dealt with architecture and other construction-related aspects of site planning, including the laying out of circulation systems and introduction of water features.

It was Downing's explanation of the aesthetic underpinnings of landscape gardening which makes this work particularly significant. Although he did not discuss the sublime in landscape,[13] perhaps realizing that it was virtually impossible to design these awe-inspiring scenes, he explained the use of beautiful and picturesque aesthetics to achieve the "harmonious, and refined imitation" of nature which was "landscaping gardening": "The Beautiful is an idea of beauty, calmly and harmoniously expressed; the Picturesque, an idea of beauty or power, strongly and irregularly expressed" (Downing, 1875, p. 54). These rather vague notions were made clearer when Downing discussed how they were to be applied to physical design:

(A)

(B)

Downing's illustrations of (A) the "beautiful" and (B) the "picturesque" aesthetic as applied to landscape design. In the "beautiful" trees are rounded, the ground plane smooth and flowing, and built elements are classical, while in the "picturesque" trees are irregular, often grotesquely shaped, the ground plane rough and rocky, and built elements Gothic in style. (Downing, 1875.)

The Beautiful in Landscape Gardening is produced by outlines whose curves are flowing and gradual, . . . in the shape of the ground, it is evinced by easy undulations melting gradually into each other. In the form of trees, by smooth stems, full, round, or symmetrical heads of foliage, and luxuriant branches. . . . In walks and roads, by easy flowing curves, following natural shapes of surface, with no sharp angles or abrupt turns. . . . The Picturesque in Landscape Gardening aims at the production of outlines of a certain spirited irregularity, surfaces comparatively abrupt and broken, and growth of a somewhat wild and bold character. The shape of the ground sought after, has its occasional smoothness varied by sudden variations, and in parts runs into dingles, rocky groups, and broken banks. The trees should in many places be old and irregular, with rough stems and bark. . . . (Downing, 1875, pp. 58–59)

Thus the beautiful was an idealized version of natural scenery in which visual complexity was simplified, while the picturesque attempted to symbolize the complexity and irregularity found in natural landscapes.

Downing did more than merely articulate the design ideals of the Romantic period. He also was one of the earliest practitioners of landscape architecture, although few works remain to illustrate how he applied the principles set forth in his books. One contemporary, author George W. Curtis, considered Downing's home, Highland Gardens at Newburgh, New York, to be "his finest work." Unfortunately now demolished, the home and grounds together were a masterpiece of compact Romantic design. On about 4 acres Downing constructed a residence in the Elizabethan Gothic style, laid out a pleasure ground of about 2 acres, and still maintained an orchard and vineyard. In commenting on the most successful features on the plan, Curtis noted that, "so skillfully were the trees

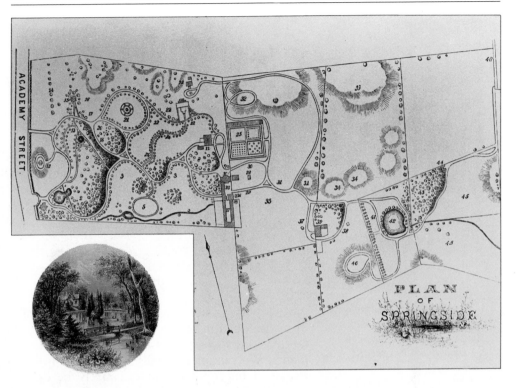

Plan of Springside, the estate of Matthew Vassar designed by Andrew Jackson Downing with Calvert Vaux as assistant. The house grounds are in the western block, with meandering roads and dense tree plantings. Inset view of the pond near the entry looking across to the Gothic cottage designed by Downing. (Lossing, 1867, pp. 62 and 65.)

arranged, that all suspicion of [nearby] town or road was removed." Downing had also enframed distant views to enlarge the grounds so well that "you fancied the estate extended to the [Hudson] river; yes, and probably owned the river as an ornament, and included the mountains beyond" (1853, p. xxxii).[14]

Downing's design for Springside, the estate of Matthew Vassar, who later founded the college which bears his name, is particularly important as the only well-documented project by Downing which remains in a preserved condition. In addition, it was a site on which he designed both the landscape and the structures, so it yields an idea of how he envisioned the relationship between buildings and their setting. Work on Springside was begun in 1850 after Vassar secured the site for an association interested in establishing it as a Rural Cemetery. When the cemetery did not materialize, Vassar developed the property as a country home and *ferme ornée*. The western, ornamental portion of the grounds had a plan which indicated its origins as a cemetery design, with a series of intertwined roads and paths separating the grounds into smaller sections. But the scheme, certainly modified to accommodate residential use, worked well by providing an extended scenic drive for visitors to the house. Downing based his plan on the site's rolling topography, preserving hilltop vegetation and locating roads in depressions that emphasized some of the dramatic rock outcrops on the property. Within this basic framework, quaint features and eclectic structures were sited, including a small pond near the site entry and a Gothic-style cottage. From the limited number of contemporaneous views of the site, it appears to have had both beautiful and picturesque characteristics. The picturesque characteristics were used to emphasize on-site views, particularly those of vistas toward the principal structures. One glaring abnormality, visible both in contemporaneous depictions and in an 1860s site plan, was the lining of roads with rows of what appear to be needle-leaf evergreens. Although Downing endorsed the use of street trees on public roads, none of his book illustrations show such a treatment on a private estate, suggesting that this feature might have been a holdover from the cemetery scheme or that it was added after his death.[15]

(A)

(B)

View of Sunnyside, Tarrytown, New York, the home of author Washington Irving. Although the designer of this estate is unknown, it was known to Downing who had certainly visited it. (A) As restored, the grounds of Sunnyside are one of the most accurate Romantic landscapes, replicating nineteenth-century views (B). (Nineteenth-century view from Harper's New Monthly Magazine, *1856, Vol. 14, No. 79.)*

Downing's involvement at Springside was one of the rare known examples of his production of a complete design. More typically, he worked as a consultant, visiting the site occasionally, making suggestions, and often supplying some plants. We cannot generally assign him full credit for these designs, since the extent of his involvement can rarely be documented. For Montgomery Place near Rhinebeck, New York, there remains substantial evidence of his design counsel in letters to its owners, the Bartons. Many of these letters are in the form of encouragement for certain proposed activities, such as construction of an arboretum, while others offer directions for solving particular design problems. This correspondence served to keep Downing informed of activities at the estate between his numerous social calls there. While visiting, he certainly gave other advice to the Bartons and may have paced off some plan improvements on the grounds. Some other properties at which Downing is known to have consulted are Wodenthe, the home of horticulturist Henry Winthrop Sargent; Blithewood on the Hudson River, which he considered a particularly well-done example of the combination of the beautiful with the picturesque; and the Fisher residence in Jenkinstown, Pennsylvania.

Although most of his work was at residential scale, Downing did complete plans for several public projects, most of which were not constructed according to his schemes. The most famous of these public projects—the Mall and White House in Washington, D.C.—was his final undertaking in several senses, for in 1852, while embarking on a trip to visit this site Downing drowned.[16] The Mall was Downing's largest project and one that was in fact a precursor to the parks movement which was shortly to commence with the establishment of Central Park in New York. For the Mall, Downing envisioned a radically different appearance than had Pierre L'Enfant, its original planner. Rather than a formal sight line across the governmental area of the city, the Mall was to be transformed into a national park which would demonstrate the Landscape Gardening style of design and also be an arboretum. To achieve these ends, he proposed creation of five separate, but adjacent, parks within the Mall. One was to be an Evergreen Garden to display needle and broadleaf evergreens, which would remain interesting during the winter. Another park would display a variety of water features, while a third would be the Botanic Garden. In spite of the rather eclectic nature of the proposed scheme, Downing's plan might have been successful were it not for this unfortunate placement of the Evergreen Garden toward the center of the Mall. This garden was to occupy over half the width of the Mall, with dense plantings organized along concentric oval paths. Had it been smaller or located elsewhere, the meandering open areas which flowed through the length of the Mall might have preserved a hint of the sight line originally planned by L'Enfant.

As part of the plan for the Mall, Downing also completed designs for the grounds of the White House. These contrasted quite sharply with those for the Mall, in the regularity of forms used. To the south of the residence, facing the proposed Washington Monument, he intended to keep a large area "open as a place for parade or military reviews, as well as public festivals or celebrations. A circular carriage drive, 40 feet wide and nearly a mile long shaded by an avenue of elms, surrounds the Parade, while a series of foot paths, 10 feet wide, winding through thickets of trees and shrubs, forms the boundary to this park, and could make an agreeable shaded promenade for pedestrians" (Downing, 1851, p. 2). Downing's interest in the design of streetscapes was reflected in his proposal for an arch, perhaps modeled after the Arc de Triomphe in Paris, at the terminus of Pennsylvania Avenue, as an entry to what he called the President's Park at the White House.

With Downing's death, though, his plans also died. John Saul, who had earlier purchased his nursery, continued as site superintendent, developing a naturalistic plan but one which differed significantly from that proposed by Downing.[17] Among Downing's other public or semipublic projects were a plan for the Cemetery of the Evergreens in Brooklyn, New York; for mental hospitals at Utica, New York, and Trenton, New Jersey; and for a Public Garden and Arboretum in Boston.

Downing's influence and writings created an atmosphere during the late 1840s and 1850s that allowed a diverse group of professionals to establish practices in landscape gardening. Although we will never know the names of all those who practiced landscape architecture during this pioneering period, the achievements of four significant individuals should be noted. These are John Notman, Howard Daniels, Robert Morris Copeland, and Horace W. S. Cleveland.

John Notman was one of the large number of practitioners whose customary work was as architects, but who also developed an interest and expertise in landscape planning and design. Following the notoriety of his design for Laurel Hill Cemetery, Notman was engaged to produce several other cemetery plans, including those for Spring Hill Cemetery in Lynchburg, Virginia, and Hollywood Cemetery in Richmond, Virginia, both of which were far more successful Romantic designs than was Laurel Hill. Following the Downing pattern of designing both house and grounds, Notman completed comprehensive plans for many estates. One example is Riverside in Burlington, New Jersey. In plan view, this work was typical of many Romantic designs of the period, with an irregularly elliptical entry drive enclosing a large open lawn area with treed areas to the outside of the drive. For other clients Notman completed only the architectural or landscape design. At the A. D. Bullock Residence near Cincinnati, he designed the house, while Strauch was commissioned for the grounds. At Mt. Holly near Camden, New Jersey, he designed only the grounds of an existing cottage.

Notman's major commission, aside from those at cemeteries, was for design of the grounds of the Virginia Capitol in Richmond. His naturalistic design replaced work previously done on a more formal plan by French architect Maximilian Godefroy. Notman did maintain some sense of symmetricality by placing tiered cast iron fountains surrounded by a low circular cast iron fence on either side of the Capitol building, but at some distance from it. Paths, although curving, did not meander. It was the planting design, particularly groves of trees, which gave the site a Romantic character.

Howard Daniels also started professional life as an architect, but there are

View in Hollywood Cemetery, Richmond, Virginia, designed by John Notman in 1848. The pond in the foreground was a typical design feature of many Rural Romantic Cemeteries although most of the ponds were constructed without the hard edge shown here.

few buildings for which he is recorded as designer. His known professional work focused on landscape architectural projects, primarily cemeteries. By 1855 he claimed to have designed fifteen cemeteries, one of which would have been Spring Grove. Other cemeteries which he is known to have worked on include Brookside in Watertown, New York; Green Lawn in Columbus, Ohio; and Oakwood in Syracuse, New York—the last being his masterwork in cemetery design. Daniels's cemetery plans differ from many others in the Romantic style by incorporating a large number of geometric forms, either circles or half circles. This practice probably facilitated the subdivision of sections into plots, and most of the geometric forms would not have been obvious at eye level when obscured by irregular tree and shrub plantings.

Daniels's most famous work, now undergoing restoration, was Druid Hill Park in Baltimore, begun in 1860. On the site of an old estate whose existing mature trees he greatly admired, Daniels adapted roads to the rolling landform while assuring that they were well constructed to withstand soil moisture. In reports to the Park Commission he sounded like a very practical and thrifty designer, first establishing a nursery at the site to cultivate seedlings and then selling trees that he had removed for road construction. Ponds, rustic structures, and a conservatory completed the Romantic landscape of Druid Hill Park.

Robert Morris Copeland was one of the few university-trained early landscape architects, but his education was in liberal arts rather than a design field. After graduation from Harvard he practiced what was known as "scientific farming," and then set himself up in practice as a landscape gardener serving primarily the Boston area. In 1854 Horace W. S. Cleveland sold his scientific farm, Oatlands, in Burlington, New Jersey, and returned to Massachusetts as Copeland's partner. During the next three years, their firm completed a series of plans for Rural Cemeteries in small towns around Boston. All these schemes were distinctive in that adaptation of roadways and lot sections to landform was the controlling design concept. Roads look as though they could logically go nowhere else.

Two of their more interesting designs were those at Sleepy Hollow Cemetery in Concord and Oak Grove in Gloucester, Massachusetts. Sleepy Hollow,

Plan of Brookside Cemetery, Watertown, New York, by Howard Daniels, 1854. This plan shows the circular geometry typical of some cemetery plans by both Daniels and Notman. Contrast this to the less regular forms more directly based upon topography in Figure 16–12. (Cornell University Library, Ithaca, New York.)

View of Boat Lake in Druid Hill Park, Baltimore, Maryland, designed by Howard Daniels in 1860.

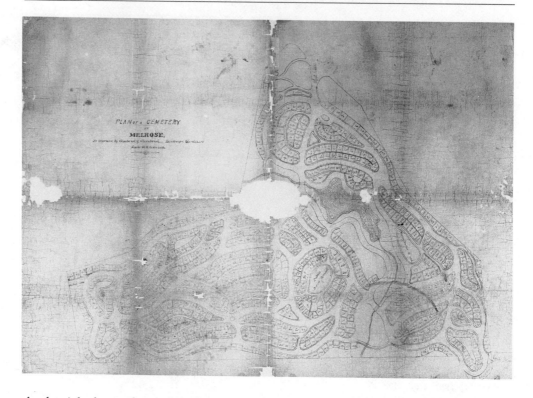

Plan of Wyoming Cemetery, Melrose, Massachusetts, 1856, by Robert Morris Copeland and H. W. S. Cleveland. Plan is typical of the work of this partnership, in that topography was the principal inspiration for site plans. Here the more regular, dispersed roads occupied a flat area, while the curving, dense road network was in a hilly section of the site. (Melrose Public Library Historical Collection.)

the burial place of noted midcentury writers such as Nathaniel Hawthorne and Louisa May Alcott, was organized so that the principal road encircled and overlooked the bowl-like depression for which the cemetery was named. This area was left relatively open, while higher areas were left more wooded. At Oak Grove, glacially deposited boulders became the principal visual feature of the design. Roads were aligned so that some boulders became focal points, while others were preserved in permanent open spaces. Other Copeland and Cleveland projects included private estates, several of them near Waltham, Massachusetts, for which documentation no longer exists. Sometime after 1857 this partnership dissolved amicably, never to be resumed. After the Civil War each man established an independent practice, with Copeland remaining in Boston and Cleveland moving to Chicago.

Although landscape architectural activities were quite limited during the early 1850s, this period was a critical one because it saw the transfer of influence from Downing to a larger group of practitioners with greater ability to implement the concepts which he had interpreted to the American public. Much of the work done during this period was undocumented and probably altered during the late nineteenth century so that our knowledge of this critical transitional decade is distorted. No project better illustrates the large number of designers interested in and practicing landscape architecture than the design competition held in 1857 for Central Park in New York City, which attracted more than thirty, mostly American, entrants. This project, because of its scale, notoriety, and eventual financial success for the city, became the single most significant event in the development of the profession of landscape architecture in North America.

CONCLUSION AND SUMMARY

By 1857 the varied social, scientific, and aesthetic interests of the 1820s and 1830s had coalesced to create a distinctive approach to landscape design in America—the Romantic style. Romantic landscapes used irregularly curvilinear forms,

TERRACE

Not all designers worked with only Romantic, curvilinear forms during the 1850s. This design for a house terrace by Eugene Baumann shows the persistence of more geometric forms, at least near buildings. (Henderson, 1869.)

were asymmetrically composed, had a direct relationship to natural landforms, used trees and shrubs in masses, and often included picturesque focal points, such as classic urns or rustic gazebos. This naturalistic treatment of landscapes was inspired by eighteenth-century English design theories, but went beyond them by combining the two principal aesthetic modes, the beautiful and the picturesque, into a unified scheme which visually linked designed and natural landscapes. While many American designers of Rural Romantic Cemeteries used and advanced this style in the 1830s, it was not until publication of *A Treatise on the Theory and Practice of Landscape Gardening* by Andrew Jackson Downing in 1841 that Romantic design was codified and popularized for adaptation to a variety of site types. Downing's widespread influence made it easier for others interested in landscape design to enter the field, thereby creating a cadre of practitioners who would firmly establish the fledgling profession over the next three decades.

NOTES

1. *Although Linden-Ward, the principal scholar of Mount Auburn Cemetery, has unequivocally denied Wadsworth's role in the design, three pieces of circumstantial evidence suggest he had a greater involvement than has been generally acknowledged. First, and least definitive as evidence, was the way in which Wadsworth listed his name on the plan. He used "by," rather than "surveyed by" as he did for projects where he merely recorded data. To illustrate: for the 1847 subdivision design that he completed for Strawberry Hill in Watertown, Massachusetts, he used "by," but for the plan of the Morse estate, also in Watertown, which he recorded prior to its sale, he used "surveyed by." Second, there is the statement by Dall that "he laid out the cemetery called Mt. Auburn, although the fact seems to have been overlooked when Dr. Bigelow published his* History of Mt. Auburn *in 1860" (1898 p. 10). Ms. Dall was obviously biased (she was a family friend of Wadsworth's) but it seems unlikely that she would have made this up on her own without some comment from Wadsworth or his family. Third, and most*

convincing to designers, is a comparison between his later cemetery designs and those of Dearborn. Harmony Grove Cemetery in Salem, Massachusetts, by Wadsworth is one of the best picturesquely designed Rural Cemeteries in America. A later design by Dearborn, Forest Hill Cemetery in Roxbury, Massachusetts, lacked the same subtle adaptation to topography.

2. Although black was the rule for all in mourning, the length of time it must be worn, the extent of its use (whether full of partial), and even such details as the type of fabric worn depended on relationship to the decreased and length of time since death, with the most intense period of mourning being the first six months. See Habenstein (1955) for a discussion of mourning practices.

3. Laurel Hill Cemetery has generally been cited as the second Rural Cemetery in Romantic style to be established in North America (see John Reps, 1965, and Linden, 1981). In fact, Mount Hope Cemetery in Bangor, Maine, was consecrated in 1834 with burials beginning that same year, thus predating Laurel Hill. Mount Hope was designed by architect Charles G. Bryant as a combined arboretum and burial place, just as Mount Auburn Cemetery had been initially planned. For further information on Mount Hope Cemetery, see Albert W. Paine, History of Mt. Hope Cemetery, Bangor, Maine. *Bangor: O. F. Knowles and Co., 1907.*

4. According to John Jay Smith, who served as a member of Laurel Hill's board, this sculpture was made "on speculation" by the artist known to him only as Thom. After the cemetery purchased the work, he moved it to Philadelphia and reworked certain figures to fit its setting.

5. The 1840 Board of Managers report attributed the plan to H. H. Krebs and William A. Pratt, while the design of the entry gate is considered the work of Robert Cary Long. The 1979 National Register of Historic Places Inventory—Nomination Form states that Long "is considered the architect of the cemetery" (p. 3).

6. In the mid-nineteenth century the typical family plot often had a large family monument, individual upright markers for each grave, and footstones to mark the bottom of each grave.

7. This decline was largely the result of a reduction in need for new cemeteries, since most older ones still had plots available. During the early twentieth century, when cemetery development again prospered, the concept of a "rural" location continued, but designs became more formalized. See Chapter 13 for a discussion of this type of cemetery, often called a Memorial Park.

8. Such rustic features as irregular tree branches became a staple garden and park amenity of the nineteenth century. The popular style was often reinterpreted in concrete in the 1920s and 1930s.

9. This was in fact his most reprinted work, with at least one edition every year from first publication in 1845 to 1867.

10. The periodical continued to be published until 1875 and contains a wealth of information related to early landscape architecture, although most material is related to horticulture. The journal will be referred to simply as The Horticulturist *in text and bibliography. In 1853 a series of editorials by Downing from* The Horticulturist *were compiled into a book,* Rural Essays.

11. For a discussion of the vast body of nineteenth-century pattern books and Downing's place in it, see Dell Upton, 1984, "Pattern Books and Professionalism," Winterthur Portfolio, *Vol. 19, No. 2/3, pp. 107–50.* Cottage Residences *included site plans and planting lists, in addition to house plans. The landscapes, which were illustrated in plan only, appear to have been more Gardenesque and geometric than the projects illustrated in* A Treatise on the Theory and Practice of Landscape Gardening, *but no explanation for this was made.*

12. Downing did not use this particular term until the fourth edition of his book. Previously he had used the term "graceful" to describe the same visual principle.

13. Among those who could agree on the meaning of "sublime" in the landscape, it represented those landscapes that produced an elevated sense of their grandeur that produced an uplifting emotion. In addition, the term suggests landscapes so startlingly spectacular as to be terrifying or awe-inspiring. These scenes were always depicted as natural landscapes which had little imprint of human alterations and were atypical for the region in which they occurred. The Hudson River valley in the early nineteenth century, Niagara Falls, and the Grand Canyon would be examples of sublime landscapes. While it might be possible to design sublime landscapes, this would be rare. An example of a designed sublime "landscape" would be Walter De Maria's environmental sculpture "The Lightning Field."

14. Contemporary critics have been less generous toward Downing's design skill, which at best seems workmanlike rather than brilliant. It may be a reflection on the limits of his landscape architectural ability that he quickly shifted interest to the more wieldy field of architectural design.

15. In 1861 John Jay Smith, as editor of The Horticulturist, *soundly criticized the estate for its grotesque statues and some inappropriate tree replacements, suggesting that after Downing's death the owner changed the character of the site. Vassar in fact did take credit for some portions of the site plan, but never clarified whether they were part of the original design or later alterations.*

16. *Downing's death at age thirty-seven was treated as a national disaster, with several memorials for him planned. A monument to Downing, designed by Calvert Vaux in the form of a vase and pedestal with commemorative inscription, was placed on the Mall in Washington, D.C., in 1856. It has recently been relocated to a more prominent position in the Haupt Garden of the Smithsonian Institution. For the story of how Downing died during the sinking of the steamboat "Henry Clay" see Curtis, 1853, and* The New York Times, *Vol. 1, No. 270, July 30, 1852.*

17. *It was this plan which was eventually removed following the plans of the Senate Park Commission of 1902. In 1976, Constitution Gardens near the Lincoln Memorial was built to commemorate the Downing Mall plan.*

17

Utopian Planning in the Romantic Period

The general attitude of experimentation that America experienced in the first half of the nineteenth century not only influenced those who sought to reform society through traditional means, but also produced a social revolution of communitarian planning. Utopian groups sought to reform the society through creation of planned communities where they would demonstrate the application of progressive social ideas.[1] Communities linked under the rubic "utopian" include some which were religious, while others were sectarian with views based on sociological rather than theological principles. What makes these communities particularly relevant to a discussion of landscapes and landscape architecture in North America was that all these groups, whether religious or nonreligious, believed explicitly that human behavior was directly influenced by the physical environment, a belief which they shared with landscape architects.

The site and city plans of utopian groups are also quite relevant to landscape architectural history for three other reasons. First, many of the innovative practices which these groups initiated became prototypes later widely followed. The Shakers, for example, were credited with inaugurating the sale of packaged, dated seeds. Second, utopian communities exemplified the physical development of a strong concept. Finally, those communities which did establish towns and farms often created inventive site plans which served as models for later, nonutopian developments. In some cases, such as the industrial suburb of Hopewell, Massachusetts, a townsite formerly occupied by a utopian group was later adapted to be a model industrial village.

While utopian philosophies and the resulting settlements were never homogeneous in their underlying beliefs, as a group they tended to share some views of life which were atypical of the larger society. They tended to favor rural life, believing that it was impossible to reform society within the corrupting realm of cities or suburbs. Many communities removed themselves to physically isolated locations, often in frontier areas. Followers of Charles Fourier, for example, established a short-lived commune at Reunion, Texas, now part of Dallas. Others sought isolation from surrounding population centers. At the Amana colonies in Iowa, town plans were turned inward by grouping villages to insulate believers from the outside world. In still other cases, behavioral change was used to reinforce pastoral ideals. Brook Farm, the famous Transcendentalist utopia near Boston, established rules of simple living, with physical labor prescribed for all residents. Later, Bronson Alcott, the father of *Little Women* author Louisa May Alcott, established an even more spartan Transcendentalist commune, Fruitlands, near Harvard, Massachusetts. Among the utopian policies followed there was proscription of enslavement of animals through domestication. Most utopian communities were agriculturally based. In fact, there was not a single mid-nineteenth-century utopian group which could be considered an industrial commune, although some groups did do some manufacturing.

Another important aspect of utopian living was its generally communal nature. In some instances, all property was owned by the community as a whole rather than by individuals. Elsewhere individuals maintained their own homes and resources, but shared certain group facilities with the community. A most extreme instance of such thinking was those groups which abolished monogamous marriage in favor of group marriage or complete freedom of sexual choice.

Utopian communities also differed from the larger population in having greater sensitivity to conservation of the natural environment. Many groups, such as the Shakers, developed innovative conservation techniques including recycling. The Mormons, in spite of prejudice against their way of life, were widely respected for their development of agriculture in the harsh conditions of Utah. This appreciation of nature usually led utopian communities to develop outdoor spaces, as well as distinctive architectural statements. At Amana villages, the rear spaces between dwellings were developed as a communal open space with paths, gardens, and play areas.

Not only did they appreciate and safeguard the natural environment, but most utopian groups regarded the undisturbed, self-perpetuating natural landscape as a symbol of Eden on Earth. This image was especially prevalent in North America, where the scope of natural resources and natural beauty was viewed, just as the Romantic philosophers had viewed it, as an expression of a perfect world uncorrupted by flawed human action. Thus, the utopians, while utilizing the land to achieve their goals, sought to exercise stewardship over it.

Three final beliefs and characteristics were common to many utopian groups. They often emphasized techniques for saving human labor, so that people could devote time to higher-level activities such as self- or otherworldly awareness and education. The Shakers were known for the development of efficient tools, while the followers of Robert Owen introduced communal activities, such as group kitchens and laundries, to make work more efficient. Many utopian groups also emphasized social equality between the sexes and among ethnic groups. Frances Wright organized the Nashoba community near Memphis, Tennessee, for emancipation of women and Afro-Americans, both slave and free. Finally, and in spite

A backstreet in an Amana community, showing the pedestrian paths that connected houses and blocks, as well as the efficient use of brick wall space for vine crops. (Photo Courtesy State Historical Society of Iowa—Special Collections.)

of good intentions and much effort, most utopian groups and the communities they founded were very short-lived. For example, Toon O'Maxwell, an Owenite community in Ontario, lasted less than three years.

To understand the theory and practice behind the multiplicity of utopian communities formed in the mid-nineteenth century, as well as to explore some of the ideas which they contributed, albeit often indirectly, to landscape architecture, four utopian groups will be reviewed here: the Shakers,[2] officially called the Millennial Church; the Fourierists, followers of the philosophy of Charles Fourier; the Mormons, members of the Church of Jesus Christ of Latter Day Saints; and Zion, the Illinois community founded by John Alexander Dowie.

CASE STUDIES IN UTOPIAN LIVING
The Shakers

The Shaker religion, founded in the late eighteenth century in England by Ann Lee, formed the first widely known utopian group in North America. Persecution led Mother Lee and her followers to emigrate to the United States in 1774, settling first in New York State. Among the beliefs which influenced both their religious and daily lives (which to Shakers were really the same thing) were belief in the impending second coming of Jesus Christ, which the establishment of their sect heralded; belief that God manifests both male and female characteristics; and belief that life on earth should be intentionally arduous, to contrast with the great ease one would experience in the next world. More closely related to their physical lives were their beliefs in the benefits of simple, communal, celibate living; pacifism; sensitivity to nature; and efficiency in labor.

These concepts were directly applied both in daily activities and in design of villages, which they established to keep themselves separate from nonbelievers, whom they termed "the world's people." Men and women, although equals in community organizations, were kept well apart from each other in work, dining, and religious ceremonies. Their clothing was quite austere in cut and in color. Building furnishings, such as the elegant ladderback chair, were simple and functional. Although dedicated to hard work, Shakers sought every opportunity to make that work more efficient. Many tasks were centralized: for example, there were community laundries where horses rather the humans provided the labor. Improvements in work systems were equally highly regarded—for example, invention of the round barn with central work area that required less worker movement.

It was the Shaker view of the difference between heavenly and worldly life that had the most direct effect on site planning in their communities. Believing as they did that the world was a place of hardship, they sought not to minimize these difficulties but to make daily life more rigid and rule-bound. A strict time schedule for waking, eating, and working was followed. Completion of daily tasks followed a regular pattern, including, for example, adherence to the "rule of the right," which required that right-side activities be done first, such as always donning the right sock before the left. In the organization of Shaker villages, this rigidity was expressed in a regular grid arrangement of structures and roads. There were no winding Romantic-style paths in Shaker villages. All were at right angles, or, in a gesture to practicality, had diagonals at 45 degree angles. At Pleasant Hill, Kentucky, one of their later villages, even the National Road was made to conform to their rectangular system.

In contrast to the Cartesian logic and austerity of worldly forms, Shakers believed that the heavenly realm was a place of great freedom, imagination, and visual richness. It was in the surrounding countryside, a portion of which was converted into a place of worship, that they expressed this heavenly freedom. A hilltop meadow near each village was set aside as a "Holy Hill." There they constructed a low, eight-sided fence in a roughly oval form. At one end a stone

Main street, formerly part of the National Highway, through the restored Shaker community of Mount Pleasant, Kentucky.

Lithograph of a Shaker Holy Hill showing the fence-enclosed sacred area with segregated lines of men and women in procession. (Lamson, 1848.)

slab identified the hill as the site of a holy, life-giving fountain and magnificent holy city that only believers could see. These hilltop enclosures were used in spring and fall as destinations in a long procession that ended with dancing—and with a feast which, like the fountain and city, appeared imaginary to nonbelievers. It was quite natural that the outdoors would be the site of this partaking of the heavenly realm. The lushness, colorfulness, and sensuousness of the natural world was a dramatic contrast to the sedate and austere world of the Shaker village.

Fourier and the Phalanx

The utopian philosophy of Charles Fourier was based on the belief that God "rules the universe by Attraction and not by Force," and that human society should operate in the same manner. Fourier believed that there were certain basic aspects of human nature, which he termed "passional attractions," that must be acknowledged and satisfied for harmonious social life. These "attractions" included the physical and the emotional; such desires as love of luxury and the need to belong. He recognized that efforts by autonomous individuals to satisfy their attractions often led to depravity, but thought that when expressed in communal situations they became beneficent and productive.

Fourier's only personal attempt to establish the type of settlement where attractions could be properly utilized, which he called "phalanxes" or "phalansteries," in his native France ended in failure. It was through two of his disciples, Victor Considerant and Albert Brisbane, that his philosophy and design concepts were implemented in North America beginning in the 1840s. The phalanstery as described in Fourier's writings and graphically depicted by Considerant was a unified dwelling and civic center complex set in a pastoral estate of several thousand acres. The phalanx building was to be constructed in a series of wings separated by ornamental courtyards. Each wing was to serve a different function; workshops and other noisy activities in one, housing in another. The center portion of this linear city was reserved for communal functions such as dining halls, chapels, a post office, and libraries. It was critical to Fourier's concept that the design allow much opportunity for both planned and accidental association among members. To accomplish this, his plans called for a covered second-story walkway, modeled on a gallery in the Louvre, which would connect all the wings and be a place for informal meetings as on any street. Courtyards between wings were also to serve vital social ends, as places to which members were drawn for passive and active recreation, as well as chance passings.

Since the phalanx was to be a self-sustaining community, the agricultural estate was of equal importance to the phalanstery and Fourier took great pains to establish criteria for its siting and arrangement. He felt that 6,000 acres was the desirable area to sustain the 1,500 to 1,600 residents he envisioned for each phalanx. Land selected was to have streams to aid in farming, and, so that a variety of crops could be grown, should have diverse landforms and vegetative cover.[3] On such a site, the phalanstery was to be centrally located. Secondary buildings, chiefly those for agriculture and industry such as greenhouses, barns, and mills, were to be located nearby. Also adjoining the main phalanx building

View of prototypical phalanx from Description du Phalanstère et Considerations Sociales sur l'Architecture *by Victor Considerant, 1848.* (Courtesy of the Newberry Library, Chicago.)

there were to be ornamental and household gardens, parks, walking trails, and bridle paths. The remainder of the site was for pasture, orchards, and cropland.

Such was the theory. Reality was far smaller, less organized, and less attractive. The North American Phalanx, the first community organized by Brisbane, in Monmouth County, New Jersey, was one of the few of the more than forty phalanxes established to construct an estate at all similar to that proposed by Fourier, but even it was a mere token of the leader's grand vision. Beginning in 1842, builders on the estate of almost 700 acres eventually constructed a frame structure which housed most residents and services.[4] This L-shaped building with three wings was eventually to have been extended, but this was not accomplished during the brief twelve-year life of the community. The agricultural estate was more successful, producing a variety of vegetables beyond the staple potato crop. As Fourier had intended, grounds around the phalanx were well designed, with a park, flower gardens, and woods.

A very different type of phalanstery was founded more than ten years later when Considerant purchased land on the Trinity River in Texas. This settlement, Reunion, was from its onset relatively small, occupying only about 320 acres. Not only was the acreage small, but due to state retention of intervening tracts of land, it was disconnected. Even the village which settlers established was dispersed, rather than being in a central structure or grouped buildings, as Fourier had directed. For a variety of reasons related to both local political conditions in Texas and ethnic frictions between French, Belgian, and American settlers, this community failed within two years.

A TALE OF TWO ZIONS

The image of a heavenly city on earth was used by two different communitarian, utopian groups—the Mormon Church and the Christian Catholic Church. Mormonism, of all the utopian groups discussed, was the only one to develop into an enduring, international religion. Founded upon revelations in ancient tablets whose location was revealed to Joseph Smith by an angel, the Mormon faith was based on communal ownership of land and goods, on a belief in the continuity of faith through relatives both living and dead, and on a hierarchical organization in which church and state were linked.[5] Smith's first followers, who joined him after publication of the angelically revealed text as the Book of Mormon in 1829, lived in western New York State. To escape prejudice and fulfill a desire for adequate land, the community moved first to Kirtland, Ohio, then on to Missouri, next to Nauvoo, Illinois, and finally in 1847 to the valley of the Great Salt Lake.

Joseph Smith promulgated many rules for life in Mormon communities, from restrictions on ingesting stimulants, such as caffeine, to the practice of polygyny—that is, one man having more than one wife. He also had a distinct, divinely inspired vision of the physical form of the Mormon settlement. The plan archetype that he designed was called the Plat of the City of Zion. It was a mile-square town in grid form with wide streets and generous half-acre lots, which were to accommodate houses and garden plots. To achieve physical order of the streetscape, building setbacks were mandated and uniform building materials were to be used. In the center of town, three blocks were reserved for community uses, especially the site of the Temple.

The form decreed by this plan was intended to achieve social cohesion by providing in-town sites for all community members, while also allowing productive activities to take place there. Symbolically, the grid illustrated the equality, in God's sight, of all Mormons, and it also allowed the town to be oriented to the cardinal directions, thereby identifying it as at the center of the Creator's universe. The condition and appearance of the landscape were also important to

VIEW of NAUVOO

View of Mormon Nauvoo, Illinois, from the Mississippi River. The temple is the large structure at the top of the slope. (Library of Congress.)

Smith and his followers. An unpolluted environment symbolized purity of spirit, while stewardship of the land in the form of verdant gardens and parks demonstrated that the Mormons were tending the Eden which had been provided by the Lord.

The prototype of Zion was implemented initially in two Mormon settlements: first at Nauvoo, then at Salt Lake City.[6] The design of Nauvoo followed the plat closely, while adapting it to hilly topography along the Mississippi River, with the town center and hence the Temple located on a high point.[7] Following the murder of Joseph Smith, the Mormons began the trek to their permanent home in the state of Desert, as they named Utah. There the Plat of Zion was enlarged for Salt Lake City, but the same land use pattern was retained. Typical blocks of about 4 acres were divided into four lots. Each lot became a small farm, with barns, orchards, and grazing areas.[8]

A second vision of Zion was that of John Alexander Dowie. Dowie's religious philosophy was based on a literal interpretation of the Bible including dietary restrictions and prohibition against divorce. In 1899 Dowie purchased a 1,000-acre tract of land on Lake Michigan a few miles south of the Wisconsin state line for his Christian Catholic Church. Unlike earlier utopian planners, Dowie wanted his community to be a true city with diverse services and businesses, rather than just an agrarian village. The plan which he developed was similar to that for Indianapolis, Indiana. At its center sat Shiloh Tabernacle, Dowie's church, surrounded by a park. Eight streets radiated from the church, four to the cardinal directions, as in Smith's Zion, and four on diagonals.[9] The remaining streets were in a grid interrupted at intervals by winding streets along ravines. Several Romantic style parks, including two at the lakefront, provided open space for this compact, urbane community.

CONCLUSION AND SUMMARY: IMPACT OF UTOPIAN THINKING ON LANDSCAPES AND LANDSCAPE ARCHITECTURE

The utopian movements of the late eighteenth and nineteenth centuries grew out of a general intellectual fervor which also indirectly fostered the development of landscape architecture in America. New attitudes toward the importance of the individual, the value of knowledge, and the natural environment as a resource to be conserved, became part of an upper-class intellectual environment familiar to all educated people—the milieu from which most landscape architects came and within which all practiced. Downing had communicated with the founders of the North American Phalanx with the intent of advising then on design issues, a project cut short by his death. Olmsted was familiar with this same community, having written a newspaper article about it. Cleveland knew members of the Transcendentalist movement through his older brother, Henry, and likely visited Brook Farm.

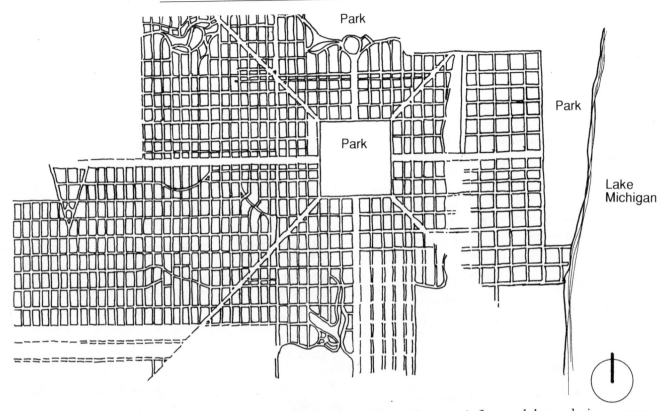

Plan of Zion, Illinois. (Data from Cook, 1970; redrawn by Rossi.)

Two general attitudes of utopian planners influenced later design movements. First, their belief in the ability of physical environments to alter human attitudes and behavior was very close to the theoretical arguments of early landscape architects for the moral and social value of large pastoral parks. Second, the concept of the value of nonindustrial labor in crafts and agriculture presaged the interest in handmade objects associated with the Arts and Crafts movement in the late nineteenth century.

Utopian communities often provided prototypes for planning that were not used by the larger society until decades later. Their concepts of town planning, particularly the notion of a pastoral village, are often considered prototypes for those of Ebenezer Howard's Garden City scheme as well as for industrial suburbs of the late nineteenth and early twentieth centuries. Certainly the idea that moral and social conditions could be improved through proper planning was one which the utopians espoused well before it became a rallying point for the participants in the City Beautiful movement. Their methods of spatial organization and land use also foreshadowed later design ideas. The notion of closely grouped dwellings to develop a sense of community influenced mid-twentieth-century planners such as Elbert Peets and Hale Walker. Fourier's phalanstery bears a surprising functional if not visual similarity to Paolo Soleri's modern unitary city of Arcosanti begun in 1970 near Cordes Junction, Arizona. Details of later site planning have also seemingly been inspired by utopian plans. The internal pedestrian courts of the Amanas foreshadowed Clarence Stein and Henry Wright's superblocks at Radburn, New Jersey, while Amana's use of speed bumps to slow through traffic has become standard for parking lots and park roads across the continent.

Utopian theoreticians and planners were merely one group that contributed to the development of the North American landscape. Their impact, though, was far greater than their numbers or the durability of their settlements might indicate. They were original thinkers who often shocked their contemporaries and challenged their standards, thereby encouraging new thoughts on old issues. In particular, their desire to save human energy for higher activities led them to develop labor–saving devices and more efficient systems of organization. This inventive mind–set certainly inspired and liberated others who, while not copying their ideas, took up the challenge of reinventing the physical environment.

NOTES

1. *Utopian communities founded on principles similar to those of nineteenth-century groups persist today. The Farm, a rural commune in Tennessee, is one of the more successful modern day examples.*

2. *This name, given them by nonbelievers, was a reference to their religious ceremonies, which included dancing and spirit-induced writhing. Aside from the appellation Millennial Church, the group had a second official title, United Society of Believers in Christ's Second Appearing.*

3. *They were also to be located near a large city, but due to land costs in near-urban areas none ever followed this suggestion.*

4. *Fourier had advocated use of inexpensive materials for buildings, so that financial resources could be used to build up the community's agricultural and industrial assets, and enhance cultural life.*

5. *The Book of Mormon also espoused the then popular theory that Native Americans were descended from one of the Lost Tribes that had been led out of Israel by God at the fall of Jerusalem. In this context North America was envisioned as a special land, a new Eden which God had prepared for his new chosen people—the Mormons.*

6. *The Plat of Zion was actually used for four cities. Two of these, Kirtland, Ohio, and Far West, Missouri, were platted but never actually developed as planned.*

7. *The Mormons left Nauvoo in 1847 and in 1849 sold the townsite to another communitarian group, the Icarians, who occupied it for a short time.*

8. *In his original plans, Smith excluded barns and stables from these in-town lots, but residents did not follow his instructions.*

9. *Cook (1970) compares the plan to the British Union Jack but does not directly state that this was Dowie's inspiration. Dowie was born in Scotland and may have been inspired by that symbolic banner.*

18

Parks Produce a New Profession

It is one great purpose of the Park to supply to the hundreds of thousands of tired workers, who have no opportunity to spend their summers in the country, a specimen of God's handiwork that shall be to them, inexpensively, what a month or two in the White Mountains or the Adirondacks is, at great cost, to those in easier circumstances.

Central Park Commission, 1858

Although much has been made—quite appropriately—of Andrew Jackson Downing's pivotal role in advancing a landscape design and planning profession, his interests were not of sufficient scope or philosophical depth to constitute the theoretical underpinnings on which the comprehensive profession of landscape architecture has been based. Up to 1857 the incipient profession remained in the repetitious doldrums of estate, cemetery, and other small-site design, with aesthetic concerns primary, and it might have lingered so for several more decades had it not been for the establishment of a large park in New York City—Central Park.

The movement to establish this park merged design with social and political goals to create an important civic amenity. Several important social forces were at work to launch public interest in open spaces. Most significant was the growth of cities and the limitations which that growth placed on access to large outdoor spaces. This growth was compounded by the new work environments—the factories and workshops—in which many people found themselves. There work schedules of ten to twelve hours a day six days a week left little time for travel to pastoral recreation areas. Urban growth also created problems of urban air, water, and solid waste pollution. While it was recognized that parks could not solve all these problems, they were considered an aid to cleaner air—"the lungs of the city."

A second factor in expediting park development was the complementary example of the Rural Romantic Cemeteries, which offered a bucolic setting for refreshing passive reflection and recreation. When Rural Romantic Cemeteries were first laid out, before many lots had been occupied and monuments erected, they looked like large, well-planted estates. Lot holders and townspeople so often used them for recreation that most cemeteries eventually established rules to curtail activities that disrupted the solemnity of the site, such as horseracing or picnicking, and limited admittance on Sundays and holidays to lot holders. These festive uses of sites dedicated to melancholy were evidence of a need expressed by many, including Frank J. Scott, who asked rhetorically, "Our parks for the dead—Greenwood, Mount Auburn, Laurel Hill, Spring Grove, and their thousand lesser imitations—are unsurpassed in the refinement of their adornments . . . but where are the parks for the living?" (1869, p 1).

Prior to 1857 those public open spaces that had been set aside for recreation were generally of two types: the small square, which was often merely a widened space at the intersection of roads, and the public garden, which was far more elaborate in plan and ornamental features. As the name suggests, these later sites were conceived as garden-like landscapes which would be available to the general public. Their garden character was reinforced by elaborate plantings in which floral and herbaceous variety rather than spatial design with plants were emphasized. They typically had small water features, usually both ponds and ornamental fountains. Public gardens were intended to be used for passive recreation, such as strolling and picnicking, and for civic and cultural events, especially small fairs and concerts. The public gardens of Boston and of Halifax, Nova Scotia, are both excellent, extant examples of this type of mid-nineteenth-century open space.

In 1836 plantings were begun in Halifax Public Garden, which was intended as a display garden for the Nova Scotia Horticultural Society. It was meant from its inception to be a place of public recreation, as well as an educational institution. Although small, Halifax Public Garden had a typical public garden's plethora of amenities and diversions: a series of ponds along a small stream, meandering paths, ornate planting beds, a cottage which was eventually used for food service, a rock garden, fountains, sculpture, and, added in 1887, a polychrome bandstand. The Boston Public Garden was larger and less saturated with features than was the Halifax garden, but it followed generally the same pattern of dense curvilinear paths used as viewing points for scattered planting, especially herbaceous display gardens, and numerous ornamental features including a pond and statuary. Separated from the Common by Charles Street, the Public Garden graphically illustrated the new perception of public outdoor spaces as attractive, rather than purely utilitarian.

While public gardens offered the urban public fairly large open spaces, they had two generally recognized shortcomings. First, they were not sufficiently large to create the illusion that one was not still in the midst of the city with its traffic, noise, and noxious odors. Second, most public gardens were really horticulturally oriented amusement parks with a variety of entertaining, but overly busy, features such as fountains, rides, vendors, and street furniture. Thus, they lacked the tranquility which was often viewed as desirable in recreational spaces. This last limitation would have been less obvious had it not been for the example of the Rural Cemetery, which offered a more bucolic setting for passive recreation, conversation, and reflection.

The Boston Public Garden circa 1861, looking toward the Common. (Souvenir Postal Cards.)

THE PARKS MOVEMENT

Central Park

While 1857, the year of the design competition for Central Park, stands out as a turning point for both urban design and landscape architecture, the parks movement had gotten underway before that event. For many years, in spite of a desperate, demonstrated need for open space, city governments had been reluctant to act. Acquisition of large areas of land by government agencies was a new, and for many questionable, act, which many politicians did not want to initiate. Fortunately, a number of socially and politically prominent individuals championed the cause of public parks. Three of the most noteworthy were Andrew Jackson Downing, William Cullen Bryant, and Ambrose C. Kingsland. Downing's interest was an obvious extension of those ideas expressed in his writings and professional work, but he recognized that the park contemplated for New York must go well beyond all existing public designs both in concept and in size. Using *The Horticulturist* as a propaganda device, he challenged the city to secure a site of at least 500 acres in which "citizens who would take excursions in carriages, or on horseback, could have the substantial delights of country roads and country scenery, and forget for a time the rattle of the pavements and the glare of brick walls" (1851, p. 317).[1] Bryant's endorsement of the idea of the park was no less critical. Beginning in 1844, he used editorials in the *New York Evening Post* to champion acquisition of large scenic sites before the best of these were developed for other purposes. As mayor of New York, Kingsland's authority and influence was pivotal to success of any public works project. Fortunately, he advocated an immediate purchase of land and petitioned the state legislature for authority to acquire land.

The original site selected for a park was a tract of 160 acres along the East River. While it had many visual advantages, particularly a waterside location, it would have been too small to effectively produce any illusion of rural scenery in the city, but this defect was recognized before any substantive work was undertaken. After considerable wrangling among park advocates and politicians, a visually undistinguished 770-acre site[2] in the middle of Manhattan Island was selected for the park. Frederick Law Olmsted later described much of this plot as having been a "vile slough," with "black and unctuous slime." Those areas not marshy were of exposed schist. In addition to these dramatic, but somewhat unencouraging, natural conditions, the tract had long been used for waste dumping and squatter housing. The contrast between the "before" and "after" condition of the Central Park site could not have been greater.

Although planning and design aspects of the park will be of greatest interest in this discussion, the primary intentions of the city were often directed toward practical ends. Evolving theories of public health focused on the need for urban open spaces to provide a clean air source. In addition, parks were a foil to crowded lower-income housing areas and the related negative health effects of slum life. Following the economic Panic of 1857, in which many workers became unemployed, park construction was viewed as a labor-intensive public relief project, which simultaneously advanced political objectives by providing patronage jobs. Equally important to those who foresaw the real estate benefits of park development, publically financed Central Park increased the value of surrounding private land. These multiple ends persisted throughout much of the life of the park, resulting in conflicts with and compromises of its original recreational purpose.

The first design for the park was completed in 1856 by the city's chief park engineer, Edward Viele, following what were then generally accepted principles of Romantic-style design and English precedent of park arrangement. This competent, but lackluster, scheme became the basis for site clearing and also likely for the design program on which the Central Park Design Competition was based.[3] The importance of this design competition and its outcome in the devel-

FIG 105.—View of Water Terrace in Central Park.

Lithographic views of Central Park: (top) looking toward Bethesda Terrace from the Ramble with key features of the Master Plan in place; (bottom) the same view of the site prior to construction. (The Horticulturist, *Vol. 14, April 1859.)*

opment of landscape architecture in North America cannot be overemphasized. It was at once a continuation of early efforts to improve public spaces and a break from the concept of designed landscapes solely as works of art lacking a cogent theoretical basis.

In late 1857 the city of New York announced the competition program, which was quite specific in requiring that designs include a parade ground, playgrounds, exhibition halls, a large fountain, a viewing tower, flower gardens, and a pond for ice skating. These program elements were, of course, typical of what one would expect a park to contain. More unusual and challenging was the provision that four cross-streets must be provided for through east-west traffic, so that the park would not impede intracity vehicular circulation. It was this condition that proved pivotal to the success of the winning entry. No direction was suggested for the visual character, perhaps due to an underlying assumption that it would have that of landscape garden-style "parking."[4]

By the close of the competition on April 1, 1858, there were thirty-three competition entries and two noncompetition submissions. There were designs by established landscape architects, such as Robert Morris Copeland with H. W. S. Cleveland, Charles Follen, and Howard Daniels, and others by park employees like engineer Viele and planting superintendents Ignaz Pilat and Samuel Gustin.[5] From this august field, the selection committee chose the scheme entitled "Greensward" for first place. The Greensward plan had been the joint effort of architect and former Downing partner Calvert Vaux, and the current park superintendent, Frederick Law Olmsted.

These two, who had met casually years earlier through Downing, were a choice pair to collaborate on the competition plan. Vaux, with his architectural training and field experience under Downing, was likely the best-trained landscape designer then in North America. Olmsted on the other hand had direct experience in management of large tracts of land through earlier ownership of a farm on Staten Island. Of greater importance, he had direct knowledge of the park site gained through daily exposure to it as superintendent. To this Olmsted added innate organizational abilities. The balance of expertise between the two men helped create a site-specific plan that solved the practical problems of circulation across the park, while at the same time preserving the illusion of rural scenery.

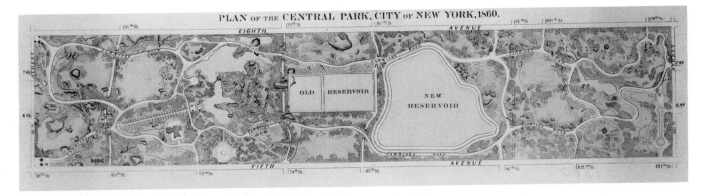

"Plan of the Central Park, City of New York, 1860." Design by Olmsted and Vaux, plan drawn by George Hayward for Valentine's Manual. *(The Historical Society of Pennsylvania.)*

Judging from emphasis in the report which accompanied their plan, circulation both from without and within the park was central to the Vaux and Olmsted concept. They proposed that the transverse roads for east to west through traffic be sunk below the grade of the park itself, so that rocks and vegetation could screen them from view of park users. This system of grade separation for traffic was then extended into the park itself through a system of separate routes for carriages, horseback riders, and pedestrians. While many members of the competition jury might not have been able to sort out the aesthetic advantages of one plan over another, most were practically minded and could easily understand the benefits which this system would provide for park users.

The Olmsted and Vaux plan was not simply a circulation plan, though. It provided a carefully orchestrated sequence of spaces that would lead visitors from the structured, crowded urban world through an active, socially oriented space and on to an intricate but convincingly designed naturalistic landscape. Although the competition plan was revised by the designers as it was implemented, the completed park's principal features and spaces generally followed the original master plan, which will be the primary basis for this discussion.[6] Central Park was intended to be experienced principally by entry from the south, then the only developed area of the city. The southeast corner was defined by an enlarged road space at which the curving road and path systems of the park began. At the southwest a single drive provided access. These original entry designs were quickly refined, apparently at the behest of the Park Commissioners, to provide official "main entrances"—Grand Army Plaza and Columbus Circle—where Fifth and Eighth Avenues crossed 59th Street.

From these entrances, pedestrians were channeled to the principal promenade, a tree-lined space a quarter of a mile long, known as the Mall. Although this was not obvious to most viewers, this space was angled to draw attention from the park's rectangular boundary lines and form a line of sight toward its principal lake and the naturalistic landscape beyond. Two rows of American elms arranged to appear in formal lines from the path, but when viewed from elsewhere in the park to look like part of an irregular mass, lined the Mall's walkway. In the 1870s, against the wishes of the designers, larger than life-size sculptures of literary figures such as Shakespeare and Schiller, which reduced the apparent size of the space, were set out on stone bases along the walk.

The Mall terminated at a lakeside plaza, Bethesda Terrace, that Vaux considered an open-air reception hall. There a tiered fountain, originally quite simple with central jet, but later replaced by a larger fountain in the form of an angel, served as focal point and linked the formal terrace with the Romantic lake at its edge. Bethesda Terrace was intended as a lively gathering place. Benches, wide staircases, and balustrades provided a choice of seating, gonfalons hung with brightly colored banners added color and movement to the scene, the fountain added sound, and the lake reflected activity and provided a setting for boating and ice skating. From Bethesda Terrace or the adjacent road overpass, one could gain a view of the area that was the symbolic and physical center of the park—the picturesque, naturalistic forest and rock area called the Ramble.

While appearing to be a preserved natural area, the Ramble was in fact purposely contrived to look undesigned. Relocated boulders suggested mountain effects, trees and shrubs hid through views, and structures, such as the bridges that carried paths across hollows, were rusticated. To maintain the illusion of the Ramble as a country place, access was purposely limited: it could only be reached by walking around the ends of the lake, by boat across the lake, or via picturesque Bow Bridge. Once within the Ramble, visitors became part of a woodland world mental miles from the rest of the park and the city. So convincing was the enclosure achieved by placement of rocks and trees that even today, with skyscrapers surrounding the park, a sense of seclusion in a country forest is maintained.

Beyond the Ramble was the viewing tower required by the competition program, designed by Vaux as a castle-like series of high walls, terraces, and small pavilions set atop Vista Rock, the highest point in the park. This Belvedere gave an overview of both the Ramble to the south and two huge reservoirs to the north. The older rectangular tank was eventually removed and replaced with a large, elliptical lawn known as the great Meadow, so that all views from the Belvedere are today equally effective.

Although New York was committed to providing a large landscape park for residents, the city could not resist the opportunity to use "undeveloped" park land for a dual purpose—as sites for reservoirs. In addition to the preexisting rectangular Croton Reservoir, a second and larger structure, although one with a more pondlike outline, was planned for the park, with its site and outline determined prior to the competition. The position and size of this new Croton Reservoir created an internal barrier within the park which has plagued its design up to this day. The Greensward plan attempted to address the reservoir's devisive

View of the Mall looking toward Bethesda Terrace, in the late nineteenth century. (The Hugh C. Leighton Postcard Company.)

The Mall, Central Park, New York.

Bethesda Terrace as seen from the pond, with the Mall in center background. The view clearly illustrates the original planting concept for the Mall with two parallel tree rows linked to the naturalistic plantings beyond by a third, less regular tree row. (Minutes of Proceedings of the Board of Commissioners of the Central Park for the Year Ending April 30, 1863.)

"View of Central Park Taken from the Ramble above the Cave Across the North End of the Lake Toward Central Park West Near 76th Street; Taken during construction." Unidentified photographer circa 1859. (Courtesy of the New-York Historical Society, New York City.)

character by surrounding it with drives elevated to water level, but these could not provide a convincing visual linkage between north and south. The southern area developed first, because it was originally closer to the center of population, received most design attention and included the most amenities. The northern portion of the site was originally left to be open fields, with the only designated use areas being those set aside for an arboretum and a hilltop observatory. Later, when the park site was extended northward, a system of ponds and streams was enlarged, but the division of the park persists today in spite of the northward shift in population.[7]

The park was, of course, not a nature preserve but a place for fun and games. Olmsted and Vaux planned its animation as well as its physical design by pro-

An example of the intricate
rustic structures typical in
Central Park, here from an
undated stereograph by E. &
H. Anthony & Company.
(Courtesy of the New-York
Historical Society, New
York City.)

"Central Park"; lithograph by
John Bachmann, printed by F.
Heppenheimer, 1863. This
aerial view from the south
illustrates site development
below the reservoirs. (Courtesy
of the New-York Historical
Society, New York City.)

CENTRAL PARK.

viding a plethora of amenities, including a Dairy to serve refreshments, boats and a boathouse on the lake near the Ramble, goat carts for children, a bandstand for concerts, and the Casino, which served as a restaurant.

The preparation of the winning plan was merely the beginning of Olmsted and Vaux's design work at Central Park. Such a large undertaking, of course, took years to complete, but the basic structure and much of the detail of the park was in place by 1860. The first area was opened to the public in June 1859. Each man was connected with the park for years afterward—Olmsted was named Architect in Chief, a position which he held until 1878 (with a hiatus during the Civil War), while Vaux worked on the park in both official and unofficial capacities as a Consulting Architect and Landscape Architect until the time of his death.[8]

While the winning master plan was certainly the work of Vaux and Olmsted only, its implementation and refinement required the collaborative efforts of many, including architects, engineers, and horticulturists. Among the most prominent people associated with the design of the park were George Waring, Jacob Wrey Mould, Ignaz Pilat, and Samuel Parsons. Waring, shortly to become a pioneering sanitary engineer, planned the system of soil underdrainage, then a commonly used technique to reduce soil saturation and improve plant growing conditions.[9] He developed a complete system of underground pipes more than 95 miles in length to remove both surface and subsurface water. He also planned the hydraulics of ponds and streams. Mould collaborated with Vaux on the design of structures within the park and was best known as designer of the intricate patterns chiseled into stone bridges or molded into cast-iron lampposts. Both Pilat and Parsons supervised the detailed planting designs of the park. Pilat, as the original planting superintendent, conducted a survey of existing plants and later oversaw design and plant installation in such key areas as the Mall and the Ramble. Parsons, although a latecomer to the park, worked with Vaux in the 1880s to complete the planting and maintain materials already in place. After Vaux's untimely death Parsons campaigned for preservation of the original plan in the face of ever mounting calls for additions, especially of large buildings, and changes in land uses toward more active recreation.[10]

In spite of problems and criticisms, especially of its perceived exorbitant cost of over $16 million, Central Park was an unmitigated success for the city of New York, with estimated annual attendance at more than 3 million by 1866.[11] It provided needed work up to and after the Civil War; it established the city's stature as a trendsetter in city planning; and most critically it demonstrated that parks did not cost cities money, but in the long term actually made money through increased real estate tax assessments.

Central Park was also *the* pivotal event in development of the multifaceted profession of landscape architecture. It made the leap in scale from the small, generally private or semiprivate sites that had previously been the staple of practice to a scale that approached that of a small region. Further, it demonstrated that function as well as appearance was important in the arrangement of outdoor spaces. It proved that properly designed landscapes were not merely civic amenities, but critical to both the physical and economic development of cities. Finally, through the publicity which the park and its designers received, it popularized the professional services that landscape architects could offer and created a cross-continental demand for these services.

Prospect Park

The first designers to benefit from the popularity of professionally designed parks were Olmsted and Vaux themselves. In 1859 New York City's neighbor, the then autonomous city of Brooklyn, seeking to keep up with its larger rival began development of a scenic landscape park all its own—Prospect Park. While Central Park was the joint and likely equal work of Vaux and Olmsted, the design of Prospect Park, especially its basic spatial concept, was principally the work of Vaux.[12] Although authorized by the state legislature in 1859, with land purchased in the early 1860s, development of the park was delayed due to the Civil War. In January 1865 the Brooklyn Park Board contacted Vaux with a request to supply a plan for development of the site which had been acquired. After one visit, he made the single most significant recommendation for the park's future: that its boundaries be reconfigured so that major through roads, which then divided it into two tracts of roughly 200 acres and a third tiny triangle, be used as park boundaries. In a sketch plan that accompanied his report, Vaux suggested these new park boundaries—as well as an overall spatial concept, including location of a principal entrance at its present location at Flatbush and Prospect Park West.[13] The sketch also illustrated that part of his rationale for extending the park southward was to incorporate a swampy tract of land suitable for a large pond. The final master plan of the park was a development and elaboration of the key principles which Vaux presented to the Board just days after his first official site visit.

At that time, Olmsted was working in California, principally as a manager for the Mariposa Mining Company, but also consulting with the state on plans for the natural area near Yosemite Valley. Although there is no evidence that the Brooklyn Park Board expected both Olmsted and Vaux to work on the plan, since they surely knew that Olmsted was not in New York, Vaux immediately wrote to him to report on his meetings and recommendations. Later in this correspondence, Vaux admonished Olmsted to return so that they could work on the park together. Shortly after Olmsted returned east in December, the partners were formally hired to prepare a plan for the park with boundaries as set out by Vaux.

The design which the two men created for Brooklyn was considered more successful than that for Central Park, principally because there were fewer constraints on the work. Certainly the fact that one of the designers had picked site boundaries which enclosed land suitable for a variety of landscape developments was a significant factor in this success. In addition, three limitations which had influenced the Central Park design were absent here: the need to disguise rectilinear boundaries, the problem of how to treat through roads, and the division of Central Park into two parts, caused by the reservoir.

Prospect Park had four major areas: the entry plaza, a long curved meadow, an area of mixed hills and meadows, and a large lake. Grand Army Plaza, the entry plaza, was one of the most remarkable outdoor spaces of the nineteenth century and a precursor to the Beaux Arts designs of the City Beautiful Movement. The Plaza had both an appropriate scale and configuration to provide an effective transition from the irregular, gridlike street pattern of Brooklyn, and also incorporated the two diagonal streets, Flatbush Boulevard and Prospect Park West, that were park boundaries.[14] By using an ellipse with its longest distance aligned to the actual park entry, distortions in the pattern of surrounding streets were concealed and a line of sight into the park suggested. Tree-filled medians separated an outer drive around the ellipse from the plaza center. At the park end there were no medians, so that views to park gates and plantings beyond were exposed. In the middle of the plaza, a circle was set aside for a focal feature, originally a fountain with central jet, but changed in 1892 to a far larger and more elaborate Soldier and Sailors Monument in the form of a triumphal arch.

The principal open area of the park, called the Long Meadow, was as refined as the entry plaza. This gently curving field gave the illusion of a space extending on to infinity. By bending the long, narrow meadow and disguising its edges with carefully placed tree masses, its full extent could never be perceived from

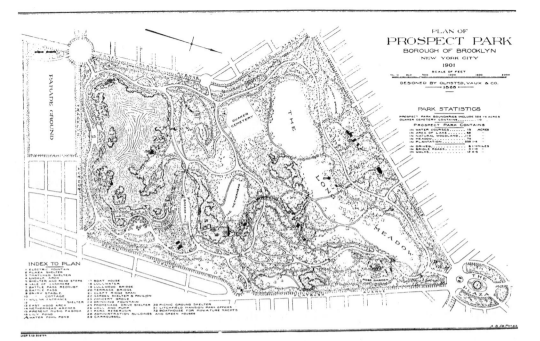

Plan of Prospect Park in 1901 based on design by Olmsted and Vaux, 1868. (Architectural Record, Vol. 44, No. 5.)

any vantage point, making it appear far larger than its actual 75 acres. Long Meadow skirted the entire northeastern edge of the park, but was separated from the city, as was the entire park, by densely planted berms. The meadow also gave form to the principal park drives, which forked at its head and then meandered along its edges.

Beyond Long Meadow a complex landform of hills and valleys offered many opportunities for different recreational areas and scenic views. Here the designers located major entertainment spaces, including the playground, which came to be called the Vale of Cashmere; the Deer Paddock which eventually became the Zoo; and the Boathouse. Rambling topography in this area also lent itself to the type of picturesque scenery which Olmsted favored. There the designers sited the Ravine, a naturalistic landscape of rock, hills, dense forests, and meandering paths, much like the Ramble in Central Park although smaller. Nearby a prominent high point was exploited as a site for the Lookout Tower.

In the southernmost portion of the park was 60-acre Prospect Lake—curved, like Long Meadow, to disguise its true size. Along this shore was sited the sole formal area within the park, a stone terrace positioned at the focal intersection of Prospect Lake and the smaller pond called Lullwater. Later plans altered this arrangement, with the formal area moved westward to a grove set aside for concerts. Although this new design was effective in itself, Vaux and Olmsted's original idea would have provided a stronger terminus to the major arm of the lake and also related the terrace to another architectural form, the building of the Refectory.[15]

As the discussion above suggests, there are many parallels between the designs for Prospect Park and Central Park. Like Central Park, Prospect Park was given a system of traffic separation with a full complement of overpasses and underpasses. In addition, principal picturesque areas of both parks were quite appropriately located in central areas away from the busiest active use areas. In spite of these likenesses, Prospect Park was not a mirror image of Central Park. Key differences included: that Prospect Park, at 526 acres, was only two-thirds the size of Central Park; Prospect did not have the same highly structured interior spatial sequence as Central Park; Prospect Park had a far more intelligible

Rustic bridge and pavilion on the lake in Prospect Park circa 1890.

and powerful entry; and Prospect Park had a more balanced distribution of use areas, so that one portion of the site did not appear to have been more blessed with amenities than another. The overall visual characters of the parks also differ markedly: in general terms, Central Park was picturesque in character, while Prospect Park represented the beautiful. Both designed and preexisting natural features contributed to this difference. The rugged, rock-covered landscape of Central Park lent itself to the picturesque treatment, while the large number of use areas required by the competition program tended to divide the site into small areas, making it impossible to achieve what was then referred to as "park," that is "beautiful," scenery. Prospect Park, on the other hand, had more rolling topography, which the designers had greater liberty to adapt to park uses. These differences in character were magnified over the years, as maintenance at Central Park fostered the spread of trees and reduction of open space, while the undulate landforms of Prospect Park were enhanced by twentieth-century lawn maintenance techniques.

Other Olmsted-Designed Parks

The Central Park competition began an era of park building across the continent. This movement not only gave us some of the most lasting and beneficial public works produced in North America, but also began the drive for urban improvement and planning to increase the liveability of cities. Druid Hill Park, discussed in Chapter 5, was the second major nineteenth-century park constructed in the Americas, but its design was in many ways more similar to that of estates than to the type of landscape park that Central Park initiated, perhaps because that was the site's original function. The real beginning of the park movement had to await an end to the Civil War, when the cities of the East were revitalized and new cities were built in the West.

Fame from their early design successes made Vaux and Olmsted, and later Olmsted in his own firm, the premier park designers on the continent. Although many parks have improperly been credited to Olmsted, he with Vaux or others was involved with hundreds of parks and park systems. Olmsted and Vaux developed plans for the South Parks [Washington and Jackson] in Chicago; for Downing Park in Newburgh, New York; and for the Buffalo, New York, park system. Working with Jacob Weidenmann, Olmsted designed Mount Royal Park in Montreal, while later as Olmsted, Olmsted and Eliot, the firm worked on parks in Hartford, Connecticut, and Cambridge, Massachusetts.[16]

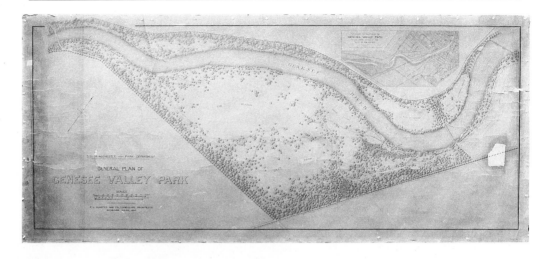

Plan of Genesee Valley Park, Rochester, New York, by Olmsted and Company, 1880. (The City of Rochester, New York, Municipal Archive, Engineering Records Collection.)

Two of the later park systems on which the Olmsted firm worked were those at Rochester, New York,[17] and Boston, Massachusetts. The Rochester system was relatively small, composed of two large scenic parks, a smaller park for horticultural displays, and numerous small squares. This group does, though, represent the full range of park types which the firm designed. At the heart of this system were two parks set astride the Genesee River, Seneca Park and Genesee Valley Park, each with a distinctive visual character. Genesee Valley Park, in the south, was located on rolling land at a point where the river floodway became quite broad. The name which Olmsted originally gave it, Meadow Park, described the appearance of both the natural and the designed landscape. Most park areas were large open fields with scattered trees placed to suggest, rather than physically define, separation from adjoining fields. The only dense tree plantings at park edges screened out adjoining uses. At both Genesee Valley and Seneca parks the river separated active and passive areas—with those to the east, in each park the larger area, reserved for passive recreation and naturalistic imagery.[18]

Seneca Park afforded breathtaking overlooks up and down a gorge of the Genesee River. In fact, much of the land within the park tract was too steep for uses other than paths, but this steepness also preserved the vegetation. The designers utilized three distinct topographical areas to suggest natural subdivisions of park uses. Plateaus above the gorge became the most developed areas of the park: those on the west bank were for active and cultural uses, while those to the east were for passive recreation, but included a pond and a small menagerie, which was set up during the summer.[19] Steep banks of the gorge held only pathways and a few rustic shelters. The riversides themselves were used for a linear path system and for water-related sports such as boating.

To complement these two larger, naturalistic landscape parks, a smaller park nearer to town was built as an informally designed botanical display garden. Highland Park, with land and plants donated by the nursery firm of Ellwanger and Barry, combined a formal entry through an allée of trees with irregular masses of trees and shrubs in horticultural displays. This park was widely known for its collections of conifers and rhododendrons, each of which made the park particularly attractive at different seasons. To complete the Rochester system of parks Olmsted, Olmsted and Eliot designed six of the small squares that dotted the city, including Plymouth Park and Franklin Square. In each case the plans called for a symmetrical series of flowing, elliptically formed paths. Areas be-

Looking up the Gorge, Seneca Park, Rochester, N.Y.

View of the Genesee River as seen from Seneca Park, Rochester, New York, circa 1900. (The Valentine and Sons Publishing Company, Ltd.)

Rhododendron displays in Highland Park, Rochester, New York, circa 1900.

tween paths and their adjoining seating were planted either in turf or ornamental flower beds with a few shade trees in lines or as specimens edging paths.

The Boston Park System was developed not just to serve recreational purposes, but to solve drainage problems in the city. What distinguishes the Boston system plan from any proposed earlier, with the exception of H. W. S. Cleveland's 1872 suggestions for Minneapolis and St. Paul, was that it advocated a completely linked system, with parks connected by parkways or riverside paths. Boston's park system, as originally conceived by Olmsted, looped from Boston Common, down Commonwealth Avenue, along Muddy River, around the boundary between Boston and Brookline, and thence back to the waterfront. This final portion of the loop ending at the harbor was never completed, but the system of five major parks and three linkage corridors enveloped much of the

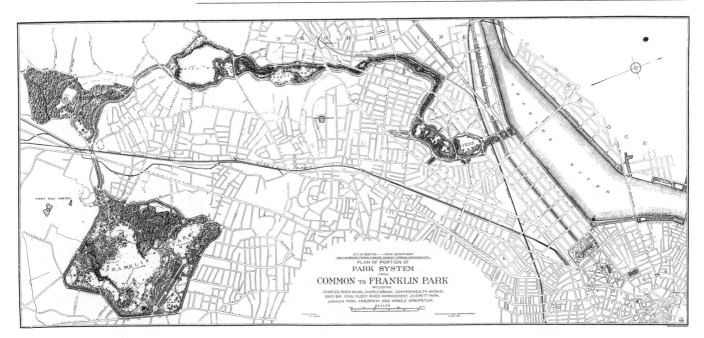

Plan of the Boston Park System from the Common to Franklin Park by Olmsted, Olmsted and Eliot, 1894. Plan shows location of the principal components of the system planned by Olmsted in the 1880s. (Courtesy National Park Service, Frederick Law Olmsted National Historic Site.)

northern and western edges of the city. Termed an "emerald necklace," the park system had its jewels—the large parks of Back Bay Fens, Leverett Park, Jamaica Park, Arnold Arboretum, and Franklin Park—while the corridors, Charlesgate, Fenway, the Riverway, Jamaicaway, and the Arborway, comprised the strand of the necklace.

Charlesgate, Back Bay Fens, and the Riverway were built along tidal salt marshes. Charlesgate was the name given the narrow strip of marsh and shoreline that connected the Fenway and Back Bay Fens with Commonwealth Avenue and the Charles River beyond it. The Back Bay itself, a 115-acre wetland, was regraded to provide retention areas for the seasonal floodwaters of tributary streams. In addition to storing excess water, the reservoirs helped to prevent pollution by retaining the sewage-contaminated water of the Charles River, which often backed up into that area of the city. Back Bay Fens was designed so that during most of the year it had a meandering stream flowing near low, grassed fields, with about half the park water-covered. Its waterway was very irregular in outline, an irregularity reinforced with naturalistic plantings, including marsh grasses used to slow the flow of water. When floods came, the fields would be inundated and only the higher ground where the paths, roads, and buildings were sited remained dry.

The Riverway and the Muddy River area were the longest, most naturalistic stretch of connecting park and parkway, but this naturalism was an illusion, for the river corridor had been completely transformed from its original condition. Not only was the channel relocated and the old one filled, but its water was changed from brackish to fresh by channeling of spring and stream water to it. Simply designed with riverside paths and seating areas, vegetation was its principal design material, essential to screening surrounding land uses which were urban even in the nineteenth century.

Leverett Park, which with adjacent Jamaica Park was renamed Olmsted Park in tribute to its designer, centered on Leverett Pond, a small freshwater pool formed from a swamp. Although it was one of the larger spaces within the park chain, few specific use areas were designated because it was anticipated that the area would eventually become a zoo. Thus, the principal design differences between this area and the Riverway and Muddy River were scale of paths and

View of the Riverway, Boston, from Longwood Bridge circa 1920. (American Society of Landscape Architects, 1931.)

plantings and the presence of two open fields. Above Leverett Park was Jamaica Park, composed primarily of Jamaica Pond. Its shores were encircled with rows or masses of trees, paths, and a parkway. The size of the pond lent itself to boating and a boathouse was provided. Leverett and Jamaica parks were linked by that portion of the necklace's strand called Jamaicaway.

The Arborway was the most regular portion of the park system. With a swath of land only 200 feet wide, it served as an ornamental parkway connecting Jamaica Park with Arnold (then Harvard) Arboretum, and then Franklin Park, the large preserve which terminated the necklace. The Arborway provided three tracks for different types of travel: a bridle path, a drive for vehicles, and a promenade for pedestrians. Each group was separated from adjoining paths by trees and shrubs in masses and hedges. The Arborway formed one edge of the arboretum, a scientific plant collection adjoining the Bussey Institute of Harvard University, which then offered training in horticulture and landscape architecture.

The crowning jewel of the emerald necklace was Franklin Park, an urban open space the equal of Central Park or Prospect Park. In a report accompanying the plan for Franklin Park, Olmsted outlined features of its two main zones. To the northeast, nearest centers of population, would be the more artificial areas, what could be called the Urban Park. Olmsted considered this zone analogous to the reception area of a building. The southwestern two-thirds of the site was the Country Park, a refuge of rural and naturalistic scenery. An east to west through road conveniently separated these two parts. This division allowed access around the clock to the Urban Park, which was illuminated at night. Within each zone, areas appropriate to its function were assigned. The Urban Park contained a promenade and recreational drive system known as the Greeting, now the zoo. Although similar in its linear form to the Mall at Central Park, the Greeting provided parallel paths for carriage and pedestrian traffic. Directly adjoining the half-mile length of the Greeting were entertainment areas, including the semicircular Music Court, the Little Folks Fair—an amusement park for children—and the Deer Park. North of the Greeting sat the Playstead, a 30-acre field reserved for athletic events and for occasions which would draw crowds. Nearby a small wooded tract was set aside for a future zoo.[20]

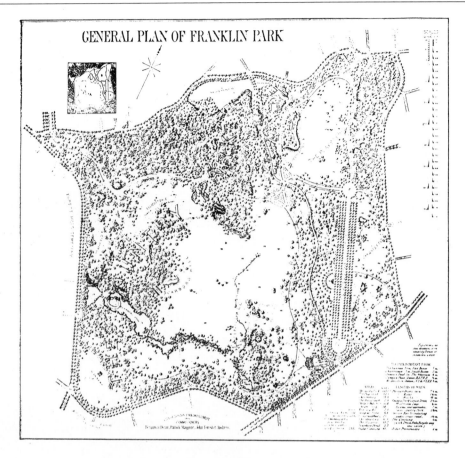

GENERAL PLAN OF FRANKLIN PARK

*Plan of Franklin Park as designed by Olmsted with the "Urban Park" to the right and the "Country Park" to the left. (*Architectural Record, *Vol. 44, No. 5.)*

The Country Park centered on a large open space ringed with tree masses or rock outcroppings. From School Master's Hill in the northeast an overview of the whole meadow, now used as a golf course, was gained. Olmsted reserved rock ledges of the Hill for picnic terraces of native stone shaded by trellises. Near the Hill a small, curved, open space—a miniature Long Meadow—called the Ellicottdale provided unstructured space for lawn games like tennis and croquet. Above the large meadow and School Master's Hill an impressive natural rock outcrop area covered with dense vegetation was preserved as the Wilderness, a picturesque woodland similar to the Ramble. Further around the edge of the big meadow sat a rocky projection, Scarboro Hill, intended to be the site of a refectory and another scenic overlook. Below the hill Scarboro Pond, later added to the original plan, provided a small pool for fishing and skating. Most of the perimeter of parkland surrounding the Country Park was densely wooded, providing an effective screen from the city.

In spite of extensive twentieth-century intrusions and extremely poor past maintenance, Franklin Park preserves the character which Olmsted sought to achieve in all his parks, but which he could hardly describe in mere words. Writing in the report accompanying the Franklin Park plan, he argued the need for rural beauty as a counterbalance to the artificiality of cities. This scenery, though, was "more than an object or a series of objects; more than a spectacle, more than a scene or a series of scenes, more than a landscape, and other than a series of landscapes"; rather, it was scenes of such beauty that they created an uplifting emotional impulse which can be found in no other daily experience (Olmsted, 1886, p. 43).

View of the Ellicottdale in Franklin Park with temporary tennis courts set up. (Architectural Record, Vol. 44, No. 5.)

Pavilion and rocky landscape on School Master's Hill, Franklin Park.

Other Parks and Park Systems in Massachusetts

As comprehensive as the Boston Park system plans were, they were quickly superseded in scope through the efforts of Charles Eliot.[21] Eliot proved to be one of the most effective proponents of open space protection. Within two years of his initial plea for preservation of natural areas in Massachusetts he had guided establishment of two quasi-governmental conversation groups, the Trustees of Reservations and the Metropolitan Park Commission. The Trustees of Reservations were dedicated to preservation of both natural and historical sites in Massachusetts. To do this, they acquired properties through purchase or donation and then managed them for nondestructive visitation. Virginia Woods, a 20-acre hemlock grove, now part of the much larger Middlesex Fells Reservation, was the first property they acquired. Today the society cares for more than sixty-five sites and manages deed restrictions on a like number. Among sites controlled by the Trustees are the William Cullen Bryant Homestead, Naumkeag,[22] and Coskata-Coatue Wildlife Refuge. Beyond these practical conservation achievements, the Trustees of Reservations were significant as the first regional, landholding preservation body. As such, the group influenced formation of national preservation organizations in both England and the United States.

The Metropolitan Park Commission was established to preserve natural areas and provide recreation within the urban and suburban area of Boston. Shortly after its organization in 1892, Eliot was appointed landscape architect and set to work developing a regional park system master plan. His plan stressed the importance of protecting natural scenic areas, such as the Outer and Inner Island of Massachusetts Bay, the value of waterfronts and wetlands, the need for public beaches, and the value of the region's few remaining woodlands, such as Middlesex Fells and the Blue Hills. This plan became the basis for the early work of the Commission.

The Commission not only acquired land to preserve from commercial development, but also built recreational parks. Eliot participated in this aspect of the Commission's work, with his most important contribution being the site plan for Revere Beach in Revere, Massachusetts. There he solved the problem of how to provide facilities for hordes of bathers, while preserving the beautiful strand which they had come to enjoy. Eliot's strategy was to organize a series of parallel zones beyond the beach, with each reserved for a particular function. A promenade with large, covered sitting areas separated the waterfront from an avenue along which bathhouses and private lots for commercial buildings were sited. Behind these beach-related activities, arterial roads, a street railway line, and railroad tracks and station formed a transportation center. To the modern eye, accustomed to the planned beaches of the 1930s and later, this solution does not appear remarkable, but in Eliot's day such spaces had been haphazardly arranged and jammed with shanties that often contributed to serious water pollution.

The Parks Movement in the Midwest

Throughout English-speaking portions of North America, pastoral parks became the civic norm and an expected part of the infrastructure for any progressive city. These parks and park systems also became a mainstay of landscape architectural practice. While the work of all noteworthy landscape architects of this period cannot be reviewed here, a few significant practitioners and projects will illustrate the scope of work. Following the earliest parks developments in the East, Chicago became the first "western" city to design and implement a park system through its three local park commissions. On the north side, Lincoln Park, the first large city park, was designed by local contractor and nursery professional Swain Nelson in the manner of a public garden. West side parks were laid out by the architectural and engineering partnership of Jenney, Schermerhorn and Bogart, with William Le Barron Jenney usually credited as the

Revere Beach as redesigned by Eliot to remove undesirable construction from the beach edge, at right, and organize it along a promenade. (Eliot, 1924.)

actual park designer. Jenney, knowledgeable about park design through travel in Europe and correspondence with Olmsted, designed the three parks of this system as naturalistic landscapes centered on large water features that often occupied a quarter or more of the site.[23] The South Park system was planned by Olmsted and Vaux, with their master plan executed and adapted to changing financial conditions by H. W. S. Cleveland, whose original contribution to the work was detailed planting designs. Positioned beyond the outer edges of the developed city, these three systems, later linked by parkways, were large-scale real estate development schemes aimed at attracting residents to land acquired at low cost by developers. Chicago thus became the first in a long series of North American cities where park development was used to manage and direct residential growth.

H. W. S. Cleveland had moved to Chicago in 1869 to take advantage of urban expansion in the Midwest. His first serious opportunity to implement his own comprehensive views of park systems planning came when he visited the Minneapolis–St. Paul area in 1872. There he instantly foresaw future merging of the Twin Cities of Minnesota and advocated a joint park planning effort to preserve the impressive natural scenery of the region, particularly that along the Mississippi River and the small, glacially formed lakes which have given the state its appellation, "land of 10,000 lakes."

While the sister cities were slow to follow his highly progressive advice, each did within a short time form a separate park system planned by Cleveland. His 1883 plan for Minneapolis parks merely put into concrete form those concepts which he had been discussing with city officials for a decade. The system included small, in-town squares, larger parks at the periphery of the developed areas, formal boulevards to connect these parks, and a pleasure drive through a linear park proposed for the banks of the Mississippi. While his plan detailed only those areas currently within the city limits, he cleverly extended the perimeter of his plan to include those areas outside the city that he would later press to have included in the system, such as Minnehaha Creek and Shingle Creek.

The St. Paul park system plan, begun five years later, was similar in concept to that for Minneapolis. Its larger parks surrounded lakes or were along the Mississippi River shoreline, with linkage of these sites accomplished by an extensive parkway system. The principal large park was Como Park on Lake Como, which in addition to the natural water feature had extensive oak groves. Around

The Lagoon in Washington Park, Chicago, designed by Olmsted and Vaux with planting design by H. W. S. Cleveland.

Washington Park, Lagoon, Chicago.
Oldest South Side Park. Area 371 Acres.

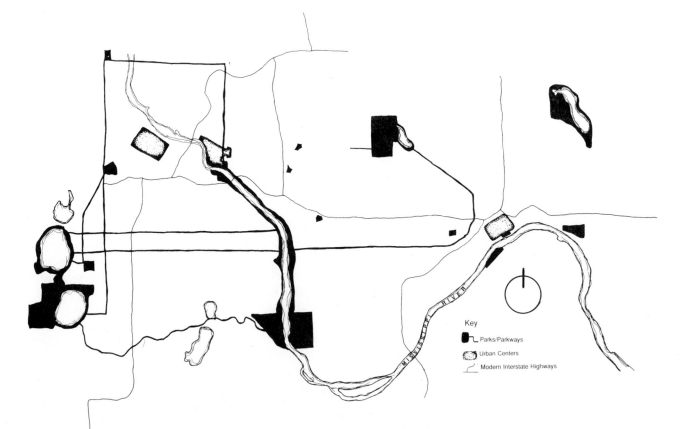

Key

Parks/Parkways

Urban Centers

Modern Interstate Highways

Key components of the park systems for Minneapolis (to the west) and St. Paul (to the east), Minnesota, as proposed by H. W. S. Cleveland. While some components, such as the lakeside parks in St. Paul, were developed, others such as the east to west boulevard across both cities were never completed. (Data from Cleveland, 1883; Cleveland, 1885; and Cleveland, 1888.)

these two natural features Cleveland composed simple masses of trees, meadows, and lakeside recreation areas. Although the design of this 257-acre site was certainly important to Cleveland, the areas for which he expressed the greatest concern were the small open spaces of the city—the squares and boulevards. Addressing the Board of Park Commissioners in 1888 he quickly pointed out that in most cities small urban squares were little more than pedestrian shortcuts: "The paths become simply thoroughfares for the rushing crowds who would otherwise be kept upon the sidewalks, and whose presence is fatal to the idea of restful refreshment [in the square].... The paths and open spaces should be disposed so as not only to invite repose but to offer no inducement to anyone who is in a hurry to think he can save time by entering it" (1889, p. 20). In the design for these small squares, Cleveland used wide paths arranged in broad curves to invite strolling and relaxing. Ample paved areas provided plenty of room for benches.

Of even greater importance to Cleveland than the squares were the linking boulevards of the city, because he had long been interested in both the visual and functional contributions that boulevards could make to urban plans. For St. Paul, with its long riverfront, Cleveland proposed a parkway loop to connect all the parks, as well as riverfront and bluff-top drives which preserved the best river overlooks. Thinking ahead to a metropolitan system for the Twin Cities, he positioned St. Paul parks and parkways in relation to significant natural areas on the Minneapolis side of the river. For example, he sited Hiawatha Park on the eastern side of the Mississippi River directly opposite the outfall of Minnehaha Creek, along which, under Cleveland's guidance, Minneapolis later developed a parkway.

Cleveland also believed that boulevards were an effective way to introduce parkland into every neighborhood, so that people could use open spaces daily rather than only on occasions when they had time to travel to a large landscape park. Parks also performed significant functional roles in urban plans. They helped define neighborhoods and manipulate land uses by influencing real estate valuation. Cleveland, among others, thought of parks and boulevards as areas where polluted air could be cleansed. Finally, Cleveland advocated the use of extensive parkway systems as a way to control urban fires, a major hazard of the nineteenth century.

Minneapolis and St. Paul had ideal natural amenities upon which to develop an integrated park system, which preserved natural features while making them accessible for use. For other midwestern cities, Cleveland produced equally effective park systems from far less impressive natural landscapes. One such city was Omaha, Nebraska. Here, as typical of almost all his design work, topography was the principal formgiver, but it was not dramatic high points or rock outcroppings which were central to the Omaha concept. Rather, Cleveland used natural depressions as the focal park areas. Concave land surfaces had the advantage of making small spaces appear larger, because the eye was drawn down and across a greater expanse of terrain. Thus, by centering parks around hollows, even tiny parks could be visually enlarged.

The Omaha park system was more balanced in composition than those for the Twin Cities, because each park was of a slightly different type to serve a different form of recreation. Those differences were based primarily upon park size and distance from the city center. At one end of the scale was Jefferson Square, the oldest remaining open space within the city, redesigned as a public plaza with ample walks and seating areas shaded by randomly dispersed trees. Tiny Bemis Park became a tranquil resting spot set in the valley of a small stream. Larger parks were located at the edge of or beyond the developed areas of the city. Hanscom Park, then the city's principal park, became a social gathering space with many entertainment features and a dense path system. A larger park proposed by Cleveland, Elmwood, became the principal naturalistic space in the city, with emphasis placed on preservation of landscape features, large-scale open spaces and tree plantings, and protection of undergrowth to separate use areas. With the exception of Elmwood Park, all of the parks were linked via a parkway system that also led to a parksite intended to be developed later along the Missouri River.

Bemis Park in Omaha, Nebraska, shown in the 1980s, illustrates Cleveland's use of concave landforms for park sites in that city.

Bushnell Park, Hartford, Connecticut, designed by Weidenmann circa 1861, with the State Capitol in the distance at right. The memorial Soldiers and Sailors Monument with twin towers was added to the park in 1885. (Souvenir Postcard Company.)

Another of the more widely recognized early landscape architects, Jacob Weidenmann, also engaged in parks design work. While much of this, such as the designs for Mount Royal Park and Congress Park, in Saratoga Springs, New York, was completed by Weidenmann while in the employ of Olmsted, Hartford's Bushnell Park was designed solely by Weidenmann. Beginning in 1861, he transformed what had been a marshy, riverside site generally considered undevelopable into a park on the scale of a Public Garden, but having more sophisticated open space and planting arrangements. To compensate for the small site size, he limited plantings to path edges, leaving large open meadows. The largest of these meadows created an informal line of sight from downtown Hartford to Trinity College, now replaced by the State Capitol, on a high point above the park. At the lowest point in the park, a small picturesque pond furnished a focal point for the entire strolling experience. Weidenmann, trained as an architect and engineer, also designed the major structures—bridges and a viewing terrace—that linked the park with the city.[24]

St. Louis had quickly followed Chicago in the establishment of large naturalistic parks. Beginning in the mid-1870s, under the design leadership of Maximilian Kern, several city parks were built, the most important of which was Forest Park.[25] More than 1,300 acres in size, this was then the largest designed park in North America. As its name suggests, dense woodland, augmented with features such as ponds and rustic shelter, was its principal attraction. Kern also envisioned the park as a place for recreational driving, so he planned a 2-mile circuitous scenic drive through an arboretum-like tree planting.

Further west, San Francisco contemplated setting aside land for a scenic park. In 1865, Olmsted was consulted on plans for a proposed park in the city, but being unfamiliar with the potentials of the hilly, stark landscape and dry climate of northern California he concluded that ornamental, parklike vegetation would not grow well there, and recommended against developing a Central Park-style landscape park.[26] Fortunately for the city, Olmsted's judgement did not deter others from acting. Construction for Golden Gate Park, on a site occupied by windswept sand dunes, was begun in 1870. The park and its site had a number of significant similarities to New York's Central Park: most obvious

View of Drexel Boulevard, Chicago, designed by Cleveland in the 1870s. Creation of the Boulevard, which linked Washington Park with the center of the city, quickly made Drexel the most fashionable address in the city.

was its long, narrow, rectilinear shape, conforming to the adjoining grid of the city plan. Its designer, engineer William Hammond Hall, magnified these similarities by replicating many motifs that had been used at Central Park, including the proposed but never built below-grade transverse roads. Golden Gate Park did not merely copy its more famous East Coast forerunner. Hall adapted the design to local conditions—for example, sinking paths and planting many needle-leaf evergreens to screen visitors from blustery ocean winds. Small lakes throughout the park were used to collect tidal overflow and drain lowlands between the former dunes. Although much altered by addition of buildings and theme gardens over the decades, Golden Gate Park remains a confirmation of Hall's design and engineering proficiency as applied to an unyielding natural setting.

Similar park development continued throughout the 1880s and into the early 1890s. Later park systems of note included that for Quincy, Illinois, with design work begun by Cleveland but later continued by Ossian Simonds, who designed more than ten parks for the city using the native midwestern plants and plant compositions which he favored. Quincy was thus the first American city to have parks designed in what would later be called the "Prairie Style."[27] In the East, Samuel Parsons took up the mantle of New York City parks development, but his work was generally confined to small tracts of land such as St. Nicholas and Jeannette parks. In Cleveland, Ernest Bowditch was commissioned to perfect the existing park system of small squares and gardens by siting and designing large pastoral parks, such as linear Rockefeller Park along Doan Brook. But the culminating plan of forty years of park development in North America was the system of open spaces and boulevards that George Kessler designed for Kansas City, Missouri. This system owed much to the landscape park movement pioneered by Daniels, Olmsted, Vaux, Cleveland, and others, but was also a sign of things to come in the near future. Not only were there large naturalistic parks, and smaller squares and boulevards, but these spaces, especially the squares and boulevards, were designed with more architectonic spatial geometry. Thus, where irregular masses had been used in Cleveland's design for Drexel Boulevard in Chicago, Kessler arranged walks, planting areas, and trees to conform with the boulevard's linear parkway form. In addition, he added many classically styled structures, such as pergolas, and ornately patterned flower beds to the nine-block-long boulevard park known as the Paseo. The novelty of Kessler's

11067
PERGOLA ON THE PASEO,
KANSAS CITY, MO.

The linear park promenade known as The Paseo, in Kansas City, Missouri, designed by Kessler.

work, and its impact on landscape design for the thirty years which followed, has been overshadowed by the influences toward formality of the World's Columbian Exposition, held in Chicago in 1893, the same year Kessler issued his first planning report and designs. Yet in the 1890s and the early twentieth century, Kansas City parks were as widely publicized as Central Park had been thirty-five years earlier.

As this new type of urban open space, which emphasized social spaces above naturlistic ones, was presented to the public, other forces were at work to alter the nature of park planning and design. First, as pastoral parks became the norm in large cities, their novelty wore away. Second, parks and boulevards had long been advocated as a way to ameliorate urban problems, but they proved insufficient remedies for problems resulting from industrialization, pollution, and increasing population. Third, improved inexpensive transportation, especially the street railway, made access to rural and undeveloped areas possible for all but the poorest urban residents. These factors, coupled with changing design preferences—they were moving away from the naturalistic and toward contrived, highly ornamented landscapes—signaled a rapid decline in the development of large pastoral parks. While such open spaces have remained part of every city's park repertoire up to the present day, their naturalistic and rural qualities were increasingly compromised with the addition of floral displays, amusement areas, zoos, new buildings, and overgrown vegetation.

PARKS BUILD A PROFESSION

More than any other design and planning activity, the parks movement created the profession of landscape architecture. Earlier projects such as Rural Cemeteries and estates had, of course, allowed designers employment in their chosen field of specialization, but these projects were small in scale and largely dominated by aesthetic concerns. Park design, on the other hand, demanded a more comprehensive philosophy to guide the social, environmental, political, and technological planning required for sites so vast and significant to cities. In particular, a coherent rationale for the value of parks as a public responsibility was required to justify the costs of such developments and the effort required. This partly explains why certain practitioners were propelled to the forefront, while others perhaps more skilled as designers were less well known to the public. Persuasive writers and speakers such as Olmsted and Cleveland were able to address public concerns about landscape development by establishing theories about the underlying value of design to society; that is, they were able to justify it as a logical expression of the welfare role of city governments.

Olmsted focused on the social role of park design:

> There are certain forms of recreation, a large share of the attraction of which must, I think, lie in the gratification of the gregarious inclination, and which . . . are so popular as to establish the importance of the requirement. If I ask myself where I have experienced the most complete gratification of this instinct in public and out of doors, among trees, I find that it has been in the promenade of the Champs Elysées. As closely following it I should name other promenades of Europe, and our own upon the New York parks. I have several times seen fifty thousand people participating in them; and the more I have seen of them, the more highly have I been led to estimate their value as means of counteracting the evils of town life . . . [for] I have looked studiously but vainly among them for a single face completely unsympathetic with the prevailing expression of good nature and light-heartedness. (1870, pp. 18–19)

Cleveland on the other hand focused particularly on functional and environmental aspects of park design:

> The landscape gardener has no other duty than to serve as the high priest of Nature. The highest function of his art is to interpret her language, and develop her suggestions, and in so doing he should only dare to touch with very reverent hands, the symbols through which she addresses her worshippers. He may so arrange the approaches which give access to her sanctuaries, as to afford the most impressive views . . . [and] conceal incongruous objects. . . . But the man who could look down from these rocky heights, through the gorgeous forest which lines their side, upon the mighty [Mississippi] river which flows at their feet, and talk of 'improving' them by the introduction of such artificial decorations as constitute the stock in trade of most of the so called landscape gardeners, who can see no beauty in Nature till they have washed her face and combed her hair and put her in stay—should be hurled headlong from the precipice whose features he would thus desecrate. . . . Preserve above all the wild and picturesque character of the river banks, and do not suffer them to be stripped of their foliage or scarred and seamed by excavations. The day is not distant when the thickly wooded banks, the deep and dark ravine, the rugged and precipitous rocks, and the picturesque cascades which form the shores of the majestic river, will be regarded as your choicest possessions for the unique character they will confer upon the city. No money could purchase what nature has here provided, and its value when contrasted to the architectural display of the great metropolis, will be proportionate to the degree of wild grandeur and beauty they display, and which no art can imitate. (1885, pp. 23–24)

As theory advanced, concern grew among many landscape designers and planners to find an appropriate term by which their unique and eclectic mixture of professional skills could be designated. Although widely used into the 1850s, the title "landscape gardener" was apparently even then not universally popular since some practitioners preferred the more erudite title of "landscape engineer" or the more picturesque name of "rural architect."[28] The first known use of the term "landscape architecture" was in the title of an 1828 book on landscape painting. As used there, it meant specifically architecture placed in landscape scenes, particularly those suitable for painting. In spite of this limited intended definition, the author, Gilbert L. Meason, suggested a quite comprehensive view of the relationship between built form and landscape form as that which "may at once enrich and restrain invention . . . to adapt the house to the site, and to unite the building to the ground, and both to the surrounding style of scenery"

(1828, p. 72). Whether such supportive sentiments encouraged later designers to adopt Meason's term is unknown, but his book was certainly widely know in nineteenth-century art and design circles.

The first use of "landscape architecture" in the modern sense to identify a landscape management, planning, design, and research discipline is credited to Olmsted and Vaux, although opinions as to the date of first usage differ. Whatever the precise date of its implementation, "landscape architecture" has always been a debatable phrase. Writing to Vaux from California in 1865, Olmsted reflected unfavorably upon this new professional title. "I am all the time bothered with the miserable nomenclature of landscape architecture. Landscape is not a good word. Architecture is not; the combination is not. Gardening is worse. . . . The art is not gardening, nor is it architecture. What I am doing here in Cala. [sic] especially is neither. It is the sylvan art, *fine* art in distinction from agriculture, or sylvan useful art. We want a distinction between a Nurseryman and a market gardener and a orchardist and an artist. . . . If you are bound to establish this new art—you dont [sic] want an old name for it" (Vaux, Papers, August 1, 1865). Yet in the end Olmsted bowed to what was Vaux's choice of nomenclature and called himself a landscape architect, perhaps realizing that to be called a "sylvan artist" was even less explicit.

Other designers accepted the new terminology less readily. H. W. S. Cleveland, for example, vacillated throughout his life, using each title, landscape gardener and landscape architect, on occasion. Many, such as Maximilian Kern and Adolph Strauch, perhaps remaining true to their European origins, used "landscape gardener" exclusively. Even into the twentieth century practitioners continued to use the older term. Beatrix Jones Farrand, although a founding member of the American Society of Landscape Architects, always described herself as a landscape gardener. This lack of consensus on an appropriate appellation

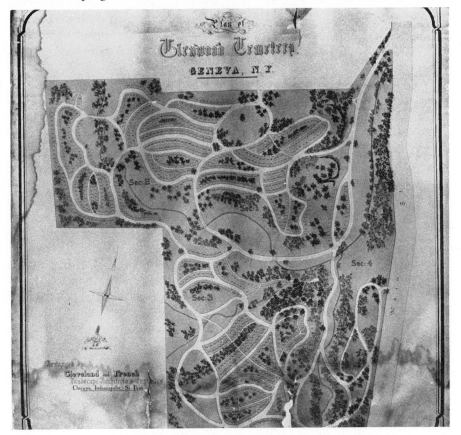

Plan of Glenwood Cemetery, Geneva, New York, by Cleveland circa 1872. (Collection of the Geneva Historical Society.)

Computer-animated view of the entry drive to Glenwood Cemetery looking from the south. View based on the plan shown in Figure 18–26. (Animation by Ed Cunnius; project funded by College of Architecture, Texas A&M University.)

for the profession has troubled practitioners to the present day, as witnessed by a spate of letters to the editors of *Landscape Architecture* magazine during the 1980s on the issue of a name change. By whatever term practitioners preferred to be called or in whatever specialty they practiced, all remained bound by the underlying philosophy of land utilization based on fit to human physical, psychological, and social needs coupled with perpetuation of natural systems in altered but stable states, which was first promulgated by the pioneer landscape architects of nineteenth-century North America.

DIVERSITY OF PROFESSIONAL PRACTICE IN THE LATE NINETEENTH CENTURY

While parks were the most significant and acclaimed projects on which landscape architects worked in the second half of the nineteenth century, their practices remained diverse. Typical projects included cemetery site plans; design of institutional grounds such as hospitals, schools, and government buildings; estate designs; and regional resource plans.

Cemeteries

Cemetery design continued to be a mainstay of professional practice after the Civil War, as cities in the West and Midwest built new burial grounds and eastern cities expanded existing sites. Within this vast body of work only a few projects and designers stand out as having made distinctive contributions. Frederick Law Olmsted designed one of the first Rural Romantic Cemeteries west of the Rocky Mountains—Mountain Grove Cemetery in Oakland, California. Mountain Grove Cemetery uniquely combined a formal, geometric area with a typically Romantic, naturalistic area. The design placed formal area on a portion of the site which was a level surface, for such landforms were "as far as possible . . . from being suggestive of picturesque treatment . . . whereas, on the hill-sides, to secure ease of ascent and descent, and to avoid rocks and sharp declivities, it is more natural and easy to proceed by curved and sinuous courses" (Mountain Grove Cemetery Association, 1865, p. 48). Plantings further reinforced the form established by roads and paths, for in the formal area each plot was surrounded

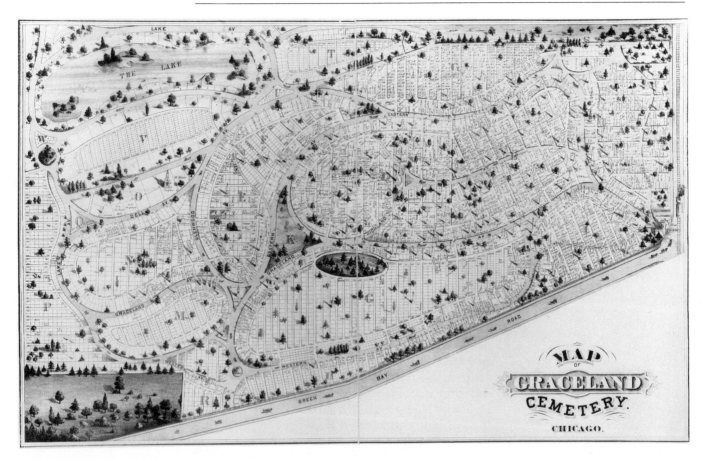

Plan of Graceland Cemetery in 1876 predates the known involvement of Ossian Simonds, who redesigned the cemetery in what came to be known as the Prairie style beginning in 1878 (see Chapter 24). This plan is unattributed, but may represent the individual or joint design efforts of William Saunders, Adolph Strauch, H. W. S. Cleveland, and Bryan Lathrop, an official of the cemetery. (Chicago Historical Society.)

by a hedge, while in the naturalistic area asymmetrical masses were used to separate plots.

Jacob Weidenmann was considered the premier cemetery designer of his day. Perfecting the "lawn style" cemetery originated by Strauch, Weidenmann promoted the concept of an open ground plane unencumbered by numerous monuments. In his book *Modern Cemeteries,* he outlined the design approach at the many cemeteries he had designed, the most famous of which was Cedar Hill in Hartford, Connecticut.

H. W. S. Cleveland continued to design Rural Romantic Cemeteries throughout the country, including Glenwood Cemetery in Geneva, New York; Eastwood Cemetery in his boyhood hometown of Lancaster, Massachusetts; Highland Cemetery in Junction City, Kansas; and Lakewood Cemetery in Minneapolis, where he would later be buried. These later works differed from those he had produced in partnership with Copeland prior to the Civil War and demonstrated the relatively modest, but noticeable, changes that had occurred in cemetery design in the ensuing years. Earlier Rural Romantic Cemeteries were relatively crowded, with some parallel drives being less than 45 feet apart and road curves often very tight. These features, coupled with the abundance of individual headstones and footstones, gave cemeteries a crowded look even when otherwise well designed. Largely through Strauch's influence, later Rural Romantic Cemeteries became more graceful in design, with broadly curving roads enclosing large areas of turf unbroken by monuments. Thus, the work of Cleveland and others during the late nineteenth century acquired a more restful and elegant quality under the lawn-style influence.

Spring Grove Cemetery not only influenced changes in cemetery design,

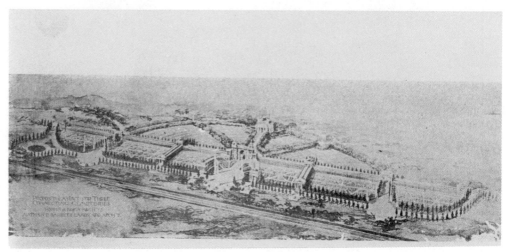

Although Romantic designs were typical for most cemeteries in the mid- and late nineteenth century, Nathan Barrett presaged early twentieth-century trends toward more architectonic landscapes in this apparently unimplemented 1876 scheme for three connected cemeteries. (The American Architect, Vol. 129, No. 2488.)

but also became a training ground for a number of landscape designers who spread the lawn style across much of the continent. The most successful of these pupils were members of the Earnshaw family, who designed cemeteries throughout the Midwest. Working under the firm name of Earnshaw and Punchon, they laid out Linwood Cemetery in Dubuque, Iowa, and Forest Lawn Cemetery in Omaha, Nebraska. Others who likely worked at Spring Grove and learned design principles through its example were H. A. Engelhardt, the designer of Mount Pleasant Cemetery in Toronto, Ontario, and Leo Weltz, who planned an addition to Oak Hill Cemetery in Lawrence, Kansas.

One of the most important cemeteries of this period—important because of its later influence on the twentieth-century style known as the Prairie Style—was Graceland Cemetery in Chicago, Illinois. Although earlier plans have been attributed to William Saunders and H. W. S. Cleveland, it is the more famous and still extant scheme for which Ossian Simonds is credited.[29] In plan, the cemetery was much the same as other Rural Romantic Cemeteries, with curving roads adapted to what landform existed in Chicago and a small pond as an ornamental feature. But what made Simonds's design unique was use of native plants. While not religiously opposed to exotics, he believed that natives could adapt better to a variety of difficult growing situations such as steep hillsides or wetlands. Further, he appreciated the beauty of the layered natural woodland with its canopy trees, shrubs of varied height and texture, and groundcover of wildflowers, believing that "nature is the best teacher" for designers (1932).

Later in the nineteenth century, cemeteries underwent a significant transformation, as did parks and boulevards. The meandering curves and irregular planting masses of the Romantic style were gradually replaced with a more regular geometry. Curves were often preserved, but as parts of circles, and formal axial spaces became more prominent. In addition, the trend begun with the introduction of Strauch's lawn concept was taken to its logical conclusion when upright monuments were prohibited. This style of cemetery would later, in the early twentieth century, be called the "memorial park." One of the earliest designers to use this approach was Nathan Barrett. In the 1880s Barrett laid out Hillside Cemetery in Anniston, Alabama, as a mosaic-like composition of circles, rectangles, and triangular forms. This arrangement divided the small burial ground into many isolated plots and emphasized the road pattern over green spaces. It was so simple as to be naive. Earlier, though, Barrett had demonstrated greater polish in the use of formal plans in an apparently unbuilt scheme for three linked cemeteries in which diagonal roads were used as principal visual linkages.[30]

Design of Institutional Sites

The nineteenth century was a period of growth in the number of public and private institutions, as well as of evolution in their approach to services, particularly for those associated with health and education. Several new types of healthcare facilities were widely developed, including veterans' residential hospitals and mental hospitals, each of which had specific site-planning and design requirements. Veterans' hospitals to serve needs of aging Civil War veterans, both the ill and the homeless, were built throughout the northern United States in the 1880s. These "hospitals" were in fact rest homes intended for permanent, as well as temporary, residence. Thus their sites had to accommodate long-term social and recreational needs. One such hospital site designed by a landscape architect was the Western Branch of the National Military Home in Leavenworth, Kansas, designed by H. W. S. Cleveland. There, dormitories were aligned along a crescent-shaped ridge to take advantage of natural ventilation and afford views to distant hills and the Missouri River. Service buildings were sited on the sides and downhill to preserve uninterrupted vistas. The Home's "frontyard" was a sloping swath of lawn across which entry drives angled. The general character of the site and its amenities, such as the ornamental pond named Lake Jeannette, were intended to provide a homelike atmosphere for residents, while affording a variety of visual and recreational opportunities.

Treatment of the mentally ill was revolutionized in the nineteenth century through the efforts of physicians such as Thomas Kirkbride and Isaac Ray. Among the innovations that they pioneered was the introduction of intimate, homelike environments in mental hospitals. While most design efforts to achieve this goal focused on architecture, design of grounds played a significant role in creating a residential atmosphere. As early as 1859, Cleveland pioneered this type of design work with his plan for Butler Hospital in Providence, Rhode Island. Later, Olmsted and Vaux made a significant advance in refinement of this therapeutic environment with their site and architectural plans at the Retreat for the Insane at Hartford, Connecticut. The grounds there included outbuildings and gardens for patient recreation, such as the Conservatory with its winter garden. At each of these hospitals, in keeping with their residential character, the grounds were designed like those of a private estate, with looping drives, paths, scenic vistas

View of Cleveland's arrangement for dormitory residences at the Western Branch National Military Home, now the Veterans Administration Center, Wadsworth, Kansas, circa 1895. (South–West News Company.)

through woodlands, garden pavilions, and, at Butler, small ponds created by weirs along a stream.

Hospital sites, however, made up only a small part of landscape architectural practice. Far more significant in terms of number of sites and size of the geographical area in which the designers were active were schools, particularly colleges and universities. The period from the late 1860s to the 1880s was a boom time for public university development. Passage of the Morrill Act of 1862 put in place the mechanism for financing university construction and expansion through sale of public lands granted by the federal government to states.[31] Among the schools that were developed during this period were the University of California at Berkeley, the University of Minnesota in Minneapolis, Kansas State University at Manhattan, and University Park in Toronto, Ontario.

The first plan for the University of California was executed by Olmsted and Vaux following Olmsted's post-Sanitary Commission stint in California.[32] In concept, it owes much to Thomas Jefferson's "academical village" idea, for Olmsted and Vaux also envisioned the university as a complete town rather than simply a collection of classrooms, dormitories, and libraries. In their view, as expressed in the report written by Olmsted,

> Scholars should be prepared to lead, not to follow reluctantly after, the advancing line of civilization. To be qualified as leaders they must have an intelligent appreciation of and sympathy with the real life of civilization, and this can only be acquired through a familiarity with the higher and more characteristic forms in which it is developed. For this reason it is desirable that scholars, at least during the period of life in which character is most easily moulded, should be surrounded by manifestations of refined domestic life, these being unquestionably the ripest and best fruits of civilization. (1866b, p. 335)

To accomplish these lofty goals, the plan provided both a campus and an adjoining townsite. Within the wooded campus different use areas were allocated in large tracts. Of these the university complex was the most structured, with buildings set on both sides of a sight line carved through tree masses to direct views toward the Golden Gate of San Francisco. Adjoining the campus proper were residential areas for faculty and students, with student housing to be like large residences rather than dormitories. South of campus the village of Berkeley was laid out in a perfunctory grid, but with a public garden at the end of the main street. Recreation in a more natural setting was provided in a mountainside park connected to the university and town by a winding hillside drive.[33]

Cleveland's plan for the University of Minnesota was less ambitious, but perhaps this simplicity allowed it to be implemented while Olmsted and Vaux's plan was not. Like the Berkeley plan, Cleveland's sought to exploit the natural setting of the campus, in this case on a bluff above the Mississippi River, by positioning all buildings in a broad curve overlooking the river. A service drive ran behind the buildings at a lower elevation, but was screened by landform and vegetation. The principal drive formed a curve directly in front of this row of buildings and separated them from the large lawn which was foreground to the campus. Vegetation, other than the lawn, consisted of simple masses of native and introduced trees, which created a small park in front of the buildings.[34]

Kansas State University was planned in the 1880s by Maximilian Kern as the academic equivalent of a *ferme ornée,* having study and living areas integrated with the agricultural tracts so important to the mission of land grant colleges. The entry driveway passed through a large lawn edged with dense tree plantings, then under a grove of trees, and finally spread out into smaller drives that linked buildings and fields. At the center of the campus, buildings formed a loose, irregular cluster, while areas beyond this ring were reserved for fields, orchards,

5152. General View of University of Minnesota.

View of the University of Minnesota in Minneapolis, circa 1900, designed by Cleveland, showing the entry and parklike foreground to campus buildings which overlooked the Mississippi Valley to the rear. (Photo by C. J. Hibbard & Company; published by the Acmegraph Company.)

a vineyard, nurseries, and pasture, all in small tracts often separated from each other by tree masses.[35]

In Canada, fewer campuses were developed in the mid- and late nineteenth century, but in general their designers favored naturalistic design concepts similar to those detailed above, as did most of their American contemporaries. William Mundie's plan for University Park in Toronto sought to make the entire campus an urban park as well as a study center. A creek corridor reserved as open space separated the campus into two zones, but also gave its otherwise naturalistic plan a clear spatial structure. Plant arrangements were similar to those in English Landscape Gardening schemes, rather than to the picturesque designs which most designers in the United States favored. Principal tree plantings were boundary masses, with only a few scattered clumps punctuating open fields, rather than creating spaces. Mundie's plan was earlier than the other work discussed here, having been started in about 1853. Thus, he had few predecessors from whom to draw inspiration, making this an important transition project between the early campus designs of Jefferson and Ramée and the more mature works that were to follow in the next three or four decades.

Private universities, many organized by religious denominations, were also founded during this period. The most famous of the private universities was Leland Stanford Junior University in Palo Alto, California, established by railroad developer and ex-governor Leland Stanford, Sr., in honor of his deceased son. Stanford was well known not only for the quality of its scholarship, but also for the innovative, regionally responsive plan on which its original development was based. There, Olmsted reapplied the comprehensive concept of a complete community, with both "town and gown," which the University of California had earlier rejected.

In Olmsted's original plan, the Stanford campus, its associated village, and open spaces were organized in a regularized but curvilinear pattern, with university buildings clustered in a semicircular row around an oval plaza. Directly in front of this area, large blocks were reserved for a woodland which linked the campus and adjoining planned residential neighborhood. Although similar in land-planning concept to later plans, this first sketch differed markedly in form from the final quadrangle plan for which Stanford became so well known. Turner et al. (1976) credit Leland Stanford himself, rather than Olmsted, with suggesting the more formal, but regionally contextural concept of linked plaza-like quadrangles.[36]

As the plan finally evolved, a series of linked quadrangles completely enclosed by buildings were the modules of design. Arcaded walkways protected pedestrians from sun and rain, while providing transitions from total enclosure in buildings to the openness of outdoor courtyards. These quad courtyards had designs similar to those of Spanish patios, with large paved areas suitable for many uses, but having dense central plantings in elevated circular planters as well. Three such quadrangles were built, with the central one being the heart of campus. At the main entry to the central quadrangle, a large commemorative arch was placed, framing the sight line to the Romanesque-style chapel by architects Rutan & Coolidge that was the focal piece of the entire space. The two flanking quadrangles were more simply designed. Beyond these two quads, space was retained for the addition of future modules, which never occurred. Outside the campus proper, the woodlands and village so essential to Olmsted's original concept were retained, but the form of the village restructured to a regular arrangement of straight streets angled toward the central quadrangle. Through a woodland park sited in front of the main quadrangle ran the principal entry drive to the campus. To the north, hillside land was to be preserved for a large park.[37]

Government-sponsored design works included the grounds of national and state capitols, as well as universities. The most successful and well known of these projects was Olmsted's design for the U.S. Capitol grounds in Washington, D.C. Following in the footsteps of Andrew Jackson Downing, who as the premier landscape designer of *his* day was commissioned to plan the most important public project executed in Washington, Olmsted was selected to redesign the unfinished grounds on Capitol Hill. This work proved important not only because of its national prominence, but because it was one of Olmsted's most sophisticated small-site plans.[38] Here he clearly integrated built form with the preexisting naturalistic design of the Mall, while still preserving within his own Romantic plan some of the axiality intended by L'Enfant in the original master plan for the city.

Olmsted's principal design problem was how to visually and physically integrate the western facade of the building, much elevated above the surrounding grade, with the adjacent landscape. Terraces had previously been suggested for

View of Stanford University, Palo Alto, California, from the entry park circa 1900. (R. J. Waters & Company.)

Plan for the grounds of the U.S. Capitol, by Olmsted. (Collection of the Architect of the Capitol.)

this linkage, but none put in place. Olmsted proposed construction of three massive terraces with broad flights of steps. The upper terrace formed a pedestal the entire length of the Capitol, extending the building's visual weight into the landscape. The lower terraces were smaller and served primarily as intermissions between stair flights, but also as a visual transition from the imposing structure to the more intimately scaled grounds. On-site circulation was critical to site use. Olmsted maintained the eastern side of the building as a transportation center, with a large paved area directly in front of the Capitol set aside for waiting vehicles and several alternative driveways for entry and exit. The western side, adjoining the Mall, became a small park with tree-shaded walks and secluded grotto enclosing a spring-fed water fountain. Arrangement of plantings on this side of the building was critical to preserving the sight line and vista that L'Enfant had so carefully composed toward the Potomac River. While Olmsted grouped trees so that the edges of masses were irregular, he carefully balanced the mass north of the sight line with an equal and symmetrical mass to the south.

He thus demonstrated that naturalistic Romantic plantings could be adapted to create a similar spatial structure as could more architectonic plantings.

An equally successful plan for an equally difficult siting of a government building was Vaux's plan for the Canadian Parliament in Ottawa, Ontario. Working under the hardship of not being able to visit the site (the design committee did not wish to pay for a trip), Vaux cleverly resolved the problem of adjacent buildings set at different elevations. He introduced a broad terrace with steps and ramps similar in concept, but with far less elevation change, to that at Washington, D.C. To further disguise irregularities in position, the grounds in front of the buildings were arranged as a paved and turfed plaza, with paths from sides and corners directed toward a central fountain. These angled paths drew the eye to the principal tower of Parliament, emphasizing the symmetry of the site and its buildings.[39]

State capitol grounds usually did not receive the same professional design treatment as did the U.S. Capitol and the Canadian Parliament. One exception was the statehouse grounds in Topeka, Kansas, although the design for these was never implemented. The designer, Cleveland, developed a plan with Romantic plantings and curvilinear but symmetrical circulation system.[40] Along the perimeter, staggered rows of trees separated the elegant statehouse from the rough and muddy streets of this frontier town. Other plantings were more random and generally less dense, most likely to allow good views of the Capitol. To achieve balance between this huge, soon to be domed structure, and its relatively small site, large areas of lawn were set between the building and surrounding streets.

Residential Design

While site-planning projects such as hospitals and cemeteries exposed the general public to landscape architectural work, many designers continued an active practice in private residential design. Ironically, this work, which may have constituted the greatest percentage of completed projects by many nineteenth-century designers, was the least well documented area of professional practice. There are two reasons for this. First, many of these projects were considered commonplace in their day—not notable enough to record. Second, most of these works have undergone such alteration over the years that, even when a site location is known, it may no longer even approximate the original design.

Therefore our best sources of information on nineteenth-century residential design are the plethora of pattern books published during this era. Although many of these were written by individuals of little known ability, several landscape architects published significant treaties. Among the more noteworthy of these works were *Rural Taste* by Maximilian Kern, *Pacific Rural Handbook* by Charles Shinn, *Beautifying Country Homes* by Jacob Weidenmann, and *Country Life* by Robert Morris Copeland. Each work made its own contribution, but the last two are most useful in understanding nineteenth-century design for residences.

Weidenmann's book was the quintessential pattern book, with a written text of helpful hints coupled with design and construction vignettes. A portfolio of more than twenty color plates, principally of residences by various designers, rounded out the volume. These plates illustrated potential arrangements for the fashionable suburban home with a half-acre or more of ground. Typically, in these plans the site was informally divided into two areas; one the ceremonial "frontyard" via which visitors entered the home, the other a work yard with service outbuildings, animal pens, and productive gardens. Arrangement of each portion was equally important, but the front was designed for style and handsome effect, while the rear was arranged for efficiency, to avoid domestic pollution, and to maintain screening of the area. These designs are only illustrated in plan, and it is difficult to assess the quality of the overall site plans since all have a sameness of curving roads, masses of trees, flower beds, and the odd pond

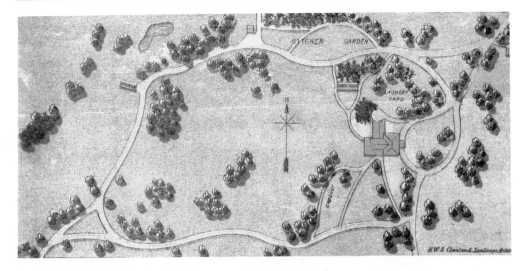

"Design of Grounds for the Hon. J. Y. Scammon, Hyde Park [now Chicago], Illinois," by Cleveland, circa 1871. (Art Institute of Chicago.)

or gazebo. Also, in the absence of graphic indicators of landform, the only significant differences between the work of various designers appear to be in the arrangement and composition of planting plans. Some designers—for example, E. F. Miller and Michael Butler—favored more scattered planting, while others—for example, W. L. Fisher and Eugene Bauman—used tight, dense masses especially at site edges. Weidenmann's own residential work fell somewhere between these two extremes, being generally more diverse than that shown for others.

Copeland's *Country Life* dealt with far more technical issues related to development of house grounds and farms. It was in fact the most comprehensive work of the period, with discussions ranging from general design issues to the construction of subsurface drainage systems. It was also far less of a pattern book, with its illustrations used to demonstrate principles which could be adapted to different sites, rather than to show plans to be followed precisely.

One noticeable trend in residential design in the 1860s and after was inclusion of Gardenesque elements, such as flower beds in the form of circles or arabesques, in plans which were otherwise Romantic in character. This represented the increasing influence of J. C. Loudon's writings on American public taste and, after 1876, the example of the grounds design at the Centennial Exposition held in Philadelphia. Even the works of Weidenmann, considered a proponent of Romantic style, displayed a similar but less frequent Gardenesque component. For example, his plan for Terrace Hill in Des Moines, Iowa, included a prominent circular flower bed set in the middle of open lawn.

Many designers did hold more steadfastly to unadulterated Romantic design principles. Donald Mitchell, best known for his literary works under the nom de plume Ik Marvel, also briefly practiced as a landscape gardener. However, his most successful design work was not the professional projects, such as parks in Allegheny, Pennsylvania, or East Rock Park in New Haven, Connecticut, but his own estate, known as Edgewood. There he created a Romantic *ferme ornée* on a very picturesque wooded tract. This design epitomized the picturesque landscape, with natural plantings modeled to create vistas toward Mitchell's modest farm home.

In the Midwest, Cleveland claimed to have laid out dozens of estates, but few were noted by name. A documented one was the residence of J. Y. Scammon in Hyde Park, located off the Midway, a boulevard connecting Washington and Jackson parks in Chicago. This 20-acre site was laid out with a highly developed zone near the house for lawn games and flower beds. By using massed trees to encircle and screen work areas such as the laundry yard, they could be located near the house without being visible from it. Most of the site was given over to a parklike area with a circuit drive around it.

One of the most famous Romantic residences of the nineteenth century was Olana, home of Hudson River School painter Frederick Church. There Church, assisted by Calvert Vaux, designed and built a fantastic Moorish-inspired residence, with a panoramic overlook of the Hudson River valley. On a magnificent hilltop site Church and Vaux planned unsurpassed picturesque and beautiful scenes, which were revealed to visitors as they wound their way up and down the serpentine entry drive.

Regional and Resource Planning

The area of professional practice that most distinguished the true landscape architect of the late nineteenth century from earlier landscape gardeners was the concern for regional and resource planning. This usually took the form of preservation of scenic natural areas, but also extended to concerns for large urban regions, and development of renewable resources. The protection of natural areas from uncontrolled development had long been a concern among the educated in the East. In the early 1850s, Cleveland warned fellow Bostonians of the need to protect the lake and hill district known as Middlesex Fells. Later, in an effort to forestall piecemeal development, he suggested that it be set aside as a resort similar to that which he had recently designed at the Natural Bridge in Virginia.

While in California Olmsted participated in the process which created the first state park in the United States—Yosemite. This work was, of course, a logical outcome of his belief in the psychological value of natural landscapes, but his views on the specific value of Yosemite and nearby Mariposa Big Tree Grove went beyond this single benefit. He also saw such natural areas, unexcelled in sublime pictorial qualities by any others in the world, as being a resource for tourism, of course at a much smaller scale than that which occurs today; and of value as the source of pure water for drinking and abundant water for navigation. In the report through which Olmsted articulated the philosophical basis for their preservation, he also outlined a simple plan for the addition of amenities to accommodate visitation: simple roads, a few cabins for semipermanent residents, and space for a superintendent. He envisioned state preserves as places where human activities remained dwarfed by the grandeur of the natural environment.

Later Olmsted, working with Vaux in an informal partnership, was called upon to apply these principles at a far less pristine site—the Reservation at Niagara Falls. The challenge there was to restore at least the appearance of a natural backdrop to the Falls in an area that had been compromised by industrialization. Mills and other industrial buildings that marred the shoreline and contributed to pollution were to be removed. Landforms, particularly exposed limestone ledges, and native vegetation were to be restored. While simple visitor amenities— primarily rustic bridges, paths, and seating—were to be added, the only significant structures were to be in the Upper Grove, farthest from the Falls. In this way Olmsted and Vaux sought to reinstate the simple natural character of the land, so that the Falls themselves would be the focus of attention.

Unfortunately, the park preserve was small, about 200 acres, with most of this on islands above the Falls. Only a narrow strip of land along the shore could be acquired, making it impossible to create a large enough buffer between the town and the Falls. Today the naturalistic image which the designers intended is achieved only on the islands when looking toward the Falls. Viewed from the Canadian side, where the view of the Falls is best, garish private construction overwhelms it. The simple treatment proposed by Olmsted and Vaux was not accepted on the Canadian side, where a public garden landscape of lawn and patterned planting beds was developed instead. Although just as touristically

Modern aerial view of Niagara Falls from the Canadian side, showing the small park area around the Falls on the American side, which Olmsted and Vaux designed to preserve the natural setting of the Falls. American Falls is in the center of the photo, and Horseshoe Falls to the right. (Copyrighted view courtesy Royal Specialty Shops, Toronto, Canada.)

inclined as the American side, the Canadian promenade had a neater, trimmer appearance which visitors over the years appear to have preferred to the contrast between naturalistic and commercial in Niagara, New York.

One of the most impressive and farsighted projects of the nineteenth century was Olmsted's regional plan for Staten Island, New York. Working from the intimate environmental knowledge acquired when he had earlier farmed on the island, Olmsted proposed the first comprehensive resource-based urban development plan. The principal problem which his report addressed was the need for improved drainage and control of land uses to counter the spread of disease, particularly malaria. By suggesting that not all land uses were appropriate to all potential sites, Olmsted went beyond then current practice to imply the need for restriction of development, thereby antedating the legal controls initiated under the city planning movement of the early twentieth century.

George Perkins Marsh's widely influential book *Man and Nature,* published in 1864, made the public aware of the possibility of environmental damage and the exhaustibility of resources.[41] A number of landscape architects utilized this realization to encourage planning and management schemes for critical resources. Among those who engaged in this work were Cleveland and William Hammond Hall. Cleveland's principal interest lay in the protection and management of forests. He argued that improper management of second-growth forests, not lack of forests, had reduced the supply of useful timber. Existing trees went uncared for, and sound management principles based on study of natural processes were neglected. He urged that scientific practices such as mulching and techniques for wind control be used under the guidance of trained forest professionals.

In the West, resource concerns focused on water, not timber. Hall, also a pioneer in development of mining control legislation, was among the pioneers in the scientific management of water. While Hall believed in the value of irrigation to "reclaim" the fertile but arid lands of California, he recognized that environmental problems could result. His principal justification for use of irrigation lay in social rather than economic need, though, for he concluded that irrigation allowed small farmers to compete effectively with large landowners. To make irrigation economically and environmentally profitable, he urged the use of methods appropriate to the landform and soil of each farm. The use of such methods, he believed, would prevent environmental problems such as standing water, which brought mosquitoes and malaria, and saturation of soil, which decayed crops and native plants alike.

CONTEMPORANEOUS REACTIONS TO THE ROMANTICISM OF THE PARKS MOVEMENT

The link between the Romantic style of design and the development of the profession of landscape architecture in the second half of the nineteenth century was strong. Romanticism, though, was more than a set of aesthetic preferences to designers such as Vaux and Olmsted. It was a world view in which the intuitive, humanized outlook of Romantic philosophers toward both people and nature was given physical and verbal expression. This complex, holistic viewpoint was not easily understood by everyone, whether designer or not. Thus, there were those who found the work of professional landscape architects to be uninspired and repetitive. Such criticism focused on three principal areas: the folly of trying to copy nature, the lack of any definite skill required to lay out curving roads and massed plantings, and the lack of entertaining variety in naturalistic landscapes. The first two criticisms were based on a lack of understanding of the precepts on which later Romantic design was based, or possibly on examination of only mediocre design works. As we have seen, nature was not to be copied, but to serve as a source of inspiration for works that were admittedly as contrived as any Renaissance garden. Just as in Renaissance gardens, the purpose of this contrivance was creation of an illusion, but one that served the needs of an urban, industrializing society. Landscape architects believed these to be needs for rest and refreshment rather than for stimulating, novel experiences. Time would prove that the public did not share this assessment, but that it was indeed based on a sound intuitive understanding of mental health needs.

The assertion that naturalistic design was as simple to execute as scribbling wavy lines on paper was as fallacious as the belief that it copied nature. Work of the highest quality, such as that of Cleveland, Hall, Olmsted, and Weidenmann, only appeared to come easily because it attained such a flawless fit between built form and natural form. This, though, resulted from careful study, years of experience, and sensitivity to the nuances of landscape form and process. Yes, anyone could produce curving forms, and many wretched examples of inept "Romantic" designs were produced, but these were like mass-produced copies of Michelangelos or Cézannes—they lacked the vigor and subtlety of the true masterpieces.

Finally, the "amusements" which naturalistic designs were intended to provide were subtle in character. People were to enjoy the songs of birds, the crunch of fallen leaves underfoot, the excitement of a child launching a toy boat, or the romance of a secluded intimate moment with a loved one. The stimulus for these experiences was to be as much from within the park visitor as from without. Landscape architects erred, though, in their assessment of public preference, failing to recognize that they were part of a social and intellectual elite whose view of the world dated from simpler times. The post-1860s public actively sought diversion and activity, enjoyed urban life so did not feel a need for relief from it, and was increasingly interested in active rather than passive recreation. Paradoxically, the period in which some of the most widely recognized masterpieces of landscape architecture were created was also a period from which would spring a very different perception of how the designed landscape should be treated.

CONCLUSION AND SUMMARY

The late Romantic period in which the profession of landscape architecture emerged as a multifaceted discipline that addressed social, ecological, and aesthetic concerns is a difficult period to assess, for it is filled with contradictions. It was a period in which a select, but growing number of designers were able to focus almost exclusively on landscape issues; but it was also a period in which their new profession was dominated by one individual—Frederick Law Olmsted. Observing his pivotal role in a positive way, he could be credited with enlarging the scope and influence of the profession beyond what it would have had without his success and motivation. Certainly, the fame of the Central Park design and his cogent writings on the philosophical rationale for public parks were critical to the parks movement. He also supported other designers, including Cleveland and Weidenmann, by recommending them for projects that he could not accept. However, looking from a negative perspective, we could say that Olmsted's notoriety overshadowed other equally talented, but perhaps less outgoing, designers. This may have led to a suppression of diversity in designing and planning, as clients demanded only that which was deemed Olmstedian.

Yet the design works that remain from this period are classics. When people speak of "parks," the image which comes to mind is of the large, pastoral landscape parks of the nineteenth century, not the modern ballfield. This heritage, of course, goes beyond mere planting design. An 800-acre open space in the middle of Manhattan would be of inestimable value even if it had no vegetation at all. Thus the parks movement represents as important an era in planning as it does in design.

Much North American design of the nineteenth century was disparaged as solely derivative from European, especially English, prototypes. While there is, of course, a direct stylistic and aesthetic link between the two, American design was based on a more solid social and environmental theoretical base. This was, in fact, the most significant contribution of the pioneers of landscape architecture—the articulation of defensible principles that included appearance but went well beyond it to include other site functions.

One of the faults, though, of the pioneer landscape architects was reluctance to compromise their views with both public preferences and the need to adapt form to specific purposes. Romantic designs, which they viewed as the principal positive way to address social and environmental concerns, could not fit all needs. When their own well thought out programmatic concerns were compromised to suit a stylistic preference, the final product was ultimately weakened. It is quite telling that naturalistic designs persisted beyond the nineteenth century in the design of certain site types such as parks and residences, suggesting an appropriateness to these uses, while elsewhere Romantic designs were quickly engulfed in more structured site plans. In spite of these limitations, the theories, professional standards, work methods, and design approach of this critical era of parks continues to influence modern professional practice.

NOTES

1. Although Downing shared this rural image with the eventual designers of the park, Olmsted and Vaux, he felt that 500 acres was sufficient area for the multitude of functions, including commemorative buildings, monuments, conservatories, and zoos. Experience has shown that to create a pastoral contrast to urban life, such secondary amenities must be kept separate from the park itself.

2. Additional land was later added to the park to make up its total present acreage, which is 843 acres.

3. Since Viele's plan was used as a starting point for the competition program, it should not be surprising that many entries had spatial organizations similar, at least in part, to his design. This resulted primarily from the limited number of potential sites suitable for specific requirements.

After the competition, Viele, who had always felt ill treated by the Commission, sued for payment of his services in preparing a site survey and the original plan. In the course of this trial, Viele charged that of the thirty-three competition entrants nearly half, including Olmsted and Vaux, had merely copied his plan and submitted it as their own. This charge is not substantiated by examination of the Olmsted-Vaux plan, which differs in all particulars except the general location of open fields from Viele's.

4. *The term "parking" was used even into the early twentieth century to describe landscapes that were a naturalistic combination of open woods and rolling meadows.*

5. *For a complete list of those known to have submitted plans (all submissions were anonymous and unless identified later the designers remain unknown), see Stewart, 1973, and Central Park Commission, 1859.*

6. *Modifications to the design came almost immediately. See the* New York Times, *May 27, 1858, p. 8, for a seventeen-point list of proposed changes.*

7. *Those facilities added to the "top" of the park generally date to the 1920s to 1940s, the Robert Moses era.*

8. *Both Olmsted and Vaux were fired and rehired by the Park Board several times over the course of their associations with the park.*

9. *Underdrainage was an important if dull topic in the history of land use. It was a common technique for agricultural, residential estate, and parks work. In addition to assuring speedy removal of runoff, it was considered important in promoting plant growth. See Waring, 1876, and French, 1859, for discussions of various applications of underdrainage.*

10. *Vaux died, as had Downing, by drowning in a boat accident.*
     If every addition proposed for the park had been built there would not be a park today; rather it would be a housing development, museum district, and public amusement park. See Wheelwright, 1910, for a listing of the extensive additions proposed in the nineteenth century alone and Rogers, 1987, for a horrifying illustration of what could have been, but for the preservation efforts of people such as Parsons.

11. *Criticisms appear to have come from those who favored a more uniformly "beautiful" aesthetic than did Vaux and Olmsted. Several commentators criticized plantings as being too close together and said that groupings were too uniform. Another critic observed that "real park scenery," that is, rolling meadows, was limited to only a few scattered patches. Although the designers certainly responded to these critics at the time of their comments, Olmsted much later synthesized his reply to these criticisms by discussing crucial aspects of the planning concept in* Observations on the Treatment of Public Plantations *(Olmsted and Harrison, 1889).*
     Various estimates of the park's cost, including both land and improvements, were made. The numbers used here are from Olmsted and Kimball, 1928. The estimate of visitation is from Devlin and Company, 1871.

12. *During their lifetimes, Olmsted was given greater public credit for the work which the two did in collaboration, a misconception which caused friction between them as early as the 1860s. That they were able to work together on later projects is confirmation of the mutually self-supporting nature of each man's skills. For recent assessments of the Vaux-Olmsted credit controversy see Graff, 1985, and Leech, 1987.*

13. *In a letter dated the following day, Vaux further developed his concept for the main entrance by illustrating a large elliptical plaza, similar in form to the present Grand Army Plaza.*

14. *Actually, a small portion of the park, now a museum and library district, lay east of Flatbush, but even in the original Olmsted and Vaux plan this was a separate area to be used primarily for a reservoir and pedestrian linkage.*

15. *Of course the Concert Grove area does today terminate in a building, but an unsympathetic one—the Wollman Ice Rink.*

16. *Olmsted participated in various partnerships throughout his professional career. Besides that with Vaux, Olmsted had the following partnerships (data from Anonymous, 1952):*

1878–84	*With John Charles Olmsted as associate (John was his adopted son—the natural son of Olmsted's deceased brother.)*
1884–89	*F. L. Olmsted and J. C. Olmsted; with John as full partner, Frederick, Jr., as associate*
1189–93	*F. L. Olmsted and Company; with John, Frederick, Jr., and Henry Codman*
1893–97	*Olmsted, Olmsted and Eliot; with John and Charles Eliot*
1897	*F. L. and J. C. Olmsted*

After Olmsted senior's retirement his sons formed the Olmsted Brothers partnership, which officially lasted until 1955.
     In the text "Olmsted firm" is used as a generic term to refer to any of these partnerships.

17. *Although the Rochester parks are generally credited to Olmsted senior, John C. Olmsted was as much involved in the project and likely served as principal designer. He continued to consult on the parks into the twentieth century. Frederick Law Olmsted, Jr., also made recommendations for the parks in conjunction with a city plan which he coauthored in 1911.*

18. *At both parks this distinction was quickly circumvented and uses became mixed. For example, the major meadow at Genesee Valley Park was converted to a golf course within ten years of the park's opening.*

Today each bank of Seneca Park has a separate title, with that to the east retaining the original name and that to the west named Maplewood.

19. *The Seneca Park Menagerie was a typical example of how originally minor additions to landscape parks eventually overwhelmed them. As first conceived in 1896, a few species of native animals were displayed in temporary enclosures. These cages gradually became permanent park fixtures. In the 1930s, as part of nationwide public works improvements, new, larger buildings were constructed and more, larger animals added to the collection. In the 1960s, the zoo filled almost one-third of the park plateau on the east side of the river, and recently there has been pressure to expand it down the hillside toward the river.*

20. *Of course the zoo when built went in the Greeting, whose design retrofit was completed in the early 1900s by Arthur Shurcliff (see endnote 7 in Chapter 12 for spelling change to his last name). Although the allocation of zoo use areas follows very closely the original spatial concept, it intensifies uses beyond anything intended by Olmsted.*

21. *Eliot was associated directly with Olmsted twice in his life; once during an apprenticeship which began in 1883, and then from 1893 until his death in 1896, when under the firm name Olmsted, Olmsted and Eliot he was a full partner.*
   Among smaller-scale projects to his credit were the Norton Estate Subdivision in Cambridge, Massachusetts; White Park, Concord, New Hampshire; and the estate of "Oakwoods," Peace Dale, Rhode Island.

22. *See Chapter 13 for discussion of this site.*

23. *These three parks, Central (now Garfield), Douglas, and Humboldt, were redesigned in the twentieth century by Jens Jensen (see Chapter 13), but the overall proportions of water and land in Jenney's original concept were retained.*

24. *Even less is known of Weidenmann's architectural work than of his landscape architectural projects. The principal source of information on architecture was his superb portfolio of etchings,* American Garden Architecture *(1876). This work indicates that he favored eclectic, historically derived designs popularized earlier by Downing. Only the Prints Department of the New York Public Library and the Columbia University Library are known to have this portfolio in their collections.*

25. *Not to be confused with the adjoining private subdivision known as Forest Park Addition laid out by Julius Pitzman.*

26. *Instead of a large landscape park, Olmsted proposed a three- to four-mile-long garden-like promenade with footpaths and carriageways, along the present route of part of Van Ness Avenue.*

27. *See Chapter 13 for discussion of this style.*

28. *The term "landscape gardener" had itself been coined just a century earlier. Poet William Shenstone, designer of Leasowes, is believed to have been the first to use it, in 1764.*

29. *Vinci (1977) concluded that Strauch also completed a plan or gave suggestions for Graceland, but cites no source for such information. Runion (1869) claimed William Saunders, a Philadelphia designer, laid out the cemetery. An anonymous pamphlet from 1871 credits the section layout and plat to Nelson Swain and "improvements" to Cleveland.*

30. *See Leavitt, 1926, for an illustration of this plan. Barrett often credited himself with reintroduction of formal styles to North America. Evidence does suggest that he used axial arrangements at a time when most landscape architects remained enamored of the Romantic and nonprofessionals were interested in Victorian eclecticism. Among his nineteenth-century projects which have clearly formal arrangements of spaces are Naumkeag itself (See Chapter 13 for discussion), an unimplemented plan for three cemeteries, and the Ponce-de-Leon Hotel in Florida. Barrett was then far ahead of his time, and few, if any other, landscape architects shared his view that "the formal garden is a gem" (quoted in Schermerhorn, 1920). Of course, as we have seen, many naturalistic parks included formal areas, suggesting that others could also design in that way but chose to emphasize other spatial arrangements.*

31. *In the United States, each state was allowed to claim 30,000 acres for each senator and representative that they had in Congress for the purpose of establishing colleges directed toward technical studies in "agricultural and mechanics." States that had no existing unclaimed public lands within their own borders were granted scrip allowing land claims in those states with available public lands. Thus most of the land grants actually sold to finance universities were in central and western states. Canada, under a somewhat different program, also made land grants for university development.*

32. *During the first part of the Civil War Olmsted served as executive secretary (essentially its director) to the U.S. Sanitary Commission, the forerunner of the American Red Cross. He was responsible for organizing medical and humanitarian relief, as well as camp hygiene for the Union Army.*

33. *This plan was never implemented, and later the Board of Regents commissioned another from William Hammond Hall, which was implemented. From about 1880 until about 1900 no master plan was followed, and additions were made somewhat haphazardly, although Warren Manning was consulted on plantings. In the early 1900s John Galen Howard developed the formal plan which most of the campus now follows.*

34. *While this portion of the campus remains relatively intact, subsequent additions did not follow its Romantic character. In the early 1900s architect Cass Gilbert developed a formal master plan which has had far more influence on twentieth-century planning on this campus.*

35. *Kern's was not the first plan for the campus, nor was its character preserved in later replannings. One later plan, by Frank Waugh, maintained some irregular planting clusters, but organized buildings in more regular alignments that created rectangular interbuilding spaces.*

36. *If that evaluation and this author's conclusions regarding credit for the formal design at the World's Columbian Exposition (see Chapter 11) are correct, they call into question previous assessments of Olmsted's design versatility and adaptation to local conditions. It seems most likely that he championed the Romantic style throughout his life and was unable or unwilling to design as well using more regular, less site-adapted forms. Much of the more formal work of his later life was likely primarily the work of others within his firm, particularly his son John, who demonstrated facility with both naturalistic and architectonic styles as well as the critical ability to link the two.*

37. *Of this plan only the first three quadrangles were completed. After Stanford's death the plan was largely abandoned and the campus developed somewhat haphazardly. In the 1980s the quadrangles were restored to an approximation of their original appearance following plans by Anthony M. Gussardo and Associates.*

38. *Jacob Weidenmann worked on this project for Olmsted and may also be responsible for significant aspects of the design.*

39. *Vaux's plan was executed in concept only, although the present ramp, step, terrace composition seems quite close to his described plans.*

40. *Interestingly, this plan was in many ways similar to Olmsted's slightly later plan for the U.S. Capitol, especially in the treatment of the "main" entrance side, where both plans included a straight, tree-lined drive and curving side roads.*

41. *See Chapter 25 for further discussion.*

19

Urban Planning in the Nineteenth Century

To use the term "urban planning" for city and town planning in the nineteenth century suggests modern concerns for spatial and service organization which, in most instances, did not exist before the planning revolution that began in the 1890s under the rubric of the City Beautiful Movement. While there certainly were urban areas that were "planned" in the comprehensive contemporary sense of the word before that date, most notably Washington D.C., these were the exception.[1] Most "planning" in the nineteenth century should more appropriately be considered real estate speculation; those few plans of higher design quality would today be considered site, rather than city, planning scale. Only those improvements and as much ambiance as were absolutely necessary to attract the well-to-do segment of the market were provided.

In Chapter 9 we will examine one particular form of real estate speculation—the railroad town—but other forms of urban development also existed. Most important in terms of area and number of people served were residential additions to existing cities. Of secondary importance were new suburbs—that is, outlying towns where most families lived in "detached dwellings with sylvan surroundings yet supplied with a considerable share of urban convenience . . ." (Olmsted, 1871, p. 9). While each of these types of development often responded to various market forces, there were broader social and technological forces at work that influenced *all* urban and suburban expansion.

Three forces particularly affected the configuration of urban and suburban areas in the nineteenth century: economics, transportation technology, and demographics. Added to these was the endemic American preference both for independent living, usually associated with having an individual, free-standing home for one's family, and for rural living. Economics affected urbanization in two ways: First, economic considerations influenced location decisions for business and industry, which often preempted choice sites. Second, industrial growth generated higher incomes for large segments of the population, which in turn provided more money for larger homes and commuter transportation. Related to economics, since costs to individuals always played a role, were improvements in transportation, from the first horse-drawn omnibuses of the 1820s to electrified street railways at the end of the century. Each transport innovation extended the distance that a person could reasonably travel as a commuter or shopper, while constant system improvements and increased ridership lessened costs. Demographic patterns also affected urbanization in two ways: urban populations grew steadily throughout the century due to immigration from rural areas, principally by those seeking factory work, and emigration from abroad. Therefore cities expanded as new housing had to be provided. At the same time that new residents were surging into cities, many native-born American urbanites, particularly those of the middle class, attempted to flee. While a preference for rural living explained part of this exodus, it was also due to the prejudiced perception that lower-income, ethnically alien populations caused urban problems.

Main Street, Overbrook, Kansas.

The typical frontier town of the nineteenth century was as planned or, more accurately, unplanned as any other American city of the period. Commerce, rather than public needs, produced such urban scenes. (Barker Texas History Center, University of Texas, Austin, Texas.)

Many nineteenth-century urban problems were those which continue to plague cities today—crime,[2] pollution, noise—while others were the direct result of lack of planning and regulation, such as the threat of fire, poor sanitation, and shoddy building construction. Fire was a significant problem in urban areas of North America from the time of the first European settlement. Construction with combustible materials coupled with close placement of buildings and the use of open flames in heating, cooking, and lighting meant that the potential for raging fires was ever present. Lack of sanitation, and the ensuing public health problems which it created, was a more constant, if less dramatic, urban issue. It was not until the 1860s, following the Civil War activities of the Sanitary Commission, that any serious, concerted effort was made to develop proper systems for water delivery and sewage removal. In spite of remarkable strides made in the 1870s and 1880s by the newly established profession of sanitary engineering, the common nineteenth-century pattern of individual, unprofessionally planned and installed cesspools continued. This led to water contamination and the spread of disease by rodents and insects. Problems of fire and poor sanitation were inextricably linked with the last major urban problem of the nineteenth century—lack of coordination in the physical expansion of cities and their infrastructure systems. Typically, development was both unplanned and unrestricted, with landowners making all choices of lot size, services, and street arrangement based only on their individual needs in the marketplace.[3] Distortions and offsets of streets in urban areas, which so clearly delineate where one development ended and another began, were just the most obvious problem which this lack of coordination created.

EARLY EFFORTS AT "CITY PLANNING"

The fact that speculation, rather than planned urban development, was the norm for most cities throughout the nineteenth century should not suggest that attempts at introducing organized thought into this chaotic process did not occur. In many ways the parks movement discussed in Chapter 7 can be thought of as representing an early form of city planning, one in which land use was passively regulated by artificially manipulating an adjoining land use through park dedication. The South Park Commissioners of Chicago, most of whom owned land

Even in state capitals, nineteenth-century growth was unplanned. View of the "urban sprawl" of Austin, Texas circa 1895. (Barker Texas History Center, University of Texas, Austin, Texas.)

near the parks, engaged in just such a scheme when they developed the Olmsted and Vaux plan for Washington Park. While parks could effectively draw people to an area, and in most instances assured higher land values for lots adjoining parks and boulevards, they could not guarantee either land use or quality of construction in areas beyond the park edge.

Park system plans, though, did help to give some structure to cities, especially when developed with an understanding of the needs for housing and businesses. Robert Morris Copeland's 1872 plan for Boston was an example of a well thought out plan for an integrated system of parks and boulevards that should be considered an urban plan as well as merely a parks plan. In setting the stage for the master plan he was to propose, Copeland outlined a rationale for urban planning: "If the [business] group can be planned for, why not the town or city? . . . The sole difference or hindrance to such planning is, that we have not been accustomed to plan in this way. We have supposed that, for some unnamed reason, planning for a city's growth and progress could only be done as it grows; that no one can foresee sufficiently the future requirements of business to widely provide for them. This is a fallacious belief" (p. 10). Copeland's specific and far-sighted suggestions for predevelopment planning included city-wide survey of conditions, development of a comprehensive plan, and creation of a zoning system, of which one feature would be the transfer of development rights. Other recommendations, which did not gain widespread acceptance until the 1960s, were urban renewal through adaptive reuse of buildings and the preservation, although for active public use, of wetlands.

So park system plans were certainly one indirect form of city planning in nineteenth-century North America. Other precedents for comprehensive planning can be seen in the schemes and theories of those who saw the need to consciously plan new additions to cities. One of the most imaginative of these proto-city planners was the scientific farmer, social reformer, and eccentric Robert Gourlay.[4] Although Gourlay was apparently not taken seriously during his lifetime except by equally unconventional early landscape architects, his words were remarkably prophetic. In an 1844 pamphlet outlining plans for improving New York City and expanding Boston, he anticipated both details of Boston's physical development and general trends in urban design and planning, which in

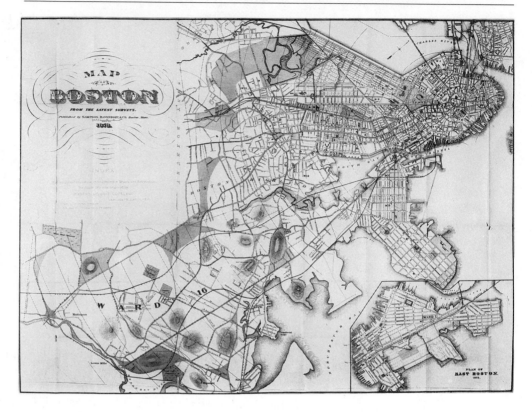

Plan of Robert Morris Copeland's suggested improvements to Boston entitled, "Map of Boston from the Latest Survey," 1872, published in Boston by Sampson Davenport and Company to accompany Copeland's booklet The Most Beautiful City in America. *(Courtesy Essex Institute, Salem, Massachusetts.)*

many cases would not arise for another fifty years. His principal concern for Boston was development of the Charles River mud flats, west of downtown, known as Back Bay. In two plans, one accompanying the 1844 report and an 1857 refinement, he proposed that large areas of Back Bay be filled for a new town, with a large, crescent-shaped basin formed from the river to divide it from the older part of Boston. This basin was to be the site of an island park, called Elysian Fields, surrounded by boulevards and other open spaces.

In setting forth this specific plan for Boston, Gourlay explained, in a rambling way, his general principles for what he called "The Science of City Building." Of greatest importance was the concept of prior planning, so that both immediate and future needs could be addressed. Gourlay was particularly interested in the arrangement of streets, both from the functional standpoint and as it related to urban aesthetics. He advocated use of street railways as a link between suburbs and central city, with a central train station at the heart of downtown. In addition, he suggested connecting scenic areas surrounding the city via parkway, prefiguring the park system of the 1880s. This man of new ideas also saw the value of the old, and advocated the preservation of old structures—in the case of Boston, the Statehouse. Finally, in many ways his ideas heralded concepts of the later City Beautiful Movement: he discussed the need for a "grand approach" boulevard to downtown, while also recognizing the importance of well-placed buildings and monuments as focal points at street termini.

Although Gourlay's plan for Boston's Back Bay did not materialize in the form he had envisioned, by 1855 the area was in the process of becoming what Lewis Mumford called an "outstanding achievement in American urban planning for the nineteenth century" (1969, p. 18). Inspired by Gourlay, but based on plans by architect Arthur Gilman, a grid of rectangular blocks centered on a boulevard, Commonwealth Avenue, were laid out from the Public Garden westward. As filling of the mud flats advanced, so too did street and house devel-

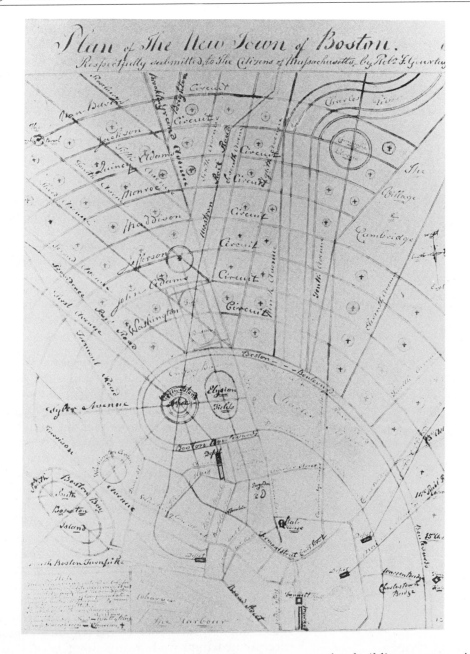

Robert Gourlay's first plan for the city of Boston, 1844. (Landscape Architecture, Vol. 6, No. 1.)

opment. A unique feature of the Back Bay district was that building construction restrictions set a uniform standard. Limitations included a setback of 20 feet for structures and prohibition against industries within the district. These checks on building location and land use were rudimentary zoning restrictions, the success of which ensured Back Bay an elegantly simple visual character and a more healthful standard of life than any other area of the city.

While the established city of Boston benefited from many specific planning recommendations, the problems of urban development in new cities of the West inspired H. W. S. Cleveland to develop rudimentary theories and recommendations for sound planning. Although best known for his book, *Landscape Architecture as Applied to the Wants of the West,* Cleveland had earlier explored the relationship of planned cities to health, safety, and welfare in a series of letters and essays aimed at improving life in his new home city, Chicago. Recommendations concerned the importance of circulation design as an integral, functional aspect of urban design rather than merely an aesthetic matter. In particular, Cleveland believed that a system of boulevards and related local streets could serve to control urban conflagrations, one of which had recently destroyed much of Chicago. Cleveland argued that boulevards would serve as firebreaks, trap windblown debris, divide the city into recognizable quadrants to aid in locating fires,[5] and provide direct access for fire-fighting equipment. While these specific recommendations may have had less impact than he anticipated, his advocacy of urban planning for functional reasons signaled an important change in the role of design in cities. At a lecture to an engineer's club in Chicago he outlined a rudimentary theory of city planning:

> [W]e as a nation enjoy such opportunity as was never before offered, for the development of the scientific and artistic principles which should be observed in the laying out of towns and cities, in order to secure all the advantages which the situation affords, for the promotion of convenience, safety, and health, as well as beauty and attractive interest. There is probably scarcely a single city of any importance in existence which is not subjected to greater or less inconvenience and often to continual suffering and taxation, from causes which might have been avoided by timely forethought and the exercise of judgment in the original design of arrangement, but which it is almost hopeless to attempt to retrieve by subsequent alterations. (1874, p. 12)

In *Landscape Architecture as Applied to the Wants of the West,* Cleveland continued his discussion of the opportunity for and importance of planning, devoting two of the six chapters in this brief book to city planning issues.[6] His arguments were simple and directed toward two principal issues. First, Cleveland asserted that planning should be more than the mindless application of grid street patterns to the landscape, but should be based on "sanitary, economic and esthetic laws." He elaborated this idea by discussing why "designing with nature," particularly landform, was not merely aesthetically important, but contributed to clearer air and improved drainage, among other advantages. Second, he reinforced the importance of well thought out prior planning, but still placed this activity in the hands of landowners rather than cities. While these messages seem obvious to readers today, the steps which Cleveland advocated in the 1870s would not find widespread acceptance for almost forty years.

Urban spatial and land use planning would take years to become realities, in spite of the efforts of individuals such as Gourlay and Cleveland. There were urban problems, though, that were so critical as to demand immediate action. These were the problems of public sanitation that led to creation of a new engineering specialty, that of the sanitary engineer. While urban growth clearly necessitated improved treatment of wastes, which by then had been demonstrated to affect health, it was not until 1871 when Edwin Chadwick invented self-cleaning sewage pipes that improved communal urban systems began to be installed. So rapid were the technical advances in toilets, water systems, and sewage systems after that date that a writer could state in 1879 that "older plumbing" installed a mere five years before was not up to contemporary standards.

In many instances, water and sewers were the first planned urban systems, requiring location coordination for adequate service, to avoid poor soils, and to assure proper fall for pipes. Equally important were outfall location and methods of disposal of accumulated wastes. This too required planning, principally in the form of site selection for disposal in water (often a local river) or on land (either in tanks or through crop irrigation). Disposal into a body of water was usually the preferred municipal solution, although in the long run it could prove more costly. The pollution problems that challenged Olmsted as he developed Boston's park plan were just one example of the consequences of poorly thought out sewage disposal. Equal in cost and scope was the Chicago solution—to block off and redirect the flow of the Chicago River, so that what by 1880 was an open sewer would not pollute Lake Michigan, the city's water source. Sanitary engineering gradually expanded in scope, so that by 1900 it included the entire gamut of urban construction concerns, including streets, communications, and lighting. As a profession, it later played an important role in the City Beautiful Movement, and many of its practitioners were later among those who first embraced the title of City Planner.

Aside from sanitary engineering, the principal form of planning in nineteenth-century cities was that based on economic need of businesses and industries. Prime locations were often given over to businesses that required resources such as water and transportation access. In this approach, which equated planning with private profit, housing, especially low-priced housing, was often relegated to locations surrounded by undesirable land uses or prone to environmental problems such as flooding.

Nineteenth-century North American cities were testing places for a few revolutionary concepts related to planned, large-scale environments, which were developed by diverse professionals in design and engineering. In certain instances, these new ideas were accepted, but they were rarely applied to cities as wholes. Certainly the rapidity of urban growth, coupled with the political power of land speculators, did much to slow acceptance of ideas which would have improved the quality of urban life and reduced the number of problems with which later planners had to contend. That this did not happen was at least in part due to the perception that North America continued to be a place with more land always available if one area became unlivable. In the nineteenth century, those who had wealth and who sought to avoid urban problems but still maintain an urbane lifestyle could easily do so by moving to suburbs.

SUBURBANIZATION

Although suburbs, those small, mostly residential villages within daily travel distance of a city, had existed in some form for at least one hundred years, the beginning of American suburbanization as both a development and residential trend is usually dated to 1815, when Brooklyn Heights, New York, across the East River from Manhattan, was established. Thus began what was the principal nineteenth-century form of city planning—development of new towns. Two particular types of suburbs, to serve two different populations, dominated nineteenth-century suburban development: industrial suburbs for workers with particular companies and rural or Romantic suburbs for upper-middle-class families.

Industrial Suburbs

Industrial suburbs began to be developed in the mid-nineteenth century as factory owners sought to isolate their workers from urban distractions—and especially from labor unionists—and to find large, inexpensive sites on which to develop modern mass-production facilities. The towns of Lowell and Lawrence, Massachusetts, exemplify both the rationale for independent industrial towns and the form which some early ones took. Lowell and Lawrence were both model industrial centers with sites for textile factories. Each town also had a full complement of modest amenities for workers, including housing, often in the form of dormitory-like boarding houses; schools; churches; and shops. In the case of these and other early New England factory towns, what planning did occur was directed solely toward efficiency of production, and was directed to features such as road and canal locations, rather than provision of open space.

As the continent became more industrialized, a few visionary manufacturers began to develop suburbs that were better planned. Again motives were often mixed, with some following the utopian ideals of men like Fourier, while others saw managed environments as a business investment—that is, they believed that healthy and happy workers would be more productive employees. Hopedale, Massachusetts, was one of the first of this new type of industrial suburb. Founded in 1841 as a religious commune, Hopedale had the appearance of a small country hamlet on a grid plan with dispersed housing. The Draper brothers, who acquired the town in 1856 for their textile machinery company, maintained this character even as they expanded the factory and townsite as the company grew after the Civil War. This small-town character, although not professionally planned, was one reflection of a paternalistic attitude on the part of the Drapers and was quite in contrast to the more forbidding urban character of contemporaneous industrial towns such as Fall River, Massachusetts. In the 1880s, Hopedale, probably influenced by the notoriety of a new industrial suburb, Pullman, Illinois, became a designed and planned town. Warren Manning, then working for Olmsted, completed planting plans for several sites in town, including the high school. Later, he contributed more directly to the city plan by developing a Romantic-style subdivision quite different from the rest of the town, with its rectilinear plan.[7]

While Hopedale achieved its noninstitutional character largely through a village-like character and some consciously designed amenities, the most famous industrial suburb of the nineteenth century was a completely planned new town. Pullman, Illinois, to the south of Chicago on Lake Calumet, was envisioned by railroad car builder George Pullman as a complete industrial and residential center. With building beginning in 1880 on a swampy plain to the plans of landscape architect and planner Nathan Barrett and architect Solon Beman, Pullman became an urbane small town which provided healthful living conditions, educational and recreational amenities, and social services then unknown to industrial workers. Pullman's physical plan was simple and efficient, yet embodied some critical planning standards. There was a clear separation of land uses, a circulation hierarchy, open spaces, and a centralized community center. The town spine was Florence Boulevard, which separated the factory buildings and supply yards from nonindustrial areas of town. Adjacent to the boulevard stood the town center, with hotel, shops, a cultural center, and town square. This square was only one of several open spaces in the community. Along an artificial lake, walkways provided strolling areas, while nearby a large park with playground, racetrack, and boating facilities served other recreational needs. In addition, workers had access to the surrounding open countryside since horses and vehicles could be rented at the community stable. Most of the town was composed, of course, of housing. This was arranged in long, rectangular blocks separated by generously sized streets. The Pullman company strictly segregated housing based on status in the corporate hierarchy. Managers occupied large, detached single-family homes near the town center, while laborers were housed in row houses or, for single men, in dormitories. Row houses, which today would be considered suitable for only a single family, often held more than one family per floor. Such housing, though, was a great improvement over that which workers in similar circumstances would have found in Chicago. Dwellings had a minimum front setback to allow light and air to all rooms. Each house had a private rearyard, then an unheard of amenity for laborers' homes. Residential streets were paved and tree-lined, giving them a suburban character.

Pullman was a completely organized community in which site planning, architecture, engineering, and landscape design were completely coordinated to create an efficient, livable, and profitable industrial community. Aesthetics and practicality went hand in hand. For example, the artificial lake in front of the

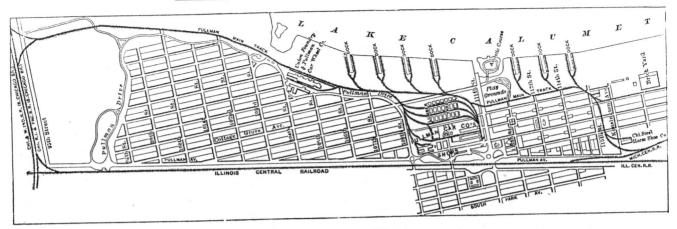

PLAN OF PULLMAN CITY.

Plan of Pullman, Illinois, by Nathan Barrett, 1885. (Harper's New Monthly Magazine, Vol. 70, No. 416.)

Park near Florence Hotel and railroad depot at Pullman, Illinois, in the 1980s.

factory served not only as a park and an ornamental backdrop for the town's railroad depot, but also as a cooling pond for the enormous Corliss engine that powered the factory. Sewage from the community fertilized an agricultural tract nearby, which in turn provided fresh foods to residents.

In spite of Pullman's seemingly utopian qualities, it was an industrial town. George Pullman eschewed any humanitarian rationale for the community's form, citing instead its potential to attract better-skilled, more loyal workers. In addition, the fame of the town itself came to be an advertisement for its product—the luxurious Pullman Palace Cars. From the beginning, the town's physical design and social amenities were heralded by American and international critics—one of whom went so far as to call it a perfect town—as models of modern planning. Pullman's utopian image, though, was not destined to be long-lived. Within fourteen years of its founding, labor unrest sparked by company policies during the depression of 1893 led to one of the most violent strikes in American history.[8] As a result of the strike both the town's and the company's reputation were damaged, resulting in an 1898 court action to dissolve corporate ownership of the townsite.

Although few industrial towns of the nineteenth century had the design character or systems organization of Pullman, the concept of improved housing for workers in a corporate-controlled setting proved very popular. Many other new towns, most of them suburbs of larger cities, were established by manufacturers. South Omaha, Nebraska, was a meat-processing center; Marysville, New Brunswick, was a mill town, often called the "Canadian Pullman"; Ivorydale, Ohio, was home to the Proctor and Gamble Company; Anniston, Alabama, was the philanthropy of industrialist Samuel Noble;[9] and LeClaire, Illinois, was the company town of the Nelson Plumbing Fixture Company.[10]

Romantic Suburbs

Industrial suburbs of one form or another were quite numerous in North America, with estimates that hundreds of varying quality were developed. More famous, but less numerous, were suburbs planned to house middle-income and upper-middle-income families: the Romantic suburb. The transfer of Romantic design principles from cemeteries to residential subdivisions was a logical transition, in which only scale and lot use were significantly altered. In every other way, such as street pattern and planting, these cities for the living mimicked the Romantic cities of the dead. Romantic suburbs became enclaves populated by native-born Caucasian Americans fleeing the influx of European immigrants and, after the Civil War, Afro-American ex-slaves. Thus these communities represent an elite ideal of the residential landscape, and one from which a significant portion of the population was unfairly excluded.

While no definitive study has established which community could claim a "first" as a Romantic suburb, three early examples stand out as prototypes: Clifton, Ohio; Glendale, Ohio; and Evergreen Hamlet, Pennsylvania. Of the three Clifton, near Cincinnati, was the earliest, having been laid out in 1843, although not officially incorporated as a town until seven years later. Clifton was a village of large lots, all more than 10 acres in size, with few roads. Those that provided access to estates were rambling, and more like country roads than suburban streets. On the other hand, Glendale, also near Cincinnati, was a true suburb, connected to the city by rail. Founded by an association of lot owners in 1851, the town had smaller lots that varied in size and a clearly defined road pattern related to the area's hilly topography. As planned by Cincinnati city engineer R. C. Phillips, the organizing feature of these roads was that most radiated from a large park located at the center of the townsite. This park, and other smaller ones located in bowl-like forested depressions, gave the community a very picturesque character. Evergreen Hamlet near Pittsburgh, laid out in the same year as Glendale, was a small subdivision for sixteen families. In concept, its plan was similar to those of modern cluster lot subdivisions. Lots were located along the principal street, Rock Ridge Avenue, with the remaining areas of the site retained as open space, farm, and school grounds. Of these three communities, Glendale was most like later Romantic suburbs due to its parks and curvilinear road system, while Clifton and Evergreen Hamlet had a more rural, village-like character.

The first large suburb widely discussed in the nineteenth-century literature as a suburban model was Llewellyn Park in West Orange, New Jersey. Begun in 1853 by industrialist Llewellyn Haskell, this picturesque subdivision became and remains one of the most elite of the Romantic suburbs, having been home to such notables as architect Alexander Jackson Davis and inventor Thomas Edison.[11] Llewellyn Park stands out from other suburbs of the period because of the scope of its concept, its level of design detail, and the perfection with which its plan was adapted to the topography. The site, initially about 400 acres, but later enlarged, was conceived as a series of complete country estates, each of which had some distinguishing feature, whether a rock outcropping, a grove of

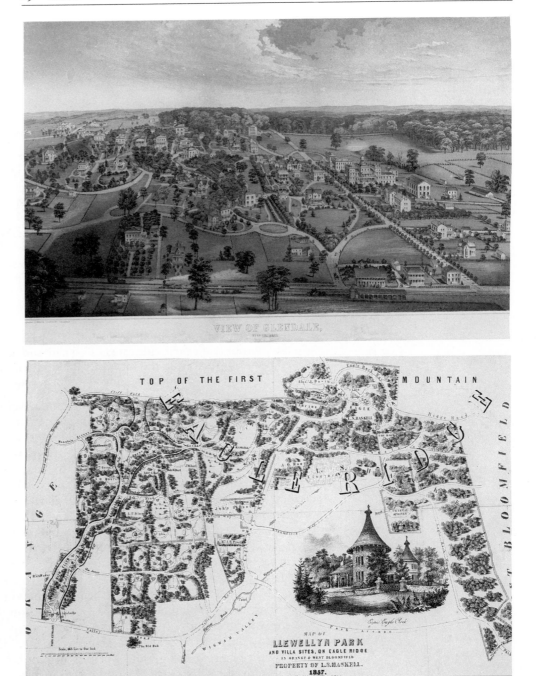

View of Glendale, Ohio, in the mid-nineteenth century. (Reproduced from the Collections of The Cincinnati Historical Society.)

Plan of Llewellyn Park, West Orange, New Jersey, 1857. (The Metropolitan Museum of Art, Harris Brisbane Dick Fund, 1924.)

trees, or some panoramic view. In addition, all residents had access to a central picturesque 50-acre park called the Ramble.

Writing in 1858, Howard Daniels gave a description of an ideal "villa park," as he called the Romantic suburb. This description was certainly based on his knowledge of Llewellyn Park, for it fits perfectly:

> [V]illa sites should be well wooded, have fine views of the park, and, if possible, command views of fine distant scenery.... The park should be centrally situated, well wooded, and if a stream of water is embraced within its limits, which can be expanded into a lake, or made to dash over a ledge of rocks, or play a fountain, it will form one of the greatest attractions.... The park should be laid out as the grand central feature of the enterprise, having fine drives, broad walks, verdant

View of the stone gatehouse lodge at Llewellyn Park, West Orange, New Jersey. On the opposite side of the drive, grateful residents erected a memorial bust of the Romantic Suburb's founder, Llewellyn Haskell, but the sculpture has here been overgrown with vegetation and is not visible.

lawns, play grounds for the children, etc., [sic] and should contain the finest trees and shrubs that can be cultivated. . . . There should be provided shady promenades, cool resting-places, in the form of pavilions, temples, kiosks, rustic covered seats, etc.,[sic] either commanding fine views or terminating vistas.[12] (1858, pp. 495–96)

Ironically, in spite of much recent scholarly interest in Llewellyn Park, no definitive attribution of the plan and design can be made. Variously credited have been Llewellyn Haskell himself, Alexander Jackson Davis, Howard Daniels, Eugene Baumann, and James MacGall. As proprietor, Haskell certainly had some part in the concept, having been the one to select the area for his own homesite. Davis was called in to design this residence and may have collaborated with Haskell on the concept or plan. Both Daniels and Baumann were credited in a contemporaneous article as having "assisted" Haskell "as landscape gardeners," while in this century MacGall's daughter claimed that he had worked at Llewellyn Park. What makes any attribution particularly difficult is that the site plan far surpasses in sophistication and detail any other known works by these individuals. Of the five only Daniels was known to have completed large-scale site plans, yet those cemetery and park plans of his which remain appear less picturesque than that of Llewellyn Park. Davis, although practicing as an architect, was knowledgeable about landscape issues, but is known to have applied that knowledge only at the scale of a single residence. Baumann's name is generally linked with planting design and horticulture, rather than site planning, while no other design work by Haskell or MacGall is known.

Following Llewellyn Park closely in date of establishment were the Romantic suburbs of Rosedale, near Toronto, Ontario, and Lake Forest, Illinois. Rosedale, although far smaller than Llewellyn Park, had an equally picturesque, ravine-cut site. Laid out in 1854 to plans by surveyor John Stoughton Dennis, its relatively small lots were given character and visual separation from their neighbors by use of the ravines and woodlands as divides. As was typical in Romantic suburbs, some ravine areas were unlotted, and were preserved as common open space, with access provided by a path system.

Lake Forest began life in 1856 as the site of a Presbyterian college, Lind University. The town's Romantic site plan, now credited to Almerin Hotchkiss, was centered on the large park to be used for the University's site.[13] The entire 1,300-acre townsite was pierced by steep-sided ravines, which were used to separate the university site and other parks from residential lots. Some ravines also inspired road locations, although much of the boldly sweeping street plan did not closely follow topography. The large size of house lots assured that much of the natural forest cover would be preserved and the town live up to the allusion of its name.

Few if any Romantic suburbs were begun during the ten years after 1857; this was due initially to the business downturn following the Panic of 1857 and then to the Civil War. When building did resume, Romantic suburbs and suburban additions proved popular with developers who wanted to attract affluent customers. The most famous of this second generation of suburbs was Riverside, Illinois, designed by Olmsted and Vaux.[14] Located along an oxbow bend in the Des Plaines River, Riverside was conceptualized as a complete suburban community. In the words of Olmsted and Vaux, it would have the convenience of the city but "with the conditions which are the peculiar advantage of the country, such as purity of air, umbrageousness, facilities for quiet out-of-door recreation and distance from the jar, noise, confusion, and bustle of commercial thoroughfares" (1868, p. 7).

With this goal in mind, the firm designed the 1,600-acre site owned by the Riverside Improvement Company as a Romantic suburb with gracefully curving roads, large open areas such as the Long Common and the linear riverside park, and generous lots with minimum building setbacks. Such features had become fairly typical of Romantic suburbs by 1869, when the Master Plan of Riverside was completed. More unusual was the attention that the designers, working with architects William Le Baron Jenney and Frederick Withers and engineer L. Y. Schermerhorn, paid to assuring convenient circulation, housing for various income groups, and complete services, including infrastructure. Although Riverside was a stop on the Burlington and Quincy Railroad, Olmsted and Vaux

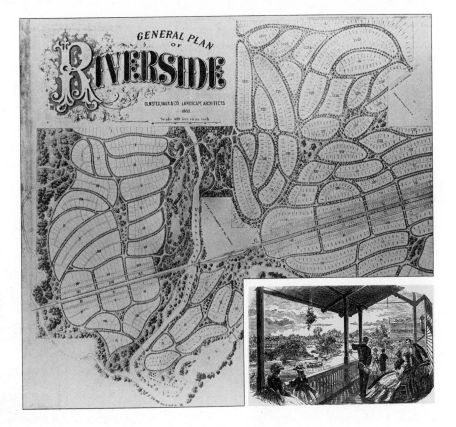

Plan of Riverside, Illinois, by Olmsted and Vaux, 1869, with inset view of the Des Plaines River. (Plan from Landscape Architecture, *Vol. 22, No. 4; view from Riverside Development Company, 1871.)*

believed that this was an insufficient link with Chicago and planned a boulevard, with separate lanes for equestrians and carriages, to the city limits, a distance of a little more than 6 miles.[15] Unlike most Romantic suburbs, which were intended for middle- and upper-income families only, Riverside had lots which could be afforded by people of varying incomes. Along the railroad tracks small lots of about an eighth of an acre were planned for the cottages of the town's laborers and service workers. As distance from the railroad increased, so did lot size, with some being almost an acre. These lots were intended for larger, more costly residences. To be a complete community, Riverside required a commercial center. One was planned for an area adjacent to the railroad depot. There, sites for community facilities including the water storage tower, a business block—a three-story building with shops, offices, and apartments—churches, and the famous Riverside Hotel were allotted.[16] Olmsted and Vaux also believed that a successful suburb required complete utilities prior to housing construction, and planned a system of lot and street drainage, as well as sewage removal.

The most obvious formgiver in the town plan was the road system. As the designers intended, its rambling, curvilinear character discouraged through traffic, so that residential character was preserved. Only Long Common Road was expected to be a direct thoroughfare to surrounding roads. The railroad line and Des Plaines River also gave some structure to the plan, primarily by dividing it into zones of slightly different character. One zone, that to the west of the river, was never even developed according to the Olmsted and Vaux plan, but was later annexed to the suburb of Brookfield. The area east of the river and north of the rail line became the principal townsite, with the largest and most varied lots. Of the two smaller, remaining zones, that south of the tracks was largely given over to smaller lots with modest homes, while the area within the bend of the river was developed into some of the most picturesque homesites of the community.

Although Riverside is today a very successful suburb of superb homes, with building and planting restoration in progress, it was far from successful in the nineteenth century. Following business losses in the Chicago Fire of 1871 and the economic Panic of 1873, Riverside Improvement Company went bankrupt, a misfortune which also affected the designers. In a typical arrangement for that time, Olmsted and Vaux had agreed to accept lots in lieu of a cash fee. When the company folded, lots became impossible to sell and most which could be sold depreciated to less than 25 percent of their previous value. So devastating were these financial setbacks to the community that it was not until the 1920s that lot sales escalated and the town took on its present character.

The Long Common in Reverside circa 1870. (Riverside Development Company, 1871.)

View of Long Common and Junction of Roads.

While Riverside, with its broadly curving streets and carefully composed tree masses, represented an aesthetically "beautiful" landscape, Highland Park to the north of Chicago was an example of a "picturesque" Romantic suburb. Done in 1872 as a redesign for an existing, more regular plat, the plan for Highland Park, by H. W. S. Cleveland with partner William Merchant French, was the epitome of a new town plan based almost entirely on adaptation to topography. A central area, which sloped gradually toward Lake Michigan, was laid out as a linear boulevard linking the downtown near the railroad depot to a lakefront park. One Highland Park historian attributed this feature to French, inspired by the design of Commonwealth Avenue in Boston's Back Bay.[17] Most of the townsite was deeply incised by wooded ravines, through which small streams flowed to the lake. Local streets were laid out based upon this very rough topography. Those nearest the lake were most asymmetrical, often with abrupt curves which revealed landform and vegetation at every turn. Farther away, as the eroded ravines were depleted, road curves became more gentle and undulating. Since no copy of the designers report has come to light, little is known of intended plantings, although it would seem likely from other planting plans that some formal allée was planned for the boulevard, Central Avenue, while elsewhere native woods were merely reinforced with introduced trees and shrubs.

Romantic suburbs became the fashionable form of suburban development throughout English-speaking North America. In 1872, Copeland began work on the Philadelphia suburb of Ridley Park, a very eclectic plan with both curvilinear and straight streets, for a site cut by two small streams that were dammed to make ponds. In 1877, Short Hills, New Jersey, credited to Jacob Weidenmann by his daughter, although generally attributed to developer Stewart Hartshorn, became a later day Llewellyn Park. At Grindstone Neck, Maine, in 1890, Nathan Barrett designed a seaside community with an extensive boulevard system. Less well designed, but still attractive, Romantic suburbs such as Park Hill in Yonkers, New York, and Wychwood Park near Toronto, sprang up around major cities. In the 1890s, this suburban concept spread to the South and West, as the Olmsted firm developed a preliminary plan for Druid Hill Park in Atlanta[18] and William Hammond Hall laid out Burlingame Park south of San Francisco.

But more common than the Romantic suburb was the small subdivision addition to an existing suburb designed in the Romantic style. These additions proliferated as towns grew and developers sought to use design as a sales gimmick that would distinguish their additions from those of competitors. Most such additions differed from complete new suburbs only in size and scale of features offered. Typical additions were the Polk and Hubbel Addition to Des Moines, Iowa, by Weidenmann; Robbins Park Addition, Hinsdale, Illinois, by Cleveland and French; Tarrytown Heights, Tarrytown, New York, by Olmsted and Vaux; Norton Subdivision, Cambridge, Massachusetts, by Charles Eliott; and Compton Heights, St. Louis, Missouri, by Julius Pitzman.

Some suburban developers, while not embracing either Romantic visual imagery or progressive planning standards, did attempt to control haphazard building. Civil engineers and surveyors were often employed by these developers to produce healthful and safe plans. These schemes typically rationalized the design process so that it could be replicated in rubber stamp fashion across the landscape with little regard to distinctive local conditions. On the positive side, some engineers aided in establishing minimum health and safety standards, which would be widely adopted following the advent of organized city planning in the early twentieth century.

Writing in 1872, a civil engineer named Gerard suggested a prototypical urban plan in grid form, but with a street hierarchy related to use. He then went

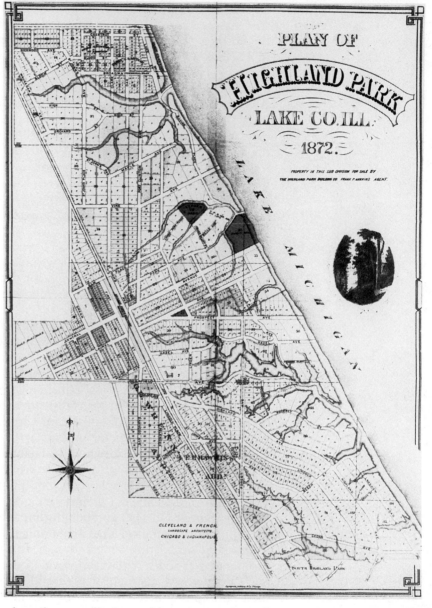

Plan of Highland Park, Illinois, by Cleveland and French, 1872. (Illinois State Historical Society.)

on to describe a well-planned streetscape in which "every house should have fronting the street a garden 40 feet in depth, in which a tree of the largest species should be planted, at 10 feet from the sidewalks, and in the centre line of the grounds. Between a sidewalk of 20 feet and the street should be a belt of ground, in which should be planted another line of trees" (Gerard, p. 6). While such standards were far too restrictive for all cases, they did suggest an emerging consensus on certain minimal urban amenities, such as setbacks and street trees, which landscape architects had advocated for decades. Some typical non-Romantic suburbs of high quality included Hyde Park near Chicago, Roxbury Highlands near Boston, Idlewild in Memphis, Tennessee, and Garden City, New York. So closely did the designs of these subdivisions follow typical nineteenth-century urban patterns that few are distinguishable today from the urban milieu within which they have been absorbed.

Romantic suburbs and suburban additions were stylish new suburban town forms, but they were not the majority of suburbs developed during the period. Most suburbs continued to be developed on patterns very similar to those of

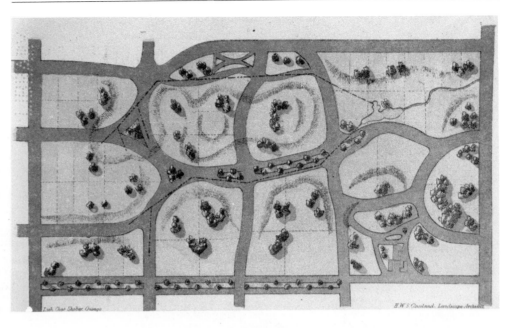

Plan of Robbins Park Subdivision, Hinsdale, Illinois, by Cleveland and French, 1870. (Art Institute of Chicago.)

central cities: that is, they were grid in plan, had uniform houses sited on small lots, had few amenities, were built on speculation, and had few constraints on development. In fact, many suburbs owed their existence to the desire of home-owners to escape any type of siting or construction restriction. When Chicago established limitations, called the "fire limits," on construction of wooden buildings within the city, developers proudly advertised their subdivisions as being "Outside Fire Limits!—You Can Build Wooden Houses!" Other suburban advantages on which these developers capitalized were freedom from city taxes in unincorporated areas, freedom from sewage regulations, and, of course, lower land costs. The result was that, in seeking escape from urban problems, home-owners often generated the same health and safety problems at their new homes.

THE ROMANTIC RESORT

The Romantic design idiom fit well for a special type of community—the resort town. Three quite different examples, Wesleyan Grove and Oak Bluffs on Martha's Vineyard in Massachusetts and the Jekyll Island Club on Jekyll Island, Georgia, suggest the diversity of Romantic-style resorts. Wesleyan Grove, the earliest of these three communities, was a religious resort for the outdoor summer revivals known as "camp meetings." Begun in 1835 as a tent encampment in an oak grove, its popularity led to continuous expansion. By 1860 permanent structures had been added, and a system of narrow streets in a circular pattern with connecting radials had been laid out. A handbill used to promote the camp showed this plan as being very regular, while more accurate as-built plans revealed a more random, Romantic scheme. Two features distinguished the camp site. First was the diminutive scale of its lots, streets, and buildings. Second was the festive Gothic cottage architecture of the permanent dwellings which gradually replaced the tents. Wesleyan Grove looked like a cozy village of elaborately detailed playhouses.

The success of Wesleyan Grove not only fostered its own growth but encouraged commercial investors to develop a compatible, but secular, resort adjoining it—Oak Bluffs. Oak Bluffs was designed by Robert Morris Copeland for the Oak Bluffs Land and Wharf Company beginning in 1866. Over the next five years, Copeland completed three different site plans, with the first being most intimate in scale and most like the existing camp meeting area. In the second

View of Oak Bluffs on Martha's Vineyard, Massachusetts, in the 1980s. To the left is the oceanfront park planned by Copeland.

plan, of 1867, the scheme was radically altered through introduction of a large oceanfront park, ringed by a semicircle of lots. As finally implemented, the site plan had two distinct areas—one with tiers of roads and lots concentric to the park and the other a rather gridlike arrangement similar to parts of Ridley Park. Copeland must have made something of a specialty of resort plans, as he is known to have designed two others, Katama, also on Martha's Vineyard, and Dering Harbor, New York. Katama, although never built, had a unique lot and open space pattern in areas adjoining the Atlantic Ocean: by widening the open space at the ocean end, all lots were assured at least minuscule vistas to the water.

Jekyll Island Club was a very different type of resort, as its popular name, "Millionaire's Village," suggests. It was begun as a private club in 1885, and its wealthy members purchased one of the Sea Islands and hired H. W. S. Cleveland to develop plans for a village of vacation cottages on the leeward side of the island. Cleveland's site plan focused on the Club House, which was a community center and hotel, with the intent that most of the island would remain wooded and undisturbed by development. The simple plan arranged curving streets to preserve the best trees and provide a waterfront drive. In an accompanying report Cleveland suggested that no formal plantings be used, but that existing woodland be supplemented with trees for color and texture contrast. As built, only the area near the Club House, and the concept of a waterfront drive, followed Cleveland's plan, but the wooded character which he so cherished was preserved.

CONCLUSION AND SUMMARY

As Frederick Law Olmsted observed in surveying American ambivalence toward the city, "There can be no doubt, then, that, in all our modern civilization . . . there is a strong drift townward. But some seem to regard [this as] . . . a sort of moral epidemic, the crisis and reaction of which they constantly expect to see. They even detect already a growing disgust with the town and signs of a back-set towards rural simplicity" (1871, p. 4). The vacillating attitude Olmsted described certainly delayed any concerted effort at improving urban health and safety through physical planning. Thus, the nineteenth century was a period in which unrestrained real estate markets and the effects of recent technology, such as railroad development, rather than community well-being were the primary forces organizing city and suburb alike. In spite of or because of this situation there were some individuals and professions that did attempt to develop a theory and practice of urban planning. These took the form of plans for specific cities, such as Gourlay's for Boston; general speculative works, like Cleveland's on planning in the developing West; or technical plans and texts dealing with sanitary engineering, including the many by George Waring, Jr.

While the status of design in cities proved discouraging, progressive developers and designers saw greater opportunities in the untainted rural areas surrounding cities. Suburban planning allowed landscape architects to apply spatial, functional, and aesthetic concepts as a total package, as well as to coordinate site planning with architectural design in many instances. The success of industrial and Romantic suburbs, as prototypes for more extensive suburbanization in the twentieth century, suggests how effective plans such as those for Pullman and Riverside really were.

NOTES

1. A comprehensive planning approach, but one focused almost entirely on downtown areas, was often taken in county seats, such as those of Ohio and Texas, where the courthouse square became the focus of downtown planning.

2. Although there is a nostalgic notion that burglary, rape, drug addiction, and other crimes were not part of nineteenth-century urban life, such is far from the case. Murder, theft, and mysterious disappearances filled the newspapers of every city. Added to this, police departments were far less professional than today, with most officers appointed for political reasons, rather than on merit. A number of historians consider the mid-nineteenth century equal to our own age in urban lawlessness.

3. Not all developers laid out subdivisions without character or open space. Early nineteenth-century New York urban additions such as that around Union Square, at 14th Street, included private parks for use of residents.

4. Among Gourlay's more unusual claims was the one which accompanied his plans for New York and Boston: that the work of developing these plans was made possible because he had not slept for "five years and eight months, with the exception of two hours" (1844, p. 10).

5. At that time Chicago and many other cities had a nighttime fire detection system which relied on a spotter located in a tower. If the spotter incorrectly identified the fire location, as it would be easy to do in areas with few landmarks, firefighters would be misdirected. Just such a problem was believed to have contributed to the Chicago Fire of 1871.

6. Landscape Architecture as Applied to the Wants of the West is the only professional publication by Cleveland which can correctly be called a book, although he is often credited with other "books" as well. Some of these, such as A Few Hints on the Central Park, were really brief essays in pamphlet form, while others, like Rural Cemeteries, were promotional brochures for his practice.

7. Manning also designed other sites at Hopedale, working there for more than ten years. Arthur Shurcliff later completed site plans and designs for this industrial suburb.

8. George Pullman's practical view of the townsite as a business operation led him to make some harsh, and for workers unacceptable, decisions. When product demand fell, Pullman laid off some workers and lowered wages for others, but at the same time raised rents on company-owned houses, placing employees in a doubly powerful vise. It was then that many workers began to realize the pitfalls of corporate paternalism.

9. Nathan Barrett was also connected with Anniston, although he is not known to have completed an urban plan. His documented projects include a street beautification plan, landscape plans for two estates, and a very formal, geometric plan for part of Hillside Cemetery.

10. The concept of the industrial suburb continued to be popular into the twentieth century. Later suburbs are discussed in Chapter 12.

11. The site design for Edison's residence, known as Glenmont, has been attributed to Jacob Weidenmann.
   One of the reasons for current preservation of the suburb's character was that Haskell established development restrictions, such as a prohibition against industrial or commercial land uses within the subdivision, a prohibition on the fencing of lots, and a requirement that all house lots must be at least 1 acre in size.

12. From the high point, Eagle Rock, where Haskell located his own home, one could reportedly see to the Hudson River and beyond. Views are now obscured by intervening development and air pollution.

13. For many years the town plan was attributed to engineer Jed Hotchkiss, who like Almerin was from St. Louis, but recent research has presented a more plausible justification for Almerin, designer of Bellefontaine Cemetery in St. Louis and Chippinnok Cemetery in Rock Island, Illinois. See Ebner (1988) for discussion of evidence.

14. *Ironically, Olmsted and Vaux saw little potential for the site when first visiting it, because of marshy ground and little woody vegetation except at the Des Plaines River. There was so little landform variation that the giant loops of the street plan were based on views rather than topography, as would have been the typical Romantic design approach.*

15. *About a mile of this boulevard, now Riverside Drive in Berwyn, Illinois, was completed as an extension of Long Common Road before the development company went bankrupt.*

16. *The water tower and hotel were designed by Jenney; the shopping block was by Withers.*

17. *Cleveland and French were in partnership for more than five years, following an introduction through Olmsted. French was trained as an engineer. From correspondence and later statements by French it appears that he practiced this technical specialty in the partnership, rather than being a designer. Although he has been credited with specific parts of the Highland Park plan, this attribution may be due to his later fame in Chicago as first director of the Art Institute. There are no known works of landscape planning on which he worked independently.*

18. *Final plans for Druid Hill were not developed until 1905, when with John Olmsted in charge, the present scheme was implemented.*

20

Impact of Railroads on the American Landscape

"[T]he railroad—that great monster, ironhearted, relentless, and infinitely powerful. Always it had issued triumphant from the fight . . . symbol of a vast power, huge and terrible; the leviathan with tentacles of steel . . ."

Frank Norris, The Octopus, *1899*

The full impact of technological developments is rarely sensed by those who invent and promote them. This is particularly true of the railroad, which began existence as a short-distance, horse-driven hauling system for coal. Within the first decades after its invention, it made canals obsolete and accelerated industrialization and settlement in North America. Although not a North American invention,[1] the use of rail lines quickly became the quintessential form of long-distance transport on the continent.

Several factors can account for this rapidity of development. In the East, competition among coastal cities to become the premier port of entry and export for European goods, as discussed earlier regarding canals, also affected development of railroads. Baltimore, which had seen its commercial position erode after construction of the Erie Canal, was constantly alert for a new transportation weapon in its battle with New York City. The railroad provided just such a weapon. It was Baltimore's business community that promoted the first long-distance freight and passenger line in the nation, the Baltimore and Ohio Railroad.

A second factor in the East was the limitations of river travel. River travel was slow, especially upstream as required in any round trip. And the difficulties of river travel became extreme when transport across major watershed divides, such as the Appalachians, was required.

In the West equally compelling forces were at work to encourage development of railroads. After the War of 1812, interest in settlement of the Central Plains accelerated.[2] At first environmental uncertainty, especially difficulty in cutting through the fibrous, deep-rooted prairie sod, was a deterrent to settlement. After development of the self-scouring steel plough in the 1830s, this obstacle was overcome and distance to marketplaces became the new limiting factor. Although navigable rivers and the Great Lakes provided some access, these systems were unreliable due to weather and were at a distance from the richest agricultural land. Rail lines could provide rapid systems of transport, could be located where need existed, and would haul large volumes of produce efficiently, although as farmers later learned, these services were not always inexpensive.[3] Another economic incentive for rail development came from the desire to exploit the mineral wealth of the Far West. The California gold rush of 1849 had alerted the country to this need. Civil War in the United States produced a turning point in rail building because it made clear the necessity of a quick, reliable link to all parts of the country to serve both political and commercial needs. Specifically, the tenuous physical linkage of California to the Union was emphasized.[4]

"Across the Continent: 'Westward the Course of Empire Takes Its Way,'" by Fanny F. Palmer, 1868, colored lithograph. The railroad in the landscape was a favorite theme of mid-nineteenth century artists. Palmer's image was more realistic than most romanticized views in contrasting the developed frontier landscape left of the tracks with that of primeval grandeur to the right. (Amon Carter Museum, Fort Worth. Acquisition number 1970.187.)

ACROSS THE CONTINENT.
WESTWARD THE COURSE OF EMPIRE TAKES ITS WAY.

DEVELOPMENT OF RAIL-BASED TRANSPORTATION

In the first half of the nineteenth century, railroad development, although rapid, was spotty. Several lines claimed to be the first on the continent, but the one opened in 1827 between Quincy and Boston, Massachusetts, appears to have actually been the first. Like many early lines, it was built for a very specific task, in this case to haul granite used in constructing the Bunker Hill Monument. Until the 1850s most lines were short, detached segments, many only a couple of miles in length, with 50 miles being a great distance for a track to span. Eventually, the wisdom of linking these became apparent, and existing lines were joined with new roads, so that the average road extended to several hundred miles.[5]

The first real step toward creating an intracontinental system was construction of a 13-mile segment of the Baltimore and Ohio Railroad (B&O) linking Baltimore to Ellicott City, Maryland, beginning in 1828. Incrementally, this line extended to Frederick, Maryland (1831); Harper's Ferry, Virginia (1834); Cumberland, Maryland—where it connected with the National Road (1842)—Wheeling, West Virginia (1853); and finally, to Chicago (1874). The importance of the B&O lies in its having been the first company to test the use of European-invented railroad components in the rugged North American landscape, where, through slow trial and error, improvements necessary for steep topography and long distances were improvised. The prominence of the B&O endured for just over twenty years, for in spite of its head start, it was not even the first line to connect directly to the rich Ohio River valley, having been preceded by both the Erie and Pennsylvania Railroads.

Not until 1869, when the famous golden spike merged the Central Pacific with the Union Pacific at Promontory, Utah, was the cross-continental bond envisioned during the Civil War produced. In 1883 three additional transcontinental routes, the Southern Pacific, the Northern Pacific, and the Atcheson, Topeka, and Santa Fe were opened. In Canada a variety of problems, particularly

*Map showing principal railroad
routes discussed in text.*
(Drawn by Rossi.)

difficulties in building across boggy soils in the Lake Superior region, delayed
inauguration of the Canadian Pacific until 1885. These intracontinental railroads
transformed the frontier cities through which they passed. Chicago, with a sea
link via the Great Lakes, became a natural transfer point as well as a center of
agricultural processing, emerging in Carl Sandburg's words as "hog butcher to
the world." Villages that did not even exist before the war were transformed
into regional commercial centers. Omaha, the eastern depot for the Union Pacific
and terminus for many connecting eastern lines, such as the Chicago and Northwestern, grew from about 2,000 people in 1860 to more than 140,000 in 1890.

Nationwide the rate of increase in the number of miles of railroad track was
remarkable, as the figures below indicate:[6]

Year	Miles of track
1830	23
1850	9,021
1870	52,914
1890	159,271
1910	236,422
1920	250,983

These numbers represent the growth of a hierarchical system which began with
city-regional, centered, short-distance lines. Then connecting lines to more isolated areas were added, until finally a weblike network had covered much of the
continent. The declining rate of increase after 1910 was due as much to a saturated transportation market as to competition from other circulation systems.

CONSEQUENCES OF RAILROAD DEVELOPMENT

When railroad development boomed after 1865, the availability of rail transportation generated both intended and unanticipated results. The most important of these was certainly the rapid rise in rate of interior settlement. Ease of access, coupled with promotional activities of the railroad companies, such as employment of emigration agents in Europe to lure new settlers to the West, caused this population growth. Many historians believe that rail expansion, which was promoted to foster agriculture, actually hastened industrialization of the continent, especially in the United States and Canada. The same freight cars that carried wheat and corn east to market could just as easily transport iron ore and lumber to factories. Railroads also opened up new domestic markets for factory goods in interior settlements, altering both shopping and merchandising practices. Consumers no longer needed to rely on local merchants, since they could order goods themselves directly using rail delivery. Early mail order companies, first Montgomery Ward and later Sears Roebuck, built commercial dynasties around this opportunity.

In the West, especially in Texas, railroads made large cattle operations economically practical. Construction of the Union Pacific and later the Atchinson, Topeka, and Santa Fe through Kansas to the market at Chicago made long-distance transfer of cattle possible in an age before refrigeration. This tradition gave the nation romantic legends of the trail drive, but it also concentrated and industrialized meat processing, which like other food processing, had previously been a strictly local activity.

Railroads changed not only economic life, but social and political life as well, by reducing contact time between East and West. The West especially benefited from the rapid spread of ideas and inventions. The lecture tour by a distinguished professor or writer, such as that of Charles Dickens in 1867, became a popular form of adult education, with rail routes being standard itineraries. Of course, the railroad facilitated visits between family and friends, making the great distances of the continent seem less a barrier to contact. Politicians quickly took advantage of these opportunities and used "whistle stop" campaign tours just as the 30-second television advertisement is used today. A geographical reorientation occurred as well. Inland cities for the first time became potential rivals to

108—Union Stock Yards, Chicago

The end of the line for rail-transported cattle. Union Stock Yards in Chicago was the world's largest food-processing center until its dismantling in the 1950s.

those of the seaboard. Chicago eventually benefited from this realignment, becoming by 1900 the "Second City" in population in the United States. Finally, in the United States, railroads are sometimes credited with causing a definite and permanent change in national attitude away from international issues, toward an inward-looking self-sufficiency and isolation. In Canada and colonial Central America political alliances prevented this, while in Mexico changing political conditions and limited resources made such an attitude unfeasible.

RAILROADS AS A FORCE OF CHANGE IN THE LANDSCAPE

Massive changes wrought by the railroads affected the North American landscape as a whole, including the planned and designed landscape. Many of the impacts that railroads had can be attributed to constraints on their layout, particularly the need for straight rights-of-way and low gradients. The turning radius of a rail car was about 400 feet. The maximum gradient for a long-distance line was 4 percent, but typically every effort was made to keep gradients below 1 percent. In addition, to extend the effective life of wooden ties by avoiding moist soil, the entire track system was constructed on natural or artificial berms. These design constraints had several impacts on the environment. Need for a relatively straight alignment meant that there was little sensitivity to natural patterns of topography or drainage.[7] Instead, awkward relationships of track to landform were resolved by "remodeling" the landscape, sometimes rather drastically. Denny Hill in Seattle, Washington, with over 7 million cubic feet of rock and soil, was dynamited to oblivion in 1907 to facilitate track installation. Less sensationally, at the local scale, additions of berms for the tressels altered small watersheds and led to changes in plant species.

Many environmental impacts attributed to railroads cannot be tied to the needs of the system itself. The rapid annihilation of the American bison is an example of such an indirect effect. Popular Currier and Ives views of sharpshooters standing on a train roof and taking easy aim depict what sometimes occurred. But the far more serious threat to the buffalo was the economically attractive transport the railroad provided for the vast number of hides collected throughout the prairie with ox-drawn wagons. Once collected, hides were driven to the railroad for transport to tanneries on the East Coast and in Europe. Demand for the product and availability of powerful rifles actually allowed the hunts to occur, but presence of railroads certainly made it more profitable and thereby accelerated the process of reducing what were in 1800 an estimated 75 million animals to about 100 by 1890.

Not all the alterations caused by railroads are viewed today as environmentally negative. Railroad rights-of-way became, in many places, a preserve for native species which were otherwise ploughed under by farmers. This was especially true in the prairie lands, were almost every square foot of soil not in a right-of-way was converted to crop or grazing land. Many prairie plant species used in recent ecological restorations were retrieved from unintended conservation zones along railroad lines.

Just as patterns created by railroads influenced the natural environment, so too did they influence human land use. In many parts of the continent railroad companies dominated urban and rural land development because they became major landowners and promoters. Beginning with the Illinois Central (IC) charter of 1851, incentives of several types were given by federal and state governments to increase the number of lines built, as well as the speed of construction.[8] Primary incentives were in land ownership, but loans were also made. The typical land grant was for a 400-foot-wide right-of-way along the tracks[9] plus a square mile section of land adjoining that right of way, alternating as to side, for the entire length of the route. The Union Pacific, for example, received about

7 million acres, while nationwide over 130 million acres of land came under railroad ownership. Thus, railroad companies controlled much of the most desirable land near lines and depots, as well as having first access to it.[10] They used this early access to dictate later settlement patterns through the founding of towns along the route.

Many of these railroad towns began life as end-of-route service centers for construction workers. Prefabricated structures and supplies were railed to the site on existing track and then assembled into towns, following plans laid out by engineers in the home office. Town location was chosen for one of three reasons: first, to capture an important local or regional market not currently being served; second, to compete with the townsite and depot of another line; and finally, to fill a specific railroad service need, such as a stop for fuel or water needed for steam engines. Environmental or aesthetic considerations did not enter into the site selection process. These new towns were uniformly grid in arrangement, with the railroad station as a community focus. For some lines, prototype plans, devoid of any adjustment to local conditions, became the sole mode of urban design. Throughout the Midwest and West the results of this urban mass production can be seen in towns such as Urbana, Illinois; Beatrice, Nebraska; and Cheyenne, Wyoming.

Railroads not only built new towns, but often decided the fate of existing ones. It was a common practice for company representatives to require compensation in cash or land for routing lines through an established town. Many communities refused to cooperate, either resenting attempted blackmail or failing to see the absolute need to be on a line. In any case, few of the uncooperative towns are well known today, as most quickly died, while nearby a more tractable competitor blossomed. At Booneville, Texas, when bypassed by a rail route, the citizenry simply moved their buildings to the new community of Bryan, accomplishing virtually overnight what the lack of a railroad did elsewhere in several years.

Whether running through newly built or existing towns, railroads affected the towns' physical appearance. In new towns, orientation of streets and lots followed consistent patterns because of centralized design and platting. When railroads passed through existing settlements, their location often led to a juxtaposition of two or more patterns. Typically, the older portion of the town was in a grid pattern, often following the matrix established by the Public Land Survey. The railroad, of course, was laid out to different parameters and could literally bisect an established plan. When this happened, newer portions of a town were laid out to follow the railroad or the downtown was realigned to parallel it. Thus, in many midwestern towns like Dwight, Illinois, planning, as well as architecture, distinguished the commercial core from the rest of the community.

There were several characteristic patterns of town orientation to the railroad. Hudson (1982) has identified three of these, based on relationship of main street to the tracks, as the "T-town pattern," the "symmetric pattern," and the "orthogonal pattern." In the T-town, main street was perpendicular to the tracks, with the depot usually serving as street terminus. This produced a consistent and concentrated downtown with hotels, major stores, and offices clustered near the tracks. The "other side of the tracks," if developed at all, often became a poorer residential area. Oklahoma City is an example of a T-town. The symmetric arrangement is one in which the railroad ran down the middle of a double main street with businesses located parallel to the line on one or both sides. The advantage of this scheme was that all shopfronts were seen by rail passengers. Its chief problems were that main street became merely an extension of the railroad; and in small towns with few commercial enterprises one side of the road often became a derelict area. That problem was compounded in the third pattern, the

McKinney, Texas, was an example of the T-town pattern identified by John Hudson, but was unusual because downtown was at a distance from the depot, adjoining courthouse square. (Barker Texas History Center, University of Texas, Austin, Texas.)

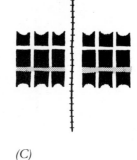

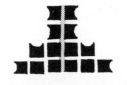

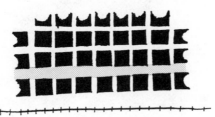

Diagrams of five typical plans of railroad towns. (A) T-town; (B) symmetric; (C) orthogonal; (D) behind commercial street; and (E) riverfront. (In sketches Main Street indicated by gray tone.) (A, B, C adapted from Hudson, 1982; drawn by Rossi.)

orthogonal. In this plan, main street was perpendicular to the tracks but divided by them into two parts. The orthogonal pattern permitted a centralized downtown with intensive uses nearest to the railroad, even though the tracks presented a barrier to movement. Hondo, Texas, is an example of a symmetric plan, while Laredo, Texas, is its complement the orthogonal.

In addition to these three, there were several other typical railroad town arrangements. In a variation of the symmetric, the railroad ran parallel to but behind the commercial area, either in the next block or several blocks away. In such plans the railroad was treated as merely a service system to be kept as much out of sight as possible. New Braunfels, Texas, and Santa Monica, California, both illustrate this arrangement. Another common pattern was for the railroad to bear little direct relationship to the town plan but to be sited on low, flat land, most commonly along a river. This pattern was typical in Mississippi Valley towns where the floodplain was considered a perfect topographic setting to accommodate the railroad, and to link it with river transportation. As a result of this practice, some of the most scenic areas adjacent to cities were given over to industrial functions.[11] Cities that illustrate this pattern were Omaha, Nebraska, and Sacramento, California. The general predictability of organization in railroad towns was a comfort to town visitors, who would find familiar patterns wherever they went, but also a source of visual monotony.

While railroad companies and most other western land developers laid out only prosaic grids for towns, there were a few creative individuals who saw in railroads an opportunity to create novel urban forms. The Romantic and industrial suburbs that have already been discussed are two examples of this. But a far more revolutionary urban vision was Roadtown, the dream of Edgar Chambless. Roadtown was an Arcosanti-like amalgamation of housing, shops, and transportation into a linear city built over and around rail lines. In Chambless's rather utopian view this urban form combined advantages of the suburb with city living. Clustering of buildings preserved nearby open space, while proximity to the rail line reduced commuting time. Chambless's idea was ahead of its time, perhaps of any time, and was never given a trial, although today many dense urban centers have much the same character without the amenities.

Bird's-eye view, with foreground cross-section, of Edgar Chambless's Roadtown concept. The subway was to be a noiseless gyroscopic monorail invented by William Boyes. (The Independent, Vol. 68, No. 3205.)

What bit of character was added to homogeneous railroad towns was often associated with the railroad station itself. These depots became centers of social life as well as symbols of community and corporate identity and pride.[12] Essayist and landscape architect Donald E. Mitchell was among the first to advocate the potential of the depot as visual amenity. In his 1867 book *Rural Studies, with Hints for Country Places,* two chapters were devoted to the design and planting of stations and lines.[13] From that time until the turn of the century many landscape architects were involved in railroad design, sometimes designing all the stations for a single line. Some examples of their work are Beverly Station by Charles Eliot and Brookline Hills Station by the Olmsted firm, both in Massachusetts, and stations at Roselle and Fanwood, New Jersey, by Nathan Barrett. This beautification was an early manifestation of one aspect of the later City Beautiful Movement and brought the benefits of designed public landscapes to towns with few other amenities.[14] About 1900, landscape architects generally ceased to be involved in this work, although the Olmsted firm was an exception. This seems to be due less to a shift in the interests of professional designers, as Stilgoe (1983) has proposed, than to the dominance of late Victorian concepts of design, which emphasized patterning of the ground plane rather than spatial design. Popular Victorian carpet-bedding and parterre schemes became increasingly stereotyped both in arrangement and in planting design, leaving little for the creative designer to contribute. In Canada, the role of professional designers was not large; they were superseded by professional railroad gardeners, skilled in practical horticulture, particularly the requirements of the often hostile physical environments of the depots, but with little sensitivity to spatial design.[15]

Railroads opened several other areas of opportunity for the emerging profession of landscape architecture. In managing their large landholdings, railroad companies often sought the expertise of people such as Maximilian G. Kern, Horace Cleveland, and Frederick Law Olmsted. Their chief tasks were the planning of forest plantations to be used as sources of steam engine fuel and the siting, and occasionally design, of towns. The Northern Pacific sought to employ Cleveland to organize their Minnesota forests and hired Olmsted, along with civil engineer G. K. Radford, to prepare an unimplemented plan for Tacoma, Washington, the line's Pacific terminus.

N. P. Station and Park, Fargo, N. D.

This Northern Pacific depot in Fargo, North Dakota, had a planting scheme typical of many designed by professional railroad gardeners. Floral beds, some quite elaborate, were the principal design feature, with trees and shrubs used as adornments rather than to create space.

In contrast to floral schemes, landscape architects designed naturalistic parks for railroad depots. This depot at Waban, Massachusetts, was one of many that the Olmsted firm designed for the Boston and Albany Railroad. (Robinson, 1903.)

An integrated transportation network circa 1875. The horse-drawn street rail line in the foreground was a forerunner of electric trolleys that hastened suburbanization later in the century. (Barker Texas History Center, University of Texas, Austin, Texas.)

Finally, railroads opened up vast new markets for landscape architectural services by making travel so much quicker. Professional announcements by both Cleveland and Eliot refer specifically to their fees for services in towns accessible in half a day by rail. In this way, professional design services became available to smaller towns as well as large cities, increasing national awareness of the benefits of thoughtful design and planning. Within local urban areas, the progeny of the railroad, the streetcar, facilitated commuting for professional work and allowed development of numerous middle-class towns known as "streetcar suburbs," which included subdivisions occasionally designed by landscape architects, such as Washburn Park in Minneapolis, designed by Cleveland.

CONCLUSION AND SUMMARY

Railroads were at their most influential in development of the North American landscape during the late nineteenth century. The rails continued to be the most important form of long-distance transportation until the 1950s, although a notable decline in expansion and use began as early as 1925. The legacy of the tracks has remained with us in the form of urban plans and industrial locations. Since the 1960s rail lines have begun to be removed from the landscape, but the rights-of-way persist, often kept intact to be used as linear parks or to serve a less polluting form of transportation—the bicycle.

The physical impact of railroads is their most obvious legacy, but other effects may have just as great an impact on how we treat the landscape today. This revolutionary transportation system actually created what might be called a "railroad culture," with emphasis on speed and efficiency. Although the trend had begun with industrialization, railroads made it imperative that a logical and relentless schedule be maintained. Among the specific changes initiated were standardization of packaging for ease of movement and to fit boxcars, creation of regional time zones, creation of a professional managerial class to assure that scheduling was maintained, and standardization of construction techniques and materials. Railroads also ushered in the age of instantaneous communications, with telegraph wires strung as track was laid to allow centralized monitoring of track and schedule conditions. American railroads, created to provide economic and political cohesion, became the rational, efficient beast which dominated nation and individual alike—the "octopus" which affected all facets of the landscape.

NOTES

1. The invention of the railroad as a passenger and freight system is generally credited to George Stephenson of Great Britain. In 1814 he developed the first locomotive capable of hauling cargo and then went on, in 1825, to construct the first common carrier railroad line, the twelve-mile long Stockton & Darlington.

2. Settlers from the United States would have moved into this area earlier than they actually did had British presence not lingered. In spite of the Treaty of Paris, the English continued to occupy some northern forts in territory ceded to the United States at the conclusion of the Revolution. Their major purposes were to maintain trade contacts with Indians and use the Indians as a barrier to settlement by Americans.

3. Agriculturalists initially viewed the railroad as a boon to crop marketability, but quickly found that where a monopoly existed the purchaser of services was at a disadvantage. The perceived high cost of transport coupled with railroad inflexibility was a significant factor in the 1867 formation of the Grange or, as it was officially known, the Patrons of Husbandry. This organization for farmers and their families led a fight in the 1870s to bring down freight costs and limit railroad control of rural areas through pricing policies.

4. The Civil War has been referred to as the Railroad War for several reasons. First, rails were the major supply systems transport for troops. Second, some of the most important action in the struggle was directed against railroad facilities, as in John Brown's prewar assault on Harpers Ferry, Virginia, and Sherman's capture of the Southern rail center at Atlanta. Finally, the war belatedly forced the country to think of railroads as a national utility rather than merely a private enterprise.

5. The earliest railroads not only differed from modern systems in their extent, but also in some particulars of their design. Initially most were not engine-driven but used real horsepower. Placing carriages on rails merely reduced friction and allowed horses to be more productive than on a road. Coaches were not the luxurious parlor cars later built by George Pullman, but were stage coaches equipped with flanged wheels. Spacing between rails was not uniform and could vary on different lines by several feet. The Erie Railroad had tracks six feet apart, while those of the Denver & Rio Grande were only three feet apart, to illustrate two extremes. Fortunately for the system in the United States a standard gauge of four feet, eight and a half inches was mandated for the transcontinental line and thereafter became the national standard.

6. 1830–70 from Thompson, 1925; 1880–1920 from Clarke, 1976.

7. Railroads did seek high ground if possible, but would not sacrifice grade or alignment to do so. Thus, in relatively flat landscapes routes followed ridgelines, but did not do so in steeper areas.

8. Legislation specifically prohibited the IC from town development along its route. This limitation was creatively circumvented through a legally separate, but economically related, development company. After this charade, the government dropped restrictions against other railroads with land grants platting towns.

9. *As the earliest grantee, the Illinois Central received only a 100-foot right-of-way. In general, later railroads got larger grants, especially those in the more rugged parts of the continent, where costs were higher. The Northern Pacific was originally given a right-of-way of 20 miles on each side of the track in states and 40 miles in territories, but later an additional 10 miles was added to each side to compensate the line for undevelopable lands in the first grant. It must be noted that even this expanse of real estate was not sufficient to save railroad developer Jay Cooke from financial ruin.*

10. *Henry (1968) pointed out, though, that nationwide only 8 percent of all railroad track miles laid received grants. Locally this percentage could be much higher. Hudson (1985) cites 25 percent of North Dakota as having been in grants to the Northern Pacific. In addition, after 1880 those grantees who did not fulfill their development obligations were required to forfeit all or part of their grants (Ellis, 1946).*

11. *This problem of ugly, unusable riversides that were polluted by adjacent uses continues to be a problem today, but a declining one. With the reduction in rail use after World War II many waterfront lines began to be removed, eventually leading to relocation of industries. In the last 20 years there has been a remarkable renaissance of interest in the amenity value of urban waterfronts. This phenomena and its most successful exemplars will be reviewed in Chapter 18.*

12. *Plantings were functional as well, particularly in the north where they were planned as living snow fences and as windbreaks.*

13. *As to the first designed station, Arnold (1905) credits Newtonville, Massachusetts, baggagemaster E. A. Richardson as the first to have actually installed a planting design in the early 1880s. This late date, if correct, suggests that it was not really the first, but the one that made the practice fashionable and widespread.*

14. *See Chapter 11 for discussion of the City Beautiful Movement and Chapter 10 for discussion of the Late Victorian period.*

15. *The Railroad Gardening Movement became so popular that in 1907 professional gardeners created an association which met annually for about 20 years. Their chief activities were education and the recognition of outstanding floral displays.*

21

Design for Ostentation:
The Late Victorian Eclectic Landscape

In terms both of overall cultural history and of landscape history, the Victorian period presents a series of contradictions: simple in its controlling principles, yet complex in details; exuberantly self-confident yet emphasizing personal modesty; highly moral and often considered prudish, yet materialistic and decadent; an age when science and technology were revered and employed to improve life, yet one that emphasized traditional symbols and forms. Perhaps it is these very contradictions that make this period so popular today; Victorian simplicity balancing what we consider our more complex age or its materialism justifying our own. In landscape history, much of the work of the period could be easily dismissed, as it sometimes is, as mere "exterior decoration" with little serious design content. Two factors make this impossible. First is the sheer popularity today of the Victorian period as a design phase. In English-speaking North America, much of the built fabric now being preserved dates from this period, which suggests that some of its design features remain meaningful. Second, and of far greater significance, is the period's pivotal position as a transition phase, although not necessarily the most logical one, between Romantic design in the nineteenth century and the revival of Renaissance-inspired planning and design in the early twentieth century.

As its name suggests, the sixty-four-year period of the reign of Queen Victoria of England (1837–1901) is considered a fairly homogeneous era characterized by similar social, economic, and style standards throughout much of Europe and the English-speaking world. The Queen, although obviously a dynamic force in establishing this model, cannot be solely credited (or blamed) for the beneficence and excesses of the age which bears her name. A number of other forces were at work to produce the distinctive qualities of this period. Most important among these were (1) industrial development; (2) coinciding with industrialization and related to it, an increase in the number of urban places and the total percentage of people living in cities; (3) growth of a business and professional middle class; and (4) changing attitudes toward family life and the home.

For a meaningful discussion of landscape history in North America during the Victorian period, it is important that phases of this period be distinguished and the contrasts during each of these phases between architecture and landscape design be clarified. Three generally cited phases of the Victorian period are the Early, High, and Late Victorian.[1] The Early Victorian is dated from the 1820s to the 1850s and corresponds quite well to the formative period of Romantic design. Early Victorian architecture employed themes from several historic periods, especially the Gothic and Greek, but never mixed styles in one building.

The High Victorian, from the 1850s to the 1880s, was a time of dramatic changes in architecture. New historical styles were introduced and features from various periods were combined in a single building. The name Queen Anne was

The J. M. Day Residence in Austin, Texas, circa 1905, was typical of many middle-class homes of the Late Victorian period in scale and design of the house, as well as size and design of the lot on which it sat. Only the presence of a rudimentary foundation planting "modernized" this house and distinguished it from typical late nineteenth-century homes. (Barker Texas History Center, University of Texas, Austin, Texas.)

coined to describe the style of these eclectic facades, which had turrets, porches, oriel windows, clapboard or fish-scale siding, ionic columns, and some feature from almost every preceding style of architecture. Landscape design remained grounded in the Romantic for some time as building design changed, but gradually landscape elements as elaborate and varied as those in structures appeared. These landscape features emphasized variety rather than site unity, buildings rather than landscape, and strong contrast between horizontal and vertical planes rather than transitions.

It was in this High Victorian phase that public design preferences began to differ from those of landscape architects. The public, for reasons to be discussed later, desired features with obvious, novel changes and elaborate detail, while landscape architects preferred the infinitely more subtle and varied effects of naturalistic design. The difference in viewpoint was well expressed by H. W. S. Cleveland, who was insulted that floral displays by a local gardener were credited to him by the public.[2] The opposite point of view was expressed by horticulturalist Peter Henderson, who found the shrub and tree masses of Romantic designs to be tiresomely uniform. This difference in design preference grew even greater during the final phase of the Victorian period, the Late Victorian.[3]

The Late Victorian phase, from the 1880s to about 1900, was one in which architectural design returned to the use of single, rather than mixed, historical styles. Neighboring houses might have quite different appearances, with one a Norman chateau and the next a Gothic castle, but each was clearly of one motif. This architectural trend was variously called Academic Eclecticism, Picturesque Eclecticism, or Single-Tract Eclecticism. Throughout this phase Romantic landscape design or elements from it remained popular. As late as 1899, Frank Waugh, a landscape architect trained in the Olmsted firm, wrote that "the natural style is unquestionably the favorite in England and America . . ." (p. 15). Professor Waugh's declaration notwithstanding, there had been a definite shift in public taste during the last twenty years of the nineteenth century. This shift replaced picturesque vistas with elaborate floral displays and simple massed tree plantings with arboretum-like groupings of eclectic specimen trees.

As this summary of Victorian design phases suggests, two somewhat contradictory concepts of landscape design coalesced at the end of this period. The earlier concept, that of the Romantic landscape, never completely lost acceptance, but was so compromised by the spatial structure and contrived aspects of the new eclecticism that a composite style replaced it in popular taste. It is the period in which this composite approach to design was prominent—dating from the 1860s to about 1900 and thus overlapping architectural periods—that will be referred to here as the "Victorian period."

DESIGN AND SOCIAL INFLUENCES IN THE VICTORIAN PERIOD

The shifts that occurred during the Victorian period can be explained by trends both in landscape architecture and in society as a whole. Landscape design was dramatically influenced by the plethora of books written by British horticulturalist J. C. Loudon. Although much of this work dealt with technical aspects of planting, Loudon also advocated a style of design, called Gardenesque, that emphasized horticultural variety and display rather than unity or spatial sequence. The concept underlying his designs was that landscapes should be obviously artificial in appearance, rather than seeming to be copied from nature. He did not advocate architectonic arrangements, but rather ones in which each plant was separated from others to assure perfection of form. He also believed that plants native to a region should *not* be used, again so the planting would appear to be "artistic" rather than natural. So persuasive and replicable were Loudon's ideas that from the 1840s on they began to influence American garden designers, including Downing.

Industrial mass production provided new opportunities to use materials and to market goods. This opportunity did not lead, as might be expected, to great innovation in design styles. Rather, emphasis was on the traditional, with innovation taking the form of innumerable elaborations and surface patterning variations within a conventional, usually historical theme. It was as though the very pace of technological innovation forced a reactionary ambivalence toward its products. In design, particularly architecture, this was reflected in the revival of various historical styles for facades even when modern materials, such as steel, created the substructure.

A number of social changes were also at work to promote interest in a new design order. Most of these can be linked with industrial development and the political maturation of North America in the 1860s. Industrialization revolutionized the lifestyles of many in English-speaking North America, changing work habits, place of residence, family structure, income, and the design and production of goods. These changes in a society that had previously been largely agricultural generated a conservative reaction, which further emphasized the traditional, the stable, and the socially acceptable.

Industrialization also led to urbanization, since workers needed to live near their centralized place of employment. At its best, urban expansion provided more people with adequate housing, steady employment, and education options. At its worst, it led to serious urban congestion, with masses of low-paid workers crowded into substandard housing. The process of industrialization not only helped to create new cities and expand old ones, but also to change urban character. It led to differentiation of land use within cities as certain sections became production centers, others low-cost housing, and still others more expensive housing. Further, it increased urban pollution, by adding industrial waste products and concentrating large numbers of people. Industrialization also fostered suburbanization by bringing into being a well-paid entrepreneurial and managerial class which could afford both new homes and the expense of commuting.[4]

Family structure also changed as a result of industrialization and urbanization, from the extended multigenerational family of rural areas toward the two-generation nuclear family. At the same time, this reduced-scale family and the home in which it dwelt were idealized. The home was to be a sanctified and pure environment within which to nurture the young and to refresh those who must, for economic reasons, labor in the dehumanized industrial jungle.[5] As originally conceived in the Early Victorian phase, this home was a center of upright and forthright thought and behavior. In the words of authors Catherine Beecher and Harriet Beecher Stowe, "a home contrived for the express purpose of enabling every member of a family to labor with the hands for the common good, and by modes at once healthful, economical, and tasteful" (1869, p. 24). Later in the Victorian period, the home became a place to display wealth, status, and fashionable taste. William Dean Howells created just such a home for his fictional March family in *A Hazard of New Fortunes*. It "had some good pictures, which her aunt had brought home from Europe . . . and it abounded in books on which he spent more than he ought. They had beautified it in every way. . . . They felt with a glow almost of virtue, how perfectly it fitted their lives. . . ." (1889, p. 23).

In this paradise[6] that was the home, the grounds played no small part. They were to be functional, providing sources of food but also places for wholesome recreation and hobbies. Equally important, these grounds were a fittingly tasteful frame to display the house. For the middle class, which especially espoused this home-centered style of life, suburbs became the ideal residential setting. Suburbs were isolated from contaminating influences of the city, while being close enough to preserve economic and social links.

The Victorians, though, were not solely interested in ostentatious display of wealth or the pursuit of consumer pleasures. The excesses of industrialization and urbanization also brought an awareness of the social evils that accompanied them. This social consciousness has been termed the New Humanism by Arthur Schlesinger (1951). It included reform movements such as those for women's political rights, children's social and physical rights, and the temperance movement. In each of these can be seen the beginnings of awareness of social issues which continue to dominate public thought today. Thus, it is not surprising that the Victorian period is often considered the beginning of our modern era.

VICTORIAN CONCEPTS OF DESIGN

Victorian design was exuberant, bold, and self-confident. What was considered beautiful by Victorians was that which was highly detailed. Design and pattern were equated, with patterns and textures applied to every surface. This *horror vacui* (Latin for "fear of voids") in surface treatment was the most obvious and telling characteristic of Victorian design. Beyond that, lines were highly articulated and broken. Color was rich and used to highlight details. Historical detailing was more important than the historical spirit of an object or its function. These characteristics were expressed in various themes and motifs used in all forms of design from architecture to bookbinding to landscape design.

Victorian design also expressed the desire to capture and control natural beauty. Stuffed animals, particularly birds, often decorated fashionable parlors. Cattle horn and hide chairs and settees were used to give a rustic or "masculine" air to a room. If no picturesque vista was naturally framed by the window of a suburban home, a miniature landscape of equal beauty could be captured for year-round delight in a "Wardian case," as the first terrariums were called. At a larger scale, treasured tropical plants could be overwintered in a window garden or greenhouse, ready to decorate the yard the following summer. Not content to manipulate only living materials, the Victorians made plant and animal motifs popular in facade ornamentation or interior furnishings, such as the cast-iron facades of a Louis Sullivan-designed building or the leaded-glass wisterias of a Tiffany lamp.

THE ECLECTIC VICTORIAN LANDSCAPE

Victorian landscape design applied these principles of Victorian "taste" to outdoor spaces, and in the process generated one of the most rule-bound and visually limited styles in design history. The wealth of detail found in Victorian design belies this fact, but an overview demonstrates that a few rather simple motifs were repeatedly applied in many different circumstances. Just as this period was one of mass-produced consumer goods, it was also one of mass-produced landscapes, especially gardens, created by following a few influential design guide books.

The overriding feature of Victorian landscape design was that it dealt with objects set in space, rather than the design of the spaces themselves. From this principle six general design "rules" followed, and were applied to the vast majority of garden and site designs of this period:

1. The principal structure on the site was to be the dominant visual element, with other features designed to maximize its scale and ornateness.

2. All lines and forms were exaggerated both in layout and detailing.

3. Forms used were realistic, rather than abstract.

4. Details from foreign historical styles were incorporated into sites that were in other particulars solely Victorian in style.

5. The ground plane was the most significant surface.

6. Individual features were isolated visually and physically from others on the site.

In Victorian site design, structures, such as the house, were intended to be the dominant visual feature. Surrounding grounds emphasized the size and grandeur of the building, rather than tying it to the site. Hence, the typical Victorian home was elevated both through grading and use of a raised basement. Access from the grounds to the house was via a short flight of steps that ended at a porch, a semi-outdoor space that extended the structure into the landscape without integrating the two. Vertical forms such as columns and peaked dormers were used to further emphasize building height. Homeowners were often advised that large plants, such as trees, should be set well away from the structure, so as not to diminish its apparent size. Those few plants placed near the structure were either small in size or had relatively fine textures. It was only after 1900 that homeowners tried to "tie the house to the site" through foundation plantings.

Exaggeration of forms and lines was expressed in the size of features, the clarity of their outline, and the use of ornate or "arabesque" patterns. Although the structure was the largest site feature, site amenities were often oversized to make them more obvious. Sculptures and fountains often had several components, such as tiers, to increase their size. In planting, the use of tropical plants with massively scaled texture achieved the same result. Exaggeration of outline was produced by the eclectic assembly of plant forms that had irregular and asymmetric silhouettes. The effect produced by positive forms, usually planting beds, boldly set against a contrasting background of lawn achieved the same end. The greatest exaggeration of line occurred in patterns applied to surfaces. Arrangements of geometric or other motifs were often quite elaborate, having patterns within other patterns. Swirling, interlaced lines suggestive of activity were especially favored.

Realism in landscape design took several forms. In planting design, bed shapes were often simple geometric outlines such as circles or diamonds. In other

Victorian porches were turn-of-the-century equivalents of modern patios—the principal outdoor living space. From this porch can be seen preferred Victorian planting design characteristics, including vines growing up house columns, freestanding planting beds, and the use of lawn as a background for scattered planting areas. (Scott, 1881.)

instances, plants or planted forms represented common objects or human figures. The floral clock was a favorite motif, but everything from dogs to boats was depicted in topiary or floral outlines. Likewise a fence was not merely an upright barrier, but through cast-iron technology could be a row of corn stalks or inter-twined grapevines. In general, there was no consistent theme expressed in the realistically designed features of a given landscape; rather, the features were intended to add variety to the design. An exception to this was that constructed features such as fences and out-structures were often related in architectural style, details, or materials to the main structure.

Historicism, especially interest in pre-eighteenth-century European culture, led to incorporation of foreign features, such as Italian statuary or Oriental stone lanterns, into site designs. These features were diverse, ranging from spatial arrangements, such as a Renaissance-inspired axial plan for a rose garden, to individual features like a summerhouse in the Chinese style, or to statuary, such as a "David" replica (cum fig leaf, of course) purchased while on the Grand Tour of Europe. These features were generally used like museum pieces: isolated from their artistic or spatial context, on display rather than incorporated into the overall design.

Importance of the ground plane resulted in turf being the principal design material of the Victorian landscape. All do-it-yourself guides advised, as did Frank Scott, that, "of all the external decorations of a home, a well kept LAWN is the most essential. Imagine the finest trees environing a dwelling, but everywhere beneath them only bare ground: then picture the same dwelling with a velvet greensward . . . without a tree or shrub upon it, and choose which is the most pleasing to the eye" (1881, p. 102). The choice would have been quite different in the Victorian period than it had been in the Romantic. Lawn was a living carpet[7] upon which all the "furnishings" of the Victorian landscape, be they plants, gazebos, or the main structure itself, could be set out. The lawn was

Turf, here kept free from all plants except at edges, was the most important plant material of the Victorian period. (Scott, 1881.)

Eclectic plantings of columnar, weeping, and dwarf trees were popular in the Late Victorian period, for as Scott expressed the popular taste, "a variety is better than any one." (Scott, 1881, p. 102.)

at once the primary, and often only, unifier of the site, and the homogeneous background that emphasized just how diverse and scattered were the elements set out upon it.

Victorian landscapes emphasized variety of detail within very uniformly open spaces. These diverse details, whether an accent piece, a planting bed, or a small specialty garden, were not linked either spatially or through related motifs. Every features was intended to stand out as a separate, internally unified element. Thus, a planting bed to the right of a walkway might be circular, while that to the left was shaped like a star. The circular form itself would be further defined by concentric bands of different plants, with plant heights carefully coordinated to produce a high point at the center.

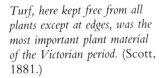

Importance of Planting in Victorian Period Landscapes

Victorian site design *was* planting design. Trees and shrubs were usually located as specimens, except when used as hedges or masses at property lines. These specimen plants were often of an unusual or new variety having distinctive form, texture, or color characteristics. Weeping or contorted forms were particularly popular. Massive or spiky exotic tropical plants, such as banana or dracaena, added contrast to the temperate landscape, while variegated leaves, double flowers, and red foliage on plants added another level of detail.

Grouped plants were usually seen in beds of herbaceous materials. This "bedding out," as these plantings were called, was done in borders or freestanding beds set out in the lawn.[8] Often the plant arrangement within beds was random, but it was more common to arrange the plants in single-species bands, or "ribbons." These patterned beds usually had a definite shape such as a circle or diamond, with the edge of the form outlined by a low plant of distinctive color, like dusty miller. Within this border roughly concentric bands, increasing in height toward the center, were arranged for maximum color and texture contrast. In the center there was often an upright focal feature of much greater height than the surrounding plants, such as a tropical shrub, a weeping mulberry, or a sundial. Beds were frequently graded—either terraced, with each terrace corresponding to a band, or sloped so the center point was raised—to better display the plant arrangement.

"Carpet bedding" was a special form of bedding out in which elaborate realistic motifs were executed in annuals and perennials. As the name suggests, these patterns gave outdoor ground planes the ornamental detail of a floor covering. They were intended as floral displays to be renewed several times a season with new plants. Patterns varied with the interests of the owner and skill of the gardener, but some popular ones were fleurs-de-lis, family crests, and signs of the zodiac. The design difficulty in laying out carpet beds was "to choose the proper plants to harmonize," so as to give the best effects (Solly, 1887, introduction). True carpet beds were probably far less common, usually confined to public parks, than surviving photographs would suggest. The designs were popular and their images made good souvenirs, hence many of those created on the ground were preserved on glass.

The most elaborate form of bedding out was the parterre. To create parterres, the entire garden had to be cut up into small planting beds, each edged and having its own pattern. The grouping of these small beds and intervening gravel path created another pattern. These parterres were the most unified type of bedding system used in the Victorian period, since they defined and filled an entire space, rather than merely punctuating a ground plane.

Just as important to Victorian design as lawn, annuals, and perennials were vines. No other period has used this material as effectively and consistently.[9] Views often show vines climbing up porch columns or rambling across lintels to enframe an entry. Vines were the sole plant material used to create a link between the grounds and buildings which sat upon them. In this they were a precursor to the ubiquitous foundation plantings of the early twentieth century. Vines, though, were rarely used to hide the foundation,[10] but more typically became another vertical element emphasizing building height. Need for physical support shaped vines to the form of the structure to which they were attached, so that even when covering an entire wall, its upright plane met the ground plane at an unconcealed 90 degree angle.

Roses, whether climbing or in shrub form, were another important Victorian plant. In fact, it was during this period, with its emphasis on novelty and variety, that the mania for rose hybridization reached a peak. It became increasingly popular toward the end of the century to set aside special areas as rose gardens to display a collection of prized specimens and the newest cultivars. The rose garden was often an isolated feature set out as a cookie-cutter-shaped bed in the lawn. When more sensitively designed, they became enclosed outdoor rooms with rectangular beds and rudimentary internal sight lines, but still with little relationship to the house or other parts of the grounds.

"Gates Ajar," named after a popular sentimental novel of the era, was a frequent theme for three-dimensional carpet beds such as this one in Como Park, St. Paul, Minnesota, circa 1890.

Several other specialty gardens were also popular. Rock gardens displayed succulents, cacti, alpine plants, and other small, colorful exotics. Low, shaded portions of a site were ideal for exhibiting fern collections. To the control-conscious Victorians, these gardens were "natural gardens," in which plants grew in more normal conditions and configurations than in the other beds on the site.

Although Victorian design relied primarily on plants, there were a number of essential site amenities. Fencing defined the boundaries of one's suburban "estate," as well as framing the grounds. Wooden fencing was used, but cast and wrought iron were more popular because they were durable, could be shaped in ornate patterns, and could be fashioned into styles which were compatible with architectural detail. Many ornamental focal points were spotted around the grounds, often surrounded by a planting bed. Realistic sculptures of classical or picturesque figures, gnomes, or animals were common. Fountains and pools were less common features, but where these were used, tiered fountains and amorphously shaped lily and fish ponds were favored. Gazebos, freestanding trellises, and summerhouses added shady sitting areas to larger properties. Many garden structures were executed in the rustic twig-work of the Romantic period, while other more formal structures were of sawn lumber or cast iron. Stone or concrete urns were prominent front lawn features, but in the Victorian period they were planting pots for a mixture of trailing and upright flowering plants, rather than sculpture, as they had been in the Romantic era.

Victorian gardens were not just places of display, but were used for all sorts of recreation. Gardening itself, as a horticultural and design hobby, was popular. Of course the high level of maintenance required to retain the precisely mowed lawn and the perfectly edged beds was also a form of exercise. Organized sports like croquet, tennis, softball, and badminton put expanses of manicured lawn to some healthful use. Yards also served as outdoor rooms for social functions—parties, weddings, receptions, poetry readings, and the like.

**Typical Victorian
Residential Sites**

Most Victorian residential grounds were developed by middle-class homeowners, with lots varying in size from a half-acre to an acre: those people to whom Frank Scott addressed *The Art of Beautifying Suburban Home Grounds* (1881).[11] Being so commonplace in their day, few of these sites were documented and we must now rely on a composite example of this type. Fortunately, botanist and keen landscape observer May T. Watts has vividly recalled what the grounds of the "Stylish House," owned by the fictitious couple David and Mary, were like in her childhood.

On Sunday afternoons, when David and Mary went for their walk around town after dinner . . . they looked at other people's circular flower beds. So they planted red cannas in the center, encircled by nasturtiums, with a final edging of dwarf low lobelias. With the snowball bush gone [a plant from an earlier design], the sweet shrub looked wrong, standing there in the center of the lawn, so they took it out, and made another circular bed. In this one they planted castor beans, encircled by red geraniums and outlined with sweet alyssum.

These gay beds were so much admired that David and Mary decided to outdo themselves for the ice-cream sociable, which was to be held in their yard under strings of Japanese lanterns.

First they planted a weeping mulberry in the side yard. Then they formed a big star-shaped bed around it. The center was massed with red cockscombs. Each point of the star was filled with golden-foliaged coleus, and outlined with variegated-leaved coleus. Then the whole was outlined with hens and chickens.

Then they put in the fountain—the one with the little girl and boy under the iron umbrella, with water shooting out of the tip of the umbrella and dripping down the sides into a little circular pool. The pool was surrounded by green- and white-leaved plantain lily, encircled by abalone shells side by side, with one edge thrust into the ground so that they made an upright pearly scalloping.

May T. Watts' sketch of the "typical" Victorian residence of her fictitious couple David and Mary. Potted plants shown in the margins illustrated some favored ways of bringing nature indoors, although the most stylish means, the terrarium, or "Wardian case" as it was originally called, is not shown. (Watts, 1957.)

The Kuehne Homestead, Austin, Texas, circa 1900, was a slightly more rustic version of the typical Victorian landscape described by Watts and probably a more typical example of common residential designs of the period. (Barker Texas History Center, University of Texas, Austin, Texas.)

The garden really looked like an embroidery piece under the Japanese lanterns, especially so since the lawn was clipped more closely now, with the new lawn mower.

Later, when the strawberry sociable was held on the lawn of another home, David and Mary admired the iron deer, and the iron dog standing guard over a sleeping iron child. . . .[12]

In contrast to such a small homesite, residences of the upper middle class had larger grounds, more amenities, and were somewhat less crowded with features. The David Davis Mansion in Bloomington, Illinois, was an example of a homesite at this scale. Davis, a lawyer by profession, was appointed in 1869 to serve on the U.S. Supreme Court. As members of the post-Civil War professional elite, his family had both the finances and "taste" to build a home in the highest fashion on the 10 acres selected out of a 1,000-acre farm for a homesite. In 1872 Davis replaced a modest frame farmhouse which had stood on the site with a far more stylish three-story brick mansion in Second Empire style. The conditions of the grounds prior to this construction have not been established through archaeological investigations, but they likely suited a working farm rather than the estate envisioned by Davis to complement his new house.

The house sat in a large lawn encircled by an oval drive, which gave access to the service yard with its barns, pens, and carriage house in the rear. Large trees were arranged informally at the inner edge of the drive, while a few specimen trees punctuated the lawn. Few shrubs were used, except for masses planted on the outside of the drive. Vines enveloped porch columns and shaded the house as they climbed to an upper porch. The principal ornamental feature of the grounds was a hedged garden located to the southeast of the house on the opposite side of the drive. This flower garden was divided into planting beds by straight paths which radiated from the center in a wagon-wheel spoke pattern. Plantings within its pie-shaped beds were irregular and random except that walks were lined with a low-growing plant border. Although quite unified internally, this rather formal flower garden lacked convincing linkages to the rest of the grounds. The Davis Mansion demonstrated application of Victorian design principles in a restrained manner, quite typical of the design of large residential grounds.

*David Davis Mansion,
Bloomington, Illinois, undated.
The Upper Garden for roses
and other flowers is in the
foreground with a low hedge
separating it from the driveway
and expanse of lawn beyond.
(David Davis Mansion State
Historic Site.)*

While the homes of upper-class Victorians continued to exhibit elaborate but spatially and thematically disorganized design, there were residential projects of large scale which showed an emerging unity of architectural and landscape architectural styles. Designs for these projects were based on reinterpretation of historical motifs with great attention to accuracy of detail, hence their designation as Academic Eclectic designs. The masterpiece of this type of site design was the Asheville, North Carolina, estate of George W. Vanderbilt, called Biltmore. Begun as a winter home in the Great Smokey Mountains, Biltmore quickly became a grand land-planning scheme that helped both to popularize formal styles of design and to establish professional forestry in the United States.[13] In spite of its trendsetting features, Biltmore was a Victorian estate, with eclectic details and a design based on site and architectural symbolism. The house, by architect Richard Morris Hunt, closely followed designs of sixteenth-century French chateaux such as Chambord. The site plan and design, by Frederick Law Olmsted, Sr., assisted by Henry Codman, John C. Olmsted, and Frederick Law Olmsted, Jr., for whom this project served as an apprenticeship, were conceived as a hybridization of the French Grand Style and the Romantic style, adapted to a ruggedly picturesque site on the French Broad River. The symbolism of the son of a nouveau riche industrialist usurping the elegant designs of European royalty surely appealed to Vanderbilt, as it did to his contemporaries.

The estate eventually totalled over 125,000 acres, with most of this area developed as forest, largely at Olmsted's urging.[14] Of this, about 8,000 acres were retained for nonforestry uses including the 250 acres nearest the house that became formal grounds. It was this formal area to which most attention has been given in discussions of the design, but it was the roads, particularly the entry drive, that were Olmsted's masterpiece. It is impossible to reduce the experience of this drive to words or to still photographs, since it is the subtle sequence of changes in alignment, plantings, internal views, and woodland features that make this the most perfect Romantic design preserved today. Olmsted chose to tie the entry drive to the landscape by winding it through stream-cut ravines. These

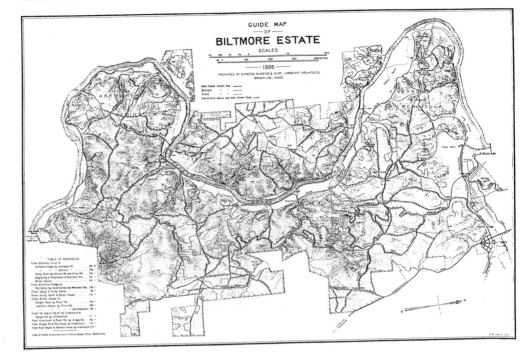

Plan of Biltmore Estate, Asheville, North Carolina, 1893, by Frederick Law Olmsted. The house and formal gardens are at right center, while Biltmore Village is to the far right toward the bottom of the plan. Plan shows the extent to which the forestry plantations dominated the site. (Courtesy National Park Service, Frederick Law Olmsted National Historical Site.)

streams were then damned to create ponds, rills, and waterfalls. It was only vistas across some of the more extensive ponds that provided glimpses of the larger landscape. The visitor experienced enclosed, intimately scaled, naturalistic woodlands before entering the architectonic spaces around the house. The contrast between the drive and the formal grounds was dramatic and abrupt, as if Olmsted wanted the distinction between the two realms to be so clear that the artificiality of the house and grounds would appear as an aberration from the overall naturalistic scheme of the estate.

The Esplanade, as the entry court to the formal grounds and the house was called, was a simply designed space of turf and trees. At the far end of the Esplanade a stone retaining wall, with ramp to the upper level, led the eye toward an eastern vista, a sight line carved from woodlands in the French manner. The retaining wall, which had concealed the vista as one entered the Esplanade, also served to visually balance the facade of the house.

Formal gardens near the house displayed various Renaissance design themes, but with an overall French character most clearly expressed in the way that the space for these grounds was enclosed by woodlands. Due to steep site topography and a need to shelter this area from winds, the garden areas to the south of the house were terraced, but more broadly than most Italian gardens. These terraces gave Olmsted an opportunity to design a series of "rooms" following various historical styles. The upper terrace, although called the "Italian Garden," was largely inspired by French design. Three flat pools of water, panels of turf, broad gravel paths, and sculpture composed this open terrace. A hedge at the downhill side separated it from lower terraces, so that distant scenery was emphasized, a feature that constituted the garden's closest similarity to Italian precedents.

Below the Italian Garden was a naturalistic garden, but one more contrived in appearance than Olmsted's typical work. This garden was arranged as a small arboretum of unusual cultivars,[15] an area for strolling that did not have the same native woodland appearance as the rest of the estate. At the lowest level was a

View along the Biltmore entry drive circa 1925 showing how natural woods were supplemented with flowering tree and shrub plantings. (Postcard by CVC.)

View of Biltmore looking from the main drive toward the chateau-style residence. To the right beyond the gates is the linden-lined Esplanade, while to the left is the terrace of the Italian Garden with its three pools.

large flower garden, the walled or English garden, which terminated in a line of equally large conservatories, a requisite of any Victorian garden.[16]

The collaborative design effort between Olmsted, his associates, and Hunt produced a site design that integrated structure, designed landscape, and naturalistically restored woodlands. The siting of the house and its out-buildings, for example, were derived from Olmsted's analysis of topography and microclimate. More specifically, Olmsted concluded that the ravine edge offered the most impressive view of the surrounding landscape and that the out-buildings could be useful in screening parts of the Esplanade from cold winter winds. Not only was the ravine edge best for views from the house, but it also provided a magnificent setting for the house when viewed from the river and bottomlands. Grounds below the ravine were given a completely different character from those at house level. They became a woodland-enclosed meadow known as the Deer Park. From the house, this space created an open vista and transition between the formal grounds and the working farm.

Biltmore became, as Olmsted had predicted in the 1880s, important as both a public work and a private estate. In its physical planning and operations, resource concerns such as forest management and scientific dairying were combined with the huge scale and ornate displays typical of this so-called Gilded Age. Through the successes of its timber management program, Biltmore was instrumental in establishing the profession of forestry in North America, while through displays at the World's Columbian Exposition in 1893, Biltmore also became a stylistic trendsetter for both the City Beautiful Movement and the Neoclassicist Revival.[17]

Although very different in scale, all three of the Victorian landscapes discussed here—David and Mary's residence, the Davis Estate, and Biltmore—demonstrate the period's interest in eclectic, detailed ornamental features and patterns. They also demonstrate the value that was placed on the home environment. Few other ages have lavished such attention on the mundane objects of daily life. Perhaps this is the Late Victorian era's greatest legacy: that design at the residential scale became at least as significant as grand schemes for cities, parks, or natural preserves.

VICTORIAN LEISURE LANDSCAPES

To Victorians, leisure represented the opportunity for educational and morally uplifting travel, social contacts, and physical recreation. Parks of the period generally continued as large, Romantic landscapes that offered a variety of spaces from formal promenades to the "rural scenery" so favored by nineteenth-century landscape architects. But, just as in the residential setting, the public no longer found relaxing naturalistic environments sufficient for recreation. They demanded entertainment, organized activity, and variety. As the nineteenth century progressed, park administrators increasingly dealt with demands for new amenities. Favored features included conservatories, bandshells, and most disruptive of all to landscape parks, menageries that usually grew into full-scale zoos.[18] In older parks, such as Lincoln Park in Chicago, these were added as afterthoughts where space allowed (or at times really did not), often destroying the original concept of a pastoral retreat. Elsewhere, zoos were added to design programs as work progressed, producing more compatible solutions, but still subverting the real value of a large park.

Aside from these rather dramatic and costly additions, park design was altered in subtle ways through changes in planting design, particularly emphasis on floral display. Many parks came to be botanic centers for viewing the latest flower introductions or for following the progress of a newly grafted weeping specimen tree. Of course, elaborately detailed carpet bedding, often in three dimensions, was particularly popular. The influential periodical *Garden and Forest* reported with dismay on the "extraordinary construction in a Chicago park, where, for the admiration of the public, was displayed a gigantic vegetable globe, bearing upon its face a map of the world delineated in Echeverias upon a ground of Sedum" (Anonymous, 1891, p. 529). The themes executed in plants were unlimited, and gardeners vied to see who could create the most-photographed beds.

The immediate inspiration for this new view of the park as an ornamental garden was the Centennial Exposition of 1876. This fair, envisioned as the opportunity for the United States to display its economic and cultural status, became the quintessential Victorian environment. Exhibit rooms glutted with displays, elaborate facades and cast iron details, and intermixing of Romantic and Late Victorian landscape features created a design standard that was followed for almost twenty years. Warren Manning attributed the popularity of carpet bed-

Another typical carpet bed design so popular for parks; here Humbolt Park, Chicago, as it was in the late nineteenth and early twentieth centuries.

ding directly to its use in the grounds of the Exposition. The most famous of these bedding areas was the Sunken Garden of the Horticultural Hall. This was a well-executed linear parterre-style bed, which had been set several feet below the surrounding walkways for better viewing. This garden was also one of the few at the fair grounds to be successfully related to the overall site plan. It was unfortunate that most people took from this example only the most obvious pattern features, rather than its more thoughtful site-related qualities.[19]

As parks were being "improved" with more interesting displays and activities, there was a contemporaneous movement for added active recreational facilities, as a means to improve health and character. The playground movement emerged as a result of urban growth and the crowding of poorer residents into cramped and unsanitary housing. Until the later part of the nineteenth century, even the poor could afford single-family dispersed housing, although it was often a frame hovel surrounded by a muddy stable yard. As the century progressed and urban land values skyrocketed, such housing proved too costly for the masses of poorly paid workers. New forms of mass housing—the tenements—were developed to nominally shelter these people. This early form of high-rise housing created dense neighborhoods, often at great distances from any open spaces. Children were confined to play spaces in streets or on stairs, sometimes with disastrous consequences. Concurrent with rising social concern for the well-being of poor urban children, active sport and exercise became a middle-class fad. This era saw the emergence of organized baseball, football, and gymnastics, all sports that required special facilities and spaces. Last, and of equal importance to growth of the playground movement, was the perception that through organized recreation, as through public schools, non-English-speaking immigrants could be taught values of hard work and self-reliance.

The first playgrounds of the movement were usually connected with schools, offering after-school and summer activities that continued character-building activities of the schools themselves. These playlots were usually small in size, often little more than a barren piece of ground on which play equipment such as swings and teeter-totters had been placed. Emphasis was on efficient muscle development and the building of coordination. Vocational activities such as digging and carrying materials were also sometimes incorporated into the exercise

Sunken Garden, Horticultural Hall, Centennial Exposition site, Philadelphia, in the early twentieth century. The original design for this bed became the basis for the reconstructed Victorian garden at the Smithsonian Institution's Arts and Industry Building in Washington, D.C. (Souvenir Postcard Company, New York.)

program. Play experiences were usually segregated by sex, especially those exercises considered too strenuous or inappropriately aggressive for girls. Progressive churches and social welfare facilities such as Jane Addams's Hull House also incorporated playgrounds into their facilities. Eventually city park departments began to construct playgrounds in existing parks and to add playgrounds and playlots to the system of small sites distributed throughout the city.

Independent playgrounds not associated with schools were often designed by landscape architects and had a visual and functional character that the earlier school playgrounds lacked. These designs were generally quite simple, with a central locker room/pavilion area set among trees, a large lawn area for ball games, an area for exercise apparatus, an encircling path, and perimeter trees. In plan, playgrounds were often symmetrical and formal with little of the spatial sequencing and mystery of larger urban parks. Most landscape architects engaged in some playground design, but the Olmsted firm was particularly active in this area, designing sites throughout the eastern United States.

There were two specialized recreational landscapes that developed during the Victorian period. These were vacation resorts and amusement parks. Amusement parks were not "parks" at all in the nineteenth-century meaning of the term, but commercial facilities providing novel, exciting, and technologically innovative experiences for the entire family. The lure of the amusement park for many people was that it was a fantasy environment that provided a host of different recreation opportunities, from water chutes to popular music performances, on one site. Most visitors to these parks were urban workers and their families who made a day trip to the park as a substitute for a vacation out of the city. Few amusement parks were as carefully designed as modern theme parks. More typically they were ad hoc collections of structures and attractions organized as the park expanded. This does not mean that the park developers failed to add visual amenities. In fact, garish and entertaining features were considered a principal form of amusement. For example, owners of Willow Grove Park, which described itself as "Philadelphia's Fairyland," installed a very costly illuminated ornamental fountain. Most amusement parks also incorporated some of the features of urban parks, with areas for picnicking and trails for hiking. This

Typical Late Victorian playground shows the emphasis placed on pure athletic exertion during play. Such outdoor gymnasiums were a mainstay of the parks movement into the 1920s.

new type of recreational site clearly demonstrated public interest during the Victorian period in new and thrilling forms of recreation.

While amusement parks met the need of the less well-to-do for a break from daily experience, those with more money and leisure favored the rural resort. These resorts were the descendants of the mineral spas and revival encampments, such as Hot Springs, Arkansas, and Oak Bluffs, Massachusetts, that had been popular throughout most of the century. During the Victorian period, resorts combined genteel social interaction with the opportunity for a variety of active recreational experiences through an entire season—the summer for northern resorts, the winter for those in the south. Resorts generally were developed to appeal to a certain social class. Saratoga Springs, New York, was an upper-class resort, while simpler sites such as Windsor Beach near Rochester, New York, appealed to the middle class. The very wealthy often created resort communities in which one built an individual home rather than staying in a hotel. Newport, Rhode Island, originally popularized in the 1820s as a resort for planters and merchants from Charleston and Savannah escaping oppressive Sea Coast summers, became in the late nineteenth century the favored summer resort of northern industrialists. There, along the rugged coast, they could find suitable sites to build their "summer cottages," such as Cornelius Vanderbilt's famous residence, The Breakers. Other resort communities were developed by the wealthy as elite enclaves. The Jekyll Island Club in Georgia (see Chapter 8) was one such resort, originally planned as a rustic winter resort for wealthy easterners.

THE UNIFIED STREETSCAPE

If Victorian home and small-site landscapes lacked unity and were often overly detailed, it was in Victorian street environments that unified, elegant, unambiguous spaces were created.[20] The Victorian streetscape was typically well constructed, with a smooth surface either paved or well graded, and with solid curbing to define roadway edges while vertically separating vehicular and pedestrian spaces. Sidewalks were present in all but the poorest neighborhoods or small communities.[21] Often the sidewalk was set back from the street, creating a planting strip usually filled with grass and single-species rows of street trees.

The practice of planting lines of trees along streets had not originated in the Victorian period, of course. There were innumerable examples in North America from colonial times, with Philadelphia's citywide plantings being among the bet-

Street scene in East Orange, New Jersey, before 1908, shows a typical Late Victorian streetscape with closely spaced trees lining the road and unifying the very diverse architectural and landscape designs of adjoining residences.

ter known. Jefferson is credited with popularizing the use of Lombardy poplars as street trees in the early nineteenth century when he had them planted along Pennsylvania Avenue in Washington, D.C. Until the late nineteenth century, though, such tree plantings were usually confined to main streets or park boulevards, with few organized plantings on residential streets. In the Victorian period, with its reverence for the home, residential streets became worthy of the design attention heretofore confined to commercial avenues or wealthy neighborhoods. Street trees were usually planted at the time a subdivision was laid out,[22] with trees of only one species, or at least only one species per block. In most areas, the size of the median between street and sidewalk limited planting to a single row parallel to the street, but where there was more space, staggered parallel rows were often used. American elms, which created a vaulted street space when mature, were a favored species as they had been for over a hundred years. Other popular trees included several types of maples, plane trees, and lindens. Although Victorians favored needle-leaf evergreens, especially those which wept, in their garden plantings, these were not considered appropriate in most street settings.[23]

Grading patterns also played a role in creating a distinctive streetscape. Most Victorian houses were elevated above levels required for adequate drainage by being set on a low terrace (usually 2 feet or less above the street level). Transition between street level and house level was usually made in one of three ways: with a low retaining wall set in toward the house about 6 to 8 feet from the sidewalk; by an architectonic slope angled at 45 degrees at the same position as the retaining wall; or by a similar slope moved closer to the structure.[24] The primary purpose of these grading schemes was to keep the building site flat by taking up the grade change in as little space as possible, thereby retaining the carpet-like effect of the lawn. This grading pattern also set the road apart spatially by depressing it below nearby structures.

Street views from the turn of the century show the clear contrast between the public streetscape and the private frontyard. The street was a unified space, well defined both at the sides and overhead by tree trunks and crowns. Both the design and the space are so easy to comprehend that they might appear boring except for the almost excessive variety offered by the frontyards, which could be glimpsed through breaks in the trees. Thus, although quite different in arrangement, the Victorian streetscape and home grounds were complementary features that balanced each other.

The most unified streetscapes of all were those of the special subdivisions, known as Private Places, that became popular in the Victorian period. The earliest Private Places were Westmoreland and Portland Places in St. Louis, established in 1888.[25] Later the Private Place concept spread to other cities, such as Indianapolis with Woodruff Place, and Houston with Courtlandt Place. As their name suggests, Private Places were privately owned streets in which purchase of a lot also brought ownership of part of the street space or membership in a lot owners' corporation. These privately owned streets were designed as boulevards with planted medians. At Audubon Place in New Orleans the median was lined with impressive palms. At Courtlandt Place dense masses of shrubs marked the ends of esplanades, serving to visually separate the residences on either side. Private Places were small, often no more than a city block long, and lots were not large for their day. What they lacked in size they assured in exclusivity, for Private Places were among the earliest subdivisions to have restrictive covenants. Some of these were racially or ethnically motivated, but others were directed toward design issues and specified uniform house setbacks, materials, or cost. These covenants have helped to protect the physical character of most Private Places.

CONCLUSION AND SUMMARY

The Victorian period is most meaningfully studied not for its particular design and planning features, but as a transition era between the Romantic period of the nineteenth century and the early twentieth-century movements in planning—the City Beautiful Movement—and design—the Neoclassicist Revival. This transition points up the limitations of Romantic design in addressing those very spatial, social, and environmental problems which its key practitioners—Copeland, Cleveland, and Olmsted among others—had hoped it could resolve. Further, an examination of Victorian trends shows us that Americans did not want to search for a distinctive New World approach to environmental design, but preferred to express their position as a world power economically, militarily, and culturally on a par with their European peers by demonstrating that they were participants in and to some extent leaders in the resurrection of traditional European styles of design and planning.

While much of the discussion here has tended to suggest that Victorian landscape design was venial and superficial, these features were part of a comprehensive societal experimentation process that eventually produced the urban, suburban, corporate, and industrial landscapes which have dominated much North American experience during the present century. It must be noted that during the Victorian period there was an underlying core of concern for serious social issues that were then beginning to influence physical design and planning. It is the legacy of these concerns which lead directly to the most significant offspring of the Late Victorian phase, the City Beautiful Movement.

NOTES

1. From Lynes, 1980.

2. From a letter to the editor of Garden and Forest, July 31, 1889, p. 370. The actual designer of the beds was most likely G. Kern, a German gardener who did this sort of work in the Chicago parks for many years.

3. Revisionist interpretations of Victorian aesthetics, such as that of Schmiechen, often consider modern dislike of the style to be grounded in the Bauhaus revolution. While there is certainly some credibility to this, it is an overstatement. Review of the late nineteenth-century literature demonstrates that there were many who questioned or berated these designs in their own day. Rather than being a result of temporal differences in preference, these attitudes toward Victorian design are merely one example of contrast between high-style, professional design biases and the tastes of the wider population.

4. *Suburbanization cannot be understood simply as a reaction to deteriorating urban conditions in the late nineteenth century since the urge for spacious residential environments has always been present in North America. There were, though, specific urban disasters that pushed people to exercise this preference for suburban living. The Chicago Fire of 1871 is often cited as an event that encouraged many in the middle class to abandon that city. Likewise, labor unrest in the 1880s and 1890s made suburbs seem more desirable than central cities.*

5. *This contrast between home and outside workplace was formalized in the sex role standards of the Victorian period. Women were expected to staff the home and be its high-minded guardians. Considered both too fragile and too pure to deal with the crass ambitions of the work world, they were to preserve the purity of children and elevate the spirits of men corrupted in the pursuit of money. These views produced some interesting by-products. The first was the "domestic science" movement promoted by women such as Beecher and Stowe, who sought to make home management an efficient form of employment. In the process, they became pioneers in making the home functional and labor-saving. Use of outdoor spaces became part of this movement, leading to what Richardson Wright termed the "feminization of American gardening."*

6. *An analogy of the home to a paradise garden would not be inappropriate, as many Victorians viewed their small landscapes in that way. An essay in Vick's Illustrated Magazine of February 1880 (Vol. 3, pp. 33–36) equates home grounds to the garden of Eden: "Man may be happy without a garden; he may have a home without a tree, or shrub, or flower; yet when the Creator prepared a home for man, made in his own image, He planted a garden, and in this placed the noblest specimen of creative power, to dress and to keep it, and there he remained during his life of innocence and happiness . . . the refinement, and innocence, and happiness of the people may be measured by the flowers they cultivate." This interest in the appearance of home grounds was furthered by the growth of a large, well-organized, transcontinental nursery and seed industry. Firms such as those of Charles Hovey or Ellwanger and Barry had by this time become modern businesses engaged in experimentation, propagation, and sale of plants both to other nurseries and to homeowners.*

7. *Lawn had been a prominent feature of designed landscapes since the Middle Ages when turf seats were popular garden amenities. The turf used from that time into the mid-nineteenth century had the appearance of a rough meadow grass and was often mixed with wildflowers. It was cut with long knives or scythes or grazed by livestock. The technical innovation of the rotary lawnmower in the 1830s (widely introduced in North America in the 1860s), coupled with commercial cultivation of refined turfs, led to introduction of lawn-quality turf at that same time.*

8. *Victorians were so enamored of the extravagant displays which could be produced by bedding out that they apparently disregarded the fact that in much of the continent beds were bare for almost half the year. The author knows of no nineteenth-century discussion of this natural phenomenon as a problem, even among those who did not favor bedding out.*

9. *The scoring system used by a Canadian homeowners' association in home beautification competitions indicated the importance of vines. Out of 100 points available, 35 were allocated to vines, including climbing roses, while trees were not given any individual points, and shrubs, including hedges, were worth only 20 points. (System quoted in Crawford, 1981.)*

10. *There were those in this period who found the lack of foundation screening problematic. Charles Eliot's 1891 article in Garden and Forest was among the earliest to suggest that "the appearance of nakedness [around houses be] removed by massing shrubs along the bases of the walls or piazzas" (p. 184).*

11. *Scott's book was one of the few of its day to balance good design with popular taste.*

12. *Quoted (with permission from Watts' heirs) from "The Stylish House" in Reading the Landscape: An Adventure in Ecology, by May Theilgaard Watts, New York: Macmillan, 1957, pp. 201–3. More recent editions of this work are titled Reading the Landscape of North America.*

13. *Biltmore was so large and comprehensive that it required a complete service infrastructure. For example, during the construction phase a spur railroad line was built to the house site to haul materials, especially the limestone blocks of which it was made. Biltmore also had its own village, located about 3 miles from the house, to serve the residential needs of the vast professional and service staff which ran the estate. The village was laid out by Olmsted on a variation of a grid with its own shopping and civic areas. Today this village serves the needs of hungry, souvenir-seeking tourists.*

14. *Biltmore's site was no pristine woodland when first developed for forestry. Neither Olmsted nor pioneer forester Gifford Pinchot was impressed when they first visited the site. The land had been used for farming, pasture, and wood collection prior to purchase. What woods remained were second growth. The modern forest is the result of a hundred years of intensive management.*

15. *Olmsted may have designed it in this way to preserve a remnant of a rejected portion of his site plan. The driveways throughout the estate were to have been planted as a linear arboretum, but Vanderbilt chose not to have this scheme executed. According to Schenck (1974) many species were already in a nursery and these may merely have been transferred to the terrace.*

16. *In the plan, the area covered by these conservatories almost equals that of the house itself.*

17. *See Chapter 11 for discussion of the City Beautiful Movement and Chapter 13 for discussion of the Neoclassicist Revival.*

18. *The problems that this fashion for zoos produced cannot be overemphasized, as many cities continue to be affected by them. The problem is really threefold. First, zoos disrupt other park activities because they are popular and usually expand, displacing other use areas. Second, because of the small spaces available, facilities for animals are often minimal at best and inhumane at worst. Recent litigation against several major zoos has begun to improve this condition. Third, the presence of large animals in the midst of an urban park often causes serious environmental problems such as water pollution from uncontrolled sewage and vermin. The notion that zoos are merely a special type of recreational facility, and not a distinctly different institution, was disproved long ago when proposals for a large one in Central Park were turned down. (There is, of course, a small children's zoo.)*

19. *The site plan and planting designs for the Exposition are attributed to C. H. Miller. Robert Morris Copeland was originally consulted about this work, but died before it could be completed. Had he lived, the plan would certainly have been of a more integrated character.*

20. *Streetscape design may be considered by some to be a feature of the City Beautiful Movement, which is generally dated to about 1900. While it does relate closely to the movement, there is ample evidence that interest in street arrangement was common by the early 1880s, and thus can be considered an element of Victorian design.*

21. *Sidewalks continued to be made of diverse materials into the Victorian period. Many were plank or wood ends set on end as modular units. Stone of various types, from large ashlar blocks to gravel, was also used. Concrete was just coming into use. It was not until the spread of the City Beautiful Movement after 1900 that concrete, the most level and uniform of sidewalk materials, began to be the pavement of choice.*

22. *Street trees in fact were often a marketing device used by subdivision owners to suggest that their development would be of high quality with many amenities. They were put in place before roads were paved or sidewalks laid and for some unfortunate homeowners became the sole amenities supplied by the developer. This practice should not detract from their value since some of the most beautiful streets in North America owe their character to this turn-of-the-century practice.*

23. *An exception was the bald cypress, of course not an "evergreen" but much like one, which was effectively used as a street tree in some parts of the South.*

24. *Frank Scott illustrated several similar, but less architectonic, schemes in* The Art of Beautifying Suburban Home Grounds of Small Extent, *but these patterns are rarely seen in photographs and may represent his attempt to "soften" and "romanticize" a Victorian feature.*

25. *The Private Place movement, as do other aspects of Victorian street design and planning, presages the design concerns of the City Beautiful Movement of the early twentieth century. This is but one indication of the role of this period as a link between the two centuries.*

St. Louis was the center of Private Place development, having the first ever developed in the United States— Lucas Place, laid out in 1851. Westmoreland Place and Portland Place are actually two separate streets within one development known as Forest Park Addition.

22

Noble Realities and Ignoble Pretenses:[1]
The City Beautiful

At my feet lay a great city. Miles of broad streets, shaded by trees and lined with fine buildings, for the most part not in continuous blocks but set in larger or smaller enclosures, stretched in every direction. Every quarter contained large open squares filled with trees, along which statues glistened and fountains flashed in the late-afternoon sun. Public buildings of a colossal size and architectural grandeur unparalleled in my day raised their stately piles on every side.

Edward Bellamy, Looking Backward, *1887*

When Edward Bellamy penned this utopian vision of Boston in the year 2000, the imagery was drawn from no contemporary American city. In fact, the North American city of this period was far from even approaching such splendor. In the South, the devastation caused by the Civil War, although being repaired, continued to limit urban development. In the northeastern United States and Canada, industrialization threatened to overwhelm cities with pollution, commercial congestion, and burgeoning population. In the West, fast growth rather than creation of utopianized cities was the goal of developers and town boosters as well. Perhaps it was because of these very contrasts between late nineteenth-century urban reality and ideals that change was inevitable. As we have seen in previous chapters, the ideals of the late nineteenth century had two significant threads—one the physical improvement of the environment, the other the moral improvement of society. It was not until the 1890s that these came together to create an urban planning approach which came to be known as the City Beautiful Movement.

WORLD'S COLUMBIAN EXPOSITION AS AN URBAN DESIGN TURNING POINT

All the forces leading to the City Beautiful Movement were crystallized into a single idealized vision of urban grandeur in the design for the world's fair scheduled to commemorate the four hundredth anniversary of the "discovery" of the New World by Columbus—the World's Columbian Exposition of 1893.[2] The eventual selection of Chicago as the Exposition site over other cities, notably New York, St. Louis, and Washington, D.C., signaled significant, but paradoxical attitude changes in American culture. On the brink of becoming an international imperial power, the United States began to focus increasingly inward. At the same time, the rough, unsophisticated culture upon which the American character was often believed to have been built was rejected in favor of a European-inspired historical associationalism. Chicago, the railroad hub of midcontinent and frontier metropolis run on entrepreneurialism and pragmatism, was transformed into an urban design and planning trendsetter for the North American continent.[3]

In early 1890, Chicago was designated by the U.S. Congress and President Harrison as the official fair site. The practical work of financing and construction

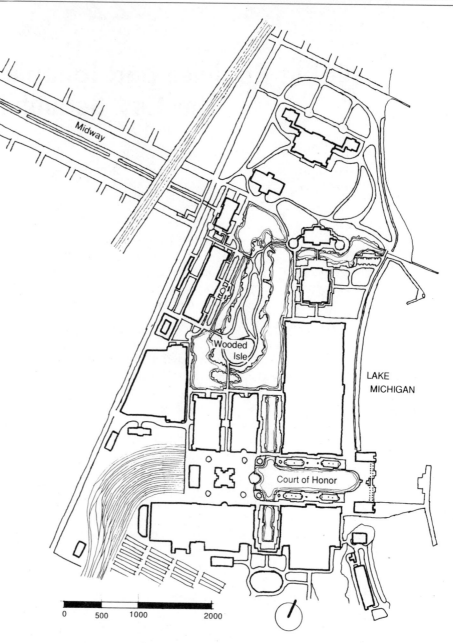

Plan of the World's Columbian Exposition held in 1893, site plan by Frederick Law Olmsted, Sr., and Henry S. Codman. (Data from Garden and Forest, Vol. 9, No. 430; drawn by Rossi.)

was then begun by the local corporation of Illinois businessmen. Their first charge was selection of a site to meet two critical criteria: first, size, with more than 150 acres required to accommodate all the planned uses, and second, access to mass transportation, especially a railroad. Equally important to the business community was that the grounds be near downtown to increase their trade. To accommodate their interests, the initial site proposal was for *two* sites, one adjacent to downtown and the other on the north or south side.[4] Needless to say, any such dual site arrangement would have created both anticipated and unanticipated problems. It was at this critical juncture that the committee took its most effective action—it decided to hire a group of design experts and *to actually follow their advice.*[5]

The multidisciplinary panel of experts assembled to plan the Exposition was a who's-who of late nineteenth-century design and fine arts. Among the principals were architects Daniel Burnham, his partner John Wellborn Root, painter

Francis D. Millet, sculptor Augustus Saint-Gaudens, engineer Abraham Gottlieb, and Frederick Law Olmsted with his associate Henry S. Codman. This stellar group would later be assisted by others of equal talent such as Daniel Chester French, Richard Morris Hunt, Charles Atwood, and Charles F. McKim. Although early planning decisions were a group effort, it was clearly Olmsted who championed an originally unpopular south side site adjacent to Lake Michigan for the fairgrounds. This site was one with which he was intimately familiar, having completed, along with Vaux, the Jackson Park master plan for it almost twenty years earlier. Although some park amenities, such as a ballfield, had been developed there, no part of the far more extensive water-based pastoral landscape which Olmsted and Vaux had planned had been implemented. In 1890, the site remained an incomplete park at the edge of a wetland with shallow lagoons, sandbars, and grassy plains. Many considered the site unappealing, but this location was one to which access could be assured and which allowed Chicago's major scenic feature, Lake Michigan, to be fully exploited. To Olmsted, temporary use of the site for the fair may have appeared the only way in which his earlier plan would ever be implemented: one of the conditions that the South Park Commissioners put on use of the site was that at the fair's close the land be reconfigured for park use.

Although various aspects of the site selection process consumed six months of negotiations between administrative bodies, fair directors, and professionals, the seemingly more complex process of developing a site design concept was largely completed in one day in November 1890. On that day Burnham (who as Director of Works was in charge of design and construction), Root, Olmsted, and Codman completed the conceptual "Brown Paper Plan" which became the basis for all later development.[6] As Olmsted (1893) explained in a magazine article, this plan had three key features: a great architectural court was to serve as site entry; lagoons were to be the major open space, with one being the center of the architectural court and another extending north from it; and in the northern lagoon there was to be a sylvan island "free from conspicuous buildings."[7] As a review of the final site plan will show, these three features remained intact in spite of later changes.

To even the most casual observer of Olmsted's work, the Exposition's plan had a distinctively architectonic appearance quite in contrast to the naturalistic Romantic designs for which he was generally known. While Olmsted was obviously aware of public preferences for some highly structured outdoor spaces— the Greeting at Franklin Park was one such space incorporated into an otherwise pastoral park—what was markedly different at the fair was the reversal of emphasis: limited naturalistic areas within otherwise architectonic spaces. Contemporary accounts suggest that the design of these spaces should be at least equally credited to Codman as to Olmsted. Burnham certainly implied that Codman's contributions were more than those of a mere assistant to the master. Writing while the Exposition was still in progress, Burnham attributed much to Codman, whom he described as "a man well trained in all matters relating to the setting and surroundings of buildings. . . . The general scheme of land and water was suggested by Mr. Codman . . ." (1893, p. 5). Twenty years later his recollection of Codman's contributions remained unchanged. He wrote, "Harry [sic] Codman's knowledge of formal settings was greater than that of all the others [designers] put together . . . Codman took the plan to Brookline [the location of the Olmsted office] and seriously set to work on exact dimensions, terraces, placing of bridges, and the general laying out of a piece of formal work" (Moore, 1913, p. 39). These comments, as well as the notable divergence from Olmsted's other works, suggest that the site plan and design for the Exposition grounds was far more of a collaboration between Olmsted and Codman than is generally recognized. Perhaps this explains the unique composition of the site—a mingling of the Romantic preference for naturalism with the emerging preference for the formal and geometric. Unfortunately, both creative geniuses behind this brilliant hybrid would be lost to the design world within less than three years—Codman prematurely dead and Olmsted incapacitated by mental fatigue caused by years of strenuous work.[8]

Many of the spatial and design concepts from the Brown Paper Plan and its innumerable reiterations were derived from the classically oriented style popularized by the Ecole des Beaux Arts in Paris. Most critical to this style was the concept of functional and spatial relationships between all portions of the site. This was most often achieved through a series of axes extending through interior spaces into the site as a means to create a visual or physical sequence of design events. This sequence was a series of diverse spaces, each of which was part of a clearly articulated functional and symbolic hierarchy. In Beaux Arts design, symmetry—particularly bilateral symmetry—was often employed, proportions of spaces followed classical norms, and details of structures were derived from historical prototypes. Heretofore, these concepts had been implemented for single structures and their adjoining sites rather than at sites with multiple structures and functions. The Columbian Exposition demonstrated that Beaux Arts principles formerly limited to glorification of architecture were in fact equally or even more suited to the creation of structured outdoor spaces.

It was the unique interrelationship of structures and structured space, together forming a designed whole, which most impressed Exposition visitors. Among those who commented, this idea was expressed in several ways: "The real art work—the design—was the ensemble"; "I could not help of thinking at every turn of the *breadth of the conception as a whole*"; and "What genius instigated the idea of these magnificent buildings and their groupings?" (Ives, 1893, p. 1; Coffin, 1897, p. 515; Truman et al., 1976, pp. 605–6). In spite of the plethora of photographs and photographic compilations in books, it is difficult for the modern reader, having experienced imposing spaces from Disney World to the Empire State Plaza, to fully appreciate the effect of these monumental spaces on even the most sophisticated nineteenth-century visitor. There really had been no site of such scale or unity of image in modern American history.

For most visitors, this experience of a lifetime began at the arrival court adjoining the Illinois Central station, built on a special spur line to serve the Exposition. At that point, only the tallest structure, the domed Administration Building designed by Hunt, was visible. Once beyond this building, visitors entered the western end of the Exposition's most famous space, the Court of Honor—the architectural court first delineated on the Brown Paper Plan. The Court, a space more than 600 feet wide and 1850 feet long, was completely enclosed by a series of massive exhibition halls.[9] An architectonically formed lagoon filled the center of the space between these structures, with paths and sunken turf panels occupying the remaining area directly in front of halls. Beyond the eastern end of the Court of Honor, through a colonnaded peristyle 60 feet in height, glimpses of the regularized but less architectonic shoreline of Lake Michigan could be seen. What was critical in this assemblage was the balance of space and structures, which unified the entire composition.

The grand space of the Court of Honor was a perfect setting for the huge commemorative sculptures popular at the turn of the century. Two such pieces were major focal points within the Court of Honor. Set in the lagoon at its eastern, Lake Michigan, end was Daniel Chester French's tribute to democracy in America, the "Republic," a classically clothed female figure which stood 95 feet above water level. At the lagoon's opposite end sat a fountain tribute to Columbus sculpted by Frederick MacMonnies in the form of a barge oared by

View of the Court of Honor, World's Columbian Exposition, looking from the east. The sculpture is French's "Republic" and the domed building in the background is the Administration Building. (Arnold and Higinbotham, 1893.)

allegorical boatmen. This was said to be the largest fountain then in existence. Other features in the Court were of a more decorative nature and planned to add detail and suggest scale. These included Venetian-style obelisks with planters, balustrades surrounding the lagoon, and occasional ornamental plantings, primarily in pots. The overall effect of the Court of Honor was of grandeur of scale, which did not overwhelm, but did impress.

The 25 acres of the Court of Honor had several other unifying design features: cornices of all structures were to be at 60 feet; 25-foot modules were specified for all building bays; and no portion of any building, even a tower extension, was to be higher than the Administration Building dome. Two final criteria were added somewhat later than these, but became architectural themes for which the Exposition became famous—or to some infamous—use of neoclassical architectural styles, with all facades in pure white. Thus the fair came to be called the White City, an idealized vision of urban perfection which one writer compared to the Black City[10]—the real Chicago of poverty, ethnic segregation, and unhygienic housing.

From the Court of Honor lagoon, canals extended north and south linking other areas of the fairgrounds. Of these, the southern area was smaller in size and less elegant in design, being largely devoted to livestock exhibits. Two of the more interesting areas on this side of the site were a reconstruction of La Rabida convent, where Columbus had taken refuge when persecuted in Spain, near which floated replicas of his caravels, and an area for ethnographic exhibits,[11] probably the most popular display at the fair. The North Canal led to an area which exceeded the Court of Honor in size, but was so designed as to appear smaller in scale. This was the lagoon of the Wooded Island—the sylvan island of the Brewn Paper Plan. At the southern end nearest the Court of Honor, this lagoon had a geometric outline, but because of the distance between structures appeared less enclosed and confined by them than did the Court. Further north the edges of the lagoon became less regular and more indented. Similarly the Wooded Island had its most intensive use—a 1¼-acre formal rose garden with densely intertwining paths—at the southern end, and its least visually obtrusive use—the Japanese Ho-o-den Palace and Tea House—at the northern end. Structures surrounding the lagoon followed this same general pattern, decreasing in scale and percentage of site occupied toward the north. At the southern end of the lagoon there were extensions of the major display halls, such as the Manufacturers' and Liberal Arts Building, and Louis Sullivan's famous Transportation Building. Smaller display halls for horticulture and for the U.S. government occupied the mid-area around the lagoon. At the northern end and extending well beyond the limits of the lagoon were sites for the exhibition buildings of the individual states; most of these were at the scale of very large residences. The one exception to this northward decrease in structural scale was the elegant Fine Arts Building which sat at the terminus of the North Pond.[12]

The professionally planned areas of the Wooded Island and the Court of Honor were the urbane fair that its directors and designers intended visitors to see. But any successful exposition had to provide entertainment as well as education and culture. In a bow to public and financial pressures, fair planners created an amusement zone that to their way of thinking could be fortuitously confined to a spatially distinct area. This was the Midway Plaisance, a strip of land originally planned as a boulevard-like connection between Washington and Jackson Parks. The Midway was planned to house those semi-seedy and uncultured uses that would have conflicted with the high tone of the fair grounds. If the formal fair site was brilliantly white, the Midway was a grimy brown; if the fair was grand, the Midway was pedestrian; if the fair was Venice, the Midway was Calcutta. These comparisons should not suggest that the Midway was either unpopular or uninteresting. In fact, it had great vitality both in terms of design and of the originality of exhibits. Here were found a Turkish coffee house, an aviary of exotic birds, an Egyptian shop and restaurant district known as the "Streets of Cairo," and the first Ferris Wheel, which towered more than 250 feet above the crowd. This assortment of ethnic, zoological, and technological displays produced a rich, exciting, and slightly risqué atmosphere.

The entire Midway occupied a strip over half a mile in length and 600 feet wide. Attractions were arranged along a central, alley-like corridor about 100 feet wide. Some exhibits fronted directly on this aisle, but many were organized

View of the Wooded Island, World's Columbian Exposition, looking from the northeast. The area with dense paths is the Rose Garden. (Ives, 1893.)

View of the Midway, World's Columbian Exposition, looking west toward the Ferris Wheel. (Arnold and Higinbotham, 1893.)

around courtyards set off from the flow of traffic.[13] This arrangement was favored by the larger, more multifaceted exhibits such as that of Ireland, which included a scaled-down Blarney Castle. Beyond all this frantic activity stood Washington Park, essentially unaltered by the Exposition and offering a place for less intensive activities.

The World's Columbian Exposition was the most written-about site plan since Central Park. Reaction began even before opening day. Some critics, such as architect Louis Sullivan, rebuked management for settling on safe, but dull, historicist designs. But in the context of the Exposition's intent and development time frame, use of one style was both understandable and reasonable. The directors had decided to employ as many different architects as possible, and limited design time necessitated that they be facile with the system chosen. On a less practical note, neoclassical themes were chosen because they were thought to convey the all-important notion that the United States and Chicago were no longer backwater mavericks among nations and cities, but full participants in the emerging international culture then dominated by Europe. Sullivan, along with others, felt that the architecture of the fair should demonstrate Chicago's emerging role as a place of design innovation.[14] These opinions, although vocally expressed, represented the minority view. Most who saw the fair reacted to it with unrestrained enthusiasm and saw in it a turning point in both American culture and design. The oft quoted essayist Henry Adams captured the essence of the fair's influence when he wrote in his autobiography that "here was a breach of continuity—a rupture in historical sequence . . . the first expression of American thought as a unity . . ."[15] Of course he was referring to far more than mere appearance, and rightly so, for the fair represented political, social, and industrial changes then in the process of transforming the continent, but which had previously had no clear expression to the public.[16] Others reacted equally favorably. H. W. S. Cleveland writing to Olmsted commented that "the effect of the whole scene was to me such a vision of beauty as I had never dreamed of. . . . Indeed I cannot tell you how much I enjoyed the study of all the various effects and how it rejoiced my heart to think that you should have been so largely the creator of

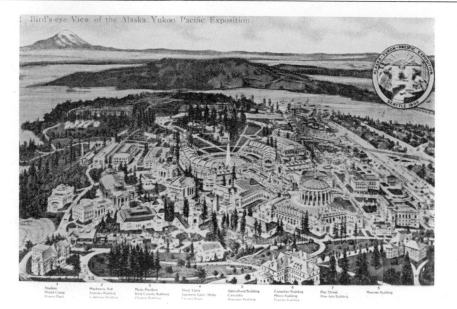

Aerial view of the Alaska-Yukon Exposition held in Seattle, Washington, in 1909. The landscape design has been attributed to Olmsted Brothers.

such a magnificent work."[17] All of the pages of text written about the fair during the early 1890s overwhelmingly concluded that it was a monumental feat both of organization and design.

What were the direct and immediate results of the fair?[18] Surprisingly they were few in number and slow to materialize, a fact which has led some to conclude, erroneously, that the fair had little impact on the subsequent urban planning movement known as the City Beautiful. As so often has occurred with a major design or planning innovation, a series of feeble copies of the original concept immediately began to sprout up around the country. In the ten years after the Exposition, most major cities in the United States held fairs based on the "Columbian" model—that is, with site plans organized around water features both artificial and natural, with large architectural courts as central spaces, and employing neoclassicist architecture, usually all in white. The fair that began this trend was the California Midwinter International Exposition of 1894.[19] This was followed by the Tennessee Centennial Exposition of 1897, the Trans-Mississippi and International Exposition at Omaha in 1898, the Pan-American Exposition at Buffalo in 1901, and the Louisiana Purchase Exposition at St. Louis in 1904. Fair mania ended in 1916, when the Panama-California Exposition closed at San Diego.[20]

Each of these extravaganzas followed religiously the details of the Columbian Exposition, but none could capture its simple vitality. Two critical but interrelated flaws contributed to this problem. First, each succeeding fair tried to be more visually elaborate than its predecessor so that it could attract the fairgoing public. Showiness was substituted for spatial design. Second, and more significant, none of the designers or organizers of these fairs recognized the critical relationship between scale of space and structures. In general, buildings were too close together in relationship to their size and ostentatiousness. Thus, the overall effect, rather than of grandeur, was of excessive display—Victorian clutter in neoclassical garb. The principal positive contribution of this series of Columbian clones was that they reproduced throughout the continent a version of the new urban ideal of beauty, shortly to be systematized as the City Beautiful Movement.

THE CITY BEAUTIFUL MOVEMENT

Inspiration and Theory

The City Beautiful Movement was an approach to urban planning that emphasized the value of highly structured, formal, historicist aesthetics for their own sake, but more importantly saw this type of urban beauty as a way to morally uplift society. As Charles Mulford Robinson, a major theorist of the movement, explained, "Social problems are to a large degree problems of the environment . . . with municipal art [an aspect of City Beautiful] the utilitarian advantages and social benefits become so paramount that they are not forgotten. . . . This art, which serves so many social ends, is municipal, in the sense of communal. . . . It is not a fad. It is not merely a bit of aestheticism. . . . Altruism is its impulse . . ." (Robinson, 1903, pp. 245, 25–36, and 28). Accordingly, just as pioneer landscape architects such as Olmsted and Cleveland had used Romantic design to further humanitarian social goals, so did turn of the century designers use revived classical planning.

We should note that there were earlier antecedents of the City Beautiful than the fair, some of which date to as far back as the immediate post-Civil War period. These would include some monumental spaces in Beaux Arts style associated with urban parks, such as the Grand Army Plaza at Prospect Park. Other precursors would include the Private Places, with their emphasis on setbacks, designed streetscapes with street trees, and other planning standards. An important contemporaneous event, which demonstrated that there were multiple forces leading toward the Movement, was the plan and designs for the park system for Kansas City, Missouri. As developed under George Kessler, the system was "Romantic" in site selection and planning, using areas of greatest natural beauty for the parks then unifying them physically through a boulevard system, but the design of these spaces had the scale and details of the Exposition, with grand vistas and classical structures. This important park system design was the first to apply such approaches to a citywide design theme.

The City Beautiful Movement is often thought to have addressed only large, high-style design projects in major cities, but this is not the case. The movement had four components that applied at all urban scales. The first component was what could be called Civic Art, that is, the beautification of cities through addition of public or semipublic works of art, including buildings. Civic Art emphasized urban unification through the use of impressive, generally Renaissance-inspired, architectural styles. Civic Art also included the addition of elaborate artistic pieces such as murals, fountains, frescoes, mosaics, and decorative light fixtures to the streetscape or to public buildings.

The second component was Civic Design, in which the city was regarded as a unit which could be organized for societal rather than solely individual goals. Civic Design emphasized monumental outdoor spaces both as appropriate expressions of this sense of community and as the best way to organize civic and commercial functions. The City Beautiful Movement recognized that architecture alone, without an appropriate spatial setting related to use and image, could never create the inspiring stateliness desired. This aspect of the City Beautiful Movement was the first recognition since the Renaissance that outdoor space itself could be a planning material and that such spaces could be as architectural as any structure.

The third component was Civic Reform, which combined both social and political reform. Corruption that occurred in large cities after the Civil War had done much to shake public confidence in the vitality of the cities. Lincoln Steffens's *The Shame of the Cities* and other "muckraking" publications helped to make urban corruption a prominent issue and so galvanized the public that reformers were bolstered by popular opinion. Many business and civic leaders feared that this threatened continued urban development and took action to reform government through the voting process. An equally serious problem was

The City Beautiful Movement's idea of "Civic Art" included ornamental streetscape features such as this lamppost. (Robinson, 1903.)

the presence of urban slums, which expanded in both area and population as cities became industrialized. Factory workers were poorly housed in compact districts often lacking in basic amenities. Reforms, such as the settlement house movement, were organized on both humanitarian and practical grounds, for these crowded districts were sources of infectious disease, crime, and labor unrest, all problems which made cities increasingly unpleasant places in which to live. The infamous New York tenements whose haunting images Jacob Riis captured were the most dismal of worker housing, but elsewhere less dramatic crowding made urban life equally repugnant.

The final aspect of the City Beautiful Movement was Civic Improvement, which emphasized the "clean-up, paint-up, fix-up" approach to creating urban beauty. Although often neglected as an aspect of the movement, it was in many ways its most significant contribution because improvements such as construction of sidewalks, street paving, and dedication of public squares led to the upgrading of towns everywhere. Further, it helped to establish local civic improvement associations that encouraged the removal of debris from lots, sweeping of streets, painting of structures, and planting of trees. Some groups, such as the General Federation of Women's Clubs, provided the only planning leadership available in their communities. Many of these organizations were the precursors of later local planning bodies.

Each of these four components, Civic Art, Civic Design, Civic Reform, and Civic Improvement, dealt to a greater or lesser degree with ten general objectives of City Beautiful planning:

• To centralize services and related uses in such a way that a hierarchical land use structure was achieved

- To establish convenient and efficient commercial and civic core districts
- To establish hygienic urban conditions, especially for residential areas
- To express the individuality of towns through exploitation of scenic features
- To treat composition of building groups as a more important functional and aesthetic concern than architectural design
- To create focal points in the streetscape to visually unify the city
- To integrate regional circulation systems into a clear hierarchy
- To treat open spaces as critical urban needs, but emphasizing active rather than passive recreation
- To preserve some historic urban elements[21]
- To provide a unified system for incorporation of modern urban features, such as industrial facilities and skyscrapers, into the existing city

The City Beautiful Movement did have some notable negative aspects which belied its underlying social concerns. In its enthusiasm to rid cities of undesirable housing and slum areas, it led to an early form of urban renewal in which families were displaced without alternative low-cost housing being made available. Although most theoreticians of the City Beautiful emphasized no particular design style for architecture or outdoor spaces, the movement came to be associated with Neoclassicist Revival styles, which many interpreted as elitist and out of place in the egalitarian societies of North America.[22] Finally, the City Beautiful Movement failed to appeal to most North Americans because the elegant style with which it was associated seemed antithetical to American tastes as being extravagant and costly.

That previously dissociated design and planning ideas could come together in the last decade of the nineteenth century in the form of the organized approach to urban design known as the City Beautiful Movement was due to several factors. First, and probably of greatest importance, was consolidation of what might be called middle-class standards of urban propriety—principally interest in the display of proper visual taste, abhorrence of squalor and crowdedness, and fear of social unrest, particularly crime and political anarchy. City organization was seen as a way to ameliorate all of these problems with one collaborative series of actions. Second, extensive European travel by well-off Americans in the second half of the century had exposed them to monumental designed spaces both dating from the Renaissance and of their own age. Paris's urban plan by Baron von Haussmann had a particular appeal. Third, growth of a wealthy and influential business class provided a design constituency that could both support large-scale projects and appreciate their long-term value. While these entrepreneurs idealized the aesthetic amenities of the City Beautiful, it was the movement's emphasis on spatial efficiency and hierarchical circulation which most suited their economic needs. Finally, growing out of sanitary engineering efforts begun in the 1870s, there was a concerted effort to improve urban health and order. Public health organizations such as Boston's Board of Survey and New York City's Commission of Street Improvements evolved by 1900 into rudimentary planning bodies that dealt with single planning concerns, rather than the comprehensive planning to follow in the twentieth century.

McMillan Commission Plan for Washington, D.C.

The first true urban (as opposed to pseudo-urban of the expositions) plan to apply City Beautiful principles at any large scale was the Senate Park Commission Plan, more commonly called the McMillan Plan, for the city of Washington, D.C. Based on L'Enfant's 1791 plan, it sought to restore the order and grandeur which over the years had been diluted by innumerable omissions and intrusions. Three of the more damaging adjustments were transformation of the Mall from an axial open space to a cluttered Downingesque Romantic garden, presence of railroad tracks and a depot on the Mall near the Capitol, and failure to complete focal points that defined major axes of the entire scheme.

Beyond the obvious influence of the Columbian Exposition, there were three other catalysts which promoted this replanning for Washington. First, the L'Enfant plan, long lost amongst other government papers, had been recently rediscovered. Second, the centennial of the Capital's relocation from Philadelphia to the District, which had occurred in 1800, was being commemorated. Finally, a design competition held in conjunction with the American Institute of Architects convention in Washington in 1900 inspired residents and politicians alike with the prospects of a real and permanent "White City" at the capital.

Under the auspices of U.S. Senator James McMillan, the Commission, consisting of Daniel Burnham, Frederick Law Olmsted, Jr., Charles McKim, Augustus Saint-Gaudens, and later Charles Moore, was assembled in 1901. Their work method involved travel, models, and drawings, particularly bird's-eye perspectives. Burnham recommended that the best way to resurrect the L'Enfant plan was to experience the same spaces that had inspired him. The Commission first traveled to American sites such as James River plantations and Annapolis, then spent five weeks traveling in Europe, drawing as they went.

Recommendations emerged rapidly. To achieve maximum effect, the com-

McMillan Commission model of Washington, D.C., as it appeared in 1900. The Mall is in the center with the Washington Monument at the far end. (Moore, 1902.)

McMillan Commission model of the planning proposal for Washington, D.C., 1900, showing redesign of the Mall to re-accentuate the axis from the Capitol to the Potomac River, located beyond the Lincoln Memorial. View taken from same position as Figure 22–7. (Moore, 1902.)

View of the Lincoln Memorial, one of the memorial locations recommended by the McMillan Commission, but not implemented until the 1920s as the plan of Washington, D.C., was carried out. (Anonymous.)

mission members demonstrated these ideas in two huge models, one of the federal core as it then existed and the other of proposed design changes. Perspectives and plans added detail to the models, but conveyed the same message: Washington D.C. as then experienced was but a hint of its real self trapped under the remnants of a century of ad hoc design and planning decisions. Among the more significant recommendations of the plan were relocation of the Washington Monument slightly off center to avoid the swampy soils which had plagued its construction, completion of the sight lines leading from it by establishing new sites for memorials to Lincoln and Jefferson, development of the federal office block known as the Federal Triangle, relocation of the railroad tracks and station away from the Mall, reestablishment of a formal planting scheme on the Mall, creation of parkways to link important surrounding sites such as Mt. Vernon directly with the city, and creation of an extensive park system along stream corridors within the District. In many ways, this plan was an embryonic regional plan. The last recommendation, for parks, largely the work of Olmsted, was the most underappreciated aspect of the McMillan plan. It gave the city both new open spaces and a road system that complemented the formal boulevards then dominating the city plan. Rock Creek Park, in places not much wider than a city block, was the major area set aside. Its key contribution to public recreation was its location in the midst of the city and its woodland appearance. In this way a remnant Romantic landscape was sited in the middle of the continent's most neoclassicist city.

Although the Senate Park Commission started out to reestablish the L'Enfant plan, it ended up by producing a *reinterpretation* of the plan. The difference is significant. Although plans for the two look similar in pattern, the visual character of the "McMillan" city was far denser, more architectural, and more elaborated in details than had been L'Enfant's. It has been speculated that L'Enfant's conception of Washington D.C. was structured in plan, but Romantic in view. As envisioned after 1901, the architectonic character extended to both plan and view.[23]

View of the Mall in the 1980s. looking toward the Washington Monument.

Not everyone appreciated City Beautiful-inspired renovations. Here an editorial cartoonist gives his view of recent changes to the grounds of the Capitol and Mall in Washington, D.C. Elbert Peets later decried both nineteenth- and twentieth-century "mutilations" of the original plan for altering key unifying features. ([Washington] Evening Star, January 14, 1908.)

Other City Beautiful Plans

The McMillan Commission Plan for Washington D.C. revitalized an earlier scheme based on planning principles similar to those of the City Beautiful. A greater challenge came when City Beautiful concepts were applied to cities that had little spatial planning beyond a perfunctory grid. The first such plan was the Cleveland Mall Plan of 1903, proposed by Burnham with fellow architects John Carrere and Arnold Brunner. The Columbian Exposition was unequivocally the inspiration for this plan, which entailed placement of a new railroad station and relocation of key civic buildings. New buildings were sited around a road-encircled central open turf area lined with trees, called the Mall.[24] Even the proportions of the open spaces and structures were very close to those of the Exposition. The chief spatial difference

Aerial perspective of the Cleveland Mall Plan by Daniel Burnham, 1903, showing the railroad depot and plaza in the foreground. (F. L. Ford, 1904.)

was that the Mall was "filled" by trees, whereas the Court of Honor had been visually open. The railroad depot, located along Lake Erie, served as the northern focal point, with the sunken tracks in front of it creating an open crossing much like the canals of the fair. Cleveland's plan was less significant for its design innovations, which were few, than for its application of "Columbian" principles on a large scale in a city previously incompatible with City Beautiful standards. On a less positive note, it was also the first plan to incorporate wholesale removal of the poor for purposes of urban renewal.

The accomplishments of Burnham and his associates in Cleveland were dwarfed in six short years by presentation of the most comprehensive City Beautiful plan developed—that for Chicago. In many ways this work was the culmination of Burnham's professional life, a commission which he had been working out in his mind for more than ten years. Begun in 1907 at the request of two business clubs, the plan had five key elements:

- Development of a regional highway, railroad, and water transportation system which included improvements to intracity links
- Development of a lakeside cultural center adjacent to downtown
- Development of a civic center to the west of downtown and the Chicago River
- Development of the lakefront and river as scenic amenities
- Extension of the park and boulevard systems, especially incorporation of outlying Forest Preserves into the system

Although a forerunner of later scientific city plans, the plan of Chicago was largely humanistic in its recommendations, emphasizing sequencing of urban spaces, appropriate designs for each land use, and urban art. Visually it achieved four goals: it relieved the existing grid pattern by adding diagonal streets; it introduced artistic focal points, on the scale of modern Buckingham Fountain; [25] it proposed unified, albeit neoclassicist, architectural styles for new buildings; and it developed water as the central theme to unify diverse areas of the city, well ahead of the current wave of waterfront revitalizations.

The Chicago Plan became the city's planning bible. Under the guidance of a key group of business leaders, notably Charles Wacker and Walter Moody, lectures, exhibits, fundraisers, and projects based on the plan ran continuously into the 1920s. Wacker went so far as to publish an abbreviated version of the plan for free distribution to schoolchildren. It became a part of the sixth-grade

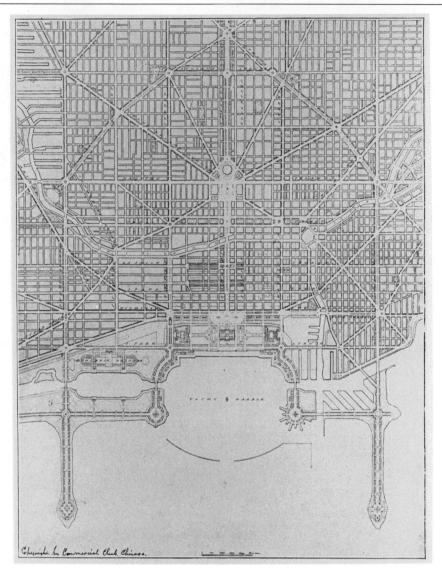

Plan of Daniel Burnham's proposed street system for central Chicago, 1907. (Moody, 1920.)

Aerial perspective of the Chicago transportation center, to be located west of the Chicago River, proposed by Daniel Burnham. The building with a tower is the post office flanked by railroad depots. (Moody, 1920)

curriculum for every school in the city—certainly the first widespread effort at public education in planning.

This plan was also a remarkable document in two regards—one artistic, the other legalistic. To illustrate the proposed planning and design concepts, Burnham and his associate Edward Bennett hired noted French illustrator Jules Guerin. Guerin's color renderings of proposed views and plans gave a subtle, impressionistic quality to otherwise hard urban images. In spite of poor reproductions in the report, they made the plan attractive to even the planning "illiterate." Of more lasting import were two sets of recommendations, which in retrospect signaled a transition in planning from visual and social concerns to legal implementation of urban planning standards. The first recommendations were that the city explore creation of a regional plan coordinating commission to oversee development of facilities, such as those for transportation, which transcended city boundaries. The second series of recommendations, written by attorney Walter Fisher, dealt with legal aspects of plan implementation. This concern with legal approaches would increasingly dominate urban planning in the twenty years following the Chicago Plan.

Burnham's admonition to "make no little plans" was one that he and other City Beautiful practitioners followed most diligently.[26] Burnham proposed an extensive redesign for San Francisco (not followed) and one for Manila in the Philippines (partially followed). At the new U.S. colonial summer capital in Baguio, Philippines, he transformed a mountain village into a city worthy of any imperial power. Although Burnham and those who associated with his firm dominated much City Beautiful planning, it should not be thought that no other equally talented designers were at work. In the first decade of the twentieth century almost every major city in the United States and Canada[27] had some type of City Beautiful plan completed. Among the more significant plans were those by Charles Mulford Robinson for Denver, Fort Wayne, and Dubuque; by John Nolen for San Diego and Madison; by Frederick Todd for Ottawa; by Thomas

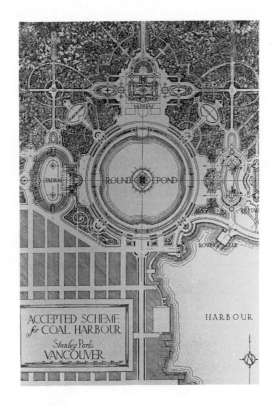

Thomas Mawson's City Beautiful scheme for Coal Harbor in Vancouver, British Columbia. (Mawson, 1927.)

Mawson for Calgary; by the Olmsted Brothers for Pittsburgh and Boulder; and by Warren Manning with assistance from J. Horace McFarland, a nationally known nonprofessional advocate of the City Beautiful, for Harrisburg.

CONCLUSION AND SUMMARY

Dominance of the City Beautiful Movement lasted for a very brief period. If we consider the World's Columbian Exposition of 1893 to be a starting point and the First National Conference on City Planning of 1909[28] to signal at least the beginning of the end, the movement spanned only sixteen years. Its importance, then, was not really in its own achievements, many of which remain today merely plans on paper, but in the transition which it provided between the Romantic planning of the nineteenth century and the scientific planning of the twentieth century. It was also the period during which many important planners, such as John Nolen, Warren Manning, and Frederick Law Olmsted, Jr., were trained. Those City Beautiful spatial ideals which they absorbed continued to inspire the work of many landscape architects and planners throughout the twentieth century.

Current opinions as to the lasting value of the City Beautiful Movement vary. At one end of the spectrum are those who view it as a fad that left much monumental urban design, but contributed little of lasting value; at the other are those who see it as the beginning of the modern age of planning. A more reasonable view than either would be that this late Victorian/early modern period produced a significant transition between nineteenth- and twentieth-century theory and practice in land use and design. In North America the popularity of both the fairs and the City Beautiful grew out of public disaffection with naturalistic design, which had begun over twenty years before. In a sense, these design and planning changes were what the late Victorians had been struggling to find—a showy, structured, morally simple approach to physical planning. Until the Columbian Exposition no one had been able to put these concepts into a coherent physical form. Once that occurred, it should not be surprising that the world seized it and reapplied its concepts universally.

Today as cities continue to struggle with issues that the City Beautiful Movement sought to resolve, its naive and simplistic belief that urban problems could be easily solved through design may cause us to ignore the positive changes it fomented. The City Beautiful Movement emphasized the inherent opportunities of urban design and planning, rather than merely addressing specific prob-

A City Beautiful "subdivision," aptly named Versailles, as envisioned by architect Thomas Hastings. A cooperative complex planned for Long Island, New York, it included a high rise "chateau" for apartments, shown in the distance, and community buildings including a yacht club and theater, shown in the foreground. (Anonymous, 1916.)

lems of land use or circulation. Further, it treated cities as metaphysical and corporeal wholes in which design and social issues could not be separated if lasting improvements were to be made. But as we shall see in the next chapter, the City Beautiful Movement failed to properly address those social concerns which it had espoused. This failure eventually led to a reaction, in which urban design was deemphasized and scientific urban planning put in its place.

NOTES

1. This phrase comes from Charles Eliot Norton's impressions of the World's Columbian Exposition as presented in a lecture on "Art in America" and quoted by Moore, 1921, p. 87.

2. Particularly in the early stages, these two planning groups, a national commission and a local corporation, were often at odds, a situation which delayed actual construction for about six months. Hence the fair opened in 1893, rather than in 1892 as intended. Progress of work on the fair suffered additionally from economic and labor problems associated with the Panic of 1893.

3. It is both ironic and fitting that the paper which first suggested the seminal importance of the frontier in American culture, as well as declaring that frontier effectively closed—Frederick Jackson Turner's "The Significance of the Frontier in American History"—was presented at the fair during the World's Congress of Historians and Historical Students on July 12, 1893. It was Turner's thesis, now generally disparaged, that the existence of free available land and the advance of American settlement westward explained American social and cultural development.

4. The Scientific American *of August 2, 1890 (Vol. 63, pp. 70–71), has an interesting article with illustration of the design proposals for the downtown site had this approach been implemented. A major argument against dual sites was that they would be inherently separate and unequal, with the "glamorous" commercial and industrial exhibits located downtown, while agricultural exhibits would be consigned to the more distant location.*

5. Although sarcasm may seem to be implied in this comment, only irony was intended. Frederick Law Olmsted must also have felt that the relationship between the committee and the professionals was somewhat unusual, as he commented upon it, using much these same words, in his Inland Architect *(1893) article.*

6. The plan was so named because it was drawn on rough, kraft-type brown paper in pencil.

7. Quoted from Olmsted, 1893, p. 20. In this article Olmsted also discussed the role of the original Jackson Park plan. He commented that "the question at once came up how far the general theory of the old plan for a public pleasure ground to be formed upon it could be made available to the special purpose of the Exposition. As a result of this consideration, we came to the conclusion that the element of the waterways in the original plan being carried out, retaining walls being built in various places for holding up the excavated material to be piled upon the shores so that in these places terraces would be formed, the necessary buildings of the Fair could be advantageously distributed upon the surrounding sandy ridges" (p. 19).

    Attempts to develop the Wooded Island, as the "sylvan island" came to be known, were endless. If not for Olmsted's pertinacity it would have become filled with structures of all sorts. Occasionally, and with reluctance, he accepted some nonintensive features such as the Japanese complex or the log cabin which Theodore Roosevelt sponsored.

8. Codman died on January 13, 1893, of complications from an appendectomy. Thus the impress of his ideas was largely upon spatial concepts and early construction of the grounds rather than its details. His brother Philip continued the site design work. Olmsted had been in physical and mental decline throughout the early 1890s. Letters to his sons and partners indicate that he was aware of his decline and imminent incapacitation. In November 1895 he made a doctor-recommended trip to England with family members, during which his mental condition degenerated to senility. The following year he returned to a Deer Isle, Maine, retirement home. Finally in fall of 1898 he became a resident of McLean Hospital, a mental hospital for which he had completed a site design years before. He died on August 28, 1903.

9. The appearance of these halls belies the fact that all but one were intended from the beginning as temporary structures. Rather than being of marble or granite, they were constructed of frame forms over which was applied a material called "staff." This was a plaster mixture to which jute fibers had been added. The foundations for most halls were pilings driven into the marshy soil and easily removed at the close of the fair.

10. Term used in the London Spectator *as cited by Keeler (1950).*

11. This area would appear to have been as much an "ethnographic zoo" as an exhibit. The displays featured unusual cultural and tribal groups in replicas of traditional housing and performing traditional skills.

12. The Fine Arts Building was the sole structure of the Exposition to be given a permanent use. Immediately after the fair it was reconstituted with permanent building materials and became the home of the Field Museum of Natural History, which remained there until 1920. After a period of disuse it became the Museum of Science and Industry, which it remains. Over the years there have been many additions and renovations, but the facade of the structure, although far larger than during the fair, continues to give some idea of the Exposition's architectural flavor. The only other architectural remnant of the fair is a recently reconstructed Japanese tea house on Wooded Island.

13. Rubin (1979) has theorized that the Midway became the prototype for the modern commercial strip because of its arrangement and architectural eclecticism. Although an interesting concept, it is clearly unsupported. First, the Midway was not striplike in arrangement but was actually quite "classical" in its arrangement of a central axis with outdoor rooms arranged off axes to its side. Second, the form of this site was not developed specifically for the fair, but for park linkage.

14. The first skyscrapers—in particular the one with non-load-bearing walls, William Le Baron Jenney's Home Insurance Building—were constructed in the city by Chicago architects. Burnham and Root were also in the forefront of innovation with their designs for the Monadnock Building and the Rookery, both in Chicago. Other Chicago-inspired architectural developments were the Chicago window and "floating raft" foundations.

15. 1918, pp. 340 and 343.

16. There are a variety of different interpretations of the sociopolitical meaning of the Exposition and the City Beautiful Movement which it stimulated, but these largely fall into two camps: those who viewed the fair as the beginning of planned, socialistic society in America and those who saw it as the ultimate expression of capitalism on the verge of imperialistic expansion. The first view is summarized by Manieri-Elia, 1979, and Neufeld, 1935—the second by Mumford, 1931, and Boyer, 1983.

17. Cleveland to Olmsted, November 8, 1893, FLO Papers.

18. The Exposition closed on October 30, 1893, by which time over 27 million people had paid to see it. The buildings continued to stand, but fires in January and July of 1894 damaged or destroyed many of these. Over the next two years, reusable parts of the built fabric were removed. By the middle of 1896 all salvageable materials had been removed, and what remained was dismantled. The site was then regraded and laid out as Jackson Park.

19. The connections between this fair and the Columbian are quite direct. It was organized by M. H. de Young, who had served as a California Commissioner to the Chicago exposition. In addition many of the exhibits from that Exposition were transported directly to San Francisco.

20. Several fairs had some skilled professional guidance in their planning. George Kessler worked on the Louisiana Purchase Exposition, but according to Francis (1913), this work was largely decorative. The Olmsted Brothers briefly assisted with planning of the Panama-California Exposition, but were replaced by Bertrand Goodhue.

21. Boyer (1983) has pointed out the irony of both Beaux Arts and City Beautiful designs, which ostensibly were derived from historical precedents, but which were philosophically ahistorical. They offered "detached fragments of the city . . . a plurality of copies stood in the place of unique experience" (p. 56). This fragmentation of idea and form would in part contribute to swift disillusionment with City Beautiful plans.

22. The reason for this association is unclear, and it apparently should not be attributed solely to the influence of the Columbian Exposition as is usually done. As late as 1897 Coffin could write that "it was said [at the time of the Exposition] that the influence of the Exposition would be so great that thereafter every courthouse, capitol, and post office in the land would be a Greek or Roman temple. . . . No such consequences have appeared thus far, and the World's Fair seems to be estimated as a thing apart" (p. 520).

23. The McMillan Commission Plan has been the key planning document for Washington during this century. Significant aspects which have been completed are the Lincoln and Jefferson Memorials, the Arlington Memorial Bridge across the Potomac, and restoration of the Mall. Two important components not yet completed are the streetscape for Pennsylvania Avenue (now in progress) and a plaza at the base of the Washington Memorial.

24. Although this name would suggest that the space was inspired by the Mall in Washington, the influence of the Columbian Exposition was clearly implied by Burnham. In an article he referred to the space as "the Court of Honor or Mall" (1903, p. 14). Brunner (1916) likewise used the Court of Honor as a model to explain placement of buildings in Cleveland.

25. This fountain in its present location was not part of the original plan, but two fountains similar to it were proposed for the termini of Jackson and Hubbard Streets.

26. In context: "Make no little plans, they have no magic to stir men's blood, and probably themselves will not be realized. Make big plans, aim high in hope and work, remembering that a noble logical diagram once recorded will never die . . ." (quoted in Journal of the Society of Architectural Historians, Vol. 4, No. 1 [1944], p. 3).

27. The City Beautiful Movement in Canada was generally behind that in the United States, with major plans not developed until after 1909. Meek (1979) outlined five periods of the Canadian City Beautiful as:

1890–1909	*"Pre-planning Phase" of small plans*
1910–1913	*City Beautiful*
1914–1918	*Incipient city planning*
1919–1924	*City planning*
1925–1930	*Reawakening of City Beautiful ideals*

Mexico was less affected by the City Beautiful Movement than the English-speaking countries. The forces in effect in urban planning there derived from recent political and labor revolutions.

28. Lubove (1962) and Scott (1969) have both cited this date as the close of the City Beautiful Movement. Boyer (1983) believes the year 1907 was more critical.

23

The City Scientific

It would be an overstatement to say that the City Beautiful Movement ended at a given point in time. Rather its aims and methods were redirected after 1909 and merged with those of social reform movements that aspired to create a managed, publically oriented society in which planning played a key role. Nothing did more to alienate the leaders of these movements from the aesthetic themes of the City Beautiful Movement than the perception that they were inextricably linked with elitist neoclassical forms and spatial organization, as well as being dominated by business interests. But whatever the validity of these perceptions, which were only partially accurate and failed to recognize any interrelationship between business and public interest, there were problems of far greater substance with the City Beautiful Movement. Five problems were particularly significant: the difficulty of "mending" poorly conceived urban plans; changing demographic patterns; an ongoing revolution in transportation systems; the housing needs of those of limited economic means; and limitations of existing legal authority for land use control.

The sixteen or more year trial given the urban revitalization ideas of the City Beautiful had demonstrated that it was far easier to conceive plans for rearranging existing cities than it was to have those plans executed. While implementation of some aspects of the Washington, D.C., Cleveland, and Chicago plans demonstrated that changes could be made, these changes were often difficult to accomplish, incompletely executed, and destructive of established social patterns. In a 1910 article in the popular magazine *The American City,* Frederick Law Olmsted, the younger, continuing in his father's role as the most prominent landscape architect of his day, hit on the essence of both the problem and the opportunity.[1] "Radical and extensive changes in the street plan of built up cities practically never take place, . . . [but] growth creates opportunities for improvement" (1910*b,* p. 209). This statement reflected the belief that it was more appropriate to devote concern to those cities or portions of cities being developed, than to the time-consuming task of rebuilding in older areas.

Cities were changing rapidly under the weight of sheer population numbers and densities. The 1920 census showed that for the first time the United States had more than 50 percent of its population residing in urban areas. Particularly problematic in this regard was the City Beautiful's usage of large tracts of land at the city center for public purposes, thus removing them from other functions that also demanded central locations. This encouraged even greater population compression in poorer districts. Another significant demographic change was in the nature of inner city dwellers. After 1900, foreign immigrants, increasingly from Eastern and southern Europe, found employment in industrial occupations and housing in concentrated neighborhoods near large factories. Migration within the United States was dominated by Afro-American movement out of rural districts in the South to inner city neighborhoods in the North. Both foreign and native urban newcomers found economic and environmental conditions not different in type, but different in magnitude, from the ones encountered by those who came earlier. Prior to 1900, for example, the type of horribly cramped tenements depicted by Jacob Riis were largely confined to New York City, while afterward they dominated the housing stock in many cities.

There were two innovations in transportation that also influenced city planning in the early twentieth century. The first to have an impact was the street railway, and the second was the automobile. Ironically, although one was a quasi-public form and the other strictly private, both fostered urban decentralization and the growth of lower-middle-class suburbs. Street railways were a common form of transportation after 1870. At first horse-drawn trolleys ran on tracks, then steam power replaced horsepower, and after 1890 electricity replaced steam, increasing the speed of the street railways, and therefore their range. Street railways made outer residential locations available to larger numbers of people and encouraged recreational and institutional development at urban fringes.[2] Although street railways continued in use in some cities until after World War II, usually with buses replacing track-mounted trolleys, the automobile quickly replaced them in the early twentieth century as a force stimulating urban planning.[3]

The final impetus toward city planning was the realization that cities lacked sufficient legal authority to actualize planning. Cities in fact had few legal tools beyond condemnation, nuisance law, building code, and infrastructure development that they could use to direct comprehensive urban revitalization. Lack of control over private land uses threatened to undermine the few improvements that cities had struggled to realize.

Three intellectual efforts were also underway which strongly influenced thinking on urban problems. The first was related to the growing interest in ecology, as expressed in the embryonic conservation movement.[4] In particular, conservationists articulated the need for management of limited resources based on scientific knowledge of how systems operated. The philosophical relationship between ecology in natural systems and the planning of human-made ones in the urban setting was frequently cited by writers. Olmsted used such an analogy to describe urban change when he said, "We thus conceive a city plan as a live thing, as a growing and gradually changing aggregation of accepted ideas or projects for physical changes in the city, all consistent with each other, and each surviving, by virtue of its own inherent merit and by virtue of its harmonizing with the rest" (1913, p. 5). The second significant intellectual influence was the growth of the social sciences, particularly the Chicago School of urban sociology. The method of this school incorporated an objective research approach with ecologically based models to explain and predict urban patterns.

Finally, the early twentieth century saw increasing emphasis on professionalism—that is, personnel educated and trained in application of standard procedures to the solution of specific problems conceived in the context of a certain body of expertise. This emphasis on professionalism in disciplines had been growing throughout the second half of the nineteenth century—establishment of professional organizations such as the American Institute of Architects and the American Medical Association attest to that—but reached a peak after 1900. In urban planning, the success of earlier collaborative efforts such as that at the World's Columbian Exposition or the one for the Chicago Plan did much to increase respect for this area of specialized skill. Three trends after 1908 demonstrated that planning had emerged as a distinctive professional activity: growth of professional organizations, proliferation of publications, and development of the first degree program in planning. Proceedings of the National Conference on City Planning, the earliest professional planning organization, established in 1909, were so important that the U.S. Senate published them as part of a document on city planning in the District of Columbia. As the professionalization of urban planning proceeded, the Conference came to be considered too general a forum for those actually working in the field, and the American City Planning Institute (now the American Institute of Planners) was formed in 1917. Later, in 1923, as planning began to look at geographical areas larger than cities, the Regional Planning Association of America was organized.

The literature of planning was broad, but a few significant works established the discipline and disseminated its accomplishments to the public. The first important North American book on scientific city planning was *City Planning* by Benjamin Marsh, published in 1909. Marsh's work, although it may seem very general today, was influential in underscoring the need for functional planning as being more critical to urban viability than then popular aesthetic approaches. He also called for zoning as the key tool to achieve health and safety in the city, citing his extensive study of European—particularly German—precedents in planning.[5] The period from 1909 to 1914 was a frenetic one in planning, and its achievements to that date were summarized in *Carrying Out the City Plan,* by attorney Flavel Shurtleff working with F. L. Olmsted. This publication, sponsored by the Russell Sage Foundation as a guide for local governmental and civic groups, reported legislation and reviewed court decisions on planning questions. *City Planning,* edited by John Nolen, with papers by leading planners, focused on philosophical issues then challenging the discipline. A plethora of planning reports from individual cities documented the practical planning experiments then in progress. Theodora Kimball aided landscape architects interested in planning by regularly reporting on recent planning reports and trends in *Landscape Architecture* magazine.

Planning became established as a formal academic discipline at approximately the same time that an extensive literature developed. The first college-level courses in urban planning were organized in the Landscape Architecture Department at Harvard by James Sturgis Pray in 1909. The following year Charles M. Robinson assumed the first chair in Civic Design at the University of Illinois. Later a chair in city planning, first occupied by Henry V. Hubbard, was instituted at Harvard, where in 1929 the first American department of planning was founded.

THE CITY PLANNING MOVEMENT

The underlying philosophy of city planning differed in several significant ways from that of the City Beautiful. "City planning" was considered to be the application of scientific methods to the survey and analysis of existing conditions and future prospects. Data gathered scientifically were then to serve as the basis of recommendations on physical arrangements and legal restrictions on development. Planning was to be systematic, practical, and rational. It was to go beyond mere physical planning—to be a form of systems organization in which standards, rather than idiosyncratic features, generated urban order and unity. What was beautiful was henceforth that which was efficient.

Emphasis on scientific methods, which in the case of planning meant statistical and natural features data, was a product of the period in which urban planning evolved. Development of the scientific method, technological successes which grew from it, and application of scientific methods to the study of social and environmental phenomena were all important factors in encouraging at least a nominally "scientific" approach. Systematic or scientific management of industrial work also gained popularity in the early 1900s as a way both to increase production and to build a more specialized work force. When Frederick Winslow Taylor published his influential book, *The Principles of Scientific Management,* in 1911, he outlined a methodology to survey and analyze industrial tasks that was very similar to, and certainly helped to codify, an evolving planning methodology.

The scientific approach to planning addressed three principal urban concerns: circulation and infrastructure development, distribution and treatment of public property, and control of development on private property. Of these only the last differed significantly from those concerns addressed by the City Beautiful Movement. Demand for control of private property signaled an important change in thinking about the rights of landowners versus public need, that in effect created the new planning era of the twentieth century. Typical "scientific" city plans dealt with the physical organization of a city's railroads, roads, street railways, waterborne transportation systems, sewer and water systems, electricity distribution, open spaces, location of industry and other land uses, and financial and legal strategies to reach objectives. Many elements of City Beautiful methods persisted in these plans, specifically emphasis on the importance of imposing focal civic centers and railroad stations as a vital gateway and imagemaker for any city.

After about 1920, the city planning movement developed two principal branches, with practitioners generally based in one but not so exclusively as to preclude interest and involvement in the other.[6] The two branches can be differentiated as physical planning and conceptual planning. Physical planners were those most closely tied to landscape architecture. They drew their inspiration for proper management of urbanization from the Garden City model of Ebenezer Howard. This model, although strongly based in the reformist social motivations of the late nineteenth century, could also be interpreted as a transformation of Romantic town planning to meet the needs of the lower middle class. With stress on adaptation to topography, site-specific planning, and provision of open spaces, such an approach was ideally suited to both the inclinations and skills of those, such as John and Frederick Law Olmsted, John Nolen, Catherine Bauer, Warren Manning, Arthur Shurcliff,[7] and George Ford, who had been trained in the design professions.

Conceptual planning emphasized management approaches to plan implementation; the study of minimum and maximum standards for sizes, areas, and densities; and the development of law. Although less directly linked to any single preceding discipline, it was an indirect offshoot of sanitary engineering, and relied heavily on emerging methodologies from the social sciences. Most of those whose work fell under this branch of planning—for example, Alfred Bettman, Harlean James, Harland Bartholomew, and Flavel Shurtleff—were trained in law, public administration, engineering, or real estate. It was the symbiotic relationship between these two groups that assured execution of physical plans within a protective regulatory structure, but without allowing standardization to suppress creative problem solving. Unfortunately, after 1940, as planning and design became somewhat estranged, this lesson in the value of collaboration was often overlooked.

THE NEW TOWNS OF "SCIENTIFIC" PLANNING

While the city planning movement did not completely abandon existing cities, its greatest emphasis and greatest successes were in the development of new towns, usually at the outer edge of an existing city. These new towns differed from the typical bungalow, gridiron suburbs then being developed in that their planners stressed what one writer called the "neighborhood concept" and others referred to as the "garden suburb" concept.[8] These towns were characterized by carefully developed, site-specific plans that included a mixture of land uses, typically residential, commercial, and institutional. Although often quite large, they were composed of smaller units, usually centered on a community facility such as a school or park. Developer-produced amenities were key features in these new towns. These typically included recreation complexes, plantings on streets or lots, and communal open spaces, which compensated for relatively high densities of land use elsewhere in the project. New towns on this model were generally developed in three ways: by commercial developers for the well-to-do; by philanthropic developers, usually foundations, for lower income families; and by industrialists for their employees.

Developer Suburbs

The most successful and famous of the developer suburbs was the Country Club District in Kansas City, Missouri.[9] Constructed by Jesse C. Nichols over more than forty years beginning in 1908, the district typified a suburban town based on sound planning principles, engendering a strong visual image, and creating through the interplay of these two elements real estate values in excess of mere land and location values.[10] The Country Club District was a community made up of almost forty different neighborhoods, each laid out according to a comprehensive plan that was protected through community design control. The earliest of these neighborhoods would today appear to have few special feaures, but Nichols learned as he developed, adding more controls and amenities, ranging from deed restrictions to sites for public buildings, in successive developments.

To make the district a complete community, the first large-scale auto-oriented shopping center on the continent—Country Club Plaza—was developed. The plaza occupied a twelve-block area within which almost half the land was set aside for auto use, either in roads, in on-street parking, or in garages. The design, though, did not slight pedestrians. Using Spanish-inspired design motifs, then in vogue, pedestrian spaces took on the aura of plazas, with fountains, plantings, seating areas, sculpture, and intricately detailed building facades. To-

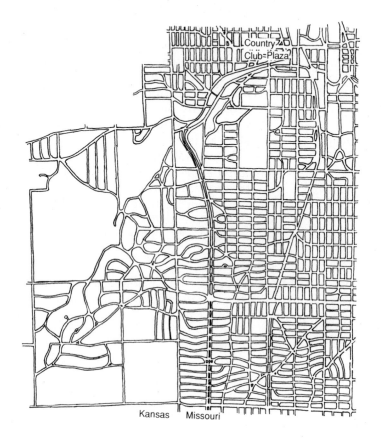

Plan of the Country Club District, Kansas City, circa 1940. (Data from Newton, 1971; drawn by Rossi.)

Kansas | Missouri

This view of a small fountain and seating area at Country Club Plaza, in the 1980s, is typical of the streetscape amenities which animate the shopping experience.

day it is these ornamental features—rather than the site plan, which appears as little more than a typical downtown—that seem most noteworthy.

Two landscape architects worked directly with Nichols to achieve this successful and visually innovative new suburb. George Kessler was employed on various projects from 1910 until his death in 1923. He worked first as a design consultant for the public spaces included in the master plan and later on the site plan for Country Club Plaza. He also indirectly influenced the district through planning of Kansas City's boulevards, three of which extended into the site. In 1913, Nichols employed the local firm headed by Sidney J. Hare to complete a comprehensive neighborhood plan. This began a more than thirty year working relationship during which Hare & Hare designed nine subdivisions, consulted on fifteen others within the district, and completed planning and design studies for the plaza. While Nichols considered the major source of inspiration for the Country Club District to have been Olmsted-designed Roland Park in Baltimore,[11] the District itself became a prototype for countless other high-quality subdivisions throughout the continent.

In Canada, English landscape architect Thomas Mawson designed Borden Park outside Ottawa for the Great Eastern Realty Company. Although following Beaux Arts design principles much like those underlying earlier City Beautiful schemes, this 1914 town plan incorporated quite farsighted land use controls that made it part of the new city planning movement. Infrastructure features were to be developed prior to land sales, with generous rights-of-way maintained. All houses were to have a common setback, thus allowing a large street space suitable for the size house to be built there. House designs had to be approved by a review committee and houses had to be sited in such a way that they would not block views to the Ottawa River. The plan also emphasized retention of community public spaces, particularly along the river shoreline, where existing vegetation was to be preserved. A modern amenity, a golf course around which homes would be clustered, rounded out the recreational opportunities for this elegant community.[12]

In the first decades of the twentieth century, the Sunbelt boom began, with California and Florida being especially favored for development. One of the most famous of the new towns founded to accommodate a growing flock of wealthy

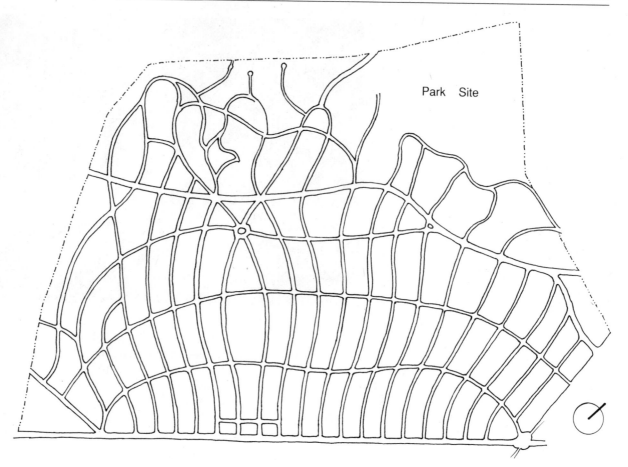

Park Site

Plan of Beverly Hills, California, by Cook, Hall, and Cornell, 1928. (Data from Cornell, 1933; drawn by Rossi.)

sunseekers was Beverly Hills, California, planned in 1909 by landscape architect Wilbur D. Cook, an alumnus of the Olmsted firm. The plan, sited on relatively flat land adjacent to the foothills, used a modified grid of subtly curving roads through most of the town, but as topography steepened varied this pattern with looped roads and cul de sacs. A sense of spaciousness was maintained by large lot sizes, immediate street tree plantings, and development of a water garden and several small scenic parks. Although not an exceptional design when compared to earlier and contemporaneous work in the East, Beverly Hills was the first large subdivision in the West with a plan based on principles of the city planning movement.

Developer suburbs sprang up everywhere that population and economy could support them. In Ohio, Shaker Heights became the most fashionable of Cleveland suburbs, with others such as Euclid Heights and Cleveland Heights being only slightly less popular. Brentwood Park in St. Louis, Missouri, designed by Henry Wright, housed the wealthy of that city on large lots. Broadacres in Houston transformed open coastal plain into a subtropical garden.[13] California had other suburbs such as St. Franciswood and Palos Verdes Estates, both by Olmsted Brothers, which were the equal of Beverly Hills. A Florida plan by the Olmsteds, for Coral Gables, featured neighborhoods, each with a different architectural theme ranging from Moorish to Oriental. That there was demand for these privately developed, highly designed, land-use-controlled, and expensive subdivisions was demonstrated by their almost universal success and their continued reputation into this decade.

Aerial view of the street layout and landform of Palos Verdes Estates in California by the Olmsted Brothers circa 1925. (Olmsted, 1927.)

Philanthropic Suburbs

A major tenet of the city planning movement was the need to extend the benefits of quality housing, particularly that of the garden suburb type, to all socioeconomic groups. Thus, it should not be surprising that a significant number of new towns were developed by reform-minded philanthropic organizations or public corporations for middle- and low-income families. Several factors differentiated these new towns from developer suburbs: first, density was always high to reduce costs; second, there was greater emphasis on variety of housing types to accommodate a wider range of income groups; and finally, innovative housing design, particularly interior space planning, was vital to accomplish the most in the smallest area.

The first new town of this type was Forest Hills Gardens on Long Island in New York. Begun in 1910 under sponsorship of the Russell Sage Foundation, it was intended to become a model of both socially responsible design and profitable low-cost housing. The Olmsted Brothers developed this site plan based on three principles: ample and direct major vehicular circulation ways, with most radiating from the commuter railroad depot; local streets that were domestic in scale, short, and indirect; and provision of a variety of public open spaces, ranging from the Village Green commercial center near Station Square to playlots on individual blocks. From the beginning, Forest Hills was to be a garden suburb, not city. Industrial and other large-scale commercial uses were specifically excluded in the extensive restrictions that the foundation established. The subdivision was given a "medieval" character by small, enclosed yard spaces and rusticated Tudor architecture, with towers and turrets silhouetted on the skyline. Architectural integrity was to be preserved through a review process supervised by Grosvenor Atterbury, the architect for most public buildings and many residences. The architect and landscape architect also paid great attention to visual details, in a sense compensating for space restrictions with richness of texture, pattern, and color.

The Forest Hills Gardens site plan allocated land for several house types, generally arranged with the highest density types nearest the station. At Station Square three- and four-story mixed-use structures included small apartments on

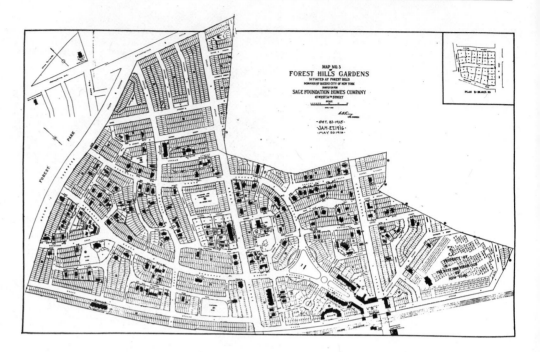

Plan of Forest Hills Gardens, New York, by Olmsted Brothers and Grosvenor Atterbury, 1916. (May, 1916.)

the upper floors, with shops occupying the ground floor and offices on the second. Beyond the Square were rows of two-story townhouses with staggered setbacks. Further from the station were groupings of attached single-family homes entered through a common front court. Traditional detached single-family homes on lots of less than an eighth of an acre completed the housing inventory. All of these housing types had only small yard spaces, with the scale of the rear yards being particularly restrictive by American standards. To compensate for this, the designers utilized novel space-saving devices, such as retractable clotheslines, and extensive planting schemes which relied on shrubs, vines, and groundcover to create the illusion of suburban gardens in courtyard-size spaces.

Although a great deal of attention was given to circulation in the Forest Hills Gardens site plan, it proved less successful than intended for two reasons—one visual, the other practical. With a mixture of curving and straight streets, the expected hierarchy was often less clear than anticipated. Shortness of blocks and the fact that many local streets, especially those in the single-family area to the north, were through streets rather than purely local tended to make circulation more dominant than it should have been for the scale of lots and buildings. The location of Forest Hills—it was a small subdivision in a large and expanding metropolitan area—exacerbated these problems. Major arterial streets, necessary to convenient regional circulation, divided the town into three zones, with the smallest, eastern area seemingly disconnected from the rest. With the growth of automobile transport later in the decade, this rather moderate problem became a major threat to spatial unity. Finally, the equally unanticipated growth of the West Side Tennis Club and its annual tournament generated local street traffic much heavier than planners could have anticipated. In spite of these shortcomings, Forest Hills Gardens became a popular place of residence, attracting a slightly more affluent group than intended. Today Forest Hills maintains its visual integrity, enclosed from the far denser surrounding housing by a railroad embankment to the south, which, in keeping with the area's medieval theme, protects it like a castle fortification.

Philanthropic Garden City-inspired housing schemes proliferated in the New

View of Station Square, Forest Hills Gardens, New York, from the railroad embankment circa 1915. (May, 1916.)

York City area into the 1920s, with the team of Clarence Stein and Henry Wright becoming specialists in this form of planning. Their first endeavor was the design of Sunnyside Gardens in Queens, begun in 1924, and meant to be a trial run for a full-scale Garden City to follow. Although modest in scale, only 55 acres, it went well beyond the Forest Hills Gardens model in being truly affordable, addressing the needs of the automobile age, and providing more usable outdoor spaces. As with Forest Hills, architectural design of the row houses which composed Sunnyside was critical. Architects Stein and Frederick Ackerman took pains to reduce costs through simplified construction, space-efficient design, and limited house frontage. Among innovations in arrangement of interior spaces was realignment of rooms so that service rooms, such as kitchen and bath, faced the street while family living spaces, such as bedrooms and living room, faced the quieter, more scenic internal garden courts. Had the preexisting grid street plat been vacated, an even more inventive site plan would surely have evolved. Despite the imposed restriction of fixed streets, Sunnyside's spatial arrangement proved successful enough that it was amplified and expanded in later projects, such as Chatham Village in Pittsburgh and Baldwin Hills Village in Los Angeles.[14]

Although much garden suburb design took place in the East, especially New York, there were garden suburbs in other locations as well. Construction of Mariemont, a new suburb on the outskirts of Cincinnati, Ohio, was begun in the same year as Sunnyside Gardens. In many ways Mariemont was a later, improved version of Forest Hills Gardens, which differed from that model in two notable aspects. First, it was designed as an automobile suburb, with local and through traffic clearly defined, but integrated within the town plan. Second, the plan included both residential and industrial uses, and in that way followed the Garden City concept more closely than did Forest Hills.

Financed by Mary Emery, a wealthy Cincinnati industrialist, Mariemont was a mixed philanthropic and real estate development. It was intended as a town of mixed socioeconomic groups, providing, in the words of its designer John

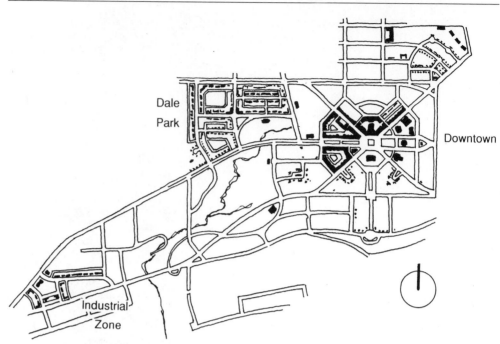

Plan of Mariemont, Ohio, by John Nolen circa 1925. (Data from Nolen, 1927a; drawn by Rossi.)

View of Dale Park shopping area in Mariemont, Ohio, in the 1980s. The small square in the foreground links the neighborhood commercial area with a park.

Nolen, "not merely the house for the family, but the whole of the family's social life—schools for the children, indoor and outdoor recreation for all, shops, entertainment and amusement" (Mariemont Company, 1925, p. 39). This goal—establishment of a self-sufficient residential suburb—was achieved, although the quality of design attracted more affluent residents than expected, thereby pricing lower-income families out of the development. Mariemont also failed to become a complete new town with living and workplaces in balance, because its industrial estate never did develop fully.

Mariemont was planned as a collection of small neighborhoods with their own parks and local shopping. In the first of these, Dale Park, the original design and planning concepts were more successfully adhered to than in some areas developed later. Dale Park housed residents primarily in row houses ("group houses," as Nolen and other planners liked to call them) of several types and price ranges, although the duplexes, apartments, and detached houses planned for other neighborhoods were present here as well. A small shopping area and community center near the center of the community served as neighborhood focal point. Community facilities were located to the north of a large open space, Dale Park. This park occupied about 20 percent of the entire neighborhood and had both naturalistic areas, in the stream valley which ran through its center, and a formal garden near the boulevard.

Mariemont has been considered Nolen's most successful plan because he integrated the rational planning standards which he considered essential to efficient housing with visual amenities important to creating comfortable and enjoyable environments. His plan also demonstrated that the automobile could be accommodated in a positive way—at Mariemont he made a focal point of the juncture of six main roads at the town's civic and commercial center, thus assuring its economic vitality.

Plan of the first built section of Radburn, New Jersey, by Clarence Stein and Henry Wright, circa 1929, illustrating the arrangement of garden and parking courts as well as the pedestrian circulation system. (Cautley, 1930.)

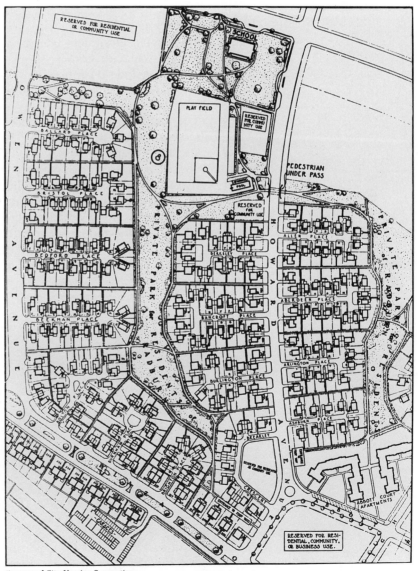

Courtesy of City Housing Corporation

A SECTION OF RADBURN

A completely different dream of the garden suburb than that developed at Forest Hills Gardens or Mariemont was Frank Lloyd Wright's Broadacre City. His concept combined technological innovations of the "machine age" with what he termed "democratic planning" and "organic" site design and architecture. His city was a dispersed suburb of large lots, with numerous internal open spaces and an encircling greenbelt. Although dispersed, civic, commercial, and recreational land uses were to be centrally positioned so that they were within ten to fifteen minutes of homes by auto. Broadacre City was completely oriented to the car: it was to be located adjacent to at least one major highway and to have a modern linear shopping center. Two significant innovations in Wright's proposal were his plans for what he called "quadruple housing," actually zero lot line or attached houses that met at one corner of each of four lots. This spatial efficiency in single-family lots was particularly important to Wright since he envisioned that each site would be used to produce food for the family or to be sold locally. Unfortunately Wright's garden suburb vision was too large in scale and radical in concept for its time, and was never implemented.

The culmination of early efforts toward developing the consummate scientifically planned new town was the design of Radburn, New Jersey, begun in 1928. Radburn was to have been the Garden City for which Sunnyside Gardens served as prototype. Designers Henry Wright and Clarence Stein planned it to be a complete town with homes, shops, workplaces, and community facilities, eventually to house 25,000 people. Radburn's housing was conceptually organized so that vehicular and pedestrian circulation were kept in exclusive zones—the superblock spatial concept. The essence of the concept was that neighborhoods composed of many large, solely residential blocks were separated from other neighborhoods only by arterial streets. From these streets projected short, local cul de sacs termed "parking courts," which served both the auto and household service needs. Row houses or duplexes backed up to these courts. The other side of the house faced a garden court, which was devoted to private frontyards, planted[15] to afford maximum privacy, and a linear public open space whose central feature was a walkway. Vehicles were completely excluded from this garden court, which was connected at one end to a much larger park—the spine around which the superblocks were arranged. Paths continued through the park, leading to community facilities, such as schools and shops. Where paths crossed arterial

Typical garden court in Radburn, New Jersey. (Anonymous, 1930b.)

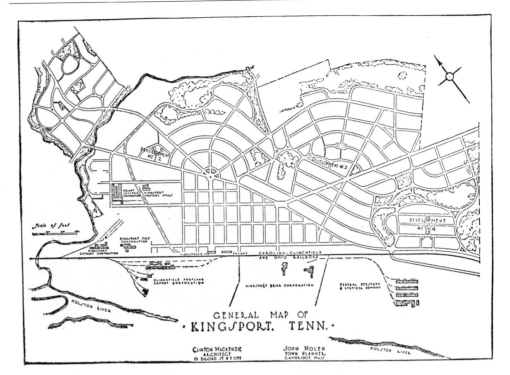

GENERAL MAP OF
·KINGSPORT. TENN.·

Plan of Kingsport, Tennessee, by John Nolen circa 1925. (Nolen, 1927a.)

streets, they became tunnels, so that pedestrians walked unhindered through underpasses. This system of superblocks with complete separation of walkers and drivers was termed the "Radburn idea."

The initial concept behind Radburn was quickly eroded, a victim of the financial realities of the period when its development began. The first idea to go was that of an industrial zone. As early as 1928, factories in the region were closing and Radburn's then rural location offered few advantages for industrial sites. This lack of nearby employment slowed initial purchases, so that at the time of the stock market crash in 1929 few superblocks had been established. In the end only one neighborhood unit was put in place. Unfortunately, Stein and Wright had not foreseen how residents would actually use Radburn. As it turned out, the garden courts were rarely used, except as circulation ways. Most active outdoor living, including play, took place in the parking courts. Although Radburn itself was not a financial success, it inspired a series of government-funded new towns during the Depression era, remained a site-planning ideal for several decades, and continues to influence contemporary residential planning.

Industrial Suburbs

The final form that garden suburbs took in the first half of the twentieth century was that of the industrial suburb developed by an employer to provide improved housing for workers.[16] While industrial suburbs did not have the design qualities of either the developer or philanthropic suburbs, they were clearly better planned than most worker housing—most workers were still living in tenements or crowded bungalows in jerry-built subdivisions, often lacking adequate infrastructure. The appearance of these suburbs varied widely, from the very typical grid plan of United States Steel's Gary, Indiana, to the romantically inspired subdivisions of the Akron, Ohio, rubber barons, Firestone Park and Goodyear Heights.

Kingsport, Tennessee, was unique among factory new towns in having been developed by a railroad to create business for its line, rather than by a single

*Downtown Longview,
Washington, by Hare and Hare
circa 1925.* (Hare, 1927.)

industrial company. Originally planned in 1906 following the very rigid grid
and radial street plans of developer George L. Carter, it was not until it was
redesigned by John Nolen in 1915 that the city was constructed in its present
form. Kingsport followed contemporary planning standards by providing an established infrastructure, a variety of open spaces, and a circulation hierarchy. As
with most of the industrial new towns, the plan was not particularly innovative
in terms of housing, providing primarily for small, but traditional, single-family
lots for detached homes. Nolen retained the rather formal arrangement of spaces
in the downtown, but altered residential areas to fit the undulating topography
more sensitively. In so doing, he maintained a clear use and image distinction
that contributed to the visual and functional integrity of the plan.

Downtown, although laid out prior to Nolen's involvement, was reorganized by him in a City Beautiful-like arrangement. At the south end of Broad
Street was the railroad depot, the only structure actually set across the sight line
of main street. At the opposite, north, end, a large, planted traffic circle provided
a focal point from which radiated five angled streets. Beyond this circle were
small public squares and wedge-shaped lots set aside for semipublic uses such as
churches. To the south of the circle, four large blocks, arranged around public
squares, were to be devoted to civic buildings. Lining Broad Street between this
civic center and the railroad station stood the commercial district.

Nolen's plan for Kingsport succeeded in achieving most goals. The town
quickly prospered, becoming home to many heavy industries drawn by the variety of resources available in the region. Commercial and residential areas developed as designed, with the most glaring omission being an incomplete civic
center.[17] Only the churches and city hall were built in planned locations. Public
squares and other public sites were later occupied by private development. Today
Kingsport continues as an industrial center, its principal problem being the industrial pollution trapped by its valley location.

Although most new industrial communities were built in the eastern part of
the continent to serve manufacturing interests, Longview, Washington, served
the extensive resource-processing industries of the northwest coast. Strategically

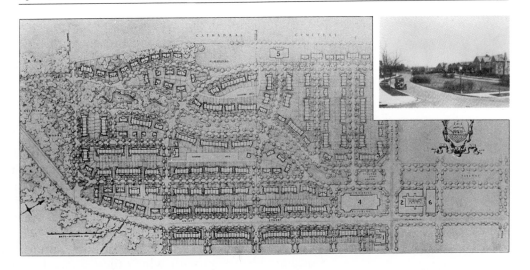

Plan of Union Park Gardens by John Nolen circa 1919. The inset view shows the parkway and adjacent houses. (Plan, Groben, 1919; View, Nolen, 1927a.)

placed at the confluence of the Cowlitz and Columbia Rivers, this town developed by the Long-Bell Lumber Company was not unique in design but was exceptional in its completeness and balance. It had a central business and civic center from which radiated the principal arterial streets. A 100-acre parkway, in places up to 800 feet wide, separated the town center from adjoining single-family residential areas and provided nearby recreational sites for residents. Mount Solo, which dominated the surrounding landscape view, became the site for a larger park. The Kansas City team of Kessler, the Hares, and Nichols were responsible for planning Longview, with the master plan of 1922 being the work of Hare & Hare.

Industrial new towns proved to be an important form of urban development in the early twentieth century. Many achieved the ideal of self-sufficiency and isolation from existing cities, something that most developers or philanthropic developments did not achieve. Industrial towns flourished throughout the continent. Some of the more successful ones were Chicopee, Georgia; Ojibway, Ontario; Indian Hill in Worcester, Massachusetts; Kistler, Pennsylvania; and Kohler, Wisconsin. These towns provided experience in practical planning for designers like Nolen, Warren Manning, George Atterbury, and Earle S. Draper that prepared them to make significant contributions to housing development during two periods of crisis—first World War I and later the Depression.

City Planning during World War I

Housing of emergency civilian and military workers during the First World War demonstrated that city planning was no longer merely an aesthetic concern of the well-to-do, but was an important aspect of healthy living. War housing was initiated by both the federal government and private corporations set up to assist military suppliers. As part of the federal effort, Frederick L. Olmsted established a planning division, designated town planners, and prepared plans for military camps (or "cantonments," as they were called) under the Quartermaster Corps of the U.S. Army. Among camps planned for the military were Camp Gordon, Georgia, by Charles D. Lay; Camp Sherman, Ohio, by Manning; and Camp Funston, Fort Riley, Kansas, by James S. Pray. The necessity of sound organization of these temporary cities was underscored by the fact that many were quite populous—Camp Funston, for example, when fully occupied was the second largest city in Kansas.

Equally important was adequate housing for industrial workers in support services, particularly ship and munitions manufacturing. Many new suburban subdivisions were built, primarily on the East Coast, to house this work force. At Wilmington, Delaware, Nolen planned Union Park Gardens as a garden suburb only a few minutes travel time from the shipyards that employed workers. Although small (only 58 acres) compared to most nonwartime subdivisions, Union Park was well planned, with tree-lined streets, adequate private yard space for its townhouses, and a park-boulevard corridor that connected to an adjacent city park. At Bridgeport, Connecticut, Arthur Shurcliff planned five different subdivisions to house munitions plant workers. Although similar to Union Park Gardens in density, they differed in having more varied outdoor spaces and housing types. Blocks were shorter and many units faced small common yards or crescent-shaped driveway courts rather than streets. Many other landscape architects and planners, including A. D. Taylor, Ferrucio Vitale, and Charles Lowrie, were employed by the U.S. Housing Authority to prepare plans for wartime housing. The speed with which these and other communities were constructed encouraged public belief that well-planned housing could be a universal reality for the industrial middle class.

Professionally planned housing developed during the first two decades of the city planning movement, whether by developers for well-to-do families, by philanthropic organizations as moderate-cost housing, or for industrial workers, shared the ideal that housing was to be more than mere shelter. Those who planned and developed this housing saw their task to be that of "community building"[18]—that is providing facilities that served public health, safety, and welfare, in addition to constructing buildings for people to live in. These groups assumed that housing would meet certain sanitary and density standards, but they went beyond that to provide residents with both tangible assets, such as parks and architectural unity, and intangible benefits, such as community identity. They viewed modern planning standards, both voluntary and enforced by law, as an aid in assuring persistence of quality—and therefore economic value—in subdivisions. In essence, community builders sponsored physical planning and design experiments that demonstrated the validity of planning concepts formulated by professionals.

Plan of Sunnyside Gardens, designed by Clarence Stein and Henry Wright, based upon the principles of Ebenezer Howard's Garden City. The Garden Court was actually a park for residents, with a pool, tennis court, playground, and garden areas. (Data from Stein, 1925; Drawn by Hodge.)

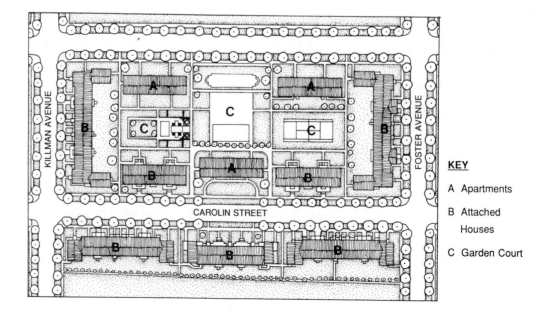

REGULATION TO CONTROL THE CITY SCIENTIFIC

One of the key lessons learned during the City Beautiful period was that even the most successful city plans could never assure an urban image consistent with the grandeur of planned city centers. The chief problem was that City Beautiful planning controlled land and structures in public ownership, but offered no incentive other than that of good example for improvement of private land. By 1910, the inadequacy of this approach and the problem of costly city plans undermined by shoddy private development encouraged cities to experiment with land use controls, principally zoning. After 1920, comprehensive planning became the principal basis and rationale for zoning and other land use regulations. At the same time, partially influenced by the elaborate designs of residential estates, imagery of the City Beautiful regained some popularity.[19] Later, in the 1930s, the urban decentralization favored by many planners began to be discredited. One of the earliest to reject unhampered suburbanization, Harland Bartholomew, contended "that decentralization, as now practiced, is economically unsound, more or less destructive in fundamental character and may ultimately produce social disadvantages as great as those found in the centralized city" (1932, p. 3).[20] Thus, the city planning movement returned its attention to the city.

The simple appeal of land use control through division of cities into zones, first developed in Europe, was hard for both planners and city officials to resist. Zoning was based on the belief that certain land uses were inherently unsuited for juxtaposition, especially with regard to public health and safety. Usually seen as being of benefit for housing, zoning served equally the need of commerce and industry to maintain compatible surrounding land uses. The first rudimentary zoning scheme was that developed in Los Angeles in 1909. In part motivated by a desire for racial segregation, this ordinance created distinct residential and industrial zones, with residential zones protected from some commercial service industries.[21]

The first comprehensive zoning ordinance was enacted in New York in 1916, under pressure from Fifth Avenue merchants who feared that the spread of garment industry workshops would destroy their fashionable district. This ordinance also responded to growing concern that vertical congestion from towering skyscrapers would reduce the streets of Manhattan to sunless, stagnant chasms. To assure some openness above street level, the ordinance set limits on building height and mass. An unintended result of these provisions was the distinctive "wedding cake" building silhouettes that were prominent in the city's skyline into the 1950s.

In 1917 Berkeley, California, passed a comprehensive ordinance with even more limiting provisions. It designated more than twenty-five different use zones, with different residential uses separated by density. From that point on, zoning became a standard tool for city government. In 1921, to facilitate zoning implementation at the local level, the U.S. Department of Commerce issued a Standard City Planning Enabling Act, authored by Alfred Bettman and F. L. Olmsted among others. By 1927, the National Conference on City Planning reported that more than 500 towns and cities had enacted some form of zoning.

In spite of the popularity of zoning among city governments, it was not universally accepted as a justifiable form of urban control. Until 1926, the legal basis for zoning legislation was tentative and constantly challenged by those unhappy with what they saw as an infringement of their property rights and those simply seeking to avoid what they considered an undesirable zoning designation for their property. The right of cities to control future development through zoning was finally assured in 1926, when the Supreme Court of the United States decided the famous case of *Euclid v. Ambler Reality*. In a cogently reasoned amici curiae brief to the court, Bettman debated not merely the case at hand but the entire conceptual and legal basis for zoning. A key component of this argument was that zoning must be areawide and based on a comprehensive plan.

"Comprehensive planning," that is, the scientific study and analysis of a community to establish goals for its future physical growth, was far more complicated an undertaking than merely cutting cities up into use zones. It required a thorough understanding of the relationship between natural systems and development, knowledge of efficient infrastructure layout, and the ability to predict the kind and amount of future growth. The first city to initiate comprehensive planning, through formation of a planning commission, was Hartford, Connecticut, in 1907. By 1910 the state of Massachusetts required a plan for all cities of 10,000 or more. These early events suggested that comprehensive planning would progress at a rate equal to legislated growth control, but this did not occur. By 1927, zoning had raced ahead of prior planning, so that only 25 percent of cities with zoning also had a comprehensive plan. This situation generally continued until after 1945, when courts began to insist on a plan as the only sound legal basis for zone designations.

In spite of the relatively small number of comprehensive plans, some quite important and influential ones were developed between 1910 and 1930. The earliest of these continued to have City Beautiful-inspired objectives, especially creation of elaborate civic centers, but concerns went well beyond creation of these public spaces. One of the most important of these early comprehensive plans was that by Warren Manning for Bangor, Maine. When a cataclysmic fire destroyed 55 acres in the heart of the city, Manning demonstrated that disaster could be turned to advantage through replanning. Recognizing that the automobile was about to transform cities, his report predicted future vehicle numbers and how that volume could be incorporated within a nineteenth-century city. Recommendations called for opening of new streets, including a tree-lined mall near the crowded market area.

In Canada, the most significant early city plan was that for the Federal district at Ottawa, by Edward Bennett in 1916. Inspired by the success of the McMillan Plan in Washington, D.C., Canada initiated a regional plan for its

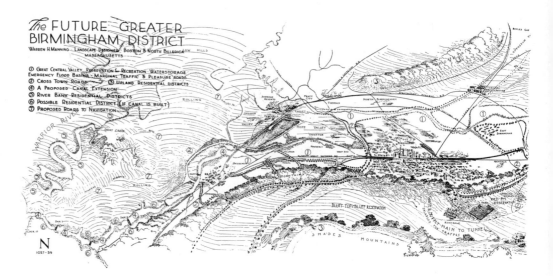

Schematic drawing of the regional plan for the Birmingham, Alabama, area by Warren Manning. (Manning, 1919.)

9) AN ANCIENT CASTLE AND RETAINERS' VILLAGE. REPRE-SENTING THE DOMINANCE AND PROTECTION OF FEUDAL DAYS

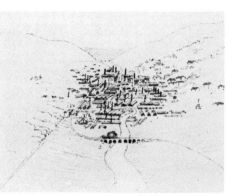

(10) THE DOMINANCE OF THE FACTORIES IN THE VALLEY HOMES ON THE HILLSIDE ABOVE

Typical illustrations assessing visual character, which accompanied Manning's Hudson-Mohawk River Plan. (Manning, 1917.)

capital, which included urban redevelopment to create grand ceremonial spaces near the government center, linkage of the city with Hull across the Ottawa River, and development of recreational areas including a National Park in the nearby Laurentian Hills. This plan, although superseded by later ones, began Ottawa's metamorphosis from town to city.

In 1919 Manning completed a plan for the Birmingham, Alabama, area that presaged later interest in regional planning. This plan was unique in embracing industry as a central theme, rather than as a use to be sequestered. Manning wrote, "Beauty is comparative. The beauty of women, or pictures, is one kind. There is a beauty in strength, and in usefulness.... The blue flame under the pot, the sparkling beauty as the slag is run out, and later the glowing hotness as the molten iron is run into the pigs, [molds] lighting up the gigantic furnaces and the steel frame buildings, is a beauty such as no artist can put on canvas" (1919, p. 14).

Comprehensive plans came to follow a fairly predictable pattern that involved mapping existing features; collecting statistical data; planning for circulation networks, parks, and civic center; and suggestions for zoning categories and district locations. The plans of Dallas, Texas (1910 and 1920), by Kessler; Sacramento, California (1916), by Nolen; Des Moines, Iowa (1920), by Bennett; and Wichita, Kansas (1923), by Bartholomew followed this approach. The plan of Cincinnati in 1925 by George B. Ford and Ernest Goodrich was a landmark for the depth of its research and the detail of its recommendations.[22]

REGIONAL PLANNING

By 1923 the dissatisfaction of planners with planning confined within the limits of city boundaries had become obvious. At the Fifteenth National Conference on City Planning, a number of papers dealt with the need for planning at the regional level. In the same year, Lewis Mumford, Clarence Stein, and environmentalist Benton MacKaye, among others, founded the Regional Planning Association of America. Members of this association believed that city planning had to be considered in the context of a balance between city and country, human and natural systems, and conservation and development.

The first plan with a truly regional focus was that for New York developed between 1921 and 1924 under the direction of five key planners: F. L. Olmsted, Nolen, Bennett, George B. Ford, and Bartholomew. This plan had many traditional features, such as designated open space systems, but also dealt with what was seen as New York City's greatest problem—residential congestion—by identifying potential sites for "garden suburb" new towns. Such a comprehensive approach was far ahead of its time, and was not implemented.

One of the most farsighted regional plans was Warren Manning's visual and physical plan for the Hudson and Mohawk River Corridor. Although nominally a proposal for a 500-mile scenic highway, the plan also included zones for other transportation systems, for public open spaces, and for a linear industrial area near the proposed highway. The most intriguing aspect of Manning's plan was discussion of the visual character of the river valley's landscape. In particular, the placement and design of buildings was considered in light of landscape scale, focal points, and symbolism. Manning's report was among the first, if not the first, to include visual assessment as a key factor in regional planning.

More radical approaches to regional planning sought to organize large areas, sometimes as defined by natural, and sometimes by political boundaries. In 1936 the Columbia Basin Report for Washington State examined the issue of resource planning for energy production in the Pacific Northwest. Wisconsin organized a State Regional Planning Committee in 1929 to coordinate local efforts and to assure that interregional issues were resolved. Regional planning as envisioned in the 1920s has yet to become truly comprehensive. It has been effectual, though, in dealing with two areas of concern: transportation and resource allocation. Regional transportation authorities were developed around many large cities, such as New York and Chicago. Resources—especially that essential and finite one, water—have been managed through regional agencies, such as the Colorado River Authority.

CONCLUSION AND SUMMARY

At the end of the nineteenth century a group of visionary designers demonstrated that urban design need not be a haphazard activity based on the whims or avarice of a few individuals. Rather, urban environments could be carefully planned, as one planned one's home or office. The visual and spatial approach adopted in that City Beautiful period failed, though, to address critical functional problems of urban living. Rather it metamorphosed into a new system of planning in which physical form and legal techniques were merged. Proponents of the city planning movement, focusing on congestion and poor housing as the greatest urban "sins," hoped to cure them by decentralizing population through development of lower-middle-class suburbs.

Ironically, in this effort the city planning movement returned to a mid-nineteenth-century residential form, the Romantic suburb, as reinterpreted in the Garden City concept, to create livable, uncongested new towns. What differed under the city planning approach was that the ideal of decentralized living in a town with complete social and recreational amenities was retooled to be affordable to a wider range of income groups. Thus, at the close of the third decade of the twentieth century, housing ideals formulated by the first professional landscape architects were finally embodied in a form that achieved the social goals which these men had advocated.

The period of the city planning movement brought a second generation of professional landscape architects into prominence. Among all those who worked in this period, three emerged as leaders—John Nolen, Frederick L. Olmsted, and Warren Manning Nolen directed his efforts almost exclusively toward planning, and he came to be considered the father of the movement. Olmsted focused on planning, especially regional planning, but through his firm continued to work at smaller, more visually oriented projects, such as the large estate designs then in vogue. Manning had the most diverse practice of the three. He engaged in city planning, regional planning, visual resource assessment, and small-scale design for projects varying in scale from estates to town squares. All three made significant contributions to the profession and to the environment through writing and public service. Through these activities they also moved the profession to the forefront of national consciousness, creating opportunities for those who would follow.

NOTES

1. From this point on in the text "Frederick Law Olmsted" will refer to the son, Frederick, Jr. (1870–1957). References to the father will designate him "Olmstead, Senior." Within the Olmsted family the son was called "Rick" to avoid confusion.

2. The relationship between street railways and popular forms of recreation is a particularly close one, as railway companies often developed amusement parks, dance halls, or other amusements at the terminus of their line, both as a way to increase weekend and holiday ridership, and thus to expose large numbers of urbanites to the ambiance of suburban life.

3. See Chapter 16 for a discussion of the impact of automobiles on design and planning.

4. See Chapter 14 for a discussion of the growth of this movement.

5. Marsh was in no way opposed to City Beautiful ideals or plans, but found some of them, particularly Burnham's Cleveland Group Plan, to deal insufficiently with hygiene and health concerns. He cited other plans, principally the work of Nolen, the Olmsted Brothers, and Robinson, in a more favorable light.

6. See DeBoer, 1943, for a satirical view of the family tree of planning.

7. In 1930 Arthur changed the spelling of his last name from Shurtleff to Schurcliff. To avoid confusion, Shurcliff will be used in the text, while in citations whichever spelling was originally used will be listed.

8. "Neighborhood" from Whitten, 1927; "garden suburb" from Unwin, 1911. "Garden suburbs" referred to towns which followed the Garden City scheme in many features, but could not be called cities either because of small size or lack of industrial workplaces.

9. Actually the district stretches over the state line into Kansas, but the original areas, including the Plaza, are in Missouri. See Figure 12-1 for location of state boundary.

10. The Country Club District was located away from the eastward development thrust of Kansas City when Nichols first purchased the land. Far from being a fashionable area, it was considered by many undesirable and unserviceable. Through the amenities which the Nichols Company added, such as site planning, a street railway, prior infrastructure development, and control of design, they created an unexpected demand for homes.

11. Roland Park was a new town, now part of Baltimore. Although usually credited to Frederick Law Olmsted, Sr., the project, which dated from 1891, was really the work of George Kessler. Later, in 1897, the Olmsted Firm was hired to design a second phase. See Schalck, 1970, for discussion of these credits. The quality of the site plan, which in many sections bears little relationship to topography, also supports this conclusion.

12. For other examples of early twentieth-century golf course subdivisions see Hubbard, 1927.

13. This Broadacres shares only a name with the suburban planning concept developed by Frank Lloyd Wright and discussed later in this chapter.

14. See Chapter 17 for discussion of Baldwin Hills Village.

15. Radburn's planting design was by Marjorie S. Cautley.

16. In spite of the labor unrest which had undone Pullman as a company town, it continued to be the model for a social and promotional ideal favored by many corporations. The industrial suburbs of the twentieth century were more numerous and generally larger than those of the nineteenth century.

17. Nolen's plan provided "separate but equal" planned housing for Afro-American workers in a geographically remote subdivision. Although it had smaller lots than most of Kingsport, it was to include sites for public neighborhood amenities. Unfortunately, in the atmosphere of the region at that time, neither this nor a later planned village was ever completely developed, forcing many black workers to live in less well planned, possibly substandard, housing. See Nolen, 1927a, for discussion of this subdivision.

18. Term used by Weiss, 1987.

19. Hegemann and Peet's (1922) monumental compilation of urban design, The American Vitruvius: An Architect's Handbook of Civic Art, was very influential in reasserting the relationship between design and well-organized urban spaces.

20. Further evidence that dispersed land uses were on the way out was the report "Planning for Residential Districts" issued in 1932 by the President's Conference on Home Building and Home Ownership. It called for implementation of what it termed "double" and "triple" lots—that is, rear lots whose only street frontage was the

space required for a driveway. These lots were essentially alley lots, which planners a mere twenty-five years earlier had deemed anathema to sound urban health.

21. Whether accurate or not, the purpose of this ordinance was often attributed to a desire to keep laundries run by Chinese out of Euroamerican neighborhoods.

22. A complete list of cities with either a comprehensive plan or a zoning ordinance up to 1927 can be found in an appendix to Nolen, 1927b.

24

The Revival of Classicism: Landscape Architecture in an Era of Conspicuous Consumption

It was a matter of chance that I should have rented a house in one of the strangest communities in North America. It was on that slender riotous island which extends itself due east of New York.... My house was at the very tip of ... the Sound, and squeezed between two huge places that rented for twelve or fifteen thousand a season. The one on my right was a colossal affair by any standard—it was a factual imitation of some Hotel de Ville in Normandy, with a tower on one side, spanking new under a thin beard of raw ivy, and a marble swimming pool, and more than forty acres of lawn and garden. It was Gatsby's mansion.

F. Scott Fitzgerald, The Great Gatsby, *1925*

Forces similar to those at work in revolutionizing city planning during the 1890s had equally dramatic effects on the design of smaller sites in the early twentieth century. These changes effectively ended the domination of Romantic design concepts and resurrected historically derived approaches that emphasized geometric spatial organization in the landscape. Coupled with this design transformation was the trend for landscape architects to concentrate on privately owned sites, especially residences, rather than public spaces such as the large landscape parks of the nineteenth century. These two trends, emphasis on residential work and return to formal design, were results of the Country Life Movement and the Neoclassicist Revival.

The Country Life Movement was an intellectual and applied movement founded by leaders in "rural" life issues, especially academic and extension professionals at land grant universities. Its philosophical purpose was to extol the virtues of rural living, which was seen as inherently superior to urban life. One country life proponent went so far as to write that the city was "the burial place of health, as well as youthful ambitions and hopes ..." (Fiske, 1913, p. xii). At an applied level the movement aimed to raise standards of rural social and economic life to that of the cities, as a means of halting emigration to urban areas. Cornell University horticulturist Liberty Hyde Bailey, the principal organizer of the movement, envisioned a romanticized agrarian culture in which people lived symbiotically with one another and with the natural world on which they depended. While the Country Life Movement produced some quite practical results, such as improved farmer education through extension courses and improved systems for economic self-determination, its principal impact was to glamorize rural living to the majority of Americans, then living in urban areas. By making rural life attractive it encouraged a return to the country for those who could afford large estates, or to suburbs for those with less wealth.

Bailey himself considered the Country Life Movement to be "sharply distinguished from the present popular back-to-the-land agitation. The latter is primarily a city or town impulse ..." (1911, p. 2). In spite of this idealistic view, the movement quickly came to be equated with the "gentleman farmer" image of middle- and upper-class country life. The popular periodical *Country Life in America* clearly expressed this sublimation of the movement's original purpose. It became a fashionable guide to such "country" activities as pheasant raising, show dog breeding, flower arranging, and design of estate grounds. What the agrarian movement shared with its middle-class usurper was the idealistic notion of human spiritual and physical purity in rural settings.

The interests of Bailey and his cohorts in rural living coincided with several other trends that also encouraged movement to the country. The large middle class, which had emerged during the late Victorian period as a dominant force in political and social life, favored rural environments because lower land costs there allowed purchase of large lots required for the type of home which could properly display one's social status. A final force in fostering country life—both for rural residents and urban expatriates—was the automobile. This new mode of transportation dramatically improved commuter travel and also allowed easy access to picturesque rural areas, such as the Berkshire and the Blue Ridge Mountains, thereby engendering a realistic rural experience for many Americans.

The Neoclassicist Revival was less a way of life than a change in design taste away from the stylized naturalism of Romanticism and toward the geometric formality of historic styles from classical times or the Renaissance. What forces altered American design preferences so drastically? Once again the influence of the World's Columbian Exposition, with its axiality and architectonic spaces, was foremost. In addition, growth of a wealthy class of industrialists, business-people, and professionals generated a market for large, architect-designed homes with spacious grounds. Architects, following the lead of France's Ecole des Beaux Arts, generally practiced a historic eclecticism which differed from Victorian eclecticism in that different styles were not combined in a single structure.[1] Historical allusion certainly suited the tastes of the well-to-do, whose homes conveyed their status as a "capitalist nobility." Beaux Arts-trained architects favored not only historicist architecture, but formal revival landscape designs as well. Such styles offered two advantages to them. First, axes and outdoor structures, such as pergolas and balustrades, extended the house by integrating interior and exterior spaces. Second, a design "system" relying on lines of sight and rectilinear forms made it possible to achieve acceptable results without clearly understanding outdoor spaces, plants, or landforms, thus allowing architects with no particular aptitude for landscape design to complete this part of the project along with the house.

Neoclassicist design was further fostered by growth in the number of North Americans traveling to Europe. Atlantic steamships and continental railroads made the Grand Tour available to an increasing number of people, who could see key sights in a short period of time. Anglophiles were, of course, drawn to Great Britain, where they viewed the great Tudor manors, but following the English fashion, most American tourists were drawn to Italy. There, recently excavated Roman sites and preserved villas of the Renaissance, many with gardens intact, were favorite destinations.

Interest in Italian design precedent was further encouraged in 1894 when the American School of Architecture, later the American Academy, opened in Rome. The Academy was conceived by its founder Charles F. McKim, of the architectural firm of McKim, Mead, and White, as an interdisciplinary study center for students and practitioners of the fine and applied arts. Initially open only to architects, the Academy recognized Landscape Architecture in 1915.[2] The Rome Prize, as the fellowship that the Academy granted came to be known, opened up opportunities for landscape architects to immerse themselves in the study of Italian villas, with early fellows producing the measured drawings which first documented these gardens. Among the distinguished landscape architects who have received this fellowship were Norman Newton, Ralph Griswold, and Alden Hopkins.

DEVELOPMENT OF THE PROFESSION

Other forms of professional development, beyond foreign study, were also underway in this period. Of critical importance were the founding of the American Society of Landscape Architects in 1899 and establishment of the first professional curriculum at Harvard in 1900.

The American Society of Landscape Architects, more commonly known by its acronym ASLA, was founded by a core group of eleven landscape architects, who practiced primarily on the East Coast. Samuel Parsons, the key organizer, convened the first ASLA meeting in the office which he shared with partner George Pentecost on January 4, 1899. Founding members were Nathan Barrett, Beatrix Farrand (then Jones), Daniel W. Langston, Charles Lowrie, Warren Manning, Frederick L. Olmsted, Jr., John Olmsted (who was voted first Society president), Parsons, Pentecost, Ossian Simonds, and Downing Vaux, the son of Calvert Vaux. The ASLA was intended from its inception to be a formal professional organization which provided technical information for members and established minimal standards of professional competency.

Harvard University was the first to develop a professional curriculum in landscape architecture.[3] Inaugurated in 1900, the program originally offered a bachelor's degree, but this was quickly changed to a master's. Frederick Law Olmsted, Jr., and Arthur Shurcliff served as original instructors, with Olmsted assuming the first endowed chair in Landscape Architecture in 1903. The scope of courses required was very similar to that of accredited programs today, including sciences and humanities in addition to technical courses in surveying, architecture, and design.[4] This curriculum aimed both at producing competent entry level professionals and at educating amateurs to be informed clients and civic leaders.

Other educational programs quickly followed Harvard's lead. In 1902 the University of Massachusetts became the first land grant college to include landscape architecture as a technical program. In 1904 Cornell established a comprehensive professional program, based in part on the individual curriculum which had been developed seven years earlier for Bryant Fleming, who became the program's first director. By 1920 six other programs were recognized: University of Illinois (1907), University of California, Berkeley (1913), Iowa State University (1914), Ohio State University (1915), University of Wisconsin (1915), and the Cambridge School (1916).[5] These early programs, usually housed in colleges of agriculture, continued to use the outdated nineteenth-century terms "landscape gardening" or "landscape design" to identify programs which, by and large, included the complete spectrum of professional landscape architectural skills and issues.

Less formalized educational activities helped to promote landscape architecture among its potential consumers. The Garden Club of America, founded in 1913, established education in both the horticultural and design aspects of landscape as one of its key goals. Individual garden clubs also directly improved professional education. One such effort, the Post Graduate Institute of Architecture and Landscape Architecture, was sponsored by the Lake Forest, Illinois, Garden Club. This program provided an intensive, interdisciplinary, advanced education for honor students from five midwestern universities working under the direction of a distinguished University of Illinois educator, Stanley White, during the late 1920s.

The Garden Club and its member clubs also educated the public by example. Throughout the country, clubs sponsored public design projects ranging in size from small traffic islands to parks. Many projects were organized in the form of competitions, thereby giving obscure designers opportunity to publicly demonstrate their abilities. Several clubs made restoration projects their special emphasis. The Garden Club of Virginia was best known for this type of community service. The Lawn at the University of Virginia with restoration plans by Alden Hopkins, and Kenmore Plantation by Charles F. Gillette were restorations organized and financed through the club.

While the Garden Club of America brought design information to well-to-do urban and suburban residents, extension services at land grant colleges communicated similar information to rural areas of the United States. The Extension Service was authorized in 1914, and worked to disseminate both basic and applied research which could be useful to rural citizens. Although all states introduced extension services for disciplines such as agriculture and home economics, landscape architects in extension work were and continue to be more limited in number. In the first decades of the Service, some landscape architects did make significant contributions both to their rural constituency and to the profession as a whole. In Illinois, for example, Wilhelm Miller promoted use of native plants and acquainted the public with the emerging regional design style known as the Prairie style.

Education can take many forms. Garden literature of the 1890s and early 1900s did much to promote rural, "villa" style living and classically derived design. Several early works contributed to the popularity of Neoclassicist design, of which the most important was certainly Charles Platt's 1894 record of his European travels, entitled *Italian Gardens*.[6] A magnificently illustrated work, its views and descriptions exemplified the design principles of the Columbian Exposition applied at residential scale. Platt's travels and monograph inspired both his own design work and a host of other design travelogues, most notably Edith Wharton's *Italian Villas and Their Gardens*. Nostalgia for garden experiences of the past was not limited to Italy. Histories of various areas, especially England, France, and Asia, became favorite "parlor-table" books. Marie L. Gothein's monumental compendium of garden history, first published in Germany as *Geschichte der Gartenkunst,* was by far the most comprehensive and scholarly work on garden history written during this period. All of these works, well illustrated with photographs, became the pattern books for a new design age.

Another type of literature also began to emerge—the professional "text." Although related to nineteenth-century publications on landscape architectural issues, such as those of Copeland, Cleveland, and Olmsted, this literature was more explicit in detail without being "how-to" literature for the masses. It attempted to integrate aesthetic and functional aspects of design, planning, and construction in such a way as to create a theory or philosophy of the discipline. While many books vie for being the first of this type, Frank Waugh's *Landscape Gardening* probably should be considered the prototype for many later works. The masterpiece of this genre, though, is certainly Hubbard and Kimball's *An Introduction to the Study of Landscape Design,* a work which has much to offer the modern reader on both design theory and small-site design. Other influential books of this period included Thomas Mawson's *Art and Craft of Garden Making,* Marjorie Seawell Cautley's *Garden Design: The Principles of Abstract Design as Applied to Landscape Composition,* and Florence Robinson's *Planting Design.*

A very different sort of publication than either the historical works or the texts was the popular photographic book illustrating great estates of the world or of North America. The earliest, such as Barr Ferrée's *American Estates and Gardens,* emphasized architecture, with supplementary material on gardens and site planning. Later, in the 1920s, the ASLA realized the value of such books as promotional devices and published a series of annual *Illustrations of Work of the Members,* which highlighted outstanding and innovative projects from recent years. While these books were certainly intended to advertise professional design services, they also became pattern books which influenced designs by other landscape architects, contractors, and homeowners.

EARLY NEOCLASSICIST ESTATES

The Neoclassicist approach to design as practiced in the first part of the twentieth century was variously described as "formal," "architectural," "geometric," or "Italian." Formality derived from axial arrangement of sight lines; the architectural quality from use of structured outdoor spaces, similar to those of interiors, and the inclusion of many built features, like balustrades and gazebos; the geometric from its reliance on rectilinear forms; and the Italian from its use of Renaissance Italian garden characteristics, such as terracing and columnar plants.

Frank Waugh (1927) identified six key features to be used in composing formal, Neoclassicist gardens. First, they were to have definite proportions of width to length, with his recommendations being a proportion of 7 or 8 to 5. Second, the garden was to be on different levels, with changes in grade taken up through terracing, rather than through free-flowing landforms. Third, the structure of the garden was to be based on alignment of the major axis. Next, and related to the previous requirement, there had to be at least one minor axis set at right angles to the major axis. Fifth, these axes, major and minor, were to be visually reinforced through other garden elements such as paving, walls, and planting. Finally, each axis had to have a terminus, whether a piece of art, a specimen tree, or an overlook to a lower or distant landscape. As we will see in the examples to be discussed, these features were present in some form in virtually every garden designed during the Neoclassicist period.

Norman Newton termed the Neoclassicist period the Country Place Era because of the dominance of large estate work in design practice. Hubert Owens, longtime head of the landscape architecture program at the University of Georgia, estimated that between 1900 and 1930 at least 90 percent of all landscape architectural projects were residences at various scales, with many large enough to be termed "estates" by American standards. This estate work of the early 1900s generally fell into one of three types: (1) early attempts at adding some architectonic garden spaces within a generally Romantic site plan; (2) eclectic sites with a variety of small gardens in different historical styles all linked by tenuous sight lines; and (3) completely Neoclassicist arrangements inspired by the best European examples and having great unity of plan and view.

An example of the early type of Neoclassicist site was the grounds of the Sloan House in Rochester, New York, with site plan and design by Olmsted Brothers.[7] When work on this plan began in 1905 as part of a larger land subdivision project, the grounds of the Sloan house were dominated by a broad, deep frontyard with a simple Romantic-style lawn framed by several large trees. At the house itself a more formal arrangement began to take shape, with a wide front terrace linking the grounds and structure. To the west and north, small gardens with geometric plans were sited. The one to the west adjacent to the living room was a hedge-enclosed floral court with beds defined by simple axial cross-walks. This garden was completely self-contained, with no direct visual relationship to the house or to other small gardens on the site. In the rear, at the end of a long sight-line path which began at the back door, was the Sundial Garden, with a more elaborate axial arrangement. This garden was an isolated

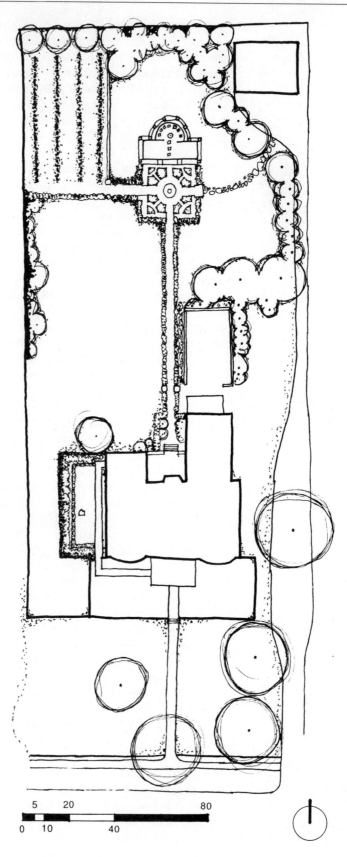

Plan of the Sloan Garden, Rochester, New York, by Olmsted Brothers (possibly with Claude Bragdon). (Data from Olmsted plan; drawn by Rossi.)

area set in an expanse of lawn. While not particularly effective by comparison to later work of the Olmsted firm, this garden was typical of those early projects through which designers began to explore the potential of Neoclassicist spatial organization and forms.

Sonnenberg Gardens in Canandaigua, New York, designed by Ernest Bowditch's firm under the direction of John Handrahan, beginning in 1902, was one of the most complete and complex of the eclectic Neoclassicist gardens.[8] Although it is views of the classically derived portions of the design that are usually seen in photographs, most of the site plan and design was Romantic in inspiration. This was most evident when looking from the entry drive, which edged an open vista known as South Lawn. Irregular tree masses framed the lawn, creating an informal line of sight from the drive across a small reflecting pond to the main facade of the house. Within this Romantic site plan a collection of eclectic gardens with Romantic, Late Victorian, Neoclassicist, and Japanese-inspired motifs was arranged around three sides of the house and linked with others by curvilinear paths.

On a direct sight line from the house were the elaborate floral fleur-de-lis parterres of the sunken Italian Garden, inspired as much by Victorian carpet bedding as by any Italian villa; a pergola linked this space with the adjoining Rose Garden. Tucked up against the house at one end of the Italian Garden was the tiny Blue and White Garden, designed as an intimate, screened sitting area. Of all the eclectic gardens on the estate it is only these three, the Italian, Rose, and Blue and White Gardens, that had any clear spatial relationship to the house or to each other, thus making this the most successful portion of the grounds.

Other theme gardens at Sonnenberg included the Rock Garden, a picturesque composition of water and puddingstone arranged to provide a variety of zones for naturalistic plantings of wildflowers and shrubs. There were two additional major garden areas, the Colonial Garden and the Japanese Garden. The Colonial Garden was a large-scale version of box-edged annual and perennial gardens. To achieve authenticity in the Japanese Garden, Sonnenberg's owner, Mary Thompson, employed a Japanese designer, K. Wadamore, both to design and to oversee construction. In spite of the spatial disunity of the estate as a

Japanese Garden at Sonnenberg Gardens, Canandaigua, New York, in the 1980s.

whole, these eclectic theme gardens are in themselves quite interesting and coherent.

The entire body of landscape architectural work by Charles Platt embodied the final type of early neoclassicist garden, characterized by clarity of concept and spatial integration. Platt's diverse art and design interests, including etching, painting, and architecture, gave him the experience to recognize the importance of site unity. As Royal Cortissoz wrote in his "Introduction" to a monograph on Platt's work, "His houses, which begin by fitting their sites, have invariably a quiet and distinguished way of looking as though he conceived them with the invention that goes to the making of a good picture or statue. Each has a personality, which is the more beguiling and stays the more delightfully in the mind because it discloses no single salient feature but is 'all of a piece' " (1913, p. VII).

Two Platt site designs with distinguished and distinctive personalities were Faulkner Farm, the estate of Charles F. Sprague, and Weld, the Larz Anderson estate, both in Brookline, Massachusetts. The plan for Faulkner Farm has been compared to that of Villa Gamberaia in Italy, the key similarity being a long, narrow, enclosed streetlike space set parallel to the slope. At Villa Gamberaia the turf panel is a symbolic "street"; at Faulkner Farm this space served as a literal street—an entry drive, with large parking court midway down its length. At both estates this linear space separated upper and lower gardens which differed in character. The heavily wooded upper garden at Faulkner Farm had promenade walks and an ironwork gazebo, called the Belvedere because it overlooked most of the estate, as principal designed features. The lower areas, screened by retaining walls from driveway views, were a formal flower garden and a turf terrace. A pergola-flanked pavilion with arched openings enclosed the formal garden at its far end. Gumdrop-shaped clipped bay trees near the pavilion repeated the form of the arches and extended the architectural theme into the garden. The turf terrace, arranged in rectangular panels, formed a transition between the house, its formal grounds, and the rural landscape beyond.

Architect Aymar Embury considered Weld "the most perfect garden in the world" (1909, p. 243). It certainly embodied an exquisitely simple but refined concept of the garden as a sequence of different visual experiences linked by

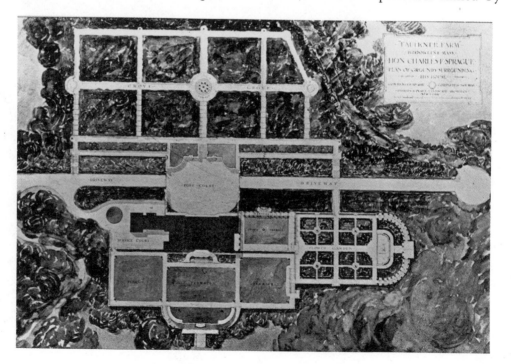

Plan of Faulkner Farm, Brookline, Massachusetts, by Charles Platt, 1897. (Baker, 1906.)

The formal garden at Faulkner Farm, as seen from the casino, circa 1905. (Baker, 1906).

equally interesting transition spaces. Weld has three principal parts: a turf panel, known as the Bowling Green, immediately adjoining the house; a wooded area which defined the Green, as woodland defined open garden in French Renaissance designs; and the formal garden, with a central panel of turf and side planting beds for flowers. As at Faulkner Farm, the view through this portion of the garden terminated at a gazebo.

Both Faulkner Farm and Weld were sites at which Platt added gardens to extant houses. When he was given the opportunity to site and design both structure and gardens, the resulting arrangements were often far more adventurous, using Italian details but creating uniquely place-specific plans. The design of the Mather estate, Gwinn, on the shore of Lake Erie near Cleveland was famous for its curving retaining walls, which protected a small harbor below the house. At Villa Turicum, the McCormick estate in Lake Forest, Illinois, Platt departed radically from his typical tripartite arrangement of woods, turf panel, and formal garden. Built on a bluff above Lake Michigan, the entire composition was fitted to a topographic prominence defined by the lakeshore and a stream ravine, with the house set at the highest point. The entry experience via a large forecourt defined by woods was kept purposely simple to heighten the drama of lake views, which were experienced on passing through the house. At lakeside a sheltered terrace overlooked the steep hillside. Access from terrace to shore was down an elaborate staircase and landing system, seemingly inspired by that at Villa Farnese at Caprarola. Formal gardens were limited to areas of secondary visual importance and screened from the entry and rear terrace by dense natural cover.

It should not be surprising that the work of the individual credited with fostering Neoclassicist design concepts in residential design was also the most accomplished of its period. Platt traveled to Italy with an open mind and all-seeing eye. He absorbed both the detail and spirit of truly great Renaissance landscapes, brought these back to North America, and in the best Renaissance spirit adapted them to specific local conditions.

Formal garden of the Garden of Weld, Brookline, Massachusetts, by Charles Platt circa 1905. (Baker, 1906.)

View of a portion of the lakeside water chain at Villa Turicum, Lake Forest, Illinois, by Charles Platt circa 1925. (Smith, 1930.)

LATER ESTATES

After 1910, design work at large residences generally became more sophisticated, but also more uniform. Years of experience amassed by individual designers, combined with publication of distinguished projects such as those of Platt, contributed to this refinement. Client demand contributed to the sameness, for as Hubbard and Kimball noted, "In the great majority of designs for private places which the landscape architect makes, in our time and country, the owners are not very widely different one from another in their ways of living and in their more important requirements in use and enjoyment for living on their land" (1917, p. 248). Certainly one form of "enjoyment" for the owners of such large properties was the display of wealth and taste, which professionally designed grounds demonstrated.

In the large body of work in this genre executed during the two decades from 1910 to 1930, that of several landscape architects was particularly important. The Olmsted firm probably completed more estate designs than any other, with work located in most states. As might be expected after reading Hubbard and Kimball's statement, much of this work was undistinguished, and some has even been described as quite mediocre. Two successful estates by the firm, though, are Krisheim in the Chestnut Hill neighborhood of Philadelphia and Beacon Hill House in the fashionable resort town of Newport, Rhode Island.[9]

At Krisheim, a formal terrace and gardens were used as a foreground to direct views toward the natural woodlands which surrounded the house and extended beyond the actual site into a public park. With adaptation to topography as its central feature, the garden began at a terrace next to the house and then extended west toward a rock retaining wall. Parallel to both the wall and the terrace, a narrow pool could most effectively be viewed from above. The formal garden below this pool was a simple composition of rectangular flower and turf beds centered on a smaller pool, with columnar evergreens defining the space around the pool and crabapples arching over brick pathways. Below this garden a walled grass panel, the Bowling Green, served as an open space transition to the wooded areas beyond, noted for their springtime dogwood displays. At Krisheim, Neoclassicist spaces were incorporated into a site which was otherwise designed in a naturalistic way. Unlike many of the earlier estates which combined the two approaches, here neither is compromised. Each part of the garden appeared perfectly suited to both its natural and created setting, because transitions were subtly and logically handled by sight-line linkage and repetition of visual themes.

Beacon Hill House was a quite different design for a quite different natural setting—a windy site with dramatic outcroppings of granite. As at Krisheim two rectangular pools, here linked by runnels, were the principal features of the main garden. Elaborately planted beds of annuals and perennials, bordered with lanes of grass, surrounded these pools. To shelter this formal garden from more naturalistic areas of the estate and protect from gusty winds, a wooden, gridded trellis enclosed it. At one end of the trellis a simple pergola shaded an elevated sitting area and enframed a bold granite outcropping, thus linking the formal garden with the naturalistic landscape between it and the hilltop house.

As well known as the Olmsted partnership was Warren Manning, who had left that office to start his own practice in 1896. Although Manning's personal

View of the garden looking toward the house, Beacon Hill House, Newport, Rhode Island, by Olmsted Brothers, circa 1917. (Boyd, 1918.)

concerns inclined more toward urban and regional planning issues, his firm name was tied to some of the more elegant estates of this period. Stan Hywet Hall in Akron, Ohio, recently restored, is certainly one for which he should justly be famous. This 70-acre estate,[10] part of which was formerly a sandstone quarry, sat at the edge of an escarpment created when the Wisconsin glaciation retreated to the present shoreline of Lake Erie. The site design took advantage of both the natural and human-made landforms: a walk lined with paper birch trees, and terminating at paired pavilions, defined the sight line to the escarpment and lake overlook, while an interconnected series of Japanese-inspired lagoons turned the lower, mined areas of the site into a woodland fantasy. Closer to the rambling Tudor-style house were formal terraces and intimate gardens, such as the walled English Garden and the Japanese Garden. In contrast to these intricate and small-scale spaces near the house was the open lawn, called the Great Meadow, which was encircled by the entry drive. The dissimilarity between the openness of this area and the intimacy of the formal gardens was one of the most dramatic designed contrasts at Stan Hywet.

Manning, son of a nursery professional and himself trained as a plantsperson, emphasized the use of native plants in estate work. At Stan Hywet he planted spring-flowering redbuds to add bright color to the neutral blacks and greys of the naturalistic lagoon woodlands, and hawthorns for their winter berry color. For the trees that lined the Great Meadow, he chose stately American chestnuts and American elms, most now lost to disease, and incorporated part of an existing apple orchard into the ornamental landscape by directing the entry drive through it. But Manning's most complete use of native plants was at "Dolobran," the Griscom residence near Philadelphia. Here not only woody natives, such as dogwood and mountain laurel, were preserved and planted, but less frequently used wildflowers, like boneset and trillium, ornamented the ground plane.

View of the Birch Walk at Stan Hywet, Akron, Ohio, by Warren Manning as restored in the 1980s.

Evergreen Garden of the Bullock Estate, Oyster Bay, New York, by Warren Manning circa 1925. (Boston Society of Landscape Architects [1935?])

Manning's personal preference for naturalistic landscapes was clear at other estates where Neoclassicist alignments and forms were integrated into an otherwise naturalistic woodland. Both the Bullock Estate in Oyster Bay, New York, and the Lambert Estate near St. Louis, Missouri, combined typically Neoclassicist features, such as direct lines of sight and classical elements like sculpture or water cascades, with plantings which were distinctive for this period in relying on preserved forests rather than elaborate flower beds or clipped woody plants.

A landscape architect equally well known for designing with native plants was Beatrix Jones Farrand. Out of personal preference and necessity, most of her professional work was residential. Farrand worked closely with her clients, often spending a week or more visiting a site, then developing alternative site plans or design features for their consideration. This attention to the unique qualities of a site and to perfection of detail was the most distinctive aspect of Farrand's work, the best-known example of which is Dumbarton Oaks in the Georgetown section of Washington, D.C. Now a research center and library operated by Harvard University, Dumbarton Oaks, originally built in the early nineteenth century, was acquired by Robert and Mildred Bliss in 1920.[11] Farrand spent the following thirty years working closely with Mrs. Bliss to produce what is often considered the best American Neoclassicist garden.

More than most estates of this period, Dumbarton Oaks was a collection of varied garden rooms arranged along sight-line paths. The most successful areas were those related directly to the landform: the North Vista and the descending series of small gardens to the east of the house. The North Vista progressed very gradually down a series of four turf-surfaced terraces which stepped along a ridge above picturesque Rock Creek. The terrace nearest the house was partially enclosed by building wings, including the Music Room added to the structure in consultation with Farrand. The three lower terraces, although appearing to be regular rectangular shapes were not: their sides converged slightly toward the horizon so as to accentuate the vista's apparent depth. Plants were chosen to further distort perspective. Those that framed the view, for example, the paired cedar of Lebanon (now replaced with deodar cedar) at the top of the second terrace, were of fine texture so as to appear more distant. The vista which these

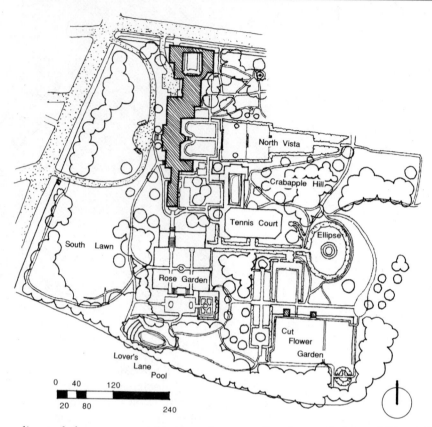

Plan of Dumbarton Oaks, Washington, D.C., by Beatrix Farrand as completed circa 1940. (Data from Masson, 1968; drawn by Rossi.)

terraces directed the eye toward was native woodland on adjoining hills. A linear clearing called "the tunnel" was cut through these trees in the French manner to visually link the terraces with the woods, once part of the estate but now a public park.

Gardens to the east of the house were critical to Farrand's goal of fitting her design to existing topography while preserving existing old oaks and beeches. Here she created a sequence of six intimate gardens of different character, each at a slightly different elevation. Adjoining the Orangery (greenhouse), the easternmost portion of the house, a small grassed terrace enclosed by a low wall of open arch-shaped brickwork preserved a magnificent beech and its dense system of dendritic surface roots. Tucked immediately below this level was the Urn Terrace, originally a simple garden of box hedges and grass. From there, one could look down on the beds of the Rose Garden with its summer display of color. At the east end of the Rose Garden an overlook and split steps led to Fountain Terrace, with its two French lead fountains of cherubs holding dolphins that spewed water into stone basins. To the north a fifth terrace, the Arbor Terrace, emphasized a cross-axis which linked the formal east side terraces with working gardens to the north. For those seeking more seclusion than these open, formal terraces provided, two meandering paths led from the Fountain Terrace to Lover's Lane Pool. This oval, brick-lined pool sat in a natural depression around which seating for an open-air theater had been built into the hillside.

In Farrand's original scheme, areas northeast of the house, located on slopes running diagonal rather than perpendicular to it, did not have formal gardens, but served recreational uses—a swimming pool and tennis courts were sited there. While the swimming pool has remained, the courts were converted to a shallow ornamental pool with an ornate pebble mosaic floor. Alteration in use made the Pebble Garden visually part of the formal gardens, but not part of the spatial sequence intended by Farrand. This is especially critical since neither the pool

Looking toward the house along the eastern sight line from the Rose Terrace, Dumbarton Oaks in the 1980s.

Lover's Lane Pool, Dumbarton Oaks.

nor the former tennis court areas worked as well with the topography as did other areas of the estate. By making one of these features part of the "garden experience," unintended emphasis has been placed on this lack of fit to the site.

Although it is the formal gardens to the north and east of the house that are most often pictured when discussing Dumbarton Oaks, the south garden, which faced the house facade, was in fact one of the most impressive compositions at the site. As was the pattern of other Neoclassicist estates such as Sonnenberg and Stan Hywet, this entry area was naturalistic, with a broad lawn framed by large trees, some dating to the original nineteenth-century estate, arranged in irregular groupings. Farrand planned both the spatial arrangement and planting design to create an impressive setting for the house when seen from R Street:

The east lawn is an important part of the design of the south front of Dumbarton Oaks as it is the one large open space, and it should always be kept open for the future. Otherwise there will be no contrast between the wooded or planted parts of the property and the broad sweep of green turf. . . . The planting on the south side of the house has been chosen from material with foliage of small scale in order to give apparent size and importance to the building. . . . As a general principle, approximately one-third of the spring line of the building should be unplanted, as the effect is unfortunate where a building seems to be totally submerged beneath a line of plants which muffle the architectural lines. . . ." (Farrand, quoted in McGuire, 1980, p. 3).

Dumbarton Oaks is one of the few great gardens for which we know much about design intent and details of planting design. In addition to the wealth of drawings preserved at the Garden Library, Farrand wrote a design essay to serve as a maintenance and restoration guide at the time the site was given to Harvard. This book both outlined general principles of composition and listed specific plant species planned for various locations. It was at once a guidebook and a planting design text, illustrating Farrand's love of native vegetation, seasonal color, and the structural qualities of plants.

While Farrand's chief interests in the garden were adaptation to topography and planting design, her client, Mildred Bliss, was interested in architectural detail. She "wished to incorporate into the garden a wealth of ornament executed in a variety of media to illustrate the wide range of decorative architectural detail and ornament available to the gardener" (Bliss, 1960, p. 22). Thus the garden was decked with a variety of decorative features: finials in the shape of pineapples, baskets of fruit, and urns; sculpture both ancient and modern; benches; gazebos; ornamental gates of wood, gilt wrought iron, and split bamboo; and fountains, from the simple jet originally used in the Ellipse to the more elaborate Provençal fountain later moved there.

Farrand considered Dumbarton Oaks her greatest work—the one that was "most deeply felt and the best of fifty years' practice" (Masson, 1968, p. 6). Two other residential projects, though less famous, are an equally significant part of her achievement. These are the Abby Aldrich Rockefeller Garden in Seal Harbor, Maine, and Farrand's own family estate, Reef Point, at Bar Harbor, Maine.

The design process for the Abby Aldrich Rockefeller garden was similar to that for Dumbarton Oaks, but it produced very different visual results. Begun in 1926, most of the structure of the garden was complete within three years, but some portions of the planting design evolved almost annually into the 1940s. The Rockefeller Garden is actually two parallel, but unique, landscapes, linked by only the most subtle of connections: a single cross-axial path. In one part of the garden, the Guardian or Spirit Path, Oriental features and design philosophy were employed to create a shaded woodland path where paired Korean tomb figures watched over visitors. A glimpse of the second garden came halfway down the Guardian Path, when the cross-path revealed a sunken, walled annual and perennial garden to the east. This space was Neoclassicist in spatial arrangement and planting design, but continued the Oriental theme in garden features, particularly the circular Moon Gate set into the north wall.

While Farrand certainly considered all of these designs experiments to be refined over time, it was her own summer home, Reef Point, that really served as her horticulture and design laboratory.[12] Located on a rocky stretch of coast, the principal parts of the garden were on a steep slope between house and water. Irregularly spaced paths created informal sight lines downhill from the house terrace and separated the garden into beds for different plant groupings. Areas of distinct visual character and ecological significance were included to illustrate that gardens need not merely be places to grow annuals and perennials. For

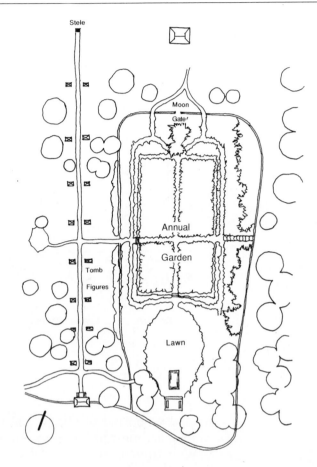

Plan of the Eyre Garden of the Abby Aldrich Rockefeller estate, Seal Harbor, Maine, by Beatrix Farrand. Work on the Rockefeller garden began in 1926. (Data from University of California, Berkeley, Department of Landscape Architecture, Documents Collection; drawn by Rossi.)

example, a low, wet area became a Bog Garden, while the shore was lined with white spruce and massed shrubs to create a windbreak. Reef Point, among the most informally composed of Farrand's designs, surely reflected her personal taste for naturalistic designs using plants as the focal point.

Emphasis on residential projects during the Neoclassicist period opened up professional opportunities in landscape architecture not previously available to women.[13] Two talented designers who took advantage of this opportunity were Ellen Shipman and Marian Coffin. Shipman was self-trained in landscape architecture, having had an informal apprenticeship under Charles Platt. Later, working through her own firm, she continued to consult with him on plantings for homes which he designed. Shipman's professional emphasis on residential work reflected a personal belief in its importance as a fine art. She once commented, "Until women took up landscaping, gardening in this country was at its lowest ebb. The renaissance of the art was due largely to the fact that women, instead of working over their boards, used plants as if they were painting pictures, and as a artist would."[14] Although Shipman's plans were quite formal, she followed no single historical pattern. A typical residential project, the Campbell residence in East Aurora, New York, linked the house with outlying recreation areas, accentuated the landform, and provided a series of formal gardens with planting beds for spectacular color arrangements. Construction drawings for this site, including an electrical plan and entry road layout, demonstrate that although Shipman may have viewed landscape architecture as a fine art, she was fully aware of the technical requirements necessary to create that art.

Marian Coffin's professional attention was equally focused on residential projects. Hers were noted for dramatic contrasts in color, inclusion of wildflow-

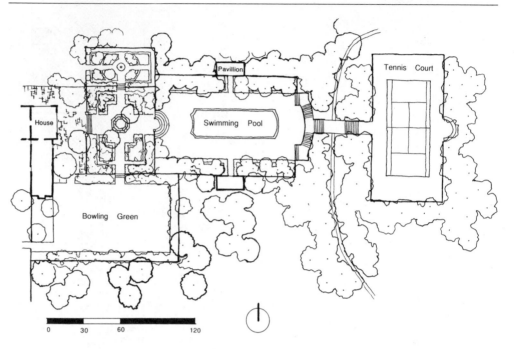

*Plan of the Campbell Estate,
East Aurora, New York,
by Ellen Shipman. (Data
from Cornell University
Archives; drawn by Rossi.)*

ers and woodland plantings, and site unity through effective transition spaces.
Among her most prominent projects were the collaboration with Henry du Pont
at Winterthur Gardens in Delaware and the E. F. Hutton estate, Hillwood, on
Long Island, New York, now part of Long Island University. Hillwood was a
series of independent gardens, conceptually inspired by the rambling Tudor-style
house, all integrated through a gridlike pattern of sight lines. The principal line
of sight was Magnolia Walk, an allée of twelve magnolias enclosed from surrounding spaces by an upright, clipped cedar hedge. Path sight lines which
crossed the walk led to gardens and recreation areas. At the Hutton estate Coffin
was particularly skillful at incorporating modern functional areas, such as a tennis
court and putting green, and formal ornamental areas like the magnolia allée into
a historically inspired site plan.

During the Neoclassicist period, professional landscape architecture came to
be practiced throughout most English-speaking parts of the continent, with each
region or large city having a locally prominent practitioner. Near Rochester,
New York, Alling de Forest planned many private residences and public sites,
including the George Eastman residence; in Dallas, Texas, Arthur and Marie
Berger designed some of the finest estates for that city's business elite, such as
the Degolyer estate, now the Dallas Arboretum and Botanical Garden; in the
Cornish area of New Hampshire, Rose S. Nichols was prominent; in Louisville,
Kentucky, Bryant Fleming dominated practice; in Kansas City and the Central
Plains, Hare and Hare; in Ontario, Canada, it was first Frederick Todd, later the
Dunington-Grubbs; in Virginia, Charles Gillette; in Santa Barbara, California,
Lockwood de Forest; in Cleveland, Ohio, A. D. Taylor; and in the Philadelphia
area, Oglesby Paul. With the vast numbers of practitioners and the demands of
their clients, it is not surprising that much of this work, at least as recorded in
photographs, displays a monotonous repetition of terraces, sight lines down
paths, sculpture as focal points, pergolas, and Gertrude Jekyll-inspired herbaceous borders.[15] One particularly noteworthy individual design effort did

Evergreen Garden at the Marshall Field Estate, Long Island, New York, by Marian C. Coffin. (ASLA, 1932.)

emerge—the work of a gifted, slightly eccentric landscape architect, Fletcher Steele.

Steele's work conveyed an originality of spirit and image which made his type of eccentricity a desirable quality for a designer. The Stockbridge, Massachusetts, estate called Naumkeag,[16] Steele's best known work, illustrated both his inventiveness and his limitations. Naumkeag had originally been laid out in the 1880s by Nathan Barrett as a series of formal gardens and allées in an otherwise wooded and pastoral landscape.[17] Steele and his client Mabel Choate believed that some of the old-fashioned character should be retained, but adapted to modern functions. Working incrementally over a thirty-year period beginning in 1926, they added five major gardens to the estate. In so doing, a very ordinary landscape was transformed into a series of fanciful outdoor rooms which combined medieval, Baroque, Abstract, Art Nouveau, Oriental, and Art Deco motifs and features.

The first space on which Steele worked was a patio off the library, called the Afternoon Garden. Here he created one of the best-scaled and "furnished" outdoor rooms in modern design. The space was enclosed on two sides by colorful Venetian-style posts connected by thick, vine-draped ropes. The garden floor was paved with random flagstones set around a parterre-like composition executed in low plants, fine gravel, and scallop-rimmed water basins with an oval reflecting pool in the center, in an arrangement that Steele compared to paving at the Garden of the Generalife in Spain. A corner sculpture by Frederick MacMoinnes provided the focal point, which drew the eye to distant Bear Mountain. The Afternoon Garden was Steele's work at its best, demonstrating infinite attention to details of scale, color, and enframement. It was a dramatic stage set for entertaining or for quiet reflection on the landscape beyond the garden.

View of the Afternoon Garden, Naumkeag, Stockbridge, Massachusetts, by Fletcher Steele; photo taken in the 1980s.

Steele's work at Naumkeag continued in spurts, with the hillside area to the south of the Afternoon Garden the next section to receive attention. As was typical of Steele's work at Naumkeag and elsewhere, the South Lawn, although adjacent to the Afternoon Garden, had few direct visual links with it. This lack of connection was not obvious from the Garden, where sweeping lines, velvet-textured turf, and an exotic pavilion reminiscent of a Middle Eastern tent created interest. However, looking back toward the house the abruptness of change from rolling grass to the stone retaining walls of the garden made the lack of linkage apparent.

In the late 1930s two other gardens were added to the estate. The first built was a walled Chinese-style garden with a tile-roofed "temple." Shortly afterward the famous Blue Stairs were added to the hillside below the Afternoon Garden. The Blue Stairs were a skillful combination of short ramps, short flights of steps, and landings, with a water cascade set in alcoves under the stairs. A linear grove of paper birch, used to repeat the color of gracefully curving metal railings, framed the entire composition. Intended merely as an improved link between the house at hilltop and a cutting garden below, the Stairs became a flight of fancy as well as a functional circulation system.

Steele's final major addition to Naumkeag was a rose garden on a south-facing slope directly below the house terrace. As always, he sought new forms through which to execute this most traditional of garden types. Rather than a bed and path system, Steele created an abstract, Op Art-like composition with ribbons of pink gravel punctuated by singly planted specimen roses, all set against a backdrop of lawn.

Steele's work at Naumkeag illustrates his experimental attitude toward design. He often searched for unique, exotic forms and features, and some of them could be quite bizarre—such as the flag-holding rodent he suggested for a finial at the Standish estate in Grosse Point, Michigan. Others were quite brilliant, like the use of chain mail to replace fabric in a pool shelter at the Allen Garden in Rochester, New York. In the late 1920s he became fascinated with the Modernist movement emerging in Europe—in fact, Steele was one of the few American landscape architects of the Neoclassicist period to appreciate the freedom of form the Modernist approach gave to designers.

The Blue Stairs and birch allée at Naumkeag in the 1980s.

During the Neoclassicist period, California's unique climate, landform, and plant communities became the basis for a distinctive regional approach to estate design. These California gardens were inspired by three principal historical styles, each of which had some cultural or environmental link to the region. The dominant approach derived from Mediterranian precedents, both Italian and Spanish. A second favored style was based on Middle Eastern gardens, particularly the walled Paradise garden of Persia. The final influence came from across the Pacific: inspired by the Japanese gardens exhibited at the various world's fairs held in the late 1800s and early 1900s, especially those at San Francisco and San Diego, gardens often included Oriental-style plantings, pavilions, and sculptural features.

A consistent theme in these California gardens was use of regionally unique plant material. Many, such as horticulturist Kate Sessions and landscape architect Lockwood de Forest, favored the rich native palette of materials so well adapted to dry conditions and often thin soils. Others, like designers A. E. Hanson and Paul Thiene and horticulturist Francesco Franceschi, saw the equal potential of introductions from parts of the world with similar climates, such as South Africa and Australia. This diversity of available materials allowed for lush and colorful plantings yielding year-round screening and color.

Neoclassicist approaches to arrangement of grounds came early to California. In 1896 architect Bertram Goodhue began work in the exclusive Santa Barbara suburb of Montecito on El Fureidis, an estate with a Middle Eastern design inspiration.[18] There, features which would later be considered prototypical of the California garden were first combined in an axial, formal plan. Terraces and steps integrated the designed landscape with the site and house. Pools, channels, and small fountains were used as focal features and site unifiers; columnar trees, especially Italian cypress, added emphasis to sight lines. Exotic and tropical plants such as banana, palms, and figs were used as specimens and in masses. Pastel-colored materials were used for walls and paths. And pergolas provided shade and enclosure.

This style of design quickly became popular with well-to-do eastern and midwestern emigrés, thereby creating a demand for landscape architectural ser-

Paul Thiene's design for the Cascades in Beverly Hills, California, circa 1930, was typical of much of the estate design in California during the Neoclassicist period. (ASLA, 1931.)

vices which had not existed in California before 1900. Among those who took advantage of this opportunity to develop practices specializing in residential work were Paul Thiene, Florence Yoch, Lucille Council, A. E. Hansen, Katherine Bashford, Lockwood de Forest, Thomas Church,[19] and, seasonally, Beatrix Farrand.

Hansen designed and built some of the largest estates in southern California. The Beverly Hills estate which he designed in the late 1920s for Harold Lloyd was among his most complex projects. For this hilltop site Hanson combined elaborate formal gardens with a picturesque landscape garden, complete with stone bridges, dovecote, and old mill, to be used as a golf course. Each of the estate areas was a convincing composition when considered alone, but the whole lacked logical linkages between the varied and unique spaces that constituted the site. Less grand in scale and elaborate in features, but far superior in site planning and design, was Hansen's scheme for the Young Garden in Pasadena. Inspired by Moorish gardens of Spain, this garden centered on a long sight-line path bordered with rows of mature olives set in beds of ivy. The only formal beds in the garden were tucked away behind the sunken circular bench which terminated the main axis.

Florence Yoch might be termed "landscape architect to the stars," because many of her clients, including David O. Selznick and Jack Warner, were associated with the film industry. From this work she also gained commissions to design outdoor sets for five movies, including the classics *Gone with the Wind* and *How Green Was My Valley*. Yoch, working with partner Lucille Council, designed landscapes similar in style and features to others of the period, but distinguished by attention to the detail of landscape structures and by inclusion of very livable outdoor living areas within the overall formal arrangement.

Beatrix Farrand was involved in some important projects in California following her husband's appointment in 1927 as director of the Huntington Library and Art Gallery in San Marino. Although not actively involved in the famous Huntington Gardens, she did complete a design for the grounds of the director's home.[20] Other projects included residences in the fashionable towns of Santa Barbara and Montecito. But her most important project in California was for the Santa Barbara Botanic Garden. This was a work in progress when she became associated with it, Lockwood de Forest having already completed plans which were then being implemented. When de Forest entered the military during World War II, Farrand assumed complete responsibility, adding gardens that were more formal than he had envisioned in his naturalistic landscape plan. Farrand's approach to planting design, though, was completely compatible with the original concept of the garden as a research center and display garden for native California plants.

Whether the distinctive features of Neoclassicist designs in California are unique enough to identify this as a regional style is open to question. What the experience of landscape architects there during this period did suggest was that interest in utilizing local features of the landscape, from climate to vegetation, could stimulate designers toward creative designs for livable outdoor spaces. It also demonstrated that historicist design approaches could be suitable when tied to local context.

REACTION TO NEOCLASSICISM

In spite of the popularity of Neoclassicist historicism and formality among designers and clients alike, some contemporaries were not uncritical of this style of design. Criticism generally related to three areas: lack of unity between house and grounds, in some designs; use of hackneyed spatial arrangements and features; and excess in elaboration of details and in variety of features. Lack of unity would certainly be the most critical of these problems, since integration of house and grounds through continuation of sight lines and repetition of forms and materials was the critical advantage which this approach offered over more naturalistic schemes. While individual garden designs might be guilty of this lack of unity, most sites of the Neoclassicist period did use its potentials, although with widely varying degrees of success, as we have seen in the work reviewed.

More common was the problem of repetitious use of garden elements and axial site plans in designs of spatially and geographically varied gardens. Writers other than Hubbard and Kimball, quoted earlier, commented on this almost unavoidable limitation. Henry Preston White felt that use of standard manufactured garden features was a cause of this problem, as was the popularity of design magazines which clients used to "shop" for just what they wanted. He aptly commented, though, that the limitations imposed by standardization could be overcome when a site's natural character was exploited and stock features adapted to it.

Finally, some gardens of this period were simply overdone, perhaps a throwback to the excesses of the Victorian period. Two quite different gardens illustrate these excesses. The site of Butchart Garden in Victoria, British Columbia, located in an area with mild climate and varied topography, would seem to have been an ideal garden site. Butchart, of course, is not the work of a professional. Its owner and creator, Jenny Butchart, in fact knew nothing about either gardening or design when she began to plant the grounds around her home near the family quarry. Through experimentation she learned a great deal about horticulture, but less about design. As viewed today, the garden is a 50-acre collection of eclectic theme gardens, most with little spatial relationship to each other. Many areas compete visually with others, since screening is often limited. The importance of such separation in eclectic gardens is clearly illustrated by the success of the first area created, the sunken garden. Enclosed by the escarpment of a former quarry, this area of the garden has a visual integrity and scale which most of the other spaces lacked.

For quite different reasons, Vizcaya, the Deering estate in Miami, Florida, is also an extreme example of Neoclassicist design. Its excesses lay in the level of ornamentation and detail created by designer Diego Suarez; the grounds, modeled after Baroque Italian gardens, had a surplus of architectural and planting details. Today much of the elaborate planting, particularly parterres, no longer exists, so that the grounds have a less busy appearance. As originally conceived, however, every surface, from rusticated retaining walls to the smallest planting bed, was an intricately patterned surface.

There is little to indicate that design problems such as these affected popular taste in any way. Neoclassicist formality dominated design throughout the first three decades of the twentieth century and influenced public works projects of the 1930s. Not all designers, though, were enamored of the historicism and architectonic character of neoclassicism. Their search for other responses to site design problems resulted in the development of two new approaches, each of which differed both philosophically and visually from the Neoclassicist. These were known as the Prairie and Modern styles.

THE PRAIRIE STYLE

Although best known as an architectural style, particularly through the work of Frank Lloyd Wright, the Prairie style was actually an attempt to create an over-arching regional theory of design. Its inspiration came from the visual and ecological character of prairie landscapes in the Midwest.[21] From typical prairie landforms came the style's principal visual concept—the use of horizontal lines. As further developed in landscape design, the Prairie style had several other important characteristics. First, it emphasized regionally distinctive character and sought to preserve both natural and cultural features typical of the Midwest. Equally important was contemporary site character, which Prairie style designs achieved by linking buildings to the grounds through placement of enframing planting masses. The style also stressed distinctive prairie proportions in the scale of plants and in the relative size of open and wooded spaces. Typical prairie scenes were symbolized by vistas to the horizon, called "long views," which gave depth to compositions. Finally, the Prairie style advocated use of native plants, both in designed landscapes and in restorations of true prairie plant communities.

Most landscapes in the Prairie style appeared naturalistic, but its concepts could as readily be applied, at least in part, to formal designs. Wilhelm Miller, whose writings popularized this style, outlined three general ways in which Prairie landscapes could be created: they could be idealized, conventionalized, or symbolized. "Idealized" landscapes were contrived recreations of Prairie scenery where none had ever naturally existed, such as a display in a conservatory. A "conventionalized" Prairie landscape was one in which certain aspects of the style, usually native plants and horizontality, were used in nonnaturalistic settings. Jens Jensen's design for a Rose Garden at Humboldt Park in Chicago was an example of this approach. While beds and paths of the garden were geometric and some plants were nonnatives, the two major spaces were level, and native roses, which were viewed from above as spring-blooming prairie flowers would be, alluded to the prairie. "Symbolized" landscapes were the most common application of the Prairie style. This approach took a number of forms, from simple but prominent planting of a single native species as a representation of the natural landscape to the design of miniaturized versions of key aspects of the prairie landscape. When Miller or other Prairie style proponents referred to "prairie" they did not mean merely the vegetative community dominated by grasses and forbs, but the entire landscape of the Prairie Region, particularly northern and central Illinois, which included dense woodlands, distinctive limestone rock outcroppings, and dramatic landform contrasts from the flatness of the plains to the bluffs of major rivers. Most Prairie style designs actually relied more on these features than on true prairie imagery.

As these descriptions of the Prairie style suggest, it was related, at least visually, to Romantic landscapes of the nineteenth century. The Prairie style might well be considered a transformation of the Romantic style to satisfy twentieth-century interests in preservation of the natural landscape.[22] The key link between Romanticism and the Prairie style is Ossian Simonds, a self-trained landscape architect who practiced chiefly in Chicago and the Midwest beginning in the 1880s. Best known for his plan of Graceland Cemetery in Chicago, Simonds's chief design innovation was the purposeful use of native plants rather than introduced species. Use of most of the principles later to be identified with the Prairie style can be seen in his earliest projects—horizontality, the long vista, prairie-scale proportions, and integration of structures with their surroundings. All that his work really lacked was a distinctive name, perhaps because he recognized it to be not a totally new approach, but a local refinement of the Romantic style.

Another less direct antecedent of the Prairie style was the Arts and Crafts Movement. Beginning in England in the mid-nineteenth century, the Movement became well known in North America in the late 1870s, following an exhibit of its craft products at the Centennial Exposition. The Arts and Crafts Movement emphasized four principles: an aesthetic inspired by natural forms; use of simple, natural materials and traditional, rather than mechanized, production methods; the social value of handcrafting, as a way to counter dehumanizing conditions of mechanized labor; and the egalitarian principle that well-designed, well-made products should be available to every one. This movement established philosophical precedents for many late nineteenth- and early twentieth-century architectural styles, from Art Nouveau to Bauhaus, but its greatest influence was on production of handcrafted household items, such as textiles and pottery. The best known American Arts and Crafts exponents were Louis Comfort Tiffany, famed for his handmade Favrile glass, which his studio transformed into glimmering lamps and windows, and Gustav Stickley, whose studio produced rustic furniture in what is known as the Mission style.

View in Graceland Cemetery, Chicago, Illinois, circa 1932, designed principally by Ossian Simonds. See Figure 18–28 for the pre-Simonds cemetery plan. (American Landscape Architect, Vol. 6, No. 1.)

Few landscapes in true Arts and Crafts style were produced in North America. Of these few, the most noteworthy were the work of the Greene brothers, architects from Pasadena, California, known for their magnificently detailed and crafted residential bungalow designs. Gardens designed by the Greenes to complement these houses followed one of two general patterns. For small sites the brothers, particularly Charles, favored miniature landscape scenes of rock, water, and plants that produced a Japanese visual character. Among their earliest commissions to include a Japanese garden was the courtyard-like rear garden of the Tichenor House in Long Beach, California. A series of larger homes on which Greene and Greene worked after 1907 had more extensive gardens with Japanese-inspired motifs. The Blacker and Gamble houses in Pasadena were superb examples of this type of garden. Large pools surrounded by carefully composed rock groupings, wooden gates, Oriental features such as lanterns, and lush, but small-scale and carefully managed, plants were all organized into a composition which set each structure into its site. The most obvious differences between these California gardens and the ones in Japan which inspired them were the openness of the gardens, which had few trees, and the large areas of turf which set off planted areas.

The second and less common type of garden designed by Greene and Greene was that illustrated at the estate known as Green Gables in Woodside, California. Here Charles Greene added rustic Arts and Crafts construction details to animate a plan which was otherwise an abstraction of then popular Neoclassicist designs. It differed from these though in its spatial simplicity, its use of lawn rather than planting beds as the major garden area, and in its reliance on water as the principal focal feature. Use of local materials, especially stone used for paths and the rustic arcades of the Water Garden, and use of native plants made Green Gables the most successful Arts and Crafts estate in America.

The influence of the Arts and Crafts Movement on the Prairie style was principally through emphasis on native materials, both building materials and

Oriental-inspired Arts and Crafts garden at Gamble House, Pasadena, California, by Greene and Greene as restored, in the 1980s.

plants. Building materials, even those used outside, were to be composed in ways that suggested handcrafted construction. Prairie school practitioners merely took this philosophy one step further, by suggesting that local materials should be used in ways which reflected the landscape from which they were taken.

The best-known and most prolific Prairie style designer was Jens Jensen. Jensen, trained in his native Denmark as an agriculturalist, came to Chicago in 1885 and found employment as a laborer on the West Parks, then being developed under the plans of local architect William Le Baron Jenney and others. Over the next ten years he gradually rose in the park organization, finally becoming chief designer. His biographer, Leonard Eaton, contended that his early experiences as a soldier in the German army forever left formal designs tainted as symbols of a repressive imperial political system. In contrast to that, "The plains speak of freedom—earth and sky meet on the far horizon" (Jensen, 1939, p. 28). From personal study of landscapes in northern Illinois, he developed a design approach that relied on prairie scene compositions, plant associations, and landforms as an alternative to the formal spatial organizations which he detested.

Jensen's earliest design works were public parks in Chicago. Three west side parks were redesigned and constructed under his guidance—Humboldt, Garfield, and Columbus. At Humbolt Park he achieved a complete expression of the Prairie concept in a designed landscape. The park had small meadows, originally planted with wildflowers, a lagoon system which Jensen called a "prairie river," several formal gardens, and active recreation areas, with masses of trees used to screen these areas from each other and surrounding streets. A particularly bold design decision was the use of lagoons, instead of more extensive tree planting, to organize the park spatially while maintaining the open character so essential to conveying a prairie image.

Among other public sites for which Jensen prepared plans were the Racine, Wisconsin, park system; Lincoln Memorial Garden in Springfield, Illinois; and an unbuilt west side boulevard system for Chicago. His greatest contribution to open space development was advocacy for establishment of the Cook County Forest Preserve District around Chicago. The District successfully preserved

The Rose Garden at Humbolt Park, Chicago, Illinois, by Jens Jensen circa 1925—an example of what Wilhelm Miller termed the "conventionalized" Prairie style.

much of the land along the Des Plaines River and its major tributaries, which now constitutes an extensive linear park.

Jensen pursued a private practice during a six-year period when the Park Commission, whose corruption he exposed, refused to employ him. This work, largely residential, allowed him to refine his design philosophy in more intimate settings and usually with less interference. Most of this work was for large estates in the northern suburbs of Chicago, projects such as the Harold Rubens Estate in Glencoe and the A. G. Becker Estate in Highland Park. At the Rubens estate Jensen laid out a meandering meadow with forest edge, for Jensen considered meadows "the bright spot of the North, reflecting light and sunshine" (1906, p. 28). The Becker estate was typical of many which Jensen designed in the wooded, ravine-cut landscape along the shores of Lake Michigan. There too, a meadow-like clearing, which gradually receded into the surrounding trees, was the principal designed space. At the edges of the woods he added trees with horizontal habit, such as the hawthorn, and trees with dramatic fall color, such as the sugar maple, to enhance seasonal visual change, a feature so critical to the prairie.

Other residential designs included those for the Ryerson estate in Lake Forest, Illinois;[23] the Edsel Ford estate in Seal Harbor, Maine; and three sites in Highland Park, Illinois: the residence of botanist May T. Watts, the Rosenberg estate (now Rosewood Park), and his own home and studio. It was at this home that he first experimented with a feature which would later become a trademark of his work—the stone council ring. The ring, intended as a gathering place, was a symbol of egalitarianism, of a society in which "there is no social caste. . . . A ring speaks of strength and friendship and is one of the great symbols of mankind. . . . These rings are the beginning of a new social life in the gardens of the America of tomorrow" (Jensen, 1939, p. 66).

Others using the Prairie style of landscape design included Frank Lloyd Wright, who, in spite of a friendship with Jensen, preferred to attend to all details of the houses which he designed.[24] His landscape work at the Darwin D. Martin residence in Buffalo, New York, and the site-planning masterpiece Fallingwater in Pennsylvania, were all inspired by the Prairie style. Walter Burley Griffin, educated as a landscape architect, but better known as a city planner for his plan of Canberra, the Australian capital city, also used the Prairie approach in a series of small residences in Oak Park, Illinois, and in his plan for a Cook County Forest Preserve District park at Hubbard's Woods, near Chicago. Griffin, with his wife, landscape architect Marion Mahoney, designed the only Prairie style housing complex, Rock Glen Subdivision in Mason City, Iowa, using dense vegetation to completely screen dwellings from each other. Other landscape architects certainly experimented briefly with the style, but returned to more conventional approaches.

Although the Prairie style had almost no impact outside the Midwest, and even there was overshadowed by public preference for the Neoclassicist, it became an important link between nineteenth-century Romantic style and the ecological approaches to design which became significant in the 1960s. Further, the Prairie style was and remains the most complete example of a regional, nonhistoricist style which responded to characteristics of the natural landscape, but interpreted and stylized them to meet site conditions and social needs.

TRENDS TOWARD MODERNISM

An end to Neoclassicist dominance in design effectively began in October 1929, with the stock market crash, but even before this economic catastrophe there were signs from Europe that a new design movement, variously called the Modern, Modernist, Moderne, Cubist, Geometric, Contemporary, or New Movement was emerging. The Modern style of design had a number of characteristics, which when combined, gave it a distinctive visual image. Its principal organizing rationale was that space should be envisioned as a single unit. This concept produced sites in which the distinction between interior and exterior spatial sequencing and scale were virtually eliminated. Patterning of the ground plane was emphasized, with patterns usually being combinations of simple geometric forms. To prevent distortions in perspective views of these patterns that would occur if they were set out on flat terraces, Modern designers often used elevated and tilted planes, even in planting beds. Ground patterning was the primary form of ornamentation in gardens since surface embellishment, such as the intricately carved balustrades and filigreed fences of the Neoclassicist period, were eliminated in favor of severely simple geometric planes.

Although rectilinear geometry continued to be used in Modern designs, there was increasing interest in other forms, particularly those with angles. Forms were also combined more freely. Adding to the variety created by this unconstrained use of shape was asymmetric composition. In spite of the use of occult balance, Modern gardens at times continued to have axes, but these were often angled or deemphasized with zigzag edging or asymmetrical plantings. In general, planted areas were small compartments in which vegetation was restricted to very architectonic configurations. One of the more lasting contributions of Modern design was the introduction of innovative, machine age materials into the landscape. Although some of these materials had been used earlier as structural components, such as concrete for walls, they had then been covered over with a more "finished" veneer. Designers became free to experiment with new materials, such as cinder block and aluminum, as well as to introduce fresh uses for old materials such as stucco and mirrors. The overall appearance of Modern designs was of starkly architectonic landscapes with subtly implied, rather than explicitly axial, spatial organization.

In the late 1920s a small group of American landscape architects became actively interested in this new style, with Fletcher Steele being its principal advocate in print. The relative merits of this approach to design were frequently discussed in *Landscape Architecture,* with a 1932 issue devoted almost entirely to differing views on the subject.[25] Three opinions predominated in these discussions. Some held that the "Modern" was really nothing new at all, just lines and forms in slightly different arrangements, but still following the basic geometry of Neoclassicist design. Most writers agreed that the style was in fact something new, but those who shared this viewpoint often disagreed as to whether the innovations had any merit for landscape architecture. Those who thought that it did *not,* criticized Modern design for lack of relationship to natural topography. Since many of the sites that had been designed up to that time were quite small— often walled courtyards—they had created their own landform patterns regardless of surrounding terrain. In spite of this limitation, other designers saw great potential for modernism to break away from the stale axial site plans which were then ubiquitous in landscape design. The new freedom which it allowed was seen by Lockwood de Forest as providing the perfect opportunity to introduce native plants to design, while Fletcher Steele, understanding the relationship of Modern design to contemporary experiments in painting, saw it as an opportunity to rescue landscape architecture from what he pejoratively termed "landscape engineers and conservers" and restore it to the status of a fine art.

Steele attempted to implement the lessons of modernism in several of his gardens, but it was only in three projects that he actually produced designs which were consistently inspired by the Modern: Branch garden in Seekonk, Massachusetts; Smithwick garden in Gloucester, Massachusetts; and Ellwanger Rose Garden in Rochester, New York. Neither of the former is extant today, and of the latter only a few walls remain. The Ellwanger Rose Garden was a tour de

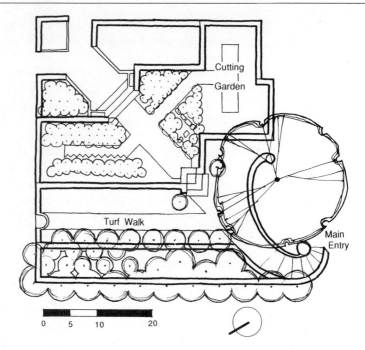

Cutting
Garden

Turf Walk

Main
Entry

0   5   10   20

Plan of the Ellwanger Garden, Rochester, New York, by Fletcher Steele, circa 1935. (Data from Karson, 1989; drawn by Rossi.)

force of innovation in form and materials. Principal entry to this walled space was via steps enclosed by elliptically curving walls, which were often a feature of Steele's work. The garden's geometric plan was influenced by Bauhaus architecture, with raised concrete beds divided by a diagonal sight line. The beds were filled with roses, many of them old and rare specimens from the Ellwanger collection. Steele's choice of building materials was unusual for its day, particularly for a private garden. The curving walls were of cinder block surfaced with pink plaster, while windbreak fences were made of fluted glass panels. To add an eclectic quality to the garden, Steele also used more traditional rustic features, such as a stake fence combined in places with a base of openwork cinder blocks and tiered trellises for clematis and other vines, in a style reminiscent of a Chinese pagoda.

Modern influences had relatively little impact on the expensive estates typical of the pre-Depression era, whose owners preferred more conservative and conspicuous landscapes. Few designers in North America, other than Steele, even attempted to implement the entire spectrum of Modern motifs, although specific individual ideas were often used. Serious investigation of the potential of Modern design had to await the 1930s, when public rather than private employment of landscape architects took the profession in new directions, or, more accurately, returned it to the full range of activities which its founders had initiated in the nineteenth century.

COMMON LANDSCAPES IN THE NEOCLASSICIST PERIOD

Grounds of the average small home underwent a complete transformation in the early twentieth century from the eclectic clutter of Late Victorian design to a simple geometry, which drew its chief inspiration from the formal, Neoclassicist designs of large estates. Perhaps the most drastic design change was removal of scattered specimen shrubs from the lawn to mass planting areas at the base of houses. This foundation planting, a ubiquitous feature of twentieth-century homes, began to appear in the late 1890s and was a requirement for refined grounds within a decade. Foundation plantings were intended to link the house

These models illustrate some of the typical frontyard arrangements for residential landscapes in the Neoclassicist period. (Taylor, 1916.)

and grounds visually, to "soften" architectural lines, to screen undesirable features, and to give the house a snug and cozy appearance. An endless series of pattern books were available to help homeowners avoid aesthetic or functional errors, such as the all too common problem of planting large evergreens very close to the house or paths. While many foundation plantings were just as busy as the lawn plantings they replaced, good designs used plants to balance the house's size and draw the eye to important features of its architectural design.

Other changes also began to appear in the grounds of small properties. Ornate fences at property lots were removed, often to be replaced with hedges. Increasingly, these hedges and other plants were clipped into geometric shapes. Linear planting borders around the perimeter of the yard replaced free-floating Victorian carpet beds, so that lawns became continuous, with only a few strategically planted trees providing shade.

After automobiles replaced horses as family transportation, the backyard also took on a new character. No longer merely a work area, it often became a private family area very similar in character to the frontyard, but with a designated outdoor "room"—usually a patio. Formal gardens, especially the popular rose garden, were also usually set in the rear. The sole vestigial nineteenth-century use of rear yards was for vegetable gardens and tool sheds.

Although small-scale residential architecture followed the general trend toward historicism common to large estates, the designs for grounds of typical small houses were not varied to relate them to building style. So similar were the suggested patterns for small residences that Frank Waugh was able to develop a "Domestic Formula" with a dozen points to guide homeowners. The one exception to this repetitive pattern was found in grounds associated with some bungalow residences. Often these followed a naturalistic pattern similar to that of nineteenth-century Romantic landscapes or else had elements inspired by Japanese gardens, such as miniature pools and rock compositions. The Japanese approach was especially popular on the West Coast.

As in earlier periods, professional assistance was available to the homeowner-turned-designer through various publications. Magazines such as *Country Life in America* and *House and Garden* carried innumerable illustrated articles about successful small properties, usually with plans which could be easily copied. Landscape architects also offered assistance. Fletcher Steele's *Design in the Little Garden* introduced readers to general principles of design, as they could be implemented at small sites. Elsa Rehmann's *The Small Place: Its Landscape Architecture* was a straightforward pattern book, but one which illustrated how various designers approached specific types of sites. It was from sources such as these that the archetypical suburban "yard" of the twentieth century emerged.

SITE PLANNING IN THE NEOCLASSICIST PERIOD

Although residential work dominated private practice during the Neoclassicist period, there were, of course, other types of projects with which landscape architects were involved. Parks continued to be a mainstay of many offices, although this work usually involved individual parks within a system or the addition of some new area to an existing park, rather than development of entire park systems as was common in the nineteenth century. Four sites of different scales exemplify park planning and design during the first decades of the twentieth century: Burr Playground; Forest Hill Park; Brackenridge Park Sunken Garden; and Lake Springfield. Burr Playground in Newton, Massachusetts, was designed by Arthur Shurcliff on a 6-acre estate donated to the city. While few structures from the site's former residential use were retained, preserved specimen trees produced an instant sense of completion for the playground, which in all other ways was quite typical of others designed during this period. Intended as a site for active recreation, the park had an open field for ball games, tennis courts, a wading pool, and a fieldhouse. Burr Playground illustrated the progress made in playlot design since the turn of the century: sports areas were separated physically and visually from each other; small areas for passive recreation, with benches and ornamental plantings, were incorporated into the grounds; and the entire site composed as a park rather than an outdoor gymnasium.

Forest Hill Park in East Cleveland and Cleveland Heights, Ohio, was the work of A. D. Taylor. Like Burr Playground, Forest Hill Park was on a site donated by a wealthy citizen, in this case John D. Rockefeller, rather than acquired through public purchase. The parksite, a woodland of over 250 acres, was developed for both active and passive recreation. In addition to the problem of combining these uses, a road and private development around the perimeter of the park divided the site into two roughly equal parts. Taylor dealt with these constraints directly, following the pattern which they suggested. Active recreation—such as the football field, tennis courts, and other ballfields—and parking were kept to the periphery near existing and future development. Dense tree masses separated these uses from open meadows on the interior of the tract. The divisive through road was realigned into a meandering, tree-lined pleasure drive which skirted the edge of the largest meadow. The skill with which Taylor organized these diverse features made Forest Hill Park a superior example of twentieth-century park design, in which naturalistic and highly developed areas were integrated to create a multifunctional park.

Specialty ornamental gardens became popular additions to parks in the early 1900s, as zoos had been at the turn of the century, with rose gardens, rock gardens, and Oriental gardens being just some of the fashionable themes. An example of an Oriental specialty garden was the Japanese Sunken Garden of Brackenridge Park in San Antonio, Texas.[26] Originally a limestone quarry, the site was "recycled" for park use in 1915 when Kimi E. Jingu began design of the ponds and islands which made up the garden. Its reigning feature was an upper-level thatch-roofed pavilion linked with the gardens below by limestone columns two stories high. Steep quarry walls were planted with native, drought-tolerant plants including mesquite and various cactus species. At the sunken level, tropicals, especially waterlilies and bamboo, gave the garden an exotic character, quite different from other areas of Brackenridge Park.

Large regional parks were the principal type of recreational site developed by public authorities during the second and third decades of this century. These sites often had an underlying economic function to which recreation was appended, as occurred at Lake Springfield in Springfield, Illinois. Planned as a water development project, this artificially created lake, formed by damming Sugar Creek, was also intended to provide water-related recreational facilities for several counties. More than 2,000 acres of shoreline were developed, with athletic fields, beaches, picnic grounds, woodlands, and docking facilities.

College and university campuses were another important site for landscape architectural services. In the first three decades of the twentieth century many older institutions expanded, requiring additional planning. Also, in the flush times up to 1929, new colleges, primarily private, were built. Campuses lent themselves readily to use of formal site plans typical of the Neoclassicist period, which at this scale also demonstrated the continuing influence of the City Beautiful Movement. On many campuses site plans were the sole feature unifying eclectic architecture and haphazardly organized outdoor features.

One university with a long history of twentieth-century planning by distinguished landscape architects was the University of Illinois at Champaign-Urbana. The campus was originally developed as a Romantic landscape within an urban grid, and the university first sought professional advice in 1906, when the Olmsted Brothers were consulted. It was they who suggested that the campus spine, already tentatively in place, be developed as the principal space organizer. Limited planning which occurred between 1909 and 1917 was controlled by a commission headed by Daniel Burnham; then, after World War I, when expansion extended the campus southward, Charles Platt was employed to plan this new section. His plan acknowledged Olmsteds' earlier recommendation, while adding a new cross-axis from east to west. It was also Platt who recommended exclusive use of Georgian architectural styles for future buildings, with his design for

Sunken Garden at Brackenridge Park, San Antonio, Texas, circa 1920. (Frances Marion Behns Collection, Barker Texas History Center, University of Texas, Austin, Texas.)

Mumford Hall being the prototype.[27] This recommendation gave the southern part of the campus visual harmony, at least until nonconforming structures were added after 1950. Platt's formal site plan was reinforced by the planting recommendations of Ferruccio Vitale, assisted by Stanley White. First, there would be architectonic terraces adjoining buildings. These would be paved or in turf, with no small-scale plants, other than hedges used for enclosure. Larger, linear open areas, principally the central mall and its connecting avenues, were to be lined with double or single rows of trees. Finally, inner courtyards and small spaces between buildings were to be treated in a garden-like fashion with shade trees, small flowering trees, shrubs, seating, and sculpture. The planning and planting schemes of Platt and Vitale were so successful that they continue to influence aspects of the campus plan today.

Some of the most exemplary pieces of work done by a landscape architect at university sites were Beatrix Farrand's planting designs for campuses, including Princeton and Yale Universities and Oberlin College in Ohio. Princeton, both her first and most continuous university commission, involved work over a thirty-year period ranging from site planning to grading to planting design. Three concepts influenced the planting design, which covered about one-quarter of the campus: that plants must be those which were most vivid during the academic year; that planting should emphasize architecture, but at the same time disguise its flaws, particularly awkward grade changes; and that upright and clinging plants should be used so that small spaces between buildings would not be further reduced in scale. The Princeton designs became masterpieces in the use of vines, groundcovers, upright trees and shrubs, and espaliered plants to create dynamic visual effects in small spaces.

Campuses throughout the continent offered employment to landscape architects of both local and national reputation. Among the most noteworthy examples were site plans by Thomas Mawson for the University of Saskatchewan, in Regina, Saskatchewan; Bremer Pond for Southern Methodist University in Dallas, Texas; Warren Manning for Lake Forest University, Lake Forest, Illinois, and Richmond College, Richmond, Virginia (with Charles Gillette, then in his employ); Kenneth Johnson for Graceland College, Lamoni, Iowa; and the Olmsted firm for the replanning of Harvard University, Cambridge, Massachusetts.

Pyne Hall at Princeton University, Princeton, New Jersey, showing the way in which Beatrix Farrand used vines, small trees, shrubs, and ground covers in very limited areas to unify the campus. (ASLA, 1932.)

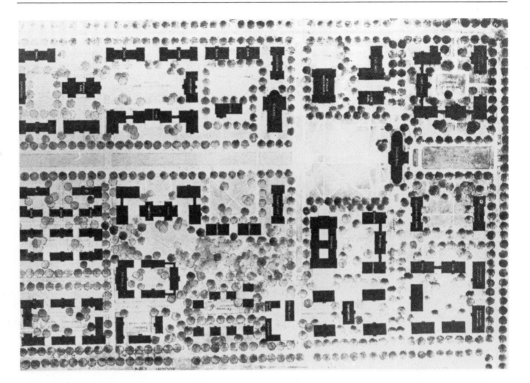

Plan of Southern Methodist University, Dallas, Texas, by Bremer Pond circa 1930 illustrates the typical axial arrangement of a campus reorganized in the Neoclassicist style. (ASLA, 1931.)

Institutional sites, such as universities, were the principal publically funded projects which employed landscape architects from 1900 until 1930. Other institutions using landscape architectural services included primary and secondary schools, medical and social service complexes, cemeteries, museums, arboretums, and botanical gardens. In general, designs for schools, residential institutions such as hospitals, and horticultural parks continued to follow naturalistic patterns, with only heavily used areas in more geometric patterns. Rose Greeley's site plan for Madeira School and Alling de Forest's plan of the Rochester, New York, Orphan Asylum are both typical of this approach.

More formal plans, such as those we have seen for estates, were common for cemeteries (which after 1900 were often called "memorial parks"), museums, and urban institutional sites. Central Memorial Park, in southern California, by Cook, Hall & Cornell exemplified Neoclassicist formality in cemetery design through use of axial boulevards and enclosure of sight lines with rows of trees.

At the Cleveland Museum of Art, Olmsted Brothers attempted to link a neoclassical building with its adjoining, less formal park using terraces, steps, and a pool. So effective was the sight line created by the terraces and stairs that even an intervening street did not seriously compromise it. Less successful was the park itself, which, while intended to suggest a naturalistic scene, had as its chief feature a hard-edged pond in an ambivalent amorphous shape. While only a few major museums got the extensive landscape treatment of the Cleveland Museum, many provided smaller outdoor areas in the form of courtyards used as sculpture gardens and to admit natural light to interior galleries. The Boston Museum of Fine Arts courtyard by Arthur Shurcliff was one of the most prominent museum courtyards. It had a very simple arrangement of broad stone walkways, hedged turf panels, columnar evergreens, a central pool with water jets, and selected pieces of sculpture, generally set around the periphery. What made this plan distinctive was use of grade changes, including an elevated entry terrace and sunken walks set behind stone balustrades, to create the illusion of greater space and depth.

Cleveland Museum of Art, Cleveland, Ohio, by Olmsted Brothers circa 1920. (Boston Society of Landscape Architects [1935?].)

Courtyard garden of the Boston Museum of Fine Arts by Arthur Shurcliff. (Boston Society of Landscape Architects [1935?].)

Landscape architects, to judge from periodicals, were also keenly interested in a new type of site—the airport. Concerns ran the gamut of landscape architectural interests, from regional planning questions such as how to scientifically determine the most appropriate locations for airports to very specific questions of site design, particularly what the aesthetic character of airports should be. Many discussions of design ended with proposals for large formal gardens to be associated with airports, principally as entry features. Few such plantings were ever implemented, but the proposals themselves illustrated that many landscape architects saw the need to bring the products of modern technology within their field of influence, but often failed to take any new inspiration from that technology, preferring instead to apply somewhat hackneyed ideas to these sites associated with the latest transportation revolution.

Airport design "in which the hangars and buildings set back from the surrounding roads, thus affording opportunity for [formal] landscape treatment." (Spoon, 1930, p. 33.)

CONCLUSION AND SUMMARY

Twentieth-century neoclassicism was actually a revival of a revivial—resurrecting Renaissance design concepts which themselves had been inspired by Imperial Rome. Such historicism had been common in the past—in the early nineteenth century, Greek revival architecture had been popular, while Downing had fostered new interest in Gothic themes. What differentiated the Neoclassicist period from these earlier revivals was that complementary architectural and landscape architectural styles were for the first time linked to produce complex, unified sites.

This revival of classicism was just one of the myriad consequences attributed to the World's Columbian Exposition. Other factors such as travel, education of American designers in Europe, especially at the Ecole des Beaux Arts, interest in country estate living, and greater personal wealth also played a part. Professional education may also have encouraged the diffusion of neoclassicism, since it was a "teachable" system that could produce acceptable, albeit obtuse, designs.

Neoclassicism represents the most extreme deviation from both the spirit and visual character of landscape architecture as established in North America by its nineteenth-century founders. Of course the difference in appearance is of little serious consequence, since stylistic change is merely one part the constantly changing response of design to social and environmental conditions. More serious was the change in perspective, away from the socially responsive concerns of romanticism and toward concern with the needs and desires of only a small portion of the population. The perceived elitism of these concerns limited landscape architecture for several decades after the 1920s, for the public associated "landscape architecture" almost solely with "estate design." Although an unfortunate and inaccurate characterization of the profession, it would take a great deal of more publicly oriented work to both redirect the profession and change public perceptions. The first opportunity to do so came as a result of the calamitous economic and social events of the Depression.

NOTES

1. *This type of eclecticism was known variously as Single-Tract Eclecticism, Academic Eclecticism, or Historical Eclecticism. Architect and critic Aymar Embury (1909) categorized eleven stylistic "types" of country house, of which ten were historic revivals: Elizabethan, Southern Colonial, New England Colonial, Classic Revival, Dutch*

Colonial (which Embury himself seemed to favor), Spanish or Mission, American Farm House, Modern English (which despite its name included any revival style other than Elizabethan), Japanesque, and Italian.

2. The Academy has also offered fellowships in environmental design, music, literature, painting, classical studies, art history, and sculpture to artists and scholars. Most of these were added within a couple of years of the establishment of the original architecture fellowships.

3. There had been earlier individual courses or diploma programs in landscape architecture, both at Harvard through the Bussy Institute and Lawrence Scientific School, and elsewhere, for example, at the University of Illinois and Cornell University. Steiner and Brooks (1986) consider the course offered at Michigan State University in 1863 to be the first formal university-level course in landscape architecture. None of these, though, granted either academic or professional degrees. The first Canadian program was founded at the University of Guelph in 1964.

4. It might be of interest to those who have completed degrees in a less rigorous age to understand what was required of early graduates. "Not only must the candidate for the M. L. A. degree already possess a bachelor's degree or evidence of its equivalent, from some institution in good standing, but he [only men were admitted] should have equipped himself in certain ways. Before he can begin work in Landscape Design, he should have acquired respectable ability to draw freehand in pencil and in wash, experience in making and using topographical surveys and drawings in projection and perspective of simple architectural and landscape forms, and a sound elementary knowledge of Physics, Geology, and Physiography, of Botany (including a familiarity with the plants commonly used in Landscape Design) and the History and Principles of the Fine Arts, especially Architecture and Landscape Architecture" (Pray, 1911, pp. 60–61).

5. The Cambridge School was a private professional design school opened to accommodate women, who at that time were not admitted to Harvard. The school, though, was scholastically affiliated with Harvard, since most of its instructors, including director Henry A. Frost, were Harvard professors. The school eventually became part of Smith College Graduate School, before closing in 1942.

6. Platt made this trip with his brother, William, who up to that time had worked in the Olmsted office.

7. Several sketch plans for this house, in the library of Rochester University, are unsigned, making attribution imprecise. One area of the grounds, the Sundial Garden, has been attributed to architect Claude Bragdon, but the source of this attribution is not documented.

8. Sonnenberg is often described as a "Victorian" garden, for several reasons. First, the house, in the "Queen Anne" style, dates from the late Victorian period. Second, some garden development was begun in the 1890s. Finally, one of the most visually dominant areas, the "Italian Garden," is in fact an elaborate carpet bed. There are several reasons why this "Victorian" designation is inaccurate and why we therefore include Sonnenberg here as an example of early Neoclassicist design. First, professional design work did not begin until 1902 and continued for over a decade, placing it definitely in that era. Second, the "Italian" carpet bed garden is a small part of the total complex, which includes other garden areas more typical of the Neoclassicist period, such as a Japanese Garden, and several axially arranged spaces including the Rose Garden and the Colonial Garden. Finally, the arrangement of gardens immediately west of the house is far too well organized on sight lines to be truly Victorian.

9. At Beacon Hill House the Olmsteds did the site plan and some garden design. Later, additional gardens and plantings were added by others, including Harriet Foote, credited with design of the Rose Garden, and John Greatorex.

10. The site was originally about 4,000 acres and included forested areas and a farm, as well as the ornamental grounds. About half of this area is now part of the Akron Metropolitan Park System.

11. Among the research specialties at Dumbarton Oaks is History of Landscape Architecture. The library collections contain rare books and manuscripts from around the world, which can be used by request or through grant of a fellowship. This author can testify that there is no more stimulating and congenial research environment than that provided at the Garden Library of Dumbarton Oaks.

12. Farrand had intended Reef Point to become an endowed educational center with outdoor plant collections and indoor library and archival collections. She acquired Gertrude Jekyll's plans and papers as the keystone of the archives, but her extensive collections also included rare garden books from the Renaissance and a large collection of garden prints. Regrettably, conditions did not allow her to continue this effort. In 1955 the corporation and fund set up for the gardens were dissolved. Her papers and collections were then donated to the University of California at Berkeley. The house and gardens found no such safe haven and were demolished, but many of the plants were relocated to a nearby estate, Asticou Gardens, in Northeast Harbor, Maine.

13. According to Anderson (1980), at that time there were two objections to women in the profession. First, that office "morale" would be disrupted in predominantly male-staffed offices. Second, that women could not as readily superintend projects or work with contractors. There was also the general attitude, expressed in much educational literature, that "women did better work than men in the residential field, partly because . . . they had a flair for design related to the human scale and partly because they paid more attention to detail" (p. 41).

14. *Quoted in her obituary in the* New York Times, *March 29, 1950, p. 29.*

15. *Jekyll is known to have designed only a few gardens in North America, but her influence was almost universal.*

16. *This unusual word, the original name for the town of Salem, Massachusetts, came from a name given to a local Native American community. The name is interpreted to have meant either "safe haven" or "north river."*

17. *Barrett often credited himself with reintroduction of formal styles to North America. Evidence does suggest that he used axial arrangements at a time when most landscape architects remained enamored of the Romantic and nonprofessionals were interested in Victorian eclecticism. Among his nineteenth-century projects which have clearly formal arrangements of spaces are Naumkeag itself, an unimplemented plan for three cemeteries, and the Ponce-de-Leon Hotel in Florida. Barrett was then far ahead of his time, and few, if any, other landscape architects shared his view that "the formal garden is a gem . . ." (quoted in Schermerhorn, 1920). Of course, as we have seen, many naturalistic parks included formal areas, suggesting that others could also design in that way but chose to emphasize other spatial arrangements.*

18. *Goodhue was architect for the house and is usually credited with the garden design as well. One contemporaneous article, though, gives the owner of the estate, James Gillespie, credit for the garden design (Anonymous, 1903).*

19. *Thomas Church is usually associated with post-World War II design innovations, but much of his early work was formal in plan. His work of this period differed somewhat from that of his contemporaries in its simplicity, with emphasis placed on spatial development and sequence rather than elaborate details. Among early works in California by Church was the Dobbins Garden in Berkeley.*

20. *The Henry Huntington estate, later bequeathed as a semipublic library and garden, was designed by William Hertrich.*

21. *The term "prairie" properly refers only to a distinctive plant community of grasses and forbs, with few woody species. "Prairie" is often equated with the geomorphological term "plain" and used to describe relatively flat landforms. Although Prairie style designers certainly knew the difference between the two, they were combined in the theories of the style, so that "prairie" signified landform as well as plant community.*

    In architecture, this design approach was referred to as the Prairie School, a term occasionally used for landscape architecture as well. In this discussion the term "style" rather than "school" will be used in keeping with the nomenclature of Wilhelm Miller.

22. *According to associate Alfred Caldwell, Jensen felt that his approach to design was opposed to the Romantic, which he believed was a "style" just like classical or Baroque. In his view the Romantic was a "simulation of nature" while the Prairie approach dealt with "living nature" (Caldwell, 1961). How this concept meshed with the three ways Miller outlined for presenting the Prairie ideal was never clarified.*

23. *This estate had an existing axial site plan by Rose S. Nichols at the time Jensen began site renovation.*

24. *Wright and Jensen are known to have collaborated at only two sites, the Cooley residence in River Forest, Illinois, and the Roberts residence in Marquette, Michigan.*

25. *Vol. 22, No. 4, July 1932.*

26. *In December 1941, the San Antonio City Council, influenced by anti-Japanese-American hysteria after Pearl Harbor, changed the name of the Garden to Chinese Sunken Garden, its official name until the original was restored in 1984. There was no corresponding change in the design of the site.*

27. *Platt also designed many other buildings for the campus, including the graduate library, the architecture building, and the President's residence.*

25

To Preserve and Conserve:
Protection of Natural and Cultural Resources

North America, that "Garden of the World," had been considered, since the first European settlement, as an illimitable land of infinite resources just waiting to be plucked from the earth. Whether based on religious beliefs in human sovereignty over the natural world or nationalistic concepts such as Manifest Destiny—which defined the environment as just another force to be subdued as the land claims of other nations were eliminated across the continent—the imperative to control and modify the landscape dominated thinking in North American until the late nineteenth century. Dominion over nature was viewed as "environmental reform"[1]: not a subjugation for the exercise of power alone but a way to make the earth more fruitful through human intervention.

Reacting against this dominant concept, small but significant group of nineteenth-century naturalists and writers began to rethink attitudes toward the American environment. They realized that unbridled exploitation of resources destroyed or threatened the quality of life that the continent had supplied. As early as 1819, horticulturist and explorer François André Michaux commented on the high rate of forest demolition and the likelihood that it would increase. With great foresight, he suggested that the government require any recipient of a land grant charter, such as a canal company, to plant "useful trees . . . along both sides of its route" (1871, p. 19). Speculation over possible pollution from the mixing of Lake Erie and Atlantic Ocean water via the Erie Canal was another early environmental concern. More commonly, early environmentalists voiced concern over the disappearance of uniquely beautiful scenic areas, such as the Blue Hills outside Boston, or visual changes to scenery, such as the reforestation of Yosemite Valley meadows when settlers suppressed fires.

Fueling these concerns were the lasting impacts of two philosophical systems—the thought of the Enlightenment and Romantic concepts of nature. From the rationalization of the Enlightenment emerged the scientific preservation and conservation movement of the late nineteenth century.[2] Romantic philosophy had an even more far-reaching influence. Sentimental attachment to natural and historic features was promoted through popular literature—books like Hawthorne's *The House of the Seven Gables* or Thoreau's *Walden*. Attitudes toward nature spread through such literature helped inspire middle-class interest in preservation and conservation at all levels.

It was after the Civil War that issues of environmental degradation and resource depletion became prominent. One of the earliest areas of concern was loss of the forest. This was not only tied to its use as a raw material for fuel and construction, but to its perceived role in maintaining regional rainfall. The Great Plains, for example, was believed by many to be a region once lushly forested, which through Indian-induced burning and buffalo overgrazing, had been reduced to grassland. As erroneous as these views were, they led to early legislation which had a limited conservation basis, such as the Timber Culture Act of 1873.

Another key resource was water. It presented two very different problems—in the East a seasonal overabundance that led to flooding, and in the West, both floods and perennial shortages. Water control schemes abounded across the country. No body of water on the continent had been subjected to more modifications for a longer period than the Mississippi River. Large-scale levee construction in the early 1800s began a series of adjustments which later included dams, channelization, and rerouting of some channels. In the West, competition for a seasonally limited resource led to development of appropriative, as opposed to riparian, water rights, that is, to a system in which the prerogative of exploitation was based on first beneficial utilization and could be divested from the land. As with physical modification of the Mississippi, these legal modifications often generated endless environmental and human problems, as has been demonstrated since the early 1900s in the California conflict for water between the residents of the Owens River valley in the central part of the state and the city of Los Angeles, which had acquired rights to the valley's water.[3]

The pace of change in the twentieth century only made preservation and conservation efforts more urgent. New technology only hastened the rate of visual and physical change to the environment. Heavy agricultural equipment required extensive clearing of previously wooded areas, such as small woodlots and fence rows, for efficiency. Use of pesticides to protect crops and forests brought mass kills of birds and other small animals. Widespread use of the automobile assured that larger numbers of people had access to scenic and historic areas outside their hometown or county, generating a demand for more places to visit. At the same time, heavy visitation created the ultimate paradox in preservation and conservation, for, as Schrepfer has noted, "regions set aside for protection have been subject to much heavier use and wear than would be the case had the areas not been set aside . . ."(1983, p. 5).

CONSERVATION OF NATURAL RESOURCES

The Nineteenth and Early Twentieth Centuries

Two important events in the incipient movement toward preservation and conservation of natural resources occurred in 1832. First, Hot Springs Reservation, now Hot Springs National Park, in Arkansas was set aside from private development by the U.S. government. Although a relatively small site, originally about 2,600 hundred acres, now only 265, it was the first landscape so preserved on the continent. Second, painter George Catlin, having just observed the wasteful slaughter of more than a thousand buffalo, summed up what would become a guiding rationale for preservation of natural areas:

> Many are the rudenesses and wilds in Nature's works, which are destined to fall before the deadly axe and desolating hands of cultivating man; and so amongst her ranks of *living*, of beast and human, we often find noble stamps, or beautiful colours, to which our admiration clings; and even in the overwhelming march of civilized improvements and refinements do we love to cherish their existence, and lend our efforts to preserve them in their primitive rudeness. Such of Nature's works are always worthy of our preservation and protection; and the further we become separated . . . from that pristine wildness and beauty, the more pleasure does the mind of enlightened man feel in recurring to those scenes, when he can have them preserved for his eyes and his mind to dwell upon. (Catlin, 1926, pp. 292–93)

He then proposed that some wild lands should be preserved for the future in a "nation's Park" where "the world could see for ages to come, the native Indian in his classic attire, galloping his wild horse, with sinewy bow, and shield and lance, amid the fleeting herds of elks and buffaloes" (Catlin, 1926 pp. 294–95). Of course Catlin's proposal was far too comprehensive for his own day and had little impact at that time.

There were, though, small groups and influential individuals, both amateur and professional, who did manage to achieve a part of Catlin's vision, albeit without the Amerindians. Among the earliest areas to receive widespread attention from conservationists, in the 1850s, was Middlesex Fells near Boston, Massachusetts. The Fells, eventually incorporated into the Metropolitan Park System, was the object of an unusual early effort to conserve land in a developing urban area. More typical was interest in preservation of lands in the undeveloped West. In 1864, the state of California established a natural reserve in the Yosemite Valley area, inspired in part by Olmsted senior's report on the environmental and scenic significance of the area. In 1872 Yellowstone National Park, the first site so designated, was established. With its surrealistic geysers and hot springs set against verdant boreal forests, it quickly came to symbolize the sort of exotic landscape deserving of preservation. Land for Canada's first national park at Banff was set aside in 1885. That same year a proposal for international preservation of Niagara Falls, suggested by Canada's governor-general Lord Frederick Dufferin, moved toward achievement.[4]

New York State, which had sponsored development of the American side of Niagara Falls, was also active in other areas. In 1885 it established the Adirondack Forest Preserve, now State Park, to preserve one of the few wilderness areas in the state from imminent development, particularly lumbering.[5] The preserve originally consisted of slightly less than 700,000 acres, intermixed with privately held lands. This mosaic of public and private lands caused problems for the park throughout its history, but these became especially intense in the late 1960s, when highway improvements made the area a more viable location for second homes. Since 1971 the state has attempted to purchase land or acquire scenic easements to assure a wild character to the park.

"Conservation of natural wealth" has a far broader meaning than merely setting aside certain areas of land as preserves. It also includes the protection of

The Upper Falls in Yosemite Valley were just one of the scenic features that made this area the focus of both nineteenth-century conservation efforts and environmental controversy.

all resources from depletion or irreparable degradation. The first challenge to American complacency toward environmental problems caused by human activities was the 1864 publication *Man and Nature; or Physical Geography as Modified by Human Action* by George Perkins Marsh. Marsh argued his case from the standpoint of cultural and economic decay. Citing examples from antiquity and the nineteenth century, he reasoned that there were limits to the alterations humans could make without permanently threatening life on earth. He was specifically concerned with the destruction of trees, but also discussed the consequences of damming waterways and draining wetlands. The significance of Marsh's book cannot be overestimated. It was the first encyclopedic, but readable, publication to make a case that resource exploitation, then accepted as an American birthright, was a short-term road to long-term problems. His work was among the most discussed in the nineteenth century, and was undoubtedly known to every early landscape architect.

Concern for the environment led to formation of a number of preservation and conservation organizations in the late nineteenth and early twentieth centuries. As a response to belief in the necessity of forests to avoid desertification, the continent's first environmental commemoration day—Arbor Day—was established in 1872 by Jay Sterling Morton. Love of trees was celebrated through the planting of seedlings, often supplied to schools or civic organizations by local businesspeople. Taking a different approach, protection rather than creation, the Sierra Club acquired wilderness tracts in the Sierra Nevada Mountains, especially those in the vicinity of Yosemite, for permanent preservation. Founded in 1892 by John Muir, Warren Olney, J. H. Senger, and William Arnes, the Sierra Club became a model for other preservation-oriented groups such as the American Scenic and Historic Preservation Society, established in 1895; the Audubon Society, 1905; and Save-the-Redwoods League, 1918.

This proliferation of environmental organizations around the turn of the century coincided with the beginning of serious interest on the part of the federal government in conservation issues. Theodore Roosevelt could be termed the "Conservation President," for it was during his administration that both professionals and amateurs who pioneered the movement were first given official credence. Among Roosevelt's advisors, forester Gifford Pinchot was one of the most respected. Through his influence National Forests were placed under authority of the same agency that employed foresters, the Department of Agriculture; the fundamental operating policies of the Forest Service were initiated; and the "conservation" philosophy of managed use "of the earth for the good of man" became firmly fixed as government policy (Pinchot, 1947, p. 322).

Just as the conservation movement was beginning to have these successes in both private and public arenas, a controversy arose which exposed the two intrinsically disparate philosophies to which conservationists subscribed. The controversy was over the fate of Hetch Hetchy Valley on the Tuolumne River just north of Yosemite Valley. The two conflicting philosophies might be termed the "preservationist" and the "exploitationist."[6] Preservationists believed absolutely in the inherent good of natural systems and the need to keep natural areas unaltered regardless of what other needs existed. They viewed the natural environment as a resource whose sole value was in its pristine contrast to altered landscapes. Exploitationists were environmental managers who believed that a few exceptional areas should remain inviolate, but that to assure this trade-offs necessary for economic development should be made. They viewed nature as a resource to be used, but wisely and within limits.

Hetch Hetchy, a miniature but less imposing version of Yosemite Valley, was targeted by the city of San Francisco in the early 1900s as a suitable site for a reservoir to supply much of the city's water. So bitter was the controversy that it divided the Sierra Club into factions which never really coalesced after this confrontation. Preservationists like Muir believed that the valley was significant in itself, but further, that to allow an engineering work of such scale anywhere in the Yosemite area could threaten all of the region. F. L. Olmsted, citing the earlier work of his father, also favored preservation and prophetically observed that "the number of people who now visit Hetch-Hetchy, or even the portions of the Yosemite Park which have been rendered more easily accessible, is no measure of the extent to which its scenery will be enjoyed throughout the twentieth century, and the crowded centuries to follow it" (1914, p. 45). Exploitationists, such as Olney, a former mayor of Oakland, believed that the needs of the Bay Area justified this loss and that it was only through such compromises that truly significant areas could be guaranteed protection. This difference in attitude toward natural resources has continued to be a key theme in the environmental movement, with groups and individuals who often share common overall interests polarized into intransigent factions.

This kind of factionalism, although precipitated by different issues, also caused a split between the two principal federal agencies administering natural areas: the National Forest Service and the National Park Service.[7] National Forests were first established in the United States in 1891 as part of a much broader land law reformation bill—the General Revision Act.[8] The National Forests, although often termed "reserves," were never intended as permanent protection zones; rather they were established to conserve trees for future managed harvests. Management of the forests was to assure that poor logging practices, which had caused untold problems for other vital resources, such as the siltation and blocking of navigable rivers, would be limited. Their existence would also guarantee that reserves would not be depleted, but constantly restocked. The Forest Service, established in its present form in 1905, was charged with research and management to reach these goals. After the 1920s, the economic function of the National Forests was often overshadowed and their mission clouded as the public began to see them as another form of recreational park.

The National Parks, on the other hand, were always intended to serve recreation as well as pure preservation, although just what was meant by "recreation" could vary considerably. Preservationists viewed recreation as passive, educational activities carried out by individuals or small groups with limited impact on the natural environment. Others, certainly the larger group, saw the parks as enlarged and exceptionally scenic playgrounds. These two viewpoints have caused friction from the time of the first National Parks director, Stephen Mather, to more contemporary controversies during the tenure of Secretary of the Interior James Watt.

Although the first National Park had been established in the 1870s, it was not until 1916 that Congress took action to establish a separate agency to manage these lands. By that time there were fifteen parks and more than thirty national monuments.[9] Formation of the National Park Service resulted from the efforts of innumerable individuals, but two names were most directly associated with the endeavor: Stephen Mather and Horace Albright. Mather, a successful Chicago businessman, took on the job of organizing the Park Service and moving the legislation for it through Congress. In less than two years he accomplished both these goals, although the initial 1916 authorization failed to provide funds for the Service and the entire experience left Mather mentally exhausted. During his recuperation it was his assistant, attorney Albright, who took over the task of directing operations when the Service was finally funded in 1917.[10] Parks Canada, the agency which administers that country's natural areas, was established in 1930 to manage a system originally consisting of eleven parks, including Georgian Bay and Jasper, but intended to increase to an eventual forty-eight.

Legislation instituting the Park Service stated its mission, in words composed by F. L. Olmsted, as being "to conserve the scenery and the natural and historic objects and the wild life therein and to provide for the enjoyment of the same in such manner and by such means as will leave them unimpaired for the enjoyment of future generations"[11] (Albright, 1985, p. 36). Early experiences of the Service demonstrated just how difficult it would be to both utilize and protect parklands. Among the earliest issues were conflicts with nearby residents over land uses, disagreements about how to develop visitor amenities in parks, funding limitations, questions as to how to develop a professional staff for the parks, and concerns related to transportation—all of which continue to be debated to this day.

One of the earliest land use conflicts occurred over ecological needs of the parks and desire of livestock owners to graze on what they saw as unused range. Today, it is often the park that is seen as a threat to surrounding grazing operations. Ranchers view parks as havens for predators such as coyotes or wolves, while some wild animals, such as brucellosis-infected buffalo, can be disease carriers to domesticated cattle. Quite different problems developed in visitor services, which Mather decided were to be handled by private concerns called "concessioners." Operating for profit, these businesses constantly sought to expand and to locate in the most heavily used spots, which generally also corresponded to the most impressive natural features.

Funding for the parks was always low, and in times of economic downturn or an insensitive administration would be lowered even further. This made it difficult to keep qualified employees, and to complete needed projects. Often the Service's original field employees were themselves a source of problems. Some had been political appointees, with no particular interest in parks but with allegiances to local ranchers or concessioners. As rapidly as he could, Mather had these people removed and conscientious superintendents like John White at Sequoia and Albright, who took over at Yellowstone in 1919, appointed.

What types of vehicles are suitable for use in natural areas has also been a vexing question. Initial problems involved automobiles, which were considered too intrusive and threatening to traditional horsepower to be admitted. It was not until 1919 that the first cars rumbled into Yellowstone, and at other parks lack of all-weather roads delayed this even longer. Thus began a long history of vehicular conflict—from cars in the first decade of the century to travel trailers in the 1950s to off-road vehicles (ORVs) in the 1980s. Passage of the Multiple Use Act for National Forests in 1960 further complicated potential conflicts on these federal lands. This law established as policy that land or resources on that land should not be reserved for a sole use, but for the most advantageous present and future combination of sustainable resource applications. While conceptually workable, the concept of multiple use, particularly when mixture and levels of use are mutually incompatible, has never been satisfactorily resolved.

A critical issue, related to each of these individual problem areas, has been to what extent natural areas should be preserved in an unaltered condition—as what are generally termed "wildernesses." Prior to the 1920s, when access to and within the parks was limited, the ability to protect natural areas from intrusion was not viewed as a significant problem. In fact, the greater concern was with how areas set aside could be developed for recreation. It was this concern which led to Frank Waugh's 1917 report on recreational opportunities in the National Forests. It did not take long, though, for quite opposite concerns to emerge, for it was quickly realized that even a relatively small number of users could irreversibly alter a natural area. Among the first to plead for nonrecreational areas of national lands were naturalist Aldo Leopold and landscape architect Arthur Carhart, both of the Forest Service. In particular, they argued against development of new roads, which admitted people to previously unopened land, and grazing, which altered natural vegetation. Early efforts at setting aside wilderness areas were slow, in part due to local demand for use of the lands and the antiquated perception that wild land remained abundant. It was not until 1964 with passage of the Wilderness Act that a sizable portion of national lands, initially over 9 million acres, was set aside to be preserved in a "wild" condition, a status that has been given widely varying interpretations.

Landscape architects and other design and planning professionals were active in the conservation movement from its inception. Horace J. McFarland of the American Civic Association was as forceful an advocate for National Parks as he had been for the revitalization of his hometown, Harrisburg, Pennsylvania. Warren Manning suggested a system of interconnections for National Parks and Monuments, via continuous public roads and trails, and also scenic drives along the seashore and major water bodies. As he had done in an earlier report on the Hudson-Mohawk River valleys,[12] he emphasized the importance of scenic views and viewpoints in visitor experience of the land. Genevieve Gillette helped launch a state park system for Michigan. F. L. Olmsted was directly involved with National Parks, both in formulating authorizing legislation and as a consultant on projects such as Lafayette National Park in Maine (now part of Acadia National Park) and a study of concession locations in Sequoia National Park.

In 1919 the National Park Service formed a division of landscape engineering, with Charles Punchard as the first landscape architect hired. His successor Thomas Vint organized what became an essential planning system, that of the Master Plan, to guide all future planning within each park. Conrad Wirth, to date the only landscape architect to head the Park System (from 1951 to 1964), described the comprehensive nature of a National Park Master Plan: "[It] contains an inventory of what we know about an area; why the area is important to the American people; how its significant story may be told to the visitor; where we may permit man-made developments and where developments shall be excluded; and how we shall provide for the preservation and protection of the park" (1955, p. 14). To implement these Master Plans through natural resource plans, design, and construction, the Park Service has employed since 1919 a steadily growing number of landscape architects, becoming in the 1980s their single largest employer.

As important as the Forest and Park Services were in preserving and conserving natural resources, they were not the only U.S. agencies which impacted the environment. In 1899 the Rivers and Harbors Act was passed, authorizing greater federal involvement in navigable waterways. Under provisions of this law, the Army Corps of Engineers began a series of major engineering works such as dams, locks, and channelizations, which permanently altered the largest waterways in the country. The value of these actions remains a constant subject of debate, but their environmental impacts cannot be doubted. Extensive restructuring of the Mississippi, for example, has been credited with siltation at the delta in Louisiana and the ensuing problems for navigation and fisheries.

Lack of water in the West was the rationale for the Reclamation Act of 1902. Its intent was to "reclaim" arid regions through government-sponsored irrigation projects of regional scale. Most of the large dam and lake projects west of the Mississippi, such as those on the Colorado and Platte Rivers, were initiated under this law and its later revisions. Once again an environmental intrusion of great magnitude brought contradictory consequences—cultivation of fertile land with abundant harvests which presumably kept consumer food costs down, but also salinization of both water and land, alterations in fishery cycles, and, as recent droughts along the Platte have shown, potential disruption of other economic activities such as tourism and transportation.

The Later Twentieth Century

During most of the twentieth century exploitationist philosophy has dominated the conservation movement. But beginning in the 1930s when government-sponsored conservation projects were placed under the jurisdiction of professional naturalists and scientists, a preservationist attitude was resurrected. Among the first both to articulate and to practice ecological preservation of resources was Aldo Leopold. His classic book *A Sand County Almanac* presented the conservation ethic in a form that made the natural world personal to every reader and transformed sensibilities regarding the wild. Professionally, Leopold promoted ecological restoration, beginning with his 1930s prairie restoration at the University of Wisconsin arboretum in Madison. Later, in the 1960s, "ecology" became a buzzword for a host of environmental issues, in an era when greater appreciation for the intrinsic value of natural systems began. Just as *Man and Nature* had triggered interest in the environment in the late 1800s, it was another book, *Silent Spring* by Rachel Carson, that is often credited with provoking these changes in public attitudes in the 1960s. Terming environmental degradation "blight," she focused on damage done through indiscriminant application of the legion of new chemicals that became available after World War II. What most alarmed the public was not the individual tales of horror which she recounted, but the carefully developed message that these were simply links in a vast, but unseen, chain that was progressively strangling the earth. Much of the success of environmental legislation in the 1970s must be credited to the influence of the small but pithy work, which Udall called "the first global environmental impact statement prepared by a scientist" (1988, p. 202).

During the presidential administration of Lyndon Johnson, landscape appearance was promoted as an important aspect of environmental quality. In 1965 the President and Lady Bird Johnson hosted a White House Conference on Natural Beauty which emphasized the need to preserve land itself as a resource, but also to protect those visual qualities which give it meaning and value for people. This conference inaugurated a far-reaching program of urban beautification, billboard control, and roadside planting. This new Johnsonian conservation ethic moved ecology from the realm of scientists and ecology devotees to mainstream consciousness.

The late 1960s and early 1970s were a particularly active time for passage of environmental legislation, particularly laws aimed at controlling pollution. During that period a slew of laws which became the basic framework of an environmental policy for the United States were passed. Important laws included the Air Quality Act of 1967 and the Water Pollution Control Act of 1972, both of which set standards for "acceptable" levels of industrial and municipal pollutants. Legislation passed in 1965 establishing the Land and Water Conservation Fund set aside federal money to be granted to states and local governments for the purchase of parklands. The Endangered Species Act of 1973 gave some protection to the most threatened flora and fauna. But probably no one law had a greater effect on environmental quality or on the profession of landscape architecture than the National Environmental Policy Act (NEPA), passed in 1970.

NEPA's requirements were far-ranging in scope and affected every project for which any federal government funding was used.[13] NEPA established as national policy prevention of damage to the physical environment. At a more practical level the legislation established a Presidential advisory panel called the Council on Environmental Quality to make environmental policy recommendations. An even more significant provision of NEPA was that all federal agencies were required to submit reports on any of the projects that they funded which had potential environmental consequences, whether natural, social, or economic. These reports, known as Environmental Impact Statements (EISs), became a method by which agencies considered the potential results of their activities, but also a means by which the public could comment on government projects. While the EIS process has been criticized for delaying or halting important projects, its provisions have been beneficial in forcing project organizers to consider alternative solutions that in the end may have benefited the agencies, the taxpayers, and certainly the environment.

Landscape architects responded to concerns such as these by reemphasizing the environmental basis for design that had been critical to the profession's founders in the nineteenth century. Using more scientific data and new approaches of data manipulation and analysis, designers incorporated natural process as one of the underlying functional bases for design. This "design with nature" approach recognized anew that "form and process are indivisible aspects of a single phenomenon. The ecological method allows one to understand form as an explicit point in evolutionary process"[14] (McHarg, 1967, p. 107).

Communities such as the Village Homes subdivision in Davis, California, had plans based upon the concept of limiting human impact on natural processes.

Also in the 1960s, Philip Lewis and Ian McHarg began to apply land use analysis systems, which many considered design by environmental determinism, to the study of natural and cultural phenomena. Lewis's method entailed looking at the landscape from the perspective of its intended human use and then seeking to identify planning criteria that would minimize the impact of that use on the natural environment, which had been assessed in terms of "resource patterns." Lewis used this approach in his seminal study of the recreational potential of Wisconsin landscapes. McHarg's approach was similar in methodology, which relied on overlays of individual resource analyses, but differed in focusing first on the characteristics of site and then determining which potential land uses were inherently suited to landscape capability. The *Plan for the Valleys* which his firm of Wallace McHarg Roberts and Todd produced in 1963 to guide development of two rural valleys near Baltimore demonstrated the potential of this process to adapt intensive land use to sensitive environments.[15] These methods became standard practice for those professionals whose emphasis was in landscape ecology.

Village Homes in Davis, California, is a subdivision where ecological principles of land use have been employed. In addition to compact building placement, pedestrian corridors such as the one shown here are used as detention areas so that no additional runoff will be generated by site development.

More recently landscape architects have begun to specialize in areas of practice directed specifically toward conservation and preservation of natural systems. Two such areas are reclamation of altered landscapes and planning and design for water management. "Reclamation" was traditionally equated with the rehabilitation of lands mined for minerals such as coal fields. Reclamation can include, though, any analysis and planning activities aimed at restoring land to a semblance of a past condition. Today reclamation includes the rehabilitation of toxic waste sites, sanitary landfills, and wetlands.

In North America the first organized reclamation of mined lands occurred in 1914 on Indiana coal fields cosmetically planted with fruit trees as a public relations tactic. Legislative efforts to control surface mining, usually the most damaging to the landscape, began in West Virginia in 1939; however, little substantive reclamation began until 1977, with passage of the Federal Surface Mining Control and Reclamation Act. This law was the first to regulate environmental aspects of the industry, establishing guidelines that required regrading the site to original contours and revegetation. In spite of such legislation, which has provided opportunities for landscape architects to specialize in mine planning and reclamation, significant environmental damage continues either from lands mined prior to legislation or unmonitored contemporary mining. An estimated 50 percent of Colorado watersheds have been contaminated by heavy metals and biological oxygen demand from over a century of mineral exploitation.

Planning for water management involved floodplain protection and development of landscape designs based on the principles of xeriscape. Under the National Flood Insurance Program, mandated in 1973, property in flood hazard areas could not be insured against floods unless the community in which they were located participated in flood zone protection. This provision effectively required that comprehensive plans exclude floodways from intensive development, and, at a smaller scale, that site plans utilize nondisruptive design features to preserve the function of floodways. Xeriscape, which is related to smaller-scale site development, involved proper plant selection, efficient irrigation methods, water-retaining grading, soil improvement, and use of mulches to reduce the moisture demand of designed landscapes. It often emphasized use of native or naturalized plants, with only small or no cultivated turf areas. This approach holds particular promise for water conservation in hot, arid regions of the continent, where as much as a third of all domestically used water has gone to maintain gardens and lawns.

Many believe that now, in the last decade of the twentieth century, we are finally on the verge of a fresh and more comprehensive conservation era. Fuel conservation, recycling of consumer products such as newspaper and aluminum, and use of natural rather than chemically produced products are often considered signs of a significant change in public attitude toward the environment. The popularity of the concepts of sustainable development suggest a changing public mindset. However, numerous past failures in seizing conservation opportunities, such as the lack to date of any significant application of solar heating technology or the low rates of voluntary recycling in some communities, suggest that conservation falls low on a scale of American concerns when measured by actions. It remains to be seen, then, if problems such as nuclear waste storage and global warming can be resolved or whether a writer of the third millennium will write, as Marsh did, that "the decay of these once flourishing countries is partly due . . . [to] man's ignorant disregard of the laws of nature . . ." (1965, pp. 10–11).

CONSERVATION OF CULTURAL RESOURCES

The Nineteenth and Early Twentieth Centuries

Philosophies underlying conservation of cultural resources have differed only in application from those for protecting natural resources. Growth of this movement followed closely in both timing and pace the progress of the environmental movement. Loss of culturally important sites began almost immediately upon settlement. European colonists had no appreciation for the works of Native Americans, and wholesale destruction, even of cities the size of Tenochtitlán, was the rule. But Euroamericans were no more sensitive to their own past, often seeing it only as an impediment to a more prosperous future. After the American Revolution, the United States entered a particularly antihistoric phase, in which the new nation saw itself as the embodiment of a future that should be unencumbered by political, social, and historical baggage representing repressive and elitist European traditions. Only in the second generation, when the country sought an identity as a world power, did its past, especially that of the "glorious revolution," become important.

Therefore, earliest attention of those in the United States interested in historic preservation was focused on those sites associated with the founding of the nation. In 1816, Philadelphia acquired Independence Hall, which was already in ruinous condition and threatened with demolition. The first landscape-oriented preservation effort was the purchase of a large portion of Mount Vernon in 1853 by an organization formed for just that purpose: the Mount Vernon Ladies Association of the Union. Although the Association's first energies were directed at restoration of structures, they did preserve agricultural lands of the plantation and garden areas, allowing their restoration and reconstruction in this century. The first landscapes preserved as such were Civil War battlefields, most of which became National Monuments in the 1890s, due to pressure from sentimental Union veterans then approaching old age. At about the same time, scientific exploration of Native American sites in the Southwest, such as Chaco Canyon and Mesa Verde, led to demand that these sites be protected. Other isolated landscape preservation activities also occurred, sponsored by private initiative. For example, in the 1890s John Bartram's home and part of his arboretum were set aside as a historic park through efforts of his descendants and industrialist Andrew Eastwick.[16]

As with the environmental movement, the turn of the century and the first decades afterward were a period of intense activity in historic preservation. The first historic preservation legislation passed the U.S. Congress in 1906: the Antiquities Act authorized the President to proclaim certain sites, in addition to southwestern Native American sites and battlefields, of historical and scientific importance as National Monuments. Monument status was to be designated for natural sites not large enough or of required quality to be in the National Park System. Private preservation efforts resulted in formation of several important organizations, such as the Society for the Preservation of New England Antiquities and the Hudson River Conservation Society. While most of these early efforts focused on historic preservation as a means to retain and communicate local identity, the economic potential of preservation activities was quickly realized.

The first to grasp the role of history as a draw for tourists was William A. R. Goodwin, the minister of Williamsburg, Virginia's historic Bruton Parish Church. In the shabby streets and decaying buildings of his economically depressed Tidewater town he saw potential both to re-create its more glorious past and to assure its economic future. His concept was the complete restoration and reconstruction of the town as it had existed in the late eighteenth century. Financing such a colossal effort was, of course, his first challenge, but the scale of his vision and the power of his arguments were sufficient to entice John D.

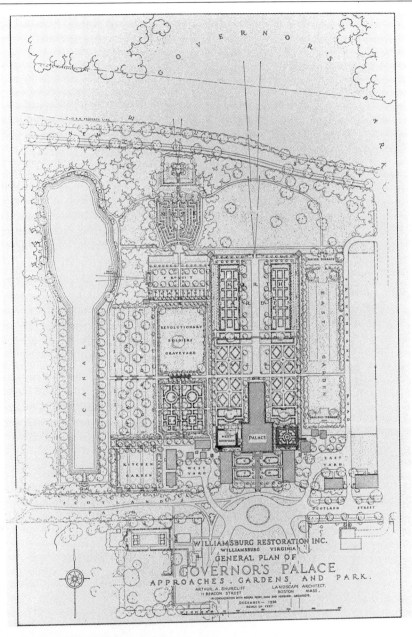

Shurcliff's reconstruction plan for the Governor's Palace at Williamsburg, Virginia. (Landscape Architecture, Vol. 27, No. 2.)

Rockefeller to contribute the initial funds and eventually bankroll most of the research and construction that followed.

Williamsburg's pivotal contribution to the preservation movement was its holism. Earlier preservation had focused on isolated structures and landscape fragments, but the Williamsburg project was conceived as a complete environment, in which all of the parts would combine not just to present physical reality, but to create an ambiance.[17] A guiding principle of the project was historical accuracy *in appearance* based on documentary and archaeological research. According to Goodwin, three principal information sources were used for garden restorations: comparison to existing contemporaneous colonial Virginia gardens and English gardens; old maps and plans of both Williamsburg and other colonial sites; and remnant features, such as steps, discovered during excavation. Unfortunately, at that time garden or landscape archaeology was a relatively unsophisticated specialization, and landscape restorations, completed under Arthur Shurcliff, the first landscape architect employed by the Colonial Williamsburg Foundation, were based more upon period representations than site-specific features. Reconstruction of the urban landscape, though, did convey the scale and spatial organization which were hallmarks of Governor Nicholson's original plan.

The example of Williamsburg, literally a phoenix rising from the ashes of two centuries, inspired other cities with preserved sites and structures to protect and restore them. Efforts such as those of the San Antonio Conservation Society, Charleston's Society for the Preservation of Old Dwellings, and the Vieux Carré Commission in New Orleans demonstrated that the past was best preserved intact as neighborhoods. The San Antonio Conservation Society, founded in 1924, initially managed single structures of architectural or civic importance, such as the Spanish Governor's Palace or the Spanish missions near the city. In the early 1930s, they realized that significant historic areas within the city also needed preservation attention. Their first effort in a historic district involved restoration and reconstruction of the eighteenth-century settlement known as La Villita on a bluff above the San Antonio River, now part of the Riverwalk area.[18]

In 1931 Charleston put into law the first zoning ordinance that designated a historic district as one of its land use zones. Nine years later a city committee engaged F. L. Olmsted to complete the first comprehensive survey and plan for this district. This plan wisely dealt with issues beyond the mere appearance of structure, and especially it addressed problems generated by automobile traffic. This pioneer work, which designated one of the largest historic districts on the continent, became a model for other cities and initiated many of the recording procedures now regularly used in Historic Site Surveys.

The Vieux Carré Commission of New Orleans, authorized in 1936, advised the city on preservation issues in the historic French Quarter.[19] It established one of the most stringent sets of architectural requirements for both old and new structures. Further, it could block demolition of historic structures. The Vieux Carré Commission thus became one of the most influential historic preservation organizations in North America.

View of the restored La Villita area of San Antonio, Texas, preserved through efforts of the San Antonio Conservation Society. (Barker Texas History Center, The University of Texas at Austin, Austin, Texas.)

While many cities took action to preserve their cultural resources, another preservation-related site type, the museum village, became popular. The earliest of these were assemblages of structures, usually those threatened with demolition at their original site, brought together into simulated villages representing some particular time period. Greenfield Village, Henry Ford's tribute to progress and invention in America, was the earliest and most eclectic of these, being a generalized nostalgic representation of a small nineteenth-century town. Later, in the 1920s, museum villages such as Sturbridge Village in Massachusetts and Farmer's Village in Cooperstown, New York, used more limited themes of time and place, although they too represented fictitious places. Sturbridge Village was one of the few to re-create a historic site plan as well as architecture. As laid out by Shurcliff, Sturbridge Village has a central town green about which commercial and public buildings are arranged. More recently developed museum villages have placed greater emphasis on accuracy of siting and site planning. At Plimouth Plantation, a simulation of the colony in 1627, a site similar to the original was developed according to an archaeologically determined plan. Realism extended to interpretation, with each docent playing the role of an original colonist, and the pungent smells of waste and decay reestablished along with structures.

Gardens were the landscapes most frequently restored by early preservation groups. The Garden Club of Virginia was particularly active in this area, funding and overseeing restorations throughout the state, such as the walled gardens of the University of Virginia, the grounds of Gunston Hall, and the Woodlawn. Arthur Shurtcliff, Alden Hopkins, his successor at Colonial Williamsburg, and Ralph Griswold were longtime consultants to the Garden Club. In the Northeast, Shurtcliff and Fletcher Steele were the principal landscape architects engaged in early garden preservations. Steele's most famous work was the garden of the relocated colonial Mission House in Stockbridge, Massachusetts. Although the accuracy of these restorations, or more precisely reconstructions, was often questioned and many have been "re-reconstructed" in light of more complete recent research, these initial efforts were critical in establishing landscapes as preservable cultural resources.

The Late Twentieth Century

Until the 1930s, most historic preservation projects in the United States were the result of private initiative. While the federal government did control some important prehistoric and historic sites, these were often given little attention beyond simply being protected from vandals and natural forces, because administrators in the National Park Service directed most of their attention to natural features. This imbalance began to change during the 1930s when intensive Federal "make-work" projects addressed both natural and cultural resources.[20]

Finally, in 1949 a quasi-governmental agency sponsored by numerous professional organizations including the ASLA—the National Trust for Historic Preservation—was authorized by Congress to coordinate preservation efforts. Its earliest endeavors were in public education and in funding purchase of threatened properties. It later directly acquired some significant structures and properties, beginning with Woodlawn Plantation in Virginia. Focusing initially on residential sites of architectural significance, the Trust has only recently taken a serious interest in the settings of these homes. Garden restorations at Trust properties include those at Chesterwood, the home of sculptor Daniel Chester French.

Passage of the National Historic Preservation Act of 1966 created the most important governmental tool for preservation, the National Register of Historic Places. The Register, administered by the National Park Service, was a system to document and recognize nationally significant sites of all types. Following passage of the Economic Recovery Tax Act, historic status also carried with it certain tax reduction benefits. Most of them were lost in subsequent tax reform legislation, but although short lived, these tax benefits are credited with encouraging restoration of over 18,000 structures throughout the country and were particularly significant in downtown revitalizations.

Small-town commercial districts were the focus of the Trust's Main Street Program, initiated in 1977 and still in operation. The Main Street project emphasized revitalization and adaptive reuse of downtown structures while maintaining facade detail and scale. It was unusual among preservation programs in that it included attention to marketing as well as physical appearance. Galesburg in Illinois, Georgetown in Texas, and Hot Springs, South Dakota, are all examples of the positive outcomes from this project. Recently the Trust has begun the Heritage Tourism program that links regional tourism with historic preservation.

In Mexico preservationists have focused on excavations, stabilization, and restoration of pre-Columbian structures and landscapes. Extensive preservation legislation gave at least token protection from vandalism and removal of artifacts from the country. In addition, technical training for conservationists was highly developed, and local restorers carried out such painstaking work as the stabilization of murals at Bonampak. Many urban sites from the early colonial period have been passively preserved due to slow economic growth. Towns such as Merida in Yucatan and Patzcuaro in Michoacan retain both their eighteenth-century scale and the compact urban density of Spanish colonial towns. The chief threats to historic preservation in Mexico ironically come less from human than from natural sources. In Mexico City subsidence threatens many old buildings, while throughout the country earthquakes endanger them.

Urban growth and renewed traditionalism after the Second World War stimulated the Canadian preservation movement. Administered by the National Historic Park and Sites Branch of Parks Canada, sites as varied as L'Anse Aux Meadows Viking settlement and Rideau Canal are preserved under the encompassing concept of national "heritage." Heritage Canada, a nonprofit foundation, was founded in the 1970s to encourage local preservation ventures. Landscapes are well represented in the accomplishments of both organizations. Agricultural

Main street in Galesburg, Illinois, one of the original community participants in the National Trust for Historic Preservation's Main Street Program. Streetscape improvements, such as the pedestrian crossings and tree plantings shown here, were typical of downtown design changes that the program encouraged.

areas, such as Motherwell Farmstead in Saskatchewan; forts, including Louisburg in Nova Scotia; and gardens, such as the Halifax Public Garden and Vaux's Parliament grounds in Ottawa, are all now protected sites.

In the last half of the 1970s and the 1980s, historic preservation moved well beyond its early concerns with buildings and small sites to embrace the whole of the designed and cultural landscape. Recognition of the Green Springs Rural Historic District in Virginia in the 1970s was one of the earliest signs of interest in large, active landscapes to preserve historic features and character. A movement that merges historic preservation and conservation was that directed toward the preservation of agricultural lands. This effort had its origins in the 1960s when significant tracts of prime agricultural land began to be lost to other types of development such as trailer parks, subdivisions, highways, and recreational sites. Agricultural lands preservation recognizes farmland as both a resource and a cultural landscape. Through techniques such as establishment of agricultural districts, purchase of easements, and transfer of development rights land is kept in agriculture for an extended period of time, although its absolute preservation is not guaranteed. The Federal Farmland Protection Policy Act of 1981 has gone beyond those generally local preservation methods to require a specific assessment of the impact of any federally funded project that might convert farmland to another use. More recently the National Agricultural Lands Study has developed a thorough database for future study of agricultural land use and conservation.

The increasing importance of landscape preservation was demonstrated by the consideration given it in recent legislation and regulation. The so-called Olmsted Bill,[21] still pending at the time of this writing, would provide documentation and evaluation for National Register status of works associated with important early practitioners such as Frederick Law Olmsted, F. L. Olmsted, Jr., J. C. Olmsted, Kessler, Cleveland, and Weidenmann. Perhaps more encouraging than this focus on the work of a few landscape architects were two National Register Bulletins[22] written in the late 1980s that outlined requirements and procedures by which designed and cultural landscapes can be included on the Register, and thus receive full recognition of their artistic and historic value.

Plaza of the Three Cultures in Mexico City.

CONCLUSION AND SUMMARY

A conservation ethic has always been a part of the philosophy of landscape architecture—Lancelot Brown's site "capabilities" could even be interpreted as a loose reference to some inherent natural or cultural character. Certainly, as landscape architecture developed into a profession in North America, awareness of the value of the environment, whether that created by natural forces or by culture, has always been a guiding theme. In the nineteenth century, the conservation ethic was bolstered largely by subjective assessments and Romantic sentiments about the landscape. By the late twentieth century, scientific studies gave more substance to conservation arguments, yet it was in the domain of political decision making that the most significant advances were made—legislation which has mandated amelioration of environmental damage, protection of natural resources, and preservation of historic and cultural landscapes. This reality suggests both the limits of the landscape architecture profession to influence the macro-scale environment, and also the need for those educated in the stewardship tradition of the profession to exercise greater leadership in the political process.

NOTES

1. Term from Tichi, 1979.

2. The use of any single term to describe complex attitudes is fraught with problems. "Conservation" is one term which has a variety of meanings and inferences. To scientific foresters such as Gifford Pinchot, it meant supervised exploitation. To others, including environmental preservationists like W. J. McGee, it meant management for maximum protection of natural or cultural features. It is used here in its most generic sense to include all conditions in which sites are purposefully administered to protect them for some purpose, whether complete preservation or controlled use.

3. For balanced discussion of the issues in this particular water controversy see Nadeau, 1950, and Hoffman, 1981. For an overview of the western water issue see Reisner, 1986.

4. See Chapter 7 for discussion of Niagara Falls.

5. After the Civil War development pressure on this landscape increased dramatically, and much of it was a "wilderness" only in contrast to the rest of the state. By the 1890s the landscape was dotted with what were euphemistically called "camps," really rustic estates for the same barons of industry with "cottages" in Newport, Rhode Island.

6. The latter group preferred to use the term "conservationist," but since this term is here used more generally, and the contrast between preservation and utilization more accurately identifies differences between the groups, "exploitationist" is used here; the term is used in a nonpejorative sense.

7. Part of this difference in philosophy between the services grows out of assigned functions, competition for limited funds, and the complex administrative histories of both agencies. For example, prior to 1900 foresters were employed by the Department of the Interior, where Parks was also housed, but the National Forests themselves were to be managed by the Department of Agriculture. Under Pinchot, the Forest Service employees and sites were brought together in the Department of Agriculture. Later, some monument sites administered by the Forest Service were transferred unamicably to Parks.

8. Prior forestry legislation, such as the Timber Culture Act, dealt with tree planting in the plains, not forest management. Planting was directed by a predecessor of the Service, known as the Division of Forestry.

9. National Parks were designated by Congress. Monuments, on the other hand, were named by the President and intended to preserve some single natural or cultural feature of small extent, such as Devil's Tower in Wyoming or Aztec Ruin in New Mexico. Some monuments, such as Glacier, later became parks. Prior to the establishment of the Park Service, monuments and parks were managed by three different departments—Agriculture, War, and Interior—depending on the type of site.

10. A most readable and personal history of the founding of the National Park Service is Albright's The Birth of the National Park Service.

11. According to Albright (1985), these lines had originally been written by Olmsted in a letter to the American Civic Association, but the committee formulating the bill, including Albright, Senator William Kent who introduced it, and Gilbert Grosvenor of the National Geographic Society, found the words to reflect as well as could be done a balance between opposing needs for preservation and use.

12. See Chapter 16.

13. *Many individual states later passed a local version of this law, which effectively extended its provisions to state-funded projects as well.*

14. *Specific projects based on this approach are discussed in Chapters 17 and 18.*

15. *The overlay approach seems to have been first used by Warren Manning as early as 1912. See Chapter 17 for discussion of another McHargian design—the Woodlands.*

16. *It is indicative of the level of preservation practice at this time that when Eastwick, a railroad man, bought much of the site, intending to memorialize Bartram, he also routed a line of his railroad through it, although in a well-depressed trench. At that time this concealment of the line was considered a rather sensitive treatment.*

17. *There were of course limits to what this approach could reasonably accomplish, and Williamsburg has always been criticized for a certain sterile quality to its interpretations. At a superficial level there is an excessive level of maintenance. More serious was the avoidance, until recently, of controversial social issues, such as slavery, indentured servitude, and the status of women.*

18. *The Society was also involved in preservation of the river bend, which became the original Riverwalk. It was to have been converted to a covered drainageway when the river was straightened. It was architect Robert Hugman, not the Society, though, who mobilized the city to revitalize the area in its present form.*

19. *The Commission, as a named body, had actually been inaugurated eleven years earlier, but its advice carried no authority and it became during this early period little more than a civic beautification organization.*

20. *See Chapter 14 for discussion of the 1930s.*

21. *Officially titled the Olmsted Heritage Landscapes Act.*

22. *Bulletins 18 and 30: Keller and Keller (1987) and McClelland, et. al. respectively.*

26

The 1930s: Era of Public Works

Little by little the sky was darkened by the mixing dust, and wind felt over the earth, loosened the dust, and carried it away. The wind grew stronger, the rain crust broke and the dust lifted up out of the fields and drove gray plumes into the air like sluggish smoke. The corn threshed the wind and made a dry, rushing sound. The finest dust did not settle back to earth now, but disappeared into the darkening sky. The wind grew stronger, whisked under stones, carried up straws and old leaves, and even little clods, marking its course as it sailed across the fields. The air and the sky darkened and through them the sun shone redly, and there was a sting in the air. . . . Men and women huddled in their houses, and they tied handkerchiefs over their noses when they went out, and wore goggles to protect their eyes. . . . Houses were shut tight, and cloth wedged around doors and windows, but the dust came in so thinly that it could not be seen in the air, and it settled like pollen on the chairs and tables, on the dishes.

John Steinbeck, The Grapes of Wrath, *1939*

Few changes have affected North American society as drastically and immediately as the events of late October 1929. In that month economic problems that had been disguised during the entire decade came to a catastrophic head, producing the disaster popularly called "the Crash." But the stock market crash and the ensuing economic calamity was just one problem that would alter priorities and redirect the profession of landscape architecture during the 1930s. Environmental problems and their inescapable social consequences also changed the direction of concern toward conservation of resources and comprehensive land use planning.

The 1930s was a short but significant period of time in the history of design and planning in North America.[1] Five Depression-era trends were particularly significant for landscape architecture. First, there was a striking change in attitude toward industrial progress, in which the private institutions and individualistic belief systems that had formerly produced widespread prosperity were questioned. In part this led to appreciation and conservation of both natural and cultural resources. Of equal importance were changing views toward an appropriate role for the federal government. Earlier most Americans would have agreed with the maxim which says that the government governs best that governs least. As the Depression deepened though, many people came to accept, even expect, high levels of government involvement in both economic and social problems. Third, landscape architects were returned to public practice, either through direct employment by the government or through federal projects on which private firms consulted. In a sense this shift reestablished concerns which many in the profession had abandoned in the early twentieth century. Fourth, in this new arena of practice, problems requiring creative, nontraditional solutions were presented to designers, hence many old notions of scale, materials, and construction were replaced with innovative approaches. Finally, since the purposes of public projects differed so radically from those of 1920s estate work, the break from private to public employment led to stylistic freedom.

TWIN DISASTERS OF THE 1930s

This era of government involvement in planning and design resulted from two disasters—one natural, the other economic—and the social upheavals that followed them. The defining event for this period was the stock market crash of October 29, 1929. Although the Crash has been attributed to various causes, most authorities agree that a significant factor was the high level of stock speculation during 1929. This speculation led to inflated prices for almost all stocks sold on the New York exchange, at a time when the general economy was not particularly strong. There were also specific industries with high rates of unemployment, and American goods were costly on world markets. And even the artificial prosperity of the 1920s had not been universal. In the southern United States, tenancy and sharecropping continued, with a significant part of the population at poverty level. Throughout rural North America many farm families lived under nineteenth-century conditions. An estimated 90 percent of farms lacked electricity, and an even greater number likely lacked modern sanitary systems.

Many knew that artificial prosperity could not continue indefinitely, but the decline once begun seemed endless. The most dismal conditions in fact did not occur until the second half of 1930. At that time rates of bank failure, with the ensuing loss of lifetime savings, became acute. Wages also began to drop significantly for those who remained employed. An estimated 15 to 20 percent of workers in the United States became unemployed, with smaller but still significant proportion out of work in Canada. As a result, more than 2 million people became homeless drifters, hopping rides on trains and sleeping in vacant areas and public parks. As whole families became displaced, squatter encampments, called Hoovervilles after then President Herbert Hoover, sprang up on public lands. Central Park became one of the more notorious of these settlements, ironically returning the site to a land use that had occurred there in the 1850s prior to park development.

The second tragedy to hit the continent during the 1930s was the environmental catastrophe known as the Dust Bowl. The Dust Bowl was a windblown erosion event on the Great Plains which began in 1932 and continued until 1940, with peak destruction occurring in mid-decade. The Dust Bowl and other agricultural problems of the decade resulted in part from a series of droughts which had begun in 1930. In that year, a severe dry spell lasting one year began in the southern and lower midwestern United States. In many areas rain was only 50 to 60 percent of the average, with some states being even harder hit. Arkansas, for example, saw only 35 percent of its anticipated rainfall. As a result of the dryness forest fires became rampant in the Southeast, destroying large areas of National Forests such as Pisgah in North Carolina. Transportation was also affected as the water level of the Mississippi and its tributaries dropped dramatically, reportedly to only 4 feet where the river flowed between Missouri and Tennessee.

The dust storms that decimated Great Plains agriculture in the 1930s resulted from a combination of market and environmental situations. Droughts were certainly a major factor. A significant contributing problem was that there were large tracts of land in agriculture on which no or poor soil conservation techniques were being applied. In addition, hot temperatures associated with the drought fueled high winds across a virtually treeless plain. The mix of desiccated, exposed soil, with winds unmodified by any breaks, produced a nightmarish landscape in which millions of acres of land were lost to cultivation, millions of head of livestock killed, and normal life disrupted.

The economic and environmental problems caused by the twin disasters of depression and disrupted agriculture resulted in equally serious social problems. Both produced widespread privation and displacement. Frustration and lack of

Clouds of dust such as this engulfed farms and towns across the Great Plains during the Dust Bowl of the 1930s. (Barker Texas History Center, The University of Texas at Austin, Austin, Texas.)

basic human services often resulted in crime, riots, and looting. For many groups of people, health declined due to poor nutrition, unavailability of medical treatment, and respiratory congestion caused by dust. Rates of marriage and childbirth declined, since people felt incapable of supporting a family and many probably feared to bring new life into a world in chaos. Finally, in the United States obsession with national problems led to renewed political isolationism, a factor sometimes cited as contributing to World War II.

LANDSCAPE ARCHITECTS IN THE PUBLIC EMPLOY

Much of the history of the 1930s, especially in the United States,[2] was the history of government response to the financial and environmental problems which shaped the era. In the earliest days of the Depression, that is during Herbert Hoover's presidency, the federal government's principal technique for economic recovery was encouragement of private sector activity—bank financing of loans and private infusions of capital into stocks. After two years of this passive encouragement, the need for direct public action was finally realized. Hoover, who it will be remembered was responsible for the standard zoning enabling act, broadened his involvement in housing issues, supporting a modern system of home mortgages designed to encourage home ownership. In addition, his administration organized the Reconstruction Finance Corporation, an agency that was to loan money to banks, businesses, and industries for economic recovery. These measures, unfortunately, were too little, too late, and public perception of their inadequacy was illustrated by the 1932 presidential election returns.

With the inauguration of Franklin D. Roosevelt in 1933, the public works and employment programs that were part of the reform movement known as the New Deal went into effect, with an explosion of federal activity. During Roosevelt's first nine months in office many of the most successful programs of the administration were conceptualized, planned, and implemented. Two programs which began in 1933 and had direct repercussions for landscape architecture were the Civilian Conservation Corps (CCC) and the Public Works Administration (PWA).

The CCC was to serve two purposes. As the name suggests, it was to engage in activities related to preservation and management of resources. Its other key function was to provide regular, constructive employment for men from disadvantaged families. Originally these men were youths, but as the program developed, adults—principally Native Americans working on their own reservations and World War I veterans—also became eligible to participate. The Corps was organized along military lines, with members living in camps and following a daily regimen of work and education. Projects that Corps teams carried out were diverse. They fought forest fires, planted trees in reforestation areas, dug drainage ditches, rebuilt historic structures, and constructed park roads, among other activities.

The PWA was formed to resolve urban housing problems. Among its particular charges were slum clearance and urban development. In the early days of the New Deal, the agency financed more construction—everything from public buildings to highway tunnels—than any other. As an omnibus funding organization the PWA made possible many projects that utilized professional design services.

Other agencies affecting landscape and landscape architecture were the Works Progress Administration (WPA), the National Resources Planning Board, and the Resettlement Administration. While the WPA filled many roles, key missions were to build or refurbish public facilities such as hospitals, airports and urban infrastructure; to help communities improve basic services such as education and public health; and to fund programs in the arts such as the Federal Writers' Project. The National Resources Planning Board organized planners to advise government agencies. Recommendations were made on social and economic, as well as physical, planning issues. The purpose of the Resettlement Administration was related to the early twentieth century Country Life Movement idealization of rural life. It sought to ameliorate the material life of farmers through improved housing, especially in new villages located at edges of urban areas.

These programs individually and as a group had significant impacts on the direction that the profession of landscape architecture took, particularly where training of young professionals was concerned. By the mid-1930s A. D. Taylor reported that there was full employment of landscape architects and that there was "probably no other profession [that] has had a greater demand for its services."[3] This high level of employment resulted from 90 percent of all landscape architects being in government service. Prior to 1929 the ratio would have been reversed, with fewer than 10 percent in public practice. The employment boom though, was not without its pitfalls. Taylor also noted that inexperienced students or recent graduates were often sent to design and supervise projects. In his view this produced shoddy work. Funding limitations resulted in many projects having very simplified designs, quite in contrast to the ornate details favored during the Neoclassicist period. Under good conditions, with skilled designers and foremen, this limitation became a boon. Many structures were given a rustic quality through use of local, nonmanufactured materials organized so that texture, relief, and mass were substituted for superficial embellishments.

The loss of so much private work forced those offices that remained open to adopt more businesslike practices and attempt to achieve economy of scale. These remaining offices often were consulted by government programs, particularly for small-scale projects, such as urban parks. Many traditionally oriented practitioners were unable to adjust to the new regime. Fletcher Steele was particularly vocal about the corruption of the profession's artistic base resulting from public employment.[4]

The majority of landscape architects, who viewed federal programs as godsends, at least financially, engaged in four principal areas of work during the 1930s. Large-scale planning, both for regional physical development and conservation of resources, developed rapidly under the New Deal. At the more site-specific level, landscape architects worked across the country on the planning and design of national and state parks. The government also endorsed the reformist attitudes of the city planning movement, employing landscape architects and planners in a variety of housing programs. Finally, designers continued to develop schemes for small sites, particularly those for urban recreation.

Large-Scale Planning

Government-sponsored regional and resource planning projects allowed landscape architects to apply principles of large-scale planning that had been difficult to implement without sanction from a central authority. Work in this area was primarily in historic preservation, soil conservation, land use planning, and watershed management. Two significant laws passed by Congress in the mid-1930s established historic preservation programs which continue to this day. The first was the Historic American Building Survey (HABS), established in 1933. HABS was a program intended to employ designers, historians, and photographers with the mission of researching and recording historic sites and structures. At each site, built features were measured and then documented by as-built drawings. Since early recording projects were limited to the period before 1840, all landscapes originally recorded were gardens. The first of these was The Lindens in Danvers, Massachusetts. HABS continues today as an active historic preservation program with recently recorded landscapes including Meridian Hill Park, to be discussed shortly, and Mount Auburn Cemetery. A second law, the Historic Sites Act, established preservation as a national policy. It also authorized specific projects, which often became prototypes for later work.

Soil conservation was a particular concern during the New Deal because of the ravages of the Dust Bowl. Hugh H. Bennett, a soil surveyor in the Department of Agriculture, led the crusade to develop and apply erosion control techniques. In 1933 under the Soil Erosion Service, the predecessor of the Soil Conservation Service (SCS) set up two years later, he began a program of demonstration projects using CCC laborers. At these demonstration sites farmers

Contour plowing such as practiced here in Hall County, Texas, was one of the soil conservation techniques advocated by Hugh Bennett and taught to farmers following the Dust Bowl. (Barker Texas History Center, The University of Texas at Austin, Austin, Texas.)

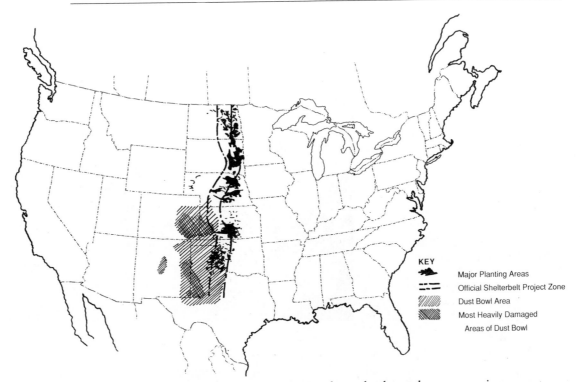

Map showing extent of Dust Bowl and zone of shelterbelts. (Data from Droze, 1977, and Butler, 1934; drawn by Rossi.)

KEY
Major Planting Areas
Official Shelterbelt Project Zone
Dust Bowl Area
Most Heavily Damaged Areas of Dust Bowl

were shown how to use erosion control methods such as terracing, contour plowing, strip planting, and tilling with a lister plough. Later in the decade, as the erosion problem diminished, the SCS began to focus on soil management rather than merely problem solving.

The largest conservation project of the 1930s was the controversial Prairie States Forest or Shelterbelt Project of the Forest Service.[5] Conceived by Roosevelt while traveling in Montana, the project was intended to provide work, like other 1930s public works projects. However, the goal of the project was unique and ambitious: to reduce the rampant winds which had been a principal cause of dust storms on the Great Plains. The shelterbelt zone was a strip 100 miles wide running north from Amarillo, Texas, to the U.S. border with Canada. Within this zone were to be planted dense north to south running windbreaks about 100 feet wide and at least one-half mile long. Individual breaks were to be a mile apart and planted with their centers on section lines. The Shelterbelt Project became a massive forestry endeavor in which native seed was collected, germinated in regional nurseries, 200 million seedlings planted, and the belts maintained, principally using CCC labor. In all, over 40,000 acres of land was taken out of agricultural production, but the compensating benefits included reduced winds and thereby less moisture and soil loss, as well as the addition of wooded recreational areas to otherwise stark plains.[6]

Land use planning during the New Deal was directed primarily toward agricultural lands, particularly the removal of low-yield, submarginal lands from cultivation. Once again, Dust Bowl experiences prompted these concerns, since it was determined that some of the worst-hit areas were those that were poorly suited to agriculture in the first place. Under programs administered by the Agricultural Adjustment Administration (AAA), poor land was purchased by the federal government, planted in forage grasses, and then leased for grazing. Much of the land secured was so marginal for agriculture that its owners had long since abandoned it.

Watershed management projects were among the most comprehensive ventures undertaken by the federal government, and some are still in progress. In

Bird's-eye perspective of Great Plains shelterbelts showing the solid north to south lines of vegetation intended by planners, but never achieved. (Butler, 1934.)

addition to providing employment, these projects were to control floods, generate electricity, improve navigation, and permanently improve the standard of living in disadvantaged regions. The Tennessee Valley Authority (TVA) was the agency mandated to oversee the largest regional planning scheme then in existence—the region being the 41,000 square miles of the Tennessee River watershed. During the Depression the TVA was best known for construction of a series of dams through which waters of the river could be managed for energy production. The first of these was Norris Dam above Knoxville, Tennessee. While the environmental consequences of this mammoth reshaping of the river system are still being assessed, response to human changes came rapidly because the TVA affected the lives of many people, from landowners to tenant farmers to small-town shopkeepers. While some anticipated great financial advantage from land sales and an improved climate for business, many people, especially landless farm laborers and tenant farmers, were permanently displaced from the land and migrated to cities.

Parks Projects

The second principal area of work in which landscape architects were involved during the Depression was the improvement of national and state parks. The need for design services at the parks opened up an area of work for landscape architects with which only a select few, such as Frank Waugh, had been involved prior to 1929. At the state level, Depression-era projects often brought landscape architects into public agencies when none had been previously employed.

The National Park System (NPS) increased in number of properties and in influence during the 1930s, as new parks, such as Everglades, were dedicated and existing parks previously administered by other jurisdictions, such as the historic battlefields, were transferred to its administration. In addition, the Park Service was assigned the task of supervising all CCC park work, whether national, state, or local.[7] It was in this capacity that the Service came to employ several hundred landscape architects as designers and project supervisors. In state and national parks, work generally related to site development such as alignment of roads and trails, planning of campsites, and design of visitor facilities. Most of the actual site and construction work planned by landscape architects was carried out by the CCC. At Yellowstone, for example, there were often multiple camps, each working in a different area. One camp cleared and graded for a road, while another built a ranger station. Other National Parks which had significant new facilities added included Yosemite, Grand Canyon, and Shenandoah, but almost every park had at least one New Deal project. These projects benefited the unemployed, and made the parks accessible to more people, but the increased public use sometimes compromised the viability of parks as ecological systems. This legacy of development for recreation continues to plague some parks today.

While the work of NPS landscape architects and CCC workers was important in providing new visitor facilities and needed service areas in national parks, their contribution was even more critical at state parks. Many states took advantage of the virtually free services provided to them by the federal government to begin park systems. Texas, Virginia, Arkansas, and Georgia were just four states which reaped rewards from the Depression in the form of a state park system. Design and construction projects in state parks were similar to those at national parks, with the work being implemented by CCC squads. At newly established Palo Duro State Park in Texas, the Corps built roads, constructed the lodge and cottages, and developed hiking trails. At Lacey-Keosaugua State Park in Iowa, an existing park reserve was made accessible to the public through construction of campsites and bridges. In the West, in addition to design and construction of facilities, much park work was directed toward protection of resources through firefighting and construction of firebreaks, but this work rarely involved landscape architects.

One of the most distinctive qualities of park design work in the 1930s was the Arts and Crafts-inspired rustic, vernacular appearance of structures such as lodges or entry gates made of local materials. At Starved Rock State Park in Illinois, the limestone so beautifully exposed along the Illinois River became the principal material for buildings. At Lake Corpus Christi State Park in Texas, caliche block was used to construct a stylized "mission" dining hall. In spite of poor standards in some parks, much of this work was first rate in both design and construction, providing some of the most attractive and appropriate park structures yet built.

This small earthen dam, faced with limestone, was typical of the rustic park structures designed by landscape architects such as A. D. Taylor, whose work this was, during the Depression era. (Landscape Architecture, Vol. 25, No. 3.)

Housing Schemes

Housing for both urban and rural citizens was a third government priority area on which landscape architects worked under the New Deal. Urban housing problems became more acute as people lost jobs and wages were lowered. The PWA, in its role as clearer of slums, became responsible for replacing them with quality public housing. Langston Terrace, the first federally funded public housing project in Washington, D.C., set a standard for others to follow. Built to resemble a large private residential complex, apartment buildings and row houses encircled a large turf entry court. As designed by architect Hilyard R. Robinson and landscape architect David A. Williston, one of the first Afro-Americans in practice, residents were provided with modest but comfortable housing within a community atmosphere.

Private housing was to be encouraged through federally guaranteed loans. The agency which administered this program was the Federal Housing Administration (FHA) established in 1934, in part through lobbying efforts of large-scale developers. Planning and construction standards set by the FHA favored large developments and planned communities, thus benefiting both developers and landscape architects. The agency had only a minor impact during the Depression, but became a significant force in the post-World War II housing boom.

The Subsistence Homesteads Project in the Department of the Interior was established to find new housing for rural families displaced by lack of work or through AAA purchases of marginal agricultural land. It was the idealistic notion of those establishing these programs that small rural villages were the best place to relocate families, both because costs would be lower than for urban renewal and because of prevailing antiurban sentiment. Hence, throughout the country, but particularly in the South, small communities, usually with names including the word "homesteads" or "gardens," were constructed. Arthurdale, West Virginia, the first of these, was distinctive in that it was built to house miners instead of farmers. Although innovative in the use of prefabricated housing, the town was poorly planned and failed to achieve the bucolic village character intended by the agency. More successful was Penderlea Homesteads in North Carolina. Its purpose, in the words of its landscape architect, was "to provide, in a healthful location and in an agreeable environment, means whereby owners of small farms may supply themselves with a good living and a profitable occupation through the practice of scientifically directed, intensive, and diversified agriculture."[8] The city plan by John Nolen was based on the same organizational concept he had used at Kingsport, with community facilities at the hub of radial arterial streets.

(A) Plan and (B) aerial perspective of park for migrant agricultural worker community near Harlingen, Texas, by Garrett Eckbo, 1940. (Eckbo, 1950.)

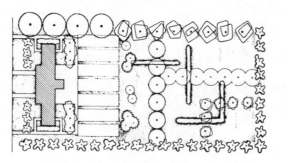

(A)

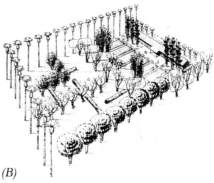

(B)

Here, though, town scale differed from that at Kingsport, because the house lots, intended as small farms, were all at least 10 acres in size. Other, less noted subsistence homesteads, most now absorbed within expanded cities, included Greenwood, Alabama; Houston Gardens, Texas; and El Monte, California.

The TVA also participated in construction of new towns with experimental housing. This program began because of the need to house those building, and later working at, water control projects. The first model town planned was Norris, Tennessee, to serve workers at Norris Dam. Begun in 1933 with Earle S. Draper and Tracy Augur as planners, the community was designed so that both the site plan and architectural design would harmonize with the rugged, wooded country in which it was located. Its overall arrangement was inspired by the Garden Cities, but executed as a more rural community, with single-family homes designed to resemble Appalachian cottages on lots of one-half to one-third of an acre. To make a complete community, a town center and Common were planned, with the school as focal point. In plan the town's curvilinear roads appeared completely haphazard, but only because they so closely related to landform, with roads set in valleys and house lots on higher ground. Although some components of Norris, such as the industrial park, were never completed, the community plan proved successful enough to be used as the basis for other TVA towns, including Wheeler, Tennessee. Today much of the distinctive planning and thoughtful architectural design is concealed by the low density of development and dense woods: Norris looks more like a town forgotten by time than the product of a revolutionary experiment in regional planning.[9]

The most successful group of communities developed during the New Deal were the renowned Green Cities, planned and constructed by the Resettlement Administration to provide quality housing in new towns located near the edge

Street scene in Norris, Tennessee. In Earle S. Draper's words, "Undue 'site improvement' was carefully avoided at Norris so as to preserve the interesting character of the natural setting." (Draper, 1938, p. 186.)

of an existing city. By purchasing large tracts, often over 10,000 acres, and then developing a master plan, program developers believed they could assure low costs and progressive physical plans.[10] The planning concept of Green Cities was based on a combination of Ebenezer Howard's Garden City, particularly its use of an open space buffer zone, with the Radburn idea of superblocks and circulation separation.[11]

In the heady and optimistic early days of the program, director Rexford Tugwell, who is credited with originating the project, envisioned twenty-five such communities, but then the realities of land acquisition, planning, and operation set in, and in the end only three towns were developed. The first was Greenbelt, Maryland, located between Baltimore and Washington, D.C. Begun in 1935, Greenbelt's first experimental city plan, completed by project engineers, was rejected by consultants Tracy Augur and John Nolen as unsympathetic to both topography and sense of community. It was after this failure that the Resettlement Administration put a team of planning and design professionals in place, setting a precedent for later projects. Hale Walker was appointed chief planner, with Douglas Ellington and R. J. Wadsworth as principal architects.

The plan of Greenbelt was based on adaptation of roads to topography and the creation of a family-oriented small town, organized into superblocks connected by pedestrian routes. A crescent-shaped loop road which wrapped around the town center and recreation area was the main entry into town. Housing, primarily row houses, was located between the two branches of this road, with the remaining housing to its south and west. Pedestrian paths were in open space corridors on which the row houses fronted. Where these paths crossed busy roads, pedestrian underpasses kept cars and residents at different levels. The focal point of the community was Roosevelt Center, a combination shopping, civic, and recreational zone. The shopping area was an auto-oriented mall with stores facing the street or a narrow interior court. Adjacent to the shopping area was the civic center, with town offices and a school. Directly north of this was a park that had ballfields, wooded areas for hiking and picnicking, and an artificial lake. All these facilities were quite accessible to everyone in the community, because the looped street plan put houses within a short distance of the center.

Greenhills, near Cincinnati, Ohio, was the next town initiated. Although similar in plan concept to Greenbelt, it was to have fewer apartments and more single-family homes, although row houses remained the dominant type of housing. In addition, it was located on a site bisected by existing streets that were allowed to remain. This street arrangement was particularly advantageous for the town's shopping center, which was sited prominently along the main north to south road. Justin Hartzog, the planner for Greenhills, compensated for intrusion of this road by leaving wider areas of open space between housing units than had been achieved at Greenbelt. In architectural style, the housing at Greenhills, designed under Roland Wank, resembled that of Greenbelt; it was boxlike in the Modern style, and fabricated of inexpensive materials.

Greendale, outside Milwaukee, Wisconsin, had the least Radburn-like plan of the Greenbelt towns. Rather its planner and landscape architect, Jacob Crane and Elbert Peets, were inspired by the plan of Williamsburg, Virginia, then prominently in the news due to its in-progress restoration. Greendale was also given a much higher percentage of single-family homes than the other towns, in an attempt to create a rural village character. Even the architectural designs executed under principal architects Harry H. Bentley and Walter G. Thomas were interpretations of colonial architecture built in modern materials, such as cinder block. In many ways, Greendale had a more sophisticated site plan than either

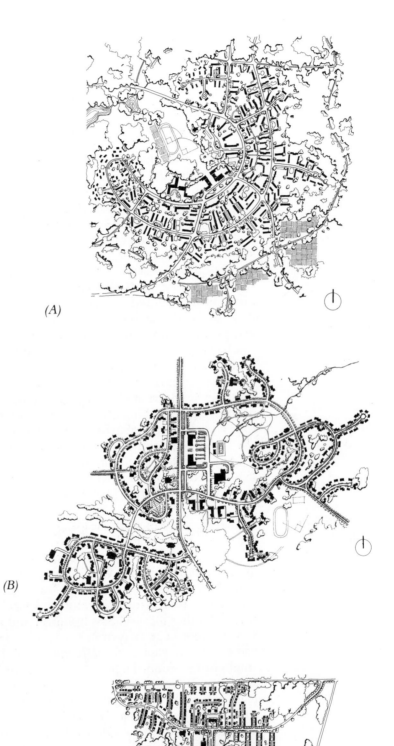

(A)

(B)

Plans of the three Green City towns at uniform scale: (A) Greenbelt, (B) Greenhills, (C) Greendale. (From data in Conkin, 1959; Architectural Record, Vol. 80, and Architectural Forum, Vol. 68; drawn by Larry Sullivan.)

(C)

Greenbelt or Greenhills. Its residential streets were oriented north to south so that each dwelling was assured solar access. Peets also manipulated widths along the principal street to distort perspective, in the Renaissance manner, when viewing the Village Hall.

Like most New Deal programs Green City towns were often very controversial, both in general concept and as new suburbs in specific areas. One proposed town for which significant planning had been completed, Greenbrook in New Jersey, failed to be built because local residents resisted selling land for the project. Concerns about these communities included fears that suburbanization, especially that subsidized by the government, would compete with central cities, leading to their ruin; or that the towns would bring the poor or racial minorities, then virtually confined to cities, to suburbs. Some viewed the Greenbelt project as a socialistic conspiracy to reduce local autonomy. Serious objections arose from the seemingly high cost per housing unit of the towns, which was in part a result of the need for immediate, rather than incremental, infrastructure development.

Local circumstances and the philosophy of its particular design team affected the quality of each Greenbelt town. While Greenbelt and Greendale were quite different in plan and appearance, each was successful in its own way. Greenbelt demonstrated that the Radburn idea could be readily adapted to any landform and planning program, while Greendale proved that moderate-cost housing need not be lackluster. Of the three, Greenhills was the least successful. Planning failed to account for the potential for increased traffic on through roads, which today effectively cleaves the town into two very separate parts. The spacing of units also decreased the appearance of a tight, visually cohesive community. Few people traveling by Greenhills today would note it to be anything other than a lower-cost, older suburban development.[12] While many social historians value the Greenbelt towns for their social contribution—that is, the attempt to encourage a sense of community—and as economic experiments in low-cost housing, designers continue to value the planning and design concepts implemented so successfully there.

Small-Site Design

A final area in which landscape architects found government employment during the New Deal was in the design of small-scale sites, especially recreational areas. As with improvements to national and state parks, much of this work provided quality public facilities which, without the Depression, might have never been built. New York City, under the leadership its "emperor" of public works, Robert Moses, took greater advantage of subsidized park design and construction than any other locality. Seventy thousand workman and several thousand professionals were kept busy transforming the urban landscape, with both good and bad results. Bryant Park, adjacent to the New York Public Library, was an example of the good. Here a small park for strolling and lunching was created on an elevated terrace. Its design, by Gilmore Clarke, was a simplified Neoclassicist plan with a large central lawn, its surrounding paths shaded by a bosque of trees.[13] The bad, and some would also say the ugly, were intrusive playgrounds and gardens added to Central Park. Twenty playlots were scattered across the park, some well planned but others quite haphazardly arranged. Formal gardens such as that near the Conservatory were built with little concern for the sequencing of space intended in the original design. Under the Moses administration Central Park became a crazy-quilt amusement park, and lost the rural character so valued by Olmsted and Vaux.[14]

Zoos and botanical gardens across the country were also beneficiaries of federal make-work programs. At Boerner Botanical Garden in Hales Corner,

Terrace and Shelter House in Trinity Park (formerly Rock Springs Park), Fort Worth, Texas, by Hare and Hare.

Wisconsin, CCC and WPA workers installed displays of all plants native to the state. In San Francisco and Chicago, federally financed workers constructed modern open zoo exhibits with artificial rock made from gunite. Urban parks also benefited from federal funding. Meridian Hill Park in Washington, D.C., and Trinity Park Rose Garden in Fort Worth, Texas, were both excellent examples of the type of project built under the New Deal. In both instances formal plans with Italianate detailing were used to create elegant public gardens. Meridian Hill Park is particularly famous for its exposed aggregate concrete—the first extensive use of this material in the country—employed as a substitute for costly carved stone.

To fill the gap between small, easily accessible urban parks and larger, but often remote, state parks, Recreational Demonstration Projects were instituted, using some of the submarginal land acquired by the AAA. These sites emphasized family-oriented passive types of recreation such as camping, swimming, and picnicking. With projects in more than twenty states, recreational areas were found near most large cities. Lake of the Ozarks near Jefferson City, Missouri, and Versailles State Park in Ripley County, Indiana, are just two of the better-known areas established under this program.

CONCLUSION AND SUMMARY

The 1930s do not constitute a planning or design period in the same sense as those discussed earlier. Rather the period was one of social, economic, and political reorientation, in which the progressive ideas of previous decades, including those from planning, finally received official recognition and implementation. In both landscape architecture and urban planning, the 1930s were a period of consolidation and integration of sound ideas developed earlier. Specifically, this period saw rekindled interest in conservation of natural resources, in the concept of planned urban environments developed for the good of residents, and in design as a response to site and user conditions rather than solely as application of historical styles.

While most Americans saw the Depression as a black cloud over social and economic life, the period proved to have the proverbial silver lining for the profession of landscape architecture. Working conditions increased the variety of project types on which designers worked, forced them to be innovative with materials and forms, encouraged greater concern for social and environmental issues, and provided work for all those educated as landscape architects. Historians often consider the Depression to be the first truly critical event, since the Civil War, to alter life in the United States. While its consequences were less radical for landscape architecture, they were such that the profession, as constituted today, was set in place with its multiplicity of concerns and approaches to practice.

NOTES

1. *For all practical purposes, "the 1930s" extended from late 1929 to late 1945. While there were significant changes during the war years, particularly the end to public works projects due to the dearth of workers, some programs and projects continued. More important, the degree of government involvement in activities related to landscape architecture remained at the same high level, although most activities switched in emphasis from civilian to military.*

2. *The economic depression affected both Canada and Mexico, but in neither was there a dramatic government response to the catastrophe. The Canadian Prairie provinces, especially Saskatchewan, were hard hit by Dust Bowl droughts, and farmers experienced problems similar to those of American farmers.*

3. *Taylor, 1934, p. 135.*

4. *Statement of Norman Newton in "Fletcher Steele: His Contributions to American Landscape Architecture," Jo Ann Dietz Beck, 1980, Master's thesis, State University of New York, College of Environmental Science and Forestry, Syracuse, N.Y. Steele was one landscape architect who maintained a successful practice during the Depression. Some large projects begun in the late 1920s, such as the Backus Estate and the Ellwanger Garden, continued into the next decade, and projects for new clients, like the Stoddards of Gloucester, Massachusetts, were begun. At an ASLA Annual Meeting, Steele declared "vehemently that he would never yield to the call of any level of government as a client."*

5. *The project was controversial principally among two groups. Foresters questioned the efficacy and practicality of the massive plantings proposed. For a variety of professional views see Journal of Forestry, 1934, Vol. 32, No. 9, pp. 959–72. Farmers were worried that they would loose acreage with no direct financial compensation. Government payments eased this concern.*

6. *Some shelterbelt plantings still remain, but many have been removed or have diminished in size and density. Decline began in the 1940s when there was insufficient labor available for routine maintenance. During the booming agricultural market of the 1960s and early 1970s many landowners cleared away the belts to increase tillable acreage.*

7. *After the Depression and World War II, NPS continued to advise states through the State Park Assistance Program, established by Conrad Wirth.*

8. *Van Schaack, 1935, p. 79.*

9. *Norris, like the Greenbelt towns, was sold to a private developer in the late 1940s.*

10. *In general, the Greenbelt towns were far more successful in physical planning than in keeping costs low—a statement which applies equally to other New Deal housing projects. Many projects cost two or more times what was estimated, so the housing was far from being "low budget" and would not have been price-competitive in a commercial market.*

11. *When the idea of developing suburban new towns was first proposed, two designers whose works were discussed earlier suggested their concepts as being more progressive than either the Garden City or Radburn plans: Frank Lloyd Wright proposed that Broadacre City be used as a prototype, while Edgar Chambless recommended consideration of Roadtown (Arnold, 1971).*

12. *During World War II the federal government began trying to sell off the Greenbelt towns. In 1949, the Greenhills townsite was sold to a homeowners group. Later, part of Greenbelt was sold to homeowners and part to a real estate corporation, while Greendale also went private. In all three instances, the greenbelts themselves were not sold with the town, and were eventually developed as other than open space.*

13. In recent years the park has become a problem area, overrun with rats and drug users. In an effort to remedy this condition, the park was closed and redesigned. The new design will afford greater visibility into the park from the street.

14. Of course, many of these "amusements" have since been removed, redesigned, or will be removed as the park is restored.

27

The Automobile Age

Few changes, other than population growth and expansion, have had the dramatic impact on landscapes of transportation innovations, particularly in North America. As we have seen, improvements in roadway construction, development of canals, and construction of railroad lines were all transportation improvements that brought with them a host of social, economic, and environmental changes. None of these, though, had the intensity and scale of impact of the invention of motorized vehicles, particularly the automobile.

When automobiles were first manufactured for public consumption in the early 1900s, the prevailing view was that they were and would remain toys for the wealthy, not that they would become the agents of a momentous transportation revolution. Numbers tell the story of the automotive epoch. In 1900 there were only about 10,000 registered passenger cars in the United States. By 1920 that number had increased almost a thousandfold to more than 8 million; and in 1930 to about 23 million.[1] While motorized vehicles offered certain traffic advantages over horse-drawn vehicles, such as requiring less roadway space per vehicle and speedier movement, they also caused new problems. In particular, great speed made street crossing hazardous to pedestrians; vehicles required greater turning radii; and more traffic management, through devices such as lane separation and signalization, was required. Had the motor been used solely in public transport vehicles, advantages would have far outweighed problems. It was the introduction of relatively inexpensive personal vehicles which added immensely to the traffic dilemma.

Proliferation of automobiles brought many changes to North America: it affected travel patterns, urban design, suburban development, pollution, and rural life. The car offered almost unlimited travel options, with door-to-door service, choice of schedule, and control over one's traveling companions. Recreational travel was immediately affected. Urban planning was also radically altered by automotive needs, particularly for improved traffic control and parking space. Nineteenth-century photographs document the confusion of traffic which then dominated urban streets—lanes were poorly defined, most intersections were not signalized, there was no enforced separation of directional traffic, and vehicles parked where convenient rather than conforming to an established pattern. This lack of order, which was certainly confusing when there were only horse-drawn vehicles, was deadly when high-speed mechanized horsepower was added.

While the car was a mixed blessing in the urban areas, it was an unrestrained aid in the development of suburbs. Street railroads had fostered many suburban developments, but by the early 1900s these systems had reached their effective range. Without a new transportation system it was unlikely that suburbs could continue to expand. The car, especially when made affordable by mass production, provided just the right tool at the right time to continue the ongoing process of suburbanization. Not only was the auto rapid transportation, but it also appealed to that same sense of independence and individuality which encouraged ownership of single-family homes. Rural life was even more dramatically affected by motorized vehicles than urban and suburban life. In fact, for many isolated farm families it revolutionized both social and economic life. A family car, or even one owned by neighbors, increased visitation among dispersed farmsteads and regular trips to town.

While few early planners envisioned the magnitude of the environmental problems that automobiles would eventually generate, there was always an awareness that they were significant sources of pollution. In the early days though, these pollutants were in fact less threatening than the disease and water-contaminating wastes produced by animals. It was not until the huge proliferation of cars after World War II, coupled with increased urban density, that the effects of auto waste on air and water were clearly seen.

THE CAR IN URBAN PLANNING

The principal problems associated with cars in the city were two—how to store cars when not in use and how to create a road system that would accommodate an ever increasing number of vehicles, safely and at reasonable speeds. Much of the literature of "municipal engineering," as "sanitary engineering" had been reconstituted and renamed, dealt with issues such as the best parking angle to accommodate the most vehicles and the proper width of driving lanes. In the early days of automotive expansion planners resisted altering well-established patterns of vehicular movement. In part this was due to the perception of motorized vehicles as only *one* of several types of vehicles to be served in urban plans. For example, as late as 1915 John C. Olmsted discussed how to integrate true horse-powered vehicles with those having gasoline-generated horsepower. Only the realization that motorized vehicles were going to replace all other types forced invention of new traffic management systems. Open, undefined traffic lanes were clarified and limited to the minimum space required for vehicles. Painted lines to define individual lanes were introduced in 1911. Acute angles, designed for ease of turning for carriages, were altered to right angles so that cars had to slow down. Curves were banked and radii increased to facilitate car turning. Physical separation of opposing traffic and signalization further controlled traffic movement. In many instances, such innovations necessitated complete redesign of intersections. Copley Square in Boston, possibly the most redesigned space in America, was an example of such a response to the need to accommodate for the automobile. In 1915, Arthur Shurcliff suggested a complete renovation of this square, the heart of Boston's Back Bay district, to solve its principal problems: undefined lanes, excessively large roadway spaces, rounded corner intersections, and the lack of protected spaces for pedestrians. Within the area of the square, Shurcliff introduced a rectangular plaza with central fountain surrounded by a circle of trees to create 90-degree street intersections. The plaza, although bisected by an electric railway line, gave the space a more pedestrian-oriented character than did the existing plan.

Parking was as problematic as auto movement for urban planners. This was not due strictly to vehicle design, but to the popularity of cars as vehicles of convenience, to be available at a moment's notice. The perennial problem of how to park as close to one's destination as possible was born. Into the second decade of the century, experimentation often dealt with comparisons between various angles of parking relative to safety, convenience, and number of vehicles stored. Initially, much parking space was in stables converted to garages, but when these proved inadequate for demand, curbside parking became the norm. A common solution, which had the negative impact of slowing through traffic, was to use edges of an existing roadway for parking. In only a few innovative projects, such

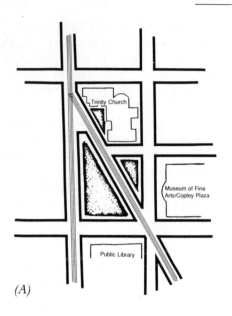

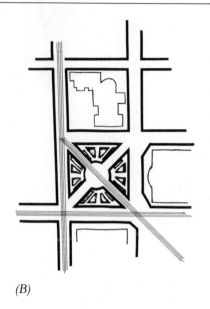

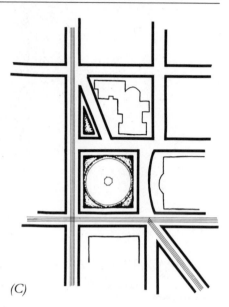

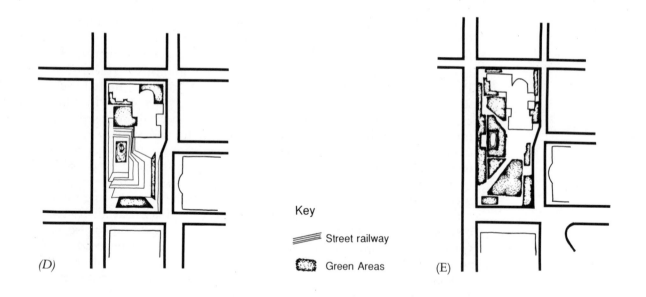

A selection of various design proposals for Copley Square, Boston, over a period of more than one hundred years. Copley Square has been redesigned to reflect changing circulation needs as well as altered perceptions of just what a "square" should be. (A) The basic plan of Copley Square from the mid-nineteenth century to the 1960s; (B) unbuilt 1897 redesign proposed by C. Howard Walker; (C) unbuilt 1917 proposal by Arthur Shurcliff called for removal of street railroad that ran through square; (D) competition winning design by Sasaki Walker that guided redevelopment of the square in the late 1960s; (E) 1985 competition-winning design by Dean Abbott, which guided redevelopment in the late 1980s. (Data from Boston Public Library, Fine Arts Department and Prints Room, Boston, Mass.; Chabrier, 1985.)

as Country Club Plaza, was the parking problem rethought and parking integrated into a comprehensive urban design solution.

After about 1915, planning for automobiles and other motorized vehicles tended to dominate city planning. John Nolen's plan for Little Rock, Arkansas, was typical in beginning with a report on traffic problems. He noted that the city's system was more than adequate in terms of number of streets, but that many did little to facilitate traffic flow because of erratic jogs in alignment. A more serious problem was lack of a street hierarchy, with major collectors near the town center no wider than those in outlying areas. Nolen's solutions for Little Rock were as typical as the problems: widen certain critical streets, reduce the number of road and railroad intersections, and introduce mechanical traffic control devices.

In the auto-oriented post-World War II period, commercial areas were reshaped from centralized business nodes into linear marketplaces, whose often vacant parking frontage became more critical to success than displays of merchandise. The road and automobile produced the shopping strip—much like Main Street in concept, but so different in scale. Dominance of automobile travel also produced new types of businesses: the motel (that is, motor hotel), the drive-in movie theater, the gas station, the fast-food restaurant, and the drive-through bank. These often decentralized, nearly autonomous facilities limited driver contact with other people, just as motor traffic limited driver contact with the landscape.

RURAL AND INTERCITY ROUTES
Rural Routes

As the importance of cars to rural residents increased, so too did demands for improved routes over which to run those cars. Urban roads might have been inefficient in organizing traffic, but many rural roads were actually seasonally impassable. Although car-haters may have exaggerated stories of horses being used to pull a fashionable roadster from a quagmire, such problems were a commonplace part of the adventure of motoring. Efforts to improve rural roads had actually begun in the late 1890s, when, inspired by the popularity of bicycling for recreation, the Good Roads movement began in the United States. Organizations that were part of the movement encouraged federal government action in road research and construction, since few country or state governments had the financial ability to carry out the large-scale work involved. Early improvements advocated by the Office of Road Inquiry, the first U.S. government agency concerned with roads, included roadbed grading, route straightening, bridge improvement, and paving, although this was often with loose stone rather than a hard surface material. Roadbed conditions were not the only problems faced by rural motorists. Routing and lack of services were equally problematic. So arduous were early trips that the first cross-country auto trip from San Francisco to New York in 1903 took over two months. Since each jurisdiction had their own road designation system, it was often difficult for drivers to follow a through route even where one existed. The Good Roads Association and other driver advocacy groups, such as the Lincoln Highway Association, encouraged development of a cross-county road, the Lincoln Highway, and a nationwide road numbering system—the system of "U.S." highway designations which continues in use today along with state and county systems for lesser roads.[2]

Rural areas also benefited from the introduction of motorized farm equipment. This increased production of individual farmers, and also made harvesting faster, but sometimes more wasteful. Of course mechanization also brought unanticipated problems, which included large capital expenditures to buy necessary equipment, overproduction, and destructive exploitation of soil productivity.

Intercity Routes

Two road systems were developed to address the needs of intercity travelers. The first was the "informal parkway," to use the term of J.C. Olmsted, and the second was the superhighway.[3] Parkways were rural descendants of those nineteenth-century boulevards that had linked urban parks; street spaces such as the Midway uniting Chicago's south side parks. While informal parkways were inspired by historic precedent, their designs addressed specific requirements of high-speed vehicles. Many of their features became prototypes for features of later superhighway systems. Parkways had large rights-of-way which were used to physically separate and visually screen the roadway from surrounding areas. The road itself was adapted to landform through a curvilinear alignment that preserved scenic features, such as streams and hills. Parkways introduced to North America the concepts of limited points of access, grade separation for crossing routes, and separate alignment of lanes running in opposite directions. In addition, commercial traffic was excluded, and amenities such as roadside parks were included for travel comfort. As all of these planning and design components suggest, parkways were intended to give drivers a recreational as well as transit experience.

The first scenic parkway in North America was Bronx River Parkway in New York, begun in 1907 but not completed until 1923. Its principal function was as an attractive and safe link between New York City and suburban Westchester County, New York. It also served urban renewal and pollution control functions, for one of the project's objectives was removal of polluting shanty residences that had been built along the river's banks. One of the largest intercity parkway systems was that developed by Westchester County, in part planned by Gilmore Clarke. The first segment of this system was an extension of the Bronx River Parkway northward along the Hudson River. Later, other linked parkways were added to connect parks and other parkways. The Westchester

A portion of the Westchester County, New York, parkway system illustrating the integration of roadway with natural features such as the stream that runs beside it. (ASLA, 1932.)

system was known for its broad road alignment, which gave the parkway a more rural character and made driving even more comfortable than on earlier parkways.

Other early parkways included Mount Vernon Memorial Highway and George Washington Parkway, both near Washington, D.C.; Natchez Trace in Mississippi; and the Blue Ridge Parkway, down the entire spine of the Appalachian Mountains. Mount Vernon Memorial Highway was a portion of the George Washington Memorial Parkway built specifically to link Mount Vernon with Washington, D.C., as planned earlier by the McMillan Commission.[4] Running through the lower Potomac River valley, the roadway linked many historic and natural areas, while providing visitors with an entry to Washington's plantation uncluttered by signage or tourist-oriented businesses. As designed by a team under Gilmore D. Clarke, much of whose professional practice was in parkway design, the highway was a divided roadway with grade-separated crossing roads deemphasized through the use of simple bridges faced in native stone, with abutments screened by trees. The George Washington Memorial Parkway was a longer road system with routes on both sides of the Potomac River from Mount Vernon in the south to the Great Falls of the Potomac at the north. Much of the right-of-way skirted the river itself, providing exceptional views down its valley and vistas into Washington. The parkway was not merely a road but a linked system of small parks as well. These parks preserved both historic sites, like Fort Washington, located on the eastern shore of the Potomac across from Mount Vernon, and natural preserves. The Parkway remains not only one of the most beautiful entries into the national capital, but also one of its most efficient.

The modern Natchez Trace parkway commemorated the history of emigration and trade by following, at least in part, the original route of the Trace. Unlike the Mount Vernon or George Washington parkway, this road had only two lanes within an uncleared right-of-way to preserve its historic character as a trace or trail.

Skyline Drive in Virginia, part of the Blue Ridge Parkway, was designed with an unusually narrow right-of-way to minimize disruption of landform and vegetation.

The Blue Ridge Parkway, developed as a public works project during the 1930s, was an extension of the original Blue Ridge Highway. The spectacular natural scenery and rugged topography of the Appalachians guided both routing and roadway design. Unlike most other parkways, much of the Blue Ridge was two-lane undivided highway, so that its impact on the landscape was minimized.

Throughout the 1920s and 1930s parkways proliferated, particularly in the eastern United States. New York City developed more parkways than any other city. These included the Henry Hudson and Cross Bronx Parkways. New York State was equally active, building the Taconic State, Wantaugh State, and Meadowbrook State Parkways, among others. The Garden State and Palisades Interstate Parkways crossed New Jersey and connected with New York parkways. In Tennessee, the TVA constructed Norris Freeway in parkway style to link the town of Norris with Norris Dam. In the Midwest the longest parkway ever proposed, the Mississippi River Parkway, was to have alignments on both sides of the river from Canada to the Gulf of Mexico. Modern parkways continue to be built, although they are usually much shorter than older ones. The award-winning parkway design for the Miami International Airport by Stresau, Smith, and Stresau demonstrates that roads as parks still offer an alternative to "roads as alleys."

Superhighways

Although parkways and superhighways have some similarities in terms of layout, there is a critical difference between the two: parkways are designed highways where safety, efficiency, and quality of the driving experience are all equally important factors, while superhighways are engineered roads for which cost, safety, and traffic volumes are the principal controlling factors. Superhighways are intended to be efficient rather than pleasurable.

The first proposal for a series of such highways in North America was for Detroit. In 1924, planners proposed a comprehensive transportation corridor with a commuter rail line in the center, a lane for express traffic, a separate lane for local traffic, and generous sidewalks for pedestrians, all within a 204-foot right-of-way. Fortuitously, this plan was not implemented, for it would have been obsolete in terms of traffic volume before it was even begun. The plan was prophetic, though, in identifying the need for separate lanes of rapid, through traffic, a concept that eventually culminated in the 1950s with construction of the Interstate Highway System.

Interest in high-speed limited-access highways increased, and in the 1930s a number of proposals for an integrated cross-continental system were produced. None was as convincing as that developed by Norman Bel Geddes for the Futurama Exhibit at General Motors' New York World's Fair building. Illustrated by a giant model which depicted a modern highway running through a composite American landscape of mountains, prairie, seashore, and river valley, the design achieved the four goals of safety, comfort, speed, and economy through sweeping curves, superelevation, controlled access, and, in cities, separation of pedestrian traffic in a second-story pedestrian causeway system. A unique part of the Bel Geddes plan called for three separate road alignments—one for 100-mile-per-hour through traffic, a second for slower 75-mile-per-hour through traffic, and a third for recreational traffic, which meandered through the landscape. This exhibit also linked superhighways to a model image of "Tomorrow's City," in which highways, skyscrapers, and generous open spaces replaced inner cities and blighted housing.

It was not until after World War II that North America was able to follow the example pioneered by German autobahns establishing an integrated system of high-speed through roads. By that time, increased traffic volume and demand for improved long-distance travel necessitated such a system. In the late 1940s and early 1950s, many large cities and urbanized counties, particularly around New York, Chicago, and Los Angeles, built their own short sections of limited-access, divided, high-speed highway. This work was done to meet immediate need in preparation for a system of national highways which had been planned since 1939.

The Pennsylvania Turnpike was the earliest long-distance road in North America to use alignment and construction standards that would be adopted later for national superhighways. Originally built with two lanes in each direction, divided by a small median, in a 200-foot right-of-way, the road was noted for

"Futurama," a model of highways for the future displayed at the New York World's Fair of 1939. Shown here are the three separate roadways for traffic of different speeds. (Bel Geddes, 1940.)

its sweeping curves and long sight distances. With only eleven original points of entrance and exit, roadside services were an important secondary consideration. Gas station-restaurant complexes were built 15 miles apart on alternate sides of the road. While road alignment conformed somewhat to the landform, massive cutting and filling was commonplace, with very abrupt vertical cuts along many segments. In contrast to many later superhighways, on the Pennsylvania Turnpike designed plantings were used to control erosion, control snow drifting, and equalize uneven winds at deep cuts. Screening of off-road clutter and roadway structures integrated the highway with surrounding land use.

The National System of Interstate and Defense Highways, as the U.S. Interstate system was officially called, was finally initiated under the Highway Act of 1956. This law outlined a system of more than 40,000 miles of roads from coast to coast and border to border, to link major cities and most state capitals. Later a similar system of Dominion Highways was formed in Canada. These highways, over 95 percent complete by 1990, had some important advantages over traditional long-distance routes. Speed was the most obvious one, with a coast to coast auto trip that had taken fifty or more days in 1900 down to four or fewer by 1990. Equally important in urban areas was the high volume of traffic that the roads could carry, even during congested peak commuting hours. Safety was a third critical advantage. Since cross traffic was eliminated and opposite direction traffic separated, there were fewer opportunities for collision. This safety factor was countered though by increased speed, which made those accidents that did occur more serious. In rural areas interstates dramatically increased safety, since there high speed and crossing traffic had always gone hand in hand to produce serious accidents.

There were limitations to the Interstate Highway system. While speed was increased, route choice was decreased, since there were so few roads planned. Often it became more time-efficient for drivers to drive out of their way on an Interstate than take a shorter but less speedy local route. This, of course, increased fuel consumption and its ensuing pollution. Interstates also limited access

Interstate 35 in Austin, Texas, was typical of the system of grade-separated roadways constructed under provisions of the Highway Act of 1956. (Barker Texas History Center, The University of Texas at Austin, Austin, Texas.)

to desired locations, such as businesses or even entire communities, due to locations of entrances and exits. High-speed travel also brought a new, blurred image of the landscapes through which drivers passed.

Perhaps the most serious change caused by the Interstate Highway system was the new order which it brought to the built landscape. Residential patterns were altered as suburbs extended farther into the urban hinterland. Commuting distances of 60 or more miles became possible, if not acceptable, to everyone. This, coupled with other government-sponsored programs, hastened the post–World War II urban exodus. Businesses were equally affected, particularly neighborhood shopping areas and small-town downtowns. Commercial areas reoriented to points of traffic concentration—Interstate interchanges and routes leading to them. Just as nineteenth-century downtowns had clustered near railroad depots, the new dispersed "main street" of the commercial strip concentrated at road entry and exit points. Interstate Highways also allowed certain businesses, such as light industry, greater freedom of locational choice. Many former inner city enterprises relocated to suburbs or small towns as a result.

This new urban order had a negative effect on older, poorer, minority-occupied areas, for two reasons. First, many planners viewed highway development as a federally funded[5] method to renew run-down areas under the guise of "progress." Thus, older neighborhoods were often the first targeted for rights-of-way. Secondly, these roads were planned based on "objective" criteria of traffic capacity, cost, and scientific safety standards by federal and state level engineers. These plans did not account for local goals other than those associated with prime travel destinations, nor was there serious examination of the social consequences of right-of-way location.

This lack of comprehensive planning allowed serious and permanent damage to occur, including destruction of viable urban neighborhoods, destruction of much of the historic fabric of small towns and cities alike, permanent occupation of waterfronts by highways, and unnatural segmentation of cities into zones unrelated to function. More positively, Interstates assured cities access to those skilled workers who preferred suburban living, fostered some local planning movements, provided permanent buffers to those neighborhoods that remained intact, and increased weekend recreational travel into cities.

The modern commercial strip was a product of increased automobile usage after World War II. It has only recently been seriously studied as an important modern landscape.

As in cities, the Interstate Highways brought both good and ill to rural areas. The highways meant better access to urban amenities, better roads for crop and livestock transport, but then construction removed millions of acres from production and also divided farms into uneconomic parcels.

While Interstate Highways and their related intra-urban alternate routes have often been criticized for destroying public transportation, in many instances public and private transit were integrated within a single right-of-way. In Chicago, for example, the city's existing subway system was extended along with construction of superhighways into the suburbs. A center portion of the highway right-of-way was reserved for electric railway lines and stations. At suburban terminals large parking areas assured that passengers could access the system, thereby guaranteeing ridership for the line. More recently, lanes for express buses and multiple-user cars have been designated on highways in cities from Houston to Washington, D.C., as a way to encourage more efficient commuter use of the Interstate Highway System.

HIGHWAYS AS DESIGNED LANDSCAPES

It is ironic that the concept of the highway as a designed landscape, so unquestionably demonstrated by early twentieth-century parkways, should have failed to influence the Interstate system. That this occurred was certainly not due to a lack of research and literature on the subject. As early as 1914 Ossian Simonds realized that public interest in automobile travel could be used as an argument to improve roadside landscapes. Later Jens Jensen wrote about the importance of the highway as viewpoint for experiencing the landscape. By the 1920s landscape architects had become actively involved in highway design, emphasizing the relationship of roadway alignment and design to safety, environmental preservation, and landscape aesthetics. While engineering studies focused on the construction mathematics of road alignment, known as "geometrics," and the design of pavements, landscape architects viewed highways as linear landscapes in which safe use and enjoyment were related to the integration of the roadway and its setting. These concerns began to be implemented during the 1930s, when landscape architects working for the federal government became more directly involved in road development. Landscape architects were particularly sensitive to excessive cutting to maintain flat road grades. While this did make driving easier and more efficient, particularly for trucks, it often caused permanent problems with falling rock or landslides. The sequence of road closures along California's scenic Highway 1 was just one of the better-known examples of this problem.

Highway departments and engineers often did look to landscape architects for help with highways—to "beautify" them after construction. This image of landscape architecture and horticulture as ornamentation for a poorly planned road was of course abhorrent to landscape architects. S. Herbert Hare expressed the opinion of most professional designers when he wrote that "the real opportunity [in road design] . . . is the application of the principles of landscape design in an organic way to the problems of location, alignment, and cross-section grading of roads . . . [to design] beauty into the highway rather than adding it superficially afterward" (1940, p. 118).

While planting design alone could never fully represent the possible contributions of landscape architecture to highway planning, there was a significant contribution which planting could make to road safety. Dense plantings between roads of a divided highway could screen oncoming headlights and prevent vehicles from crossing the median. Plants could perceptually narrow the apparent width of a roadway to slow traffic. At curves, trees seen from a distance signaled the upcoming change in alignment.

Landscape architects were also interested in the impact of roads on the larger landscape. Frank Waugh and Elsa Rehmann wrote about a distinctive roadside ecology which developed as a result of road-related conditions of sunlight and soil. Waugh found that even simple country lanes produced distinctive bands of naturalized plants. Particularly important was the effect of graded and scraped roadways and shoulders, which provided a perfect environment for invading weeds, both native and introduced. While these weeds stabilized disturbed soils, they also often contaminated nearby fields or woodlands, as the rampant spread of kudzu in the South demonstrated.

In the 1960s, under the leadership of First Lady "Lady Bird" Johnson, a national commitment to highway beautification began. The Highway Beautification Act provided guidelines for billboard construction and roadside planting. Years of experience had suggested the most useful, road-tolerant plants were usually natives, as well as a few hardy imports like juniper and Russian olive. At the same time, research demonstrated the advantages of reduced roadside maintenance, particularly mowing, in allowing volunteer plants to vegetate and stabilize roadsides. Later, when higher maintenance costs mandated less intensive maintenance, highway officials remembered these early experiments, which had also demonstrated that fallow roadsides often become more attractive than cultivated ones.

A more comprehensive approach to roadway design was suggested by the classic study *The View from the Road.* Donald Appleyard and his coauthors emphasized the role of spatial sequence in driving, rather than mere "beautification." Inventing a notation system to evaluate urban landscapes viewed at high speed, the study suggested that landscapes have meaning which is communicated to the driver—and that these meanings influence both highway safety and sense of place.

Recent highway site plans have attempted to make an amenity out of the roadway, rather than treat it merely as a service corridor. In Seattle, Washington,

Freeway Park, Seattle, Washington, by Lawrence Halprin Associates made new use of otherwise wasted airspace above an inner city highway. (Department of Landscape Architecture slide collection, Texas A&M University.)

"Crossing the Plains" by Bradford Graves, one of the sculptures sited along Interstate 80, commemorates pioneer travel using celestial navigation by aligning its four points to compass directions. (Nebraska Department of Economic Development.)

Model of "Blue Shadows," the winning entry in the Freeway as Art competition. In the center a large mast served as conductor for the "music" produced by the highway and the ever changing sunlight. Design and model by John L. Brown, Michael Knudsen, and Mark Hults. (Photo courtesy of Harlow Landphair.)

Freeway Park was literally "built on thin air." Designed by the Halprin firm, with Angela Danadjieva as project manager, the parksite included two strips of land on either side of Interstate 5 plus the far larger intervening airspace over the highway. While the most intriguing experience of the park is for pedestrians, who can climb through its abstracted mountain landscape of steep canyons and cascading waterfalls, the park also introduced variety to the highway corridor. Modular concrete planters with dense masses of trees and shrubs hang over the roadway, creating the illusion that cars were entering a mountain tunnel.

In 1973, Nebraska, as a special project to commemorate the upcoming Bicentennial of the American Revolution, commissioned ten original monumental outdoor sculptures to be placed in rest areas of Interstate 80. The completed works included themes inspired by the landscape, like the kinetic "Nebraska Wind Sculpture" by George Baker. While these artworks certainly enlivened the rest areas, most were also positioned to be viewed from the road.

This concept of "the highway as art" was the theme of a recent design competition, in which the entire site of an interstate highway in Houston, Texas, was transformed into an environmental sculpture. The winning design, entitled "Blue Shadows" and produced by John L. Brown, Michael Knudsen, and Mark Hults, explored "the road as music, or more specifically, the road and its physical elements as instruments with which music is made" (quoted in Landphair, 1989). In this scheme trees, masts placed at roadside, and wavelike forms served as instruments that were "played" by the movement of the sun across the land. Such imaginative interpretations of the highway are but one way in which transportation can become more than just a functional part of the landscape.

CONCLUSION AND SUMMARY

Automobile travel and the related highway systems are just the most recent events in a two-hundred-year-long sequence of transportation innovations that have altered the North American landscape. More than just a technological innovation, private automobiles reflect in motorized form American preferences for independent modes of travel in which individual choice is maximized. As one automobile advertisement sums it up, "It's not just your car, it's your freedom." Such freedom did not come without a significant environmental price. Roads, parking, and auto services consumed large areas of land, estimated in some urban areas at 50 per-cent. High traffic volumes increased travel times and reduced the efficiency of the system, while adding serious pollutants—particularly carbon monoxide—to the environment.

The problems produced by automobiles, followed by high gas costs in the 1970s, produced a backlash in favor of public transportation. Local bus and rail systems, often subsidized because they were unprofitable, were constructed with mixed results. The Bay Area Rapid Transport system, which has been plagued by inefficiency and excessive cost, more than fifteen years after completion does not carry the ridership projected for the late 1960s. The Washington, D.C., system, although more successful, has not dramatically reduced congestion during peak travel hours. Still, cities seeking ways to relieve congestion without further highway intrusions have few equally effective tools currently available. Houston and Los Angeles, both cited as quintessential automobile cities, have recently considered comprehensive rail systems. Los Angeles has gone so far as to revive one route of the Pacific Electric Railway, prematurely closed in the 1920s as the car conquered Southern California. More radical solutions to the transportation dilemma have been tested, with some success, in towns and small cities. Davis, California, for example, has an extensive bicycle path system that makes pedaling quicker for short, in-town trips than driving. Perhaps from such experiments an efficient, integrated transportation system, which relies on a variety of transportation forms from the bicycle to the auto to the street railway to the airplane, may eventually emerge.

NOTES

1. Data cited in Rae, 1971, from U.S. government sources.

2. In the federal system, roads running east to west are even-numbered, while those running north to south are odd. Low numbers began at the Canadian border and got higher southward. The odd/even system was maintained for later Interstate Highway Systems.

3. The term "informal" was used to suggest that they were designed in a naturalistic, Romantic manner rather than as formal boulevards.

4. Such a route, though, was not a new idea on the part of the Commission. Several plans and routes for such a road, at least the southern segment, had been formulated in the late 1800s. It was commemoration of the two-hundredth anniversary of Washington's birth in 1932 which moved these plans toward implementation.

5. Part of the attraction for local governments was that road construction for the Interstate system was funded at about 90 percent by the federal government.

28

The Modern City

The bucolic atmosphere of the new San Francisco can perhaps best be seen in the fact that, down Market Street and some other streets, creeks now run. These had earlier, at great expense, been put into huge culverts underground, as is usual in cities. The Ecotopians spent even more to bring them up to ground level again. So now on this major boulevard you may see a charming series of little falls, with water gurgling and splashing, and channels lined with rocks, trees, bamboos, ferns. . . . Market Street, once a mighty boulevard striking through the city down to the waterfront, has become a mall planted with thousands of trees. The "street" itself, on which electric taxis, minibuses, and delivery carts purr along, has shrunk to a two-lane affair.

Ernest Callenbach, Ecotopia, *1975*

The period from the beginning of the Depression in 1929 to the end of World War II in 1945 created a significant break in the design continuum of the early twentieth century. That break allowed a new generation of designers to experiment with innovative responses to the social, economic, and environmental issues that resulted from the upheavals of the Depression and the war. While none of these reforms produced an urban milieu as strikingly unconventional as Callenbach's novelistic impression of an ecologically rebuilt San Francisco, the changes were notable. In particular there were four major differences that affected the natural and built environment at all scales:

1. Changes in the means of financing investment and development

2. Increase in number and type of regulations affecting planning

3. Changes in demographics and lifestyle

4. The impact of modernism

The Depression era had introduced people in the United States to a level of government involvement in daily affairs that was unprecedented in North America. In particular, the concept that the federal government should be directly involved with financing previously nonpublic projects, such as housing, led to a redirection of government priorities. After the war, the government extended its financial support, which during the Depression had served to provide a minimal livelihood, to projects intended to speed national economic recovery and to help meet public demand for goods and services. One of the most important areas of government financial support was in programs to guarantee home loans, such as those authorized under the Housing Act of 1949—the so-called Fannie Mae loan program—and under the Veterans' Administration loan program. Not only did such programs make it easier and quicker for people to secure home loans, but through standards established to ensure the security of government investments, sound principles of subdivision site planning and housing design improved the national housing stock.

A second change in consumer loans was influenced by government policy, but operated in the private sector. This was introduction of the long-term home loan. Previously cash purchase or short-term loans, five or ten years at the maximum, were the norm. This system required that individuals acquire substantial cash savings before home purchase, with the result that many simply could not buy homes, or could only buy them relatively late in life. Particularly in large cities, it was not uncommon for many middle-class families to be renters, rather than have the preferred status of homeowner, simply because of the difficulty of saving enough to purchase a home. With government guarantees, lending institutions were no longer reluctant to loan money for longer periods of time, since unforeseen personal circumstances would not affect repayment.

The combination of some direct government home loans; government guarantees on many other private loans; and a longer loan period, generally coupled with a dramatic reduction in the required down payment, ensured that most employed people could acquire homes. This ability to purchase residential property was coupled with a pent-up demand for new, larger, and better housing, since relatively little had been built since 1929. General economic prosperity following the war also led to an increase in marriages and births—the so-called baby boom—further encouraging a demand for homes.

This sequence of events triggered by government entry into the private loan arena not only benefited the individual purchaser, but also commercial developers. In some instances they became eligible to receive loans directly, but more typically their knowledge of the loan process and the types of housing that could qualify for it allowed them to produce marketable products for which prospective home buyers were all but assured loans. Since, like private lenders, they were almost assured a market, they too were more readily able to acquire start-up investment funds and develop large, highly profitable communities.

Concurrent with government involvement in financing came an increase in regulation, both regulation related to government-financed programs and to general environmental quality. Much of this regulation grew from the city planning tradition—for example, zoning restrictions and improved building codes. Later, regulatory control was extended beyond the limits of local jurisdictions to include special environments such as wetlands, floodplains, and historic districts. While such legislation increased development costs, it also protected valued landscapes and provided employment for specialists in these areas of planning.

Social change, related to the distribution of population and to economic prosperity, also affected post-1945 design. The four most significant demographic trends were population concentration in urban areas; the population bulge known as the "baby boom," for the exceptionally large birthrate from 1945 to 1960; increase in the relative number of older people in the population, a trend which has continued to accelerate; and, after 1960 in the United States, population movement from the Northeast and Midwest to the South and West, the area generally termed the Sunbelt.

These demographic changes, coupled with high incomes, produced significant changes in the way people lived—affecting such areas as preferences in residential type and location, travel patterns, preferred recreational activities, household composition, and family size. Each of these lifestyle changes had a corresponding influence on the landscape. Among the important changes in lifestyle were increased dependence, in some areas becoming complete reliance, on the automobile for transportation; greater interest in actually using outdoor spaces, particularly the backyard, for activities rather than as a showplace; growth of suburbs and large suburban subdivisions; and finally, in the more recent past, interest in ecology, nonpolluting and energy-conserving landscapes, and sustainable development.

A final influence of importance was the Modernist design philosophy, which had both aesthetic and functional components. Modern design was first expressed in architectural design through the work of Europeans such as Le Corbusier, Aalto, and members of the Bauhaus. While the influence of the aesthetic aspects of modernism has recently waned, the functional components have had a lasting and significant impact on the built environment, changing the focus of designers away from mere form and appearance to an examination of the purposes of design and planning for both human and environmental well-being.

MODERN URBAN PLANNING

Economic revival following World War II caused a rebirth of interest in improvement of cities. The need for such refurbishment came after nearly two decades in which private buildings and public infrastructure had decayed due to lack of funding. The city planning of the second half of the twentieth century was not different from that of earlier decades in concept, but only in particulars. One interesting phenomenon was a renewed interest in the integration of objective planning with visual design—the City Beautiful and the City Scientific merged for a new urban order.

Postwar planning addressed four major issues. The first was urban blight, that is, the physical disintegration of buildings and infrastructure. Blighted neighborhoods, according to a planning report for Chicago in 1943, were those in which 50 percent of residential structures were built prior to 1895 *and* at least 50 percent of units in those structures were substandard. These twin indicators of age and condition had a significant impact on programs to deal with blight, which generally involved demolition and replacement rather another option—renovation. A second problem was the continuing one of how to accommodate the auto in the city. By 1950, though, the problem had reached critical proportions as the car-for-every-family ideal became a reality. Adequate parking continued to be difficult, but in large cities a more crucial issue was how to accommodate huge numbers of commuter vehicles at peak travel times. The solution involved construction of limited-access superhighways, often part of the Interstate Highway system.[1] What remedy these roads brought for the traffic dilemma was offset by the problems that they caused: breaking established lines of circulation, decimating older neighborhoods, and erasing needed low-cost housing. The perception that cities were blighted, substandard places to live, coupled with easy access to the urban job market via superhighways, led to the third major postwar urban problem—flight to the suburbs. Of course not everyone could flee, generally only those of some affluence. As they left the city, so too did tax revenues, neighborhood service businesses, and often the most vocal, watchful segment of society. The final urban problem of this period was how to integrate New Deal-inspired, government-sponsored urban planning and social welfare programs into a prosperous, private-enterprise-driven economy. For over two decades, up to and including the Great Society programs of the Johnson administration, American cities were subjected to constant experimentation in a utopian effort to "perfect" them.

By the 1960s urban and suburban growth had created three additional problems—the bonus of growth. One was the phenomenon referred to as "conurbation" or "megalopolis," that is, the continuous urbanization of previously agricultural areas between cities. The principal megalopolis in North America was, of course, the Boston–New York–Philadelphia–Baltimore–Washington, D.C., corridor. Middle-class flight to the suburbs led to development in each city's hinterland until intervening rural land had effectively been suburbanized. Secondly, as developers began to construct larger, more complex subdivisions—sometimes the size of small towns—local systems such as infrastructure, schools, and transportation became so overwhelmed that it took years to raise the quantity to standard. Finally, in the aftermath of planning and design modifications to modernize cities came the realization that they had often been so sanitized that the most vibrant aspects of urban living were eliminated. Critic Jane Jacobs chided conventional planning because "the rebuilt portions of cities and the endless new developments spreading beyond the cities are reducing city and countryside alike to a monotonous, unnourishing gruel. . . . It all comes, first-, second-, third- or fourth-hand, out of the same intellectual dish of mush, a mush in which the qualities, necessities, advantages and behavior of great cities have been utterly confused with the qualities, necessities, advantages and behavior of other and more inert types of settlements" (1961, p. 6).

THE ROLE OF LEGISLATION IN URBAN PLANNING

These problems and concerns did not lead to completely experimental urban planning strategies, but to modification of tried and tested ones. Thus the late twentieth century was not a period of planning innovation, but one of the persistence and refinement of basic approaches pioneered in earlier decades. In general, planning extended to more cities, so that by the 1980s few cities and towns lacked some form of master planning. Even Houston, the perennial antizoning city, is now contemplating this form of land use control. In addition, planning became more scientific, standardized, and professionalized. The most important "pattern books" of the late twentieth century were those which outlined criteria for planning, such as those published by the Urban Land Institute. Comprehensive planning became increasingly important as the means to justify land use decisions. Planning jurisdictions also increased in scale, with more regional planning bodies being formed, many of them to address the problems of major metropolitan areas. The most influential regional planning boards in the United States have been the National Capital Planning Commission and National Capital Regional Planning Commission for the Washington, D.C. area. Some states, such as California and Oregon, have initiated statewide plans.

While older planning concepts continued to influence modern urban patterns, some innovations have been made in how those concepts are applied. For example, several new zoning strategies have been introduced to supplement the standard use, height, and bulk ordinances. Performance zoning established standards of usage for large tracts that could be achieved through different types of development rather than through a specified land use. For example, for residential development a performance standard of five dwelling units per acre could be implemented through single-family lots at five per acre, townhouses at ten per developed acre with half the site reserved for open space, or high-rise apartments at one hundred units per acre with most of the site retained as open area. Transfer of development rights is a strategy devised specifically to help preserve historic structures; a site development value, usually the number of square feet allowed on that lot by the zoning ordinance, is calculated. An owner of a historic structure who agrees to preserve the structure has the right to sell the unused development potential of the site—that is, the square footage of a new building that could be constructed on the site minus the footage of the existing building. The purchaser of these rights can then use them in a special "transfer" district, allowing developers in that area to build more and higher than their zoning would otherwise allow.

Legislation has also influenced other aspects of urban planning and design, particularly in the United States. The first significant postwar urban legislation was the Housing Act of 1949, with major amendments in 1954 and 1961. This federal law required that all cities have what was indecisively termed a "general plan" before proceeding with local plan implementation or legislation. Although the term was weak, comprehensive planning based on well thought out prior intentions was bolstered. The law also provided significant funding for public housing, set standards that local public housing had to meet to receive that funding, and subsidized some privately developed low-cost housing. This Housing Act became an important force in shaping the modern inner city.

In 1966 the Demonstration Cities and Metropolitan Development Act established the Model Cities Program. This program differed significantly from the thrust of previous urban legislation. It mandated citizen input into planning decisions and required that neighborhood preservation, rather than demolition, be part of urban improvement. Finally, the Act established in principle the need for urban regional planning. The last major federal legislation to transform designed urban landscapes was the Housing Act revision of 1971, particularly the section called Title VII. This act differed from earlier housing legislation in looking at housing as one part of a total urban development package. It established loan and grant programs to help fund what were known as "New-Towns in-Town"—essentially completely new, compact neighborhoods with housing, shopping, offices, and open space. Cedar-Riverside in Minneapolis, Minnesota, one of the best known of these new towns, will be discussed later.

In the 1970s and 1980s federal tax legislation also affected urban conditions. Specifically, tax credits and exemptions intended to foster historic preservation aided the restoration of older neighborhoods. These tax credits made it financially feasible for new owners to purchase older, run-down residences considered to be blighted and renovate them to modern standards of safety and comfort. Entire districts such as the Old Town area of Chicago became "Renewed Towns in Town" through the efforts of innumerable new homeowners. This process, though, was not without its drawbacks. Often referred to as "gentrification," these renovations often removed housing from the stock available to low-income families.

URBAN RENEWAL AS CITY PLANNING

Although the term "urban renewal" was not officially used until the Housing Act of 1954, the concept of urban planning through razing of older or run-down buildings or districts was not new. As early as Burnham's plan for Cleveland, land had been cleared of unwanted uses to provide sites for new construction. What differed after 1945 was not the concept but the extent to which it was applied and the methods used.

Urban renewal had four original rationales: slum clearance, improved low-cost housing, nonresidential urban redevelopment, and public control of private development. Renewal was authorized and funded by federal agencies, principally the Urban Renewal Administration, but instigated and managed by local planning bodies to address local problems. Large tracts of land that it would almost certainly have been financially unfeasible to acquire by other means were condemned through eminent domain proceedings by planning boards. Once acquired, these public agencies resold the land to private developers who had agreed to redevelop the site to a particular plan. The federal role involved compensating local governments 50 to 75 percent of the difference between actual costs of land acquisition and clearing, and the price that developers would pay for that site.

In theory urban renewal benefited everyone. Local planners gained direct control over land use; developers in effect received land subsidies; residents got new housing, as well as more efficient infrastructure services; and the federal government could enforce minimal planning and construction standards. Theory, though, rarely became practice, especially regarding new affordable housing. Urban renewal generated as many problems as it solved. It often replaced horizontal slums with vertical high-rise ones. In other instances, development costs mitigated against housing becoming low cost when completed. Although renewal projects were required to have a relocation plan for even temporarily displaced residents, none were adequate in scope or timeliness. Relocation problems also more drastically affected poorer segments of the population, for whom housing options were already very limited. Further, clearing of blighted zones often proceeded before concrete plans and reliable redevelopment funding had been finalized. Many cities were left with large, deserted tracts that remained undeveloped for several decades. Finally, urban renewal addressed only physical planning, with few complementary programs to address social and economic issues that had as much, if not more, impact on cities.

The story of urban renewal involved both successful and unsuccessful projects, and many that were quite controversial. One of the most effective, at least in terms of city government goals, was the redevelopment of the civic center in Hartford, Connecticut, with its centerpiece Constitution Plaza. Redeveloped in the late 1950s and early 1960s to replace a district of nineteenth-century stores and warehouses, the civic center included a coliseum, exhibit hall, hotel, offices, plazas, and parking garages. The Hartford project, financed jointly by the city and Aetna Life and Casualty Company, was one of the first renewal projects to reject traditional streetscape development and move pedestrians to a second-story system of walks and plazas. Constitution Plaza, designed by Sasaki, Walker Associates, provided beautifully articulated, well-maintained terraced plazas for office workers and hotel guests. Although attractive in themselves, these upper-level walks relegated street level to the role of alley.

Less widely well regarded was the government center at the Governor Nelson A. Rockefeller Empire State Plaza in Albany, New York. This 100-acre site with elevated central plaza was a complex of state government offices, a performing arts center, a museum, and sites for memorials, such as the state's Vietnam Memorial. All of these massively scaled spaces and buildings were in distinct contrast to the scale of dilapidated downtown Albany that they replaced. An unintentionally self-deprecating description of the plaza, with which no critic would disagree, was provided in the site brochure: "The architecture is overwhelming. The [forty-two story] Tower . . . speaks for itself. The four smaller towers are called 'Agency Buildings' and house many state departments. . . . You

View of Constitution Plaza, Hartford, Connecticut, in the 1980s. Street level with its entry to the first-story garage is hidden by the foreground shrubs.

*Empire State Plaza, Albany,
New York, looking toward the
old state Capitol, in the 1980s.*

might be particularly interested in the concrete building perched on stilts like a flying saucer [known locally as 'The Egg']. . . . It is a Performing Arts Center. . . . Observe the monumental contemporary sculpture in several outdoor areas . . ." (General Services, n.d., pp. 3–5). All of these "overwhelming" structures were organized around a monolithic 25-acre mall with three giant reflecting pools in a line down the center. At one end, the late nineteenth-century state Capitol served as a focal point, while at the other sat the Brutalist-inspired Cultural Education Center. Peter Blake labeled the plaza complex "a neofascist assemblage of skyscraper and paved and windswept plazas" (1979, p.7).

Recently, urban renewal has taken a less destructive approach that involves redevelopment of existing buildings and neighborhoods with minimal disruption of residential patterns. In New York City, M. Paul Friedburg, working with architect I. M. Pei, revitalized two streets of a Bedford Stuyvesant neighborhood by renovating townhouses and apartments, as well as redesigning the streets for pedestrians. One street, modeled after *Woonerfs* in the Netherlands, was turned into a pedestrian-oriented space, with driving lanes reduced in width, parking limited to central, angled slots, and newly created pedestrian zones designed as plazas with trees, benches, and lighting. In other cities, abandoned industrial districts have been converted into new residential neighborhoods. In the Printer's Row District of Chicago existing multistoried factories and warehouses became low-rent galleries, studios, and apartments.

THE MODERNIST CITY

One of the principal influences on postwar urban design was Modernist urban planning and design theory, particularly that of architects such as Le Corbusier and Victor Gruen. While no North American city embraced modernism as wholeheartedly as did Brazil's new national capital at Brasilia, its biases were given form at a smaller scale in cities throughout the continent (for example, at the Empire State Plaza). The notion of the Modernist city, first proposed as a unified theory at the Congrès Internationaux d'Architecture Moderne in the late 1920s, was rooted in reformist notions of that era. In particular its advocates used planning to advance public, rather than private, goals—a process in which planned form would be used to achieve egalitarian social objectives. Machines were the model of efficiency that Modernist planners sought to implement in built form by allocating land uses based on a balance of basic functions. While these ideas were not completely novel, the form chosen to achieve them was quite different from earlier urban prototypes. Specifically, Modernist practitioners advocated high-rise cities in which population concentration allowed large areas of land to be retained for open space immediately adjacent to buildings.

Modernist planning theory had the greatest direct impact on the design of public housing facilities, for two reasons. First, the scale of postwar need for low-cost housing suggested that a new approach was needed. Second, space- and facility-efficient Modernist housing was viewed as a cost-efficient way to provide this housing quickly. Unfortunately, the archetypes proposed by upper-income intellectuals and professionals were not well suited to the needs of lower-income families. Many of these Modernist housing complexes were part of the urban renewal movement and replaced older, poorly maintained low-rise apartments and townhouses. It was theorized that by housing families in multistory towers, land that would not otherwise be acquired could be preserved nearby for parks and recreation. What was not foreseen were the social and functional problems created by grouping people at such high densities and separating them from the street-level environment: parents were unable to supervise children at play unless they accompanied them. Elevators used to access upper-level apartments became sites of crime—that is, if they worked at all. Finally, residents lost much of the close and supportive contact that they had had when able to visit regularly with neighbors across the street or passing by. In addition, there were financial problems with public housing development, largely due to the limitations of government programs. Federal project managers concerned themselves only with construction costs, repayment schedules for local housing authorities, and rental conditions, but failed to consider that the complete cost of housing development included site acquisition or that poor maintenance would reduce the life of housing.

The symbol for the failure of this type of housing was the Pruitt-Igoe public housing high rises in Saint Louis, Missouri. After less than two decades of occupancy, they had proved to be so unlivable that they were demolished in a spectacular explosion. Unfortunately, it took so long for the fact that such types of housing did not work to sink in that similar, and similarly problematic, public housing had already been constructed in every major city.

In the 1960s, with the renewed interest in social issues, designers and philanthropists alike returned to the issue of truly low-cost urban housing. By that time it had been realized that public/private joint ventures were more realistic than solely public housing. Programs of government subsidy for poorer residents in private housing became an alternative to the "project." With passage of the New-Town in-Town provisions of the Housing Act of 1971, a direct experiment in public/private joint ventures began. The first new development begun under this program was Cedar-Riverside in Minneapolis, Minnesota, planned and designed by Lawrence Halprin and Associates; Sasaki, Walker Associates; and architect Ralph Rapson. This new town was to be a multifunctional neighborhood with an eventual 350 people for each of its 340 acres. To accommodate this density, much of the housing was to be in high-rise apartment towers like those that dominated the first phase of the project, Cedar-Riverside West. Although primarily residential, a local commercial area, office space, and cultural facilities such as a theater were planned. Pedestrian and vehicular traffic were separated by level, with parking provided in garages below buildings. Although widely acclaimed in the 1970s, Cedar-Riverside has not yet been completed and remains primarily a large apartment house complex, rather than a total community.

A more successful urban new town, Battery Park City, was developed in Manhattan during the 1970s and 1980s. Originally planned in the Modernist

The main plaza with surrounding high-rise buildings at Cedar-Riverside, Minneapolis, Minnesota, in the late 1970s.

mode, but recently enlarged and reconceptualized as a humanized urban village by the architectural firm of Cooper, Eckstut Associates, Battery Park City may eventually become a balanced community with a high-profile commercial area centered on the World Trade and World Financial Centers, residential nodes with a variety of housing types, and almost a third of its area reserved for open spaces, including the award-winning riverfront Esplanade designed by Hanna/Olin with Cooper, Eckstut.[2]

REEMPHASIS ON THE SOCIAL ROLE OF PLANNING AND DESIGN

The failure of government-sponsored urban planning, the insensitive severity of Modernist planning and architecture, pent-up demands for racial equality, and the maturing of liberal-minded baby boomers were all forces that led to greater social responsiveness in the design professions beginning in the 1960s. These responses took a number of forms: citizen participation in the design process was encouraged and fostered; greater attention was paid to the needs of special populations such as the elderly, children, and the mentally ill; community sense of place and sense of image were encouraged as a means to dispel environmental anomie; and serious study of the effect of the designed environment on its users was begun.

Citizen involvement in the planning and design process, although resisted by some designers, proved to be a professional boon to others who pursued it as a specialty. New techniques for group input and decision making were developed. The public meeting became a standard part of every major public project and many private ones as well. While design by committee would never produce unified site plans, input from potential users helped to reveal key issues and potential problems, which were then addressed in design and planning programs along with other project requirements.

One of the most famous user-designed spaces was People's Park in Berkeley, California. Taking over a lot cleared of housing by the University of California in preparation for new construction, the land was quickly expropriated by residents for recreation. Organized with assistance from local landscape architects and students, the park provided everything that the community wanted from an in-town open space including garden plots and a pit for barbecues.[3]

The growing public advocacy for input into design was particularly important in designing for those with special physical or psychological needs. As the population aged, as the handicapped gained greater freedom through technological advances, and as the mentally ill were integrated with the larger society, recognition of their environmental needs grew. For example, special construction features helpful to the elderly, such as nonslip pavements and low pathway slopes, have become standard features of housing projects. More universally, the right of access for all has been recognized, with national legislation mandating handicapped access standards. While implementation of all of these planning and design concerns is at a fundamental level of refinement, the acknowledgment that safe, functional, and attractive environments can serve the entire population has produced a needed sensitivity to special user groups.

Far less success has been achieved in dealing with the needs of specific ethnic communities. Many omissions have been at an obvious level—for example, building of passive recreational facilities in neighborhoods with a preponderance of teens and preteens. Other omissions have negated key aspects of community social life. Gans's classic study *The Urban Villagers* pointed out the incompatibility of suburban streetscapes with the social interaction needs of working-class Italian-American families. In public housing the provision of built-in furnishings such as beds and dressers created a sense of institutionalization for individuals whose self-worth was tied to those personal possessions that they could afford to acquire.

In his classic study of urban plazas, Whyte pointed out that even the needs of the general population were rarely recognized in designed spaces, simply because designers did not observe how people actually used space. Belatedly, renewed interest in the social role of design has produced an important body of research, most not yet fully implemented in practice, that explores user preferences and needs. Among the classic studies was that by Kiyoshi Izumi that clearly articulated the psychosocial importance of the built environment. Later John Zeisel, Robert Sommer, Edward Hall, and others conducted experiments in which the influence of simple designed arrangements, such as the placement of interior furnishings, on human behavior was demonstrated. Landscape-scale studies of social behavior include William Whyte's classic analysis of friendship patterns in suburbs, and studies by Sue Weidemann and James Anderson on types of outdoor spaces preferred by residents of public housing projects.

This research has produced a number of usable theories to aid design and planning. Oscar Newman's concept of "defensible space"—that is, the idea that the arrangement of buildings, doorways, and windows can give residents greater control over their neighborhood—has been used in a number of housing projects to control crime. Ideas about territoriality, derived from animal behavior studies, have informed planned spatial hierarchies in small sites and cities alike. The concept of the "behavior setting"—that is, the notion that patterns of behavior are associated with certain related times, places, and events—has been used as the organizing principle for many formal and informal studies of landscape use.

While emphasis on the social role of landscape design and planning is not new—Olmsted and Vaux were adamant about the stress-reducing effects of naturalistic scenery and Cleveland wrote about the importance of parks for children's well-being—contemporary interest has been more far-reaching and permanent, although far from universal. When government-financed research and design implementation were available, into the 1970s, academics and practitioners alike were motivated to pursue and implement socially based design research. Unfortunately, reduced funding, redirected research programs, and the difficulty of translating theory into practice have slowed progress in this vital aspect of design and planning.

Example of defensible space in a Minneapolis public housing project. Here the private frontyards of each unit were separated from the walkway by low fences to clearly establish the bounds of public and private space.

SUBURBAN PLANNING

The most significant type of postwar site planning and design, in terms of volume of work, was that for housing.[4] Particularly in the 1970s and 1980s, master planning of suburban residential communities or mixed-use developments with housing as a key component became a mainstay of many professional offices. The boom in housing during the entire period was a result first of population growth and then of financial incentives for home ownership. Later, growth of local planning control increased demand for defensible, professionally prepared plans that could pass the necessary legislative hurdles for permitting. The first modern subdivision plans were those for the Levittown developments in New York, New Jersey, and Pennsylvania. The Levitt company set the pattern for most later development by offering a fixed number of housing floor plans and facades, subdividing into small lots, providing homeowners with rudimentary modern conveniences as part of a package, and building to established standards of government loan programs. Thus, the potential buyer was assured not only a minimally livable home, but also that the house could be easily financed. The first Levittown, begun in 1948 on Long Island, had a simple grid plan with few amenities beyond street trees and infrastructure. Later developments were adapted to preferred taste in subdivision design, to include a less geometric street plan, more preoccupancy planting, and shopping facilities.

Although criticized by professional designers and social scientists alike, the three Levitt-built communities were very successful with lower-middle-income purchasers. For them the assembly-line system of subdivision development and house construction used at Levittown generated sufficient savings to allow many to afford a first home. The principal problems with these developments were the uniformity of "ticky-tacky boxes" down miles and miles of streets,[5] the lack of many basic services within reasonable distance, and the complete automobile orientation of the development. But these conditions appear to have kept few buyers away from the towns, where sales were always brisk. Levittown in Pennsylvania eventually was home to about 90,000 people, and only recent industrial downturns have threatened its stability.

Levittowns provided the prototype for residential subdivisions large and small in every part of the country, most just as successful financially as the originals. With such success innovation was often difficult to sell to potential developers. But gradually as purchasers became more sophisticated and the first-time homeowners of the 1950s sought to upgrade their residences, more amenity-oriented subdivisions began to appear. Among the first ideas to gain widespread popularity was a rather old one, houses on a cul-de-sac. The cul-de-sac—a dead end street with a generous turnaround—made streets more private by curtailing through traffic, created a social node for residents, and usually allowed a larger portion of the lot to become a rear yard. Although often employed merely as a way to get additional lots out of any odd-shaped tract of land, these closer streets came to be used as a circulation theme in expensive subdivisions where they offered the cachet of being semiprivate courts.

The development of subdivision plans based on criteria related to site character signaled a trend toward considering the quality of life provided to residents. In the 1970s, the quality of life was directly linked to availability of open space in a subdivision, and this linkage led to a number of site-planning innovations. One of the most significant was the cluster lot plan. In this approach lots were kept small so that land between lots or tiers of lots could be retained as community open spaces. Cluster lots were also generally more efficient in terms of infrastructure costs. Often the common areas were preserved in natural plant cover, so that they provided natural screening between units, places for wildlife food and cover, as well as passive recreation areas. The best-known cluster lot community was Village Homes in Davis, California, where emphasis was placed on preservation of open space, energy-efficient site planning, and on-site management of surface water.

More typical of cluster lot housing projects was Straw Hill in Manchester, New Hampshire. There George Matarazzo grouped housing units to retain a complex system of natural drainageways. Subdivisions utilizing cluster lot principles reflected growing interest in adapting development to conservation of ecological systems. More typically landscapes were treated as visual amenities—sales tools to attract more affluent purchasers—rather than as inherently worthwhile. Although this approach lacked the theoretical underpinnings of places such as Village Homes, many sound designs with merit resulted from this fashion. One of the myriad of developments in this mode was Greenbrook near Danville, California. There a central greenway along a creek became an attenuated, diffused downtown. Community facilities including a school, park, and clubhouse were all located within this green corridor. Most local loop streets bent at the greenway, so that the corridors also became street termini, as well as uninterrupted pedestrian passageways.

The most significant change to affect new housing developments was the creation of a special zoning designation that allowed large tracts of land to be planned to respond most efficiently to both site and economic needs. This new zoning category was the Planned Unit Development, or PUD.[6] PUDs allowed developers to request suspension of existing land use designations for large tracts, usually at least 50 acres, and instead develop unique plans that met city requirements but allowed the site to be designed as a whole with a variety of housing types and amenities as part of the package. An agreement between a planning commission and developer for a planned development was essentially a contract that allowed the developer greater freedom of action, but retained for the commission rights to accept, reject, or modify any proposed plan. PUDs rapidly became the normal way of developing high-quality residential subdivisions, whether for a few hundred homeowners or the size of new towns. At the smaller end of the scale, PUDs of 100 acres were often developed to provide housing of various types and costs. They typically included some traditional single-family lots, usually sited on the most desirable land, townhouses, and multifamily units either as condominiums or rental apartments.

At the scale of a new town were PUDs such as Rancho Bernardo near San Diego.[7] There AVCO Development Company began in 1962 to develop more than 6,000 acres as a residential community to accommodate an ultimate population of 40,000. As with many PUDs, emphasis in both design and marketing was on quality of life in an attractive community. In Rancho Bernardo, as might be anticipated from the name, architectural themes alluding to the area's Spanish past were used; red tile roofs, for example, were required on all structures. Life-style features also included provision for active leisure activities, such as jogging and bike paths that connect the entire community. Boulevards, well screened from surrounding homes, functioned as collectors to serve neighborhoods and control the location of heavy traffic. As was typical in most residentially oriented PUDs, a shopping center served as community center, with public buildings such as the post office located adjacent to it. Other large, regionally significant Planned Unit Developments included Kingsmill on the James River near Williamsburg, Virginia, and Ancient Tree in Northbrook, Illinois.

Another approach to providing housing at reasonable cost involved use of new housing types in subdivisions. While most studies confirmed American preference for detached single-family homes, cost prevented many from achieving this dream. Since the late 1960s, developers have sought to tap the market of those unable to buy detached homes by marketing less land-intensive types of housing. The first type to gain widespread popularity was the townhouse. Of course, this was a very traditional type of housing but had usually been confined to urban areas. When moved to suburbia, the attached townhouse allowed greater density of land development, thereby reducing costs. In addition, the modular nature of townhouses allowed them to be more easily adapted to difficult sites and created variety in facade alignment, which gave such developments attractive characters. Patio homes also allowed intensive land use because units could be attached to prevent waste of space. The principal difference between townhouses and patio homes was in the location of private outdoor space. As their name suggests, patio homes were modeled after the Spanish colonial house to include an interior courtyard enclosed by the building or by a wall. A final important innovation in housing design was the zero lot line house. Where approved, this

The main shopping center at Rancho Bernardo near San Diego illustrates the use of thematic facades to unify an otherwise typical strip shopping center.

form of housing allowed units to be placed at or very near one side lot line so that setbacks, usually located on two sides, were grouped into one larger, more usable side yard. Many of the first subdivisions to use this planning innovation merely moved traditional, wide single-family homes to one side of a lot. Later it was realized that even greater cost reductions in land and infrastructure could be achieved by reorienting the house so that it had a narrow street width and ran deep into the lot. As with patio houses, one of the problems with zero lot line development was that it often created a dismal streetscape—one saw little more than driveways leading to bare garage doors.

Of course, not all housing projects have been made up of of single-family housing. Growing out of the concerns of the Depression era, but planned by private developers as economic conditions improved in the late 1930s, were a number of well-designed apartment subdivisions, such as Interlaken Garden Apartments outside New York City and Baldwin Hills Village in Los Angeles. In both complexes, developers tried to reduce housing costs by increasing unit per acre density. At the same time, to compensate for density, apartments were laid out around courtyard-like open spaces linked with a larger open area. Auto penetration of both sites was limited to arterial streets and parking courts. Designed by Clarke and Rapuano, Interlaken Garden Apartments was organized so that as many units as possible had views to an on-site lake. At Baldwin Hills Village, by Clarence Stein and Fred Barlow, views and community life focused inward to courts and the "village green."

As family types change, the population ages, economic conditions and banking practices change, and population density shifts to new areas of the continent, housing both as shelter and as a form of planning will change accordingly. It is

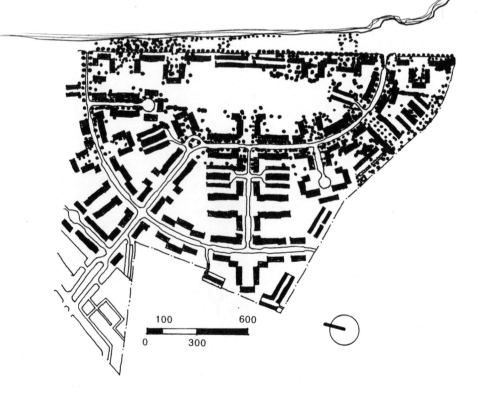

Plan of Interlaken Gardens apartments near New York City, designed by Clarke and Rapuano. (Data from Architectural Record, Vol. 86, No. 3; drawn by Rossi.)

100   600

0   300

likely that it will remain an important form of practice both in the private sector, where plans are generated, and in the public sector, where land use requirements are enforced. Just as in the past, landscape architects will play a significant role in adapting housing to both environmental needs and those of residents. While subdivision additions to existing cities and large residential communities will be one way to do this, more ambitious planners foresee the need to create complete new towns.

NEW TOWNS: SUBURBS AS CITIES

As the pace of suburbanization quickened in the 1950s and after, designers, planners, developers, and local governments alike became alarmed at the proliferation of identityless bedroom communities that taxed local resources, but often provided an insufficient tax base to compensate for their own needs for roads, schools, and utilities.[8] Looking backward, these groups took inspiration from sources such as Romantic suburbs, early twentieth-century industrial new towns, Radburn, and the Green Cities, and proposed imaginative solutions to the creation of sustainable new communities. Several consistent characteristics typify most of these postwar new towns: location near a major city, but at the outer edge of its suburbs; complete master planning prior to construction; neighborhoods fused into larger villages as the principal unit of planning; site plans adapted to natural landscape systems and character; and restricted intrusion of the automobile on physical and visual character of the development.

Having all of these characteristics, Reston, Virginia, was one of the most successful of the new towns, although this success meant that the community served a more affluent population than was originally intended. Begun in 1961, Reston, located 18 miles west of Washington, D.C., near Dulles Airport, was planned as a complete community to accommodate an eventual population of about 90,000 on more than 7,000 acres. The master plan on which the town has been based, by the architecture and planning firm of Wittlesey and Conklin, was the first for a PUD approved in Fairfax County, Virginia, and Reston was probably the largest PUD existing or planned on the continent at that time.[9]

Reston was to be a new "hometown" in which residents could live, work, and ultimately retire. The plan included two major town centers; seven villages, each with its own community and commercial center; a large industrial/office zone, and a variety of leisure activity areas including parks and a cultural center. To suit the diverse housing needs of such a new town, Reston's planners utilized almost every conceivable type of housing, including high-rise and mid-rise apartments, townhouses, traditional single-family detached homes, single-family clustered homes, and patio homes.

Individual villages, separated from each other by greenbelts, were the core of Reston's spatial concept. The first and most distinctive of these villages, Lake Anne Village, centered on a large artificial lake. Lake Anne Village had a very urbane character, with a European-inspired downtown plaza encircled on two sides by a J-shaped three-story commercial/office/apartment building and opening on one remaining side onto Lake Anne. The plaza was expected to be a hub of daily activity for shopping, relaxing at cafes, or boating. Around this village center, housing was zoned by density with multistory apartments directly off the plaza, townhouses in more secluded areas nearby, and single-family houses at the periphery of the village. Motorized vehicles were kept to the exterior of all housing areas, which faced pedestrian pathways linking major use areas. Residents of Lake Anne Village could reach the village center along these footpaths in less than ten minutes.

The original Reston master plan, now three decades old, has been followed in outline to a remarkable degree. The circulation hierarchy remains in place,

View of the shopping area at Lake Anne Village, Reston, Virginia.

lakes have been constructed as planned, and recreational facilities, such as golf courses and parks, provide intended leisure opportunities. But contemporary Reston is not exactly like the town envisioned in the early 1960s. Its housing has generally become more "suburbanized," with traditional arrangements of single-family homes and townhouses now more numerous than earlier innovative housing. Village Centers, although still well screened from surrounding roads, now have the character of well-designed strip shopping centers, rather than the urbane personality of Lake Anne Village Center. These changes, though, should not detract from the importance of Reston as the first successful, internationally recognized model for postwar American new towns.

While the planning of Reston was based chiefly on lifestyle concerns, planning of another new town, The Woodlands, begun in 1972 near Houston, was geared to preserving critical on-site environmental conditions, particularly dense vegetative cover and drainage patterns. Site planners Wallace, McHarg, Roberts and Todd, working with William L. Pereira, based development recommendations on an exhaustive ecological inventory and analysis. Their principal concern was protection of the critical watershed serving Houston that lay below parts of the 18,000-acre tract. The plan that evolved over a number of revisions kept roads to ridgelines, sited built areas on midslopes, and preserved valleys and recharge areas for open space. To reduce runoff, native cover rather than turf was retained over much of the site, including lots of single-family homes. In the process the designers managed to create a true "tree-city U.S.A.," with few buildings ever visible at one glance.

Human needs were not neglected at The Woodlands, though. The new town was to be composed of seven[10] villages, with more than twenty small shopping/community areas, a regional shopping mall, two golf courses, a University of Houston branch, and an outdoor theater. Unfortunately, as at Reston, some of the solid planning concepts originally developed for The Woodlands have been neglected in recently constructed areas—roads have been widened, grass allowed to replace native groundcovers, and previously preserved zones built upon.

Almost every major city was the beneficiary of some suburban new town scheme during the 1960s and 1970s. Among the more significant have been Columbia, Maryland, located between Washington, D.C., and Baltimore; Jona-

Housing along one of the many ponds at The Woodlands, Conroe, Texas, that store runoff and recharge aquifers.

than near Minneapolis; Park Forest South near Chicago; Litchfield Park near Phoenix; Erin Mills near Toronto; Las Colinas near Dallas; and California Springs in southern California. Columbia, Jonathan, and Park Forest South are all similar in planning concept to Reston, but have maintained greater income diversity. Columbia, initiated by the legendary developer James Rouse, was organized around a hierarchy of neighborhood zones set into a fabric of preserved open spaces that account for about 20 percent of the site. Jonathan, in addition to residential, commercial, and industrial land uses, was to be a center of higher education, with sites reserved for colleges, libraries, and technical centers. In addition, Jonathan was the only new town to qualify for guaranteed loans under a federal program that encouraged new town development.[11] The planners of Park Forest South designed a linear, multileveled town center as the community's focal point, but kept the rest of the town in relatively low-density uses with access from zone to zone via a network of foot and bicycle paths.

Litchfield Park was conceived as a town of neighborhoods just like the new towns discussed thus far, but differed from them in circulation and town center organization. Major streets within the community, which separated neighborhoods, followed a fairly traditional modified grid pattern. More ingenious was the communitywide path system, designed to eliminate intracity travel by auto and replace it with golf carts and bicycles. A linear town center, equally close to all neighborhoods, brought together community facilities including schools, convention center, and shopping inside a green corridor.

Erin Mills was an ecologically planned community, with planning based on concerns similar to those that influenced the design of The Woodlands. Primary concern, though, was not for drainage but with preservation and restoration of diversity of flora and fauna. To accomplish this, the most sensitive ecosystems, as determined by scientific study, were set aside for open spaces or other low-intensity uses.

The rationale at Las Colinas was image, not ecology. Intended to be an urbane corporate utopia, the town was planned for security, homogeneity, and perfection of detail. Its high-rise downtown, centered on the waterway system called the Mandalay Canal, was an amalgamation of eclectic built images col-

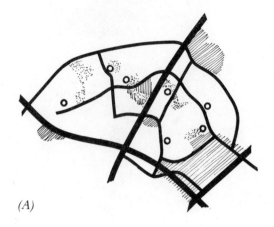

(A)

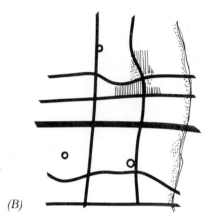

(B)

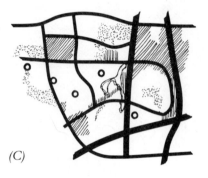

(C)

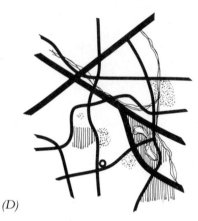

(D)

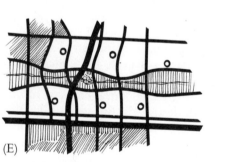

(E)

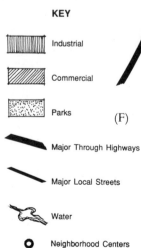

(G)

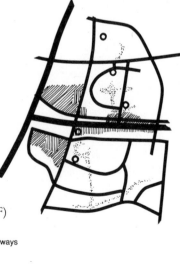

(F)

KEY

	Industrial
	Commercial
	Parks
	Major Through Highways
	Major Local Streets
	Water
◯	Neighborhood Centers

Schematic plans of seven contemporary new towns, drawn to approximately uniform scales; (A) Columbia, Maryland; (B) Erin Mills, Ontario; (C) Jonathan, Minnesota; (D) Las Colinas, Texas; (E) Litchfield, California; (F) Reston, Virginia; (G) The Woodlands, Conroe, Texas.

lected by developer Ben Carpenter during years of travel. What this eclectic scene lacked was the vitality of a site-specific design and the unifying elements needed to create a unique whole out of its disparate parts.

California Springs, the most recently developed of the new towns discussed here, is really little more than a plan on paper at the time of this writing. Located almost 100 miles north of Los Angeles, California Springs will be more than three times as far from a central city as the most distant new town built so far. The developers' strategy has been to use distance from the city to assure affordability of its homes. California Springs will also be different in design, with a grid street pattern[12] and less pastoral landscape than towns such as Reston and Columbia. Only time will tell if this new formula will prove as successful under current economic and buyer preference conditions as did the new towns established two decades ago.

The most unusual new town of the post-World War II era was certainly Paolo Soleri's Arcosanti. It is really an understatement—like thinking of a nuclear bomb as merely a weapon—to consider Arcosanti just a new town, for in Soleri's vision it was the physical manifestation of a new urban order based on egalitarianism and ecological balance. In the megastructure that is Arcosanti, a space- and resource-efficient community for tens of thousands has been planned and is under construction. Soleri believes that his new city, grounded in sound social and environmental principles, will resolve urban problems as diverse as suburban sprawl, drug addiction, and recycling—those same problems that planners and social reformers have attempted to work out through city reorganization throughout the twentieth century.

CONTEMPORARY URBAN DESIGN

City beautification through urban design in the last half of the twentieth century has focused on development of specific sites or areas within the city, rather than the comprehensive civic planning of the first decades of the century during the City Beautiful period. Four specific site types have been especially important during this era: the mixed-use center, the downtown mall, the plaza, and the redeveloped waterfront. Mixed-use centers were privately built complexes similar in concept to some urban renewal schemes, but with greater emphasis on commercial and office facilities than on housing. A model for later developments was Rockefeller Center in New York City. Begun in the 1930s on a master plan by L. A. Reinhard and Henry Hofmeister, the project gradually evolved over about twenty years as experience suggested modifications to original plans. Rockefeller Center replaced more than twelve midtown blocks with high-rise office towers connected to the celebrated sunken plaza by planted concourses. As originally designed, this plaza was nothing more than a paved forecourt for shops and restaurants, but that use did little to entice patrons to the lower level and was quickly replaced by the winter skating rink and summer cafe that now animate the space. While fiscal concerns limited open space, every available outdoor area became a garden. This included rooftops, which were to have a series of small landscapes, designed by Arthur Shurcliff, based on the "Gardens of Nations" theme.

A more recently constructed mixed-use center, Rainbow Center in Niagara Falls, New York, replaced the preexisting downtown core with a suburban, mall-like complex. Its indoor shopping mall, convention center, and parking garages for tourists to the nearby falls focused inward toward a 5-acre plaza, which has been unflatteringly dubbed "Piazza del Kroger" by one author. The center, planned by Victor Gruen Associates, had one important landscape design, that for the modern public conservatory called Wintergarden designed by M. Paul Friedburg. Wintergarden has an intimately scaled tropical garden with

In summer the sunken plaza of Rockefeller Center, famous as a wintertime skating rink, is used as a cafe. (Technical Reference Center, Texas A&M University.)

waterfalls and ponds, envisioned, as its name suggests, as a place of escape during long upstate New York winters.

The most ambitious mixed-use centers have been those by developer/architect John Portman, which he called "coordinate units." His success with this type of project began with Peachtree Center in Atlanta. That highly urban complex was developed as a three-zone system located across parts of eight city blocks. Uses included the Merchandise and Apparel Marts, a shopping center, office buildings, and two hotels—one of which, the Hyatt, had trademark Portman features of glassed elevators, dramatic water fountains, and interior spaces designed like outdoor plazas. The success of Peachtree Center, and later Embarcadero Center in San Francisco, helped make Portman one of the most sought after developers of mixed-use centers in the United States during the 1970s and 1980s.

Coal Harbor in Vancouver, British Columbia, is an as yet incomplete mixed-use center with a larger number of functions than either Rockefeller Center or Rainbow Center. Planned to include housing of several types, a hotel site, a retail marketplace, and a marina, Coal Harbor will be the first large-scale, high-density development in the dispersed city plan of Vancouver. To compensate for this density, developers plan to provide significant areas of waterfront open space including a public green, plaza, and promenade.

Downtown shopping areas that suffered, and continue to suffer, economically when competing with auto-oriented shopping centers have undergone two types of redevelopment in an attempt to revitalize them. The earliest solutions transformed downtown itself into a version of the shopping mall, by closing off streets to through traffic and redesigning them as pedestrian malls. Among the first cities to use this strategy was Fresno, California. Fresno Mall, planned by Victor Gruen Associates and designed by Eckbo, Dean, Austin and Williams, transformed a six-block-long segment of Fulton Street and adjoining cross-streets into a linear plaza. Irregular angular and curvilinear paving bands in dark tones

Embarcadero Center, San Francisco, with Isamu Noguchi's fountain of large water chutes in the foreground.

set against a light background that filled the space between storefronts created a dynamic ground-plane pattern against which was set a variety of site amenities, such as fountains, seating areas covered with pergolas, and a clock tower. A key feature of the mall's plan was an undelineated open lane through the center of the pavement that allowed a colorful motor-driven mini-trolley to provide public transit within the otherwise pedestrian mall, to compensate for removal of automotive traffic from the street. In the first years of operation, after its opening in 1964, the mall was successful in attracting the affluent shoppers desired by merchants, but this success was relatively short-lived. By the mid-1970s shop vacancies had increased, but the area continues to support considerable retail activity and, as Garrett Eckbo has recently observed, the active street life that the mall was designed to facilitate.

Main street malls have also been successful in larger cities. For the Nicollet Mall in Minneapolis, an innovative site plan was used to maintain the vitality that street traffic provides, while increasing pedestrian spaces. As planned by Barton-Aschman Associates and designed by Lawrence Halprin Associates, a narrow serpentine roadway reserved for buses and emergency vehicles replaced the original street. This allowed more space for walkways and the various amenities that made Nicollet Street one of the continent's best furnished streetscapes. Each block was designed with a distinctive theme of fountains and a specific tree species. Larger structures along the transitway included bus shelters with services such as stamp machines or newspaper dispensers, a central clock tower, and a sculpture by Alexander Calder.

The pedestrian quality of the mall was reinforced by redevelopment of surrounding buildings, as well as new construction, the most important of which was construction of the IDS Center.[13] At street level the Center was an open plaza known as the Crystal Court for the faceted glass panels that enclosed it up to its 120-foot ceiling. This court, surrounded by shops and balconies used for restaurants, was a principal point of access to the city's system of second-story skywalks, which provided enclosed pedestrian access to major buildings downtown. Although the mall and skywalk systems were often inappropriately copied in other cities, the plan provided a practical solution for downtown redevelopment in cold climates where extensive outdoor plazas can have only limited year-round use.

Nicollet Mall in Minneapolis, circa 1980, showing how pedestrian spaces were doubled in size by reducing driving lanes.

The design and early economic successes of downtown malls like those in Fresno and Minneapolis inspired small towns and large cities across the country to close off their main streets for pedestrian use. Unfortunately, most of these schemes were poorly conceptualized, and although well designed, failed to meet community economic needs. The mall in Burlington, Iowa, by Barton-Aschman, was imaginatively designed on themes that emphasized the city's importance as a port of call for Mississippi riverboats, such as a planter in the shape of a paddlewheel. Unfortunately, all of this clever design failed to bring business back to downtown, in part because the buying public had moved to the outskirts of the city and because parking was *perceived* to be too distant and inadequate. Elsewhere, mall designs intended to improve the downtown business environment themselves contributed to its downturn. In Champaign, Illinois, for example, the principal shopping street was closed to through traffic, a move which led to rerouting of traffic around rather than toward shopping areas. In addition, the pedestrian space thus created was dominated by a sunken plaza area covered with a black-painted space-frame canopy. Rather than creating a lively, cheerful atmosphere, this space darkened the street, obscured parts of storefronts, and provided better amenities for idlers than for shoppers.

A second, and generally more successful, strategy to revitalize downtown shopping was the adaptive reuse of existing but underutilized older buildings or building complexes as shopping centers. Abandoned industrial buildings, with their large interior spaces and service yards, proved especially popular for reuse. The best known of such developments was Ghirardelli Square in San Francisco. Long the landmark factory for Ghirardelli Chocolates, the site was located adjacent to the booming tourist area around Fisherman's Wharf and offered spectacular vistas of San Francisco Bay. Lawrence Halprin Associates developed a site plan and design in which new buildings were added to the existing factory structures to enclose a central mall. This space had the character and scale of a residential patio, with movable furniture, potted plants, a fountain surrounded by steps which provided additional seating, and carefully selected specimen trees with unique sculptural forms. Although the square has undergone cycles of decline and vitality, it is a testament to the quality of the design that it remained popular as a pedestrian plaza even when its commercial functions were in a downturn.

The main street mall at Burlington, Iowa, in the 1980s.

The principal shopping level at Ghirardelli Square in San Francisco, in the 1980s.

Plazas have become a ubiquitous addendum to all major urban buildings constructed during the last three decades. Not only do they give personality to often unremarkable structures, but urban zoning also encouraged their inclusion in projects by allowing addition of extra stories for open space retained at ground level. Chicago's City Hall plaza was typical of many first-generation postwar plazas in the tedious simplicity of its design. Really little more than a paved surface with rectangular pool and Picasso sculpture set out upon it, the plaza's most fitting function was as setting for the public demonstrations and protests so common during the 1960s. Of the same period but more sophisticated in concept was Chase Manhattan Bank Plaza in New York. Designed by Isamu Noguchi on two levels, the plaza had both public open space and sculpture. The unexceptional upper level, a paved void, served as an overlook for the sunken

Chicago's Civic Center Plaza with its principal amenity, a sculpture by Pablo Picasso, circa 1980.

area of the plaza. This lower-level abstraction of a Japanese dry garden, which Noguchi considered his version of Ryoanji, was composed of wavy bands of granite setts in concentric circles broken by an irregular arrangement of four large black boulders and three smaller stones.

As part of a search for usable urban open space, many plazas were sited on rooftops of low inner city buildings, where they could be viewed from surrounding high rises, as well as used by pedestrians. The most acclaimed of these roof gardens was Mellon Square in Pittsburgh's Golden Triangle area. Built over a multistory garage, the plaza's simple arrangement of rectangular planting beds and pools against a bold triangular-patterned terrazzo pavement grew out of the need to limit the weight of plaza features to the roof's bearing capacity. As designed by John O. Simonds the square was as attractive at night, when illumination dramatized plants, as during the day when the paving pattern was its chief visual highlight. Other successful roof plaza designs included Kaiser Center Roof Garden in Oakland and Tower Square in Hartford.

As designers experimented with more refined, articulated urban plazas they veered from sterile paved voids and toward active, people-oriented gathering places with seating, fountains, and a planned program of activities. One of the most thriving of these plazas was the First National Bank Plaza in Chicago. Built on three levels, its broad stairways became popular seating spots from which to view activities in the lowest level. At that sunken level a large pool, with automatically adjusted fountain jets to compensate for the city's famous winds, served as a focal point and backdrop to the regular schedule of summer performances held there. Just as important as this lowest level with its amphitheater-like arrangement were the smaller upper and middle levels. The upper streetside tier served as an extended sidewalk from which to view street life. It also accommodated a summertime cafe and the freestanding wall covered with a Marc Chagall mosaic. The middle level provided secluded spaces for conversation, reading, or game playing, yet visitors there could still observe both street and lower-level activities.

A very different concept for the urban plaza was the type termed a "vest pocket park." Vest pocket parks were tiny plazas tucked between buildings for use as public outdoor living rooms. The first, and in many ways still the best,

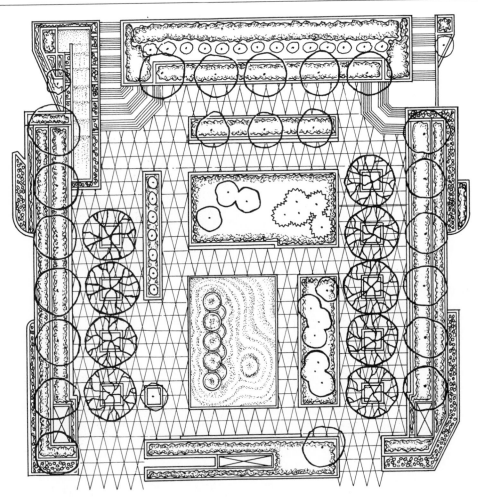

Plan of Mellon Square, a parking garage roof garden in Pittsburgh, designed by John O. Simonds. (Drawn by Hodge.)

First National Bank Plaza, Chicago, Illinois, from the mid-level plaza.

Paley Park, New York City, with its simple water-wall in the background. (Technical Reference Center, Texas A&M University.)

of these parks was Paley Park in New York, designed by Zion and Breen in 1965.[14] Built on a 4,000-square-foot lot vacated by demolition of a building, the park's simple beauty was achieved through a perfect balance of only the most essential features. Separation from the street was implied through slight elevation above the sidewalk. At the rear a cascading wall of water insulated visitors from jarring street clamor with soothing white noise. A canopy of branches from a honey locust bosque admitted only dappled sunlight, and scaled the towering open air ceiling to comfortable interior proportions. Finally, visitors were provided with comfortable, movable furniture and a refreshment kiosk. Paley Park's effective combination of elements, which square foot for square foot have made this the most heavily used public plaza in North America, became a formula repeated in other vest pocket parks across the continent.

Two Washington, D.C., squares that adjoin each other along Pennsylvania Avenue illustrate the variety of modern plaza design—Freedom Plaza (formerly Western Plaza) and Pershing Plaza. Freedom Plaza was an urbane plaza originally intended to serve as an outdoor cafe and wintertime skating rink. Designed by Robert Venturi and John Rauch, the plaza was a large-scale, three-dimensional version of L'Enfant's plan for the city; on the plaza were to be two huge marble pylons that when viewed from the east sighted on the White House, now hidden from Pennsylvania Avenue by the Treasury building. The Mall and White House garden were of turf, while streets were carved into the pavement. Although never completed according to the designers' intentions with the pylons and model buildings, the plaza illustrates application of an intellectual, historical concept as the basis for an urban open space. Pershing Plaza is conceptually more closely related to nineteenth-century landscape parks in that it created an urban oasis with lush plantings that separate the plaza from the street and pools and fountains to provide diversions from daily activities. As designed by M. Paul Friedburg, Pershing Plaza is also like a giant patio, with tables and chairs set in secluded niches for conversation and other passive relaxation.[15]

Three other recently developed plazas merit mention for their unique conceptions of urban open space: Levi Strauss Plaza in San Francisco; Williams Square in Las Colinas; and Piazza de Italia in New Orleans. Levi Strauss Plaza was

Pershing Plaza on Pennsylvania Avenue in Washington, D.C., can justifiably be termed an "urban oasis."

actually two distinctive spaces in one unified composition, an example of the new eclecticism in which juxtaposition of forms accentuates each. The site plan by Hellmuth, Obata and Kassabaum (HOK) included a dynamic carved boulder fountain designed by Lawrence Halprin. This fountain creates the focal point of what could be called the formal part of the plaza, an open paved court intimately surrounded by buildings. This area was linked by paving across a through street to the more informal area of the park, an Oriental-inspired garden of rock-sided channels and naturalistic tree groves. Only the lack of a convincing transition between the two areas marred this remarkable integration of distinct designed zones.

Williams Square had no such split personality to contend with. Its 6,000 square feet were designed by the SWA Group solely as an abstraction of a north Texas prairie-savannah landscape. The space itself was enclosed on three sides by office buildings, but with open corners to give views of a distant lake, and double rows of native live oaks. A sculptural group of 1½ times life size mustangs by artist Rob Glen gave the plaza a surreal sense of the landscape before the nineteenth century. Although it was this focal sculpture, made more real by the illusion of hooves galloping across the stream,[16] that received most publicity, the design's real achievement was in treatment of the stream course, with subtle variation in profile, edge treatment, and water speed.

Piazza de Italia has been called the first Postmodern landscape design. The plaza, centerpiece of an as yet incomplete mixed-use development, was planned as a setting for public meetings and festivals of the neighboring Italian-American community. The imagery chosen by designers Charles Moore and Perez Associates was rooted in this link to Italy. At the plaza's center were concentric bands of gray and black granite and slate that broke where they touched a set of irregular steps in the shape of the Italian peninsula. "Sicily" became a rostrum. A theatrical backdrop of neon-edged arches and pediments from which gargoyle-like heads, one modeled on Charles Moore's, spewed water to the "Mediterranean" pool surrounding the boot continued the theme. Unfortunately, all of the designers' inventiveness and giddy play on themes could not compensate for inappropriate selection of material,[17] incompletion of surrounding buildings, and poor site maintenance that have combined to leave the plaza in a forlorn state.

Lawrence Halprin's massive stone fountain with surrounding pools and falls at Levi Strauss Plaza in San Francisco.

The stylized plain and creek at Williams Square, Las Colinas, Texas.

A final type of plaza that has become quite popular in the last fifteen to twenty years is the fountain plaza, in which a water feature became sole or controlling feature of the design. Two leading examples of this type of plaza were Embarcadero Center Plaza, with gigantic water chutes designed by Isamu Noguchi, and Lawrence Halprin's Portland, Oregon, Forecourt Fountain. Each of these was really a water play environment. More recently, at Tanner Fountain at Harvard University, uncomplicated natural materials were used to create a sensuously surreal counterpoint to the functional routine of the campus plan. The fountain itself is a circle of rounded stones 60 feet in diameter set over existing grass and asphalt. A mist of water from jets set in the ground hovers in a cloud over the rocks, producing seasonally unique effects. This collaborative design by the Peter Walker/Martha Schwartz Group and artist Joan

The central fountain area of Piazza de Italia in New Orleans, with fountains not operating.

Ira Keller (also known as Auditorium Forecourt) Fountain, Portland, Oregon, succeeds in providing both active and passive recreation within one city block.

Brigham demonstrated that mystery can often be just as intriguing as adventure.

Quite opposite in concept is the almost baroque use of water at aptly named Fountain Place in Dallas. With almost three-quarters of its surface in water, the plaza, designed by Dan Kiley, displays almost every popular water feature seen in other urban plazas, along with several new inventions. The principal water feature is what Kiley called a "swamp in the city"—pools with bubbling jets into which is set a bosque of bald cypress. Other fountains in the composition include a maze of geysers that spray upward through the pavement and a cascade of terraced pools. While there are obvious questions about such generous use of water at the edge of a semi-arid region, this plaza has demonstrated once again that water is an instant attraction.

A bayou-inspired planting of bald cypress in a bosque at Fountain Place, Dallas, Texas. (Elizabeth McGreevey.)

The Riverwalk, San Antonio, Texas, is just one flight of stairs below street-level congestion.

While some cities have brought water artificially to ornament their urban plazas, other cities have sought to utilize natural waterways that for years had been treated as industrial or sewage facilities. The renewal of riverfronts and lakefronts has probably been the most significant innovation in contemporary urban design, as cities from coast to coast discovered that their principal scenic amenities need not be channelized, covered over, or polluted. Inspiration for much of this waterfront renewal was the San Antonio, Texas, Riverwalk first improved in the 1930s through the efforts of local architect Robert Hugman. Using WPA labor, simple additions of sitting areas, planters, and stairways to street level created a linear park that later attracted shops and restaurants. More recently, amenities of the Riverwalk have been extended out from downtown and into residential areas. Additional artificial canals link the river with civic and retail facilities, including the Convention Center and Rivercenter shopping mall. While the original Riverwalk loop had an earthy, rustic character, these areas have a more urbane, architectonic appearance.

In St. Louis a more dramatic alteration of a riverfront occurred with development of the Jefferson National Expansion Memorial to commemorate the Louisiana Purchase. Here nineteenth-century warehouses, including several historic structures originally to be preserved, were cleared to make way for a 500-acre commemorative park. Of course, the most obvious feature of this park was the enormous arch observatory designed by Eero Saarinen to symbolize the role of St. Louis as a gateway to the West. As a setting for this dynamic form, Dan Kiley developed a simple scheme of massed tree plantings and sculptural landforms. Although subsequently criticized for its insensitivity to the historic fabric of the city's riverfront, the park scheme was an important forerunner to the riverfront revitalization boom of the 1970s and 1980s.

The quintessential waterfront of this urban revival was Baltimore's Inner Harbor, planned by Wallace, McHarg, Roberts and Todd. Again a nineteenth-century warehouse district was partially cleared, but in this instance it was replaced not with a park but with an urbane shopping and entertainment district. Along the waterfront were a science museum, an aquarium, a Trade Center, and the Harbor Place market, all of which front on a promenade that served as a public park. Adjoining the waterfront center are new in-town residential areas. The success of Inner Harbor stems both from its simple design, which places emphasis on human activity, and its linkage with downtown Baltimore via an elevated crosswalk and fountain plaza. Waterfront revivals such as that in Baltimore have energized cities, while encouraging private developers across the continent to open up waterways for public use. Charleston's Waterfront Park, Philadelphia's Penn's Landing, Omaha's Riverwalk, and Houston's Buffalo Bayou redevelopment are just some of the results of this trend.

Inner Harbor, Baltimore, Maryland, has a simple design that emphasizes lively activity and thus attracts crowds.

(A)

(B)

Buffalo Bayou in Houston, Texas, illustrates the recent changes that cities have made in waterfronts.
(A) The bayou circa 1904 as an industrial canal; (B) 1991 as a greenway. (Left: Barker Texas
History Center, University of Texas at Austin, Austin, Texas.)

CONCLUSION AND SUMMARY

Four cities illustrate the variety of different approaches to planning that have characterized the last half of the twentieth century: Ottawa, Canada; Columbus, Indiana; Houston, Texas; and Detroit, Michigan. Ottawa pursued a City Beautiful ideal of the city as a work of art. In keeping with its role as national capital, it was planned with the impressive government center and scenic natural features of the area as its foci. At the heart of the city was Confederation Square, a formal focal point that provided a transition between the commercial and residential city, and that of the national capital, including Parliament, the museum district, and the government conference center in a revitalized train depot.

In Columbus, Indiana, design was also central to planning, but here it was privately initiated site by site design. In a program funded by a local organization, the Cummings Engine Foundation, design fees were paid for those projects that used the services of architects or landscape architects. Thus, Columbus, a town of about 30,000 people, has more "world class" design than cities many times its size. Among well-known sites there are North Christian Church and Irwin Union Bank, both by Eero Saarinen with Dan Kiley.[18] But Columbus was really an outdoor museum of late twentieth-century architecture and landscape architecture, rather than a truly "planned" city: not only do architectural masterpieces adjoin undesigned sheds, but little attention had been paid to overall visual character or innovative land use planning.

Houston was the quintessential late twentieth-century boomtown, rebuilt in the 1970s and early 1980s as a high-rise downtown with satellite office/commercial districts on loop superhighways. What planning did occur was based solely on development of infrastructure and private deed covenants, which until recently enforced by city agencies did little more than give mental solace to residents. Although the large-scale land use pattern produced by these quasi-planning methods did not differ markedly from that of other more conventionally planned cities, glaring land use juxtapositions did occur—for example, a forty-story office tower on a tiny lot abutting a single-family subdivision. Lack of comprehensive planning also complicated the delivery of urban services, since the city could not control the order of development or its density.

Detroit was an example of a city beset by every major urban problem from suburban flight to budget deficits and equally plagued by ill-conceived application of federal law and poor use of federal subsidies. During the 1950s and 1960s the city eagerly consumed urban renewal funding, beginning first with a 100-acre site near downtown cleared for a new civic center and moving on by 1958 to the larger Mack-Concord neighborhood. The city's most prominent redevelopment scheme has been the Renaissance Center, a riverfront complex of high-rise offices, hotels, and apartments, eventually to include twenty-three buildings, designed by John Portman and Associates. This was the new downtown as "urban fortress," which, in the words of William Whyte, said "Afraid of Detroit? Come in and be safe" (1980, p. 88). Unfortunately, Detroit has yet to reap many long-term positive results from four decades of urban redevelopment.

These four case studies illustrate that city planning has taken a number of different forms in the late twentieth century, but most combine functional planning with efforts to improve urban appearance. Thus we have moved into an era in which cities and metropolitan regions are treated as complex wholes, rather than one in which planners address a limited number of specific issues as had occurred earlier in the City Beautiful and City Scientific periods. Yet in spite of this synthesis the most significant urban problems remain unsolved because social trends have outstripped the ability of physical design to respond in a timely way, and because so many problems will never be solved merely through better form or law.

NOTES

1. See Chapter 16 for further discussion.

2. This Esplanade returned the area to its original park function during the Dutch colonial period.

3. Later, there were serious confrontations between police and residents when the university imposed its right to use the land for other purposes. Use, though, was eventually returned to an informal park space.

4. See also Chapter 18 for discussion of housing in new towns.

5. Some would also comment that this physical sameness was reinforced by the social sameness of residents. There were few if any ethnic or racial minorities represented in the population. Most original purchasers were also young families whose income came from similar trade or white collar occupations.

6. In subdivision marketing jargon PUDs are often termed "Master Planned" communities.

7. There is no absolute cutoff point to distinguish a large subdivision from a new town. For the purposes of discussion here, the author has used intent of the developer and innovation in the scope of the plan to distinguish these two types of development. In addition, those sites discussed as new towns in Chapter 18 were intended to serve more diverse functions, rather than merely housing and related services, as were those developments discussed here as large subdivisions.

8. More recently planners have become concerned about a particular type of suburb, the colonia, that is anything but the bucolic environment that most people associate with the term suburb. Colonias are large (often up to 10,000-person), rural subdivisions built in unincorporated areas of the southwestern United States that offer lower-cost, but completely unimproved, lots to purchasers, many of whom are recent immigrants from Mexico. They lack the most basic services such as sewer, water, and paved streets. Thus communities with densities of ten to twenty people per acre must rely on septic systems and community wells.

9. Reston's original developer, Robert Simon, first hired Harland Bartholomew and Associates to complete a plan that conformed to then existing use zones. This plan lacked unity, as well as having awkward neighborhood arrangements, and was rejected by the planning commission. In the late 1960s Simon sold Reston to Gulf Oil Company, which has continued its development.

Innumerable landscape architects have worked at Reston over the years including John Simonds and Meade Palmer.

10. Seven seems to be a lucky number for new town neighborhoods, with many following the Reston pattern for no apparent reason other than tradition.

11. This program was established under the Housing Act of 1968, but was so poorly conceived and implemented that it was rescinded within two years.

12. *The recent critical success of Seaside, Florida, with a gridlike plan related to city designs of the City Beautiful era, has encouraged a reexamination of the potential of checkerboard street schemes.*

13. *Named for Investors Diversified Services, the building developer, and designed by Philip Johnson and John Burgee. The building became nationally known when used as a set for opening credits of the* Mary Tyler Moore Show, *a television program that aired in 1970s.*

14. *Interestingly, the park concept had been developed several years earlier as a hypothetical open space design for an exhibit. All of the particulars applied in specific form, such as use of a water-wall to screen street noise and movable furniture to facilitate socializing, were present in the earlier scheme.*

15. *Interestingly, when these two plazas were first commissioned, the site assigned to Friedburg was the one where Freedom Plaza now stands, while Venturi and Rauch were to design the other. Venturi and Rauch produced a design that was reportedly considered unsuitable to the smaller triangular site of Pershing Plaza, and so design assignments were reversed.*

16. *The illusion is far more effective in photographs than in life.*

17. *To give an example, polished black marble slabs were chosen to face the bases of columns, but corners were left unsupported and were quickly broken off.*

18. *Kiley's work is the most widely represented of any landscape architect, with at least eight projects to his credit in Columbus.*

29

Modern Garden Design and Site Planning

Since the end of the war the horizon of the landscape architect has continued to expand. In private practice, with both private and public clients, or as an employee of government at all levels, he is successfully meeting the demand for any specific purpose or purposes desired, from the smallest house lot to the largest city.

Compared with any similar period in history the changes in social and economic conditions which we have witnessed during the past fifty years, and which in turn have affected the teaching and practice of landscape architecture, have been truly kaleidoscopic. Perhaps the wonder is not so much that, in the midst of so many opportunities open to us, we find ourselves whirling a little in our uncertainty as to what we are and what we shall call ourselves, as that we have kept our balance as well as we have and have not ridden off in all directions. For this we should be thankful. (Stevenson, 1948, pp. 136–37)

The opportunities of which Markely Stevenson spoke in his address to the forty-ninth annual ASLA meeting were principally those presented by economic, demographic, and social changes following the return to more normal conditions after 1945. These shifts affected small-scale design and planning even more forcefully than they did urban and regional projects. In part this was the result of new economic conditions that allowed a greater number of people to become either directly or indirectly consumers of landscape architectural services. In the 1950s the suburban ranch-style home could receive the same careful design attention, although with very different visual results, that had previously been reserved for large estates. New marketing practices encouraged the construction of professionally designed shopping environments and private recreational facilities. To deal with concerns about land use efficiency, preservation of open space, and observance of regulatory constraints, the services of experienced land planners were often required. Thus, landscape architecture was propelled from its limited areas of concern in the 1920s to grapple with the diverse and ever changing issues that confront modern designers, including aesthetics, balance between human and environmental needs, and landscapes usable by all.

THE IMPACT OF MODERNISM

As we saw when discussing the work of Fletcher Steele—whose influence inspired a number of the designers to be discussed here, including Thomas Church—the Modernist aesthetic became an issue in American landscape design at least by the 1920s. The modernism of that period, in both Europe and North America, was simply an aesthetic system of simplified line and asymmetrical form that still dealt with the landscape as a static artistic composition rather than as functional space. Without strong theoretical underpinnings, modernism was no more appropriate to American land uses than was Beaux Arts-inspired neoclassicism. Although many designers played with modernism and explored its underlying rationale in the twenties and thirties, it was not until a group of young designers studying together at the Harvard Graduate School of Design began to

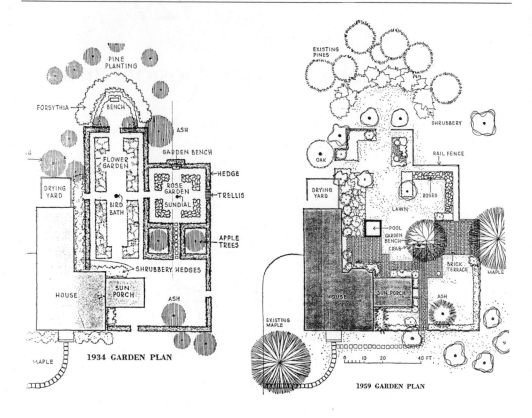

In the early 1960s a popular magazine used these two plans of the same garden in different years to exemplify what they called "the essence of the recent garden revolution." (A) The garden as it appeared in 1934; (B) as it was redesigned in 1957. Both designs were by Charles Middeleer. (Reprinted by permission House Beautiful, copyright © June 1961. The Hearst Corporation. All rights reserved.)

apply Modernist design theory to practical land use problems that this approach became widely accepted.

In a pivotal series of articles for the journals *Pencil Points* and *Architectural Record,* Garrett Eckbo, Daniel Kiley, and James Rose, at times writing as coauthors and at other times singly, proclaimed a manifesto of the new design theory in which human needs, the character of the natural environment, and the fit between these two became the principal stimuli for design. The authors decried both Romantic design, which they viewed as the arbitrary application of wiggly lines in a futile attempt to copy nature, and Neoclassicist design, for its emphasis on decorative, formal spaces that often served as backdrops for buildings rather than meeting the very real needs of people for usable outdoor spaces. The catchword that came to convey this idea of usefulness in outdoor spaces was "functionalism." Functionalism implied that site uses, rather than arbitrary patterns, determined site form; that the site was an outdoor room or rooms, rather than a sequence of axially organized visual experiences; and that the landscape's principal role was to support human social activity, rather than merely create settings for structures. In *Landscape for Living,* Eckbo later summarized these tenets of modernism that began "with the rejection of pre-conceived academic systems of form as being stale and irrelevant, and proceeds with a re-analysis of basic elements and problems, and an attempt to derive from that analysis principles of organization which are truly relevant and not superficial or shallow" (1950, p. 48). It is a testament to the persuasiveness and pervasiveness of Modernist thought in the late twentieth century that these ideas seem commonplace today.

Modernism took its inspiration from several sources, both contemporary and traditional. It was particularly influenced by both the theories and practices of Modern art, in particular the reliance on nonrepresentational forms to express purely visual principles. Like Cubist theory, Modern design simplified forms and intended scenes to be observed from changing viewpoints. Technology, with its pure relationship of form to function, was also a source of inspiration. This inspiration took several directions, including streamlining of form to express purpose and use of modern high-tech materials in construction. Science, particularly the emerging science of ecology, influenced the way in which fit between human environmental needs and natural systems was analyzed and interpreted. Finally, traditional non-Western design also inspired modern design, with Japanese design particularly revered for its compactness and spatial efficiency, for its subtle asymmetry, for its use of plants as sculpture, and for its simplicity of line.

These influences were not to be assembled into a standardized, rule-bound form, as similar inspirations had produced the very predictable neoclassicism of the early twentieth century.[1] Instead they became a stimulus for highly individual approaches to landscape design that were similar only in underlying principles. Common characteristics of Modern design included use of strong geometric lines in composition; free use of a variety of forms, often within a single design; use of plants as *one* possible garden material, rather than as the principal purpose of the garden; use of plants for their natural form, rather than controlling them to create artificial forms; complete integration of spaces through the use of flowing forms (that is, the spaces themselves were integrated) rather than through sight lines; emphasis on economy of scale and flexible use of space; in residential design, emphasis on the rear outdoor space as an extension of the house through the use of related materials, extended spaces, and large windows; preference for asymmetrical compositions; emphasis on the creation of human-scale outdoor rooms; and use of nontraditional materials.

One event which crystallized the public acceptance of Modern design in America was the widely publicized World's Fair held in New York in 1939. There most architecture and much landscape architecture had a Modernist flavor, giving both designers and the general public an image of how these principles could be applied at a scale larger than the small residential property.[2] Among those landscape designs at the Fair that helped popularize modernism were the Ford Motor Company's Garden Court by Clarke and Rapuano and the Budd Manufacturing display garden by Alfred Geiffert, Jr.

One of the gardens at the Ford Motor Company exhibit, 1939 World's Fair, New York. (Anonymous, 1939.)

While the impact of modernism was felt at all scales of design, as examples reviewed later will show, it had its greatest impact on the small property. Modernism specifically reconsidered the small, residential site as a work of art in which functions directed development but allowed expression of visual principles. This emphasis on small-scale residential work was best developed in the work of some leaders in contemporary design such as Thomas Church, Garrett Eckbo, and Lawrence Halprin.

Thomas D. Church's work has proved transitional between the neoclassicism of the early twentieth century, modernism of midcentury, and the recent development of postmodernism. As we saw in Chapter 13, Church began professional practice in the heyday of neoclassicism, but although influenced by the Beaux Arts principles to which he was exposed at Harvard and through European travel, he applied the axial, formal arrangements of the Beaux Arts in a simplified manner always adapted to the unique California landscape in which he worked. Church's real inspiration, though, was never stylistic precedent but the language of design itself—line, form, texture, movement, and scale. Modern design, which gave designers freedom to experiment with these elements unencumbered by fixed spatial standards, was thus a natural focus of his innate inclinations. Although Church certainly took inspiration from Modern architecture and art, he went well beyond those models by adapting modernism to landscape design in a manner which embraced the new, without rejecting appropriate design concepts of the past. It was Church's abstraction and simplification of classical design themes, from sight lines to parterres to trompe l'oeil, through which he foreshadowed Postmodern adaptation of historic precedent to create contextual references for the landscape.

Church's name has been closely associated with what is generally called the "California style": that is, modernism adapted to informal outdoor living, in which areas such as pools, patios, and decks provided exterior rooms. Many of his garden plans and features, such as trees penetrating decks, amorphously shaped pools, and native rocks as pool edging, became prototypes copied across the country. Yet few could capture the essence of Church's design work—an absolute, essential, pure relationship between the design itself, the site, and the client's needs. While others copied *his* work, Church viewed each design as a unique statement of place and use, which his fluid mind could form into a coherent whole.

The one aspect of Church's work which remained rooted in tradition was the manner in which he worked with clients. Descriptions of his design process suggest that concepts were formulated through on-site charrettes in which Church, his client, architects for site structures, and contractors all took part. Working from basic site requirements or design themes already present in architecture or existing features, Church often developed a series of alternative schemes. Each of these addressed functional and visual issues, but demonstrated that they could be dealt with in a variety of ways to achieve different spatial arrangements and images.

One of Church's earlier designs illustrated this fluidity with form and function, as well as his ability to create spatial illusion. The Sullivan garden designed in 1937 typified many of Church's early commissions for small courtyard-sized gardens in San Francisco. Church developed four spatially distinctive concepts for the Sullivan garden, three of which relied on distortion of perspective through the use of strong diagonal lines. In the Modernist scheme selected for execution, two bold perpendicular lines set at an angle from the lot lines led the eye across the small space, suggesting a greater width than actually present. This angle also allowed Church to screen a far corner of the garden, where he set a small, private patio with pool. Here, at a smaller scale and in Modernist forms, Church used

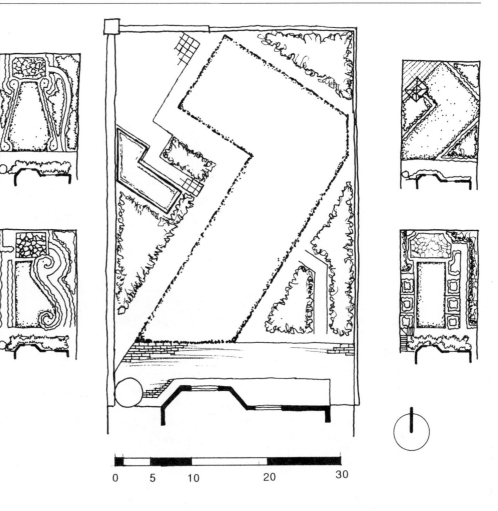

Sullivan Garden, San Francisco, California, by Thomas Church. The larger central plan is the one implemented, while the four smaller ones show alternative spatial concepts which Church considered. (Data from Church, 1983; drawn by Rossi.)

0	5	10		20	30

the curved or angled space as effectively as Olmsted and Vaux had done decades earlier at Long Meadow in Prospect Park, to create the illusion of unbounded space.

Two of Church's most influential garden designs were created in 1948—the Donnell Garden in Sonoma, California, and the Martin Residence in Aptos Beach, California. Although quite different in scale and overall concept, the designs share two characteristics often found in his work: integration of the site with the surrounding natural landscape through repetition of forms or materials, and careful use of a variety of forms to link the hard, geometric lines of buildings with the more irregular, flowing lines of natural landscapes.

The Donnell garden was a quintessential California-style residential landscape—the garden as a patio, with swimming pool as both the recreational and visual focal point.[3] Built prior to construction of a house on the site, the garden was sited on high ground affording a magnificent overview of the Sonoma River valley. Existing oaks at the edge of the plateau were retained and brush cleared so that trees framed the distant view, yet enclosed the garden. Much of this enclosed space was a concrete patio articulated with a simple pattern of gridded joints. In one corner, where a grove of oaks grew, concrete was changed to redwood decking perforated to wrap around the tree trunks. The bathhouse pavilion in Modern style perfectly complemented the patio and pool area by emphasizing horizontal vistas through its prominent, projecting flat roof.

The Donnell garden, Sonoma County, California, by Thomas Church. (Church, 1983.)

The centerpiece of the Donnell garden, though, was its swimming pool, at once a space, a water feature, a recreational area, and a piece of sculpture. Church used the fashionable kidney shape, but adapted it to create two separate usable pool areas within one form—a deep, long area with diving board at one end for serious swimming and a sheltered, shallow alcove for children's play or relaxing. To symbolically separate these two pool wings, a sinuous sculpture by Adaline Kent was set at their crux. Like the pool itself this sculpture contributed many activities in one form: an underwater recess made it a swim-through toy; its flat curving surface made it an in-pool lounge; and, most important, it was a sculpture, which through repetition of other landscape unified the garden itself and linked it with the distant landscape of rounded hills.

The Martin residence, a weekend beach house overlooking Monterey Bay, itself defined the site and enclosed three sides of a tiny garden, thereby directing all views toward the beach and bay beyond it. The garden, really an abstract ground-plane design, was composed of simple materials arranged to replicate surrounding landscape forms. A wooden deck filled those areas nearest the house and provided a large usable patio. Arranged of modular panels forming a diagonally set grid, this deck linked structure and site. Adjacent to one side of the deck, an irregularly shaped planting bed with salt-tolerant native plants and some ornamentals linked the garden with natural vegetation of nearby dunes. The area between this bed and a seat with a zigzag shape at the edge of the deck was filled with sand—an intimate, private beach for the Martins. Visually, this sand area served a dual purpose. It continued the beach into the garden, and provided a formless transition between the geometric deck and curving bed of the gardens.

In spite of Church's association with innovative, Modern-inspired gardens, such as at the Donnell and Martin sites, throughout his life the early lessons of European, especially Italian, design continued to inspire much of his work. Among the many gardens designed with simplified axial plans using historical garden themes was one built in 1969 in Hillsborough, California. At this small site, Church transformed a simple pool area into a terraced outdoor room, while turning a previously unexploited stream into a ferny woodland that became part of the ornamental landscape.

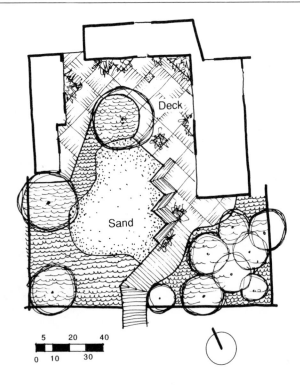

Plan of the Martin residence by Church. (Data from Church, 1983; drawn by Rossi.)

Church's adroitness with the basic elements and principles of design, as well as his fluency with historical precedent as inspiration for three-dimensional form, makes it difficult to synthesize an overview of what made a "Church" garden. However, an overriding characteristic of all his work, regardless of scale, site type, or client preference, was always a focus on integration of parts to create site unity. This integration could be achieved in many ways. At the broadest conceptual scale Church's work always attempted to integrate interior and exterior spaces, so that the spaces themselves and the activities carried out in them were part of a continuous pattern of living. Likewise, designs linked created spaces with the natural landscape by intermixing the two, as was done with the trees puncturing the Donnell deck or through enframement or repetition of a distant view. At the smaller scale different site functions were often linked in one feature—for example, a raised bed edge which also doubled as a seating wall or platform for potted plants. But Church's designs were far more than any objective verbal assessment can communicate—they were three-dimensional works of art that used landscape as their principal material.

Garrett Eckbo was just as committed as Church to fully exploring the boundless new world of form, materials, and function that modernism opened up. His projects and writings addressed both the formal and visual aspects of modern design—and they did more: they embodied the first complete treatment of the theoretical basis of modern American landscape design and planning. Eckbo viewed design as a universal human process, only recently professionalized, in which the underlying relationship between people and the natural world, and between one person and another, could be expressed through physical form. He also reemphasized the significance of space itself as the principal material with which designers created visual illusions and improvisations. Eckbo's design philosophy emphasized those intuitive aspects of the design process that had been obscured by the Beaux Arts historicist tradition of the early twentieth century and were in his own day being overshadowed by objective, analytical approaches

A more Neoclassicist-inspired Church garden in Hillsborough, California. (Church, 1983.)

to design problem solving. He believed that "creative design is a constant balancing of fantasy and practicality. We must not avoid even the wildest hunches or notions—but we must immediately project these into the realm of practical application to see what the results may be. We don't abstract and categorize the world as does science" (Eckbo, 1965, p. 113).

As important as all these philosophical points were in establishing a modern basis for landscape architecture, Eckbo's greatest contribution was in reemphasis on the social role of design. Although this had been a central, if not the most critical, focus of the nineteenth-century founders of the profession, the ideal of design as a social service through which individual lives and the entire society could be improved had been all but lost during the early twentieth century, as landscape architecture became a *design business* rather than the personal quest that it often seemed to be for people like Copeland, Vaux, and Olmsted. Depression-era planners had, through their new town experiments, certainly done much to promote the role of urban planning in public welfare. Design, though, was still often considered to be mere beautification—a luxury with little underlying social rationale. At a very fundamental level Eckbo viewed the designed environment as the stage set upon which actors performed their chosen role. Just as in the theater where props and sets supported and enhanced these actions, it was the role of the designer to provide a supportive stage for the daily acts of life.

Among Eckbo's earliest designs for private clients were a large number of small garden sites where he experimented with ideas about the manipulation of space and the use of innovative materials. His own residence in Los Angeles, designed as a display of aluminum as an outdoor material, was one of the most imaginative of these sites. There aluminum in various forms and colors was used for pavilions, privacy, and shade screens and even for a fountain basin.

At the Slater residence, Eckbo's trademark combination of angled, rectilinear, and curved lines distorted the unusual triangular shape of a small lot. To increase the apparent size of the lot, provide screened private space, and deemphasize an unusable lot corner, he separated the yard into two areas with a broadly curving fence of redwood slats. On the house side of the fence, panels of concrete and turf created interesting ground-plane forms that reinforced view depth. Be-

The Slater residence designed by Garrett Eckbo used a variety of forms to focus attention on living areas, and away from triangular lot shape. (Eckbo, 1956.)

hind the fence, a stand of preserved trees with their lower trunks screened created the illusion of a far denser and deeper mass than actually existed.

The Eckbo and Slater sites demonstrated Eckbo's ability to transform the small residential site from a mere backyard into a multifunctional landscape. His work on larger properties demonstrated how similar principles could be adapted to more complex requirements and site conditions. At a bayside residence with two dwellings and a guest house located in Marin County, California, Eckbo designed a pool, bathhouse, and lawn area that tied these buildings together, while at the same time emphasizing a dramatic vista across San Francisco Bay. Set in a natural bowl-shaped landform, the pool became a centerpiece around which other features, such as the bathhouse, fences, and plantings revolved. This arrangement emphasized the pool's importance, of course, but also created an intimately enclosed area within an otherwise undefined area of the site. Breaks in the concentric enclosing forms, particularly plant groups, were used as frames to emphasize the bay view.

Eckbo's body of work also brought modernism beyond the garden gate to address problems of complex site organization, demonstrating the freedom that this mid-twentieth century approach allowed designers. Many of these projects were designed through one of the two firms with which he has been associated— Eckbo, Dean, Austin and Williams (EDAW), of which he was a cofounder, and more recently a smaller firm under his own name. Among the more important of these larger works were Ambassador College, Pasadena, California; Baylands Park, Palo Alto, California; and the University of New Mexico, Albuquerque.

One of Eckbo's contemporaries in the so-called "Harvard Revolution" of the 1930s pursued similar design ideas. James Rose was as innovative a designer, but chose to deemphasize theory in his work for a total emphasis on site character: "from Rose's point of view it is fatal to theorize about [underlying design theory] . . . because even the best theory is only a substitute for the reality of what is actually happening at that time and in that place" (Snow, 1967, p. 9). This visceral approach to design was clearly expressed in the series of portfolio-like books Rose authored. There the emphasis was on image and mood rather than clinical analysis of the components that create that image.

This lack of an expressed theory should not suggest that Rose's work was arbitrary; rather he felt that overemphasis on parts signaled a failure to look at

Ambassador College, Pasadena, California, where a modern line of sight connects upper and lower campus areas.

design in the holistic way in which the finished work is actually perceived. Rose believed that projects evolved from a collaboration of the site, the client, and himself as designer, with the mechanics of this synergism being less important than the physical outcome. The physical design, though, was not merely a study in form and texture, for he believed that "form is a result and not a predetermined element of the problem. . . . [Form] has no other basis than the psychology of the artist or the people who created it" (Rose, 1939*b*, pp. 98, 100). This approach, of course, emphasized the singularity of each designed site. In spite of this emphasis on the unique, Rose's work as a whole does display his personal interest in several issues.

Rose considered the design of the landscape itself to be a form of sculpture. To create these living, changing sculptures he worked either directly on site or through models, believing that two-dimensional representations of three-dimensional reality created artificial abstractions. His works show particular emphasis on the three-dimensional manipulation of the ground plane, particularly through terracing and systems of ramps and steps to create fluid linkages between spaces. Plants likewise contributed to the sculpting of the landscape by molding those spaces, and, through their texture, color, and movement, animating them.

Rose's interest in landscape design as sculpture led naturally to an interest in the use of sculpture in the landscape. These sculptures ranged from formal works of art displayed in carefully composed outdoor galleries to uniquely shaped trees set against contrasting backgrounds. The Wurtburger Garden in Baltimore, Maryland, designed as a gallery for a modern sculpture collection, is often considered one of Rose's most successful works. There works by Henry Moore, Lachaise, and Lipschitz were displayed on terraces set into an existing woodland. Although more than one work is visible when overviewing the garden, each has a distinctive position, chosen to dramatize that work but also place it in a suitable

"Where does the sculpture end? Where does it begin? In the rocks? In levels? Texture? Or does it disappear into the water? Or is it all one thing—a process—becoming something new while remaining just the same as the viewer moves?" A James Rose garden. (Quotation and photo from Snow, 1967, pp. 70–71.)

relationship to those nearby. A female figure by Maillol, for instance, was positioned on a pedestal set in a flat pool of water. The piece appears to hover magically above the water, while its upright form repeats the mass and verticality of the woodland which is its backdrop.

Dan Kiley, the final member of the Harvard trio, was less reactionary toward Beaux Arts historicism than his colleagues, yet was equally determined to build a design philosophy based on something more solid than use of form and proportion. The essence of his theory of design was both the topic and title of a 1963 essay, "Nature: The Source of All Design." In his view, in nature one observed "the simplification of organization in continuity," and through design adapted this to human needs and the physical requirements of the site (Kiley, 1963, p. 127). This simplified organization of which he wrote was to be based on the underlying processes of nature, which he considered to be change and growth. Using the principles of simplicity, unity, integration of landscape and built structure, and appropriateness to setting, Kiley developed a highly individual and consistent approach to design that transcends the experimental eclecticism of many of his contemporaries.

Among post-World War II designers Kiley was somewhat unusual in that he embraced historical precedents as inspiration for his work. Among the rather eclectic examples to which he has referred for inspiration were designed Japanese landscapes, the work of André Le Notre, and that of Fletcher Steele. At a more intuitive level Kiley's work reflected a primordial historicism rooted in the psychic need for order in the world. As he has commented, "Man has always made more or less straight lines" (Karson, 1986, p. 50).

These inspirations have led Kiley to appreciate geometric order in the landscape. The plan forms of typical projects, whether residences such as the Miller residence in Columbus, Indiana, or urban plazas such as the Third Block of

A garden designed by Rose expressly to display a modern sculpture. (Snow, 1967.)

Independence Mall in Philadelphia, are grids of varying scale and articulation, but each very specific to its setting. These works are equally distinctive at eye level, where spaces diffuse into each other through tree trunks or fountain jets with few visual barriers other than those screening off-site views. This openness emphasizes the unity achieved through repetition of rectilinear form, but also gives the impression that the site is a picture being viewed through a series of translucent panels.

Another example of Kiley's approach is the design for the Hamilton residence in Columbus, Indiana. Here, in a redesign of a small lot for an existing house, Kiley created a series of outdoor pavilions linked by allées or arbors, all of which wrap around a central panel of lawn. The lawn is central to the composition not merely in physical terms, but because it is the simple background which separates and clarifies the various use areas, such as the gazebo or the Spanish fountain, that otherwise might overwhelm in scale if not in diversity this fairly small site.

Much of Kiley's work, even that for public uses, has been of a residential scale in its detailing and spatial sequencing. One of the most successful of these designs is that for the Oakland Museum in Oakland, California. The structure, designed by Kevin Roche, with whom Kiley has often worked, was a masterpiece of architecture as landscape. Built partially underground, galleries were organized as a series of terraces that extended out onto rooftop gardens used as settings for sculpture. The garden terraces were also points for viewing magnificent vistas of the city, Lake Merritt, the foothills, and San Francisco Bay. Because of its rooftop setting, much of the planting was lawn or groundcover. Where depth allowed sufficient space for deeper-rooting plants, large, dense masses were planted to create a lush, overgrown urban island—much like a modern Hanging Gardens of Babylon.

As influential as Church, Eckbo, Rose, and Kiley have been in post-World War II design, the landscape architect who seems best to personify the scope of design and environmental concerns during this era has been Lawrence Halprin. His work embodies all aspects of modernism as it evolved in America, including the social role of design, emphasis on adaptation to natural systems, and the

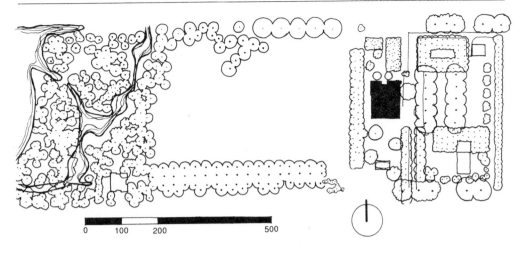

Plan of the Miller Residence, Columbus, Indiana, by Dan Kiley. (Data from Byrd and Rainey, 1982; drawn by Rossi.)

The largest of the roof gardens at the Oakland Museum, Oakland, California, by Kiley. (Department of Landscape Architecture Slide Collection, Texas A&M University.)

importance of function and process in yielding form. Among leading designers Halprin has most directly embraced the sequence of social changes that influenced design and planning in the half-century or so since World War II. In particular, during the 1960s when design, along with other aspects of social life, was revolutionized by the new level of public involvement in decision making, it was Halprin who adapted his firm's design process to the new social reality. Public participation in design through workshops and feedback sessions became a means through which he incorporated human process into landscape design.

The work of Halprin and his firm was equally focused on the use of natural systems as a formgiver in design. At the planning level, in projects such as the master plan for the Navajo Nation in Arizona, ecological systems were used as a rationale for allocation of needed human use areas. More typically, natural systems became the inspiration for site plans in which dramatic landscapes, such as mountains or valleys, were abstracted to form urban sculpture. Since the late 1950s Halprin's work at all scales has explored the role of water in the landscape, including systems derived from Middle Eastern prototypes, from water as a form of moving sculpture, and from water as it shapes the natural landscape.

It is the very variety of Halprin's approaches, coupled with his sincere and keen interest in human landscape experience, that has made his works timely across four decades and continues to do so into a fifth, the 1990s. While garden designs are only a small portion of his total body of work, more of which will be discussed later, two of his early works at garden scale remain masterpieces which illustrate his versatility. The Simon Roof Garden in San Francisco, begun in 1951, was perhaps his most simple and direct work. Composed of 4-foot-square modular units, the garden juxtaposed textures found in succulents, small grasses, rounded river rocks, and gravel, to create a ground-plane bas-relief from natural materials. Its character was like that of an expanded Oriental tray garden—a contrived composition that suggested a natural landscape while maintaining its carefully articulated artistic balance.

Equally simple in concept, but sophisticated in articulation, was the McIntyre Garden in Hillsborough, California. The "garden" really consisted of two parts, one a small, partially sunken courtyard inspired by Islamic design and the other a surrounding wood and meadow. In this courtyard, Halprin explored the role of water in creating both unity and movement. With flow beginning at an elevated, table-like concrete fountain, the water moved through two narrow channels and down a set of steps to a large pool surrounding a tree-shaded island patio. The rectilinear geometry of the court itself and pools, along with the variety of ways in which water was treated, all reflect inspiration from the Is-

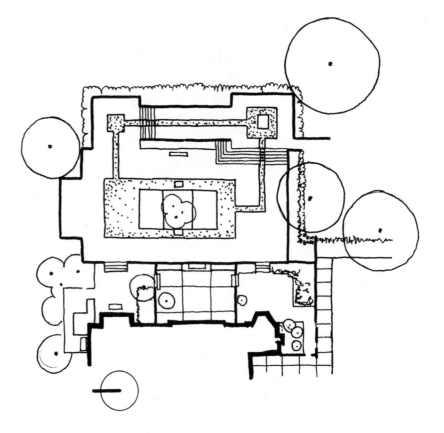

Plan of McIntyre Garden, Hillsborough, California, by Lawrence Halprin. (Data from House and Garden, Vol. 122, No. 2; drawn by Rossi.)

lamic garden, but an interpreted inspiration adapted to modern California. The themes, both visual and conceptual, that Halprin explored here were models that informed later works like Heritage Park in Fort Worth, Texas.

While Halprin chose to use Middle Eastern precedent as inspiration for gardens in semi-arid California, Luis Barragan found inspiration in the vernacular tradition of his native Mexico. Inspired by pre-Columbian, Spanish, and natural landscape forms, Barragan's designs, created over more than half a century of practice in architecture and landscape architecture, which he considered "architecture without ceilings," displayed a consistency of concept unrivaled in modern design. His works were intended to create feelings of solitude, reflection, and serenity in outdoor spaces by reducing natural landscape features to human scale. Barragan's typical palette of materials and finishes has often been compared to the surrealistic landscapes of a Giorgio de Chirico painting. Masonry planes, either walls of structures or freestanding, were the chief formgivers. Color, often bright sherbert or rich earth tones, modulated walls and created specific relationships of linkage or depth. The principal contrasting material in Barragan designs was water, used both in flat pools to replicate the masonry planes, and also in dynamic, moving streams in complete contrast to the placid masonry backdrop. To Barragan, the sound of moving water was a kind of music in the landscape. One of his most famous water systems, the elevated water chute first used in a park at El Pedregal de San Angel near Mexico City, became so popular for its drama and playfulness that it was copied throughout the world.

Much of Barragan's design work has been for residences, including the individual residences that he planned in various subdivisions. For these commissions he often designed the house and garden as a unit, with the garden having a patio or plaza-like character. These simple compositions of turfed panels and terraces enclosed like courtyards became dramatic transitions between the built and natural landscapes. Among his more important garden designs were those for model houses in El Pedregal, one of the most dramatic sites on the continent. Developed on an old lava field, El Pedregal de San Angel was a speculative residential development for which Barragan was both designer and developer. Low areas of lava fields were filled to create flat expanses of lawn or tile-edged pools. At the edges of these filled areas the richly textured, erratic lava masses provided a primal base from which emerged buildings constructed of similar lava. To term the resulting compositions dramatic is an understatement, for the contrast of textures, colors, and forms—all set against the deep blue of the Mexican sky—created an unforgettable image of landscape as theatrical set.

Barragan's use of vernacular themes presaged a recent trend toward new regional approaches to design, especially small-scale site design and planting design. While many factors can account for this new regionalism, the example of Robert Burle Marx in South America demonstrated that native or naturalized materials can be used to create bold design statements that reflect the natural environment and are well adapted to its conditions. Three particular regional trends have been evident: one in the Southwest for drought-tolerant landscapes, another in the Midwest and Plains regions for prairie restorations, and a last in the South for revival of cottage gardens.

The new southwestern garden replaced turf with sand, gravel, and boulders. Native cactus, succulents, and water-conserving materials were used, instead of imported hybrids or exotics. Shade was created with trellises rather than with high-maintenance shade trees, and voluminous water fountains were replaced by graveled arroyos that merely suggested water. Prairie restorations took the form of either a scientific regeneration of prairie plant associations or less rigorous plantings of typical grasses and forbs. Of equal importance to the plants installed was the type of maintenance. Grasses were no longer mowed on a weekly basis,

View of the natural lava flows as integrated into the designed landscape by Luis Barragan at El Pedregal de San Angel. (Landscape Architecture, Vol. 43, No. 2.)

Federal Reserve Gardens designed by James van Sweden and Wolfgang Oehme of Oehme, van Sweden and Associates using ornamental grasses and native wildflowers. Sculpture is by Raya Bodnarchuk. (Photograph by James van Sweden.)

but only once or twice seasonally to allow vegetative growth and reseeding. Cottage gardens were really a traditional form that had been replaced by the modern front lawn. As now revived, cottage gardens are an eclectic crazy-quilt of traditional plants and new varieties, organized so that constancy of bloom and intricacy of detail give the garden its character.

A less strictly regional approach to garden design that utilizes some of the visual characteristics as these three regional garden types is the style referred to as "the new American garden." Popularized in large measure through the work of James Van Sweden and Wolfgang Oehme, this style uses naturalistic plant compositions, with emphasis on texture and color contrasts of annuals, perennials, grasses, and some shrubs. Massed plantings are generally omitted in favor of an impressionistic melange of natives and exotics. It is this type of planting design that has revived use of grasses and prairie flowers such as liatris or coneflower as ornamentals.

A great deal of recent small-scale design has been inspired by the style known as postmodernism, in architectural vogue during the 1970s and much of the 1980s. Postmodernism was a reaction to the perceived sterility and intellectualism of Modern design. It attempted to return to the built environment contextual references—references to use or site or cultural milieu—that modernism had removed in its quest for functionalism. While this noncontextual, antiseptic quality had never characterized designed landscapes, with the exception of some urban plazas, many landscape designers embraced the playful use of historical precedent and liberating use of eclectic materials that are features of Postmodernism. In their own way Postmodern designs became just as intellectually obtuse and stereotyped as had Modern design—for example, the use of ancient measurements such as the cubit to infer a linkage with the past in a synagogue design or the unlimited stylizations of classical columns. Such excesses were fortunately more common to architecture than to landscape architecture.

Extended discussion of postmodernism in landscape design began in 1980 with publication of the infamous Bagel Garden by Martha Schwartz, which became the most comment-generating project ever published in *Landscape Architecture*. In Schwartz's words, "The Bagel Garden is intended to be humorous but also artistically serious. The irony of the garden is created by the juxtaposition of the formal geometry (imperial and elite) with the bagels (homey and domestic)" (1980, p. 44). This garden at SWA's Boston office was a minification of Postmodern ideals, with its historically based parterre of hedge, purple gravel, and varnished bagels related both to its neighborhood context of brick row houses (with nearby bagel-dispensing delicatessen) and to its user context of academically and artistically oriented designers.

More stylized in its historicism was the Harlequin Plaza rooftop square designed by the SWA Group for an office complex in Greenwood Village, Colorado. Designed as a surrealistic Renaissance plaza, its effects were achieved using asymmetry to disguise the irregular placement of buildings and utility fixtures as well as distortion of perspective with mirrors to increase perceived scale and depth of view. As with the Bagel Garden, materials were unusual for an exterior design, including mirrored glass and colored plastic walls and clown-checked black and white terrazzo paving.

While postmodernism did not become widely accepted among landscape architects, in part because its relationship to "context" was often tenuous by the standards of the profession, it has resulted in an increased interest in and reliance on historical precedent as inspiration for design. Unfortunately, this "inspiration" has often taken the form of insipid replications of historical plans or details, rather than a truly inspired spark of new life from the old.

An important influence on landscape design of the past decade has been Modernist visual art, particularly that branch known as "earthworks" or "environmental art." In this type of sculpture the earth itself or materials from the earth become the principal materials used to execute the piece. There are three different approaches to earthworks art. The first involves large works set into or upon the land in such a way that the landscape and created piece are inextricably merged as one artistic work. "Valley Curtain" by Christo is one example of this approach to earthworks art. A second approach uses natural materials directly as the material for artistic expression. Robert Smithson's "Amarillo Ramp" made of earth, stone, and water; Michael Heizer's water strider mounds used as landforms in a design for a reclamation project on mined land; and Heizer's subtractive sculpture "Double Negative" all typify this approach. The final approach is one in which the made parts of the artwork interact with an ephemeral natural process to produce the artistic product. Walter de Maries's "Lightning Field," which uses an alignment of stainless steel poles to "capture" lightning, and Nancy Holt's "Sun Tunnels" are two classic works in this genre.

Environmental artworks such as these have had their principal influences on designed landscapes of relatively small scale, particularly monuments and gardens. In fact, this influence has generated a now widely accepted new approach to commemorative monuments that are more symbolic than representational. The most important of these monuments, in terms of its influence on later works, was the United States Vietnam Veterans Memorial designed in 1981 by Maya Y. Lin. Sited on the Mall northeast of the Lincoln Memorial, the Vietnam Veterans Memorial is a black granite two-segment wall almost 500 feet long that slices into the earth. Into the shiny granite surface are carved the names of every member of the military who died in action in Vietnam, in order of their death. The materials and design were chosen to contrast with the typical white, classical monuments of the capital. In addition, the reflective granite was to be a mirror that linked the visitor with those who had died. The design for this poignantly

*United States Vietnam
Veterans Memorial,
Washington, D.C., designed
by Maya Lin.*

elegant monument, unfortunately, became one of the most misunderstood and misinterpreted of the twentieth century. The black granite was criticized as reflecting negative attitudes toward the war. Likewise, its depression into the ground was viewed as an antiwar comment. While the monument does have limitations—for example, a reference book is needed to locate a names on the wall—it has allowed both personal and public commemoration of the war dead, and it has also become a prototype for war memorials throughout the United States.

At a more intimate scale, earthworks art has inspired a new, visually creative approach to small-site design akin in spirit to that which occurred immediately after World War II. In these works, by designers such as Michael van Valkenburg and George Hargreaves, space itself is the material to be visually manipulated through placement of line and form, as well as through contrasts of texture and use of asymmetrical balance. In innovative works such as the "Isaacs Water Wall," van Valkenburg has experimented with using natural processes, in this case rain, as an integral part of the composition, with the water causing intended but random changes in the surface color of copper wall panels. Whether such art-inspired improvisations will influence more conventional designs, as modernism did four decades ago, remains to be seen.

SITE PLANNING

While modern design and post–World War II social forces affected design at the garden scale, even more significant effects were reflected in larger site plans. In fact, postwar trends actually produced whole new categories of site type. One of the most important of these was a new retailing environment, the auto-oriented shopping center. While there had been pre-1940s precedent for the shopping center—such as the shopping block at Roland Park, Maryland, and the regional-scale shopping area in the Country Club District of Kansas City—these had only tentatively dealt with circulation changes resulting from automobile use. It was not until the economic rebirth of the late 1940s that increased population, increased buying power, economic demands for efficient retail operations, and shifting residential patterns created the conditions necessary to support strip shopping malls and the more design-sophisticated regional shopping mall.

Site planners experimented with a number of organizational patterns for regional shopping malls. Some, such as Hudson's New Center near Detroit, accommodated close-in parking by placing it both on the outside of stores and in the interior court space. A major drive actually separated the court space, so that pedestrian circulation was limited to walks in front of stores and an overpass across the central drive to link the two halves of the mall. Such an arrangement, similar in spatial concept but far higher in traffic density, was reminiscent of older Main Street shopping districts. A significant leap in shopping center design occurred when the court enclosed by store buildings was transformed into a pedestrian mall, designed like a garden or plaza. One of the earliest malls with this type of arrangement was Shoppers' World in Framingham, Massachusetts, completed in 1951. Located off a major highway, parking remained the dominant site land use but wide sidewalks located between every three or four parking lanes facilitated pedestrian access to the shopping area. Two parallel shop wings flanked a central open-air court which was enclosed at either end by anchor department stores, one of which had a futuristic circular form. All buildings were connected on the court side by a covered walkway. At the court's interior, paths and plantings in a Modernistic arrangement of angles, zigzags, and asymmetrical forms provided a pleasant setting for crosswalks and seating areas.[4] More important to retailers, these plantings forced shoppers to the periphery of the space next to stores, rather than allowing them to move anywhere across the open space. The spatial concept developed by Arthur and Sidney Shurcliff for Shoppers' World became a model for countless malls across the country.

While the basic planning concept of regional shopping malls—location near a major highway, use of a loop drive, parking surrounding the shopping area, and an ornamental open air court—remained unchanged into the 1960s, courtyard designs were significantly upgraded when Lawrence Halprin and Associates designed many elegant malls across the country. One of these, Oakbrook Center near Chicago, combined a plethora of water fountains linked by channels with

The pedestrian court at Shoppers' World, Framingham, Massachusetts, designed by Shurcliff and Shurcliff. (Landscape Architecture, Vol. 42, No. 2.)

The pedestrian court at Oakbrook Center, Oakbrook, Illinois, by Lawrence Halprin and Associates.

residential-scale plantings including mature specimen trees and beds of seasonal flowers to create a shopping environment as popular with strollers as with serious shoppers. More recently this suburban imagery was supplanted by urbane, if surreal, whimsy at Rio Shopping Center in Atlanta. This new image of shopping mall as art may become the new way to market consumer goods.

In the late 1970s the advantage of complete enclosure for shopping malls became apparent. In spite of this, their plans remained unchanged except that the formerly exterior garden was transformed into an interior one, which could be planted with tropicals as well as annuals and perennials. This new practice of "interiorscaping" became a specialty for some practitioners and was used in many different types of buildings. While much of this work was quite undistinguished, other interior gardens were brilliantly executed miniature landscapes that created a real illusion of being out of doors. At the Bradford Exchange office in Deerfield, Illinois, Joe Carr used magnolias as a canopy for a year-round courtyard. At the IBM Garden Plaza in New York City, Zion and Breen's bamboo-dominated design for the glassed gallery suggested tropical jungle. More recently, at Battery Park City in New York City, Diana Balmori and M. Paul Friedberg designed a bosque of towering Washington palms to define the elegantly simple Winter Garden at the World Financial Center.

Population dispersal to suburbs and increasing dependence on the automobile affected the location and design of corporate offices in ways similar to those of shopping areas. Corporate headquarters relocated to urban outskirts to be near pools of highly trained workers and at the same time take advantage of the transportation convenience of location on major highways, particularly Interstates. These new suburban headquarters or "campuses," as they have been quite appropriately termed, were intended to communicate corporate image, take advantage of lower land acquisition costs, provide space for expansion, and provide a desirable work environment for employees.

Ironically, many of the earliest corporate campuses used iconography from nineteenth-century parks to serve the needs of modern business and industry. At the John Deere headquarters in Moline, Illinois, a site on which later headquarters were modeled, Sasaki Associates juxtaposed a bucolic landscape of willow-edged

A modern "Romantic" landscape—John Deere headquarters, Moline, Illinois.

ponds and rippling lawns against the steel box designed by Eero Saarinen for offices. Set across a wooded valley, this building was sited like a pavilion in an English country estate to allow views of the restful pastoral scenery, but to be distinct from it. Equally exemplary was Deere's use of the site as an enlarged sculpture garden, where large-scale pieces by Henry Moore and Isamu Noguchi replaced the "garden follies" that one might have found in an eighteenth-century landscape.

The desire of corporate developers to project a unique image for their site often allowed designers to experiment with distinctive forms for site plans. At Squibb headquarters in New Jersey, Dan Kiley applied his distinctive vision of the natural to set buildings in bosques of plane trees and honey locusts. Although regular and gridlike in plan, these masses created a forest that screened and sheltered buildings from their surroundings to create a sequestered corporate estate.

A quartet of recent corporate headquarters and business parks—Codex, Frito-Lay, Dulles Corners, and HEB—illustrate the variety of concepts that have informed contemporary projects. Codex World Headquarters outside Boston reflected concern for the relationship of site to setting. Designed by Hanna/Olin to fit complex contextual demands, including preservation of an existing horse farm and of uninterrupted, uncompromised views to the picturesque Blue Hills nearby, the site plan used restated regional design themes to convey a distinctive sense of place: the headquarters building reflected industrial architecture of nearby mill towns; a glass-covered court provided a space likened to a New England town common; and materials including granite and native trees such as sugar maples created an instantly identifiable regional character. At a more subtle level, the stepped form of the building facade and the gentle berming of intrusive structures like the parking garage echo local topography, to which the site clearly relates.

Equally strong regionally related themes, although very different ones, tie the Frito-Lay corporate headquarters near Dallas to its north Texas prairie site. Using an existing farm pond as the focal point of the composition, the office building was located across its narrow end in such a way that the wings of this triangular structure created a limestone-edged pond courtyard. As designed by Sasaki Associates with Howard Garrett, those areas of the site not used for well-

At the University of California-Santa Cruz, many entry drives are through dense woodlands, which also serve as buffers between the distinctive colleges. (Ed Cunnius.)

screened and well-planted parking areas or roads were retained for meadows and turf areas, with only a small portion in manicured lawn. While not a true prairie restoration, plantings like native wildflowers and grasses such as Mexican hat and little bluestem replicated a site image lost from Texas since the late nineteenth century.

Very different concepts guided development of Dulles Corner office park in northern Virginia. Taking its themes from designed urban landscapes, the site was replete with pedestrian walkways, sitting areas, and axial tree plantings in a central open air corridor that functioned to link the various buildings of the park. The most significant aspect of this site plan by WZMH Architects and EDAW was the development of outdoor spaces through placement of buildings with fixed setbacks and space-enveloping wings. Less successful and less suitable was the direct use of spatial sequences from a historical design—Central Park in New York City. So direct was the inspiration that the largest open area at Dulles Corner was actually called Central Park. While there are differences in scale and surrounding relationships, anyone familiar with the original Central Park would recognize it as prototype for Dulles Corners' tree-lined axial promenade overlooking a naturalistic pond surrounded by miniaturized Romantic parklands.

A quite different approach to use of historical precedent in corporate campuses has been the trend, analogous to the reuse of older building developments for retail uses, to revitalize abandoned structures. At HEB headquarters, located along a recently improved portion of the Riverwalk in San Antonio, Texas, a former arsenal became offices for a large supermarket chain. Outdoor areas formerly used to store ordinance and vehicles became service and recreational courts for employees. Eschewing any sentimental glorification of the past, the site design used simple modern forms and elements reflecting the rectilinear forms of the buildings.

True campuses—for colleges and universities—also underwent remarkable changes after World War II. Expansion of the student population, first due to government-financed veteran's education and later due to the baby boom, and the proliferation of commuter-oriented campuses at both junior colleges and universities were the principal factors that influenced campus design. Junior colleges offering two-year programs and community-oriented adult education rather than the traditional four-year degree to young people were themselves the product of postwar social trends. Most were nonresidential and located in suburbs or small cities that previously had no local access to postsecondary education. Because of their location, most of these campuses were auto-oriented, with space devoted to parking equaling that set aside for academic uses. This need to accommodate high levels of automobile traffic often overwhelmed other planning concerns and led to dispersed campus schemes that lacked the spatial cohesion of the traditional campus.

One innovative campus plan which demonstrated that junior college design need not be unimaginative or bland was that for Foothills Junior College in Los Altos, California, by Sasaki Walker Associates with Ernest Krump, architect. Sited adjacent to an expressway for ease of access, the campus itself controlled auto traffic by separating vehicular and pedestrian circulation. Site topography zoned land uses. Academic and physical education buildings were located on two hills, while drives and parking were confined to areas below the hills. The academic campus had the character of a medieval hill town, with the many small classroom and administration buildings forming a wall-like perimeter along hill edges. The "city gates" to campus were the steep hillside paths that formed a transition from vehicular areas to the pedestrian campus core. Within that core spatial development was far from medieval, with three major open courts and innumerable smaller nodes providing outdoor study and visiting spaces. Covered walkways made movement around campus more comfortable in any season. The enclosure and development of these courts gave the campus an inward focus and human scale that most junior colleges lacked. The Foothills Junior College plan not only inspired later campus designs, but foreshadowed, if not stimulated, the trend to pedestrianize campuses by closing streets to vehicles.

The concept of an inward-focused, pedestrian-oriented campus inspired larger, more traditional universities as well. At the University of California-Santa Cruz, developed in the 1970s as one of three new campuses for the University of California system, this idea was translated into a version of Jefferson's "academical village" suitable both to the auto age and to the environmental sensitivity of the 1970s. The planning concept for UC-Santa Cruz, developed by architect John Warnecke and Thomas Church, made the campus experience one of driving through a park dotted with villages. On 2,000 redwood-covered acres overlooking the Pacific Ocean, individual colleges, termed "cluster colleges," were sited to exploit topography and the screening potential of the forest. Each college was semi-independent in its operations and in its design character. One of the most famous, Kresge College, was designed as a Postmodern European village; with a compact, L-shaped main street and its buildings painted in bright whites, oranges, and yellows, the human educational environment of Kresge contrasted vividly with the surrounding woodland. In contrast, the design for Merrill College used bold, simplified, angular forms and earth-toned materials for buildings carefully set in amongst tree groves, in a manner very popular with ecologically oriented Californians in the 1970s.

At the University of Wisconsin at Kenosha ecological analysis was the principle rationale for the campus plan, by Hellmuth, Obata and Kassabaum. Not only did the design preserve existing forests and prairies, but it incorporated them into the site plan to become living laboratories as well as definers of campus units.

Not all post-World War II campus plans were for large sites where dispersed, low-rise schemes were practical. At inner city universities, urbane high-rise complexes with intensively developed plaza-scale open spaces created an "academical metropolis." The most famous and controversial of these urban campus designs was that for the new University of Illinois opened in Chicago in 1965. Chicago Circle, as the campus was called to distinguish it from the older campus in Champaign-Urbana, raised criticism both for its planning process and hard-edged urbane design. Built on a site west of downtown Chicago near the location proposed in Burnham's Plan for Chicago as the site for a Civic Center, the project was as much urban renewal as university development.[5]

The multiblock site was, before development of Chicago Circle, a densely settled Italian-American community housed in small frame buildings dating from the late nineteenth century. This neighborhood was also home to internationally known Hull House. For a number of years the city had proposed various renewal projects in the area, and some land had already been cleared, but these had never materialized. When the university's Board of Trustees threatened to develop in the suburbs if the city did not provide a large contiguous tract near good transportation, the centrally located neighborhood near Halsted Street was designated as the university site. Most of the controversy attached to the planning process related to displacement of residents and the annihilation of an old neighborhood. The University allayed some of this criticism by restoring the original Hull House building and incorporating it, albeit in a very unsympathetic manner, into the campus design.

The campus itself was a dense city, organized, in plans by Skidmore, Owings and Merrill, around its principal functional components, rather than traditional academic subject matter. Thus, there was no physical structure for a "college of science," but laboratory facilities of all types were grouped together to be used as needed. Faculty and administrative offices were grouped in the high-rise tower that identified the campus to drivers on the adjacent expressway. Most mid-rise structures on campus were linked by street-level plazas and second-story causeways, which also provided access to the surrounding parking areas. The principal plaza of this complex was the Great Court, a rooftop patio with four small amphitheaters and large undifferentiated paved areas, all surrounding an at-grade outdoor arena. What vegetation ameliorated the architectonic character of campus open spaces was generally limited to trees in grates, which did little to alter scale or provide more intimate and usable outdoor spaces.[6] The architectonic image of Chicago Circle was as controversial as its urban renewal plans. Those who associated "campus" with the pastoral, rural settings of the state universities or Ivy League schools found the hardness and lack of student amenities degrading to the academic experience. It was only recently, as the campus reached a kind of "middle age," that the value of its design, as an alternative campus concept, has been appreciated and applied at other campuses.

If the University of Illinois-Chicago Circle was a campus with an urban image, the national university of Mexico was a campus that really was a city. The Universidad National Autonoma de Mexico, known by the acronym UNAM, opened in 1954 as a university new town with zones for academic, recreational, special event, and residential uses.[7] Covering approximately 3 square miles in the lava-rock-strewn Pedragal district, this sprawling campus was unified through modern architecture and public art, especially the bold murals by artists such as Diego Rivera for which Mexico is so well known. Although quite monumental in overall appearance, the campus site plan incorporated many gathering spaces at both the plaza and patio scale. As at Pedregal Gardens, the UNAM campus incorporated on-site lava flows into the ground-plane design—their irregular, uncontrolled forms contrasting dramatically with the Cartesian geome-

Some of the antiquated industrial machinery reused as sculpture and play equipment at Gas Works Park in Seattle.

try of Modern style structures. This huge campus, with its student population now nearing 100,000, is segmented by an internal road system. The largest zone, set aside solely for pedestrians, was the academic portion, organized around a large open turf area. Adjacent to it was an almost equally large sports area, also undissected by drives. Across a major highway sat the sports arena built for the 1968 Olympics and the residential area with dorms and apartments for students, as well as a housing subdivision for faculty and administration.

While new campuses were being constructed across the continent, existing schools were struggling with the need to add facilities and at the same time maintain a cohesive campus plan. Some, like Princeton University, abandoned the old order in favor of modern asymmetry in plans, a solution which at best created two distinct campus areas, and at worst caused a visual schizophrenia. Elsewhere, as at the University of Illinois-Champaign-Urbana or the University of Minnesota, underground structures were built in an attempt to preserve openness and views to important buildings or spaces. In any event few campus plans of the 1950s, 1960s, or 1970s followed either the concepts or intentions of earlier schemes, which had given campuses great spatial and architectural consistency. More recently there has been renewed attention to the ordered planning of the early twentieth century. The University of Illinois for example, in a 1986 plan for the northern campus area by Sasaki Associates, reintroduced the general concepts of Charles Platt's plan for the south campus. In particular, the Sasaki scheme extended the historic campus spine northward to terminate in a grassed oval court similar in concept, although much smaller in scale, to the malls in the southern part of campus.

RECREATION

Just as commercial and campus needs changed in the post-World War II period, so too did recreational needs and preferences. The baby boom led to greater emphasis on small, local play spaces and less on larger regional parks. As house lots became smaller, public recreation became more important. In general, the park of the later twentieth century was no longer a multifunctional landscape

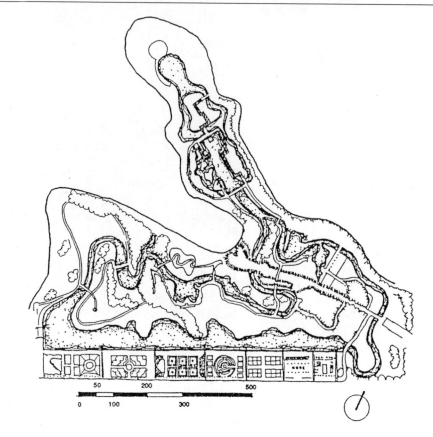

Schematic plan of Moody Gardens in Galveston, Texas. (Data from Jellicoe, 1989; drawn by Rossi.)

park, but a place for active recreation, with facilities such as ballfields and tennis courts. Larger parks that were created often were justified in terms of serving functions in addition to recreation, an important one being flood control. Particularly after passage of flood control legislation in the United States, cities sought cost-effective ways to store runoff and use floodplain land without allowing permanent development. Parks provided a perfect land use for this purpose because impermanent, inexpensive facilities such as paths and open fields could be built in areas subject to inundation.

This multiple use of land coupled with reuse of "found" space has been a key theme in recent park design. Among the most creative examples of adaptive reuse was Richard Haag's scheme for Gas Works Park in Seattle. Built on a derelict peninsula on Lake Union, the park centered on gas-generating machinery remaining from the site's former industrial use. This equipment, renovated for safety and enclosed, became play equipment for children of all ages. Most of the site of more than 20 acres was regraded into sweeping landforms suitable for playing catch, picnicking, or flying a kite. Although most often recognized for its fanciful use of industrial equipment, it is really these earthen sculptures that are the masterwork of the design.[8]

Smaller in scale, but literally "built on thin air" was Freeway Park, also in Seattle. Designed by the Halprin firm with Angela Danadjieva as project manager, the park site included two strips of land on either side of Interstate 5 and the air space over the intervening portion of highway. The park thus served as needed open space in the heart of the city and also as a pedestrian connection from downtown to nearby residential areas. Although urbane in concept, the design was intended to mimic a natural landscape of evergreen-covered mountains, steep canyons, and cascading waterfalls. This though was not mere illusionism, but an attempt to cut the park user off from the freeway and block sounds with falling water. It was also an adventurous experience, as visitors were challenged to walk into the stylized canyons and under the pounding water. The design also dealt effectively with the question of views from the freeway below by stepping modular planting boxes down the freeway-facing sides of the park.

In the last fifty years, many of the great landscape parks of the nineteenth century have undergone significant changes. In many cases, these changes have included unfortunate filling of open spaces with new uses, which often served only one specialized use. In other cases, and at an increasing rate, these parks are being restored to some semblance of their original design, an example being the recent restoration of Central Park. One of the greatest challenges to modern park planners and designers has been how to sensitively integrate new uses into the living fabric of a great park. An outstanding recent example of successful integration was Bruce Kelly's redesign of the Strawberry Fields area of Central Park as a memorial to John Lennon. Kelly followed the general concept of the Olmsted and Vaux master plan, integrated subsequent alterations such as a pathway, and created a lasting memorial to the musician's message in the focal "Imagine" mosaic.

A key change influencing modern recreational design has been new theories about play. One of these new approaches, the "theory of loose parts," emphasized the need to engage a child's mind as well as body. This was to be accomplished by providing play spaces with the maximum number of variable parts, including movable elements and choice of order in which parts were used. Thus, the turn-of-the-century gymnasium-style fixed playground of hanging rings and jungle gyms was replaced with play equipment that could be organized in different configurations and used in more than one way by children. The most extreme form of loose parts play space was the adventure playground, in which scavenged or donated materials were constantly reassembled by children to suit the needs of the moment. The adventure playground, which originated in Europe, was always a radical play alternative that never became widely accepted in America, in part because its helter-skelter, unmanicured image was at odds with most adults' perceptions of a suitable designed landscape. Modern timber play equipment with cargo nets and tire swings is a commercial offspring of earlier free-play parks.

A persistent planning problem—how to link dispersed recreational areas—has recently been resolved through the use of abandoned vehicular transportation corridors as linear parks. These greenways now cross North America, including former canal towpaths such as the C&O Towpath in Washington, D.C., and in Maryland, former railroad rights-of-way such as Prairie Path through the western suburbs of Chicago, and abandoned industrial areas along waterfronts such as the Central Mississippi Riverfront Regional Park in Minneapolis and St. Paul. Typically, these greenways serve pedestrians, bicyclists, and recreational boaters. In many communities they form the sole pedestrian-oriented route and are used for both commuting and recreation.

In the last two decades, recreational and conservation needs have come together as park agencies established small parks to protect important local natural environments such as woodlands, endangered species, wetlands, and wildlife corridors. A unique form of the natural park has been the underwater park, usually established to protect a marine ecological system or archaeological site. Fort Jefferson National Monument in the Florida Keys was the first park to include a significant marine area in its boundaries. Nations in Central America and the Caribbean have been particularly active in establishing this type of park—including Utila Park in Honduras and Exuma Cays Land and Sea Park in the Bahamas.

While outdoor recreation has generally been the province of public agencies, the post-World War II period saw tremendous growth in specialized private recreational facilities—everything from theme parks to miniature golf courses. Theme parks have not only set new standards for recreational facilities, but have also reinforced the role of careful site planning and design in improving the quality of recreational experience. Although not the first theme park, Disneyland in Anaheim, California, opened in 1954, established an ideal of public expectation. The Disney parks are masterpieces of a new genre—carefully designed commercial sites in which the chief product for sale is fantasy.

Disneyland and Disney World are places that one either loves or hates, and judging by their financial success most people love them. Regardless of which view one takes, the sites merit study. On the positive side, they are very successful systems of circulation in which pedestrian movement is integrated with a variety of vehicular systems from the family car in which one arrives to the monorail. They are also excellent examples of the physical development of specific design themes, albeit somewhat hackneyed ones. Detail was also carefully addressed, from the precise five-eighths scale reduction of Main Street and Town Square to the image-making accessories in each of the different theme "lands." But crucial problems do exist. Aside from questions of artificiality, large theme parks, particularly the "theme region" the Disney Corporation has developed in Orlando, Florida, create serious environmental problems ranging from excessive seasonal demands on infrastructure to pollution of easily degraded Florida groundwater. Perhaps it is time for the level of theme park regional planning to catch up to its level of site planning and design.

The modern recreating public is not interested only in fantasy recreation, but also seeks what could be called educational recreation activities. Particularly popular in the last two decades have been places to learn about the natural environment and gardening. New arboretums have been constructed and older ones enlarged. Botanical centers have become popular visitor amenities in larger park systems. Zoos have been enlarged and redesigned to emphasize an "ecological" approach to the display and management of animals. Morton Arboretum in Lisle, Illinois, is an example of a revitalized outdoor museum of plant material. Founded in 1922, the arboretum has always served as a site of plant research, including early ecological restorations, but has more recently introduced new display gardens oriented toward suburban homeowners. Botanical centers of all sizes demonstrate the latest horticultural innovations and instruct the public on grounds management and gardening, with increasing emphasis on environmentally sound management such as composting. The most extravagant of these botanical centers is the as yet unfinished Moody Gardens in Galveston, Texas. Following a master plan by Geoffrey Jellicoe, a 250-acre wetland site will be transformed into a combination museum of garden history, botanical research center, and wetland reserve, based on the concept of "landscapes of civilization."

Animals are also a focus of educational recreation sites. In their modern conservation role, zoos have become centers of protection and propagation for endangered wildlife. In keeping with this role, and in response to demand for more humane treatment of animals, many zoos have been redesigned to house and display their charges in social and environmental groupings similar to those found in their natural habitat. The Seattle firm of Jones & Jones has become nationally known for this type of work. One of their most significant projects was the ASLA award-winning redesign for Woodland Zoo Park in Seattle.[9] Ten world bioclimatic zones were simulated, and in each zone display areas depict the landscape character of an animal's home region, provide the type of cover critical to each species, and allow unobtrusive human observation of animals.

Improved aviation service has made long-distance travel an important type of modern recreation. As a result destination resorts have increased in number, size, and geographical distribution. Today entire regions are planned for tourism. Typically, destination resort planning and design have been based on one of two concepts. The first produces what can be called the "image-oriented" resort, much like a theme park in its use of ersatz images to create ambiance. The second produces what could be termed the "place-oriented resort," in which local character, particularly that of the natural environment, is emphasized in planning and design. Many of each type exist throughout the continent, but examples of image-oriented resorts abound in ski areas in the United States. One newly opened resort community of this type is Beaver Creek near Vail in Colorado. Said to be modeled on Alpine villages of northern Italy, Beaver Creek's intensive development is as at odds with its Rocky Mountain environment, as is its architectural theme. Place-oriented resorts attempted to adapt to natural environmental or cultural themes. The best of these are planned to minimize destruction of the setting that has drawn people to that location. At Amelia Island Resort in Florida a portion of the site with a unique plant community called the Sunken Forest was preserved by limiting access to a boardwalk. At Sea Ranch, a second-home community on the coast in Sonoma County, California, the entire development was planned to protect existing flora and fauna, along with the region's wild, brooding seaside character. Following an ecological study by Halprin and Associates, housing and community facilities were clustered in areas where they would have the least impact, as well as fit best with existing site modifications. For example, areas previously cleared by logging became the principal areas of new construction, while hedgerows that formerly shielded sheep meadows protected and screened housing.

The problems of the use impacts on resort landscapes are particularly acute where resort and tourism planning become a form of regional planning. The Mexican islands of Cancun and Cozumel, developed as destination resorts within the past twenty years, are an excellent example of this process. The principal types of environmental analysis completed during planning were related to the capacity of the islands to provide materials and services necessary to support large resort hotels. Choice sites were set aside for major hotels, but far less attention was paid to creating a total resort environment, so the islands have become resort strips with few additional amenities for visitors or employees. In addition, high water tables have been easily contaminated by waste and runoff from paving.

CONCLUSION AND SUMMARY

The modern era has demonstrated that whatever the inversions in design over time, landscape architecture returns to three underlying concerns that give substance to its practice: aesthetics, environmentalism, and social need. In this, the post-World War II period has been more like the formative nineteenth-century period of landscape architecture than like the age that immediately preceded it. Just as in the nineteenth century, late twentieth-century designers have been inspired by the visual arts; they have viewed the natural environment as both an inspiration for form and a resource to be conserved; and they have recognized that design could be a small but necessary force for the improvement of society and individuals. That such similarities could persist through the political and cultural upheavals, through the shift from a rural to an urban continent, and from landscape architecture as a personal credo to an organized profession attests to the vigor and consequence of these issues.

Modern design has reemphasized both the importance of the individual visionary in creating unique environmental statements, as well as the need for sound functional bases for design. Vision allows these functional concerns to be treated as opportunities rather than as the constraints that a less creative assessment might make of them.

POSTSCRIPT   Whether rightly or wrongly, the study of the past is often considered a vehicle to predict the direction of future events. If the past can suggest what direction the discipline and profession of landscape architecture may take, what in fact is foretold? First, we must recognize that there are cycles of change in popularity and importance of landscape issues, in the scale at which they operate, and in preferred design and planning approaches. Thus, the mid-nineteenth century was a period when the public was particularly sensitive to landscape concerns, especially at the small-site level, and preferred a naturalistic appearance in designed landscapes, while the 1950s was a period in which the landscape was important only as a setting in which rapid, technologically advanced development could occur, with obviously artificial designed spaces preferred. Second, these cycles tend to bounce back and forth between extremes—one very formal, the other informal, one very aware of environmental concerns, the other minimizing human environmental impacts, one socially conscious, the other aesthetically conscious; and one in which the profession is viewed as a science, the other in which it is viewed as an art. Third, regulation has a significant effect on directions the profession takes, and regulation is constantly increasing. Ironically, early landscape architects of the nineteenth century who had virtually no legal constraints to deal with advocated many of the legislated standards that some landscape architects now feel constrain creative design and planning. But conversely, regulation increases employment of landscape architects in areas such as plan review, wetlands restoration, mined land reclamation, master plan development, and historic preservation. Fourth, social and demographic changes directly influence the types and scope of projects landscape architects are selected to work on, and the specific direction these changes will take are often difficult to predict before they are established trends. Twenty-five years ago, who would have anticipated massive entry of women into the workplace, or, conversely, who would have thought that we could have made so little progress in improving urban transportation. The only certainty is that population will increase, placing greater pressure on environmental systems and causing urbanization of more areas. Political decisions, economic modifications, and technological advances will also affect the profession and the landscape in ways equally unpredictable. In the late 1960s and 1970s, environmental concern appeared on the verge of becoming a way of life, but this trend was broken by political events of the 1980s, only to be revived in the late 1980s and early 1990s. Announcements of advances in electrical superconductivity generated great speculation on what a landscape with fewer high-power transmission lines or hydroelectric dams would be like, but early optimism was quickly quashed by scientific and engineering realities. Sixth, like all human experience, design practice is becoming increasing global, in particular with western work methods and spatial arrangements being exported worldwide. This should not suggest that local or regional patterns will die out completely, for many are being revived, but usually in a context that integrates them with modern western traditions.

With these six factors in mind, what might be the speculative future of landscape architecture? As a discipline it will certainly grow as the types of issues landscape architects deal with become part of accepted practice in landscape design or planning. Whether this will translate into a comparable growth in the profession under its present title is less sure. The split off of planners, many of whom were nominally part of the profession, in the early twentieth century suggests a scenario, often repeated at a smaller scale, of landscape architecture providing the inspiration for a specialty, which later splits off as a separate, more circumscribed profession. It does seem certain that as regulation and general environmental complexity grow, specialization, either within the profession or as outgrowth from it, will increase. At the same time the need for generalists will continue, but perhaps with their work at any given point in time specialized to target a specific market such as land development or environmental restoration. The current historicism in design, an outgrowth of postmodernism, and particularly of the Postmodern emphasis on architectonic spaces, is likely to subside, to be replaced by a neonaturalism, either derived from historical precedent or more likely inspired by increasing concerns for the condition of the environment. Of course, as these cycles go, this will then eventually be replaced by a return to formality and structure in the landscape. At a larger scale, the world will eventually become a planned environment in which both land uses and management strategies are applied at regional and even national levels. California's state plan and Florida's recent requirement that all incorporated and unincorporated urban places have comprehensive plans are just two early examples of the broad level at which physical and systems planning will eventually operate.

While all of these practical changes occur, there will remain one constant within the profession of landscape architecture: that the skills of problem solving in both physical alteration of environments and the systems through which they are controlled will be the most significant activity of the profession. Regardless of types of projects, scale of projects, or stylistic fashions, the ability to creatively manipulate multiple criteria, issues, and physical solutions will remain the most critical skill which the profession has to offer. If a study of the past has any value it is to demonstrate that solutions change, but that the so elusive creative process remains the object of greatest value.

NOTES

1. *Of course, this generality refers to innovative early Modern work. Later, many motifs considered typical of Modern design became just as hackneyed as the turf panel had been in the 1920s.*

2. *The Fair's site plan was somewhat traditional, with a series of axial avenues radiating from a central focal point—the Trylon and Perisphere. The grounds even included a space similar in concept to the Court of Honor at the World's Columbian Exposition, called the Court of Peace, where national exhibit halls were sited.*

3. *Lawrence Halprin, while an associate of Church's firm, also worked on this design.*

4. *The designers were quick to point out that seating was to be temporary and that benches were "purposely provided without backs so that loiterers will not be attracted" (Shurcliff, 1952, p. 149). Fortunately, developers and designers quickly learned that "loitering" encouraged longer shopping trips.*

5. *See Chapter 17 for a discussion of urban renewal.*

6. *Part of the reason for this very open, almost foreboding design was the need to make this inner city campus appear safe and secure.*

7. *The UNAM is the oldest school of higher education in North America, having been founded in the sixteenth century. Until the development of University City, it had been housed in separate buildings spread across Mexico City.*

8. *The original 1972 Master Plan included additional facilities for active recreation, never built. Thus the park has a more simple, more pastoral character than originally envisioned, but these omissions do not seem to have detracted from its popularity with visitors.*

9. *The original plan was by the Olmsted firm, but this had already been drastically altered.*

References

PART 1
Chapter 1

Bradford, M. A. 1957. *Ancient Landscapes.* Westport, Conn.: Greenwood.

Butzer, Karl W. 1971. *Environment and Archaeology: An Ecological Approach to Prehistory.* Chicago: University of Chicago Press.

———. 1976. *After Australopithecines: Statigraphy, Ecology and Culture in the Middle Pleistocene.* Chicago: Aldine Press.

Clark, Graham. 1977. *World Prehistory in New Perspective.* Cambridge: Cambridge University Press.

———. 1980. *Mesolithic Prelude: The Paleolithic-Mesolithic Transition in Old World History.* Edinburgh: Edinburgh University Press.

Leakey, Richard, and Alan Walker. 1985. "Homo Erectus Unearthed," *National Geographic* 168(5):624–73.

Prideaux, Tom. 1973. *Cro-Magnon Man.* New York: Time-Life Books.

Schoeninger, Margaret Jean. 1980. *Changes in Human Subsistence Activities from the Middle Paleolithic to the Neolithic Period in the Middle East.* Ann Arbor: University Microfilms Press.

Soffer, Olga, ed. 1987. *The Pleistocene Old World: Regional Perspectives.* New York: Plenum Press.

Weaver, Kenneth. 1985. "The Search for Our Ancestors," *National Geographic* 168(5):560–83.

Wenke, Robert J. 1980. *Patterns in Prehistory.* New York and Oxford: Oxford University Press.

Wymer, J. 1982. *The Paleolithic Age.* London: Croom Helm.

Chapter 2

Bender, Barbara. 1975. *Farming in Prehistory.* New York: St. Martin's.

Eickelman, Dale F. 1981. *The Middle East: An Anthropological Approach.* Englewood Cliffs, N.J.: Prentice-Hall.

Frankfort, Henri. 1951. *The Birth of Civilization in the Near East.* Bloomington: Indiana University Press.

Fussell, G. E. 1968. *Farming Technique from Prehistoric to Modern Times.* New York: Pergamon.

Mallart, James. 1975. *The Neolithic of the Near East.* New York: Scribners.

Sauer, Carl. 1952. *Agricultural Origins and Dispersals.* New York: George Grady.

Schoeninger, Margaret Jean. 1980. *Changes in Human Subsistence Activities from the Middle Paleolithic to the Neolithic Period in the Middle East.* Ann Arbor: University Microfilms Press.

Singh, Purushottam. 1974. *Neolithic Cultures of Western Asia.* London and New York: Seminar Press.

Stigler, R., ed. 1974. *The Old World: Early Man to Development of Agriculture.* New York: St. Martin's.

Todd, Ian A. 1976. *Catal Huyac in Perspective.* Menlo Park, Calif.: Cummings.

Wenke, Robert J. 1980. *Patterns in Prehistory.* New York and Oxford: Oxford University Press.

Chapter 3

Adams, Robert McC. 1965. *Land behind Bagdad: A History of Settlement on the Diyala Plains.* Chicago: University of Chicago Press.
——. 1968. "The Natural History of Urbanism," *Smithsonian* Annual II, *The Fitness of Man's Environment.* 2:18–26.
Contenau, George. 1962. *Everyday Life in Babylon and Assyria.* London: Edward Arnold.
Dani, Ahmed Hasan, ed. 1981. *The Indus Civilization: New Perspectives.* Islamabad: The Center for the Study of Civilizations of Central Asia.
Downing, Theodore E., and Mcguire Gibson, eds. 1974. *Irrigation's Impact on Society.* Tucson: University of Arizona Press.
Ellis, Marie de J. 1976. *Agriculture and the State in Ancient Mesopotamia.* Philadelphia: The Babylonian Fund University Museum.
Jacobsen, T. and R.M. Adams. 1958. "Salt and Silt in Ancient Mesopotamian Agriculture." *Science,* 128:1251–8
Lamberg-Karlovsky, C. C. 1968. *Hunters, Farmers, and Civilizations: Old World Archaeology.* San Francisco: W. H. Freeman.
Leanard, Jonathon N. 1976. *The First Farmers.* New York: Time-Life Books.
Possehl, Gregory. 1979. *Ancient Cities of the Indus.* Durham, N.C.: Carolina Academic Press.
——. 1982. *The Harappan Civilization: A Contemporary Perspective.* Warminster: Ans & Phillips.
Reed, Charles A. 1977. *Origins of Agriculture.* Paris: Mouton.
Shand, Richard. 1969. *Agricultural Development in Asia.* Berkeley: University of California Press.
Trow-Smith, Robert. 1967. *Life from the Land.* London: Longmans.
Walters, Stanley D. 1970. *Water for Larsa.* London: Yale University Press.

Chapter 4

Abdel-Salam, Mamoun. 1937. *An Outline of the History of Agriculture in Egypt.* Cairo: Grunberg.
Bratton, F. G. 1968. *A History of Egyptian Archaeology.* New York: Crowell.
Casson, Lionel. 1965. *Ancient Egypt.* New York: Time, Inc.
Erman, Adolf. 1971. *Life in Ancient Egypt.* New York: Dover.
Hayes, William C. 1964. *Most Ancient Egypt.* Chicago: University of Chicago Press.
Hoffman, Michael, A. 1979. *Egypt before the Pharoahs: The Prehistoric Foundations of Egyptian Civilization.* New York: Knopf.
James, T. G. H. 1988. *Ancient Egypt.* Austin: University of Texas Press.
Johnson, Paul. 1978. *The Civilizations of Ancient Egypt.* New York: Atheneum.
Ludwig, Emil. 1937. *The Nile.* New York: Viking.
Moorehead, Alan. 1960. *The White Nile.* New York: Harper & Brothers.
Murname, William J. 1983. *The Guide to Ancient Egypt.* London: Penguin.
Romer, John. 1984. *Ancient Lives.* London: Weidenfeld and Nicolson.
Smith, Grafton. 1970. *The Ancient Egyptians and the Origin of Civilization.* New York: Books for Libraries Press.
Trigger, Bruce G. 1976. *Nubia under the Pharaohs.* London: Thames and Hudson.

Chapter 5

Attenborough, David. 1987. *The First Eden: The Mediterranean World and Man.* Boston: Little, Brown.
Bowra, C. M. 1965. *Classical Greece.* New York: Time, Inc.
Branigan, J. J. 1969. *The Mediterranean Lands.* London: Macdonald and Evans.
Finley, Moses. 1985. *Studies in Land and Credit in Ancient Athens, 500–200 B.C.* New Brunswick, N.J.: Rutgers University Press.
Hawkes, Jane. 1974. *Atlas of Ancient Archeology.* New York: McGraw-Hill.

Hunter, John Michael. 1985. *Land into Landscape.* London and New York: Goodwin.

Jellicoe, Geoffrey and Susan. 1975. *The Landscape of Man.* New York: Viking.

Milhoefer, A. 1977. *Ancient Athens, Piraeus and Phaleron.* Chicago: Ares.

Newton, Norman T. 1971. *Design on the Land: The Development of Landscape Architecture.* Cambridge, Mass.: Harvard University Press.

Russell, Bertrand. 1945. *A History of Western Philosophy.* New York: Simon and Schuster.

Semple, E. C. 1971. *The Geography of the Ancient Mediterranean.* New York: AMS Press.

Trump, D. L. 1980. *Prehistory of the Mediterranean.* New Haven and London: Yale University Press.

Chapter 6

Bailey, Cyril. 1962. *The Legacy of Rome.* Oxford: Clarendon.

Blake, Marion Elizabeth. 1947. *Ancient Roman Construction in Italy from the Prehistoric Period of Augustus.* Washington, D.C.: Carnegie Institution.

Boren, Henry C. *Roman Society: A Social, Economic and Cultural History.* Chapel Hill: University of North Carolina Press.

Brehaut, E. 1933. *Cato the Censorer on Farming.* New York: Columbia University Press.

Chevalier, Raymond. 1976. *Roman Roads.* London: B. T. Batsford.

Collingwood, R. G., and Ian Richmond. 1979. *The Archaeology of Roman Britain.* London: Methuen.

Farmer, V. 1913. *Cato-Varro: Roman Farm Management.* New York: Macmillan.

Heichelheim, Fritz M., and Cedric A. Yeo. 1962. *A History of the Roman People.* Englewood Cliffs, N.J.: Prentice-Hall.

Liversidge, Joan. 1970. *Everyday Life in the Roman Empire.* New York: Putnam.

Norberg-Schulz, Christian. 1975. *Meaning in Western Architecture.* New York: Praeger.

Percival, John. 1987. *The Roman Villa.* Los Angeles: University of California Press.

Potter, T. W. 1987. *Roman Italy.* Los Angeles: University of California Press.

Rivet, A. L. F. 1969. *The Roman Villa in Britain.* New York: Praeger.

Stambaugh, John. 1988. *The Ancient Roman City.* Baltimore and London: Johns Hopkins Press.

Veyne, Paul, ed. 1987. *A History of Private Life: From Pagan Rome to Byzantium.* Cambridge: Harvard University Press.

White, K. D. 1970. *Roman Farming.* New York: Cornell University Press.

Chapter 7

Duby, George, ed. 1988. *A History of Private Life: Revelations of the Medieval World.* Cambridge, Mass.: Harvard University Press.

Eco, Umberto. 1986. *Art and Beauty in the Middle Ages.* New Haven and London: Yale University Press.

Heer, Friedrich. 1961. *The Medieval World.* New York: Harry N. Abrams.

Hunter, John Michael. 1985. *Land into Landscape.* London and New York: Goodwin.

Morris, A. E. J. 1979. *History of Urban Form.* New York: Wiley.

Mumford, Lewis. 1961. *The City in History.* New York: Harcourt, Brace and World.

Newton, Norman T. 1971. *Design on the Land: The Development of Landscape Architecture.* Cambridge, Mass., Harvard University Press.

Power, Eileen. 1963. *Medieval People.* New York: Barnes and Noble.

Rowling, Marjorie. 1979. *Life in Medieval Times.* New York: Perigee.

Russell, Bertrand. 1945. *A History of Western Philosophy*. New York: Simon and Schuster.

Smith, Clifford T. 1978. *An Historical Geography of Europe Before 1800*. London: Longman.

White, I. D. et. al. 1984. *Environmental Systems*. London: George Allen.

Whittlesey, Derwent. 1949. *Environmental Foundations of European History*. New York: Appleton-Century-Crofts.

Wood, Margaret. 1965. *The English Medieval House*. London: Phoenix House.

Chapter 8

Arberry, Arthur J. 1967. "Muslim Cordoba." in *Cities of Destinies*. New York: McGraw-Hill

Bacon, Edmond. 1978. *Design of Cities*. New York: Penguin.

Benevolo, Leonardo L. 1971. *The Origins of Modern Town Planning*. Cambridge, Mass.: MIT Press

———. 1980. *The History of the City*. Cambridge, Mass.: MIT Press.

Brucher, Adam Gene. 1984. *Florence: The Golden Age, 1138–1737*. New York: Abbeville.

Clout, H. D. 1977. *Themes in Historical Geography in France*. London and New York: Academic Press.

Dodgshon, R.A. and R.A. Butlin. eds. 1978. *An Historical Geography of England and Wales*. London: Academic Press.

Hibbert, Christopher. 1975. *The House of the Medici*. New York: Morrow.

———. 1989. *Venice: The Biography of a City*. New York: Norton.

Johnson-Marshall, Percy. 1966. *Rebuilding Cities*. Chicago: Aldine.

Lane, Frederic C. 1973. *Venice: A Maritime Republic*. Baltimore: Johns Hopkins University Press.

Magi, Giovanne. 1983. *Cultura Contadina in Toscana*. Florence: Casa Editrice Editore.

Morris, James. 1974. *Venice*. London: Faber and Faber.

Russell, Josiah. 1972. *Medieval Regions and Their Cities*. Plymouth: David and Charles Publishers.

Shackleton, Margaret Reid. 19xx. *Europe—A Regional Geography*. New York: Praeger.

Tout, Thomas F. 1968. *Medieval Town Planning*. Manchester: Manchester University Press.

Waley, Daniel. 1969. *The Italian City Republics*. New York: McGraw-Hill.

Chapter 9

Appleton, Jay. 1975. *The Experience of Landscape*. London and New York: Wiley.

Argan, Giulio C. 1969. *The Renaissance City*. New York: George Braziller.

Baudel, Ferdinand. 1982. *Civilization and Capitalism, 15th–18th Centuries*, Vol II: *The Wheels of Commerce*. London: Collins

Burke, Peter. 1986. *The Italian Renaissance: Culture and Society in Italy*. Princeton: The Princeton University Press.

Cochrane, Erwin W. 1973. *Florence in the Forgotten Centuries, 1527–1800*. Chicago: University of Chicago Press.

Giedeon, Sigfried. 1961. *Space, Time and Architecture*. Cambridge, Mass.: Harvard University Press.

Gutkind, Erwin A. 1969. *International History of Urban Development in Southern Europe: Italy and Greece*. New York: Free Press of Glencoe.

Masson, Gorgina G. 1966. *Italian Gardens*. London: Thames and Hudson.

Miskimin, Harry A. 1975. *The Economy of Early Renaissance Europe 1300-1460*. Cambridge: Cambridge University Press.

Moholy-Nagy, Sibyl. 1969. *Matrix of Man*. London: Pall Mall Press.

Partne, Peter. 1976. *Renaissance Rome, 1500–1559: A Portrait of a Society.* Berkeley: University of California Press.

Relph, E. 1981. *Rational Landscapes and Humanistic Geography.* London: Croom Helm.

Schmal, H., ed. 1981. *The Patterns of European Organization Since 1500.* London: Croom Helm.

Slicher van Bath, B. H. 1963. *The Agrarian History of Western Europe, A.D. 500–1850.* London: Edward Arnold.

Wittkower, Rudolf R. 1962. *Architectural Principles in the Age of Humanism.* London: Alec Tiranti.

Wolfflin, Heinrich. 1975. *Renaissance and Baroque.* New York: Cornell University Press.

Zucker, Paul. 1959. *Town and Square.* Cambridge: MIT Press.

Chapter 10

Bacon, Edmond. 1978. *Design of Cities.* New York: Penguin.

Berrall, Julia. 1966. *The Garden.* New York: Viking.

Burke, James. 1978. *Connections.* Boston: Little, Brown.

Carter, Harold. 1983. *An Introduction to Urban Geography.* London: Arnold.

Clark, Kenneth. 1956. *Landscape into Art.* Hormondsworth: Penguin Books.

East, Gordon. 1935. *An Historical Geography of Europe.* New York: E. P. Dutton.

French, Jere S. 1978. *Urban Space.* Dubuque: Kendal/Hunt.

Fussell, G. E. 1972. *The Classical Tradition in Western European Farming.* Rutherford, N.J.: Fairleigh Dickinson University Press.

Glacken, C.J. 1967. *Traces on the Rhodian Shore: Nature and Culture in Western Thought from Ancient Times to the End of the Eighteenth Century.* Berkeley: University of California Press.

Goudie, Andrew. 1986. *The Human Impact on the Natural Environment.* Oxford: Blackwell.

Hunter, John Michael. 1985. *Land into Landscape.* London: Goodwin.

Lavendan, Pierre. 1979. *French Architecture.* Dallas: Southwest Book Services.

Mellor, Roy E. H., and E. A. Smith. 1979. *Europe: A Geographical Survey of the Continent.* New York: Columbia University Press.

Tobey, G. B. 1973. *A History of Landscape Architecture.* New York: American Elsevier.

Trow-Smith, Robert. 1967. *Life from the Land.* London: Longmans.

Whittlesey, Derwent. 1949. *Environmental Foundations of European History.* New York: Appleton-Century-Crofts.

Williamson, Tom, and Liz Bellamy. 1987. *Property and Landscape.* London: Philip.

Chapter 11

Ashby, Eric B. 1978. *Reconciling Man with the Environment.* London: Oxford University Press.

Batterberry, Michael. 1973. *Twentieth Century Art.* New York: McGraw-Hill.

Burke, G. C. 1971. *Towns in the Making.* London: Edward Arnold.

Carter, D. W. G. 1988. *Coastal Environments.* London: Academic Press.

Chadwick, George F. 1966. *The Park and the Town: Public Landscape in the 19th and 20th Centuries.* London: Architectural Press.

Detwyler, Thomas R. 1971. *Man's Impact on the Environment.* New York: McGraw-Hill.

Goudie, Andrew. 1986. *The Human Impact on the Natural Environment.* Oxford: Blackwell.

Gregory, Derek D. 1978. *Ideology, Science and Human Geography.* London: Hutchinson.

Howard, Ebenezer. 1946. *Garden Cities for Tomorrow.* London: Faber and Faber.

Simmons, Ian G. 1989. *Changing the Earth: Culture, Environment and History.* Oxford: Basil Blackwell.

Thirgood, J. V. 1981. *Man and the Mediterranean Forest—A History of Resource Depletion.* London: Academic Press.

Thomas, William L., ed. 1956. *Man's Role in Changing the Face of the Earth.* Chicago: University of Chicago Press.

Wagner, Richard H. 1974. *Environment and Man.* New York: Norton.

PART 2

Chapter 12

Arreola, Daniel D. 1986. "The Atrio in the Mexican Bario: Speculations on a Vernacular Landscape Symbol." Paper presented to the Annual Meeting of the Association of American Geographers. Minneapolis, Minn. May 3–7, 1986.

Berry, Michael S. 1982. *Time, Space, and Transition in Anasazi Prehistory.* Salt Lake City: University of Utah Press.

Brose, David S., and N'omi Greber. 1979. *Hopewell Archaeology: The Chillicothe Conference.* Kent, Ohio: Kent State University Press.

Calloway, Colin G. 1991. *Dawnland Encounters: Indians and Europeans in Northern New England.* Hanover, N.H.: University Press of New England.

Coe, Michael, Dean Snow, and Elizabeth Benson. 1986. *Atlas of Ancient America.* New York: Facts on File.

Coleman, Kenneth, ed. 1977. *A History of Georgia.* Athens: University of Georgia Press.

Cordell, Linda S. 1984. *Prehistory of the Southwest.* Orlando, Fla.: Academic.

Fagan, Brian M. 1987. *The Great Journey: The Peopling of Ancient America.* London: Thames and Hudson.

Fowler, Melvin. 1989. *The Cahokia Atlas: A Historical Atlas of Cahokia Archaeology.* Springfield: Illinois Historic Preservation Agency.

Frazier, Kendrick. 1986. *People of Chaco: A Canyon and Its Culture.* New York: W. W. Norton.

Hallowell, A. Irving. 1959. "The Backlash of the Frontier: The Impact of the Indian on American Culture," in *Annual Report of the Board of Regents of the Smithsonian Institution (1958).* Washington, D.C.: U.S. Government Printing Office. Publication 4354.

Hardoy, Jorge. 1968. *Urban Planning in Pre-Columbian America.* New York: Braziller.

Havry, Emil W. 1974. "The Problem of Contacts between the Southwestern United States and Mexico," in *The Mesoamerican Southwest: Readings in Archaeology, Ethnohistory and Ethnology,* Basil C. Hedrick, J. Charles Delley, and Carrol L. Rivey, eds. Carbondale: Southern Illinois University Press.

Jones, Dewitt, and Linda S. Cordell. 1985. *Anasazi World.* Portland, Ore.: Graphic Arts Publishing.

Judd, Neil M. 1925. "Everyday Life in Pueblo Bonito." *National Geographic,* Vol. 48, No. 3, pp. 227–62.

———. 1959. "The Braced-up Cliff at Pueblo Bonito," in *Annual Report of the Board of Regents of the Smithsonian Institution (1958).* Washington, D.C.: U.S. Government Printing Office. Publication 4354.

Kincaid, Chris, ed. 1983. *Chaco Roads Project, Phase I: A Reappraisal of Prehistoric Roads in the San Juan Basin.* Albuquerque: Department of the Interior, Bureau of Land Management.

★King, Leslie J. 1984. *Central Place Theory.* Beverly Hills, Calif.: Sage.

Kolata, Alan L. 1982. "Tiwanaku: Portrait of an Andean Civilization." *Field Museum Bulletin,* September.

★Indicates references given in one chapter and cited throughout Part 2.

Lagasse, Peter F., William B. Gillespie, and Kenneth G. Eggert. 1983. "Hydraulic Engineering Analysis of Prehistoric Water-Control Systems at Chaco Canyon," in *Recent Research on Chaco Prehistory.* W. James Judge and John D. Schelberg, eds. Albuquerque: National Park Service.

———. 1984. *Great Pueblo Architecture of Chaco Canyon, New Mexico.* Albuquerque: University of New Mexico Press.

Lekson, Stephen H. 1983. "Standing Architecture at Chaco Canyon and the Interpretation of Local and Regional Organization," in *Recent Research on Chaco Prehistory.* W. James Judge and John D. Schelberg, eds. Albuquerque: National Park Service.

Lister, Robert H., and Florence C. Lister. 1981. *Chaco Canyon: Archaeology and Archaeologists.* Albuquerque: University of New Mexico Press.

Metress, James F. 1981. "The Place of the Amerindian in the Origin of the Southern Appalachian Grass Balds," in *Geobotany II.* Robert C. Romans, ed. New York: Plenum.

Millon, René. 1973. "The Teotihuacan Map," in *Urbanization at Teotihuacan,* Vol. 1, Part 1, *Text,* and Part 2, *Maps.* Austin: University of Texas Press.

———. 1980. "Teotihuacan," in *Readings from Scientific American: Pre-Columbian Archaeology.* Gordon R. Wiley and Jeremy A. Sabloff, eds. San Francisco: W. H. Freeman.

Morgan, William N. 1980. *Prehistoric Architecture in the Eastern United States.* Cambridge, Mass.: MIT Press.

Morse, Dan F., and Phyllis A. Morse. 1983. *Archaeology of the Central Mississippi Valley.* New York: Academic.

Mullen, William. 1983. "Secrets of Tewanaku." *Chicago Tribune Magazine,* Nov. 23, p. 10.

Myer, William E. 1928. "Indian Trails of the Southwest," in *Forty-Second Annual Report of the Bureau of Ethnology to the Secretary of the Smithsonian Institution, 1924–1925.* Washington, D.C.: U.S. Government Printing Office.

Nuttall, Zelia. 1919. "The Gardens of Ancient Mexico." *Journal of the International Garden Club,* Vol. 3, Dec., pp. 573–90.

Parker, Arthur C. 1989. *Seneca Myths and Folk Tales.* Lincoln: University of Nebraska Press.

Porter, Stephen C., ed. 1983. *Late-Quaternary Environments of the United States,* Vol. 1: *The Late Pleistocene.* Minneapolis: University of Minnesota Press.

Powers, Robert P. 1984. "Regional Interaction in the San Juan Basin: The Chacoan Outlier System," in *Recent Research on Chaco Prehistory,* W. James Judge and John D. Schelberg, eds. Albuquerque: National Park Service.

Powers, Robert P., William B. Gillespie, and Stephen H. Lekson. 1983. *The Outlier Survey: A Regional View of Settlement in the San Juan Basin.* Albuquerque: National Park Service.

Rostlund, Erhard. 1957. "The Myth of a Natural Prairie Belt in Alabama: An Interpretation of Historical Records," in *Annals of the Association of American Geographers,* Vol. 47, No. 4, pp. 392–411.

Sanders, William T., Jeffrey R. Parsons, and Robert S. Santley. 1979. *The Basin of Mexico: Ecological Processes in the Evolution of a Civilization.* New York: Academic.

Smith, Bruce D., ed. 1848. *Mississippian Settlement Patterns.* New York: Academic.

Squier, E. G., and E. H. Davis. 1973. *Ancient Monuments of the Mississippi Valley Comprising the Results of Extensive Original Surveys and Explorations.* Washington, D.C.: Smithsonian Institution.

Texas Parks and Wildlife Department. 1984. "Caddoan Mounds: Temples and Tombs of an Ancient People." Austin: TPWD.

Webb, William S., and Charles E. Snow. 1974. *The Adena People.* Knoxville: University of Tennessee Press.

Wedel, Waldo R. 1961. *Prehistoric Man on the Great Plains.* Oklahoma City: University of Oklahoma Press.

Windes, Thomas. 1984. "A New Look at Population in Chaco Canyon," in *Recent Research on Chaco Prehistory.* W. James Judge and John D. Schelberg, eds. Albuquerque: National Park Service.

Wolf, Eric. 1976. *The Valley of Mexico.* Albuquerque: University of New Mexico Press.

Wyckoff, Don G., and Dennis Peterson. N.d. "Spiro Mounds: Prehistoric Gateway . . . Present-Day Enigma." Oklahoma City: Oklahoma Archaeological Survey.

Zelinsky, Wilbur. 1973. *The Cultural Geography of the United States.* Englewood Cliffs, N.J.: Prentice-Hall.

Chapter 13

Adams, Charles F., ed. 1892. *The Genesis of the Massachusetts Town, and the Development of Town-Meeting Government.* Cambridge: John Wilson and Son.

Almaraz, Felix D., Jr. 1989. *The San Antonio Missions and Their System of Land Tenure.* Austin: University of Texas.

American Society of Landscape Architects. 1932. *Colonial Gardens: The Landscape Architecture of George Washington's Time.* Washington D.C.: U.S. George Washington Bicentennial Commission.

Bailyn, Bernard. 1986. *The Peopling of British North America: An Introduction.* New York: Knopf.

Bannister, Turpin C. 1943. "Early Town Planning in New York State," *Journal of the Society of Architectural Historians,* Vol. 3, No. 1, pp. 36–42.

Baudouin, Charles. 1927. *"Plan de l'emplacement et Maison de Monsieur de Veaudreuil a Montreal."* N.p.: J. B. Angers and R. Decouagne.

Bevan, Edith Rossiter. 1950. "Gardens and Gardening in Early Maryland," *Maryland Historical Magazine,* Vol. 45, No. 4, pp. 243–70.

★Bidwell, Percy W., and John I. Falconer. 1925. *History of Agriculture in the Northern United States, 1620–1860.* Washington, D.C.: Carnegie Institution.

Bridenbaugh, Carl. 1964. *Cities in the Wilderness: The First Hundred Years of Urban Growth in America.* New York: Knopf.

Bush-Brown, Louise and James Bush-Brown. 1929. *Portraits of Philadelphia Gardens.* Philadelphia: Dorrance.

Coleman, James. 1881. *Coleman's Re-Print of William Penn's Original Proposal and Plan for the Founding and Building of Philadelphia in Pennsylvania, America, in 1683.* London: n.p.

Cooney, Loraine Meeks. 1933. *Garden History of Georgia, 1733–1933.* Atlanta: Peachtree Garden Club.

Cronon, William. 1983. *Changes in the Land: Indians, Colonists and Ecology in New England.* New York: Hill and Wang.

Crouch, Dora P., Daniel J. Garr, and Axel I. Mundigo. 1982. *Spanish City Planning in North America.* Cambridge: MIT Press.

Draper, Earle S. 1933. "Southern Plantations. II." *Landscape Architecture,* Vol. 23, No. 2, pp. 117–38.

Duncan, Frances. 1910. "An Old-Time Carolina Garden." *The Century Magazine,* Vol. 80. No. 6, pp. 803–11.

Earle, Alice Morse. 1901. *Old-Time Gardens.* New York: Macmillan.

Favretti, Rudy F. 1962. *Early New England Gardens: 1620–1840.* Sturbridge, Mass.: Barre.

———, and Gordon P. DeWolf. 1972. *Colonial Gardens.* Barre, Mass.: Barre.

Fleming, Donald, and Bernard Bailyn, eds. 1976. *Perspectives in American History,* Vol. X. Cambridge: Harvard University Press.

Fries, Sylvia D. 1977. *The Urban Idea in Colonial America.* Philadelphia: Temple University Press.

Genovese, Eugene D. 1972. *Roll Jordon Roll: The World the Slaves Made.* New York: Pantheon.

Gums, Bonnie L. 1988. *Archaeology at French Colonial Cahokia.* Springfield: Illinois Historic Preservation Agency.

Halsey, Francis Whiting. 1963. *The Old New York Frontier.* Port Washington, N.Y.: Ira J. Friedman.

Harris, Richard C. 1966. *The Seigneurial System in Early Canada.* Madison: University of Wisconsin Press.

Historic Savannah Foundation. 1968. *Historic Savannah.* Savannah: HSF.

Hubka, Thomas C. 1984. *Big House, Little House, Back House, Barn: The Connected Farm Buildings of New England.* Hanover, N.H.: University Press of New England.

Iseley, N. Jane, with Evangeline Davis. 1975. *Charleston Houses and Gardens.* Charleston: Preservation Society of Charleston.

Isham, Norman Morrison. 1928. *Early American Houses.* Boston: The Walpole Society.

Keith, Robert G. 1971. "Encomienda, Hacienda and Corregimiento in Spanish America: A Structural Analysis." *Hispanic American Historical Review,* Vol. 51, No. 3, pp. 431–46.

Kim, Sung Bok. 1978. *Landlord and Tenant in Colonial New York: Manorial Society, 1664–1775.* Chapel Hill: University of North Carolina Press.

Lanning, John H. 1935. *The Spanish Missions of Georgia.* Chapel Hill: University of North Carolina Press.

Lemmon, Kenneth. 1965. *The Golden Age of Plant Hunters.* London: Phoenix House.

Maccubin, Robert P., and Peter Martin. 1984. *British and American Gardens in the Eighteenth Century.* Williamsburg: Colonial Williamsburg Foundation.

McBride, George M. 1923. *The Land Systems of Mexico.* New York: American Geographical Society.

McCormick, Kathleen. 1990. "History Unearthed." *Historic Preservation,* Vol. 42, No. 4, pp. 58–61.

Meinig, Donald. 1971. *Southwest: Three Peoples in Geographic Change, 1600–1970.* New York: Oxford University Press.

———. 1986. *The Shaping of America: A Geographical Perspective on 500 Years of History,* Vol. 1, *Atlantic America, 1492–1800.* New Haven: Yale University Press.

Moorhead, Max L. 1975. *The Presidio-Bastion of the Spanish Borderlands.* Norman: University of Oklahoma Press.

Morrow, Baker H. 1987. *A Dictionary of Landscape Architecture.* Albuquerque: University of New Mexico Press.

Mountgomery, Robert. 1717. *A Discourse Concerning the Design'd Establishment of a New Colony to the South of Carolina . . .* London: n.p.

*Newton, Norman T. 1971. *Design on the Land: The Development of Landscape Architecture.* Cambridge, Mass.: Harvard University Press.

Powell, Sumner Chilton. 1963. *Puritan Village: The Formation of a New England Town.* Middletown, Conn., and Cincinatti, Ohio: Wesleyan University Press.

Rainbolt, John C. 1969. "The Absence of Towns in Seventeenth-Century Virginia." *Journal of Southern History,* Vol. 35, No. 3, pp. 343–60.

Reese, Trevor R., ed. 1974. *Our First Visit in America: Early Reports from the Colony of Georgia 1732–1740.* Savannah: Beehive Press.

*Reps, John W. 1965. *The Making of Urban America.* Princeton, N.J.: Princeton University Press.

———. 1972. *Tidewater Towns: City Planning in Colonial Virginia and Maryland.* Williamsburg: Colonial Williamsburg Foundation.

Riley, Edward M. 1950. "The Town Acts of Colonial Virginia." *Journal of Southern History,* Vol. 16, No. 3, pp. 306–23.

Root, R. R., and G. R. Forbes. 1911. "Notes Upon a Colonial Garden at Salem, Massachusetts." *Landscape Architecture,* Vol. 2, No. 1, pp. 16–20.

Sale, Edith T. 1930. *Historic Gardens of Virginia.* Richmond: William Byrd Press.

Sharp, Granville. 1794. "A General Plan for Laying Out Towns and Townships on the New Acquired Lands in the East Indies, America or Elsewhere." Map—no place or publisher.

Shurcliff, Arthur A. 1937. "The Gardens of the Governor's Palace Williamsburg, Virginia." *Landscape Architecture,* Vol. 27, No. 2, pp. 55–89.

Singleton, Theresa A. 1985. *The Archaeology of Slavery and Plantation Life.* Orlando, Fla.: Academic.

Snyder, Martin P. 1975. *City of Independence: Views of Philadelphia before 1800.* New York: Praeger.

South, Stanley A. 1967. " 'Russellborough': Two Royal Governors' Mansions at Brunswick Town." *North Carolina Historical Review,* Vol. 44, pp. 360–72.

Stanislawski, Dan. 1947. "Early Spanish Town Planning in the New World." *Geographical Review,* Vol. 37. No. 1, pp. 94–105.

Stilgoe, John. 1976. *Pattern on the Land: The Making of a Colonial Landscape: 1633–1800.* Ph.D. thesis. Cambridge, Mass.: Harvard University.

*———. 1982. *Common Landscape of America, 1580–1845.* New Haven: Yale University Press.

Stokes, Isaac N. P. 1967. *The Iconography of Manhattan Island,* Vol. I: *1498–1811.* New York: Arno.

Stoney, Samuel Gaillard. 1939. *Charleston: Azaleas and Old Bricks.* Boston: Houghton Mifflin.

Tate, Thad W. 1972. *The Negro in Eighteenth-Century Williamsburg.* Charlottesville: University Press of Virginia.

*Tobey, George B. 1973. *A History of Landscape Architecture: The Relationship of People to the Environment.* New York: Elsevier.

Trewartha, Glenn T. 1946. "Types of Rural Settlement in Colonial America." *Geographical Review,* Vol. 36, No. 4, pp. 568–96.

Ver Planck, Florence W., ed. 1946. *Old Salem Gardens.* Salem, Mass.: The Salem Garden Club.

Watson, John F. 1909. *Annals of Philadelphia and Pennsylvania in the Olden Time . . .* Philadelphia: Leary, Stuart and Company.

Williams, Dorothy Hunt. 1975. *Historic Virginia Gardens: Preservations by the Garden Club of Virginia.* Charlottesville: University Press of Virginia.

Winthrop, John. 1943. "Essay on the Ordering of Towns," in *Winthrop Paper,* Vol. III: *1631–1637.* Boston: Massachusetts Horticultural Society.

Zelinsky, Wilbur. 1973. *The Cultural Geography of the United States.* Englewood Cliffs, N.J.: Prentice-Hall.

Chapter 14

Adams, William Howard, ed. 1976. *The Eye of Thomas Jefferson.* Washington, D.C.: National Gallery of Art.

———. 1983. *Jefferson's Monticello.* New York: Abbeville.

American Society of Landscape Architects. 1932. *Colonial Gardens: The Landscape Architecture of George Washington's Time.* Washington, D.C.: U.S. George Washington Bicentennial Commission.

Bartram, William. 1980. *Travels.* Salt Lake City: Peregrine Smith.

Beiswanger, William L. 1984. "The Temple in the Garden: Thomas Jefferson's Vision of the Monticello Landscape," in *British and American Gardens in the*

Eighteenth Century. Robert P. Maccubbin and Peter Martin, eds. Williamsburg, Va.: Colonial Williamsburg Foundation.

Betts, Edwin Morris. 1944. *Thomas Jefferson's Garden Book, 1766–1824.* Philadelphia: The American Philosophical Society.

———, and B. Perkins Hazlehurst. 1971. *Thomas Jefferson's Flower Garden at Monticello.* Charlottesville: University Press of Virginia.

*Boas, George. 1961. *Romanticism in America.* New York: Russell & Russell.

Brogden, William A. 1983. "The Ferme Ornée and Changing Attitudes to Agricultural Improvement." Eighteenth Century Life, *Vol. 8, No. 1, pp. 39–40.*

Bruce, Philip Alexander. 1922. *History of the University of Virginia, 1819–1919,* Vol. 1. New York: Macmillan.

Bush-Brown, Louise and James Bush-Brown. 1929. *Portraits of Philadelphia Gardens.* Philadelphia: Dorrance.

Caemmerer, H. Paul. 1950. *The Life of Pierre Charles L'Enfant, Planner of the City Beautiful—The City of Washington.* Washington, D.C.: National Republic Publishing.

Carter, Edward C., II, ed. 1977. *The Virginia Journals of Benjamin Henry Latrobe, 1789–1795.* New Haven: Yale University Press.

De Forest, Elizabeth Kellam. 1983. *The Gardens and Grounds at Mount Vernon: How George Washington Planned and Planted Them.* Charlottesville: University Press of Virginia.

*Downing, Andrew Jackson. 1977. *A Treatise on the Theory and Practice of Landscape Gardening* (1875 edition). Little Compton, R.I.: Theophrastus.

Dougherty, J. P. 1974. "Baroque and Picturesque Motifs in L'Enfant's Design for the Federal City." *American Quarterly,* Vol. 26, No. 1, pp. 23–36.

Ellicott, Andrew. 1803. *The Journal of Andrew Ellicott.* Philadelphia: Thomas Dobson.

Elman, Robert. 1977. *First in the Field: America's Pioneering Naturalists.* New York: Mason/Charter.

Faris, John T. 1932. *Old Gardens in and About Philadelphia and Those Who Made Them.* Indianapolis: Bobbs-Merrill.

Fitzpatrick, John C., ed. 1925. *The Diaries of George Washington, 1748–1799.* Boston: Houghton Mifflin.

Goldman Lucien. 1973. *The Philosophy of the Enlightenment.* Cambridge: MIT Press.

Green, Constance M. 1976. *Washington: History of the Capitol, 1800–1950.* Princeton, N.J.: Princeton University Press.

*Gutheim, Frederick. 1977. *Worthy of the Nation: The History of Planning for the National Capital.* Washington, D.C.: Smithsonian Institution Press.

Heintzelman, Patricia L. 1972. *Elysium on the Schuykill: William Hamilton's Woodlands.* Master's thesis. Dover: University of Delaware.

Hislop, Codman. 1932. "The Ramée Plans." *Union Alumni Monthly,* Vol. 22, No. 2, pp. 48–53.

Hogan, Pendleton. 1987. *The Lawn: A Guide to Jefferson's University.* Charlottesville: University Press of Virginia.

Holland, Celia M. 1970. *Ellicott City, MD: Mill Town U.S.A.* Tuxedo, Md.: C. M. Holland.

Hugill, Peter J. 1986. "English Landscape Tastes in the United States." *Geographical Review,* Vol. 76, No. 4, pp. 408–23.

Kelso, William M. 1984. "Landscape Archaeology: A Key to Virginia's Cultivated Past," in *British and American Gardens in the Eighteenth Century.* Robert P. Maccubbin and Peter Martin, eds. Williamsburg, Va.: Colonial Williamsburg Foundation.

Kite, Elizabeth S., ed. 1929. *L'Enfant and Washington, 1791–1792.* Baltimore: Johns Hopkins Press.

Lambeth, William Alexander, and Warren H. Manning. 1913. *Thomas Jefferson as an Architect and a Designer of Landscapes.* Boston: Houghton Mifflin.

Langley, Batty. 1728. *New Principles of Gardening.* London.

Larrabee, Harold A. 1934. "Joseph Jacques Ramée and America's First Unified College Plan." Franco-American Pamphlet Series, No. 1. New York: American Society of the French Legion of Honor.

★Leighton, Ann. 1987. *American Gardens of the Nineteenth Century: "For comfort and affluence"* Amherst: University of Massachusetts Press.

Leone, Mark P. 1989a. "The Relationship between Archaeological Data and the Documentary Record: 18th Century Gardens in Annapolis, Maryland." *Historical Archaeology,* Vol. 22, pp. 29–35.

Leone, Mark, et al. 1989b. "Power Gardens of Annapolis." *Archaeology,* Vol. 42, No. 2, pp. 35–39 and 74–75.

Lossing, Benson J. 1871. *The Home of Washington.* New York: Virtue and Yorston.

Maccubbin, Robert P., and Peter Martin, eds. 1984. *British and American Gardens in the Eighteenth Century.* Williamsburg, Va.: Colonial Williamsburg Foundation.

Martin, Peter. 1991. *The Pleasure Gardens of Virginia: From Jamestown to Jefferson,* Princeton, N.J.: Princeton University Press.

Marx, Leo. 1974. "The American Revolution and the American Landscape." Washington, D.C.: American Enterprise Institute for Public Policy Research.

Massachusetts Subscriber. 1851. "The Rare Trees and Pleasure Grounds of Pennsylvania." *The Horticulturist,* Vol. 6, pp. 127–129.

Mayall, R. Newton. 1935. "Recording Historic American Landscape Architecture." *Landscape Architecture,* Vol. 26, No. 1, pp. 1–11.

———. 1952. "Country Seat of a Gentleman, 'The Vale.' " *Old Time New England,* Vol. 43, pp. 36–41.

Moore, Charles. 1901. "Augustus Brevoort Woodward—A Citizen of Two Cities." *Records of the Columbia Historical Society,* Vol. 4, pp. 114–127.

Nettles, Curtis P. 1962. *The Emergence of a National Economy: 1775–1815.* New York: Holt, Rinehart and Winston.

Nichols, Frederick Doveton, and Ralph E. Griswold. 1978. *Thomas Jefferson, Landscape Architect.* Charlottesville: University of Virginia Press.

Nye, Russel Blaine. 1960. *The Cultural Life of the New Nation: 1776–1830.* New York: Harper Row.

O'Neal, William B. 1976. *Pictorial History of the University of Virginia.* Charlottesville: University Press of Virginia.

Paca-Steele, Barbara. 1986. "The Mathematics of an Eighteenth-Century Wilderness Garden." *Journal of Garden History,* Vol. 6, No. 4, pp. 299–320.

★Peckham, Morse, ed. 1965. *Romanticism: The Culture of the Nineteenth Century.* New York: Braziller.

Peets, Elbert. 1928. "Famous Town Planners: III—L'Enfant." *Town Planning Review,* Vol. 18, No. 1, pp. 30–49.

Reps, John W. 1961. "Thomas Jefferson's Checkerboard Towns." *Journal of the Society of Architectural Historians,* Vol. 20, No. 3, pp. 108–14.

★———. 1967. *Monumental Washington.* Princeton, N.J.: Princeton University Press.

Savelle, Max. 1974. *Empires to Nations: Expansion in America 1713–1824.* Minneapolis: University of Minnesota Press.

Schwartz, Anne. 1986. "Jefferson's Garden Reborn." *Garden,* Vol. 6, No. 6, pp. 6–11.

Stetson, Sarah P. 1949. "William Hamilton and His 'Woodlands.' " *Pennsylvania Magazine of History and Biography,* Vol. 73, No. 1, pp. 26–33.

Vaughan, Samuel. 1976. "Plan of Mount Vernon." Mount Vernon: Mount Vernon Ladies' Association of the Union.

Washington, George. 1945. "George Washington's Map of His Mount Vernon." Mount Vernon: Mount Vernon Ladies' Association of the Union.

*Whiffen, Marcos, and Frederick Koeper. 1981. *American Architecture 1607–1976.* Cambridge: MIT Press.

Williams, Dorothy Hunt. 1975. *Historic Virginia Gardens.* Charlottesville: University Press of Virginia.

Williams, Morley Jeffers. 1938. "Washington's Changes at Mount Vernon Plantation." *Landscape Architecture,* Vol. 28, No. 2, pp. 63–73.

Woods, Mary N. 1985. "Thomas Jefferson and the University of Virginia: Planning the Academic Village." *Journal of the Society of Architectural Historians,* Vol. 44, No. 3, pp. 266–83.

Chapter 15

Agnew, Dwight L. 1941. "The Government Land Surveyor as a Pioneer." *Mississippi Valley Historical Review,* Vol. 28, No. 3, pp. 369–82.

Anderson, Patricia. 1984. *The Course of Empire: The Erie Canal and the New York Landscape, 1825–1875.* Rochester, N.Y.: Memorial Art Gallery of the University of Rochester.

Anonymous. 1869. "The Public Domain," in *Report of the Commissioner of Agriculture for the Year 1868.* Washington, D.C.: U.S. Government Printing Office.

Ayres, Harral. 1940. *The Great Trail of New England.* Boston: Meador.

Birkbeck, Morris. 1818. *Letters from Illinois.* Philadelphia: M. Carey and Son.

*Blanchard, Rufus. 1882. *History of Du Page County, Illinois.* Chicago: O. L. Baskin & Co.

Buckingham, James Silk. 1842. *The Eastern and Western States of America,* Vol. 2. London: Fisher, Son & Co.

Carstensen, Vernon R., ed. 1963. *The Public Lands: Studies in the History of the Public Domain.* Madison: University of Wisconsin Press.

Clawson, Marion. 1968. *The Land System of the United States.* Lincoln: University of Nebraska Press.

Collot, Victor. 1924. *A Journey in North America,* Vol. 1. Florence, Italy: O. Lange. (Reprint of 1826 publication by Arthur Bertrand, Paris.)

Cronon, William. 1983. *Changes in the Land: Indians, Colonists, and the Ecology of New England.* New York: Hill and Wang.

Dick, Everett. 1937. *The Sod-House Frontier, 1854–1890.* New York: D. Appleton-Century.

Durrenberger, Joseph. 1968. *Turnpikes.* Cos Cob, Conn.: John E. Edwards.

Faragher, John Mack. 1986. *Sugar Creek: Life on the Illinois Prairie.* New Haven: Yale University Press.

Flint, Timothy. 1826. *Recollections of the Last Ten Years in the Valley of the Mississippi.* Boston: Cummings, Hilliard and Company.

Franzwa, Gregory M. 1989. *Maps of the Santa Fe Trail.* St. Louis: Patrice Press.

*Friesen, Gerald. 1984. *The Canadian Prairies: A History.* Lincoln: University of Nebraska Press.

Gates, Paul Wallace. 1968. *History of Public Land Development.* Washington, D.C.: Public Land Review Commission. See NUC 1968–72, Vol. 33, p. 18.

George, Henry. 1871. *Our Land and Land Policy, National and State.* San Francisco: White & Bauer.

Haites, Erik F., James Mak, and Gary M. Walton. 1975. *Western River Transportation: The Era of Early Internal Development, 1810–1860.* Baltimore: Johns Hopkins University Press.

*Harris, Marshall. 1953. *Origin of the Land Tenure System in the United States.* Ames: Iowa State College Press.

Harris, R. Cole. 1987. *Historical Atlas of Canada,* Vol. 1. Toronto: University of Toronto Press.

Hibbard, Benjamin Horace. 1924. *A History of the Public Land Policies.* New York: Macmillan.

Hornbeck, David. 1978. "Land Tenure and Rancho Expansion in Alta California, 1784–1846." *Journal of Historical Geography,* Vol. 4, No. 4, pp. 371–90.

Hulbert, Archer. 1902–5. *Historic Highways of America,* Vols. 6, 9, and 10. Cleveland: A. H. Clark Company.

———. 1920. *The Paths of Inland Commerce.* New Haven: Yale University Press.

Johnson, Hildegard Binder. 1947. "Rational and Ecological Aspects of the Quarter Section: An Example from Minnesota." *Geographical Review,* Vol. 47, No. 3, pp. 330–48.

Jordan, Philip. 1948. *The National Road.* Indianapolis: Bobbs-Merrill.

Jordan, Terry G., and Matti Kaups. 1989. *The American Backwoods Frontier.* Baltimore: Johns Hopkins University Press.

Limerick, Patricia Nelson. 1987. *The Legacy of Conquest: The Unbroken Past of the American West.* New York: W. W. Norton.

*Marx, Leo. 1964. *The Machine in the Garden: Technology and the Pastoral Ideal in America.* New York: Oxford University Press.

Melish, John. 1815. *Traveller's Directory through the United States.* Philadelphia: G. Palmer.

Meyer, Balthasar Henry, and Caroline E. MacGill. 1917. *History of Transportation in the United States Before 1860.* Washington, D.C.: Carnegie Institution of Washington.

*Nash, Roderick. 1967. *Wilderness and the American Mind.* New Haven: Yale University Press.

National Research Council. 1956. "Rural Settlement Patterns in the U.S. as Illustrated on One Hundred Topographic Quadrangle Maps." Washington, D.C.: National Academy of Science—National Research Council. Publication 380.

Noble, Vergil E. 1986. "History and Archaeology along the I and M Canal." *Historic Illinois,* Vol. 9, No. 4, pp. 10–15.

Opie, John. 1986. "The American Grasslands: Two Centuries of Perceptions." *American Land Forum Magazine,* Summer, pp. 33–45.

———. 1987. *The Law of the Land: Two Hundred Years of American Farmland Policy.* Lincoln: University of Nebraska Press.

Powell, Lyman. 1901. *Historic Towns of the Western States.* New York: G. P. Putnam.

*Rose, Albert C. 1976. *Historic American Roads: From Frontier Trails to Superhighways.* New York: Crown.

Saxbe, William B., Jr. 1987. "Battle of the Transits: The Toledo War." *Timeline* (Journal of the Ohio Historical Society), Vol. 4, No. 5, pp. 2–11.

Searight, Thomas B. 1971. *The Old Pike: An Illustrated Narrative of the National Road.* Orange, Va.: Green Tree Press (revised reprint of 1894 publication).

Shaw, Ronald. 1966. *Erie Water West: A History of the Erie Canal, 1792–1854.* Lexington: University of Kentucky Press.

*Smith, Henry Nash. 1975. *Virgin Land.* Cambridge: Harvard University Press.

Speed, Thomas. 1886. *The Wilderness Road, a Description of the Routes of Travel . . .* Louisville: Filson Club Publications.

Thomson, Don W. 1966. *Men and Meridians: The History of Surveying and Mapping in Canada.* Ottawa: Information Canada.

Thrower, Norman J. W. 1966. *Original Survey and Land Subdivision*. Chicago: Rand McNally.

Treat, Payson Jackson. 1910. *The National Land System*. New York: E. B. Treat & Co.

Webster, Pelatian. 1969. "An Essay on the Value and Extent of Our Western Unlocated Lands . . ." in *Political Essays on the Nature and Operation of Money, Public Finances and Other Subjects*. New York: Burt Franklin.

Whitford, N. E. 1906. *History of the Canal System of New York*. Albany: Brandow Printing Company.

Woods, John. 1904–7. "Two Years Residence in the Settlement on the English Prairie," in *Early Western Travels*, Vol. 10. R. G. Thwaites, ed. Cleveland: A. H. Clark Comp.

Wyckoff, William. 1988. *The Developer's Frontier: The Making of the Western New York Landscape*. New Haven: Yale University Press.

Chapter 16

Affleck, Thomas. 1860. *Southern Rural Almanac and Plantation and Garden Calendar for 1860*. New Orleans: David Felt.

Allibone, S. Austin. 1856. "A Biographical Notice, and An Account of the Works, of Andrew J. Downing," in *The Yearbook of Agriculture . . . For 1855 and 1856*, David A. Wells, ed. Philadelphia: Childs & Peterson.

Anonymous. 1828. "Parmentier's Horticultural Garden." *New England Farmer*, Vol. 7, pp. 82–85.

———. 1840. "Report of the Board of Managers to the Proprietors and Lot-Holders of Green Mount Cemetery." Baltimore: Woods and Crane.

———. 1841. "Review of 'A Treatise on the Theory and Practice of Landscape Gardening . . .'" *North American Review*, Vol. 53, [No. 1], pp. 258–62.

———. 1844. "Guide to Laurel Hill Cemetery, Near Philadelphia." Philadelphia: G. Sherman.

———. 1849a. "Annual Report to the Lot Holders of the Cemetery of Spring Grove, and the Public 1848–1849." Cincinnati: Gazette Office.

———. 1849b. "Report of the Trustees of Green Lawn Cemetery." Columbus: Ohio State Journal Print.

———. 1852. *Rules and Regulations of the Cemetery of the Evergreens*. New York: Wm. C. Bryant & Co.

———. 1860. *The History, Incorporation, Rules and Regulations of Oakwood Cemetery at Syracuse, N.Y. . . .* Syracuse: J. G. K. Truair & Company, Printers.

Barry, Patrick. 1853a. "The Home of the Late A. J. Downing." *The Horticulturist*, Vol. 8, pp. 20–27.

———. 1853b. "Rural Cemeteries." *The Horticulturist*, Vol. 8, pp. 297–300.

Brooke, C. E. 1973. "National Register of Historic Places Inventory—Nomination Form for Mt. Hope-Highland Park Historic District." Albany, N.Y.: NYS Division for Historic Preservation.

Chadwick, Edwin. 1845. "A Report on the Results of a Special Inquiry into the Practice of Interment in Towns." Philadelphia: C. Sherman.

Christian, W. Asbury. 1900. *Lynchburg and Its People*. Lynchburg, Va.: J. P. Bell Company.

Cleaveland, Nehemiah. 1853. *Hints Concerning Greenwood; Its Monuments and Improvements*. New York: Pudney & Russell.

Coffin, John G. 1823. "Remarks on the Dangers and Duties of Sepulture or Security for the Living, with Respect and Repose for the Dead." Boston: Phelps and Farnharm.

Commission on Chicago Historical and Architectural Landmarks. 1982. "Oak Woods Cemetery." Chicago: The Commission.

Cook, Clarence. 1852. "The Late A. J. Downing." *The New York Quarterly,* Vol. 1, pp. 367–82.

Curtis, George W. 1853. "Memoir," in *Rural Essays.* (See under Downing, 1974.)

Dall, Caroline. 1898. "In Memoriam: Alexander Wadsworth." Washington, D.C.: n.p.

Dallett, Francis J. 1959. "John Notman, Architect." *Princeton University Library Chronicle,* Vol. 20, No. 3, pp. 127–39.

Daniels, Howard. 1855. "Advertisement." *The Horticulturist,* Vol. 10, p. 148.

———. 1860a. "A Public Park for Baltimore." *The Horticulturist,* Vol. 15, pp. 435–38.

———. 1860b. "1st Annual Report of the Landscape Gardener." *Baltimore Park Commission Annual Report.* n.p.

Daniels, Howard, and George R. Parsons. 1854. "Plan of Brookside Cemetery." Watertown, N.Y.: n.p.

Davison, Carolina V. 1934. "Maximilian Godefroy." *Maryland Historical Magazine,* Vol. 29, pp. 175–211.

Downing, Andrew Jackson. 1841. *A Treatise on the Theory and Practice of Landscape Gardening.* New York: Wiley and Putnam.

———. 1845. *Fruits and Fruit Trees of America.* New York: Wiley and Putnam.

———. 1849a. "On the Improvement of Country Villages." *The Horticulturist.* Vol. 3, p. 545.

———. 1849b. "Public Cemeteries and Public Gardens." *The Horticulturist,* Vol. 4, pp. 9–12.

———. 1850. *The Architecture of Country Houses.* New York: D. Appleton.

———. 1851. "Explanation Accompanying His Plan for Improving the Public Ground of the City of Washington." *Records of the Commissioners of Public Buildings—Letters Received.* Vol. 37, Letter 3158½.

———. 1853. *Rural Essays.* New York: G. P. Putnam and Company.

———. 1858a. "The New York Park." *Documents of the Board of Commissioners of the Central Park for the Year Ending April 30, 1858.* New York: Wm. C. Bryant & Co.

———. 1858b. "Downing's Landscape Gardening." *The Horticulturist,* Vol. 8 (New Series), pp. 411–13.

———. 1873. *Cottage Residences.* New York: Wiley.

———. 1875. *A Treatise on the Theory and Practice of Landscape Gardening,* New York: Orange Judd and Company.

———. 1974. *Rural Essays.* New York: Da Capo.

Duncan, Frances. 1907. "Magnolia Gardens." *The Century Magazine,* Vol. 74, No. 4, pp. 513–19.

Earnshaw, J., and Strauch, A. N.d. Plan for "Subdivision of the Blachly Farm Adjoining Avondale." N.p.

Ellwanger and Barry Papers, Department of Rare Books and Special Collections, University of Rochester Library.

Flagg, Wilson. 1853. "Rural Cemeteries." *Hovey's Horticulture,* Vol. 19, pp. 486–98.

Frothingham, Octavius B. 1876. *Transcendentalism in New England: A History.* New York: G. P. Putnam.

Gobrecht, Larry T. 1982. "National Register of Historic Places Inventory—Nomination Form for Green Wood Cemetery." Albany, NY: Historic Preservation Field Services Bureau.

Grieff, Constance M. 1979. *John Notman, Architect 1810–1865.* Philadelphia: The Athenaeum.

Greve, Charles T. 1904. *Centennial History of Cincinnati and Representative Citizens,* Vol. 1. Chicago: Biographical Publishing Company.

Grosso, Diane Holahan. 1982. "From the Genesee to the World." *The University of Rochester Library Bulletin,* Vol. 35, No. 1, pp. 2–25.

Habenstein, Robert W. 1955. *The History of American Funeral Directing.* Milwaukee: Bulfin Printers.

Haley, Jacquetta M. 1988. *Pleasure Grounds: Andrew Jackson Downing and Montgomery Place.* Tarrytown, N.Y.: Sleepy Hollow Press.

Henderson, Peter. 1869. *Practical Floriculture.* New York: Orange Judd and Company.

Howat, John K. 1972. *The Hudson River and its Painters.* New York: Viking.

★Leighton, Ann. 1987. *American Gardens of the Nineteenth Century: "For Comfort and Affluence."* Amherst: University of Massachusetts Press.

Linden, Blanche M. G. 1981. *Death and the Garden; The Cult of the Melancholy and the "Rural" Cemetery.* Ph.D. thesis. Cambridge, Mass.: Harvard University.

Linden-Ward, Blanche. 1989. *Silent City on a Hill: Landscapes of Memory and Boston's Mount Auburn Cemetery.* Columbus: Ohio State University Press.

———, and Alan Ward. 1985. "Spring Grove: The Role of the Rural Cemetery in American Landscape Design." *Landscape Architecture,* Vol. 75, No. 5, pp. 126–31, 140.

Lossing, Benson J. 1867. *Vassar College and Its Founder.* New York: C. A. Alvord.

Major, Judith K. 1986. "The Downing Letters." *Landscape Architecture,* Vol. 76, No. 1, pp. 50–57.

Mann, William. 1990. "The Hudson River Region: The Early Nineteenth-Century Source of America's Love of Natural Landscape Scenery." *CELA 89: Proceedings,* Sara Katherine Williams and Robert R. Grist, eds. Washington, D.C.: Landscape Architecture Foundation.

McKelvey, Blake. 1940. "The Flower City: Center of Nurseries and Fruit Orchards." *Rochester Historical Society Publications,* Vol. 18, Part II, pp. 121–69.

Mead, Peter B. 1861. "Another Day's Ride." *The Horticulturist,* Vol. 16, pp. 455–59.

Parmentier, André. 1828. "Landscapes and Picturesque Gardens," in *The New American Gardener.* Thomas G. Fessenden, ed. Boston: J. B. Russell.

Rotundo, Barbara. 1973. "The Rural Cemetery Movement." *Essex Institute Historical Collections,* Vol. 109, pp. 231–40.

S., J. W. 1832. "Parmentier's Garden, near Brooklyn." *Gardener's Magazine,* Vol. 8, pp. 70–72.

Scott, Mary W., and Louise F. Catterall. 1957. *Virginia's Capitol Square.* Richmond: The Valentine Museum.

Seward, W. H. Papers, Department of Rare Books and Special Collections, University of Rochester Library.

Shoken, Fred. 1979. "National Register of Historic Places Inventory—Nomination Form for Green Mount Cemetery." Baltimore: Commission for Historical and Architectural Preservation.

Schuyler, David P. 1979. *Public Landscapes and American Urban Culture 1800–1870: Rural Cemeteries, City Parks, and Suburbs.* Ph.D. thesis. New York: Columbia University.

———. 1986. *The New American Landscape.* Baltimore: Johns Hopkins University Press.

Sloane, David C. 1984. *Living and the Dead: New York State Cemetery Landscapes as Reflections of a Changing American Culture to 1949.* Ph.D. thesis. Syracuse: University of Syracuse.

———. 1991. *The Last Great Necessity: Cemeteries in American History.* Baltimore: Johns Hopkins University Press.

Smith, J. Jay. 1846. *Designs for Monuments and Mural Tables: Adapted to Rural Cemeteries, Church Yards, Churches and Chapels.* New York: Bartlett & Welford.

———. 1856. "The Downing Monument." *The Horticulturist,* Vol. 11, pp. 489–91.

———. 1892. *Recollections of John Jay Smith.* Philadelphia: J. B. Lippincott.

Smith, R. A. 1852. *Smith's Illustrated Guide to and Through Laurel Hill Cemetery.* Philadelphia: Willis P. Hazard.

Spingarn, J. E. 1938. "Henry Winthrop Sargent and the Landscape Tradition at Wodenthe." *Landscape Architecture,* Vol. 29, No. 1, pp. 24–39.

Stetson, Sarah. 1949. "André Parmentier: Little Known Pioneer in American Landscape Architecture." *Landscape Architecture,* Vol. 39, No. 4, pp. 184–86.

Strauch, Adolph. 1869. *Spring Grove Cemetery: Its History and Improvements with Observations on Ancient and Modern Places.* Cincinnati: Robert Clarke & Co.

———, and Henry Earnshaw. 1857. "Reports of the Landscape Gardener and the Superintendent." *The Cincinnati Cemetery of Spring Grove: Report for 1857.* Cincinnati: C. F. Bradley and Company.

Tatum, George B. 1949. "Andrew Jackson Downing: Arbiter of American Taste 1815–1852." Ph.D. thesis. Princeton, N.J.: Princeton University.

———, and Elisabeth Blair Macdougall, eds. 1989. *Dumbarton Oaks Colloquium on the History of Landscape Architecture, XI: Prophet with Honor; The Career of Andrew Jackson Downing, 1815–1852.* Philadelphia: The Athenaeum.

Toole, Robert M. 1989. "Springside: A. J. Downing's Only Extant Garden." *Journal of Garden History,* Vol. 9, No. 1, pp. 20–39.

Wadsworth, Alexander. 1839. "Plan of Harmony Grove Cemetery, Boston." B. W. Bouve's Litho.

Walter, Cornelia W. 1847. *Mount Auburn Illustrated.* New York: R. Martin.

Warminski, Margaret. 1989. "National Register of Historic Places Registration Form for Highland Park Cemetery." Florence, Ky.: North Kentucky Area Development District.

White, William N. 1856. *Gardening for the South; or the Kitchen and Fruit Garden with the Best Methods for their Cultivation . . .* New York: C. M. Saxton and Company.

Zellie, Carole. 1982. "An Investigation of Nineteenth Century Surveyors and Land Planners in Massachusetts: 1830–1860." *Landscape Journal,* Vol. 1, No. 2, pp. 96–103.

Chapter 17

*Benevolo, Leonardo. 1967. *The Origins of Modern Town Planning.* Cambridge, Mass.: MIT Press.

Bestor, Arthur. 1950. *Backwoods Utopia: The Sectarian and Owenite Phases of Communitarian Socialism in America: 1663–1829.* Philadelphia: University of Pennsylvania Press.

Bremer, Fredrika. 1864. *The Homes of the New World: Impressions of America.* New York: Harper Brothers.

Considerant, V[ictor]. 1846. *Description du Phalanstère et Considerations Sociales sur l'Architecture.* Paris: Librairie Societaire.

Cook, Philip L. 1970. "Zion City, Illinois: John Alexander Dowie's Theocracy." Zion: Zion Historical Society.

Dallas, Will. 1910. "The Toon O'Maxwell." *Canadian Magazine,* February 10, p. 328.

Emlem, Robert P. 1987. *Shaker Village Views.* Hanover, N.H.: University Press of New England.

Everett, Edward. 1823. "The Shakers." *North American Review,* Vol. 16, pp. 76–102.

Flanders, Robert Bruce. 1965. *Nauvoo: Kingdom on the Mississippi.* Urbana: University of Illinois Press.

Fourier, Charles. 1971. *Design for Utopia: Selected Writings of Charles Fourier.* New York: Schocken.

Fox, Feramorz Young. 1932. *The Mormon Land System: A Study of the Settlement and Utilization of Land Under Direction of the Mormon Church.* Ph.D. thesis. Evanston, Ill.: Northwestern University.

Hammond, William J., and Margaret F. Hammond. 1958. *La Reunion, a French Settlement in Texas.* Dallas: Royal.

Hayden, Dolores. 1976. *Seven American Utopias: The Architecture of Communitarian Socialism, 1790–1975.* Cambridge, Mass.: MIT Press.

Holloway, Mark. 1966. *Heavens on Earth.* New York: Dover.

Jackson, Richard H. 1978. "Mormon Perception and Settlement." *Annals of the Association of American Geographers,* Vol. 68, No. 3, pp. 317–34.

Kirchmann, George. 1979. "Unsettled Utopias: The North American Phalanx and the Raritan Bay Union." *New Jersey History,* Vol. 97, No. 1, pp. 25–36.

Koster, Donald N. 1975. *Transcendentalism in America.* Boston: Twayne.

Lamson, David R. 1848. *Two Years' Experience Among the Shakers . . .* West Boylston, Mass.: David R. Lamson.

Lifchez, Raymond. 1976. "Inspired Planning: Mormon and Fourierist Communities in the Nineteenth Century." *Landscape,* Vol. 20, No. 3, pp. 29–35.

Meinig, Donald W. 1965. "The Mormon Culture Region: Strategies and Patterns in the Geography of the American West, 1847–1964." *Annals of the Association of American Geographers,* Vol. 55, pp. 191–220.

Merk, Frederick. 1978. *History of the Westward Movement.* New York: Knopf.

Noyes, John Humphrey. 1966. *The History of American Socialism.* New York: Dover.

Olmsted, Frederick Law. 1852. "The Phalanstery and the Planansterians." *New York Tribune,* July 24.

Shambaugh, Bertha M. H. 1971. *Amana That Was and Amana That Is.* New York: Benjamin Blom.

Swan, Norma Lippincott, ed. 1975 (originally published 1853). *Exposé of the Conditions and Progress of the North American Phalanx: In Reply to the Inquiries of Horace Greeley.* Philadelphia: Porcupine Press.

Swift, Lindsay. 1900. *Brook Farm: Its Members, Scholars, and Visitors.* New York: Macmillan.

Webber, Everett. 1959. *Escape to Utopia: The Communal Movement in America,* New York: Hastings House.

Wilson, Lewis G. N.d. "Hopedale and Its Founder." Hopedale, Mass.: unattributed reprint.

Chapter 18

Alexopoulos, John. 1983. *Nineteenth Century Parks of Hartford: A Legacy to the Nation.* Hartford, Conn.: Hartford Architecture Conservancy.

Anonymous. N.d. *History of the Park System of Quincy, Illinois; 1888–1917.* n.p.

———. 1858. "Central Park Board." *New York Times,* May 27, p. 8.

———. 1871a. *The Central Park Explained and Illustrated.* New York: Devlin and Company.

———. 1871b. "Graceland Cemetery." Unidentified pamphlet. Nourse Collection, Lancaster, Massachusetts, Public Library.

———. 1874. *A Handbook of Prospect Park.* New York: E. B. Tripp.

———. 1890. "Jeannette Park, New York." *Garden and Forest,* Vol. 3, pp. 498–99.

———. 1891. "Public Gardens." *Garden and Forest,* Vol. 4, No. 42, pp. 529–30.

———. 1900. *A History and Description of the Boston Metropolitan Parks.* Boston: Wright and Potter Printing Company.

————. 1903. *Cedar Hill Cemetery, Hartford, Connecticut, 1863–1903*. Hartford, Conn.: Cedar Hill Cemetery.

————. 1952. "Olmsted Firms." One-page list in the Library of the Harvard Graduate School of Design.

"Ars Longa." 1858. "Description of the Design for Laying out the Central Park." New York: Wm. C. Bryant & Co.

Bain, David. 1985. "William Mundie, Landscape Gardener." *Journal of Garden History,* Vol. 5, No. 3, pp. 298–308.

Behnke, William A., and Associates. 1981. *Rockefeller Park.* Unpublished report.

★Blackmar, Frank W. 1890. *The History of Federal and State Aid to Higher Education.* Washington, D.C.: U.S. Government Printing Office.

Brooklyn Park Commission. 1873. *Annual Reports, 1861–1873.* Brooklyn, N.Y.

Brunner, Arnold W., Frederick Law Olmsted, Jr., and Bion J. Arnold. 1911. *A City Plan for Rochester.* Rochester: Rochester Civic Improvement Company.

Central Park Commission. 1858a. "Description of Designs for Improvement of Central Park." New York: Commissioners of the Central Park.

————. 1858b. Minutes of Proceedings. New York: Wm. C. Bryant & Co.

————. 1858c. "Document No. 5," quoted in *Forty Years of Landscape Architecture: Central Park.* Frederick Law Olmsted, Jr., and Theodora Kimball, eds., 1928.

————. 1859. Second Annual Report. New York: Wm. C. Bryant & Co.

Clary, Raymond H. 1984. *The Making of Golden Gate Park, The Early Years: 1865–1906.* San Francisco: Don't Call it Frisco Press.

Cleveland, H. W. S. 1882. *The Culture and Management of Our Native Forests.* Springfield, Ill.: H. W. Rokker.

————. 1885. *Public Parks, Radial Avenues, and Boulevards: Outline Plan of a Park System for the City of St. Paul.* St. Paul: Globe Job Office.

Commissioners of Forest Park. 1876. *Report of the Commissioners of Forest Park—1875.* Saint Louis: Jno. J. Daly, Printer.

Cranz, Galen. 1982. *The Politics of Park Design.* Cambridge, Mass.: MIT Press.

Daniels, Howard. 1858. "Plan for Central Park." Unpublished report in Codman Collection, Boston Public Library.

Devlin and Company. 1871. *The Central Park Explained and Illustrated.* New York: Devlin and Company.

Downing, Andrew Jackson. 1851. "The New-York Park." *The Horticulturist,* Vol. 6, pp. 345–49.

Dumont, Donna, Galen Cranz, and Mary Dumont. 1981. "San Francisco's Park Policy in the Nineteenth Century: Goals versus Outcomes." Working Paper 342, Institute of Urban and Regional Development, University of California, Berkeley.

Eliot, Charles. 1893. "A Report upon the Opportunities for Public Open Spaces in the Metropolitan District of Boston." Boston: Wright and Potter Printing.

★Eliot, Charles W. 1924. *Charles Eliot, Landscape Architect.* Cambridge, Mass.: Harvard University Press.

★Fein, Albert. 1972. *Frederick Law Olmsted and the American Environmental Tradition.* New York: Braziller.

Fisher, Irving D. 1986. *Frederick Law Olmsted and the City Planning Movement in the United States.* Ann Arbor: UMI Research Press.

Follen, Charles. 1859. *Suggestions on Landscape Gardening.* Boston: Phillips, Sampson and Co.

Folwell, William Watts. Papers. Minneapolis: University of Minnesota.

French, Henry Flagg. 1859. *Farm Drainage.* New York: A. O. Moore & Co.

Graff, M. M. 1985. *Central Park and Prospect Park: A New Perspective.* New York: Greensward Foundation.

Graef, H. A. 1865. *Explanatory Remarks to a Sectional Plan of Prospect Park.* Brooklyn, N.Y.: Rome Brothers.

Gray, James. 1951. *The University of Minnesota 1851–1951.* Minneapolis: University of Minnesota Press.

H., E. G. 1908. "The Man Who Made St. Louis Beautiful." *St. Louis Daily Globe-Democrat,* Vol. 34, No. 26, p. 7, Magazine.

Hall, A. Oakley. N.d. "The Birth of Central Park." Unpublished report. Philadelphia: Historical Society of Pennsylvania.

Hall, William Hammond. 1889. "Irrigation in California." *The National Geographic Magazine,* Vol. 1, No. 4, pp. 277–90.

Harvey, Robert R. 1977. "Documenting a Victorian Landscape in the Midwest." *APT Bulletin,* Vol. 9, No. 3, pp. 73–99.

Hovey, C. M. 1860. "New York Central Park." *The Magazine of Horticulture,* Vol. 26, No. 1, Fourth Series, pp. 529–34.

Jackson, John B. 1972. *American Space: The Centennial Years.* New York: Norton.

Kern, Maximilian G. 1884. *Rural Taste in Western Towns and Country Districts in its Relation to the Principles of Landscape Gardening.* Columbia, Mo.: Herald Printing House.

Kessler, George E. 1893. "Report of the Engineer." *Report of the Board of Park and Boulevard Commissioners of Kansas City, MO.* Kansas City: Hudson-Kimberly Publishing Company.

Lay, Charles Downing. 1930. "Some Opinions About Landscape Design." *Landscape Architecture,* Vol. 20, No. 4, pp. 308–10.

Leavitt, Charles Wellford. 1926. "A Half Century of Landscape Architecture." *American Architect,* Vol. 129, No. 2488, pp. 61–64.

Leech, Robert W. 1987. "The First Dilemma." *Landscape Architecture,* Vol. 77, No. 1, pp. 62–65.

Lettieri, Linda Hittle. 1986. "Updating Stanford's Inner Quad." *Landscape Architecture,* Vol. 76, No. 6, pp. 68–71.

Longstreth, Richard. 1985. "From Farm to Campus." *Winterthur Portfolio,* Vol. 20, No. 2/3, pp. 149–79.

Manning, Warren. 1898. "Landscape Phase of the University of California Plan." Boston: n.p.

Marsh, George Perkins. 1965. *Man and Nature.* Cambridge, Mass.: Harvard University Press.

McKelvey, Blake. 1949. "An Historical View of Rochester's Parks and Playgrounds." *Rochester History,* Vol. 11, No. 1, pp. 1–24.

———. 1988. *A Growing Legacy: An Illustrated History of Rochester's Parks.* Rochester: City of Rochester.

★McLaughlin, Charles Capen, editor in chief. 1977–90. *The Papers of Frederick Law Olmsted,* Vols. 1–5. Baltimore: Johns Hopkins University Press.

★McPeck, Eleanor M., Keith Morgan, and Cynthia Zaitzevsky. 1983. *Olmsted in Massachusetts: The Public Legacy.* Brookline: Massachusetts Association for Olmsted Parks.

Meason, Gilbert L. 1828. *On the Landscape Architecture of the Great Painters of Italy.* London: D. Jacques.

Mitchell, Donald G. 1869. *Pictures of Edgewood in a Series of Photographs.* New York: Charles Scribner and Company.

Mountain Grove Cemetery Association. 1865. *Organization of Mountain Grove Cemetery Association.* San Francisco: M. D. Carr & Company.

Nolen, John. 1905. "Frederick Law Olmsted and His Work: II: The Terraces and Landscape Work of the United States Capitol at Washington." *House and Garden,* Vol. 9, March, pp. 117–28.

Olmsted Brothers. 1904. *Report Upon the Development of Public Grounds for Greater Baltimore.* Baltimore: The Lord Baltimore Press.

★Olmsted, Frederick Law. Papers [cited as FLO Papers]. Library of Congress, Washington, D.C.

——. 1866a. *A Few Things to be Thought of Before Proceeding to Plan Buildings for the National Agricultural Colleges.* New York: The American News Company.

——. 1866b. "The Project for the Improvement of the College Property." *Report Upon a Projected Improvment of the Estate of the College of California.* New York: Wm. C. Bryant & Co.

——. 1870. *Public Parks and the Enlargement of Towns.* Cambridge, Mass.: American Social Science Association.

——. 1886. *Notes on the Plan of Franklin Park and Related Matters.* Boston: Park Department.

——, Elisha Hams, J. M. Trowbridge, and H. H. Richardson. 1871. *Report of a Preliminary Scheme of Improvements.* New York: Staten Island Improvement Commission.

Olmsted, Frederick Law, and Calvert Vaux. 1868. "Preliminary Report in Regard to a Plan of Public Pleasure Grounds for the City of San Francisco," New York: Wm. C. Bryant & Co.

Olmsted, Frederick, and J. B. Harrison. 1889. *Observations on the Treatment of Public Plantations.* Boston: T. R. Marvin & Sons.

Olmsted, Frederick Law, and Company. 1890. "General Plan of Genesee Valley Park." City of Rochester Vault.

——. 1893. "General Plan for Seneca Park." City of Rochester Vault.

[Olmsted, Frederick Law, and Calvert Vaux—author given as "Greensward."]. 1858. "Description of a Plan for the Improvement of the Central Park." New York: John F. Trow.

Olmsted, Frederick Law, Jr., ed. 1914. "The Beginning of Central Park: A Ragment of Autobiography." *Nineteenth Annual Report, 1914, Of the American Scenic and Historic Preservation Society.* Albany: J. B. Lyon.

——. 1921. Letter to C. Bowyer Vaux, February 18. New York Public Library.

★Olmsted, Frederick Law, Jr., and Theodora Kimball, eds. 1928. *Forty Years of Landscape Architecture: Central Park.* New York: G. P. Putnam.

Olmsted, John C. 1908. "The Boston Park System," in *Transactions of the American Society of Landscape Architects, 1899–1908,* pp. 42–55. Harrisburg, Pa.: J. Horace McFarland and Co.

Olmsted, Olmsted, and Eliot. 1894. "General Plan for Subdividing into Roads and Building Lots the Property of the Newton Boulevard Syndicate . . ." Codman Collection, Boston Public Library.

Parsons, Samuel. 1906. "The Art of Landscape Gardening." *The Outlook,* Vol. 84, pp. 223–32.

——. 1910. *Landscape Gardening Studies.* New York: John Lane Company.

Partridge, Loren W. 1978. *John Howard Galen and the Berkeley Campus: Beaux-Arts Architecture in the "Athens of the West."* Berkeley: Berkeley Architectural Heritage Association.

Pentecost, George F. 1902. "Landscape Architecture." *Inland Architect and News Record,* Vol. 39, No. 5, pp. 39–41.

Pilat, Ignaz Anton. Papers, Rare Book Room, New York Public Library.

Pond, Bremer W. 1950. "Fifty Years in Retrospect." *Landscape Architecture,* Vol. 40, No. 2, pp. 59–60.

Rauch, John H. 1869. *Public Parks: Their Effects upon the Moral, Physical and Sanitary Condition of the Inhabitants of Large Cities.* Chicago: S. C. Griggs & Co.

Reps, John W. 1989. *Saint Louis Illustrated.* Columbia: University of Missouri Press.

Rochester Park Commission. 1899. *Report of the Board of Park Commissioners of the City of Rochester, NY, 1888 to 1898.* Rochester: Union and Advertiser Press.

Rogers, Elizabeth Barlow. 1987. *Rebuilding Central Park: A Management and Restoration Plan.* Cambridge, Mass.: MIT Press.

*Roper, Laura Wood. 1973. FLO: A Biography of Frederick Law Olmsted. Baltimore: Johns Hopkins University Press.

Runion, James B. 1869. *Out of Town.* Chicago: The Western News Co.

*Schermerhorn, Richard, Jr. 1920. "Nathan Franklin Barrett Landscape Architect." *Landscape Architecture,* Vol. 10, No. 3, pp. 108–13.

*Schuyler, David. 1978. *Victorian Landscape Gardening: A Facsimilie of Jacob Weidenmann's "Beautifying Country Homes."* Watkins Glen, N.Y.: American Life Foundation.

Scott, Frank J. 1869. *Palaces of America.* Boston: The Radical.

Shinn, Charles H. 1879. *Pacific Rural Handbook.* San Francisco: Dewey and Company.

———. 1914. "Roadside Planting." N.p.: Garden Club of America.

Simonds, Ossian C. [c. 1910.] "What Trees and Shrubs Should We Plant in Cemeteries." *Cemetery Handbook.* Chicago: Allied Arts Publishing Company.

———. 1932. "Nature as the Great Teacher in Landscape Gardening." *Landscape Architecture,* Vol. 22, No. 2, pp. 100–108.

Simpson, Jeffrey, and Mary Ellen W. Hern, eds. 1981. *Art of the Olmsted Landscape: His Works in New York City.* New York: New York City Landmarks Preservation Commission.

Spreiregen, Paul D., ed. 1968. "Central Park," in *On the Art of Designing Cities: Selected Essays of Elbert Peets.* Cambridge, Mass.: MIT Press.

Stewart, Ian R. 1968. "Parks, Progressivism, and Planning: Charles Eliot in Metropolitan Context." *Landscape Architecture,* Vol. 58, No. 3, pp. 201–4.

———. 1973. *Central Park 1851–1871: Urbanization and Environmental Planning in New York City.* Ph.D. thesis. Ithaca, N.Y.: Cornell University.

Stewart, John J. 1976. "Notes on Calvert Vaux's 1873 Design for the Public Grounds of the Parliament Buildings in Ottawa." *APT Bulletin,* Vol. 8, No. 1, pp. 1–27.

Tishler, William H. 1967. "A Tree Grows in Boston." *Connection: Visual Arts At Harvard,* Summer.

Turak, Theodore. 1986. *William Le Baron Jenney: A Pioneer of Modern Architecture.* Ann Arbor: UMI Research Press.

Turner, Paul V., Marcia E. Vetrocq, and Karen Wetze. 1976. *The Founders and the Architects: The Design of Stanford University.* Palo Alto: Stanford University.

Vaux, Calvert. Papers, Rare Book Room, New York Public Library.

———. 1863. "Description of the Terrace." *Sixth Annual Report of the Board of Commissioners of the Central Park.* New York: Wm. C. Bryant & Co.

———. [1865.] "Brooklyn Park Report on Boundaries." Manuscript Report. New York: Avery Library.

———. [c. 1879]. *Official Correspondence, etc. in Reference to Plans for the Arrangement of Public Grounds in Front of the Parliament Buildings at Ottawa.* New York: G. P. Putnam.

Vinci, John. 1977. "Graceland: The Nineteenth-Century Garden Cemetery." *Chicago History,* Vol. 6, No. 2, pp. 86–98.

Waring, George E., Jr. 1876. *The Sanitary Drainage of Houses and Towns.* Boston: Houghton, Mifflin & Co.

Weidenmann, Jacob. 1870. *Beautifying Country Homes: A Handbook of Landscape Gardening.* New York: Orange Judd and Company.

———. 1876. *American Garden Architecture.* privately published.

———. 1888. *Modern Cemeteries.* Chicago: Monumental News.

*Weidenmann, Marguerite. N.d. "A Sketch of the Life and Works of Jacob Weidenmann." Manuscript in Prints Department, New York Public Library.

Weirick, Ray F. 1910. "The Park and Boulevard System of Kansas City, MO." *The American City,* Vol. 3, No. 5, pp. 211–18.

Wheelwright, Robert. 1910. "Attacks on Central Park." *Landscape Architecture,* Vol. 1, No. 1, pp. 9–21.

Wickes, Marjorie, and Tim O'Connell. 1988. "The Legacy of Frederick Law Olmsted." *Rochester History,* Vol. 50, No. 2, pp. 1–23.

Wilson, Alex. 1983. "The Public Gardens of Halifax, Nova Scotia." *Journal of Garden History,* Vol. 3, No. 3, pp. 179–92.

Wright, Ellen. 1904. *Elizur Wright's Appeals for Middlesex Fells and the Forests with a Sketch of What He Did for Both.* N.p.: Ellen Wright.

Zaitzevsky, Cynthia. 1973. "The Olmsted Firm and the Structures of the Boston Park System." *Journal of the Society of Architectural Historians,* Vol. 32, No. 2, pp. 167–74.

———. 1982. *Frederick Law Olmsted and the Boston Park System.* Cambridge, Mass.: Harvard University Press.

Chapter 19

Abbott, Carl. 1980. " 'Necessary Adjuncts to its Growth': The Railroad Suburbs of Chicago, 1854–1875." *Journal of the Illinois State Historical Society,* Vol. 73, No. 2, pp. 117–31.

Alderman, Metle N., ed. 1916. *Lake Forest: Art and History Edition.* Chicago: American Communities Company.

*Andreas, Alfred T. 1975. *History of Chicago.* New York: Arno.

Anonymous. 1852. "The Environs of Cincinnati." Western Horticultural Review, *Vol. 2, pp. 399–400.*

———. 1857. "Landscape Gardening." *The Crayon,* Vol. 4, No. 8, p. 248.

———. 1879. "The Rockwell Case." *The Plumber and Sanitary Engineer,* Vol. 2, No. 3, p. 61.

———. 1883. "The Arcadian City of Pullman." *Agricultural Review,* January, pp. 69–89.

———. 1890. "Glendale," Manuscript Map at Cincinnati Historical Society.

Archer, John. 1983. "Country and City in the American Romantic Suburb." *Journal of the Society of Architectural Historians,* Vol. 42, No. 2, pp. 139–56.

Arpee, Edward. 1963. *Lake Forest, Illinois: History and Reminiscences 1861–1961.* Lake Forest: Rotary Club of Lake Forest.

Baker, M. N. 1901. *Municipal Engineering and Sanitation.* New York: Macmillan.

Bassman, Herbert J., ed. 1936. *Riverside Then & Now: A History of Riverside, Illinois.* Riverside: N.p.

Barrett, Nathan, et al. 1890. "Sketches and Map of Grindstone Neck, ME."

Blake, Nelson, M. 1956. *Water for the Cities: A History of the Urban Water Supply Problem in the United States.* Syracuse: Syracuse University Press.

Boyer, M. Christine. 1985. *Manhattan Manners: Architecture and Style, 1850–1900.* New York: Rizzoli.

Buder, Stanley. 1967. *Pullman: An Experiment in Industrial Order and Community Planning 1880–1930.* New York: Oxford University Press.

Bunting, Bainbridge. 1954. "The Plan of the Back Bay Area in Boston." *Journal of the Society of Architectural Historians,* Vol. 13, No. 2, pp. 19–24.

Burns, Elizabeth K. 1980. "The Enduring Affluent Suburb." *Landscape,* Vol. 24, No. 1, pp. 33–41.

*Chamberlin, Everett. 1874. *Chicago and its Suburbs.* Chicago: T. A. Hungerford & Company.

Chicago Tribune. 1873. "Our Suburbs." Chicago: The Tribune Company.

Cleveland, H. W. S. 1873. *Landscape Architecture as Applied to the Wants of the West.* Chicago: Jansen, McClurg & Company.

———. 1874. "Boulevards as a Means of Checking Conflagrations." *Chicago Tribune,* September 20, pp. 12:1–2.

———. 1887. "Extract from the Report of H.W.S. Cleveland," in *Prospectus of the Jekyll Island Club.* N.p.

———, and [W. M. R.] French. 1872. Manuscript Map of the "Plan of Highland Park, Lake Co. Ill." Large colored version at Highland Park Historical Society; small black-and-white version at Illinois State Historical Society.

Copeland, Robert Morris. 1872. *The Most Beautiful City in America: Essay and Plan for the Improvement of the City of Boston.* Boston: Lee and Shepard.

Daniels, Howard. 1858. "Villa Parks." *The Horticulturist,* Vol. 13 (Vol. 8, New Series), pp. 495–96.

Davenport, F. Garvin. 1973. "The Sanitation Revolution in Illinois 1870–1900." *Journal of the Illinois State Historical Society,* Vol. 66, No. 3, pp. 306–26.

Davies, Jane B. 1975. "Llewellyn Park in West Orange, New Jersey." *Antiques,* Vol. 107, No. 1, pp. 142–58.

Dickson, Isabelle C. 1971. "Park Hill, an Idyl of the Hudson." *Yonkers Historical Bulletin,* Vol. 18, No. 2, pp. 7–13.

Doty, Mrs. Duane. 1893. *The Town of Pullman: Its Growth with Brief Accounts of its Industries.* Pullman: T. P. Struhsacker.

Ebner, Michael H. 1988. *Creating Chicago's North Shore: A Suburban History.* Chicago: University of Chicago Press.

Eliot, Charles William. 1924. *Charles Eliot, Landscape Architect.* Cambridge, Mass.: Harvard University Press.

Fales, Raymond L. 1971. "Land-Use Theory and the Spatial Structure of the Nineteenth-Century City," in *Papers of the Regional Science Association,* Vol. 28, pp. 49–80.

Fisher, Irving D. 1986. *Frederick Law Olmsted and the City Planning Movement in the United States.* Ann Arbor: UMI Research Press.

Fischer, Ron. 1983. "The Development of the Garden Suburb of Toronto." *Journal of Garden History,* Vol. 3, No. 3, pp. 193–207.

Garner, John S. 1984. *The Model Company Town: Urban Design through Private Enterprise in Nineteenth-Century New England.* Amherst: University of Massachusetts Press.

Gates, Grace Hooten. 1983. *The Model City of the New South: Anniston, Alabama, 1872–1900.* Huntsville, Ala.: Stroud.

Gerard, P. 1872. *How to Build a City.* Philadelphia: Review Printing House.

Gourlay, Robert Fleming. 1844. *Plans for Beautifying New York and for Enlarging and Improving the City of Boston.* Boston: Crocker & Brewster and Saxton, Pierce & Company.

Hartshorn, Cora L. 1979. *A Short History of the Short Hills Section of Millburn, N.J.* Millburn: Millburn-Short Hills Historical Society.

Henderson, Susan. 1987. "Llewellyn Park, Suburban Idyll." *Journal of Garden History,* Vol. 7, No. 3, pp. 221–43.

Highland Park Building Company. 1872. Manuscript Ledger of Meetings, Highland Park, Il., Historical Society.

Hubbard, Theodora Kimball, ed. 1931. "Riverside, Illinois: A Residential Neighborhood Designed Over Sixty Years Ago." *Landscape Architecture,* Vol. 21, No. 4, pp. 257–91.

*Jackson, Kenneth T. 1985. *Crabgrass Frontier: The Suburbanization of the United States.* New York: Oxford University Press.

King, Arthur G. 1959. "The Birth of the Village of Clifton." *Bulletin of the Historical and Philosophical Society of Ohio,* Vol. 17, No. 2, pp. 124–34.

Lillibridge, Robert M. 1953. "Pullman: Town Development in the Era of Eclecticism." *Journal of the Society of Architectural Historians,* Vol. 12, No. 3, pp. 17–22.

Maxwell, Sidney D. 1870. *Suburbs of Cincinnati.* Cincinnati: G. E. Stevens.

*Mayer, Harold M., and Richard C. Wade. 1969. *Chicago, Growth of a Metropolis.* Chicago: University of Chicago Press.

McCash, William Barton, and June Hall McCash. 1985. *Jekyll Club Historic District.* Jekyll Island: Jekyll Island Museum.

McDermott, J. J. 1976. *The Culture of Experience.* Prospect Heights, Ill.: Waveland.

Meakin, Budgett. 1905. *Model Factories and Villages: Ideal Conditions of Labour and Housing.* London: T. Fisher Unwin.

Menhinick, Howard K. 1932. "Riverside Sixty Years Later." *Landscape Architecture,* Vol. 22, No. 2, pp. 109–17.

Milani, Lois Darroch. 1971. *Robert Gourlay, Gadfly.* Bristol, R.I.: Ampersand.

Mumford, Lewis. 1931. *The Brown Decades.* New York: Harcourt, Brace.

———. 1969. "The Significance of Back Bay Boston," in *Back Bay Boston: The City as a Work of Art.* Boston: Museum of Fine Arts.

O'Connell, Ed. 1986. "Edwardsville's LeClaire Historic District." *Historic Illinois,* Vol. 9, No. 3, pp. 2–5.

Olmsted, Frederick Law. 1870. *Public Parks and the Enlargement of Cities.* Cambridge, Mass.: American Social Science Association.

———. 1871. *Report of a Preliminary Scheme of Improvements.* Staten Island: Staten Island Improvement Commission.

———, and [Calvert] Vaux. 1868. "Preliminary Report upon the Proposed Suburban Village at Riverside, near Chicago." New York: Sutton, Bowne & Company.

Pond, Irving K. 1934. "Pullman—America's First Planned Industrial Town." *Illinois Society of Architects Monthly Bulletin,* June/July, pp. 6–7.

Ranney, Victoria Post. 1972. *Olmsted in Chicago.* Chicago: The Open Lands Project.

[Recker, Elmus.] 1861. "Map of the Village of Clifton." Manuscript Map at Cincinnati Historical Society.

Riverside Development Company. 1871. *Riverside in 1871, With a Description of Its Improvements.* Chicago: D. & C. H. Blakely, Printers.

Rosen, Christine Meisner. 1986a. "Infrastructural Improvement in Nineteenth-Century Cities: A Conceptual Framework and Cases." *Journal of Urban History,* Vol. 12, No. 3, pp. 211–56.

———. 1986b. *The Limits of Power: Great Fires and the Process of City Growth in America.* Cambridge: Cambridge University Press.

Runion, James B. 1869. *Out of Town.* Chicago: The Western News Company.

Schuyler, David. 1986. *The New Urban Landscape: The Redefinition of City Form in Nineteenth-Century America.* Baltimore: Johns Hopkins University Press.

Spann, Edward K. 1981. *The New Metropolis: New York City, 1840–1857.* New York: Columbia University Press.

Steele, Fletcher. 1915. "Robert Fleming Gourlay, City Planner." *Landscape Architecture,* Vol. 6, No. 1, pp. 1–14.

Stilgoe, John R. 1988. *Borderland: Origins of the American Suburb, 1820–1939.* New Haven: Yale University Press.

Swift, Samuel. 1903. "Llewellyn Park, West Orange, Essex Co., New Jersey." *House and Garden,* Vol. 3, No. 6, pp. 327–35.

Taylor, Graham Romeyn. 1915. *Satellite Cities: A Study of Industrial Suburbs.* New York: D. Appleton & Co.

Thernstrom, Stephan, and Richard Sennett, eds. 1969. *Nineteenth-Century Cities: Essays in the New Urban History.* New Haven: Yale University Press.

Toft, Carolyn Hewes, and Jane Molloy Porter. 1984. *Compton Heights: A Historical and Architectural Guide.* St. Louis: Landmarks Association.

Tunnard, Christopher. 1947. "The Romantic Suburb in America." *The Magazine of Art,* Vol. 40, No. 5, pp. 184–87.

Waring, George E., Jr. 1879. *The Sanitary Drainage of Houses and Towns.* Boston: Houghton, Mifflin & Company.

Warner, Sam Bass, Jr. 1962. *Streetcar Suburbs: The Process of Growth in Boston 1870–1900.* Cambridge, Mass.: Harvard University Press.

Weiss, Ellen. 1975. "Robert Morris Copeland's Plans for Oak Bluffs." *Journal of the Society of Architectural Historians,* Vol. 34, No. 1, pp. 60–64.

———. 1987. *City in the Woods: The Life and Design of an American Camp Meeting on Martha's Vineyard.* New York: Oxford University Press.

White, Dana F., and Victor A. Kramer, eds. 1979. *Olmsted South: Old South Critic/New South Planner.* Westport, Conn.: Greenwood.

[Williams, Henry T.] 1870. "Riverside Park, Chicago." *The Horticulturist,* Vol. 25, pp. 325–27.

Wilson, Richard Guy. 1979. "Idealism and the Origin of the First American Suburb: Llewellyn Park, New Jersey." *The American Art Journal,* Vol. 11, No. 4, pp. 79–90.

Wittelle, Marvyn. 1958. *Pioneer to Commuter: The Story of Highland Park.* Highland Park: The Rotary Club.

Chapter 20

Abbott, Carl. 1980. " 'Necessary Adjuncts to its Growth': The Railroad Suburbs of Chicago, 1854–1875." *Journal of the Illinois State Historical Society,* Vol. 73, pp. 117–31.

Arnold, Frank A. 1905. "A Study in Railroad Gardening." *Suburban Life,* May, pp. 3–5.

Chambless, Edgar. 1910. *Roadtown.* New York: Roadtown Press.

Chandler, Alfred. 1965. *The Railroads: The Nation's First Big Business,* New York: Harcourt, Brace & World.

Clarke, Thomas C., et al. 1976. *The American Railway: Its Construction, Development, Management, and Appliances,* New York: Arno.

Danly, Susan, and Leo Marx. 1988. *The Railroad in American Art: Representations of Technological Change.* Cambridge, Mass.: MIT Press.

Ellis, David Maldwyn. 1946. "The Forfeiture of Railroad Land Grants." *Mississippi Valley Historical Review,* Vol. 33, pp. 27–60.

Gates, Paul W. 1934. *The Illinois Central Railroad and its Colonization Work.* Cambridge, Mass.: Harvard University Press.

Hastings, Milo. 1910. "Roadtown: A Multiple Home." *The Independent,* Vol. 68, No. 3205, pp. 974–80.

Henry, Robert S. 1968. "The Railroad Land Grant Legend in American History Texts," in *The Public Lands: Studies in the History of the Public Domain.* Vernon Carstensen, ed. Madison: University of Wisconsin Press.

Hudson, John C. 1982. "Towns of the Western Railroad." *Great Plains Quarterly,* Vol. 2, No. 1, pp. 41–54.

———. 1985. *Plains Country Towns.* Minneapolis: University of Minnesota Press.

Jensen, Oliver. 1975. *The American Heritage History of Railroads in America.* New York: American Heritage Publishing.

Kirby, Russell S. 1981. "Nineteenth-Century Patterns of Railroad Development on the Great Plains." *Great Plains Quarterly,* Vol. 1, No. 4, pp. 157–70.

Knight, Oliver. 1973. "Toward an Understanding of the Western Town." *Western Historical Quarterly,* Vol. 4, No. 1, pp. 27–42.

Meyer, Balthasar Henry, and Caroline E. MacGill. 1917. *History of Transportation in the U.S. before 1860.* Washington, D.C.: The Carnegie Institution of Washington.

[Mitchell, Donald G.] 1867. "De Rebus Ruris. No. VIII: Village Greens and Railway Gardens." *Hours at Home,* Vol. 4, No. 4, pp. 429–36.

———. 1867. *Rural Studies, With Hints for Country Places.* New York: Charles Scribner & Co.

Modelski, Andrew. *Railroad Maps of North America: The First Hundred Years.* Washington, D.C.: Library of Congress.

Norris, Frank. 1964 (originally published in 1899). *The Octopus.* New York: Signet.

Quiett, Glenn Chesney. 1934. *They Built the West: An Epic of Rails and Cities.* New York: D. Appleton-Century Co.

Railway Gardening Association. 1911. *Proceedings of the 5th Annual Meeting of the Railroad Gardening Association.* Champaign, Ill.: Railroad Gardening Association.

Reps, John W. 1975. *Cities on Stone: Nineteenth Century Lithograph Images of the Urban West.* Fort Worth: Amon Carter Museum.

Righter, Robert W. 1985. *The Making of a Town: Wright, Wyoming.* Boulder: Roberts Rinehart.

Robinson, Charles Mulford. 1902. "A Railroad Beautiful." *House and Garden,* Vol. 2, pp. 564–70.

———. 1903. *Modern Civic Art or the City Made Beautiful.* New York: G. P. Putnam's Sons.

———. 1904. "Suburban Station Grounds." *House and Garden,* Vol. 3, pp. 182–87.

Smalley, Eugene V. 1883. *History of the Northern Pacific Railroad.* New York: G. P. Putnam.

Stilgoe, John R. 1982. "The Railroad Beautiful: Landscape Architecture and The Railroad Gardening Movement, 1867–1930." *Landscape Journal,* Vol. 1, No. 2, pp. 57–66.

———. 1983. *Metropolitan Corridor: Railroads and the American Scene.* New Haven: Yale University Press.

Stover, John F. 1987. *History of the Baltimore and Ohio Railroad.* Lafayette, Ind.: Purdue University Press.

Strong, W. J. 1914. "Railway Gardening in Western Canada by the Canadian Pacific Railway Company," in *Proceedings of the 7th Annual Meeting of the Railway Gardening Association.* Nashville, Tenn.: Railroad Gardening Association.

Thompson, Slason. 1925. *A Short History of American Railroads.* Chicago: Bureau of Railway News & Statistics.

von Baeyer, Edwinna. 1984. *Rhetoric and Roses: A History of Canadian Gardening, 1900–1930.* Markham, Ontario: Fitzhenry and Whiteside.

Vance, James E. 1986. *Capturing the Horizon: The Historical Geography of Transportation.* New York: Harper & Row.

Wakely, Arthur C., ed. 1917. *Omaha: The Gate City and Douglas County, Nebraska,* Vol. 1. Chicago: S. J. Clarke Publishing Company.

[Woodward, F. W.] 1969. "Railway Gardens." *The Horticulturist,* Vol. 24, pp. 147–48.

Chapter 21

Anonymous. 1890*a.* "Jeannette Park, New York." *Garden and Forest,* Vol. 3, pp. 498–99.

———. 1890*b.* "Street Trees." *Garden and Forest,* Vol. 3, p. 137.

———. 1891. "Public Gardens." *Garden and Forest,* Vol. 4, pp. 529–30.

Baumann, Eugene. 1869. "Designs for Ornamental Grounds and Flower Gardens," in *Practical Floriculture,* by Peter Henderson. New York: Orange Judd and Company.

Beecher, Catharine E., and Harriet Beecher Stowe. 1869. *The American Woman's Home.* New York: J. B. Ford.

Carter, Tom. 1985. *The Victorian Garden.* Salem, N.H.: Salem House.

Carvey, Elizabeth. 1985. "Rock Island's Turn-of-the-Century Amusement Park." *Historic Illinois,* Vol. 7, No. 5, pp. 1–5, 13.

Cavallo, Dominick. 1981. *Muscles and Morals: Organized Playgrounds and Urban Reform, 1880–1920.* Philadelphia: University of Pennsylvania Press.

Christy, Stephen. [1987.] "Landscape Analysis [of Davis Mansion]." Unpublished report for Illinois Historic Preservation Agency.

Crawford, Pleasance. 1981. *The Ontario Home Landscape: 1890–1914.* Toronto: Department of Landscape Architecture (unpublished paper).

Dengler, Dorothy. 1945. *The Rise and Fall of White City, Windsor Beach and Summerville.* Unpublished manuscript in collection of Rochester, New York, Public Library.

De Wolf, John. 1891. "Cacti in Landscape Gardening." *Garden and Forest,* Vol. 4, pp. 592–93.

Doell, M. Christine. 1986. *Gardens of the Gilded Age: Nineteenth Century Gardens and Homegrounds of New York State.* Syracuse: Syracuse University Press.

Downing, Antoinette F., and Vincent J. Scully, Jr. 1967. *The Architectural Heritage of Newport, Rhode Island, 1640–1915.* New York: American Legacy Press.

Eliot, Charles. 1891. "Two Studies in House Plantings." *Garden and Forest,* Vol, 4, pp. 184–85.

Favretti, Rudy J., and Joy Putnam Favretti. 1978. *Landscapes and Gardens for Historic Buildings.* Nashville: American Association for State and Local History.

Friends of the Public Gardens. 1989. *The Halifax Public Garden.* Halifax, Nova Scotia: Friends of the Public Garden.

Gloag, John. 1962. *Victorian Taste: Some Social Aspects of Architecture and Industrial Design, from 1820–1900.* Newton Abbott, Great Britain: David & Charles.

Green, Harvey. 1983. *The Light of the Home: An Intimate View of the Lives of Women in Victorian America.* New York: Pantheon.

Hamlin, Talbott. 1952. "The Rise of Eclecticism in New York." *Journal of the Society of Architectural Historians,* Vol. 11, No. 2, pp. 3–8.

Henderson, Peter. 1869. *Practical Floriculture.* New York: Orange Judd and Company.

Hodges, Leigh Mitchell. 1908. *Willow Grove Park: Philadelphia's Fairyland, Season 1908.* Philadelphia.

Hoopes, Josiah. 1872. "Planting of Dooryards and Small Gardens with Ornamental Trees, Shrubs, and Evergreens." *The Horticulturist,* Vol. 27, pp. 40–43.

Howells, William Dean. 1889. *A Hazard of New Fortunes.* New York: Boni and Liveright, Inc.

Hunter, Julius K. 1988. *Westmoreland and Portland Places: The History and Architecture of America's Premier Private Streets, 1888–1988.* Columbia: University of Missouri Press.

Johnson, Joseph Forsyth. 1898. *Residential Sites and Environments: Their Conveniences, Gardens, Parks, Plantings, etc.* New York: A. T. Delamare Printing and Publishing Comp. Ltd.

Lee, Joseph. 1903. "Boston's Playground System." *New England Magazine,* Vol. 27, No. 7, pp. 520–36.

Lynes, Russell. 1980. *The Tastemakers: The Shaping of American Popular Taste.* New York: Dover.

Manning, Warren. 1902. "The Influence of American Expositions on the Out-Door Arts." Boston: Massachusetts Horticulture Society.

McCabe, James D. 1975. (John Francis Marion, ed.) *A Collector's Reprint: The Illustrated History of the Centennial Exhibition . . .* Philadelphia: National Publishing Company.

Minhinnick, Jeanne. 1970. *At Home in Upper Canada.* Toronto: Clarke, Irwin.

Moore, Evelyn R. 1985. "Bloomington's David Davis Mansion." *Historic Illinois,* Vol. 7, No. 6, pp. 4–5.

Newcomb, Peggy Cornett. 1985. *Popular Annuals of Eastern North America, 1865–1914.* Washington, D.C.: Dumbarton Oaks.

Nini, Stephen. 1989. "Courtlandt Place: Houston's Private Place." College Station, Tex.: unpublished paper.

Schenck, Carl Alwin. 1974. *The Birth of Forestry in America: Biltmore Forest School 1898–1913.* Santa Cruz, Calif.: Forest History Society and Appalachian Consortium.

★Schlesigner, Arthur. 1951. *The Rise of Modern America: 1865–1951,* 4th ed. New York: Macmillan.

Schmiechen, James A. 1988. "The Victorians, the Historians, and the Idea of Modernism." *American Historical Review,* Vol. 93, No. 2, pp. 287–316.

Scott, Frank J. 1881. *The Art of Beautifying Suburban Home Grounds of Small Extent.* New York: American Book Exchange.

Snyder, Ellen Marie. 1985. "Victory Over Nature: Victorian Cast-Iron Seating." *Winterthur Portfolio,* Vol. 20, No. 4, pp. 221–41.

Solly, George A. 1887. *Carpet and Ornamental Flower Bed Designs.* Springfield, Mass.: George A. Solly and Son.

Streatfield, David C. 1984. " 'Paradise' on the Frontier: Victorian Gardens on the San Francisco Peninsula." *Garden History,* Vol. 12, No. 1, pp. 58–80.

Thompson, R. 1892. *The Gardener's Assistant.* London: Blackie & Son Ltd.

Tunnard, Christopher. 1948. *Gardens in the Modern Landscape.* New York: Scribner.

Vaux, Calvert, and Samuel Parsons, Jr. 1881. *Concerning Lawn Planting.* New York: Orange Judd and Company.

Waugh, Frank. 1899. *Landscape Gardening: Treatise on the General Principles Governing Outdoor Art.* New York: Orange Judd and Company.

Wilson, Joseph M. 1876. *The Masterpieces of the Centennial Expositions Illustrated,* Vol. 3. Philadelphia: Gebblie & Barrie.

Wilson, Richard Guy, ed. 1982. *Victorian Resorts and Hotels.* Philadelphia: The Victorian Society in America.

Wright, Richardson. 1934. *The Story of Gardening, From the Hanging Gardens of Babylon to the Hanging Gardens of New York.* New York: Dodd, Mead.

Chapter 22

Adams, Henry. 1918. *The Education of Henry Adams.* Boston: Houghton Mifflin Co.

American Architect and Building News. 1892. "The World's Fair Buildings," *American Architect and Building News,* November 6, pp. 85–86.

Anonymous. 1894. *The Official History of the California Midwinter International Exposition.* San Francisco: H. S. Crocker Company.

———. 1890. "Chicago's World's Fair." *Scientific American,* Vol. 63, No. 5, pp. 70–71.

———. 1896. "Fate of the Chicago World's Fair Buildings." *Scientific American,* Vol. 75, No. 14, p. 267.

———. 1916. "A New Versailles." *American Architect,* Vol. 109, No. 2113, pp. 412–13.

——. 1930. *Development of the United States Capitol.* Washington, D.C.: U.S. Government Printing Office.

Appelbaum, Stanley. 1980. *The Chicago World's Fair of 1893: A Photographic Record.* New York: Dover.

Arnold, C. D., and H. D. Higinbotham. 1893. *Official Views of the World's Columbian Exposition.* Chicago: World's Columbian Exposition Company.

Badger, R. Reid. 1979. *The Great American Fair: The World's Columbian Exposition and American Culture.* Chicago: Nelson Hall.

Barnes, Sisley. 1977. "George Ferris' Wheel: The Great Attraction of the Midway Plaisance." *Chicago History,* Vol. 6, No. 3, pp. 177–82.

Bellamy, Edward. 1887. *Looking Backward.* Boston: Ticknor Publishers.

Bennett, Mark, ed. 1976. *History of the Louisiana Purchase Exposition.* New York: Arno.

Birk, Dorothy Daniels. 1979. *The World Came to St. Louis.* St. Louis: Bethany Press.

Blodgett, Harold C. 1916. *How You Can Help Make Your Hometown a Better Hometown.* St. Louis: National "Clean up" and "Paint Up" Campaign.

Bluestone, Daniel. 1988. "Detroit's City Beautiful and the Problem of Commerce." *Journal of the Society of Architectural Historians,* Vol. 47, No. 3, pp. 245–62.

★Boyer, M. Christine. 1983. *Dreaming the Rational City: The Myth of American City Planning.* Cambridge, Mass.: MIT Press.

Brunner, Arnold. 1916. "Cleveland's Group Plan." *Proceedings of the Eighth National Conference on City Planning,* Vol. 8. Cleveland: National Conference on City Planning.

Burnham, Daniel. Papers. Art Institute of Chicago.

——. 1892. "Report of the Director of Works—World's Columbian Exposition." Chicago: Rand, McNally & Company.

——. 1893. "The Organization of the World's Columbian Exposition." *Inland Architect and News Record,* Vol. 22, No. 1, pp. 5–8.

——. 1902. "White City and Capital City." *The Century Magazine,* Vol. 63, pp. 619–20.

——. 1903. "The Grouping of Public Buildings at Cleveland." *Inland Architect and News Record,* Vol. 42, No. 2, pp. 13–15.

——. 1913. "Lessons of the Chicago World's Fair." *Architectural Record,* Vol. 33, No. 1, pp. 33–44.

——, and Edward H. Bennett. 1970. *Plan of Chicago.* New York: Da Capo.

Caffin, Charles H. 1901. "The Beautifying of Cities." *The World's View,* Vol. 3, No. 1, pp. 1429–35.

Ciucci, Giorgio, et al. 1979. *The American City: From the Civil War to the New Deal.* Gorgio Ciucci, ed. Cambridge, Mass.: MIT Press.

Coffin, William Anderson. 1897. "The Fair as a Work of Art," in *A History of the World's Columbian Exposition Held in Chicago in 1893.* Rossiter Johnson, ed. New York: D. Appleton Co.

Currey, J. Seymour. 1912. *Chicago: Its History and Its Builders,* Vol. 2. Chicago: S. J. Clarke Publishing Company.

Ford, Frederick L. 1904. *The Grouping of Public Buildings.* Hartford, Conn.: Municipal Art Society.

Francis, David. 1913. *The Universal Exposition of 1904.* St. Louis: Louisiana Purchase Exposition Company.

Ginger, Ray. 1967. *Age of Excess: The United States from 1877 to 1914.* New York: Macmillan.

Hegemann, Werner. 1937. *City Planning Housing.* New York: Architectural Book Publishing.

Hines, Thomas S. 1979. *Burnham of Chicago: Architect and Planner.* Chicago: University of Chicago Press.

Ives, Halsey C. 1893. *The Dream City: A Portfolio of Photographic Views of the World's Columbian Exposition.* St. Louis: N. D. Thompson Publishing Company.

Keeler, Clinton. 1950. "The White City and the Black City: The Dream of Civilization." *American Quarterly,* Vol. 2, No. 2, pp. 112–17.

Kriehn, George. 1899. "The City Beautiful." *Municipal Affairs,* Vol. 3, pp. 594–601.

*Krueckeberg, Donald, ed. 1983. *The American Planner: Biographies and Recollections.* New York: Methuen.

Lubove, Roy. 1962. *The Progressives and the Slums: Tenement House Reform in New York City 1890–1917.* Pittsburgh: University of Pittsburgh Press.

Macomber, Ben. 1915. *The Jewel City: Its Planning and Achievement; Its Architecture, Sculpture, Symbolism and Music; Its Gardens, Palaces, and Exhibits.* San Francisco: John H. Williams.

Manieri-Elia, Mario. 1979. "Toward an 'Imperial City': Daniel H. Burnham and the City Beautiful Movement," in *The American City: From the Civil War to the New Deal.* Giorgio Ciucci, ed. Cambridge, Mass.: MIT Press.

Manning, Warren H. 1904. *The History of Village Improvement in the United States.* Syracuse: Mason Press.

*Mawson, Thomas H. 1911. *Civic Art: Studies in Town Planning, Parks, Boulevards, and Open Spaces.* London: B. T. Batsford.

———. 1927. *The Life and Work of an English Landscape Architect.* New York: Scribner.

Meek, Margaret Anne. 1979. *History of the City Beautiful Movement in Canada, 1890–1930.* Master's thesis. Vancouver: University of British Columbia.

Miller, E. Lynn. 1990. "The Influence of J. Horace McFarland on the Parks, Riverways, and Civic Improvements in America," in *CELA 89 Proceedings.* Sara Katherine Williams and Robert R. Grist, eds. Washington, D.C.: Landscape Architecture Foundation.

Moody, Walter D. 1920. *Wacker's Manual of the Plan of Chicago.* Chicago: Chicago Plan Commission.

Moore, Charles, ed. 1902. *The Improvement of the Park System of the District of Columbia.* Washington, D.C.: U.S. Government Printing Office.

———. 1913. "Lessons of the Chicago World's Fair." *Architectural Record,* Vol. 33, No. 1, pp. 33–44.

———. 1921. *Daniel H. Burnham: Architect, Planner of Cities,* Vols. 1 and 2. Boston: Houghton Mifflin.

Mullgardt, Louis Christian. 1915. *The Architecture and Landscape Gardening of the Exposition,* 2nd ed. San Francisco: Paul Elder.

Mumford, Lewis. 1931. "Two Chicago Fairs." *New Republic.* Vol. 65, No. 842, pp. 271–72.

Neufeld, Maurice. 1935. *The Contribution of the World's Columbian Exposition of 1893 to the Idea of a Planned Society in America.* Ph.D. thesis. Madison: University of Wisconsin.

Olmsted, Frederick Law. Papers [cited as FLO Papers]. Library of Congress, Washington, D.C.

———. 1893. "The Landscape Architecture of the World's Columbian Exposition." *Inland Architect and News Record,* Vol. 22, No. 2, pp. 18–21.

*Peets, Elbert, and Werner Hegeman. 1922. *The American Vitruvius: An Architect's Handbook of Civic Art.* New York: Architectural Book Publishing.

Peterson, Jon. 1983. "The City Beautiful Movement: Forgotten Origins and Lost Meanings," in *Introduction to Planning History in the United States.* Donald A.

Krueckeberg, ed. New Brunswick, N.J.: Rutgers—The State University of New Jersey.

Riis, Jacob. 1971. *How the Other Half Lives.* New York: Arno.

Robinson, Charles Mulford. 1899. "Improvement in City Life: Aesthetic Progress." *Atlantic Monthly,* Vol. 83, pp. 771–85.

———. 1903. *Modern Civic Art or the City Made Beautiful.* New York: G. P. Putnam.

———. 1906*a.* "Proposed Plans for the Improvement of the City of Denver." Denver: Art Commission.

———. 1906*b.* "A Plan of Civic Improvement for the City of Oakland, California." Oakland: Oakland Enquirer Publishing Co.

———. 1907. "Report on the Improvement of the City of Dubuque, Iowa." Unpublished report.

———. 1908. "The Improvement of Ridgewood, N.J." Ridgewood: The Ridgewood Herald.

———. 1909. "Report of Charles Mulford Robinson for Fort Wayne Civic Improvement Association." Fort Wayne: Press of Fort Wayne Printing Co.

———. 1911. *The Width and Arrangement of Streets: A Study in Town Planning.* New York: The Engineering News Publishing Co.

———. 1913. *The Improvement of Towns and Cities or the Practical Basis of Civic Aesthetics.* New York: G. P. Putnam.

Rubin, Barbara. 1979. "Aesthetic Ideology and Urban Design." *Annals of the Association of American Geographers.* Vol. 69, No. 3, pp. 339–61.

Rydell, Robert W. 1984. *All the World's a Fair: Visions of Empire at American International Expositions, 1876–1916.* Chicago: University of Chicago Press.

*Scott, Mel. 1969. *American City Planning.* Berkeley: University of California Press.

Shepp, James W. and Daniel B. 1893. *Shepp's World's Fair Photographed.* Philadelphia: Globe Bible Publishing Company.

Spreiregen, Paul D., ed. 1968. *On the Art of Designing Cities: Selected Essays of Elbert Peets.* Cambridge, Mass.: MIT Press.

Steffens, Lincoln. 1957. *The Shame of the Cities.* New York: Hill and Wang.

Truman, Benjamin C. 1976. *History of the World's Fair.* New York: Arno.

Tunnard, Christopher. 1950. "A City Called Beautiful." *Journal of the Society of Architectural Historians,* Vol. 9, Nos. 1 & 2, pp. 31–36.

Van Nus, Walter. 1977. "The Fate of City Beautiful Thought in Canada," in *The Canadian City: Essays in Urban History.* Gilbert A. Stelter and Alan F. Artibise, eds. Toronto: McClelland and Stewart.

Wilson, William H. 1964. *The City Beautiful Movement in Kansas City.* Columbia: University of Missouri Press.

———. 1980. "The Ideology, Aesthetics and Politics of the City Beautiful Movement," in *The Rise of Modern Urban Planning.* Anthony Sutliffe, ed. New York: St. Martin's.

———. 1987. "The Billboard: Bane of the City Beautiful." *Journal of Urban History,* Vol. 13, No. 4, pp. 394–425.

———. 1989. *The City Beautiful Movement.* Baltimore: Johns Hopkins University Press.

Winslow, Carleton Monroe. 1916. *The Architecture and the Gardens of the San Diego Exposition.* San Francisco: Paul Elder and Company.

Wright, P. B. 1893. "Exposition Reviewed. II." *American Architect and Building News,* Vol. 42, p. 22.

Wrigley, Robert, Jr. 1983. "The Plan of Chicago," in *Introduction to Planning History in the United States.* Donald A. Krueckeberg, ed. New Brunswick, N.J.: Rutgers—The State University of New Jersey.

Zukowsky, John, Sally Chappell, and Robert Bruegmann. 1979. *The Plan of Chicago: 1909–1979.* Chicago: Art Institute of Chicago.

Chapter 23

Anonymous, 1930*a*. *Development of the United States Capitol.* Washington D.C.: U.S. Government Printing Office.

———. 1930*b*. "Radburn: A Town Planned for Safety." *American Architect,* Vol. 87, No. 2579, pp. 42–45, 128, 130.

Atterbury, Grosvenor. 1913. *Model Towns in America.* New York: National Housing Association.

Bartholomew, Harland. 1920. "The Lansing Plan." St. Louis: unpublished report.

———. 1922. "The Principles of City Planning." *The American City,* Vol. 26, pp. 457–61.

———. 1932. "A Program to Prevent Economic Disintegration." *Proceedings of the Twenty-Fourth National Conference on City Planning.* Philadelphia: William F. Fell.

★———. 1955. *Land Values in American Cities.* Cambridge, Mass.: Harvard University Press.

Bennett, Edward H. 1922. "Zoning Chicago." *National Municipal Review,* Vol. 2, No. 3, pp. 69–71.

★Boyer, M. Christine. 1983. *Dreaming the Rational City: The Myth of American City Planning.* Cambridge, Mass.: MIT Press.

Caparn, H. A. 1906. "Parallelogram Park—Suburban Life by the Square Mile." *Craftsman,* Vol. 10, pp. 767–74.

Cautley, Marjorie Sewell. 1930. "Planting at Radburn." *Landscape Architecture,* Vol. 21, No. 1, pp. 23–29.

Comey, Arthur C. 1933. *Transition Zoning.* Cambridge, Mass.: Harvard University Press.

———. 1946. *City and Regional Planning Papers [of Alfred Bettmon].* Cambridge, Mass.: Harvard University Press.

Corell, Alwyn. 1913. "Co-operative Group Planning: A Suburban Development." *Architectural Record,* Vol. 34, pp. 467–75.

Cornell, Ralph D. 1933. "Landscape Architecture and Subdivision." *Architect and Engineer,* Vol. 112, No. 3, pp. 11–19.

DeBoer, S. R. 1943. "The Landscape Planner's Tribe: A Genealogical Study within the Profession." *Landscape Architecture,* Vol. 33, No. 4, pp. 117–18.

Draper, Earle S. 1927. "Southern Textile Village Planning." *Landscape Architecture,* Vol. 18, No. 1, pp. 1–28.

Eliot, Charles W., 2nd. 1936. "Accomplishments in Regional Planning," in *Planning for City, State, Region and Nation.* Chicago: American Society of Planning Officials.

Federal Plan Commission of Ottawa and Hull. 1916. *Report of the Federal Plan Commission on a General Plan for the Cities of Ottawa and Hull.* Ottawa: Federal Plan Commission.

Flink, James J. 1970. *America Adopts the Automobile, 1895–1910.* Cambridge, Mass.: MIT Press.

Ford, George B. 1913. "The City Scientific," in *Proceedings of the Fifth National Conference on City Planning.* Cambridge, Mass.: The University Press.

———. 1917. *City Planning Progress in the United States, 1917.* Washington, D.C.: Journal of the American Institute of Architects.

Frary, I. T. 1918. "Surburban Landscape Planning in Cleveland." *Architectural Record,* Vol. 43, No. 235, pp. 371–84.

Friedman, John, and Clyde Weaver. 1979. *Territory and Function: The Evolution of Regional Planning.* Berkeley: University of California Press.

Grey, Elmer. 1912. "The New Suburb of the Pacific Coast." *Scribner's Magazine,* Vol. 52, No. 1, pp. 36–51.

Gries, John M., and James Ford, eds. 1932. *Planning for Residential Districts.* Washington, D.C.: The President's Conference on Home Building and Home Ownership.

Groben, William E. 1919. "Union Park Gardens." *Architectural Record,* Vol. 45, No. 1, pp. 45–64.

Haar, Charles M., and Jerold S. Kayden. *Zoning and the American Dream.* Chicago: Planners Press.

Hall, George D. 1930. "Beverly Hills, California—A Subdivision That Grew Into a City." *American Landscape Architecture,* Vol. 3, No. 2, pp. 21–26.

Hancock, John Loretz. 1964. *John Nolen and the American Planning Movement: A History of Culture Change and Community Response, 1900–1940.* Ph.D. thesis. Philadelphia: University of Pennsylvania.

Hare, S. Herbert. 1927. "The Planning of the Industrial City of Longview, Washington." *Proceedings of the American Society of Civil Engineers,* Vol. 53, pp. 1178–83.

Hare & Hare. 1950. "A City Plan for Council Bluffs, Iowa." Typewritten report.

Head, Louis P. 1925. "The Kessler City Plan for Dallas." Dallas: The Kessler Plan Association.

Hegemann, Werner, and Elbert Peets. 1922. *The American Vitruvius: An Architect's Handbook of Civic Art.* New York: Architectural Book Publishing.

Hubbard, Henry V. 1927. "The Golf Course and the Land Subdivision." *Landscape Architecture,* Vol. 17, No. 3, pp. 211–24.

Lewis, Nelson P. 1918. "The Automobile and the City Plan," in *Proceedings of the Third National Conference on City Planning.* New York: Douglas MacMurtrie.

Lohmann, Karl B. 1931. *Principles of City Planning.* New York: McGraw-Hill.

Longview Company. 1923. "Longview, Washington: The City Practical that Vision Built." Longview, Wash.: The Longview Company.

Lubove, Roy. 1962. *The Progressives and the Slums: Tenement House Reform in New York City, 1890–1917.* Pittsburgh: University of Pittsburgh Press.

———. 1963. *Community Planning in the 1920's: The Contribution of the Regional Planning Association of America.* Pittsburgh: University of Pittsburgh Press.

———. 1967. *The Urban Community: Housing and Planning in the Progressive Era.* Englewood Cliffs, N.J.: Prentice-Hall.

MacKaye, Benton. 1928. *The New Exploration: A Philosophy of Regional Planning.* New York: Harcourt Brace.

Manning, Warren H. 1910. "Villages for Workingmen and Workingmen's Homes," in *Proceedings of the Second National Conference on City Planning and the Problems of Congestion.* Cambridge, Mass.: The University Press.

———. 1911. "Bangor City Plan: The Burned District." Bangor: The Civic Improvement Committee.

———. 1913. "The Billerica Town Plan." *Landscape Architecture,* Vol. 3, No. 3, pp. 108–18.

———. 1917. "The National Importance of the Hudson-Mohawk Thoroughfare and Objects in its Landscape." *Journal of the American Institute of Architects,* Vol. 5, No. 4, pp. 161–69.

———. 1918. "A Description of Estates on the Community Lands About the Mayfield Country Club." Privately printed.

———. 1919. "Warren H. Manning's City Plan of Birmingham." Birmingham, Ala.: City of Birmingham.

Mariemont Company. 1925. "A Descriptive and Pictured Story of Mariemont." Cincinnati: Mariemont Company.

Marsh, Benjamin. 1909. *An Introduction to City Planning.* New York: B. C. Marsh.

Mawson, Thomas H. 1914. *Borden Park: Report on the Development of the Great Eastern Realty Company.* Lancaster, UK: Great Eastern Realty Company.

May, Charles C. 1916. "Forest Hills Gardens from the Town Planning Viewpoint." *Architecture,* Vol. 34, No. 2, pp. 161–73.

Molyneaux, Gary O'Dell. 1979. *Planned Land Use Change in an Urban Setting: The J. C. Nichols Company and the Country Club District of Kansas City.* Ph.D. thesis. Champaign: University of Illinois.

*Mumford, Lewis. 1938. *The Culture of Cities.* New York: Harcourt Brace.

Nolen, John. 1911. "Standardized Street Widths," in *Proceedings of the Third National Conference on City Planning.* Cambridge, Mass.: The University Press.

———. 1912. *Replanning Small Cities: Six Typical Studies.* New York: B. W. Huebsch.

———, ed. 1916. *City Planning.* New York: D. Appleton Co.

———. 1927a. *New Towns for Old.* Boston: Marshall Jones Company.

———. 1927b. "Twenty Years of City Planning Progress in the United States," in *Proceedings of the Nineteenth National Conference on City Planning.* Philadelphia: William F. Fell.

Olmsted, Frederick Law, Jr. 1910a. "Introductory Address on City Planning," in *Proceedings of the Second National Conference on City Planning and the Problems of Congestion.* Cambridge, Mass.: The University Press.

———. 1910b. "The Limits of City Beautification—A Reply to an Inquiry." *The American City,* Vol. 2, No. 5, pp. 209–12.

———. 1911. "Reply in Behalf of the City Planning Conference," in *Proceedings of the Third National Conference on City Planning.* Cambridge, Mass.: The University Press.

———. 1913. "A City Planning Program," in *Proceedings of the Fifth National Conference on City Planning.* Cambridge, Mass.: The University Press.

———. 1927. "Palos Verdes Estates." *Landscape Architecture,* Vol. 17, No. 4, pp. 255–61.

Parker, Carl Rust, Bremer W. Pond, and Theodora Kimball, eds. 1922. *Transactions of the American Society of Landscape Architects, 1909–1921.* Amsterdam, N.Y.: The Recorder Press.

Pray, James S. 1917. "Planning the Cantonments." *Landscape Architecture,* Vol. 8, No. 1, pp. 1–17.

Rogers, Gardener S. N.d. "City Planning and Zoning Accomplishments." Unpublished report of the Civic Development Department of the Chamber of Commerce of the United States.

Sage Foundation. N.d. "Forest Hills Gardens." New York: Sage Foundation Homes Company.

Schalck, Harry G. 1970. "Mini-Revisionism in City Planning History: The Planners of Roland Park." *Journal of the Society of Architectural Historians,* Vol. 29, No. 4, pp. 347–49.

Shaker Heights Improvement Co. 1914. *The Shaker Heights Subdivision of SH.* Cleveland: The Shaker Heights Improvement Co.

Shillaber, Caroline. 1982. "Elbert Peets, Champion of the Civic Form." *Landscape Architecture,* Vol. 72, No. 6, pp. 54–59, 100.

Shurtleff, Flavel. 1914. *Carrying Out the City Plan.* New York: Survey Associates.

———. 1926. "City and Regional Planning Since 1876." *American Architect,* Vol. 129, No. 2488, pp. 57–60.

Smith, L. L. 1930. "The Industrial Garden City of Kohler, Wisconsin." *American Landscape Architect,* Vol. 3, No. 3, pp. 10–18.

Stein, Clarence. 1925. "A New Venture in Housing." *American City,* Vol. 32, pp. 277–81.

———. 1966. *Toward New Towns for America.* Cambridge: MIT Press.

Stilgoe, John R. 1988. *Borderland: Origins of the American Suburb, 1820–1939.* New Haven: Yale University Press.

Steele, Fletcher. 1911. "An Emergency Report for Bangor, Maine." *Landscape Architecture,* Vol. 2, No. 1, pp. 1–15.

Taylor, Graham Romeyn. 1909. "Creating the Newest Steel City." *The Survey,* April 3, 1909.

Toll, Seymour I. 1969. *Zoned American.* New York: Grossman.

Unwin, Raymond. 1911. "Discussion," in *Proceedings of the Third National Conference on City Planning.* Cambridge, Mass.: The University Press.

Veiller, Lawrence. 1915. "Protecting Residential Districts," in *Proceedings of the Sixth National Conference on City Planning.* Cambridge, Mass.: The University Press.

Weibe, Robert H. 1967. *The Search for Order, 1877–1920.* New York: Hill and Wang.

Weiss, Marc A. 1987. *The Rise of the Community Builders.* New York: Columbia University Press.

Whitnall, Gordon. 1931. "The History of Zoning." *Annals of the American Academy of Political and Social Science,* Vol. 155, Part 2, pp. 1–14.

Whitten, Robert. 1923. "Regional Zoning," in *Proceedings of the Fifteenth National Conference on City Planning.* Baltimore.

———. 1927. *A Research into the Economics of Land Subdivision.* Syracuse: School of Citizenship and Public Affairs.

Wright, Frank Lloyd. 1958. *The Living City.* New York: Horizon.

Wright, Henry N. 1971. "Radburn Revisited." *Architectural Forum,* Vol. 135, No. 1, pp. 52–57.

Chapter 24

Adams, Steven. 1987. *The Arts and Crafts Movement.* Secacus, N.J.: Chartwell.

American Society of Landscape Architects. 1933. *Illustrations of Works of the Members.* New York: The House of J. Hayden Twiss.

Anderson, Dorothy May. 1980. *Women, Design, and The Cambridge School.* West Lafayette, Ind.: PDA Publishers.

Anonymous. N.d. "The Burr Playground Deeded to the City of Newton, Massachusetts." January 27, 1920. N.p.

———. N.d. "Hillside Children's Center Architectural Drawings." Rare Book Room, Univesity of Rochester Library, Rochester, New York.

———. 1903. " 'El Fureidis.' " *House and Garden,* Vol. 4, No. 3, pp. 97–103.

———. 1909. "The House of William G. Mather." *Architectural Record,* Vol. 26, No. 5, pp. 313–17.

———. 1932. "The Cambridge School." *Landscape Architecture,* Vol. 22, No. 4, p. 344.

———. 1950. "Obituary: Mrs. Ellen Shipman, Landscape Designer." *New York Times,* March 29, 1950, p. 29.

———. 1958. *Gardens Designed by Marian Cruger Coffin, Landscape Architect, 1876–1957.* Geneva, N.Y.: Hobart College.

Appleton, Frank M. 1980. "The Butchart Gardens." *Horticulture,* Vol. 58, No. 4, pp. 34–43.

Bailey, L. H. 1911. *The Country-Life Movement in the United States.* New York: Macmillan.

Balmori, Diana, Diane Kostial McGuire, and Eleanor M. McPeck. 1985. *Beatrix Farrand's American Landscapes.* Sagaponack, N.Y.: Sagapress.

Beck, Jo Ann Dietz. 1980. *Fletcher Steele: His Contributions to American Landscape Architecture.* Master's thesis. Syracuse: State College of New York, College of Environmental Science and Forestry.

Benjamin, Susan. 1987. "Highland Park's A.G. Becker Estate." *Historic Illinois,* Vol. 9, No. 6, pp. 1–5, 7.

Bissell, Ervanna Bowen. 1926. *Glimpses of Santa Barbara and Montecito Gardens.* Santa Barbara, Calif.: Ervanna Bowen Bissell.

Bliss, Mildred. 1960. "Beatrix Jones Farrand, 1872–1959." Unpublished manuscript.

Bloomfield, Ann. 1988. "The Evolution of a Landscape: Charles Sumner Greene's Designs for Green Gables." *Journal of the Society of Architectural Historians,* Vol. 47, No. 3, pp. 231–44.

Boston Society of Landscape Architects. [1935.] *Studies in Landscape Architecture.* Boston: Bruce Humphries, Inc.

Bowers, William L. 1974. *The Country Life Movement in America, 1900–1920.* Port Washington, N.Y.: Kennikat.

Boyd, John Taylor. 1918. "The Work of Olmsted Brothers, Part II." *Architectural Record,* Vol. 44, pp. 502–21.

Bragdon, Claude. Papers. Rare Book Room, University of Rochester Library, Rochester, New York.

Burton, Kate E. 1927. "The Cleveland Museum of Art." *Bulletin of the Garden Club of America,* No. 3 (Third Series), pp. 40–41.

Bush-Brown, Louise and James Bush-Brown. 1929. *Portraits of Philadelphia Gardens.* Philadelphia: Dorrance.

Caldwell, Alfred. 1961. "Jens Jensen: The Prairie Spirit." *Landscape Architecture,* Vol. 51, No. 2, pp. 102–5.

Cantor, Jay E. 1985. *Winterthur.* New York: Abrams.

Caparn, Harold A., James Sturgis Pray, and Downing Vaux, eds. 1909. *Transactions of the American Society of Landscape Architects from its Inception in 1899 to the End of 1908.* Harrisburg: J. Horace McFarland Co.

Cautley, Marjorie Sewell. 1935. *Garden Design: The Principles of Abstract Design as Applied to Landscape Composition.* New York: Dodd, Mead.

Child, Susan. 1984. "Stan Hywet Hall, Estate of F. A. Seiberling, Esq., Akron, Ohio: Historic Preservation of Landscape and Garden." Unpublished report.

Cook, Nancy. 1982. "National Register Nomination for May T. Watts House." Unpublished nomination application.

Cornell, Ralph D. 1933. "Landscape Architecture and City Planning." *Architect and Engineer,* Vol. 113, No. 2, pp. 21–26.

Cortissoz, Royal, ed. 1913. *Monograph of the Work of Charles A. Platt.* New York: Architectural Book Publishing.

Crawford, Pleasance. 1982. "Charles Ernest Woolverton (1879–1934), Ontario Landscape Architect." *Landscape Architectural Review,* Vol. 3, No. 2, pp. 17–20.

de Forest, Lockwood. 1945. "Opportunity Knocks!" *Landscape Architecture,* Vol. 36, No. 1, p. 10.

Deitz, Paula. 1985. "The Abby Aldrich Rockefeller Garden." *House and Garden,* Vol. 157, No. 2, pp. 116–27.

Dill, Malcolm H. 1932. "To What Extent Can Landscape Architecture 'Go Modern'?" *Landscape Architecture,* Vol. 22, No. 4, pp. 289–92.

Dobyns, Winifred Starr. 1931. *California Gardens.* New York: Macmillan.

Dunington-Grubb, H. B. 1937. "The Suburban Garden." *The Journal, Royal Architectural Institute of Canada,* Vol. 14, No. 7, pp. 122–29.

Eaton, Leonard K. 1964. *Landscape Artist in America: The Life and Work of Jens Jensen.* Chicago: University of Chicago Press.

Ellis, Mary Heard. 1916. "The Beautification of Home Grounds." *Bulletin of the University of Texas,* No. 17.

Embury, Aymar, II. 1909. *One Hundred Country Houses.* New York: Century Co.

Farrand, Beatrix Jones. 1907. "The Garden as a Picture." *Scribner's Magazine,* Vol. 42, No. 1, pp. 2–11.

———. 1924. "Notes on Photographs of Planting at Princeton by Beatrix Farrand." *Landscape Architecture,* Vol. 14, No. 4, pp. 265–67.

———. 1946. "Reef Point Gardens: The Start and the Goal of a Study in Landscape Gardening." *Landscape Architecture,* Vol. 37, No. 1, pp. 12–13.

———. 1949. "Dumbarton Oaks: An Historical Setting for the Making of History." *Landscape Architecture,* Vol. 34, No. 4, pp. 131–35.

Ferrée, Barr. 1904. *American Estates and Gardens.* New York: Munn and Co.

Fiske, George Walter, 1913. *The Challenge of the Country: A Study of Country Life Opportunity.* New York: Association Press.

Fitzgerald, F. Scott. 1925. *The Great Gatsby.* New York: Scribner.

Frary, I. T. 1919. "The Sunken Garden in Brackenridge Park. San Antonio, Texas." *Architectural Record,* Vol. 40, No. 215, pp. 185–87.

Frost, Henry Atherton, and William R. Sears. 1928. "Women in Architecture and Landscape Architecture." Northampton, Mass.: Smith College.

Gothein, Marie. 1979. *A History of Garden Art,* Vol. 1. New York: Hacker.

Grundmann, William J. 1984. "Warren H. Manning's Park Work in Milwaukee, 1892–1904." Unpublished paper.

Hansen, A. E. 1985. *An Arcadian Landscape: The California Gardens of A. E. Hanson.* Los Angeles: Hennessey & Ingalls.

Henshaw, Julia W. 1923. "Wonder Gardens of the Canadian West." *Country Life,* Vol. 35, No. 3, pp. 44–47.

Howe, Samuel. 1915. *American Country Houses of Today.* New York: Architectural Book Publishing.

Hubbard, Henry Vincent, and Theodora Kimball. 1917. *An Introduction to the Study of Landscape Design.* New York: Macmillan.

Jensen, Jens. 1906. "Landscape Art—An Inspiration from the Western Plains." *The Sketchbook,* Vol. 6, pp. 21–28.

———. 1908. "Some Gardens in the Middle West." *Architectural Review,* Vol. 15, No. 4, pp. 93–95.

———. 1939. *Siftings.* Chicago: Ralph Fletcher Seymour.

Johnson, Leonard J. 1927. *Foundation Planting.* New York: A. T. De La Mare Co.

Karson, Robin. 1989. *Fletcher Steele, Landscape Architect: An Account of the Gardenmaker's Life, 1885–1971.* New York: Abrams.

Krall, Daniel W. 1990. "Ellen Biddle Shipman and Her Design for Longue Vue Gardens." *CELA 89: Proceedings.* Sara Katherine Williams and Robert R. Grist, eds. Washington, D.C.: Landscape Architectural Foundation.

Lancaster, Clay. 1983. *The Japanese Influence in America.* New York: Abbeville.

———. 1985. *The American Bungalow, 1880–1930.* New York: Abbeville.

Linden-Ward, Blanche. 1987. "Stan Hywet." *Landscape Architecture,* Vol. 77, No. 4, pp. 66–71.

Makinson, Randell L. 1977. *Greene and Greene: Architecture as a Fine Art.* Salt Lake City: Peregrine Smith.

Maney, Susan. 1987. Interview with Preservation Horticulturist, Landmarks Society of Western New York, at Ellwanger Garden, Rochester, New York.

Masson, Georgina. 1968. *Dumbarton Oaks: A Guide to the Gardens.* Washington, D.C.: Dumbarton Oaks, Trustees for Harvard University.

Mawson, Thomas H. 1901. *The Art and Craft of Garden Making,* 2nd revised edition. London: B. T. Batsford.

———. 1902. "The Unity of the House and Garden." *Journal of the Royal Institute of British Architects,* Vol. 9, pp. 357–75.

McFarland, J. Horace. 1903. "Dolobran—A Wild Gardening Estate." *Country Life in America,* Vol. 4, No. 5, pp. 338–42.

McGuire, Diane Kostial, ed. 1980. *Beatrix Farrand's Plant Book for Dumbarton Oaks.* Washington, D.C.: Dumbarton Oaks, Trustees for Harvard University.

———, and Lois Fern. 1982. *Beatrix Jones Farrand, (1872–1959): Fifty Years of American Landscape Architecture.* Washington, D.C.: Dumbarton Oaks.

Miller, Wilhelm. 1914. *The "Illinois Way" of Beautifying the Farm.* Urbana: Department of Horticulture, University of Illinois.

———. 1915. *The Prairie Spirit in Landscape Gardening.* Urbana: Department of Horticulture, University of Illinois.

Monroe, Lynn Lewis. 1985. *Sonnenberg Gardens, Canandaigua, N.Y.* Alfred, N.Y.: Lynn Lewis and Gene Monroe.

Morgan, Keith N. 1985. *Charles A. Platt: The Artist as Architect.* New York: Architectural History Foundation.

Morrill, John Barstow. 1948. "Forest Preserve District of Cook County, Illinois." *Landscape Architecture,* Vol. 38, No. 4, pp. 139–44.

Murmann, Eugene O. 1914. *California Gardens.* Los Angeles: Eugene O. Murmann.

Newton, Norman T. 1932. "Modern Trends—What Are They?" *Landscape Architecture,* Vol. 22, No. 4, pp. 302–3.

———. 1949. "Professional Training of Landscape Architects at Harvard." *Landscape Architecture,* Vol. 39, No. 4, pp. 181–83.

Northend, Mary F. 1908. "Interesting Formal Gardens." *House and Garden,* Vol. 13, No. 2, pp. 41–45.

Olmsted Brothers. 1906. "Letter to Edmund J. James, President, University of Illinois." University Board of Trustees Proceedings, Record Series 1/1/802. Champaign, Ill.: University of Illinois Archives.

Owens, Hubert B. 1983. *Personal History of Landscape Architecture in the Last Sixty Years, 1922–1982.* Athens, Ga.: University of Georgia Alumni Society.

Padilla, Victoria. 1961. *Southern California Gardens.* Berkeley: University of California Press.

Peters, William. 1980. "Lockwood de Forest, Landscape Architect: Santa Barbara, California, 1896–1949." Master's thesis. Berkeley: University of California.

Phelps, Harriet Jackson. 1979. *Newport in Flower: A History of Newport's Horticultural Heritage.* Newport, R.I.: Preservation Society of Newport County.

Platt, Charles A. 1894. *Italian Gardens.* New York: Harper and Brothers.

Pond, Bremer. 1950. "Fifty Years in Retrospect." *Landscape Architecture,* Vol. 40, No. 1, pp. 59–66.

Pray, James Sturgis. 1911. "The Department of Landscape Architecture in Harvard University." *Landscape Architecture,* Vol. 1, No. 2, pp. 53–70.

Rehmann, Elsa. 1918. *The Small Place: Its Landscape Architecture.* New York: G. P. Putnam.

★Roberts, Martha McMillan. 1962. *Public Gardens and Arboretums of the United States.* New York: Holt, Rinehart and Winston.

Robinson, Florence Bell. 1940. *Planting Design.* Champaign, Ill.: Garrard.

Shipman, Ellen McGowan Biddle. Papers 1914–1946. Cornell University Archives, Collection #1259, Ithaca, New York.

Smith, F. A. Cushing. 1930. " 'Villa Turicum' the Country Estate." *American Landscape Architect,* Vol. 2, No. 6, pp. 9–18.

Spoon, Jacob John. 1930. "Landscape Design for Airports." *American Landscape Architect,* Vol. 3, No. 6, pp. 33–35.

Steele, Fletcher. Fletcher Steele Collection. State University of New York. Syracuse, New York, Archives.

————. Papers. Rare Book Room, University of Rochester Library, Rochester, New York.

————. 1913. "The New Richmond College." *Landscape Architecture,* Vol. 3, No. 2, pp. 59–67.

————. 1924. *Design in the Little Garden.* Boston: Atlantic Monthly Press.

————. 1929. "New Styles in Gardening." *House Beautiful,* Vol. 55, pp. 317, 352–53.

————. 1930. "New Pioneering in Garden Design." *Landscape Architecture,* Vol. 20, No. 3, pp. 159–76.

————. 1947. "Naumkeag." *House and Garden,* Vol. 92, No. 1, pp. 68–71, 110–11.

————. 1964. *Gardens and People.* Boston: Houghton Mifflin.

Steiner, Frederick R., and Kenneth R. Brooks. 1986. "Agricultural Education and Landscape Architecture." *Landscape Journal,* Vol. 5, No. 1, pp. 19–32.

Streatfield, David C. 1977. "The Evolution of the California Landscape. Part 3: The Great Promotions." *Landscape Architecture,* Vol. 67, No. 3, pp. 229–39.

————. 1982. "Echoes of England and Italy 'On the Edge of the World': Green Gables and Charles Greene." *Journal of Garden History,* Vol. 2, No. 4, pp. 377–98.

————. 1985. "Where Pine and Palm Meet: The California Garden as Regional Expression." *Landscape Journal,* Vol. 4, No. 2, pp. 61–74.

Taylor, A. D. 1916. "Models for Architectural and Landscape Work—Part I." *American Architect,* Vol. 59, No. 2105, pp. 265–69.

————. 1938. "Forest Hill Park: A Report on the Proposed Landscape Development." Cleveland, unpublished report.

Teutonico, Jeanne Marie. 1983. "Marian Cruger Coffin: The Long Island Estates." Unpublished master's thesis. New York: Columbia University.

Tilton, Leon D., and Thomas E. O'Donnell. 1930. *The History of the Growth and Development of the Campus of the University of Illinois.* Champaign: University of Illinois Press.

Tinamus, C. S. 1936. "Lake Springfield: A Classic Municipal Enterprise." Kansas City, Mo.: Burns & McDonnell Engineering Company.

Turner, Paul Venable. 1984. *Campus: An American Planning Tradition.* New York: Architectural History Foundation.

Valentine, Lucia and Alan. 1973. *The American Academy in Rome.* Charlottesville: University Press of Virginia.

Vitale, Ferruccio. 1926. "The Lake Forest Institute." *Landscape Architecture,* Vol. 17, No. 1, pp. 67–68.

Waugh, Frank. 1914. *Rural Improvement.* New York: Orange Judd and Company.

————. 1915. *Landscape Gardening: Treatise on the General Principles Governing Outdoor Art,* 2nd ed. New York: Orange Judd and Company.

————. 1927. *Formal Design in Landscape Architecture.* New York: Orange Judd and Company.

Webel, Richard K. 1922. "Appreciation of Landscape Architecture: Modern Developments." *Architectural Progress,* Vol. 5, No. 11, pp. 11–22.

Wharton, Edith. 1910. *Italian Villas and their Gardens.* New York: The Century Company.

Wheeler, Stuart L. 1990. "Building for the Centuries." *University of Richmond Magazine,* Vol. 52, No. 2, pp. 2–6.

White, Henry Preston. 1913. "The Architectural Garden—II." *American Architect,* Vol. 52, No. 1934, pp. 45–48.

Yoch, James J. 1989. *Landscaping the American Dream: The Gardens and Film Sets of Florence Yoch: 1890–1972.* New York: Abrams/Sagapress.

Chapter 25

Albright, Horace M. 1985. *The Birth of the National Park Service: The Founding Years, 1913–33.* Salt Lake City: Howe Brothers.

Belknap, Raymond K., and John G. Furtado. 1968. "The Natural Land Unit as a Planning Base." *Landscape Architecture,* Vol. 58, No. 2, pp. 145–47.

Berger, John J. 1985. *Restoring the Earth.* New York: Knopf.

Buggey, Susan. 1985. "For Use and Beauty." *Canadian Collector,* Vol. 20, No. 1, pp. 27–30.

Carson, Rachel. 1962. *Silent Spring.* New York: Houghton Mifflin.

Catlin, George. 1926. *North American Indians: Being Letters and Notes on their Manners, Customers, and Conditions, Written during Eight Years' Travel amongst the Wildest Tribes in North American, 1832–1839,* Vol. I. Edinburgh: John Grant.

Chase, Alston. 1986. *Playing God In Yellowstone: The Destruction of America's First National Park.* Boston: Atlantic Monthly Press.

Chittenden, Hiram Martin. 1964. *The Yellowstone National Park.* Norman: University of Oklahoma Press.

Cleveland, Horace W. S. 1882. *The Culture and Management of Our Native Forests for Development as Timber or Ornamental Wood.* Springfield, Ill.: H. W. Bokka.

———. 1885. *Public Parks, Radial Avenues, and Boulevards: Outline Plan of a Park System for the City of St. Paul.* St. Paul: Globe Job Office.

———. 1889a. "Address to the Board of Park Commissioners for Improvement of Vacant Squares in the City, October 13, 1888," in *Second Annual Report of Board of Park Commissioners for 1888,* St. Paul, Minn.

———. 1889b. "Address to Joint Committee of Minneapolis and St. Paul on Mississippi River Park, January 12, 1889," in *Second Annual Report of Board of Park Commissioners for 1888.* St. Paul, Minn.

Copeland, Robert Morris. 1859. *Country Life: A Handbook of Agriculture, Horticulture, and Landscape Gardening.* Boston: John P. Jewett and Company.

Coughlin, Robert E., and John C. Keene. 1981. *The Protection of Farmland: A Reference Guidebook for State and Local Governments.* Washington, D.C.: U.S. Government Printing Office.

Denig, Nancy Watkins. 1985. " 'On Values' Revisited': A Judeo-Christian Theology of Man and Nature." *Landscape Journal,* Vol. 4, No. 2, pp. 96–105.

Gilliam, Ann, ed. 1979. *Voices for the Earth: A Treasury of the Sierra Club Bulletin.* San Francisco: Sierra Club Books.

Goodwin, W. A. R. 1937. "The Restoration of Colonial Williamsburg." *National Geographic,* Vol. 71, No. 4, pp. 401–43.

Grese, Robert E. 1990. "Designing with the Native Landscape: 1880–1940." Unpublished report. Ann Arbor, Mich.: School of Natural Resources, The University of Michigan.

Hackett, Brian. 1963. "Ecological Approach to Design." *Landscape Architecture,* Vol. 53, No. 2, pp. 123–26.

Halprin, Lawrence. 1962. "The Shape of Erosion." *Landscape Architecture,* Vol. 52, No. 2, pp. 87–88.

Hoffman, Abraham. 1981. *Vision or Villainy: Origins of the Owens Valley–Los Angeles Water Controversy.* College Station: Texas A&M University Press.

Hosmer, Charles B., Jr. 1965. *Presence of the Past: A History of the Preservation Movement in the United States before Williamsburg.* New York: G. P. Putnam.

———. 1981. *Preservation Comes of Age: From Williamsburg to the National Trust, 1926–1949,* Vol. 1. Charlottesville: University Press of Virginia.

Hydrick, Rick. 1984. "The Genesis of National Park Management: John Roberts White and Sequoia National Park, 1920–1947." *Journal of Forest History,* Vol. 28, No. 2, pp. 68–81.

Jordan, William R., III, Michael E. Gilpin, and John D. Aber, eds. 1987. *Restoration Ecology.* Cambridge, England: Cambridge University Press.

Keller, J. Timothy, and Genevieve P. Keller. 1987. "How to Evaluate and Nominate Designed Historic Landscapes." National Register Bulletin 18, Department of the Interior. Washington, D.C.: U.S. Government Printing Office.

Kemper, J. P. 1972. *Rebellious River.* New York: Arno.

Landecker, Heidi. 1990. "In Search of an Arbiter." *Landscape Architecture,* Vol. 80, No. 1, pp. 87–90.

Leopold, Aldo. 1949. *A Sand County Almanac.* New York: Oxford University Press.

Manning, Warren. 1924. "A National Park System." *Parks and Recreation,* [Minot, North Dakota], Vol. 71, January–February, pp. 219–29.

Marsh, George Perkins. 1965. *Man and Nature.* Cambridge: Harvard University Press.

McClelland, Linda Flint, et al. 1990. *Guidelines for Evaluating and Documenting Rural Historical Landscapes.* National Register Bulletin 30, Washington, D.C.: Department of the Interior.

McDougall, Terry. 1985. "A Celebration of Parks." *Canadian Heritage,* May–June 1985, pp. 2–3.

McGreevy, Patrick. 1988. "The End of America: The Beginning of Canada." *Canadian Geographer,* Vol. 32, No. 4, pp. 307–18.

McHarg, Ian. 1967. "An Ecological Method for Landscape Architecture." *Landscape Architecture,* Vol. 57, No. 2, pp. 105–7.

———. 1969. *Design With Nature.* Garden City, N.Y.: Doubleday.

Michaux, Francois A[ndré]. 1871. *The North American Sylva . . .* Philadelphia: Rice and Rutter.

Muir, John. 1901. *Our National Parks.* Boston: Houghton Mifflin Company.

Mulloy, Elizabeth D. 1976. *The History of the National Trust for Historic Preservation, 1963–1973.* Washington, D.C.: Preservation Press.

Murtagh, William J. 1988. *Keeping Time: The History and Theory of Preservation in America.* Pittstown, N.J.: Main Street Press.

Myers, Phyllis. 1988. *State Grants for Parklands, 1965–1984.* Washington, D.C.: The Conservation Foundation.

Nash, Roderick. 1967. *Wilderness and the American Mind.* New Haven: Yale University Press.

———, ed. 1968. *The American Environment: Readings in the History of Conservation.* Reading, Mass.: Addison-Wesley.

Nadeau, Remi. 1950. *The Water Seekers.* Garden City, N.Y.: Doubleday.

Niagara Falls Gazette. 1878. Untitled article. October 2, 1878, p. 3:2.

———. 1879. "The International Park." October 1, 1879, pp. 2–3.

Olmsted, F. L., Sr. 1880. "Notes by Mr. Olmsted," in *Special Report of the New York State Survey on the Preservation of the Scenery of Niagra Falls for the Year 1879.* Albany: Charles Van Benthuysen & Sons.

Olmsted, F. L., Jr. 1914. "Hetch-Hetchy." *Landscape Architecture,* Vol. 4, No. 2, pp. 37–46.

———. 1929. *Report of State Park Survey of California.* Sacramento: California State Printing Office.

Paige, John C., and Laura Soulleire Harrison. 1987. *Out of the Vapors: A Social and Architectural History of Bath House Row, Hot Springs National Park, Arkansas.* Washington, D.C.: U.S. Department of the Interior.

Pepper, David. 1984. *The Roots of Modern Environmentalism.* London: Croom Helm.

Petulla, Joseph. 1977. *American Environmental History.* San Francisco: Boyd & Fraser.

———. 1980. *American Environmentalism: Values, Tactics, Priorities.* College Station: Texas A&M University Press.

Pinchot, Gifford, 1947. *Breaking New Ground.* New York: Harcourt, Brace.

Pisani, Donald J. 1985. "Forests and Conservation, 1865–1890." *Journal of American History,* Vol. 72, No. 2, pp. 349–59.

Ramsdell, Charles. 1959. *San Antonio: A Historical and Pictorial Guide.* Austin: University of Texas Press.

Rehmann, Elsa. 1933. "An Ecological Approach." *Landscape Architecture,* Vol. 23, No. 4, pp. 239–46.

Reisner, Marc. 1986. *Cadillac Desert: The American West and Its Disappearing Water.* New York: Viking.

Sanborn, Margaret. 1981. *Yosemite: Its Discovery, Its Wonders, and Its People.* New York: Random House.

Schaller, Frank W., and Paul Sutton. 1978. *Reclamation of Drastically Disturbed Lands.* Madison, Wis.: American Society of Agronomy.

Schrepfer, Susan R. 1983. *The Fight to Save the Redwoods: A History of Environmental Reform, 1917–1978.* Madison: University of Wisconsin Press.

Skankland, Robert. 1951. *Steve Mather of the National Parks.* New York: Knopf.

Smith, Darrell H. 1930. *The Forest Service: Its History, Activities, and Organization.* Washington, D.C.: Brookings Institute.

Smith, Frank E. 1966. *The Politics of Conservation.* New York: Pantheon.

Steen, Harold K. 1976. *The U.S. Forest Service: A History.* Seattle: University of Washington Press.

Steinitz, Carl, Paul Parker, and Lawrie Jordan. 1976. "Hand-Drawn Overlays: Their History and Prospective Uses." *Landscape Architecture,* Vol. 66, No. 5, pp. 444–55.

Tichi, Cecelia. 1979. *New World, New Earth.* New Haven: Yale University Press.

Udall, Stewart L. 1988. *The Quiet Crisis and The Next Generation.* Salt Lake City: Peregrine Smith.

Wakeley, Arthur C., ed. 1917. *Omaha: The Gate City and Douglas County Nebraska.* Chicago: The S. J. Clarke Publishing Company.

Wiley, Peter, and Robert Gottlieb. 1982. *Empires in the Sun: The Rise of the New American West.* New York: G. P. Putnam.

Wirth, Conrad. 1955. "The Landscape Architect in National Park Work." *Landscape Architecture,* Vol. 46, No. 1, pp. 13–18.

Wirth, Theodore. 1945. *Minneapolis Park System, 1883–1944.* Minneapolis Board of Park Commissioners.

Wright, Ellen. 1904. *Elizur Wright's Appeals for Middlesex Fells and the Forests with a Sketch of What He Did for Both.* Ellen Wright.

Whyte, William H. 1959. "Landscape: A Vanishing Resource." *Landscape Architecture,* Vol. 50, No. 1, pp. 8–13.

Yee, Roger. 1974. "Planning for the Brave New World." *Progressive Architecture,* Vol. 55, No. 6, pp. 88–97.

Chapter 26

Alanen, Arnold R., and Joseph A. Eden. 1987. *Main Street Ready-Made: The New Deal Community of Greendale, Wisconsin.* Madison: State Historical Society of Wisconsin.

Allen, Frederick L. 1940. *Since Yesterday: The Nineteen-Thirties in America.* New York: Harper and Brothers.

Anonymous. 1938. "Washington, D.C.: Langston Housing Project." *Architectural Forum,* Vol. 68, pp. 378–79.

———. 1940. "Greenhills: Second Anniversary, 1940." Greenhills, Ohio: Greenhills News Bulletin Association.

Arnold, Joseph L. 1971. *The New Deal in the Suburbs: A History of the Greenbelt Town Program, 1935–1954.* Columbus: Ohio State University Press.

Bennett, Hugh H. 1939. *Soil Conservation*. New York: McGraw-Hill.

Boardman, F. W., Jr. 1967. *The Thirties: America and the Great Depression*. New York: Henry Z. Walck.

Bonnifield, Paul. 1979. *The Dust Bowl: Men, Dirt, and Depression*. Albuquerque: University of New Mexico Press.

Burggraf, Frank, and Karen Rollet. N.d. "Man-Made Elements in Natural Settings: The CCC in Arkansas." Unpublished report, University of Arkansas.

Butler, Ovid. 1934. "The Prairie Shelter Belt." *American Forests,* Vol. 40, No. 9, pp. 395–98.

Caro, Robert A. 1974. *The Power Broker: Robert Moses and the Fall of New York*. New York: Knopf.

Christensen, Carol A. 1986. *The American Garden City and New Towns Movement*. Ann Arbor: UMI Research Press.

Cigliano, Jan E. 1982. *Norris, Tennessee: American's Forgotten TVA New Town*. Master's thesis in Urban and Regional Planning. Washington, D.C.: George Washington University.

Coffin, Laurence E., and Beatriz de Winthuysen Coffin. 1988. "Greenbelt: A Maryland 'New Town' Turns 50." *Landscape Architecture,* Vol. 78, No. 4, pp. 48–53.

Conkin, Paul. 1959. *Tomorrow a New World: The New Deal Community Program*. Ithaca, N.Y.: Cornell University Press.

———. 1967. *FDR and the Origins of the Welfare State*. New York: Thomas Y. Crowell.

Coode, Thomas H., and Dennis E. Fabbri. 1975. "The New Deal's Arthurdale Project in West Virginia." *West Virginia History,* Vol. 36, No. 4, pp. 291–308.

Culley, Frank H. 1933. "Emergency Conservation Work in the National Parks, Part 2: Yellowstone National Park." *Landscape Architecture,* Vol. 22, No. 1, pp. 34–35.

Cutler, Phoebe. 1985. *The Public Landscape of the New Deal*. New Haven: Yale University Press.

Draper, Earle S. 1933. "The Landscape Architect in Public Works I: Tennessee Valley Authority." *Landscape Architecture,* Vol. 24, No. 1, pp. 24–25.

———. 1935. "Housing by the TVA." *American Planning and Civic Annual*. Washington, D.C.: American Planning and Civic Association.

———. 1936. "Regional Planning and the Tennessee River Valley Authority." Transcript of lecture given at Harvard University.

———. 1938. "Landscape Architecture in the Tennessee Valley." *Landscape Architecture,* Vol. 28, No. 4, pp. 185–90.

Droze, Wilmon H. 1977. *Trees, Prairies, and People: A History of Tree Planting in the Western States*. Denton: Texas Woman's University.

Eckbo, Garrett. 1950. *Landscape for Living*. New York: Architectural Record.

Elwood, Philip H. 1934. "The Landscape Architect in Public Works II: State Park Conservation Work, Part 1; The Central Plains and Eastern Rockies." *Landscape Architecture,* Vol. 23, No. 2, pp. 83–85.

———. 1936. "Some Landscape Architectural Problems in Government Service." *Landscape Architecture,* Vol. 26, No. 4, pp. 186–91.

Fairbanks, Robert B. 1978. "Cincinnati and Greenhills: The Response to a Federal Community." *Cincinnati Historical Society Bulletin,* Vol. 36, No. 4, pp. 223–41.

Grant, Nancy L. 1990. *TVA and Black Americans: Planning for the Status Quo*. Philadelphia: Temple University Press.

Hare, S. Herbert. 1933. "The Municipal Rose Garden at Fort Worth." *Parks and Recreation,* Vol. 17, pp. 22–23.

————. 1936. "The Prospective Field of Our Profession." *Landscape Architecture,* Vol. 26, No. 4, pp. 175–78.

Hartzog, Justin R. 1938. "Planning of Suburban Resettlement Towns: Greenhills." *Journal of the American Institute of Planners,* Vol. 4, pp. 29–33.

Held, R. Burnell, and Marion Clawson. 1965. *Soil Conservation in Perspective.* Baltimore: Johns Hopkins Press.

Howell, Glenn. 1976. *C. C. C. Boys Remember: A Pictorial History of the Civilian Conservation Corps.* Medford, Ore.: Klocker Printery.

Hurt, R. Douglas. 1981. *The Dust Bowl: An Agricultural and Social History.* Chicago: Nelson-Hall.

————. 1986. "Federal Land Reclamation in the Dust Bowl." *Great Plains Quarterly,* Vol. 6, No. 2, pp. 94–106.

Jennings, Allyn R. 1933. "Planning State Parks." *Landscape Architecture,* Vol. 23, No. 4, pp. 221–34.

Jones, Kenneth F. 1933. "Emergency Conservation Work, Part 1: U.S. Forest Service Keosauqua, Iowa." *Landscape Architecture,* Vol. 23, No. 2, pp. 29–30.

Knight, Emerson. 1934. "State Park Conservation Work, Part 2: Oregon and the California Coast Redwood Belt." *Landscape Architecture,* Vol. 23, No. 2, pp. 85–86.

Leach, Charles Bradley. 1978. "Greenhills, Ohio: The Evolution of an American New Town." Ph.D. thesis. Cleveland, Ohio: Case Western Reserve University.

Mayall, R. Newton. 1935. "Recording Historic American Landscape Architecture." *Landscape Architecture,* Vol. 26, No. 1, pp. 1–11.

McDonald, Michael J., and John Muldowny. 1982. *TVA and the Dispossessed: The Resettlement of Population in Norris Dam Area.* Knoxville: University of Tennessee Press.

Merk, Frederick. 1978. *History of the Westward Movement.* New York: Knopf.

Miller, E. Lynn. 1978. "Homesteading FDR-style at Arthurdale." *Landscape Architecture,* Vol. 68, No. 5, 418–23, 433.

Morgan, Arthur E. 1934. "The Human Problem of the Tennessee Valley Authority." *Landscape Architecture,* Vol. 23, No. 3, pp. 119–25.

Muckle, Kirk, and Dreck Wilson. 1982. "David Augustus Williston: Pioneer Black Professional." *Landscape Architecture,* Vol. 72, No. 1, pp. 82–85.

Nelson, Beatrice Ward. 1928. *State Recreation: Parks, Forests, and Game Preserves.* Washington, D.C.: National Conference on State Parks, Inc.

Olson, James S., ed. 1985. *Historical Dictionary of the New Deal.* Westport, Conn.: Greenwood.

Owen, A. L. Reisch. 1983. *Conservation under F. D. R.* New York: Praeger.

Peaslee, Horace W. 1930. "Landscape Construction Notes XXXIII: Notes on the Concrete Work of Meridian Hill Park, Washington." *Landscape Architecture,* Vol. 21, No. 1, pp. 31–38.

Peets, Elbert. 1937. "Washington, Williamsburg, The Century of Progress, and Greendale," in *City Planning Housing.* Werner Hegemann, ed. New York: Architectural Book Publishing.

————. 1949. "Studies in Planning Texture—For Housing in a Greenbelt Town." *Architectural Record,* Vol. 106, No. 2, pp. 131–37.

Potter, Barrett G. 1976. "The Dirty Thirties Shelterbelt Project." *American Forests,* Vol. 82, No. 1, pp. 36–39.

Salmond, John A. 1967. *The Civilian Conservation Corps, 1933–1942: A New Deal Case Study.* Durham, N.C.: Duke University Press.

Shillaber, Caroline. 1982. "Elbert Peets: Champion of the Civic Form." *Landscape Architecture,* Vol. 72, No. 6, pp. 54–59, 100.

Smith, Frank E. 1966. *The Politics of Conservation.* New York: Pantheon.

Steinbeck, John. 1939. *The Grapes of Wrath*. New York: Viking.

Steiner, Frederick. 1987. "Soil Conservation Policy in the United States." *Environmental Management*, Vol. 11, No. 2, pp. 209–23.

Svobida, Lawrence. 1986. *Farming the Dust Bowl: A First-Hand Account from Kansas*. Lawrence: University Press of Kansas.

Taylor, A. D. 1933. "Landscape Architecture To-Day." *Landscape Architecture*, Vol. 23, No. 2, pp. 85–96.

———. 1934. "Public Works and the Profession of Landscape Architecture." *Landscape Architecture*, Vol. 23, No. 3. pp. 135–41.

Tugwell, Rexford G. 1937. "The Meaning of Greenbelt Towns." *The New Republic*, Vol. 90, No. 1158, pp. 42–43.

Van Schaack, Gordon. 1935. "Penderlea Homesteads: The Development of a Subsistence Homesteads Project." *Landscape Architecture*, Vol. 25, No. 2, pp. 75–80.

Walker, Hale. 1938. "Some Major Technical Problems Encountered in the Planning of Greenbelt, Maryland." *Journal of the American Institute of Planners*, Vol. 4, pp. 34–39.

Weiss, Marc A. 1987. *The Rise of the Community Builders*. New York: Columbia University Press.

Williamson, Mary Lou, ed. 1987. *Greenbelt: History of a New Town 1937–1987*. Norfolk, W.Va.: The Donning Corporation.

Wirth, Conrad L. 1945. *Civilian Conservation Corps Program of the U.S. Department of the Interior*. Washington, D.C.: U.S. Government Printing Office.

Woodruff, Nan Elizabeth. 1985. *As Rare as Rain: Federal Relief in the Great Southern Drought of 1930–31*. Urbana: University of Illinois Press.

Chapter 27

Abbuehl, Edward H. 1961. "A Road Built for Pleasure." *Landscape Architecture*, Vol. 51, No. 4, pp. 233–37.

Altshuler, Alan A. 1983. "The Intercity Freeway," in *Introduction to Planning History in the United States*. New Brunswick, N.J.: Center for Urban Policy Research.

Anonymous. 1979. "Miami International Terminal Parkway." *Landscape Architecture*, Vol. 69, No. 4, pp. 384–85.

Appleyard, Donald, Kevin Lynch, and John R. Myer. 1964. *The View from the Road*. Cambridge, Mass.: MIT Press.

Bartholomew, Harland. 1949. "The Location of Interstate Highways in Cities." *The American Planning and Civic Annual*. Washington, D.C.: American Planning and Civic Association.

Bel Geddes, Norman. 1940. *Magic Motorways*. New York: Random House.

Bement, Austin F. 1923. "The Greatest Automobile Road in the World." *Country Life*, Vol. 43, No. 3, p. 96.

Blake, Peter. 1964. *God's Own Junkyard*. New York: Holt, Rinehart and Winston.

Brodsly, David. 1981. *L. A. Freeway*. Berkeley: University of California Press.

Chabrier, Yvonne. 1985. "The Greening of Copley Square." *Landscape Architecture*, Vol. 75, No. 6, pp. 70–76.

Clay, Grady. 1958. "New Highways: Number One Enemy?" *Landscape Architecture*, Vol. 48, No. 2, pp. 79–82.

Clarke, Gilmore D. 1932. "The Mount Vernon Memorial Highway." *Landscape Architecture*, Vol. 22, No. 3, pp. 179–90.

Davies, Richard O. 1975. *The Age of Asphalt: The Automobile, the Freeway, and the Condition of Metropolitan America*. Philadelphia: Lippincott.

Downer, Jay. 1917. "The Bronx River Parkway," in *Proceedings of the Ninth National Conference on City Planning*. New York: Douglas McMurtrie.

Eliot, Charles W., 2nd. 1932. "The George Washington Memorial Parkway." *Landscape Architecture,* Vol. 22, No. 3, pp. 191–200.

Forgey, Benjamin. 1989. "Parkway Design: A Lost Art?" *Landscape Architecture,* Vol. 79, No. 3, pp. 44–47.

Gubbels, Jac L. 1940. "Texas Landscapes for Safety." *Landscape Architecture,* Vol. 30, No. 2, pp. 59–63.

Hall, Peter. 1982. *Great Planning Disasters.* Berkeley: University of California Press.

Halprin, Lawrence. 1966. *Freeways.* New York: Reinhold.

Hare, S. Herbert. 1940. "Beauty Designed into the Highway, Not Added Superficially." *Landscape Architecture,* Vol. 30, No. 3, pp. 118–19.

Hugill, Peter. 1985. "The Rediscovery of America: Elite Automobile Touring." *Annals of Tourism Research,* Vol. 12, pp. 435–47.

Jensen, Jens. 1924. "Roadside Planting." *Landscape Architecture,* Vol. 14, No. 3, pp. 186–87.

Landphair, Harlow. 1989. "Final Report: Special Projects, Design Arts/Visual Arts, Collaborative Initiative; 'The Freeway as Art.' " College Station, Tex.: Unpublished report.

Lay, Charles Downing. 1919*a.* "Bronx Parkway." *Landscape Architecture,* Vol. 10, No. 2, pp. 103–4.

———. 1919*b.* "Notes on the Influence of Automobiles on Town, Country, and Estate Planning." *Landscape Architecture,* Vol. 10, No. 2, pp. 89–95.

Liebs, Chester H. 1985. *Main Street to Miracle Mile: American Roadside Architecture.* Boston: Little, Brown.

Marshall, Margaret. 1977. "Seattle's Freeway Park: How the Impossible Came to Be." *Landscape Architecture,* Vol. 67, No. 6, pp. 399–403.

McMahon, L. E., and Alice I. Bourquin. 1953. "Detroit's Evolution of an Expressway System." *Landscape Architecture,* Vol. 44, No. 1, pp. 5–10.

Munsey, Frank A. 1906. "The Automobile in America." *Munsey's Magazine,* Vol. 34, pp. 403–7.

Nichols, Arthur. 1940. "Landscape Design in Highway Development." *Landscape Architecture,* Vol. 30, No. 3, pp. 113–20.

Nolen, John. 1930. *City Plan—Little Rock, Arkansas.* Cambridge, Mass.: Unpublished report.

Nolen, John, and Henry V. Hubbard. 1937. *Parkways and Land Values.* Cambridge, Mass.: Harvard University Press.

Olmsted, Frederick Law. 1910. "Street-Traffic Studies." *Landscape Architecture,* Vol. 1, No. 1, pp. 1–8.

Olmsted, John C. 1915. "Classes of Parkways." *Landscape Architecture,* Vol. 6, No. 1, pp. 37–48.

Rae, John B. 1965. *The American Automobile: A Brief History.* Chicago: University of Chicago Press.

———. 1971. *The Road and the Car in American Life.* Cambridge, Mass.: MIT Press.

Rapid Transit Commission. 1924. *Proposed Super-Highway for Greater Detroit.* Detroit: Rapid Transit Commission.

Robinson, John. 1971. *Highways and Our Environment.* New York: McGraw-Hill.

Seely, Bruce E. 1987. *Building the American Highway System: Engineers as Policy Makers.* Philadelphia: Temple University Press.

Shurtleff, Arthur A. 1916. "Traffic Control and Its Application to the Re-Design of Copley Square, Boston." *Landscape Architecture,* Vol. 6, No. 2, pp. 61–71.

Snow, W. Brewster. 1959. *The Highway and the Landscape.* New Brunswick, N.J.: Rutgers University Press.

Stewart, Ralph A. 1942. "The Pennsylvania Turnpike and Its Landscape Treatment." *Landscape Architecture,* Vol. 32, No. 2, pp. 47–52.

Tobey, George B., Jr. 1965. "Leave Those Roadsides Alone!" *Landscape Architecture,* Vol. 55, No. 3, pp. 182–83.

Waugh, Frank A. 1931. "Ecology of the Roadside." *Landscape Architecture,* Vol. 21, No. 2, pp. 81–92.

Young, Hugh. 1923. "Day and Night Storage and Parking of Motor Vehicles," in *Proceedings of Fifteenth National Conference on City Planning.* Baltimore.

Chapter 28

Anonymous. 1971. "Superblock: New Life on the Street." *Architectural Forum,* Vol. 134, No. 1, pp. 66–75.

———. 1973. "Cedar-Riverside." *Architectural Record,* Vol. 154, No. 7, pp. 102–3.

Bailey, James. 1973. "An In-City New Town Stalled by Environmentalists." *AIA Journal,* Vol. 62, No. 6, pp. 33–35.

Bellush, Jewel, and Murray Hausknecht, eds. 1967. *Urban Renewal: People, Politics, and Planning.* Garden City, N.Y.: Anchor.

Blake, Peter. 1979. *God's Own Junkyard.* New York: Holt, Rinehart and Winston.

Chicago Plan Commission. 1943. *Master Plan of Residential Land Use of Chicago.* Chicago: Chicago Plan Commission.

Church, Thomas, Grace Hall, and Michael Laurie. 1983. *Gardens Are for People.* New York: McGraw-Hill.

Eckbo, Garrett. 1986. "Fresno Mall Revisited." *Landscape Architecture,* Vol. 76, No. 6, pp. 54–57.

———. 1990. *Garrett Eckbo: Philosophy of Landscape.* Tokyo: Process Architecture Publishing Company.

Eisinger, Peter K. 1985. "The Search for a National Urban Policy, 1968–1980." *Journal of Urban History,* Vol. 12, No. 1, pp. 3–23.

Futagawa, Yukio, ed. 1974. *Global Architecture: MLTW/Moore, Lyndon, Turnbull and Whitacker, The Sea Ranch, California.* Tokyo: A. D. A. Edita.

Futterman, Robert A. 1961. *The Future of Our Cities.* Garden City, N.Y.: Doubleday.

Gans, Herbert. 1962. *The Urban Villagers: Group and Class in the Life of Italian Americans.* New York: Free Press of Glencoe.

General Services Office. N.d. "The Governor Nelson A. Rockefeller Empire State Plaza." Albany: GSO

Glazer, Nathan. 1966. *Cities.* New York: Knopf.

Gottmann, Jean. 1961. *Megalopolis: The Urbanized Northeastern Seaboard of the United States.* Cambridge, Mass.: MIT Press.

Gruen, Victor. 1973. *Centers for the Urban Environment.* New York: Van Nostrand Reinhold.

Gump, Paul V. 1971. "The Behavior Setting: A Promising Unit for Environmental Designers." *Landscape Architecture,* Vol. 61, No. 2, pp. 130–34.

Hall, Edward T. 1966. *The Hidden Dimension.* Garden City, N.Y.: Doubleday.

Hester, Randolph T. 1975. "Warning: Ivory Tower Designers May Be Hazardous to Your Neighborhood's Health." *Landscape Architecture,* Vol. 65, No. 3, pp. 296–303.

Holston, James. 1989. *The Modernist City: An Anthropological Critique of Brasilia.* Chicago: University of Chicago Press.

Karson, Robin. 1985. "Battery Park City Takes Manhattan." *Landscape Architecture,* Vol. 74, No. 2, pp. 64–69.

Kincaid, H. Evert. 1947. "Urban Development: Chicago's Efforts to Combat the Growth of Blighted Areas." *Landscape Architecture,* Vol. 37, No. 4, pp. 135–39.

Jacobs, Jane. 1961. *The Death and Life of Great American Cities.* New York: Vintage.

Marder, Tod A. 1985. *The Critical Edge: Controversy in Recent American Architecture.* Cambridge, Mass.: MIT Press.

Martin, Roger. 1969. "Exciting Start with Nicollet Mall." *Landscape Architecture,* Vol. 59, No. 4, pp. 299–304.

Meehan, Eugene J. 1979. *The Quality of Federal Policymaking: Programmed Failure in Public Housing.* Columbia: University of Missouri Press.

National Capital Park and Planning Commission. 1964. *On Wedges and Corridors.* Riverdale, Md.: The Commission.

Portman, John, and Jonathan Barnett. 1976. *The Architect as Developer.* New York: McGraw-Hill.

Redstone, Louis G. 1976. *The New Downtowns.* New York: McGraw-Hill.

Relph, Edward. 1987. *The Modern Urban Landscape.* Baltimore: Johns Hopkins University Press.

Robertson, Kent A. 1987. "Pedestrian Skywalks: The Esthetic Impact on Downtown." *Landscape,* Vol. 29, No. 3, pp. 43–47.

Rowe, Peter G. 1991. *Making a Middle Landscape,* Cambridge, Mass.: MIT Press.

Saarinen, Thomas F. 1976. *Environmental Planning: Perception and Behavior.* Boston: Houghton Mifflin.

Sommer, Robert, and Franklin D. Becker. 1969. "The Old Men in Plaza Park." *Landscape Architecture,* Vol. 59, No. 2, pp. 111–13.

——, and Robert L. Thayer, Jr. 1977. "The Radicalization of Common Ground—People's Park, Berkeley: An Unnatural History." *Landscape Architecture,* Vol. 67, No. 6, pp. 510–14.

Spirn, Anne Whiston. 1984. *The Granite Garden: Urban Nature and Human Design.* New York: Basic Books.

Steiner, Frederick. 1981. *The Politics of New Town Planning.* Athens: Ohio University Press.

Sunderland, Lowell E. 1970. "Columbia—New Town." *Town and Country Planning,* Vol. 38, No. 7, pp. 322–26.

Thayer, Robert L., Jr. 1977. "Designing an Experimental Solar Community." *Landscape Architecture,* Vol. 67, No. 3, pp. 223–28.

Turner, Alan. 1974. "New Communities in the United States: 1968–1973." *Town Planning Review,* Vol. 45, No. 3, pp. 259–73.

Watt, Dan. ed. 1982. *Reston: The First Twenty Years.* Reston, Va: Reston Publishing Company.

Whyte, William H. 1980. *The Social Life of Small Urban Spaces.* Washington D.C.: Conservation Foundation.

Wilmers, Peter. 1971. "The Good Life in Virginia." *Town and Country Planning,* Vol. 39, No. 1, pp. 73–78.

Yaeger, David J. 1982. "Working Class: Looking for Elan in Levittown." *Landscape Architecture,* Vol. 72, No. 2, pp. 64–67.

Chapter 29

Anonymous. 1939. "Landscape Architecture at the New York World's Fair II: A Portfolio of Photographs of Modern Design." *Landscape Architecture,* Vol. 30, No. 1, pp. 1–25.

——. 1974. "Halprin Revisited in 1973: Still Changing 'To Stay Alive.' " *Landscape Architecture,* Vol. 64, No. 3, pp. 140–47.

Ambasz, Emilio. 1976. *The Architecture of Luis Barragan.* New York: Museum of Modern Art.

Appelbaum, Stanley, ed. 1977. *The New York World's Fair 1939/1940.* New York: Dover.

Baker, Geoffrey, and Bruno Funaro. 1951. *Shopping Centers: Design and Operation.* New York: Reinhold.

Bayon, Damian. 1976. "An Interview with Luis Barragan." *Landscape Architecture,* Vol. 66, No. 6, pp. 530–33.

Burle Marx, Roberto. 1954. "A Garden Style in Brazil to Meet Contemporary Needs." *Landscape Architecture.* Vol. 44, No. 4, pp. 200–208.

Byrd, Warren T., Jr., and Reuben M. Rainey, ed. 1982. *The Work of Dan Kiley: A Dialogue on Design Theory.* Proceedings of the First Annual Symposium on Landscape Architecture. School of Architecture, University of Virginia.

Eastman, Susan R. 1982. "Coining a Phrase." *Landscape Architecture,* Vol. 72, No. 1, pp. 54–57.

Eckbo, Garrett. 1937. "Small Gardens in the City." *Pencil Points,* Vol. 18, No. 9, pp. 573–86.

———. 1950. *Landscape for Living.* New York: Architectural Record.

———. 1956. *The Art of Home Landscaping.* New York: McGraw-Hill.

———. 1965. "Creative Design of the Landscape." *Landscape Architecture,* Vol. 55, No. 5, pp. 113–16.

———. 1983. "Is Landscape Architecture?" *Landscape Architecture,* Vol. 73, No. 3, pp. 64–65.

———. 1984. Untitled lecture/presentation. Texas A&M University, College Station, Texas.

Fleisher, Horace. 1953. "The Gardens of the Pedregal." *Landscape Architecture,* Vol. 43, No. 2, pp. 49–52.

Galchutt, William H., and William J. Wallis. 1972. "Disney's Other World: Mickey-Mousing with Florida's Water Supplies?" *Landscape Architecture,* Vol. 63, No. 1, pp. 28–33.

Gans, Herbert. 1967. *The Levittowners.* New York: Random House.

Goldstein, Barbara. 1983. "Harlequin Plaza." *Landscape Architecture,* Vol. 73, No. 4, pp. 56–59.

Halprin, Lawrence. 1986. *Lawrence Halprin: Changing Places.* San Francisco: San Francisco Museum of Modern Art.

Harman, Gabriel C. 1961. "New Approaches to Land Development." *Landscape Architecture,* Vol. 51, No. 3, pp. 153–57.

Jellicoe, Geoffrey. 1989. *The Landscape of Civilization.* Northiam, England: Garden Art Press.

Jencks, Charles A. 1977. *The Language of Post-Modern Architecture,* 3rd edition. London: Academy Editions.

Johnson, Jory. 1988. "Codex World Headquarters: Regionalism and Invention." *Landscape Architecture,* Vol. 78, No. 3, pp. 58–63.

———. 1990. "Pastures of Plenty: Thirty Years of Corporate Villas in America." *Landscape Architecture,* Vol. 80, No. 3. pp. 51–57.

Karson, Robin. 1986. "Conversation with Kiley." *Landscape Architecture,* Vol. 76, No. 2, pp. 50–57.

———. 1987. "A New Historicism in Campus Planning." *Landscape Architecture,* Vol. 77, No. 2, pp. 74–81.

Kassler, Elizabeth R. 1964. *Modern Gardens in the Landscape.* Garden City, N.Y.: Doubleday.

Kay, Jane Holtz. 1989. "The Green vs. The Grid." *Landscape Architecture,* Vol. 79, No. 8. pp. 74–79.

Kiley, Dan. 1963. "Nature: The Source of All Design." *Landscape Architecture,* Vol. 57, No. 2, p. 127.

Langdon, Philip. 1989. "Beyond the Cul-de-Sac." *Landscape Architecture,* Vol. 79, No. 8, pp. 72–73.

Laurie, Michael. 1967. "Foothills Revisited." *Landscape Architecture,* Vol. 57, No. 3, pp. 182–84.

Little, Charles. 1990. *Greenways for America.* Baltimore: Johns Hopkins University Press.

Marshall, Lane, ed. 1981. *Landscape Architecture into the 21st Century.* Washington D.C.: American Society of Landscape Architects.

McHenry, Dean E. 1964. "California's New Campuses: Santa Cruz Campus." *Architectural Record,* Vol. 136, No. 5, pp. 175–78.

Myers, I. M. 1952. *Mexico's Modern Architecture.* New York: Architectural Book Publishing.

Oehme, Wolfgang, James van Sweden, and Susan Rademacker Frey. 1990. *Bold Romantic Gardens.* Reston, Va.: Acropolis Books.

Rose, James. 1939a. "Freedom in the Gardens." *Pencil Points,* Vol. 2, No. 10, pp. 639–643.

———. 1939b. "Articulate Form in Landscape Design." *Pencil Points,* Vol. 2, No. 20, pp. 98–100.

———. 1958. *Creative Gardens.* New York: Reinhold.

Rosen, George. 1980. *Decision-Making Chicago-Style: The Genesis of a University of Illinois Campus.* Urbana: University of Illinois Press.

Schjetnan, Mario G. 1982. "Luis Barragan: The Influential Lyricist of Mexican Culture." *Landscape Architecture,* Vol. 72, No. 1, pp. 68–75.

Schuler, Stanley. 1967. *America's Great Private Gardens.* New York: Macmillan.

Shurcliff, Sidney. 1952. "Shopper's World." *Landscape Architecture,* Vol. 42, No. 3, pp. 43–47.

Schwartz, Martha. 1980. "Back Bay Bagel Garden." *Landscape Architecture,* Vol. 70, No. 1, pp. 43–46.

Snow, Marc. 1967. *Modern American Gardens, Designed by James Rose.* New York: Reinhold.

Stevenson, Markley. 1948. "Landscape Architecture in a Changing World." *Landscape Architecture,* Vol. 38, No. 4, pp. 135–38.

Thompson, J. Williams. 1988. "Dulles Corner." *Landscape Architecture,* Vol. 78, No. 8, pp. 82–87.

———. 1989. "Where the Freeway Ends." *Landscape Architecture,* Vol. 79, No. 10, pp. 52–57.

———. 1990. "Standard Bearer of Modernism." *Landscape Architecture,* Vol. 80, No. 2, pp. 88–95.

Tiller, Kay. 1988. "Frito Lay's Prairie Campus." *Landscape Architecture,* Vol. 78, No. 3, pp. 40–45.

Whittet, David B. 1967. "Greenways for Suburbia." *Landscape Architecture,* Vol. 58, No. 1, pp. 16–19.

Wickstead, George W. 1965. "Critique: Fresno Mall's First 12 Months." *Landscape Architecture,* Vol. 56, No. 1, pp. 44–45, 48.

Zion, Robert. 1957. "The Landscape Architect and the Shopping Center." *Landscape Architecture,* Vol. 48, No. 1, pp. 7–12.

Source Acknowledgements

The authors have made every effort to trace the copyright ownership of the illustrations used in this book. In cases where this was not possible, we would welcome the opportunity to include any omissions in subsequent editions.

Pages 14; 203: Andrew Neal. Page 17: Ann Savage. Pages 18; 127 top; 130 bottom right; 142; 177; 279 left: Benevolo, Leonardo, *History of the City*. Copyright © 1980 MIT Press. Pages 37; 42 top, bottom; 49: Lample, Paul. *Cities and Planning in the Near East*. Copyright © 1968 George Braziller, Inc. Pages 39; 149; 151; 231 top; 235 top; 236; 254 top; 255: Aerofilms. Page 48 top: The British Academy. Pages 51 top left, top right; 59; 186 top; 289: NASA. Page 55 bottom right: Thomas Jr., William L. *Man's Role in Changing the Face of the Earth*. The University of Chicago Press. Page 64: Hoffman, Michael. *Egypt Before the Pharoahs: The Prehistoric Foundations of Egyptian Civilization*. New York: Knopf. Page 67: Wreszinski, L. *Atlas zur Altaegyptischen Kulturgeschichte*. Page 71: Metropolitan Museum of Art. Page 74: John Romer. Page 76: Perrot, Georges. *A History of Art in Ancient Egypt*. Pages 83 bottom left; 105: National Remote Sensing Center, RAE. Page 84: Hans Jerrentrup. Pages 101 right; 156; 245; 246 top; 246 bottom; 282: Gallion, Arthur. *The Urban Pattern*. Page 102 top, bottom: Hughes, J. Donald. *Ecology in Ancient Civilizations*. Page 109: G. Totil. Page 115 top: Ministero della Pubblica Instruzione. Pages 115 bottom; 115; 118, 131: *Cities of Ancient Greece and Italy: Planning in Classical Antiquity*. George Braziller, Inc. Page 122: Assozione Turistica Italy. Page 125: Libyan Department of Antiquities. Page 128: White, K. D. *Roman Farming*. Page 130 top right, bottom left: Stambaugh, John E. *The Ancient Roman City*. 1988. Johns Hopkins University Press, pp. 108, 125. Page 139: S. C. Bisserot. Page 140: Hansjurgen Müller-Beck. Page 141 top: Lysbeth Drewett. Page 150: Putzger, G. *Schul-Atlas*. Page 154: Crisp. *Medieval Gardens*. Page 161: Fussell, G. E. *The Classical Tradition in Western European Farming*. Rutherford, N.J.: Fairleigh Dickinson University Press. Page 172 top: Nigel Press Associates. Page 172 bottom: Blackwell Scientific Groupe. Page 173: British Rail and Travel Association. Page 186 bottom: G. F. Zarella. Page 187: Johnson-Marshall, Percy. *Rebuilding Cities*. Chicago: Aldine. Page 193: A. Campana. Page 197: Institut Geographique, Paris. Page 203: J. Allen Cash Photolibrary. Page 211: Pijoan, J. *Historia Del Arte*. Page 235 bottom: Williams, J. *Hampton Court*. Page 243 right: Pean, P. *Jardins de France*. Page 247; 274: Society for the Diffusion of Useful Knowledge. Page 248: Hunter, J. M. *Land into Landscape*. Page 251: Tobey, G. *A History of Landscape Architecture*. Page 254 bottom: Williamson, T. and L. Bellamy. *Property and Landscape*. George Philipe Ltd., 59 Grosvenor Street, London W1X 9DA. Page 258: Airministry, RAF. Page 261 top: Hiller, Carl E. *Babylon to Brazilia—The Challenge of City Planning*. Page 262 top: Greater London Records Office. Page 262 bottom: Ernout, A. and J. C. Alphand. *L'art des Jardins*. Page 263: Gilpin, William. *Practical Hints on Landscape Gardening*. Page 264: Alphand, J. C. *Promenades de Paris*. Page 265 top: Bournville Village Trust—Works Publication Department. Page 271: Kunstmuseum, Berne. Page 74 top: Susan Jellicoe. Page 275: Amsterdam Parks Department. Page 277: Phillipe Gaignard. Page 280: Reprinted by permission of the publishers from *The Making of Urban Europe, 1000–1950,* by Paul M. Hohenberg and Lynn Hollen Lees, Cambridge, Mass.: Harvard University Press. Copyright © 1985 by the President and Fellows of Harvard College. Page 281: *AIA Journal*, July 1967. Page 288: Bruce Coleman.

Illustrations not cited in the credits or on individual pages are property of Philip Pregill and Nancy Volkman. Line Illustrations for Part One were drawn by Sam Kim; line illustrations for Part Two are credited in the captions.

Index